THE NATURE

AND

FUNCTIONS OF LAW

FOURTH EDITION

By

HAROLD J. BERMAN

Ames Professor of Law, Harvard University

and

WILLIAM R. GREINER

Professor of Law, State University of New York at Buffalo

Mineola, New York

THE FOUNDATION PRESS, INC.

1980

Berman & Greiner—Nat.Law 4th Ed.

PREFACE TO THE FOURTH EDITION

This edition is a further refinement and expansion of the topics and materials of the preceding editions. We have reorganized materials, notably in Parts Three and Four, and added new materials, primarily in Parts One, Three and Four.

In Part One, Chapter Three, Criminal Procedure Prior to Trial, has been updated in light of the evolution of the constitutional law of criminal procedure over the last decade. Administrative and legislative alternatives to judicial regulation of police practices are considered, and some new comparative law perspectives are presented in excerpts from a lively scholarly debate on the merits and limitations of French criminal procedure. Chapter Four, The Trial, has been augmented by excerpts dealing with the ethical problems of lawyers, particularly in the practice of trial advocacy.

Part Three, Law as a Process of Protecting and Facilitating Voluntary Arrangements, has been substantially revised and reorganized to reflect recent developments in legal thought about contract and contract doctrine. Common law doctrine is compared and contrasted to the Uniform Commercial Code treatment of a variety of contract problems.

Part Four, Law as a Process of Resolving Acute Social Conflict, has been expanded to follow the progress of race relations law in the United States. The bulk of the change in this part is in the last Chapter, Securing Fundamental Rights. The evolution of our modern law and policy regarding collective bargaining is compared and contrasted with recent developments regarding racial discrimination in employment. Much of this new matter relates to developments under Title VII of the Civil Rights Act of 1964, and to the role of judges, the executive, and the Equal Employment Opportunity Commission in implementing that statute. This chapter is the most speculative and perhaps the most difficult in the book, but it affords some of the richest possibilities for innovative teaching.

The original themes and purposes of the first three editions are, we think, preserved in this volume. The belief expressed in the first edition, that the undergraduate curriculum is a fertile field in which to teach and learn about law, is still strongly held by the authors. We hope that this edition of the book will prove useful to both old friends and new acquaintances who share that view.

HAROLD J. BERMAN
WILLIAM R. GREINER

Chapel Hill, North Carolina
and Buffalo, New York
December, 1979

FROM THE PREFACE TO THE THIRD EDITION

Despite some substantial changes, the present edition of this book remains in most respects the same as the first two editions. The basic topics covered are the same, with the exception of the addition of a body of materials on the law of race relations. The theoretical approach is the same, with the exception that greater emphasis has been placed on the constitutional background of American law. As in the earlier editions, approximately half of the book is comprised of case reports and approximately half of commentaries and readings. The intent remains the same—to provide a basic textbook for introductory courses in law offered to students of the arts and sciences, to students of business administration, and to others who, though not professional law students, wish to have some grasp of what a legal system is and what it is for.

The changes in the new edition are a response not only to important changes that have taken place in American law during the past six years but also to important changes that have taken place in American attitudes, and especially student attitudes, toward law. This will be apparent from the following list of major revisions:

In Part One ("Law as a Process of Resolution of Disputes"), the first chapter ("The Competence and Jurisdiction of Courts") has been changed to include recent materials on jurisdiction over so-called "political questions." Also the third chapter ("Criminal Procedure Prior to Trial") has been revised to include current leading cases on procedural due process—*Miranda* and others—as well as writings on the relation of the Fifth and Fourteenth Amendments to problems of law enforcement by police and prosecutors.

Part Two ("Law as a Process of Maintaining Historical Continuity and Doctrinal Consistency") and Part Three ("Law as a Process of Protecting and Facilitating Voluntary Arrangements") have been left substantially as they were in the second edition. However, Part Four ("Law as a Process of Resolving Acute Social Conflict") has been significantly altered by an attempt to compare and contrast the history of legal resolution of labor conflicts with the history of legal resolution of racial conflicts. Thus we have added a new chapter on the Black civil rights movement, and we have interspersed civil rights materials in the materials on labor relations—comparing, for example, the sit-in demonstrations of the 1960's and administrative enforcement of Title VII of the Civil Rights Act of 1964 with the sit-down strikes of the 1930's and administrative enforcement of collective agreements. We also attempt to compare the legal strategies of organized labor and those of the Black civil rights groups.

HAROLD J. BERMAN
WILLIAM R. GREINER

Cambridge, Mass., and Buffalo, N. Y.
May 19, 1972

FROM THE PREFACE TO THE SECOND EDITION

The first edition of this book, published in 1958, was something of an experiment. At that time relatively few colleges and universities offered liberal arts courses in law. It was hoped that the book might help to stimulate the introduction of such courses in more schools, and, in fact, a considerable number of college teachers have used the book as the basis for instituting courses in law for college undergraduates.

Since 1958, the first edition has been adopted in about forty colleges and universities. Also, in recent years, several other authors have published books designed to fulfill a similar purpose. It may be said without exaggeration that there is an important and growing movement to expand the teaching of law in the liberal arts curriculum. Moreover, some business schools and departments of business administration have liberalized their courses in business law; in the last decade, many business law teachers have moved away from the traditional approach to business law, with its emphasis on the rules of commercial and corporate law, and have sought to present a more comprehensive, and a more profound, view of legal institutions and the legal process as a fundamental part of the social, political, and economic environment of the business firm and the business system. We hope that this edition of our book will further stimulate this movement and that more liberal arts courses in law will find a place both in the arts and sciences and in the business administration curriculums.

A reviewer of the first edition of this book stated that it raised the questions, "Is there a place in the undergraduate curriculum for a course on the legal process?" and "If so, what should be its content?" [1] The experience of the past eight years, at least, would seem to give an unqualified affirmative answer to the first question. The second question, hopefully, will always be debatable.

In the summer of 1963, the author of the first edition, Mr. Berman, asked Mr. Greiner if he would collaborate in producing a second edition. Mr. Greiner had been using the book for several years as the text for his course in law in the School of Business Administration at the University of Washington in Seattle—a course offered not only to business students but also to students in the College of Arts and Sciences. Both authors were satisfied that the basic structure and style of the first edition should be preserved, but both were also convinced that substantial additions and revisions were needed. Mr. Greiner consented to take the initial responsibility for selecting new materials. Both have worked closely together in reviewing the new

---

1. Alan F. Westin, Book Review, 69 Yale Law Journal 538 (1960).

selections and in going over the original materials, and both assume joint and several responsibility for the final product.

The most obvious difference between the first and the second editions is in length : the size of the book has been increased by about two-thirds. It is now intended to be suitable for a full-year course, although it remains adaptable, with appropriate omissions, to a half-year course. In addition, a teacher's manual will be available to indicate the authors' suggestions for appropriate use of the materials.

* * *

HAROLD J. BERMAN
WILLIAM R. GREINER

Princeton, N. J., and Branford, Conn.
July 15, 1966.

FROM THE PREFACE TO THE FIRST EDITION

This book is intended primarily as a textbook for courses in law offered to undergraduate and graduate students of the arts and sciences. It may also have value as an introduction to law for people who are not enrolled in any course in the subject, provided that they are willing to study with care the materials presented and to give special attention to the questions which are interspersed at frequent intervals. It is hoped that it will have interest also for teachers of business law who are depressed by the excessive narrowness of approach, and excessive breadth of coverage, of the traditional course in business law, and who would like to present an introductory course which approaches law broadly as one of the liberal arts but at the same time treats fairly intensively a relatively few themes.

The basic need which this book attempts to meet is well expressed in the opening lecture of a series given in 1923 by Harlan F. Stone, then Dean of Columbia University Law School and later Chief Justice of the United States—a lecture entitled, incidentally, "Nature and Functions of Law." Dean Stone said:

> "It has always seemed to me to be a fact requiring some explanation on the part of our educators that the subject of law has received so little attention in our scheme of liberal education in the United States. . . . Law lies at the very root of civilization itself, for science, art, commerce, the capacity of cooperative effort by communities and peoples which we identify with civilization, have become possible only through the establishment of social order, which in turn makes law possible, and of which law is the necessary concomitant. . . . Nevertheless our educational institutions, while holding fast to the ancient classical learning, and occupying the fields of natural science, economics, and sociology, have with a few notable exceptions left the study of law to be carried on wholly by professional law schools. I would not have the layman receive professional training in law, nor would I have institutions devoted to liberal education give courses in law such as are given in law schools, but there are certain fundamental notions of the nature of law, certain facts relating to its history and development, and certain principles which underlie its efficient administration which should become a part of the intellectual equipment of every intelligent citizen." [1]

---

1. Harlan F. Stone, *Law and Its Administration* (Columbia University Lectures) (New York, 1924), pp. 1–2.

Although as a rule the study of law plays a very small part in the liberal arts curriculum, it cannot be said to be entirely neglected. In addition to courses in Constitutional Law, Administrative Law, and International Law, which are offered in most of the larger colleges, more general courses on law are occasionally presented under various titles such as "The Nature and Functions of Law," "The American Legal System," "Introduction to Law," "Law and Society," "Legal Philosophy," and the like. Moreover, such general courses have been increasing in number in recent years. The experience of many of these courses clearly testifies to the fact that a basic understanding of the nature and functions of law is by no means inaccessible to the non-lawyer, and that such a basic understanding can be of the greatest interest and value to him whether as a social scientist or simply as an educated person.

There is, however, considerable divergence of opinion concerning what subject-matter liberal arts courses in law should include and how they should be taught. Books written for laymen which attempt to present an overall picture of the legal system are usually either too technical or not technical enough, and in any case are not suitable as textbooks for a course. As a result each instructor has tended to compile his own special selection of readings. While this diversity of approach has certain advantages, there is also a need for a common effort toward creating a common discipline, through which the benefits of diverse experience may be shared.

The present book, which grows out of courses in law which the author has taught occasionally in the Social Relations Department of Harvard College since 1951 and in the School of Industrial Management at Massachusetts Institute of Technology from 1950 to 1953, is published in the belief that it is suitable for use in other colleges as well, and in the hope that it may help to stimulate further efforts to increase and improve the teaching of law in the liberal arts curriculum.

. . .

HAROLD J. BERMAN

Cambridge, Massachusetts
September 15, 1958

ACKNOWLEDGMENTS

Special acknowledgment is made of the fact that much of the material in Part Four of this book is taken from Archibald Cox, Cases on Labor Law, 3rd ed. (1953), and Archibald Cox and Derek Bok, Cases on Labor Law, 5th ed. (1962), 7th ed. (1969), and Archibald Cox, Derek Bok, and Robert A. Gorman, Cases on Labor Law, 8th ed. (1977), (The Foundation Press, Inc., Mineola, N. Y.).

We also thank Arlene Ferrick, who assisted in the preparation of new material for this edition, and O. Patricia Taylor who prepared the manuscript for publication, and who also prepared the indexes.

Acknowledgment is made of the permission of *The New Yorker* to reproduce the cartoon by Robert Day shown on page 38, and of the McNaught Syndicate, Inc., to reproduce the drawing by Frank Beck shown on page 23.

In addition, permission to quote passages from the following works is gratefully acknowledged:

The American Law Institute, Model Code of Pre-Arraignment Procedure, (1975) and Uniform Commercial Code and Official Comments (1972).

Thurman Arnold, The Symbols of Government (New Haven, Yale University Press, 1935);

Peter M. Bergman (ed.), *The Chronological History of the Negro in America* (New York, N. Y., Harper & Row Publishers, Inc., 1969);

Harold J. Berman, "Excuse for Nonperformance in the Light of Contract Practices in International Trade," 63 Columbia Law Review, 1413 (1963);

Arnold Bernhard, "The Antitrust Convictions in the Electrical Equipment Case," *The Value Line Investment Survey*, March 13, 1961 (published by Arnold Bernhard & Co., Inc., New York);

Alexander M. Bickel, *The Least Dangerous Branch*, (copyright © 1962, by The Bobbs-Merrill Company, Inc., reprinted by permission of the publisher);

Charles L. Black, Jr., "The Lawfulness of the Segregation Decisions," 69 Yale Law Journal, 421 (1960) (reprinted by permission of The Yale Law Journal Company and Fred B. Rothman & Company);

ACKNOWLEDGMENTS

Charles E. Clark, *Handbook of the Law of Code Pleading* (St. Paul, Minn., West Publishing Co., 1947);

Felix S. Cohen, "Field Theory and Judicial Logic," 59 Yale Law Journal, 238 (1949);

Morris R. Cohen, "The Basis of Contract," 46 Harvard Law Review 553 (1933), (reprinted with the permission of Harry N. Rosenfield, Esq., executor of the estate of Morris R. Cohen);

Arthur L. Corbin, *Corbin on Contracts*, one vol. ed. (St. Paul, Minn., West Publishing Co., 1952);

Charles P. Curtis, *It's Your Law* (Cambridge, Mass., Harvard University Press, copyright 1954 by the President and Fellows of Harvard College);

Kenneth Culp Davis, *Administrative Law Text* (St. Paul, Minn., West Publishing Co., 1959);

Kenneth C. Davis, *Discretionary Justice* (Baton Rouge, La., Louisiana State University Press, 1969);

Foster R. Dulles, *Labor in America*, 2d rev. ed. (New York, N. Y., Thomas Y. Crowell Company, 1960);

Emile Durkheim, *One the Division of Labor in Society* (transl. & ed. by George Simpson; New York, The Macmillan Company, 1935);

"Equity on the Campus: the Limits of Injunctive Regulation of University Protest," 80 Yale Law Journal 987, (1971) (Reprinted by permission of the Yale Law Journal Company and Fred B. Rothman and Company).

Elgin Edwards, "Hard Answers for Hard Questions: Dissenting in Part from Dean Freedman's Views on the Attorney Client Privilege," 11 Criminal Law Bulletin 478 (1975), Warren, Gorham and Lamont, Inc.

Richard H. Field and Benjamin Kaplan, *Materials for a Basic Course in Civil Procedure* (Brooklyn, N. Y., The Foundation Press, Inc., 1953);

Sidney Fine, *Sit Down* (Ann Arbor, Mich., University of Michigan Press, 1970);

Jerome Frank, *Courts on Trial; Myth and Reality in American Justice* (reprinted by permission of the Princeton University Press, copyright © 1949 by Jerome Frank);

Jerome Frank, *Law and the Modern Mind*, Anchor Books edition (New York, Doubleday & Company Inc., 1963); copyright 1930, 1933, 1949 by Coward-McCann Inc.; copyright 1930 by Brentano's Inc.;

copyright renewed in 1958 by Florence K. Frank; reprinted by arrangement with the estate of Barbara Frank Kristein;

Marvin K. Frankel, "The Search for Truth on Empircal View," 123 University of Pennsylvania Law Review 1031, (1975).

Monroe H. Freedman, "Where the Bodies are Buried: The Adversary System and the Obligation of Confidentiality," 10 Criminal Law Bulletin (1974), reprinted as the first Chapter of *Lawyers' Ethics in an Adversary System*, Bobbs-Merrill, Inc. (1975).

Lon L. Fuller, *Basic Contract Law* (St. Paul, Minn., West Publishing Co., 1947);

Lon L. Fuller, *The Problems of Jurisprudence* (Brooklyn, N. Y., The Foundation Press, Inc., 1949; temporary ed.);

Lon L. Fuller and William R. Perdue, Jr., "The Reliance Interest in Contract Damages," 46 Yale Law Journal, 52, 373 (1936);

Abraham S. Goldstein and Martin Marcus, "The Myth of Judicial Supervision in Three 'Inquisitorial System': France, Italy and Germany," 87 Yale Law Journal 240 (1978), also "Comment on Continental and Criminal Procedure," 87 Yale Law Journal 1570 (1978). (Reprinted by permission of the Yale Law Journal Company and Fred B. Rothman & Company).

Irving Goldstein, *Trial Techniques* (Chicago, Callaghan & Co., 1935);

Charles O. Gregory, *Labor and the Law*, 2d rev. ed. (New York, W. W. Norton & Co., Inc., 1958);

Henry H. Hart, Jr., and Herbert Wechsler, *The Federal Courts and the Federal System* (Brooklyn, N. Y., The Foundation Press, Inc., 1953);

Otto Kahn-Freund, Introduction to Karl Renner, *The Institutions of Private Law and their Social Functions* (London, Routledge and Kegal Paul, Ltd., 1949);

Livingston Hall, Yale Kamisar, Jerrold Israel, and Wayne LaFave, *Cases on Modern Criminal Procedure*, 3rd ed., (St. Paul, Minn., West Publishing Co., 1969);

Harry Kalven, Jr., "The Concept of the Public Forum," *The Supreme Court Review*, 1965, Philip Kurland, editor;

Harry Kalven, Jr., "The Dignity of the Civil Jury," 50 University of Virginia Law Review, 1055 (1964);

Benjamin Kaplan, "Civil Procedure: Reflections on the Comparison of Systems," 9 University of Buffalo Law Review, 409 (1960);

ACKNOWLEDGMENTS

Friedrich Kessler, "Contracts of Adhesion—Some Thoughts on Freedom of Contract," 43 Columbia Law Review, 629 (1943);

Irving Konvitz and Theodore Leskes, *A Century of Civil Rights* (Irvington-on-Hudson, N. Y., Columbia University Press, 1961);

John H. Langbein and Lloyd L. Weinreib, "Continental Criminal Procedure: 'Myth and Reality' ", 87 Yale Law Journal 1549 (1978). (Reprinted by permission of the Yale Law Journal Company and Fred B. Rothman & Company).

Edward H. Levi, *An Introduction to Legal Reasoning* (Chicago, University of Chicago Press, 1949);

Karl N. Llewellyn, *The Bramble Bush* (New York, Oceana Publications, 1951);

Ian R. MacNeil, "A Primer of Contract Planning," 48 Southern California Law Review 627, (1975).

Stewart Macaulay, "Non-Contractual Relations in Business: A Preliminary Study," 28 American Sociological Review, 55 (1963);

Lewis Mayers, *The American Legal System*, rev. ed. (copyright © 1955, 1964 by Lewis Mayers; reprinted by permission of Harper & Row, Publishers);

Loren Miller, *The Petitioners* (copyright © 1966 by Loren Miller, reprinted by permission of Pantheon Books, a Division of Random House, Inc.);

Cornelius J. Peck, "The Equal Employment Opportunity Commission. Developments in the Administrative Process 1965–1975", 51 Washington Law Review 831 (1976).

Charles A. Reich, "Police Questioning of Law Abiding Citizens," 75 Yale Law Journal, 1161 (1965) (reprinted by permission of The Yale Law Journal Company and Fred B. Rothman & Company);

Charles B. Renfrew, "The Paper Label Sentences: An Evaluation", 86 Yale Law Journal 590 (1977). (Reprinted by permission of the Yale Law Journal Company and Fred B. Rothman & Company).

Maurice Rosenberg, *The Pretrial Conference and Effective Justice* (New York, Columbia University Press, 1964);

Walter V. Schaefer, *Precedent and Policy* (Chicago, University of Chicago Press, 1956);

Sir Hartley W. Shawcross, *The Function and Responsibilities of an Advocate* (New York, Association of the Bar of the City of New York, 1958);

ACKNOWLEDGMENTS

Harry Shulman, "Reason, Contract and Law in Labor Relations," 68 Harvard Law Review, 1002 (1955);

Jerome H. Skolnick, *Justice Without Trial: Law Enforcement in a Democratic Society* (copyright © 1966 by John Wiley & Sons, Inc., reprinted by permission);

Michael I. Sovern, *Legal Restraints on Racial Discrimination in Employment*, (copyright © 1966 by The Twentieth Century Fund, New York);

Richard E. Speidel, Robert S. Summers and James M. White, Jr., *Commercial and Consumer Law*, 2d ed., the West Publishing Company (1974).

Joseph N. Ulman, *A Judge Takes the Stand* (New York, Alfred A. Knopf, 1933);

E. Clement Vose, "NAACP Strategy in the Covenant Cases," 1955 Western Reserve Law Review, 101;

Arthur I. Waskow, *From Race Riot to Sit-in* (copyright © 1966 by Doubleday & Company, Inc.; reprinted by permission of the publisher);

Herbert Wechsler, "Toward Neutral Principles of Constitutional Law," 73 Harvard Law Review, 1 (1959);

John H. Wigmore, *A Student's Textbook of the Law of Evidence* (Chicago, The Foundation Press, Inc., 1935);

James Q. Wilson, *Varieties of Police Behavior* (Cambridge, Mass., Harvard University Press, 1968);

C. Vann Woodward, *The Strange Career of Jim Crow*, 2d rev. ed., (New York, N. Y., Oxford University Press, Inc., 1966);

Charles E. Wyzanski, Jr., "A Trial Judge's Freedom and Responsibility," 65 Harvard Law Review, 1281 (1952);

"Developments in the Law: Confessions," 79 Harvard Law Review, 935 (1966);

"Patent Licensing Will be U. S. Antitrust Target," *The New York Times*, Dec. 10, 1965 (© 1965 by the New York Times Company, reprinted by permission);

"Professional Responsibility: Report of the Joint Conference," 44 American Bar Association Journal, 1159 (1958);

"Revolution in Civil Rights," (Washington, D. C., Congressional Quarterly Service, 1966).

*

SUMMARY OF CONTENTS

SUMMARY OF CONTENTS

PART FOUR

DETAILED TABLE OF CONTENTS

PART THREE

Law as a Process of Protecting and Facilitating Voluntary Ar-
rangements: Illustrations from the Law of Contract

PART FOUR

*

NATURE AND FUNCTIONS
OF LAW

INTRODUCTION

The Study of Law as Part of
Liberal Education

Is law a proper subject of study outside of law schools?

An imposing array of distinguished men—most of them, to be sure, lawyers—have said that it is not only proper but very important that "every gentleman and scholar," as Blackstone put it in 1758, should have "a competent knowledge of the laws of that society in which we live." Such a knowledge, Blackstone added, is "an highly useful, I had said almost essential, part of liberal and polite education." [1]

The famous *Commentaries on the Laws of England* comprise Blackstone's lectures given at Oxford University not primarily to prospective lawyers but to students of the liberal arts. Their influence upon the thinking of generations of Englishmen and Americans, laymen as well as lawyers, is well known. Edmund Burke referred to their impact on the American colonists in his *Speech on Conciliation with America*.

> "In no country perhaps in the world," Burke said, "is the law so general a study. The profession itself is numerous and powerful, and in most provinces it takes the lead. The greater number of the deputies sent to the congress were lawyers. But all who read, and most do read, endeavor to obtain some smattering in that science. I have been told by an eminent bookseller, that in no branch of his business, after tracts of popular devotion, were so many books as those on the law exported to the plantations. The colonists have now fallen into the way of printing them for their own use. I hear that they have sold nearly as many of 'Blackstone's Commentaries' in America as in England. . . ." [2]

---

1. Sir William Blackstone, Discourse on the Study of Law; Being an Introductory Lecture Read in the Public Schools, October 25, 1758 (Oxford, 1758), p. 3.

2. Edmund Burke, Works (London, 1852), Vol. III, p. 256.

The colonists' zeal for the study of law, Burke stated, gave them a capacity to "snuff the approach of tyranny in every tainted breeze."

It was perhaps with Burke's words in mind that the distinguished Constitution framer and Supreme Court Justice James Wilson told the young men and women who attended his lectures in law at the college of Philadelphia in 1790–1791: "The science of law should, in some measure, and in some degree, be the study of every free citizen, and of every free man.   .   .   .   The knowledge of those rational principles on which the law is founded ought, especially in a free government, to be diffused over the whole community." [3]

Some three hundred years earlier Sir John Fortescue wrote the first English book expressly intended to teach a non-lawyer the basic elements of law. This work, *In Praise of the Laws of England*, written to instruct Prince Edward, the heir apparent, was designed as a one-year course in the English common law and constitution, including a description of the professional legal training of the time.

> "But sir," Fortescue argues to the reluctant prince, "how will you have righteousness and justice unless you first acquire a competent knowledge of the law by which justice is to be learned and known?" [4]

A similar plea, though in more modern terms, was made by Woodrow Wilson in 1894, in an important address entitled "Legal Education of Undergraduates." "We need laymen who understand the necessity for law and the right uses of it too well to be unduly impatient of its restraints," Wilson stated. The function of a college course in law, he said, is to teach the student "what law is, how it came into existence, what relation its form bears to its substance, and how it gives to society its fibre and strength and poise of frame." [5]

How has it happened that in spite of the influence of men like James Wilson and Woodrow Wilson, the study of law in the United States is for the most part a matter of postgraduate professional training?

The answer is in part a historical one. In the 14th and 15th centuries a secular class of lawyers emerged in England, and the law administered by the royal courts became independent, in some important respects at least, from Roman and Canon law. To a large extent English lawyers came to receive their training in the Inns of Court, at the hands of the legal profession itself, and not in the uni-

---

3. James Wilson, Lectures on Law (1790–1791), in Works (Phila., 1804), p. 9. Wilson states that law cannot exist without liberty, nor liberty without law, and therefore the science of law is the science of both.

4. Sir John Fortescue, In Praise of the Laws of England (1468–1470; 1537)

(transl. by Francis Gigor, London, 1917), Chapter V. The chapter is entitled, "Ignorance of the Law causes a Contempt Thereof."

5. Reports of the American Bar Association, Vol. 17, p. 439 (1894).

versities. In the sixteenth and seventeenth centuries, the English universities taught Roman and Canon law—in Latin—as bulwarks of royal and ecclesiastical power, while important segments of the legal profession took a leading part in the struggle against royal and ecclesiastical prerogatives.

Blackstone's appointment to the Vinerian chair of jurisprudence in 1758 marked the first effort to make English law a university subject. Blackstone thought it would help both would-be lawyers and educated people generally to have a "system of legal education" (as he called it) which would be far broader than the practical legal training offered in the Inns of Court. Blackstone may thus be considered the founder of the modern English system of university education in law.

In the United States Blackstone's influence took a different line of development. In the late eighteenth and early nineteenth centuries, general courses in law, chiefly modelled after his, were established in many American universities; however, these courses were in time superseded by the development of university law schools—a form of professional legal education which, strictly speaking, has no counterpart either in England or on the Continent of Europe.

The transition from university courses in law as part of the liberal arts curriculum to professional law schools for training young men and women for the bar was clearly marked in the inaugural lecture of Isaac Parker, Chief Justice of the Supreme Judicial Court of Massachusetts, as Royall Professor of Law in Harvard College, in 1815. Under the conditions of his appointment, Judge Parker was required to deliver fifteen lectures on law to college seniors and graduate students. He took the occasion of his inaugural lecture to propose that "a school for the instruction of resident graduates in jurisprudence" be "ingrafted on this professorship," stating that if students were to study in such a law school prior to entering into legal practice it would "tend greatly to improve the character of the Bar of our State." Under Parker's influence the Harvard Law School was founded in 1817. By 1850 there were fifteen law schools in the United States; by 1870 there were thirty-one; today there are more than 200.

Unquestionably the professional law school as it has developed in the United States has been an extremely important instrument for improving not only the character of the bar but also the quality of the legal system itself. Yet a price has been paid for this gain, in that to a large extent the study of law has become a professional monopoly, and general education in law for non-lawyers has been sacrificed. With the emergence of professional graduate schools of law it seems simply to have been taken for granted by many people that the nature of our legal system is a subject beyond the ken or the interest of the undergraduate and the non-specialist.

Today the need for law study in the undergraduate curriculum is most acutely felt, perhaps, by teachers in law schools, since they have the opportunity to observe the misinformation and ignorance regarding law which prevails among the college graduates who enter law school each year. From this they have inferred the state of understanding that prevails among college undergraduates generally. As our society has grown more urbanized and our law ways more complex, young people have had progressively fewer opportunities to learn about the workings of our legal system; at the same time the United States has become probably the most law-run and lawyer-run country in the history of mankind. In addition, the United States is one of the few civilized countries in which the study of law is not undertaken by a substantial proportion of undergraduates, regardless of their professional aspirations. The significance of this gap in our higher education is illuminated in a statement by the late president of Yale University, A. Whitney Griswold.

> "I think that law in the United States has suffered some retrogression of recent date . . . I do not think that the full meaning and value of law are communicated to society through the law's own formal processes . . . To be effective, the rule of law must be comprehended by society, not as an esoteric concept, but as a working principle comparable to regular elections and the secret ballot; and the plain fact is that it is not so comprehended. This, I think, is an educational deficiency . . .

> "The American people do not sufficiently understand the rule of law because it has never been properly explained to them. The legal profession has not succeeded in explaining it perhaps because it has been too busy with *ad hoc* issues and winning cases. The teaching profession has not succeeded in explaining it perhaps because it has not sensed its true importance. If the two great pillars of society, law and learning, are to stand, the professional representatives of each must come to the aid of the other . . ."

The reasons for law study in the undergraduate curriculum may be stated in the most elementary terms, therefore, of the need for overcoming sheer ignorance and misinformation on the part of otherwise educated people about a subject of the greatest political, economic and social importance. Not only our educational system but also our legal system suffers. To paraphrase Clemenceau—law is too important to be left to the lawyers.

Beyond this, the need for such study may be stated in terms of the following propositions, fuller elaboration of which is left to subsequent chapters:

a. An understanding of the nature of the legal order and of legal reasoning is of significant cultural value in itself.

b. An understanding of law is essential to an understanding of the political values of American society and of the international community, and it enriches not only political science but also other disciplines such as philosophy, history, economics, sociology, and anthropology.

c. The diffusion of an understanding of law to wider segments of the scholarly community can result in a greater illumination of legal science, as scholars of other disciplines come to give more attention to legal data.

d. The study of law can be an important means of developing the student's sense of justice and capacity for responsible judgment.[6]

Proper Purposes of Law Study by Students of the Arts and Sciences

To do the right thing for the wrong reasons is sometimes worse than doing nothing. Chief among the wrong reasons for studying law in the undergraduate curriculum is in order to acquire some "know-how" in the handling of legal affairs. The student who takes a course in law, or several such courses, is no better equipped to give legal advice than the student who takes a course or courses in biology is thereby better able to perform a surgical operation. Indeed, the only "practical" benefit, in the very narrow sense of that term, which a student might derive from a liberal arts course in law is a better awareness of the kinds of situations in which he or she ought to consult a lawyer, and a better understanding of the advice which a lawyer gives. In short, such a course might prepare the student to be a better client, but it cannot ever begin to make a lawyer of him or her.

This raises the more controversial question whether it is improper for a student to take a liberal arts course (or courses) in law in order to prepare for future professional legal training. Here experience indicates that to the extent that the liberal arts course attempts to teach law from the same viewpoint as the professional law school, the law student is generally not helped by having had it. Indeed a course which purports to prepare students for law school by giving them a little bit of law in advance will be a waste of time and may even be harmful. Nothing is more misleading *from a technical point of view* than "a little bit of law."

Although a liberal arts course in law will not help a person "get through" law school, it can nevertheless, if taught right, help provide a

6. These reasons are discussed at some length in Harold J. Berman, On the Teaching of Law in the Liberal Arts Curriculum (Brooklyn, N. Y., 1957). See also the following: Paul A. Freund, "Law and the Universities," Washington Univ. Law Quarterly, p. 367 (1953); Moffatt Hancock, "Teaching Law in the Liberal Arts Curriculum," Stanford Law Review, Vol. 7, p. 320 (1955); Brainerd Currie, "The Place of the Law in the Liberal Arts College," Journal of Legal Education, Vol. 5, p. 428 (1953).

foundation for law studies, just as courses in economics, or history, or language can help provide such a foundation. To dig a foundation one goes in the opposite direction from that in which one goes to erect the structure supported by the foundation. The undergraduate curriculum is a place to raise questions about legal history, legal philosophy, legal sociology—subjects to which, unfortunately, professional law schools still generally give insufficient attention. On the other hand, it is impossible fruitfully to study the role of law in society without knowing something about law in the technical sense, that is, about contracts or torts or civil and criminal procedure, or other fields— any more than it is possible fruitfully to study the history of music without knowing what a symphony or an opera or a string quartet sounds like. Thus prospective law students take the risks of a superficial treatment of some of the subjects they will learn more thoroughly later. If these risks are called to their attention not only once but often during the course, and if they are the kind of students who aspire to broader scholarship in law than law schools generally provide, they can profit by undergraduate law study. But they will not "do better" in law school as a result of it.

A third improper purpose of law study in the undergraduate curriculum is to "learn law." "Nobody knows any law," someone has said, "until he knows it all—and nobody knows it all." By "learning law," or "knowing law," people usually mean being able to recite legal rules. To seek in a liberal arts course a summary of the vast body of legal rules which are to be found in the statute books, the court reports, the blackletter treatises, and the host of other legal materials which make up a law library, is to seek that which is unattainable and which, if it were attained, would be useless.

Understanding the Legal Order as a
Vital Part of the Social Order

Law is not *essentially* a body of rules at all. Rules are an important part of the tools which law uses. But it is foolish to approach law in the first instance through one of the devices which it employs. The student of society, above all, should study law as a social institution. "If the Law of the State be seen as in first essence not a 'code' nor a body of Rules, but as in first essence a going institution," writes Llewellyn, "it opens itself at once to inquiry by the non-technician." [7]

Law is an institution in the sense of an integrated pattern or process of social behavior and ideas. What goes on inside courts, legislatures, law offices, and other places in which law-making, law-enforcing, law-administering, and law-interpreting is carried on, together with what goes on inside the minds of people thinking with

7. Karl N. Llewellyn, "The Normative,   Problem of Juristic Method," Yale
   the Legal, and the Law-Jobs: The   Law Journal, Vol. 49, p. 1355 (1940).

reference to what goes on in those places, forms a law way of acting and thinking, which overlaps but is not identical with economic, religious, political and other social ways of acting and thinking.

As soon as law is defined in terms of a set of actions and ideas, instead of in terms of a set of rules, it becomes possible to study its interrelationships with other types of patterned behavior and thought. Thus by a study of the part which law plays in the total social process, one may acquire fuller understanding both of law and of the nature of society itself.

To speak of law as a "social institution" and as a "way of acting and thinking" invites us to take a further step toward a definition by adding the conception of "order." *Law is a form of social order; legal order is one important way of holding a society together.* It is primarily for the sake of an understanding of legal order as a vital part of social order that law should be studied in the liberal arts curriculum.

The proposition has two aspects. First, legal order is a vital part of any social order. People cannot live together in society without law of some kind. There has never been a society without some type of legal order, however rudimentary. Second, the place of law in our society—that is, in the Western tradition of thought and action—is unique. The West has exalted law as a fundamental basis of unity in society. Belief in the existence of a "fundamental law," to which governments must adhere or risk overthrow as despotisms, has been characteristic of European thought at least since the eleventh century. This belief finds expression in the English concept of the Rule of Law as well as in the German idea of the *Rechtsstaat*, not to mention the American Constitutional requirement of due process of law. It is a belief which is challenged in modern times most strikingly by totalitarian systems, but also by some currents of democratic jurisprudence.

Not only in Western political life but also in Western social and economic life generally, law plays a role far greater than in other major cultures. The law of Western nations (and of some nations that have taken over Western law) reaches into virtually every aspect of social relations. In business, in family life, in recreation, in religious affairs, and in many other types of activities, legal concepts and legal rights and duties play a far more important part than Westerners themselves generally realize. "In the West," the 19th century Russian Slavophil Kireevsky wrote scornfully, "brothers make contracts with brothers." But whether the relatively high degree of "legalization" of Western life is viewed unfavorably or favorably, it is a fact.

The student is therefore invited to study law for the sake of understanding one of the foundations not only of our social order but of our whole set of values. Such a study involves an analysis of aspects of so-called "public law," including constitutional rights of the individual against arbitrary action by state officials, and also an analysis of so-called "private law" [8] concerning legal modes and standards of making private arrangements and settling private disputes. From this study it is hoped that some light will be shed on the ultimate inquiry regarding the relationship of law, as a process of ordering human affairs, to the conceptions of order and freedom fostered by our Western traditions.

Understanding Legal Science as a Vital Part of Social Science

If the first purpose of the study of law by a student of the arts and sciences should be to understand the nature of legal order and of legal processes of creating order, the second should be to understand the science of law, that is, the body of systematic knowledge about law, and to make that body of systematic knowledge part of his or her systematic knowledge about society as a whole. More concretely, it should be the student's aim to acquire an awareness of the principles which underlie legal processes, and thereby to enrich his or her awareness of the principles underlying political, economic, historical, psychological and other types of social and personal processes of thought and behavior.

In an elementary and concrete sense, an understanding of the nature and functions of law is essential to a proper understanding of many other disciplines. A student of economics or business administration, for example, must be somewhat at a loss to understand what a corporation is, or what property means, or how a collective bargaining agreement works, without any background in the legal system from which these concepts and institutions derive. Similarly, a sociologist who studies the writings of Max Weber or Emile Durkheim must feel the need for some knowledge of the legal institutions upon which they drew so heavily in developing their sociological theories; or, to take other examples, sociology of the family, or of the factory, or of public opinion, omits an essential part of its subject matter unless it deals with family law, or labor law, or legal control of communications. In political science, the need for some background of law study is obvious: one cannot comprehend, for example, the significance of the Bill of Rights of the Constitution unless one knows a good deal about criminal and civil court procedure. Likewise, the historian who knows no law must be at a loss to understand the role of Edward Coke in the development of parliamentary government in 17th century England, or the significance of the Napoleonic Codes in 19th century European history, or the problem of the reception of English common law in the United States—not to mention whole eras such as the Anglo-Saxon

8. The phrases "public law" and "private law" have no precise meaning. Here "public law" refers to branches of law by which governmental activities are regulated, and "private law" refers to branches of law by which relations between private individuals are regulated.

period of English history, our knowledge of which is derived principally from the legal monuments which they left.

Beyond supplementing the subject matter and research materials of other disciplines, the study of law can add new dimensions to the basic perspectives of those disciplines; it can enrich insights and improve theories which are now developed by scholars without reference to legal materials. This is true even in disciplines whose subject matter does not directly overlap law: to mention one example, a student of philosophy can profitably study legal reasoning and legal processes in order to get new insights into logic, into ethics, and into philosophical theories such as those of pragmatism and natural law. Indeed, it has been said that "the sparks of all sciences are raked up in the ashes of the law." That is because legal science overlaps all the traditional social sciences—just as the legal order overlaps all other types of social order.

To illustrate, let us examine briefly the contribution which law study can make to three social sciences—political science, economics, and sociology.

Law and political science. Reference has already been made to the importance which law study can have in enriching the non-lawyer's understanding of what the Rule of Law means in our society and of what the relation of the individual to the state is and ought to be. Civil rights and civil liberties, if they are not at bottom legal in nature, at least have an essential legal aspect. Indeed, in the American system of government virtually all problems have an essential legal aspect, in the most technical sense, insofar as political acts are controlled and tested in the courts. As Alexis de Tocqueville wrote, "Hardly any political question arises in the United States that is not resolved sooner or later into a judicial question."

The contribution which law study can make to political science is more, however, than a contribution of overlapping subject matter; it is a contribution of approach and of theory. To teach the structure and functions of government *together with* the law regulating private social relations (contract law, property law, corporation law, etc.) involves a recognition of the common denominators which link politics with the regulation of social life generally.

The link between public and private law [9] is apparent. The judges who decide the constitutionality of a statute are people who are grounded not only in constitutional law but also in the law of property, of contracts, and of other branches of private law. Most important of all, they are grounded in the law of judicial procedure, which gives a common foundation to all branches of substantive law. Indeed constitutional law applies to the political structure of society a framework of processes and norms similar in nature and function to the frame-

9. The difficulty of defining public and
private law is referred to *supra*, note 8.

work which so-called private law applies to diffuse social activities. The student of constitutional law who does not know what pleadings are, how the adversary system works, how to distinguish a dictum from a holding, to what extent judges are free and not free to make law, *et cetera,* will tend to misread Supreme Court opinions on constitutional issues as essays in political theory instead of treating them as explanations of judicial decisions of specific issues in dispute.

Though less apparent than the link between public law and private law, the link between law as a whole (including both aspects) and politics as a whole is equally real. In the first place, legal limitations upon political authority may be an essential factor in the making of a political decision. The process of weighing legal against political factors in making such a decision may itself be illuminated through an understanding of the relatively greater importance of political realities in the making of constitutional legal decisions as contrasted with decisions in the field of property law, or contracts, or commercial law. Further, the differences as well as the similarities between the mode of making political decisions and the mode of making judicial decisions are themselves illuminating.

Beyond this, one's philosophy of government cannot be divorced from one's philosophy of law. "Legal positivism," "legal realism," "natural-law theory," "historical jurisprudence"—are labels which have corresponding labels in political theory; and the legal theory may serve as a check, at least, upon the political theory, since legal theory refers generally to a more specific subject matter and can be tested more easily by cases. More important, apart from labels and formal theories, the study of law by undergraduate and graduate students of political science can influence their philosophy of government in several important ways. It can illuminate current political theories which focus upon "power" and upon "values," making clear the extent to which the institutional framework for formulation and implementation of policy itself influences policy and hence limits the power struggle, and, as Lon L. Fuller has put it, the extent to which the means adopted to allocate values define the values being allocated.[10] Further, the study of law can help political scientists to steer a course between the Scylla of irrationalism and the Charybdis of excessive rationalism, showing concretely the potentialities and limitations of human reason in resolving social conflict. In addition, the study of law can give a historical dimension to political theory, for law is an instrument not only for social change but also for social continuity; in our tradition, at least, the judge in deciding a case must—in Edmund Burke's phrase—look backward to his or her ancestry as well as forward to his or her posterity. Private law, especially, changes slowly over the centuries, showing a continuous development which

10. Quoted in Harold J. Berman, On the Teaching of Law in the Liberal Arts Curriculum (Brooklyn, N. Y., 1957), p. 50.

sometimes even survives the most violent political revolutions. Thus a theory of legal development helps political theory to give proper weight to the factor of tradition.

Finally, the science of law—in the sense of a systematized body of knowledge about law—has particular significance for the political science of international relations. The whole problem of bringing order out of the chaos of international relations involves a basic question of legal theory. As Carl B. Spaeth states: [11]

> "Both the advocates of limited world government, and the members of the 'old fashioned school of diplomacy' . . . have, in my view, completely misconceived the nature of law and legal order. Both groups have large followings among our people. The one group, the advocates of world government, go to one extreme in attributing much more potential to law and legal organization than we of the legal profession would claim for the institution even on the domestic scene. The other school, which would place major reliance on diplomacy, goes to the opposite extreme in asserting little or no role for law in the development of world community."

In other words, an appreciation of what kinds of international conflicts *can* be resolved by law, and what kinds *cannot*, involves an appreciation of the nature of law, and not only of the nature of international politics.

Law and economics. That law and economics interpenetrate each other is apparent, as has already been indicated, if only from the fact that much of the very vocabulary of economics (property, corporations, credit, taxation, patents, etc.) is essentially legal in nature. That this was once well understood is evident from a book such as Adam Smith's *Wealth of Nations,* which deals with economics and law as integral parts of the same subject. Although modern textbooks in economics often touch only briefly on legal problems, many economists are now coming once again to realize that to neglect the institutional processes through which economic forces operate and by which they are controlled is to adopt an excessively artificial and narrow approach.

In some areas of inquiry law and economics are especially interrelated, *e. g.,* antitrust law and industrial organization, tax law and public finance. More basically, however, law penetrates the very foundations of economics, for it is by means of legal institutions that prices are in fact agreed upon, wages in fact set, business organizations in fact formed, and so forth. A theory of perfect competition assumes the existence of a system of contract law; a theory of socialist economics assumes the existence of a system of administrative law; a theory of international trade assumes the existence of a system of international law, or at least the existence of nations as legal entities ("sovereigns"); and so on. As soon as

11. *Id.,* p. 51.

the theory is used to explain and test the realities, the legal assumptions which it makes require examination.

The foregoing is to say that a proper purpose of the study of law in the undergraduate curriculum is to acquire an understanding of those legal institutions which overlap economic institutions and hence must be understood in order fully to grasp economics as a social science. But beyond the question of understanding *legal institutions* for this purpose is the question of understanding *legal science*—for the same purpose. It is important to know, in order to improve one's understanding of various economic theories of competition, for example, not merely what the legal institution of a contract is, and what are the differences between a contract to sell a horse and a contract not to compete, but also various theories of contract expounded by legal scholars. It is important, not only because the legal theory affects the legal institution but also because the legal theory illuminates the economic theory. Theories with respect to the effects of various kinds of public controls upon freedom of contract are in and of themselves, under different names, theories of competition. Or to take another example, the theory of the legal nature of an "escalator clause" in a collective bargaining agreement can affect economic theory with respect to the relationship of wages and prices.

Law and sociology. More than perhaps any other social science, sociology can benefit from the infusion of legal materials and legal ideas, for the reason that law provides a practical synthesis of the same subject matter of which sociology offers a theoretical synthesis.

Until recently American sociologists (though not European sociologists) have for the most part given insufficient attention to law. They have been concerned largely with informal (so-called primary) groups (such as social classes, the family, gangs, the professions); with informal social relations (such as race relations, class relations, consequences of technological change upon social habits and attitudes); and with operational concepts (such as status, role, ideologies, values, integration, disorganization) which serve to explain informal behavior patterns and ideals as well as informal power relations. The study of law by sociologists can have tremendous value in confronting them a) with formal institutional processes whereby social order is achieved, coupled with b) a framework of theory explaining and justifying those formal processes.

Sociologists sometimes speak of the ethos of a culture—its orientation, its values, and the folkways and mores which incorporate them—and of its power structure, the coercive controls imposed on customary social relations. Law falls between the two—whether it is conceived as something which is imposed downwards by an omnipotent authority or whether it is conceived as something which grows upwards from the behavior patterns and ideal patterns of the culture. Legal institutions and legal science can provide, therefore a basis for testing social controls in terms of social values, and social values in terms of social controls.

Concretely, the sociologist who deals with the family or labor relations or the business firm or public opinion or political power— can find in the legal aspects of these subjects (such as marriage and divorce, collective bargaining, powers of directors, legal control of the press, constitutional restraints upon the executive) not only valuable legal materials for sociological analysis, but also valuable legal analysis. To give one example: legal literature analyzes the question whether the arbitrator of labor disputes under collective bargaining agreements better fulfills his or her function as peacemaker in the factory by confining himself to relatively narrow issues and adopting a relatively formal procedure or, on the contrary, by extending his or her jurisdiction relatively broadly and basing his or her decision explicitly on the needs of the plant in general rather than on the terms of the contract between union and management. Such analysis by lawyers is itself sociological in nature, and is a contribution to the sociology of labor relations.

Moreover, legal science—and not only legal institutions—has a particular value for sociologists in helping to correct a tendency to underestimate the exent to which men are free, in Lon L. Fuller's phrase, "to impose social relationships on themselves." Mr. Fuller states:[12]

> "(T)here is a particular kind of decision in which the lawyer participates where he sometimes, insofar as any human being can, controls the thing, and that is those decisions which impose a framework for future dealings. (That kind of decision is) most aptly illustrated in drafting articles of partnership or setting up a society and drafting a constitution for it.

> "That is a terribly difficult responsibility to discharge, for I think sociology very rightly emphasizes the influence of our social institutions on us, so that things we think we are deciding ourselves often are being decided for us by the institutions under which we live.

> "On the other hand, sociology tends to neglect the fact that people do impose these social relationships on themselves and that lawyers have a large responsibility in drafting these little constitutions, if you will, which have such a profound influence on human relations—a profound influence in part because they are often irreversible. An illustration of that can be found in the statutes creating the various administrative agencies, statutes which often involve an irreversible decision. Once an agency is set up, it becomes a vested interest, a going concern; one could name several agencies which would obviously not be set up today as they originally were, and yet it seems impossible to start over again."

12. *Id.*, p. 61.

The value of law study in the undergraduate curriculum for the development of legal science. It is implicit in the preceding treatment of the value of law study for students of other disciplines that legal scholarship, too, has much to gain from the teaching of law in the undergraduate curriculum. Social scientists and humanists who have learned to consider law as a subject of scholarly interest to themselves will inevitably contribute insights which will help lawyers to understand their own discipline. This is especially needed at a time when many law teachers are searching for new means of interpreting legal decisions, rules and procedures in terms of their social functions.

What is needed, above all, is a realization that underlying the many social sciences, including legal science, is one science of society. The over-compartmentalization of knowledge stunts intellectual growth, for it is at the frontiers of the various disciplines that they meet. The study of law can help to overcome excessive compartmentalization, first, because law as a social institution—that is, *legal order*—overlaps and coordinates virtually all aspects of social life, and second, because the principles which legal scholarship has developed to explain law—that is, *legal science*—interpenetrates all the various existing social disciplines. By combining the insights of legal science with political, economic, historical, sociological, psychological and other insights, an important step forward can be taken in the development of the single social science which all the disciplines are striving to realize.

Understanding Legal Reasoning as a Vital Part of Responsible Social Thought

The student who seeks to understand legal order as a type of social order, and legal science as a type of social science, should also seek to understand legal reasoning as a type of responsible social thought. By legal reasoning we mean the kind of reasoning which is implicit in legal processes and legal institutions (that is, in the legal order) rather than the kind of reasoning which is characteristic of legal scholarship. By responsible social thought we mean the kind of thinking—called "thinking" rather than "reasoning," since it is not necessarily as "reasoned," that is, as elaborated—which people in positions of social responsibility use to reach decisions requiring action.

Legal reasoning is a kind of reasoning which is adapted to the reaching of decisions for action. In this respect, it is like the kind of reasoning characteristic of engineering, medicine, business administration, or any other applied, or practical, art or science. It is a quite different kind of reasoning from that which is adapted to the establishment of general principles, characteristic of mathematics or physics or any other pure science. The pure scientist seeks—primarily—truth; the applied scientist seeks—primarily—right action.

The logic of action follows different laws from the logic of analysis. In reasoning toward a decision as to what action to take in a given situation, a person thinks in terms of the consequences of the alternatives which confront him or her, and tests his or her principles in terms of those consequences. The general principles are treated as guides to action. Reasoning adapted to decisions for action is, almost by definition, pragmatic. Pure analysis, on the other hand, is concerned with the validity of inferences, not with the validity of action. It seeks principles which can explain reality, not principles which can change reality.

Legal reasoning, as a kind of reasoning adapted to decisions for action, proceeds in terms of the application of principles to fact situations and of the testing of the application in terms of potential consequences. One difference between legal reasoning and most other types of such "active" reasoning is that in law there is a tendency to attempt to spell out each step in this ratiocination; moreover, in modern times under some systems of law the reasoning process is apt to be written down at length. In other words, the person responsible for the decision gives, in writing, an official explanation of how the decision was reached.

It is proper for students of the arts and sciences, through a study of the reasons offered for their decisions by judges and other "lawmen", to seek an understanding of the nature of responsible social thought in general. Whether or not students of the arts and sciences by such study can themselves acquire a better capacity for responsible judgment, the analysis of explicit reasons given for action decisions by the people who made them opens a new dimension of reality to those who hitherto have been exposed largely to analyses of what is usually called "scientific" reasoning. Judicial opinions, states Chester I. Barnard, provide "the only body of literature up to within the last 15 years that has had anything to do with the rationality of decisions for action." [13] "We tend to forget," states Philip H. Rhinelander, "that, as Immanuel Kant said, there is no rule for applying a rule . . . (In law) every general principle has got to be applied to concrete sets of facts and this involves a kind of judgment which is not involved in formulating the principles themselves." [14]

If the undergraduate or graduate student of the arts and sciences undertakes the study of law not in order to acquire legal know-how, or to prepare for law school, or to learn legal rules, but in order to discover the significance of the legal order as a part of the social order, the significance of legal science as a part of social science, and the significance of legal reasoning as a part of responsible social

13. *Id.*, p. 22.   14. *Id.*, p. 24.

thought, he or she cannot fail to be a better educated person, a better social scientist, and a better thinker, at the end of such a study than he or she was at the beginning.

What is Law?

Purposes of a definition. The German philosopher Immanuel Kant chided lawyers with the fact that although for centuries they had been searching for a definition of the subject matter of their profession, they still were unable to agree upon one. Kant proceeded to construct his own definition of law—which, however, has found no more universal acceptance than the others that have been offered before or since.

It may be asked, Why bother with a definition at all? May we not simply assume that the meaning of the term "law" will become clear to the student as he studies "legal" materials? This indeed is the assumption made in most American law schools today, where the question, "What is law?" is usually left to be considered in a course labeled Jurisprudence, which is generally an elective course chosen by only a small proportion of the student body. The professional law student tends to define law subconsciously as what law professors teach, just as the professional lawyers tend to define law subconsciously as what they practice, what courts and legislatures do, *et cetera.*

Lawyers are not necessarily handicapped—indeed they may sometimes be aided—by the lack of an articulated definition of law. By immersing themselves in the tradition of their profession, they may acquire a sound feeling of what law is, just as a musician may acquire a sound feeling of what music is though he or she may be unable to put it in words. The tradition of law teaching and law practice embodies concepts which tend to become part of the lawyer's intellectual heritage even though they are not definitely formulated. But the students who approach law from the outside, as social scientists, and who are unwilling to immerse themselves in the legal tradition without critical analysis of that tradition, must have some sort of definition of law simply in order to know where to begin their study. A definition, that is, a hypothesis as to the essential nature of the thing defined, is a starting-point for investigation. Without a concept of what law is—however tentative—there is no assurance that the particular aspect of the subject being studied at a given time has any special importance, or even relevance, to the ultimate inquiry.

A definition may also be a finishing-point for investigation. That, of course, is its danger. It may remove from focus some areas which otherwise, by a process of free association of ideas, would come into the picture, and which in fact ought to come into the picture.

The limiting effects of a definition are especially harmful to the professional lawyer, to whose practice nothing human should be alien. The professional lawyer should not be inhibited from making any investigation, or from thinking any thought, by a definition of law which categorically excludes certain materials or certain ideas as "non-legal." For the social scientist, on the other hand, it is essential that the area of the legal be marked off from the area of the political, the economic, the moral, the customary, and so forth, so that the interrelationships of these various aspects of social life may be explained. Thus a statement of what law is can help to put law in focus not only by providing a starting-point for investigation but also by setting boundaries to the investigation.

Finally, it is important to define law in order to establish proper methods of studying law. Since different methods of study are appropriate to different subjects, one cannot determine the appropriate (the "scientific") method of studying a particular subject unless one also determines the nature of that subject. Thus if law, as some influential writers have said, is essentially a body of rules related to each other by logical consistency, then an appropriate technique for its study is that of conceptual analysis, that is, comparison of word with word, concept with concept, according to stated criteria of reasoning. If, on the other hand, to take another definition, law is essentially an instrument of political control, then an appropriate technique for its study is that of political analysis, that is, a comparison of the political consequences of alternative legal rules or legal institutions. Other definitions suggest other modes of analysis.

A definition, then, helps to provide a starting-point for investigation, boundaries of investigation, and a method of analysis.

Difficulties of defining law. The fact that law is a social institution of great complexity, with many different aspects, which varies in its nature in different societies and in different stages of historical development, places difficulties in the way of a definition. Yet complexity is not in itself a decisive obstacle to definition, especially if by "definition" we mean simply a hypothesis as to the nature of the thing defined. "Society" is more complex than "law," yet it is susceptible to definition. "Wealth" is a thing of many aspects, which varies in nature and function from society to society, but it is nonetheless definable.

However, "law" differs from "society," or "wealth," in that it is not a word invented by scholars to explain certain facts of life; it is, rather, a name—a name given by people to something which they believe in. Like "Christianity," or "democracy," "law" is a word charged with emotion, a "fighting" word. People have gone to war because "law" was violated. If confusion is to be avoided, the scholar's definition of law must correspond *in some degree* to the thing to which people give the name law.

Moreover, an additional source of difficulty lies in the existence of authoritative definitions of law declared by official law-making and law-interpreting bodies—legislatures, courts, and the like. Practically speaking, law is not what the scholars say it is but what the judges (and other officials charged with the responsibility of declaring it) say it is. If confusion is to be avoided, the scholar's definition of law must correspond *in some degree* to the thing to which such officials give the name law.

Thus any scholarly analysis of the nature of law must reckon both with popular conceptions and with authoritative declarations of what law is. Yet such conceptions and declarations cannot simply be adopted outright as scientific formulae. For one thing, there are inconsistencies both in the popular conceptions and in the authoritative declarations, as well as between the two. In addition, the scholar, by examining law in various societies and over long periods of time, and by studying the interrelationships between law and other aspects of social life, can contribute new insights into the nature of law and can thereby enrich and refine both the popular and the official definitions. In other words, a scholarly, or scientific, definition of law must be accepted as having a value, just as the popular and the official definitions have value.

Traditional concepts of law. Although law has been defined in hundreds of different ways, three general types of concepts have predominated. One type of concept emphasizes the relationship between law and moral justice; it sees both the ultimate origin of law and the ultimate sanction of law in "right reason." A second type of concept emphasizes the relationship between law and political power; it sees both the ultimate origin of law and the ultimate sanction of law in "the will of the state." A third type of concept emphasizes the relationship between law and the total historical development of the community; it sees both the ultimate origin of law and the ultimate sanction of law in "tradition," "custom" and "national character."

These types of concepts, and the social philosophies which they manifest, have vied with each other for ascendancy throughout the history of civilization, and continue to do so today. Nevertheless in different periods of Western legal development particular stress has been laid on one or another of these concepts; they are not to be understood in isolation from the total social and historical context from which they derive.

Thus in the formative era of the development of Western legal systems, from the 11th through the 15th centuries, most concepts of law centered around its relationship to moral justice and right reason. Building on the 6th century Byzantine Emperor Justinian's definitions of law as "a theory of right and wrong" (*iusti atque iniusti scientia*) and "an art of the good and the equitable" (*ars boni et aequi*), and also on Aristotle's concept of law as "reason unaffected by desire" (that is, by the passions of the individual), jurists and theologians of medieval Christendom developed the theory that human law is based on the law of human nature, which in turn reflects divine law. Because "natural law" forbids unjustified killing, commands compensation for harm caused by wrongful acts, and so forth, therefore man, in order to realize natural justice, elaborates, by the exercise of reason, rules as to when homicide is justified, what kinds of acts are wrongful, and so forth. Thus St. Thomas Aquinas defined law as "nothing else than an ordinance of reason for the common good, made and promulgated by him who has care of the community" (*Summa Theologica*, Part II, First Part, Question 90).

The belief that law is founded essentially on right reason did not go unchallenged, however, even in the Catholic Middle Ages. In 1345 in a case reported in the English Year Books—which were notes on cases tried in the royal courts—the following interchange took place:

> "Hillary, J. Plaintiff, will you say anything else . . . ?
> "R. Thorpe (who was lawyer for the plaintiff) . . .
> I think you will do as others have done in the same (kind of) case,
> or else we do not know what the law is.
> "Hillary, J. It is the will of the Justices.
> "Stonore, C. J. No; law is that which is right." [15]

Thorpe takes a characteristically professional view of "what the law is." To the lawyer whose job it is to advise and represent clients, law is apt to appear as what the courts (or other officials with power of decision) do in particular cases. Five-and-one-half centuries after Thorpe, Oliver Wendell Holmes, Jr., then not yet a justice of the Supreme Court of the United States, wrote, "The prophecies of what the courts will do in fact, and nothing more pretentious, are what I mean by law." [16]

Justice Hillary's definition, on the other hand, recalls the statement of Chief Justice of the United States Charles Evans Hughes, Jr., who shocked some people (though he was only restating in a blunt form the orthodox American constitutional doctrine of judicial supremacy) by writing that "The Constitution is what the judges say it is." To define law as the will of the justices, or what the judges say it is, suggests that what the courts will in fact do may differ from lawyers' or others' prophecies of what they will do based on past experience. Holmes's definition is, after all, an impossible one for

---

15. Langbridge's Case. Common Bench, 1345. Year Book 19 Edw. III 375. The report is in Law French, the official legal language of the time. The initial J. stands for Justice; C. J. for Chief Justice. The Chief Justice says: "Nanyl; ley est resoun." "Resoun" can also be translated "reason," but "what is right" expresses the meaning better.

16. "The Path of the Law," Harvard Law Review, Vol. 10, p. 461 (1897).

judges to adopt as a guide to their own decisions in cases, since it would place them in the position of predicting their own conduct. Thus while Thorpe urges the court to decide on the basis of what it had done in similar cases in the past, Hillary says, in effect, "We are not bound by what we did in the past; we can decide on any basis we please." [17]   The Chief Justice corrects both men in terms of a law of nature, saying, in effect, "It is true that we are not bound by past decisions, but neither can we decide the case on any basis we please. We must decide on the basis of what is right, on the basis of natural justice."

"Natural law theory"—the view that law has its origin and its ultimate sanction in the nature of man as a moral and rational creature—stresses the moral and rational elements in legal processes and in legal solutions to social problems. In contrast, "positivism"—the view that law has its origin and its sanction in the will of officials and ultimately of the state—stresses the political elements in law, and especially the political authoritativeness of legal rules. With the rise of the secular national state in the 16th century, positivist definitions of law came to the fore and by the end of the 19th century came to predominate. "Law properly is the word of him, that by right hath command over others," wrote Thomas Hobbes.[18] "Law is a command proceeding from the supreme political authority of a State, and addressed to the persons who are subjects of that authority," wrote a leading English jurist in the early twentieth century.[19] A statement of the circumstances under which the public force will be brought to bear on persons through the courts—is another definition of law by Holmes, in which the element of politics is put in the forefront.[20]

The "imperative theory of law"—that law is essentially a general command of the highest political authority, backed by coercive sanctions—has usually been associated with the theory that law is distinct from morals, and that the law as it ought to be should not affect the *interpretation* of the law as it is. It is not argued by adherents of this view that moral principles do not play a part in bringing into being the law as it is, or in changing it; but at any given moment, they state, the existing law is analytically separate from any moral ideas of what that law should be. In that sense, law is morally neutral; it is essentially a body of technical rules and concepts to be analyzed. Hence the name "analytical jurisprudence" is often given to this school, as contrasted with the "philosophical school" which adheres to natural-law theory.

17. The legal doctrine that courts are bound by their decisions in previous cases did not develop until centuries later. See *infra*, p. 586 ff.

18. Thomas Hobbes, Leviathan, or the matter, forme, and power of a commonwealth, ecclesiasticall and civill (Cambridge, England, 1935 ed.), p. 109.

Note that in the sentence quoted the phrase "by right" begs the question.

19. Sheldon Amos, The Science of Law (London, 1909), p. 48.

20. Cf. "The Path of the Law," *supra* note 16.

A third type of concept of law finds its origin and its sanction neither in reason and morals nor in political power but in the traditions, customs and character of the community. The so-called historical school of jurisprudence views law as having an organic connection with the mind and spirit of the people. Law "is developed first by custom and popular faith," wrote Savigny, "and only then by juristic activity—everywhere, therefore, by internal silently operating powers, not by the arbitrary will of the lawgiver." [21] As a people become more mature and complex, their law loses some of its simplicity and its symbolism and becomes more abstract, more technical. Hence it is a mistake to view law either as a body of ideal or "natural" propositions, or as a system of rules promulgated by the state; law is, rather, a particular expression of the common consciousness of a people at a given time and place.

Other adherents of the historical school went beyond the concept of the consciousness of the people, and sought to link the history of law with the social history of man conceived as an evolution from the primitive family group to the modern territorial state. Thus in the view of Sir Henry Maine, law has developed in all societies by certain stages, and its growth has followed certain patterns.[22] By law, then, Maine meant a whole complex of ideas, institutions and techniques seen as a developing system. By adding a historical dimension to the concept of law, the historical school of jurisprudence challenged the analytical and philosophical schools to broaden their definitions of law. At the same time historical jurisprudence laid the foundations for later sociological theories of law.

The foregoing sketch by no means lists all the various concepts of law of the various schools of legal philosophy; yet virtually all other concepts bear close enough affinity to natural-law theory, positivism, or historical jurisprudence to be considered as variations of one or more of them. Thus so-called "sociological jurisprudence," which developed at the end of the 19th and in the early 20th centuries, is an offspring of positivism and historical jurisprudence which seeks to interpret the rules of law of a given society as a balancing of various kinds of interests. Each legal decision is thus seen as the result of the weighing of the social consequences of alternatives. Indeed, "sociological jurisprudence" is not a systematic theory of law but rather a classification of interests for the guidance of those who make and interpret law. Adherents of this school oppose the wooden application of rules according to the internal logic of their concepts, and urge their application according to their social functions.[23]

21. Friedrich Karl von Savigny, Of the Vocation of Our Age for Legislation and Jurisprudence (transl. by Hayward, London, 1831).

22. See generally Sir Henry Maine, Ancient Law: Its Connection with the Early History of Society and Its Relation to Modern Ideas, with Sir Frederick Pollock's notes (London, 1906).

23. Cf. Roscoe Pound, Interpretations of Legal History (Cambridge, Mass., 1946), p. 141 ff.

Special mention should also be made of the so-called "legal realist" movement which obsessed much of American legal thinking in the 1920s and 1930s. The "legal realists" built on positivism in rejecting reason and nature as foundations of law, but departed from traditional positivism—as well as from "sociological jurisprudence" —in viewing legal realities not in terms of rules at all, but in terms of behavior, especially official behavior. "What these officials [judges, sheriffs, clerks, jailers, lawyers, *etc.*] do about disputes is, to my mind, the law itself," wrote Llewellyn, then a prominent spokesman of "realist" jurisprudence, in 1930. In searching for the underlying factors which determine official behavior various adherents of this approach turned to psychological factors, economic factors, ideological factors, and others.[24]

Criticism of traditional concepts of law. It should be apparent that each of the three principal types of concepts of law which have thus far been considered makes an important contribution to an understanding of law, and that at the time and by the same token each taken separately is open to criticism.

The positivist theory, by focusing on the political element in law, the element of legal force, tends to exclude from consideration important areas and aspects of law such as international law (which exists despite the absence of an international sovereign), ecclesiastical law (which has its origin and sanction in tradition and in the inner order of the church), and the law of primitive societies (in which the state does not exist and political authority is diffuse). Moreover, and more important, in every society people may and often do enter into legal relations with each other without reference to political commands or external sanctions. Thus, for example, when a boy agrees to mow a man's lawn for five dollars, the conduct of both may be strongly influenced by their sense of the legal character of the obligations incurred, but neither is necessarily conscious of any specific rules of law which, according to the positivist, govern the transaction, and neither would seek a legal sanction against the other. Many other examples could be given of obligations and rights which are *felt* to be legal

24. Cf. Karl N. Llewellyn, The Bramble Bush (New York, 1930, 1951), Chapter I. The literature on the various schools of legal thought indicated in the foregoing discussion is vast. Ample bibliographical references may be found in Julius Stone, The Province and Function of Law (London, 1947). In addition to the works cited in the preceding footnotes the following are valuable introductions: On natural law, A. P. d'Entrèves, Natural Law: An Introduction to Legal Philosophy (London, 1951); on historical jurisprudence, Sir Paul Vinogradoff, Outlines of Historical Jurisprudence (London, 1920–22); on positivism, John Austin, Lectures on Jurisprudence (3rd ed., London, 1869); on sociological jurisprudence, Roscoe Pound, Social Control Through Law (New Haven, 1942); on legal realism, Jerome Frank, Law and the Modern Mind (New York, 1930). See also H. L. A. Hart, The Concept of Law (Oxford, 1961) and L. L. Fuller, The Morality of Law (New Haven, 1965).

though they are outside the realm of "public force" or enforceability by the state.

All In A Lifetime   What To Do?

Drawing by Frank Beck.
Copyright, 1948. Published with permission of the
McNaught Syndicate, Inc.

If one considers the other side of positivist theory, its strict separation of law and morality, one faces the difficulty of interpreting legal principles which are explicitly derived from moral conceptions— the principle, for example, that a fair hearing requires that the accused be confronted by his accusers and that he have the right to interrogate them—independently of the morality inherent in the principles. If one asks what the principle *as it is* really means—whether, for example, it extends to a case in which the government for reasons of internal security does not wish to reveal the sources of its information—one is unavoidably led into a discussion of the purpose of the principle, what it *ought* to accomplish.

The English language is more amenable to a positivist theory than most languages, inasmuch as it uses the same word to refer to the legal order or system of justice, Law with a capital *L*, so to speak (*droit* in French, *Recht* in German, *pravo* in Russian, *jus* in Latin), on the one hand, and particular legal rules or standards (*loi*, *Gesetz*, *zakon, lex*), on the other. "We have washed our terminology in cynical acid," wrote Holmes. "Yet the ethical element is there," Pound comments, "not in the terminology, indeed, but in the body of authoritative materials, in the form of a definite body of received ideals, as well established and quite efficacious in the results in judicial decisions as in the precepts. 'Taught law,' said Maitland, 'is tough law.' This body of ideals, handed down in the law books, read by students and taught consciously or unconsciously by law teachers, as part of the fundamenta of legal thinking, is much more long lived than particular rules of law, and the ideals are much more far-reaching in their effects."[25]

It is largely because of the necessity of recognizing the importance of ideals in law—a necessity deriving in part from the assault upon legal ideals inflicted by totalitarianism and from the national effort to re-formulate those ideals especially during World War II—that the version of positivism called "legal realism" has by and large lost its hold as a fighting philosophy, though it continues to exert considerable influence. In 1951 Llewellyn stated that his oft-repeated definition (quoted above) of law as "what officials do about disputes" is "at best a very partial statement of the whole truth. For it is clear that one office of law is to control officials in some part, and to guide them even in places where no thoroughgoing control is possible, or is desired." (The Bramble Bush, 1951 ed., p. 9).[26]

"They ain't strikes, they ain't balls, they ain't nothin'," said a well known baseball umpire, "until I call 'em." But how does he know what to call 'em?

Natural-law theory, on the other hand, by focusing on the elements of reason and morality in law, tends to obscure the fact that unreasonable and unjust laws which do not conform to the "body of received ideals," may be present in a legal system—may be imposed, for example, by a tyrant, or a conqueror. To say, as many adherents of a natural-law theory do, that such laws are really not laws at all, and that only *just* law is law, seems to distort language; also it tends to remove from the scrutiny of legal theory those aspects of social control in which irrational and arbitrary goals are imposed through legal processes. Laws which condemn whole races or whole classes to destruction, or which impose ex post facto punishments for acts which were both morally just and legally justifiable when performed, do indeed violate basic principles upon which law itself is founded. To say, however, that therefore they are not laws only renders it neces-

25. Roscoe Pound, "Hierarchy of Sources and Forms in Different Systems of Law," Tulane Law Review, Vol. 7, pp. 475, 477 (1933).

26. In The Common Law Tradition: Deciding Appeals, (Boston, 1960), published shortly before he died, Professor Llewellyn attempted a systematic reconciliation of the ideas of the legal realists with the need for predictability in judicial decisions. The book is a fascinating study of the judicial process in America.

sary to invent new terminology to distinguish injustice accomplished by statutes, administrative procedures and regulations, adjudication, and other "legal" institutions from injustice accomplished by other means.

Another difficulty which plagues natural-law theory is that of finding middle terms between broad principles of equality, justice, and the like, and particular decisions or rules. One may invoke the same moral considerations, often, to reach opposite results, and where different moral considerations conflict with each other it is sometimes difficult or impossible to devise tests to determine which should prevail.

Finally, theories which derive law from the national character or common consciousness of a people, or see it as a product of historical evolution, tend to make the area of the legal so wide that it becomes impossible to encompass it, or indeed to know where to begin to analyze it. Undoubtedly a community's law reflects its values and develops out of its entire life in time and space. But there is a danger that the distinctive legal elements of a legal system will be lost in an approach which fuses law with social history. The more cautious adherents of the historical school of jurisprudence, therefore, have tended more and more to become simply historians of law. The more ambitious have tended to develop broad theories which make law virtually coextensive with regulation of any kind and, indeed, with the entire social order. Thus Eugen Ehrlich's concept of "living law" as the factual usages which determine the functions of people within the family, the local community, the church, the factory, and other associations, including the state,[27] has been termed by C. K. Allen an example of "megalomaniac jurisprudence." "Experience has shown again and again," writes Allen, "that knowledge of everything usually ends in wisdom in nothing. Jurisprudence may well be regarded as a 'social science,' but it cannot hope to be the compendium of all the social sciences."[28]

A Functional Approach to Law

Once one juxtaposes the three schools of jurisprudence which have been described, it becomes apparent that what is needed is not a choice of one to the exclusion of the others but rather a synthesis which will build on what is valid in all three. The legal aspect of social order must be approached partly in terms of the particular moral principles which it embodies, partly in terms of the particular political authorities which shape it, and partly in terms of the particu-

27. See Eugen Ehrlich, Fundamental Principles of the Sociology of Law (transl. by Moll, Cambridge, Mass., 1936). Ehrlich wrote elsewhere that law "is in reality the political, social and economic organization of mankind."

28. Carleton K. Allen, Law in the Making (Oxford, 1935), p. 35.

lar historical experience and values which it expresses. Indeed, these are not three things but one thing viewed from three different angles.

A synthesis may be achieved, and the nature of law more fully clarified, if the distinctive features of law are sought not in its *origins* and *sanctions* but in its *functions*.

We have stressed earlier that law is a social institution, that is, an integrated pattern or process of behavior and ideas, which helps to restore, maintain and create social order.[29] The fact that law helps to give order to social life does not, of course, distinguish it from other social institutions. The factory, the market, the state, the family, the church, the school, the club—these too, each in its own fashion, are integrated ways of acting and thinking which contribute to the resolution, prevention and control of social disorder. But we can best understand law, it is submitted, if we consider it primarily as one of the order-creating, or ordering, processes, and compare it, from that point of view, with other ordering processes.[30]

If we consider the various kinds of threats to social order, and the various kinds of ways in which such threats are met in a given society, we can distinguish between kinds of disorder (or potential disorder) which call forth relatively spontaneous, speedy and unformulated social responses, on the one hand, and kinds of disorder which call forth relatively deliberate, time-consuming, and articulately defined social responses. Moreover, the latter kind of response tends to be public and objective, while the former tends to be more intimate and more personal.

If a guest spills the gravy, the good hostess may quickly divert attention; if a husband and wife quarrel they may stop speaking to each other for a time; if a man has a political enemy or a business rival he may seek secretly to undermine his reputation. These kinds of activity are part of the folkways (patterns of social behavior) and *mores* (norms of social behavior) of a given society, which include habit, convention, public opinion, tradition, and other *informal* social controls.

If, on the other hand, a *legal* solution is sought to the problems that arise from breaches of etiquette or other disruptions of the patterns or norms of social behavior, then *time* must be taken for *deliberate* action, for *articulate definition* of the issues, for a decision which is subject to *public* scrutiny and which is *objective* in the sense that it reflects an explicit community judgment and not merely an explicitly personal judgment. These qualities of legal activity may be summed up in the word *formality;* formality, in this particular sense, inheres in all kinds of legal activity, whether it be the making of laws

29. *Supra*, pp. 6–8.

30. The word "process" suggests a more mobile institutional form than does the word "pattern," a series of consecutive steps rather than a web or network.

(legislation), the issuing of regulations under law (administration), the applying of laws to disputes (adjudication), or the making of private arrangements intended to be legally binding (negotiation of a contract, drawing of a will, etc.).

Legal activity is also distinguished by some of the above-mentioned characteristics from the use of force. "Lynch law" is not law, under this definition, because it is too spontaneous, too violent, too inarticulate. A war may be legal, under rules of international law, but war is not a law-way of settling disputes. The secret administrative trial of persons charged with being "socially dangerous"—as authorized by a Soviet statute of 1934 reportedly repealed in 1953—is an example of a mixed legal-nonlegal form; an accusation was framed and presented to a group of officials who passed on it—to this extent legal formality was maintained—but the secrecy of the proceeding, the absence of opportunity of the accused to be heard, the vagueness of the offense charged, and the surrounding atmosphere of political terror, were elements which rendered the entire process a caricature of legal forms.

As part of its formality, in the sense in which that term is here used, the law way of ordering human affairs is characterized by a drive toward generality. In mature legal systems, at least, the first step in the legal solution of a social problem is explicitly to define the problem, that is, to put it in some general category. The persons who are the subject of regulation are treated as members of a general class, and the standards applied to them are general standards. The tendency toward generality, in this sense, is inherent in the objectivity of law, the fact that it reflects an explicit community judgment. Even the ancient Greek oracle, with its charismatic quality of divine ad hoc decision, was considered to reflect a hidden consistency.

Such use of the terms "law" and "legal" stresses the element of institution and the element of process, rather than the element of rules. It is not denied that rules are an important device of legal institutions and legal processes, an important technique by which law operates. But the rules, or propositions of law, must be understood as a part, only, of the patterns of interactions among the participants involved in any legal activity. Law essentially is something that is done; it is a series of steps taken. Procedure is the heart of the law— without procedure there is no possibility of the existence of law.

Law, then, is something that is done when things go wrong. Implicit in this usage is the concept that the way a society is organized and the way it functions normally is to be distinguished from the way it responds to challenge, to crisis, to disruption of the normal organization; and that law is invented to deal with actual or potential disruptions of patterns or norms of social behavior. The characteristics which we have assigned to it—its deliberateness, its expensiveness in time, its articulateness, its publicity, its objectivity, its generality—

make it suitable as a solution for some, but not all, such disruptions. Others are resolved by more informal processes, whether of friendship or of force. Law is thus seen as a special kind of ordering process, a special type of process of restoring, maintaining or creating social order—a type of ordering which is primarily neither the way of friendship nor the way of force but something in between.

Such a definition of law focuses primarily on the nature of the legal response to social problems, rather than on its origin and its sanctions. Law may be imposed downward by omnipotent authority, or it may grow upward from tradition and the ethos of the culture, or it may grow outward, so to speak, from reason. Indeed, it probably must have its origin and its sanction in one or more of these aspects of the social order. But what makes it law, as distinct from other social institutions and processes, is its formality—in the sense of that word specified above. It is the formality of legal processes which makes legal relations a special and unique type of social relations, distinct from informal (that is, undefined, spontaneous, intimate) relations.

To see law as a particular kind of institutional process is to lay the foundation for an analysis of the social functions of legal activity and legal relations. Before stating some of the social functions of law, however, it is important that the concept of social function be itself analyzed briefly.

By a social function of law is meant a tendency of law to contribute to the maintenance of social order.

We take the term *function* from the biological sciences, where it is used to refer to the "vital or organic processes considered in the respects in which they contribute to the maintenance of the organism," rather than from the mathematical sciences or from the various popular usages.[31] The analogy between biological and social functions requires clarification, however, at two principal points.

First, in law—in contrast to biology—a distinction must be made between those consequences upon the social order which are intended, those which are anticipated but unintended, and those which are unanticipated. We may say, for example, that it is an intended consequence of criminal procedure that it reduces the risk of blood feud and other forms of private vengeance—in the sense that it is the purpose of legislators, judges, and the public generally in creating and maintaining criminal procedure to achieve this consequence. There is not only a tendency of criminal procedure to produce the consequences indicated, but in a loose sense it is a purpose of criminal procedure (more strictly, of the people responsible for criminal procedure) to produce them. One might also say it is a "purpose" of the heart to aid in the circulation of blood, but clearly the heart and its processes are

31. *Cf.* R. K. Merton, Social Theory and Social Structure (Glencoe, Illinois, 1957), pp. 20–21.

related to the bodily organism in an entirely different sense from that in which a court and its processes are related to the social order. The heart is not conscious of the part it plays.

The importance of conscious purposiveness in human activity has led some writers to avoid the term "function" in dealing with legal and other social institutions. Nevertheless, we prefer to speak of the functions of law, including those which are exercised purposively, rather than of its purposes only, for the principal reason that some of the most important consequences of law are not intended or even anticipated; yet they are characteristic consequences, resulting from important tendencies of the legal system. Also the term "purpose" suggests the deliberate creation of particular results. Thus one would not say that it is a *purpose* of the jury method of trial to nullify certain rules of law which violate popular conceptions of justice, though such nullification is an anticipated consequence; yet surely this is a *function* of the jury system. In the case of the tendency of law to produce consequences which are not only unintended but also unanticipated, as, for example, the development of a class of specialists from whom political leaders may be chosen, the use of the term "purpose" seems entirely inappropriate, while the use of the term "function" is valid if one believes the consequences are characteristic and flow in fact from an important tendency. (Thus one would *not* say that it is a function of the jury trial to provide diversion for jurors from their usual occupations—though in times past, at least, it was one of its functions to provide a kind of social drama for the community as a whole.)

We use the expression "social functions of law," then, to include the purposes of law as well as its important tendencies to produce unintended consequences.

A second qualification of the analogy between social and biological functions stems from our definition of a social function as a tendency to contribute to the maintenance of *social order*—conceived as an integrated and harmonious process of interaction among the various parts of the society. By no means all the characteristic consequences of law are "functional" in that sense. The same qualities which make criminal procedure, to take the same example, a relatively satisfactory means of appeasing and controlling feelings of private vengeance also make it time-consuming and hence expensive—so expensive, indeed, that a person charged with crime may be unable to afford to retain good defense counsel and to pay for the expenses of preparing the case. Law has, indeed, many qualities or tendencies which contribute to social disorder, to disintegration, and to discontinuity. To determine what are social functions of law and what are social "dysfunctions" (to use Merton's term) requires an evaluation of what consequences are socially beneficial and what are socially detrimental. It is beyond the scope of such a volume as this to state the criteria by which such an evaluation can be made. It must be said, however, that the use of a functional analysis does not presuppose that society is an organism in the biological sense or that social order and social disorder may be tested by the same kind of criteria and methods with which bodily health and bodily disease can be tested.

By focusing attention primarily on the procedural side of law, that is, its "action" side, rather than on the substantive propositions or rules respecting rights and duties, and, secondly, by viewing legal procedures as a set of institutional ways of acting, established by society as a means of ordering social relations, we are able more easily to identify the social functions which law serves. If we were to focus attention instead on the substantive legal rules we should be led into almost every conceivable aspect of social relations, and we should find ourselves involved in the paradoxical task of formulating the social functions of society itself. For substantive legal rules embrace—in our society, at least—most aspects of social life. Not only business arrangements and political organization but family life, entertainment, and even the most informal and customary social activities, may be viewed under the aspect of some legal rule or other. To buy a package of cigarettes is to enter into the legal transaction of purchase and sale. To hold a girl's hand is to exercise a legal privilege, if she consents— and to commit a tort[32] if she doesn't. If one were to study the social functions of a rule that imposes certain duties on the seller of cigarettes, or of the rule that permits a girl to recover damages against a boy for holding her hand without her consent, we should have to do so in terms of such wide varieties of factors of social life that the analysis would become unmanageable. We should have to study the law of sales in all its aspects, and the law of torts in all its aspects, in order to determine to what extent the particular social situations involved in the two examples are subjected to standard legal norms and to what extent the norms are adapted to the particular requirements of the situation. If, on the other hand, we investigate the social functions, not of legal propositions regarding the contract of purchase and sale, or regarding the tort of unpermitted touching (called "battery"), but rather of the procedure of a civil suit for damages, or the procedure of making an administrative regulation under the Pure Food and Drug Acts governing the liabilities of sellers of cigarettes, the inquiry is restricted to more manageable limits and is directed toward issues more pertinent to an understanding of the nature and functions of law. The social functions of a civil suit for damages are similar in nature to the social functions of other types of civil suits. The social functions of administrative regulation of the sale of food and drugs are revealing of the social functions of administrative regulation in general. Adjudication, administration, legislation, as well as negotiation, are major legal processes whose social functions

32. See *infra* p. 495 for a definition of
this term.

are to an important degree independent of the social functions of the substantive definitions of rights and duties which they produce.

Even with the limitations suggested, a complete analysis of the social functions of law would impose the herculean task of describing all the tendencies of law to produce all the characteristic consequences which serve to maintain the entire social order. If we added to this an analysis of the social "dysfunctions" of law, we should come close to exhausting the entire range of human knowledge and experience. No such "megalomaniac jurisprudence," to use C. K. Allen's phrase once again, is here contemplated. Our purpose is to state the most important general social functions of law, in order to provide a framework for interpretation of the legal materials presented in this volume and at the same time to show some of the most important connections between law and other branches of social science.

We may identify three general social functions of any system of law. The first is the function of restoring equilibrium to the social order (or to some part thereof) when that equilibrium has been seriously disrupted. Since a serious disruption of the social equilibrium inevitably involves conflict, friction, and hence dispute, the function of restoring social equilibrium may be restated more simply as the function of resolving disputes. It must be understood, however, that the legal process of resolution of disputes involving individuals and groups of individuals is at the same time a process of restoring equilibrium to society.

Where there is no existing or potential dispute in society, there is no need for institutional procedures for defining and allocating rights and duties. Law arises, in the first instance, from claims made by one person or group against another—claims made in the name of the social order. The word "claim" is derived from *clamor*; the claimant "shouts" that he or she is hurt, or threatened, and that he or she wants a remedy. From the point of view of the aggrieved party, a legal remedy serves as a satisfaction of financial loss or of wounded feelings or of both; from the point of view of society, a legal remedy serves as a means of preserving peace in the face of serious private conflict which, if no legal remedy were available, might issue forth in private vengeance and self-help; and also, from the point of view of society, a legal remedy serves as a means of reaffirming the social norms which one individual or group alleges that another has violated or threatens to violate.

The legal (whether judicial, legislative, administrative, contractual, or other) process of resolution of disputes thus serves as an alternative to private vengeance, self-help and sheer force. It serves also as an alternative to informal accommodation or settlement. The disputants may themselves simply "make up," or informal pressures of family, neighbors, church, school or other social institutions may be brought to bear in order to bring about such an informal settlement.

Indeed, most types of social conflict, whether manifest or latent, are generally resolved by informal means—by custom, good will, informal pressures, and the like.

The distinction between criminal cases in which the state prosecutes and civil cases in which an aggrieved party claims a remedy should not obscure the fact that in each type of case there is both a personal conflict and a social disequilibrium calling for readjustment. The distinction between a judicial determination of the rights of the parties and a legislative or administrative determination of standards by which conduct is to be judged should not obscure the fact that in each type of determination there are interested parties—whether individuals or groups—presenting opposing claims and defenses to be resolved in the name of the community as a whole.

A second general function of law in any society is that of enabling members of the society to calculate the consequences of their conduct, thereby securing and facilitating voluntary transactions and arrangements. I can proceed through the green light with some confidence that the cars coming the other way will stop at the red—a confidence based in part upon the legal obligation imposed upon people to stop at a red light. I can with confidence make a down-payment on a car or a house, knowing that the seller is required by law to perform his or her part of the bargain. Thus law serves as a means of protecting normal expectations and of enabling people to act more efficiently.

The social function of law in enabling members of a society to calculate the consequences of their conduct is parallel to the similar social function of other agencies. The most elementary mode of creating and perpetuating patterns of behavior, with their complementary expectations, is through the family, age-groups, schools, churches, work associations, business associations, and the like. These institutions attempt to instill the desire to behave in accordance with accepted social standards, and they reinforce inner motivations by allocating rewards and punishments both of a tangible, material nature (granting or withdrawal of food, shelter, corporal punishment, *etc.*) and of an intangible, psychical nature (granting or withdrawal of prestige, social acceptance, *etc.*).

Law becomes necessary as a means of making calculable the consequences of conduct when these other means prove inadequate, either because of the complexity of the consequences and the patterns involved or because of the lack of a common will among the people concerned. We need a red light, with its attendant legal obligation to stop, only because (a) some people coming from different directions would otherwise not know when they ought to stop and when they ought to go, *or* (b) some people, though knowing what they ought to do, would risk incurring non-legal sanctions for doing what they ought not to do. In short, a red light is designed to make the obligation precise and at the same time to provide a sanction or a remedy for violation. Such sanction or remedy, incidentally, need not be external, in the sense of a money fine or a jail sentence or money damages payable to a person injured; it may be the inner sanction of not wishing to break the law.   *LAW ABIDINGNESS*

Law, then, not only has the function of settlement of dispute but also has the function of regulating social action rationally and efficiently, of enabling people to "get things done," or, more particularly, of making it possible to predict with more assurance what others will do. The two functions overlap and complement each other; however, they may also conflict with each other. The peace-making function of law emphasizes the elements of fair hearing, publicity, community participation, and equitableness in the administration of legal justice; the function of law in making calculable the consequences of one's acts emphasizes the elements of precision, definiteness, speed, and logical consistency in legal rules and legal procedures.

The second general function of law which has been stated finds striking expression in those aspects of modern legal systems whereby voluntary arrangements entered into by individuals are protected and facilitated. The use of the legal device of the limited liability company, for example, to promote overseas discovery and colonization in the 17th and 18th centuries, is a remarkable testimony to the power of legal invention to release social energy in a rational and efficient way. The legal device of contract itself, whereby two parties are able to establish a whole framework of mutual social relationships for the future, is a similar example. One might view corporation law or contract law the way one might view traffic regulations—as means of creating, maintaining or restoring social equilibrium through a system of remedies and sanctions against persons who disrupt it. This would tend to minimize, however, the most important function of these branches of law, namely, that of providing channels through which people may achieve objectives which they set for themselves.

A third general function of law in any society is to teach people right belief, right feeling, and right action—that is, to mold the moral and legal conceptions and attitudes of a society. Reference has already been made to the fact that the desire to behave in accordance with accepted social standards is taught in the first instance by the family, local community, school, church, work association, business association, and similar groups. It is primarily through these agencies that the standards and traditions of a given society are transmitted from generation to generation. We have already suggested that, in complex situations, or in situations where there is lack of a common will, these agencies may be incapable of adequately protecting expectations or adequately facilitating voluntary arrangements and that law may therefore be required, in such situations, to serve the function of rationalizing social action and making it more efficient.

It must be noted in addition that these informal primary agencies may be incapable of adequately transmitting social values, and especially *new* social values, without the help of law; and this, again, is apt to be true where the society is complex and divided.

Every system of law educates the moral and legal conceptions of those who are subject to it. This task of law is made explicit and primary in religious legal systems, such as the ancient Hebrew law, based, as it was, on the Ten Commandments and the Torah. It is also explicit and primary in totalitarian systems of law such as the Soviet.[33] But also in the modern Western states, where law has for some time been conceived in more secular terms as a means of delimiting interests, protecting rights, preventing interference by one person in the domain of another, and so forth, it has never been entirely forgotten that at least one of the functions of criminal law is to teach people what is socially dangerous, that at least one of the functions of contract law is to teach people that contracts should be kept, that at least one of the functions of judicial procedure is to teach people that disputes should be settled peacefully and rationally, and that this educational function extends throughout law as a whole.

In the 20th century the educational function of law has assumed increasing importance chiefly (though not entirely) because of the emergence of large-scale social problems which, it is generally thought, cannot be solved without large-scale governmental action and which at the same time require substantial readjustment of traditional social attitudes and beliefs. The vastly increased scope of legislation and of administrative law in virtually all countries during the past 50 years is connected with the need to make people think, feel and behave in ways different from those in which they thought, felt and behaved previously. Two concrete examples of this in American law are the provision of the Securities and Exchange Act of 1933 which makes it a criminal offense, in certain cases, to market securities without a "full and fair disclosure" of the condition of the corporation, and the provision of the National Labor Relations Act of 1947 which requires that management "bargain in good faith" with labor over conditions of employment. These two provisions are striking because they refer explicitly to standards of fairness and good faith, which are to be administered by agencies with large legal powers—the Securities and Exchange Commission and the National Labor Relations Board, respectively. Government regulation of the

---

33. Cf. Article 3 of the Soviet Law on Court Organization which states: "By all its activity a court shall educate the citizens of the U.S.S.R. in the spirit of loyalty to the Motherland, and the cause of communism, and in the spirit of exact and undeviating execution of Soviet laws, of a protective attitude towards socialist property, of observance of labor discipline, of an honorable attitude toward state and social duty, and of respect for the rights, honor, and dignity of citizens, and for the rules of socialist communal life." See generally, Harold J. Berman, Justice in the U.S.S.R., 2d ed., (Cambridge, Mass., 1963).

marketing of securities and of collective bargaining necessarily involves an effort through administrative investigations, hearings, regulations, and other procedures, as well as through adjudications, to persuade people to accept as right the beliefs, feelings, and behavior patterns implicit in the particular legislation involved, as interpreted by the administrative agencies and the courts. What is true of the two particular regulatory schemes mentioned is also true of hundreds of others that have emerged in the United States in recent decades. It is even more true of law in countries which have moved much farther in the direction of socialism than we have.

Even apart from newer forms of government control, however, the educational function of law is implicit in law as a whole, including law-making, law-administering and law-interpreting. Thus law not only (a) helps to maintain social equilibrium by giving remedies for wrongs, and (b) helps to provide channels for social action by protecting expectations; it also (c) helps to mold and remold social thought, feeling and behavior by proclaiming and enforcing standards of conduct. Its educational role is performed not only in the substantive rules it lays down but also in its procedures, including its judicial procedures, and not only by coercion but also by persuasion. Thus Thurman Arnold describes the judicial trial as a "series of object lessons and examples." "It is the way in which society is trained in right ways of thought and action, not by compulsion, but by parables which it interprets and follows voluntarily." [34]

Although the three general functions of law stated above are universal in all legal systems, different societies place different emphases upon one or another of them. The problem of satisfaction of the injured party and of the community by law is more acute in societies in which arbitrariness and violence is relatively widespread and the remedy of self-help more easily available. The problem of legal assurance of calculability of conduct and of security of transactions is more acute in societies in which there is a high degree of complexity of social and economic life. The problem of educating people's moral and legal conceptions through law is more acute in societies in which the traditional non-legal instruments of such education are relatively weak and the state is relatively paternalistic. Apart from these large differences in functional emphasis among different legal systems, there are differences within an individual legal system: our property law and commercial law place a relatively great emphasis on security of transactions; certain branches of our labor law, on the other hand, such as arbitration of grievances, place a relatively great emphasis on education of the parties; our law of murder emphasizes more than other branches of law the function of satisfaction of the community's sense of outrage.

34. Thurman Arnold, The Symbols of Government (New Haven, 1935), p. 129.

In addition to universal functions of law as such, particular legal systems have their own unique functions. Here one may be mentioned, since it is developed at length (as are the three universal functions previously discussed) in the cases and text materials that follow. In Western law, and in legal systems that have come under Western influence, there has been considerable emphasis upon *the function of law in maintaining historical continuity and consistency of doctrine*. Thus Western law must be viewed not only as a response to social conditions existing at a given moment but also as the unfolding of ideas in history.

Special types of judicial reasoning—reasoning by analogy of previous decisions (precedents), and reasoning by analogy of doctrine and statute—have been developed in the West as means of growth of the legal systems of the various nations. The underlying premise of these types of legal reasoning is that law is a unified and organically developing system which is intimately related to a unified and organically developing social system. The idea that society can develop organically, that it can make progress from year to year and from generation to generation, and the idea that the legal system also can grow and can be both a reflection and an instrument of the growth of the social order, are specifically Western ideas which have produced a specifically Western type of law.

In speaking of law, then, we have in mind a special type of process of restoring, maintaining or creating social order, characterized by formality (in the sense indicated: that is, by relative deliberateness, definiteness, etc.), whose main general functions are (a) to resolve disputes, (b) to facilitate and protect voluntary arrangements, (c) to mold and remold the moral and legal conceptions of a society and (d) in the Western tradition, at least, to maintain historical continuity and consistency of doctrine.

The foregoing discussion of the nature and functions of law is intended only as the barest introduction of a subject far too big and important to be exhausted in a few pages, or, for that matter, a few volumes. The student who comes to this discussion "cold" is bound to be confused and frustrated. "Why can't the experts agree?" "Each theory seems inadequate by itself; why not put them all together into one?" "How can a beginner answer questions which have tormented legal scholars for thousands of years?" "Must one make up his or her mind on this?" "Could not other qualities and functions of law be listed?" "What difference does it make?"

The answers to these questions are not difficult. Experts *seldom* agree. Each theory *is* inadequate by itself—and rarely, except for purposes of exposition, are they held in absolute isolation from each other. A beginner *cannot* answer these questions. It is *not* necessary to make up one's mind on this *right away, once and forever*. Other qualities and functions of law *could* be listed.

But it does make an enormous difference. What one stresses as fundamental to the nature and functions of law determines one's approach not only to the subject as a whole but also to particular legal problems. As United States Supreme Court Justice Felix Frankfurter has said, "Every [legal] decision is a function of some juristic philosophy."

The Structure and Method of This Book

Obviously no single book and no single course can teach "the law". The Harvard Law School library alone contains over a million volumes of or about law, and to attempt to digest them would be to adopt the conception of law which Oliver Wendell Holmes, Jr., attributed to the old-fashioned English lawyer—"a chaos with a full index." To attempt to summarize what lawyers, judges and other officials *do* would result in a chaos without the index.

The proper approach is not by a geological survey of the whole field but, as someone has put it, by sinking shafts into those areas which contain the richest deposits. In order to determine, however, which of the innumerable areas of law thus to explore we must first know what we are looking for. Our choice of subjects is determined by our conception of what law essentially is and what social functions it primarily performs. By the approach offered in the preceding pages we have laid a basis for selecting for fairly intensive study certain aspects of law which illuminate its nature and functions thus conceived.

The first part of the book, following the present Introduction, selects certain aspects of the law of civil and criminal procedure which illustrate the nature of law as a process of resolution of disputes. The topics chosen are not different from some of the topics which are studied in law school: jurisdiction of courts, procedure prior to trial, protection against unlawful arrest and against unreasonable searches and seizures, evidence, right to trial by jury, and others. But the emphasis is more philosophical, more historical and comparative, and more sociological than in law school courses generally.

Thus the first materials presented—on jurisdiction—are designed to raise the question, What kinds of disputes should courts decide and what kinds of disputes should they not decide? This question is one part of a more fundamental question which forms a principal theme of the entire book: What are the potentialities and what are the limits of effective legal action?

The problem of what kinds of disputes courts should or should not decide is dealt with in terms, first, of several civil cases in which the courts refused to take jurisdiction on the ground that there was not a genuine, or live, controversy involved. Notes and questions in connection with each case explore philosophical and historical aspects of the problem. Finally a passage is presented in which Thurman Arnold attacks as "irrational" the practice of courts in requir-

"What burns me up is that the answer is right here somewhere, staring us in the face."

Drawing by Robt. Day
© 1950 The New Yorker Magazine, Inc.

ing that there be a controversy and in confining their decisions to the narrow issues presented by the parties, followed by a passage in which Lon L. Fuller states that this practice is one of the conditions upon whose observance rests the "moral force" of a judicial decision.

The same basic question is seen from a different angle in the next section which treats the requirement in criminal cases that there be a law which specifically makes punishable the act with which the defendant is charged. Here the adverse parties are the State and the accused, and unless the State has, through its legislature, previously declared the act punishable—so runs one doctrine—the court has no authority to convict, though the wrong be heinous. Comparative and historical materials show the use of a different doctrine in earlier Soviet and Nazi criminal law, and in Europe prior to the French Revolution. The question is raised why American law, which gives the courts a relatively broad discretion to create new civil remedies, so jealously guards the legislature's exclusive jurisdiction to say what acts shall be criminally punishable. A possible answer to that question is then suggested by some materials which consider the differences between civil remedies and criminal sanctions.

Two other phases of the jurisdiction of courts are dealt with very briefly in the first chapter: first, the jurisdictional requirements of our federal system, in which state and federal courts have concurrent power, and second, jurisdiction of the person in civil cases.

Following the chapter on jurisdiction are two chapters on procedure prior to trial in civil cases and in criminal cases. The material on civil procedure shows the emphasis upon precise formulation of issues for decision, the emphasis upon adversary proceedings, and in general the high degree of restraint and formality characteristic of adjudication as contrasted with other means of social control. At the same time relatively new devices introducing more flexibility in the proceedings are described. The material on criminal procedure, on the other hand, raises important questions of constitutional rights, with respect to arrest, interrogation, search and seizure, and the like. The contrast is brought out between the reforms of recent decades leading to cooperation between opposing sides in civil cases prior to trial (the use of depositions, the pre-trial conference, *etc.*), and the resistance to similar proposals on the criminal side. The European criminal procedure, with its extensive preliminary investigation at the hands of an examining magistrate with very broad powers, is analyzed at some length.

Finally the analysis of law as a process of resolution of disputes is concluded by a chapter on the trial. The chapter begins with an analysis of the law of evidence and a short essay on the burden of proof. This is followed by a study of the role of the jury in which Judge Jerome Frank's broadside attack upon the jury trial is juxtaposed with Professor Harry Kalven's defense of the jury system. The role of the trial judge is discussed in essays by two trial judges; and the role of the trial lawyer is analyzed in excerpts from a number of prominent jurists and lawyers.

The materials on law as a process of resolution of disputes are mostly, but by no means entirely, a descriptive and analytical study of American court procedure. They are written or selected to provide a basis for understanding the nature and functions of adjudication in general, and, through adjudication, other types of legal processes as well.

Part Two of the book is concerned with the function of law in giving historical continuity and doctrinal consistency to social life. More particularly, attention is given to the nature and functions of legal reasoning by analogy of previous decisions—especially under the doctrine of precedents—and legal reasoning by analogy of doctrine and statute.

The introductory section analyzes some of the distinctive characteristics of legal reasoning. The technique of interpreting previous cases under the doctrine of precedent is explained in a passage from Karl N. Llewellyn. Thereafter the application of the doctrine is illustrated and tested in a series of five cases in the New York courts from 1852 to 1916 dealing with the question of the liability of a manufacturer of a defective product to a sub-purchaser injured because of the defect. At first the court accepts the rule that there is no liability because the manufacturer is not in contractual relations with the sub-purchaser, but makes an exception for "dangerous substances" like poison or a gun. Gradually the exception is extended until it in effect swallows up the rule, and in MacPherson v. Buick Motor Co. Judge Cardozo reinterprets the earlier cases and finds them consistent with the doctrine that a negligent manufacturer is liable to one injured by a defect in the product regardless of whether or not the injured person purchased the product from an intermediate distributor.

Is the doctrine of precedent more than a game of matching cases? An article by Edward H. Levi analyzes Judge Cardozo's technique of analogizing and distinguishing cases as "the" process of legal reasoning, whereby law keeps pace with historical development without running ahead of it. "The words change to receive the content which the community gives to them." Ultimately an automobile does not seem less "dangerous" than a poison.

Yet just as Cardozo was putting the law of manufacturers' liability on the track of ordinary negligence principles, other forces were at work to extend liability, in certain classes of cases, to harm caused by conduct which was not negligent. A note on so-called "strict" or "absolute" liability indicates various situations in which exceptions are made to the doctrine "no liability without fault," so that, for example, by a series of fictions manufacturers of food products are now liable in many states for injuries to consumers from hidden defects in the food even though the manufacturer has not been careless. After this note a case is presented in which a waitress was injured by the explosion of a soft-drink bottle, and one of the judges urges that the bottling company should be liable whether or not it was at fault. The judge's argument is based on the analogy of various doctrines of absolute liability applicable in other types of cases and on the analogy of various statutes imposing absolute liability such as the Pure Food and Drug Acts. This is followed by a more recent case in which the court extends the absolute liability doctrine of the food products cases to encompass a wider range of products, in this particular case a defective automobile. The judge's argument here is based on analogies from earlier cases on products liability, and on consideration of public policy drawn from statutory law and from the judge's conceptions of what is "right" in a market economy characterized by mass producers and mass marketing techniques. This is followed by a passage discussing the extent to which our courts are willing to reason from the "precedent" of a statute.

This part concludes with four sections in which is made a comparative and historical analysis of methods of legal reasoning practiced in legal systems of the West. The first three sections compare the so-called "common-law" and "civil law" types of legal reasoning and the fourth presents an historical note on the development of the doctrine of precedent, including a reference to the different roles which it plays in property law, in constitutional law and in tort law.

Both reasoning from the authority of precedent and reasoning from the authority of statute or doctrine are contrasted with reasoning directly from social policy, in which conclusions are reached on the basis of the net benefits to society, without recourse to authority in the legal sense. The question whether an "insurance" theory of liability should be adopted as a response to the problem of consumer accidents is distinguished from the question whether the courts are the proper agencies to make this change. The latter question is related to the nature and limits of the authorities by which courts are bound, and, more broadly, to the function of the courts as bearers of the community's traditions.

Part Three of the book considers the social function of law as a process of protecting and facilitating voluntary arrangements, using materials on the law of contract. Again the illustrative materials are intended to be far narrower in scope than a complete study of the broad social function would require.

Without law it would be difficult if not impossible for people to establish the complex mutual relationships required by the system of division of labor characteristic of modern societies. Without a law of property it would be impossible, for example, to borrow money on the security of one's house; without a law of tort it would be too risky financially for most people to drive automobiles; without a law of landlord and tenant it would be difficult to operate a rooming house; without a law of contract it would be impossible to hold a "permanent" position.   Law establishes conditions which make it possible for people to operate; it creates channels for activities, for "getting things done."

One important way in which law enables people to get things done is by setting a framework for voluntary agreement and by providing a process for enforcing agreements.   Contract law gives insights into the nature of the legal process of facilitating and protecting voluntary arrangements.

Part Three consists of two chapters dealing, respectively, with the protecting and facilitating functions of contract law.   In the first chapter an attempt is made to set out some basic elements of contract law and to raise some fundamental questions about the aims of contract law.   The first of the four sections in this chapter presents some cases in which the courts are faced with the problem of deciding whether they should enforce an agreement and impose liability *in contract* for the breach of promises.   These few cases illuminate the drive for consistency of doctrine in contract law, for a credit economy often requires unifying concepts which will simplify, standardize and render calculable in a single idiom a wide variety of obligations.   However, these cases also demonstrate that there are many contracts which fall outside the "standard"—normal—transaction for which a general body of contract doctrine is devised.   For example, arrangements regarding family life, and arrangements between parties possessed of vastly unequal bargaining power, may not be subject to the same rules as apply to standard commercial bargains. The first section of this chapter closes with an examination of the problems posed by the often conflicting ideals of consistency of doctrine and fairness in contractual relations.

In the next section are presented a few cases which explore the role of the individual will in the formation of contracts.   In these cases the courts struggle to set out standards for determining when to release a person from an unfortunate bargain which is based on a mistake.   In attempting to reach a good result in these cases the courts must weigh the interests of the parties in the particular transaction and also the interests of society in the general rules of contract law. In each case the party who erred in assessing the facts underlying the bargain presents a strong case for relief, but the court must also consider whether it would be just to the other party to thwart his expectations by refusing to enforce the contract.   Furthermore, the court must recognize that in a credit economy there is a general community interest in the security of transactions, which security may be weakened if objectively valid contracts may be avoided because of a unilateral mistake made by one of the parties.   This section also presents a few cases in which courts are called upon to decide how losses caused by unanticipated events should be allocated between the parties to a contract.   These cases raise issues as to the special role of judges in dealing with contract disputes where neither party has caused the loss, but where neither party explicitly bargained for the allocation of the risk of the loss in question.

The chapter then concludes with three sections which provide an overview of the theoretical foundations of contract.

The first two of these sections presents materials regarding remedies for breach of contract, and uses this subject to consider different purposes and conceptions of contract law. The last section of this chapter provides a jurisprudential postscript on the subject of contract law drawn from the writings of two of the most eminent contemporary scholars in this field.

The second chapter in Part Three is devoted to an examination of contract law as a process of planning voluntary arrangements. The suggestion is made that contract is primarily a means for planning exchange relationships. The lawyer's role in the planning process is examined. The last section in this part is devoted to an article in which Professor Stewart Macaulay presents some findings regarding the extent to which businessmen rely on their own customs and institutions to establish exchange relationships and resolve disputes which arise out of those relationships. This material provides a setting for raising some questions regarding the relationship between the legal order and private ordering techniques.

The final part of the book views law as a process of resolving acute social conflict, taking its materials from labor law and the law regarding race relations, instances where law serves to resolve or attempt to resolve serious conflicts between large groups of people and not merely between individuals.

In responding to problems of acute social conflict, law is inevitably concerned not merely with allocating rights and duties or balancing interests but also with influencing the moral and legal conceptions of the people who are the subjects of rights and duties, the people whose interests are affected. The educational function of law, its role in shaping the beliefs and attitudes of the community, comes to the fore most prominently where underlying the immediate problem or controversy is a deep cleavage in values which threatens the whole social order.

A brief introductory chapter presents some material on the rise of the labor movement after the civil war. This chapter also deals with the early exercise by the courts of their power to enjoin strikes and picketing, a power which was most effectively used to retard the spread of organized labor.

The purpose of presenting the history of the labor injunction is not primarily to show that law has changed as social, economic and political conditions have changed, but rather to test the effectiveness of the judicial response to the underlying social conflict. Therefore, materials are presented on the rise of the labor movement in the context of American social and economic development in the late 19th and early 20th centuries. On this background, the cases show a conflict of opinion between judges who adopt not only diverse economic theories but also diverse theories of the nature of law. Basically, however, the ineffectiveness of the judicial response was due to the inadequacies of traditional legal doctrines and traditional legal remedies. The courts were unable to deal with the underlying causes of the conflict.

The next two chapters chronicle the course of legislation dealing with the problems occasioned by the rise of organized labor. Beginning with the Sherman Act of 1890 and ending with the Taft-Hartley Act of 1947, the materials encompass a wide range of issues relating to the respective roles of legislatures and courts in the development of law and policy adequate to meet the problems created by massive social change. Included in these chapters is some limited introduction to that uniquely American institution, judicial review of the constitutionality of legislation. These chapters culminate with an examination of the legal and political upheaval associated with the New Deal, for the period of the New Deal witnessed not only legislative restrictions upon the powers of the judiciary in labor cases but also the creation of a system of administrative regulation of collective bargaining.

The next to last chapter turns from the history of labor law to the rise and decline of laws supporting racial segregation. Of special importance here is the opportunity to examine the use of carefully managed constitutional litigation to hasten the decline of this legal structure. This aspect of law and social change in America is treated in cases and materials regarding racially restrictive covenants in real estate transactions, and "separate but equal" public education.

The last chapter goes back to the development of labor law, and more particularly to the emergence of the new approaches to labor-management relations established by legislation in the 1930s and 1940s. Those enactments established a system of administrative controls designed not only to create a framework for peaceful negotiation and settlement of disputes between labor and management, but also explicitly to encourage new attitudes of cooperation and new conceptions of mutual rights and duties under the law. The materials present an outline of the National Labor Relations Act and its philosophy, including the reasons for enactment of the Taft-Hartley amendments in 1947 and the contribution of the Taft-Hartley Act to the national labor policy; a description of the organization and procedure of the National Labor Relations Board; a brief statement of the activity of the Board in enforcing section 8(a)(1) of the Act which declares it to be an unfair labor practice to interfere with, restrain or coerce employees in the exercise of their rights of self-organization, and section 8(a)(5) and 8(b)(3) which impose a duty on management and labor to bargain in good faith. The question is raised, "In what ways do the greater informality of the Board's procedure and its broader powers, as compared with a court, facilitate its implementation of the policy of the Act, and in what ways do they create potentialities of abuse?" Also a passage is presented outlining the nature of the collective bargaining process and stating what is required of employers and unions to make collective bargaining effective.

Woven through this final chapter are materials dealing with attempts to secure equal opportunity in employment for all, regardless of race. Comparison and contrast of the remedies to implement the victories of organized labor and civil rights organizations provides additional insight on the uses and limits of law as a means to effect social change.

The final chapter also deals with means for administering the collective bargaining contract. Some attention is paid to the judicial role in enforcing these contracts, but the primary focus is on the use of the so-called grievance procedure and the arbitration of disputes. The collective bargaining agreement is, from a legal point of view, a contract between union and management, but it is also a kind of constitution for the peaceful and orderly carrying on of labor-management relations. Inevitably disputes arise as to the rights of the parties, and in general such disputes are settled by a procedure of complaints and hearings and ultimately by decision of an impartial arbitrator. In many respects the labor arbitrator is like a judge in a court proceeding. It is his or her job to conduct a hearing, to find the facts, and to determine the rights of the parties under the contract. On the other hand, these are "parties" who are in a much closer relationship than most businessmen who enter into contracts with each other. They are members of a common enterprise, a going concern, and they must continue to live together after the dispute is settled. Arbitrators of labor disputes have been confronted with sharp questions relating to the nature and functions of the process of labor arbitration—questions which have been put in the context, often, of the comparison or contrast between arbitration and adjudication. Should the arbitrator restrict his or her decision to the issues raised by the pleadings? Should he or she simply interpret the contract? Or should the arbitrator assume the function of educating the parties as to their mutual responsibilities toward each other? To what extent are the answers to such questions as these conditional upon the type of industry involved, the stability of labor relations within it, and the maturity of the union and of management? These questions are raised by materials outlining grievance and arbitration procedure in various industries, some opinions of arbitrators in cases that have come to them for decision, and an article by the late Professor Harry Shulman, who was a leading exponent of the broad view of what may be called the "parental" function of the arbitrator.

The study of labor arbitration brings the student back to the questions raised at the very beginning of the book. At the same time, the study of arbitration illuminates the interrelationships between adjudication, legislation, administration, and contract, for labor arbitration takes place within a framework in which all these elements are explicit. Thus this seems a good point at which to close the introductory study of the nature and functions of law.

The use of cases in teaching law to students of the arts and sciences. The so-called "case method" of teaching is not one thing but many, and it may be used in a variety of ways. As used in law schools, one of its primary functions is to help the student to "think like a lawyer" and "talk like a lawyer." A liberal arts course in law must have a quite different kind of emphasis—namely, to teach students *why the law is what it is*, and, as part of that subject, *why lawyers think, talk and act the way they do*. These differences in purpose dictate a difference in teaching method. Yet class discussion of cases can also be an invaluable teaching device, if properly used, for accomplishing the purposes of the liberal arts course in law.

First, cases give the student a vicarious experience of law. The first case presented in this book, for example, involves a lawsuit between two people with apparently identical interests who made up a case and sought a ruling from the Supreme Court of the United States which would help them and which would perhaps be detrimental to others who were not parties to their lawsuit. The Supreme Court said that the controversy was a "feigned" one, and it therefore refused to decide it. These are "the facts" in a very small nutshell. But neither a digest of the facts nor a statement of rules respecting feigned controversies can provide an adequate substitute for the concrete situation as reported by the court. The student is challenged by the actual report of the case, as he or she could not be by a digest of it, to identify with one side or the other. The student sees, on the one hand, the difficult situation of the parties, which impels them to seek a ruling, and, on the other, Judge Taney's outrage at the imposition sought to be made upon the dignity of the Supreme Court. And only by having the report are we in a position to ask, "Do the reasons offered by the court justify the decision?"

Secondly, by arguing the case back and forth, whether in class discussion or among friends outside of class or simply in his or her own mind, the student begins to sense the pressure upon the judge or lawyer or legislator to reach a decision and to reach it relatively quickly—compared, for example, to the scholar who seeks truth and who can wait forever before reaching a conclusion. The student begins also to see that the decision must be made in a relatively narrow context, that of the case at hand, with all its individual peculiarities, though at the same time the repercussions of the decision may be very broad and may affect the whole society. This insight, too, is extremely difficult to convey except by the vicarious experience which the case provides. The nature of reasoning which is adapted to the reaching of right decisions is not easily grasped by those whose formal instruction is limited to reasoning adapted to the establishment of general principles.

Thirdly, the cases present the raw materials out of which a philosophy of law—or a sociology of law—can be constructed. You start with the specific facts which give rise to the suit: Mrs. Thomas is injured by taking extract of belladona which she thought to be extract of dandelion. Should she be allowed to recover damages for her pain and suffering and if so from whom? Should the retail druggist who filled the prescription be liable, or should she be allowed to recover against the apothecary who originally packaged the drug and mislabeled it? Why should either of them be liable? As soon as the question "Why" is asked the discussion may fan out into the widest areas of economics, politics, philosophy. Yet the discussion is held down to the time and place of the concrete dispute: New York state, 1852. Where should the Court of Appeals of New York go to get the law for this case? How is this case different from cases X, Y, and Z, already decided? Is it important that there be consistency in the decision of such cases? The reasoning back and forth from particular to general and from general to particular may swing in increasingly wider orbits. Thus the raw data of the cases stimulate generalization about the nature and functions of law, yet keep generalization within bounds of what law is in a technical sense.

Of course, the case method—or the various case methods—of teaching law can hardly suffice for students who seek not professional training but a broad view of the subject. In the first place, law is far more than litigation, and litigation is far more than argument in appellate courts. The student must be exposed to statutes and to administrative regulations as well as to what is sometimes called "private lawmaking," that is, negotiation of agreements which are law for the parties who make them. In the second place, not even the decided cases, much less legislation, can be understood apart from the historical, economic, political and other social factors which influence them. The student rightly seeks not only a knowledge of how law solves problems but also a knowledge of the relationship of legal solutions to the social order which is their ultimate source—a relationship which is by no means always suggested in judicial decisions or in other legal materials.

Hence in the present book large amounts of text materials have been included, not only as annotations to cases but as independent materials for study. Some of these materials are descriptive and analytical treatments of legal subjects and some of them are discussions of the social background of legal subjects. It is hoped that the juxtaposition of cases and other materials will permit a combination of the best features of the case method of teaching, as used in American law schools, and the best features of the lecture method as used traditionally in the liberal arts college.

Part One

LAW AS A PROCESS OF RESOLUTION OF DISPUTES: ILLUSTRATIONS FROM CIVIL AND CRIMINAL PROCEDURE

One of the most important ways of understanding law is to view it as a process, that is, a set of procedures, for the resolution of disputes. Such a view stresses procedure as the heart of the law, and sees substantive rules as meaningful only in the context of the settlement of some past, existing or potential controversy. "Process" means way, or method, but it connotes some degree of elaborateness in the way or method. The legal process is more elaborate than most other processes of resolving disputes. Not every process, or procedure, is legal in nature, and law is not the only process of resolving disputes; nevertheless law includes a great many more kinds of dispute-resolving processes than is generally realized.

To many, the phrase "legal procedure" connotes only procedure in court or in connection with litigation. The phrase has, however, a much broader meaning. It includes the procedure of legislation: the debate on a bill on the floor of the legislature, or even the drafting of it by a legislative committee, for example, is as much legal procedure as the examination of witnesses in a court trial. "Legal procedure" includes also the procedure of administration, such as the making of regulations for an industry under government control. As used here, it may include even the procedure of negotiation of a contract, insofar as such negotiation takes place within the framework of a set procedure.

The court, that is, an impartial tribunal for adjudication of disputes, remains, nevertheless, the greatest invention of law, and the process of adjudication is the principal model, the archetype, of other legal processes of resolution of conflict. Is not a presidential election, for example, a kind of adjudication, with the "parties" contending for a favorable verdict in the "court of public opinion?" Legislation has this in common with adjudication, that characteristically issues are formulated and submitted to the decision of the whole tribunal; decision is preceded by a hearing of opposing points of view; and so long as the legislators are free to change their minds in the light of the debate, the decision has an element of impartiality. It is no accident that originally the supreme lawmaking body of England was called "the High Court of Parliament," that the House of Lords still sits as the supreme judicial body of that country, and that in Massachusetts from colonial times until the present the legislature has been called "the General Court." Administration (that is, executive action), and even negotiation, also involve elements of adjudication, taken in this broad sense.

Since court procedure is legal procedure *par excellence*—though by no means the only type of legal procedure—it is a fruitful starting point for the study of law. Moreover, it is essential to start the study of law with court procedure if the opinions of judges in support of their decisions of litigated cases are to be used, since it is utterly impossible to understand judicial opinions without a knowledge of the procedural context in which they are written.

In Part One we shall study chiefly (though not exclusively) the American system of judicial procedure, both civil and criminal— since it is better to make a more thorough analysis of a single system than to make a superficial comparison of many systems. However, the main lesson will be lost if the American judicial procedure is studied without distinguishing those features of it which are inherent in the judicial process as such from those features which are part of the Western, and more particularly the American, legal tradition. Therefore some materials are offered which put the American system of judicial procedure in a historical and comparative perspective. The questions inserted after the cases and at various points in the materials are designed to focus attention on those matters which must be understood if the technique of law is to be seen in terms of its social functions.

Chapter 1

THE COMPETENCE AND JURISDICTION OF COURTS

SECTION 1. OUTLINE OF A "CIVIL ACTION"

A lawsuit in which the complaining party seeks personal redress in the form of money or other property, or through a judicial decree to establish, enforce, or protect a right, is called a "civil action" or "civil proceeding" in contradistinction to "prosecutions" or "criminal proceedings" in which the state moves to convict a person accused of having committed a crime. The following is a brief description of the stages in a typical civil action in an American court.

A has been injured by some act of B. A consults an attorney who advises that on the basis of the facts reported by A, B is legally obligated to compensate A for the injury. At A's request a suit against B is initiated by the attorney, who files a written complaint in a court stating that A has been wronged by B and that A desires the court to entertain the suit and award a judgment against B. B must be informed of the complaint by A before the court may proceed with the lawsuit. Therefore A's attorney will see to it that a copy of the complaint is delivered to B along with a demand (summons) that B answer the complaint within a specified time. (The minimum time within which the complaint must be answered is set by the statutes or court rules regarding procedure in civil actions.) B enlists the aid of an attorney and is advised that there may be a valid defense against A's claim. At B's request the attorney undertakes the defense. B's attorney informs the court, in writing, of B's intention to defend the suit and the grounds of B's defense. A, now referred to as the plaintiff, has entered a plea for legal redress, and B, now referred to as the defendant, has entered his plea that the court deny the claim.[1] A and B are now parties to a civil action, the case of A versus B.

A number of further preliminary steps will now be taken by the attorneys for A and B. These steps are primarily concerned with developing more detailed information regarding the case so that after the pleading and the preliminary preparation has been completed the nature of the dispute between the parties will be more clearly delineated. During this preliminary process questions may arise regarding

---

1. The statements of the parties setting out their claims or defenses are called, collectively, "pleadings"; they contain the respective "pleas" of the parties. The verb is "to plead"—as in "The defendant pleads that the time within which the plaintiff's action must be brought has expired."

the events and circumstances which support the claim of A and the defenses of B. These events and circumstances are "the facts" of the case. They relate to the question, "Who did what to whom when, how, and why?" Questions may also arise regarding the legal significance of the facts. For example, if it is assumed that the facts as stated by the plaintiff (or defendant) are correct, do those facts give rise to a good claim for relief or a good defense under the rules of law applicable to the case? These questions of fact and questions of law will then be resolved by a trial. (Note that it is not always necessary to have a trial to dispose of a lawsuit. The parties may agree to a settlement prior to trial. Or the preliminary preparation of the case may provide a basis for judicial resolution of the dispute prior to trial. This subject is considered in more detail in Chapter 2.)

The trial is a hearing at which the parties are given an opportunity to present their respective sides of the matter to an impartial tribunal. This presentation is divided into two parts: (a) the plaintiff's case and (b) the defendant's case.

(a) The plaintiff, through his or her attorney, will introduce evidence which tends to support the allegations concerning the facts on which plaintiff's suit is based. The attorney will also present an argument regarding the legal principles which will support a judgment for A. At the close of the plaintiff's case the defendant may ask that the suit be dismissed. For example, defendant may argue that the plaintiff has failed to introduce evidence sufficient to substantiate the claim or that the plaintiff has failed to show that the law provides for the relief which the plaintiff seeks. If this request (motion) is granted the trial ends; otherwise it will proceed and the defendant will be allowed to present his or her case.

(b) The defendant, through his or her attorney, may then present evidence which tends to substantiate the defendant's view of the facts or contradict the evidence presented by the plaintiff. Similarly, the defense may present an argument which tends to refute the legal argument advanced on behalf of the plaintiff and which substantiates the defendant's claim that judgment should be entered in his or her favor. Thus the opposing sides are responsible for developing the information regarding fact and law on which the court's decision is predicated.

The basic responsibility of the court is to hear the opposing sides, decide the disputed issues of fact or law, and render judgment in accord with the facts and law as found.

The chief officer of the court is the judge. Sometimes the judge will hear cases sitting alone; at other times the judge may have the assistance of a jury, usually consisting of twelve people drawn from the community at large. When the judge sits alone he or she must decide both the facts and the law and render judgment accordingly. The judge (often referred to as "the court") decides what law is applicable to the case and informs ("instructs") the jury what that law is. The jurors then must determine what are the facts and what result (verdict) should follow from applying to those facts the law which the judge has given to them. Usually the jury verdict is in a "general" form, *e. g.*, "We find for the plaintiff in the sum of $7,500," or "We find for the defendant." The judge will then—in most cases —render a judgment based on the jury verdict. The judgment in a civil case is a formal declaration of the outcome of the suit and an announcement of the remedy (if any) to which the winner is entitled. This terminates the trial phase of the litigation but is not necessarily the end of the judicial proceedings.

Either or both of the parties may not be satisfied that the judgment of the court is proper. If this is so, there may be an appeal from the decision of the trial court. The appeal will be made to an appellate court, a tribunal established expressly for the purpose of reviewing the decisions of lower courts, such as the trial court.

The function of the appellate court is to review decisions of lower courts to determine if substantial error has been committed in those courts. If an error has been committed which, in the opinion of the appellate court, actually or potentially led to a judgment adverse to the party who appealed (appellant), then the appellate court may act to correct this error. Such action will be taken only in those instances where the error was of a type which the appellate court is competent to review. We may label these errors as errors of law. For example, where a trial judge finds that rule X is applicable to a particular point in a case and the appellate court finds instead that rule Y is the appropriate rule, we may say that an error of law has been committed and the appellate court may correct this error. On the other hand, claims that a jury has erred in making findings of fact are not generally a sound basis for appeal, for the finding of fact is the special province of the trial court and appellate courts are reluctant to disturb such findings. However, if the record of the case makes it abundantly clear that the facts found by the jury (or judge) were not supported by the evidence presented in the trial, the appellate court may revise the decision, since a gross misreading of the evidence is considered an "error of law."

The party who wishes to appeal must complain to the appellate court that error has been committed and must take the necessary steps to present his or her case to the reviewing court. Upon such request an appellate hearing will be held. This hearing affords the appellant (sometimes referred to as the petitioner, or the plaintiff in error) and the other party (variously referred to as the appellee, the respondent, or the defendant in error) an opportunity to make argument to the court. The appellate court consists of a panel of three or more judges who sit to hear counsel present argument and then to decide the appeal by vote (majority rule). No new evidence is presented since the appellate court is not competent to make new findings of fact; rather the court bases its decision on the verbatim record of the trial court proceedings, on the argument of the attorneys in the appellate proceeding, and on its own understanding of the applicable law.

The oral argument in the appellate hearing is a discussion between lawyers at the bar (the attorneys) and lawyers on the bench (the judges) as to the correct legal principles which govern the case at hand. (In addition to hearing oral argument, the appellate court receives "briefs"—written arguments—from the attorneys.) If the record and the argument disclose substantial error, the appellate court may then take steps to correct the error by reversing the judgment and finding for the appellant or by sending the case back for a new trial. In most cases, the appellate court's decision is announced through a written opinion prepared by one of the judges.

When a final judgment is pronounced in a court action the issues in the case are said to be *res judicata*—"the matter is adjudged"—and will not be re-examined by the courts. This rule has exceptions but for the most part the courts adopt a policy which favors the termination of litigation between parties once they have had a full and fair hearing of their case and a judgment thereon.

This is but a rough outline of the procedure through which a civil action—a case involving the competing claims of individual parties—passes on its way to judicial resolution. It is not a totally accurate or perfect description of the process but for our purposes it provides basic information sufficient to facilitate the study of the material in Chapter 1. Chapters 2, 3, and 4 present a more thorough analysis of this aspect of legal procedure.

SECTION 2. THE REQUIREMENT OF A LIVE CONTROVERSY IN CIVIL CASES

This section presents material which has been selected and organized to serve two objectives. First, the material provides an introduction to the reading of judicial opinions which should allow the student to become familiar with the basic form in which appellate court decisions in the United States are delivered, and to develop some facility in analyzing judicial opinions. Second, the material raises numerous questions regarding the nature of the judicial function and factors which limit the exercise of the judicial function.

The issues and questions which can be developed from a careful reading and analysis of this section could carry beginning students well beyond the limits of their capacity and also beyond the bounds of relevance to the main purposes of this book.   In order that the reader may have some guidance in this beginning effort, the following questions are suggested as being particularly important and worthy of analysis during the reading and discussion of this section:

1. Can judges act as judges in situations where there is no dispute before them?

2. What is a dispute as far as judges are concerned?

3. Must judges attempt to resolve all disputes which are brought before them?

4. May judges attempt to resolve all disputes which are brought before them?

5. Who can present a dispute to a court so as to invoke judicial action to resolve that dispute?

6. Does the timing of the presentation of a dispute to a court have a bearing on the ability or willingness of a court to attempt to resolve the dispute?

7. Do the materials in this section suggest that judges perform a function beyond that of resolving individual disputes?

Since these questions provide a base on which some of the major themes of this book are developed, the following commentary on them is offered as an additional guide to the reader.

Questions 1 and 7:   Judges act to resolve disputes, but the judicial function may encompass more than the power to resolve disputes.   The reader should explore these questions as a base for formulating a definition of the judicial function, and the limits of that function.

Questions 2, 3, and 4:   It is necessary to determine what kinds of disputes are appropriate for judicial resolution.   For example, should a dispute between a mother and child regarding the child's eating habits be submitted to a court?   The answer to that question seems obvious, and most judges would have no difficulty in determining that such a matter is best left to resolution by other means, but there are many other instances where the issue of judicial competence is not so easily resolved.   The student should examine the following material with an eye to developing some notions about the guidelines which help judges determine whether or not it is appropriate for them to act on a matter presented to them.

Question 5:   Even though a particular dispute is of a type generally recognized as being appropriate for judicial resolution, there may be a question as to who is the appropriate person to bring the issue into the courts.   Should the judges themselves reach out and call into court all disputes of which they are aware, or should judges wait until someone comes to them and invokes judicial consideration of the matter?   If it is essential that judges act only when requested to act, does it matter who starts the action? For example, if Jones knows that Smith has been cheated by Brown, should judges hear a case in which Jones sues Brown to recover compensation for Smith?

The cases and materials in this first section of the book will raise the issues outlined above. The balance of the book will provide additional material bearing on these issues, for this section is an introduction to the relationship between two central issues explored in this book, namely: What are the limits of effective legal action? How does the law establish and preserve its own legitimacy?

SECTION 2.1   FEIGNED CONTROVERSIES

LORD v. VEAZIE

Supreme Court of the United States, 1850.
49 U.S. (8 How.) 251 [1]

This case was brought up, . . . from the Circuit Court of the United States for the District of Maine. . . .

In August, 1848, John W. Veazie and Nathaniel Lord executed a written instrument, which purported to be a conveyance by Veazie to Lord of 250 shares of the stock [of the Bangor and Piscataquis Canal and Railroad Company], for the consideration of $6,000. This deed contained the following covenant: [2]

"And I do hereby covenant and agree to and with the said Lord, that I will warrant and defend the said shares, and all property and privileges of said corporation incident thereto, to the said Lord, his executors, administrators, and assigns, and that the said shares, property, and privileges are free and clear of all encumbrances; and I further covenant with said Lord, that the stockholders of said company have the right to use the waters of the Penobscot River within the limits mentioned in their

---

1. "49 U.S. (8 How.) 251 (1850)" means: Volume 49 of the United States Reports (volume 8 of Howard's Reports) at page 251, decided in 1850. Howard was a private reporter of the United States Supreme Court decisions. Today those decisions are published in three sets of reports: the United States Reports (which are the reports issued by the court itself), the so-called Lawyer's Edition, published by the Lawyers Cooperative Publishing Co., and the Supreme Court Reporter, published by the West Publishing Co. The latter two are customarily abbreviated "L.Ed." and "S.Ct." There are differences in format among the three sets of reports, and minor differences in the brief account, preceding the opinion of the court, concerning who appeared as counsel on the written briefs and in oral argument and the procedure that brought the case into the Supreme Court. In the earlier days of private reporting, the reporter often made his own rather lengthy statement of the facts of the case.

2. Do not be depressed by the archaic language in which Veazie's promise ("covenant") to Lord was couched. Some of the technical terminology is unnecessary, but some that may appear unnecessary to the uninitiated is in fact vital. In this instance the meaning is clear enough for purposes of understanding the present lawsuit.

charter for the purposes of navigation and transportation by steam or otherwise."

In September 1848, this action on the above covenant was docketed by consent,[3] and a statement of facts agreed upon by the respective counsel, under which the opinion of the court was to be taken, viz. that if [the said shares are not free and clear of all encumbrances, and more specifically if it should be found that the City Bank at Boston has a valid claim to ownership of the railroad], then the plaintiff was entitled to recover; or if the canal and railroad company, or the stockholders thereof, had not a right to navigate the river, then the plaintiff was also entitled to recover. . . .

In October, 1848, the court, held by Mr. Justice Ware, gave judgment for the defendant pro forma, at the request of the parties, in order that the judgment and question might be brought before this court, and the case was brought up . . . as before mentioned.[4]

On the 31st of January, 1849, the record[5] was filed in this court, and on the 2d of February, printed arguments of counsel were filed, and the case submitted to the court on the 5th. It was not taken up by the court, but continued to the next term.

On the 28th of December, 1849, Mr. Wyman B. S. Moor [acting in his own behalf and as attorney for the City Bank, at Boston, filed a motion to dismiss the appeal in this case] upon the ground that it was a fictitious case, got up between said parties[6] for the purpose of settling legal questions upon which he, the said Moor and the City Bank [at Boston], had a large amount of property depending. The motion made by Mr. Moor upon his individual account was to dismiss the appeal; that made by him as counsel for the City Bank was in the alternative, either to dismiss the suit, or order the same back to the Circuit Court for trial, and allow the said City Bank to be heard in the trial of the same.

[In addition to the motion to dismiss, Mr. Moor filed supporting affidavits. These affidavits and the other documents filed with the court alleged the following matters of fact.]

In 1842, the Bangor and Piscataquis Canal and Railroad Company, in the State of Maine, which had been chartered by the State, executed a deed to the City Bank, at Boston, by virtue of which that bank claimed to hold the entire property of the company.[7]

3. This means that Veazie formally agreed to have Lord's suit for damages, based on Veazie's promise, placed on the court's calendar ("docket") for trial and made no objection to the statement of facts contained in Lord's complaint.

4. This means that the court, with the plaintiff's consent, without hearing argument entered a judgment for the defendant, with the understanding that the plaintiff could appeal to the Supreme Court. (This procedure is not used today, though occasionally it is possible by other procedural means to present a case immediately to the appellate court.)

5. The "record" includes all the papers filed by the parties. Where a trial or trial type hearing was part of the procedure prior to appeal, a verbatim transcript of the testimony in the trial or hearing may have to be included in the record on appeal.

6. The "parties" are Lord and Veazie.

7. The deed referred to was probably a mortgage deed issued by the railroad to secure a loan from the bank. Such a deed transfers a limited interest in specific property, called a security interest, from the borrower to the lender. In the event of default on the loan the

In 1846, the Legislature of Maine granted to William Moor and Daniel Moor, Jun., their associates and assigns, the sole right of navigating the Penobscot River.

In July, 1847, an act was passed additional to the charter of the [railroad] company, by virtue of which a reorganization took place. The City Bank claimed to be the sole proprietors or beneficiaries under this new charter, and John W. Veazie, who had held a large number of shares in the original company, claimed that the management and control were granted to the stockholders.[8]

[The major stockholder in the Bangor and Piscataquis Railroad Company was one Samuel Veazie, the father of John W. Veazie, and the father-in-law of Nathaniel Lord.]

None of the persons whose interest was adverse to that of the plaintiff and defendant had any knowledge of these proceedings, until after the case was removed to this court, and submitted for decision on printed arguments, although one or more of those most deeply interested resided in the town in which Lord, one of the parties, lived.

[In addition, Mr. Moor stated that a suit brought by him against Veazie in the Court of Maine was still pending there, and that the suit involved the same right of navigating the Penobscot River, which was one of the points in the conveyance from Lord to Veazie.]

[Mr. Moor] further stated his belief, that this case was a feigned issue, got up collusively between the said Lord and Veazie, for the purpose of prejudicing his rights, and obtaining the judgment of this court upon principles of law affecting a large amount of property, in which he and others were interested.[9]

MR. CHIEF JUSTICE TANEY [10] delivered the opinion of the court.

The court is satisfied, upon examining the record in this case, and

---

mortgaged property may be used to satisfy all or a part of the loan obligation.

8. The reorganization of a corporation is a procedure through which the ownership of a corporation may be changed or rearranged. The City Bank's claim that the reorganization gave it the ownership of the Railroad Company probably stems from the transactions involved in the execution of the deed (see note 7 *supra*). Since the railroad corporation was established (chartered) by an act of the Maine legislature, the changes affecting the reorganization also had to come through legislative action. Today the organization, reorganization, and dissolution of corporations is normally accomplished through nonlegislative proceedings.

9. All of the preceding is taken from the statement of the reporter, Mr.

Howard. See note 1, *supra*. The editors have substantially rearranged this material but have preserved, wherever possible, the language used by Mr. Howard. The brackets denote places where the editors have revised the language in the reporter's summary of the case.

10. Roger Brooke Taney (1777–1864) was the second son of an aristocratic Maryland family, who first became nationally known as Andrew Jackson's Attorney General and Secretary of the Treasury. When Jackson appointed him in 1836 to succeed John Marshall as Chief Justice of the United States, it was feared by many that Taney would bend the Court to the political purposes of "Jacksonian democracy." Once on the Court, however, Chief Justice Taney became a leading exponent of judicial self-restraint and the inherent limitations of the judicial function. Paradoxically again,

the affidavits filed in the motion to dismiss, that the contract set out in the pleadings was made for the purpose of instituting this suit, and that there is no real dispute between the plaintiff and defendant. On the contrary, it is evident that their interest in the question brought here for decision is one and the same, and not adverse; and that in these proceedings the plaintiff and the defendant are attempting to procure the opinion of this court upon a question of law, in the decision of which they have a common interest opposed to that of other persons, who are not parties to this suit, who had no knowledge of it while it was pending in the Circuit Court, and no opportunity of being heard there in defence of their rights. And their conduct is the more objectionable, because they have brought up the question upon a statement of facts agreed on between themselves, without the knowledge of the parties with whom they were in truth in dispute, and upon a judgment *pro forma* entered by their mutual consent, without any actual judicial decision by the court. It is a question, too, in which it appears that property to a very large amount is involved, the right to which depends on its decision.

It is proper to say that the counsel who argued here the motion to dismiss, in behalf of the parties to the suit, stand entirely acquitted of any participation in the purposes for which these proceedings were instituted; and indeed could have had none, as they were not counsel in the Circuit Court, and had no concern with the case until after it came before this court. And we are bound to presume that the counsel who conducted the case in the court below were equally uninformed of the design and object of these parties; and that they would not knowingly have represented to the court that a feigned controversy was a real one.

It is the office of courts of justice to decide the rights of persons and of property, when the persons interested cannot adjust them by agreement between themselves—and to do this upon the full hearing of both parties. And any attempt, by a mere colorable dispute, to obtain the opinion of the court upon a question of law which a party desires to know for his own interest or his own purposes, when there is no real and substantial controversy between those who appear as adverse parties to the suit, is an abuse which courts of justice have always reprehended, and treated as a punishable contempt of court.

The suit is spoken of, in the affidavits filed in support of it, as an amicable action, and the proceeding defended on that ground. But an amicable action, in the sense in which these words are used in courts of justice, presupposes that there is a real dispute between the parties concerning some matter of right. And in a case of that kind it sometimes happens, that, for the purpose of obtaining a decision of the controversy, without incurring needless expense and trouble, they agree to conduct the suit in an amicable manner, that is to say, that they will not embarrass each other with unnecessary forms or technicalities, and

however, in 1859 in the famous Dred Scott case he went well beyond what was necessary for the decision in stating that Congress had no right to abolish slavery in the Territories. This decision has been Taney's chief identifying mark in history, but it should be weighed against the sum total of his judicial career.

will mutually admit facts which they know to be true, and without requiring proof, and will bring the point in dispute before the court for decision, without subjecting each other to unnecessary expense or delay. But there must be an actual controversy, and adverse interests. The amity consists in the manner in which it is brought to issue before the court. And such amicable actions, so far from being objects of censure, are always approved and encouraged, because they facilitate greatly the administration of justice between the parties. The objection in the case before us is, not that the proceedings were amicable, but that there is no real conflict of interest between them; that the plaintiff and defendant have the same interest, and that interest adverse and in conflict with the interest of third persons, whose rights would be seriously affected if the question of law was decided in the manner that both of the parties to this suit desire it to be.

A judgment entered under such circumstances, and for such purposes, is a mere form. The whole proceeding was in contempt of the court, and highly reprehensible, and the learned district judge, who was then holding the Circuit Court, undoubtedly suffered the judgment *pro forma* to be entered under the impression that there was in fact a controversy between the plaintiff and defendant, and that they were proceeding to obtain a decision upon a disputed question of law, in which they had adverse interests. A judgment in form, thus procured, in the eye of the law is no judgment of the court. It is a nullity, and no writ of error will lie upon it. This writ is, therefore, dismissed.

Order

This cause came on to be heard on the transcript of the record from the Circuit Court of the United States for the District of Maine, and was argued by counsel, and it appearing to the court here, from the affidavit and other evidence filed in the case by Mr. Moor, in behalf of third persons not parties to this suit, that there is no real dispute between the plaintiff and defendant in this suit, but, on the contrary, that their interest is one and the same, and is adverse to the interests of the persons aforesaid, it is the opinion of this court, that the judgment of the Circuit Court entered *pro forma* in this case is a nullity and void, and that no writ of error will lie upon it. On consideration whereof, it is now here ordered and adjudged by this court, that the writ of error be, and the same is hereby, dismissed, each party paying his own costs, and that this cause be, and the same is hereby, remanded to the said court, to be dealt with as law and justice may require.

Notes and Questions

1. Write a brief summary of the Court's opinion, giving (a) the facts relevant to the decision, (b) the legal issue or issues which the Court considered, (c) the decision of the Court, (d) the reasons for the decision.

2. Do the facts as summarized by the reporter offer *conclusive* evidence that there was no actual controversy between Lord and Veazie? Do these facts provide a reasonable basis for an *inference* that there was no actual controversy between Lord and Veazie? Articulate a full explanation of your answers to these questions.

3.　Does the reporter's summary of the case disclose the existence of a conflict (actual or potential) between (a) the City Bank of Boston and the shareholders of the railroad, (b) Moor and the railroad, (c) Moor and the City Bank of Boston?

4.　Why did Mr. Moor make a different motion in his own behalf from that which he made as counsel for the City Bank?

5.　Now that Mr. Moor and the City Bank are notified and are in the case, wouldn't it be sensible for the court to return the case to the Circuit Court for a new trial?

6.　If the Supreme Court had decided this case in favor of Veazie, how (if at all) would that judgment adversely affect the rights of Moor or the City Bank?

7.　Compare the following case with Lord v. Veazie:

United States v. Johnson, 319 U.S. 302, 63 S.Ct. 1233 (1943). Roach, a tenant in a residential property owned by Johnson, paid rent in excess of the maximum permitted under wartime price control regulations established by the Price Administrator pursuant to the Emergency Price Control Act of 1942. Roach then sued Johnson alleging that the collection of the excessive payment was a violation of the Act and demanding treble damages and reasonable attorney's fees as provided in the Act. Johnson then filed a motion to dismiss the suit on the grounds that the Act was unconstitutional and therefore Roach had no valid cause of action, i. e., no right to recover damages for breach of a constitutionally invalid statute. The United States intervened in the case as an interested party and filed a brief in support of the constitutionality of the Act. The District Court dismissed Roach's complaint, holding that the Act was unconstitutional. The United States then moved to reopen the case on the ground that it was a collusive suit and was not a real case or controversy. That motion was denied. The United States appealed to the Supreme Court, claiming error by the District Court in its rulings on both the constitutional issue and the motion to reopen the case. The Government submitted an affidavit of the plaintiff (Roach) which was uncontradicted by Johnson and which alleged the following facts:

The suit had been brought in a fictitious name; it was instituted as a "friendly suit" at the landlord's request; the plaintiff did not employ, pay, or even meet the attorney who appeared in his behalf and he had no knowledge of who had paid the required court fees; the plaintiff had not read the complaint filed in his name and he had no knowledge of the amount demanded as damages until he read a report about the suit in a local newspaper.

The Supreme Court vacated the judgment of the District Court and remanded the case to that court with instructions that the case be dismissed "because it is not in any real sense adversary. It does not assume the 'honest and actual antagonistic assertion of rights' to be adjudicated—a safeguard essential to the integrity of the judicial process   .   .   ."

8.   Can the following case be reconciled with Lord v. Veazie and U. S. v. Johnson?

Buchanan v. Warley, 245 U.S. 60, 38 S.Ct. 16 (1917).   A municipal ordinance of Louisville, Kentucky forbade "any colored person" or any "white person" to reside on any block where the majority of houses were occupied as residences by persons of the other race. Buchanan owned a lot on a block which had ten existing residences. Eight of the houses were occupied by whites, while the two houses closest to Buchanan's lot were occupied by Negroes.

Buchanan contracted to sell the lot to Warley, who was a Negro. The contract contained the following proviso:

> "It is understood that I [Worley] am purchasing the above property for the purpose of having erected thereon a house which I propose to make my residence, and it is a distinct part of this agreement that I shall not be required to accept a deed to the above property or to pay for said property unless I have the right under the laws of the State of Kentucky and the City of Louisville to occupy said property as a residence."

Buchanan brought suit against Warley to compel him to accept a deed to the property and to pay the agreed price.   Warley answered that he was excused from performance by the proviso set out above since the Louisville ordinance barred him from using the lot for his own residence.   Buchanan replied that the ordinance was unconstitutional under the Fourteenth Amendment to the Constitution of the United States (*infra* p. 213) and therefore could not be enforced against Warley.   The trial court and the Court of Appeals of Kentucky held that the ordinance was valid and gave Warley a complete defense to the action.   Buchanan appealed this judgment to the Supreme Court of the United States.

The attorneys for Buchanan and Warley presented extensive briefs and vigorous oral argument to the Court regarding the constitutional validity of such legislative attempts to segregate the races. Numerous briefs were also presented by persons and organizations (including the National Association for the Advancement of Colored People—NAACP) appearing as *amicus curiae*, i. e., friend of the court.   The Supreme Court held the ordinance to be an unconstitutional deprivation of Buchanan's property rights without "due process of law".

SECTION 2.2   ADVISORY OPINIONS

MATTER OF STATE INDUSTRIAL COMMISSION

Court of Appeals of New York,[1] 1918.
224 N.Y. 13, 119 N.E. 1027.[2]

[In 1914, a Workmen's Compensation Law went into effect in the State of New York, establishing an insurance program to provide compensation to the victims of industrial accidents or their beneficiaries. The cost of the program was to be borne by employers who either had to purchase insurance or make their own provision, by self-insurance, for the payment of benefits. Benefits were to be paid periodically to the employee until he or she recovered or, in the event of a permanent or fatal injury, to the employee or his or her beneficiaries for a specified length of time. The responsibility for administering the program and enforcing the law was vested in a State Industrial Commission.

The 1914 law provided that in the case of a permanent though not fatal injury, the Commission could collect from the employer or insurer an amount equal to the present value of the award. In such cases the Commission then became responsible for the administration of the funds and the payment of benefits under the award. The law was amended in June 1917 to provide that the Commission should have similar authority regarding death benefit awards.[3]]

CARDOZO, J.[4] On July 2, 1917, one of the members of the state industrial commission proposed to that body a resolution that every mutual compensation insurance company and every self-insurer should pay into the state fund, under section 27 of the Workmen's Compensation Law, as amended by chapter 705 of the Laws of 1917, the present value of death benefits under every award against such insurance carriers for deaths occurring between July 1, 1914, and July 1, 1917, inclusive.

The resolution was neither adopted nor rejected. All that the commission did was to recite that there was doubt about its power, and to certify to the Appellate Division a question of law to be answered by that court. The following is the question certified: "Has the state

1. The Court of Appeals is the highest court of the State of New York. In most states, the highest court is called the Supreme Court (*cf.* Supreme Court of Ohio, Supreme Court of California); in Massachusetts, it is called the Supreme Judicial Court. In New York, by a strange quirk, the title Supreme Court is given to trial courts; the intermediate court of appeal is called the Appellate Division.

2. "224 N.Y. 13" means: Volume 224 of the New York Reports (as the volumes of reported cases of the Court of Appeals are called), at page 13. New York Court of Appeals decisions are also reported, together with those of

several other states, in the North Eastern Reporter (abbreviated N.E.), as shown by the citation, "119 N.E. 1027."

3. The two preceding paragraphs were added by the editors.

4. The author of the opinion is Benjamin N. Cardozo, member of the New York Court of Appeals from 1914 to 1932 and of the Supreme Court of the United States from 1932 to 1938. He is famous not only as a judge but also as the author of The Nature of the Judicial Process, The Growth of the Law, and other books.

industrial commission power and authority under the provisions of section 27 of the Workmen's Compensation Law, as amended by chapter 705 of the Laws of 1917, to require the payment into the state fund, in accordance with the provisions of said section, of the present value of unpaid death benefits in cases in which awards were made prior to July 1, 1917?"

At the Appellate Division the Self-Insurer's Association, an unincorporated body of insurers, was allowed to appear and file a brief. Like permission was granted to the New York Central Railroad Company. Till then the attorney-general stood before the court alone. Even afterwards there were no adverse parties. There were merely friends of the court striving to enlighten its judgment. The Appellate Division did not order anything to be done or forborne. It could not. It merely answered a question. Its order was that the question propounded be answered in the affirmative. It thereupon granted leave to the intervenors to appeal to this court. The same question that was certified to the Appellate Division has been certified to us.

The determination of such an appeal is not within our jurisdiction. The practice is said to be justified under section 23 of the act. That section authorizes an appeal to the Appellate Division from an award or decision of the commission. It then provides that "the commission may also, in its discretion certify to such Appellate Division of the Supreme Court, questions of law involved in its decision." Appeals may be taken to this court subject to the same limitations as in civil actions (Matter of Harnett v. Steen Co., 216 N.Y. 101, 110 N.E. 170).

Nothing in these provisions sustains the practice followed. The commission made no decision. There was no case or controversy before it. No summons to attend a hearing had been given to the insurance carriers. No carrier had appeared. The members of the commission, debating their powers among themselves, asked and obtained the advisory opinion of a court. Without notice to the carriers to be affected by their action, they fortified themselves in advance by judicial instruction. In such circumstances the answer of the Appellate Division bound no one and settled nothing. We do not know that the commission will ever adopt the proposed resolution. If it does, and so notifies the carriers, the legality of its action will remain open for contest in the courts. No advice that may now be given in response to a request for light and guidance can prejudge the issue or control the outcome.

In that situation our duty is not doubtful. The function of the courts is to determine controversies between litigants (Interstate Commerce Commission v. Brimson, 154 U.S. 447, 475, 14 S.Ct. 1125; Osborn v. Bank of U. S., 9 Wheat. 738, 819; Mills v. Green, 159 U.S. 651, 16 S.Ct. 132; Marye v. Parsons, 114 U.S. 325, 330, 5 S.Ct. 962; Am. Book Co. v. Kansas, 193 U.S. 49, 24 S.Ct. 394). They do not give advisory opinions. The giving of such opinions is not the exercise of the judicial function (Thayer, Cases on Constitutional Law, vol. 1, p. 175; American Doctrine of Const. Law, 7 Harvard Law Review, 153). It is true that in England the custom of the constitution makes the judges of the high court the assistants of the Lords, and requires them, upon the demand of the Lords, to give "consultative" opinions (Thayer, *supra;* Opinion of the Justices, 126 Mass. 557, 562). But that custom is a survival of the days when the judges were members of the great council of the realm (Thayer, *supra;* T. E. May, Parliamentary Practice [12th ed.], pp. 55, 56, 182; Anson, Law and Custom of the Constitution, pp. 45, 52, 449). In the United States no such duty attaches to the judicial office in the absence of express provision of the Constitution. (Dinan v. Swig, 223 Mass. 516, 519, 112 N.E. 91; Opinion of Court, 62 N.H. 704, 706; Rice v. Austin, 19 Minn. 103.) Even in those states, e. g., Massachusetts, Maine, and New Hampshire, where such provisions are found, the opinions thus given have not the quality of judicial authority. The judges then act, "not as a court, but as the constitutional advisers of the other departments" (Opinion of Justices, 126 Mass. 557, 566; Laughlin v. City of Portland, 111 Me. 486, 497, 90 A. 318). In this state the legislature is without power to charge the courts with the performance of non-judicial duties (Matter of Davies, 168 N.Y. 89, 61 N.E. 118). It has not attempted to do so by this statute. The questions to be certified under section 23 of the act must be incidental to a pending controversy with adverse parties litigant. Those limitations apply to the Appellate Division. Even more explicit are the restrictions in this court. Our jurisdiction is to be exercised subject to the same limitations as in civil actions (Workmen's Comp.Act, § 23; Code Civ.Proc. § 190). The order under review is not one which finally determines a special proceeding (Matter of Droege, 197 N.Y. 44, 50, 90 N.E. 340; Matter of Jones, 181 N.Y. 389, 74 N.E. 226). It is not an intermediate order in a special proceeding. There has been no judicial proceeding at all. There has been a tender of advice which may be accepted or rejected.

The record now before us supplies a pointed illustration of the need that the judicial function be kept within its ancient bounds. Some of the arguments addressed to us in criticism of the resolution apply to all awards for death benefits; others to awards made before June, 1916; others to awards where one of the dependents is a widow. It is thus conceivable that the proposed resolution may be valid as to some carriers and invalid as to others. We are asked by an omnibus answer to an omnibus question to adjudge the rights of all. That is not the way in which a system of case law develops. We deal with the particular instance; and we wait till it arises.

The appeal must be dismissed without costs to either party.

HISCOCK, CH. J., COLLIN, CUDDEBACK, POUND, CRANE and ANDREWS, JJ., concur.

Appeal dismissed.

Note

"Case Law; Common Law"

In the last paragraph of his opinion, Judge Cardozo speaks of "a system of case law" and the way such a system of law develops. He is referring to a special attribute of the legal systems of the United States and the British Commonwealth of nations. Each of these legal systems is rooted in the law which evolved in England following the Norman conquest, the so-called Common Law. English Common Law judges developed a heavy reliance on judicial opinions in past cases as a source of law to be followed in the resolution of live cases in court. The past cases came to be seen as "precedents" from which lawyers and judges could extract principles to guide and govern the process of resolving present disputes. Thus, in a real sense, the judges came to feel and be bound by their own (and their brethren's) decisions in past cases where the issues in the present case were the same as or similar to issues in the past cases. Note, for example, the extensive citation in Judge Cardozo's opinion of prior decisions of state and federal courts in cases dealing with the issue of the scope of appellate jurisdiction of courts. Each of these cases is put forth by Judge Cardozo as a precedent which is authority for the respective propositions asserted by him immediately prior to their citation in his opinion.

This subject is more extensively treated in subsequent sections. Suffice it to note here that the system of case law has its own imperatives which are strongly felt by judges and lawyers in the common law jurisdictions. When Judge Cardozo speaks with reference to the resolution of the case before him, he draws on the precedent of past cases *and* he knows that his words have significance for the future since his decision will itself become a precedent. Could that knowledge be a factor affecting his decision?

Questions

1. Write a short statement of the case, giving (a) the important facts, (b) the issue or issues presented, (c) the decision of the court, and (d) the reasons for the decision.

2. What is an advisory opinion? Why should courts not be eager to give advisory opinions?

3. What are adverse parties? Was not the attorney general "adverse" to the Self-Insurer's Association?

4. Suppose the commission had adopted the resolution and the association had then refused to pay. Would the court have then been required to decide the same question that was here certified by the commission? If so, why should it not be required to decide it in advance of the commission's adoption of the resolution?

5. Contrast the extensive citation of previous decisions in the opinion in this case with the total absence of such citations in Lord v. Veazie, *supra*. What reasons can you suggest for the difference between the two opinions with respect to this matter?

UNITED STATES CONSTITUTION
Article III

Section 1. The judicial power of the United States shall be vested in one Supreme Court, and in such inferior courts as the Congress may from time to time ordain and establish. The judges, both of the Supreme and inferior courts, shall hold their offices during good behavior, and shall, at stated times, receive for their services, a compensation, which shall not be diminished during their continuance in office.

Section 2.   (1) The judicial power shall extend to all cases, in law and equity, arising under this Constitution, the laws of the United States, and treaties made, or which shall be made, under their authority;—to all cases affecting ambassadors, other public ministers and consuls;—to all cases of admiralty and maritime jurisdiction;—to controversies to which the United States shall be a party;—to controversies between two or more States;—between a State and citizens of another State;—between citizens of different States;—between citizens of the same State claiming lands under grants of different States, and between a State, or the citizens thereof, and foreign States, citizens or subjects.

OPINION OF THE JUSTICES, 1793

The constitutions and laws of some states of the United States and of many foreign states give courts the power to issue advisory opinions to the legislative or executive branches in certain types of situations. The courts have tended to construe such grants of power narrowly, and to hold that such advisory opinions have no binding effect. The Supreme Court of the United States early held that the federal courts should not give formal advisory opinions. In 1793 the Justices of the Supreme Court of the United States received the following letter, sent to them in the President's behalf by the Secretary of State:

Philadelphia, July 18, 1793

Gentlemen:

The war which has taken place among the powers of Europe produces frequent transactions within our ports and limits, on which questions arise of considerable difficulty, and of greater importance to the peace of the United States. These questions depend for their solution on the construction of our treaties, on the laws of nature and nations, and on the laws of the land, and are often presented under circumstances *which do not give a cognizance of them to the tribunals of the country.* Yet, their decision is so little analogous to the ordinary functions of the executive, as to occasion embarrassment and difficulty to them. The President therefore would be much relieved if he found himself free to refer questions of this description to the opinions of the judges of the Supreme Court of the United States, whose knowledge of the subject would secure us against errors dangerous to the peace of the United States, and their authority insure the respect of all parties. He has therefore asked the attendance of such of the judges as could be collected in time for the occasion, to know, in the first place, their opinion, whether the public may, with propriety, be availed of their *advice on these questions?* And if they may, to present, for their advice the abstract questions which have already occurred, or may soon occur, from which they will themselves strike out such as any circumstances might, in their opinion, forbid them to pronounce on. I have the honour to be with sentiments of the most perfect respect, gentlemen,

Your most obedient and humble servant,

Thomas Jefferson

———

The following are some of the questions submitted by the President to the Justices:

    1. Do the treaties between the United States and France give to France or her citizens, a *right*, when at war with a power with whom the United States are at peace, to fit out originally in and from the ports of the United States vessels armed for war, with or without commission?

    2. If they give such a *right*, does it extend to all manner of armed vessels, or to particular kinds only? If the latter, to what kinds does it extend?

    3. Do they give to France or her citizens, in the case supposed a right to refit or arm anew vessels, which, before their coming within any port of the United States, were armed for war, with or without commission?

    4. If they give such a *right*, does it extend to all manner of armed vessels, or to particular kinds only? If the latter, to what kinds does it extend? Does it include an *augmentation* of force, or does it only extend to replacing the vessel in *status quo*?

. . .

    19. If any armed vessel of a foreign power at war with another, with whom the United States are at peace, shall make prize of the subjects or property of its enemy within the territory or jurisdiction of the United States, have not the United States a right to cause restitution of such prizes? Are they bound, or not, by the principles of neutrality to do so, if such prize shall be within their power?

    20. To what distance, by the laws and usages of nations, may the United States exercise the right of prohibiting the hostilities of foreign powers at war with each other within rivers, bays, and arms of the sea, and upon the sea along the coasts of the United States?

    21. Have vessels, armed for war under commission from a foreign power, a right, without the consent of the United States, to engage within their jurisdiction seamen or soldiers for the service of such vessels, being citizens of that power, or of another foreign power, or citizens of the United States?

. . .

    25. May we, within our own ports, sell ships to both parties, prepared merely for merchandise? May they be pierced for guns?

26.　May we carry either or both kinds to the ports of the belligerent powers for sale?

27.　Is the principle, that free bottoms make free goods, and enemy bottoms make enemy goods, to be considered as now an established part of the law of nations?

28.　If it is not, are nations with whom we have no treaties, authorized by the law of nations to take out of our vessels enemy passengers, not being soldiers, and their baggage?

29.　May an armed vessel belonging to any of the belligerent powers follow *immediately* merchant vessels, enemies, departing from our ports, for the purpose of making prizes of them?　If not, how long ought the former to remain, after the latter have sailed?　And what shall be considered as the place of departure, from which the time is to be counted?　And how are the facts to be ascertained?

Chief Justice Jay and the Associate Justices replied to the President directly, as follows:

August 8, 1793

Sir:

We have considered the previous question stated in a letter written by your direction to us by the Secretary of State on the 18th of last month, [regarding] the lines of separation drawn by the Constitution between the three departments of the government. These being in certain respects checks upon each other, and our being judges of a court in the last resort, are considerations which afford strong arguments against the propriety of our extra-judicially deciding the questions alluded to, especially as the power given by the Constitution to the President, of calling on the heads of departments for opinions, seems to have been *purposely* as well as expressly united to the *executive* departments.

We exceedingly regret every event that may cause embarrassment to your administration, but we derive consolation from the reflection that your judgment will discern what is right, and that your usual prudence, decision, and firmness will surmount every obstacle to the preservation of the rights, peace, and dignity of the United States.

Questions

1.　Article III of the United States Constitution provides for the establishment of a Supreme Court and enumerates specific instances in which the Court may exercise the judicial power.　The enumerated instances are situations involving cases or controversies.　There is no express limitation on the exercise of judicial power which prohibits making advisory opinions, and the terms "case" and "controversy" are not defined.　Do you think that the framers of the Constitution would have been wiser to provide a general definition of the judicial power?

2.　Assuming that the Constitution of the United States leaves open the question whether the Justices of the Supreme Court, in addition to exercising "the judicial power" of deciding various enumerated types of "cases" and "controversies," may also advise the President "extrajudicially" on the proper interpretation of treaties, international law, and the like—do you think the Justices acted wisely in refusing so to advise? Why?

3.   If the Court had answered the questions propounded by Mr. Jefferson, how would this have saved the executive from "embarrassment and difficulty"? Can you think of any reasons why the President and the Secretary of State might have been perfectly satisfied with the reply made by the Court?

4.   Does the Court's answer to Mr. Jefferson help you to define the meaning of the term "judicial power" referred to in Article III of the Constitution?

Note

Does the following note on advisory opinions help you to understand the preceding cases? It is taken from Henry M. Hart, Jr.,* and Herbert Wechsler,** The Federal Courts and the Federal System (Brooklyn, N. Y., 1953), pp. 77–79.

Notice that all legal propositions consist of general directions or arrangements about what is to be done in future situations. Notice that the situations which may arise are of infinite, or near infinite, variety, and hence can be foreseen only imperfectly. Notice that the integrity and continued workability of the arrangements depends upon having some means of settling uncertain or controverted questions about their application to particular situations as and when the situations arise. Notice, finally, that the process of settlement of such questions is different from the process of making new arrangements in general terms for the future. The difference consists, does it not, in the necessity of relating the conclusion about the particular application in question, in some intelligible and acceptable way, to previous understanding about the arrangement and its other applications?

Would it be sound to conclude that the judicial function is essentially the function (in such cases as may be presented for decision) of authoritative application to particular situations of general propositions drawn from pre-existing sources—including as a necessary incident the function of determining the facts of the particular situation and of resolving uncertainties about the content of the applicable general propositions? Would it be sound to conclude, in addition, that this function is an inescapable one in any regime of law? . . .

In considering this question, take into account:

(a) The sheer multiplication of matters to which attention must be directed, and the resulting dispersion of thought, when a legal proposition is being formulated in the abstract;

---

* Henry M. Hart, Jr. was the Dean Professor of Law, Harvard University Law School, at the time of his death in 1969.

** Herbert Wechsler is Harlan Fiske Stone Professor of Constitutional Law, Columbia University School of Law.

(b) The special disadvantages of dispersion of thought when a legal proposition is being formulated by a process of reasoned development of authoritative premises rather than by such a process, for example, as that by which statutes are enacted;

(c) The importance, in the judicial development of law, of a concrete set of facts as an aid to the accurate formulation of the legal issue to be decided—the weight, in other words, which should be given to the maxim, *ex facto ius oritur* ["law arises out of fact"];

(d) The importance of an adversary presentation of evidence as an aid to the accurate determination of the facts out of which the legal issue arises;

(e) The importance of an adversary presentation of argument in the formulation and decision of the legal issue;

(f) The importance of a concrete set of facts in limiting the scope of the legal determination and as an aid to its accurate interpretation;

(g) The diminished scope for the play of personal convictions or preferences with respect to public policy when decision is focused upon a definite legal issue derived from a concrete set of facts;

(h) The value of having courts function as organs of the sober second thought of the community appraising action already taken, rather than as advisers at the front line of governmental action at the stage of initial decision;

(i) The importance of all the factors enumerated in maximizing the acceptability of decisions, and the importance of acceptable decisions.

In relation particularly to points (c) and (f), above, recall how often there is genuine uncertainty about the meaning of an abstract proposition. Reflect that in such a situation there are only two ways in which the meaning can be clarified—by restatement in other abstract terms whose meaning is not in doubt, or by concrete example. Consider how the possibilities of confusion are multiplied when meaning cannot be interpreted in the light of such an example. Cf. Morris, Foundations of the Theory of Signs (International Encyclopedia of Unified Science, Vol. 1, No. 2, 1938) 24–25.

SECTION 2.3   MOOT CASES: UNRIPE CONTROVERSIES

COLE v. CHIEF OF POLICE OF FALL RIVER

Supreme Judicial Court of Massachusetts, 1942.
312 Mass. 523, 45 N.E.2d 400.

RONAN, J. The plaintiff, a candidate for the office of representative in Congress from the Fourteenth Congressional District of Massachusetts, equipped an automobile and trailer, both registered in his name, with signs directing attention to the record of his opponent and informing the public that he was a candidate for the office. The trailer carried a large board, approximately fifteen feet long and seven feet wide, on each of the two faces of which was a sign attacking the public record of his opponent. The automobile bore a sign approximately four feet long and three feet high which announced the candidacy of the plaintiff and referred to his opponent as an ex-congressman. On the morning of May 30, 1942, while the automobile and trailer were being operated along a public street in Fall River by an agent of the plaintiff, the said agent was informed by the defendant Verville, a captain of the police department of Fall River, that he was violating the law and, subsequently, the defendant Violette, chief of police, informed the plaintiff that he intended to enforce against him an ordinance which provided that "No person shall operate or park a vehicle on any street or highway for the primary purpose of displaying advertising signs." The plaintiff then [brought suit] against the chief of police, a police captain, the police board of the city of Fall River created by St.1894, c. 351, and the mayor. [The suit,] with the consent of the parties, was dismissed as to the mayor. The remaining defendants intend to enforce the ordinance above mentioned and various other ordinances governing traffic on the streets of Fall River, and also the rules and regulations adopted by the State department of public works, division of highways, by virtue of G.L.(Ter.Ed.) c. 93, § 29, for the control and restriction of billboards, signs, and other advertising devices. The plaintiff has appealed from a final decree dismissing the bill.

When the case was reached for argument in this court on November 10, 1942, it was properly represented by an affidavit filed by the defendants that the plaintiff had been defeated in the primary election of his party held on September 15, 1942, and that the successful candidate at this primary of the political party of which the plaintiff was a member was defeated at the election held on November 3, 1942, by the candidate of the opposing party. The plaintiff on the other hand has filed an affidavit stating that he intends to use upon the streets of Fall River in another political campaign this equipment with different messages on it.

The aim of [the suit] is a permanent injunction, restraining the defendants from interfering with the operation of the plaintiff's automobile and trailer bearing the signs described in the bill upon the streets of Fall River. The occasion for the use of such signs has passed and there is now no actual controversy based upon any factual foundation existing between the parties. While there still may be a difference of opinion as to the validity of the ordinances in question, there is no longer any present clash of contending rights. Parties are not entitled to decisions upon abstract propositions of law unrelated to some live controversy. [Citations of cases omitted.] This rule applies with special force where an adjudication is sought upon the constitutionality of some statute or ordinance as "it is almost the undeviating rule of the courts, both state and Federal—not to decide constitutional questions until the necessity for such decision arises in the record before the court." [Citations of cases omitted.] The possibility that the same issues might arise in the future and that it might be advantageous for the parties to have their rights determined in advance is not enough to call for the rendition of a judgment, which the future might show was of little practical value and merely settled a matter that had become no more than a theoretical dispute. The questions raised by the bill have become moot. [Citations of cases omitted.]

The final decree, in the opinion of a majority of the court, is to be modified by the insertion of a clause to the effect that the bill is dismissed on the ground that the questions raised have become moot, and the decree as so modified is affirmed with costs. [Citations of cases omitted.]

Ordered accordingly.

Note

"Common Law" and "Equity": an historical outline. In the majority of civil cases the plaintiff seeks "damages," that is, a money award. In the preceding case, however, the plaintiff did not seek damages but an injunction, which is a court order directing the person to whom it is addressed to do or to refrain from doing certain acts. A suit for an injunction is called a "suit in equity," as contrasted with an action for damages which is called an "action at law." Explanation of this contrast between "law" and "equity" requires a brief excursion into legal history.[1]

Prior to the Norman Conquest there was no substantial body of law which was applicable throughout England. Although the Angles, Saxons, and other kinship groups had courts, the law administered in their courts was largely a matter of custom which varied from place to place and from tribe to tribe. Royal law was sparse and did not attempt to alter the basic local and tribal character of the legal system. After the Conquest, the Normans did not immediately displace the local and tribal laws but sought to adapt them to the socio-political institutions (feudalism) which they brought with them from the continent. Eventually, however, the Anglo-Saxon legal structure was superseded by a system more suitable to the needs of the Anglo-Norman nation.

Starting in 1178, the Anglo-Norman kings instituted a system of central courts, staffed by the king's judges, who administered the king's justice in matters delegated to them. These royal courts became the regular courts of England, which sat to resolve disputes according to law. The law administered by these courts was not the local law of Anglo-Saxon days but a law common to all England. The system of procedures, remedies, and rules developed in these regular courts was later designated as "the common law" and the courts themselves came to be referred to as "courts of common law."

The term "equity," derived from the Latin *aequitas*, has the general meaning of equality or justice. As a legal concept the term had a somewhat different meaning in the legal systems of the 12th and 13th centuries. "Equity" was the principle of mercy and fairness which could be invoked to mitigate hardships ("inequities") occasioned by too strict an adherence to general legal doctrine in unusual

1. A fuller historical treatment of the larger background of legal development out of which both common law and equity emerged is given *infra*, pp. 572 ff.

cases. This concept of equity had evolved in Roman Law, especially under the influence of the Christian emperors of Byzantium, and it was perpetuated in other legal systems, particularly where the Church was influential.

Equity, in the sense of an exceptional exercise of discretion based on mercy or fairness, was a technique used by English judges during the formative years of the common law. During that period the common law courts freely adapted their procedures and remedies to the changing needs of their society, and they occasionally invoked the concepts of equity or right reason to justify adaptations and changes in the law. In time, however, reliance upon concepts of equity as a means of expanding the common law declined. This, in turn, stimulated the development in England of a special court, a "court of equity," which administered a system of procedures and remedies called "equity," in contradistinction to the system of procedures and remedies of the common law courts.

The emergence of this dual system of national courts in England may be traced to the 14th and 15th centuries. At that time the King's Bench (as the chief royal court was called) became rigid and narrow in its interpretation of its own functions and its own rules. The English legal historian T. F. T. Plucknett has set the date for the crystallization of this tendency to narrowness at 1342: it is in that year that one Justice said, "We will not and cannot change ancient usages," and another Justice laid down the rule, "Statutes are to be strictly interpreted," and that the first mention of the contrast between law and equity appeared in the law reports. "It is significant," Professor Plucknett has said, "that this is the moment when we first hear of the equitable jurisdiction of the Chancellor."[2]

The Chancellor was the most important statesman subordinate to the King. He was in a sense a deputy king, who could act on behalf of the King to assure that the machinery of government ran well and in accord with royal wishes. Pursuant to this authority the Chancellor established a special bureau in the Chancery (the Chancellor's office) to hear grievances which the King's Bench and other royal courts could not or would not handle adequately.

The handling of grievances in Chancery differed substantially from the practice in the royal courts. The Chancellor's jurisdiction was said to be a matter of "grace," i. e., review of a case in Chancery could not be demanded by a litigant as a matter of right but was invoked by petition which the Chancellor could accept or reject at his discretion. The Chancellor's jurisdiction was also said to be a matter of "conscience," meaning that the Chancellor was not bound to act according to the technicalities of the common law but instead was to

2. *Cf.* T. F. T. Plucknett, Statutes and Their Interpretation in the First Half of the Fourteenth Century (Cambridge, 1922), p. 121.

act according to the dictates of justice and mercy; he was to do "equity" when the law failed in this regard.

Since the Chancellor was almost invariably an ecclesiastic, he drew on the canon law of the Roman Catholic Church to guide him in his efforts to do "equity." His connection with the Church of Rome also caused him to draw on the law books of the Roman Empire for guidance, for Roman law was a major subject of study in the universities and monasteries of the West during the period when the equitable jurisdiction of the Chancellor was developing.

The Chancellor took jurisdiction in cases in which the royal courts would not give the kind of relief which in conscience the plaintiff should have. Thus equity became a supplementary system of justice. The Chancery did not have a general jurisdiction over all kinds of disputes; it acted—and equity continues to act—in those cases where "the legal (*i. e.*, common law) remedy is inadequate."

Although at first the Chancellor's exercise of jurisdiction in equity was but one of many tasks he performed, it came in time to be his prime function. The Chancery came to be called the High Court of Chancery and the Chancellor sat as chief judge of this court. The judicialization of the Chancery was accelerated in the 16th and 17th centuries when, for the most part, the Tudor and Stuart royalty ceased to appoint ecclesiastics to the office of Chancellor. The image of the Chancellor as a person particularly suited to decide matters according to "grace" and "conscience" no doubt suffered as a result, and the Chancellor became identified as just another lay official of the crown. The exercise of discretion by the Chancellor came to be looked upon as another means through which royal prerogative could be implemented, and the Court of Chancery became enmeshed in the struggle between the King and Parliament regarding the limits of royal authority and the role of Parliament in English government. This struggle was ultimately resolved in favor of Parliament, although only after the Puritan Revolution. The common law courts, which had sided with the Parliament, emerged as the dominant courts of England. The High Court of Chancery and the separate system of equity survived this upheaval but the discretionary powers of the Chancellor were greatly lessened as a result of the decline in royal authority.

Another factor which affected change in the working of the Court of Chancery was the religious reformation of England. The formal ties between the English monarchy and the Pope were broken by the establishment of the Church of England. This, plus cessation of the practice of appointing ecclesiastics as Chancellor, cut the informal tie between equity, on the one hand, and canon and Roman law on the other. Cut loose from this contact with other legal systems, and stripped of some of the flexibility afforded in the days when the Chancellor exercised a royal prerogative to change law, the

High Court of Chancery became in many ways as conservative as the common law courts had been. The Chancellor came to act not so much according to the notion of "grace" and "conscience" as in accord with the established practices of his predecessors. Equity became a formal and systematic body of law, in some respects more rigid and inflexible than the common law.

The dual court system of "law" and "equity" was carried to America by the colonists, and separate chancery courts were in operation in many of the states at the time of the adoption of the federal constitution. The dual system persisted in both England and the United States until the middle 19th century, at which time pressure for legal reform resulted in a reorganization of the courts in England and in many of the states.

The procedure and practice in the courts, both the common law courts and the chancery, came under severe attack. The very existence of dual court systems was criticized as an unnecessary feature of our law which tended to complicate litigation and hinder justice. Procedural reforms were undertaken and the dual court system was replaced, in most jurisdictions, by a unified court system in which judges sat to administer both "law" and "equity" as part of a unified system of procedures, remedies, and rules applicable in civil actions. But even where "equity" and "law" have been merged, in the sense that they are no longer administered by separate courts, lawyers and judges tend to think of them as distinct systems. An injunction, for example, is an "equitable remedy" and rules of equity practice—rules largely developed in the old Court of Chancery—are applied in such a proceeding. Similarly an action for damages for breach of contract, for example, is still referred to as an "action at law."

Notes and Questions

1. Write a short statement of the principal case, giving (a) the important facts, (b) the issue or issues presented, (c) the decision of the court, and (d) the reasons for the decision.

2. Does the decision in this case rest on the same principles as those reflected in Lord v. Veazie and Matter of Industrial Commission?

3. Plaintiff in this case is seeking an injunction. What specific acts of the police does he seek to enjoin? What appears to be the legal basis for his request for an injunction?

4. It is a general principle of equity that an injunction may be obtained only where the remedy "at law" is inadequate? Should that principle be controlling in this case?

5. Suppose Cole had brought suit to recover a money award under a statute authorizing civil actions for damages resulting from a denial of "civil rights" by a public official. Would this case be moot after November 3, 1942 (election day)?

Suppose the public prosecutor instituted criminal proceedings against the defendants in the principal case, based on the facts in that case, under a statute authorizing criminal proceedings to punish public officials for violating a person's civil rights. Would this prosecution be moot after election day?

What is a moot case?

6. When, and under what circumstances, might Cole present a "ripe" case to adjudicate the issues raised by him in the principal case?

7. Can you draft an injunction which would protect the right to free speech claimed by Cole but which would not interfere with the police in the performance of their duty to enforce the laws of Massachusetts or the Town of Fall River? Can you draft an injunction which would protect the right of free speech claimed by Cole, but which would not interfere with the community interest which the ordinance is supposed to protect? Can you draft an injunction which would strike some balance between the right asserted by Cole, the duty of the police, and the interests of the community?

8. A person bound by an injunction must comply scrupulously with its commands. Non-compliance is treated as an act of disrespect to the court which issued the injunction. Such disrespect, called contempt of court, is punishable in proceedings called contempt proceedings, in which the court may direct that the party in contempt pay a monetary penalty or that he be imprisoned, usually for a brief period, as punishment for the act of contempt. Such proceedings to punish for a past infraction are commonly called "criminal contempt" proceedings. In addition, most injunctions impose a continuing duty of compliance and refusal to comply with the injunction may constitute a continuing offense which calls for action to secure compliance. A common remedy in such cases is to incarcerate the offender until he "purges the contempt" by complying with the terms of the injunction. Proceedings to procure compliance with an injunction are commonly called "civil contempt" proceedings.

In 1957 during the Congressional debate on the Civil Rights Bill it was stated by some that the effect of an injunction against an election official restraining him or her from discriminating against Negroes could be nullified by delaying the initiation of contempt proceedings until the election was over, at which time the injunction would be moot. Others said that an injunction could be framed which would bind election officials in all future elections. [Note that the contempt proceedings here referred to are proceedings designed to secure obedience to the injunction.]

Do you see any good reasons against issuance of such injunctions? Assuming there are none, is the present case distinguishable on the ground that the petitioner for the injunction is not a United States Attorney (as under the Civil Rights Bill) but a private person?

9. Compare the decision in Cole v. Chief of Police with Anderson et al. v. Martin, 375 U.S. 399, 84 S.Ct. 454 (1964): Plaintiffs (Anderson and others) were candidates for election to public office in the State of Louisiana. A Louisiana statute provided that the race of each candidate be listed on the ballot. Plaintiffs, who are Negroes, sued in the Federal District Court to enjoin Martin, Secretary of State of Louisiana, from listing their race on the ballots to be used in the election in which plaintiffs were candidates. The complaint asserted that the election law violated rights guaranteed to the plaintiffs by the United States Constitution. The District Court denied the request for an injunction. Plaintiffs then moved to amend their complaint to show that the election had taken place during the pendency of the case before the District Court and that they had been defeated, but that they intended to be candidates for the same offices at the next election. The District Court denied this motion and refused to grant a permanent injunction against the enforcement of the statute. Plaintiffs appealed this decision directly to the Supreme Court of the United States. The Supreme Court found that the statute violated constitutionally protected rights of the plaintiffs and reversed the decision of the District Court.

Note

Declaratory Judgments. In countries which came under the strong influence of Roman law there has existed for many centuries a procedure whereby courts could declare the rights of parties in cases where no wrong has been done or immediately threatened and where no court order to the defendant to pay money or to do or refrain from doing something is sought. For over a century a similar procedure has existed in England, and it was subsequently introduced by so-called Declaratory Judgment Acts in the United States.

Even prior to such statutes there were certain types of situations in which American courts did nothing more than declare the law. For example, they could always grant petitions to determine the rights of adverse claimants to land and buildings—a proceeding "to remove a cloud from the title to real estate," or "to quiet title," as it is called. Also after secular courts obtained jurisdiction over marriage and divorce they acquired in most states the power to declare a bigamous marriage, for example, void from the beginning—no new status being created and no order being given, the decree being purely declaratory.

These and other examples were considered exceptional, however, until the Declaratory Judgment Acts extended the practice so that "Courts of record within their respective jurisdictions shall have power to declare rights, status, and other legal relations whether or not further relief is or could be claimed. . . . The declaration may be either affirmative or negative in form and effect; and such declarations shall have the force and effect of a final judgment or decree." [1]

In upholding the constitutionality of a Declaratory Judgment Act against the charge that it extends the jurisdiction of courts beyond the limits laid down in the federal Constitution, the Supreme Court of Pennsylvania stated that "in all jurisdictions where declaratory judgment practice obtains, the rule is established that it is a matter of judicial discretion whether or not jurisdiction will be taken to any particular case . . . and that jurisdiction will never be assumed unless the tribunal appealed to is satisfied that an actual controversy, or the ripening seeds of one, exists between parties . . . and that the declaration sought will be a practical help in ending the controversy. . . . Moreover, in a declaratory judgment proceeding the court will not decide future rights in anticipation of an event which may not happen, but, just as in the ordinary executory action, it will wait until the event takes place, unless special circumstances appear which warrant an immediate decision, as, for instance, where present rights depend on the declaration sought by plaintiff; and even then such rights will not be determined unless all parties concerned in their adjudication are present and ready to proceed with the case. . . ." [2]

SECTION 2.4   POLITICAL QUESTIONS

UNITED STATES CONSTITUTION

Article I

*   *   *

Section 8. The Congress shall have Power To lay and collect taxes, Duties, Imposts and Excises, to pay the Debts and provide for the common Defence and general Welfare of the United States;

. . .

To declare War, grant Letters of Marque and Reprisal, and make Rules concerning Captures on Land and Water;

---

1. Uniform Declaratory Judgment Act, 1922, § 1. This is one of approximately 120 "Uniform and Model Acts" which have been promulgated by the National Conference of Commissioners on Uniform State Laws and recommended for enactment by the states. The Commissioners are appointed by the Governors of their respective states. Over 100 of the recommended Acts have been enacted in verbatim or modified form in one or more of the 53 American legislative jurisdictions. The Uniform Declaratory Judgment Act has been adopted in 38 states, in the Commonwealth of Puerto Rico, and in the Territory of the Virgin Islands. Other states have adopted their own declaratory judgment acts, see e. g. New York CPLR § 3001. There is also a Federal Declaratory Judgments Act, 28 U.S.C.A. § 2201.

2. Petition of Kariher, Supreme Court of Pennsylvania, 284 Pa. 455, 131 A. 265 (1925).

To raise and support Armies, but no Appropriation of Money to that Use shall be for a longer Term than two Years;

To provide and maintain a Navy;

To make Rules for the Government and Regulation of the land and naval Forces;

To provide for calling forth the Militia to execute the Laws of the Union, suppress Insurrections and repel Invasions;

To provide for organizing, arming, and disciplining the Militia, and for governing such Part of them as may be employed in the Service of the United States, reserving to the States respectively, the Appointment of the Officers, and the Authority of training the Militia according to the discipline prescribed by Congress; . . .

To make all Laws which shall be necessary and proper for carrying into Execution the foregoing Powers, and all other Powers vested by this Constitution in the Government of the United States, or in any Department or Officer thereof.

Article II

*   *   *

Section 2. The President shall be Commander in Chief of the Army and Navy of the United States, and of the Militia of the several States, when called into the actual Service of the United States; . . .

*   *   *

AMENDMENT II. (1791)

A well regulated Militia, being necessary to the security of a free State, the right of the people to keep and bear Arms, shall not be infringed.

AMENDMENT III. (1791)

No Soldier shall, in time of peace be quartered in any house, without the consent of the Owner, nor in time of war, but in a manner to be prescribed by law.

*   *   *

AMENDMENT V. (1791)

No person shall be held to answer for a capital or otherwise infamous crime, unless on a presentment or indictment of a Grand Jury, except in cases arising in the land or naval forces, or in the Militia, when in actual service in time of War or public danger; . . .

UNITED STATES v. SISSON

United States District Court, D. Massachusetts, 1968.
294 F.Supp. 511.

WYZANSKI, CHIEF JUDGE. The grand jury indicted Sisson for wilfully refusing to perform a duty required under the Military Selective Service

Act of 1967, U.S.C. Title 50 App. § 451 et seq., in that he refused to comply with an order of his draft board to submit to induction into the armed forces of the United States.

He has moved to dismiss the indictment principally upon the ground that the draft act as applied to him violates the Constitution. He contends that there is under the Constitution of the United States no authority to conscript him to serve in a war not declared by Congress.

* * *

. . . The court has a procedural, as well as a substantive, problem. It must decide whether the question sought to be raised is in that category of political questions which are not within a court's jurisdiction and, if the issue falls within the court's jurisdiction, whether, as a matter of substance the defendant is right in his contention that the order is repugnant to the Constitution. Again, while those two aspects are technically separate, they are so close as often to overlap.

* * *

Congress in 1967 extended the Selective Service Act, Pub.L. No. 90–40, 81 Stat. 100. Congress acted with full knowledge that persons called for duty under the Act had been, and are likely to be, sent to Vietnam. Indeed, in 1965 Congress had amended the same Act with the hardly concealed object of punishing persons who tore up their draft cards out of protest at the Vietnam war. See United States v. O'Brien, 391 U.S. 367, 88 S.Ct. 1673, 20 L.Ed.2d 672.

Moreover, Congress has again and again appropriated money for the draft act, for the Vietnam war, and for cognate activities. Congress has also enacted what is called the Tonkin Gulf Resolution, which some have viewed as advance authorization for the expansion of the Vietnam war.

What the court thus faces is a situation in which there has been joint action by the President and Congress, even if the joint action has not taken the form of a declaration of war.

The absence of the formal declaration of war is not to be regarded as a trivial omission. A declaration of war has more than ritualistic or symbolic significance. What something is called has much to do with how authorities act and also with how those subject to authority respond. There is a vast difference between money exacted as a penalty for a crime and money exacted as compensation for a civil wrong. Judges require stronger evidence, and a far greater degree of certainty before assigning the badge of shame involved in a fine than when they enter a judgment of civil liability for compensatory damages. The procedural and substantive standards differ. There is a roughly similar distinction between a declaration of war and a Congressional appropriation to support military action overseas directed by the President.

But the fact that a declaration of war is a far more important act than an appropriation act or than an extension of a Selective Service Act does not go the whole way to show that in every situation of foreign military action, a declaration of war is a necessary prerequisite to conscription for that military engagement.

We are reminded by McCulloch v. Maryland, 17 U.S. (4 Wheat.) 316, 4 L.Ed. 579, and its progeny, that the national government has powers beyond those clearly stipulated in the Constitution. That the Constitution expresses one way of achieving a result does not inevitably carry a negative pregnant. Other ways may be employed by Congress as necessary and proper. Indeed, the implied powers may be not only Congressional but sometimes Presidential. In re Debs, 158 U.S. 564, 15 S.Ct. 900, 39 L.Ed. 1092. And this implication may be most justifiable in foreign affairs. United States v. Curtiss-Wright Export Corp., 299 U.S. 304, 57 S.Ct. 216, 81 L.Ed. 255. What may be involved in the present case is a choice between a limited undeclared war approved by the President and Congress and an unlimited declaration of war through an Act of Congress. The two choices may find support in different, related, but not inconsistent Constitutional powers.

If the national government does have two or more choices there are readily imagined reasons not to elect to exercise the expressly granted power to declare war.

A declaration of war expresses in the most formidable and unlimited terms a belligerent posture against an enemy. In Vietnam it is at least plausibly contended by some in authority that our troops are not engaged in fighting any enemy of the United States but are participating in the defense of what is said to be one country from the aggression of what is said to be another country. It is inappropriate for this court in any way to intimate whether South Vietnam and North Vietnam are separate countries, or whether there is a civil war, or whether there is a failure on the part of the people in Vietnam and elsewhere to abide by agreements made in Geneva. It is sufficient to say that the present situation is one in which the State Department and the other branches of the executive treat our action in Vietnam as though it were different from an unlimited war against an enemy.

Moreover, in the Vietnam situation a declaration of war would produce consequences which no court can fully anticipate. A declaration of war affects treaties of the United States, obligations of the United States under international organizations, and many public and private arrangements. A determination not to declare war is more than an avoidance of a domestic constitutional procedure. It has international implications of vast dimensions. Indeed, it is said that since 1945 no country has declared war on any other country. Whether this is true or not, it shows that not only in the United States but generally, there is a reluctance to take a step which symbolically and practically entails multiple unforeseeable consequences.

From the foregoing this Court concludes that the distinction between a declaration of war and a cooperative action by the legislative [sic] and executive with respect to military activities in foreign countries is the very essence of what is meant by a political question. It involves just the sort of evidence, policy considerations, and constitutional principles which elude the normal processes of the judiciary and which are for [sic] more suitable for determination by coordinate branches of the government. It is not an act of abdication when a court says that political questions of this sort are not within its jurisdiction. It is a recognition that the tools with which a court can work, the data which it can fairly appraise, the conclusions which it can reach as a basis for entering judgments, have limits.

Because defendant Sisson seeks an adjudication of what is a political question, his motion to dismiss the indictment is denied.

Questions

1. Do the several extracts from the United States Constitution (*supra* pp. 79–80) expressly deal with the matter of conscription into the Armed Forces in time of peace *or* in time of war?

2. If the Constitution is silent on the subject of conscription into the Armed Forces, does that mean that the United States does not have the authority to conscript in time of peace or in time of war?

Does Judge Wyzanski suggest one answer to that question?

3. In light of the several extracts from the United States Constitution (*supra* pp. 79–80), might a judge reasonably conclude that conscription into the Armed Forces is not barred by the Constitution, and that the President may deploy conscripts into combat with or without a declaration of war?   Does Judge Wyzanski outline such an argument in his opinion?

4. If the United States Constitution expressly forbade conscription into the Armed Forces except in time of war as declared by Congress, would Sisson's case present a political question?

UNITED STATES v. SISSON [1]

United States District Court, D. Massachusetts, 1968.
294 F.Supp. 515.

WYZANSKI, CHIEF JUDGE.   Defendant construes his motion to dismiss the indictment as including a contention that he is entitled to have the indictment dismissed on the ground that he is being ordered to fight in a genocidal war.

The issue of defendant's standing to raise the genocidal question and the issue whether the question is a question not within this Court's jurisdiction resemble the issues already considered by this Court in denying defendant's motion to dismiss the indictment on the ground that defendant has been ordered to fight in a conflict as to which Congress has not declared war. However, there are differences between the problems which the earlier motion presented and the ones now raised.

For argument's sake one may assume that a conscript has a standing to object to induction in a war declared contrary to a binding international obligation in the form of a treaty, in the form of membership in an international organization, or otherwise.   One may even assume that a conscript may similarly object to being inducted to fight in a war the openly declared purpose of which is to wipe out a nation and drive its people into the sea. Conceivably, in the two situations just described, the conscript would have a standing to raise the issue and the court would be faced with a problem which was not purely a political question, but indeed fell within judicial competence.

The issue now tendered by this defendant is unlike either of the two cases just mentioned.   At its strongest, the defendant's case is that a sur-

1. Cite as Sisson II.

vey of the military operations in Vietnam would lead a disinterested tribunal to conclude that the laws of war have been violated and that, contrary to international obligations, express and implied, in treaty and in custom, the United States has resorted to barbaric methods of war, including genocide.

If the situation were as defendant contends, the facts would surely be difficult to ascertain so long as the conflict continues, so long as the United States government has reasons not to disclose all its military operations, and so long as a court was primarily dependent upon compliance by American military and civilian officials with its judicial orders. It should be remembered that the tribunal at Nuremberg, probably because it had a Russian judge, was unable to face up to the problems tendered by the Katyn massacres. Moreover, neither at Nuremberg nor at Tokyo, tribunals upon which an American judge sat, was there any attempt to resolve the problems raised by the nuclear bombing of Hiroshima and Nagasaki. It is inherent in a tribunal composed partly of judges drawn from the alleged offending nation that a wholly disinterested judgment is most unlikely to be achieved. With effort, self-discipline, and judicial training, men may transcend their personal bias, but few there are who in international disputes of magnitude are capable of entirely disregarding their political allegiance and acting solely with respect to legal considerations and ethical imperatives. If during hostilities a trustworthy, credible international judgment is to be rendered with respect to alleged national misconduct in war, representatives of the supposed offender must not sit in judgment upon the nation. An analogous path of reasoning must lead one to conclude that a domestic tribunal is entirely unfit to adjudicate the question whether there has been a violation of international law during a war by the very nation which created, manned, and compensated the tribunal seized of the case.

Because a domestic tribunal is incapable of eliciting the facts during a war, and because it is probably incapable of exercising a disinterested judgment which would command the confidence of sound judicial opinion, this Court holds that the defendant has tendered an issue which involves a so-called political question not within the jurisdiction of this Court. Cf. United States v. Mitchell, 369 F.2d 323 (2d Cir.).

The motion to dismiss the indictment is again denied.

Notes and Questions

1. One commentator has suggested that "the foundation, in both intellect and instinct, of the political-question doctrine [is] the Court's sense of lack of capacity, compounded in unequal parts of (a) the strangeness of the issue and its intractability to principled resolution; (b) the sheer momentousness of it, which tends to unbalance judicial judgment; (c) the anxiety, not so much that the judicial judgment will be ignored, as that perhaps it should but will not be; (d) finally ('in a mature democracy'), the inner vulnerability, the self-doubt of an institution which is electorally irresponsible and has no earth to draw strength from." Alexander M. Bickel, The Least Dangerous Branch, p. 184 (New York, 1962, Bobbs-Merrill Inc.).

2.   Does it seem strange to you that a United States judge would suggest that his employment by, and allegiance to the United States are reasons for not passing on a challenge to the validity of action by the United States Government? Would that employment and allegiance be grounds for disqualification of federal judges in criminal cases generally, or in civil actions where the United States is a party? Why do you suppose Judge Wyzanski thinks his employment relationship and political allegiance is relevant in this case, when he would almost certainly answer "No!" to the preceding question?

3.   If there were no disputed issues of fact in Sisson II regarding the nature of United States involvement in the war in Vietnam, and if the United States Constitution, and/or United States statutes, and/or United States treaties with foreign nations *clearly* established the invalidity of United States involvement in the war in Vietnam, would Sisson II present a political question?

4.   Professor Black suggests that judicial review of legislative and executive action has been an extremely effective and useful means of validating (legitimating) the acts of legislatures and public officers. He demonstrates that historically courts in the United States have only rarely invalidated such acts, and he suggests that approval of a statute or other official action in a judicial opinion carries great weight in the court of public opinion. (See Charles L. Black, Jr. The People and the Court, Ch. III, New York 1960, The MacMillan Company.)

Does this concept of the legitimating function of judicial review give added meaning and significance to Judge Wyzanski's reasoning in Sisson II?

5.   Does the doctrine of political questions help to explain the "Opinion of the Justices" (*supra* p. 67 ff)?

6.   Sisson was tried before a jury which found him guilty as charged in the indictment. Defense Counsel then moved to arrest judgment on the verdict claiming that Sisson had been indicted and tried for a violation of a statute which, as applied to him, was unconstitutional. The grounds for this motion and the holding of the court on it are stated in the concluding paragraphs of Judge Wyzanski's opinion in United States v. Sisson,[2] 297 F.Supp. 902, 911–912 (D.C.Mass.1969):

> Sisson's case being limited to a claim of conscientious objection to combat service in a foreign campaign, this court holds that the free exercise of religion clause in the First Amendment and the due process clause of the Fifth Amendment prohibit the application of the 1967 draft act to Sisson to require him to render combat service in Vietnam.

> The chief reason for reaching this conclusion after examining the competing interests is the magnitude of Sisson's interest in not

2.   Cite as Sisson III.

killing in the Vietnam conflict as against the want of magnitude in the country's present need for him to be so employed.

The statute as here applied creates a clash between law and morality for which no exigency exists, and before, in Justice Sutherland's words, "the last extremity" or anything close to that dire predicament has been glimpsed, or even predicted, or reasonably feared.

When the state through its laws seeks to override reasonable moral commitments it makes a dangerously uncharacteristic choice. The law grows from the deposits of morality. Law and morality are, in turn, debtors and creditors of each other. The law cannot be adequately enforced by the courts alone, or by courts supported merely by the police and the military. The true secret of legal might lies in the habits of conscientious men disciplining themselves to obey the law they respect without the necessity of judicial and administrative orders. When the law treats a reasonable, conscientious act as a crime it subverts its own power. It invites civil disobedience. It impairs the very habits which nourish and preserve the law.

The Supreme Court may not address itself to the broad issue just decided. Being a court of last resort, it unlike an inferior court, can confidently rest its judgment upon a narrow issue.   .   .   . So it is incumbent on this court to consider the narrow issue, whether the 1967 Act invalidly discriminates against Sisson as a non-religious conscientious objector.

The draft act now limits "exemption from combat training and service" to one "who, by reason of religious training and belief, is conscientiously opposed to participation in war in any form" 50 U.S.C.App. Section 456(j), commonly cited as Section 6(j) of the Act as amended.

A Quaker, for example, is covered if he claims belief in the ultimate implications of William Penn's teaching.

Persons trained in and believing in other religious ways may or may not be covered. A Roman Catholic obedient to the teaching of Thomas Aquinas and Pope John XXIII might distinguish between a just war in which he would fight and an unjust war in which he would not fight. Those who administer the Selective Service System opine that Congress has not allowed exemption to those whose conscientious objection rests on such a distinction. See Lt. Gen. Lewis B. Hershey, Legal Aspects of Selective Service, U. S. Gov. Printing Office, January 1, 1969, pp. 13–14. This court has a more open mind.

However, the administrators and this court both agree that Congress has not provided a conscientious objector status for a person whose claim is admittedly not formally religious.

In this situation Sisson claims that even if the Constitution might not otherwise preclude Congress from drafting him for combat service in Vietnam, the Constitution does preclude Congress from drafting him under the 1967 Act. The reason is that this Act grants conscientious objector status solely to religious conscientious objectors but not to nonreligious objectors.

Earlier this opinion noted that it is practical to accord the same status to nonreligious conscientious objectors as to religious objectors. Moreover, it is difficult to imagine any ground for a statutory distinction except religious prejudice. In short, in the draft act Congress unconstitutionally discriminated against atheists, agnostics, and men, like Sisson, who, whether they be religious or not, are motivated in their objection to the draft by profound moral beliefs which constitute the central convictions of their beings.

This Court, therefore, concludes that in granting to the religious conscientious objector but not to Sisson a special conscientious objector status, the Act, as applied to Sisson, violates the provision of the First Amendment that "Congress shall make no law respecting an establishment of religion or prohibiting the free exercise thereof."

[Citation of authority omitted.]

To guard against misunderstanding, this Court has *not* ruled that:

(1) The Government has no right to conduct Vietnam Operations; or

(2) The Government is using unlawful methods in Vietnam; or

(3) The Government has no power to conscript the generality of men for combat service; or

(4) The Government in a defense of the homeland has no power to conscript for combat service anyone it sees fit; or

(5) The Government has no power to conscript conscientious objectors for non-combat service.

Indeed the Court assumes without deciding that each one of those propositions states the exact reverse of the law.

All that this Court decides is that as a sincere conscientious objector Sisson cannot constitutionally be subjected to military orders (not reviewable in a United States constitutional Court,) which may require him to kill in the Vietnam conflict.

Enter forthwith this decision and this court's order granting defendant Sisson's motion in arrest of judgment.

7. Suppose the Selective Service Act provided for no conscientious objector classification on any grounds, religious or otherwise. How, if at all, might that have affected Judge Wyzanski's ruling on Sisson's motion in arrest of judgment?

8. The Government appealed to the Supreme Court seeking reversal of Judge Wyzanski's decision. Both parties argued that the Court had jurisdiction of the appeal under Title 18 United States Code, § 3731, which authorizes direct appeal to the Supreme Court from an "arrest of judgment" in a criminal case. The Court, in an opinion by Justice Harlan, dismissed the appeal for lack of jurisdiction. United States v. Sisson, 399 U.S. 267, 90 S.Ct. 2117 (1970). The Court determined that Judge Wyzanski's decision was a "direct-

ed acquittal" not an "arrest of judgment" (thus disagreeing with Judge Wyzanski's own characterization of his decision.) The Court held that 18 United States Code § 3731 did not authorize appeal by the government from a directed acquittal.

Justices Brennan, Marshall, and Stewart joined in the entire opinion. Justice Black joined in only part of the opinion. Chief Justice Burger dissented in an opinion in which Justices Douglas and White joined. Justice White dissented in an opinion in which Chief Justice Burger and Justice Douglas joined. Justice Blackmun did not participate in the consideration or decision of the case.

9. Throughout the Vietnam war, attempts were made by divers of its opponents to secure a judicial determination that the conduct of that war by the United States violated either domestic or international law. The federal courts before which these claims were made invariably held that they were without authority to rule on the merits of the issue. See e. g., U. S. v. Berrigan, 283 F.Supp. 336 (1968), Davi v. Laird, 318 F.Supp. 478 (1970), and Mitchell v. Laird, 488 F.2d 611 (1973). Berrigan was a criminal prosecution of a number of prominent opponents of the Vietnam war in which the defendants were charged with injuring federal property, mutilating federal records, and hindering the administration of the Selective Service Act. The charges arose out of a demonstration in which the defendants entered federal offices and, among other things, poured blood on Selective Service records. Defendants alleged as defenses that the conduct of the war violated international law, the U.S. Constitution, and the principles underlying the judgment in the World War II war crimes trials at Nuremburg. The Court found that such defenses were not available to the defendants because the alleged violations of international and constitutional law were not directly injurious to the defendants. The Court also found that application of the Nuremberg principles presented a uniquely political question that would require findings as to the origins and nature of the war effort.

Davi was a taxpayer who sought to enjoin the further expenditure of tax monies on what he alleged to be an unconstitutional war. In Mitchell the plaintiffs were thirteen members of Congress who sought to enjoin the President, and the Secretary of Defense, from further prosecution of the war. Both cases were dismissed on the political question ground.

SECTION 2.5 STANDING TO SUE

TILESTON v. ULLMAN

Supreme Court of the United States, 1943.
318 U.S. 44, 63 S.Ct. 493.

Appeal from the Supreme Court of Errors of Connecticut.

PER CURIAM.[1] This case comes here on appeal to review a declaratory judgment of the Supreme Court of Errors of Connecticut that §§ 6246 and 6562 of the General Statutes of Connecticut of 1930—prohibiting the use of drugs or instruments to prevent conception, and the giving of assistance or counsel in their use—are applicable to appellant, a registered physician and as applied to him are constitutional. 129 Conn. 84, 26 A.2d 582, 588.

The suit was tried and judgment rendered on the allegations of the complaint which are stipulated to be true. Appellant alleged that the statute, if applicable to him, would prevent his giving professional advice concerning the use of contraceptives to three patients whose condition of health was such that their lives would be endangered by child-bearing, and that appellees, law enforcement officers of the state, intend to prosecute any offense against the statute and "claim or may claim" that the proposed professional advice would constitute such an offense. The complaint set out in detail the danger to the lives of appellant's patients in the event that they should bear children, but contained no allegations asserting any claim under the Fourteenth Amendment[2] of infringement of appellant's liberty or his property rights. The relief prayed was a declaratory judgment as to whether the statutes are applicable to appellant and if so whether they constitute a valid exercise of constitutional power "within the meaning and intent of Amendment XIV of the Constitution of the United States prohibiting a state from depriving any person of life without due process of law." On stipulation of the parties the state superior court ordered these questions of law reserved for the consideration and advice of the Supreme Court of Errors. That court, which assumed without deciding that the case was an appropriate one for a declaratory judgment, ruled that the statutes "prohibit the action proposed to be done" by appellant and "are constitutional."

We are of the opinion that the proceedings in the state courts present no constitutional question which appellant has standing to assert. The sole constitutional attack upon the statutes under the Fourteenth Amendment is confined to their deprivation of life—obviously not appellant's but his patients'. There is no allegation or proof that appellant's life is in danger. His patients are not parties to this proceeding and there is no basis on which we can say that he has standing to secure an adjudication of his patients' constitutional right to life, which they do not assert in their own behalf. Cronin v. Adams, 192 U.S. 108, 114, 24 S.Ct. 219, 220; Standard Stock Food

---

1. A per curiam ("by the court") opinion announces the decision of the court but does not identify which of the judges wrote the opinion. Per curiam opinions are rendered in cases where the issues are not deemed to be sufficiently important to warrant an extensive treatment.

2. The text of the Fourteenth Amendment is reproduced *infra* at p. 213.

Co. v. Wright, 225 U.S. 540, 550, 32 S.Ct. 784, 786; Bosley v. McLaughlin, 236 U.S. 385, 395, 35 S.Ct. 345, 348; Blair v. United States, 250 U.S. 273, 39 S.Ct. 468; The Winnebago, 205 U.S. 354, 360, 27 S.Ct. 509, 511; Davis & Farnum Mfg. Co. v. Los Angeles, 189 U.S. 207, 220, 23 S.Ct. 498, 501. No question is raised in the record with respect to the deprivation of appellant's liberty or property in contravention of the Fourteenth Amendment, nor is there anything in the opinion or decision of any question of the Supreme Court of Errors. That court's practice is to decline to answer, questions not reserved. General Statutes § 5652; Loomis Institute v. Healy, 90 Conn. 102, 129, 119 A. 31; John J. McCarthy Co. v. Alsop, 122 Conn. 288, 298, 299, 189 A. 464.

Since the appeal must be dismissed on the ground that appellant has no standing to litigate the constitutional question which the record presents, it is unnecessary to consider whether the record shows the existence of a genuine case or controversy essential to the exercise of the jurisdiction of this Court. Cf. Nashville, C. & St. L. Ry. v. Wallace, 288 U.S. 249, 259, 53 S.Ct. 345, 346.

Dismissed.

Notes and Questions

The decision in Tileston v. Ullman turned on the finding that Dr. Tileston did not have "standing" to challenge the statute on the grounds which he advanced in the Supreme Court. The notion of standing encompasses a complex of ideas regarding proper occasions for the exercise of judicial power. The following lists some situations which give rise to questions of standing.

1. A sues to recover damages for an injury done to B. Unless A is acting on behalf of B in a representative capacity recognized by the law, or as purchaser of B's claim, A has no standing to recover the damages.

2. A sues to prevent the enforcement of a law on the basis that enforcement will be injurious to the rights of others. A has no standing to bring this suit. Tileston v. Ullman is such a case.

3. A resists the application of some legal sanction, e. g., damages or an injunction, by claiming that the grant of a remedy against him will be injurious to others. As a general rule a defendant in A's position would probably be found not to have standing to raise the rights of others as a defense, but there are exceptions. Cf. Barrows v. Jackson, 346 U.S. 249, 73 S.Ct. 1031 (1953) and discussion of this case in Davis, Administrative Law Text (1959), pp. 405–406.

4. On the basis of the preceding examples, can you draw some conclusions concerning the conditions which must be met in order for a litigant to have standing to raise an issue for judicial resolution? Can you explain your conclusions in terms of a judicial philosophy concerning the role of the courts in our society?

5. The concept of standing to sue has been most fully developed by the Supreme Court of the United States in cases where the ulti-

mate issue is the constitutional validity of legislative or executive action.   How would you, as a judge, rule on the standing of the complaining party in the following cases?

(a) A state, through elected officials, brings suit to enjoin the Secretary of the Treasury of the United States from expending federal monies appropriated by Congress to support a federal health program which the state asserts is invalid under the Constitution of the United States.   The state pays no federal taxes, but residents of the state are both taxpayers and citizens of the United States. See Massachusetts v. Mellon, 262 U.S. 447, 43 S.Ct. 597 (1923), and Cf. Flast v. Cohen, 392 U.S. 83, 88 S.Ct. 1942 (1968).

(b) In a companion case a woman, who is both a taxpayer and citizen of the United States, sues in her own behalf to enjoin the Secretary of the Treasury from expending monies appropriated for the same federal public health program.   See Frothingham v. Mellon, 262 U.S. 447, 43 S.Ct. 597 (1923), and Cf. Flast v. Cohen, 392 U.S. 83, 88 S.Ct. 1942 (1968).

(c) Some states have recognized the standing of their citizens and taxpayers to challenge public expenditures in court.   In one of these states some taxpayers brought a suit in the state courts to challenge the reading of passages from the Bible in the public schools. The taxpayers complained that the reading of the Bible in the public schools was a religious exercise proscribed by the United States Constitution.   The state court found against the plaintiffs, and they appeal to the Supreme Court of the United States.   See Doremus v. Board of Education, 342 U.S. 429, 72 S.Ct. 394 (1952); contra Flast v. Cohen, 392 U.S. 83, 88 S.Ct. 1942 (1968).

(d) Parents of children enrolled in public schools sue to enjoin the conduct of officially sanctioned religious exercises in the schools. The plaintiffs' children are not required to participate in the exercises (prayer and scripture reading) and may remain silent or be excused from the classroom when such exercises are in progress. The parents allege that rights of their children secured by the first amendment of the constitution of the United States, are abridged by these exercises.   See Engel v. Vitale, 370 U.S. 421, 82 S.Ct. 1261 (1960), and School District of Abington Township v. Schempp, 374 U.S. 203, 83 S.Ct. 1560 (1963).

(e) A U.S. citizen and taxpayer made repeated attempts to secure information from the U.S. Government (in particular the Treasury Department) regarding the expenditures of the Central Intelligence Agency.   Meeting with virtually no success he brought suit seeking a declaration that portions of the Central Intelligence Agency Act contravened Article I, § 9, clause 7 of the United States Constitution (which deals with the disbursal of federal funds and publication of financial records regarding disbursal of federal funds).   United States v. Richardson, 418 U.S. 166, 94 S.Ct. 2940 (1974).

(f) A group of five law students formed an unincorporated association for the purpose of enhancing the quality of the environment. They brought suit against the Interstate Commerce Commission seeking to enjoin railroad rate increases which they alleged would tend to discourage the use of "recyclable" materials (mainly scrap) by increasing the cost of such materials relative to unprocessed raw material. The students alleged individual harm since the cost of all manufactured goods would be increased by the rate increase (a 2.5% surcharge on all commodities) and from the adverse environmental effects which would be caused by rates which encouraged the use in manufacturing of raw rather than reprocessed materials. U. S. v. SCRAP, 412 U.S. 669, 93 S.Ct. 2405 (1973).

(g) The U.S. Forest Service wished to provide recreational facilities, primarily a ski resort, in the Mineral King Valley of the Sequoia National Forest. The service solicited bids from resort developers, and determined to award a contract for the development to Walt Disney Enterprises, Inc. The plan called for a resort which could accommodate 14,000 visitors daily. The State of California proposed to build a state highway to provide access to the Mineral King Valley, which was then inaccessible to vehicular traffic. The highway and a power line for the resort were to traverse a part of the Sequoia National Park, which was administered by the U.S. Department of Interior.

A club dedicated to environmental protection and preservation of the wilderness, sued in U.S. District Court for a declaratory judgment and injunction to restrain the Interior Department from approving the Mineral King development, and from approving the construction of the proposed highway and power line. The club alleged no monetary damages to it or its members, but it claimed to have "a special interest in the conservation and the sound maintenance of the national parks, game refuges, and forests of the Country,". Sierra Club v. Morton, 405 U.S. 727, 92 S.Ct. 1361 (1972).

SECTION 2.6   JUSTICIABLE CONTROVERSIES

POE v. ULLMAN

Supreme Court of the United States, 1961.
367 U.S. 497, 81 S.Ct. 1752.

[Some footnotes by the Justices have been omitted. Others have been renumbered. Footnotes added by the editors have been placed in brackets.]

MR. JUSTICE FRANKFURTER [1] announced the judgment of the Court and an opinion in which THE CHIEF JUSTICE, MR. JUSTICE CLARK and MR. JUSTICE WHITTAKER join.

I. [The author of the majority opinion, Justice Felix Frankfurter, was ap-   pointed to the Supreme Court in 1939. Prior to that time he was a professor

These appeals challenge the constitutionality, under the Fourteenth Amendment, of Connecticut statutes which, as authoritatively construed by the Connecticut Supreme Court of Errors, prohibit the use of contraceptive devices and the giving of medical advice in the use of such devices. In proceedings seeking declarations of law, not on review of convictions for violation of the statutes, that court has ruled that these statutes would be applicable in the case of married couples and even under claim that conception would constitute a serious threat to the health or life of the female spouse.

No. 60 combines two actions brought in a Connecticut Superior Court for declaratory relief. The complaint in the first alleges that the plaintiffs, Paul and Pauline Poe, are a husband and wife, thirty and twenty-six years old respectively, who live together and have no children. Mrs. Poe has had three consecutive pregnancies terminating in infants with multiple congenital abnormalities from which each died shortly after birth. Plaintiffs have consulted Dr. Buxton, an obstetrician and gynecologist of eminence, and it is Dr. Buxton's opinion that the cause of the infants' abnormalities is genetic, although the underlying "mechanism" is unclear. In view of the great emotional stress already suffered by plaintiffs, the probable consequence of another pregnancy is psychological strain extremely disturbing to the physical and mental health of both husband and wife. Plaintiffs know that it is Dr. Buxton's opinion that the best and safest medical treatment which could be prescribed for their situation is advice in methods of preventing conception. Dr. Buxton knows of drugs, medicinal articles and instruments which can be safely used to effect contraception. Medically, the use of these devices is indicated as the best and safest preventive measure necessary for the protection of plaintiffs' health. Plaintiffs, however, have been unable to obtain this information for the sole reason that its delivery and use may or will be claimed by the defendant State's Attorney (appellee in this Court) to constitute offenses against Connecticut law. The State's Attorney intends to prosecute offenses against the State's laws, and claims that the giving of contraceptive advice and the use of contraceptive devices would be offenses forbidden by Conn.Gen.Stat.Rev., 1958, §§ 53–32 and 54–196.[2] Alleging irreparable injury and a substantial uncertainty of legal relations (a

at the Harvard Law School. His appointment to the Court was opposed by some who considered him a radical, principally because of his vigorous support of various "New Deal" policies of the Franklin D. Roosevelt administration. His judicial opinions after 1939 reflect, however, what most people would call a conservative view of the judicial function. Justice Frankfurter retired from the Court in 1963. He died in 1965.]

2. As a matter of specific legislation, Connecticut outlaws only the use of contraceptive materials. Conn.Gen. Stat.Rev.1958, § 53–32 provides:

"*Use of drugs or instruments to prevent conception.* Any person who uses any drug, medicinal article or instrument for the purpose of preventing concep-

tion shall be fined not less than fifty dollars or imprisoned not less than sixty days nor more than one year or be both fined and imprisoned."

There are not substantive provisions dealing with the sale or distribution of such devices, nor with the giving of information concerning their use. These activities are deemed to be involved in law solely because of the general criminal accessory enactment of Connecticut. This is Conn.Gen. Stat.Rev.1958, § 54–196:

"*Accessories.* Any person who assists, abets, counsels, causes, hires, or commands another to commit any offense may be prosecuted and punished as if he were the principal offender."

local procedural requisite for a declaration), plaintiffs ask a declaratory judgment that §§ 53–32 and 54–196 are unconstitutional, in that they deprive the plaintiffs of life and liberty without due process of law.

The second action in No. 60 is brought by Jane Doe,[3] a twenty-five-year-old housewife. Mrs. Doe, it is alleged, lives with her husband, they have no children; Mrs. Doe recently underwent a pregnancy which induced in her a critical physical illness—two weeks' unconsciousness and a total of nine weeks' acute sickness which left her with partial paralysis, marked impairment of speech, and emotional instability. Another pregnancy would be exceedingly perilous to her life. She, too, has consulted Dr. Buxton, who believes that the best and safest treatment for her is contraceptive advice. The remaining allegations of Mrs. Doe's complaint, and the relief sought, are similar to those in the case of Mr. and Mrs. Poe.

In No. 61, also a declaratory judgment action, Dr. Buxton is the plaintiff. Setting forth facts identical to those alleged by Jane Doe, he asks that the Connecticut statutes prohibiting his giving of contraceptive advice to Mrs. Doe be adjudged unconstitutional, as depriving him of liberty and property without due process.

[Note that the preceding analysis of the "facts" in these cases is a summary by JUSTICE FRANKFURTER of the allegations made by the appellants in the complaints they filed in the Connecticut courts. No trial was held to determine the accuracy of these allegations, because the defendant (Ullman) demurred to these complaints, that is, he filed a statement in court in which he agreed, for purposes of argument only, that the allegations of fact were true, but he contended that the facts as alleged provided no legal basis for the relief requested by the appellants. The arguments in the Connecticut courts were addressed solely to this contention, and the Connecticut courts found for Ullman on the basis that the statutes in question were constitutional and that the plaintiffs should be denied the declaratory relief they had requested.]

Appellants' complaints in these declaratory judgment proceedings do not clearly, and certainly do not in terms, allege that appellee Ullman threatens to prosecute them for use of, or for giving advice concerning, contraceptive devices. The allegations are merely that, in the course of his public duty, he intends to prosecute any offenses against Connecticut law, and that he claims that use of and advice concerning contraceptives would constitute offenses. The lack of immediacy of the threat described by these allegations might alone raise serious questions of non-justiciability of appellants' claims. See United Public Workers v. Mitchell, 330 U.S. 75, 88, 67 S.Ct. 556, 564. But even were we to read the allegations to convey a clear threat of imminent prosecutions, we are not bound to accept as true all that is alleged on the face of the complaint and admitted, technically, by demurrer, any more than the Court is bound by stipulation of the parties. Swift & Co. v. Hocking Valley R. Co., 243 U.S. 281, 289, 37 S.Ct. 287, 289. Formal agreement between parties that collides with plausibility is too fragile a foundation for indulging in constitutional adjudication.

---

3. [Poe and Doe are fictitious names used by the plaintiffs to conceal their identity. Because of the intimate details of the plaintiff's allegations, the Supreme Court of Errors allowed the plaintiffs to sue in these fictitious names, upon the assurance of counsel that they represented bona fide complainants.]

The Connecticut law prohibiting the use of contraceptives has been on the State's books since 1879. Conn.Acts 1879, c. 78. During the more than three-quarters of a century since its enactment, a prosecution for its violation seems never to have been initiated, save in State v. Nelson, 126 Conn. 412, 11 A.2d 856. The circumstances of that case, decided in 1940, only prove the abstract character of what is before us. There, a test case was brought to determine the constitutionality of the Act as applied against two doctors and a nurse who had allegedly disseminated contraceptive information. After the Supreme Court of Errors sustained the legislation on appeal from a demurrer to the information, the State moved to dismiss the information. Neither counsel nor our own researches have discovered any other attempt to enforce the prohibition of distribution or use of contraceptive devices by criminal process. The unreality of these law suits is illumined by another circumstance. We were advised by counsel for appellants that contraceptives are commonly and notoriously sold in Connecticut drug stores. Yet no prosecutions are recorded; and certainly such ubiquitous, open, public sales would more quickly invite the attention of enforcement officials than the conduct in which the present appellants wish to engage—the giving of private medical advice by a doctor to his individual patients, and their private use of the devices prescribed. The undeviating policy of nullification by Connecticut of its anti-contraceptive laws throughout all the long years that they have been on the statute books bespeaks more than prosecutorial paralysis. What was said in another context is relevant here. "Deeply embedded traditional ways of carrying out state policy . . ."—or not carrying it out—"are often tougher and truer law than the dead words of the written text." Nashville, C. & St. L. R. Co. v. Browning, 310 U.S. 362, 369, 60 S.Ct. 968, 972.

The restriction of our jurisdiction to cases and controversies within the meaning of Article III of the Constitution, see Muskrat v. United States, 219 U.S. 346, 31 S.Ct. 250, is not the sole limitation on the exercise of our appellate powers, especially in cases raising constitutional questions. The policy reflected in numerous cases and over a long period was thus summarized in the oft-quoted statement of Mr. Justice Brandeis: "The Court [has] developed, for its own governance in the cases confessedly within its jurisdiction, a series of rules under which it has avoided passing upon a large part of all the constitutional questions pressed upon it for decision." Ashwander v. Tennessee Valley Authority, 297 U.S. 288, 341, 346, 56 S.Ct. 466, 482 (concurring opinion). In part the rules summarized in the Ashwander opinion have derived from the historically defined, limited nature and function of courts and from the recognition that, within the framework of our adversary system, the adjudicatory process is most securely founded when it is exercised under the impact of a lively conflict between antagonistic demands, actively pressed, which make resolution of the controverted issue a practical necessity. See Little v. Bowers, 134 U.S. 547, 558, 10 S.Ct. 620, 623; California v. San Pablo & Tulare R. Co., 149 U.S. 308, 314, 13 S.Ct. 876, 878; United States v. Fruehauf, 365 U.S. 146, 157, 81 S.Ct. 547, 554. In part they derive from the fundamental federal and tripartite character of our National Government and from the role—restricted by its very responsibility—of the federal courts, and particularly this Court, within that structure. See the Note to Hayburn's Case, 2 Dall. 409; Massachusetts v. Mellon, 262 U.S. 447, 488–489, 43 S.Ct. 597, 601; Watson v. Buck, 313 U.S. 387, 400–403, 61

S.Ct. 962, 966–968; Alabama State Federation of Labor v. McAdory, 325 U.S. 450, 471, 65 S.Ct. 1384, 1394.

These considerations press with special urgency in cases challenging legislative action or state judicial action as repugnant to the Constitution. "The best teaching of this Court's experience admonishes us not to entertain constitutional questions in advance of the strictest necessity." Parker v. County of Los Angeles, 338 U.S. 327, 333, 70 S.Ct. 161, 163. See also Liverpool, N. Y. & P. S. S. Co. v. Commissioners, 113 U.S. 33, 39, 5 S.Ct. 352, 355. The various doctrines of "standing," "ripeness," and "mootness," which this Court has evolved with particular, though not exclusive, reference to such cases are but several manifestations—each having its own "varied application"—of the primary conception that federal judicial power is to be exercised to strike down legislation, whether state or federal, only at the instance of one who is himself immediately harmed, or immediately threatened with harm, by the challenged action. Stearns v. Wood, 236 U.S. 75, 35 S.Ct. 229; Texas v. Interstate Commerce Comm'n, 258 U.S. 158, 42 S.Ct. 261; United Public Workers v. Mitchell, 330 U.S. 75, 89–90, 67 S.Ct. 556, 564–565. "This court can have no right to pronounce an abstract opinion upon the constitutionality of a State law. Such law must be brought into actual, or threatened operation upon rights properly falling under judicial cognizance, or a remedy is not to be had here." Georgia v. Stanton, 6 Wall. 50, 75, approvingly quoting Mr. Justice Thompson, dissenting, in Cherokee Nation v. Georgia, 5 Pet. 1, 75; also quoted in New Jersey v. Sargent, 269 U.S. 328, 331, 46 S.Ct. 122. "The party who invokes the power [to annul legislation on grounds of its unconstitutionality] must be able to show not only that the statute is invalid but that he has sustained or is immediately in danger of sustaining some direct injury as the result of its enforcement.   .   .   ." Massachusetts v. Mellon, 262 U.S. 447, 488, 43 S.Ct. 597, 601.

This principle was given early application and has been recurringly enforced in the Court's refusal to entertain cases which disclosed a want of a truly adversary contest, of a collision of actively asserted and differing claims. See, e. g., Cleveland v. Chamberlain, 1 Black 419; Wood-Paper Co. v. Heft, 8 Wall. 333. Such cases may not be "collusive" in the derogatory sense of Lord v. Veazie, 8 How. 251—in the sense of merely colorable disputes got up to secure an advantageous ruling from the Court. See South Spring Hill Gold Mining Co. v. Amador Medean Gold Mining Co., 145 U.S. 300, 301, 12 S.Ct. 921. The Court has found unfit for adjudication any cause that "is not in any real sense adversary," that "does not assume the 'honest and actual antagonistic assertion of rights' to be adjudicated—a safeguard essential to the integrity of the judicial process, and one which we have held to be indispensable to adjudication of constitutional questions by this Court." United States v. Johnson, 319 U.S. 302, 305, 63 S.Ct. 1075, 1076. The requirement for adversity was classically expounded in Chicago & Grand Trunk R. Co. v. Wellman, 143 U.S. 339, 344–345, 12 S.Ct. 400, 402:

> " * * * The theory upon which, apparently, this suit was brought is that parties have an appeal from the legislature to the courts; and that the latter are given an immediate and general supervision of the constitutionality of the acts of the former. Such is not true. Whenever, in pursuance of an honest and actual antagonistic assertion of rights by one individual against another, there

is presented a question involving the validity of any act of any legislature, State or Federal, and the decision necessarily rests on the competency of the legislature to so enact, the court must, in the exercise of its solemn duties, determine whether the act be constitutional or not; but such an exercise of power is the ultimate and supreme function of courts. It is legitimate only in the last resort, and as a necessity in the determination of real, earnest and vital controversy between individuals. It never was the thought that, by means of a friendly suit, a party beaten in the legislature could transfer to the courts an inquiry as to the constitutionality of the legislative act."

What was said in the Wellman case found ready application in proceedings brought under modern declaratory judgment procedures. For just as the declaratory judgment device does not "purport to alter the character of the controversies which are the subject of the judicial power under the Constitution," United States v. West Virginia, 295 U.S. 463, 475, 55 S.Ct. 789, 793, it does not permit litigants to invoke the power of this Court to obtain constitutional rulings in advance of necessity. Electric Bond & Share Co. v. Securities and Exchange Comm'n, 303 U.S. 419, 443, 58 S.Ct. 678, 687. The Court has been on the alert against use of the declaratory judgment device for avoiding the rigorous insistence on exigent adversity as a condition for evoking Court adjudication. This is as true of state court suits for declaratory judgments as of federal. By exercising their jurisdiction, state courts cannot determine the jurisdiction to be exercised by this Court. Tyler v. Judges of the Court of Registration, 179 U.S. 405, 21 S.Ct. 206; Doremus v. Board of Education, 342 U.S. 429, 72 S.Ct. 394. Although we have held that a state declaratory-judgment suit may constitute a case or controversy within our appellate jurisdiction, it is to be reviewed here only "so long as the case retains the essentials of an adversary proceeding, involving a real, not a hypothetical, controversy, which is finally determined by the judgment below." Nashville, C. & St. L. R. Co. v. Wallace, 288 U.S. 249, 264, 53 S.Ct. 345, 348. It was with respect to a state-originating declaratory judgment proceeding that we said, in Alabama State Federation of Labor v. McAdory, 325 U.S. 450, 471, 65 S.Ct. 1384, 1394, that "The extent to which the declaratory judgment procedure may be used in the federal courts to control state action lies in the sound discretion of the Court. . . ." Indeed, we have recognized, in such cases, that " . . . the discretionary element characteristic of declaratory jurisdiction, and imported perhaps from equity jurisdiction and practice without the remedial phase, offers a convenient instrument for making . . . effective . . ." the policy against premature constitutional decision. Rescue Army v. Municipal Court, 331 U.S. 549, 573, n. 41, 67 S.Ct. 1409, 1422.

Insofar as appellants seek to justify the exercise of our declaratory power by the threat of prosecution, facts which they can no more negative by complaint and demurrer than they could by stipulation preclude our determining their appeals on the merits. Cf. Bartemeyer v. Iowa, 18 Wall. 129, 134–135. It is clear that the mere existence of a state penal statute would constitute insufficient grounds to support a federal court's adjudication of its constitutionality in proceedings brought against the State's prosecuting officials if real threat of enforcement is wanting. See Ex parte La Prade, 289 U.S. 444, 458, 53 S.Ct. 682. If the prosecutor expressly agrees not to prosecute, a suit against him for declaratory and injunctive relief is not such an adversary case as will be reviewed here. C. I. O. v. McAdory, 325 U.S. 472, 475, 65 S.Ct. 1395, 1397. Eighty years of Connecticut history demonstrate a similar, albeit tacit agreement. The fact that Connecticut has not chosen to press the enforcement of this statute deprives these controversies of the immediacy which is an indispensable condition of constitutional adjudication. This Court cannot be umpire to debates concerning harmless, empty shadows. To find it necessary to pass on these statutes now, in order to protect appellants from the hazards of prosecution, would be to close our eyes to reality.

Nor does the allegation by the Poes and Doe that they are unable to obtain information concerning contraceptive devices from Dr. Buxton, "for the sole reason that the delivery and use of such information and advice may or will be claimed by the defendant State's Attorney to constitute offenses," disclose a necessity for present constitutional decision. It is true that this Court has several times passed upon criminal statutes challenged by persons who claimed that the effects of the statutes were to deter others from maintaining profitable or advantageous relations with the complainants. See, e. g., Truax v. Raich, 239 U.S. 33, 36 S.Ct. 7; Pierce v. Society of Sisters, 268 U.S. 510, 45 S.Ct. 571. But in these cases the deterrent effect complained of was one which was grounded in a realistic fear of prosecution. We cannot agree that if Dr. Buxton's compliance with these statutes is uncoerced by the risk of their enforcement, his patients are entitled to a declaratory judgment concerning the statutes' validity. And, with due regard to Dr. Buxton's standing as a physician and to his personal sensitiveness, we cannot accept, as the basis of constitutional adjudication, other than as chimerical the fear of enforcement of provisions that have during so many years gone uniformly and without exception unenforced.

Justiciability is of course not a legal concept with a fixed content or susceptible of scientific verification. Its utilization is the resultant of many subtle pressures, including the appropriateness of the issues for decision by this Court and the actual hardship to the litigants of denying them the relief sought. Both these factors justify withholding adjudication of the constitutional issue raised under the circumstances and in the manner in which they are now before the Court.

Dismissed.

MR. JUSTICE BLACK dissents because he believes that the constitutional questions should be reached and decided.

MR. JUSTICE BRENNAN,* concurring in the judgment.

I agree that this appeal must be dismissed for failure to present a real and substantial controversy which unequivocally calls for adjudication of the rights claimed in advance of any attempt by the State to curtail them by criminal prosecution. I am not convinced, on this skimpy record, that these appellants as individuals are truly caught in an inescapable dilemma.

* Justice William Brennan, Jr., was appointed to the Supreme Court by President Eisenhower in 1956. At the time of his appointment he was a judge on the Supreme Court of New Jersey.

The true controversy in this case is over the opening of birth-control clinics on a large scale; it is that which the State has prevented in the past, not the use of contraceptives by isolated and individual married couples. It will be time enough to decide the constitutional questions urged upon us when, if ever, that real controversy flares up again. Until it does, or until the State makes a definite and concrete threat to enforce these laws against individual married couples—a threat which it has never made in the past except under the provocation of litigation—this Court may not be compelled to exercise its most delicate power of constitutional adjudication.

MR. JUSTICE DOUGLAS,** dissenting.

I.

These cases are dismissed because a majority of the members of this Court conclude, for varying reasons, that this controversy does not present a justiciable question. That conclusion is too transparent to require an extended reply. The device of the declaratory judgment is an honored one. Its use in the federal system is restricted to "cases" or "controversies" within the meaning of Article III. The question must be "appropriate for judicial determination," not hypothetical, abstract, academic or moot. Aetna Life Ins. Co. v. Haworth, 300 U.S. 227, 240, 57 S.Ct. 461, 464. It must touch "the legal relations of parties having adverse legal interests." *Id.*, 240–241, 57 S.Ct. at page 464. It must be "real and substantial" and admit of "specific relief through a decree of a conclusive character." *Id.*, 241, 57 S.Ct. at page 464. The fact that damages are not awarded or an injunction does not issue, the fact that there are no allegations of irreparable injury are irrelevant. *Id.*, 241, 57 S.Ct. at page 464. This is hornbook law.[4] The need for this remedy in the federal field was summarized in a Senate Report as follows:

> ". . . it is often necessary, in the absence of the declaratory judgment procedure, to violate or purport to violate a statute in order to obtain a judicial determination of its meaning or validity." S.Rep. No. 1005, 73d Cong., 2d Sess., pp. 2–3.

If there is a case where the need for this remedy in the shadow of a criminal prosecution is shown, it is this one, as MR. JUSTICE HARLAN demonstrates. Plaintiffs in No. 60 are two sets of husband and wife. One wife is pathetically ill, having delivered a stillborn fetus. If she

---

** Justice William O. Douglas was appointed to the Supreme Court by President Roosevelt in 1939. He was formerly a Professor of Law at Columbia University and at Yale University. He served as a member and chairman of the Securities and Exchange Commission (1934–1936). He is the author of numerous books and articles on law, U. S. foreign policy, and natural resources and conservation.

4. [Hornbooks are texts designed to provide an authoritative summary and formulation of a particular body of legal rules, e. g., Contract, Property, etc. Hornbook law is legal principle so elementary and unquestioned that it is easily formulated into the kind of authoritative statement commonly found in hornbooks.

The name hornbook was originally applied to primers used by children (16th–19th century). These primers consisted of a tablet on which was printed such things as the alphabet, numbers, etc. The tablets were covered with a thin sheet of translucent horn. Hence the name hornbooks.]

becomes pregnant again, her life will be gravely jeopardized. This couple have been unable to get medical advice concerning the "best and safest" means to avoid pregnancy from their physician, plaintiff in No. 61, because if he gave it he would commit a crime. The use of contraceptive devices would also constitute a crime. And it is alleged—and admitted by the State—that the State's Attorney intends to enforce the law by prosecuting offenses under the laws.

A public clinic dispensing birth-control information has indeed been closed by the State. Doctors and a nurse working in that clinic were arrested by the police and charged with advising married women on the use of contraceptives. That litigation produced State v. Nelson, 126 Conn. 412, 11 A.2d 856, which upheld these statutes. That same police raid on the clinic resulted in the seizure of a quantity of the clinic's contraception literature and medical equipment and supplies. The legality of that seizure was in question in State v. Certain Contraceptive Materials, 126 Conn. 428, 11 A.2d 863.

The Court refers to the Nelson prosecution as a "test case" and implies that it had little impact. Yet its impact was described differently by a contemporary observer who concluded his comment with this sentence: "This serious setback to the birth control movement [the Nelson case] led to the closing of all the clinics in the state, just as they had been previously closed in the state of Massachusetts." At oral argument, counsel for appellants confirmed that the clinics are still closed. In response to a question from the bench, he affirmed that "no public or private clinic" has dared give birth-control advice since the decision in the Nelson case.

These, then, are the circumstances in which the Court feels that it can, contrary to every principle of American or English common law, go outside the record to conclude that there exists a "tacit agreement" that these statutes will not be enforced. No lawyer, I think, would advise his clients to rely on that "tacit agreement." No police official, I think, would feel himself bound by that "tacit agreement." After our national experience during the prohibition era, it would be absurd to pretend that all criminal statutes are adequately enforced. But that does not mean that bootlegging was the less a crime. Cf. Costello v. United States, 365 U.S. 265, 81 S.Ct. 534. In fact, an arbitrary administrative pattern of non-enforcement may increase the hardships of those subject to the law. See J. Goldstein, Police Discretion Not to Invoke the Criminal Process, 69 Yale L.J. 543.[5]

When the Court goes outside the record to determine that Connecticut has adopted "The undeviating policy of nullification . . . of its anti-contraceptive laws," it selects a particularly poor case in which to exercise such a novel power. This is not a law which is a dead letter. Twice since 1940, Connecticut has re-enacted these laws as part of general statutory

---

5. [The cases considered to this point gives ample display of the judicial custom of citing material to support assertions made in an opinion. Most of the material cited has consisted of prior judicial opinions, statutes, and authoritative treatises on law. The citation of non-judicial, non-legislative material, including scholarly writings, has become more common in recent decades. The reference here is to the Yale Law Journal, edited by students at the Yale Law School. The author of the article cited is a Professor of Law at the Yale Law School.]

revisions. Consistently, bills to remove the statutes from the books have been rejected by the legislature. In short, the statutes—far from being the accidental left-overs of another era—are the center of a continuing controversy in the State. See *e. g.*, The New Republic, May 19, 1947, p. 8.[6]

Again, the Court relies on the inability of counsel to show any attempts, other than the Nelson case, "to enforce the prohibition of distribution or use of contraceptive devices by criminal process." Yet, on oral argument, counsel for the appellee stated on his own knowledge that several proprietors had been prosecuted in the "minor police courts of Connecticut" after they had been "picked up" for selling contraceptives. The enforcement of criminal laws in minor courts has just as much impact as in those cases where appellate courts are resorted to. . . .

What are these people—doctor and patients—to do? Flout the law and go to prison? Violate the law surreptitiously and hope they will not get caught? By today's decision we leave them no other alternatives. It is not the choice they need have under the regime of the declaratory judgment and our constitutional system. It is not the choice worthy of a civilized society. A sick wife, a concerned husband, a conscientious doctor seek a dignified, discrete, orderly answer to the critical problem confronting them. We should not turn them away and make them flout the law and get arrested to have their constitutional rights determined. See Railway Mail Assn. v. Corsi, 326 U.S. 88, 65 S.Ct. 1483. They are entitled to an answer to their predicament here and now.

[In the remainder of his opinion JUSTICE DOUGLAS argued that the statute was unconstitutional.]

MR. JUSTICE HARLAN,* dissenting.

Part One.

Justiciability.

There can be no quarrel with the plurality opinion's statement that "Justiciability is of course not a legal concept with a fixed content or susceptible of scientific verification," but, with deference, the fact that justiciability is not precisely definable does not make it ineffable. Although a large number of cases are brought to bear on the conclusion that is reached, I think it is fairly demonstrable that the authorities fall far short of compelling dismissal of these appeals. Even so, it is suggested that the cases do point the way to a "rigorous insistence on exigent adversity" and a "pol-

---

6. [The citation of a popular periodical, such as the New Republic, is somewhat unusual but is in keeping with the tendency of modern judges to draw on extra-legal sources of information to support their opinions. Perhaps the most famous instance of this kind was the extensive use of sociological findings and publications in support of the decision in the School Segregation Cases. See Brown v. Board of Education, 347 U.S. 483 (1954).]

* Justice John Marshall Harlan was appointed to the Supreme Court by President Eisenhower in 1955. Prior to that time he was a judge on the U. S. Court of Appeals for the second circuit. He was the grandson of John Marshall Harlan, Associate Justice of the U. S. Supreme Court (1877–1910). Justice Harlan retired from the Court in 1971. He died in 1972.

icy against premature constitutional decision," which properly understood does indeed demand that result.

The policy referred to is one to which I unreservedly subscribe. Without undertaking to be definitive, I would suppose it is a policy the wisdom of which is woven of several strands: (1) Due regard for the fact that the source of the Court's power lies ultimately in its duty to decide, in conformity with the Constitution, the particular controversies which come to it, and does not arise from some generalized power of supervision over state and national legislatures; (2) therefore it should insist that litigants bring to the Court interests and rights which require present recognition and controversies demanding immediate resolution; (3) also it follows that the controversy must be one which is in truth and fact the litigant's own, so that the clash of adversary contest which is needed to sharpen and illuminate issues is present and gives that aid on which our adjudicatory system has come to rely; (4) finally, it is required that other means of redress for the particular right claimed be unavailable, so that the process of the Court may not become overburdened and conflicts with other courts or departments of government may not needlessly be created, which might come about if either those truly affected are not the ones demanding relief, or if the relief we can give is not truly needed.

In particularization of this composite policy the Court, in the course of its decisions on matters of justiciability, has developed and given expression to a number of important limitations on the exercise of its jurisdiction, the presence or absence of which here should determine the justiciability of these appeals. Since all of them are referred to here in one way or another, it is well to proceed to a disclosure of those which are *not* involved in the present appeals, thereby focusing attention on the one factor on which reliance appears to be placed by both the plurality and concurring opinions in this instance.

First: It should by now be abundantly clear that the fact that only Constitutional claims are presented in proceedings seeking *anticipatory* relief against state criminal statutes does not for that reason alone make the claims premature. [Citations omitted] Whatever general pronouncements may be found to the contrary must, in context, be seen to refer to considerations quite different from anything present in these cases.

Thus in Alabama State Federation of Labor, etc. v. McAdory, supra, anticipatory relief was withheld for the precise reason that normally this Court ought not to consider the Constitutionality of a state statute in the absence of a controlling interpretation of its meaning and effect by the state courts. . . . these appeals come to us from the highest court of Connecticut, thus affording us—in company with previous state interpretations of the same statute—a clear construction of the scope of the statute, thereby in effect assuring that our review constitutes no greater interference with state administration than the state procedures themselves allow.

Second: I do not think these appeals may be dismissed for want of "ripeness" as that concept has been understood in its "varied applications." There is no lack of "ripeness" in the sense that is exemplified by cases such as Stearns v. Wood, 236 U.S. 75, 35 S.Ct. 229, 59 L.Ed. 475; Electric Bond

& Share Co. v. Securities & Exchange Comm., 303 U.S. 419, 58 S.Ct. 678, 82 L.Ed. 936. [Citations omitted.] In all of those cases the lack of ripeness inhered in the fact that the need for some further procedure, some further contingency of application or interpretation, whether judicial, administrative or executive, or some further clarification of the intentions of the claimant, served to make remote the issue which was sought to be presented to the Court. Certainly the appellants have stated in their pleadings fully and unequivocally what it is that they intend to do; no clarifying or resolving contingency stands in their way before they may embark on that conduct. Thus there is no circumstance besides that of detection or prosecution to make remote the particular controversy. And it is clear beyond cavil that the mere fact that a controversy such as this is rendered still more unavoidable by an actual prosecution, is not *alone* sufficient to make the case too remote, not ideally enough "ripe" for adjudication, at the prior stage of anticipatory relief. . . .

Third: This is not a feigned, hypothetical, friendly or colorable suit such as discloses "a want of a truly adversary contest." . . . Nor is there any question of collusion as in Lord v. Veazie, 8 How. 251, 12 L.Ed. 1067, or in United States v. Johnson, 319 U.S. 302, 63 S.Ct. 1075, 87 L.Ed. 1413. And there is nothing to suggest that the parties by their conduct of this litigation have cooperated to force an adjudication of a Constitutional issue which—were the parties interested solely in winning their cases rather than obtaining a Constitutional decision—might not arise in an arm's-length contested proceeding.

* * *

In the present appeals no more is alleged or conceded than is consistent with undisputed facts and with ordinary practice in deciding a case for anticipatory relief on demurrer. I think it is unjustifiably stretching things to assume that appellants are not deterred by the threat of prosecution from engaging in the conduct in which they assert a right to engage, or to assume that appellee's demurrer to the proposition that he asserts the right to enforce the statute against appellants at any time he chooses is anything but a candid one.

Indeed, as will be developed below, I think both the plurality and concurring opinions confuse on this score the predictive likelihood that, had they not brought themselves to appellee's attention, he would not enforce the statute against them, with some entirely suppositious "tacit agreement" not to prosecute, thereby ignoring the prosecutor's claim, asserted in these very proceedings, of a right, at his unbounded prosecutorial discretion, to enforce the statute.

Fourth: The doctrine of the cases dealing with a litigant's lack of standing to raise a Constitutional claim is said to justify the dismissal of these appeals. The precedents put forward as examples of this doctrine, . . . do indeed stand for the proposition that a legal claim will not be considered at the instance of one who has no real and concrete interest in its vindication. This is well in accord with the grounds for declining jurisdiction suggested above. But this doctrine in turn needs further particularization lest it become a catchall for an unarticulated discretion on the part of this Court to decline to adjudicate appeals involving Constitutional issues.

There is no question but that appellants here are asserting rights which are peculiarly their own, and which, if they are to be raised at all, may be raised most appropriately by them. Cf. Tileston v. Ullman, 318 U.S. 44, 63 S.Ct. 493. [Citations omitted.] Nor do I understand the argument to be that this is the sort of claim which is too remote ever to be pressed by anyone, because no one is ever sufficiently involved.

* * *

Thus, in truth, it is not the parties pressing this claim but the occasion chosen for pressing it which is objected to. But as has been shown the fact that it is anticipatory relief which is asked cannot of itself make the occasion objectionable.

We are brought, then, to the precise failing in these proceedings which is said to justify refusal to exercise our mandatory appellate jurisdiction: that there has been but one recorded Connecticut case dealing with a *prosecution* under the statute. The significance of this lack of recorded evidence of prosecutions is said to make the presentation of appellants' rights too remote, too contingent, too hypothetical for adjudication in the light of the policies already considered. . . . In my view it is only as a result of misconceptions both about the purport of the record before us and about the nature of the rights appellants put forward that this conclusion can be reached.

As far as the record is concerned, I think it is pure conjecture, and indeed conjecture which to me seems contrary to realities, that an open violation of the statute by a doctor (or more obviously still by a birth-control clinic) would not result in a substantial threat of prosecution. Crucial to the opposite conclusion is the description of the 1940 prosecution instituted in State v. Nelson, 126 Conn. 412, 11 A.2d 856, as a "test case" which, as it is viewed, scarcely even punctuates the uniform state practice of nonenforcement of this statute. I read the history of Connecticut enforcement in a very different light. The Nelson case, as appears from the state court's opinion, was a prosecution of two doctors and a nurse for aiding and abetting violations of this statute by married women in prescribing and advising the use of contraceptive materials by them. It is true that there is evidence of a customary unwillingness to enforce the statute prior to Nelson, for in that case the prosecutor stated to the trial court in a later motion to discontinue the prosecutions that "When this Waterbury clinic [operated by the defendants] was opened there were in open operation elsewhere in the State at least eight other contraceptive clinics which had been in existence for a long period of time and no questions as to their right to operate had been raised . . . ."

What must also be noted is that the prosecutor followed this statement with an explanation that the primary purpose of the prosecution was to provide clear warning to all those who, like Nelson, might rely on this practice of nonenforcement. . . .

Thus the respect in which Nelson was a test case is only that it was brought for the purpose of making entirely clear the State's power and willingness to enforce against "*any* person, whether a physician or layman" (emphasis supplied), the statute and to eliminate from future cases the very doubt about the existence of these elements which had resulted in eight open birth-control clinics, and which would have made unfair the conviction of Nelson.

The plurality opinion now finds, and the concurring opinion must assume, that the only explanation of the absence of recorded prosecutions subsequent to the Nelson case is that Connecticut has renounced that intention to prosecute and punish *"any* person . . . in accordance with the literal provisions of the law" which it announced in Nelson. But if renunciation of the purposes of the Nelson prosecution is consistent with a lack of subsequent prosecutions, success of that purpose is no less consistent with this lack. I find it difficult to believe that doctors generally—and not just those operating specialized clinics—would continue openly to disseminate advice about contraceptives after Nelson in reliance on the State's supposed unwillingness to prosecute, or to consider that high-minded members of the profession would in consequence of such inaction deem themselves warranted in disrespecting this law so long as it is on the books. Nor can I regard as "chimerical" the fear of enforcement of these provisions that seems to have caused the disappearance of at least nine birth-control clinics. In short, I fear that the Court has indulged in a bit of sleight of hand to be rid of this case. It has treated the significance of the absence of prosecutions during the twenty years since Nelson as identical with that of the absence of prosecutions during the years before Nelson. It has ignored the fact that the very purpose of the Nelson prosecution was to change defiance into compliance. It has ignored the very possibility that this purpose may have been successful. The result is to postulate a security from prosecution for open defiance of the statute which I do not believe the record supports.

* * *

But even if Dr. Buxton were not in the litigation and appellants the Poes and Doe were seeking simply to use contraceptives without any need of consulting a physician beforehand—which is not the case we have, although it is the case which the plurality opinion of the Court is primarily concerned to discuss—even then I think that it misconceives the concept of justiciability and the nature of these appellants' rights to say that the failure of the State to carry through any criminal prosecution requires dismissal of their appeals.

The Court's disposition assumes that to decide the case now, in the absence of any consummated prosecutions, is unwise because it forces a difficult decision in advance of any exigent necessity therefor. Of course it is abundantly clear that this requisite necessity can exist prior to any actual prosecution, for that is the theory of anticipatory relief, and is by now familiar law. What must be relied on, therefore, is that the historical absence of prosecutions in some way leaves these appellants free to violate the statute without fear of prosecution, whether or not the law is Constitutional, and thus absolves us from the duty of deciding if it is. Despite the suggestion of a "tougher and truer law" of immunity from criminal prosecution and despite speculation as to a "tacit agreement" that this law will not be enforced, there is, of course, no suggestion of an estoppel against the State if it should attempt to prosecute appellants. Neither the plurality nor the concurring opinion suggests that appellants have some legally cognizable right not to be prosecuted if the statute is Constitutional. What is meant is simply that the appellants are more or less free to act without fear of prosecution because the prosecuting authorities of the State, in their discretion and at their whim, are, as a matter of prediction, unlikely to decide to prosecute.

Here is the core of my disagreement with the present disposition. As I will develop later in this opinion, the most substantial claim which these married persons press is their right to enjoy the privacy of their marital relations free of the enquiry of the criminal law, whether it be in a prosecution of them or of a doctor whom they have consulted. And I cannot agree that their enjoyment of this privacy is not substantially impinged upon, when they are told that if they use contraceptives, indeed whether they do so or not, the only thing which stands between them and being forced to render criminal account of their marital privacy is the whim of the prosecutor. Connecticut's highest court has told us in the clearest terms that, given proof, the prosecutor will succeed if he decides to bring a proceeding against one of the appellants for taking the precise actions appellants have announced they intend to take. The State Court does not agree that there has come into play a "tougher and truer law than the dead words of the written text," and in the light of twelve unsuccessful attempts since 1943 to change this legislation, Poe v. Ullman, 147 Conn. 48, 56, note 2, 156 A.2d 508, 513, this position is not difficult to understand. Prosecution and conviction for the clearly spelled-out actions the appellants wish to take is not made unlikely by any fortuitous factor outside the control of the parties, nor is it made uncertain by possible variations in the actions appellants actually take from those the state courts have already passed upon. All that stands between the appellants and jail is the legally unfettered whim of the prosecutor and the Constitutional issue this Court today refuses to decide.

If we revert again to the reasons underlying our reluctance to exercise a jurisdiction which technically we possess, and the concrete expression of those underlying reasons in our cases, . . . then I think it must become clear that there is no justification for failing to decide these married persons' appeals. The controversy awaits nothing but an actual prosecution, and, as will be shown, the substantial damage against which these appellants, Mrs. Doe and the Poes, are entitled to protection will be accomplished by such a prosecution, whatever its outcome in the state courts or here. By the present decision, although as a general matter the parties would be entitled to our review in an anticipatory proceeding which the State allowed to be instituted in its courts, these appellants are made to await actual prosecution before we will hear them. Indeed it appears that whereas appellants would surely have been entitled to review were this a new statute, see Harrison v. N. A. A. C. P., supra, the State here is enabled to maintain at least some substantial measure of compliance with this statute and still obviate any review in this Court, by the device of purely discretionary prosecutorial inactivity. It seems to me to destroy the whole purpose of anticipatory relief to consider the prosecutor's discretion, once all legal and administrative channels have been cleared, as in any way analogous to those other contingencies which make remote a controversy presenting Constitutional claims.

In this light it is not surprising that the Court's position is without support in the precedents. Indeed it seems to me that Pierce v. Society of Sisters, 268 U.S. 510, 45 S.Ct. 571, 69 L.Ed. 1070, provides very clear authority contrary to the position of the Court in this case, for there a Court which included Justices Holmes, Brandeis, and Stone rejected a claim of prematureness and then passed upon and held unconstitutional a state statute whose sanctions were not even to become effective for more than seventeen months after the time the case was argued to this Court. The Court found allegations of present loss of business, caused by the threat of the statute's future enforcement against the Society's clientele, sufficient to make the injury to the Society "present and very real." 268 U.S. at page 536, 45 S.Ct. at page 574. I cannot regard as less present, or less real, the tendency to discourage the exercise of the liberties of these appellants, caused by reluctance to submit their freedoms from prosecution and conviction to the discretion of the Connecticut prosecuting authorities. I therefore think it incumbent on us to consider the merits of appellants' Constitutional claims.

[In part two of his opinion, MR. JUSTICE HARLAN also found that the Connecticut Statute was unconstitutional].

MR. JUSTICE STEWART,* dissenting.

For the reasons so convincingly advanced by both MR. JUSTICE DOUGLAS and MR. JUSTICE HARLAN, I join them in dissenting from the dismissal of these appeals. Since the appeals are nonetheless dismissed, my dissent need go no further. However, in refraining from a discussion of the constitutional issues, I in no way imply that the ultimate result I would reach on the merits of these controversies would differ from the conclusions of my dissenting Brothers.

Notes and Questions

1. In the instant case Justice Frankfurter announced the judgment of the Court in an opinion with which Chief Justice Warren, and Justices Clark and Whittaker concurred. Justice Brennan concurred with the judgment of the Court but he did not join in Justice Frankfurter's opinion. Justice Black dissented without opinion, Justices Douglas and Harlan dissented and wrote separate opinions, and Justice Stewart joined in both dissenting opinions and added some remarks of his own. The Court reached its result by a 5 to 4 vote but neither the majority nor the dissenters prepared opinions which could be joined in by all of the Justices who voted alike. The Court thus rendered a judgment but without a majority opinion.

In most cases where opinions are handed down there is one opinion in which all or a majority of the Justices join. This opinion is then the opinion of the Court, even though it is prepared and delivered by one of the Justices. In the absence of separate opinions, and unless special reference is made to other members of the Court to explain their participation in the case, it may be assumed that they join in the opinion of the Court.

2. Did Justice Frankfurter find that the Supreme Court did not have jurisdiction in Poe v. Ullman, or that the case did not present a justiciable controversy? Did his decision turn on a finding that the case lacked the element of adversity, or that the plaintiffs did not

---

* Justice Potter Stewart was appointed to the Supreme Court by President Eisenhower in 1958. At the time of his appointment he was a judge of the U. S. Court of Appeals for the Sixth Circuit.

have standing, or that the case was moot, or that the case was unripe, or was there some other ground for his decision?

3.　Is the disagreement between Justices Frankfurter and Harlan based on differences in their views as to the application of legal principles of jurisdiction and justiciability in this case, or is their disagreement based on different appraisals of the facts in this case?

4.　What purposes are served by the writing of a dissenting opinion?

5.　What purposes are served by Justice Brennan's concurring opinion?　Test your answer to this question in light of the following case.

GRISWOLD v. CONNECTICUT

Supreme Court of the United States, 1965.
381 U.S. 479, 85 S.Ct. 1678.

MR. JUSTICE DOUGLAS delivered the opinion of the Court.

Appellant Griswold is Executive Director of the Planned Parenthood League of Connecticut.　Appellant Buxton is a licensed physician and a professor at the Yale Medical School who served as Medical Director for the League at its Center in New Haven—a center open and operating from November 1 to November 10, 1961, when appellants were arrested.

They gave information, instruction, and medical advice to *married persons* as to the means of preventing conception.　They examined the wife and prescribed the best contraceptive device or material for her use. Fees were usually charged, although some couples were serviced free.

The statutes whose constitutionality is involved in this appeal are §§ 53–32 and 54–196 of the General Statutes of Connecticut (1938).　.　.　.

The appellants were found guilty as accessories and fined $100 each, against the claim that the accessory statute as so applied violated the Fourteenth Amendment.　The Appellate Division of the Circuit Court affirmed. The Court of Errors affirmed that judgment.　.　.　.

We think that appellants have standing to raise the constitutional rights of the married people with whom they had a professional relationship.　Tileston v. Ullman, 318 U.S. 44, 63 S.Ct. 493, 87 L.Ed. 603, is different, for there the plaintiff seeking to represent others asked for a declaratory judgment.　In that situation we thought that the requirements of standing should be strict, lest the standards of "case or controversy" in Article III of the Constitution become blurred.　Here those doubts are removed by reason of a criminal conviction for serving married couples in violation of an aiding-and-abetting statute.　Certainly the accessory should have standing to assert that the offense which he is charged with assisting is not, or cannot constitutionally be a crime.

.　.　.　The rights of husband and wife, pressed here, are likely to be diluted or adversely affected unless those rights are considered in a suit involving those who have this kind of confidential relation to them.

[Coming to the merits, the Court held the contraceptives use statute to be unconstitutional. JUSTICES GOLDBERG, HARLAN and WHITE wrote separate concurring opinions. JUSTICES BLACK and STEWART dissented in separate opinions.]

Notes and Questions

1. Does the fact that Griswold is now a defendant appealing the conviction and fine, rather than a plaintiff seeking a declaratory judgment, materially change the issues, or the factors to be considered in resolving the issues which were before the court in Poe v. Ullman? Considered in light of the subsequent developments in Griswold, was Poe a good decision? Was Poe a useful decision?

2. In Epperson v. Arkansas, 393 U.S. 97, 89 S.Ct. 266 (1968), plaintiff was a public school teacher who instituted a declaratory judgment action challenging the constitutional validity of the Arkansas "monkey law", Ark.Stat.Ann. §§ 80–1627, and 80–1628. These sections declared it unlawful "for a teacher in any state supported school or university" to teach the theory or doctrine that mankind ascended or descended from a lower order of animals, or "to adopt or use in any such institution a textbook that teaches this theory." Violation was a misdemeanor, and also was made grounds for dismissal from a teaching position.

In 1964, the Little Rock school board approved and prescribed the use of a new textbook which contained a chapter setting forth "the theory about the origin of man from a lower animal." Epperson was employed as a biology teacher at Little Rock Central High School in the fall of 1965. The new biology textbook was assigned for her use. She sued for the declaratory judgment and to enjoin enforcement of the "monkey law" by the state and by the local school officials. There was no record of any prior prosecutions under the statute. There was no indication at the time that prosecution under the statute was contemplated by any public officials.

Was Epperson v. Arkansas a justiciable controversy?

3. The trial court ruled in Epperson's favor, declaring the statute void under the free speech provisions of the First Amendment to the Constitution of the United States. The Supreme Court of Arkansas reversed on appeal in a two sentence, *per curiam* opinion. Epperson appealed to the Supreme Court of the United States. The record on appeal did not disclose whether or not she was still employed as a teacher in Arkansas at the time her appeal was argued.

Was Epperson v. Arkansas a justiciable controversy when it reached the United States Supreme Court? The Court in Epperson declared the Arkansas "monkey law" void as a violation of the "establishment of religion" provision of the First Amendment.

4. In 1971, Marco DeFunis, Jr. applied for admission to the University of Washington Law School, a state operated institution.

DeFunis' application was denied in the normal course of the Law School's admissions process. At that time, the Law School, like many other Universities, Colleges, and professional schools, employed special recruiting and admissions procedures for Black, Hispanic, Native American, and other racial minority group students. DeFunis alleged that his academic qualifications were superior to students admitted through the Law School's special admissions program. He claimed that denial of his application constituted impermissible discrimination in violation of the Equal Protection Clause of the Fourteenth Amendment to the United States Constitution. DeFunis sued the President and other officials of the University of Washington seeking admission to the Law School as a remedy for the wrong he alleged. The suit was brought in the Superior Court for King County, State of Washington. The trial judge found for DeFunis and ordered that he be admitted to the Law School. DeFunis matriculated in September 1971 while the case was on appeal to the Washington Supreme Court. By the time that appeal was heard and decided, DeFunis was in his second year of law school. The Washington Supreme Court reversed the trial court, holding that the Law School admissions policy was not invalid under the Fourteenth Amendment. DeFunis petitioned for review in the U.S. Supreme Court. By the time the case was heard by the U.S. Supreme Court, DeFunis was in his last semester in law school, and regardless of the outcome of his lawsuit, the defendants planned to let him complete his studies. ·What result in the U.S. Supreme Court? DeFunis v. Odegaard, 416 U.S. 312, 94 S.Ct. 1704 (1974).

SECTION 2.7   JUDICIAL SELF-RESTRAINT: TWO VIEWS

In his opinion in Poe v. Ullman, Justice Frankfurter used the following quotation in support of his decision: "The best teaching of this Court's experience admonishes us not to entertain constitutional questions in advance of the strictest necessity." In the following passage Thurman Arnold presents a sharply opposing view. In developing your own position on this issue, consider the points raised in the passage from Hart and Wechsler, *supra*, pp. 70–71 and the analysis of Professor Lon L. Fuller in the passage printed *infra*, p. 113, after the quotation from Thurman Arnold.

[The following passage is from THURMAN ARNOLD,* THE SYMBOLS OF GOVERNMENT (New Haven, 1935), pp. 173–174, 178, 183–185. Footnotes are omitted.]

* At the time he wrote this passage, Thurman Arnold was Professor of Law at the Yale Law School. He later served as Assistant Attorney General of the U. S. (1938–1943), and as a judge on the U. S. Court of Appeals for the District of Columbia Circuit (1943–1945). He engaged in the practice of law in Washington, D.C. from 1945 until his death in 1969. His major writings include, The Symbols of Government (1935), The Folklore of Capitalism (1937), Democracy and Free Enterprise (1942), and Fair Fights and Foul: A Dissenting Lawyer's Life (1965).

.   .   .   Courts owe their prestige to the idea that they are constantly making the law more and more certain. They owe their power to the fact that they never clarify total situations. They leave the cases which are just around the corner always undecided, and thus compel business men and legislators to be constantly in fear of their judicial veto. This is a characteristic of judicial government. Without it we would scarcely have what people call a government of law. Other countries perhaps do not extend the process so far as the United States, but the situation above described is inherent in any judicial institution.

The trick by which this strategic position of the courts is maintained is the institution of civil trial by combat which is developed in this country probably to a further extent than in any other. An analysis of this institution, technical though it may be, is necessary for an understanding of how government operates.

As the criminal trial dramatizes law enforcement as a creed, so the civil trial dramatizes the moral beauty of the noninterference of government in private affairs. Enforcement of the criminal law by policemen, is a public duty; enforcement of civil rights by policemen, or even administrative officials, tends toward bureaucracy. The whole ideology, and procedural organization of the civil trial is designed to insulate the court and the Government from taking the initiative in enforcing or even protecting the civil rights of individuals. Even the existence of injustice is preferred to the active participation of the court in private or business affairs.

This role of the civil trial as a symbol of individual freedom from active interference by the government, makes it a most important factor in preserving conservative traditions in the face of new regulatory legislation. It achieves its obstructive power not by opposing the Government, so much as by declining to decide general problems, or to give sweeping directions. In this way, courts obtain a power to keep litigants guessing; a condition which would be impossible in a body charged with the actual enforcement of law.   .   .   .

The method by which this strategic position of a court is maintained is by the application of Anglo-American legal theory that only the particular and narrow issues brought before the courts by contesting parties be made the basis of judge-made law. This theory, briefly outlined, is as follows:

A court is not supposed to regulate situations merely because regulation is badly needed. A court should never approve, disapprove, or clarify an entire set of rules governing a general business situation. A court should never answer questions. The limits of the power of the courts in this direction is to produce parables out of which further arguments may be spun.

What the issues of a case are, depends upon a printed record, beyond the limits of which no court should go. Statements of law on assumed facts, a familiar procedure to continental judges, are supposed in this country to indicate loose judicial thinking. The court may be aware, as men of common sense, that the parties desire a general rule to be adopted or rejected, or the parties may even stipulate that such is their desire. Nevertheless, the court is powerless to discuss the rule or principle if the actual facts in the record do not raise those precise issues in a way prescribed by technical rules. . . .

Assumptions Underlying the Search for Issues

The suggestion that a court should be permitted to speak without a contested case before it, has been met with an air of shocked surprise by such persons learned in the law as the writer has interviewed on the subject. It is considered dangerous in spite of the fact that in large areas of judicial participation in business, such as consent receiverships, this is exactly what the courts have been compelled to do. Courts for a long time have regulated insolvent business on the sensible lines of control instead of the romantic technique of battle. The difficulties have arisen only because the older tradition keeps courts from exercising enough control. Today, when something of the same type of regulation is being imposed upon solvent business, the notion of groups of individuals getting up plans and regulations for the approval of the court becomes a necessary development. Yet we still prefer a two-party injunction suit to test the operation of a code to a more sensible impartial examination at the request of interested groups who are not necessarily fighting each other. The reasons for this preference are worth examining.

The philosophical rationalization of why courts may not be trusted to clarify rules in confused situations, except by the hit-or-miss method of the occasional decision after a contest, is of course contradictory. If one were compelled to summarize the assumptions underlying the ideal of a law-making body, which never speaks except to settle a combat properly brought before it, the result would be somewhat as follows:

1. Every trial should be a contest over issues presented by the parties, and not an investigation of what the facts were which created the necessity of the suit.

2. If one party loses on a technicality it is his own fault because he is supposed to know the rules. Simplicity of rules is obtained by not permitting courts to clarify these rules except by penalizing one of the antagonists. To permit anyone to find out about them in advance would destroy the idea of a combat.

3. Courts are not permitted to plan their participation in a new situation, such as was presented by the recovery acts, any more than they were permitted to plan their participation in arbitration, rate-making, or administrative law. This participation is rather to be determined by a series of battles. Each particular battle is a war to end war.

4. Rules governing human conduct will be better and more consistent if only a small section of that conduct is considered at a time. It is a mistake for a rule-making body to consider a situation as a whole.

5. The best way to avoid litigation is to make the power to promulgate rules and regulations exclusively dependent upon litigation.

6. Courts should keep their eyes fixed on the past and follow precedent. Legislature should look to the future, and disregard it. Thus the two extremes will correct each other, if courts making their decisions will only keep future policies in mind, and if legislatures will only have more

respect for the past.   Thus the legislative and judicial functions will nicely balance each other, provided we set up enough administrative tribunals actually to do the work required.

These assumptions are reconciled with practical efficiency by the notion that courts are more apt to formulate or apply rules soundly if the opposite sides are prevented from sitting around a table together in friendly conference.   Mutual exaggeration is supposed to create lack of exaggeration.   Bitter partisanship in opposite directions is supposed to bring out the truth.   Of course no rational human being would apply such a theory to his own affairs or to other departments of the government.   It has never been supposed that bitter and partisan lobbying assisted legislative bodies in their law-making.   No investigation is conducted by hiring persons to argue opposite sides.   The common law is neither clear, sound, nor even capable of being restated in areas where the results of cases are being most bitterly contested.   And particularly with reference to administrative regulation does mutual exaggeration of opposing claims violate the whole theory of rational, scientific investigation.   Yet in spite of this most obvious fact, the ordinary teacher of law will insist (1) that combat makes for clarity, (2) that heated arguments bring out the truth, and (3) that anyone who does not believe this is a loose thinker.   The explanation of this attitude lies in the realm of social anthropology.

[The following passage is from LON L. FULLER,* THE PROBLEMS OF JURISPRUDENCE (Brooklyn, N. Y., 1949; temporary edition), pp. 706–707.]

Conditions under which Adjudication as a Principle of Order Achieves its Maximum Moral Force

Adjudication involves a complex of factors that may appear in various combinations and that may be present in varying degrees.   We may, however, say that the moral force of a judgment or decision will be at a maximum when the following conditions are satisfied: (1) The judge does not act on his own initiative, but on the application of one or both of the disputants.   (2) The judge has no direct or indirect interest (even emotional) in the outcome of the case.   (3) The judge confines his decision to the controversy before him and attempts no regulation of the parties' relations going beyond that controversy.   (4) The case presented to the judge involves an existing controversy, and not merely the prospect of some future disagreement.   (5) The judge decides the case solely on the basis of the evidence and arguments presented to him by the parties. (6) Each disputant is given ample opportunity to present his case.

It is seldom that all of these conditions can be realized in practice, and it is not here asserted that it is always wise to observe all of them. What is asserted is merely that adjudication as a principle of order achieves its maximum force when all of these conditions are satisfied.   Some of

---

* Lon L. Fuller is Professor of Law at Harvard University.   He is the author of numerous books and articles on jurisprudence and contract law.   Among his recent publications are The Anatomy of Law (1970), The Morality of Law (rev. ed. 1969), and Basic Contract Law (with Robert Braucher) (1964).

this moral or persuasive force may wisely be sacrificed when other considerations dictate a departure from the conditions enumerated above, and where the tribunal, as an agent of legitimated power, had the capacity to compel respect for its decision.

The connection between the conditions enumerated above and the moral force of the judgment rendered is not something irrational and fortuitous. The key to it is found in the fact that men instinctively seek to surround the process of adjudication with those conditions that will tend to insure that the decision rendered is the closest possible approximation of the common need. This obviously explains the conditions of disinterestedness on the part of the judge and the opportunity for a full hearing of both sides, that is, conditions 2 and 6 in the enumeration above. Underlying the other four conditions is a single insight, namely, that men's interests and desires form a complex network, and that to discover the most effective and least disruptive pattern of order within this network requires an intimate acquaintance with the network itself and the interests and desires of which it is composed. In other words, these conditions are designed to obviate an evil that may be broadly called "absentee management." The judge must stick to the case before him (condition 3), because if he ventures beyond it he may attempt to regulate affairs on which he is inadequately informed. The judge must work within the framework of the parties' arguments and proof (condition 5), because if he goes beyond these he will lack the guidance given him by the parties and may not understand the interests that are affected by a decision rendered outside that framework. The case must involve a present controversy (condition 4), because neither the parties nor the judge can be sure that they fully understand the implications of a possible, future controversy or the precise interests that may be affected by it when it arises. The first condition (that the judge should act on the application of the parties) is perhaps the most difficult to justify. It arises from the fact that the judge who calls the parties in and himself sets the framework of the hearing lays himself open to the suspicion of planning a general regulation in which the controversy on which he hears evidence and arguments appears as a mere detail. Thus a violation of condition 1 tends to carry with it a strong suspicion that condition 3 is being violated.

Questions

1.   What are the basic differences in the positions taken by Professors Arnold and Fuller, respectively?

2.   Is it possible for a court to "clarify total situations"? Is there not a law of diminishing returns, or what might be called a *principle of economy*, inherent in judicial decision-making, namely, that the wider the grounds upon which the court decides the case, the more difficult the application of those grounds to future cases, or to other parts of the "total situation"?

3.   If, on the other hand, a court were concerned "merely" with deciding the particular case before it, would it be likely to write an opinion setting forth the reasons for its decision? What are the various purposes that you would assign to the writing of judicial opinions?

4.   What does Fuller mean when he speaks of the "maximum moral force" of adjudication as a "principle of order"?

5.   Compare Arnold and Fuller with the excerpts from Hart and Wechsler, *supra* pp. 70–71.

6.   Review the questions presented in the introduction to this section, *supra* p. 55 and answer them on the basis of the material you have read this far.

SECTION 3.   THE REQUIREMENT IN CRIMINAL CASES OF A LAW SPECIFICALLY PROSCRIBING THE ACT CHARGED

In the preceding section we began an examination of the nature and scope of the judicial power.   We saw that the requirement of a live controversy in civil cases both defines and limits that power. Now we turn to an examination of a body of doctrine which tends to define and limit the power of courts with respect to criminal cases.

The issues raised in this section are presented as a parallel to the issues raised in the prior section.   Technically, the two topics are unrelated but for our purpose—to explore the nature and functions of law—it is useful to juxtapose them.   Each, in its own way, sheds light on the limitations which are imposed on the judicial function by the judges themselves.

The following prefatory comments on distinctive aspects of criminal procedure should provide some background and vocabulary which will prove useful in the reading and analysis of the materials presented in this section and in Chapter 3.

a.   A criminal proceeding is an action brought by a government (federal, state, municipal) against a person or persons. Thus criminal cases are denominated by such names as, State v. Nelson, United States v. McBoyle, and Ohio v. Lafferty, but in some states a criminal case is labeled as an action by the people, *e. g.*, People v. Dreares, on the theory that the real party in interest is the people and that the government is acting in the people's behalf in bringing the criminal action.

b.   The government is said to "prosecute" in criminal actions; the official who conducts the case for the government is called the prosecutor; and the opposing sides in the action are referred to as the prosecution and the defense.

c.   The rules governing the prosecution of a criminal action are said to be designed to secure great protection for the defense and to impose limits on the prosecution.   Thus the requirements of proof of guilt are stricter in a criminal case than in a civil case. See *infra* pp. 382–383.

d. The verdict in a criminal proceeding is generally announced as a finding of guilt or innocence, *i. e.*, jury verdicts may state either "We find the defendant guilty" or "We find the defendant innocent."

e. The judgment of the court follows the rendition of the verdict. Thus in the case of a finding of innocence, a judgment of acquittal is made and the defendant is discharged, while a finding of guilt will generally be followed by a judgment of conviction and the defendant is held for further proceedings in which the court pronounces sentence against the defendant.

f. The sentence is the sanction (penalty) which the judge imposes on the convicted defendant. Fines (a money payment), imprisonment, or both a fine and imprisonment, are the penalties generally applied in criminal cases. After sentence the convict is turned over to the officials responsible for carrying out the sentence. The defendant may appeal, or further proceedings on behalf of the convict may be initiated at a later date. As a general rule, the prosecutor may not appeal from a judgment of acquittal.

SECTION 3.1   "COMMON LAW CRIMES"

The term "Common Law" is used, as we have seen, to designate the system of law which evolved in the royal courts of Anglo-Norman England, and which is a foundation for the legal systems of most English speaking countries. The term "common law"—note the lower case letters—may be used in a variety of senses. In this section it is used primarily to refer to reliance on "case law" (precedents) as a source of legal rules and principles.[1] Common law in this sense is found in the reports of judicial decisions, in contradistinction to statutory law which is found in the recorded acts of legislatures.

The idea that judges make law, and that a substantial part of our law originates in judicial proceedings and is reported in judicial decisions, may seem strange. The reader is asked to accept that idea on faith, just for the time being. Part Two of the book is devoted to an extended examination of this feature of the Anglo-American legal system. Here we are concerned with a more narrow issue. If we assume that judges do have the authority to create or revise legal rules as part of the process of resolving disputes between individuals in

[1.] See the Note, "Case Law: Common Law", *supra* p. 65, and the Note "Common Law" and "Equity", *supra* pp. 73–76.

matters of property, contract, personal injuries and the like, should it follow that they have a similar authority to create or revise legal rules in the process of deciding criminal cases? Or should the making of criminal law be left solely to the legislature?

OHIO v. LAFFERTY

Court of Common Pleas of Ohio, Fifth Circuit, 1817.
Tappan (Ohio) 113.

Lafferty was convicted, on three several indictments, for selling unwholesome provisions.

Wright, for the defendant, moved, in arrest of judgment "for that there is no law of this state against selling unwholesome provisions." He observed, that the indictment was bottomed upon the common law of England, which was not in force in this state, it never having been adopted by our constitution or recognized by our laws or judicial decisions: that the 4th section of the 3d article of the constitution, limited and confined the jurisdiction of the court to offences declared such by the statute laws. He admitted that the offence charged, was an offence against the public, which at common law was indictable and punishable where the common law was in force; but that, in this state, as the common law was not in force; and no statute had declared it criminal, it was not an act which could be prosecuted criminally.

Beebe, contra. That the section of the constitution quoted and relied upon by Wright, as limiting the jurisdiction of the court to statutory offences, was not fairly construed; it should be considered as referring the courts to the statute law, for the extent or their several jurisdictions in criminal cases; and so considered the statute law which gave to the supreme court jurisdiction in all capital cases, and to the courts of common pleas jurisdiction in all cases not capital, without any specification of indictable offences; did point out the manner and the cases in which this section of the constitution intended the duties of the courts should be divided, and that it did not exclude a common law jurisdiction.

PRESIDENT (JUDGE TAPPAN). The question raised on this motion, whether the common law is a rule of decision in this state? is one of very great interest and importance, and one upon which contradictory opinions have been holden both at the bar and upon the bench.

No just government ever did, nor probably ever can, exist, without an unwritten or common law. By the common law, is meant those maxims, principles, and forms of judicial proceeding, which have no written law to prescribe or warrant them, but which, founded on the laws of nature and the dictates of reason, have by usage and custom, become interwoven with the written laws; and, by such incorporation, form a part of the municipal code of each state or nation, which has emerged from the loose and erratic habits of savage life, to civilization, order, and a government of laws.

For the forms of process, indictment, and trial, we have no statute law directing us; and for almost the whole law of evidence, in criminal as well as in civil proceedings, we must look to the common law, for we have no other guide. Can it be said, then, that the common law is not in force, when, without its aid and sanction, justice cannot be administered; when even the written laws cannot be construed, explained, and enforced, without the common law, which furnishes the rules and principles of such construction?

We may go further and say, that not only is the common law necessarily in force here, but that its authority is superior to that of the written laws; for it not only furnishes the rules and principles by which the statute laws are construed, but it ascertains and determines the validity and authority of them. It is, therefore, that Lord Hobart said, that a statute law against reason, as to make a man a judge in his own cause, was void.

As the laws of nature and reason are necessarily in force in every community of civilized men, (because nature is the common parent, and reason the common guardian of man) so with communities as with individuals, the right of self-preservation is a right paramount to the institution of written law; and hence the maxim, *the safety of the people is the supreme law,* needs not the sanction of a constitution or statute to give it validity and force; but it cannot have validity and force, as law, unless the judicial tribunals have power to punish all such actions as directly tend to jeopardize that safety; unless, indeed, the judicial tribunals are the guardians of public morals and the conservators of the public peace and order. Whatever acts, then, are wicked and immoral in themselves, and directly tend to injure the community, are crimes against the community, which not only *may,* but *must* be repressed and punished, or government and social order cannot be preserved. It is this salutary principle of the common law, which spreads its shield over society, to protect it from the incessant activity and novel inventions of the profligate and unprincipled, inventions which the most perfect legislation could not always foresee and guard against.

But although the common law, in all countries, has its foundation in reason and the laws of nature, and therefore is similar in its general principles, yet in its application it has been modified and adapted to various forms of government; as the different orders of architecture, having their foundation in utility and graceful proportion, rise in various forms of symmetry and beauty, in accordance with the taste and judgment of the builder. It is also a law of liberty; and hence we find, that when North America was colonized by emigrants who fled from the pressure of monarchy and priestcraft in the old world, to enjoy freedom in the new, they brought with them the common law of England, (their mother country) claiming it as their birth-right and inheritance. In their charters from the crown, they were careful to have it recognized as the foundation on which they were to erect their laws and governments: not more anxious was Aeneas to secure from the burning ruins of Troy his household Gods, than were these first settlors of America to secure to themselves and their children the benefits of the common law of England. From thence, through every stage of the colonial governments, the common law was in force, so far as it was found necessary or useful. When the revolution commenced, and independent state governments were formed; in the midst of hostile collisions with the mother country, when the passions of men were inflamed, and a deep and general abhorrence of the tyranny of the British government was felt; the sages and patriots who commenced that revolution, and founded those state governments, recognized in the common law a guardian of liberty and social order. The common law of England has thus always been the common law of the colonies and states of North America; not indeed in its full extent, supporting a monarchy, aristocracy, and hierarchy, but so far as it was applicable to our more free and happy habits of government.

Has society been formed and government instituted in Ohio, on different principles from the other states in this respect? The answer to this question will be found in our written laws.

The ordinance passed by the congress of the United States, on the 13th of July 1787, "for the government of the territory of the United States North West of the river Ohio," is the earliest of our written laws. Possessing the North Western Territory in absolute sovereignty, the United States, by that instrument, provide for the temporary government of the people who may settle there; and, to use the language of that instrument, "for extending the fundamental principles of civil and religious liberty, which forms the basis whereon these republics, their laws and constitutions, are erected; to fix and establish those principles as the basis of all laws, constitutions and governments, which forever hereafter shall be formed in the said territory; to provide also for the establishment of states and permanent government therein; and for their admission to a share in the federal councils, on an equal footing with the original states, at as early periods as may be consistent with the general interest," it was ordained and declared, "that the inhabitants of the said territory shall *always* be entitled to the benefits of the writ of habeas corpus, and of the trial by jury; of a proportionate representation of the people in the legislature, *and of judicial proceedings according to the course of the common law*"—as one of the articles of compact between the original states, and the people and states in the said territory, to remain forever unalterable unless by common consent. Under this ordinance we purchased lands and made settlements, in this then N. Western Territory; we became voluntary parties to this contract, and made it, by our own set, what it was intended to be, "the basis of all our laws, constitutions and government"—and thus the common law became here, as it had become in the earliest colonies, the foundation of our whole system of jurisprudence.

That these articles of compact were of perpetual obligation upon the people and states to be formed in the territory, unless altered by the mutual consent of such states and of the original states, is a position which I have never heard controverted; yet it may not be useless to advert to express recognitions of it by both the contracting parties. First: the United States, by the act of congress entitled "an act to enable the people of the eastern division of the territory North West of the river Ohio, to form a constitution and state government, and for the admission of such state into the Union, on an equal footing with the original states, and for other purposes," under the authority of which Ohio became an independent state, authorized the people of said divisions to form a constitution and state government, "provided the same shall be republican, and not repugnant to the ordinance of the 13th of July 1787, between the original states and the people and states of the territory North West of the river Ohio." Section 5th.—Second: the people of Ohio, by the preamble to their state constitution, declare, that they ordain and establish that constitution, "consistent with the constitution of the United States, the ordinance of congress of 1787, and the law of congress."

The common law being a part of the existing system of jurisprudence at the time when the state government was formed, and its continuance being expressly provided for by the 4th section of the last article or schedule to this constitution, which declares that "all laws and parts of laws now in force in this territory, not inconsistent with this constitution, shall continue and remain in full effect until repealed by the legislature;" we will next examine the power of this court to enforce it.

The 1st section of the 3d article of the constitution declares, that "the judicial power of the state, both as to matters of law and equity, shall be vested in a supreme court, in courts of common pleas for each country," &c. The 2d section declares, that the supreme court "shall have original and appellate jurisdiction, both in common law and chancery, in such cases as shall be directed by law;" and the 3d section, that "the court of common pleas shall have common law and chancery jurisdiction in all such cases as shall be directed by law." These sections refer to future legislative provision to mark the boundaries of jurisdiction between the court of common pleas and the supreme court, and to fix their extent; but they do not refer to such provision, to point out the particular wrongs which may be redressed by petition in equity, by private suit, or by criminal prosecution. Such has been the uniform construction of these sections by the legislature, since the constitution was formed, as must be evident from the fact that no statute law has ever been made or projected, to detail those wrongs, private or public, which the judicial tribunals were to redress by virtue of their chancery powers, or "according to the course of the common law;" such a statute would indeed be a phenomenon, the result of a more perfect legislation than man has yet attained to.

But it has been urged, that the 4th section of the 3d article, is the only part of the constitution which gives this court jurisdiction in criminal cases, and that it expressly refers to future statutory provision, to point out the *cases* in which such jurisdiction may be exercised. The language of this section is: "The judges of the supreme court and courts of common pleas, shall have complete criminal jurisdiction, in such cases, and in such manner, as may be pointed out by law."

The laws in existence at the time when the constitution was formed, 29th Nov. 1802, and the state government commenced, (beside those of the United States) were the common law, the statutes of other states adopted by the governor and judges of the territory, and the acts of the territorial legislatures; all which were continued in force by the constitution. This section of the constitution, by giving jurisdiction in matters of crime, "*in such cases and in such manner as may be pointed out by law,*" must mean, in such cases and in such manner as may be now, or hereafter pointed out by law; for it must either intend to give the court jurisdiction according to the then existing laws, or to require of the legislature an immediate and perfect criminal code, and so operate as a repeal of the former; it could not intend the latter, because neither a convention or legislature can ever be construed to have exceeded their power, unless such intent is clearly and positively expressed; and so far is such intent from being expressed, by the section referred to, that the utmost latitude of construction leaves the intent that way ambiguous. It must intend the former: 1st. Because the convention who framed the constitution, were limited in their powers by the ordinance and law of congress; it had not power to deprive the people of

Ohio of the benefit of judicial proceedings according to the course of the common law. 2d. Because the convention intended the constitution to be consistent with the ordinance and law. And 3d. Because the constitution expressly continues in force all existing laws.

Such seems ever to have been the opinion of the legislature of this state; for the first general assembly which sat under the constitution, passed an act to fix the extent of jurisdiction in the courts, and gave to the common pleas "cognizance of all crimes, offences and misdemeanors, the punishment whereof is not capital." 1st vol. stat. laws, 40. But neither the first or second general assembly deemed it necessary to make any material alteration in the criminal code they had received from the territorial government; nor had the state any other criminal laws, until the first of August, 1805. And when the state courts superceded the territorial, they were required, "agreeable to their respective jurisdictions," to "take cognizance of all judgments, causes and matters whatsoever, whether civil or criminal, that are now pending, undetermined or unsatisfied," in the territorial courts; and they were "authorized and required to hear and decide upon the said matters." 1st vol. stat. laws, 50. In prosecutions at common law, then depending in the territorial courts, the state courts were thus directed to take cognizance, to hear and decide upon them, "according to the course of the common law."

But suppose that the position is a correct one, that the principles of the common law have no force or authority in this state, and what are the consequences? They are these: that there are no legal forms of process, of indictments, or trial; there is no law of evidence; and the statute laws cannot be enforced, but must remain inoperative from the uncertain signification of the terms used in defining criminal offences. Beside, the constitution gives jurisdiction to this court in criminal matters, "in such cases and in *such manner as may be pointed out by law;*" and as we have no statute pointing out the manner in which such jurisdiction shall be exercised, the consequence follows that it cannot be lawfully exercised in any manner whatever.

On the whole, therefore, it may be concluded, that were the written laws wholly silent on the subject, the principles and maxims of the common law must, of necessity, be the rule and guide of judicial decision, in criminal as well as in civil cases: to supply the defects of a necessarily imperfect legislation, and to prevent "the will of the judge, that law of tyrants," being substituted in the room of known and settled rules of law in the administration of justice.

And that by the ordinance of congress, the constitution and laws of the state, a common law jurisdiction in criminal cases is established and vested in this court. The motion in arrest is, therefore, overruled.

The defendant was fined 50 dollars in each case, with costs.

Questions

1. If someone has done something which everyone agrees is wrong, shouldn't the courts have jurisdiction to punish him or her?

2. Is the sale of unwholesome provisions obviously wrong?

3. Assuming that the received common law is necessarily applicable to civil actions, is it necessarily applicable to criminal actions?

4.   Assuming that the received common law is either necessary or appropriate to establish the procedures to be followed by prosecutors and judges, e. g., "forms of process, indictment, and trial", is it therefore necessary or appropriate for judges to follow the common law insofar as it also establishes substantive criminal law, e. g., the common law offense of "selling unwholesome provisions"?

5.   If no previous case of selling unwholesome provisions had ever been decided, and hence there was no common law on the precise question, would Judge Tappan have felt compelled to dismiss the indictments?

6.   What are Judge Tappan's views regarding, (a) the source of the common law and (b) the relationship between common law and legislation? Would you expect such views to be held by judges in a country where strong monarchs have reigned, where the function of legislation has slowly and only lately passed from the monarch and his advisors to a more representative legislative body, and where judges have been attempting to establish the principle that the sovereign is bound by law just as his subjects are? Are such views appropriate in a society governed by democratically elected officials and legislatures?

7.   In the English case of King v. Manley, [1933] 1 K.B. 592, Elizabeth Manley was indicted for making certain false statements to the police to the effect that some man whose description she gave came up from behind her and struck her and stole her purse. She had given the police similar imaginary reports several times before. The accused contended that the indictment disclosed no offense known to the law. The court held that it constituted a "public mischief." There being no statute defining such an offense, the court cited previous cases in which it had been stated that "All offences of a public nature, that is, all such acts or attempts as tend to the prejudice of the community, are indictable." The decision was severely criticized by English legal scholars, and it was in effect repudiated in a subsequent case. Nevertheless, in 1961 the House of Lords reaffirmed the reasoning of the Manley case in Shaw v. Director of Public Prosecutions. (1961 All England Law Reports, Vol. 2, p. 446.) Shaw had published *Ladies' Directory*, a magazine composed almost entirely of advertisements of London prostitutes. He had been assured by counsel that his conduct was not illegal and he had delivered a copy of the first issue to Scotland Yard for police inspection. He published five more issues before he was charged with the offense of "conspiracy to corrupt public morals." Prostitution is not prohibited by English law, nor is fornication or adultery. Yet all the judges except one agreed that Shaw had conspired with others to do a criminal act. The power to determine that the act was criminal was said to derive from the fact that the court is *custos morum*, "guardian of morals"—a concept which the King's Bench in the 17th century declared that it inherited from the Court of Star Chamber.

(See Le Roy v. Sidley, 1 Sid. 168, 82 Eng.Rep. 1032 (K.B. 1663). Sidley was a young English gentleman and forerunner of modern day streakers and flashers. He was charged for having stood naked on the balcony of his townhouse before a crowd of onlookers.

8. In Germany under the Nazi regime it was made a crime punishable by imprisonment to utter "spiteful or provocative statements . . . which disclose a base disposition toward the leading personalities of the nation . . . or toward measures taken or institutions established by them, and of such a nature as to undermine the people's confidence in their political leadership." It was not uncommon that persons would inform the police, often with vindictive motives, of violations of this and similar statutes, as a result of which information the violators would be punished by imprisonment. After the overthrow of Nazism German prosecutors brought criminal actions against some of these informers, for having procured the imprisonment of another. The defense generally rested on the ground that the statements which were reported were in fact criminal under the laws then in force. Some German courts rejected this defense on the ground that the Nazi laws in question were so arbitrary and unjust as to lack the necessary moral qualities of law, and that they constituted "statutory lawlessness." Do you agree? The problem is discussed in L. L. Fuller, "Positivism and Fidelity to Law—A Reply to Professor Hart," Harvard Law Review, Vol. 71, p. 648 ff. (1958); and H. L. A. Hart "Positivism and the Separation of Law and Morals," *id.*, p. 615 ff.

9. "Treason, murder, certain sexual offenses and some serious offenses against property are fairly constant in the criminal laws of the world, with relatively similar definitions. . . . In addition to these offenses, however, the increasing complexity of social life has led to the creation by the state of a vast number of laws which strike at forms of conduct peculiar to some particular type of social organization. Roscoe Pound in his Criminal Justice in America has found in analyzing the criminal laws of Rhode Island that the revised public laws of 1822 defined 50 crimes while the title, 'Of Crimes and Punishment,' of the general laws of 1923 defined 212. More than half of the offenses that may be prosecuted by the state and punished by fine and imprisonment or both are contained in special laws passed since 1872 dealing with such problems as the protection of workers in industry, the regulation of motor vehicle traffic, the regulation of selling securities and of merchandise and the enforcement of liquor prohibition laws. He concludes that during the last hundred years the number of crimes for which one could be prosecuted in Rhode Island has multiplied by eight. This criminalization of conduct has come as a result of the social growth and differentiation of an industrial civilization. Many of these crimes are not considered antisocial by large groups within the state. . . . " Thorsten Sellin, Crime, 4 Encyclopedia of the Social Sciences 563–564, (1931).

Berman & Greiner–Nat.Law 4th Ed.—6

What does this suggest regarding: (a) the nature of crime, and (b) the judicial role in determining what constitutes a crime? Does Poe v. Ullman, *supra*, suggest that the expansion of criminal law may in some respect be more apparent than real?

10. ". . . Crime is a legal concept, although some writers have used the term indiscriminately to denote antisocial, immoral or sinful behavior. . . . What the law calls crime is merely conduct which is declared to be socially harmful to the group or groups in a state which are large enough to influence legislation . . ." Sellin, *op. cit.* Is this a satisfactory definition of crime? How would you change or qualify it? Is Sellin's definition of crime related to Holmes' predictive theory of law (see *supra* p. 19)? Would this definition be useful to a legislator who had to decide how to vote on a bill which would declare some new form of conduct to be a crime?

Note

The rule declared in Ohio v. Lafferty did not remain law in Ohio. Cf. the following passage from Walker, Introduction to American Law (Phila., 1837) § 447: "How crimes and punishments are ascertained." [Footnotes omitted.]

In England and in several of the states, the common law prevails in the punishment of crimes; and many acts are punishable from precedent, which have never been made so by legislative provision. But the manifest evil of this doctrine is, that the majority of men, unskilled in law, cannot be supposed to know beforehand, whether a given act will be criminal or not. In fact, the accumulation of precedents through the lapse of centuries, must render it difficult for the most consummate lawyer to be able to pronounce at once with certainty on the subject. And yet it is absolutely necessary to act upon the well known maxim, that ignorance of the law is no excuse for its violation; because, otherwise, ignorance would always be pretended. This consideration alone is sufficient to demonstrate the importance of requiring every offence to be defined by the legislature, together with its punishment; and accordingly it has become a fundamental doctrine in the federal courts and in the courts of this state (Ohio), that they have no common law jurisdiction of crimes; and cannot treat any act as an offence, until the proper legislature has declared it to be such, and meted out the punishment. With regard to the federal courts, this doctrine, though sometimes doubted, rests upon the absence of any power in the federal constitution to punish crimes except in certain specified cases, before enumerated, for which Congress is to provide. And with regard to this state, the doctrine rests upon the clause of the constitution, which confers criminal jurisdiction upon the courts, "in such cases and in such manner as may be pointed out by law." This is construed to refer the subject of crimes to future legislative provision; and as our legislature has not adopted the criminal part of the common law, but has provided a substitute, it has therefore abrogated it. A different opinion has been sometimes entertained; but this is now the universal sentiment; and the happy consequence is, that on a few pages of the statute books, may be found enumerated all the offences which can be punished by the federal or state government, and the measure of punishment annexed to each. So that the only use now made of the criminal part of the common law, is to furnish the outlines of criminal procedure, and define the terms employed in the statutes. If there be any evil to be apprehended from this doctrine, it is that such cases may arise in which men cannot be punished, though they richly deserve it, because the legislature has not anticipated their offences; but this objection weighs hardly a feather against the inestimable privilege of having every offence, for which punishment can be inflicted, distinctly and accurately defined; instead of being left to be collected from doubtful precedents established in a very different state of society, and scattered at remote intervals, through the reported decisions of seven or eight centuries.

The common law of crimes, which was developed in England and carried to the United States prior to the American Revolution, remains in force in more than half the states either as a result of judicial decision or by express statutory provision adopting the common law of crime. In other states, and under federal law, all crimes are established by legislation expressly defining the many various forms of criminal conduct. As a general rule modern judges are not prone to expand the common law of crimes, perhaps because the legislation of comprehensive criminal statutes has obviated any real need to do so. The definition of new crimes and appropriate sanctions for new crimes is generally left to legislative action. See "Common Law Crimes in the United States," 47 Columbia Law Review 1332 (1947).

3.2   STRICT CONSTRUCTION OF CRIMINAL STATUTES

McBOYLE v. UNITED STATES

Supreme Court of the United States, 1931.
283 U.S. 25, 51 S.Ct. 340.

MR. JUSTICE HOLMES* delivered the opinion of the Court:

The petitioner was convicted of transporting from Ottawa, Illinois, to Guymon, Oklahoma, an airplane that he knew to have been stolen, and was sentenced to serve three years' imprisonment and to pay a fine of $2,000. The judgment was affirmed by the Circuit Court of Appeals for the Tenth Circuit. 43 F.2d 273. A writ of certiorari was granted by this Court on the question whether the National Motor Vehicle Theft Act

---

* Justice Oliver Wendell Holmes, Jr. was appointed to the Supreme Court by President Theodore Roosevelt in 1902. A graduate of Harvard College in 1861, he served with distinction in the Union army and was twice wounded in battle. While recovering from his wounds he enrolled in Harvard Law School, and received his LL.B. in 1866. He practiced law in Massachusetts from 1867 to 1882, when he became Professor of Law at Harvard University. He was appointed to the Supreme Judicial Court of Massachusetts in 1883, and served as Chief Judge of that court from 1899 to 1902. Justice Holmes sat on the U. S. Supreme Court from 1902 to 1932. During his fifty years on the bench, both state and federal, he was a sometime dissenter from the opinions of his fellow judges. The strength and insight of his dissenting opinions earned him a reputation as a "Great Dissenter" but over the whole of his judicial career he generally joined in the opinions of the majority. He was a forerunner of the so-called legal realists, and he expounded a philosophy of judicial self-restraint.

applies to aircraft. Act of October 29, 1919, c. 89, 41 Stat. 324; U.S. Code, Title 18, sec. 408. That Act provides: "Sec. 2 That when used in this Act: (a) The term 'motor vehicle' shall include an automobile, automobile truck, automobile wagon, motor cycle, or any other self-propelled vehicle not designed for running on rails; . . .   Sec. 3 That whoever shall transport or cause to be transported in interstate or foreign commerce a motor vehicle, knowing the same to have been stolen, shall be punished by a fine of not more than $5,000, or by imprisonment of not more than five years, or both."

Section 2 defines the motor vehicles of which the transportation in interstate commerce is punished in sec. 3. The question is the meaning of the word "vehicle" in the phrase "any other self-propelled vehicle not designed for running on rails." No doubt etymologically it is possible to use the word to signify a conveyance working on land, water or air, and sometimes legislation extends the use in that direction, e. g., land and air, water being separately provided for, in the Tariff Act, September 22, 1922, c. 356, sec. 401(b), 42 Stat. 858, 948. But in everyday speech "vehicle" calls up the picture of a thing moving on land. Thus in Rev.Stats. sec. 4, intended, the Government suggests, rather to enlarge than restrict the definition, vehicle includes every contrivance capable of being used "as a means of transportation on land." And this is repeated, expressly excluding aircraft, in the Tariff Act, June 17, 1930, c. 997, sec. 401(b); 46 Stat. 590, 708. So here, the phrase under discussion calls up the popular picture. For after including automobile truck, automobile wagon and motor cycle, the words "any other self-propelled vehicle not designed for running on rails" still indicate that a vehicle in the popular sense, that is a vehicle running on land, is the theme. It is a vehicle that runs, not something, not commonly called a vehicle, that flies. Airplanes were well known in 1919, when this statute was passed; but it is admitted that they were not mentioned in the reports or in the debates in Congress. It is impossible to read words that so carefully enumerate the different forms of motor vehicles and have no reference of any kind to aircraft, as including airplanes under a term that usage more and more precisely confines to a different class. The counsel for the petitioner have shown that the phraseology of the statute as to motor vehicles follows that of earlier statutes of Connecticut, Delaware, Ohio, Michigan and Missouri, not to mention the late Regulations of Traffic for the District of Columbia, Title 6, c. 9, sec. 242, none of which can be supposed to leave the earth.

Although it is not likely that a criminal will carefully consider the text of the law before he murders or steals, it is reasonable that a fair warning should be given to the world in language that the common world will understand, of what the law intends to do if a certain line is passed. To make the warning fair, so far as possible the line should be clear. When a rule of conduct is laid down in words that evoke in the common mind only the picture of vehicles moving on land, the statute should not be extended to aircraft, simply because it may seem to us that a similar policy applies, or upon the speculation that, if the legislature had thought of it, very likely broader words would have been used. United States v. Bhagt Singh Thind, 261 U.S. 204, 209, 43 S.Ct. 338.

Judgment reversed.

Questions

1. In formal logic the "denotation" of a term is the class of objects to which the term refers. The "connotation" of a term is the set of attributes common to the members of the class of objects to which the term refers. Thus the term "airplane" connotes wings, engines, the ability to become airborne, *etc.*, and denotes the 747, SST, Spad, *etc.* What evidence does Justice Holmes cite to show what the term "vehicle" denotes or connotes? Is there any evidence to show that the Congress used the term "vehicle" with reference solely to things which move on land?

2. How does the court know what the term "vehicle" means in everyday speech?

3. Was it necessary for the court to classify vehicles into those that run on land and those that fly? Would it have been more sensible to have interpreted the statute not in terms of the "picture" evoked by the words used, but in terms of the purpose of giving the federal courts jurisdiction over certain crimes involving transfer of stolen objects across the state lines?

4. Is Justice Holmes saying that the Court has no jurisdiction to punish McBoyle, or is he saying that what McBoyle did is not a crime? Is there any difference between these two positions?

5. Is the court saying that the accused—or the world—should be given fair warning that the act is a crime, or fair warning of what the punishment will be, or fair warning of what courts have jurisdiction?

6. Does the "fair warning" argument provide a sufficient justification for the maxim "no crime without a law" and the policy of strict construction of criminal statutes? What more substantial reasons can you suggest for the strong judicial support of both concepts?

7. Note that the Constitution of the United States does not confer on the federal government a general power to maintain peace and order, the so-called police power, but instead delineates with some specificity the areas of national concern which are the proper subject of federal action.[1] The general responsibility and power to maintain social order through civil and criminal processes is reserved to the several states. The federal criminal statute in *McBoyle* is based on a special prerogative of the federal government, the power to regulate interstate commerce set out in Article I, Section 8, of the United States Constitution. Should the limited jurisdictional base of this statute affect its interpretation in a federal court? Should relations between the state and federal governments have a bearing on the interpretation of this statute in a federal court?

---

1. See Section 4.1 *infra*, especially at pp. 148–149.

8. Should the fact that McBoyle could be prosecuted in Oklahoma or Illinois under state law make a difference in the interpretation of the federal statute? Is your answer based on your understanding of the division of criminal jurisdiction between the state and federal governments, or on considerations of fairness to the accused, or both?

9. In 1945 Congress amended the National Motor Vehicle Theft Act to state: "Wherever motor vehicle appears in this Act it shall read motor vehicle or airplane." What does this suggest concerning the relation between the legislative and judicial functions?

10. How do you suppose Judge Tappan (Ohio v. Lafferty, *supra* p. 117) might have decided this case? Explain your answer.

11. "The general rule that a penal statute is to be strictly construed does not apply to this chapter, but the provisions herein must be construed according to the fair import of their terms to promote justice and effect the objects of the law." L.1965, c. 1030. [New York Penal Law]

Is this rule on the construction of criminal statutes a more sensible rule than that espoused in the McBoyle case? Is your answer affected by the knowledge that the New York Penal Law is a new comprehensive criminal code adopted after extensive study and upon the recommendation of a commission staffed by eminent judges, lawyers and social scientists? Would your answer be different if you knew that the penal law of a jurisdiction was not a comprehensive modern code, but a body of statutes enacted at various times over a period of some two hundred years? The penal law of the United States is of the latter type. At the time of this writing legislation to codify, revise and reform the federal criminal code was pending before the Subcommittee on Criminal Laws and Procedures of the Senate Committee on the Judiciary.

SECTION 3.3   THE DOCTRINE OF ANALOGY IN CRIMINAL CASES

Legal reasoning, like all reasoning, proceeds in part by the comparison of relationships. In legal reasoning such comparison is explicit, for the application of a rule of law to a given fact situation requires explicit consideration of its applicability to similar fact situations. Thus in the McBoyle case the Supreme Court of the United States compared the theft of automobiles and motorcycles with the theft of an airplane in order to determine whether the National Motor Vehicle Theft Act, which admittedly applied to the former, also applied to the latter. In the Lafferty case the Ohio court compared the situation in Ohio before and after the adoption of the state constitution in order to determine whether the common law of crimes, which was applicable before, was also applicable after.

Such reasoning takes the form: *A* is sufficiently like *B* so that the principle applicable to *B* is also applicable to *A*. To find such an analogy, or likeness, requires, however, more than a mere listing of similarities. All cases have characteristics in common, and yet no two are identical. The similarities and differences must be evaluated, in order to determine whether the former outweigh the latter or the latter outweigh the former. Indeed, the factor of evaluation, or weighing, enters into the determination that a similarity or a difference exists, for unless we had some criteria of evaluation, some standards of judgment, we would not know what features to identify. We would not know where to begin or where to end.

A legal system establishes a set of criteria of evaluation, or standards of judgment, appropriate to the adjudication of cases on the basis of analogy. In a later chapter specifically devoted to methods of judicial reasoning we shall study more systematically the judicial process of comparison of a particular case with cases previously decided. Our concern here is with a simpler question, namely, the use of reasoning by analogy to broaden the jurisdiction of courts in criminal cases.

No Crime Without A Law

As the immediately preceding cases indicate, there is a general requirement in American law that in *criminal* cases it is not enough, in order to establish the court's jurisdiction, that the defendant committed an offense against the public; there is in addition the requirement that the offense alleged be one which has previously been defined by law, and indeed, in the federal courts at least, by statute law; and, further, courts so jealously guard the defendant's right not to be prosecuted for an act hitherto not specifically declared to be punishable that they often refuse to extend a criminal statute by interpretation but insist on construing it "strictly."

Thus the criteria of evaluation of similarities and differences are not necessarily the same in criminal as in civil cases. If the McBoyle case had involved a statute imposing *civil* liability upon one who unlawfully took another's "self-propelled vehicle not designed for running on rails," the court might well have held that airplanes were sufficiently similar to automobiles and motorcycles to be covered. There would have been, at any rate, no concern about "giving fair warning" to the civil defendant, or about the dangers of judicial creation of a new wrong.

Chief Justice Marshall put in one sentence the policy underlying the rule that penal statutes are to be construed strictly. The rule "is founded," he wrote in U. S. v. Wiltberger, 18 U.S. (5 Wheat.) 76, 1820, "on the tenderness of the law for the rights of individuals, and on the plain principle that the power of punishment is vested in the legislative, and not in the judicial, department." By "the rights of individuals" Marshall undoubtedly meant their rights against the prosecuting arm of the state: that arm might only be used according to explicit and careful instructions *previously laid down*. The sharp division of power between the legislature and the judiciary in this area of law is a further protection of the individual, since it restrains the judges from creating new definitions of crimes in the guise of interpreting old ones.

The rule that the legislature alone has the power to define what is criminal and to prescribe the limits of punishment dates from the time of the French Revolution. Prior to that time, judges both on the Continent of Europe and in England (and America) had more or less the same power to develop new definitions of crimes as they had to develop new causes of action in civil cases. The political thinkers of the Enlightenment and of the Revolution opposed judicial law-making partly because they considered the judiciary too closely attached to the landed gentry, the nobility, and the *ancien régime;* they distrusted it—especially in the field of crimes—as a threat to the middle and lower classes. Thus the doctrine was established, "No crime without a law" (*Nullum crimen sine lege*) and "No punishment without a law" (*Nulla poena sine lege*)—the word "law" (*lex*) in both maxims meaning statute, or legislation.

The doctrine in its narrow form was never entirely accepted—as we have already seen—in England or in the United States, where especially with regard to minor offenses, general ideas of "public morals" are sometimes invoked to punish in the absence of clear statutory proscriptions. However, the reaction in England to the decision in King v. Manley (see *supra* p. 122) shows the sensitivity that exists in that country to any charge of judicial creation of new crimes; and in the United States not only is our federal criminal law entirely statutory, but by far the largest part of our state criminal law is either statutory or of such ancient judicial vintage as to have the stability of a statute.

The rule that crimes and punishments are to be defined by the legislature rather than the judiciary is distinct, of course, from the rule that statutes defining crimes and punishments are to be strictly construed. Statutes cannot be "applied" without being at the same time "interpreted," and *every new interpretation necessarily either stretches or shrinks the statute.* Thus the judiciary must of necessity share with the legislature the responsibility for creative development of the criminal law. Insofar as the judiciary construes penal statutes strictly, it compels the legislature to specify in detail and with precision its criminal proscriptions. Insofar as the judiciary construes penal statutes liberally, it enables the legislature to rely on judicial elaboration of general criminal proscriptions.

Despite continual reiteration by American judges of the rule of strict construction, the fact is that criminal statutes are sometimes construed liberally. For example, a New York statute, which made punishable a breach of the peace was extended by judicial interpretation to the making of a political speech on a street corner. The criminal sanctions of the Sherman Act of 1890 forbidding conspiracies in restraint of trade have been invoked to punish business activities, in spite of the vagueness of the statutory language.[1] Many other examples could be given. Of course no rule of construction of a statute is an end in itself; in all cases the rule is designed as an aid to discovering the proper application of the statute. There is no simple mechanical device which will tell a court at what point it should stop on the continuum which runs from the one extreme of withholding punishment for an existing crime and the other extreme of creating a new crime.

The Doctrine of Analogy: Examples from Soviet Criminal Law

In addition to the rules of strict and liberal construction, there is a third technique available to courts which are confronted with criminal charges not clearly within the express provisions of a criminal statute. That is to apply the spirit of the statute, or indeed the spirit of the legal system as a whole. More exactly, this method of interpretation involves an explicit recognition that the offense committed by the defendant has not previously been defined as a crime by the legislature either expressly or by implication; that is, it is not sufficiently similar to the acts made punishable by the particular statute under which the indictment is brought so that one could, by liberal interpretation, say that the purpose of the statute is to make this particular act punishable. Yet it is thought that the offense *is* sufficiently similar to the acts proscribed by the statute in question to warrant the conclusion that society would benefit from the application of the statute to this offense in the same way that it would benefit from the application of the statute to offenses clearly indicated therein. This third technique is sometimes called "the doctrine of analogy."

In Soviet Russia and in Nazi Germany and in countries under their influence the doctrine of analogy was adopted and the rule of *nullum crimen, nulla poena sine lege* was denounced as a "bourgeois" principle. The Soviet legislators put in their criminal code of 1926 the following provision (Article 16): "If a socially dangerous act is not directly provided for by the present code, the foundations and limits of responsibility for it shall be determined according to those articles of the code which provide for those crimes most similar to it in kind." Under Article 16 the Soviet courts were able to adapt the criminal law to their own, or their government's, conceptions of public policy. Thus in one case a Moslem who performed the religious rite of circumcision was convicted by analogy for violation of the provision of the code prohibiting rape. In another case the Soviet Supreme Court applied the code provision on "counterrevolutionary crimes" to acts disruptive of the economic order, creating by analogy a new concept of "economic counterrevolution."

Soviet writers expressly distinguish the doctrine of analogy from extension of a statute by liberal interpretation. With increased

---

1. See Section 3.4 *infra.*

emphasis upon "stability of laws" since the mid-1930s, however, the Soviet courts began to place limitations upon Article 16 which virtually nullified this distinction. It was held that the similarity between the act prohibited under the code provision which is invoked and the act which the defendant committed must be a similarity in importance as well as in kind, and that the act committed must be one which is generally prohibited by law but not directly mentioned in a particular code provision (or statute). The kind of case that was cited as a typical instance for the application of the doctrine of analogy is that of a theft performed in the marketplace to which collective farmers bring their produce; there was no article in the Criminal Code (which was enacted before collectivization of agriculture) directly providing for punishment of that particular form of theft (though it is punishable under the article proscribing theft generally), but there was an article providing for punishment for thefts committed in railroad stations, on wharves, on steamboats, in baggage-cars and in hotels, and the Soviet courts held that since that article deals with thefts committed in crowded places it should be applied by analogy to a theft performed in the collective farm marketplace. Contrast this decision with that of the United States Supreme Court in the McBoyle case.

In the late 1930s Article 16 came under the criticism of some Soviet writers. One jurist wrote, in 1938: "The legislators, in revising the final text of the Criminal Code of the U.S.S.R., should provide for all forms of crime. This is a possible and also a necessary task. Every member of society should know not only his duties . . . but also the measures of social influence which can be applied for any breach of the Socialist legal order. Analogy is especially incompatible with Article 112 of the Constitution, which speaks of the independence of the court and its subjection only to law." [2] The limitations on Article 16 which were developed in the late 1930s were dropped, however, during the war, when it was felt that emergency situations not specifically provided for in the criminal law needed to be dealt with by judicial action. After the war the doctrine of analogy again came under attack. Thus the 1948 textbook of the Ministry of Justice of the U.S.S.R., Criminal Law, General Part, pp. 245–247, states:

In the first years of development of Soviet criminal law, when the codification of criminal legislation was absent and socialist justice was based on individual decrees of the Soviet authorities and on revolutionary legal consciousness of judges, the question of analogy did not arise. The declaration of conduct as criminal and punishable depended entirely on the judge, who in such case referred to the decrees of the Soviet authorities and to the circulars and instructions of the penal organs, [and] to his own revolutionary

2. Quoted in Harold J. Berman, "Principles of Soviet Criminal Law," Yale Law Journal, Vol. 56, p. 810 (1947).

legal consciousness. . . . The necessity of introducing analogy was clear already in the drafting of the Criminal Code in 1922. At the session of the All-Union Central Executive Committee which issued the draft Criminal Code of the R.S.F.S.R. in the first edition, it was indicated that no single code can embrace all the many forms of crimes. . . . [The article on analogy] helped the court authority to react quickly to new crimes still not provided for by the Code, not waiting until new criminal codes would be issued.

. . . The presence of analogy in Soviet criminal law was conditioned by the practical needs of the socialist state in a particular phase of its development. . . . After the acceptance of the Stalin constitution of the U.S.S.R. the limits of application of analogy were still further narrowed in connection with the realization of the principle of stability of laws. The preparation of a draft Criminal Code of the U.S.S.R., in correspondence with the instruction of the Constitution of the U.S.S.R., produced in 1939–1940 a lively discussion in Soviet criminal-legal literature relating to whether analogy should be preserved or excluded from the future uniform Criminal Code . . . [Some argued that] in the struggle against the existence of "one law for *Kazan* and another for *Kaluga*" it would be difficult at the same time to preserve analogy in the criminal legislation . . . since each judge would proceed from his own conception of the social danger of this or that act. With the appearance of new forms of crimes the legislator always has the opportunity to react quickly by the issuance of a corresponding criminal statute or decree. . . .

In December 1958, the Supreme Soviet of the U.S.S.R. enacted comprehensive criminal legislation which eliminated the doctrine of analogy from Soviet criminal law and provided expressly that no one could be punished for an act which was not prohibited by criminal statute. (See Harold J. Berman, Justice in the U.S.S.R.: An Interpretation of Soviet Law, 1963 ed., pp. 35–36, 56, 73; but see also pp. 86, 290, 403; and Harold J. Berman and James W. Spindler, Soviet Criminal Law and Procedure: the RSFSR Codes, 1966.)

SECTION 3.4 REPRESSIVE AND RESTITUTIVE SANCTIONS. REMEDIES FOR VIOLATIONS OF THE ANTITRUST LAWS

Under the doctrine of *nullum crimen sine lege*, courts have no jurisdiction in criminal cases unless there is a statute specifically making the defendant's act a crime. This doctrine has no counterpart in civil cases. Courts often accept jurisdiction of civil cases although the legislature has not specifically declared that the wrong allegedly committed by the defendant is the basis for a civil action. Moreover, judges are far more free in civil cases than in criminal cases to construe statutes broadly and to remedy wrongs not previously recognized as such. This power is, of course, limited by many factors, including the requirement that judges act only with respect to justiciable controversies. (See Section 2, *supra* p. 54 ff.) But that requirement is itself subject to judicial revision, since judges are deemed competent to determine what matters are appropriate for adjudication.

The contrast between the severe, and often self-imposed, limitation of a court's jurisdiction in criminal cases and its broad powers under the doctrine of justiciability in civil cases may be illuminated and explained by the following materials on legal sanctions.

[The following is taken from EMILE DURKHEIM,* ON THE DIVISION OF LABOR IN SOCIETY, translated and edited by George Simpson (New York, 1933), pp. 69, 80, 85, 111–112.]

[The sanctions attached to juridical rules] are of two kinds. Some consist essentially in suffering, or at least a loss, inflicted on the agent. They make demands on his fortune, or on his honor, or on his life, or on his liberty, and deprive him of something he enjoys. We call them repressive. They constitute penal law. It is true that those which are attached to rules which are purely moral have the same character, only they are distributed in a diffuse manner by everybody indiscriminately, whereas those in penal law are applied through the intermediary of a definite organ; they are organized. As for the other type, it does not necessarily imply suffering for the agent, but consists only of *the return of things as they were*, in the reestablishment of troubled relations to their normal state. . . . We must then separate juridical rules into two great classes, accordingly as they have organized repressive sanctions or only restitutive sanctions. The first comprise all penal law; the second, civil law, commercial law, procedural law, administrative and constitutional law, after abstraction of the penal rules which may be found there. . . .

. . . an act is criminal when it offends strong and defined states of the collective conscience. . . .

. . . punishment consists of a passionate reaction. . . .

What distinguishes [the restitutive] sanction is that it is not expiatory, but consists of a simple *return in state*. Sufferance proportionate to the misdeed is not inflicted on the one who has violated the [civil] law or who disregards it; he is simply sentenced to comply with it. If certain things were done, the judge reinstates them as they would have been. He speaks of law; he says nothing of punishment. Damage-interests have no penal character; they are only a means of reviewing the past in order to reinstate it, as far as possible, to its normal form.[1] . . .

Neglect of these rules is not even punished diffusely. The pleader who has lost in litigation is not disgraced, his honor is not put in question. We can even imagine these rules being other than they are without feeling any

---

* Emile Durkheim was both sociologist and philosopher. He was born and was educated in France and taught sociology and pedagogy in Paris. His insights on the relationship between law and society in general are scattered throughout his writings.

1. Durkheim in this statement has in mind French law and other legal systems which have no doctrine of puni-tive damages. Under American law a plaintiff in an action for negligence, for example, may recover, in addition to compensation for harm, additional damages if the defendant's act was "malicious," and these additional damages are explicitly designated as "puni-tive." Even in French law, however, the award of money damages may in fact be a kind of punishment, as, for example, in a suit for libel.

repugnance. The idea of tolerating murder arouses us, but we quite easily accept modification of the right of succession, and can even conceive of its possible abolition. It is at least a question which we do not refuse to discuss   .   .   .

[The following is taken from JAMES STEPHENS, THE CROCK OF GOLD (London, 1913), p. 163.]

Justice is the maintaining of equilibrium. The blood of Cain must cry, not from the lips of the Avenger, but from the aggrieved earth herself who demands that atonement shall be made for a disturbance of her consciousness. All justice is, therefore, readjustment. A thwarted consciousness has every right to clamour for assistance, but not for punishment.

The Sherman Antitrust Act of 1890, and the Clayton Act of 1914 are the basic antitrust statutes of the United States. They reflect congressional concern about the size, power, and restrictive practices of business firms. Pertinent sections of the two Acts are reproduced below.

THE SHERMAN ANTITRUST ACT OF 1890

(Public Law 51–190, 26 Stat. 209, approved July 2, 1890.)

Sec. 1.   Every contract, combination in the form of trust or otherwise, or conspiracy, in restraint of trade or commerce among the several States, or with foreign nations, is declared to be illegal. Every person who shall make any such contract or engage in any such combination or conspiracy shall be deemed guilty of a misdemeanor, and, on conviction thereof, shall be punished by fine not exceeding fifty thousand dollars, or by imprisonment not exceeding one year, or by both said punishments, in the discretion of the court.

Sec. 2.   Every person who shall monopolize, or attempt to monopolize, or combine or conspire with any other person or persons, to monopolize any part of the trade or commerce among the several States, or with foreign nations, shall be deemed guilty of a misdemeanor, and, on conviction thereof, shall be punished by fine not exceeding fifty thousand dollars, or by imprisonment not exceeding one year, or by both said punishments, in the discretion of the court.

* * *

Sec. 4.   The several district courts of the United States are invested with jurisdiction to prevent and restrain violations of this Act; and it shall be the duty of the several district attorneys of the United States, in their respective districts, under the direction of the Attorney General, to institute proceedings in equity to prevent and restrain such violations.

CLAYTON ACT OF 1914

(Public Law 63–212, 38 Stat. 730, approved October 15, 1914.)

Sec. 4. . . . any person who shall be injured in his business or property by reason of anything forbidden in the antitrust laws may sue therefor in any district court of the United States . . . and shall recover threefold the damages by him sustained, and the cost of the suit, including a reasonable attorney's fee.

[The following is taken from A. D. NEALE,* THE ANTITRUST LAWS OF THE U. S. A. (Cambridge, England, 1960), pp. 369–371, 393–396. Footnotes are omitted.]

The choice between criminal prosecution and civil action

. . . Once the Department of Justice is in possession, by one means or another, of the information needed for making a case, it has to decide whether to proceed by criminal prosecution or by civil action. There are two aspects of this decision. The first is the question of what the action is to achieve.

The criminal case can do no more and no less than punish offenders for past offences. After the punishment has been exacted, the situation is exactly as it was before the case was brought. The punishment no doubt acts to some extent as a deterrent against further offences but this is all that has been achieved. The Department of Justice in most important cases wants to do more than this. It wants in effect to regulate the industry so that its practices may conform with the law and with the policy lying behind antitrust.

The nature of some types of offence is such that punishment has virtually no effect on the situation. If, for example, a monopoly has been illegally obtained in some important line of commerce, the mere imposition of a fine (unless the fine were of impossible severity) would leave the situation exactly where it was. The Department cannot regard the situation as improved unless the company concerned is no longer in a position to exercise monopoly power. In such a case, therefore, it wants to secure the dissolution or divestment of the monopoly concerned. . . . Regulatory remedies of this kind may be obtained only as a result of civil proceedings in which the court acts as a chancellor dispensing equity. For this reason most of the biggest cases in antitrust history have been civil proceedings.

On the other hand, a flagrant breach of one of the established *per se* [1] offences cannot usefully be tackled by civil proceedings, for to secure from

---

* Mr. Neale was Undersecretary for the Board of Trade of the United Kingdom at the time the book from which this extract is taken was published. The book was written under the auspices of the Board of Trade and was intended primarily as an introduction to American antitrust law for British civil servants and businessmen.

1. Certain violations of the Sherman Act, e. g., price fixing, and boycotts, have been held to be absolutely forbidden by the law. The courts will not hear any defense which attempts to justify these practices. They are per se (intrinsically) unlawful.

a court of equity an injunction against repeating the offence would merely be repeating in the injunction what is already contained in the statute. Such offences must therefore be prosecuted criminally so as to invoke the sanction of punishment.

It frequently happens, of course, that the same situation encompasses both a flagrant breach of the law and the need for some remedy of a regulatory type. In such situations it is common for the Department of Justice to bring concurrent criminal and civil proceedings. Then the court in the criminal case may impose a penalty and another court in the civil case may hand down a decree containing injunctions regulating the industry for the future. The criminal proceeding can never affect the future; the civil proceeding can never affect the past. The one punishes past offences; the other lays down a model of conduct for the future.

The second aspect of the choice between criminal and civil proceedings is simply that of doing justice to those who are subject to antitrust discipline. The Congress of 1890 enacted—and no subsequent Congress has repealed— the criminal provisions of the Sherman Act and there would probably be no wide public support for any proposal to abandon them. On the other hand, it is widely felt that criminal proceedings are not appropriate in cases near the borderline of the law where there may be no precedents and no reasonable expectation on the part of business that a given line of conduct is actionable. The Attorney General's National Committee, which sympathized with this view, put it that the criminal process "should be used only where the law is clear and the facts reveal a flagrant offense and plain intent unreasonably to restrain trade". The actual practice of the Department of Justice is not far removed from this prescription and the Committee felt able generally to endorse the Department's practice as expounded to it.

* * *

Criminal and civil remedies: fines in practice the only criminal penalty

The last topic in this description of antitrust is that of remedies; the impact of these laws on business cannot be assessed without knowing what happens to those who break them. It has already been noted that the Government's choice between criminal and civil proceedings cannot be guided simply by the gravity of supposed offences and is to some extent artificial. The real guide is the expected end-result of the legal process. A flagrant price-fixing conspiracy must be made the subject of a criminal case. A civil proceeding ending in a set of injunctions for the future could do no more in such a case than repeat the injunctions of the statute itself. The only end-result worth having from the point of view of the authorities is the punishment of the wrongdoer.

On the other hand, a flagrant and cynical seizure of monopoly power by a single enterprise or by a conspiracy between a few large firms may involve an altogether more serious degree of restraint of trade. Punishment may be just as apt as in the former case and indeed criminal proceedings may be brought and fines imposed. But in such a case it would be highly unsatisfactory to the authorities if fines of a few thousand dollars ended the matter. The monopoly would still be in control and the fines might be regarded simply as a not unreasonable licence fee for monopoly power. In such a case, therefore, those who enforce the law must have recourse to civil proceedings in order to obtain control over the future behaviour of the monopolist and, if possible, to secure a decree of dissolution so that its power may be dispersed or diluted. Yet the decree in a civil proceeding is not in theory punitive.

All this is somewhat artificial. People who have built up a successful business will regard a decree breaking it up as punitive, whatever the legal textbooks may say. Even injunctive relief, when it is extensive and detailed, will be regarded as punitive, especially when activities are prohibited in a particular industry while in other industries, not yet in the toils of antitrust, similar activities may be carried on without let. Injunctions requiring, for example, the compulsory licensing of patents to competitors are felt to be punitive in just this way.

On the other hand, civil remedies do not carry the odium of criminal penalties, and for this reason, even when they are drastic in effect, do not touch the public sense of justice in the same way as severe criminal penalties. Criminal sanctions are notoriously difficult to administer when divorced from moral indignation. As already noted, antitrust offences are *mala prohibita*, not *mala in se*.[2] There are, of course, other fields of criminal law in which offences do not carry any great degree of moral obliquity. Public opinion is notably less apt to applaud the punishment of parking offences or of offences against obscure sections of finance acts than the punishment of thieves or blackmailers. Antitrust offences certainly come into the same category and those who commit them tend to be respectable persons not easy to associate with deliberate moral failing.

It is this fact which has largely prevented the imposition of jail sentences on antitrust offenders. The Sherman Act provides for sentences of imprisonment up to one year, but in practice such sentences are hardly ever imposed. The very few cases in which jail sentences have been imposed have mostly featured some special element of rackteering or fraud which aroused moral indignation. From time to time the Government presses strongly for jail sentences in very flagrant cases of *per se* offences, in particular pricefixing, and some courts have served warning that they may take this step. It is still most unlikely to become common.

* * *

In practice the only criminal sanction in antitrust is the fine. Until 1955 the maximum fine for a violation of the criminal provisions of the antitrust laws was five thousand dollars. It is now fifty thousand dollars, as a result of legislation passed in that year. It has, of course, always been possible for a number of separate charges to be laid in the same case and fines imposed for each, so that the amounts may go up to three or four times the nominal maximum in practice. The most serious threat to the businessman arises when he is named as an independent defendant apart from his company. If antitrust offences can be brought home to his individual responsibility, large fines can be a serious punishment. (It has been held that fines may not count as a tax-deductable expense and that they may not be reimbursed by the company employing the offender.)

2. Some acts are said to be criminal because they are naturally wrong in and of themselves (*mala in se*), other acts are said to be criminal only because they are prohibited by the law (*mala prohibita*).

So far as companies are concerned, the old maximum rate of five thousand dollars was not likely to have any spectacular deterrent effect. Even twenty thousand dollars on four charges was not a vast amount for a large corporation to pay, particularly if the violations concerned had enhanced profits. The five thousand dollars maximum was written into the law in 1890 when the purchasing power of the dollar was substantially greater than at the present day. It was for this reason that many proposals were made in recent years for increasing the maximum. Some people even argued in favour of having no maximum but leaving the fine to the discretion of the court. The majority view of the Attorney General's National Committee was that the maximum should be increased to ten thousand dollars, but Congress adopted the minority view that fifty thousand dollars was more appropriate as a maximum, given the discretion of the courts to impose a lesser figure.

Even with the new maximum it is probable, however, that the real sanction of the criminal provisions of the antitrust laws will still lie not so much in the risk of financial penalty as in the sheer fact of criminal indictment as it affects businessmen who have a respected place in their communities. Criminal proceedings under the Sherman Act involve "going quietly" with the policeman, having your fingerprints taken and all the other unattractive incidents of any other crime, together, of course, with a considerable amount of unfavourable publicity and the heavy costs of defending the suit.

Questions

1. There is no statutory definition of the terms "restraint of trade" and "monopolization." These terms have been given meaning through judicial interpretation in civil and criminal cases. Does the imposition of criminal sanctions in Sherman Act cases violate the principle of *nullum crimen sine lege*? Does the imposition of criminal sanctions in Sherman Act cases accord with the policy of strictly construing criminal statutes? (See McBoyle v. U. S., *supra* p. 125) What does Neale mean when he refers to the "borderline of the law?" (*Supra* p. 137)

2. Can you see any connection between the concept of acts "mala in se" and the common law of crimes relied on in Ohio v. Lafferty (*supra* p. 117)?

3. Can any legal remedy affect the past? Can a criminal proceeding affect the future?

4. If the community does not display any moral indignation at violations of the antitrust laws, if jail sentences are rarely meted out to violators, if violators are well able to pay the fines assessed, and if the civil antitrust remedies are often more punitive than the criminal sanctions, then what is the purpose of preserving the criminal jurisdiction under the antitrust laws? Consider the following:

> "Mr. Donald F. Turner, the head of the Justice Department's antitrust division . . . plans to de-emphasize criminal antitrust convictions on the grounds that they accomplish little towards making business more competitive.

* * *

"Mr. Turner rejects the criminal suit approach for all but the most flagrant cases of willful violation of the laws, because he does not believe conviction of criminal violations actually improves competition. Criminal prosecutions probably do have some deterrent effects on other potential violators, he said, but the fines imposed by law are so small as to be meaningless to large companies. On the other hand, he said, when civil suits are filed, much more effective remedies, such as mandatory patent licensing and prohibitions against price cutting and other predatory activities, can often be much more effective. Thus, Mr. Turner said, he may actually pass up some opportunities to file criminal suits and file civil suits instead.

"Mr. Turner takes a similar view of Government assistance on obtaining convictions in such criminal cases as are filed. He does not intend, in general, to press for convictions where the suit can be brought to a close by Government acceptance of nolo contendere pleas. Under these the defendant does not admit guilt, but does not contest the suit. Penalties, including jail sentences—may be imposed just as if a conviction had been obtained. The key difference is that any private individuals who may have been injured by the antitrust violation have to prove there was an illegal action before they can collect damages. If a conviction or guilty plea has been obtained by the Government, the private litigants can use that as proof of illegality in their suits.

"Mr. Turner, against the arguments of many of his staff . . . accepted a nolo plea in the recent price fixing case involving almost all the major steel companies. His belief was that there was no certainty that the Government could obtain a conviction and, in any event, that the major private parties who might have been injured by the alleged price-fixing conspiracy were big companies, such as auto manufacturers, who have plenty of lawyers of their own to fight their damage cases.

"Mr. Turner argues that juries generally have been most reluctant to convict businesses of criminal antitrust violations and this is a major reason to accept nolo pleas rather than insist on convictions." The New York Times, December 10, 1965, p. 31.

[The following is taken from ARNOLD BERNHARD, "THE ANTITRUST CONVICTIONS IN THE ELECTRICAL EQUIPMENT CASE," The Value Line Survey, March 13, 1961.]

The Antitrust Convictions in the Electrical Equipment Case

On Feb. 6 and 7, 1961, Judge J. Cullen Ganey of the United States District Court for the Eastern District of Pennsylvania, imposed fines of $1,-787,000 on 29 electrical equipment manufacturers, most prominent among which were General Electric and Westinghouse, and sentenced 7 executives in the industry to prison for conspiring to violate the antitrust laws against price fixing. Twenty-three others received suspended sentences. The executives sentenced to prison, until then respected senior citizens of their communities and nation, were thereupon manacled like common felons and led off to jail in full glare of the publicity that passes for journalism these days.

Judge Ganey said, "Before imposing sentence, I want to make certain observations . . . what is really at stake here is the survival of the kind of economy under which America has grown to greatness, the free enterprise system. The conduct of the corporate and individual defendants . . . has flagrantly mocked the image of that economic system of free enterprise which we profess to the country and destroyed the model which we offer today as a free world alternative to state control and eventual dictatorship."

General Electric, although it found itself compelled to plead guilty to some of the indictments as a matter of practical expediency, vigorously and on the whole successfully, disassociated itself and its chief officers and directors from its guilty agents in the lower echelons, and clearly proved that it had honestly tried to enforce its own regulations against price fixing upon the executive heads of its more than one hundred departments and twenty-odd divisions, which regulations were even more stringent in certain respects than the antitrust laws themselves.

The whole country was immediately aroused to a high pitch of moral indignation, sensing as it did, that the very soul of America, its free enterprise system, the bulwark against communism and the only alternative to state control and dictatorship, to use Judge Ganey's words, had been betrayed.

The Attorney General, Mr. Robert F. Kennedy, writing on this case in Life Magazine under date of February 24, 1961, said, "Our antitrust laws were written in an attempt to control business monopoly . . . but in . . . earlier trust cases . . . the punishment was usually in the form of fines, and after it was over, business went on as usual. The businessman who participated was not treated as though he had really done anything wrong. He was just following the accepted practices of big business in the Twentieth Century, U.S.A. He was accepted as usual at the country club, he was appointed as usual to be the chairman of the community charity drive . . . more and more often, corruption and dishonesty have been excused because 'everyone does it'." . . . Judge Ganey's decision had great impact because it showed that somebody is willing to say *"I am not going to accept this. We can do better."* In the same tone, Life Magazine declared in its editorial columns, " . . . The crooks in the electrical industry have set back the progress of the modern corporation toward public acceptance of its claims to wider social responsibility and a quasi-political role"; and then, in a burst of sadistic exultation, published a picture of one of the condemned executives behind prison bars, his downcast, bald head and spectacled eyes a portrait of shame; and it pilloried the other condemned by publishing their pictures for public recognition.

What is the truth of the matter? Were a few little fellows thrown to the wolves to protect the higher-ups? Has America's image of a free economy been betrayed by crooks? What about the laws that were so long breached in Twentieth-Century U.S.A. without meaningful penalty, thus ascribing to them the sanction of custom?

Notes and Questions

1. If the antitrust laws have been "so long breached . . . without meaningful penalty" that "the sanction of custom" has been

ascribed to the practice of only assessing fines for criminal violations, then was it a breach of the policy of *nulla poena sine lege*
(no punishment without a law) to send the electrical equipment conspirators to jail?

2.   Is it immoral, or only illegal, to violate the antitrust laws?
Does the distinction between acts *"mala in se"* and acts *"mala prohibita"* make sense to you?

3.   In 1974 five corporate executives were convicted of conspiring to fix prices in the paper label industry.   The trial judge, Charles
B. Renfrew of the Federal District Court for the Northern District of
California, imposed sentences which he later characterized as "unorthodox and somewhat controversial."   The sentences and Judge Renfrew's reasons for employing them are described in the following passages.

[The following is taken from RENFREW, "THE PAPER LA-
BEL SENTENCES: AN EVALUATION," 86 Yale Law Journal 590,
590–594 (1977).   Some footnotes omitted; others are renumbered.]

In October 1974, I imposed unorthodox and somewhat controversial sentences upon five corporate executives convicted of conspiring to fix prices
in the paper label industry [1] in violation of § 1 of the Sherman Act.   Besides giving the defendants suspended jail sentences ranging from three to
six months and fining them from $5,000 to $15,000 each, I required, as a
special condition of probation, that each defendant "make an oral presentation before twelve (12) business, civic or other groups about the circumstances of this case and his participation therein" and "submit a written report to the Court giving details of each such appearance, the composition of
the group, the import of the presentation, and the response thereto." [2]

* * *

The paper label case involved a classic violation of the antitrust laws.
The paper label industry manufactures the paper labels that are affixed to
the containers of a variety of canned and bottled products.   Many of the
companies in the industry are small in comparison to their customers.   The
possibility that purchasers will shift to another more competitive supplier
forces companies in the industry to keep their costs and prices as low as
possible.   In general, this is the type of economic situation that the competitive economic model predicts and that the antitrust laws seek to encourage.

Although such a market structure engenders remarkable efficiency, it
places the businessmen involved under constant pressure to retain their
market positions.   As a result, no matter how strongly businessmen support
competition in theory, they often tend to be considerably less enthusiastic

1.   See, e. g., Judgment and Order of
Probation and Fine, United States v.
Blankenheim, No. CR–74–182–CBR (N.
D.Cal., filed Nov. 1, 1974) (on file with
Yale Law Journal).   The case from
which these sentences arose is herein-
after referred to as the "paper label
case."

2.   Judgment and Order of Probation
and Fine, United States v. Blankenheim, No. CR–74–182–CBR (N.D.Cal.,
filed Nov. 1, 1974) (on file with Yale
Law Journal).   The pertinent language
in the Judgment and Order of Probation and Fine against each defendant
is identical.

when the competition is directed against their own companies. Manufacturers of paper labels responded to the competitive conditions in their industry by expanding casual social contacts at trade association meetings to include the exchange of increasingly explicit information concerning pricing decisions and policies. These exchanges of information eventually resulted in a division of the market through pricing agreements. The scheme collapsed when a disgruntled former employee revealed the illegal practices, leading to a number of private treble damage actions and a criminal indictment.

* * *

For me, this classic violation posed an extremely difficult sentencing decision. A sentencing judge's recognition that imprisonment may be a necessary response to criminal activity often creates a tension between his sense of duty to society and his concern for the individual defendant. In the instant case, this tension was especially great because, in my view, the only theory of punishment that could justify imprisoning the defendants was one of general deterrence.

All of the defendants were community leaders of previously unsullied reputation who held top executive positions in their corporations. My personal observation of the impact of the prosecution on these defendants convinced me that they did not present a threat of continued violations. Thus, imprisonment could not be justified in terms of such typical sentencing objectives as specific deterrence and isolation. Similarly, in-prison rehabilitation was not at issue because the defendants needed neither psycholigical counseling nor vocational training.

Retribution did not mandate the incarceration of the defendants because the hardship resulting from the prosecution itself and the fines that I intended to impose constituted sufficient expiation for the violations that had occurred. Being prosecuted placed a considerable emotional burden on the defendants. Furthermore, the cost of counsel had been great and had been borne individually, and the fines that I would impose were large relative to the defendants' ability to pay. According full weight to the societal importance of the antitrust laws—an importance emphasized by the recent enactment of the Antitrust Procedures and Penalties Act, which makes such violations felonies rather than misdemeanors [3]—I believed that the monetary exactions alone constituted firm and proportionate punishment.

---

3. See 15 U.S.C.A. § 1.

Despite the seriousness of antitrust violations, I find a blanket comparison between these crimes and other felonies inappropriate. I believe that crimes of violence are, in general, much more destructive of the fabric of society than are nonviolent commercial crimes. The butcher who routinely charges his customers an extra quarter for the weight of his thumb on the scale surely abuses his position. Over time, his activities may result in an economic loss to his customers far exceeding the "take" of an average bank robbery, and, if discovered, his dishonesty would undoubtedly create mistrust and anger among his customers. Yet, however reprehensible the butcher's conduct may be, I feel certain that it entails a smaller social cost than would result if each of his customers were stopped at gunpoint and robbed of a quarter several times a week for the same period of time. Violent crime massively disrupts and distorts the daily social intercourse among human beings upon which any viable society depends. While the two kinds of crime may have a similar economic impact, and may both instill some apprehension in the public, the psychological effect of violent crime is clearly more pernicious.

Determining whether these fines would best serve general deterrence was for me the hard issue. Given the difficulty of detection and proof of criminal violations of the antitrust laws, a judge must use every sentencing opportunity to maximize the deterrence of potential violators. The sentences should be sufficiently harsh to discourage similar criminal activity; too lenient a sentence might depreciate the seriousness of the offense and encourage other violations.

Prior to sentencing in the paper label case, I tried to gauge the impact the imposition of fines would have on the community at large, and particularly on the business community, where other price-fixing violations might occur. Although I considered the prospective monetary penalties punitive, I was concerned that the leniency of the fines, compared to incarceration, might actually have a provocative effect on those who learned of the sentences. This possibility troubled me, particularly because the potential offenders were primarily businessmen, individuals who customarily calculate expectation of profit as compared to risk of loss. To the extent that certain of these individuals are otherwise disposed to violate the law, a perceived diminution in the sanction could have the effect of encouraging violations.

General deterrence requires both that an unpleasant punishment be imposed upon wrongdoers and that the public have a relatively high degree of knowledge about the activities proscribed by law and the sentences imposed for its violation. After careful consideration, although not without reservation, I decided that the sentences I eventually imposed met these requirements. The emotional and financial burden of the prosecution, the fines imposed, and the defendants' embarrassment in appearing before groups of their peers as convicted criminals would supply the deterrent sting. The requirement that the individual defendants give speeches about their experiences promised greater public awareness of the demands of the law and the consequences of its violation. I expected that media coverage of the sentences would convey the same message to an even wider audience. Indeed, the communicative possibilities of the sentences struck me as their most desirable feature.

* * *

The paper label sentences are discussed and critiqued in a series of comments published contemporaneously with the Renfrew article. See Baker, Reeves, Dershowitz, Simon and Wheeler, "The Paper Label Sentences: Critiques," 86 Yale Law Journal 619 *et seq.* (1977).

SECTION 4. JURISDICTIONAL REQUIREMENTS OF A FEDERAL SYSTEM

We have seen that there are some kinds of disputes which courts will not undertake to resolve, and there are some kinds of wrongs which courts will not undertake to punish. There are matters—to put it in other words—which courts are not *competent* to decide. Yet even if a civil case is justiciable, or a criminal prosecution authorized by statute, a court may decline to take *jurisdiction* of it. "Jurisdiction" originally meant "law-speaking"; in modern usage one might call it "the say." If a person presented a petition for a divorce to the Supreme Court of the United States, he or she would be told that that court does not have jurisdiction—does not have "the say"—to hear such a case; that this is not the particular kind of court which is authorized to decide the particular kind of case presented.

The question of which court has jurisdiction over a particular matter is closely related to the political question of which sovereign has the power and the right to decide the case and to enforce the judicial remedies or sanctions with respect to it. The courts are, after all, an arm of a sovereign whose reach is limited by the existence of other sovereigns.

This aspect of jurisdiction—the choice of the right court—is common to all modern legal systems, but it is particularly significant in the United States, where each of the fifty states has its own court system and where, in addition, there is a separate system of United States (federal) courts. The fifty state systems are independent of each other for most purposes, although they are related by common ancestry. The state courts are also largely independent of the federal courts, although the two systems are tied together, for some purposes, by national bonds which emanate from the United States Constitution. This proliferation of courts is exacerbated by the fact that in both the state and federal systems judicial authority is divided among various courts exercising different functions. This section presents a brief survey of jurisdictional relationships among the multitude of courts in the United States.

SECTION 4.1   THE DIVISION OF JUDICIAL AUTHORITY BETWEEN STATE AND FEDERAL COURTS

Let us start with a few rough rules of thumb and some supporting examples, in order to indicate some of the dimensions of state and federal jurisdiction.

1. *A primary function of the state courts is to enforce the laws of their respective states.* This is particularly true as regards penal and regulatory laws.

Example: A commits a robbery in New York City. A can be tried for this crime only in the courts of New York, which will apply the New York (state) law.

Example: The laws of state X require all trucking companies operating in the state to acquire a license from the state Public Utilities Commission. B has been operating a trucking business in X, but he has not been licensed to do so. The courts of state X will take jurisdiction of a proceeding in which the Commission seeks to enjoin B from continuing to operate in state X without a license.

2. *A primary function of the state courts is to adjudicate cases involving persons resident in their respective states.* This jurisdictional element is often intertwined with the element set out in item 1 above, for most of the cases coming before the courts of any state will involve residents of the state *and* will also call for the application of the laws of the state.

Example: Doe and Roe, residents of New York state, collide while driving their automobiles in New York City. An action for damages arising out of this collision may be brought in the courts of New York, which will apply the New York law regarding standards of careful driving.

Frequently a state court will be presented with a case in which one or both of the parties is a state resident *but* the cause of action is based on the laws of another state.

Example: Same facts as in the preceding example, except Doe and Roe are residents of New Jersey. Doe may sue Roe in the New Jersey state courts, which have jurisdiction to hear the case, but the New Jersey courts will probably apply the New York law regarding standards of careful driving to settle the issue of liability.

Example: Same facts as above except Doe is a resident of New York, and Roe is a resident of New Jersey. Doe may sue Roe in the New Jersey state courts. The applicable law will probably be the law of New York.

The responsibility of state courts to decide cases arising under the laws of another sovereign rests on several bases. First, the most convenient forum for the adjudication of a case is often a state different from the state where the cause of action arose (as in the preceding example). Second, there is a principle of comity or mutuality in the relations between sovereigns. Thus state A gives effect to state B's law in return for B's courts according similar respect to A's law. (This is a principle of international law but it is also relevant to relations between states in the United States.) Third, the United States Constitution, Article IV, section 1, requires that "full faith and credit . . . be given in each State to the public acts, records and judicial proceedings of every other State."

Note that these principles of convenience, comity, and full faith and credit extend only to civil proceedings. State criminal proceedings can be brought only in the courts of the state where the criminal acts were committed.

3. *A subsidiary function of the state courts is to adjudicate cases in which some or all of the claims or defenses raised by the parties are based on the laws of the United States.* This, in a sense, is an extension of principles discussed in item 2 above. However it is of such signal importance as to warrant independent treatment.

Example: A railroad employee is injured on the job while on a train traveling between New York and Connecticut. The Federal Employer's Liability Act (FELA) provides that the employee may bring suit to recover damages for his injuries, and the act also establishes standards for determining liability and assessing the damages. The FELA also provides that such a suit may be brought in either a state or federal court. If the employee brings his FELA suit in a state court, that court must hear the case and decide it according to the FELA standards.

Example: A person is brought before a state court on a state criminal charge. The defendant alleges in the trial court that some or all of the state's evidence was gathered through procedures which violate the due process clause of the Fourteenth Amendment to the United States Constitution (see *infra* at p. 213 *et seq.*). The trial court has primary jurisdiction to rule on the federal constitutional issues; state appellate courts may hear appeals from the trial court ruling(s) on the federal issues; the Supreme Court of the United States may hear an appeal from the state court rulings on the federal issues.

Article VI, section 2, of the United States Constitution provides that: "This Constitution, and the laws of the United States which shall be made in pursuance thereof, . . . shall be the supreme law of the land; and the judges in every state shall be bound thereby, anything in the Constitution or laws of any state notwithstanding."

This "supremacy" clause, perhaps more than any other part of the Constitution, establishes the United States as a nation that is independent of and superior to the several states. While the states retain some independence as sovereigns, theirs is a sovereignty which is severely limited by the powers granted to the United States in the Constitution. Thus when the Congress legislates on matters properly subject to federal control, the states and their courts are as much bound by that legislation as are the federal courts. This supremacy of federal law is the doctrinal basis for the requirement that state courts adjudicate certain types of civil cases brought by a plaintiff whose claim for relief is based on federal law. (In many types of cases based on federal law, however, Congress has given the federal courts exclusive jurisdiction, so that state courts are precluded from hearing them at all.)

Although it is an almost absolute rule of international law that one sovereign will not provide a forum for the prosecution of violations of the criminal law of another sovereign, it is possible in the United States—under the supremacy clause—for federal crimes to be prosecuted in state courts. As a matter of practice, however, prosecutions for violation of federal law are almost always brought in federal courts.

4. *The prime function of the federal courts is to enforce the laws of the United States.* The source of the federal judicial power is Article III of the United States Constitution (reprinted in part *supra* at p. 66). Section 2(1) of Article III provides that the judicial power of the United States "shall extend to all cases . . . arising under this Constitution, the laws of the United States, and treaties made, or which shall be made, under their authority." This proviso is the basis for the so-called "federal question" jurisdiction of the federal courts. Thus it is constitutionally proper for the federal courts to undertake to resolve cases in which some substantial issue of federal law is raised by way of claim or defense. (Note that the precise jurisdictional limits on the federal courts are established by statute. All the federal courts are established, and their jurisdiction determined, by the Congress in acts implementing Article III.)

Example: The Internal Revenue Service of the United States Treasury Department claims that Roe has failed to pay some federal taxes due on his earnings. A suit to recover the tax deficiency is a case arising under the laws of the United States. This case will be tried in the federal courts. Not only is it constitutionally proper for the federal courts to hear this case, but Congress has decreed that the federal courts have exclusive jurisdiction over such cases.

Example: A railroad employee is injured, as in the first example under item 3 above. In that case the injured employee could also bring suit in the federal courts. The FELA provides that cases under the Act may be brought in either state or federal courts. (This is called concurrent jurisdiction.)

Example: Doe kidnaps a child in New York and takes the child to New Jersey. The transportation of the victim between the states is a federal crime, punishable in the federal courts. Note that the kidnapping violates New York law, and Doe may *also* be tried and punished by the courts of New York state.

5. *A subsidiary function of the federal courts is to adjudicate cases in which the parties are residents of different states.* Section 2(1) of Article III provides that the judicial power of the United States extends to cases "between citizens of different states." This is the so-called "diversity of citizenship" jurisdiction of the federal courts. The theory underlying this jurisdiction is that state courts may be prejudiced against out-of-state residents, and that the federal courts should be available to provide an unbiased forum. The statute implementing this constitutional provision states that the federal courts may hear civil actions involving citizens of different states, if the amount in controversy exceeds $10,000.

Example: Doe and Roe collide, as in the examples in item 2 above. Assume that Doe is a resident of New York, and Roe is a resident of New Jersey. Doe wishes to sue Roe for $25,000 (an amount alleged by Doe to be sufficient to compensate him for his injuries). This suit may be brought in the federal courts sitting in New Jersey. The case will be decided according to state law regarding standards of careful driving. In this instance, since the collision took place in New York, the relevant state law is probably that of New York. Note that this is another case where the state and federal courts have concurrent jurisdiction.

The foregoing is a very brief and incomplete survey of jurisdictional relationships between the state and federal courts, but it serves to outline some of the more salient features of federal-state jurisdiction. It also provides the foundation for some additional observations on the jurisdictional requirements of our federal system.

First, note that the jurisdiction of the state courts is, in a sense, more general than that of the federal courts. The state courts may hear civil cases based on state law (including the law of other states) and on federal law and they may hear criminal cases based on their own state law and on federal law. The jurisdiction of the federal courts, on the other hand, is limited by Constitution and statute primarily to cases in which some substantial question of federal law is raised. The "diversity of citizenship" cases are an exception to the federal question rule, in that state law is applied in such cases, but this exception rests on a specific constitutional grant of jurisdiction.

Second, the state courts have a general jurisdiction to hear cases where the only applicable law is common law, *i. e.*, judge-made law. The federal courts, on the other hand, have no general common law jurisdiction. The law applied in federal courts, insofar as it is federal law and not the application of state law, is almost wholly statutory or constitutional law.

These distinctions between state and federal court jurisdiction reflect one theory of American federalism. According to this theory, the states are sovereigns which exercise the complete and general powers incident to sovereignty, except for specific limitations placed on them by their own constitutions and the Constitution of the United States. The United States, on the other hand, is said to be a limited sovereign which may exercise only those powers specifically delegated to it in the Constitution. In fact, the division of power between the present federal government and the state governments does not accord with this theory. Nevertheless, the theory continues to have potency with respect to jurisdictional relations between state and federal courts. Concern for the independence and integrity of the state judiciaries has prompted the federal courts to be especially strict in requiring that the would-be litigant in the federal courts clearly establish the grounds on which he invokes their jurisdiction. These strict requirements add another complicating element to the already complex questions of state-federal jurisdiction.

SECTION 4.2   THE DIVISION OF JUDICIAL POWER WITHIN STATE AND FEDERAL COURT SYSTEMS

The judicial power of government, whether state or federal, is vested in a system of courts in which there are several classes of courts to hear different classes of actions and/or to perform different functions in the adjudication of cases. The development, within a court system, of many courts each having some limited and special authority may be explained partly on the basis of convenience and efficiency.

It is convenient in a big city, for example, that violations of traffic regulations be tried in a special court, and it would be ridiculous for a Traffic Court to take jurisdiction of a murder case (even if the murder occurred in a dispute over a ticket for speeding). Special Juvenile Courts are often established to deal with juvenile offenders, and less often special Domestic Relations Courts are established to deal with matters of divorce and support of children. All matters of probate of wills and administration of estates of decedents are generally handled by a special Probate Court (called in New York a Surrogate's Court).

Apart from special courts which handle special kinds of cases, there is usually in each city a court which can handle various kinds of civil cases involving small amounts of money—generally called Town Court, or Municipal Court, or City Court; and another court which can try various kinds of criminal cases involving minor charges —generally called Police Court or Magistrate Court. In smaller localities there is apt to be a Justice of the Peace, with jurisdiction over minor civil and criminal matters.

The most important trial courts of a state are the courts of "general jurisdiction," often called Superior Courts, which can try civil and criminal cases of all kinds.

There are in all states not only trial courts but also appellate courts, which hear appeals taken from the decisions of the trial courts. In many states there is both a final appellate court, called usually the Supreme Court, and an intermediate appellate court, called usually a Court of Appeals. (As previously noted, in New York the final appellate court is called the Court of Appeals, the trial court of general jurisdiction is called the Supreme Court, and the intermediate appellate court is called the Appellate Division of the Supreme Court.)

The system of courts within a particular state is often not as simple as the above description would indicate. The organization of the courts of a state is generally determined more by historical factors than by abstract logic, and once a court is established it is extremely difficult to abolish it in the interest of efficiency. In some states the complexity of the court system, the existence of a large number of specialized courts, and the lack of coordination among courts, may result in serious delays in the administration of justice.

A schematic description of a state court system is presented in the chart on page 152.

STATE COURT ORGANIZATION

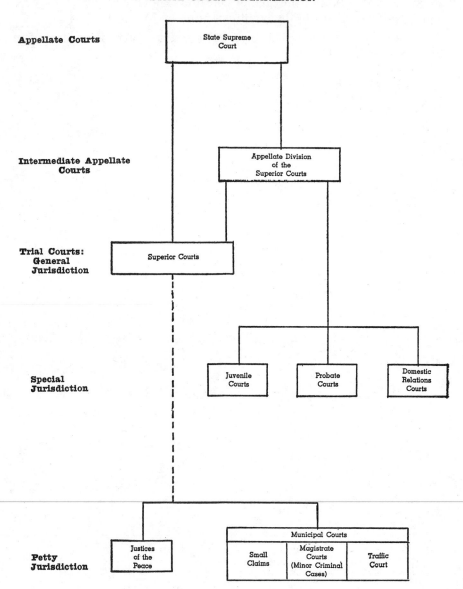

Note: Each of the states has its own system of organizing its courts. The names and the number of courts, and the appellate relationships, vary from state to state. This chart does not describe the court system of any state but is a composite designed to indicate, generally, how a state court system may be organized. The schema shown here is a bit more elaborate than that of many states in that it includes an intermediate court of appeals. This is a feature of the court systems in some of the more populous states, e. g., California and New York, but many states have only one appellate court.

Key: ————— Appeal
- - - - - - - - Transfer for a new trial in lieu of appeal.

The federal court system has a considerably more complex structure than that of any state system. The chief reason for this is the need to establish a great many special courts and agencies to administer law which is applicable on a national basis and to adjudicate cases stemming from the affairs of more than 200 million people spread out over a whole continent.

Although there are a greater number of specialized courts and agencies in the federal system than in state systems, the form of organization is basically the same. There are a series of courts and agencies in which legal proceedings are commonly initiated. Some of these have jurisdiction only over special classes of action; others have a more general jurisdiction. Superior to the courts and agencies which have "original" jurisdiction, that is, jurisdiction over the origination of legal proceedings, there are intermediate appellate tribunals, some of which hear appeals in limited classes of cases while others have a more general appellate jurisdiction. The Supreme Court of the United States is at the head of the system, sitting primarily as an appellate court to hear cases which arise in both the state and the federal courts and which involve important questions of federal law. The appellate organization of the federal court system will be examined in greater detail below; for the moment we need only observe that it is a complex system but one which is somewhat similar in form to the state court system.

The litigant who has made the proper selection of a court system in which to institute legal proceedings is thus faced with an array of courts from which he or she must select the court most appropriate to hear the case. This is an important choice, for selection of the wrong court is wasteful of time and money and, in some cases, a wrong choice may prove fatal to the plaintiff's action. Further elaboration of this problem is not necessary for our purposes; suffice it to say that this aspect of the jurisdiction of courts is illustrative of the complex and difficult issues which judges, lawyers and litigants face when trying to determine when and under what circumstances a particular court is competent to adjudicate a dispute.

SECTION 4.3   APPELLATE ORGANIZATION OF THE FEDERAL COURT SYSTEM

Article III, section 1 of the United States Constitution provides that "the judicial power of the United States"—as contrasted with the judicial power of the several states—"shall be vested in one Supreme Court and in such inferior courts as the Congress may from time to time ordain and establish." The scope of the judicial power of the United States is set out in section 2 of Article III (reprinted *supra* p. 67) as a power to adjudicate specified classes of cases and controversies.

Article III of the Constitution provides the basis for, but does not itself establish, the federal judiciary. All federal courts, including the Supreme Court, have been established by Congress in accordance with the constitutional mandate that there be one Supreme Court and such other courts as the Congress deems necessary. Once the federal judiciary was established, the judicial power was vested in that judiciary by the Constitution, but the allocation of the judicial power among the various courts in the system is made by the Congress through legislation (e. g., the Judicial Code of the United States) in accordance with constitutional requirements. The following is a brief sketch of the court system which has been devised by the Congress.

For purposes of law enforcement and administration, the United States is divided into judicial districts. Within each state there is at least one federal district, served by a United States District Court; in addition, there are United States District Courts in the District of Columbia and the Commonwealth of Puerto Rico. The District Courts are the principal trial courts in the federal system. They are courts of general jurisdiction in that they may hear a broad range of cases which arise in their respective districts. Thus almost all federal criminal cases are brought in the District Courts as are most civil cases which arise under federal law.

Appellate review of the decisions of the District Courts is the primary responsibility of the Courts of Appeals. There are 11 Courts of Appeals in the federal system, one for each of ten federal judicial circuits and one for the District of Columbia. The circuits are composed of three or more states, and the Court of Appeals for each of the circuits hears appeals from the District Courts which sit in their respective circuits; e. g., New York, Connecticut, and Vermont comprise the Second Circuit and appeals from the District Courts sitting in those states are heard by the Court of Appeals for the Second Circuit which sits in New York City. The Courts of Appeals are intermediate appellate courts; their decisions may be submitted to the Supreme Court of the United States for review.

The Supreme Court of the United States is the court of last resort in the federal system. It has jurisdiction to hear some original proceedings but by far the greatest bulk of its work is the review of decisions from the lower federal courts and from the highest state courts in cases where a substantial issue of federal law has been raised in the state court proceedings.

The usual method of invoking review by the Supreme Court of the United States is through a petition for "certiorari"—that is, for a certification of the case to the Supreme Court; such a petition is granted at the discretion of the Supreme Court and "only where there are special and important reasons therefor" (Rule 38(5) of the Supreme Court Rules). The fact that the result reached in the court below was erroneous is not in itself such a reason. In a 1949 address to the American Bar Association, Chief Justice Vinson said, "The Supreme Court is not, and never has been, primarily concerned with the correction of errors in lower court decisions. . . . To remain effective, the Supreme Court must continue to decide only those cases which present questions whose resolution will have an immediate importance far beyond the particular facts and parties involved."

A party may, however, secure review by the Supreme Court on "appeal"—as contrasted with "certiorari"—as a matter of right, when the highest state court finds a statute or treaty of the United States to be invalid, or when it upholds a state statute whose constitutionality under the United States Constitution is challenged, or when a federal court finds a state statute repugnant to the treaties, laws or Constitution of the United States. In such cases the Supreme Court will restrict its inquiry to the important questions of federalism which such appeals raise.

Finally, a case may be brought before the Supreme Court of the United States upon certification of a United States Court of Appeals which seeks instructions as to how a question of law should be decided. This device is rarely used.

The District Courts, the Courts of Appeals, and the Supreme Court are the courts of general authority in the federal system. There are also some special courts which have been established to hear particular classes of cases: a United States Customs Court to hear cases arising out of the imposition of customs duties on imported goods; a United States Court of Customs and Patent Appeals, to hear appeals from the Customs Court and, in patent cases, from the United States Patent Office; a United States Court of Claims, to hear certain claims against the United States; a United States Tax Court, to hear cases relating to the imposition of federal taxes; a United States Court of Military Appeals, to hear appeals from courts martial; Municipal Courts of the District of Columbia; and Territorial Courts for Guam, the Virgin Islands, and the Canal Zone.

One other feature of the federal system deserves mention here. The Congress has established a large number of boards, commissions, and agencies to administer and enforce federal law, particularly law respecting the regulation of business activity. These so-called administrative agencies have a special and limited authority with respect to particular federal statutes. For example, surface transportation between the several states (by rail, highway, and water) is subjected to regulation by the Interstate Commerce Act and it is the responsibility of the Interstate Commerce Commission to administer and enforce this law. The Civil Aeronautics Board, the Federal Trade Commission, the U. S. Patent Office, the National Labor Relations Board, *etc.*, exercise similar authority with respect to other legislation. In the performance of their duties these administrative agencies make many decisions regarding the application of the law to activities of firms and individuals. Congress has provided for review of some of these decisions in appellate proceedings in the federal courts.

The chart on page 157 presents a schematic view of the appellate organization of the federal court system.

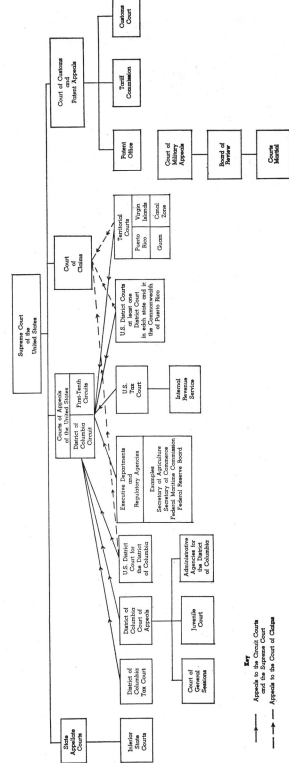

APPELLATE ORGANIZATION OF THE FEDERAL COURTS

Notes: 1. There are some occasions for appeals from the federal trial courts directly to the Supreme Court of the United States. This is not indicated on the chart since it is much more common for appeals from the trial courts to be made to Courts of Appeals or the Court of Claims.

2. The decisions of the military courts may not be reviewed, by appeal, in the civilian courts. The Court of Military Appeals is staffed by civilian judges.

Notes and Questions

1.   Why should there be a system of appeals from decisions of trial courts?   Is it because the judges of trial courts are considered truly "inferior"?   Is it because justice requires that the losing party be given a second chance?   Why is the appellate court generally limited to a review of errors of law, as contrasted with errors of fact?

2.   Other federal systems, e. g., Canada and Switzerland, do not have a dual system of state and federal courts.   In these systems local law and federal law are administered through one court system. Note that the United States Constitution does not require the establishment of a separate system of federal courts.   The Constitution provides for the establishment of a Supreme Court, but all other federal courts are established and maintained by Congress at its discretion, as authorized in Article III, Section 1.   Instead of establishing a separate system of federal courts, Congress might have required the state courts to hear all cases arising under federal law, and empowered the Supreme Court to exercise appellate jurisdiction over the state court decisions involving federal law.

Do you think this system would have been more or less complex than the present system?   Would such a system have led to more or less uniformity in our legal system?   Would such a system have tended to strengthen or weaken the independence of state governments?   Would the introduction of such a system today improve or harm the quality of adjudication?   Does the existence of a plurality of courts increase the opportunity to secure judicial protection of the rights of an aggrieved person?

3.   Diversity of citizenship jurisdiction was provided for when the relations between the states, and between citizens of different states, were more nearly like international relations.   In spite of the tremendous physical growth of the United States and its population, a multitude of unifying factors have eliminated most of the strangeness or hostility that sometimes characterized relations between citizens of different states in earlier times.   In the light of the unification of the country, do you think the diversity of citizenship jurisdiction of the federal courts should be retained?

SECTION 5.   JURISDICTION OF THE PERSON IN CIVIL CASES

We now consider very briefly another aspect of jurisdiction: the authority of the court over the person of the defendant in civil cases.

Suppose a citizen of Massachusetts, living in Boston, brings suit in a Massachusetts court against a citizen of Argentina, living in

Buenos Aires. If the defendant makes no statements and does not appear, can the Massachusetts court properly enter a judgment against him or her?

Suppose the defendant is a citizen not of Argentina but of Massachusetts, and is living in that state in the city of Springfield? Should that make a difference in the answer?

Upon reflection it should be apparent that there are two broad problems here. One is the problem of assuring that the defendant has an opportunity to know that a lawsuit is being brought against him, so that he can defend against it. The second is the problem of protecting persons against judgments of a foreign state with which they have no real connection.

Service of process. Ordinarily a defendant is subjected to the jurisdiction of a court by the presentation to him of a proper notice that an action in that court is being brought against him. The presentation of such notice is called "service of process." In England at common law the plaintiff generally obtained a document called a "writ" issued by a royal official ordering the sheriff to notify the defendant to be before the particular court at a particular time to answer the particular complaint. In America today it is generally the clerk of the court itself who issues the writ (or summons), at the plaintiff's request, either to the sheriff or directly to the defendant; and in some states the process served upon the defendant is simply a notice signed by the plaintiff's attorney.

The court's process extends normally throughout the territorial jurisdiction of the state in which it sits, and no farther. If the defendant is in the state and a summons is served upon him or her there, he or she becomes subject to the jurisdiction of the court, even though he or she is a nonresident simply passing through the state— unless for some reason he or she is privileged to be exempt from service of process (as, for example, where he or she has been brought into the state by force, or has come for the purpose of giving testimony in a judicial proceeding).

Jurisdiction over residents; substituted service. If the defendant is a resident of a state, that state's courts may take jurisdiction over him or her even though he or she is not personally served with process within the state. State statutes often provide that service upon a resident may be made by leaving the process at his usual place of abode, or by some other form of "substituted service", including in some cases publication in a newspaper. The courts have held that it is not necessary under the Constitution of the United States that the defendant actually have notice of the action being brought against him or her, in order for the court to have jurisdiction, so long as the method of service prescribed and used is one which is reasonably calculated to give notice and an opportunity to defend.

Jurisdiction over property. It must be mentioned also that even though a court is without jurisdiction to render a judgment over the defendant personally, it may render a judgment affecting his or her interest in property if it has jurisdiction of the property. Thus a so-called *in rem* ("against the thing," as contrasted with *in personam,* "against the person") suit may be instituted against a defendant by an attachment of the defendant's property within the state, and the court may order that the property be sold and the proceeds applied to the discharge of the plaintiff's claim against the defendant—even though the defendant has not been served with process and indeed the court has no jurisdiction over the defendant personally. Similarly, in a suit called *quasi-in-rem,* one who owes the defendant money may be compelled to pay that money to the plaintiff in satisfaction of the claim against the defendant—in an action in which the court has no jurisdiction over the person of the defendant.

Jurisdiction obtained by consent. If the defendant consents to the jurisdiction of the court, that is enough, though he or she be a nonresident and no process has been served on him or her. Such consent may be manifested by the defendant's appearing in the action (provided the appearance is for some other purpose than that of raising the objection of lack of jurisdiction over him). The defendant may consent also by appointing an agent to accept service or by agreeing to service by any other method, or by waiving service.

Constitutional requirements for jurisdiction over non-residents. If a valid judgment is rendered in one state and thereafter an action is brought under it in another state, the second state is bound to enforce the judgment, under Article IV, section 1, of the Constitution of the United States, which states that "full faith and credit shall be given in each state to the public acts, records, and judicial proceedings of every other state."

If, however, the judgment in the first state was rendered by a court which had no jurisdiction over the defendant it cannot be enforced in the second state without a violation of the Fourteenth Amendment of the Constitution of the United States, which declares that no state shall "deprive any person of life, liberty or property without due process of law."

Since Constitutional principles are involved, the question of the validity of the jurisdictional requirements to be met by the states is subject to the determination of the Supreme Court of the United States.

The Supreme Court has often said that personal jurisdiction is based upon the power of the state over the person of the defendant. "The foundation of jurisdiction is physical power," is a phrase often quoted. "Can the Island of Tobago pass a law to bind the rights of the whole world? Would the world submit to such an assumed jurisdiction?" asked an English judge. Mr. Justice Field, speaking for the Supreme Court of the United States, in the leading case of Pennoyer v. Neff,[1] said:

> "The authority of every tribunal is necessarily restricted by the territorial limits of the state in which it is established. Any attempt to exercise authority beyond those limits would be deemed in every other forum, as has been said by this court, an illegitimate assumption of power, and be resisted as mere abuse."

Thus, even though the defendant has notice of the action and an opportunity to be heard, the general rule has been that no liabilities can be imposed upon him or her for failure to appear before the courts of a state in which he or she is not a resident—unless he or she can be found and personally served with process in that state, or unless he or she has consented to its jurisdiction.

Yet with the extension of business activity and of communications across state boundaries the notion that the state has jurisdiction over a nonresident only if it can catch him or her, so to speak, seems less and less valid. Indeed in Pennoyer v. Neff, the Supreme Court left open the question whether a state may not constitutionally require a nonresident entering into a business partnership or association within its limits, or making contracts enforceable there, to appoint an agent or representative in the state to receive service of process in legal proceedings instituted with respect to such partnership, association, or contracts; and whether it might not provide, further, that if the nonresident fails to do so, service may be made upon a public officer designated for that purpose. In fact, many states have enacted such requirements, and their validity has been uniformly upheld.

Similarly, it is established that a state may rightly direct that nonresidents who operate automobiles on its highways shall be deemed to have appointed the Secretary of State as agent to accept service of process, provided there is some provision making it reasonably probable that notice of the service on the Secretary will be communicated to the nonresident defendant who is sued.

The colorful but descriptive term "long arm statutes" has been applied to the variety of state laws authorizing state courts to take jurisdiction over non-residents who are not physically present in the state at the time a civil action is commenced against them. In such statutes, fundamental rules of fairness are observed. The "long arm" jurisdiction usually rests on some substantial activity conducted by or for the defendant in the state where the action is brought, and the plaintiff is required to use reasonable and effective means to put the

1. 95 U.S. 714 (1877).

defendant on notice regarding commencement of the action. The key to the validity of the long arm jurisdiction is that it is based on some substantial "contacts, ties or relations" between the defendant and the state where the action is brought. That jurisdictional standard was first announced by the U.S. Supreme Court in 1945 in a case involving state taxation of interstate business, International Shoe Co. v. Washington, 326 U.S. 310, 66 S.Ct. 154 (1945). The Court has recently embraced the International Shoe standard as the norm for all determinations of the propriety of a state court's exercising jurisdiction in legal proceedings involving non-resident defendants, Shaffer v. Heitner, 433 U.S. 186, 97 S.Ct. 2569 (1977).

Notes and Questions

1. Is the theory that "the foundation of jurisdiction is physical power" supported by the nonresident motorist and nonresident business association statutes? Or are these examples of the Island of Tobago passing a law to bind the rights of the whole world?

2. Should not the rule for personal jurisdiction be the same for both residents and nonresidents, namely, that if the defendant has actually been notified the court should have jurisdiction over him or her, and if he or she has not been notified it should not have jurisdiction?

3. Should the rule be that a person can be sued without his or her consent only in the state in which he or she resides or in a state in which he or she has property or is doing business?

4. Why should there be any general rule regarding jurisdiction over the person except that of fairness or justice in the individual case?

5. The same rules regarding jurisdiction over the person and property of nonresidents apply to citizens of foreign countries and citizens of other states of the United States. Is that fair to citizens of foreign countries? Is your conclusion affected by the fact that only in the (rare) event of a treaty so providing are judgments of American courts generally enforceable in foreign countries, and judgments of foreign courts generally enforceable in American courts?

6. Suppose a person is induced to come into the jurisdiction by false statements made for the sole purpose of service of process: should the court take the view that how he or she happened to be in the jurisdiction is immaterial? In Wyman v. Newhouse, 93 F.2d 313 (2d Cir. 1937), Mr. Newhouse, a resident of New York, had had meretricious relations over a period of years with Mrs. Wyman, a widow resident in Florida. Mrs. Wyman wrote Mr. Newhouse that she was leaving the United States to visit her mother in Ireland, who was dying, that she would not return, and that she loved him and wanted

him to come to Florida for a last visit.　Upon his arrival at Miami airport, Mr. Newhouse was served with process in a Florida action by Mrs. Wyman for money loaned to him and for seduction under promise of marriage.　Mr. Newhouse did not appear in the action and a judgment was entered against him on his default.　Subsequently Mrs. Wyman sued in the federal court in New York to collect the Florida judgment, and Mr. Newhouse set up as a defense that the Florida court had not had personal jurisdiction over him and therefore its judgment was void.　Should the court have held (as it did) that the defense was valid?

7.　The following is taken from the opinion of Mr. Justice Black,* writing for the court, in Frisbie v. Collins, 342 U.S. 519, 72 S.Ct. 509 (1952):

> Acting as his own lawyer, the respondent Shirley Collins brought this habeas corpus [1] case in a United States District Court seeking release from a Michigan state prison where he is serving a life sentence for murder.　His petition alleges that while he was living in Chicago, Michigan officers forcibly seized, handcuffed, blackjacked and took him to Michigan.　He claims that trial and conviction under such circumstances is in violation of the Due Process Clause of the Fourteenth Amendment and the Federal Kidnaping Act, and that therefore his conviction is a nullity.

> The District Court denied the writ without a hearing on the ground that the state court had power to try respondent "regardless of how presence was procured."　The Court of Appeals, one judge dissenting, reversed and remanded the cause for hearing.　6 Cir., 189 F.2d 464.　It held that the Federal Kidnaping Act had changed the rule declared in prior holdings of this Court, that a state could constitutionally try and convict a defendant after acquiring jurisdiction by force.　To review this important question we granted certiorari.　342 U.S. 865, 72 S.Ct. 112.

*　*　*

> This Court has never departed from the rule announced in Ker v. Illinois, 119 U.S. 436, 444, 7 S.Ct. 225, 229, 30 L.Ed. 421, that the power of a court to try a person for crime is not impaired by the fact that he had been brought within the court's jurisdiction by reason of a "forcible abduction."　No persuasive reasons are now presented to justify overruling this line of cases.　They rest on the sound basis that due process of law is satisfied when one present in court is convicted of crime after having been fairly apprized of the charges against him and after a fair trial in accord-

---

* Justice Hugo L. Black was appointed to the Supreme Court by President Roosevelt in 1937.　He served as U. S. Senator from Alabama from 1927 to 1937.　He was reputed to be the intellectual leader of the so-called liberal wing of the Supreme Court from 1950 through 1970.　With Justice Doug- las and Chief Justice Warren, in particular, he did much to establish the Supreme Court as a guardian of "civil liberties" in criminal cases.　Justice Black died in 1971, shortly after he retired from the Court.

1.　*Habeas corpus* is discussed *infra* at p. 261.

ance with constitutional procedural safeguards. There is nothing in the Constitution that requires a court to permit a guilty person rightfully convicted to escape justice because he was brought to trial against his will.

The court could find no basis in the Kidnaping Act to grant the relief requested by Collins and affirmed the judgment of the District Court.

Compare Wyman v. Newhouse and Frisbie v. Collins. Why were different results reached in these cases? What remedy did Collins seek from the federal courts? How, if at all, would that remedy be effectuated? What remedy did Newhouse seek from the Federal Court? How, if at all, would that remedy be effectuated? Is it significant that Collins could not have been tried in Illinois for the alleged murder, while Mrs. Wyman could have brought suit against Newhouse in New York state basing her claim for relief on the law of Florida regarding both the loan of money and seduction under the promise of marriage? Is it significant that criminal prosecutions are tried in the courts of the sovereign whose officers will carry out the sentence of the court, while civil actions are often tried in the court of one sovereign (*e. g.*, Florida) while the judgment in the case may be enforced in the courts of another sovereign (*e. g.*, New York, or the United States)?

Do you think that the judgments of the federal courts in Wyman v. Newhouse *and* Frisbie v. Collins further legitimate interests of the United States and the several states regarding the balance of political and judicial power in a federal system?

8. *Extradition* is the formal process through which a person may be removed from one state in order to be tried on criminal charges pending against him in another state. That process commonly provides a hearing in the state where the person is found, at which time the accused is afforded an opportunity to show cause why he should not be extradited. (The grounds for preventing extradition are relatively narrow, since it is generally presumed that the accused will be afforded a fair trial in the state which seeks extradition, and that he will be able to present his defenses in those proceedings.) The accused may waive the extradition process and return voluntarily to stand trial.

A state's duty to deliver a fugitive to the authorities of another state is imposed by the United States Constitution. Article IV, Section 2(2) provides that "A person charged in any State with treason, felony, or other crime, who shall flee from justice, and be found in another State, shall, on demand of the executive authority of the State from which he fled, be delivered up, to be removed to the state having jurisdiction of the crime." The governors of the respective states are responsible for the implementation of this provision, that duty having been imposed upon them by Congress in an Act passed in

1793. However, the Act did not provide for a judicial remedy for non-compliance and the Supreme Court has held that it is not empowered to command compliance; thus performance of the statutory and constitutional duty is discretionary with the state governors. Consequently state governors have often refused to allow extradition in cases where they have believed that extradition would work an injustice.

Does Article IV, Section 2(2), and the Act of 1793 establish the right of one state to have extradition of a fugitive from another state?

Does it appear from the Constitution, Article IV, Section 2(2) that the process of extradition is concerned primarily with protecting the interests of the states in the enforcement of their criminal laws? Could the United States Supreme Court, in Frisbie v. Collins, have created a right in persons to the benefits, if any, of the extradition process provided for in state laws?

Is your reaction to the decision in Frisbie v. Collins (*supra* p. 163) affected by the fact that state criminal procedure is closely regulated by constitutional provisions, both state and federal, designed to insure fairness to the accused in the trial of criminal cases? (See Chapter 3, *infra*.)

9. One federal court has waivered regarding the propriety and present vitality of the *Ker-Frisbie* rule regarding jurisdiction over the defendant in federal criminal cases. In Toscanino v. U. S., 500 F. 2d 267 (1974), the U.S. Court of Appeals for the Second Circuit heard an appeal in which the appellant alleged that his conviction on narcotics charges was constitutionally invalid. Toscanino, a citizen of Italy, alleged that he had been kidnapped from Uruguay by Brazilian officials, who took him to Brazil where he was imprisoned and tortured; that Brazilian officials then took him to the U.S. where he was turned over to officials of the U.S.; and that U.S. officials were complicit in the acts of the Brazilian officials. The U.S. invoked the *Ker-Frisbie* doctrine claiming that even if what he alleged was true, that did not deprive the U.S. District Court of jurisdiction to the criminal charges against him. The Court of Appeals held that Toscanino was entitled to offer proof to support his allegations, and remanded the case to the District Court for further proceedings "not inconsistent with [the Court of Appeals] opinion." No specific relief was directed by the Court in the event Toscanino proved his allegations. That was left to the discretion of the District Court. The clear implication of the Court of Appeals opinion was that if Toscanino succeeded in proving his allegation, his conviction should be vacated and the indictment against him dismissed. Presumably the District Court could have also directed that he be returned to Uruguay (or at least given a head start to Kennedy International Airport). The result in Toscanino rested on the Court of Appeals belief that *Ker-Frisbie* had

been undercut by decisions of the U.S. Supreme Court which had clarified or extended the protections to be afforded under the "due process" provisions of the U.S. Constitution.

On the remand the District Court found that Toscanino had no credible evidence to support his allegation that officers of the United States were complicit in his abduction, imprisonment, torture, and removal to the United States. The District Court therefore declined to hold a full evidentiary hearing, and dismissed his motion to vacate the judgment and to dismiss the indictment against him. U. S. v. Toscanino, 398 F.Supp. 916 (U.S.D.C., E.D.New York, 1975). Subsequently, the Second Circuit Court of Appeals limited Toscanino to "outrageous" situations, and held it not to apply to merely high-handed action by government officials. U. S. ex rel. Lujan v. Gengler, 510 F.2d 62 (1975). Other Circuits have rejected Toscanino outright, see U. S. v. Herrara, 504 F.2d 859 (5th Cir. 1974); U. S. v. Mazzaro, 537 F.2d 257 (7th Cir. 1976); U. S. v. Lara, 539 F.2d 495 (5th Cir. 1976). The Supreme Court recently affirmed the *Ker-Frisbie* doctrine in Gernstein v. Pugh, 420 U.S. 103, 95 S.Ct. 854 (1975).

Chapter 2

CIVIL PROCEDURE PRIOR TO TRIAL

In the Introduction (p. 26), we stated that if a *legal* solution is sought for problems that arise from disruptions of the patterns or norms of social behavior, then *time* must be taken for *deliberate* action, for *articulate definition* of the issues, for a decision which is subject to *public* scrutiny and which is *objective* in the sense that it reflects an explicit community judgment and not merely personal judgment. These qualities of legal activity may be summed up in the word *formality*. The balance of Part One of this book is devoted to an examination of some aspects of the *formality* of law.

The material in Chapter 2 has been selected and arranged to outline some elements of modern pre-trial procedure. The student should analyze this material to attempt to determine how, if at all, pretrial procedure provides *formality* which assures that *time* will be taken for *deliberate* action and for an *articulate definition* of the issues.

SECTION 6. CATEGORIZATION OF FACTS

[The following is taken from KARL N. LLEWELLYN,* THE BRAMBLE BUSH (New York, 1951), p. 48 ff.]

. . . What are the facts? The plaintiff's name is Atkinson and the defendant's Walpole. The defendant, despite his name, is an Italian by extraction, but the plaintiff's ancestors came over with the Pilgrims. The defendant has a schnautzer-dog named Walter, red hair, and $30,000 worth of life insurance. All these are facts. The case, however, does not deal with life insurance. It is about an auto accident. The defendant's auto was a Buick painted pale magenta. He is married. His wife was in the back seat, an irritable somewhat faded blonde. She was attempting back seat driving when the accident occurred. He

---

* Karl N. Llewellyn served on the law faculty at Yale University and at Columbia University, and, at the time of his death in 1962, he was Professor of Law at the University of Chicago. He wrote extensively on contract law, commercial law, and jurisprudence. The Bramble Bush is based on a series of lectures by Professor Llewellyn which were delivered to first year law students at Columbia University. Other major works by Professor Llewellyn are The Cheyenne Way (with E. A. Hoebel, 1941), and The Common Law Tradition: Deciding Appeals (1961).

had turned around to make objection. In the process the car swerved and hit the plaintiff. The sun was shining; there was a rather lovely dappled sky low to the West. The time was late October on a Tuesday. The road was smooth, concrete. It had been put in by the McCarthy Road Work Company. How many of these facts are important to the decision? How many of these facts are, as we say, legally relevant? Is it relevant that the road was in the country or the city; that it was concrete or tarmac or of dirt; that it was a private or a public way? Is it relevant that the defendant was driving a Buick, or a motor car, or a vehicle? Is it important that he looked around as the car swerved? Is it crucial? Would it have been the same if he had been drunk, or had swerved for fun, to see how close he could run by the plaintiff, but had missed his guess?

Is it not obvious that as soon as you pick up this statement of the facts to find its legal bearings you must discard some as of no interest whatsoever, discard others as dramatic but as legal nothings? And is it not clear, further, that when you pick up the facts which are left and which do seem relevant, you suddenly cease to deal with them in the concrete and deal with them instead in *categories* which you, for one reason or another, deem significant? It is not the road between Pittsville and Arlington; it is "a highway." It is not a particular pale magenta Buick eight, by number 732507, but "a motor car," and perhaps even "a vehicle." It is not a turning around to look at Adoree Walpole, but a lapse from the supposedly proper procedure of careful drivers, with which you are concerned. Each concrete fact of the case arranges itself, I say, as the *representative* of a much wider abstract *category* of facts, and it is not in itself but as a member of the category that you attribute significance to it. But what is to tell you whether to make your category "Buicks" or "motor cars" or "vehicles"? What is to tell you to make your category "road" or "public highway"?   .   .   .

Note

In the preceding passage, Professor Llewellyn addressed himself to one of the central questions of legal procedure, namely, "how is a dispute, a complex matter of facts and applicable norms, to be prepared for adjudication?" His suggestion is that the preparation involves a process of classification in which the raw data of the case are reformulated in terms of legally significant categories. This process of categorization is necessary if the court is to resolve the case in accordance with standards applicable to other similar cases, that is, other cases in the same category. Thus categorization of the concrete realities of the dispute is an essential aspect of the fundamental requirement of law that like cases be treated in a like manner. Moreover, since the standards, that is, the norms applicable to the case, are themselves stated in a general form, it is often necessary to state the particular circumstances of the case in a similar form in order to perceive the interrelationship of the circumstances and the applicable norms. In addition, categorization is a means of simplifying the task of adjudication; professional judges who must handle a large volume of cases, can dispose of them far more efficiently if they are presented in terms of familiar, regularly used concepts and categories rather than as unique situations.

Nevertheless, the impulse to categorize also has its dangers. In the interests of achieving generality the distinctive qualities of a case may be obscured. Where particular circumstances may fall within several different general categories, the lawyers and judges may be tempted to choose one at the expense of others. The following materials explore some aspects of the problem of steering between excessive generalization and excessive particularization in the preparation of a case for judicial trial and decision.

SECTION 7. PLEADING

Civil suits are initiated by a process called pleading. This section examines some rudiments of that process and demonstrates how categorization of facts takes place from the earliest stages of a lawsuit.

SECTION 7.1 WHAT IS PLEADING?

[The following is taken from CHARLES E. CLARK,* HANDBOOK OF THE LAW OF CODE PLEADING, 2d ed. (St. Paul, Minn., 1947), pp. 1–4. Footnotes are omitted.]

Before any dispute can be adjusted or decided it is necessary to ascertain the actual points at issue between the disputants. Conceivably this may be done in several ways. Perhaps the simplest is a process of direct questioning of the parties by the arbitrator or judge. Another method is the exchange of written statements in advance of a direct hearing of the parties. Under our Anglo-American system of legal procedure we are committed by tradition and history, by present practice, and probably, by general inclination, except in exceptional cases, to the latter method. Our system calls for the development of issues *by the parties themselves* in formal manner in advance of the actual trial. This is accomplished by requiring the serving on the opposing party or the filing in court alternatively by the parties of *pleadings*—written instruments wherein are set forth the statements and contentions of each as to the points and facts in dispute. These *pleadings* are to be distinguished from the lawyer's oral argument or *"plea"* made to the court or jury at the trial of the case. Originally under the common-law system the pleadings were oral, but for several centuries they have

---

* The author was formerly a judge of the U.S. Court of Appeals, 2nd Circuit, prior to that he had been Dean of the Yale Law School. Judge Clark died in 1964.

been written and have become technical legal documents, carefully framed by the attorneys of the parties. The content of these documents and the manner in which they are to be employed in the litigation have become the subject of rules in general of a highly refined nature. *Pleading* is the name given to the legal science which deals with these rules.

The *pleadings* therefore serve the primary purpose of acquainting the court and the parties with the facts in dispute. In so doing they should point out the actual issues to be settled. Several other purposes may also be served by the pleadings. Thus a Committee of the American Bar Association classified the main purposes to be achieved by the pleadings as follows: (1) To serve as a formal basis for the judgment to be entered; (2) to separate issues of fact from questions of law; (3) to give the litigants the advantage of the plea of res adjudicata if again molested; (4) to notify the parties of the claims, defenses, and cross-demands of their adversaries. As hereinafter pointed out . . . the purpose especially emphasized has varied from time to time. Thus in common-law pleading especial emphasis was placed upon the *issue-formulating* function of pleadings; under the earlier code pleading like emphasis was placed upon *stating the material, ultimate facts* in the pleadings; while at the present time the emphasis seems to have shifted to the *notice* function of the pleading. . . .

Notes

1. *Code Pleading.* During the nineteenth century many states attempted to codify aspects of their law. Common law principles and random statutes were drawn together in what were intended to be systematic internally consistent bodies of statutory law setting out the law of the state on such matters as contracts, real property, personal property, and crimes. Reform of civil procedure was a special object of the codification movement and codes of procedure were promulgated with an eye to simplifying the preparation and trial of lawsuits. Code pleading is the term generally used to describe the type of pleading prescribed for civil actions in those states which adopted codes during the 19th century.

2. According to Judge Clark, code pleadings were to contain statements of "ultimate facts". This requirement follows from the distinction drawn between "ultimate facts" and "evidence" in a legal proceeding. Simply stated the ultimate facts in a lawsuit are the conclusions reached by the fact finder about what happened in the situation which gave rise to the suit. Evidence, on the other hand, is the intermediate facts from which the findings of ultimate facts are drawn. Put another way, the ultimate facts are the conclusions which the pleader believes the fact finder can be persuaded to reach after hearing the evidence.[1] Thus a requirement that ultimate facts are to be pleaded means that the pleader is not expected to and is

---

1. The subject is considered further in Chapter 4 at p. 361 *et seq.*

not supposed to plead (state) evidence, but rather to plead the ultimate facts which the pleader will attempt to establish through the proof (evidence) to be presented in the trial.

SECTION 7.2   MODERN PLEADING: EXAMPLES FROM THE FEDERAL RULES OF CIVIL PROCEDURE

This section sets out examples of modern pleadings under the Federal Rules of Civil Procedure. Consider the following questions as you examine these pleadings.

(a) Do these pleadings suggest that the Federal Rules emphasize "the *issue formulating* function of pleadings," or the purpose of *"stating the material, ultimate facts,"* or "the *notice* function of the pleading?"

(b) What is "a formal basis for the judgment to be entered", and how might these pleadings provide such a basis?

(c) Do these pleadings separate issues of fact from questions of law, and, if so, in what sense are those matters separated?

(d) How might the pleadings be used in order "to give the litigants the advantage of the plea of *res adjudicata* . . ."?[1]

The Federal Rules of Civil Procedure, adopted for the federal courts in 1938, reflect the modern, advanced system of "code pleading".[2] The Federal Rules attempt to reduce formalism in pleading to a minimum. Rule 2 states that "There shall be one form of action, to be known as a civil action." Rule 3 states that "A civil action is commenced by filing a complaint." Under Rule 8(a), a complaint must contain "(1) a short and plain statement of the grounds upon which the court's jurisdiction depends . . . , (2) a short and plain statement of the claim showing that the pleader is entitled to relief, and (3) a demand for judgment for the relief to which he deems himself entitled."

Although the Federal Rules speak of "one civil action", they nonetheless distinguish between various forms of complaints, such as a complaint for breach of contract, complaint for negligence, *etc.* Examples of a Complaint for Negligence (taken from Form 9 of the Federal Rules), of a Summons, and of an Answer to a Complaint for Negligence follow. The complaint and answer relate to a hypothetical case which is the subject of Section 8, *infra.*

---

1. See p. 170 *supra.*   **2.** See text at pp. 169–170 *supra.*

COMPLAINT

MORRIS and NANCY BROWN,
Plaintiffs,

    v.

MUNICIPAL TRANSIT CO.,
Defendant.

TO THE ABOVE–NAMED DEFENDANT:

    1. Jurisdiction is founded upon plaintiff's and defendant's residence within the District of Columbia and that the relief sought exceeds $10,000.

    2. On September 4, 1949, at the intersection of public highways Nebraska Ave. and Connecticut Ave., defendant's servant negligently drove a motor vehicle against plaintiff's automobile.

    3. As a result Plaintiff 1 suffered a sacroiliac sprain and fracture of the skull. Plaintiff 2 suffered permanent injury of a fractured left femur and contusions and abrasions to her body and also nervous shock and mental anguish. Plaintiffs also incurred medical expense and $457.25 property damage.

    Wherefore the plaintiffs demand judgment against the defendant in the sum of $15,000 and costs.

_____

[Attorney for the Plaintiffs]

_____

[Address]

_____

    The complaint is served upon the defendant along with a Summons issued by the Clerk of the Court.

SUMMONS

United States District Judge
For
The District of Columbia

Civil Action, File Number 500–50

MORRIS and NANCY BROWN,
Plaintiffs

    v.

MUNICIPAL TRANSIT CO.,

Defendant.

TO THE ABOVE–NAMED DEFENDANT:

    You are hereby summoned and required to serve upon _____, plaintiffs' attorney, whose address is _____, _____, an answer to the complaint which is herewith served upon you, within 20 days of service of summons upon you, exclusive of the day of service. If you fail to do so, judgment by default will be taken against you for the relief demanded in the complaint.

_____

Clerk of Court

[*Seal of the U. S. District Court*]

Dated _____

After the complaint is served the defendant is required within a certain time period to assert defenses and objections. Failure to do so will subject the defendant to a judgment by default.

Under the Federal Rules of Civil Procedure, certain defenses must be made, if at all, in an "answer", which the defendant serves upon the plaintiff; certain other defenses may be made either in an answer or, at the defendant's option, by a "motion" directed to the court. Thus in an action for negligence if the defendant wishes to state that he or she was not negligent, he or she must make such defenses in the answer. If the defendant wishes to contend that the court does not have jurisdiction over the case, or that the complaint fails to state a claim upon which (even if all allegations are proved) relief can be granted, he or she may apply directly to the court for an order dismissing the action.

With certain exceptions, if the defendant fails to present any defense or objection (whether by motion or answer), he or she loses (waives) the right to do so on trial. On the other hand, the defendant does not waive any defense or objection by joining it with other defenses or objections.

ANSWER

MORRIS and NANCY BROWN,
Plaintiffs

       v.

MUNICIPAL TRANSIT CO.,
Defendant.

To the above-named Plaintiffs, Defendant alleges as follows:

First Defense

Defendant denies allegations of negligence in Paragraph 2 of complaint; that the accident occurred due solely to the negligence of plaintiff 1.

Second Defense

Plaintiff was guilty of negligence which was a contributing cause of the accident.

Third Defense

Plaintiff 2 had knowledge of and assumed the risks incident to riding in the car driven by plaintiff 1.

Fourth Defense

Plaintiffs 1 and 2 were on a joint venture making plaintiff 1 the agent of plaintiff 2 and therefore the negligence of plaintiff 1 should be imputed to plaintiff 2.

Counterclaim

Based upon defendant's allegations in paragraph 1 of its answer, the defendant demands a judgment against plaintiffs of $295.25.

_____

[Attorney for Defendants]

_____

[Address]

Date _____   _____

A complaint such as the preceding example by no means gives the defendant notice of all the allegations against him or her. It does not contain an allegation that the plaintiff was free from contributory fault.[1] It does not contain an allegation that the defendant is not a government agency and hence not immune from liability. It does not contain an allegation that the time period within which suit may be brought has not elapsed, or that the same case has not previously been adjudicated. These and a host of other relevant matters, if they exist, are left for the defendant to raise. Thus the burden of allegation is divided between the parties. In technical terms, contributory negligence of the plaintiff, governmental immunity, and the statute of limitations are affirmative defenses. (You will note that the answer set out above does specifically assert affirmative defenses, including contributory negligence.) The line dividing what the plaintiff must allege in order to succeed and what the defendant must allege in order to succeed is drawn in part on the basis of what the plaintiff and defendant, respectively, must prove on trial. In a state in which the burden of proof[2] in a negligence action is on the plaintiff to show freedom from contributory fault, for example, the rules of procedure would probably require that the plaintiff allege such in the complaint. Thus the pleadings serve the function, in part,

---

1. Contributory fault or contributory negligence may be asserted as a defense to a negligence action in many common law jurisdictions. The gist of this defense is that if the plaintiff's injury is attributable at least in part to his own fault (*i. e.*, negligence, lack of due care) then the plaintiff may not recover even if the injury is also attributable in part to negligent conduct of the defendant.

2. This subject is discussed *infra*, at p. 380 ff.

of distinguishing where the burden of proof lies on the various issues. Put otherwise, the plaintiff need only state in the complaint those allegations which, if proved will entitle the plaintiff to succeed.

The purpose of the requirements for pleading are not simply to allocate burden of proof, however. They also are designed to prevent the fraudulent litigant from getting away with ambiguity and trickery, as well as to avoid surprise and expense on the part of the defendant. Thus Rule 9(b) of the Federal Rules states that where "fraud or mistake" is alleged, the circumstances constituting fraud or mistake shall be stated with particularity. On the other hand, the same rule states that "malice, intent, knowledge, and other condition of mind of a person may be averred generally."

Thirdly—in addition to considerations of proof, and, of surprise, expense and trickery—there is, underlying the requirements of pleading, the consideration of relevancy to the substantive rights of the parties, that is, to the rules of law which will be invoked upon trial. The rule of law that a person is liable for harm caused to another by negligent act sets the framework of Form 9. Similarly rules of law regarding defenses to a negligence claim set the framework for the Answer to a Complaint for Negligence.

Replying to defenses. Under the older common law procedure and under many State codes, the plaintiff is required to reply to defenses, other than denials, which the defendant sets up in the answer. The Federal Rules do not permit the plaintiff to reply to any defenses unless the court orders a reply (which it will not ordinarily do); at the same time, the Rules provide that "Averments in a pleading to which no responsive pleading is required or permitted shall be taken as denied or avoided." Thus, for example, if the complaint alleges that the defendant negligently ran down the plaintiff with an automobile, and the answer (a) denies that the running down was negligent and (b) asserts that the statute of limitations has run (*i. e.*, the time period within which suit may be brought has elapsed), then, on trial, it is taken as admitted that the defendant ran down the plaintiff; what remains in dispute is whether that act was negligent and whether the statute of limitations has run. With respect to the latter, the plaintiff has the opportunity of showing either (a) that the statute of limitations has not run, or (b) that even if it has run, there is some reason why that fact should not bar the action.

Questions

1. Do paragraphs 2 and 3 of the complaint (*supra* p. 172) and the enumerated defenses in the answer (*supra* pp. 173–174) assert matters of fact, or issues of law, or both?

2. Are the allegations of fact in the complaint and answer "categorized facts", and, if so, what basis did the attorneys have for categorizing the facts?

DIOGUARDI v. DURNING

United States Court of Appeals, Second Circuit, 1944.
139 F.2d 774.

CLARK, CIRCUIT JUDGE. In his complaint, obviously home drawn, plaintiff attempts to assert a series of grievances against the Collector of Customs at the Port of New York growing out of his endeavors to import merchandise from Italy "of great value," consisting of bottles of "tonics." We may pass certain of his claims as either inadequate or inadequately stated and consider only these two: (1) that on the auction day, October 9, 1940, when defendant sold the merchandise at "public custom," "he sold my merchandise to another bidder with my price of $110, and not of his price of $120," and (2) "that three weeks before the sale, two cases, of 19 bottles each case, disappeared." Plaintiff does not make wholly clear how these goods came into the collector's hands, since he alleges compliance with the revenue laws; but he does say he made a claim for "refund of merchandise which was two-thirds paid in Milano, Italy," and that the collector denied the claim. These and other circumstances alleged indicate (what, indeed, plaintiff's brief asserts) that his original dispute was with his consignor as to whether anything more was due upon the merchandise, and that the collector, having held it for a year (presumably as unclaimed merchandise under 19 U.S.C.A. § 1491), then sold it, or such part of it as was left, at public auction. For his asserted injuries plaintiff claimed $5,000 damages, together with interest and costs, against the defendant individually and as collector. This complaint was dismissed by the District Court, . . . on the ground that it "fails to state facts sufficient to constitute a cause of action."

Thereupon plaintiff filed an amended complaint, wherein, with an obviously heightened conviction that he was being unjustly treated, he vigorously reiterates his claims, including those quoted above and now stated as that his "medicinal extracts" were given to the Springdale Distilling Company "with my betting [bidding?] price of $110: and not their price of $120," and "It isn't so easy to do away with two cases with 37 bottles of one quart. Being protected, they can take this chance." An earlier paragraph suggests that defendant had explained the loss of the two cases by "saying that they had leaked, which could never be true in the manner they were bottled." On defendant's motion for dismissal on the same ground as before, the court made a final judgment dismissing the complaint, and plaintiff now comes to us with increased volubility, if not clarity.

It would seem, however, that he has stated enough to withstand a mere formal motion, directed only to the face of the complaint, and that here is another instance of judicial haste which in the long run makes waste. Under the new rules of civil procedure, there is no pleading requirement of stating "facts sufficient to constitute a cause of action," but only that there be "a short and plain statement of the claim showing that the pleader is entitled to relief," Federal Rules of Civil Procedure, rule 8(a), 28 U.S.C.A. following section 723c; and the motion for dismissal under Rule 12(b) is for failure to state "a claim upon which relief can be granted." The District Court does not state why it concluded that the complaints showed no claim upon which relief could be granted; and the United States Attorney's brief before us does not help us, for it is limited to the prognostication—unfortunately ill founded so far as we are concerned—that "the most cursory examination" of them will show the correctness of the District Court's action.

We think that, however inartistically they may be stated, the plaintiff has disclosed his claims that the collector has converted or otherwise done away with two of his cases of medicinal tonics and has sold the rest in a manner incompatible with the public auction he had announced—and, indeed, required by 19 U.S.C.A. § 1491, above cited, and the Treasury Regulations promulgated under it, formerly 19 CFR 18.7–18.12, now 19 CFR 20.5, 8 Fed. Reg. 8407, 8408, June 19, 1943. As to this latter claim, it may be that the collector's only error is a failure to collect an additional ten dollars from the Springdale Distilling Company; but giving the plaintiff the benefit of reasonable intendments in his allegations (as we must on this motion), the claim appears to be in effect that he was actually the first bidder at the price for which they were sold, and hence was entitled to the merchandise. Of course, defendant did not need to move on the complaint alone; he could have disclosed the facts from his point of view, in advance of a trial if he chose, by asking for a pre-trial hearing or by moving for a summary judgment with supporting affidavits. But, as it stands, we do not see how the plaintiff may properly be deprived of his day in court to show what he obviously so firmly believes and what for present purposes defendant must be taken as admitting. . . . In view of plaintiff's limited ability to write and speak English, it will be difficult for the District Court to arrive at justice unless he consents to receive legal assistance in the presentation of his case. The record indicates that he refused further help from a lawyer suggested by the court, and his brief (which was a recital of facts, rather than an argument of law) shows distrust of a lawyer of standing at this bar. It is the plaintiff's privilege to decline all legal help, United States v. Mitchell, 2 Cir., 137 F.2d 1006, 1010, 1011; but we fear that he will be indeed ill advised to attempt to meet a motion for summary judgment or other similar presentation of the merits without competent advice and assistance.

Judgment is reversed and the action is remanded for further proceedings not inconsistent with this opinion.

Questions

1. Dioguardi's "home drawn" complaint, though inartistic, contained ample allegations of "facts". Does it appear from the extracts reprinted in the opinion, that he stated "material, ultimate facts" as required in code pleading? [See text p. 170 *supra* at fn. 1] What determines whether or not the facts pleaded are material facts? How would the United States Attorney determine whether or not the facts pleaded are material facts? How would the trial judge determine whether or not the facts pleaded were material facts?

2. Does it appear to you that Dioguardi's pleading provided ". . . a short and plain statement of the claim showing that the pleader is entitled to relief, . . ." as required by Rule 8(a) FRCP? How would the defense attorney or the trial judge determine whether or not Dioguardi has stated a "claim" showing that he is "entitled to relief"?

3. How did Judge Clark determine that Dioguardi had satisfied Rule 8(a), and how do you suppose Judge Clark gathered the information upon which he based that determination?

4. Did the United States Attorney act reasonably, in your opinion, when he moved for dismissal of the complaint in this case? Did the District Court Judge act reasonably, in your opinion, in dismissing the complaint in this case?

5. Does it appear that the facts in Dioguardi's complaint were "categorized facts"? Did Judge Clark categorize the facts in Dioguardi's complaint? If Dioguardi had hired a lawyer, do you suppose the lawyer would have categorized Dioguardi's facts when drafting the complaint?

Fortified by his victory in the Circuit Court and unmindful of Judge Clark's advice that he obtain the assistance of counsel, Dioguardi persisted with his suit against Durning. A trial was held after which the complaint was dismissed. Dioguardi appealed to the Circuit Court demanding reversal of the judgment.

DIOGUARDI v. DURNING

United States Court of Appeals, Second Circuit, 1945.
151 F.2d 501.

PER CURIAM.   .   .   .   [Dioguardi] appeals upon a record showing that he has had a fair and complete trial, after which the District Court has found upon substantial evidence   .   .   .   that the goods destroyed were done so according to law when they showed signs of spoiling and that the bid accepted was actually the highest bid received.   .   .   .   On plaintiff's own showing and the facts now of record, it is clear that his lively sense of injustice is not properly directed against the customs officials, and that his grievance is against his vendors in Italy, whose charges against the goods he refused to pay at the outset, thereby precipitating the chain of events leading to the present futile suit.

Judgment affirmed.

Question

Does the subsequent history of Dioguardi v. Durning demonstrate that the Circuit Court's first opinion in the case was wrong?

SECTION 7.3   INCONSISTENT PLEADINGS AND
SHAM PLEADINGS

Rule 8(e)(2) of the Federal Rules expressly provides that "A party may set forth two or more statements of a claim or defense alternately or hypothetically   .   .   .   A party may also state as many separate claims or defenses as he has regardless of consistency . . . All statements shall be made subject to the obligations set forth in Rule 11."

Rule 11 states: "Every pleading of a party represented by an attorney shall be signed by at least one attorney of record in his individual name, whose address shall be stated. A party who is not represented by an attorney shall sign his pleading and state his address. . . . The signature of an attorney constitutes a certificate by him that he has read the pleading; that to the best of his knowledge, information, and belief there is good ground to support it; and that it is not interposed for delay. If a pleading is not signed or is signed with intent to defeat the purpose of this rule, it may be stricken as sham and false and the action may proceed as though the pleading had not been served. For a wilful violation of this rule an attorney may be subjected to appropriate disciplinary action. Similar action may be taken if scandalous or indecent matter is inserted."

In connection with these two rules Professors Field and Kaplan recall the famous, if legendary, Case of the Kettle.[1] "The plaintiff claimed damages for a kettle which he asserted that the defendant had borrowed from him and allowed to become cracked while it was in his possession. The defendant was supposed to have pleaded (1) that he did not borrow the kettle, (2) that it was never cracked, and (3) that it was cracked when he borrowed it."

Notes and Questions

1. Would or should this pleading be possible today under the Federal Rules of Civil Procedure?

2. Was the lawyer in the Kettle case a liar? Consider the following passage taken from Felix S. Cohen, "Field Theory and Judicial Logic," 59 Yale Law Journal 238 (1949):

Are Lawyers Liars?

Anyone who has read the statement of facts in a large number of briefs of appellants and appellees is likely to conclude that any resemblances between opposing accounts of the same facts are purely fortuitous and unintentional. The impression that opposing lawyers seldom agree on the facts is strengthened if one listens to opposing counsel in almost any trial. Now, as a matter of simple logic, two inconsistent statements cannot both be true. At least *one* must be false. And it is always possible that *both* are false, as, for example, when the plaintiff's attorney says the defendant speeded into the zone of the accident at sixty miles an hour and the defendant's counsel insists his client was jogging along at twenty miles an hour, while, in fact, he was moving at forty miles an hour. Thus, a logician may conclude that either (1) at least half of our practicing lawyers utter falsehoods whenever they open their mouths or fountain

1. Richard H. Field and Benjamin Kaplan, Materials for a Basic Course in Civil Procedure (Brooklyn, N. Y., 1953), p. 21.

pens, or (2) that a substantial majority of practicing lawyers utter false-hoods on a substantial number of such occasions. If we define a liar as a person who frequently utters such falsehoods, it would seem to follow logically that most lawyers are liars.

How the edifice of justice can be supported by the efforts of liars at the bar and ex-liars on the bench is one of the paradoxes of legal logic which the man in the street has never solved. The bitter sketch of "Two Lawyers" by Daumier still expresses the accepted public view of the legal profession. So, too, does the oft-told story of Satan's refusal to mend the party wall between Heaven and Hell when it was his turn to do so, of St. Peter's fruitless protests and threats to bring suit, and of Satan's crushing comeback: "Where do you think you will find a lawyer?"

Of course, lawyers know that the popular opinion on these subjects is inaccurate. Lawyers have ample opportunity to know how earnestly two litigants will swear to inconsistent accounts of a single event. Lawyers thus have special opportunities to learn what many logicians have not yet recognized: that truth on earth is a matter of degree, and that, whatever may be the case in Heaven, a terrestrial major league batting average above .300 is nothing to be sneezed at.

The difference between the lawyer's and the logician's view of truth is worth more attention than it has had from either lawyers or logicians.

From the standpoint of rigorous logic, a proposition is either true or false. There is no middle ground. A statement such as "It is raining," which is true at one time and place and not at another, is ambiguous, and an ambiguous sentence is not a proposition, though each of its possible meanings may constitute a proposition. Indeed, the characteristic of being either true or false is commonly utilized in modern logic as the defining characteristic of propositions.

Life, unfortunately, is not so simple. Logicians may define proposi-tions, but whether they can find or create propositions is another matter. Even if we convince ourselves that there *are* propositions, it does not necessarily follow that we can actually create them or find them; we may convince ourselves that there is, somewhere, an oldest man on earth, without ever being sure who he is.

3.   Two propositions are inconsistent if they are so related that both of them cannot be true. If the three pleas in the Kettle case are propositions (see Cohen's definition of a proposition *supra*) then they are obviously inconsistent. But is it proper to treat statements in the pleadings as asserting propositions? Would it not be equally proper to treat the pleadings as raising questions which are to be resolved in court?

4.   "A question is really an ambiguous proposition; the answer is its determination." Felix S. Cohen, "What is a Question?", 39 The Monist 350–364 (1929).

Can you think of any reason why a lawyer, as advocate, might phrase a question in such a way that it appears to be a proposition?

5.   It should not be forgotten that even in the preliminary prep-aration of a case for trial the participants are engaged in an adversary

process in which the lawyer must function in the role of advocate. Consider the following admonition to young attorneys. (Quoted in full from Trial Techniques by Irving Goldstein, p. 123, published by Callaghan & Company, 6141 North Cicero Ave., Chicago, Illinois, 60646.)

"It has been found that attorneys are in the habit of making too many motions to strike pleadings. It seems as though their first impulse upon the examination of an opponent's pleading is to rush into court on a motion to strike. In most instances, this is a grave error. Motions to strike should never be made unless the object to be gained far overshadows the harm that may be done. An impulsive ill-considered motion to strike will only result in a harmful education of the opponent. He may have improperly or imperfectly pleaded his cause of action or his defense, but an improvident motion to strike will educate him to a realization of the defects and also teach him, as a result of the argument of the motion, just how to remedy the defects. He proceeds to do so by filing an amended pleading. Far greater harm than just a waste of time may result, however. During the argument on the motion before the Court, there is usually some discussion as to the facts involved in the case, the elements to be proved, the method of proof, with the citation of authorities, and an argument on the law involved. In a short while the maker of the motion to strike begins to realize that not only has he educated his opponent on the intricacies of proper leading, but he has awakened his opponent to the necessity of really preparing his case for trial. In all probabilities, by this time the trial attorney has so displayed his 'hand' that the opponent for the first time really realizes just what he must meet .   .   .   In other words the 'sleeping lion' has been aroused . . .   He may then so thoroughly prepare himself for trial that it will result in his winning the case. This happens so frequently that it is a pretty good rule to usually decide against the impulse to make a motion to strike."

Is this advice outmoded by the Federal Rules of Civil Procedure?

SECTION 7.4 SUPPLEMENTING THE PLEADINGS: DEPOSITIONS AND DISCOVERY

By generally excluding replies, the Federal Rules leave the issues to be decided on trial much less sharply narrowed and defined than under the older system of pleading. On the other hand, the Federal Rules also establish a much more elaborate system of discovering the facts and of simplifying the issues in advance of trial. The system of pleading must be understood in relation to the system of eliciting information prior to trial by means of depositions and discovery and to the system of simplifying the issues through a pre-trial conference.

After all the pleadings are filed, each side prepares its case for trial. The lawyer for each party talks with the witnesses, collects documents and other things which he or she may need to present as evidence, and in general digs up—or hires an investigator to dig up—both the facts upon which he or she may rely at the trial and the facts upon which his or her opponent may rely and with which he or she must therefore be prepared to deal.

Under the old-fashioned combat theory of trial procedure neither side is bound in any way to help the other prepare its case, and indeed strictest secrecy may be maintained in each camp. Only at the trial may an adverse party, or a person friendly to an adverse party, be compelled by subpoena to give testimony or surrender papers or other evidence. This system gives unjustified advantage to the side with the cleverer lawyer or the wider facilities for investigation.

In recent decades means have been provided to reduce the element of secrecy prior to trial by enabling each party, subject to certain safeguards, to question the other, or the other's witnesses, under oath, to compel the production of books or documents or other tangible things in the control of others, to permit entry onto land or other property for purposes of inspecting or measuring or photographing objects of relevance to the lawsuit, and to compel the other party in proper cases to submit to a physical or mental examination by a physician.

Under the Federal Rules of Civil Procedure, "Any party may take the testimony of any person, including a party, by deposition upon oral examination or with written interrogatories for the purpose of discovery or for use as evidence in the action or for both purposes . . . The attendance of witnesses may be compelled by the use of subpoena . . . " (Rule 26(a)). Further, "the deponent may be examined regarding any matter, not privileged, which is relevant to the subject matter involved in the pending action . . . " (Rule 26(b)).

Upon oral examination the deponent is interrogated by counsel for the other party or parties. A stenographer takes down the questions and answers. The testimony is given under oath administered by a person who presides over the taking of the deposition. In the case of written interrogatories, the answers need not be returned until 15 days, and there is no opportunity for cross-examination.

"There are many reasons why a party may wish to take a deposition," write Professors Field and Kaplan.[1] "We shall suggest a few of the possibilities.

"1. He may have a witness with whose story he is fully familiar so there is no occasion to 'discover' it. But the witness may be old and likely to die before trial, or he may be young and about to join the armed forces, or for some other reason there is a danger that he may be unavailable to testify at the trial. A deposition

---

1. Richard H. Field and Benjamin Kaplan, Materials for a Basic Course in Civil Procedure (Brooklyn, N.Y., 1953), pp. 50–51.

will serve to record his testimony and, as we shall see, it may be used at trial upon a proper showing that the witness is unavailable.

"2.　He may be left genuinely in the dark by his adversary's pleadings and want to take his deposition to uncover the nature of the claim or defense which he must be prepared to meet at trial.

"3.　He may hope that he can by a deposition expose a fatal weakness in his adversary's claim or defense and thus be able to avoid a trial altogether by a motion for 'summary judgment.'

.　.　.

"4.　He may know enough of what the story of his adversary or some other witness will be for purposes of his own preparation. But he nevertheless may want a deposition to pin the witness down by sworn testimony well in advance of trial.　If, as sometimes happens, the story told at trial is different, the deposition may be used to discredit the witness.

"5.　He may know or suspect that his adversary or some other person has information which would aid him in his own investigation and preparation for trial.　The test of relevance for the purpose of the deposition is broad.　It is possible to elicit on deposition testimony which would not be admissible at the trial, so long as it 'appears reasonably calculated to lead to the discovery of admissible evidence.'　(Rule 26(b)).　Thus a deponent may be required to reveal the names and addresses of other witnesses.　He may also be required to recount what he has been told by them, even though, as we shall learn shortly, such a second-hand story would at trial run afoul of the rule excluding hearsay evidence."

SECTION 8.　PRE–TRIAL CONFERENCES: FORMULATING THE ISSUES

FEDERAL RULES OF CIVIL PROCEDURE

Rule 16

Pretrial Procedure; Formulating Issues.　In any action, the court may in its discretion direct the attorneys for the parties to appear before it for a conference to consider

(1) The simplification of the issues;

(2) The necessity or desirability of amendments to the pleadings;

(3) The possibility of obtaining admissions of fact and of documents which will avoid unnecessary proof;

(4) The limitation of the number of expert witnesses;

(5) The advisability of a preliminary reference of issues to a master for findings to be used as evidence when the trial is to be by jury;

(6) Such other matters as may aid in the disposition of the action.

The court shall make an order which recites the action taken at the conference, the amendments allowed to the pleadings, and the agreements made by the parties as to any of the matters considered, and which limits the issues for trial to those not disposed of by admissions or agreements of counsel; and such order when entered controls the subsequent course of the action, unless modified at the trial to prevent manifest injustice. The court in its discretion may establish by rule a pre-trial calendar on which actions may be placed for consideration as above provided and may either confine the calendar to jury actions or to non-jury actions or extend it to all actions.

The following is a report of a mock pre-trial conference held for the instruction of lawyers in the courtroom of the United States Court of Appeals for the District of Columbia, September 20, 1950, as reported in Federal Rules Decisions, Vol. 11, p. 15 ff. (1952).]

BROWN v. MUNICIPAL TRANSIT CO.

Alexander Holtzoff, Judge, United States District Court for the District of Columbia, and a supporting cast of members of the District of Columbia Bar:

The Court: The case of Brown v. Municipal Transit Company.

Mr. Horning: Ready for the defendant.

Mr. Bulman: Ready for the plaintiff.

The Court: Mr. Joseph Bulman appears for the plaintiff; and Mr. George Horning, for the defendant.

Mr. Bulman, will you state your case, please?

Mr. Bulman: If it please the court: This is Civil Action 500–50. This is a case wherein Morris Brown and Nancy Brown, his wife, are the plaintiffs, and the Municipal Transit Company is the defendant.

This accident, as Your Honor will note from the complaint, occurred on September 14, 1949. Morris Brown, the operator and owner of the car, was operating his automobile in a westerly direction on Nebraska Avenue, Northwest, and with him at the time was his wife, Nancy, who is a plaintiff.

At the corner—I am sure Your Honor is familiar with it—there are traffic lights, and they were in operation at that particular time. This accident happened at 3 p. m. The weather was clear. It is our contention that Mr. Brown, in the operation of his automobile, entered the intersection with the go, or green, light, and that before he was able to cross the intersection he was struck by a Municipal Transit Company bus which was being operated in a northerly direction.

Our allegations of negligence are that the operator of the bus was negligent in that he failed to keep a proper lookout, failed to apply his brakes, he violated the traffic regulations then and there in operation, and specifically he failed to observe the red light.

The Court: (Dictating to pretrial typist) Action for personal injuries and property damage.

Plaintiff No. 1 was the owner and driver of an automobile in which Plaintiff No. 2, his wife, was a passenger.

Plaintiffs claim that the automobile was proceeding westerly on Nebraska Avenue and was struck by defendant's bus proceeding northerly on Connecticut Avenue, the collision taking place in the intersection between Nebraska and Connecticut Avenues.

Plaintiffs claim that the automobile was crossing on a green light and that the bus ran against a red light.

Mr. Horning, what is the defense?

Mr. Horning: This is a rather unusual negligence case if it please Your Honor. We have a number of defenses and include also a counterclaim.

The Court: Well, do you admit that the collision took place in the intersection?

Mr. Horning: I do, sir, but not in the manner in which the plaintiffs claim.

The Court: (Dictating to pretrial typist) Defendant admits that the collision took place in the intersection.

Mr. Horning: We maintain that the bus was proceeding in a northerly direction, on this wide highway—Connecticut Avenue—and that it entered the intersection with the green light for it; that the automobile of the plaintiff Morris Brown, in which his wife was a passenger, was proceeding as alleged, in a westerly direction along Nebraska Avenue, but that it entered the intersection on a red light and struck the bus on the right front of the bus at about the number one door.

So we claim, first of all, a general denial of the allegations of negligence asserted.

Secondly, as far as Morris Brown, the owner of the automobile is concerned, we claim that the accident occurred solely and entirely due to his negligence; or, in the alternative, certainly to his contributory negligence. Of course, that would not bar any recovery by his wife, but here is where the unusual aspects of this case come in.

The Court: Before you proceed, suppose we get the issues as far as you have stated them.

(Dictating to pretrial typist) Defendant claims that the automobile ran through a red light; that the bus was proceeding on a green light and that the collision was due to the sole negligence of plaintiff No. 1, or, in the alternative, that plaintiff No. 1 was guilty of contributory negligence.

Mr. Horning: As far as plaintiff No. 2 is concerned, we assert two principal defenses: First, that she assumed the risk of injury and damage in riding in her husband's automobile under the circumstances then existing; secondly, that they were on a joint venture, which made him the agent of her in the operation of the automobile, so as to preclude any recovery by her in either event.

Before coming to this pretrial, we took depositions of both plaintiffs, and we learned these facts therefrom: that these parties had been to a cocktail party. The accident did not occur, as my friend says, at 3 p. m., but it occurred, our evidence will show conclusively, in the neighborhood of 6 o'clock. They had been to this cocktail party and to the knowledge of Mrs. Brown she saw her husband imbibing quite freely in intoxicating liquor. We do not claim, of course, that he was so intoxicated that he could not operate his car, but under the facts and circumstances his judgment was certainly impaired.

In addition to that, we say that by reason of those facts and circumstances, her attendance at this party, knowing that he was imbibing in intoxicating liquor that was sufficient in quantity to impair his judgment, she assumed any risk of injury and damage while riding in the car with him as driver under those conditions.

The pretrial deposition further shows that this accident occurred at an intersection which is not on a direct route at all from the scene of the cocktail party to their home over in Southeast Washington; in fact, it was in the opposite direction; and the reason they were going along the route that they were then following was that she was anxious to get to Woodward & Lothrop's department store at Nebraska and Wisconsin Avenues, about a mile west of this location, before that store closed at 6 o'clock, in order that she might pick up some purchases which she had made in the morning and left for alteration.

In view of that situation, we claim that the husband was driving the automobile then with her on a joint enterprise, on a mission for her, so he was her agent.

Now, another defense is asserted, and that is—

The Court: Suppose we get this put down in the pretrial order before you proceed.

(Dictating to pretrial typist) Defendant claims that plaintiff No. 1 had imbibed intoxicating liquor shortly prior to the accident and that plaintiff No. 2 was aware of that fact.

Defendant claims that plaintiff No. 2 assumed the risk of her husband's negligence.

Defendant further claims that the car was being driven on a mission for plaintiff No. 2 and that, therefore, the negligence of plaintiff No. 1 should be imputed to her.

Mr. Horning: That is correct, sir.

Another defense that we have is negative in character. As Your Honor well knows, that intersection is broad and the streets are wide.

The Court: I recall the intersection.

Mr. Horning: There is scarcely an excuse for an accident to occur there.

We assert that after the operator of the bus, on the proper green light and at the proper speed, had entered that intersection and had seen that automobile coming at a high rate of speed very close to the intersection and from his right—that when confronted with that sudden emergency he did everything in his power to bring his bus to a stop prior to the collision and was unable so to do.

The Court: (Dictating to pretrial typist) Defendant further claims that the bus driver made every effort to avoid the collision.

(Addressing counsel) Is that correct?

Mr. Horning: That is correct.

Then, on the aspects of our counterclaim, we have counterclaimed against Morris Brown for property damage to the bus as the result of the collision, in the sum of $295.25.

The Court: (Dictating to pretrial typist) Defendant counterclaims against plaintiff No. 1, for damages to the bus.

Mr. Bulman, what damages do you claim?

Mr. Bulman: If Your Honor please, on behalf of the plaintiff Nancy Brown, the wife in this case, we claim that as the result of this collision she sustained permanent injuries, consisting of a fractured left femur— Your Honor knows that that is the long bone in the leg—and also contusions and abrasions to her body; and, of course, she has made claim for nervous shock and mental anguish.

The Court: I want to segregate the permanent from the temporary injuries.

Mr. Bulman: The permanent injuries are the fractured left femur and a fracture of the pelvis.

The Court: (Dictating to pretrial typist) Plaintiff No. 2 claims permanent injuries to her left femur and pelvis.

Mr. Bulman: Your Honor, while I am on the subject of claims by the plaintiff Nancy Brown, I should like to have leave of the Court at this time to amend my complaint to include for loss of consortium by the husband of the wife.

Your Honor is familiar with the recent decision handed down by our Court of Appeals in the Hightower case, which was a momentous decision, in which the Court allowed damage to the wife on the claim for loss of consortium.

The Court: Yes. Is there any objection to granting leave to amend?

Mr. Horning: There certainly is, yes, as violent an objection as I can interpose. As Your Honor recalls, having read that decision, it just flew in the face of every decision from every State supreme court in the United States which was cited in the opinion. The Court of Appeals said it recognized that the law was 100 percent against it, but that it was creating this cause of action here because it felt that it was right and proper. In view of that situation, counsel who were involved in that case—and I have conferred with them—have applied to the Supreme Court of the United States for certiorari.

As Your Honor knows, the Supreme Court does not convene until October 1, and we shall then know whether certiorari will be granted. If granted, of course, the case will be reviewed. This seems to me to be a very late day for counsel to come into court and ask leave of the Court to institute a new cause of action when there can be no proper claim for it, and when we have already had her examined. He just waits until after the decision in the Hightower case and says, "I want to amend and ask for more money."

Our Court of Appeals is filled with decisions that the right of consortium is not a derivative action. It is something separate and distinct. I say the fair thing to do is not to complicate the issues in this case which are already sufficiently complicated, but to require the plaintiff to file a new suit, a suit as of today, and then by that time we will have had a decision from the Supreme Court, if it grants certiorari, which would mean that that case would either be tried or would not be tried. Certainly no damage or harm could result to the plaintiff Nancy Brown as the result of that action by the Court but harm and detriment could result to us and probably cause a mistrial of the whole thing, because this case will be tried, as Your Honor knows, shortly after court opens on the first Tuesday of October; in fact, it is right at the head of the list.

The Court: It seems to the Court that all the issues should be tried in the one action. The Court will grant leave to amend.

(Dictating to pretrial typist) Plaintiff No. 2 is granted leave to amend the complaint by asserting a claim for loss of consortium.

Mr. Horning: Specifically, Your Honor will note in the pretrial order that I have an exception to that ruling. It is necessary because I feel that no matter which way this case goes, it has got to go to the Court of Appeals.

The Court: (Dictating to pretrial typist) Defendant objects to this.

I suppose you also include various temporary injuries?

Mr. Bulman: Yes, but I am reminded by Mr. Horning, in his remarks to the Court, that this would increase the claim of Nancy Brown, and we are seeking more money. For that reason, having this additional claim, I ask leave of the Court to amend my *ad damnum* clause and to increase the amount from $15,000 to $20,000.

The Court: Yes, that follows as a matter of course. I will grant leave to amend.

Mr. Horning: In connection with this amendment Your Honor has just granted, do you wish at this time to take up the matter of physical examination in connection with the allegations of loss as claimed?

The Court: Yes. Obviously you are entitled to a further medical examination. Is there any objection to that?

Mr. Bulman: I think, Your Honor, if we pass to the next claim, Mr. Horning's demand of the Court might also include further examination. I have other elements here which I think the Court should be apprised of —and I will do so—in the claim of plaintiff number one, insofar as additional requests of the Court are concerned.

The Court: (Dictating to pretrial typist) Plaintiffs are granted leave to amend their complaint so as to increase the demand for damages to $20,000.

Defendant is granted the right to a medical examination of the plaintiffs on this additional issue.

Mr. Horning, this case will be reached for trial in about three weeks, so I think you should proceed to your additional medical examination right away, because failure to do so will not be a ground for a continuance.

Mr. Horning: I shall be very glad to do that, sir.

The Court: Does this complete the statement of the claim for damages of plaintiff No. 2?

Mr. Bulman: Yes.

The Court: How about plaintiff No. 1?

Mr. Bulman: Insofar as plaintiff number one is concerned, as the result of this accident he sustained a sacroiliac sprain and suffered a fracture of the skull and numerous bruises and contusions.

Of course, we are also making claim for property damage to his automobile.

The Court: Which of those injuries do you claim were permanent in their effect?

Mr. Bulman: We claim permanent effect to the spine, Your Honor, and also a fractured skull.

I might say this to the Court: Recently it has been brought to my attention that Mr. Brown, as the result of trauma that he has suffered as the result of this accident, has been suffering from arthritis, and I have obtained a statement from an eminent orthopedic surgeon to the effect that as the result of the blow that he sustained in this accident he has an aggravation of a preexisting arthritic condition. So for that reason I should like to include a claim for that at this time and ask leave of the Court to include that as an item of damage.

The Court: Is there any objection?

Mr. Horning: Yes. This, similarly, is another of those claims that comes at the last minute. I have already had him examined on the basis of injuries which I understood he was alleged to have sustained. Now he comes in with something new and different, so I am again compelled to ask Your Honor to grant us the right to have him examined by an arthritic specialist of our choice.

The Court: I think that is fair.

Mr. Bulman: We have no objection, Your Honor.

The Court: (Dictating to pretrial typist) Plaintiff No. 1 claims permanent injuries to his spine—

Is there anything else?

Mr. Bulman: To his spine and to his head, this arthritic condition.

The Court: (Continuing dictating) And an aggravation of his arthritic condition.

Mr. Horning: In that connection, Your Honor, may I also ask you to include that I will have the right to take his deposition again, strictly limited to these additional claims which he is now asserting?

The Court: (Dictating to pretrial typist) Defendant will have the right to a medical examination and to take the deposition of plaintiff No. 1 on the claim of aggravation of arthritic condition.

Plaintiff is granted leave to amend his complaint so as to embrace this additional claim.

Does that complete the statement of issues, gentlemen?

Mr. Bulman: It does, Your Honor.

The Court: It seems to me there ought to be a great deal that can be stipulated, so as to reduce the time to be taken by the Court at the trial. I presume it will be stipulated that plaintiff No. 1 was the owner and operator of the car and that plaintiff No. 2 was his wife?

Mr. Horning: Yes, sir.

The Court: (Dictating to pretrial typist) It is stipulated that plaintiff No. 1 was the owner and driver of the automobile and that plaintiff No. 2 was his wife and a passenger in the automobile.

Is there any dispute, gentlemen, as to whether this intersection was controlled by traffic lights and whether the traffic lights were in operation?

Mr. Bulman: No, Your Honor.

The Court: (Dictating to pretrial typist) It is stipulated that the intersection was controlled by traffic lights and that the traffic lights were in operation at the time of the collision.

Now, Mr. Bulman, have you any other suggestions as to what might be stipulated?

Mr. Bulman: Yes. I would like to have Mr. Horning stipulate that the traffic regulations which were applicable in this case may be admitted.

Mr. Horning: I shall be happy to do so.

The Court: (Dictating to pretrial typist) It is stipulated that the following evidence may be admitted without formal proof subject to objections as to relevancy and competency: (1) Traffic regulations.

Mr. Bulman: Your Honor, both of these plaintiffs were confined to the hospital for some period of time. I would like to have the hospital records stipulated subject to relevancy and competency.

The Court: Yes. Of course, under the Federal Shopbook Rule as construed in this jurisdiction, only routine records will be admissible, and not opinions that might be contained in the records.

Mr. Bulman: Yes, Your Honor.

The Court: Will it be agreeable to you to stipulate the hospital records, Mr. Horning?

Mr. Horning: No objection, Your Honor.

The Court: (Dictating to pretrial typist) (2) Hospital records, insofar as they are otherwise admissible.

Mr. Bulman: Your Honor, the plaintiff Morris Brown was employed by the United States Government. As the result of the injuries he was forced to take sick leave and annual leave. I have submitted to Mr. Horning a copy of a report from his immediate chief, and he has agreed with me that the amount of leave therein claimed will be stipulated.

Mr. Horning: That is correct, Your Honor.

The Court: (Dictating to pretrial typist) It is stipulated that plaintiff's Government leave records may be admitted in evidence without formal proof.

Shall we have them marked as exhibits?

Mr. Bulman: I think we can arrange that between ourselves, Your Honor.

The Court: Very well.

Mr. Bulman: I have here X-rays which were taken, and Mr. Horning has seen them. We would like to have Your Honor mark them.

The Court: Have you seen these X-rays, Mr. Horning?

Mr. Horning: Yes, I have, and I stipulate them.

The Court: (Dictating to pretrial typist) X-ray photographs which are being marked may be admitted in evidence without formal proof.

Mr. Bulman: Now, Your Honor, shortly after the accident a photograph was taken of the intersection, which shows the topography as well as weather conditions that then obtained there. I have the photograph, and I have shown it to Mr. Horning. It is understood that any vehicles thereon are not to be considered as evidence; the photograph shows merely the locale. I would like to have that photograph stipulated.

The Court: Is that agreeable to you, Mr. Horning?

Mr. Horning: It is.

The Court: If you will hand me the photograph, I shall mark it.

(Dictating to pretrial typist) It is stipulated that the photograph number 1, so marked, may be admitted in evidence without formal proof, merely for the purpose of showing the locale.

Mr. Bulman: Your Honor, also a photograph was taken of the vehicle that was involved—that is, the vehicle of the plaintiff—and I am merely asking Mr. Horning to stipulate that it is being offered to show where the point of impact took place rather than to show the damage that ensued as the result.

The Court: Is there any objection to that?

Mr. Horning: Well, I think he has me that time. Normally I would object to the introduction in evidence, as something to inflame the jury, of any picture of an automobile; but since he has claimed that it is limited to show only the point of impact, I will stipulate that and admit it subject to that strictly qualified limitation.

The Court: (Dictating to pretrial typist) It is stipulated that photograph number 2, which will be marked, may be admitted in evidence without formal proof, merely for the purpose of showing the point of impact.

Is there anything else?

Mr. Bulman: Yes, Your Honor. I am showing Mr. Horning a picture of plaintiff number one, which shows certain contusions and bruises about his head. I would like to have the picture in evidence to show what his condition was immediately after the accident, because those bruises have since disappeared. I ask Mr. Horning to stipulate as to that.

Mr. Horning: I could not so stipulate. First of all, at the time of trial I would object. I have never seen this before. I have never had an opportunity to check up as to what his condition was. At the time I took his deposition, he did not look anything like this. So I am afraid I cannot stipulate.

The Court: I think you will have to make proof of this item.

Mr. Bulman: May I ask Mr. Horning, if Your Honor please, whether he will require me to bring the photographer who took the picture, or whether he will put me to proof as to the plaintiff's condition?

Mr. Horning: I think you had better prove it in its entirety.

The Court: I think you had better prove the accuracy of the photograph. Of course, you do not have to have the photographer, if you have some other witness who can testify it is an accurate photograph of the condition that it purports to represent.

Mr. Bulman: If Your Honor please, I have here a weather report from the United States Weather Bureau, which sets forth the condition of the weather on that particular afternoon.

The Court: Will you stipulate that, Mr. Horning?

Mr. Horning: Yes, sir.

The Court: (Dictating to pretrial typist) It is stipulated that the Weather Bureau report, which is being marked may be admitted in evidence without formal proof.

Is there anything else, Mr. Bulman?

Mr. Bulman: I have a list of all the expenses that were incurred by the plaintiffs—hospital bills, doctor bills, and so forth—and I have furnished a list of those to Mr. Horning prior to the pretrial, but I have the actual bills here.

The Court: Will you look at these bills and see if you will stipulate to their introduction?

Mr. Horning: I have seen them, Your Honor. I am perfectly willing to stipulate to them and that they total $1,676, as set forth.

The Court: (Dictating to pretrial typist) It is stipulated that the medical and hospital bills which are being marked may be introduced in evidence without formal proof.

Mr. Bulman: I might say that Mr. Horning has run a tape on these bills.

Mr. Horning: I have to watch our dollars.

The Court: Is there anything further?

Mr. Bulman: We have a paid bill for the property damage in the amount of $457.25. I wonder if Mr. Horning will stipulate to that as the value of the repairs.

The Court: I think perhaps you ought to be able to stipulate as to the amount of property damage. Have you seen this bill?

Mr. Horning: Yes, I have seen the bill, and I will so stipulate, and also that it was a fair and reasonable cost of repair; but similarly I would ask him to stipulate as to the amount of the counterclaim for damage to the bus in the sum of $295.25, as alleged.

Mr. Bulman: We are so willing.

The Court: I think that is fair.

(Dictating to pretrial typist) It is stipulated that the cost of repairs to the automobile was $457.25 and that this was a reasonable cost.

It is further stipulated that the reasonable cost of repairs to the bus was $295.25.

Have you anything further?

Mr. Bulman: Your Honor, Mr. Horning and I have exchanged names and addresses of witnesses that both of us have—at least, at the time request was made. I would like to ask Mr. Horning at this time whether or not his claims department has turned up any additional witnesses since that list was made; and if so, I would like to have the names of those witnesses prior to trial.

Mr. Horning: No, we have no additional witnesses. I turned the list over to him. But we would similarly like to ask if he has found any additional witnesses on his behalf.

Mr. Bulman: We have found one additional witness, who we think will be important. I will furnish the name of that witness to Mr. Horning.

The Court: Mr. Horning, do you have any matters to suggest by way of stipulation?

Mr. Horning: Only one, and that is a plat of the intersection. I have had a plat prepared and have exhibited it to Mr. Bulman. I can assure Your Honor it is a transcript taken off the official city records and will show the locale and the traffic lights and their location and synchronization. I would like Mr. Bulman to stipulate to the admissibility of the plat.

The Court: Have you seen this, Mr. Bulman?

Mr. Bulman: Yes, Your Honor, I have, and I have no objection.

The Court: (Dictating to pretrial typist) It is stipulated that the plat which is being marked as Defendant's Exhibit 1 may be admitted in evidence without formal proof.

Is there anything further so far as the pretrial is concerned, gentlemen?

Mr. Bulman: I do not believe so.

The Court: I think we have eliminated a great deal of trial time by these stipulations.

Have you gentlemen explored the possibility of an adjustment of this matter?

Mr. Bulman: Your Honor, I have made demand upon the company since I have filed suit, but I am frank to admit that there has been no offer forthcoming.

Would Your Honor be interested in the amounts I claim for the respective plaintiffs?

The Court: I would be very glad to have you state what you are asking in compromise.

Mr. Bulman: Your Honor can see from the claims here that both plaintiffs suffered severe permanent injuries.

On behalf of the plaintiff Nancy Brown—that is, the wife—I ask $7,500. On behalf of the husband, I ask $9,500. I think those amounts are fair and reasonable in view of the fact that we have over $2,000 worth of special expenses and that medical care may continue in the future by reason of these permanent injuries. I think that is a very fair offer.

The Court: What do you say, Mr. Horning?

Mr. Horning: I am somewhat surprised at a settlement demand of $17,-000 which is now made, when during the negotiations for settlement prior to the suit, and even at the time of the taking of the deposition, my file indicates that Mr. Bulman was willing to settle those claims for $5,000. So at this time, when he comes up with a $17,000 offer, it seems that it puts us further apart than we ever were.

I might state to Your Honor that, as Your Honor knows, we have a board that appraises the value of these cases. The board carefully considered this case. We felt that there was not any liability at all; that our bus was being operated in a proper manner; that it had entered the intersection on a green light; and that it had the right-of-way. The automobile struck the bus at the right front door.

We have two passengers who were seated in the front of the bus, where they had a grandstand view of it, both of whom have given statements, and whose names and addresses I furnished to Mr. Bulman. I assume he has interviewed them. They substantiate the claim of the bus driver.

We have, on the other hand, Mr. Brown driving his automobile, certainly feeling gay from this cocktail party, at a high rate of speed, anxious to get to Woodward & Lothrop's, a mile away, before 6 o'clock, when it closed, and entering this wide intersection on a red light.

We feel in view of that situation that the case is one which should be tried. Of course, if Mr. Bulman were to come down to something more reasonable, I might resubmit it. In fact, at this time I might state to Your Honor that I would recommend that we forego our counterclaim of about $300 and perhaps pay, just as nuisance value, what it would cost us to try the case, in the neighborhood of $500, making a total out-of-pocket of around $800 as the result of the accident, rather than to try the case.

The Court: Well, the settlement value of a case like this, of course, depends on the extent to which there are disinterested witnesses to substantiate the claims of the parties. You say you have two passengers to support the contention that it was the plaintiff's car which ran through the red light.

Mr. Horning: Yes, Your Honor.

The Court: Have you any disinterested witnesses?

Mr. Bulman: Yes. First, I would invite the attention of the Court to the fact that the board which Mr. Horning speaks of is not a jury. They have proven wrong in the past. This is something Your Honor knows of. Secondly, I am rather amazed in this case that they have only two witnesses, because it was early in the afternoon, and the bus was fully loaded, and they show up with two witnesses.

I interviewed both of those witnesses and found they were seated somewhere about in the middle of the bus, and the bus was rather crowded, so I think their positions of observation were not any too good.

On the other hand, luckily for my clients, on that corner there is a gas station, and there was a gas station attendant there. He was not doing anything at the moment. He had a grandstand seat of this entire thing, and he tells us—and we have a statement from him—to the effect that our car entered on the green light, and he is positive.

I think, Your Honor, that that spells out a distinct question of fact to go to the jury. Because of that Your Honor, I do not think that our demands are so far fetched. They may be a little high, but I have never known the Municipal Transit Company to give me any more money than I have demanded. If Mr. Horning is willing to take it up with the company, I will be very happy to talk to my clients.

The Court: This is a case with disinterested witnesses on both sides. There is a conflict on a crucial issue. No one can tell what the outcome may be.

There is this about it, Mr. Horning. This is the kind of case where, if you get a verdict against you, it can be a very heavy verdict because of the nature of the injuries. As you know, juries in this jurisdiction have been giving very heavy verdicts if they decide for the plaintiffs and if there are serious permanent injuries.

But, of course, Mr. Bulman, it seems to me you run a very serious risk of having the jury decide for the defendant. It is one of those uncertain cases. It might go either way, depending on the impression made by the disinterested witnesses. It seems to me, under the circumstances, that it might behoove you to abate your demand somewhat.

Mr. Bulman: Your Honor, I do not feel we are taking any risk with a $500 offer.

The Court: No; I am sure Mr. Horning would be willing to pay considerably higher than that.

Mr. Horning: Well, it is $800, Your Honor, waiving the counterclaim.

Mr. Bulman: I am fully appreciative of the risks my clients entail in this case, Your Honor, but I am governed by the fact that they have in the neighborhood of $2,000 worth of out-of-pocket expenses.

Of course, Mr. Horning is not concerned with this, but the plaintiffs do have to pay me a fee, and the result is that what we get in settlement is not net to themselves.

However, if Mr. Horning is serious in trying to get this case out of the way, I think I would be willing to recommend $7,500 for both cases.

The Court: What do you say to that, Mr. Horning? I think that is more within the bounds of reason than the original demand.

Mr. Horning: As Your Honor knows, I have worked before you for a long time. You have helped us to settle many cases in pretrial. I would like to ask Your Honor what your candid view about the case is and what we should do.

The Court: Well, before I do that, I would like to know whether you are willing to go substantially higher than $800.

Mr. Horning: Yes, Your Honor; if Your Honor feels that it is a case we should settle, and should settle for more than that, I am willing.

The Court: It seems to me that this is a case where a fairly substantial settlement would be warranted, because you run a very serious risk of having a very heavy verdict against you if the plaintiff prevails, because of the nature of damages.

On the other hand, Mr. Bulman, I think that if the case is to be settled, the plaintiffs must be reasonable also. I recall there was a case tried before me not so long ago in which the plaintiffs rejected a substantial offer, and then the jury brought in a verdict for the defendant. I think your clients should bear that possibility in mind.

Mr. Bulman: That was not my case, Your Honor.

The Court: Would you be willing to pay $5,000, Mr. Horning?

Mr. Horning: Does Your Honor feel that that is fair and reasonable, in view of the circumstances?

The Court: I think it is. Of course, I am not trying to force my views on you, gentlemen. I do not have to repeat that you gentlemen are entitled to have a jury determine the issues. But in view of the fact that you invited my comments, it seems to me that $5,000 would be a reasonable amount to pay, because it would be insurance against a very heavy verdict. Would your client be willing to accept $5,000?

Mr. Bulman: Your Honor, I do not think they would go that low; but if Your Honor could manipulate his thoughts to the price of $6,000, we might be very much interested in that.

The Court: What do you say about that?

Mr. Horning: Of course, as Your Honor knows, I have great respect for Your Honor's judgment in these cases. You have wide experience in them. I will be happy to go back to my client and to the board and report what has transpired here today; and further, I will state to Your Honor that I will recommend settlement in the figure Your Honor has set. I trust we will be able to effect a settlement and avoid a lengthy trial.

The Court: Well, apparently we are only a thousand dollars apart at this moment.

What do you say about that?

Mr. Bulman: Your Honor, I will tell my clients Your Honor's view. They have great respect for the Court's view, more than for counsel's. If Your Honor thinks $5,000 is a reasonable sum, I am sure they will go along.

The Court: I think that is a reasonable sum, considering the possibilities of this case and its uncertainties.

Well, gentlemen, in the meantime, will you please sign the pretrial memorandum?

The case will go on the trial assignment and will be reached in about three weeks. But I hope you will come back and report within the next few days that you have settled this case for the amount we have tentatively agreed upon.

Notes and Questions

1. What are the express purposes of the pre-trial conference as stated in Rule 16 and as manifested in the case of Brown v. Municipal Transit Co.?

2. What are the implicit functions of the pre-trial conference as evidenced in the case of Brown v. Municipal Transit Co.?

3. Does it appear that the evidence known to each of the attorneys directly affected their choices of the legal categories they deemed

appropriate to the resolution of this case? Does it appear that the legal categories selected by the attorneys directly affected their view of the "facts" in the case? (Recall in this regard, question 2 p. 175 *supra.*)

4. Should the judge have urged a settlement upon the parties? Should he have introduced the question at all?

5. It has been generally assumed that the pre-trial conference is a highly desirable innovation in civil practice in that it both improves the quality of adjudication and increases the efficiency of the courts. Furthermore, the pre-trial conference has been viewed as a desirable means to encourage settlement prior to trial. Perhaps it is too much to expect that any one procedure can serve so many · ends. A study of the use of pre-trial conferences in New Jersey has suggested that this may be a valid reservation. A pertinent portion of the report from that study is set out below.

[The following is taken from MAURICE ROSENBERG,* THE PRETRIAL CONFERENCE AND EFFECTIVE JUSTICE (New York, 1964), pp. 113–116.]

Any procedure that saddles litigation with added costs in time, effort, and inevitably, money has the burden of showing that it yields more than it costs. The pretrial conference is no exception to that rule. If soundness in theory could discharge the burden of proof, pretrial would easily make the showing, satisfying all its critics save those who are hypersensitive about damage to the adversary tradition. But ideal theory is not the only test, and the fact that pretrial indisputably looks good on paper does not mean that it assuredly works well in the courtroom. In this study the effort has been to learn how much of value pretrial actually yields in practice, and primarily how well it does in gaining either or both of its major objectives—to improve the quality of the trial process, and to enhance the efficiency of court operations.

It is an article of faith with pretrial's supporters that a pretrial conference achieves both goals at once. Implicit in that conviction is the assumption that if a conference has done all it should to prepare the case for a good trial it will *ipso facto* have cultivated the ground for settlement. The idea that a proper pretrial conference is a two-in-one exercise is a meretricious yet tenacious one. It loses its attractiveness when examined closely in the light of the actual steps that should logically be taken for each of the purposes in question.

If one were to give names to the steps designed to achieve each purpose, one might say that the activities at pretrial that are calculated to promote a good quality litigation process by mapping the course of the proceedings en route to the trial courtroom and inside it are "trial oriented." Those mainly aimed at fostering efficiency by inducing compromise short of trial are "settlement oriented." It seems to us that each object calls for various sorts

---

* Maurice Rosenberg is Professor of Law
at Columbia University.

of actions by the judge and lawyers involved, that some of the actions are identical for both purposes but some are not, and that this means a single conference will not automatically do double duty. In large measure this is because there will be a change in what issues are relevant as the object of the conference changes. But even in dealing with the same issue or subject matter a judge might proceed by widely divergent paths depending on whether his object is to shape the case for trial or to ease its settlement. Let us look at the specifics of a personal injury pretrial.

In an accident case there are a half-dozen subjects that plainly ought to be treated whether the aim of the conference is to promote trial quality or to improve the chances for settlement. The nature of the action must be outlined. Factual contentions of each side as to how the accident happened should be explored for their bearing on issues of liability. The judge should try to draw from the attorneys any admissions and stipulations they will agree to. The plaintiff ought to make known what injuries and money damages he claims, and the defendant ought to make known his responses to the claims. Before the conference is over the lawyers should specify which, if any, law questions are still open for determination and state which have been abandoned.

Each of those items is important to understanding what the case is about and what is in dispute. Each seems indispensable, whatever the objective of the conference, and they can therefore be called "common" subjects or items.

Even so, wide variations are possible in the way in which the conference might endeavor to develop a common subject. For example, while in either event the judge ought to encourage a precise definition of the issues that are open, in a settlement conference it is not vital for the judge to make a decisive ruling that a particular question is an issue for trial; whereas he ought to do exactly that in a trial-oriented proceeding. Again, a settlement conference would be little concerned with having the attorneys prepare beforehand meticulous written statements as to their admissions, but a trial-oriented proceeding insists on it. In general, admissions, statements, and positions at a settlement conference can be tentative or hypothetical; but at a trial conference they must be exact and definitive. Thus, the end in view will shape the treatment of the subject matter.

Moreover, a trial-oriented conference when carefully conducted will include many steps that would have no place in a settlement conference. The court should insist that each side tender a precise formulation of its factual contentions, including the specific respect in which the plaintiff claims the defendant was negligent or in which the defendant claims the plaintiff was contributorily negligent. The pleadings should, if necessary, be formally amended to add, drop, or modify allegations to reflect the litigants' current posture. Legal issues remaining open should be formulated word-for-word, to leave no ambiguities as to the parties' positions, much as if the judge were devising instructions for the jury. The same care should feature the reduction of stipulations to writing. Exhibits should be marked in evidence when this can be done appropriately. Quite exact plans for trial should be made, including if possible setting a day, estimating its length, directing exchange of needed briefs, limiting the number of witnesses, and providing, in the case of experts, for advance exchange of summaries of their testimony. In a proper case, the judge should make dispositive rulings as, for instance, striking allegations unsupported by any suggestion of evidence, or granting partial summary judgment.[1] Actions such as those listed are essential predicates to a pretrial order definitively shaping a case for trial, but not for a settlement.

Conversely, a judge takes many steps to promote settlements that would be out of place in mapping a comprehensive plan for the future course of the litigation. For example, to brighten chances of settlement he should review prior efforts by the litigants to reach a compromise and then discuss the dollar value of particular items of injury and analyze the dollar gap between the amount the plaintiff demanded and the defendant offered. Very likely he should outline the risks to each side of various elements of liability and damage. Perhaps he should disclose his own reaction to the factual and legal issues presented. No doubt he should explore the costs to be anticipated if the case were to be litigated to the finish.

From the foregoing sampling it can be seen that many lines a judge should follow at a settlement conference would be irrelevant to an orderly trial, and some might be actively prejudicial. In a one-judge county, for instance, there would be the problem of who should preside at the trial of a case in which the judge at pretrial had indicated his belief that the plaintiff's damage claims were much exaggerated or that a tendered defense was sham or dubious.

That sketch of some of the differences in content and emphasis in the two types of conferences is not an analysis that will be found in existing pretrial rules or manuals. Generally, they draw no distinctions because they are based on the two-in-one credo. The analysis is intended to suggest that if rationally performed, the steps at a pretrial conference will be responsive to previously stated ends.

Question

Professor Rosenberg's research suggests that one form of process may not perform different functions equally well. Does that finding offer insights applicable to your evaluation of the Arnold and Fuller extracts *supra* at pp. 110, 113?

---

1. [When it appears from the pleadings and the preliminary proceedings that there is no dispute as to the facts, the judge may, on motion, grant a judgment in accordance with the law applicable to the undisputed facts. This is the so-called summary judgment.]

Chapter 3

CRIMINAL PROCEDURE PRIOR TO TRIAL

Preceding sections of the book have adverted to distinctions between civil and criminal law. We have seen that criminal law deals primarily with acts which are deemed so reprehensible and disruptive of social order that the state may prosecute and seek to punish persons who commit them. We have seen further that the competence and jurisdiction of courts in criminal actions is somewhat different from their competence and jurisdiction in civil cases. The following materials should extend the student's comprehension of the similarities and differences between civil and criminal law—both in their objectives and in their techniques—by affording some opportunity to compare and contrast procedure prior to trial in criminal cases with procedure prior to trial in civil cases. Such comparison and contrast should shed additional light on the crucial role of procedure (and in a slightly broader sense, process) as the matrix within which substantive rights and duties are defined.

In considering pre-trial procedure in criminal cases, we shall pay special attention to relationships between the judicial process and the less formal processes of the police and the prosecutor. Two central questions will emerge in this inquiry: (1) As a matter of principle, should judges attempt to regulate those phases of the criminal process which are conducted by police and prosecutor; (2) As a matter of practice, can judges effectively regulate those phases of the criminal process?

SECTION 9. CRIMINAL JUSTICE IN AMERICA: PRELIMINARY OBSERVATIONS

[The following is taken from LIVINGSTON HALL,* YALE KAMISAR,** JERROLD ISRAEL,† and WAYNE LA FAVE,†† MODERN CRIMINAL PROCEDURE (St. Paul, Minn. 1969), pp. 3, 8–12. Some footnotes omitted; others are renumbered.]

* Professor, Harvard University Law School.

** Professor, University of Michigan Law School.

† Professor, University of Michigan Law School.

†† Professor, University of Illinois College of Law.

THE STEPS IN THE CRIMINAL PROCESS

It should be emphasized that criminal procedure varies not only from state to state, but often from locality to locality within a state. In particular, practices followed in rural or semi-rural communities are often different from those utilized in metropolitan areas. Also, the basic procedural steps depend to some extent upon the level of the charged offense, i. e., whether a misdemeanor or felony. The following description concentrates upon felony prosecutions in metropolitan courts.

1. *Pre-arrest Investigation.* Police investigation of a specific crime may be instituted in various ways, including a citizen's complaint, an observation in the course of patrolling, or an informant's "tip." The most common techniques of investigation include observation at the scene of the crime and interviews with witnesses. In some areas, e. g., vice crimes, police frequently employ other, more "aggressive" methods of investigation, such as the use of undercover agents or continuous surveillance.

Sooner or later, the police will contact a suspected offender. Of course, where the officer acts upon the basis of direct observation at the scene of the crime, this may be the first step taken. Most police-suspect encounters do not involve arrests. By "arrest" we refer to the act of taking a person into custody (i. e., transporting him to the station) for the purpose of charging him with a crime. Irrespective of its validity as a legal definition, this is the definition used in most statistical surveys, and therefore will be used here.

Most police-suspect encounters involve temporary detention, often lasting less than five minutes. Based on available figures, it seems likely that the number of annual police-suspect encounters in a city the size of Chicago exceeds one million (excluding traffic offense encounters). The vast majority of these encounters, possibly 85%, will relate only to possible misdemeanors. Most occur on the street, but a substantial number take place at a home or place of business. Recent studies indicate that, in about one-third of their encounters with suspects, patrolmen engage in "questioning of a probing nature that goes beyond mere identification of the person and that [leads] to defining the person as a suspect or offender." In about one out of every five encounters, at least in high crime areas, the officer will engage in some form of search. In most circumstances this will be a search of the person (often a "frisking"), although approximately 15% of the searches involve an inspection of a vehicle or home. On rare occasions, the officer might have previously obtained a search warrant from a magistrate's court. Ordinarily, however, the officer will seek to search on the basis of the suspect's consent, or the search will be accompanied by an arrest. Thus, less than 150 search warrants will be issued in a major city, such as Detroit, during an entire year.

2. *The Arrest.* Only 10–15% of all police-suspect encounters will result in arrests. The total number of arrests in a city of two million will approach 100,000 per year (excluding traffic offenses).[1] The number of ar-

I. This does not include arrests of juveniles which constitute a substantial portion of the total arrests, particularly in the felony range. For example, Chicago in 1964 reported 50,-000 arrests of persons under 18 out

rests may vary considerably from city to city according to police policy in dealing with drunkenness. Where all drunks are regularly arrested, they may account for 30–50% of all arrests. In any event, only a small percentage of arrests, ranging from 10–25%, are based on probable felony charges.

In a limited number of situations, e. g., where the suspect's whereabouts were previously unknown, an arrest may be based upon a warrant issued by the local magistrates' court. Ordinarily, however, arrests are made without a warrant, and the decision to arrest is made by the individual officer at the point of contact with the suspect. Occasionally, the officer will confer, typically by radio, with a superior at the precinct or district headquarters before making an arrest.

Arresting officers commonly exercise considerable discretion in determining whether to make an arrest. Quite frequently, in situations involving minor misdemeanors, e. g., assault, an officer may refuse to make an arrest even though the offense was committed in his presence. On the other hand, in felony situations, the officer will usually make an arrest if he believes he has sufficient grounds. Even here, however, there are certain exceptions, e. g., statutory rape.

3. *"Booking."* The suspected offender will usually be "booked" shortly after his arrival at the precinct or district station. Booking is essentially a clerical process, involving nothing more than an entry on the police "blotter" or arrest book indicating the suspect's name, the time of the arrest and the offense involved. Depending upon the severity of the offense, the suspect may be fingerprinted, photographed and requested to supply a handwriting sample. Not all persons brought to the station are detained for possible prosecution. In some instances, the "desk sergeant" or precinct duty officer may decide that the arresting officer does not have sufficient evidence to detain the suspect or that the offense involved (usually a misdemeanor) does not call for prosecution. In the latter situation, there frequently may be some sort of "station house adjustment," e. g., a participant in a fight may be "handed over" to his wife after a proper lecture. Persons may also be released after in-station interrogation establishes that no crime was committed. Thus, police frequently find that forcible rape charges, or charges of attempted forcible entry involving relatives, are baseless. In some jurisdictions, where the booking process is delayed, these persons will never be booked. In others, they are first booked and then released, often with no further notation than "insufficient evidence."

4. *The Decision to Prosecute.* After the suspect is booked, a report of the offense, based chiefly on the arresting officer's report, is made to a member of the prosecutor's staff. In cases where considerable investigation preceded the arrest, the prosecutor may have been consulted previously. Ordinarily, however, this is the prosecutor's first contact with the case, and, at this point, he decides whether the defendant should be charged with an offense. In making this decision the prosecutor may consider various factors including the weight of the evidence, the nature of the crime, the nature of the defendant, and the alternative remedies available.

The prosecutor will decide against charging in a substantial number of cases. Not infrequently, 30–50% of the persons arrested in a major city

of a total of 255,000 arrests. Of the 35,000 arrests related to what FBI characterizes as Class I (more serious) crimes, 16,000 involved persons under 18.

on felony and misdemeanor charges are not prosecuted. It is frequently impossible, however, to determine how many of these informal "dismissals" were made by the police and how many by the prosecutor. Generally, the smaller the community, the more likely the prosecutor will be consulted before dismissal of persons arrested on any significant charge. Available evidence indicates, however, that even in most major cities, the "dismissal" of felony suspects is primarily the responsibility of the prosecutor. Moreover, the felony dismissal rate often is only slightly less than the total dismissal rate (although it is not clear how many felonies are "converted" into misdemeanors at this stage).

If the prosecutor decides that a case has been made and it should be prosecuted, he prepares a complaint, identifying the defendant and specifying the charge against him. Depending upon the nature of the charge, the complaint will be signed either by the officer or the complaining witness. In some jurisdictions, the prosecutor proceeds solely on the complaint, but, in most, he must also obtain an arrest warrant, which serves as the basis for defendant's continued detention. The warrant is issued by a local magistrate on the basis of the complaint and is usually obtained immediately after the prosecutor makes the decision to charge.[2]

5. *The Initial Appearance or "Presentment".* Statutes in most states require that an arrested person be taken without unreasonable delay to the nearest local magistrate. In most major cities, the felony suspect will not be taken before the magistrate for at least several hours. The exact length of the delay depends upon various factors, such as: (1) the timing of the arrest, i. e., whether made at a time, e. g., Sunday, when neither magistrate nor prosecutor is readily available; (2) the desire of headquarter detectives to interrogate the suspect; and (3) the number of arrested persons presently being processed by the police. Quite frequently, a substantial portion of the persons arrested on felony charges, perhaps as many as 50%, are detained more than 12 hours before being presented before the magistrate.

When the defendant is presented, the magistrate informs him of the charges against him and his constitutional rights. This process is commonly termed the "arraignment on the warrant" although it is not technically an arraignment since no plea is made (see step 8, infra).[3] The mag-

---

2. The decision to prosecute in minor misdemeanor charges may be left almost entirely in the discretion of the police. In some jurisdictions, the police will draft the misdemeanor arrest warrant—if one is used—and the case will be prosecuted before the magistrate by a police officer. The prosecutor will only come into contact with the case if special problems arise or a conviction is later appealed.

3. Since the magistrate has jurisdiction to try misdemeanor cases, they are handled quite differently. The defendant will be asked to plead at his initial appearance. If he pleads guilty, as the great majority do, he often will be sentenced immediately. If he pleads not guilty, and the arresting officer is present, he will be tried immediately unless he requests a delay. In a city with a population of two million, the lower courts will dispose of approximately 25,000 non-traffic misdemeanors each year. [The figure may be considerably higher, depending upon prosecutor's policy in dealing with public drunkenness cases.]

About 5% of the misdemeanor cases will be dismissed by the prosecutor on his own motion. Of the remainder, 75–85% will plead guilty. Of the defendants who go to trial, 15–25% will be acquitted. Over 75% of these convicted (including both guilty pleas and trial convictions) will be fined and released or placed on probation.

istrate generally will inform the defendant of his right to have a preliminary examination and his right to be represented by counsel at the examination. If the defendant is indigent, many states will appoint counsel at this point—at least if the defendant requests a preliminary hearing. The majority of states, however, apparently do not appoint counsel prior to the formal arraignment on the information or indictment.

The magistrate also sets bail at the initial appearance.[4] Frequently, bail is determined by a set schedule which varies in amount according to the crime charged (i. e., the more serious the offense, the higher the bond). In other jurisdictions, the magistrate will make some attempt to evaluate each case individually, but the primary factor considered is still the nature of the offense. Ordinarily, the defendant will not post the security himself, but will obtain a bond from a bondsman at a cost of 10% of the face amount of the bond. Very frequently the defendant will not have sufficient funds to secure a bond. Although the proportion of persons who fail to make bail varies widely from place to place, several studies indicate that it frequently exceeds 50% of the felony defendants. However, various communities have recently experimented with bail reform projects designed to deemphasize the use of money bail. Recent federal and state legislation has sought to achieve the same end. As a result, most indigent defendants are able to obtain their release in an increasing number of metropolitan areas (though still a distinct minority).

6. *Preliminary Hearing.* The preliminary hearing is designed to protect against unwarranted prosecutions. At the hearing, the prosecutor must produce sufficient evidence to satisfy the magistrate that there is probable cause to believe the defendant committed a felony. Defendant may cross examine witnesses and introduce evidence in his own behalf, although very few defendants, especially if represented by counsel, go beyond cross-examination. If the magistrate finds probable cause, he will then "bind over" the defendant for trial before the court of general jurisdiction. Ordinarily, the magistrate refuses to "bind over" in only a small percentage of the cases before him. Moreover, in many jurisdictions, preliminary hearings are held in less than half of all cases. In some, defendants waive their right to a preliminary hearing in as many as 70% of all cases. In others, where the grand jury is utilized to screen prosecutions, the preliminary hearing ordinarily is not available if the grand jury indicts prior to the scheduled hearing. When preliminary hearings

The quality of trials before magistrates courts varies considerably according to the court. Some of the more common defects are described in Task Force Report: *The Courts* 30: "An observer in the lower criminal courts ordinarily sees a trial bearing little resemblance to those carried out under traditional notions of due process. There is usually no court reporter unless the defendant can afford to pay one. Also in some cities trials are conducted without counsel for either side; the case is prosecuted by a police officer and defended by the accused himself. One result is an informality in the proceedings which would not be toler-

ated in a felony trial. Rules of evidence are largely ignored. Speed is the watchword. Trials in misdemeanor cases may be over in a matter of 5, 10, or 15 minutes; they rarely last an hour even in relatively complicated cases."

4. In many jurisdictions, a person arrested on a minor misdemeanor charge may be released on bail by the police. The amount of such "station-house" bail is sometimes committed to police discretion, sometimes regulated by a schedule established by the magistrate, and sometimes set by statute.

are held, counsel frequently employ the hearing primarily as an informal discovery device, since formal discovery is considerably more restricted in criminal than in civil cases.

After the judge "binds over", the prosecutor will prepare the official accusation against the defendant. In some states the prosecutor can do this himself by preparing an information (a written accusation, signed by the prosecutor, and setting forth facts which charge the defendant with a criminal offense).

7. *Grand Jury Indictment.* In many jurisdictions, the decision to prosecute must be approved by a grand jury. This body ordinarily consists of 16 to 23 private citizens who meet behind closed doors to receive evidence presented by the prosecutor. The defendant has no right to offer his own evidence or to be present before the grand jury. If twelve of the grand jurors find that the prosecutor has established probable cause, the grand jury will issue an indictment (a written accusation, prepared by the prosecutor and signed by the grand jury, charging the defendant with the commission of a specified crime). In most jurisdictions, the grand jury refuses to indict in only a small percentage of cases.

8. *Arraignment on the Information or Indictment.* Adding the limited screening of the grand jury and preliminary examination to that done by the police and prosecutor, the net result frequently is that only half of the persons arrested on felony charges will be formally charged with commission of a felony. Of course, that statistic varies somewhat among major cities. In some jurisdictions, the prosecutor screens more carefully before charges are filed; in others, the screening is performed later, usually after defense counsel has conferred with the prosecutor, and a substantial percentage of cases filed (e. g., 15–20%) are dismissed on the prosecutor's motion. In a city of two million, with fairly careful initial screening, approximately 4,000 felony charges will be filed in a single year.

After the indictment or information is filed, the defendant is arraigned. He is brought before the trial court, informed of the charges against him and the pleas he might enter (usually guilty, not guilty, and nolo contendere). If the defendant is indigent and counsel has not previously been appointed, that will be done at this point. Where defendant either waves counsel or previously had counsel, he will ordinarily enter his plea.

Putting aside the cases dismissed by the prosecutor on his own motion, approximately 70–80% of all the remaining defendants plead guilty. Ordinarily, this decision is based on negotiations between the prosecutor and the defense counsel, and defendants frequently plead guilty to lesser offenses than those originally charged.

9. *Pretrial Motions.* Assuming the defendant pleads "not guilty," various procedural objections are likely to be raised before trial. Ordinarily, objection to the sufficiency of indictment or information will be made even before the plea is entered. This is also true of objections based upon prior jeopardy, the statute of limitations, and the improper composition or irregular procedure of the grand jury. After the plea is entered, defendant may seek a change in venue (particularly in cases involving substantial publicity) or request the severance of his trial from that of a codefendant. While raising interesting legal questions, reported decisions indicate that these motions are made in only a small proportion of the cases

that go to trial. Motions relating to discovery, e. g., requests for a bill of particulars, are more common. Probable the most significant pretrial motion, at least in terms of its immediate impact on the dismissal rate, is the motion to suppress illegally obtained evidence. In certain types of cases, e. g., narcotics, such motions offer considerably better chance for a dismissal than possible acquittal at trial. A survey of a six-day period in Cook County revealed, for example, that motions to suppress were made in 41% of all narcotics cases and were successful in 75% of those cases. Where the motions were sustained, the cases were usually dismissed for lack of evidence.

10. *Trial.* Although the percentage of trials is small, the total number may be quite substantial. A court of general jurisdiction in a major city may have 700–800 criminal trials per year. This may account for 20–30% of all cases tried in that court.

Although felony defendants have a right to jury trial, a substantial number waive that right. The percentage of waiver varies considerably throughout the nation, but the national average is approximately 40%. Whether the case is tried by judge or jury, the statistical likelihood of gaining an acquittal is not very good. The acquittal rate for most major felonies is below 33%. The over-all acquittal rate for all felony trials in a major city may easily fall below 20%.

The trial itself resembles the civil trial in many respects. There are, however, several important distinctions (as well as certain common features that have special significance in the criminal case). These include (1) the presumption of innocence, (2) the requirement of proof beyond a reasonable doubt, (3) the right of the accused not to take the stand, (4) exclusion of evidence obtained by the state in an illegal manner, and (5) the more frequent use of defendant's admissions.

11. *Sentencing.* Ordinarily the judge has substantial discretion in determining the appropriate sentence. For most crimes, he has the alternative of imposing imprisonment or probation. Where imprisonment is selected, the legislature usually has set a maximum sentence, but not a minimum (although the minimum may be limited to a certain percentage of the maximum). Also, some states permit the judge to set a maximum within the statutory limit.

Sentencing patterns vary substantially even within the same state. The pattern in Detroit, however, is fairly typical for major metropolitan areas. Approximately 40% of the convicted defendants are placed on probation or given suspended sentences. Of those incarcerated, the vast majority are sentenced to the state maximum security prison, where the average time actually served is about two years.

12. *Appeals.* Approximately 20–40% of the defendants found guilty after trial appeal their convictions. The rate of reversals varies substantially, but it is not unusual for an appellate court to reverse in 20% of its criminal cases. Of course in many instances the defendant may be retried and subsequently convicted.

13. *Post-conviction Remedies.* Post-conviction remedies are very rarely successful although frequently utilized. In 1964, approximately 9% of the adult felony prisoners in federal institutions petitioned for col-

lateral relief. The percentage of state prisoners filing petitions is probably lower since collateral relief generally is more readily available in the federal system. However, the number of petitions from both state and federal prisoners has been steadily rising in the last several years.

[The following is taken from "THE CHALLENGE OF CRIME IN A FREE SOCIETY," Final Report of The President's Commission on Law Enforcement and the Administration of Justice, (Washington, D.C., 1967) pp. 7–8.]

A general view of The Criminal Justice System

This chart seeks to present a simple yet comprehensive view
of the movement of cases through the criminal justice system.
Procedures in individual jurisdictions may vary from the
pattern shown here. The differing weights of line indicate
the relative volumes of cases disposed of at various points
in the system, but this is only suggestive since no nationwide
data of this sort exists.

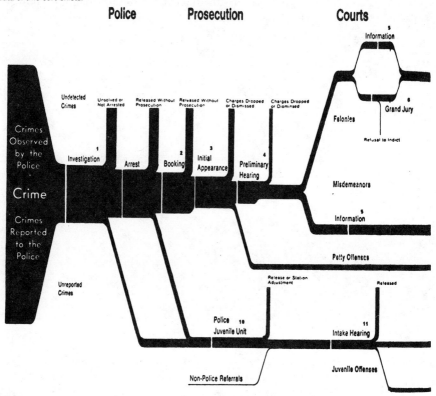

| **Police** | **Prosecution** | **Courts** |

1   May continue until trial.

2   Administrative record of arrest. First step at
    which temporary release on bail may be
    available.

3   Before magistrate, commissioner, or justice of
    peace. Formal notice of charge, advice of
    rights. Bail set. Summary trials for petty
    offenses usually conducted here without
    further processing.

4   Preliminary testing of evidence against
    defendant. Charge may be reduced. No
    separate preliminary hearing for misdemeanors
    in some systems.

5   Charge filed by prosecutor on basis of
    information submitted by police or citizens.
    Alternative to grand jury indictment; often
    used in felonies, almost always in
    misdemeanors.

6   Reviews whether Government evidence
    sufficient to justify trial. Some States have no
    grand jury system; others seldom use it.

[A4863]

Note

The preceding outline concentrates on the steps which may be
followed in the handling of major crimes, *i. e.*, felonies. It should be
noted however, that a large proportion (probably the majority) of
criminal cases involve minor crimes, *i. e.*, misdemeanors, which are
commonly disposed of in less elaborate proceedings than those available in felony cases. Cf. footnotes 2 and 4 at pp. 203 and 204 *supra*.

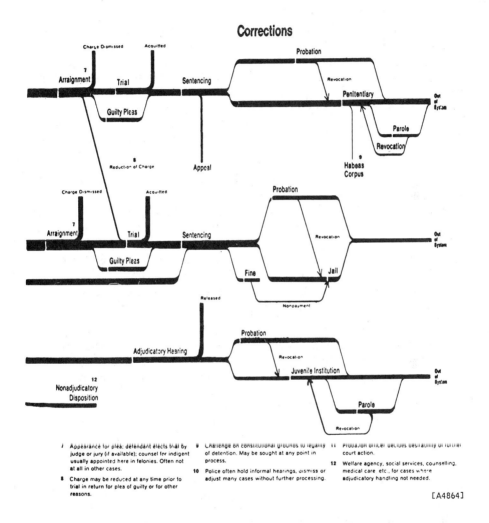

Corrections

In a relatively small number of cases, usually involving organized crime or "white collar" crime such as embezzlement or corruption of public officials, the initial investigation may be done by the prosecutor, sometimes with the aid of the police, sometimes through a grand jury, and formal criminal charges are prepared as a first step in the process. Following this a warrant of arrest based on the allegations in the formal charge may be issued by a magistrate, or in some cases, the prosecutor may waive arrest and request that the defendant merely be summoned for the initial appearance on the charges and then be admitted to bail or released on his or her "own recognizance" (so-called release on O. R., i. e., without posting bail). This special type of procedure, ordinarily controlled from the start by the prosecutor and generally reserved for "elite" crime, is analogous to civil proceedings in which preparation of a formal charge, the complaint, is the first step against the defendant. The accused is afforded the maximum benefit of the screening elements of our system of criminal justice, i. e., prosecutorial review, grand jury indictment, and warrant for arrest (or summons) issued by a magistrate on a showing of probable cause that a crime has been committed. This is in sharp contrast with the bulk of criminal cases in which arrest precedes the preparation of formal charges and in which the accused is subject to a form of official detention (not unlike the end result of a successful prosecution) before formal charges are even prepared.

Note finally that the above description of the steps in the criminal process pays little attention to the use of arrest warrants. A warrant is a document issued by a magistrate, or a judge, which authorizes public officials to search places or seize persons or things in a criminal investigation. The theoretical purpose of an arrest warrant is to provide an independent magisterial review in order to afford protection against unlawful arrests. In point of fact, arrest warrants are issued in relatively few cases, and, as we shall see, judicial review of police action is almost always a post-arrest occurrence.

> "It is often assumed that in the absence of any need for immediate action the normal and desirable method for determining whom to arrest is by the police presenting the facts to a magistrate, who is removed from the competitive task of detecting crime and bringing about the arrest of offenders. However, in current practice arrest warrants are seldom used, and when they are used the participation of the judicial officer is usually a formality with little or no attention given by him to the question of whether an adequate basis exists for making an arrest. . . ." Wayne R. LaFave, Arrest (Boston, 1965), p. 8.

Arrests made without a warrant are permissible under the United States Constitution, so long as the arrest is based on a determination by the arresting official that there is probable cause that the person to be arrested has committed a crime. See U. S. v. Watson, 423 U.S. 111, 96 S.Ct. 820 (1976), and Section 11.2 infra at pp. 225–229.

SECTION 10. THE CONSTITUTION AND THE RULE OF LAW: PRELIMINARY COMMENTS ON JUDICIAL SUPERVISION OF CRIMINAL PROCEDURE PRIOR TO TRIAL

The first ten amendments to the United States Constitution make up the so-called Bill of Rights. These amendments assert certain basic protections of persons against arbitrary and unreasonable acts of public officials. Their adoption soon after the ratification of the Constitution reflects the fundamental nature of the guarantees set out in them and also discloses some of the basic complaints against governmental action which precipitated the American Revolution. Many of those complaints were directed against the administration of criminal law during the colonial period.

The Fourth, Fifth, Sixth, and Eighth Amendments deal specifically with criminal procedure. The texts of these amendments are set out below, together with some explanatory notes.

Amendment IV. The right of the people to be secure in their persons, houses, papers, and effects, against unreasonable searches and seizures, shall not be violated, and no Warrants shall issue, but upon probable cause, supported by Oath or affirmation, and particularly describing the place to be searched, and the persons or things to be seized.

The seizures here mentioned include both seizures of property and persons (arrest).

Amendment V. No person shall be held to answer for a capital, or otherwise infamous crime, unless on a presentment or indictment of a Grand Jury, except in cases arising in the land or naval forces, or in the Militia, when in actual service in time of War or public danger; nor shall any person be subject for the same offence to be twice put in jeopardy of life or limb, nor shall be compelled in any criminal case to be a witness against himself, nor be deprived of life, liberty, or property, without due process of law; nor shall private property be taken for public use, without just compensation.

A "capital, or otherwise infamous crime" is a crime punishable by death or imprisonment for a term of more than one year. The first proviso of this amendment requires a particular mode of preparing the formal charges on which a person may be tried in such cases. This subject is considered *infra* at p. 305 ff.

The second proviso of this amendment establishes protection against "double jeopardy" and guarantees the "privilege against self incrimination."

Amendment VI. In all criminal prosecutions, the accused shall enjoy the right to a speedy and public trial, by an impartial jury of the State and district wherein the crime shall have been committed, which district shall have been previously ascertained by law, and to be informed of the nature and cause of the accusation; to be confronted with the witnesses against him; to have compulsory process for obtaining Witnesses in his favor, and to have the Assistance of Counsel for his defence.

The districts herein referred to are the federal judicial districts. See *supra* at p. 153 ff.

"Compulsory process" is the subpoena power which a court uses where necessary, to bring witnesses into court.

Amendment VIII. Excessive bail shall not be required, nor excessive fines imposed, nor cruel and unusual punishments inflicted.

Bail is one means an accused may use to obtain release from custody during the period between arrest and the final judicial disposition of pending charges. The procedure generally requires the accused to put up money, property, or other security which will be forfeited upon failure of the accused to return and stand trial.

The primacy of these guarantees is underscored by their inclusion in our written Constitution, for they are there recorded in permanent verbal form as a statement of supreme law. Of course, their real meaning is determined not only by their verbal form but also by the ways in which they have been understood and applied.

What, in practice, is the extent of the constitutional limitation on a public official's exercise of the powers of office, and what is the extent of the protection afforded private persons against official action? When officer and private person come into confrontation regarding the constitutional propriety of official action, how is such a dispute to be resolved?

In the American system, judges are the arbiters of such disputes, for the Constitution is law, and as such is a fit subject for judicial inquiry and interpretation in the context of a case or controversy. As judges interpret and apply the expressions in the Constitution to the facts before them, the law of the Constitution passes from abstraction into reality. Its meaning is made known with respect to past conduct and its impact in the future is made more clear.

For a long time the Bill of Rights was understood as establishing limitations only upon the federal government, and not upon the states. Indeed, the first 10 Amendments were added to the Constitution as part of the price for its ratification by the original states. Recollections of arbitrary actions by officers of a remote central government were fresh in the minds of a people who had just forcibly severed their political ties with England, and so protection was sought against similar occurrences at the hands of officers of the new central government.

The understanding that the Bill of Rights was a specific limitation only upon the federal government was supported in Barron v. Baltimore, 32 U.S. 243 (1833), in which Chief Justice Marshall writing for a unanimous Supreme Court, held that the Fifth Amendment did not apply to the States but only to the federal government.

This does not mean, however, that only the federal criminal process has been subjected to constitutional limitations. Many of the procedural requirements of the Bill of Rights are incorporated in state law by state constitutions; a steady process of nationalization of fundamental rights, in both civil and criminal matters, has occurred since the late nineteenth century. The constitutional basis for the latter is the Fourteenth Amendment to the United States Constitution.

Amendment XIV. Section 1. All persons born or naturalized in the United States, and subject to the jurisdiction thereof, are citizens of the United States and of the State wherein they reside. No State shall make or enforce any law which shall abridge the privileges or immunities of citizens of the United States; nor shall any State deprive any person of life, liberty, or property, without due process of law; nor deny to any person within its jurisdiction the equal protection of the laws.

[Sections 2, 3 and 4 are omitted.]

Section 5. The Congress shall have power to enforce, by appropriate legislation, the provisions of this article.

[The following is taken from LEWIS MAYERS,* THE AMERICAN LEGAL SYSTEM, rev. ed. (New York, 1964), pp. 12–15. Footnotes are omitted.]

Although there is a copious body of rules, both traditional and statutory, designed to protect the individual against unfairness and oppression at the hands of law-enforcement officers or courts, that protection rests basically on constitutional provisions. Hence, in advance of an examination of particular features of our criminal procedure, it is essential to understand the constitutional framework within which that procedure operates. That framework varies as between federal and state criminal justice.

In federal criminal proceedings, the constitutional position is simple. From the beginning there have been the prohibitions against unreasonable searches and seizures, double jeopardy, and compulsory self-incrimination; the requirements of grand jury indictment and of trial by a jury of the district; the right of confrontation of witnesses and of the assistance of counsel; and the prohibition of excessive bail, of excessive fines, and of cruel and unusual punishments. The specific application of these provisions has been established by a long series of pronouncements by the Supreme Court. In the last two decades the Court has had the further opportunity to express its views through its power, conferred by Congress, to make rules for the conduct of all federal criminal proceedings.

The constitutional framework of state criminal proceedings is more complex, and can best be understood in the light of its historical development. During the century and a half of the colonial regime, criminal justice was almost solely the affair of the individual colony. Nevertheless, certain basic English statutes applied to all the colonies; and in serious cases the

---

* Mr. Mayers was formerly a member of the faculty at the City College of New York, where he taught law. His other writings include, Shall We Repeal the Fifth Amendment (1954), and The Machinery of Justice (1963).

possibility did exist of a check by the Privy Council, acting on appeal. For almost a century following the Revolution, however, no corresponding national check existed. Except for the prohibition against state ex post facto laws, the Constitution embodied no restriction on the criminal procedures of the state. Nor (contrary to what is so often popularly assumed) did the Bill of Rights—*i. e.*, the ten amendments to the Constitution adopted in 1791—add any restriction whatever on the states; it applied only to the newly created federal government. In the field of criminal justice each state remained undisputed sovereign.

This sovereignty of the state continued unimpaired until 1868, when a provision was added to the Constitution which was in due course to subject the entire criminal procedure of the states (and indeed their civil procedure and much of their substantive law as well) to the supervision of the Supreme Court. The Fourteenth Amendment, adopted in that year, contained among other provisions, the injunction that "no state shall deprive any person of life, liberty or property without due process of law, or deny to any person within its jurisdiction the equal protection of the laws."

The phrase "equal protection of the laws" was novel; but the phrase "due process of law"—far the more important in the event—was a familiar one. It had been employed in an English statute as early as the fourteenth century, apparently in the same sense as the phrase "the law of the land," which had been employed in Magna Carta in the previous century; and the two phrases occur in subsequent English statutes and in colonial statutes and documents. Neither phrase appears in the Constitution as originally adopted, but the requirement of "due process of law" as to federal action was added to the Constitution in 1791 (in the Fifth Amendment). Precisely what was in the mind of the draftsmen, or what was understood to be the significance of the phrase by the Congress which proposed it or by the state legislatures which ratified the amendment embodying it, is impossible to discover; there is no contemporary discussion that has come down to us. Certain it is however that half a century later, when Joseph Story, a justice of the Supreme Court and one of America's great jurists, published his commentary on the Constitution, destined to become a classic, the phrase was considered of so little significance that he devoted only a few lines to its discussion, treating it indeed as auxiliary to the prohibition against compelling one to be a witness against himself in a criminal case.

Meanwhile, a similar requirement (employing in every case the phrase "law of the land") had been embodied in most of the eleven state constitutions adopted during the Revolution; in the decades that followed, the same requirement, usually in the phrase "due process of law" was incorporated in the new constitutions of perhaps all the states created during that period. When, therefore, the corresponding language was embodied in the Fourteenth Amendment, its effect was apparently simply to reinforce by federal authority a principle already in force throughout the states; the federal power was to be invoked because the Negro, newly emancipated, could not safely be remitted for "due process of law" solely to a state officialdom dominated by his late masters.

Up to that time, the phrase, now five centuries old, and made familiar by the usage of three-quarters of a century in the federal Constitution and later in state constitutions, had as applied to criminal prosecution simply meant that each person was entitled to have the established legal procedure followed in his case. The phrase did not import that the procedure was fair or rational; for it had come into use at a time when trial by ordeal and by combat still prevailed, and had grown old during a period when the most crucial essentials of a fair procedure—the right of the accused to be informed in advance of the accusation against him, to confront his accusers, to have the assistance of counsel—had not yet been firmly established. At the time this phrase was incorporated in the Constitution as a limitation on federal proceedings, the accused was still denied the elementary right to testify on his own behalf; yet no one thought of suggesting that "due process of law" required that he should be given that right, nor was that suggestion made during the decades that followed. Indeed, when the Fourteenth Amendment was adopted, that right was still denied him in almost every state.

It is not surprising therefore that the inclusion in the Fourteenth Amendment of the requirement that the states afford "due process of law" attracted but little attention; far less indeed than did the provisions contained in the same amendment for extending citizenship to the Negro and for reducing the congressional representation of any state which disfranchised him. Yet, the incorporation in the Constitution of this seemingly subsidiary restriction upon the states laid the foundation for the development of that supervisory power of the federal courts, and particularly of the Supreme Court, over all the operations of state government, which has revolutionized our federal system. Here we are concerned, however, with only one phase of that revolutionary process—that related to criminal procedure. In that field the process may be said to have begun in 1884, when the Court was asked to declare it to be a denial of due process of law for a state to put one on trial for a felony on an information filed by the prosecutor, without indictment by a grand jury. The Court rejected this contention, as it did other contentions made in a steadily growing stream of criminal cases in the next half century. As late as 1915 the Court declared that "it is perfectly well settled that a criminal prosecution in the courts of a State . . . conducted according to the settled course of judicial proceedings as established by the law of the State . . . is 'due process' in the constitutional sense."

It was not indeed until 1927 that a state court conviction was for the first time set aside on the ground that the unfairness of the procedure employed rendered the conviction void for want of due process. In recent decades there has been a marked increase in the number of state convictions carried to the Court, and a substantial number of them have been set aside by it. In addition, the lower federal courts, under a greatly expanded power accorded them by the Court in habeas corpus proceedings, have also set aside numerous state convictions.

Note

The decade 1960 to 1970 saw a stream of landmark opinions issue from the Court regarding the meaning of "due process of law" in state criminal proceedings. These opinions established that it is a denial of due process of law for a state to: (a) allow property seized in an unlawful search to be used as evidence in criminal proceedings, Mapp v. Ohio, 367 U.S. 643, 81 S.Ct. 1684 (1961) (see *infra* p. 243);

(b) impose cruel and unusual punishments, Robinson v. California, 370 U.S. 660, 82 S.Ct. 1417 (1962); (c) fail to provide adequate legal counsel to the accused in a felony case, Gideon v. Wainwright, 372 U.S. 335, 83 S.Ct. 792 (1963); (d) deny a person the protection of the privilege against self incrimination, Malloy v. Hogan, 378 U.S. 1, 84 S.Ct. 1489 (1964); (e) deny an accused the right to confront the witnesses against him, Pointer v. Texas, 380 U.S. 400, 85 S.Ct. 1065 (1965), and Douglas v. Alabama, 380 U.S. 415, 85 S.Ct. 1074 (1965); (f) deny an accused a speedy trial, Klopfer v. North Carolina, 386 U. S. 213, 87 S.Ct. 988 (1967); (g) deny an accused a jury trial in a serious criminal case (including all felony and at least some misdemeanor cases), Duncan v. Louisiana, 391 U.S. 145, 88 S.Ct. 1444 (1967); (h) try a person more than once for the same offense (double jeopardy), Klopfer v. North Carolina, 386 U.S. 213, 87 S.Ct. 988 (1967), and Benton v. Maryland, 395 U.S. 784, 89 S.Ct. 2056 (1969); (i) to allow persons to be convicted of a crime upon a lesser standard of proof than "proof beyond a reasonable doubt" that a crime has been committed, In re Winship, 397 U.S. 358, 90 S.Ct. 1068 (1970).

Since 1970 the Supreme Court has clarified and refined some of its holdings on these issues. For example, the Court has held that states may use juries of less than the traditional 12 persons in criminal trials, Williams v. Florida, 399 U.S. 78, 90 S.Ct. 1893 (1970); that less than unanimous jury verdicts are permissible in criminal cases, Apodaca v. Oregon, 406 U.S. 404, 92 S.Ct. 1628 (1972); and that although the state must prove each and every element of a crime beyond a reasonable doubt, the state may provide for affirmative defenses to crimes, and require that the defendant bear the burden of proof on affirmative defenses, Patterson v. New York, 432 U.S. 197, 97 S.Ct. 2319 (1977).

Much of the remainder of this chapter will explore aspects of judicial intervention in the criminal process through the explication of the due process concept. A chief concern will be with the availability and adequacy of judicial remedies for violations of the due process requirement by public officials.

SECTION 11. THE POLICE PHASE OF THE
CRIMINAL PROCESS

SECTION 11.1 LAW AND/OR ORDER: THE DILEMMA OF
POLICE WORK IN A DEMOCRATIC SOCIETY

[The following is taken from JEROME SKOLNICK,* JUSTICE WITHOUT TRIAL (New York, 1966), pp. 1, 17–18. Some footnotes

* Professor of Sociology, University of
California at Berkeley.

omitted; others are renumbered; others have been amended by the editors.]

For what social purpose do police exist? What values do the police serve in a democratic society? Are the police to be principally an agency of social control, with their chief value the efficient enforcement of the prohibitive norms of substantive criminal law? Or are the police to be an institution falling under the hegemony of the legal system, with a basic commitment to the rule of law, even if this obligation may result in a reduction of social order? How does this dilemma of democratic society hamper the capacity of the police, institutionally and individually, to respond to legal standards of law enforcement?

* * *

. . . .: *The police in democratic society are required to maintain order and to do so under the rule of law. As functionaries charged with maintaining order, they are part of the bureaucracy. The ideology of democratic bureaucracy emphasizes initiative rather than disciplined adherence to rules and regulations. By contrast, the rule of law emphasizes the rights of individual citizens and constraints upon the initiative of legal officials. This tension between the operational consequences of ideas of order, efficiency, and initiative, on the one hand, and legality, on the other, constitutes the principle problem of police as a democratic legal organization. . . .***

Law and Order: The Source of the Dilemma

If the police could maintain order without regard to legality, their short-run difficulties would be considerably diminished. However, they are inevitably concerned with interpreting legality because of their use of *law* as an instrument of order. The criminal law contains a set of rules for the maintenance of social order. This arsenal comprises the *substantive* part of the criminal law, that is, the elements of crime, the principles under which the accused is to be held accountable for alleged crime, the principles justifying the enactment of specific prohibitions, and the crimes themselves. Sociologists usually concentrate here, asking how well this control system operates, analyzing the conditions under which it achieves intended goals, and the circumstances rendering it least efficient.

Another part of the criminal law, however, regulates the conduct of state officials charged with processing citizens who are suspected, accused, or found guilty of crime. Involved here are such matters as the law of search, the law of arrest, the elements and degree of proof, the right to counsel, the nature of a lawful accusation of crime, and the fairness of trial. The procedures of the criminal law, therefore, stress protection of individual liberties *within* a system of social order.

This dichotomy suggests that the common juxtaposition of "law and order" is an oversimplification. Law is not merely an instrument of order, but may frequently be its adversary. There are communities that appear disorderly to some (such as bohemian communities valuing diversity), but which nevertheless maintain a substantial degree of legality. The contrary may also be found: a situation where order is well maintained, but where the policy and practice of legality is not evident. The totalitarian social

** Emphasis in the original.

system, whether in a nation or an institution, is a situation of order without rule of law. Such a situation is probably best illustrated by martial rule, where military authority may claim and exercise the power of amnesty and detention without warrant. If, in addition, the writ of habeas corpus, the right to inquire into these acts, is suspended, as it typically is under martial rule, the executive can exercise arbitrary powers. Such a system of social control is efficient, but does not conform to generally held notions about the "rule of law."

Although there is no precise definition of the rule of law, or its synonym, the principle of legality, its essential element is the reduction of arbitrariness by officials—for example, constraints on the activities of the police—and of arbitrariness in positive law by the application of "rational principles of civic order." A statement expressive of the rule of law is found in a report on police arrests for "investigations." The authors, who are lawyers, write, "Anglo-American law has a tradition of antipathy to the imprisonment of a citizen at the will of executive officers." A more explicit definition of the rule of law in the administration of criminal law has been presented as follows:

> The principle of *nulla poena sine lege* imposes formidable restraints upon the definition of criminal conduct. Standards of conduct must meet stringent tests of specificity and clarity, may act only prospectively, and must be strictly construed in favor of the accused. Further, the definition of criminal conduct has largely come to be regarded as a legislative function, thereby precluding the judiciary from devising new crimes. The public-mischief doctrine and the sometimes over-generalized "ends" of criminal conspiracy are usually regarded as anomalous departures from this main stream. The cognate principle of procedural regularity and fairness, in short, due process of law, commands that the legal standard be applied to the individual with scrupulous fairness in order to minimize the chances of convicting the innocent, protect against abuse of official power, and generate an atmosphere of impartial justice. As a consequence, a complex network of procedural requirements embodied variously in constitutional, statutory, or judge-made law is imposed upon the criminal adjudicatory process—public trial, unbiased tribunal, legal representation, open hearing, confrontation, and related concomitants of procedural justice.[1]

Thus, when law is used as the instrument of social order, it necessarily poses a dilemma. The phrase "law and order" is misleading because it draws attention away from the substantial incompatibilities existing between the two ideas. Order under law suggests procedures different from achievement of "social control" through threat of coercion and summary judgment. Order under law is concerned not merely with the achievement of regularized social activity but with the means used to come by peaceable behavior, certainly with procedure, but also with positive law. It would surely be a violation of the rule of law for a legislature to make epilepsy a crime, even though a public "seizure" typically disturbs order in the community. While most law enforcement officials regard drug addicts as menacing to the community, a law making it a crime to *be* an ad-

---

1. Sanford H. Kadish, "Legal Norm and Discretion in the Police and Sentencing Process," Harvard Law Review, 75 (1962), 904–905.

dict has been declared unconstitutional.** This example, purposely selected from substantive criminal law, indicates that conceptions of legality apply here as well as in the more traditional realm of criminal procedure. In short, "law" and "order" are frequently found to be in opposition, because law implies rational restraint upon the rules and procedures utilized to achieve order. Order under law, therefore, subordinates the ideal of conformity to the ideal of legality.

. . . [A] democratic society envisions constraint upon those who are granted the right to invoke the processes of punishment in the name of the law. They must draw their rules clearly, state them prospectively. The rules themselves must be rational, not whimsically constructed, and carried out with procedural regularity and fairness. Most important of all, rule is from below, not above. Authorities are servants of the people, not a "vanguard" of elites instructing the masses. The overriding value is consent of the governed. From it derives the principle of the accountability of authority, accountability primarily to courts of law and ultimately to a democratically constituted legislature based upon universal suffrage.

[The following is taken from JAMES Q. WILSON, VARIETIES OF POLICE BEHAVIOR (Cambridge, Mass., 1968), pp. 16–17, 19–22, 29–31. Footnotes are omitted.]

The patrolman's role is defined more by his responsibility for *maintaining order* than by his responsibility for enforcing the law. By "order" is meant the absence of disorder, and by disorder is meant behavior that either disturbs or threatens to disturb the public peace or that involves face-to-face conflict among two or more persons. Disorder, in short, involves a dispute over what is "right" or "seemly" conduct or over who is to blame for conduct that is agreed to be wrong or unseemly. A noisy drunk, a rowdy teenager shouting or racing his car in the middle of the night, a loud radio in the apartment next door, a panhandler soliciting money from passersby, persons wearing eccentric clothes and unusual hair styles loitering in public places—all these are examples of behavior which "the public" (an onlooker, a neighbor, the community at large) may disapprove of and ask the patrolman to "put a stop to." Needless to say, the drunk, the teenager, the persons next door, the panhandler, and the hippies are likely to take a different view of the matter, to suggest that people "mind their own business," and to be irritated with the "cop" who intervenes. On the other hand, a fight, a tavern brawl, and an assault on an unfaithful lover are kinds of behavior that even the participants are not likely to condone. Thus, they may agree that the police have a right to intervene, but they are likely to disagree over who is to blame and thus against whom the police ought to act.

Some or all of these examples of disorderly behavior involve infractions of the law; any intervention by the police is at least under color of the law and in fact might be viewed as an "enforcement" of the law. A judge, examining the matter after the fact, is likely to see the issue wholly in these terms. But the patrolman does not. Though he may use the law to make an arrest, just as often he will do something else, such as

[** United States v. Robinson, 361 U.S. 220, 80 S.Ct. 282 (1959).]

tell people to "knock it off," "break it up," or "go home and sober up." In his eyes even an arrest does not always end his involvement in the matter. In some sense he was involved in settling a dispute; if and how he settled it is important both to the parties involved and to the officer himself. To the patrolman, "enforcing the law" is what he does when there is no dispute—when making an arrest or issuing a summons exhausts his responsibilities. Giving a traffic ticket is the clearest case: an infraction of the law is observed and familiar, routinized steps are taken to make the offender liable to the penalties of the law. Similarly, if the patrolman comes upon a burglary in progress, catches a fleeing robber, or is involved in apprehending a person suspected of having committed a crime, he is enforcing the law. Other agencies will decide whether the suspect is in fact guilty; but *if* he is guilty, then he is to blame. Guilt is at issue in both order-maintaining and law-enforcing situations, but blame is at issue only in the former. The noisy neighbor or the knife-wielding lover may say, "Don't blame me"; the fleeing robber, on the other hand, will say, "I'm not guilty."

The problem of order, more than the problem of law enforcement, is central to the patrolman's role for several reasons. First, in at least the larger or more socially heterogeneous cities, the patrolman encounters far more problems of order maintenance than opportunities for law enforcement, except with respect to traffic laws. . . .

Second, the maintenance of order exposes the patrolman to physical danger, and his reaction in turn may expose the disputants to danger. Statistically, the risk of injury or death to the patrolman may not be great in order maintenance situations but it exists and, worse, it is unpredictable, occurring, as almost every officer interviewed testified, "when you least expect it." In 1965 there were reported over twenty thousand assaults on police officers, nearly seven thousand of which resulted in injury to the officer; eighty-three officers were killed and only thirty of these by auto accidents. There is no way to tell what proportion of these deaths and injuries occurred in the restoring of order as opposed to the pursuit and subduing of a criminal, but patrolmen almost universally contrast the random, unexpected nature of danger involved in handling, say, a domestic quarrel with the "routine" and taken-for-granted nature of danger when chasing a bank robber. Jerome Skolnick considers the preoccupation with danger an important element of the police officer's "working personality." I would add that the risk of danger in order maintenance patrol work, though statistically less than the danger involved in enforcing traffic laws or apprehending felons, has a disproportionate effect on the officer partly because its unexpected nature makes him more apprehensive and partly because he tends to communicate his apprehension to the citizen.

* * *

But most important, the order maintenance function necessarily involves the exercising of substantial discretion over matters of the greatest importance (public and private morality, honor and dishonor, life and death) in a situation that is, by definition, one of conflict and in an environment that is apprehensive and perhaps hostile.

Discretion exists both because many of the relevant laws are necessarily ambiguous and because, under the laws of many states governing arrests for certain forms of disorder, the "victim" must cooperate with the patrolman if the law is to be invoked at all. Statutes defining "disorderly conduct" or "disturbing the peace" are examples of laws that are not only ambiguous, but necessarily so. In New York State, disorderly conduct is a breach of the peace occasioned by, among other things, offensive behavior or language, disturbing other people, begging, having an "evil reputation" and "consorting with persons of like evil reputations," and "causing a crowd to collect." In California disturbing the peace includes "maliciously and wilfully" breaching the peace of a neighborhood or person by, among other things, "loud or unusual noise," "tumultuous or offensive conduct," or using "vulgar, profane, or indecent language within the presence or hearing of women or children." One might object, as some have, that such statutes are vague and one might expect the courts to rule (again, as some have) all or parts of them unconstitutional for failing to specify a clear standard, but one would be hard pressed to invent a statute that would cover all possible cases of objectionable disorder in language that would leave little discretion to the officer. Most criminal laws define *acts* (murder, rape, speeding, possessing narcotics), which are held to be illegal; people may disagree as to whether the act should be illegal, as they do with respect to narcotics, for example, but there is little disagreement as to what the behavior in question consists of. Laws regarding disorderly conduct and the like assert, usually by implication, that there is a *condition* ("public order") that can be diminished by various actions. The difficulty, of course, is that public order is nowhere defined and can never be defined unambiguously because what constitutes order is a matter of opinion and convention, not a state of nature. (An unmurdered person, an unraped woman, and an unpossessed narcotic can be defined so as to be recognizable to any reasonable person.) An additional difficulty, a corollary of the first, is the impossibility of specifying, except in the extreme case, what degree of disorder is intolerable and who is to be held culpable for that degree. A suburban street is quiet and pleasant; a big city street is noisy and (to some) offensive; what degree of noise and offense, and produced by whom, constitutes "disorderly conduct"?

Occupations whose members exercise, as do the police, wide discretion alone and with respect to matters of the greatest importance are typically "professions"—the medical profession, for example. The right to handle emergency situations, to be privy to "guilty information," and to make decisions involving questions of life and death or honor and dishonor is usually, as with a doctor or priest, conferred by an organized profession. The profession certifies that the member has acquired by education certain information and by apprenticeship certain arts and skills that render him competent to perform these functions and that he is willing to subject himself to the code of ethics and sense of duty of his colleagues (or, in the case of the priest, to the laws and punishments of God). Failure to perform his duties properly will, if detected, be dealt with by professional sanctions—primarily, loss of respect. Members of professions tend to govern themselves through collegial bodies, to restrict the authority of their nominal superiors, to take seriously their reputation among fellow professionals, and to encourage some of their kind to devote themselves to adding systematically to the knowledge of the profession through writing and research. The police are not in any of these senses professionals. They acquire most of their knowledge and skill on the job, not in separate academies; they are emphatically subject to the authority of their superiors; they have no serious professional society, only a union-like bargaining agent; and they do not produce, in systematic written form, new knowledge about their craft.

In sum, the order-maintenance function of the patrolman defines his role and that role, which is unlike that of any other occupation, can be described as one in which *sub-professionals, working alone, exercise wide discretion in matters of utmost importance (life and death, honor and dishonor) in an environment that is apprehensive and perhaps hostile.* The agents of various other governmental organizations may display one or two of these characteristics, but none or almost none display all in combination. The doctor has wide discretion over matters of life and death, but he is a professional working in a supportive environment. The teacher works alone and has considerable discretion, but he may be a professional and in any case education, though important, is not a matter of life or death. A welfare worker, though working alone among apprehensive clients, has relatively little discretion—the laws define rather precisely what payments he can authorize to a client and supervisors review his written reports and proposed family budgets.

This role places the patrolman in a special relationship to the law, a relationship that is obscured by describing what he does as "enforcing the law." To the patrolman, the law is one resource among many that he may use to deal with disorder, but it is not the only one or even the most important; beyond that, the law is a constraint that tells him what he must *not* do but that is peculiarly unhelpful in telling him what he *should* do. Thus, he approaches incidents that threaten order *not in terms of enforcing the law but in terms of "handling the situation."* The officer is expected, by colleagues as well as superiors, to "handle his beat." This means keeping things under control so that there are no complaints that he is doing nothing or that he is doing too much. To handle his beat, the law provides one resource, the possibility of arrest, and a set of constraints, *but it does not supply to the patrolman a set of legal rules to be applied.* A phrase heard by interviewers countless times is "You can't go by what the book says."

Notes and Questions

1. How does Professor Wilson define the terms "order" and "maintaining order" for purposes of his discourse?

2. Professor Skolnick's discussion of police work does not include precise definitions of the terms "order" and "to maintain order". Is there a concept of order and maintenance of order implicit in the extract from Professor Skolnick? If so, are these implicit definitions like or unlike Wilson's definition of those terms?

3. Do Skolnick or Wilson suggest that a policeman's conception of "order" and of his role in "maintaining order" may influence his conception of law? Is that conception of law likely to be different from a judge's conception of law?

4. Professor Skolnick has commented further on the policeman's conception of order:

"The policeman, because his work requires him to be occupied continually with potential violence, develops a perceptual shorthand to identify certain kinds of people as symbolic assailants, that is, as persons who use gesture, language, and attire that the policeman has come to recognize as a prelude to violence. This does not mean that violence by the symbolic assailant is necessarily predictable. On the contrary, the policeman responds to the vague indication of danger suggested by appearance. Like the animals of the experimental psychologist, the policeman finds the threat of random damage more compelling than a predetermined and inevitable punishment. ·. . .

"[A] young man may suggest the threat of violence to the policeman by his manner of walking or strutting, the insolence in the demeanor being registered by the policeman as a possible preamble to later attack. Signs vary from area to area, but a youth dressed in a black leather jacket and motorcycle boots is sure to draw at least a suspicious glance from a policeman.

"However complex the motives aroused by the element of danger, its consequences for sustaining police culture are unambiguous. This element requires him . . . to live in a world straining toward duality, and suggesting danger when they are perceived. Consequently, it is in the nature of the policeman's situation that his conception of order emphasize regularity and predictability. It is, therefore, a conception shaped by persistent suspicion . .". Justice Without Trial, pp. 45–46.

5. What special problems of *legality* (in Skolnick's sense *supra* p. 216) are posed by the element of discretion in police work (discussed by Wilson, *supra* p. 219)?

NEW YORK PENAL LAW

§ 240.20 Disorderly conduct

A person is guilty of disorderly conduct when, with intent to cause public inconvenience, annoyance or alarm, or recklessly creating a risk thereof:

1. He engages in fighting or in violent, tumultuous or threatening behavior; or

2. He makes unreasonable noise; or

3. In a public place, he uses abusive or obscene language, or makes an obscene gesture; or

4. Without lawful authority, he disturbs any lawful assembly or meeting of persons; or

5. He obstructs vehicular or pedestrian traffic; or

6. He congregates with other persons in a public place and refuses to comply with a lawful order of the police to disperse; or

7.   He creates a hazardous or physically offensive condition by any act which serves no legitimate purpose.

Disorderly conduct is a violation.

[The penalty for conviction of a violation may be a fine or imprisonment for up to fifteen (15) days.   N.Y.Penal Law § 55.00.]

Questions

1.   What problems of legality are posed by this statute?

2.   How would you revise this statute?   Why?

The problems of police work are further complicated by what Professor Sanford Kadish has termed "overcriminalization" of conduct.[1]   His thesis, simply stated, is that our society imposes extraordinary burdens on the criminal process by declaring criminal many forms of ".   .   .   moral deviancy among consenting adults   .   .   .," e.g., homosexual intercourse, prostitution, gambling, and the use of drugs and alcohol.   These laws pose enormous problems of law enforcement.   These are, in many ways, victimless crimes in which there can be no complaining party to assist in law enforcement.   Moreover, the very fact that such behavior is declared unlawful encourages development of an extensive organized criminal apparatus which, in addition to providing these illicit goods and services, attempts to corrupt public officials.   Professor Kadish also points out that criminal law is often used to perform tasks which might better be provided by social service agencies.   For example, public drunkenness is made criminal behavior and the drunk tank at the local lock up provides a poor substitute for an alcoholic ward or clinic in a medical facility.

This proliferation of the criminal law and its attempted use for a wide variety of social purposes has been noted earlier in our materials in the extract from Thorstin Sellin, note 9, supra at p. 123.

The ubiquity and more than occasional ambiguity of substantive criminal law adds another dimension to the discretion of police and prosecutor.   Not only is there a choice regarding whether or not to bring charges, there is often a substantial range of choice regarding what charges will be laid if a prosecution is undertaken.

The potential for official abuse of authority is enlarged by this aspect of criminal law.   Obscure and infrequently used laws may be brought to bear, or charges may be laid under a statute broad enough to encompass conduct which most people would not consider to be criminal.   The remedies for this use of criminal law may not be adequate.   Judges may strike down outmoded statutes or vague statutes under various constitutional provisions, or they may interpret such statutes narrowly to exclude the conduct complained of, but the defendants in such cases will have had to bear the indignity of

1.   Sanford H. Kadish, "The Crisis of
     Overcriminalization", 374 Annals 157
     (1967).

arrest and prosecution, with the attendant psychic and monetary costs. This is an especially difficult issue in times of political unrest when social change may unleash both civil disorder and a "law and order" reaction in the public at large and in officials charged with the maintenance of order.

SECTION 11.2   ARREST AND SEARCH: LEGAL STANDARDS TO GUIDE AND CHECK OFFICIAL ACTION

This and the following section treat briefly some controversial problems of criminal procedure raised to high visibility as a result of United States Supreme Court decisions during the decade 1960 to 1970 (see note, *supra* p. 215)." These cases demonstrate the tension between the police who are charged with maintaining order under the substantive criminal law, and judges who are bound to maintain the rule of law as prescribed in the United States Constitution.

Probable cause. The Fourth Amendment asserts "the right of the people to be secure in their persons, houses, papers and effects against unreasonable searches and seizures   .   .   .". But what is the measure of reasonableness, and who is to establish the standard? Perhaps some guidance on these issues is found in another provision of the Fourth Amendment which states that "no Warrants shall issue but upon probable cause, supported by Oath or affirmation   .   .   .". Observe, however, that there is no requirement that a warrant issue in every case of arrest or search (see p. 209 *supra* and pp. 229–232 *infra*). Nevertheless, if an arrest can be approved by a magistrate only when there is probable cause, i. e., reasonable grounds to believe that a crime has been or is being committed, is it not logical to suppose that an officer who arrests (or searches) without a warrant must have the same probable cause? Legislatures and judges have answered that question affirmatively. But what constitutes probable cause? Consider the following taken from Draper v. U. S., 358 U.S. 307, 79 S.Ct. 329 (1959):

> " 'In dealing with probable cause,   .   .   .   as the very name implies, we deal with probabilities. These are not technical; they are the factual and practical considerations of everyday life on which reasonable and prudent men, not legal technicians, act.' Brinegar v. United States, ... Probable cause exists where 'the facts and circumstances within [the arresting officers'] knowledge and of which they had reasonably trustworthy information [are] sufficient in themselves to warrant a man of reasonable caution in the belief that' an offense has been or is being committed. Carroll v. United States, 267 U.S. 132, 162."

The difficulty of working out the practical meaning of the probable cause standard may be demonstrated by considering a few examples drawn from cases in which courts have had to decide whether or not there was probable cause to support official action against suspected criminals.

1.   "Petitioner was convicted of knowingly concealing and transporting narcotic drugs in Denver, Colorado, in violation of 35 Stat. 614, as amended, 21 U.S.C. § 174. His conviction was based in part on the use in evidence against him of two 'envelopes containing [865 grains of] heroin' and a hypodermic syringe that had been taken from his person following his arrest, by the arresting officer.

"The evidence offered [on the issue of probable cause] was not substantially disputed. It established that one Marsh, a federal narcotic agent with 29 years' experience, was stationed at Denver; that one Hereford had been engaged as a 'special employee' of the Bureau of Narcotics at Denver for about six months, and from time to time gave information to Marsh regarding violations of the narcotic laws, for which Hereford was paid small sums of money, and that Marsh had always found the information given by Hereford to be accurate and reliable. On September 3, 1956, Hereford told Marsh that James Draper (petitioner) recently had taken up abode at a stated address in Denver and 'was peddling narcotics to several addicts' in that city. Four days later, on September 7, Hereford told Marsh 'that Draper had gone to Chicago the day before [September 6] by train [and] that he was going to bring back three ounces of heroin [and] that he would return to Denver either on the morning of the 8th of September or the morning of the 9th of September also by train.' Hereford also gave Marsh a detailed physical description of Draper and of the clothing he was wearing, and said that he would be carrying 'a tan zipper bag,' and that he habitually 'walked real fast.'

"On the morning of September 8, Marsh and a Denver police officer went to the Denver Union Station and kept watch over all incoming trains from Chicago, but they did not see anyone fitting the description that Hereford had given. Repeating the process on the morning of September 9, they saw a person, having the exact physical attributes and wearing the precise clothing described by Hereford, alight from an incoming Chicago train and start walking 'fast' toward the exit. He was carrying a tan zipper bag in his right hand and the left was thrust in his raincoat pocket. Marsh, accompanied by the police officer, overtook, stopped and arrested him. They then searched him and found the two 'envelopes containing heroin' clutched in his left hand in his raincoat pocket, and found the syringe in the tan zipper bag. Marsh then took him (petitioner) in custody". Draper v. U. S., 358 U.S. 307, 79 S.Ct. 329 (1959).

Did the officers have probable cause to make an arrest?

2.   F.B.I. agents applied to a United States Commissioner for a warrant to authorize the search of premises controlled by one

William Spinelli. The agents submitted an affidavit in support of their application which asserted the following:

"1. The FBI had kept track of Spinelli's movements on five days during the month of August 1965. On four of these occasions, Spinelli was seen crossing one of two bridges leading from Illinois into St. Louis, Missouri, between 11 a.m. and 12:15 p.m. On four of the five days, Spinelli was also seen parking his car in a lot used by residents of an apartment house at 1108 Indian Circle Drive in St. Louis, between 3:30 p.m. and 4:45 p.m. On one day, Spinelli was followed further and seen to enter a particular apartment in the building.

"2. An FBI check with the telephone company revealed that this apartment contained two telephones listed under the name of Grace P. Hagen, and carrying the numbers WYdown 4–0029 and WYdown 4–0136.

"3. The application stated that 'William Spinelli is known to this affiant and to federal law enforcement agents and local law enforcement agents as a bookmaker, an associate of bookmakers, a gambler, and an associate of gamblers.'

"4. Finally it was stated that the FBI 'has been informed by a confidential reliable informant that William Spinelli is operating a handbook and accepting wagers and disseminating wagering information by means of the telephones which have been assigned the numbers WYdown 4–0029 and WYdown 4–0136'." Spinelli v. U. S., 393 U.S. 410, 89 S.Ct. 584 (1969).

Should the Commissioner have issued a search warrant?

3. "The arresting officer testified at the trial that on the afternoon of September 23, 1964, the defendant was standing on a street corner in Brooklyn. During a period of more than 20 minutes, from a vantage point 50 to 60 feet away in a parked automobile, the officer observed six unknown persons approach the defendant. Each of these persons engaged the defendant in a short conversation, and, at the conclusion thereof, each was seen to hand him money in bill form. On three of these occasions the defendant was observed making notations on a slip of paper. Then, at approximately 1:30 P.M., the officer approached the defendant, identified himself as a police officer, and placed him under arrest. The officer testified that prior to the arrest he had not overheard any of the conversations between the defendant and the unknown persons, nor was he able to see the notations made by the defendant on the piece of paper.

"Following the arrest, the officer seized a slip of paper from the defendant's hand and took him to his car where he was searched. At this time two more pieces of paper were found on the defendant's person. All three pieces of paper bore numbers of three digits which the officer, conceded to be an expert in policy operations, testified to be mutual race horse policy numbers." * * * People v. Valentine, 17 N.Y.2d 128, 269 N.Y.S. 111, 216 N.E.2d 321 (1966).

Was there probable cause to arrest?

4. Three federal agents went to an apartment house to investigate the activities of one McDonald, whom they suspected of participating in a gambling operation known as "numbers" or "policy". When they arrived outside the building one officer thought he heard an adding machine in operation. The officers entered the building through a window in another apartment and went into the hallway leading to McDonald's apartment. One of the officers peeked through a transom over the door to the apartment and observed McDonald performing clerical operations such as would be common in a numbers operation. The officers entered, arrested McDonald and confiscated material used in numbers gambling. McDonald v. U. S., 335 U.S. 451, 69 S.Ct. 191 (1948).

Was the arrest lawful?

5. An investigator for the internal revenue service obtained a search warrant based on a sworn affidavit which alleged that: a) agents had been maintaining surveillance of a described premise and had observed numerous deliveries of such items as large bags of sugar and empty tin drums; b) agents had walked past the premises and had smelled the odor of fermenting mash and had heard the sounds of a pump motor, such as would be used in distilling operations. U. S. v. Ventresca, 380 U.S. 102, 85 S.Ct. 741 (1965).

Should the United States Commissioner have issued this warrant?

6. An officer observed two men, both known to have prior convictions for larceny, carrying a console type record player in a commercial area at 6:30 p. m. The player was observed to be new and bearing store tags. When questioned, one suspect stated that the machine belonged to his brother and that he was taking it to be repaired. When the officer pointed out the tags, the suspect changed his story and said the machine had been given to him by an unknown person whom he could not describe. The officer then arrested both men. Brooks v. U. S., 159 A.2d 876 (D.C.Mun.App. (1960)).

Was there probable cause to make the arrest?

7. In 1967 a federal tax investigator and a local constable entered the premises of respondent Harris, pursuant to a search warrant issued by a federal magistrate, and seized jugs of whiskey upon which the federal tax had not been paid. The warrant had been issued solely on the basis of the investigator's affidavit, which recited the following:

> "Roosevelt Harris has had a reputation with me for over 4 years as being a trafficker of nontaxpaid distilled spirits, and over this period I have received numerous information [sic] from all types of persons as to his activities. Constable Howard Johnson located a sizeable stash of illicit whiskey in an abandoned house under

Harris' control during this period of time. This date, I have received information from a person who fears for their [*sic*] life and property should their name be revealed. I have interviewed this person, found this person to be a prudent person, and have, under a sworn verbal statement, gained the following information: This person has personal knowledge of and has purchased illicit whiskey from within the residence described, for a period of more than 2 years, and most recently within the past 2 weeks, has knowledge of a person who purchased illicit whiskey within the past two days from the house, has personal knowledge that the illicit whiskey is consumed by purchasers in the outbuilding known as and utilized as the 'dance hall,' and has seen Roosevelt Harris go to the other outbuilding, located about 50 yards from the residence, on numerous occasions, to obtain the whiskey for this person and other persons."

Should the magistrate have issued the search warrant? U. S. v. Harris, 403 U.S. 573, 91 S.Ct. 2075 (1971).

Questions

1. If you found that any of the preceding fact situations demonstrated probable cause to arrest, to search, or to issue a warrant for those purposes, why did you make that determination?

2. If you found that any of the preceding fact situations did not demonstrate probable cause to support either arrest, search or issuance of a warrant, why did you make that determination?

3. Which of these situations seem to you to present the strongest basis for finding probable cause, and which present the weakest basis for finding probable cause? Why?

4. Is there a common problem linking situations 1, 2, 3 and 7, and differentiating them from situations 4, 5 and 6?

5. Reconsider situations 1, 3, 4 and 6 in the following light. Assume that you are a magistrate, and that in each case the officers came to you before they made the arrest and asked you to issue a warrant. On the basis of what the officers knew and could present at that time, would you have held that there was probable cause to arrest or search? Suppose instead that the arrests had been made, and the incriminating evidence had been discovered in that process, and then the issues of probable cause to arrest and search were raised in proceedings before you. How, if at all, might that affect your judgment on the probable cause issue?

Most American jurisdictions specify in their codes or rules of criminal procedure that arrests without warrants may be made only where there is "probable cause" or "reasonable grounds" for believing that the suspect is committing or has committed a crime. For example, the power of federal marshals and deputies to arrest without a warrant is set out in Title 18 United States Code, Section 3053.

"United States marshalls and their deputies may . . .
make arrests without warrant for any offense against the United
States committed in their presence, or for any felony cognizable
under the laws of the United States if they have reasonable grounds
to believe that the person to be arrested has committed or is committing such felony."

The authority to arrest without a warrant is granted to other
federal officers, e. g., F.B.I., Bureau of Narcotics, in virtually identical language in other sections of the United States Code. A variety
of common law and statutory rules regarding arrest without a warrant is summarized below.

[The following is taken from THE AMERICAN LAW INSTI-
TUTE, OFFICIAL DRAFT, CODE OF CRIMINAL PROCEDURE
(1930), pp. 231–241.]

Both at common law and under the statutes of all the states having legislation on the subject, it is settled that an officer may arrest without a warrant for a felony committed in his presence. . . .

With regard to arrest by an officer without warrant for a misdemeanor
two different rules are laid down in the statutes and decisions of the various
states.

I. An officer may arrest without warrant for a breach of the peace
committed in his presence. . . .

II. An officer may arrest without warrant for any misdemeanor committed in his presence. . . .

The phrase "in his presence," in connection with arrest without warrant, has been extensively interpreted by the courts. In the first place it is
to be noted that it is not confined to what occurs in his immediate presence
but includes offenses which he sees committed. . . .

It is likewise held that an offense is committed in the officer's presence
when he hears the offense committed. . . .

It has also been held that an offense, of which the officer receives information by smell, was committed within his presence. In M'Bride v. United States, C.C.A.Ala., 284 F. 416, and State v. Quartier, 114 Or. 657, 236 P.
746, prohibition officers who smelled whiskey in process of distillation arrested the person operating the still.

In the case of arrest for a misdemeanor the arrest must be made immediately or after fresh pursuit. . . .

The settled rule at common law in this country is that an officer may
arrest without a warrant on suspicion of felony where he has reasonable
ground to believe (a) that a felony has been committed and (b) the person
arrested committed it.

There are six types of statutes to be found in the various states:

I. Like the common law rule, that arrest may be made by an officer
without warrant where he has reasonable cause to believe (a) that a felony
has been committed and (b) that the person arrested committed it. . . .

II.   Officer may arrest without warrant:

"On a charge made, upon a reasonable cause, of the commission of a felony by the party arrested.

"At night when there is reasonable cause to believe that he has committed a felony." .   .   .

III.   Officer may arrest without warrant:

"On a charge, made upon reasonable cause, of the commission of a felony by the person proposed to be arrested."

IV.   Officer "may at night without a warrant arrest any person whom he has reasonable cause for believing to have committed a felony, and is justified in making the arrest, though it afterward appear that a felony had been committed, but that the person arrested did not commit it."

V.   Where it is shown by satisfactory proof to a peace officer, upon the representation of a credible person, that a felony has been committed, and that the offender is about to escape, so that there is no time to procure a warrant, such peace officer may, without a warrant, pursue and arrest the accused.

VI.   "Upon certain information that a felony has been committed .   .   . any person may arrest."

At English common law it was well established that a private person may arrest without a warrant for a felony committed in his presence. .   .

In the case of offenses below the grade of felony the rule at English common law was that a private person may arrest without a warrant only for a breach of the peace committed or about to be committed in his presence. .   .   .

Regarding the right of a private person to arrest without warrant for a misdemeanor there seems to be no exception in this country to the rule that he may not arrest for a misdemeanor not committed in his presence. For misdemeanors committed in his presence four different rules are to be found.

I.   A private person may not arrest for any misdemeanor. .   .   .

II.   A private person may arrest for petit larceny. .   .   .

III.   A private person may arrest for a breach of the peace committed in his presence. .   .   .

IV.   A private person may arrest without warrant for any misdemeanor committed in his presence. .   .   .

It is the almost universal rule in this country, either by decision or statute, that a private person is justified in arresting without warrant upon suspicion of felony where the felony was in fact committed by the person arrested. .   .   .

As to whether a private person is justified in arresting without warrant on suspicion where the person arrested did not commit the felony there is a wide divergence of opinion in this country. Following are the four different rules on this point:

I.   A private person is only justified in arresting without warrant for a felony not committed in his presence when the felony was committed by the person arrested. .   .   .

II.   A private person is justified in arresting for a felony not committed in his presence where the felony was in fact committed, and the person arresting had reasonable ground to believe the person arrested committed it, although he did not in fact do so.   .   .   .

III.   .   .   .   when the person arrested has committed a felony, although not in his presence.   .   .   .

IV.   A private person may arrest for a felony not committed in his presence where he has reasonable grounds to believe the person arrested committed a felony, although no felony was in fact committed.   .   .   .

Notes and Questions

1.   Should there be different standards regarding: (a) a peace officer's right to arrest without a warrant; and (b) a private person's right to arrest without a warrant?

2.   An improper or unlawful arrest may be grounds for imposing civil liability or criminal sanctions on the arresting officer. Since an arrest made subject to a valid warrant is presumed to be lawful, the procedure for obtaining warrants affords a substantial protection to the officer.

3.   Should there be a rule that "in the absence of any need for immediate action" the police should obtain arrest warrants before making arrests? How would you enforce such a rule?

4.   In a more recent work on this subject, the American Law Institute (ALI) proposes the following formulation of the rules regarding arrest without a warrant.

ALI MODEL CODE OF PRE–ARRAIGNMENT PROCEDURE

ARTICLE 120.   ARREST

Section 120.1   Arrest Without a Warrant

(1) **Authority to Arrest Without a Warrant.** A law enforcement officer may arrest a person without a warrant if the officer has reasonable cause to believe that such person has committed

(a) a felony;

(b) a misdemeanor, and the officer has reasonable cause to believe that such person

(i) will not be apprehended unless immediately arrested; or

(ii) may cause injury to himself or others or damage to property unless immediately arrested; or

(c) a misdemeanor or petty misdemeanor in the officer's presence.

(2) **Reasonable Cause.** "Reasonable cause to believe" means a basis for belief in the existence of facts which, in view of the circumstances un-

der and the purpose for which the standard is applied, is substantial, objective, and sufficient to satisfy applicable constitutional requirements. An arrest shall not be deemed to have been made on insufficient cause hereunder solely on the ground that the officer is unable to determine the particular crime which may have been committed.

(3) **Determining Reasonable Cause.** In determining whether reasonable cause exists to justify an arrest under this Section, a law enforcement officer may take into account all information that a prudent officer would judge relevant to the likelihood that a crime has been committed and that a person to be arrested has committed it, including information derived from any expert knowledge which the officer in fact possesses and information received from an informant whom it is reasonable under the circumstances to credit, whether or not at the time of making the arrest the officer knows the informant's identity.

5.   Would you support the adoption of the ALI standards regarding arrest without a warrant if you were

     (a)   a policeman?
     (b)   a prosecutor?
     (c)   a magistrate or judge?
     (d)   a legislator?

Explain your answer in each case.

SECTION 11.3   UNLAWFUL POLICE WORK: A PROBLEM OF REMEDIES

The preceding materials disclose an elaborate, complex, conflicting and difficult set of issues regarding the legal standards to guide police work. At least two sets of fundamental questions can be raised about these standards. First, why should we have them; what purposes do they serve; what is the problem they attempt to solve? Second, if we have such standards, what should we do to remedy a breach of such standards? In the balance of this section we will deal with the problem of remedies for breaches by public officers of legal standards regarding arrests, searches, and interrogation of persons suspected of having committed crimes. Before doing that, however, we should address, at least briefly, the first set of questions regarding the purposes for establishing standards to guide police work.

The primary reason for establishing such standards apparently is because we believe that the powers to arrest, to search, and to interrogate may intrude upon basic personal freedoms, and that such intrusions are potentially and seriously injurious to persons. The essence of the injury is the deprivation of liberty, privacy, and dignity which is occasioned by arrest, search or interrogation. The seriousness of the injury depends upon the extent to which arrest, search or interrogation can intrude on these values. If, for example, an arrest (or search or interrogation) entailed only brief detention, by polite and very discrete officials, in pleasant surroundings, and under the watchful eye of observers appointed to represent and/or protect the interests of a suspect, then our rules regarding arrest (or search or interrogation) might be quite lenient, and our remedies for an unlawful arrest (or search or interrogation) might be quite lenient. If, however, arrest, search or interrogation entail more than brief detention, under unpleasant circumstances, in unpleasant surroundings, and with hostile officials and observers in attendance, then our views as to the proper ground rules and remedies for breach may be quite different. Our views in this regard will also be tempered by our sense as to the public injury occasioned by criminal activity, the extent to which police work may avoid or limit that injury, and the extent to which police work may be hampered by legal regulation. Regrettably, we have precious little empirical evidence to help us answer all the questions in this area, though social scientists have done much in recent years to help in this regard. But, as we shall see, the tentative resolution of these issues has had to be worked out in courts, where judges have had to fashion doctrine and remedies without full and systematic empirical and theoretical bases for their decisions. They have proceeded by trial and error, but informed by their sense that the context of arrest, search and interrogation is a hostile and unpleasant environment in both street and station house. As we shall see, the judges have attempted to fashion rules which attempt both to limit the power to arrest, search or interrogate and to alter the environments in which those activities occur. As we shall also see, those efforts have not succeeded, and other legal means and processes are now being sought to deal with these issues.

Unlawful Arrest

PEOPLE v. DREARES

Supreme Court of New York, Appellate Division, First Department, 1961.
15 A.D.2d 204, 221 N.Y.S.2d 819.

[The defendant was arrested for loitering in a subway station. He resisted the arrest and injured one of the arresting officers. He was tried on the loitering charge and was acquitted. Defendant was then charged with third degree assault for having forcibly resisted the aforementioned arrest. Defendant was convicted of this charge and this appeal was taken.]

BREITEL, JUSTICE PRESIDING.

* * *

The prior acquittal for loitering, which is not disputed, is determinative that defendant was not guilty of the underlying offense for which he was arrested. This follows from and is simply a special application of the principle that as to each element in a criminal case, and not only on the whole case, the People must establish guilt beyond a reasonable doubt. . .

Such acquittal, then, raises the issue as to the lawfulness of the arrest in which defendant forcibly resisted the transit officers. The rule in this State is that an arrest without a warrant for an offense less than a felony must be posited upon the actual commission of the crime or offense in the presence of the arresting person. . . . Defendant's prior acquittal of the crime for which he was arrested consequently established the arrest to have been unlawful, and he was therefore entitled to resist such an arrest with reasonable force. . . .

* * *

Under the rule in People v. Bell, 306 N.Y. 110, 115 N.E.2d 821, the provision in the loitering statute for calling upon a suspected person to explain his presence has been construed as merely establishing a condition precedent to prosecution. The insufficiency or incredibility of the explanation given at the time of arrest, or even the failure to give any explanation, is not an element of the crime, and, presumably, the police officer must proceed at the risk that the arrest may prove to be unlawful. This may mean, then, that in certain circumstances a police officer may be duty bound to make an arrest on facts known to him, and be subsequently found in the ensuing prosecution (or even in a civil case which might arise from the transaction) to have made an unlawful arrest ascertained and ascertainable only after the arrest. However, because of the explanation defendant made to at least one of the officers, the Court does not reach the very difficult question whether a person suspected of loitering may resist arrest, made on objectively valid grounds, even though he has declined, upon request, to provide a true explanation for his presence which he knows would or should dispel such apparent grounds for lawful arrest.

Judgment of conviction unanimously reversed on the law only, and the information dismissed. All concur.

Notes and Questions

1.   Does People v. Dreares assert the existence of a right to resist an unlawful arrest? What, precisely, is the scope of that right, in theory and in practice? As a member of the New York bar, would you advise clients that such a right exists and, if so, that they could exercise it?

Does the right to resist an unlawful arrest afford a practical remedy for an unlawful arrest? Or is its effect only to discourage the police from making unlawful arrests?

2.   Does People v. Dreares suggest one very practical effect of the existence of a right to resist an unlawful arrest?

3.   Why might a judge in a case like People v. Dreares wish to say no more than he absolutely has to in order to resolve the case before him, even though this keeps people guessing about the outcome of other similar cases?

4.   Do you think a decision like People v. Dreares might tend to reinforce a policeman's respect for the rule of law?

5.   Does a decision like People v. Dreares tend to maintain a rough equilibrium, a "balance of advantage" based on uncertainty, between police and citizens in street encounters?

6.   New York Penal Law § 240.35 Loitering "A person is guilty of loitering when he:

* * *

"6.   Loiters, remains or wanders in or about a place without apparent reason and under circumstances which justify suspicion that he may be engaged or about to engage in crime, and, upon inquiry by a peace officer, refuses to identify himself or fails to give a reasonably credible account of his conduct and purposes;

* * *

"Loitering is a violation."

What questions does § 240.35 pose for you? How do you answer those questions?

7.   New York Penal Law § 240.35(6) has been held void for vagueness under the due process provisions of the New York and U.S. Constitutions. See People v. Beltrand (Criminal Court of the City of New York, New York County), 63 Misc.2d 1041, 314 N.Y.S.2d 276 (1970); People v. Villaneuva (City Court of Long Beach, Nassau County), 65 Misc.2d 484, 318 N.Y.S.2d 167 (1971); People v. Berck, 32 N.Y.2d 567, 347 N.Y.S.2d 33, 300 N.E.2d 411 (1973).

In 1968 the following provision, a so-called no-sock law, was added to the New York Penal Law.

New York Penal Law, § 35.27.   Justification; use of physical force in resisting arrest prohibited.   A person may not use physical force to resist an arrest, whether authorized or unauthorized, which is being effected or attempted by a peace officer when it would reasonably appear that the latter is a peace officer.

Notes and Questions

1.   What is the likely effect of § 35.27 on the outcome of a case like People v. Dreares?

2.   What do you think will be the impact, if any, of § 35.27 on the behavior of police and citizens in encounters on the street?

3.   Which is better, the law on resisting arrest exemplified in People v. Dreares or the law as stated in § 35.27? Explain your answer.

4.   "The decision to resist arrest is the work of a moment rather than the result of carefully considered alternatives. The real question is whether for this act of resistance the citizen ought to be convicted of a crime . . . . The right to resist unlawful arrest memorializes one of the principal elements in the heritage of the English

revolution: the belief that the will to resist arbitrary authority in a reasonable way is valuable and ought not to be suppressed by the criminal law. In the face of obvious injustice, one ought not to be forced to submit and swallow one's sense of justice. More importantly, it is unconscionable to convict a man for resisting an injustice. This is indeed a value judgment, but the values are fundamental." Paul G. Chevigny, "The Right to Resist an Unlawful Arrest", 78 Yale Law Journal 1128, 1138 (1969).

Are there other values at stake in this matter?

5. Courts have given a limiting construction to New York Penal Law § 35.27. If a defendant is arrested, and then is charged with resisting that arrest, the defendant is still free to offer as a defense that the arrest was unlawful in its inception. See People v. Lyke, 72 Misc. 2d 1046, 340 N.Y.S.2d 357 (1973), People v. Ailey, 76 Misc.2d 589, 350 N.Y.S.2d 981 (1974), People v. John Doe*, 85 Misc.2d 592, 380 N.Y.S. 2d 549 (1976). However, if the resistance to an unlawful arrest amounts to an assault on the arresting officer, then the defendant may not invoke the defense that the arrest was unlawful. People v. Lyke, *supra*, and *accord*, U. S. ex rel. Horelick v. Criminal Court of the City of New York, 366 F.Supp. 1140 (1973).

New York Penal Law § 205.30 defines the defense of resisting arrest:

"A person is guilty of resisting arrest when he intentionally prevents or attempts to prevent a peace officer from effecting an authorized arrest of himself or another person.

"Resisting arrest is a class A misdemeanor."

In New York, a necessary element of an assault is that the defendant caused physical harm to a person. New York Penal Law §§ 120.00, 120.05, 120.10.

After a careful reading of the language of both § 205.30 and § 35.-27, can you offer a rationale for the courts' holding regarding the relationship of § 35.27 to § 205.30? In light of the cases cited above, what appears to be the practical significance of § 35.27?

6. Does the New York law on resisting unlawful arrest, described above, seem to you to provide adequate guidance to arresting officers regarding the limits of their authority? Does it pose practical limits on their authority?

7. Does that law seem to you to provide a suitable remedy for an unlawful arrest? What remedy does that law provide?

8. What alternative would you suggest? Is a civil action for damages likely to provide satisfaction to a victim of an unlawful arrest? Whom should the victim sue? The arresting officers, or the mu-

* The defendant was a youthful offender (between the ages of 16 and 19). A pseudonym was used in the court papers and title to the case pursuant to New York law which attempts to shelter youthful offenders from adverse publicity.

nicipality for whom they work? Would criminal prosecutions for unlawful arrests be a better alternative to self help by the victim? Why? Why not?

Stop and Frisk

The preceding materials regarding probable cause and unlawful arrest may have left the impression that the steps leading up to an arrest call for very conscious and deliberate actions in which the arresting officer must weigh legal standards against observed behavior and make very fine determinations regarding the law, the facts, and the consequences of acting or not acting. In practice, police work on the street appears to be more spontaneous and intuitive. That fact further complicates the problem of formulating standards of conduct and remedies for breach of standards. Consider the following materials in this regard.

[The following is taken from CHARLES A. REICH*, "POLICE QUESTIONING OF LAW ABIDING CITIZENS," 75 Yale Law Journal 1161 (1965), pp. 1161–1162.]

. . . In this article, I am not concerned with police investigations after a crime has been reported, or with circumstances which suggest that the individual who has been stopped may be doing something illegal. My problem is this: no crime has been reported, no suspect has been described, there is no visible sign of an offense, there is nothing whatever to direct police attention to this particular individual. I am concerned with what is called *preventive* police work.

. . . The increasing preventive activities of the police present an issue of first importance. What happens when the person stopped is a Negro, or poor, or frightened? What intrusions upon privacy, what affronts to dignity, occur? How much discretion do the police have to invent an offense for anyone who objects to being questioned? May the police establish a regular routine of requiring pedestrians to carry identification and explain their presence, or of requiring motorists to stop and tell where they are going? I do not have answers, but I have some questions. Let us focus on the moment of contact between the citizen and the police.

The first issue that troubles me is whether the police have any power at all to stop a law abiding person on a public street. Of course any individual has a right to approach any other individual—to ask him the time, to ask him how to find the Yale Divinity School, or to ask his opinion about foreign policy. But it is not quite the same when the police stop someone. There is authority in the approach of the police, and command in their tone. I can ignore

* Formerly Professor of Law Yale University; author of The Greening of America.

the ordinary person, but can I ignore the police? Police officers tell me that they have a *right* to stop anyone in a public place, without having a reason. I think I have a *right* not to be stopped. So far as I know, reported court decisions do not supply us with an answer.

The next issue is what questions the police may ask. Name? Address? Occupation? Age? Marital status? Explanation of presence and destination? Documentary proof of identity? Many people might have no objection to giving out any or all of these facts about themselves. But I have a strong sense that however innocuous the facts may be, some things are nobody's business. I do not particularly like to be probed, and I like it much less when the probing is official. I certainly do not think that every police officer has a roving commission to satisfy his curiosity about anyone he sees on the street.

Closely related to questioning is the issue of the individual's replies. May he refuse to answer? May he demand to know the identity of the officer? May he demand to know why he is being stopped? May he lie to the officer about his age, or why he is out on the street? May he turn and go on his way? I submit that very few people know what their rights are under such circumstances. I do not even know how to find out.

The next issue is what *actions* the officer may take if the individual attempts to claim some rights. May the officer detain him? Frisk him? Search him? Take him to the police station? Hold him there for questioning? Here the law does supply an answer in general terms, for we know that arrests and searches can be made only upon probable cause. But concrete answers really depend upon what we conclude about the right to stop and to ask questions.

The last issue is what remedies are available to the citizen to test out the law in the circumstances I have described. There is always the right to defend against any criminal charge that may result. There is always a tort action for false arrest. Perhaps in some extreme circumstances there might be grounds for an action under one of the civil rights statutes, or for an injunction against a continuing police practice. But these remedies are often costly, time-consuming, and ultimately unsuccessful. No one effectively "polices the police."

* * *

ALI MODEL CODE OF PRE–ARRAIGNMENT PROCEDURE

ARTICLE 110. PRE-ARREST CONTACTS OF POLICE OFFICERS WITH INDIVIDUALS

Section 110.1 Requests for Cooperation by Law Enforcement Officers

(1) **Authority to Request Cooperation.** A law enforcement officer may, subject to the provisions of this Code or other law, request any person to furnish information or otherwise cooperate in the investigation or prevention of crime. The officer may request the person to respond to questions, to appear at a police station, or to comply with any other reasonable

request. In making requests pursuant to this Section, no officer shall indicate that a person is legally obliged to furnish information or otherwise to cooperate if no such legal obligation exists. Compliance with a request for information or other cooperation hereunder shall not be regarded as involuntary or coerced solely on the ground that such request was made by one known to be a law enforcement officer.

(2) **Questioning of Suspects: Required Warning.** If a law enforcement officer, acting pursuant to this Section, suspects or has reasonable cause to suspect that a person may have committed a crime, he shall, as promptly as is reasonable under the circumstances and in any case prior to engaging in sustained questioning of that person, take such steps as are reasonable under the circumstances to make clear that no legal obligation exists to respond to the questioning. If the questioning takes place at a police station, prosecutor's office, or other similar place, the person to be questioned shall first be informed that he may promptly communicate with counsel, relatives or friends, and that counsel, relatives or friends may have access to him as provided in Section 140.7.

(3) **Warning to Persons Asked to Appear at a Police Station.** If a law enforcement officer acting pursuant to this Section requests any person to come to or remain at a police station, prosecutor's office or other similar place, he shall take such steps as are reasonable under the circumstances to make clear that there is no legal obligation to comply with such request.

Questions

Does § 110.1 of the ALI Model Code afford answers to some or all of the issues and questions posed by Professor Reich? Are those answers adequate, in your judgment, to deal with Professor Reich's concerns? What purposes are served by this section of the Model Code?

In 1968, the Supreme Court of the United States was called upon to deal with some of the issues posed by Professor Reich, and addressed in the ALI standards. The case was Terry v. Ohio, 392 U.S. 1, 88 S.Ct. 1868 (1968). In that case, Terry appealed from his conviction upon a charge of carrying a concealed weapon. Terry had been arrested by Cleveland Police Detective Martin McFadden. The events leading up to the arrest were described by the Court as follows.

[At a pre-trial hearing] Officer McFadden testified that while he was patrolling in plain clothes in downtown Cleveland at approximately 2:30 in the afternoon of October 31, 1963, his attention was attracted by two men, Chilton and Terry, standing on the corner of Huron Road and Euclid Avenue. He had never seen the two men before, and he was unable to say precisely what first drew his eye to them. However, he testified that he had been a policeman for 39 years and a detective for 35 and that he had been assigned to patrol this vicinity of downtown Cleveland for shoplifters and pickpockets for 30 years.

He explained that he had developed routine habits of observation over the years and that he would "stand and watch people or walk and watch people at many intervals of the day." He added: "Now, in this case when I looked over they didn't look right to me at the time."

His interest aroused, Officer McFadden took up a post of observation in the entrance to a store 300 to 400 feet away from the two men. "I get more purpose to watch them when I seen their movements," he testified. He saw one of the men leave the other one and walk southwest on Huron Road, past some stores. The man paused for a moment and looked in a store window, then walked on a short distance, turned around and walked back toward the corner, pausing once again to look in the same store window. He rejoined his companion at the corner, and the two conferred briefly. Then the second man went through the same series of motions, strolling down Huron Road, looking in the same window, walking on a short distance, turning back, peering in the store window again, and returning to confer with the first man at the corner. The two men repeated this ritual alternately between five and six times apiece—in all, roughly a dozen trips. At one point, while the two were standing together on the corner, a third man approached them and engaged them briefly in conversation. This man then left the two others and walked west on Euclid Avenue. Chilton and Terry resumed their measured pacing, peering, and conferring. After this had gone on for 10 to 12 minutes, the two men walked off together, heading west on Euclid Avenue, following the path taken earlier by the third man.

By this time Officer McFadden had become thoroughly suspicious. He testified that after observing their elaborately casual and oft-repeated reconnaissance of the store window on Huron Road, he suspected the two men of "casing a job, a stick-up," and that he considered it his duty as a police officer to investigate further. He added that he feared "they may have a gun." Thus, Officer McFadden followed Chilton and Terry and saw them stop in front of Zucker's store to talk to the same man who had conferred with them earlier on the street corner. Deciding that the situation was ripe for direct action, Officer McFadden approached the three men, identified himself as a police officer and asked for their names. At this point his knowledge was confined to what he had observed. He was not acquainted with any of the three men by name or by sight, and he had received no information concerning them from any other source. When the men "mumbled something" in response to his inquiries, Officer McFadden grabbed petitioner Terry, spun him around so that they were facing the other two, with Terry between McFadden and the others, and patted down the outside of his clothing. In the left breast pocket of Terry's overcoat Officer McFadden felt a pistol. He reached inside the overcoat pocket, but was unable to remove the gun. At this point, keeping Terry between himself and the others, the officer ordered all three men to enter Zucker's store. As they went in, he removed Terry's overcoat completely, removed a .38-caliber revolver from the pocket and ordered all three men to face the wall with their hands raised. Officer McFadden proceeded to pat down the outer clothing of Chilton and the third man, Katz. He discovered another revolver in the outer pocket of Chilton's overcoat, but no weapons were found on Katz. The officer testified that he only patted the men down to see whether they had weapons, and that he did not put his hands beneath the outer garments of either Terry or Chilton until he felt their guns. So far as appears from the record, he never placed his hands beneath Katz' outer garments. Officer McFadden seized Chilton's gun, asked the proprietor of the store to call a police wagon, and took all three men to the station, where Chilton and Terry were formally charged with carrying concealed weapons.

* * *

Questions

1. Did Officer McFadden have probable cause to arrest Terry at any time prior to discovering the concealed weapon?

2. What authority did Officer McFadden have for stopping Terry and Chilton and addressing questions to them? Did he need any special authority to do that? Did he have "reasonable grounds" for accosting Chilton and Terry and addressing questions to them?

3. When Chilton and Terry could not respond adequately to McFadden's questions, did he have "reasonable grounds" for pursuing the investigation further? If so, did he have "reasonable grounds" for grabbing Terry and patting him down?

4. After patting down Terry, did McFadden have probable cause to arrest Terry? To search his overcoat? Did he have reasonable grounds to pat down Chilton and Katz?

5. What criteria and values have you invoked to this point to help you answer the preceding questions?

6. Assume that you were an attorney appointed to defend Terry against the charge that he was unlawfully carrying a concealed weapon. Assume further that Terry had no legal authority or privilege to carry the pistol, and that he was unlawfully carrying the pistol. What defense would you offer in his behalf?

7. Assume that Officer McFadden's conduct in seizing and patting down Terry was unlawful, i. e., that it violated legal standards regarding arrest and search of persons. What remedy or remedies would you pursue on Terry's behalf?

8. If you were Terry, what remedy or defense would you think most appropriate to solve the problem posed by your unfortunate contact with Officer McFadden?

———

As far as we can tell, Terry was clearly guilty of carrying a concealed weapon in violation of Ohio law, and he had no substantive defense to the crime. His attorney, however, had a procedural ground on which to defend Terry. He moved prior to trial to suppress the evidence of the crime, on the grounds that it was illegally seized in that McFadden did not have probable cause to detain Terry, or to search his person. Moreover, Terry's attorney was aware that federal courts had held that the use in a criminal trial of illegally taken evidence is a violation of due process of law. In order to remedy that problem, the federal judges have fashioned an exclusionary rule barring the use of such illegally seized evidence in federal trials, Weeks v. U. S., 232 U.S. 383, 34 S.Ct. 341 (1914). That rule was subsequently extended, via the Fourteenth Amendment, to cover state trials. Consider in this regard the following excerpts from Mapp v. Ohio, 367 U.S. 643, 81 S.Ct. 1684(1961).

There are those who say, as did JUSTICE (then JUDGE) CARDOZO, that under our constitutional exclusionary doctrine "[t]he criminal is to go free because the constable has blundered." People v. Defore, 242 N.Y. at page 21, 150 N.E. at page 587. In some cases this will undoubtedly be the result. But, as was said in Elkins, "there is another consideration—the imperative of judicial integrity." 364 U.S. at page 222, 80 S.Ct. at page 1447. The criminal goes free, if he must, but it is the law that sets him free. Nothing can destroy a government more quickly than its failure to observe its own laws, or worse, its disregard of the character of its own existence. As MR. JUSTICE BRANDEIS, dissenting, said in Olmstead v. United States, 1928, 277 U.S. 438, 485, 48 S.Ct. 564, 575, 72 L.Ed. 944: "Our government is the potent, the omnipresent teacher. For good or for ill, it teaches the whole people by its example. * * * If the government becomes a lawbreaker, it breeds contempt for law; it invites every man to become a law unto himself; it invites anarchy." Nor can it lightly be assumed that, as a practical matter, adoption of the exclusionary rule fetters law enforcement. Only last year this Court expressly considered that contention and found that "pragmatic evidence of a sort" to the contrary was not wanting. Elkins v. United States, *supra*, 364 U.S. at page 218, 80 S.Ct. at page 1444. The court noted that

"The federal courts themselves have operated under the exclusionary rule of Weeks for almost half a century; yet it has not been suggested either that the Federal Bureau of Investigation has thereby been rendered ineffective, or that the administration of criminal justice in the federal courts has thereby been disrupted. Moreover, the experience of the states is impressive * * *. The movement towards the rule of exclusion has been halting but seemingly inexorable." 364 U.S. at pages 218–219, 80 S.Ct. at pages 1444–1445.

The ignoble shortcut to conviction left open to the State tends to destroy the entire system of constitutional restraints on which the liberties of the people rest. Having once recognized that the right to privacy embodied in the Fourth Amendment is enforceable against the States, and that the right to be secure against rude invasions of privacy by state officers is, therefore, constitutional in origin, we can no longer permit that right to remain an empty promise. Because it is enforceable in the same manner and to like effect as other basic rights secured by the Due Process Clause, we can no longer permit it to be revocable at the whim of any police officer who, in the name of law enforcement itself, chooses to suspend its enjoyment. Our decision, founded on reason and truth, gives to the individual no more than that which the Constitution guarantees him, to the police officer no less than that to which honest law enforcement is entitled, and, to the courts, that judicial integrity so necessary in the true administration of justice.

The trial court denied Terry's suppression motion on the ground that Officer McFadden, on the basis of his experience, "had reasonable cause to believe . . . that the defendants were conducting themselves suspiciously, and some interrogation should be made of their action." Purely for his own protection, the court held, the officer had the right to pat down the outer clothing of these men, who he had reasonable cause to believe might be armed. The court distinguished between an investigatory "stop" and an arrest, and between "frisk" of the outer clothing for weapons and a full-blown search for evidence of crime. The "frisk," it held, was essential to the proper performance of the officer's investigatory duties, for without it "the answer to the police officer may be a bullet, and a loaded pistol discovered during the frisk is admissible."

Terry and Chilton then waived jury trial, pleaded not guilty, and were convicted as charged. They appealed their convictions to an intermediate appellate court, and the Supreme Court of Ohio, both of which affirmed the convictions. Subsequently Chilton died, but Terry sought relief by petition for certiorari in the United States Supreme Court. The Court granted certiorari, heard Terry's appeal, and decided to affirm his conviction. Following are excerpts from Chief Justice Warren's * opinion for the Court.

If this case involved police conduct subject to the Warrant Clause of the Fourth Amendment, we would have to ascertain whether "probable cause" existed to justify the search and seizure which took place. However, that is not the case. We do not retreat from our holdings that the police must, whenever practicable, obtain advance judicial approval of searches and seizures through the warrant procedure, see e. g., Katz v. United States, 389 U.S. 347, 88 S.Ct. 507 (1967); Beck v. Ohio, 379 U.S. 89, 96, 85 S.Ct. 223, 228 (1964); Chapman v. United States, 365 U.S. 610, 81 S.Ct. 776 (1961), or that in most instances failure to comply with the warrant requirement can only be excused by exigent circumstances, see, e. g., Warden v. Hayden, 387 U.S. 294, 87 S.Ct. 1642 (1967) (hot pursuit); cf. Preston v. United States, 376 U.S. 364, 367–368, 84 S.Ct. 881, 884 (1964). But we deal here with an entire rubric of police conduct—necessarily swift action predicated upon the on-the-spot observations of the officer on the beat—which historically has not been, and as a practical matter could not be, subjected to the warrant procedure. Instead, the conduct involved in this case must be tested by the Fourth Amendment's general proscription against unreasonable searches and seizures.

---

* Justice Warren was appointed to the Supreme Court in 1953. His appointment by President Eisenhower came after a distinguished career in public service and politics. He was twice governor of California, and he was the Republican nominee for Vice-President of the United States in 1948. During his tenure as Chief Justice the Supreme Court was extremely active in the areas of Civil Rights and Criminal Procedure. Some of the most famous and controversial decisions of the "Warren Court" are reprinted in this chapter.

Nonetheless, the notions which underlie both the warrant procedure and the requirement of probable cause remain fully relevant in this context. In order to assess the reasonableness of Officer McFadden's conduct as a general proposition, it is necessary "first to focus upon the governmental interest which allegedly justifies official intrusion upon the constitutionally protected interests of the private citizen," for there is "no ready test for determining reasonableness other than by balancing the need to search [or seize] against the invasion which the search [or seizure] entails." Camara v. Municipal Court, 387 U.S. 523, 534–535, 536–537, 87 S.Ct. 1727, 1735 (1967). And in justifying the particular intrusion the police officer must be able to point to specific and articulable facts which, taken together with rational inferences from those facts, reasonably warrant that intrusion. The scheme of the Fourth Amendment becomes meaningful only when it is assured that at some point the conduct of those charged with enforcing the laws can be subjected to the more detached, neutral scrutiny of a judge who must evaluate the reasonableness of a particular search or seizure in light of the particular circumstances. And in making that assessment it is imperative that the facts be judged against an objective standard: would the facts available to the officer at the moment of the seizure or the search "warrant a man of reasonable caution in the belief" that the action taken was appropriate? Cf. Carroll v. United States, 267 U.S. 132, 45 S.Ct. 280 (1925); Beck v. Ohio, 379 U.S. 89, 96–97, 85 S.Ct. 223, 229 (1964). Anything less would invite intrusions upon constitutionally guaranteed rights based on nothing more substantial than inarticulate hunches, a result this Court has consistently refused to sanction. See, e. g., Beck v. Ohio, supra; Rios v. United States, 364 U.S. 253, 80 S.Ct. 1431 (1960); Henry v. United States, 361 U.S. 98, 80 S.Ct. 168 (1959). And simple " 'good faith on the part of the arresting officer is not enough.' . . . If subjective good faith alone were the test, the protections of the Fourth Amendment would evaporate, and the people would be 'secure in their persons, houses, papers, and effects,' only in the discretion of the police." Beck v. Ohio, supra, at 97, 85 S.Ct. at 229.

Applying these principles to this case, we consider first the nature and extent of the governmental interests involved. One general interest is of course that of effective crime prevention and detection; it is this interest which underlies the recognition that a police officer may in appropriate circumstances and in an appropriate manner approach a person for purposes of investigating possibly criminal behavior even though there is no probable cause to make an arrest. It was this legitimate investigative function Officer McFadden was discharging when he decided to approach petitioner and his companions. He had observed Terry, Chilton, and Katz go through a series of acts, each of them perhaps innocent in itself, but which taken together warranted further investigation. There is nothing unusual in two men standing together on a street corner, perhaps waiting for someone. Nor is there anything suspicious about people in such circumstances strolling up and down the street, singly or in pairs. Store windows, moreover, are made to be looked in. But the story is quite different where, as here, two men hover about a street corner for an extended period of time, at the end of which it becomes apparent that they are not waiting for anyone or anything; where these men pace alternately along an identical route, pausing to stare in the same store window roughly 24 times; where each completion of this route is followed immediately by a conference between the two men on the corner; where they are joined in one of these conferences by a third man who leaves swiftly; and where the two men finally follow the third and rejoin him a couple of blocks away. It would have been poor police work indeed for an officer of 30 years' experience in the detection of thievery from stores in this same neighborhood to have failed to investigate this behavior further.

The crux of this case, however, is not the propriety of Officer McFadden's taking steps to investigate petitioner's suspicious behavior, but rather, whether there was justification for McFadden's invasion of Terry's personal security by searching him for weapons in the course of that investigation. We are now concerned with more than the governmental interest in investigating crime; in addition, there is the more immediate interest of the police officer in taking steps to assure himself that the person with whom he is dealing is not armed with a weapon that could unexpectedly and fatally be used against him. Certainly it would be unreasonable to require that police officers take unnecessary risks in the performance of their duties. American criminals have a long tradition of armed violence, and every year in this country many law enforcement officers are killed in the line of duty, and thousands more are wounded. Virtually all of these deaths and a substantial portion of the injuries are inflicted with guns and knives.[5]

In view of these facts, we cannot blind ourselves to the need for law enforcement officers to protect themselves and other prospective victims of violence in situations where they may lack probable cause for an arrest. When an officer is justified in believing that the individual whose suspicious behavior he is investigating at close range is armed and presently dangerous to the officer or to others, it would appear to be clearly unreasonable to deny the officer the power to take necessary measures to determine whether the person is in fact carrying a weapon and to neutralize the threat of physical harm.

We must still consider, however, the nature and quality of the intrusion on individual rights which must be accepted if police officers are to be conceded the right to search for weapons in situations where probable cause to arrest for crime is lacking. Even a limited search of the outer clothing for weapons constitutes a severe, though brief, intrusion upon cherished personal security, and it must surely be an annoying, frightening, and perhaps humiliating experience. Petitioner contends that such an intrusion is permissible only incident to a lawful arrest, either for a crime involving the possession of weapons or for a crime the commission of which led the

---

5. Fifty-seven law enforcement officers were killed in the line of duty in this country in 1966, bringing the total to 335 for the seven-year period beginning with 1960. Also in 1966, there were 23,851 assaults on police officers, 9,113 of which resulted in injuries to the policemen. Fifty-five of the 57 officers killed in 1966 died from gunshot wounds, 41 of them inflicted by handguns easily secreted about the person. The remaining two murders were perpetrated by knives. See Federal Bureau of Investigation, Uniform Crime Reports for the United States—1966, at 45–48, 152 and Table 51.

The easy availability of firearms to potential criminals in this country is well known and has provoked much debate. See e. g., President's Commission on Law Enforcement and Administration of Justice, The Challenge of Crime in a Free Society 239–243 (1967). Whatever the merits of gun-control proposals, this fact is relevant to an assessment of the need for some form of self-protective search power.

officer to investigate in the first place.   However, this argument must be closely examined.

Petitioner does not argue that a police officer should refrain from making any investigation of suspicious circumstances until such time as he has probable cause to make an arrest; nor does he deny that police officers in properly discharging their investigative function may find themselves confronting persons who might well be armed and dangerous.   Moreover, he does not say that an officer is always unjustified in searching a suspect to discover weapons.   Rather, he says it is unreasonable for the policeman to take that step until such time as the situation evolves to a point where there is probable cause to make an arrest.   When that point has been reached, petitioner would concede the officer's right to conduct a search of the suspect for weapons, fruits or instrumentalities of the crime, or "mere" evidence, incident to the arrest.

There are two weaknesses in this line of reasoning, however.   First, it fails to take account of traditional limitations upon the scope of searches, and thus recognizes no distinction in purpose, character, and extent between a search incident to an arrest and a limited search for weapons.   The former, although justified in part by the acknowledged necessity to protect the arresting officer from assault with a concealed weapon, Preston v. United States, 376 U.S. 364, 367, 84 S.Ct. 881, 883 (1964), is also justified on other grounds, ibid., and can therefore involve a relatively extensive exploration of the person.   A search for weapons in the absence of probable cause to arrest, however, must, like any other search, be strictly circumscribed by the exigencies which justify its initiation.   Warden v. Hayden, 387 U.S. 294, 310, 87 S.Ct. 1642, 1652 (1967) (MR. JUSTICE FORTAS, concurring). Thus it must be limited to that which is necessary for the discovery of weapons which might be used to harm the officer or others nearby, and may realistically be characterized as something less than a "full" search, even though it remains a serious intrusion.

A second, and related, objection to petitioner's argument is that it assumes that the law of arrest has already worked out the balance between the particular interests involved here—the neutralization of danger to the policeman in the investigative circumstance and the sanctity of the individual.   But this is not so.   An arrest is a wholly different kind of intrusion upon individual freedom from a limited search for weapons, and the interests each is designed to serve are likewise quite different.   An arrest is the initial stage of a criminal prosecution.   It is intended to vindicate society's interest in having its laws obeyed, and it is inevitably accompanied by future interference with the individual's freedom of movement, whether or not trial or conviction ultimately follows.   The protective search for weapons, on the other hand, constitutes a brief, though far from inconsiderable, intrusion upon the sanctity of the person.   It does not follow that because an officer may lawfully arrest a person only when he is apprised of facts sufficient to warrant a belief that the person has committed or is committing a crime, the officer is equally unjustified, absent that kind of evidence, in making any intrusions short of an arrest.   Moreover, a perfectly reasonable apprehension of danger may arise long before the officer is possessed of adequate information to justify taking a person into custody for the purpose of prosecuting him for a crime.   Petitioner's reliance on cases which have worked out standards of reasonableness with regard to "seizures" constituting arrests and searches incident thereto is thus misplaced. It assumes that the interests sought to be vindicated and the invasions of personal security may be equated in the two cases, and thereby ignores a vital aspect of the analysis of the reasonableness of particular types of conduct under the Fourth Amendment. See Camara v. Municipal Court, supra.

Our evaluation of the proper balance that has to be struck in this type of case leads us to conclude that there must be a narrowly drawn authority to permit a reasonable search for weapons for the protection of the police officer, where he has reason to believe that he is dealing with an armed and dangerous individual, regardless of whether he has probable cause to arrest the individual for a crime. The officer need not be absolutely certain that the individual is armed; the issue is whether a reasonably prudent man in the circumstances would be warranted in the belief that his safety or that of others was in danger. Cf. Beck v. Ohio, 379 U.S. 89, 91, 85 S.Ct. 223, 226 (1964); Brinegar v. United States, 338 U.S. 160, 174–176, 69 S.Ct. 1302, 1311 (1949); Stacey v. Emery, 97 U.S. 642, 645 (1878). And in determining whether the officer acted reasonably in such circumstances, due weight must be given, not to his inchoate and unparticularized suspicion or "hunch," but to the specific reasonable inferences which he is entitled to draw from the facts in light of his experience. Cf. Brinegar v. United States, supra.

* * *

. . . The sole justification of the search in the present situation is the protection of the police officer and others nearby, and it must therefore be confined in scope to an intrusion reasonably designed to discover guns, knives, clubs, or other hidden instruments for the assault of the police officer.

The scope of the search in this case presents no serious problem in light of these standards. Officer McFadden patted down the outer clothing of petitioner and his two companions. He did not place his hands in their pockets or under the outer surface of their garments until he had felt weapons, and then he merely reached for and removed the guns. He never did invade Katz' person beyond the outer surfaces of his clothes, since he discovered nothing in his pat-down which might have been a weapon. Officer McFadden confined his search strictly to what was minimally necessary to learn whether the men were armed and to disarm them once he discovered the weapons. He did not conduct a general exploratory search for whatever evidence of criminal activity he might find.

We conclude that the revolver seized from Terry was properly admitted in evidence against him. At the time he seized petitioner and searched him for weapons, Officer McFadden had reasonable grounds to believe that petitioner was armed and dangerous, and it was necessary for the protection of himself and others to take swift measures to discover the true facts and neutralize the threat of harm if it materialized. The policeman carefully restricted his search to what was appropriate to the discovery of the particular items which he sought. Each case of this sort will, of course, have to be decided on its own facts. We merely hold today that where a police officer observes unusual conduct which leads him reasonably to conclude in light of his experience that criminal activity may be afoot and that the persons with whom he is dealing may be armed and presently dangerous, where in the course of investigating this behavior he identifies himself as a policeman and makes reasonable inquiries, and where nothing in the initial stages of the encounter serves to dispel his reasonable fear for his own or others' safety, he is entitled for the protection of himself and others in the area to conduct a carefully limited search of the outer clothing of such persons in an attempt to discover weapons which might be used to assault him.

Questions

1. What purposes seem to you to be served by the use of an exclusionary rule as a remedy for unlawful police work? Is the primary purpose to deter the police? To vindicate the interests of specific defendants like Terry? To vindicate judicial interests regarding the integrity of the trial process?

2. What problems are posed by the use of an exclusionary rule? Does Justice Warren recognize and attempt to deal with such problems in the excerpts from his opinion?

3. Assume that you are an attorney who regularly represents defendants in criminal cases. How would you formulate the rule underlying the decision in Terry v. Ohio?

4. Assume that you are a Deputy District Attorney who regularly tries criminal cases including many "possession" offenses. How would you formulate the rule underlying the decision in Terry v. Ohio?

5. Assume that you are a detective assigned to robbery detail. How would you formulate the rule underlying the decision in Terry v. Ohio?

6. Does it appear that the majority in Terry anticipates that a strict application of the exclusionary rule is likely to significantly alter the behavior of police or citizens in encounters such as the occurrence in Terry?

7. Which would you think might most significantly affect police behavior on the street, a strict exclusionary rule or a flexible— "keep them guessing"—approach?

8. How, if at all, do judges determine the effects of their decisions on official behavior?

9. Can you think of any reasons why judges might tend to fashion strict rules regarding the propriety of arrests or stops in cases where the alleged offense is possession of contraband, e. g., a gun or narcotics?

––––––––––

The issues posed in Terry v. Ohio had been considered in other forums prior to the decision in that case. For example, the following "stop and frisk" provision was part of the law of New York prior to the decision in Terry.

§ 180–a. Temporary questioning of persons in public places; search for weapons.

1. A police officer may stop any person abroad in a public place whom he reasonably suspects is committing, has committed or is about to commit a felony or any of the crimes specified in section five hundred fifty-two of this chapter, and may demand of him his name, address and an explanation of his actions.

2. When a police officer has stopped a person for questioning pursuant to this section and reasonably suspects that he is in danger of life or limb, he may search such person for a dangerous weapon. If the police officer finds ·such a weapon or any other thing the possession of which may constitute a crime, he may take and keep it until the completion of the questioning, at which time he shall either return it, if lawfully possessed, or arrest such person.

Section 180–a has since been amended to extend the stop and frisk authority to court officers, in order to allow court officers to search courtroom spectators for weapons, and it has been renumbered, but its essential features remain unchanged in the present law. See New York Penal Code § 140.50.

The U.S. Supreme Court had an opportunity to comment on § 180–a at the time it decided Terry. Two companion cases, Sibron v. New York and Peters v. New York, were decided with Terry, see 392 U.S. 40, 88 S.Ct. 1889 (1968). The facts in these two cases are summarized in the following excerpts from the opinion of the Court.

"Sibron, . . . was convicted of the unlawful possession of heroin. He moved before trial to suppress the heroin seized from his person by the arresting officer, Brooklyn Patrolman Anthony Martin. After the trial court denied his motion, Sibron pleaded guilty to the charge, preserving his right to appeal the evidentiary ruling. At the hearing on the motion to suppress, Officer Martin testified that while he was patrolling his beat in uniform on March 9, 1965, he observed Sibron 'continually from the hours of 4:00 P.M. to 12:00, midnight . . . in the vicinity of 742 Broadway.' He stated that during this period of time he saw Sibron in conversation with six or eight persons whom he (Patrolman Martin) knew from past experience to be narcotics addicts. The officer testified that he did not overhear any of these conversations, and that he did not see anything pass between Sibron and any of the others. Late in the evening Sibron entered a restaurant. Patrolman Martin saw Sibron speak with three more known addicts inside the restaurant. Once again, nothing was overheard and nothing was seen to pass between Sibron and the addicts. Sibron sat down and ordered pie and coffee, and, as he was eating, Patrolman Martin approached him and told him to come outside. Once outside, the officer said to Sibron, 'You know what I am after.' According to the officer, Sibron 'mumbled something and reached into his pocket.' Simultaneously, Patrolman Martin thrust his hand into the same pocket, discovering several glassine envelopes, which, it turned out, contained heroin."

"Peters, the appellant in No. 74, was convicted of possessing burglary tools under circumstances evincing an intent to employ them in the commission of a crime. The tools were seized from his person at the time of his arrest, and like Sibron he made a pretrial motion to suppress them. When the trial court denied the motion, he too pleaded guilty, preserving his right to appeal. Officer Samuel Lasky of the New York City Police Department testified at the hearing on the motion that he was at home in his apartment in Mount Vernon, New York, at about 1 p. m. on July 10, 1964. He had just finished taking a shower and was drying himself when he heard a noise at his door. His attempt to investigate was interrupted by a telephone call, but when he returned and looked through the peephole into the hall, Officer Lasky saw 'two men tiptoeing out of the alcove toward the stairway.' He immediately called the police, put on some civilian clothes and armed himself with his service revolver. Returning to the peephole, he saw 'a tall man tiptoeing away from the alcove and followed by this shorter man, Mr. Peters, toward the stairway.' Officer Lasky testified that he had lived in the 120-unit building for 12 years and that he did not recognize either of the men as tenants. Believing that he had happened upon the two men in the course of an attempted burglary, Officer Lasky opened his door, entered the hallway and slammed the door loudly behind him. This precipitated a flight down the stairs on the part of the two men, and Officer Lasky gave chase. His apartment was located on the sixth floor, and he apprehended Peters between the fourth and fifth floors. Grabbing Peters by the collar, he continued down another flight in unsuccessful pursuit of the other man. Peters explained his presence in the building to Officer Lasky by saying that he was visiting a girl friend. However, he declined to reveal the girl friend's name, on the ground that she was a married woman. Officer Lasky patted Peters down for weapons, and discovered a hard object in his pocket. He stated at the hearing that the object did not feel like a gun, but that it might have been a knife. He removed the object from Peters' pocket. It was an opaque plastic envelope, containing burglar's tools."

Both Sibron and Peters were convicted in the New York courts. The U.S. Supreme Court reversed in Sibron, holding both that patrolman Martin had insufficient grounds for stopping Sibron, and that the search incident to the stop was not a protective search for weapons, but was in fact a search for evidence that would support Martin's suspicion that Sibron had narcotics on his person. The Court suggested that even if the stop of Sibron had been justifiable under Terry, the search in Sibron was too extensive in that it went well beyond the limits of a protective pat down intended to assure that the suspect was not armed with a deadly weapon.

In Peters, the Court affirmed on the grounds that Officer Lasky had probable cause to believe that Peters was committing a crime, and that when Officer Lasky literally collared Peters in the hallway, that was a full arrest, not just an investigatory stop. The Court found that the search in Peters was limited at first to a precautionary pat down to protect against weapons; that the search became more extensive only after the officer found some evidence that Peters might be armed; and the Court also suggested that a limited search for evidence of the crime of burglary was reasonable in a case where the defendant was already under arrest on suspicion of the commission of that crime.

The Court expressly declined to consider any issue as to the validity of § 180–a of the New York Penal Law. In Sibron the Court found that the search was clearly in violation of the Fourth Amendment strictures on searches and seizures, thus § 180–a was not relevant to the outcome of the case. In Peters, § 180–a was found inapplicable since the defendant was not held under a § 180–a stop, but was under arrest at the time he was searched.

Terry v. Ohio, and its companion cases Sibron and Peters, came before the Supreme Court when it was engaged in a thoroughgoing probing and reassessment of the constitutional standards governing the criminal process, and especially the police phase of that process. The decision in Terry was something of a departure from the trend of the Court's decisions in this area during the 1960s. The trend of those cases had been to require police to observe punctiliously the strictures of the Bill of Rights and the Due Process provisions of the U.S. Constitution. Terry gave a Supreme Court imprimatur to common investigative procedures the legality of which had theretofore been somewhat ambiguous, and at the same time found that "reasonable suspicion", rather than "probable cause", would privilege limited detentions and searches. Justice Douglas alone dissented from the Court's attempt at compromise between the strict words of the Fourth Amendment and what the majority apparently felt to be the requirements of police work on the street.

In subsequent cases the Court has had to deal again with issues of stop and frisk.

1.   The following is from the opinion of the court in Adams v. Williams, 407 U.S. 143, 92 S.Ct. 1921 (1971).

> "Police Sgt. John Connolly was alone early in the morning on car patrol duty in a high-crime area of Bridgeport, Connecticut. At approximately 2:15 a. m. a person known to Sgt. Connolly approached his cruiser and informed him that an individual seated in a nearby vehicle was carrying narcotics and had a gun at his waist.
>
> After calling for assistance on his car radio, Sgt. Connolly approached the vehicle to investigate the informant's report. Connolly tapped on the car window and asked the occupant, Robert Williams, to open the door. When Williams rolled down the window instead, the sergeant reached into the car and removed a fully loaded revolver from Williams' waistband. The gun had not been visible to Connolly from outside the car, but it was in precisely the place indicated by the informant. Williams was then arrested by Connolly for unlawful possession of the pistol. A search incident to that arrest was conducted after other officers arrived. They found substantial quantities of heroin on Williams' person and in

the car, and they found a machete and a second revolver hidden in the automobile."

Williams was convicted of unlawful possession of both the handgun and the narcotics. He sought relief via *habeas corpus* proceedings in federal court. The District Court denied his petition; the Circuit Court of Appeals for the Second Circuit, sitting *en banc*, granted the relief requested by Williams; the Supreme Court reversed the Circuit Court, and denied Williams' petition.

The Court in an opinion, per Mr. Justice Rehnquist, held that although the unverified informant's tip was insufficient to support an arrest, it was nonetheless sufficient to justify a forceable stop because the informant was known by Sergeant Connolly and had provided him with information prior to the night in question. Justice Rehnquist then concluded that since the frisk for the gun was justified, the arrest on the gun charge was lawful, and once the defendant was lawfully under arrest that privileged the search which turned up the narcotics.

Chief Justice Burger, and Justices Stewart, White, Blackmun, and Powell joined in the majority opinion. Justices Douglas, Brennan, and Marshall dissented. In his dissent, Justice Marshall pointed out that the trial court record disclosed that the only information the informant had provided Sergeant Connolly dealt with alleged homosexual behavior in the Bridgeport railroad station, and Sergeant Connolly had been unable to corroborate that tip.

2. The following is from the opinion of the Court in U. S. v. Robinson, 414 U.S. 218, 94 S.Ct. 467 (1973).

"On April 23, 1968, at approximately 11 p.m., Officer Richard Jenks, a 15-year veteran of the District of Columbia Metropolitan Police Department, observed the respondent driving a 1965 Cadillac near the intersection of 8th and C Streets, N.E., in the District of Columbia. Jenks, as a result of previous investigation following a check of respondent's operator's permit four days earlier, determined there was reason to believe that respondent was operating a motor vehicle after the revocation of his operator's permit. This is an offense defined by statute in the District of Columbia which carries a mandatory minimum jail term, a mandatory minimum fine, or both. D.C.Code Ann. § 40–302(d) (1967).

"Jenks signaled respondent to stop the automobile, which respondent did, and all three of the occupants emerged from the car. At that point Jenks informed respondent that he was under arrest for 'operating after revocation and obtaining a permit by misrepresentation.' It was assumed by the Court of Appeals, and is conceded by the respondent here, that Jenks had probable cause to arrest respondent, and that he effected a full-custody arrest.

"In accordance with procedures prescribed in police department instructions, Jenks then began to search respondent. He explained at a subsequent hearing that he was 'face-to-face' with the respondent, and 'placed [his] hands on [the respondent], my right-hand to his left breast like this (demonstrating) and proceeded to pat him down thus [with the right land].' During this patdown, Jenks felt an object in the left breast pocket of the heavy coat respondent was wearing, but testified that he 'couldn't tell what it was' and also that he 'couldn't actually tell the size of it.' Jenks then reached into the pocket and pulled out the object, which turned out to be a 'crumpled up cigarette package.' Jenks testified that at this point he still did not know what was in the package:

> 'As I felt the package I could feel objects in the package but I couldn't tell what they were. . . . I knew they weren't cigarettes.'

"The officer then opened the cigarette pack and found 14 gelatin capsules of white powder which he thought to be, and which later analysis proved to be, heroin. Jenks then continued his search of respondent to completion, feeling around his waist and trouser legs, and examining the remaining pockets. The heroin seized from the respondent was admitted into evidence at the trial which resulted in his conviction in the District Court."

Robinson was convicted on narcotic charges. The U.S. Court of Appeals for the D.C. Circuit, sitting *en banc*, reversed holding that the heroin had been unlawfully seized and could not be used in evidence against Robinson; on appeal, the U.S. Supreme Court reversed the Circuit Court and affirmed Robinson's conviction.

The Court, per Mr. Justice Rehnquist, held that once Robinson was validly under arrest on the motor vehicle charge Officer Jenks was privileged to search Robinson's person for weapons or evidence. The Circuit Court had held that the principle of Terry v. Ohio applied as well to searches incident to arrest as to stop and frisk cases. Accordingly, the Circuit Court held that while Officer Jenks was privileged to conduct a protective pat down for weapons, there was no basis in the facts before him to continue a search where no weapons were found, and where the object recovered from Robinson's pocket had no discernible evidentiary relationship to the offense for which Robinson was arrested. Justice Rehnquist pointed out that Terry was not controlling, since its rules regarding the limited nature of protective searches were posed in the context of a stop not an arrest. After examining the precedents regarding searches incident to arrest, Justice Rehnquist concluded that "It is the fact of the lawful arrest which establishes the authority to search, and we hold that in the case of a lawful custodial arrest a full search of the person is not only an exception to the warrant requirement of the Fourth Amendment, but is also a 'reasonable search' under that Amendment", 414 U.S. 218 at 235.

Chief Justice Burger and Justices Stewart, White, Blackmun, and Powell joined in the majority opinion. Justices Douglas and Brennan joined in the dissenting opinion of Justice Marshall.

3.   The following is from the opinion of the Court in Gustafson v. Florida, 414 U.S. 260, 94 S.Ct. 488 (1973).

"At approximately 2 a.m., on January 12, 1969, Lieutenant Paul R. Smith, a uniformed municipal police officer of Eau Gallie,

Florida, was on a routine patrol in an unmarked squad car when he observed a 1953 white Cadillac, bearing New York license plates, driving south through the town. Smith observed the automobile weave across the center line and back to the right side of the road 'three or four' times. Smith testified that he observed the two occupants of the Cadillac look back; after they apparently saw the squad car, the car drove across the highway and behind a grocery store, and then headed south on another city street.

"At that point Smith turned on his flashing light and ordered the Cadillac over to the side of the road. After stopping the vehicle, Smith asked petitioner, the driver, to produce his operator's license. Petitioner informed Smith that he was a student and that he had left his operator's license in his dormitory room in the neighboring city of Melbourne, Florida. Petitioner was then placed under arrest for failure to have his vehicle operator's license in his possession. It was conceded by the parties below and in this Court that the officer had probable cause to arrest upon learning that petitioner did not have his license in his possession, and that he took petitioner into custody in order to transport him to the stationhouse for further inquiry.

"Smith then proceeded to search the petitioner's person. Smith testified that he patted down the clothing of the petitioner, 'outside and inside, I checked the belt, the shirt pockets and all around the belt, completely around inside.' Upon completing his patdown, he testified, he placed his hand into the left front coat pocket of the coat petitioner was wearing. From that pocket he extracted a 'long chain' and a Benson and Hedges cigarette box. Smith testified that he then 'opened [the cigarette box] and it appeared there were marihuana cigarettes in the box. I had been shown this in training at the police department and these appeared to be marihuana to me.' "

Gustafson was convicted in a Florida trial court for unlawful possession of marijuana. His conviction was reversed on appeal to an intermediate appellate court, but on appeal of that decision the Florida Supreme Court affirmed the conviction. Gustafson petitioned for certiorari in the United States Supreme Court. His case was argued and decided with Robinson (*supra*). The Supreme Court affirmed the conviction.

Justice Rehnquist wrote the opinion in Gustafson, joined by all of the other members of the majority in Robinson. The Robinson dissentters also dissented in Gustafson.

This capsule history should convey some sense of the difficulty the Court has had in dealing with the use of an exclusionary rule as a remedy for breaches of the vague standards of "probable cause" and "reasonable suspicion".

Questions

Would a comprehensive code, adopted by a legislature, provide effective means to regulate the conduct of stops, frisks, arrests, and searches of persons arrested? Would such a code be preferable to a set of judges' rules worked out case by case in appellate courts? If so, why?

———

ALI MODEL CODE OF PRE–ARRAIGNMENT PROCEDURE
ARTICLE 110

Section 110.2   Stopping of Persons

(1) **Cases in Which Stop is Authorized.** A law enforcement officer, lawfully present in any place, may, in the following circumstances, order a person to remain in the officer's presence near such place for such period as is reasonably necessary for the accomplishment of the purposes authorized in the Subsection, but in no case for more than twenty minutes:

(a) *Persons in suspicious circumstances relating to certain misdemeanors and felonies.*

(i) Such person is observed in circumstances such that the officer reasonably suspects that he has just committed, is committing, or is about to commit a misdemeanor or felony, involving danger of forcible injury to persons or of appropriation of or damage to property, and

(ii) such action is reasonably necessary to obtain or verify the identification of such person, to obtain or verify an account of such person's presence or conduct, or to determine whether to arrest such person.

(b) *Witnesses near scene of certain misdemeanors and felonies.*

(i) The officer has reasonable cause to believe that a misdemeanor or felony, involving danger of forcible injury to persons or of appropriation of or danger to property, has just been committed near the place where he finds such person, and

(ii) the officer has reasonable cause to believe that such person has knowledge of material aid in the investigation of such crime, and

(iii) such action is reasonably necessary to obtain or verify the identification of such person, or to obtain an account of such crime.

(c) *Suspects sought for certain previously committed felonies.*

(i) The officer has reasonable cause to believe that a felony involving danger of forcible injury to persons or of appropriation of or damage to property has been committed, and

(ii) he reasonably suspects such person may have committed it, and

(iii) such action is reasonably necessary to obtain or verify the identification of such person for the purpose of determining whether to arrest him for such felony.

(2) **Stopping of Vehicles at Roadblock.** A law enforcement officer may, if

(a) he has reasonable cause to believe that a felony has been committed; and

(b) stopping all or most automobiles, trucks, buses or other such motor vehicles moving in a particular direction or directions is reasonably necessary to permit a search for the perpetrator or victim of such felony in view of the seriousness and special circumstances of such felony,

order the drivers of such vehicles to stop, and may search such vehicles to the extent necessary to accomplish such purpose. Such action shall be accomplished as promptly as possible under the circumstances.

(3) **Use of Force.** In order to exercise the authority conferred in Subsections (1) and (2) of this Section, a law enforcement officer may use such force, other than deadly force, as is reasonably necessary to stop any person or vehicle or to cause any person to remain in the officer's presence.

(4) **Frisk for Dangerous Weapons.** A law enforcement officer who has stopped any person pursuant to this Section may, if the officer reasonably believes that his safety or the safety of others then present so requires, search for any dangerous weapon by an external patting of such person's outer clothing. If in the course of such search he feels an object which he reasonably believes to be a dangerous weapon, he may take such action as is necessary to examine such object.

(5) **Questioning of Suspects.**

(a) *Warnings.* If a law enforcement officer stops any person who he suspects or has reasonable cause to suspect may have committed a crime, the officer shall warn such person as promptly as is reasonable under the circumstances, and in any case before engaging in any sustained questioning

(i) that such person is not obliged to say anything, and anything he says may be used in evidence against him,

(ii) that within twenty minutes he will be released unless he is arrested,

(iii) that if he is arrested he will be taken to a police station where he may promptly communicate by telephone with counsel, relatives or friends, and

(iv) that he will not be questioned unless he wishes, and that if he wishes to consult a lawyer or have a lawyer present during questioning, he will not be questioned at this time, and that after being taken to the stationhouse a lawyer will be furnished him prior to questioning if he is unable to obtain one.

(b) *Limitations on Questioning.* No law enforcement officer shall question a person detained pursuant to the authority in this Section who he suspects or has reasonable cause to suspect may have committed a crime, if such person has indicated in any manner that he does not wish to be questioned, or that he wishes to consult counsel before submitting to any questioning.

(6) **Action to Be Taken After Period of Stop.** Unless an officer acting hereunder arrests a person during the time he is authorized by Subsections (1) and (2) of this Section to require such person to remain in his presence, he shall, at the end of such time, inform such person that he is free to go.

(7) **Records Relating to Persons Stopped.** In accordance with regulations to be issued pursuant to Section 10.3, a law enforcement officer, who has ordered any person to remain in his presence pursuant to this Section, shall with reasonable promptness thereafter make a record of the circumstances and purposes of the stop.

ARTICLE 230.   SEARCH AND SEIZURE INCIDENTAL TO ARREST

Section SS 230.1   General Authorization

(1) **Permissible Purposes.** Subject to the limitations in the other provisions of this Article, an officer who is making a valid arrest under Section 120.1 or 120.3 of Part I of this Code may, without a search warrant, conduct a search of the person or property of the arrested individual, for the following purposes only;

(a) to effect the arrest with all practicable safety of the officer, the arrested individual, and others;

(b) to furnish appropriate custodial care, if the arrested individual is jailed; or

(c) to obtain evidence of the commission of the offense for which the individual is arrested or to seize contraband, the fruits of crime, or other things criminally possessed or used in connection with the offense.

(2) **Things Subject to Seizure.** In the course of a search conducted pursuant to this Article, the arresting officer may seize only things which he reasonably believes to be subject to seizure as provided in Section SS 210.3 hereof. The provisions of Subsection SS 220.3(7) and Section 220.6 shall be applicable to searches and seizures undertaken pursuant to this Article.

(3) **Intermingled Documents.** If in the course of a search conducted pursuant to this Article the arresting officer discovers documents specified in Subsection SS 220.2(4), and if he has reason to believe that intermingled with them are documents or portions thereof which are subject to seizure under Section SS 210.3 and connected with the offense for which the arrest is made, the officer shall handle such documents in accordance with the provisions of Section SS 220.5, and a hearing, in accordance with the provisions of Subsection SS 220.5(3), shall be held before a judicial officer having jurisdiction of the offense for which the arrest was made.

Section SS 230.2   Search Incidental to Arrest for Minor Offenses

The searches and seizures authorized by the other Sections of this Article shall not be authorized if the arrest is on a charge of committing a "violation" as defined in Section 1.04(5) of the Model Penal Code, or a traffic offense or other misdemeanor, the elements and circumstances of which involve no unlawful possession or violent, or intentionally or recklessly dangerous, conduct: *Provided*, That this Section shall not be construed to forbid the search for dangerous weapons authorized by Subsection 110.2(4) of Part I if the circumstances described in Subsection 110.2(1) thereof are present at the time of the arrest.

Section SS 230.3   Search of the Person

(1) **Permissible Scope.** An officer making an arrest on a charge other than as described in Section SS 230.2 and the authorized officials at the police station or other police building to which the arrested individual is brought, may conduct a search of the arrested individual's garments and personal effects ready to hand, the surface of his body, and the area within his immediate control.

(2) **Search of Body Cavities.** Search of an arrested individual's blood stream, body cavities, and subcutaneous tissues may be conducted as incidental to an arrest only if there is a strong probability that it will disclose things subject to seizure and related to the offense for which the individual was arrested, and if it reasonably appears that the delay consequent upon procurement of a search warrant would probably result in the disappearance or destruction of the objects of the search, and that the search is otherwise reasonable under the circumstances of the case, including the seriousness of the offense and the nature of the physical invasion of the individual's person.

(3) **Privacy.** The searches authorized by Subsections (1) and (2) shall be carried out with all reasonable regard for privacy, and unless exceptional circumstances otherwise require, search of the arrested individual prior to his arrival at the police station shall be limited to such search as is reasonably necessary in order to effect the arrest with all practicable safety, or prevent destruction of evidence relating to the crime for which he is arrested.

Questions

1.   Were the stops, frisks, and/or searches incidental to arrest in Terry, Sibron, Peters, Adams v. Williams, Robinson, and Gustafson, *supra* pp. 252–255, proper under the rules laid down in the preceding excerpts from the ALI Model Code.

2.   Does the ALI Model Code select a middle ground between the limitations on searches suggested in Terry and the broader authorization to search in Robinson and Gustafson? Explain your answer.

Problem

"The question is whether it is an unreasonable seizure under the Fourth and Fourteenth Amendments to stop an automobile, being driven on a public highway, for the purpose of checking the driving license of the operator and the registration of the car, where there is neither probable cause to believe nor reasonable suspicion that the car is being driven contrary to the laws governing the operation of motor vehicles or that either the car or any of its occupants is subject to seizure or detention in connection with the violation of any other applicable law.

"At 7:20 p.m. on November 30, 1976, a New Castle County, Del. patrolman in a police cruiser stopped the automobile occupied by respondent. The patrolman smelled marihuana smoke as he was walking toward the stopped vehicle, and he seized marihuana in plain

view on the car floor.   Respondent was subsequently indicted for illegal possession of a controlled substance.   At a hearing on respondent's motion to suppress the marihuana seized as a result of the stop,
the patrolman testified that prior to stopping the vehicle he had observed neither traffic or equipment violations nor any suspicious
activity, and that he made the stop only in order to check the driver's
license and registration.   The patrolman was not acting pursuant to
any standards, guidelines, or procedures pertaining to document spot
checks, promulgated by either his department or the State Attorney
General.   Characterizing the stop as 'routine,' the patrolman explained, 'I saw the car in the area and was not answering any complaints so I decided to pull them off.'   The trial court granted
the motion to suppress finding the stop and detention to have been
wholly capricious and therefore violative of the Fourth Amendment.

"The Delaware Supreme Court affirmed, noting first that '[t]he
issue of the legal validity of systematic, roadblock-type stops of a
number of vehicles for license and vehicle registration check is *not*
now before the Court,' 382 A.2d 1359, 1362 (1978) (emphasis in
original).   The court held that 'a random stop of a motorist in the
absence of specific articulable facts which justify the stop by indicating a reasonable suspicion that a violation of the law has occurred is
constitutionally impermissible and violative of the Fourth and Fourteenth Amendments to the Constitution.'   382 A.2d, at 1364.   We
granted certiorari to resolve the conflict between this decision, which
is in accord with decisions in five other jurisdictions, and the contrary
determination in six jurisdictions that the Fourth Amendment does
not prohibit the kind of automobile stop that occurred here."

From the opinion of the Court, per Mr. Justice White, in **Prouse
v. State of Delaware,** —— U.S. ——, 99 S.Ct. 1391 (1979).

If you were the attorney for the accused, what argument(s)
would you make in support of the motion to suppress?

If you were the attorney for the State of Delaware, what argu-
ment(s) would you make in opposition to the motion to suppress?

The Court held "that except in those situations in which there
is at least articulable and reasonable suspicion that a motorist is unlicensed or that an automobile is not registered, or that either the
vehicle or an occupant is otherwise subject to seizure for violation of
law, stopping an automobile and detaining the driver in order to check
his driver's license and the registration of the automobile are unreasonable under the Fourth Amendment.   This holding does not preclude the State of Delaware or other States from developing methods
for spot checks that involve less intrusion or that do not involve
the unconstrained exercise of discretion.   Questioning of all oncom-
ing traffic at roadblock-type stops is one possible alternative.   We
hold only that persons in automobiles on public roadways may not

for that reason alone have their travel and privacy interfered with at the unbridled discretion of police officers."

. . .

Justice Rehnquist dissented.

Query: Is this case likely to significantly affect police behavior? Explain your answer.

The Writ of Habeas Corpus

The writ of habeas corpus provides an expeditious procedure to test the propriety of official detention of persons. The person in custody or someone on his behalf may present a petition for a writ of habeas corpus (a Latin phrase meaning literally "have the body"), and if the petition is in proper form presented to a proper court or judge and if it states grounds which, if true, would entitle the prisoner to be released, then it must be granted. That is, the court or judge must direct a writ to the person who has the petitioner in custody ordering him to "have the body" of the prisoner before the court or judge at a specified time and also to be present himself to explain by what authority the prisoner is being held. If the custodian's answer does not state an adequate cause of detention, the court or judge will order the prisoner's discharge forthwith; if it does state an adequate cause of detention, there will be a hearing to determine the question.

"The most celebrated writ in the English law," according to Blackstone, habeas corpus was used by the common law courts in their running battle with the Star Chamber and other "prerogative courts" of the 16th and 17th centuries. In 1641 Parliament authorized the use of the writ of habeas corpus to prevent restraint by an order of the King or the King's Council without "probable cause" (that is, reasonable grounds to believe the defendant committed the offense charged). By a federal statute of 1867 the writ is available to all persons for any detention in violation of the constitution or laws of the United States.

In most legal systems other than the Anglo-American, an official who unlawfully detains a person is subject to prosecution or disciplinary action after the event, and to a civil suit, but there is no equivalent of habeas corpus whereby a court may intervene to order the prisoner released for purposes of a hearing as to whether his detention is lawful. Such a power of judicial intervention is probably not consonant with the more elaborate system of criminal investigation characteristic of French, German, Swiss, Russian and other Continental European legal orders. A person in detention who wishes to challenge the legality of that detention may do so, typically, only by appeal to administrative authorities superior to the officials who are responsible for the detention.

Interrogation of Suspects

The preceding materials on unlawful arrest and "stop and frisk" indicate some of the difficulties posed by efforts to develop norms and procedures to regulate police work "on the street." The Supreme Court's record on these issues, commencing with its opinion in Terry v. Ohio, shows how hard it is for judges to develop adequate means to balance the competing demands for vigorous police work, the safety of police officers, and preservation of the personal security and dignity of citizens in encounters with investigating or arresting officers. The exclusionary rule evolved since Weeks may satisfy a desire for preserving the integrity of the trial process by barring "tainted" evidence which would otherwise be used to secure a conviction, but it hardly serves the purpose of controlling police behavior or of vindicating the interests of innocent persons whose rights and dignity have been abused by unlawful police behavior.

The problem of developing norms to regulate police behavior on the street is surpassed, both in difficulty and emotional impact, by the problem of regulating police work in the station house, namely during post-arrest interrogation of suspects.

FEDERAL RULES OF CRIMINAL PROCEDURE

Rule 5 *

INITIAL APPEARANCE BEFORE THE MAGISTRATE

(a) **In General.** An officer making an arrest under a warrant issued upon a complaint or any person making an arrest without a warrant shall take the arrested person without unnecessary delay before the nearest available federal magistrate or, in the event that a federal magistrate is not reasonably available, before a state or local judicial officer authorized by 18 U.S.C. § 3041. If a person arrested without a warrant is brought before a magistrate, a complaint shall be filed forthwith which shall comply with the requirements of Rule 4(a) with respect to the showing of probable cause. When a person, arrested with or without a warrant or given a summons, appears initially before the magistrate, the magistrate shall proceed in accordance with the applicable subdivisions of this rule.

* * *

(c) **Offenses Not Triable by the United States Magistrate.** If the charge against the defendant is not triable by the United States magistrate, the defendant shall not be called upon to plead. The magistrate shall inform the defendant of the complaint against him and of any affidavit filed therewith, of his right to retain counsel, of his right to request the assignment of counsel if he is unable to obtain counsel, and of the general circumstances under which he may secure pretrial release. He shall inform the defendant that he is not required to make a statement and that any statement made by him may be used against him. The magistrate shall also inform the defendant of his right to a preliminary examination. He shall allow the defendant reasonable time and opportunity to consult counsel and shall admit the defendant to bail as provided by statute or in these rules.

* As amended through July 1, 1977.

A defendant is entitled to a preliminary examination, unless waived, when charged with any offense, other than a petty offense, which is to be tried by a judge of the district court. If the defendant waives preliminary examination, the magistrate shall forthwith hold him to answer in the district court. If the defendant does not waive the preliminary examination, the magistrate shall schedule a preliminary examination. Such examination shall be held within a reasonable time but in any event not later than 10 days following the initial appearance if the defendant is in custody and no later than 20 days if he is not in custody, provided, however, that the preliminary examination shall not be held if the defendant is indicted or if an information against the defendant is filed in district court before the date set for the preliminary examination. With the consent of the defendant and upon a showing of good cause, taking into account the public interest in the prompt disposition of criminal cases, time limits specified in this subdivision may be extended one or more times by a federal magistrate. In the absence of such consent by the defendant, time limits may be extended by a judge of the United States only upon a showing that extraordinary circumstances exist and that delay is indispensable to the interests of justice.

MALLORY v. UNITED STATES

Supreme Court of the United States, 1957.
354 U.S. 449, 77 S.Ct. 1356.

[Mallory had been arrested on suspicion of having committed a rape. (The crime was committed and the arrest was made in the District of Columbia; thus all the proceedings were administered by federal officers acting under federal law.) Mallory was held for seven hours and interrogated during that time. He confessed to the crime. After this interrogation and confession he was presented before a United States Commissioner as provided for in Rule 5(a).** He was convicted after trial in the United States District Court. The Court of Appeals for the District of Columbia affirmed the conviction. The case came before the Supreme Court on a writ of certiorari.]

MR. JUSTICE FRANKFURTER delivered the opinion of the Court.

* * *

The scheme for initiating a federal prosecution is plainly defined. The police may not arrest upon mere suspicion but only "probable cause." The next step in the proceeding is to arraign the arrested person before a judicial officer as quickly as possible so that he may be advised of his rights and so that the issue of probable cause may be promptly determined. The arrested person, may, of course, be "booked" by the police. But he is not to be taken to police headquarters in order to carry out a process of inquiry that lends itself, even if not so designed, to eliciting damaging statements to support the arrest and ultimately his guilt.

The duty enjoined upon arresting officers to arraign "without unnecessary delay" indicates that the command does not call for mechanical or au-

---

** At the time of Mallory's arrest Rule 5 of the Federal Rules of Criminal Procedure was somewhat different in form and content than the present version which is reprinted above. Former Rule 5(a) and (c) did contain the requirements in present Rule 5(a) and (b) reprinted above.

tomatic obedience. Circumstances may justify a brief delay between arrest and arraignment, as for instance, where the story volunteered by the accused is susceptible of quick verification through third parties. But the delay must not be of a nature to give opportunity for the extraction of a confession.

* * *

We cannot sanction the extended delay, resulting in confession, without subordinating the general rule of prompt arraignment to the discretion of arresting officers in finding exceptional circumstances for its disregard. In every case where the police resort to interrogation of an arrested person and secure a confession, they may well claim, and quite sincerely, that they were merely trying to check on the information given by him. Against such a claim and the evil potentialities of the practice for which it is urged stands Rule 5(a) as a barrier. Nor is there an escape from the constraint laid upon the police by that Rule in that two other suspects were involved for the same crime. Presumably, whomever the police arrest they must arrest on "probable cause." It is not the function of the police to arrest, as it were, at large and to use an interrogating process at police headquarters in order to determine whom they should charge before a committing magistrate on "probable cause."

[The case was remanded to the District Court with the instruction that in a new trial the confession and any other information gathered as a result of the interrogation would be inadmissible due to the application of the exclusionary rule regarding unlawfully obtained evidence.]

Note

Justice Frankfurter refers to the proceeding contemplated in Rule 5(a) as the arraignment. This is technically not correct. In the federal system arraignment is a different procedure which occurs at a later stage; its purpose is to allow the accused to hear the exact charges against him, and to plead in answer to those charges. See *infra* p. 319.

The Rule 5(a) appearance is intended solely to inform the accused of his rights, particularly his right to counsel. At this proceeding the accused may be admitted to bail.

In addition to the 5(a) appearance, the accused may request a preliminary examination, provided for in Rule 5(c). The purpose of this procedure is to allow the accused to test the sufficiency of the complaint against him by requiring the prosecutor to demonstrate to the Commissioner that there is "probable cause" to hold the accused. If the Commissioner finds against the prosecutor, the accused is entitled to be released. If the Commissioner finds probable cause to hold the accused for trial—"bind him over for trial"—he may admit the accused to bail, or review the bail—if any—set earlier. The preliminary examination may be waived by the accused.

Questions

1. What legislative purposes could be reasonably inferred from Rule 5(a)?

2. What purpose does Judge Frankfurter see in Rule 5(a)?

3. What would be the likely effect of a rigorous enforcement of Rule 5(a) on the ability of federal officers to conduct post-arrest interrogations?

4. What are Judge Frankfurter's apparent views regarding the legality of the arrest in this case? Does he suggest that there is a connection between the propensity of police to make arrests "on suspicion" and the availability of a suspect for interrogation after arrest?

5. What impact, if any, might rigorous enforcement of Rule 5(a) have on the propensity of police to make arrests "on suspicion"?

Constitutional limits to the use of interrogations and confessions in criminal cases. Mallory v. U. S. states the basic legal requirements regarding the use of post-arrest interrogation as an investigative technique in federal criminal cases. Note, however, that the Mallory rule is based on the interpretation of a statute (Rule 5(a) F.R.Cr.P.). Mallory, like the decision in McNabb v. United States, 318 U.S. 332, 63 S.Ct. 608 (1943), in which the opinion was also written by Justice Frankfurter, carefully avoids any constitutional issue. The McNabb case turned solely on the issue of the admissibility of a confession obtained during an unnecessary delay between arrest and presentment under Rule 5.[1] Justice Frankfurter's opinion asserted that Rule 5(a) expressed a Congressional purpose to prevent "third degree" tactics in obtaining confessions.

The McNabb-Mallory rule is assumed to have severely limited the use of post-arrest interrogations in federal criminal investigations.

Does that seem to you to be a reasonable assumption? How should the McNabb-Mallory doctrine affect the interaction of Rule 5(a) and Rule 5(c)? Would you suppose that the proceeding before a magistrate, as provided in Rule 5(c), would be likely to limit or eliminate interrogations of suspects by federal officers?

Except for the McNabb-Mallory doctrine, the rules for admission of confessions in federal prosecutions were developed primarily on a non-statutory base of judge made "common law" rules. The thrust of these rules was to bar the admission in evidence of confes-

---

1. The case was remanded for a new trial. The prosecution proved that the defendants had, in fact, been promptly presented before a magistrate, and the defendants were convicted. McNabb v. United States, 142 F.2d 904 (6th Cir.), cert. denied 323 U.S. 771, 65 S.Ct. 114 (1944).

sions deemed unreliable due to the use of threats or improper induce-ments by the interrogator. In one case, Bram v. U. S., 168 U.S. 532, 18 S.Ct. 183 (1897) the Supreme Court suggested that the rules for admission of confessions should be based on a Constitutional ground, the Fifth Amendment privilege against self-incrimination, and that the test for admission of a confession should be whether or not the confession was made voluntarily. In subsequent cases the Court de-clined to pursue the constitutional theory of Bram and instead pur-ported to rely on the common law test regarding the use of threats or inducements. However, in a later case, Ziang Sun Wan v. United States, 266 U.S. 1, 45 S.Ct. 1 (1924), the Court, per Justice Brandeis, apparently extended the common law rules to mean that any involun-tary confession, not merely those produced by threats or inducements, should be excluded. The Court cited Bram v. United States for that proposition.

This reliance on a voluntariness test became the hallmark of a much more significant group of cases in which the use of confes-sions was reviewed under the "due process" provision of the Four-teenth Amendment.

[The following is taken from "DEVELOPMENTS IN THE LAW: CONFESSIONS," 79 Harvard Law Review 935, 961–964 (1966), an unsigned note prepared by student members of the Har-vard Law Review staff. Some footnotes omitted; others are re-numbered.]

Due Process and Confessions.—At common law the circumstances un-der which a confession was made were relevant to its admissibility only in-sofar as they affected its probative value. Yet implicit in this, as in many other rules of evidence, was a basic belief that fundamental notions of fair-ness require a trial to be conducted according to procedures that ensure a high degree of accuracy in fact-finding. Even among rules of evidence, the confessions rules were especially strict, perhaps embodying the notion that the greatest certainty should be required of evidence so likely to pro-duce a conviction. There was, however, no conception that the interroga-tion that yielded the confession should conform to a standard of procedural regularity, or that institutional safeguards had to be provided during inter-rogation as they were at trial, or that the extent to which such regularity or safeguards were lacking bore directly on the admissibility of a confes-sion.

But in a series of decisions beginning in 1936 with Brown v. Mississip-pi, the Supreme Court radically changed the law; it has imposed limitations on the admissibility of confessions, deriving from the fundamental notion that the interrogation at which a confession is obtained is a part of the process by which the state procures a conviction, and therefore subject to the requirements of the due process clause of the fourteenth amendment. The necessity and justice of some such control is rarely disputed, but the Court has encountered great difficulties in deciding just what process is due at interrogation. Its decisions in this area prior to [1964] were based on the premise that "the public interest requires that interrogation, . . . at a police station, not completely be forbidden, so long as it is conducted fairly   .   .   .   ."   For this reason the Court concluded that institutional safeguards are not an appropriate means of protecting suspects' rights at interrogation since they are likely to be too obstructive to the solution of crimes.   Instead of requiring production before a magistrate on arrest or provision of counsel, the Court sought to develop a definition of the process due to persons subjected to interrogation, and expected the lower courts to scrutinize the record of an interrogation to decide whether these interests had been impaired.[1]   But the Court has been less than successful in describing the specific interests of the defendant deemed to be secured against state infringement.   Indeed, on occasion the Court has exhibited a surprising disinterest in the task.   In Blackburn v. Alabama, for example, it held that a madman's confession was inadmissible, declaring that use of the confession at trial affronted "a most basic sense of justice," and continuing on to say that "this judgment can without difficulty be articulated in terms of the unreliability of the confession, the lack of rational choice of the accused, or simply a strong conviction that our system of law enforcement should not operate so as to take advantage of a person in this fashion." [2]   Such pronouncements were bound to leave lower courts without a clear idea of which circumstances surrounding an interrogation are especially relevant to the due process issue.   The vacuum has been filled by a great variety of attempts by lower federal courts, state supreme courts, and commentators to state the requirement of due process in this context.

*   *   *

The Supreme Court's pre-[1964] confession cases are usually described as voluntariness cases, because the Court has frequently used that term in enunciating the requisites for admissibility under the due process clause and also, perhaps, because the inquiry called for by these opinions is reminiscent of that employed in applying the common law voluntariness rules—an examination of the circumstances surrounding the making of a confession. In Culombe v. Connecticut, the due process voluntariness analysis was described by Mr. Justice Frankfurter as a "three-phased process": [3]

> First, there is the business of finding the crude, historical facts, the external "phenomenological" occurrences and events surrounding the confession.   Second, because the concept of "voluntariness" is one which concerns a mental state, there is the imaginative recreation, largely inferential, of internal, "psychological" fact. Third, there is the application to this psychological fact of standards for judgment informed by the larger legal conceptions ordinarily characterized as rules of law but which, also, comprehend both induction from, and anticipation of, factual circumstances.

Mr. Justice Frankfurter noted that " 'voluntariness' is   .   .   .   an amphibian.   It purports at once to describe an internal psychic state and

---

1. Not all the Justices have accepted this approach.   Mr. Justice Douglas has long believed that something like the McNabb rule should be applied to the states, see, e. 'g., his concurring opinion in Watts v. Indiana, 338 U.S. 49, 56–57, 69 S.Ct. 1347 (1949).   He and other Justices have also maintained that a confession given after refusal of a request for counsel should be inadmissible.   See, *e.g.*, Culombe v. Connecticut, 367 U.S. 568, 637–41, 81 S.Ct. 1860 (1961) (opinion of Douglas, J.).

2. 361 U.S. 199, 207, 80 S.Ct. 274, 280 (1960).

3. 367 U.S. 568, 603, 81 S.Ct. 1860, 1879 (1961).

to characterize that state for legal purposes." [4]   But without a clear understanding of the applicable "legal purposes" as a guide, the fact of voluntariness is extremely difficult to find, since it represents not an observable
physical phenomenon but a characterization of varying concatenations of
facts.   The purposes that dictate a requirement of voluntariness must
determine when that requirement is satisfied.   The Court's cases suggest
that the due process voluntariness standard has three possible goals: (1)
ensuring that convictions are based on reliable evidence; (2) deterring improper police conduct; or (3) assuring that a defendant's confession is the
product of his free and rational choice.   The sections immediately following attempt to assess the extent to which the Court's decisions are consistent with these goals.

    As suggested above, a primary judicial concern in the decision
to admit a confession is whether or not it is reliable evidence.   The
facts in Brown v. Mississippi are instructive in this regard.   The
defendants in Brown, all Negroes, had been convicted of the murder
of a white man solely on the basis of confessions which had been
given after policemen whipped the defendants with steel studded
belts.   The effect of such an egregious form of coercion clearly deprives a confession of those elements which go to make up a voluntary admission of guilt.   Such an involuntary statement is clearly
unreliable.   The truth of the statement is suspect since the admissions of guilt may have been the price paid for relief from physical
or psychological mistreatment.

    The notions of voluntariness and reliability are closely related
but they are not inextricably bound together.   For example, a purely
voluntary confession, i. e., one made without any coercion or inducements by an interrogator, may be quite unreliable if made by a person
who is psychologically pre-disposed to abnormal feelings of guilt and
the desire for punishment to expiate such guilt feelings.   Similarly, an
involuntary, i. e., officially coerced, confession may be shown by
other evidence (corroboration) to be quite reliable.   Nevertheless
there is probably a sound basis for assigning a high positive correlation between the voluntariness (or involuntariness) and reliability
(or unreliability) of a confession in light of the generally fragmentary
nature of proof in legal proceedings.   Where there is ample extrinsic
evidence of guilt, a confession may not be a crucial element in the
proof.   Confessions are likely to be most important as proof in cases
where extrinsic evidence is limited, and in such a case the check on reliability afforded by the corroborating extrinsic evidence is also limited.   Accordingly, courts might well adopt a presumption that an
involuntary confession is an unreliable confession.   Many decisions
of the Supreme Court, lower federal courts, and state courts in the
years since Brown v. Mississippi can be explained in terms of this
voluntariness/reliability interaction.   It is also clear, however, that
the Court was moving in the 1950s and early 1960s to a more pure

---

4. *Id.* at 605, 81 S.Ct. at 1880.

voluntariness test in which the concern for reliability was, at best, secondary.[1]

Moreover, during this period the standards regarding what constituted coercive practices were considerably broadened to encompass much more than physical mistreatment such as that in Brown. For example, prolonged questioning, Ashcraft v. Tennessee, 322 U.S. 143, 64 S.Ct. 921 (1944), and questioning by relays of interrogators, Haynes v. Washington, 373 U.S. 503, 83 S.Ct. 1336 (1963), were held to be sufficiently coercive to justify suppression of resulting incriminating statements. Finally, the Court manifested increasing concern over the psychological aspects of interrogation and the possibility that a "weak" or "inexperienced" suspect might be induced to confess because his will could be overborne by the blandishments, cajolery and/or superior intellect of a trained interrogator in the confines of the station house. Concern for the psychological aspects of interrogation was probably heightened by the reported "brainwashing" of captured United States soldiers during the Korean War. Then, too, the potential immorality of interrogations as a police technique was pointed up by experiences in Nazi Germany and Stalinist Russia, and judges indicated full awareness of that history.

By the mid-1960s the Supreme Court had fashioned a complex and highly sophisticated body of doctrine regarding the use of confessions. The test was said to be that of "voluntariness," and in each case where the admissibility of a confession was challenged on that ground, a court hearing the case had to examine the facts carefully to determine whether the confession was voluntary as that term was defined in the numerous cases decided by the Supreme Court. This type of case-by-case analysis of facts, and the search for the guiding doctrine of previous cases is a commonplace in common law jurisdictions. In this instance, however, the courts were not merely developing common law doctrine, they were instead applying and defining constitutional law, the due process requirement of the Fourteenth Amendment. As a result, the U.S. Supreme Court, as final arbiter in such matters, bid fair to become a court of criminal appeals as defense lawyers sought to press the limits of the voluntariness doctrine on behalf of their clients in appeals to the Court. At the same time, police reliance on interrogations and confessions did not appear to lessen appreciably. In terms of its impact on the efficiency of judicial administration, the voluntariness test was becoming a burdensome legal doctrine. Moreover, to the extent that it was an attempt to affect police practices, the voluntariness test seemed to be singularly unsuccessful. Then in 1964 and 1966 the United States Supreme Court embarked on a new course regarding the use of confessions taken in post-arrest interrogations.

1. Rogers v. Richmond, 365 U.S. 534, 81 S.Ct. 735 (1961).

The first step in this new direction came in Escobedo v. Illinois, 378 U.S. 478, 84 S.Ct. 1758 (1964).

Escobedo had been arrested in connection with the investigation of the fatal shooting of his brother-in-law. He was taken to police headquarters for interrogation. He later testified that on at least one occasion after arrest and prior to interrogation he asked and was denied permission to consult an attorney who had been retained by his family shortly after the shooting. The attorney attempted to see Escobedo at the station house after being notified of the arrest. The police refused to allow the attorney to see Escobedo until they "'were through interrogating him." During the interrogation Escobedo made admissions implicating himself in the shooting. Ultimately he made and signed a statement that he had accompanied another man who had actually done the shooting.

Escobedo was convicted of murder. His conviction was affirmed in the Supreme Court of Illinois. He petitioned the U.S. Supreme Court, which reversed the conviction in an opinion by Mr. Justice Goldberg.*

This Court also has recognized that "history amply shows that confessions have often been extorted to save law enforcement officials the trouble and effort of obtaining valid and independent evidence . . . ." Haynes v. Washington, 373 U.S. 503, 519, 83 S.Ct. 1336, 1346.

We have also learned the companion lesson of history that no system of criminal justice can, or should, survive if it comes to depend for its continued effectiveness on the citizens' abdication through unawareness of their constitutional rights. No system worth preserving should have to *fear* that if an accused is permitted to consult with a lawyer, he will become aware of, and exercise, these rights. If the exercise of constitutional rights will thwart the effectiveness of a system of law enforcement, then there is something very wrong with that system.

We hold, therefore, that where, as here, the investigation is no longer a general inquiry into an unsolved crime but has begun to focus on a particular suspect, the suspect has been taken into police custody, the police carry out a process of interrogations that lends itself to eliciting incriminating statements, the suspect has requested and been denied an opportunity to consult with his lawyer, and the police have not effectively warned him of his absolute constitutional right to remain silent, the accused has been denied "the Assistance of Counsel" in violation of the Sixth Amendment to the Constitution as "made obligatory upon the States by the Fourteenth Amendment," Gideon v. Wainwright, 372 U.S., at 342, 83 S.Ct., at 795 and that no statement elicited by the police during the interrogation may be used against him in a criminal trial. Escobedo v. Illinois, at p. 490–1. Footnotes omitted.

* Justice Arthur J. Goldberg was appointed to the Supreme Court by President Kennedy in 1962. He had been General Counsel of the United Steelworkers of America (1948–1961), and Secretary of Labor of the U.S. (1961–1962). He resigned from the Supreme Court in 1965 to become U.S. Ambassador to the United Nations.

On remand Escobedo was released. Apparently the state's attorney did not institute a second prosecution since without the incriminating statement there was insufficient evidence to substantiate the charge of murder against Escobedo.

Chief Justice Warren and Justices Douglas, Black, and Brennan joined in the majority opinion. Justices Harlan and Stewart dissented in a separate opinion. Justice White dissented in an opinion in which Justices Stewart and Clark joined.

Escobedo v. Illinois was a judicial *tour de force*. Never before, the dissenters were quick to point out, had the right to counsel been extended to include proceedings prior to arraignment. Moreover, it was apparent that the right to counsel (like the McNabb-Mallory doctrine and Rule 5(a)) was here being used in an attempt to limit police interrogations of suspects, and that the Court was moving in a different direction from that reflected in the voluntariness test.

> "By abandoning the voluntary-involuntary test for admissibility of confessions, the Court seems driven by the notion that it is uncivilized law enforcement to use an accused's own admissions against him at his trial. It attempts to find a home for this new and nebulous rule of due process by attaching it to the right to counsel guaranteed in the federal system by the Sixth Amendment and binding upon the States by virtue of the due process guarantee of the Fourteenth Amendment. . . . The right to counsel now not only entitles the accused to counsel's advice and aid in preparing for trial but stands as an impenetrable barrier to any interrogation once the accused has become a suspect. From that very moment apparently his right to counsel attaches, a rule wholly unworkable and impossible to administer unless police cars are equipped with public defenders and undercover agents and police informants have defense counsel at their side. I would not abandon the Court's prior cases defining with some care and analysis the circumstances requiring the presence or aid of counsel and substitute the amorphous and wholly unworkable principle that counsel is constitutionally required whenever he would or could be helpful. . . .
>
> "These cases dealt with the requirement of counsel at proceedings in which definable rights could be won or lost, not with stages where probative evidence might be obtained. Under this new approach one might just as well argue that a potential defendant is constitutionally entitled to a lawyer before, not after, he commits a crime, since it is then that crucial incriminating evidence is put within the reach of the Government by the would-be accused. Until now there simply has been no right guaranteed by the Federal Constitution to be free from the use at trial of a voluntary admission made prior to indictment.
>
> * * *
>
> "The Court chooses to ignore these matters and to rely on the virtues and morality of a system of criminal law enforcement which

does not depend on the 'confession.' No such judgment is to be found in the Constitution. It might be appropriate for a legislature to provide that a suspect should not be consulted during a criminal investigation; that an accused should never be called before a grand jury to answer, even if he wants to, what may well be incriminating questions; and that no person, whether he be a suspect, guilty criminal or innocent bystander, should be put to the ordeal of responding to orderly noncompulsory inquiry by the State. But this is not the system our Constitution requires. The only 'inquisitions' the Constitution forbids are those which compel incrimination. Escobedo's statements were not compelled and the Court does not hold that they were.

"This new American judges' rule, which is to be applied in both federal and state courts, is perhaps thought to be a necessary safeguard against the possibility of extorted confessions. To this extent it reflects a deep-seated distrust of law enforcement officers everywhere, unsupported by relevant data or current material based upon our own experience. Obviously law enforcement officers can make mistakes and exceed their authority, as today's decision shows that even judges can do, but I have somewhat more faith than the Court evidently has in the ability and desire of prosecutors and of the power of the appellate courts to discern and correct such violations of the law.

* * *

"I do not suggest for a moment that law enforcement will be destroyed by the rule announced today. The need for peace and order is too insistent for that. But it will be crippled and its task made a great deal more difficult, all in my opinion, for unsound, unstated reasons, which can find no home in any of the provisions of the Constitution."

[Justice White dissenting in Escobedo v. Illinois.]

Like many landmark cases Escobedo left many questions unanswered. The public press and scholarly journals both carried numerous publications speculating on the scope of the now expanded Sixth Amendment right to counsel, and debating the wisdom of the Escobedo decision. Another unresolved issue was the relationship of the Escobedo decision to the scope of the Fifth Amendment privilege against self-incrimination.†

---

† The *Escobedo* case was argued on April 29, 1964, and decided on June 22, 1964. On March 5, 1964, Malloy v. Hogan, *supra* p. ——, was argued, and on June 15, 1964, a week before *Escobedo*, the Court announced its decision in *Malloy*, namely that the Fifth Amendment privilege applied in state proceedings.

MIRANDA v. ARIZONA (No. 759) *

Supreme Court of the United States, 1966.
384 U.S. 436, 86 S.Ct. 1602.**

MR. CHIEF JUSTICE WARREN delivered the opinion of the Court.

The cases before us raise questions which go to the roots of our concepts of American criminal jurisprudence: the restraints society must observe consistent with the Federal Constitution in prosecuting individuals for crime. More specifically, we deal with the admissibility of statements obtained from an individual who is subjected to custodial police interrogation and the necessity for procedures which assure that the individual is accorded his privilege under the Fifth Amendment to the Constitution not to be compelled to incriminate himself. . . .

We start here, as we did in Escobedo, with the premise that our holding is not an innovation in our jurisprudence, but is an application of principles long recognized and applied in other settings. We have undertaken a thorough re-examination of the Escobedo decision and the principles it announced, and we reaffirm it. That case was but an explication of basic rights that are enshrined in our Constitution—that "No person * * * shall be compelled in any criminal case to be a witness against himself," and that "the accused shall * * * have the Assistance of Counsel"—rights which were put in jeopardy in that case through official overbearing. These precious rights were fixed in our Constitution only after centuries of persecution and struggle. And in the words of Chief Justice Marshall, they were secured "for ages to come and * * * designed to approach immortality as nearly as human institutions can approach it," Cohens v. Virginia, 6 Wheat. 264, 387 (1821). . . .

Our holding will be spelled out with some specificity in the pages which follow but briefly stated it is this: the prosecution may not use statements, whether exculpatory or inculpatory, stemming from custodial interrogation of the defendant unless it demonstrates the use of procedural safeguards effective to secure the privilege against self-incrimination. By custodial interrogation, we mean questioning initiated by law enforcement officers after a person has been taken into custody or otherwise deprived of his freedom of action in any significant way.[1] As for the procedural safeguards to be employed, unless other fully effective means are devised to inform accused persons of their right of silence and to assure a continuous opportunity to exercise it, the following measures are required. Prior to any questioning, the person must be warned that he has a right to remain silent, that any statement he does make may be used as evidence against him, and that he has a right to the presence of an attorney, either retained or appointed. The defendant may waive effectuation of these rights, provided the waiver is made voluntarily, know-

---

* Together with No. 760, Vignera v. New York . . . and No. 761, Westover v. United States . . . and No. 584, California v. Stewart . . . .

** Some footnotes are omitted, others are renumbered.

1. This is what we meant in Escobedo when we spoke of an investigation which had focused on an accused.

ingly and intelligently.   If, however, he indicates in any manner and at any stage of the process that he wishes to consult with an attorney before speaking there can be no questioning.   Likewise, if the individual is alone and indicates in any manner that he does not wish to be interrogated, the police may not question him.   The mere fact that he may have answered some questions or volunteered some statements on his own does not deprive him of the right to refrain from answering any further inquiries until he has consulted with an attorney and thereafter consents to be questioned.

I.

The constitutional issue we decide in each of these cases is the admissibility of statements obtained from a defendant questioned while in custody and deprived of his freedom of action.   In each, the defendant was questioned by police officers, detectives, or a prosecuting attorney in a room in which he was cut off from the outside world.   In none of these cases was the defendant given a full and effective warning of his rights at the outset of the interrogation process.   In all the cases, the questioning elicited oral admissions, and in three of them, signed statements as well which were admitted at their trials.   They all thus share salient features— incommunicado interrogation of individuals in a police-dominated atmosphere, resulting in self-incriminating statements without full warnings of constitutional rights. . . .

Again we stress that the modern practice of in-custody interrogation is psychologically rather than physically oriented. . . . Interrogation still takes place in privacy.   Privacy results in secrecy and this in turn results in a gap in our knowledge as to what in fact goes on in the interrogation rooms.   A valuable source of information about present police practices, however, may be found in various police manuals and texts which document procedures employed with success in the past, and which recommend various other effective tactics.   These texts are used by law enforcement agencies themselves as guides.[2]   It should be noted that these texts professedly present the most enlightened and effective means presently used to obtain statements through custodial interrogation.   By considering these texts and other data, it is possible to describe procedures observed and noted around the country. . . .

From these representative samples of interrogation techniques, the setting prescribed by the manuals and observed in practice becomes clear. In essence, it is this: To be alone with the subject is essential to prevent

---

2.   The methods described in Inbau and Reid, Criminal Interrogation and Confessions (1962), are a revision and enlargement of material presented in three prior editions of a predecessor text * * *.   The authors and their associates are officers of the Chicago Police Scientific Crime Detection Laboratory and have had extensive experience in writing, lecturing and speaking to law enforcement authorities over a 20-year period.   They say that the techniques portrayed in their manuals reflect their experiences and are the most effective psychological stratagems to employ during interrogations.   Similarly, the techniques described in O'Hara, Fundamentals of Criminal Investigation (1959), were gleaned from long service as observer, lecturer in police science, and work as a federal criminal investigator.   All these texts have had rather extensive use among law enforcement agencies and among students of police science, with total sales and circulation of over 44,000.

distraction and to deprive him of any outside support. The aura of confidence in his guilt undermines his will to resist. He merely confirms the preconceived story the police seek to have him describe. Patience and persistence, at times relentless questioning, are employed. To obtain a confession, the interrogator must "patiently maneuver himself or his quarry into a position from which the desired object may be obtained." When normal procedures fail to produce the needed result, the police may resort to deceptive stratagems such as giving false legal advice. It is important to keep the subject off balance, for example, by trading on his insecurity about himself or his surroundings. The police then persuade, trick, or cajole him out of exercising his constitutional rights.

Even without employing brutality, the "third degree" or the specific stratagems described above, the very fact of custodial interrogation exacts a heavy toll on individual liberty and trades on the weakness of individuals. . . .

In the cases before us today, given this background, we concern ourselves primarily with this interrogation atmosphere and the evils it can bring. In No. 759, Miranda v. Arizona, the police arrested the defendant and took him to a special interrogation room where they secured a confession. In No. 760, Vignera v. New York, the defendant made oral admissions to the police after interrogation in the afternoon, and then signed an inculpatory statement upon being questioned by an assistant district attorney later the same evening. In No. 761, Westover v. United States, the defendant was handed over to the Federal Bureau of Investigation by local authorities after they had detained and interrogated him for a lengthy period, both at night and the following morning. After some two hours of questioning, the federal officers had obtained signed statements from the defendant. Lastly, in No. 584, California v. Stewart, the local police held the defendant five days in the station and interrogated him on nine separate occasions before they secured his inculpatory statement.

In these cases, we might not find the defendants' statements to have been involuntary in traditional terms. Our concern for adequate safeguards to protect precious Fifth Amndment rights is, of course, not lessened in the slightest. In each of the cases, the defendant was thrust into an unfamiliar atmosphere and run through menacing police interrogation procedures. The potentiality for compulsion is forcefully apparent, for example, in Miranda, where the indigent Mexican defendant was a seriously disturbed individual with pronounced sexual fantasies, and in Stewart, in which the defendant was an indigent Los Angeles Negro who had dropped out of school in the sixth grade. To be sure, the records do not evince overt physical coercion or patented psychological ploys. The fact remains that in none of these cases did the officers undertake to afford appropriate safeguards at the outset of the interrogation to insure that the statements were truly the product of free choice.

It is obvious that such an interrogation environment is created for no purpose other than to subjugate the individual to the will of his examiner. This atmosphere carries its own badge of intimidation. To be sure, this is not physical intimidation, but it is equally destructive of human dignity.[3] The current practice of incommunicado interrogation is at odds with one of our Nation's most cherished principles—that the individual may not be compelled to incriminate himself. Unless adequate protective devices are employed to dispel the compulsion inherent in custodial surroundings, no statement obtained from the defendant can truly be the product of his free choice.

From the foregoing, we can readily perceive an intimate connection between the privilege against self-incrimination and police custodial questioning. . . .

II.

The question in these cases is whether the privilege is fully applicable during a period of custodial interrogation. . . . We are satisfied that all the principles embodied in the privilege apply to informal compulsion exerted by law-enforcement officers during in-custody questioning. An individual swept from familiar surroundings into police custody, surrounded by antagonistic forces, and subjected to the techniques of persuasion described above cannot be otherwise than under compulsion to speak. As a practical matter, the compulsion to speak in the isolated setting of the police station may well be greater than in courts or other official investigations, where there are often impartial observers to guard against intimidation or trickery. . . .

* * *

It is impossible for us to foresee the potential alternatives for protecting the privilege which might be devised by Congress or the States in the exercise of their creative rule-making capacities. Therefore we cannot say that the Constitution necessarily requires adherence to any particular solution for the inherent compulsions of the interrogation process as it is presently conducted. Our decision in no way creates a constitutional straitjacket which will handicap sound efforts at reform, nor is it intended to have this effect. We encourage Congress and the States to continue their laudable search for increasingly effective ways of protecting the rights of the individual while promoting efficient enforcement of our criminal laws. However, unless we are shown other procedures which are at least as effective in apprising accused persons of their right of silence and in assuring a continuous opportunity to exercise it, the following safeguards must be observed.

3. The absurdity of denying that a confession obtained under these circumstances is compelled is aptly portrayed by an example in Professor Sutherland's recent article, Crime and Confession, 79 Harv.L.Rev. 21, 37 (1965): "Suppose a well-to-do testatrix says she intends to will her property to Elizabeth. John and James want her to bequeath it to them instead. They capture the testatrix, put her in a carefully designed room, out of touch with everyone but themselves and their convenient 'witnesses,' keep her secluded there for hours while they make insistent demands, weary her with contradictions and finally induce her to execute the will in their favor. Assume that John and James are deeply and correctly convinced that Elizabeth is unworthy and will make base use of the property if she gets her hands on it, whereas John and James have the noblest and most righteous intentions. Would any judge of probate accept the will so procured as the 'voluntary' act of the testatrix?"

[Chief Justice Warren then stated, in greater detail, the procedural requirements set out in the summary statement of the Court's holding—*supra* pp. 273–274.

* * *

The warnings required and the waiver necessary in accordance with our opinion today are, in the absence of a fully effective equivalent, prerequisites to the admissibility of any statement made by a defendant. No distinction can be drawn between statements which are direct confessions and statements which amount to "admissions" of part or all of an offense. The privilege against self-incrimination protects the individual from being compelled to incriminate himself in any manner; it does not distinguish degrees of incrimination. Similarly, for precisely the same reason, no distinction may be drawn between inculpatory statements and statements alleged to be merely "exculpatory." If a statement made were in fact truly exculpatory it would, of course, never be used by the prosecution. In fact, statements merely intended to be exculpatory by the defendant are often used to impeach his testimony at trial or to demonstrate untruths in the statement given under interrogation and thus to prove guilt by implication. These statements are incriminating in any meaningful sense of the word and may not be used without the full warnings and effective waiver required for any other statement. In Escobedo itself, the defendant fully intended his accusation of another as the slayer to be exculpatory as to himself.

The principles announced today deal with the protection which must be given to the privilege against self-incrimination when the individual is first subjected to police interrogation while in custody at the station or otherwise deprived of his freedom of action in any way. It is at this point that our adversary system of criminal proceedings commences, distinguishing itself at the outset from the inquisitorial system recognized in some countries. Under the system of warnings we delineate today or under any other system which may be devised and found effective, the safeguards to be erected about the privilege must come into play at this point.

Our decision is not intended to hamper the traditional function of police officers in investigating crime. . . . When an individual is in custody on probable cause, the police may, of course, seek out evidence in the field to be used at trial against him. Such investigation may include inquiry of persons not under restraint. General on-the-scene questioning as to facts surrounding a crime or other general questioning of citizens in the fact-finding process is not affected by our holding. It is an act of responsible citizenship for individuals to give whatever information they may have to aid in law enforcement. In such situations the compelling atmosphere inherent in the process of in-custody interrogation is not necessarily present.

In dealing with statements obtained through interrogation, we do not purport to find all confessions inadmissible. Confessions remain a proper element in law enforcement. Any statement given freely and voluntarily without any compelling influences is, of course, admissible in evidence. The fundamental import of the privilege while an individual is in custody is not whether he is allowed to talk to the police without the benefit of warnings and counsel, but whether he can be interrogated. There is no requirement that police stop a person who enters a police station and states that he wishes to confess to a crime, or a person who calls the police to offer a confession or any other statement he desires to make. Volunteered statements of any kind are not barred by the Fifth Amendment and their admissibility is not affected by our holding today.

To summarize, we hold that when an individual is taken into custody or otherwise deprived of his freedom by the authorities and is subjected to questioning, the privilege against self-incrimination is jeopardized. Procedural safeguards must be employed to protect the privilege, and unless other fully effective means are adopted to notify the person of his right of silence and to assure that the exercise of the right will be scrupulously honored, the following measures are required. He must be warned prior to any questioning that he has the right to remain silent, that anything he says can be used against him in a court of law, that he has the right to the presence of an attorney, and that if he cannot afford an attorney one will be appointed for him prior to any questioning if he so desires. Opportunity to exercise these rights must be afforded to him throughout the interrogation. After such warnings have been given, and such opportunity afforded him, the individual may knowingly and intelligently waive these rights and agree to answer questions or make a statement. But unless and until such warnings and waiver are demonstrated by the prosecution at trial, no evidence obtained as a result of interrogation can be used against him.

* * *

Therefore, in accordance with the foregoing, the judgments of the Supreme Court of Arizona in No. 759, of the New York Court of Appeals in No. 760, and of the Court of Appeals for the Ninth Circuit in No. 761 are reversed. The judgment of the Supreme Court of California in No. 584 is affirmed.

[Justice Clark dissented in a separate opinion. Justice Harlan dissented in an opinion in which Justices Stewart and White joined him.]

Questions

1. What exactly are the Miranda rules regarding police interrogation?

2. The following statement is taken from a card carried by all patrolmen and detectives of a metropolitan police force in New York State:

RULES OF INTERROGATION

1. You have the right to remain silent.
2. Anything you say can and will be used against you in a court of law.
3. You have the right to talk to a lawyer, right now, and have him present with you while you are being questioned.
4. If you cannot afford to hire a lawyer one will be furnished to represent you before any questioning, if you wish one.

WAIVER

1. Do you understand each of these rights I have explained to you?

2. Having these rights in mind, do you wish to talk to me/us now?

The same message is also printed on the card in Spanish. The officers are under standing orders to read the message (in the appropriate language) to the suspect at the time of arrest. Does the instruction satisfy the Miranda requirements concerning the duty to inform suspects of their rights?

3. What are the abuses Miranda attempts to avoid? Do you think it likely that Miranda can be successfully implemented to substantially eliminate any of these abuses?

4. Assume, *arguendo*, that Miranda in fact will be largely ineffective in curtailing official abuses and preserving Fourth and Fifth Amendment rights. Assume also that Miranda has been a major ground for extensive public criticism and official attacks on the Supreme Court. Given these assumptions, would you say that Miranda was a wise decision? Was it a good decision?

5. Would a rule barring the use of any confessions unless made after advice of counsel and in the presence of a magistrate be preferable to the Miranda rules?

———

[The following is taken from RICHARD AYRES, "CONFESSIONS AND THE COURTS," Yale Alumni Magazine, Dec. 1968, pp. 21–22. The article summarizes the results of research by staff members of the Yale Law Journal regarding the impact of the Miranda decision on police practices.]

Our data and impressions . . . converge to a single conclusion: Despite the dark predictions by critics, the impact of the *Miranda* decision has apparently been negligible. This is true for two reasons. First, interrogations are simply not very important in solving crimes. Second, the *Miranda* rules, even when applied (as they often are not) affect interrogations only slightly because the police can still question suspects virtually at will.

How, then, shall we assess *Miranda,* and how does our assessment bear on the current furor over the criminal procedure decisions of the Supreme Court? I think our study shows, on the one hand, that too much energy has been wasted claiming the Court has "swung the balance in favor of the criminal." On the other hand, it also illustrates the Court's powerlessness to protect the rights of citizens in the face of determined opposition from other institutions, such as the police.

The state objectives of the *Miranda* decision were to assure that suspects were informed of their legal rights and that they would be allowed to exercise them if they chose to. Yet the only penalty the Court could impose for violations of its rules was that information gathered illegally could not be admitted into evidence at a trial. But as we learned in New

Haven, this penalty seldom has any operational meaning, because the police usually have ample evidence to convict without a confession.

Then why did the Court promulgate the *Miranda* rules? I think the police have perceived the meaning of *Miranda* accurately. The decision was a last-ditch effort by the Court to control the conduct of the police. It reflects the Court's dismay at the inability or lack of desire of other social institutions to oversee the police. The Court has had ample evidence in the cases which have come before it over the last 35 years that policemen are often all too willing to engage in manifestly unfair behavior.

Numerous studies, beginning with the massive Wickersham Commission Report of the early 1930s, have documented police practices which no citizen would feel were fair if they were applied to him. Yet there has been little sign that state legislatures, city governments, or police departments themselves are willing to take effective action to assure that all citizens are treated fairly and equally by policemen.

Decisions such as *Miranda* also reflect the paucity of devices which the court has to "police the police." Unlike a local police chief, the Supreme Court cannot fire or fine an officer who refuses to abide by the law of the land. The only weapon—a pitifully weak one—is to deprive him of one of the objects of his labors if he refuses to implement the law as he was sworn to. This is a roundabout, undesirable, and ineffective method of disciplining police forces.

* * *

The full report of this research is found in Interrogations in New Haven: The Impact of Miranda, 76 Yale L.J. 1519 (1967), an unsigned student note. Reports of similar findings in other research on the impact of Miranda is found in Griffiths & Ayres, A Postscript to The Miranda Project: Interrogation of Draft Protestors, 77 Yale L.J. 300 (1967), Seeburg & Wettick, Miranda in Pittsburgh—A Statistical Study, 29 U.Pitt.L.Rev. 1 (1967), Medalie, Leitz & Alexander, Custodial Police Interrogation in Our Nation's Capitol: The Attempt to Implement Miranda, 66 Mich.L.Rev. 1347 (1968), Leiken, Police Interrogation in Colorado, 47 Denver Law Journal 1 (1970).

According to Mr. Leiken, the Denver, Colorado police department adopted the practice of submitting the following form to suspects, after reading from it the summary Miranda warnings:

DENVER POLICE DEPARTMENT ADVISEMENT FORM

Name _____Birthdate_____
Date_____Time_____Location_____

You have a right to remain silent.

Anything you say can be used as evidence against you in court.

You have a right to talk to a lawyer before questioning and have him present during questioning.

If you cannot afford a lawyer, one will be appointed for you before questioning.

Do you understand each of these rights I have read to you?

Answer _____

Signature of Person Advised _____

Knowing my rights and knowing what I am doing, I now wish to voluntarily talk to you.

Signature of the Person Advised _____

Witnessed by _____

Signature of the Advising Officer _____

The Denver police procedure was then to encourage the suspect to sign the form, preferably in both the part acknowledging the warnings, and the part waiving the right to remain silent. Leiken, *supra* p. 9.

There is a great emphasis on the reading of the advisement form, and this procedure is almost never omitted during interrogations by members of the Denver Police Department. The findings in this study differ in this respect from those of the Yale study of the New Haven Police Department, conducted shortly after *Miranda* had taken effect. At that time in New Haven, less than half the suspects had received a warning which included more than half of the specific warnings required by *Miranda*.

Leiken, *supra* p. 10. Footnotes omitted.

Query: Why do you suppose the Denver police demonstrated this preoccupation with the advisement form?

————

Although the social scientific evidence on the practical impacts of Miranda rather strongly suggests that it has had little if any effect on police practices, it has proved to be a highly emotional issue with the police, who have rather consistently viewed it and related cases dealing with search and seizure (see e. g., pp. 240–256, *supra*) as a serious threat to their law enforcement efforts. Since Miranda left many unanswered questions as to its scope and applications, the Court has not wanted for opportunities to elaborate the Miranda doctrine. In a number of post-Miranda cases the Court has rather substantially limited the Miranda rule to situations in which the suspect is in custody, against his or her will, and in a setting where the interrogation is likely to have the adverse psychological effects described in Chief Justice Warren's opinion in Miranda.

For example, in Oregon v. Mathiason, 429 U.S. 492, 97 S.Ct. 711 (1977), the Court held that the Miranda warnings were not required in a case where a suspect in a burglary voluntarily came to the station house at the request of an investigating officer, met with and was interviewed by a detective but was not placed under arrest, and confessed to the crime in the course of the interview.

In U. S. v. Harris, 401 U.S. 222, 91 S.Ct. 643 (1971), and Oregon v. Hass, 420 U.S. 714, 95 S.Ct. 1215 (1975), the Court held that statements taken from a suspect in violation of Miranda, and which would be inadmissible if the prosecution attempted to include them as part of its case, might nevertheless be used to impeach the testimony of a defendant who took the stand to testify in his or her defense.

In Beckwith v. U. S., 425 U.S. 341, 96 S.Ct. 1613 (1976), the Court held that the Miranda warnings were not required where Internal Revenue agents conducted an interview of a suspected tax evader in the suspect's own home before the suspect was arrested.

In U. S. v. Mandujano, 425 U.S. 564, 96 S.Ct. 1768 (1976), the Court upheld the perjury conviction of a grand jury witness who was called to testify regarding criminal activity in which he was probably involved. The witness was not informed of his right to counsel and privilege against self-incrimination. Four justices held that the Miranda warnings should not be required in grand jury proceedings. Four other justices concurred in the result but without endorsing the implication that the grand jury interrogation was not a custodial interrogation within the meaning of Miranda.

In Michigan v. Mosley, 423 U.S. 96, 95 S.Ct. 321 (1975), the Court found that a suspect who had been read his rights and who had then specifically invoked his right to remain silent could nonetheless be subjected to a subsequent interrogation unless he again specifically invoked the right to remain silent. The case presented the Court an opportunity to develop some clearer standards regarding what constitutes an acceptable waiver of rights by the suspect. In dissent Justice Brennan urged the adoption of a rule that once the defendant had invoked the right to remain silent, no further questioning could occur prior to arraignment before a magistrate or until counsel is appointed and consults with the suspect.

Some commentators have argued that in the absence of clearer guidelines than the Court has yet evolved regarding the implementation of Miranda, lower court judges will generally admit confessions in cases where the allegations as to the nature of the police conduct and the suspect's exercise of rights "are contradictory, ambiguous, or ambivalent." See Elsen and Rosett, "Protections for the Suspect Under Miranda v. Arizona," 67 Columbia L.Rev. 655 (1967), and Leiken, *supra* at p. 42.

Although the post-Miranda opinions summarized above may be viewed as rather closely limiting the application of the Miranda rules, it is clear that the Court still adheres to a core concept of Miranda that police interrogation must be regulated in order to protect the right to counsel and the privilege against self-incrimination.

The following is taken from the opinion of Mr. Justice Stewart, for the majority, in Brewer v. Williams, 430 U.S. 387, 97 S.Ct. 1232 (1977):

On the afternoon of December 24, 1968, a 10-year-old girl named Pamela Powers went with her family to the YMCA in Des Moines, Iowa, to watch a wrestling tournament in which her brother was participating.

When she failed to return from a trip to the washroom, a search for her began. The search was unsuccessful.

Robert Williams, who had recently escaped from a mental hospital, was a resident of the YMCA. Soon after the girl's disappearance Williams was seen in the YMCA lobby carrying some clothing and a large bundle wrapped in a blanket. He obtained help from a 14-year-old boy in opening the street door of the YMCA and the door to his automobile parked outside. When Williams placed the bundle in the front seat of his car the boy "saw two legs in it and they were skinny and white." Before anyone could see what was in the bundle Williams drove away. His abandoned car was found the following day in Davenport, Iowa, roughly 160 miles east of Des Moines. A warrant was then issued in Des Moines for his arrest on a charge of abduction.

On the morning of December 26, a Des Moines lawyer named Henry McKnight went to the Des Moines police station and informed the officers present that he had just received a long distance call from Williams, and that he had advised Williams to turn himself in to the Davenport police. Williams did surrender that morning to the police in Davenport, and they booked him on the charge specified in the arrest warrant and gave him the warnings required by Miranda v. Arizona, 384 U.S. 436, 86 S.Ct. 1602. The Davenport police then telephoned their counterparts in Des Moines to inform them that Williams had surrendered. McKnight, the lawyer, was still at the Des Moines police headquarters, and Williams conversed with McKnight on the telephone. In the presence of the Des Moines Chief of Police and a Police Detective named Leaming, McKnight advised Williams that Des Moines police officers would be driving to Davenport to pick him up, that the officers would not interrogate him or mistreat him, and that Williams was not to talk to the officers about Pamela Powers until after consulting with McKnight upon his return to Des Moines. As a result of these conversations, it was agreed between McKnight and the Des Moines police officials that Detective Leaming and a fellow officer would drive to Davenport to pick up Williams, that they would bring him directly back to Des Moines, and that they would not question him during the trip.

In the meantime Williams was arraigned before a judge in Davenport on the outstanding arrest warrant. The judge advised him of his *Miranda* rights and committed him to jail. Before leaving the courtroom, Williams conferred with a lawyer named Kelly, who advised him not to make any statements until consulting with McKnight back in Des Moines.

Detective Leaming and his fellow officer arrived in Davenport about noon to pick up Williams and return him to Des Moines. Soon after their arrival they met with Williams and Kelly, who, they understood, was acting as Williams' lawyer. Detective Leaming repeated the *Miranda* warnings, and told Williams:

> ". . . we both know that you're being represented here by Mr. Kelly and you're being represented by Mr. McKnight in Des Moines, and . . . I want you to remember this because we'll be visiting between here and Des Moines."

Williams then conferred again with Kelly alone, and after this conference Kelly reiterated to Detective Leaming that Williams was not to be questioned about the disappearance of Pamela Powers until after he had consulted with McKnight back in Des Moines. When Leaming expressed some reservations, Kelly firmly stated that the agreement with McKnight was to be carried out—that there was to be no interrogation of Williams during the automobile journey to Des Moines. Kelly was denied permission to ride in the police car back to Des Moines with Williams and the two officers.

The two Detectives, with Williams in their charge, then set out on the 160-mile drive. At no time during the trip did Williams express a willingness to be interrogated in the absence of an attorney. Instead, he stated several times that "[w]hen I get to Des Moines and see Mr. McKnight, I am going to tell you the whole story." Detective Leaming knew that Williams was a former mental patient, and knew also that he was deeply religious.

The Detective and his prisoner soon embarked on a wide-ranging conversation covering a variety of topics, including the subject of religion. Then, not long after leaving Davenport and reaching the interstate highway, Detective Leaming delivered what has been referred to in the briefs and oral arguments as the "Christian burial speech." Addressing Williams as "Reverend," the Detective said:

> "I want to give you something to think about while we're traveling down the road. . . . Number one, I want you to observe the weather conditions, it's raining, it's sleeting, it's freezing, driving is very treacherous, visibility is poor, it's going to be dark early this evening. They are predicting several inches of snow for tonight, and I feel that you yourself are the only person that knows where this little girl's body is, that you yourself have only been there once, and if you get a snow on top of it you yourself may be unable to find it. And, since we will be going right past the area on the way into Des Moines, I feel that we could stop and locate the body, that the parents of this little girl should be entitled to a Christian burial for the little girl who was snatched away from them on Christmas Eve and murdered. And I feel we should stop and locate it on the way in rather than waiting until morning and trying to come back out after a snow storm and possibly not being able to find it at all."

Williams asked Detective Leaming why he thought their route to Des Moines would be taking them past the girl's body, and Leaming responded that he knew the body was in the area of Mitchellville—a town they would be passing on the way to Des Moines. Leaming then stated: "I do not want you to answer me. I don't want to discuss it further. Just think about it as we're riding down the road."

As the car approached Grinnell, a town approximately 100 miles west of Davenport, Williams asked whether the police had found the victim's shoes. When Detective Leaming replied that he was unsure, Williams directed the officers to a service station where he said he had left the shoes; a search for them proved unsuccessful. As they continued towards Des Moines, Williams asked whether the police had found the blanket, and directed the officers to a rest area where he said he had disposed of the blanket. Nothing was found. The car continued towards Des Moines, and as it approached Mitchellville, Williams said that he would show the officers where the body was. He then directed the police to the body of Pamela Powers.

Williams was indicted for first-degree murder. Before trial, his counsel moved to suppress all evidence relating to or resulting from any statements Williams had made during the automobile ride from Davenport to Des Moines. After an evidentiary hearing the trial judge denied the motion. He found that "an agreement was made between defense counsel and the police officials to the effect that the Defendant was not to be questioned on the return trip to Des Moines," and that the evidence in question had been elicited from Williams during "a critical stage in the proceedings requiring the presence of counsel on his request." The judge ruled, however, that Williams had "waived his right to have an attorney present during the giving of such information."

The evidence in question was introduced over counsel's continuing objection at the subsequent trial. The jury found Williams guilty of murder, and the judgment of conviction was affirmed by the Iowa Supreme Court, a bare majority of whose members agreed with the trial court that Williams had "waived his right to the presence of his counsel" on the automobile ride from Davenport to Des Moines. State v. Williams, 182 N.W.2d 396, 402. The four dissenting justices expressed the view that "when counsel and police have agreed defendant is not to be questioned until counsel is present and defendant has been advised not to talk and repeatedly has stated he will tell the whole story after he talks with counsel, the state should be required to make a stronger showing of intentional voluntary waiver than was made here." *Id.*, at 408.

Williams then petitioned for a writ of habeas corpus in the United States District Court for the Southern District of Iowa. Counsel for the State and for Williams stipulated "that the case would be submitted on the record of facts and proceedings in the trial court, without taking of further testimony." The District Court made findings of fact as summarized above, and concluded as a matter of law that the evidence in question had been wrongly admitted at Williams' trial. This conclusion was based on three alternative and independent grounds: (1) that Williams had been denied his constitutional right to the assistance of counsel; (2) that he had been denied the constitutional protections defined by this Court's decisions in Escobedo v. Illinois, 378 U.S. 478, 84 S.Ct. 1758, and Miranda v. Arizona, 384 U.S. 436, 86 S.Ct. 1602; and (3) that in any event, his self-incriminatory statements on the automobile trip from Davenport to Des Moines had been involuntarily made. Further, the District Court ruled that there had been no waiver by Williams of the constitutional protections in question. Williams v. Brewer, 375 F.Supp. 174.

The Court of Appeals for the Eighth Circuit, with one judge dissenting, affirmed this judgment, 509 F.2d 227, and denied a petition for rehearing en banc. We granted certiorari to consider the constitutional issues presented. 423 U.S. 1031, 96 S.Ct. 561.

Twenty-two states, through their chief legal officers, petitioned the Court in Brewer v. Williams requesting that the Court reconsider its decision in Miranda. (New York Times, March 24, 1977 at p. 1). The Court did not reconsider Miranda. It ruled, in an opinion by Mr. Justice Stewart, that Williams' petition for habeas corpus was meritorious, and it affirmed the District Court and Circuit Court of Appeals determinations that Williams was entitled to a new trial. The Court found that Detective Leaming's "Christian burial speech" had been tantamount to an interrogation; that this was a clear violation of the terms of the agreement between the police and Williams' attorneys; that the "interrogation" during the car trip effectively deprived Williams of the assistance of counsel; and that Williams had not waived his right to counsel when he made the incriminating statements.

The majority opinion concluded with the following remarks:

The crime of which Williams was convicted was senseless and brutal, calling for swift and energetic action by the police to apprehend the perpetrator and gather evidence with which he could be convicted. No mission of law enforcement officials is more important. Yet "[d]isinterested zeal for the public good does not assure either wisdom or right in the methods it pursues." Haley v. Ohio, 332 U.S. 596, 605, 68 S.Ct. 302, 306 (Frankfurter, J., concurring in the judgment). Although we do not lightly affirm the issuance of a writ of habeas corpus in this case, so clear a violation of the Sixth and Fourteenth Amendments as here occurred cannot be condoned. The pressures on state executive and judicial officers charged with the administration of the criminal law are great, especially when the crime is murder and the victim a small child. But it is precisely the predictability of those pressures that makes imperative a resolute loyalty to the guarantees that the Constitution extends to us all.

The judgment of the Court of Appeals is affirmed.

Vigorous dissents were written by Chief Justice Burger, and Justice White, who was joined by Justices Blackmun and Rehnquist. The Chief Justice argued that Miranda/Escobedo should not require exclusion of the evidence elicited by Detective Leaming where the circumstances disclosed that the evidence was "of unquestioned reliability" and Williams' "disclosures were voluntary and uncoerced." He argued that the purpose of the exclusionary rule is to "safeguard the fairness of the trial and the factfinding process," and under that standard the facts in Brewer v. Williams did not warrant exclusion of the evidence as to how the victim's body was found.

Justice White thought that the facts warranted a finding that Williams had voluntarily waived the right to further assistance of counsel during the car trip with Detective Leaming.

Problem

"On March 26, 1971, the proprietor of a pizza parlor in Rochester, N.Y. was killed during an attempted robbery. On August 10, 1971, Detective Anthony Fantigrossi of the Rochester Police was told by another officer that an informant had supplied a possible lead implicating petitioner in the crime. Fantigrossi questioned the supposed source of the lead—a jail inmate awaiting trial for burglary—but learned nothing that supplied 'enough information to get a warrant' for petitioner's arrest. App., at 60. Nevertheless, Fantigrossi

ordered other detectives to 'pick up' petitioner and 'bring him in.'
Id., at 54. Three detectives located petitioner at a neighbor's house
on the morning of August 11. Petitioner was taken into custody;
although he was not told he was under arrest, he would have been
physically restrained if he had attempted to leave. People v. Dunaway, Monroe Cty. Ct., App. 116, 117 (Mar. 11, 1977). He was driven
to police headquarters in a police car and placed in an interrogation
room, where he was questioned by officers after being given the warnings required by Miranda v. Arizona, 384 U.S. 436 (1966). Petitioner
waived counsel and eventually made statements and drew sketches
that incriminated him in the crime.

"At petitioner's jury trial for attempted robbery and felony murder, his motions to suppress the statements and sketches were denied,
and he was convicted. On appeal, both the Appellate Division of the
Fourth Department and the New York Court of Appeals initially affirmed the conviction without opinion. People v. Dunaway, 42 A.D.
2d 689, 346 N.Y.S.2d 779 (1973), aff'd, 35 N.Y.2d 741, 320 N.E.2d 646
(1974). However, this Court granted certiorari, vacated the judgment, and remanded the case for further consideration in light of the
Court's supervening decision in Brown v. Illinois, 422 U.S. 590 (1975).
Dunaway v. New York, 422 U.S. 1053 (1975). The petitioner in
Brown, like petitioner Dunaway, made inculpatory statements after
receiving Miranda warnings during custodial interrogation following his seizure—in that case a formal arrest—on less than probable
cause. Brown's motion to suppress the statements was also denied
and the statements were used to convict him. Although the Illinois
Supreme Court recognized that Brown's arrest was unlawful, it affirmed the admission of the statements on the ground that the giving
of Miranda warnings served to break the causal connection between
the illegal arrest and the giving of the statements. This Court reversed, holding that the Illinois courts erred in adopting a *per se* rule
that Miranda warnings in and of themselves sufficed to cure the
Fourth Amendment violation; rather the Court held that in order
to use such statements, the prosecution must show not only that the
statements meet the Fifth Amendment voluntariness standard, but
also that the causal connection between the statements and the illegal
arrest is broken sufficiently to purge the primary taint of the illegal
arrest in light of the distinct policies and interests of the Fourth
Amendment.

"In compliance with the remand, the New York Court of Appeals
directed the Monroe County Court to make further factual findings
as to whether there was a detention of petitioner, whether the police
had probable cause, 'and, in the event there was a detention and
probable cause is not found for such detention, to determine the further question as to whether the making of the confessions was rendered infirm by the illegal arrest (see Brown v. Illinois, 422 U.S. 590,

supra).'   People v. Dunaway, 38 N.Y.2d 812, 813–814, 345 N.E.2d 583, 584 (1975).

"The County Court determined after a supplementary suppression hearing that Dunaway's motion to suppress should have been granted. Although reaffirming that there had been 'full compliance with the mandate of Miranda v. Arizona,' the County Court found that 'this case does not involve a situation where the defendant voluntarily appeared at police headquarters in response to a request of the police . . . .' App., at 117. The State's attempt to justify petitioner's involuntary investigatory detention on the authority of People v. Morales, 22 N.Y.2d 55, 238 N.E.2d 307 (1968)—which upheld a similar detention on the basis of information amounting to less than probable cause for arrest—was rejected on the grounds that the precedential value of Morales was questionable, and that the controlling authority was the 'strong language' in Brown v. Illinois indicating 'disdain for custodial questioning without probable cause to arrest.' The County Court further held that 'the factual predicate in this case did not amount to probable cause sufficient to support the arrest of defendant," that "the Miranda warnings by themselves did not purge the taint of the defendant's illegal seizure. Brown v. Illinois, supra . . . and [that] there was no claim or showing by the People of any attenuation of the defendant's illegal detention," App., at 121. Accordingly petitioner's motion to suppress was granted. *Ibid.*

"A divided Appellate Division reversed. Although agreeing that the police lacked probable cause to arrest petitioner, the majority relied on the Court of Appeals' reaffirmation, subsequent to the County Court's decision, that "[l]aw enforcement officials may detain an individual upon reasonable suspicion for questioning for a reasonable and brief period of time under carefully controlled conditions which are ample to protect the individual's Fifth and Sixth Amendment Rights." People v. Dunaway, 61 A.D.2d 299, 302, 402 N.Y.S.2d 490, 492 (1978), quoting People v. Morales, 42 N.Y.2d 129, 135, 366 N.E.2d 248, 251 (1977). The Appellate Division also held that even if petitioner's detention were illegal, the taint of his illegal detention was sufficiently attenuated to allow the admission of his statements and sketches. The Appellate Division emphasized that petitioner was never threatened or abused by the police and purported to distinguish Brown v. Illinois. The Court of Appeals dismissed petitioner's application for leave to appeal. App., at 134.

"We granted certiorari, —— U.S. —— (1978), to clarify the Fourth Amendment's requirements as to the permissible grounds for custodial interrogation and to review the New York court's application of Brown v. Illinois. . . ."

From the opinion of the Court, per Mr. Justice Brennan, in Dunaway v. New York, —— U.S. ——, 99 S.Ct. 2248 (1979).

What is the basis for the motion to suppress the confession? Is it that the accused's Fourth Amendment rights were violated? Since the arresting officers read the accused the Miranda warnings, shouldn't that be enough to make the confession admissible? If not, why not?

If you were the attorney for the State of New York, would you argue that Terry v. Ohio supports denial of the motion to suppress? If so, why?

The Court reversed the New York courts' denial of the motion to suppress. Justice Rehnquist and the Chief Justice dissented.

SECTION 11.4 CONTROL OF POLICE BEHAVIOR BY JUDICIAL REVIEW: A CRITIQUE

The Supreme Court has not lacked for critics of its recent decisions regarding the application of the Bill of Rights to state criminal procedure. A notable contribution to that literature was made by Judge Henry J. Friendly (United States Court of Appeals—Second Circuit) in his article "The Bill of Rights as a Code of Criminal Procedure", 53 California Law Review 929 (1965). The concluding paragraphs of that article follow.

> My submission—no less respectful for having been occasionally vigorous—is that in applying the Bill of Rights to the states, the Supreme Court should not regard these declarations of fundamental principles as if they were a detailed code of criminal procedure, allowing no room whatever for reasonable difference of judgment or play in the joints. The "specifics" simply are not that specific.
>
> . . .
>
> Professor Frankfurter, as he then was, showed remarkable prescience when, in paying contemporary tribute to Powell v. Alabama more than thirty years ago, he included the caveat that the fourteenth amendment "is not the basis of a uniform code of criminal procedure federally imposed. Alternative modes of arriving at truth are not—they must not be—forever frozen. There is room for growth and vitality, for adaptation to shifting necessities, for wide differences of reasonable convenience in method."
>
> Here too, in . . . Chief Justice [Marshall's] words, the Justices "must never forget that it is a *constitution* we are expounding." The consequences of constitutional adjudication are not less awesome in criminal procedure than elsewhere. As a wise judge of our own times warned: "Constitutions are deliberately made difficult of amendment; mistaken readings of them cannot be readily corrected. Moreover, if they could be, constitutions must not degenerate into vade mecums or codes; when they begin to do so, it is a sign of a community unsure of itself and seeking protection against its own misgivings." The Bill of Rights ought not to be read as prohibiting the development of "workable rules," or as requiring the states forever to conform their criminal procedures to the preferences of five Justices, reached on a record whose extreme

facts may have induced the rapid formulation of a principle broader than empirical investigation would show to be wise and without the illumination such a study would afford. . . . The Justices are too sophisticated really to believe that the first eight amendments speak so clearly on every issue as to make irrelevant the hard facts of life. The wisdom of Mr. Justice Brandeis' observation, "It is one of the happy incidents of the federal system that a single courageous State may, if its citizens choose, serve as a laboratory," cannot be sloughed off by denying "power to experiment with the fundamental liberties of citizens safeguarded by the Bill of Rights"; the very question is how far these safeguards extend. Five to four divisions within the Court afford no more impressive evidence on that score than did those of thirty years ago with respect to the due process and equal protection clauses. In the long run the people could hardly be expected to be more tolerant of judicial condemnation of reasonable efforts by state governments to protect the security of their lives and property than they were of nullification of efforts to advance their economic and social welfare. In that area we arrived at reasonable compromises of those conflicts of "right and wrong—between whose endless jar justice resides"; we must find them here too.

The revered and supreme guardian of the Bill of Rights, the Court, happily does not stand alone. It should welcome the aid that legislatures may now be ready to offer in discharging the grave responsibilities of the due administration of criminal justice.

SECTION 11.5   LEGISLATIVE REGULATION OF POLICE INTERROGATION: A FOOTNOTE TO MIRANDA

In Miranda, Chief Justice Warren solicited the formulation of legislative rules which would provide "effective ways of protecting the rights of the individual while promoting efficient enforcement of our criminal laws (*supra* p. 276).

Justice Warren's invitation has been virtually ignored by state legislatures. An attempt at a comprehensive statement of legislative rules regarding police interrogation has been proposed by the American Law Institute.

ALI MODEL CODE OF PRE–ARRAIGNMENT PROCEDURE
Article 120

Section 120.8   Procedures on Arrest: Warnings; Questioning

(1) **Warnings.** Upon making an arrest, a law enforcement officer shall

    (a) identify himself as such unless his identity is otherwise apparent;

    (b) inform the arrested person that he is under arrest;

    (c) as promptly as is reasonable under the circumstances, inform the arrested person of the cause of the arrest, unless the cause appears to be evident; and

(d) as promptly as is reasonable under the circumstances, and in any case before engaging in any sustained interrogation, warn such person

(i) that he is not obligated to say anything, and anything he says may be used in evidence against him,

(ii) that he will promptly be taken to a police station where he may promptly communicate with counsel, relatives or friends,

(iii) that he will not be questioned unless he wishes, and that he may consult a lawyer before being questioned and may have a lawyer present during any questioning, and

(iv) that if he wishes to consult a lawyer or to have a lawyer present during questioning, but is unable to obtain one, he will not be questioned until a lawyer has been provided for him.

(2) **Limitations on Questioning.** No law enforcement officer shall question an arrested person if such person has indicated in any manner that he does not wish to be questioned, or that he wishes to consult counsel before submitting to any questioning.

* * *

ARTICLE 130

Section 130.1 Procedures Upon Arrested Persons' Arrival at Police Station

(1) **Appearance Before Station Officer.** Any person arrested and brought to a police station shall forthwith be presented before the station officer, who shall make a record of the time when such person was brought before him. The chief officer of each law enforcement agency shall assure that at all times there will be one or more officers in each police station specifically designated as station officers who are qualified to perform the duties provided in this Code.

(2) **Warning.** The station officer shall immediately inform the arrested person of the crime for which he has been arrested and how long he may be held prior to the time he is to be released or charged; and the station officer shall then advise the arrested person in plain and understandable language

(a) that if charged with crime, he will be released on bail or taken before a judicial officer;

(b) that he is not obliged to say anything and that anything he says may be used in evidence against him;

(c) that he may promptly communicate by telephone with counsel, relatives or friends and that, if necessary, funds in reasonable amounts will be provided to enable him to do so; and

(d) that counsel or a relative or friend may have access to him as provided in Section 140.7.

[Note: the station officer shall here inform the arrested person of the arrangements in the jurisdiction for providing counsel to persons in his circumstances, and shall inform him how soon counsel is likely to be available to him.]

The arrested person shall also forthwith be given a printed form which in plain and understandable language contains the substance of the matters listed in paragraphs (a)–(d) above, and he shall be asked to read it and to sign a statement at the bottom of such form which shall state: "I have read the warning given above and understand it." The station officer shall then countersign the form, recording thereon that he duly gave the warning required by this Section and return a copy of the signed form to the arrested person. If the arrested person refuses to sign, the station officer shall make a written record, which he shall sign, that he gave the warning required by this Section and that the arrested person refused to sign the form.

(3) **Warning to Illiterate Persons.** If the arrested person is unable to read or write, the station officer shall give the oral warning required by Subsection (2) of this Section in the presence of a witness; and the station officer shall make a written record, which he and such witness shall sign, that he gave the oral warning required by Subsection (2) of this Section and that no written warning was given on account of the illiteracy of the arrested person.

(4) **Incapacity to Understand Warning.** In any case where an arrested person is in such condition, on account of illness, injury, drink, or drugs, that, in the judgment of the station officer, he is incapable of understanding the warning, such warning shall be given as soon as such person is able to understand it.

(5) **Assistance in Communication.** Promptly after the warning the station officer shall make reasonable effort to assist the arrested person in communicating with (1) a relative or friend and (2) other persons reasonably needed to obtain the services of a lawyer, including, if appropriate, the [public defender's office] [legal aid service] [lawyer referral service], and to meet any terms of pre-appearance release. If necessary the station officer shall provide funds in reasonable amount to enable the arrested person to use the telephone.

(6) **Information Concerning Location of Arrested Persons.** Information concerning the location of any arrested person upon his appearance at a police station under this Section shall promptly be made available to a relative, attorney or friend upon a single inquiry at a centralized location.

* * *

ARTICLE 140

Section 140.8   Conditions on Questioning Arrested Persons

(1) **No Questioning Prior to Warning or Access to Telephone.** No law enforcement officer shall question an arrested person after he has been brought to the police station or otherwise attempt to induce him to make a statement unless he has been advised by the station officer in plain understandable language

(a) that he is not obliged to say anything and that anything he says may be used in evidence against him;

(b) that he will not be questioned unless he wishes, and that he may consult a lawyer before being questioned and may have a lawyer present during any questioning; and

(c) that if he wishes to consult a lawyer or to have a lawyer present during questioning, but is unable to obtain one, he will not be questioned until a lawyer has been provided for him; such advice shall also include information on how he may arrange to have a lawyer so provided.

No law enforcement officer shall question any arrested person who has been brought to a police station until he has been afforded an opportunity to use the telephone pursuant to Subsection 130.1(5).

(2) **Waivers.** Unless an arrested person is represented by counsel, and his counsel is present or he and his counsel have consented thereto, such person shall not be questioned after he has been brought to the police station unless he waives his right to counsel in accordance with the following procedures:

(a) After giving the warnings of rights required by Subsection (1), the station officer may then inquire whether the arrested person wishes to waive his right to counsel and to make a statement or consent to questioning in the absence of counsel.

(b) If the arrested person in response to such inquiry indicates that he wishes to make a statement or consents to questioning in the absence of counsel, he shall be asked to sign a writing to that effect which the station officer shall countersign.

(c) The arrested person shall be informed that any waiver given hereunder may be revoked by him at any time.

(d) No waiver shall be sought from an arrested person at any time after he has indicated in any manner that he does not wish to be questioned or that he wishes to consult counsel before submitting to questioning.

(3) **Revocation of Waiver.** If at any time after an arrested person has waived his right to counsel pursuant to Subsection (2), such person indicates in any manner that he wishes to revoke such waiver, or that he does not wish to be questioned or to make a statement, or that he wishes to consult counsel before submitting to further questioning or making a statement, such waiver shall be deemed revoked.

(4) **Period of Lawful Questioning.** No law enforcement officer shall seek a waiver of the right to counsel from an arrested person, or question such person pursuant to such a waiver, after the later of (a) the end of the [two] hour period provided for in Subsection 130.2(1) or (b) the end of the period of screening authorized by Subsections 130.2(2) and (3).

(5) **Non-Investigative Questioning.** As used in this Code "questioning" refers to questioning designed to investigate crimes or the involvement of the arrested person or others in crimes. Compliance with the procedures for questioning set forth in this Code is not required in connection with other conversation between the arrested person and law enforcement officers.

(6) **Questioning to Obtain Information Not for Use Against Arrested Person.** A law enforcement officer may question an arrested person without complying with this Section if prior thereto the prosecuting attorney has determined that he will not use against the arrested person in any proceeding any statement obtained by such questioning or any other evidence obtained as a result of such statement. Such determination by the prosecuting attorney shall be communicated to the arrested person prior to such questioning and a written record thereof shall be furnished to him. No statement or other evidence obtained as a result of a statement obtained

pursuant to this Subsection shall be used in any proceeding against the arrested person.

The Model Code Article 150 provides for the suppression of evidence taken in violation of these provisions.

Question

Review the facts in Brewer v. Williams, supra pp. 282–285. How would that case have been decided under the Model Code?

The Congress has legislated on the subject of police interrogation.

Title 18 United States Code § 3501. Admissibility of Confessions

(a) In any criminal prosecution brought by the United States or by the District of Columbia, a confession, as defined in subsection (e) hereof, shall be admissible in evidence if it is voluntarily given. Before such confession is received in evidence, the trial judge shall, out of the presence of the jury, determine any issue as to voluntariness. If the trial judge determines that the confession was voluntarily made it shall be admitted in evidence and the trial judge shall permit the jury to hear relevant evidence on the issue of voluntariness and shall instruct the jury to give such weight to the confession as the jury feels it deserves under all the circumstances.

(b) The trial judge in determining the issue of voluntariness shall take into consideration all the circumstances surrounding the giving of the confession, including (1) the time elapsing between arrest and arraignment of the defendant making the confession, if it was made after arrest and before arraignment, (2) whether such defendant knew the nature of the offense with which he was charged or of which he was suspected at the time of making the confession, (3) whether or not such defendant was advised or knew that he was not required to make any statement and that any such statement could be used against him, (4) whether or not such defendant had been advised prior to questioning of his right to the assistance of counsel; and (5) whether or not such defendant was without the assistance of counsel when questioned and when giving such confession.

The presence or absence of any of the above-mentioned factors to be taken into consideration by the judge need not be conclusive on the issue of voluntariness of the confession.

(c) In any criminal prosecution by the United States or by the District of Columbia, a confession made or given by a person who is a defendant therein, while such person was under arrest or other detention in the custody of any law-enforcement officer or law-enforcement agency, shall not be inadmissible solely because of delay in bringing such person before a commissioner or other officer empowered to commit persons charged with offenses against the laws of the United States or of the District of Columbia if such confession is found by the trial judge to have been made voluntarily and if the weight to be given the confession is left to the jury and if such confession was made or given by such person within six hours immediately following his arrest or other detention: *Provided,* That the time limitation contained in this subsection shall not apply in any case in which the delay in bringing such person before such commissioner or other officer beyond such six-hour period is found by the trial judge to be reasonable considering the means of transportation and the distance to be traveled to the nearest available such commissioner or other officer.

(d) Nothing contained in this section shall bar the admission in evidence of any confession made or given voluntarily by any person to any other person without interrogation by anyone, or at any time at which the person who made or gave such confession was not under arrest or other detention.

(e) As used in this section, the term "confession" means any confession of guilt of any criminal offense or any self-incriminating statement made or given orally or in writing.

Notes and Questions

1.   Section 3501 was added to United States Code by Public Law 90–351, the "Omnibus Crime Control and Safe Streets Act", (82 Stat. 210, June 19, 1968).

2.   Does Section 3501 alter the McNabb-Mallory doctrine regarding the interpretation of Rule 5(a), Federal Rules of Criminal Procedure? Would it be appropriate for Congress to attempt to alter the McNabb-Mallory doctrine?

3.   How does Section 3501 relate to the Miranda rules regarding the admissibility of confessions?

4.   Does Section 3501 provide a legislative alternative to Miranda for protecting the privilege against self-incrimination?

5.   At the date of this writing, no federal court had yet ruled on the constitutional issues presented by § 3501.

6.   What is the function of the privilege against self-incrimination? Should there be a privilege against self-incrimination?

7.   What values seem to you to underlie the Bill of Rights provisions regarding arrests, searches, and interrogations? Do those values conflict with other social interests and values? By whom and by what means should such conflicts be resolved? How, in fact, does it appear that such conflicts are resolved in the United States?

SECTION 12.   THE PROSECUTOR'S PHASE OF THE CRIMINAL PROCESS

SECTION 12.1   PROSECUTORIAL DISCRETION

The importance of the police and prosecutor in American criminal law is magnified and at the same time made more problematic by the substantial discretion they exercise with respect to law enforcement.

As we have seen, the police have very significant powers regarding the initiation and conduct of investigations. There are theoretical checks on the exercise of those powers, derived from constitutions and statutes, but the checks are difficult to implement in cases where the police act improperly. On the other side of the coin, the police and the prosecutor have a very significant power in their ability to choose not to act, not to investigate, not to arrest, or not to prosecute cases presented to them. The legal limits on the exercise of this discretionary authority are perhaps even weaker than the legal limits on affirmative exercises of the police power. The following excerpts explore some of the issues posed by this aspect of American criminal justice.

UNITED STATES v. COX

United States Court of Appeals, Fifth Circuit, 1965.
342 F.2d 167.

Before TUTTLE, CHIEF JUDGE, and RIVES, JONES, BROWN, WISDOM, GEWIN and BELL, CIRCUIT JUDGES.

JONES, CIRCUIT JUDGE. On October 22, 1964, an order of the United States District Court for the Southern District of Mississippi, signed by Harold Cox, a judge of that Court, was entered. The order, with caption and formal closing omitted, is as follows:

"THE GRAND JURY, duly elected, impaneled and organized, for the Southern District of Mississippi, reconvened on order of the Court at 9:00 A.M., October 21, 1964, in Court Room Number 2 in Jackson, Mississippi, for the general dispatch of its business. The grand jury was fully instructed as to their duties, powers and responsibilities and retired to the grand jury room number 538 in the Federal Building at Jackson to do its work. The United States Attorney (and one of his assistants) sat with the grand jury throughout the day on October 21 and explained in detail to the grand jury the perjury laws and the Court's construction of such laws for their information. The grand jury heard witnesses throughout the day on October 21, 1964. On the morning of October 22, 1964, the grand jury, through its foreman, made known to the Court in open court that they had requested Robert E. Hauberg, United States Attorney, to prepare certain indictments which they desired to bring against some of the persons under consideration and about which they had heard testimony, and the United States Attorney refused to draft or sign any such indictments on instructions of the Acting Attorney General of the United States; whereupon the Court ordered and directed said United States Attorney to draft such true bills or no bills as the grand jury may have duly voted and desired to report and to sign such instruments as required by law under penalty of contempt. The United States Attorney was afforded one hour within which to decide as to whether or not he would abide by the instructions and order of the Court in such respect. At the end of such time, the Court re-convened and the United States Attorney was specifically asked in open court as to whether or not he intended to conform with the order and direction of the Court in said respects whereupon the United States Attorney answered that he respectfully declined to do so on instructions from Nicholas deB. Katzenbach, Acting Attorney General. He was thereupon duly adjudged by the Court to be in civil contempt of the Court and was afforded an opportunity to make any statement which he desired to make to the Court before sentence; whereupon the United States Attorney reiterated his inability to comply with the order of the Court upon express and direct instructions from Nicholas deB. Katzenbach, Acting Attorney General of the United States.

"WHEREFORE, IT IS ORDERED AND ADJUDGED by the Court that Robert E. Hauberg, United States Attorney, is guilty of civil contempt of this Court and in the presence of the Court for his said refusal to obey its said order and he is ordered into custody of the United States Marshal to be confined by him in the Hinds County, Mississippi, jail, there to remain until he purges himself of this contempt by agreeing to conform to said order by performing his official duty for the grand jury as requested in the several (about five) pending cases before them on October 21 and October 22, 1964.

"IT IS FURTHER ORDERED by the Court that a citation issue to Nicholas deB. Katzenbach, Acting Attorney General of the United States, directing him to appear before this Court and show cause why he should not be adjudged guilty of contempt of this Court for his instructions and directions to the United States Attorney to disregard and disobey the orders of this Court in the respects stated.

"The United States Attorney requested a stay of enforcement of this order and further proceedings herein for five days after this date to enable him to apply to the United States Court of Appeals for the Fifth Circuit for a writ of prohibition and such request is granted; and these proceedings and enforcement of this order in its entirety is stayed for five days, subject to the further orders of the United States Court of Appeals on said application; and for the enforcement of all of which, let proper process issue."

The United States Attorney, Robert E. Hauberg, and the Acting Attorney General, Nicholas deB. Katzenbach, have appealed from the order and they, joined by the United States, seek a writ of prohibition against the District Judge from enforcing the Court's order, and from asserting jurisdiction to require the Attorney General or the United States Attorney "to institute criminal prosecutions or to take any steps in regard thereto." The facts recited in the order are uncontroverted. No further facts are essential to a decision of the issues before this Court. Although the issues here presented arose, in part at least, as an incident of a civil rights matter, no civil rights questions are involved in the rather broad inquiry which we are called upon to make.

The constitutional requirement of an indictment or presentment as a predicate to a prosecution for capital or infamous crimes has for its primary purpose the protection of the individual from jeopardy except on a finding of probable cause by a group of his fellow citizens, and is designed to afford a safeguard against oppressive actions of the prosecutor or a court. The constitutional provision is not to be read as conferring on or preserving to the grand jury, as such, any rights or prerogatives. The constitutional provision is, as has been said, for the benefit of the accused. . . .

The judicial power of the United States is vested in the federal courts, and extends to prosecutions for violations of the criminal laws of the United States. The executive power is vested in the President of the United States, who is required to take care that the laws be faithfully executed. The Attorney General is the hand of the President in taking care that the laws of the United States in legal proceedings and in the prosecution of offenses, be faithfully executed. The role of the grand jury is restricted to a finding as to whether or not there is probable cause to believe that an offense has been committed. The discretionary power of the attorney for the United States in determining whether a prosecution shall be commenced or maintained may well depend upon matters of policy wholly apart from any question of probable cause. Although as a member of the bar, the attorney for the United States is an officer of the court, he is nevertheless an executive official of the Government, and it is as an officer of the executive department that he exercises a discretion as to whether or not there shall be a prosecution in a particular case. It follows, as an incident of the constitutional separation of powers, that the courts are not to interfere with the free exercise of the discretionary powers of the attorneys of the United States in their control over criminal prosecutions. The provision of Rule 7, requiring the signing of the indictment by the attorney for the Government, is a recognition of the power of Government counsel to permit or not to permit the bringing of an indictment. If the attorney refuses to sign, as he has the discretionary power of doing, we conclude that there is no valid indictment. It is not to be supposed that the signature of counsel is merely an attestation of the act of the grand jury. The signature of the foreman performs that function. It is not to be supposed that the signature of counsel is a certificate that the indictment is in proper form to charge an offense. The sufficiency of the indictment may be tested before the court. Rather, we think, the requirement of the signature is for the purpose of evidencing the joinder of the attorney for the United States with the grand jury in instituting a criminal proceeding in the Court. Without the signature there can be no criminal proceeding brought upon an indictment. Substantial compliance rather than technical exactness meets the requirement of the rule. There seems to be no authority for the statement that the absence of a signature is not fatal. 4 Barron & Holtzoff Federal Practice & Procedure 61, § 1913.

* * *

Because, as we conclude, the signature of the Government attorney is necessary to the validity of the indictment and the affixing or withholding of the signature is a matter of executive discretion which cannot be coerced or reviewed by the courts, the contempt order must be reversed. It seems that, since the United States Attorney cannot be required to give validity to an indictment by affixing his signature, he should not be required to indulge in an exercise of futility by the preparation of the form of an indictment which he is unwilling to vitalize with his signature. Therefore he should not be required to prepare indictments which he is unwilling and under no duty to sign.

Notes and Questions

1.   Does the separation of powers argument strike you as a particularly solid footing for the result reached in United States v. Cox? Consider the following:

"One main reason that seems to actuate federal courts in holding that discretion of prosecutors may not be reviewed to protect against abuse has been stated by the Fifth Circuit in a 1965 opinion: '. . . it is as an officer of the executive department that he [the U. S. Attorney] exercises a discretion as to whether or not there shall be a prosecution in a particular case. It follows, as an incident of the constitutional separation of powers, that the courts are not to interfere with the free exercise of the discretionary powers of the attorneys of the United States in their control over criminal prosecutions.' This reason is so clearly unsound as to be almost absurd. If separation of powers prevents review of discretion of executive officers, then more than a hundred Supreme Court decisions spread over a century and three-quarters will have to be found contrary to the Constitution! If courts could not interfere with abuse of discretion by executive officers, our fundamental institutions would be altogether different from what they are. If the statement just quoted from the Fifth Circuit were true, the courts would be powerless to interfere when executive officers, acting illegally, are about to execute an innocent person!" Kenneth C. Davis, Discretionary Justice, p. 211 (Baton Rouge, La., University of Louisiana Press, 1969).

2.   Who was suing whom in United States v. Cox and what relief was sought by the plaintiff?

3.   Would the reasoning of the Circuit Court in United States v. Cox apply as well to a case where the victim of an alleged kidnapping invoked the aid of a United States District Court to force the United States Attorney to prosecute after an indictment was returned against the alleged kidnapper?

4.   Can you offer practical reasons for judicial reluctance to review the exercise of prosecutorial discretion.

5.   The following is taken from the special concurring opinion of Judge Wisdom in United States v. Cox, *op. cit*:

. . . [T]he facts . . . demonstrate, better than abstract principles or legal dicta, the imperative necessity that the United States, through its Attorney General, have uncontrollable discretion to prosecute.

The crucial fact here is that Goff and Kendrick, two Negroes, testified in a suit by the United States against the Registrar of Clarke County, Mississippi, and the State of Mississippi, to enforce the voting rights of Negroes under the Fourteenth Amendment and the Civil Rights Act. United States v. Ramsey, 5 Cir. 1964, 331 F.2d 824; rev'd on reh'g, 331 F.2d 838.

Goff and Kendrick testified that some seven years earlier at Stonewall, Mississippi, the registrar had refused to register them or give them application forms. They said that they had seen white persons registering, one of whom was a B. Floyd Jones. Ramsey, the registrar, testified that Jones had not registered at that time or place, but had registered the year before in Enterprise, Mississippi. He testified also that he had never discriminated against Negro applicants for registration. Jones testified that he was near the registration table in Stonewall in 1955, had talked with the registrar, and had shaken hands with him. The presiding judge, Judge W. Harold Cox, stated from the bench that Goff and Kendrick should be "bound over to await the action of the grand jury for perjury".[1]

In January 1963 attorneys of the Department of Justice requested the Federal Bureau of Investigation to investigate the possible perjury. The FBI completed a full investigation in March 1963 and referred the matter to the Department's Criminal Division. In June 1963 the Criminal Division advised the local United States Attorney, Mr. Hauberg, that the matter presented "no basis for a perjury prosecution". Mr. Hauberg informed Judge Cox of the Department's decision. Judge Cox stated that in his view the matter was clearly one for the grand jury and that he would be inclined, if necessary, to appoint an outside attorney to present the matter to the grand jury. (I find no authority for a federal judge to displace the United States Attorney by appointing a special prosecutor.) On receiving this information, the Criminal Division again reviewed its files and concluded that the charge of perjury could not be sustained. General Katzenbach, then Deputy Attorney General, after reviewing the files, concurred in the Criminal Division's decision. In September 1963 General Katzenbach called on Judge Cox as a courtesy to explain why the Department had arrived at the conclusion that no perjury was involved. Judge Cox, unconvinced, requested the United States Attorney to present to the grand jury the Goff and Kendrick cases, which he regarded as cases of "palpable perjury".

In October 1963 Goff and Kendrick were arrested, jailed for two days, and placed on a $3,000 bond for violations of State law for falsely testifying in federal court. After their indictment by a state grand jury, the Department of Justice filed suit against the State District Attorney, United States v. Warner, (Civ. No. 1219, S.D.Miss.), seeking to enjoin the state prosecution on the grounds that: (1) the States have no authority to prosecute for alleged perjury committed while testifying in a federal court; (2) the pur-

---

1. When counsel for the State, Mr. Riddell, completed Mr. Ramsey's direct examination, and before his cross-examination, respondent Judge W. Harold Cox, who was presiding, stated:

"I want to hear from the government about why this Court shouldn't require this Negro Reverend W. G. Goff and his companion Kendrick to show cause why they shouldn't be bound over to await the action of the grand jury for perjury. I want to hear from you on that.

* * * * * *

"I think they ought to be put under about a $3,000.00 bond each to await the action of a grand jury. Unless I change my mind that is going to be the order.

"BY MR. STERN [Government counsel]: I will be happy to reconcile their testimony.

"BY THE COURT: I just want these Negroes to know that they can't come into this Court and swear to something as important as that was and is and get by with it. I don't care who brings them here.

"BY MR. STERN: I understand.

"BY THE COURT: Yes, sir. And I mean that for whites alike, but I am talking about the case at hand. I just don't intend to put up with perjury. That is something I will not tolerate. All right."

pose and effect of the State's prosecution was to threaten and intimidate Goff and Kendrick and to inhibit them and other Negroes from registering to vote. See United States v. Wood, 5 Cir. 1961, 295 F.2d 772; Harvey v. State of Mississippi, 5 Cir. 1965, 340 F.2d 263. The district court (per Mize, J.) ruled in favor of the United States, citing In re Loney, 1890, 134 U.S. 372, 10 S.Ct. 584, 33 L.Ed. 949, and 42 U.S.C. § 1971(b) prohibiting intimidation for the purpose of interfering with voting rights.

The Federal Grand Jury, originally convened on September 9, 1963, was reconvened on September 21, 1964. September 28, 1964, the Foreman of the Grand Jury advised the Government Attorney who was presenting matters to the Grand Jury that Judge Cox had asked the Foreman to hear several witnesses. September 29, 1964, Mr. Riddell, attorney for the Registrar, and the district attorney for the Second Circuit District for the State of Mississippi, Mr. Holleman, came to the courthouse to appear before the Grand Jury. Judge Mize, in a special charge to the Grand Jury stated—in open court— that Judge Cox had informed him, before leaving for his vacation, that:

> "* * * he wanted the Grand Jury to call before it Mr. Boyce Holleman of Gulfport, Mississippi and Mr. Talley [sic] Riddell of Quitman, Mississippi as witnesses, because it was his impression that they had some matters that ought to be investigated at least and that they should be permitted to appear."

Against the backdrop of Mississippi versus the Nation in the field of civil rights, we have a heated but bona fide difference of opinion between Judge Cox and the Attorney General as to whether two Negroes, Goff and Kendrick, should be prosecuted for perjury. Taking a narrow view of the case, we would be justified in holding that the Attorney General's implied powers, by analogy to the express powers of Rule 48(a), give him discretion to prosecute. Here there was a bona fide, reasonable exercise of discretion made after a full investigation and long consideration of the case—both sides of the case, not just the evidence tending to show guilt. If the grand jury is dissatisfied with that administrative decision, it may exercise its inquisitorial power and make a presentment in open court. It could be said, that is all there is to the case. But there is more to the case.

This Court, along with everyone else, knows that Goff and Kendrick, if prosecuted, run the risk of being tried in a climate of community hostility. They run the risk of a punishment that may not fit the crime. The Registrar, who provoked the original litigation, runs no risk, notwithstanding the fact that the district court, in effect, found that Ramsey did not tell the truth on the witness stand. In these circumstances, the very least demands of justice require that the discretion to prosecute be lodged with a person or agency insulated from local prejudices and parochial pressures. This is not the hard case that makes bad law. This is the type of case that comes up, in one way or another, whenever the customs, beliefs, or interests of a region collide with national policy as fixed by the Constitution or by Congress. It is not likely that the men who devised diversity jurisdiction * expected to turn over to local juries the discretionary power to bring federal prosecutions. This case is unusual only for the clarity with which the facts, speaking for themselves, illuminate the imperative necessity in American Federalism that the discretion to prosecute be lodged in the Attorney General of United States.

---

* See p. 148 *supra*.

The decision not to prosecute represents the exercise of a discretion analogous to the exercise of executive privilege. As a matter of law, the Attorney General has concluded that there is not sufficient evidence to prove perjury. As a matter of fact, the Attorney General has concluded, as he pleaded in United States v. Warner, that trial for perjury would have the effect of inhibiting not only Goff and Kendrick but other Negroes in Mississippi from registering to vote. There is a conflict, therefore, between society's interest in law enforcement (diluted in this case by the Attorney General's conclusion that the evidence does not support the charge of guilt) and the national policy, set forth in the Constitution and the Civil Rights Acts, of outlawing racial discrimination. It is unthinkable that resolution of this important conflict affecting the whole Nation should lie with a majority of twenty-three members of a jury chosen from the Southern District of Mississippi. The nature of American Federalism, looking to the differences between the Constitution and the Articles of Confederation, requires that the power to resolve this question lie in the unfettered discretion of the President of United States or his deputy for law enforcement, the Attorney General.

My memory, too, goes back to the days, pointedly referred to by the dissenters, when we had "an Attorney General suspected of being corrupt." But I am not aware that we have had more lawless Attorneys General than lawless juries.

Notes

1. The non-interventionist policy evinced in U. S. v. Cox has prevailed in cases where prosecutors refuse to prosecute even though the petitioners raise serious questions "as to the protection of the civil rights and physical security of a definable class of victims of crime and as to the fair administration of the criminal justice system. See, *e. g.*, Inmates of Attica v. Rockefeller, 2d Cir. 1973, 477 F.2d 375. Inmates of a correctional facility where a prisoner riot had occurred alleged that state officers had committed a variety of criminal acts, including assault and manslaughter or murder, in quelling the prisoner uprising. 32 inmates and 11 prison employees held hostage by the inmates had died of gunshot wounds inflicted by police officers in the assault to retake control of the prison from the inmates.

2. The equal protection clause of the Fourteenth Amendment to the U.S. Constitution affords a potential basis for controlling some abuses of discretion by police or prosecutor. Yick Wo v. Hopkins, 118 U.S. 356, 6 S.Ct. 1064 (1886), established that selective and discriminatory enforcement of an otherwise valid regulatory statute may violate the equal protection clause. (In Yick Wo Chinese laundrymen in California alleged that a San Francisco ordinance regulating the hand laundry business was enforced in a systematic discriminatory effort to drive the Chinese out of the hand laundry business.) The burden of proving discriminatory enforcement is on the defendant, and the difficulty of discharging that burden has made the equal protection ground a theoretical but not practical means of limiting official discretion, but see U. S. v. Falk, 2 Cir. 1973, 479 F.2d 616. Appellant Falk had been convicted for a violation of the Selective Service Law, *i. e.*,

failing to carry his registration and classification cards on his person. Falk alleged that the prosecution was lodged against him solely because he was a known and vociferous opponent of United States policy in Southeast Asia and to U.S. military involvement in Vietnam. At trial Falk offered to prove that in a conversation with defense counsel the U.S. attorney had admitted this motivation for bringing the criminal charges. A divided Circuit Court vacated the judgment of conviction and remanded to the District Court to afford Falk an evidentiary hearing on the allegation of discriminatory enforcement. The majority opinion held that Falk had made out a *prima facie* case of discriminatory enforcement, and the burden of proof would thus rest on the government to present clear and compelling evidence to the contrary. The Court also held that Falk would be entitled to compel the U.S. attorney to testify under oath in the evidentiary hearing in the District Court.

[The following is taken from KENNETH C. DAVIS,* DISCRETIONARY JUSTICE (Baton Rouge, La., 1969), pp. 188–191.]

Must the prosecutor's discretionary power be uncontrolled? Viewed in broad perspective, the American legal system seems to be shot through with many excessive and uncontrolled discretionary powers but the one that stands out above all others is the power to prosecute or not to prosecute. The affirmative power to prosecute is enormous, but the negative power to withhold prosecution may be even greater, because it is less protected against abuse.

The prosecuting power is not limited to those who are called prosecutors; to an extent that varies in different localities the prosecuting power may be exercised by the police, and a goodly portion of it is exercised by regulatory agencies, licensing agencies, and other agencies and officers. The prosecuting power is not limited to the criminal law; it extends as far as law enforcement extends, including initiation of proceedings for license suspension or revocation, and even to enforcement of such provisions as those requiring that rates or charges be reasonable.

Even though the many prosecuting powers at all levels of government obviously vary widely in the extent and manner of confining, structuring, and checking, the major outlines are almost always governed by a single set of universally accepted assumptions. The principal assumptions are that the prosecuting power must of course be discretionary, that statutory provisions as to what enforcement officers "shall" do may be freely violated without disapproval from the public or from other officials, that determinations to prosecute or not to prosecute may be made secretly without any statement of findings or reasons, that such decisions by a top prosecutor of a city or county or state usually need not be reviewable by any other administrative authority, and that decisions to prosecute or not to prosecute are not judicially reviewable for abuse of discretion.

Why these various assumptions are made is not easy to discover; the best short answer seems to be that no one has done any systematic thinking

* Professor, University of Chicago Law
School and author of Police Discretion,
1975.

to produce the assumptions, but that the customs about prosecuting, like most other customs, are the product of unplanned evolution. Whatever caused the assumptions to grow as they did, prosecutors usually assert that everybody knows that they are necessary.

But I wonder: Why should a prosecutor—say, a county prosecutor— have discretionary power to decide not to prosecute even when the evidence of guilt is clear, perhaps partly on the basis of political influence, without ever having to state to anyone what evidence was brought to light by his investigation and without having to explain to anyone why he interprets a statute as he does or why he chooses a particular position on a difficult question of policy? Why should the discretionary power be so unconfined that, of half a dozen potential defendants he can prove guilty, he can select any one for prosecution and let the other five go, making his decision, if he chooses, on the basis of considerations extraneous to justice? If he finds that A and B are equally guilty of felony and equally deserving of prosecution, why should he be permitted to prosecute B for felony but to let A off with a plea of guilty to a misdemeanor, unless he has a rational and legal basis for his choice, stated on an open record? Why should the vital decisions he makes be immune to review by other officials and immune to review by the courts, even though our legal and governmental system else-where generally assumes the need for checking human frailties? Why should he have a complete power to decide that one statute duly enacted by the people's representatives shall not be enforced at all, that another statute will be fully enforced, and that a third will be enforced only if, as, and when he thinks that it should be enforced in a particular case? Even if we assume that a prosecutor has to have a power of selective en-forcement, why do we not require him to state publicly his general policies and require him to follow those policies in individual cases in order to pro-tect evenhanded justice? Why not subject prosecutors' decisions to a sim-ple and general requirement of open findings, open reasons, and open prece-dents, except when special reason for confidentiality exists? Why not strive to protect prosecutors' decisions from political or other ulterior influence in the same way we strive to protect judges' decisions?

The unthinking answer to such questions as these is that the prosecu-tor's function is merely to do the preliminary screening and to present the cases, and that the decisions that count are made on the basis of the trial. But public accusation and trial often leave scars which are not removed by proof of innocence. Mr. Justice Jackson was talking realism when he said, as Attorney General:

> The prosecutor has more control over life, liberty, and reputation than any other person in America. His discretion is tremendous. He can have citizens investigated and, if he is that kind of person, he can have this done to the tune of public statements and veiled or unveiled intimations. Or the prosecutor may choose a more subtle course and simply have a citizen's friends interviewed. . . . He may dismiss the case before trial, in which case the defense never has a chance to be heard. . . . If the prosecutor is ob-liged to choose his cases, it follows that he can choose his defend-ants. . . . [A] prosecutor stands a fair chance of finding at least a technical violation of some act on the part of almost any-

one. . . . It is in this realm—in which the prosecutor picks some person whom he dislikes or desires to embarrass, or selects some group of unpopular persons and then looks for an offense, that the greatest danger of abuse of prosecuting power lies. It is here that law enforcement becomes personal. . . .[1]

Mr. Justice Jackson was discussing what a prosecutor does affirmatively; the damage done by public accusation may be permanent even when innocence is proved in a later proceeding. What a prosecutor does negatively is almost always final and even less protected—withholding prosecution, nol pros of a case, acceptance of a plea of guilty to a lesser offense—even when such decisions are irrational or improperly motivated and even when the result is unjust discrimination against those who are not similarly favored. The notion that the tribunal that holds the trial corrects abuses of the prosecuting power is obviously without merit.

Nor will the other usual justification for uncontrolled discretionary power of prosecutors stand analysis—that the intrinsic nature of the prosecuting function is such that the only workable system is uncontrolled discretion. True, the habit of assuming that *of course* the prosecutor's discretion must be uncontrolled is so deeply embedded that the usual implied response to questions as to whether the prosecuting power can be confined or structured or checked is that the questioner must be totally without understanding. Inability of those who are responsible for administering the system to answer the most elementary questions as to the reasons behind the system is itself a reason to reexamine.

Questions

What issues of legality (see Skolnick and Wilson, *supra* pp. 216–222) are raised by the discretionary authority of police and prosecutor not to prosecute? How and by whom should those issues be resolved?

SECTION 12.2 PREPARATION AND PRESENTATION OF FORMAL CRIMINAL CHARGES

We have seen that an essential element of pre-trial procedure, either civil or criminal, is notification to the defendant of the claims or charges made against him. The complaint performs this function in a civil case and also initiates the action and provides a basis for further proceedings prior to trial. Criminal cases entail a somewhat more elaborate process to serve the same ends. First of all, the initial complaint which invokes official action is often made by a person who has been witness to or injured by criminal conduct. The police and prosecutor are responsible for reacting to this complaint first by investigating the matter and then by prosecuting, if this seems advisable. If the prosecutor does decide to prosecute, formal written charges must be presented on behalf of the state. These charges may be made

1. 24 J.Amer.Jud.Soc. 18–19 (1940).

in alternative forms, depending on the procedural requirements of the jurisdiction where the prosecution is lodged.

FEDERAL RULES OF CRIMINAL PROCEDURE
Rule 7
THE INDICTMENT AND THE INFORMATION

(a) Use of Indictment or Information. An offense which may be punished by death shall be prosecuted by indictment. An offense which may be punished by imprisonment for a term exceeding one year or at hard labor shall be prosecuted by indictment or, if indictment is waived, it may be prosecuted by information. Any other offense may be prosecuted by indictment or by information. An information may be filed without leave of court.

(b) Waiver of Indictment. An offense which may be punished by imprisonment for a term exceeding one year or at hard labor may be prosecuted by information if the defendant, after he has been advised of the nature of the charge and of his rights, waives in open court prosecution by indictment.

(c) Nature and Contents. The indictment or the information shall be a plain, concise and definite written statement of the essential facts constituting the offense charged. It shall be signed by the attorney for the government. It need not contain a formal commencement, a formal conclusion or any other matter not necessary to such statement. Allegations made in one count may be incorporated by reference in another count. It may be alleged in a single count that the means by which the defendant committed the offense are unknown or that he committed it by one or more specified means. The indictment or information shall state for each count the official or customary citation of the statute, rule, regulation or other provision of law which the defendant is alleged therein to have violated. Error in the citation or its omission shall not be ground for dismissal of the indictment or information or for reversal of a conviction if the error or omission did not mislead the defendant to his prejudice.

(d) Surplusage. The court on motion of the defendant may strike surplusage from the indictment or information.

(e) Amendment of Information. The court may permit an information to be amended at any time before verdict or finding if no additional or different offense is charged and if substantial rights of the defendant are not prejudiced.

(f) Bill of Particulars. The court for cause may direct the filing of a bill of particulars. A motion for a bill of particulars may be made only within ten days after arraignment or at such other time before or after arraignment as may be prescribed by rule or order. A bill of particulars may be amended at any time subject to such conditions as justice requires.

The Constitution of the United States provides in Amendment V that "No person shall be held to answer for a capital or otherwise infamous crime"—which in practice means any crime punishable by imprisonment for one year or more—"unless on a presentment or indictment of a Grand Jury." Thus the use of the grand jury in federal cases is guaranteed, though it has been abandoned in about half the states and in England.

An ancient English institution, the grand jury at common law is a body of at least twelve and not more than 23 persons which is charged with the investigation of crimes and with the indictment of persons to be tried for crimes. In the case of grand jury investigations leading to indictments, a bill of indictment is usually drawn by the prosecuting attorney ("district attorney," "county attorney," or, in the federal system, "United States attorney"), and if the grand jury finds the bill of indictment to be a "true bill," it then becomes an indictment and the accused stands indicted. At common law an indictment required the favorable vote of twelve grand jurors—hence the limitation of grand jurors to twenty-three, so that there could not be an indictment by a minority of them.

If the grand jurors of their own knowledge, or of their own motion on information from others, take notice of a public offense, they may make a "presentment." Usually such a presentment is considered an instruction to the prosecuting attorney to draw a bill of indictment, which must then be submitted to the grand jury.

Proceedings before the grand jury are generally secret, and the defendant may have no knowledge of the charges, or of the fact that an investigation involving him is being made, until he is required to appear to hear the indictment or information.

In states which do not have a grand jury procedure, and in cases of federal crimes which are not "infamous," a criminal prosecution is instituted by a so-called information, which is a written accusation made by the public prosecuting officer. The constitutions of some states require that prosecution by information shall be only after examination and commitment of the accused by a magistrate, or the waiver of such examination.

[The following pages contain excerpts from HANDBOOK FOR FEDERAL GRAND JURORS, Issued as a Public Service by the Federal Grand Jury Association for the Southern District of New York (3rd ed., 1953)]:

Selection of the Grand Jury

Selection of the grand jury begins when a number of names, usually fixed at seventy-five, are publicly drawn from a box containing ballots naming at least three hundred people previously chosen by lot from the voting lists and found qualified after being interviewed by the jury clerk at the United States Court House, Foley Square, New York. Notices are sent to the names drawn. When the prospective jurors assemble in Court on the specified day, their attendance is checked, and the names of all except those excused are again placed in a box. Twenty-three are drawn by the Clerk of the Court and, if none of these are disqualified or challenged, they are impaneled as the jury. The remaining prospective jurors are excused.

(Federal Judicial Code, § 1864).

Before the grand jury is sworn any person held on a criminal charge may challenge through his counsel the right of the panel to sit as a grand jury on the ground that it was not lawfully selected, and may challenge any individual juror on the ground that he is not legally qualified to serve.

(Rule 6(b), Federal Rules of Criminal Procedure.)

When the panel is ready to be sworn, the Court appoints one of the jurors as foreman who must administer the oath to witnesses, sign all indictments, and preside over the deliberations of the jury. The Court also appoints a deputy foreman who will assume these functions in the absence of the foreman.

* * *

The Grand Jury in Session

The Foreman

The foreman presides over the deliberations of the grand jury, signs all indictments, and administers the oath to the witnesses . . .

Prior to each meeting of the grand jury, the United States Attorney will hand a notice to the foreman or the secretary indicating the appearances scheduled for that day.

The normal procedure in considering a case is as follows:

     a. The United States Attorney will first outline the case to be presented and explain the criminal statutes which may apply to the facts presented.

     b. The first witness is then called. As the witness enters the room, the foreman administers the oath. Two witnesses should never be allowed in the grand jury room at the same time. The foreman should never permit discussion of the case by the grand jury in the presence of a witness.

     c. When the United States Attorney has questioned the last witness and concluded presentation of the case, he and the grand jury stenographer leave the room, for the grand jury must deliberate and vote in secret. The foreman will then ask for a discussion of the case and, at the conclusion of the discussion, for a vote on whether or not to indict.

     d. Following the vote, the secretary should record the result, and when an indictment is voted, should also record the number of votes for indictment. When the foreman has advised the United States Attorney of the disposition of the case, the grand jury is ready for presentation of the next matter.

Scope of the Investigation

The United States Attorney or one of his assistants will usually present the evidence and question witnesses before the grand jury. When the United States Attorney is through questioning the witness, any member of the grand jury may also ask questions of the witness. To save time and for the sake of orderly procedure, all questioning should be controlled by the foreman. If not satisfied with the evidence produced, the grand jurors may ask that other witnesses be called. In the absence of the United States Attorney, the interrogation would be conducted by the foreman.

The grand jury will first consider the cases which the United States Attorney brings to their attention. In addition it has unlimited authority to inquire, on its own initiative, into offenses which have come to the attention of any one or more of the grand jurors. As a practical matter such independent investigation can best be carried forward by requesting the United States Attorney to call and question the desired witnesses. But the grand jury also has authority, although it is rarely exercised, to exclude the United States Attorney and to compel the presence of its own witnesses through a subpoena which is sealed by the Clerk of the Court and signed by the foreman, who would then conduct the questioning.

The scope of such independent investigation has no limit, for the grand jury is authorized to conduct an inquiry even where it has no particular defendant and no particular crime in view and may summon any person in the country who in its judgment may throw light on the investigation of the violation of Federal penal laws. This power to conduct independent investigation in secrecy constitutes beyond question the most effective weapon available to any group of private citizens for compelling diligent law enforcement and for attacking corruption in public office.

Appearance of the Defendant

A grand jury is not bound to hear the defendant, but it can suggest to the United States Attorney that the defendant be called to testify, or the defendant himself may submit a written request to the grand jury asking for permission to appear before it. In the latter event, the grand jury grants or denies the request, as it sees fit.

A defendant should never be allowed to testify unless he has first waived the right to claim immunity from prosecution. Under the Fifth Amendment of the Federal Constitution, no person can be "compelled in any criminal case to be a witness against himself," and anyone who testifies under compulsion may claim immunity from prosecution as to any matters discussed in his testimony. Before a defendant is allowed to testify, therefore, the United States Attorney and the foreman must be sure that the defendant is appearing before the grand jury voluntarily; that he understands that he is not compelled to testify; and that if he does choose to testify, any statements he makes may be used against him in court.

When the defendant appears, before he is sworn, the foreman should inform him of his rights, in substantially these words:
"The Grand Jury is willing to hear what you have to say in regard to the charge against you. Understand clearly that you come before us of your own free will; you are not forced to appear nor forced to testify. Anything you say is said freely and at your own instance. But if you do choose to testify, everything you say is recorded here, and may be used as evidence against you.
"After this explanation, do you wish to testify?

Secrecy

Every member of the grand jury is sworn to secrecy. When voting on an indictment, only members of the grand jury may be present, and neither their deliberations nor the vote of any individual grand juror should ever be revealed by them. When evidence is being presented to the grand jury only attorneys for the government, an interpreter when needed, a stenographer for recording the evidence, and the witness under examination may be present.

These individuals with the exception of the witness are also bound to secrecy, and should never reveal the deliberations of the grand jury except on order of the Court. The witness under examination is not bound to secrecy for he cannot be obliged to keep his own testimony secret. The failure to adhere rigidly to the restrictions on the admission of outsiders to grand jury proceedings has been held sufficient to invalidate an indictment, and failure to obey the requirement of secrecy whether on the part of a juror, a stenographer or an attorney for the government constitutes a breach of trust.

(Rule 6(e), Federal Rules of Criminal Procedure.)

Voting on Indictment

When the grand jury has heard as many witnesses as seem necessary, or all that are available, the United States Attorney and the stenographer leave the room. Under no circumstances must anyone other than the members of the grand jury be present when a case is being discussed or a vote is being taken. The foreman invites discussion on a motion, "A True Bill is moved against the defendant John Doe on the charge of ————." After discussion (and every member of the grand jury has the right to comment on the evidence) a vote is taken. If there are 12 affirmative votes, the foreman declares that "A True Bill" or "Indictment" has been found. The foreman will so advise the United States Attorney who will prepare an indictment for the foreman's signature. All such indictments must be returned to a Judge in open Court in the presence of at least 16 grand jurors, and the secretary's record of the voting filed with the Clerk of the Court at the proper time.

If less than 12 grand jurors vote affirmatively, a "No True Bill" should be recorded. If the defendant has already been arrested, the foreman should report promptly to the Court that a "No True Bill" has been voted.

(Rule 6(f), Federal Rules of Criminal Procedure.)

The grand jury should not indict unless persuaded by hearing the evidence that a crime has been committed and that the individual charged should stand trial for the offense. The grand jury is free to decide as it sees fit and is responsible to no one for its decisions unless corruptly made. It may properly refuse to indict, even where a clear violation of law has been shown, without giving any reason for its decision.

When an indictment is voted, the Court may direct that the indictment be kept secret until the defendant is in custody or has given bail, in which event the indictment will be sealed by the Clerk of the Court so that it will not become a matter of public record until released by the Court. As long as an indictment is sealed in this manner, no member of the grand jury may disclose the fact that an indictment has been voted.

(Rule 6(e), Federal Rules of Criminal Procedure.)

Although the primary function of a grand jury is to decide whether to indict or not in a particular case, many courts have also recognized that the grand jury has power to present to the Court a report relating to evil conditions in the District, provided that no individual is expressly or implicitly identified and criticized in the report. The filing of any such report is subject to the discretion of the Court which will refuse to make public a document which violates the grand jurors' oath of secrecy by criticizing an individual on evidence insufficient to find an indictment. Such reports can become a valuable by-product of grand jury investigations but should be employed with great restraint and only on occasions where benefit to the community will clearly result.

The United States Attorney

The United States Attorney is charged with the duty of prosecuting all crimes against the United States committed within his District. To fulfill this obligation, the United States Attorney and his assistants must rely heavily on informed and efficient grand juries.

The United States Attorney or one of his assistants usually presents the evidence to the grand jury, both as to matters originating with his office and as to additional matters requested by the grand jury acting on its own initiative. If in an extreme case the grand jury should decide to exclude the United States Attorney and conduct an independent investigation, it would call, and through its foreman question, its own witnesses.

The United States Attorney is the legal advisor of the grand jury. He is always prepared to explain the law, but should never be asked for his opinion as to the facts unless as to the legal effect of testimony or other evidence. The grand jury may also apply to the Court for instructions as to the law and it has even been suggested that under special circumstances a grand jury may seek legal advice from an attorney in private practice. Under the Federal Rules of Criminal Procedure, however, it is clear that such an attorney could be called before the grand jury only as a witness. He would not be permitted to question other witnesses nor be present in the grand jury room when any other witness was being questioned. It is also clear that under the requirement of secrecy, the grand jury would be forbidden to make known to the attorney, whether in the grand jury room or outside, the testimony of other witnesses or any part of its deliberations.

(Rule 6(d), Federal Rules of Criminal Procedure.)

The United States Attorney must prepare the indictments voted by the grand jury. In no case may he be present when a grand jury votes upon an indictment, but after an indictment is voted and filed with the Court, the further prosecution of the indictment is entirely within his control. The grand jury has no further authority over it, nor any power to withdraw it.

In the case of offenses punishable by death, prosecution may be had only upon an indictment returned by the grand jury. However, in cases punishable by more than one year imprisonment, if the defendant signs a written statement in Court waiving the right to prosecution by indictment, the United States Attorney is permitted to prosecute without presenting the case to a grand jury. Instead he will file with the Court an "information," which is nothing more than a statement of the offense charged.

Offenses punishable by one year imprisonment or less may be prosecuted by "information" without a waiver of indictment. In practice an "information" is employed if it appears from the outset that the defendant will plead guilty to the charge and desires a speedy disposition of his case.

(Rule 7, Federal Rules of Criminal Procedure.)

Discharge of the Grand Jury

At such time as the business before it is finished, the grand jury will be discharged by the Court. When so discharged, the functions and powers of a grand jury cease entirely. Its members are no longer grand jurors, and nothing remains of their official character, except the obligation to secrecy as to the proceedings of the grand jury to which they belonged.

This obligation attaches at the moment when the oath is taken, and remains binding always and everywhere. A grand juror or anyone having served as a grand juror may disclose matters occurring before the grand jury only when so directed by the Court in connection with a judicial proceeding, or when permitted by the Court at the request of a defendant who has shown that grounds may exist for dismissing the indictment because of matters occurring before the grand jury.

(Rule 6(e), Federal Rules of Criminal Procedure.)

――――――

UNITED STATES v. COX

United States Court of Appeals, Fifth Circuit, 1965.
342 F.2d 167.

[Review the majority opinion which is reprinted at p. 296 *supra.*]

RIVES, GEWIN and GRIFFIN B. BELL, CIRCUIT JUDGES (concurring in part and dissenting in part):

[T]he basic issue before this Court is whether the controlling discretion as to the institution of a felony prosecution rests with the Attorney General or with the grand jury. The majority opinion would ignore the broad inquisitorial powers of the grand jury, and limit the constitutional requirement of Amendment V to the benefit of the accused.

We agree with Professor Orfield that:
"The grand jury serves two great functions. One is to bring to trial persons accused of crime upon just grounds. The other is to protect persons against unfounded or malicious prosecutions by insuring that no criminal proceeding will be undertaken without a disinterested determination of probable guilt. The inquisitorial function has been called the more important."

* * *

The grand jury possesses plenary and independent inquisitorial powers. The Supreme Court has held that an Executive Order and a Circular Letter of the Department of Justice requiring approval of the Attorney General before any evidence could be presented in certain cases "was not intended to curtail or limit the well-recognized power of the grand jury to consider and investigate any alleged crime within its jurisdiction. . . .

A federal grand jury has the unquestioned right to inquire into any matter within the jurisdiction involving violations of law and to return an indictment if it finds a reasonable probability that a crime has been committed. This it may do at the instance of the court, the District Attorney, the Attorney General or on its own initiative, from evidence it may gather or from knowledge of its members.

The majority holds that: "The provision of Rule 7, requiring the signing of the indictment by the attorney for the Government, is a recognition of the power of Government counsel to permit or not to permit the bringing of an indictment."

With deference we call attention that no authority is cited in support of that holding and we submit that it ignores the history of the grand jury and of the Rules of Criminal Procedure. . . .

The Fifth Amendment adopted the grand jury as it had then been developed in England over the course of many centuries, and made it a part of the fundamental law of the United States for the institution of prosecutions for crime. Thus the grand jury originated long before the doctrine of separation of powers was made the constitutional basis of our frame of government. The same Constitution which separated the three powers of government adopted the institution of the grand jury. It follows that no nice distinction need be drawn as to whether the grand jury may perform some function of the executive department. As well said by the Seventh Circuit:

> "While the grand jury is, in a sense, a part of our court system, when exercising its traditional functions it possesses an independence which is unique. Its authority is derived from none of the three basic divisions of our government, but rather directly from the people themselves."

In re April 1956 Term Grand Jury, 1956, 239 F.2d 263, 269.

Moreover, in point of law and reality, the plenary inquisitorial power of the grand jury does not impinge in the slightest upon the executive function of the Attorney General to prosecute or not to prosecute offenses against the United States, for as soon as the indictment is returned, "The Attorney General or the United States Attorney may by leave of court file a dismissal . . . ." Rule 48(a), F.R.Crim.P.

* * *

Judge Weinfield in United States v. Greater Blouse, Skirt & Neckwear Contractors Ass'n, S.D.N.Y.1964, 228 F.Supp. 483, 489–490, well described the situation which might arise after indictment where the Attorney General or the United States Attorney does not wish to prosecute and where the district court denies dismissal:

> "The Attorney General is the head of the Department of Justice, a part of the Executive branch of the Government. Even were leave of Court to the dismissal of the indictment denied, the Attorney General would still have the right to adhere to the Department's view that the indictment cannot be supported by proof upon a trial of the merits, and accordingly, in the exercise of his discretion, decline to move the case for trial. The Court in that circumstance would be without power to issue a mandamus or other order to compel prosecution of the indictment, since such a direction would invade the traditional separation of powers doctrine. And if the indictment continues to remain in status quo, each defendant would be in a position to move for dismissal of the indictment under Rule 48(b)."

The grand jury may be permitted to function in its traditional sphere, while at the same time enforcing the separation of powers doctrine as between the executive and judicial branches of the government. This can best be done, indeed, it is mandatory, by requiring the United States Attorney to assist the grand jury in preparing indictments which they wish to consider or return, and by requiring the United States Attorney to sign any indictment that is to be returned. Then, once the indictment is returned, the Attorney

General or the United States Attorney can refuse to go forward. That refusal will, of course, be in open court and not in the secret confines of the grand jury room. To permit the district court to compel the United States Attorney to proceed beyond this point would invest prosecutorial power in the judiciary, power which under the Constitution is reserved to the executive branch of the government. It may be that the court, in the interest of justice, may require a showing of good faith, and a statement of some rational basis for dismissal. In the unlikely event of bad faith or irrational action, not here present, it may be that the court could appoint counsel to prosecute the case. In brief, the court may have the same inherent power to administer justice to the government as it does to the defendant. That question is not now before us and may never arise. Except for a very limited discretion, however, the court's power to withhold leave to dismiss an indictment is solely for the protection of the defendant.

* * *

By way of precaution, let us state that nothing here said is intended to reflect upon the present Acting Attorney General, in whose integrity we have the utmost confidence. Memory goes back, however, to days when we had an Attorney General suspected of being corrupt. There is no assurance that that will never again happen. We are establishing a precedent for other cases; we are construing a Constitution; we should retain intact that great constitutional bulwark, the institution of the grand jury.

* * *

WISDOM, CIRCUIT JUDGE (concurring specially):

Too many opinion-writers are like too many cooks. I brave the danger of spoiling *our* broth only because the savory aroma of the competing dish the dissenters offer conceals its indigestible ingredients.

The dissenters show judicial craftsmanship of the highest order in writing persuasively about "the traditional sphere" of the grand jury while not turning up one case holding that a court may compel a prosecutor to prepare and sign a bill of indictment requested by a grand jury. Not one case in all the years between 1166 and 1965! I submit that the result reached in the dissent is the product of a misunderstanding of the historical meaning of "presentment and indictment", a failure to give effect to the difference between the sword and the shield of the grand jury,[1] and an abstract approach that disregards the factual setting in which the issue is presented.

Nothing in the position of any of the judges in the majority "ignores" or tends to diminish the purely inquisitorial role of the federal grand jury. But when that role goes beyond inquiry and report and becomes accusatorial, no aura of traditional or constitutional sanctity surrounds the grand jury. The Grand Jury earned its place in the Bill of Rights by its shield, not by its sword.

1. The Federal Grand Jury Handbook, p. 8, describes the functions of the Grand Jury in these words:

"The Grand Jury is both a sword and a shield of justice—a sword because it is the terror of criminals, a shield because it is the protection of the innocent against unjust prosecution. But these important powers obviously create equally grave responsibilities to see that such powers are in no wise perverted or abused. With its almost limitless powers, a Grand Jury might, unless motivated by the highest sense of justice, find indictments not warranted by the evidence and thus become a source of oppression to our citizens."

I.

.   .   .   there is nothing in my view or in that of the other judges in the majority that would, as the dissenting judges assert, authorize Government counsel to "radically reduce the powers of the grand jury". *The grand jury never had a plenary power to indict.* It had a limited power to indict—after accusation by the Crown or the Government in the form of a bill of indictment preferred to the grand jury. The common law oath of a grand juror, as Justice Vanderbilt has pointed out, "says not a single word about indictments; on the contrary, at common law the grand jury swore to 'diligently inquire and true presentments made'. See Shaftesbury Trial, 8 St.Tr. 759." The oath a federal grand juror takes today is identical with the common law oath in its avoidance of any reference to "indictment".

The decision of the majority does not affect the inquisitorial power of the grand jury. No one questions the jury's plenary power to inquire, to summon and interrogate witnesses, and to present either findings and a report or an accusation in open court by presentment.

Finally, the decision does not affect the power of the grand jury to shield suspected law violators. By refusing to indict, the grand jury has the unchallengeable power to defend the innocent from government oppression by unjust prosecution. And it has the equally unchallengeable power to shield the guilty, should the whims of the jurors or their conscious or subconscious response to community pressures induce twelve or more jurors to give sanctuary to the guilty.

II.

Because recognition of the grand jury's shield-like function is lodged in the Bill of Rights, the bedrock of basic rights, it is fair to say that national policy favors a liberal construction of the power of the grand jury to protect the individual against official tyranny. No such policy favors the grand jury in its accusatorial role. Accordingly, we look for and should expect to find a check on its unjust accusations similar to the grand jury's check on the government's unjust accusations.

If there is one aspect of the doctrine of Separation of Powers that the Founding Fathers agreed upon, it is the principle, as Montesquieu stated it: "To prevent the abuse of power, it is necessary that by the very disposition of things, power should be a check to power". Taking their institutions as they found them, the framers wove a web of checks and balances designed to prevent abuse of power, regardless of the age, origin, and character of the institution. At the same time, the framers were too sophisticated to believe that the three branches of government were absolutely separate, airtight departments. It does not matter, therefore, whether the grand jury is regarded as an arm of the court, as the Federal Grand Jury Handbook states, or is regarded as a *sui generis* institution derived from the people. What does matter is that the power of the executive not to prosecute, and therefore not to take steps necessarily leading to prosecution, is the appropriate curb on a grand jury in keeping with the constitutional theory of checks and balances. Such a check is especially necessary, if there is any question of the grand jury's and the district court's being in agreement; if they differ, of course the district court may dismiss the grand jury. The need is rendered more acute if there is a possibility that community hostility against the suspected offenders, individually or as a race, may jeopardize justice before the petit jury. In short, if we give the same meaning to "presentment or indictment" that Madison and others gave to these terms when Madison introduced the Bill of Rights in the First Congress, the grand jury provision in the Bill of Rights cuts both ways: it prevents harassment and intimidation and oppression through unjust prosecution—by the Grand Jury or by the Government.

III.

The prosecution of offenses against the United States is an executive function within the exclusive prerogative of the Attorney General. . . . That official, the chief law-enforcement officer of the Federal Government is "the hand of the president in taking care that the laws of the United States in protection of the interests of the United States in legal proceedings and in the prosecution of offenses be faithfully executed." Ponzi v. Fassenden, 1922, 258 U.S. 254, 262, 42 S.Ct. 309, 311, 66 L.Ed. 607. He "has the authority, and it is made his duty, to supervise the conduct of all suits brought by or against the United States", including the authority "to begin criminal prosecution". United States v. San Jacinto Tin Co., 125 U.S. 273, 278–279, 8 S.Ct. 850, 31 L.Ed. 747. He "is invested with the general superintendence of all such suits, and all the district attorneys who do bring them in the various courts in the country are placed under his immediate direction and control." Id., p. 279, 8 S.Ct. at p. 853, and see In re Neagle, 135 U.S. 1, 66, 10 S.Ct. 658, 34 L.Ed. 55.

"[T]he district attorney has absolute control over criminal prosecutions, and can dismiss or refuse to prosecute, any of them at his discretion. The responsibility is wholly his." United States v. Woody, D.C.Mont.1924, 2 F.2d 262. The determination of whether and when to prosecute "is a matter of policy for the prosecuting officer and not for the determination of the courts". District of Columbia v. Buckley, 1942, 75 U.S.App.D.C. 301, 128 F. 2d 17. As another court has stated it:

"All of these considerations point up the wisdom of vesting broad discretion in the United States Attorney. The federal courts are powerless to interfere with his discretionary power. The Court cannot compel him to prosecute a complaint, or even an indictment, whatever his reasons for not acting. The remedy for any dereliction of his duty lies, not with the courts, but, with the executive branch of our government and ultimately with the people." Pugach v. Klein, S.D.N.Y.1961, 193 F.Supp. 630, 635.

"Congress, well aware of this discretion has never challenged its existence." Schwartz, Federal Criminal Jurisdiction and Prosecutors' Discretion, 13 L. & Cont.Prob. 64, 83 (1948).

* * *

The reason for vesting discretion to prosecute in the Executive, acting through the Attorney General is two-fold. First, in the interests of justice and the orderly, efficient administration of the law, some person or agency should be able to prevent an unjust prosecution. The freedom of the petit jury to bring in a verdict of not guilty and the progressive development of the law in the direction of making more meaningful the guarantees of an accused person's constitutional rights give considerable protection to the individual before and after trial. They do not protect against a baseless prosecution. This is a harassment to the accused and an expensive strain on the machinery of justice. The appropriate repository for authority to prevent a baseless prosecution is the chief law-enforcement officer whose duty, *unlike the grand jury's duty, is to collect evidence on both sides of a case.*

Second, when, within the context of law-enforcement, national policy is involved, because of national security, conduct of foreign policy, or a conflict between two branches of government, the appropriate branch to decide the matter is the executive branch. The executive is charged with carrying out national policy on law-enforcement and, generally speaking, is informed on more levels than the more specialized judicial and legislative branches. In such a situation, a decision not to prosecute is analogous to the exercise of executive privilege. The executive's absolute and exclusive discretion to prosecute may be rationalized as an illustration of the doctrine of separation of powers, but it would have evolved without the doctrine and exists in countries that do not purport to accept this doctrine.

[The balance of the opinion is reprinted at Note 5, p. 299 *supra.*]

Questions

1. What is the "accusatorial" function of the Grand Jury? What is the "inquisitorial" function of the Grand Jury?

Does the extract from the Federal Grand Juror's Handbook, *supra* pp. 307–312, indicate which of these functions is the more important?

2. The Grand Jury developed in England at a time when there was no professional police force, and when the prosecution of criminal cases was conducted largely by private parties. Does this help to explain why the Grand Jury has both an accusatorial and an inquisitorial authority? Does this help to explain why the Grand Jury was supposed to be both a sword and a shield?

3. The investigation of crime in England is now the responsibility of public officials. Does this help to explain why the Grand Jury has been abolished in England?

4. In England it is still permissible for private parties to institute criminal proceedings on behalf of the Crown. What are the advantages and disadvantages of such a system? Do you prefer the more limited public participation in the criminal process which is characteristic of American practice? If so, why?

The indictment is a formal statement of the charges against the accused. It must set out the elements of the offense charged—this is commonly done by quoting the language of the statute under which the charge is brought—and it must set out the essential facts constituting the offense.[1]

1. See e. g., Rule 7(c), Federal Rules of Criminal Procedure, *supra.*

In the past the indictment was often a prolix document full of formal language and subject to many technical requirements, but under modern systems of pleading the tendency is to make the indictment brief and simple. For example, one of the forms appended to the Federal Rules of Criminal Procedure is the following: [2]

IN THE UNITED STATES DISTRICT COURT
FOR THE _____ DISTRICT OF _____,
_____ DIVISION

UNITED STATES OF AMERICA
v.

JOHN DOE

No. _____
(18 U.S.C. §§ 1111, 1114)

The grand jury charges:

On or about the _____ day of _____, 19__, in the _____ District of _____, John Doe with premeditation and by means of shooting murdered John Roe, who was then an officer of the Federal Bureau of Investigation of the Department of Justice engaged in the performance of his official duties.

A True Bill.

_____,
Foreman.

_____
United States Attorney.

Question: Do you think that this form satisfies the requirements of Rule 7(c) of the Federal Rules of Criminal Procedure? [3]

This simplication of the form for indictment parallels the simplification of pleading in civil cases, however, other aspects of the two procedures differ markedly.

The Federal Rules of Civil Procedure provide for liberal amendment to the pleadings. Thus in a civil case the plaintiff will be allowed to cure deficiencies in his pleading which are pointed out prior to trial. A different practice is followed in criminal cases. If the indictment is defective and this is disclosed prior to trial, the prosecution may be dismissed and the prosecutor may have to secure a new indictment in order to proceed further.

If the proof offered in a civil trial discloses that the plaintiff is proceeding on the wrong legal theory, he or she may be allowed to amend the complaint to conform its allegations to the proof. Liberal amendment of indictments is not allowed. A variance between the charge laid in the indictment and the charge made out in the trial can-

---

2. The form for an information is the same except the words "the United States Attorney charges" are substituted for "the Grand Jury charges." The information is signed only by the United States Attorney.

3. *Supra* p. 306.

not be cured by amendment. Instead the indictment will be dismissed on motion by the defense and the prosecutor will have to begin again. Thus in criminal procedure there are substantial elements reminiscent of the practice at common law.

Question: Is there anything in Amendments V and VI of the United States Constitution which explains this remainder of common law practice in spite of the modern rules of procedure which are applicable in federal trials?

Where a prosecution proceeds on an information rather than an indictment the criminal procedure is much more like civil practice, and amendment of the information will be allowed so long as this does not work any real hardship on the defense.

Question: Why this difference between indictment and information?

After indictment the accused is brought before the court ("arraigned")—by means of a warrant of arrest or a summons—to answer to the charges. At the arraignment the court reads the indictment or information, or else states the substance of it to the defendant, and calls upon him or her to plead to it. Three pleas are open: "not guilty," "guilty," or "nolo contendere" ("I do not wish to contest"). At one time in English law if a person indicted for felony "stood mute," and it was found that his refusal to plead was wilful, he was pressed by irons until he pleaded—or died.[4] Later the obstinate refusal to plead was treated as a plea of guilty. Today it is considered a plea of not guilty.

If the defendant pleads guilty (or nolo) nothing remains for the court to do but to sentence him or her, except that the plea of guilty in capital cases is in many states not permitted.

Question: What reasons can you suggest for that exception?

In addition to the three pleas named above, it is also possible in some jurisdictions to plead "not guilty by reason of insanity." Also in some jurisdictions it is possible to raise by means of the plea certain matters which under more modern procedure are raised by various motions, such as the motion to dismiss the indictment because it is defective or because the court has no jurisdiction over the defendant or over the subject matter of the charges, or because the defendant has already been convicted once for the crime charged.

Once the defendant has made a plea, he or she cannot legally be compelled prior to trial to answer questions, produce documents or other materials, or submit to physical or mental examination. Moreover, although under Rule 16 of the Federal Rules of Criminal Procedure the defendant can compel the prosecution in advance of trial to produce for inspection and copying designated books, papers, documents or oth-

4. By dying without pleading he avoided a conviction of felony with consequent forfeiture of all his belongings to the Crown.

er tangible objects, there is nothing he or she can do to compel testimony by deposition from prosecution witnesses, as in civil cases. Also there is no general provision for advance disclosure of the witnesses to be produced at the trial, though a statute of 1790 provides that in treason and other capital cases an accused may have a list of the jury and of the witnesses to be produced at trial. As a matter of judicial discretion, however, federal district courts have sometimes ordered the government to furnish the accused a list of its witnesses.

No provision for pre-trial conference is made in the Federal Rules of Criminal Procedure—in contrast to the Federal Rules of Civil Procedure. Such a provision was recommended by the Advisory Committee established to aid the Supreme Court in the drafting of the Rules. The recommendation was based in part on the practice which had developed in some district courts, especially in lengthy and complex cases. Even without a rule, of course, there is nothing to stop a court from requesting the prosecuting attorney and the defendant's counsel to appear to discuss the possibility of narrowing issues, eliminating uncontested issues of fact, and agreeing upon other matters.

"The rule recommended by the Advisory Committee sought to avoid any element of compulsion of the defendant, having in mind the obvious differences between criminal and civil proceedings in respect of the relationship of the defendant to the court as well as to the adverse party. Participation in the conference was to be upon 'invitation' rather than by 'direction'; the defendant was to have the right to be present in person; and the rule was not to be invoked in the case of any defendant not represented by counsel. But the proposal nevertheless encountered resistance. Some took the position that it would encourage 'fishing expeditions' by defendants, and some feared that it might result in forcing concessions and stipulations to which a defendant would not otherwise agree. In any event, the Court rejected the proposal." [5]

The opposition to a provision for pre-trial conferences in criminal cases should be viewed together with the various restrictions upon the powers of police investigation as part of a system designed to keep the prosecution and the accused as far apart as possible prior to trial. As a result of the insulation of the defendant from the prosecution and also the limited discovery procedures, the outcome of the criminal trial is far more apt to be affected by dramatic surprises in testimony and by the forensic skill of the lawyers than is the outcome of the civil trial. The crucial question is, to what extent are these defects inherent in the safeguards which we have erected against unlawful detention and compulsory self-incrimination?

5. George Dession, Criminal Law and Administration (Brooklyn, N. Y., 1949), p. 917.

SECTION 12.3   PLEA BARGAINING

[The following is taken from "THE CHALLENGE OF CRIME IN A FREE SOCIETY," Final Report of the President's Commission on Law Enforcement and the Administration of Justice, *op. cit.*, pp. 9–11. Footnotes are omitted.]

The Negotiated Plea of Guilty

The question of guilt or innocence is not contested in the overwhelming majority of criminal cases. A recent estimate is that guilty pleas account for 90 percent of all convictions; and perhaps as high as 95 percent of misdemeanor convictions. But the Commission has found it difficult to calculate with any degree of certainty the percentage of cases disposed of by guilty plea, since reliable statistical information is limited. Clearly it is very high. The following statistics indicate the number and percentage of guilty plea convictions in trial courts of general jurisdiction in States in which such information was available.

State (1964 statistics unless otherwise indicated)	Total convictions	Guilty Pleas	
		Number	Percent of total
California (1965)	30,840	22,817	74.0
Connecticut	1,596	1,494	93.9
District of Columbia (year ending June 30, 1964)	1,115	817	73.3
Hawaii	393	360	91.5
Illinois	5,591	4,768	85.2
Kansas	3,025	2,727	90.2
Massachusetts (1963)	7,790	6,642	85.2
Minnesota (1965)	1,567	1,437	91.7
New York	17,249	16,464	95.5
Pennsylvania (1960)	25,632	17,108	66.8
U.S. District Courts	29,170	26,273	90.2
Average [excluding Pennsylvania] [1]			87.0

[1] The Pennsylvania figures have been excluded from the average because they were from an earlier year, and the types of cases included did not appear fully comparable with the others.

A substantial percentage of guilty pleas are the product of negotiations between the prosecutor and defense counsel or the accused, although again precise data are unavailable. Commonly known as "plea bargaining," this is a process very much like the pretrial settlement of civil cases. It involves discussions looking toward an agreement under which the accused will enter a plea of guilty in exchange for a reduced charge or a favorable sentence recommendation by the prosecutor. Even when there have been no explicit negotiations, defendants relying on prevailing practices often act on the justifiable assumption that those who plead guilty will be sentenced more leniently.

Few practices in the system of criminal justice create a greater sense of unease and suspicion than the negotiated plea of guilty. The correctional needs of the offender and legislative policies reflected in the criminal law appear to be sacrificed to the need for tactical accommodations between the prosecutor and defense counsel. The offense for which guilt is acknowledged and for which the sentence is imposed often appears almost incidental to keeping the business of the courts moving.

The system usually operates in an informal, invisible manner. There is ordinarily no formal recognition that the defendant has been offered an inducement to plead guilty. Although the participants and frequently the judge know that negotiation has taken place, the prosecutor and defendant must ordinarily go through a courtroom ritual in which they deny that the guilty plea is the result of any threat or promise. As a result there is no judicial review of the propriety of the bargain—no check on the amount of pressure put on the defendant to plead guilty. The judge, the public, and sometimes the defendant himself cannot know for certain who got what from whom in exchange for what. The process comes to look less rational, more subject to chance factors, to undue pressures, and sometimes to the hint of corruption. Moreover, the defendant may not get the benefit he bargained for. There is no guarantee that the judge will follow the prosecutor's recommendations for lenient sentence. In most instances the defendant does not know what sentence he will receive until he has pleaded guilty and sentence has been imposed. If the defendant is disappointed, he may move to withdraw his plea, but there is no assurance that the motion will be granted, particularly since at the time he tendered his guilty plea, he probably denied the very negotiations he now alleges.

A more fundamental problem with plea bargaining is the propriety of offering the defendant an inducement to surrender his right to trial. This problem becomes increasingly substantial as the prospective reward increases, because the concessions to the defendant become harder to justify on grounds other than expediency. There is always the danger that a defendant who would be found not guilty if he insisted on his right to trial will be induced to plead guilty. The defendant has an absolute right to put the prosecution to its proof, and if too much pressure is brought to discourage the exercise of this right, the integrity of the system, which the court trial is relied upon to vindicate, will not be demonstrated. When the prosecution is not put to its proof and all the evidence is not brought out in open court, the public is not assured that illegalities in law enforcement are revealed and corrected or that the seriousness of the defendant's crimes are shown and adequate punishment imposed. Prosecutors who are overburdened or are insufficiently energetic may compromise cases that call for severe sanctions.

Despite the serious questions raised by a system of negotiated pleas, there are important arguments for preserving it. Our system of criminal justice has come to depend upon a steady flow of guilty pleas. There are simply not enough judges, prosecutors, or defense counsel to operate a system in which most defendants go to trial. Many of the Commission's proposals, such as the recommendation to expand appointment of counsel for the indigent, will strain the available resources for many years. If reliance on trial were increased at this time, it would undoubtedly lower the quality of justice throughout the system. Even were the resources available, there is some question whether a just system would require that they be allocated to providing all defendants with a full trial. Trial as we know it is an elaborate mechanism for finding facts. To use this process in cases where the facts are not really in dispute seems wasteful.

The plea agreement if carried out, eliminates the risk inherent in all adversary litigation. No matter how strong the evidence may appear and how well prepared and conducted a trial may be, each side must realistically consider the possibility of an unfavorable outcome. At its best the trial process is an imperfect method of factfinding; factors such as the attorney's skill, the availability of witnesses, the judge's attitude, jury vagaries, and luck will influence the result. Each side is interested in limiting these inherent litigation risks. In addition, the concessions of a negotiated plea are also commonly used by prosecutors when a defendant cooperates with law enforcement agencies by furnishing information or testimony against other offenders.

Confining trials to cases involving substantial issues may also help to preserve the significance of the presumption of innocence and the requirement of proof beyond a reasonable doubt. If trial were to become routine even in cases in which there is no substantial issue of guilt, the overwhelming statistical probability of guilt might incline judges and jurors to be more skeptical of the defense than at present.

Because of the invisibility of the plea bargaining system, the essential issues involved have generally not received adequate consideration by the courts. Some courts have, however, begun to look at the system for what it is and to focus on the need to regulate it to assure that neither public nor private interests are sacrificed. As a Federal Court of Appeals noted in a recent case:

> In a sense, it can be said that most guilty pleas are the result of a "bargain" with the prosecutor. But this, standing alone, does not vitiate such pleas. A guilty defendant must always weigh the possibility of his conviction on all counts, and the possibility of his getting the maximum sentence, against the possibility that he can plead to fewer, or lesser, offenses, and perhaps receive a lighter sentence. The latter possibility exists if he pleads guilty . . .

> No competent lawyer, discussing a possible guilty plea with a client, could fail to canvass these possible alternatives with him. Nor would he fail to ascertain the willingness of the prosecution to "go along." . . .

> The important thing is not that there shall be no "deal" or "bargain," but that the plea shall be a genuine one, by a defendant who is guilty; one who understands his situation, his rights, and the consequences of the plea, and is neither deceived nor coerced.

Some jurisdictions appear to be able to deal with their caseloads without reliance on negotiated guilty pleas. The discussion in this chapter should not be taken as suggesting that plea bargaining should be introduced in courts that have satisfactory alternatives. Particularly in single judge courts it may not be feasible to introduce the safeguards that would enable a negotiated plea system to operate fairly and effectively. Indeed this chapter does not resolve the issue whether a negotiated guilty plea system is a desirable method of dealing with cases. Rather the discussion is directed to improving the operation of the plea bargaining system in those jurisdictions where negotiations are ordinary occurrences.

Forms and Uses of Negotiated Pleas

The plea agreement follows several patterns. In its best known form it is an arrangement between the prosecutor and the defendant or his lawyer whereby the accused pleads guilty to a charge less serious than could be proven at trial. "Less serious" in this context usually means an offense which carries a lower maximum sentence. The defendant's motivation is to confine the upper limits of the judge's sentencing power. Similar results are obtained when the plea is entered in return for the prosecutor's agreement to drop counts in a multi-count indictment or not to charge the defendant as a habitual offender. In some situations the benefits obtained by the defendant may be illusory, as when he bargains for a reduction in counts unaware that local judges rarely impose consecutive sentences.

Charge reduction is tied to the exercise of the prosecutor's discretion as to what offenses he will charge originally. Although the charge process is distinct from the plea negotiation, the two are closely related by the prosecutor's expectations at the time of charge as to the likely course bargaining will take, and by the important role bargaining for reduced charges plays in the exercise of the prosecutor's discretion.

Plea negotiations concerning charges provide an opportunity to mitigate the harshness of a criminal code or to rationalize its inconsistencies and to lead to a disposition based on an assessment of the individual factors of each crime. The field over which these negotiations may range is broad; the defendant's conduct on a single occasion may justify separate charges of robbery, larceny, assault with a deadly weapon, assault, or disorderly conduct. Some of these offenses are felonies, while others are misdemeanors, and the maximum sentences may range from 30 years to less than 1 year. Conviction of a felony may involve serious collateral disabilities, including disqualification from engaging in certain licensed occupations or businesses, while conviction of a misdemeanor may not. The prosecutor often has a wide range of penal provisions from which to choose. His choice has enormous correctional implications, and it is through charge bargaining that in many courts he seeks to turn this discretion to his own advantage.

Charge reduction may be used to avoid a mandatory minimum sentence or a restriction on the power to grant probation. In these instances the agreed plea becomes a way of restoring sentencing discretion when it has in part been eliminated from the code. Charge reduction is also used to avoid the community opprobrium that attaches to conviction of certain offenses. Thus to avoid being labeled a child molester or homosexual, the defendant may offer to plead guilty to a charge such as disorderly conduct or assault.

The plea agreement may take forms other than a reduction of charges. A defendant may plead guilty to a charge that accurately describes his conduct in return for the prosecutor's agreement to recommend leniency or for a specific recommendation of probation or of a lesser sentence than would probably be imposed if the defendant insisted upon a trial. Although in theory the judge retains complete discretion as to sentence, in reality the negotiations are conducted by the prosecutor and the defendant or his attorney on the assumption that the recommended sentence will be imposed. The practices of individual judges vary, but they are likely to be known to the parties. Some judges neither request nor accept sentencing recommendations, and others give them differing weight in different cases. But many judges feel obligated to accept such recommendations, because they know that it is essential to the plea negotiation system. In some instances the judge may indicate explicitly that he will impose a particular sentence if the defendant pleads guilty. This can lead to the undesirable involvement of the judge as an active participant in negotiations, lending the weight of his power and prestige to inducing the defendant to plead guilty.

Other forms of plea bargaining may involve judge shopping. In places where there are wide sentencing disparities, a plea of guilty may be entered in exchange for the prosecutor's agreement that the defendant will appear before a particular judge for sentencing.

Problems in Current Plea Bargaining Practices

There are many serious problems with the way that the plea bargaining system is administered. In the first place bargaining takes place at a stage when the parties' knowledge of their own and each other's cases is likely to be fragmentary. Presentence reports and other investigations into the background of the offender usually are made after conviction and are unavailable at the plea bargain stage. Thus the prosecutor's decision is usually made without the benefit of information regarding the circumstances of the offense, the background and character of the defendant, and other factors necessary for sound dispositional decisions. In too many places the acceptance of pleas to lesser offenses, which began as a device to individualize treatment, becomes routine, with a standard reduction for certain charges.

The informality and wide variation in practice among prosecutors and trial judges regarding plea bargains often cause bewilderment and a sense of injustice among defendants. Some may be denied the opportunity to participate in the bargaining process and the benefits which may accrue because they or their counsel are unaware of the customary practices of plea negotiation. Others may come away from a system which invites judge shopping with justifiable feelings that they have been treated improperly.

Too often the result may be excessive leniency for professional and habitual criminals who generally have expert legal advice and are best able to take full advantage of the bargaining opportunity. Marginal offenders, on the other hand, may be dealt with harshly, and left with a deep sense of injustice, having learned too late of the possibilities of manipulation offered by the system.

The most troublesome problem is the possibility that an innocent defendant may plead guilty because of the fear that he will be sentenced more harshly if he is convicted after trial or that he will be subjected to damaging publicity because of a repugnant charge. The danger of convicting the innocent obviously must be reduced to the lowest possible level, but the fact is that neither trial nor plea bargain is a perfectly accurate procedure. In both, the innocent face the risk of conviction. The real question is whether the risks are sufficiently greater in the bargaining process to warrant either abandoning it entirely or modifying it drastically. Such improper practices as deliberate and unwarranted overcharging by the prosecutor to improve his bargaining position, threats of very heavy sentences if the defendant insists on a trial, or threats to prosecute relatives and friends of the defendant unless he pleads guilty may, on occasion, create pressures that can prove too great for even the innocent to resist. The existence of mandatory minimum sentences aggravates this problem since they exert a particularly heavy pressure on defendants to relinquish their chance of an acquittal. Inadequate discovery procedures often impair counsel's ability to appraise the risks of trial. Clearly those courts that continue to use a negotiated plea system must take vigorous steps to reduce these potential abuses.

Both Congress and the federal courts have attempted to deal with issues and problems noted in the preceding excerpt from the Report of the President's Commission.

FEDERAL RULES OF CRIMINAL PROCEDURE

Rule 11

PLEAS

(a) **Alternatives.** A defendant may plead not guilty, guilty, or nolo contendere. If a defendant refuses to plead or if a defendant corporation fails to appear, the court shall enter a plea of not guilty.

(b) **Nolo contendere.** A defendant may plead nolo contendere only with the consent of the court. Such a plea shall be accepted by the court only after due consideration of the views of the parties and the interest of the public in the effective administration of justice.

(c) **Advice to defendant.** Before accepting a plea of guilty or nolo contendere, the court must address the defendant personally in open court and inform him of, and determine that he understands, the following:

(1) the nature of the charge to which the plea is offered, the mandatory minimum penalty provided by law, if any, and the maximum possible penalty provided by law; and

(2) if the defendant is not represented by an attorney, that he has the right to be represented by an attorney at every stage of the proceeding against him and, if necessary, one will be appointed to represent him; and

(3) that he has the right to plead not guilty or to persist in that plea if it has already been made, and that he has the right to be tried by a jury and at that trial has the right to the assistance of counsel, the right to confront and cross-examine witnesses against him, and the right not to be compelled to incriminate himself; and

(4) that if he pleads guilty or nolo contendere there will not be a further trial of any kind, so that by pleading guilty or nolo contendere he waives the right to a trial; and

(5) that if he pleads guilty or nolo contendere, the court may ask him questions about the offense to which he has pleaded, and if he answers these questions under oath, on the record, and in the presence of counsel, his answers may later be used against him in a prosecution for perjury or false statement.

(d) **Insuring that the plea is voluntary.** The court shall not accept a plea of guilty or nolo contendere without first, by addressing the defendant personally in open court, determining that the plea is voluntary and not the result of force or threats or of promises apart from a plea agreement. The court shall also inquire as to whether the defendant's willingness to plead guilty or nolo contendere results from prior discussions between the attorney for the government and the defendant or his attorney.

(e) Plea agreement procedure.

(1) In general. The attorney for the government and the attorney for the defendant or the defendant when acting pro se may engage in discussions with a view toward reaching an agreement that, upon the entering of a plea of guilty or nolo contendere to a charged offense or to a lesser or related offense, the attorney for the government will do any of the following:

> (A) move for dismissal of other charges; or

> (B) make a recommendation, or agree not to oppose the defendant's request, for a particular sentence, with the understanding that such recommendation or request shall not be binding upon the court; or

> (C) agree that a specific sentence is the appropriate disposition of the case.

The court shall not participate in any such discussions.

(2) Notice of such agreement. If a plea agreement has been reached by the parties, the court shall, on the record, require the disclosure of the agreement in open court or, on a showing of good cause, in camera, at the time the plea is offered. Thereupon the court may accept or reject the agreement, or may defer its decision as to the acceptance or rejection until there has been an opportunity to consider the presentence report.

(3) Acceptance of a plea agreement. If the court accepts the plea agreement, the court shall inform the defendant that it will embody in the judgment and sentence the disposition provided for in the plea agreement.

(4) Rejection of a plea agreement. If the court rejects the plea agreement, the court shall, on the record, inform the parties of this fact, advise the defendant personally in open court or, on a showing of good cause, in camera, that the court is not bound by the plea agreement, afford the defendant the opportunity to then withdraw his plea, and advise the defendant that if he persists in his guilty plea or plea of nolo contendere the disposition of the case may be less favorable to the defendant than that contemplated by the plea agreement.

(5) Time of plea agreement procedure. Except for good cause shown, notification to the court of the existence of a plea agreement shall be given at the arraignment or at such other time, prior to trial, as may be fixed by the court.

(6) Inadmissibility of pleas, offers of pleas, and related statements. Except as otherwise provided in this paragraph, evidence of a plea of guilty, later withdrawn, or a plea of nolo contendere, or of an offer to plead guilty or nolo contendere to the crime charged or any other crime, or of statements made in connection with, and relevant to, any of the foregoing pleas or offers, is not admissible in any civil or criminal proceeding against the person who made the plea or offer. However, evidence of a statement made in connection with, and relevant to, a plea of guilty, later withdrawn, a plea of nolo contendere, or an offer to plead guilty or nolo contendere to the crime charged or any other crime, is admissible in a criminal proceeding for perjury or false statement if the statement was made by the defendant under oath, on the record, and in the presence of counsel.

(f) Determining accuracy of plea. Notwithstanding the acceptance of a plea of guilty, the court should not enter a judgment upon such plea without making such inquiry as shall satisfy it that there is a factual basis for the plea.

(g) Record of proceedings. A verbatim record of the proceedings at which the defendant enters a plea shall be made and, if there is a plea of guilty or nolo contendere, the record shall include, without limitation, the court's advice to the defendant, the inquiry into the voluntariness of the plea including any plea agreement, and the inquiry into the accuracy of a guilty plea.

Notes and Questions

1. Which issues and problems noted in the excerpt from the Report of the President's Commission, *supra* p. 321, are dealt with in Rule 11?

2. What should be done if the government reneges on a plea bargain?

In Santobello v. New York, 404 U.S. 257, 92 S.Ct. 495 (1971), the defendant/petitioner had been indicted on two felony counts involving gambling offenses. A plea bargain was struck in which the defendant, upon advice of counsel, withdrew his initial plea of innocent and pleaded guilty to a lesser included offense. The maximum sentence on the lesser offense was one year in a correctional facility. The prosecutor agreed to make no recommendation to the trial judge regarding sentencing of the defendant.

Subsequently, the defendant acquired new counsel who moved to withdraw the guilty plea on the grounds that crucial evidence against the defendant had been taken in violation of his rights, and that the defendant was unaware of that fact when he made the plea bargain. The motion was denied. During the time the motion was pending, the original presiding judge retired, and a new prosecutor took over the case. At the sentencing hearing the new prosecutor recommended imposition of the maximum sentence of one year. The new presiding judge imposed that sentence, citing defendant's extensive criminal record. Defense counsel objected that the prosecutor's recommendation was a violation of the plea bargain, but to no avail. The conviction and sentence were affirmed on appeal in New York and the defendant petitioned for review in the U.S. Supreme Court. The Court, in an opinion by Chief Justice Burger, held that the prosecutor was obligated to abide by the terms of the plea bargain. Accordingly, the case was remanded to the trial court. The relief to be accorded in the trial court was not specified.

> "The ultimate relief to which petitioner is entitled we leave to
> the discretion of the state court, which is in a better position to

decide whether the circumstances of this case require only that
there be specific performance of the agreement on the plea, in
which case petitioner should be resentenced by a different judge,
or whether, in the view of the state court, the circumstances require granting the relief sought by petitioner, i. e., the opportunity
to withdraw his plea of guilty. We emphasize that this is in no
sense to question the fairness of the sentencing judge; the fault
here rests on the prosecutor, not on the sentencing judge."

Justice Douglas joined the majority and filed a separate concurring opinion in which he argued for a constitutional rule that prosecutorial breach of a plea bargain should always result in vacation of the
sentence and remand to the lower courts for them to decide whether
the circumstances of the case call for specific performance on the plea
bargain, or for the defendant to be given the option of going to trial
on the original charges. Justice Marshall, joined by Justices Brennan
and Stewart, concurred in the vacation of judgment and remand, but
argued that the lower courts should be instructed to allow the defendant to withdraw the guilty plea.

If you were the trial judge on the remand of Santobello, what
would you do if the defense counsel asked to withdraw the guilty plea?
If you were Santobello's attorney, would you ask to withdraw the
plea? Would your answer be different if you knew that your motion
to withdraw the plea would be heard by the same judge who would
sentence Santobello in the event the motion on the plea was denied?

3.   What should be done if the defendant enters a negotiated plea
of guilty to a lesser charge, but then informs the sentencing judge that
he or she is not in fact guilty, but is pleading guilty only to avoid the
risk of more severe punishment if tried and found guilty of the more
serious charge?

This issue was posed in North Carolina v. Alford, 400 U.S. 25, 91
S.Ct. 160 (1970). Alford had been indicted on a charge of first degree
murder (then punishable by death under North Carolina law). There
was strong evidence of guilt, and defense counsel advised Alford to
enter a negotiated plea of guilty to second degree murder (a crime then
not punishable by death under North Carolina law). Alford informed
the trial judge in open court that he was not guilty, but he nonetheless
would plead guilty on the advice of counsel. He was sentenced to 30
years in prison. Subsequently he petitioned for habeas corpus in Federal District Court. The District Court denied the petition, but a divided panel of the Fourth Circuit Court of Appeals granted his petition, holding that the guilty plea was involuntary. The state appealed
to the Supreme Court, which reversed and remanded to the Circuit
Court for further proceedings. The majority of the court started
their analysis from the proposition that a plea of nolo contendere is
constitutionally permissible in federal criminal proceedings.

"The issue in Hudson v. United States, 272 U.S. 451, 47 S.Ct.
127 (1926), was whether a federal court has power to impose a

prison sentence after accepting a plea of nolo contendere, a plea by which a defendant does not expressly admit his guilt but nonetheless waives his right to a trial and authorizes the court for purposes of the case to treat him as if he were guilty. The Court held that a trial court does have such power, and except for the cases which were rejected in *Hudson*, the federal courts have uniformly followed this rule, even in cases involving moral turpitude. Bruce v. United States, *supra*, at 120 n. 20 (dictum). See, *e. g.*, Lott v. United States, 367 U.S. 421, 81 S.Ct. 1563 (1961) (fraudulent evasion of income tax); Sullivan v. United States, 348 U.S. 170, 75 S.Ct. 182 (1954) (ibid.); Farnsworth v. Zerbst, 98 F.2d 541 (CA5 1938) (espionage); Pharr v. United States, 48 F.2d 767 (CA6 1931) (misapplication of bank funds); United States v. Bagliore, 182 F.2d 714 (EDNY 1960) (receiving stolen property). Implicit in the *nolo contendere* cases is a recognition that the Constitution does not bar imposition of a prison sentence upon an accused who is unwilling expressly to admit his guilt but who, faced with grim alternatives, is willing to waive his trial and accept the sentence.

"These cases would be directly in point if Alford had simply insisted on his plea but refused to admit the crime. The fact that his plea was denominated a plea of guilty rather than a plea of *nolo contendere* is of no constitutional significance with respect to the issue now before us, for the Constitution is concerned with the practical consequences, not the formal categorizations of state law. See Smith v. Bennett, 365 U.S. 708, 712, 81 S.Ct. 895, 897 (1961); Jones v. United States, 362 U.S. 257, 266, 80 S.Ct. 725, 733 (1960). Cf. Kermarec v. Compagnie Generale Transatlantique, 358 U.S. 625, 630–632, 79 S.Ct. 406, 409–411 (1959). Thus, while most pleas of guilty consist of both a waiver of trial and an express admission of guilt, the latter element is not a constitutional requisite to the imposition of criminal penalty. An individual accused of crime may voluntarily, knowingly, and understandingly consent to the imposition of a prison sentence even if he is unwilling or unable to admit his participation in the acts constituting the crime.

"Nor can we perceive any material difference between a plea which refuses to admit commission of the criminal act and a plea containing a protestation of innocence when, as in the instant case, a defendant intelligently concludes that his interests require entry of a guilty plea and the record before the judge contains strong evidence of actual guilt. Here the State had a strong case of first-degree murder against Alford. Whether he realized or disbelieved his guilt, he insisted on his plea because in his view he had absolutely nothing to gain by a trial and much to gain by pleading. Because of the overwhelming evidence against him, a trial was precisely what neither Alford nor his attorney desired. Confronted with the choice between a trial for first-degree murder, on the one hand, and a plea of guilty to second-degree murder, on the other, Alford quite reasonably chose the latter and thereby limited the maximum penalty to a 30-year term. When his plea is viewed in light of the evidence against him, which substantially negated his claim of innocence and which further provided a means by which the judge could test whether the plea was being intelligently entered, see McCarthy v. United States, *supra*, at 466–467, 89 S.Ct. at 1170, 1171 (1969) its validity cannot be seriously questioned. In view of the strong factual basis for the plea demonstrated by the State and Alford's clearly expressed desire to enter it despite his professed belief in his innocence, we hold that the trial judge did not commit constitutional error in accepting it."

The issue in Alford was made more difficult by the fact that Alford had pleaded guilty in order to avoid the risk of the death penalty, and after he entered his plea and was sentenced, the Court in another caes held that the death penalty was unconstitutional, at least as it was then being utilized in most states. Alford's habeas corpus petition to review his sentence was almost surely prompted by this subsequent change in the status of the law regarding the death penalty.

Justices Brennan, Douglas, and Marshall dissented in North Carolina v. Alford, arguing that the facts clearly demonstrated that Alford's plea was not voluntary but was coerced by fear of the death penalty.

Query: What if the trial judge in Alford had refused to accept Alford's equivocal plea of guilty, but had required that Alford stand trial, with the result that Alford was convicted of murder in the first degree, and was sentenced to death or to life imprisonment? Would Alford have good grounds to allege on appeal or in a habeas corpus review that the refusal of his plea denied him "due process of law"? Consider Rule 11(b) in this regard. What if the judge had refused to accept Alford's plea because he or she was not satisfied "that there [was] a factual basis for the plea"? If trial and conviction on the first degree charge had followed, would Alford have good grounds for relief on an appeal of the conviction?

What is the central problem underlying the Alford case? Is it a weakness in the plea bargaining process, or is it a more fundamental problem in criminal trials and in sentencing?

Alford was accused of causing the death of another person. In the most general terms, he was accused of having committed a homicide. Within that general category of crime there are discrete levels or degrees of culpability. For example, Alford was charged with murder in the first degree, an intentional and premeditated homicide, but as a result of the plea bargain he was allowed to plead to a lesser offense, second degree murder, an intentional but not premeditated homicide. Had the prosecutor wished, he might have allowed Alford to plead to even lesser offenses, such as manslaughter or criminally negligent homicide. The theory underlying the different degrees of crimes such as homicide is that there are different degrees of culpability associated with the motivation and state of mind of the accused.

That theory also leads to the general practice of assigning different penalties for the different degrees of crime. Thus in Alford, the maximum sentence for first degree murder was the death penalty, while the maximum sentence for second degree murder was thirty years imprisonment.

This range of discretion regarding possible sentences for a crime is extended by the modern practice of allowing the sentencing judge to choose a broad range of sentences for each degree of a crime. Accordingly, although the maximum sentence for second degree murder might be set by a legislature as thirty years imprisonment, the legislature might also authorize a judge to impose much lesser sentences of a few years imprisonment or even to allow the defendant to be freed on probation. The judge's choice in this regard would be guided by his or her view of the defendant's culpability, past criminal record, and prospects for rehabilitation. The judge might also be guided by recommendations from the prosecutor.

The prosecutor's discretion regarding charges, and the judge's discretion regarding sentencing are major factors in the plea bargaining process. Where that discretion is regularly exercised to induce or reward guilty pleas, appellate courts have indicated concern regarding the fairness of the plea bargaining and sentencing processes, see, e. g., U. S. v. Stockwell, 9 Cir. 1973, 472 F.2d 1186, and Scott v. U. S., D.C. Cir. 1969, 419 F.2d 264.

In Scott, the defendant had elected to stand trial, was convicted, and then was sentenced to from five to fifteen years in prison. The record of the sentencing hearing showed that the trial judge had probably imposed a higher than normal sentence because the defendant had chosen to stand trial, and would make no admission of guilt after his conviction.

The Circuit Court remanded the case for resentencing, in spite of the Court's expressions of general reluctance to review the sentencing decisions of the lower courts, but Judge Bazelon's majority opinion in Scott included the following commentary on differential sentencing and plea bargaining (some footnotes renumbered, others omitted):

Two arguments inevitably appear whenever differential sentencing is discussed. The first is that the defendant's choice of plea shows whether he recognizes and repents his crime. One difficulty with this argument is that no court or commentator has explained why a defendant's insistence upon his self-incrimination privilege is not also evidence of a lack of repentence. Or his insistence that evidence unconstitutionally seized should not be admitted.

Repentance has a role in penology. But the premise of our criminal jurisprudence has always been that the time for repentance comes after trial. The adversary process is a fact-finding engine, not a drama of contrition in which a prejudged defendant is expected to knit up his lacerated bonds to society.

There is a tension between the right of the accused to assert his innocence and the interest of society in his repentance. But we could consider resolving this conflict in favor of the latter interest only if the trial offered an unparalleled opportunity to test the repentance of the accused. It does not. There is other, and better, evidence of such repentance. The sort of information collected in presentence reports provides a far more finely brushed portrait of the man than do a few hours or days at trial. And the offender while on probation or in prison after trial can demonstrate his insight into his problems far better than at trial.

If the defendant were unaware that a proper display of remorse might affect his sentence, his willingness to admit the crime might offer the sentencing judge some guidance. But with the inducement of a lighter sentence dangled before him, the sincerity of any cries of *mea culpa* becomes questionable. Moreover, the refusal of a defendant to plead guilty is not necessarily indicative of a lack of repentance. A man may regret his crime but wish desperately to avoid the stigma of a criminal conviction.[1]

The Supreme Court was careful to point out in Sherbert v. Verner that "no showing merely of a rational relationship to some colorable state interest would suffice" to justify an infringement of First Amendment rights.[2] Even if we assume that the right to a fair trial may in some circumstances be made costly, the required justification here also must be a paramount goal achievable in no other way. The supposed value of a guilty plea in demonstrating repentance does not meet this test.

The second argument for differential sentencing is necessity. Most convictions, perhaps as many as 90 per cent in some jurisdictions, are the product of guilty pleas.[3] Unless a large proportion of defendants plead guilty, the argument runs, the already crowded dockets in many jurisdictions would collapse into chaos. Since most defendants are indigent, the only price they can be forced to pay for pleading innocent is time in jail. Ergo, differential sentences are justified for those who plead guilty and those who plead innocent.

When approached from this perspective, the problem inevitably becomes entwined with that of plea bargaining. And the difficulties that practice presents are exceeded only by its pervasiveness. In many areas such bargaining dominates the criminal process. Its format may vary. The prosecutor may agree to reduce the charge in exchange for a guilty plea, or he may agree to recommend a lighter sentence. The judge may be aware of the agreement or he may not. If aware that a bargain has been struck, the court may or may not ratify the agreement before a plea is offered and accepted.

When a defendant pleads guilty in exchange for the promise of the prosecutor or court, a subsequent challenge to the voluntariness of his plea

---

1. In fact, a colorable argument can be made that a glib willingness to admit guilt in order to "secure something in return" may indicate quite the opposite of repentance, and that a reluctance to admit guilt may in fact reflect repentance. *See* Alschuler, The Prosecutor's Role in Plea Bargaining, 36 U.Chi.L. Rev. 50, 57 n. 24 (1968).

2. 374 U.S. at 406, 83 S.Ct. at 1795.

3. *See* The President's Comm'n on Law Enforcement and Administration of Justice, Task Force Report: The Courts 9 (1967) [hereinafter Task Force Report]; D. J. Newman, Conviction: The Determination of Guilt or Innocence Without Trial 3 n. 1 (1966).

raises a recognized constitutional issue. When the accused refuses to plead guilty and subsequently receives a heavier sentence, the invisibility with which the system operates in individual cases too often conceals the constitutional issue. But the problem is the same in both contexts. Whether the defendant surrenders his right to a trial because of a bargain with court or prosecutor, or exercises his right at the cost of a stiffer sentence, a price has been put on the right.

The two sides of this coin are related in a practical sense as well. At least when only a single charge is involved, the effectiveness of plea bargaining depends upon the willingness of the court to impose a lighter sentence when a defendant pleads guilty. If such is the custom within a jurisdiction, the prosecutor enjoys credibility. Indeed, if the custom is sufficiently well known, actual bargaining may be unnecessary: enough defendants will be cowed into guilty pleas simply by the force of their lawyers' warnings that defendants convicted after demanding a trial receive long sentences.

Thus, to the extent that the appellant here received a longer sentence because he pleaded innocent, he was a pawn sacrificed to induce other defendants to plead guilty. Since this is so, to consider the price he paid for the exercise of his right without regard for the process of which it is but one instance would be to ignore reality. 419 F.2d 264, at pp. 270–272.

* * *

If inducements are to be offered for guilty pleas, there are strong reasons why the court should not be the party to offer them. The trial judge may sacrifice his ability to preside impartially at trial by becoming too involved with pre-trial negotiations. Even if he does not, it may so appear to the defendant. It is important not only that a trial be fair in fact, but also that the defendant believe that justice has been done. The accused may fairly doubt this if he thinks the judge begrudges him the exercise of his right to trial. Moreover, the defendant's uncertainty concerning the expectations or wishes of the judge will prevent his exercise of the best judgment in deciding upon a plea.

Judge Weinfeld has concluded in two careful opinions that whatever the propriety of plea bargaining between prosecutors and defendants, the peculiarly sensitive position of the trial judge renders involuntary any guilty plea induced by a commitment from the bench.[4] His vivid portrayal of the "unequal positions of the judge and the accused, one with the power to commit to prison and the other deeply concerned to avoid prison" presents a compelling brief for demanding that the judge not become a participant in the bargaining process.

In this case the trial judge did not bargain with the defendant. Indeed he did not even point out that he might be more lenient with a defendant who pleaded guilty until after trial. But in so stating at the sentencing hearing he announced to all future defendants the guidelines in his court room. We cannot approve of these guidelines for the same reasons that we could not condone actual plea bargaining by a trial judge. The policy announced by the trial judge may not endanger his actual impartiality at

---

4. United States ex rel. Elksnis v. Gilligan, 256 F.Supp. 244 (S.D.N.Y.1966); United States v. Tateo, 214 F.Supp. 560 (S.D.N.Y.1963); *see also* Euziere v. United States, 249 F.2d 293 (10th Cir. 1957).

trials as much as his participation in plea bargaining sessions might. And we certainly do not criticize the impartiality displayed by the experienced trial judge in this case. But we cannot ignore the impact of such a policy on the appearance of justice to criminal defendants and their ability to choose wisely between a plea of guilty and an exercise of their right to trial.

In recognizing that an announced policy of differential sentencing presents some of the same dangers as conventional plea bargaining, we do not, as the concurring opinion suggests, equate the two practices. Overt plea bargaining by a trial judge places direct and immediate pressure upon the defendant to forego his right to a trial. An announced policy of differential sentencing which distinguishes between defendants who demand a trial and those who do not presents an inducement to plead guilty which may be less coercive in the individual case, but which nevertheless must affect the decision to exercise the constitutional right to a trial. 419 F.2d 264, at pp. 273–274.

Question

Does Rule 11 of the Federal Rules of Criminal Procedure deal with the issues posed in Scott v. United States, and North Carolina v. Alford? See particularly Rule 11(d) and (e).

[The following is taken from ABRAHAM BLUMBERG*, "LAWYERS WITH CONVICTIONS," 3 Criminal Law Bulletin 384 (1967).]

The "cop-out" ceremony is not only invaluable for redefining the defendant's perspectives of himself, but also in reiterating his guilt in a public ritual. The accused is made to assert his guilt of a specific crime, including a complete recital of its details. He is further made to say that he is entering his plea of guilt freely and that he is not doing so because of any promises that may have been made to him. This last is intended as a blanket statement to shield the court bureaucrats from any charges of coercion. This cuts off any appellate review on grounds that due process was denied as well as cutting off any second thoughts the defendant may have about his plea.

This affirmation of guilt is not a simple affair. Most of those who plead guilty are guilty and may be willing or even eager to say so in order to be charged with a lesser crime or receive a lesser sentence. The system serves the guilty better because they are glad to get half a loaf in return for playing along. But the innocent—subject to precisely the same pressures— get no reward from a negotiated plea. In any case, the defendant's conception of himself as guilty is ephemeral; in private he will quickly reassert his innocence. The "cop-out" . . . is a charade. The accused projects the appropriate amount of guilt, penance, and remorse; his hearers engage in the fantasy that he is contrite and merits a lesser punishment.

* * *

Based on data which are admittedly tentative and fragmentary, the furor over confessions, whether forced or voluntary, is not statistically

* Abraham S. Blumberg is Associate Professor of Law and Sociology at the John Jay College of the City University of New York.

meaningful. Criminal law enforcement has always depended, and will continue to do so in the foreseeable future, on judicial confessions—that is, pleas of guilty—rather than confessions hammered out in the squeal room of a police station.

The Gideon, Miranda, and Escobedo decisions were greeted with such lively delight or anguished dismay that outsiders must have thought that the Supreme Court had wrought some magnificent transformation in the defense lawyer. Actually, the Court in these cases was perpetuating the Perry Mason myth of an adversary trial, while in the lesser courts of the nation, the dreary succession of 90 percent negotiated pleas continued.

SECTION 12.4 LIMITING PROSECUTORIAL DISCRETION: A COMPARATIVE VIEW

[The following is taken from KENNETH C. DAVIS, DISCRETIONARY JUSTICE, *op. cit.*, pp. 191–195. Footnotes are renumbered.]

Lawyers all over the continent of Europe know that a prosecuting system can be viable without uncontrolled discretion. A quick look at a prosecuting system in one such country will show that the basic assumptions Americans have long made about the prosecuting power are not the only possible ones.

The prosecuting system in West Germany. Some knowledge of continental attitudes about the prosecuting power is useful, not because those attitudes should be transplanted to America, but because Americans need to realize that the assumptions on which our system is built are not inevitable.

Alexander Pekelis, who, with a European background, examined in depth both European and American legal institutions, observed that

. . . under the American system criminal prosecution is simply a right and never a duty of the federal or state attorney. Its exercise is wholly within the discretion of the prosecuting officers and the grand jury. In Italy . . . prosecution [is] a duty of the attorney general; in France and in Germany the prosecuting agency had but a slight degree of discretion, and this pertained to minor offenses and was subject to review by the court. . . . Thus the practical administration of criminal justice [in the United States], at least in its negative aspect, becomes an administrative rather than a judicial activity. . . . In brief, then, comparative investigations thus far seem to reveal that in the administration of justice the common-law countries have traditionally relied upon a wide exercise of discretionary power to an incomparably greater extent than any civil-law country in Europe.[1]

Although no two continental systems of prosecuting are the same, all stand in contrast with the Anglo-American systems in the fundamental attitude about discretionary power of prosecutors. The continental countries

1. Alexander Pekelis, Law and Social Action (1950), 81–83.

seem in general to reflect the Pekelis background remark that "the European Rechtsstaat was planned and organized with the very purpose of reducing the human element in the administration of justice to its imaginable minimum. . . . The less discretion, the more justice." [2] British and American attitudes seem the opposite: Uncontrolled discretionary power of prosecutors is simply assumed.

American assumptions that a prosecutor must in the nature of things have a broad and largely uncontrolled discretionary power run so deep that I have found extreme skepticism on the part of any Americans to whom I have tried to explain the European attitudes about prosecuting. The almost universal reaction is along this line: "The prosecuting power intrinsically involves broad discretion because (1) in the nature of things all law can't be enforced, (2) the prosecutor has to interpret uncertain statutory provisions, and (3) the prosecutor has to exercise discretion in deciding whether the evidence is sufficient." But the plain fact is that viable systems exist in which prosecutors have almost no discretionary power. Let us look more closely at one of them, that of West Germany.

Like the realities of the American prosecuting power, the realities of the German prosecuting power are beyond the statutes and the published reports of cases. The crucial element is the customary practices of prosecutors. To get the facts, I have sought help from five informants, all of whom have a German legal education and experience in the German system, and two of whom have had experience in prosecuting German cases: A distinguished legal scholar in comparative law who has worked in America since 1933,[3] a judge of the Supreme Administrative Court,[4] a young legal scholar in a German university who has taught as a visiting professor in two American law schools,[5] and two younger legal scholars who have come to America from Germany.[6] In the facts I am about to relate, the five are

---

2. Id. at 80. Although some major features of the prosecuting systems of the continental countries stand in contrast with those of the English-speaking nations, still some differences from one continental country to another are significant. For instance, prosecutors in Denmark and Norway have a very wide discretion to waive prosecution, but such waivers are generally limited to less serious offenses and are exceptional for serious crimes. In Sweden and Finland, the "principle of legality" means that prosecutors have a legal duty to prosecute if they find guilt sufficiently established; the main exceptions relate to young offenders. See Andenaes, The Legal Framework, 9, 10.

The contrast between England and the continent is brought out by a British writer, Glanville Williams, "Discretion in Prosecuting," [1956] Crim.L.Rev. 222: "It is completely wrong to suppose (as is sometimes done) that the institution of prosecution is an automatic or mechanical matter. This is, indeed, the theory in some Continental countries, such as Germany, where the rule is that the public prosecutor must take proceedings for all crimes that come to his notice for which there is sufficient evidence, unless they fall within an exception for petty offences, in respect of which he is given discretion. In England, however, there is discretion in prosecuting in respect of all crimes."

3. Professor Max Rheinstein of the University of Chicago.

4. Dr. Ernst K. Pakuscher.

5. Professor Fritz Scharpf of the University of Constance, who was visiting professor at the Yale Law School 1964–66 and at the University of Chicago during 1966.

6. Associate Professor Gerhard Casper and Assistant Professor Peter Schlechtriem, both currently teaching at the University of Chicago Law School.

unanimous; omitted from my description is one facet about which they are not unanimous.

A German lawyer who is asked whether or not a German prosecutor has discretionary power is likely instinctively to say no. This is because students in German law schools are taught that prosecutors do not have discretionary power. The practice for the most part conforms to the theory that is taught, although some deviations from the theory can be found.

The American will immediately ask: "How on earth can a prosecutor interpret vague or ambiguous statutes and pass upon sufficiency of evidence without exercising discretionary power?" The German answer to that question is one that deserves to be understood by Americans. A crucial part of the answer is that some of the discretion exercised by American prosecutors is exercised by German judges.

The most important difference between the German system and the American system is this: *Whenever the evidence that the defendant has committed a serious crime* [7] *is reasonably clear and the law is not in doubt, the German prosecutor, unlike the American prosecutor, is without discretionary power to withhold prosecution. This means that selective enforcement, a major feature of the American system, is almost wholly absent from the German system.* The German prosecutor does not withhold prosecution for such reasons as that he thinks the statute overreaches, that justice requires withholding enforcement because of special circumstances, that the statute ought to be enforced against some violators and not others, that he lacks time for bringing a marginal prosecution, or that he finds political advantage in not prosecuting. Hence the German prosecutor never has discretionary power to engage in plea bargaining.

The German and American systems also differ when the evidence or the law or both seem to the prosecutor to be doubtful. When a doubt seems to require a discretionary choice, the German prosecutor does not resolve the doubt; he almost always presents a doubtful case to the judge, who determines the sufficiency of the evidence and the proper interpretation of the law. Of course, in America the prosecutor makes a discretionary determination in every doubtful case, either to prosecute or not to prosecute.

Even when the prosecutor finds prosecution of a suspect clearly inappropriate, the German system, unlike the American system, provides protection against abuse of power. When a crime is reported by the police or by a private party, a file is opened and registered; the file can be traced at any time. A German prosecutor can never simply forget about the case as his American counterpart may do. The file cannot be closed without a statement of written reasons, which in important cases must be approved by the prosecutor's superior, and which must be reported to any victim of the crime and to any suspect who was interrogated. Every prosecutor is supervised by a superior in a hierarchical system headed by the Minister of Justice, who is himself responsible to the cabinet. The supervision is real, not merely a threat; files are in fact often reviewed. Availability to victims of crimes of procedure to compel prosecution constitutes still another check.

---

7. With respect to certain small misdemeanors, including traffic offenses, both the police and the prosecutors in Germany have a substantial power of selective enforcement. This exception is explicitly recognized in the statutes.

Departures from the theory that prosecutors lack discretionary power in Germany are few and slight. Determining whether to make an investigation of a suspect, or whether to investigate further, or whether innocence is so clear that the case should not be presented to the judge may involve some element of discretion. And a little play in the joints is probably inevitable. One of my German informants has the impression, for instance, that the statute against homosexual practices is not fully enforced in Hamburg, but he thinks that the method of withholding prosecution is usually by finding the evidence insufficient; if his impression is correct, some discretionary power even about policy may in fact be exercised. During the Weimar Republic the Minister of Justice, with Cabinet approval but in violation of the statutes, openly refused to prosecute for certain political crimes. Although a statute makes it a crime not only to perform an abortion but for a woman to have one performed, women are seldom prosecuted for having abortions performed. But these examples of deviations from the theory are highly exceptional. With respect to the great bulk of crimes, the German prosecutor ordinarily has no power of selective enforcement. In this he stands in contrast with his American counterpart, who, with respect to the great bulk of crimes, ordinarily has a power of selective enforcement.[8]

SECTION 12.5   SELF REGULATION OF POLICE AND PROSECUTION: ADMINISTRATIVE RULES AS A SUBSTITUTE FOR JUDGE'S RULES

The extract from Davis, Discretionary Justice, reprinted in Section 12.4 is but a part of a widely acclaimed inquiry regarding the scope and impact of executive and administrative discretion exercised, under law, in American government. Professor Davis there presented a compelling case for the proposition that unfettered administrative discretion is pervasive in our society, and ought to be limited and channeled by the legal process. One of Davis' prescriptions for reform is to channel the exercise of discretion by imposing much more extensive requirements that decision making by public officials and agencies be made in accordance with general principles, i. e., rules, promulgated and published by the agency both to guide its own actions and inform the public of agency policy.

8. A case which is not typical of German attitudes shows how extreme the German theory can be when carried into practice. A judge found a woman guilty of stealing four diapers. The statute required a severe penalty because of a prior conviction of theft. The judge by strained interpretation imposed a lighter sentence, as he thought justice required. The judge was then prosecuted for violating the statute requiring the severe sentence! The answer to my question whether the prosecutor of the judge had discretionary power to withhold prosecution was, "None whatsoever."

ALI MODEL CODE OF PRE–ARRAIGNMENT PROCEDURE

Section 10.3 Regulations

(1) **Duty to Issue Regulations.** The chief law officer of the state [attorney general of the state] [   ] shall provide for the preparation and issuance of regulations implementing the provisions of this Code within each law enforcement agency and prosecution office in the state. Such regulations shall clearly designate the subordinate officers who are responsible for the enforcement of this Code in relation to persons in custody at each stage from arrest to release or court appearance. Such regulations shall provide, so far as practicable, for uniform practices throughout the state.

(2) **Local Regulations.** The regulations issued pursuant to Subsection (1) of this Section shall provide, where appropriate, for the preparation and issuance of additional local regulations for use within particular law enforcement agencies. Such local regulations shall be subject to review and revision by the chief law officer of the state [attorney general of the state] [   ].

(3) **Public Documents.** Regulations issued under this section shall be public documents.

(4) **Procedure for Adoption of Regulations.** [Reference to State Procedures for Approval and Effectiveness of Administrative Regulations.]

Questions

[Review the excerpts from Skolnick and Wilson, *supra* pp. 216–222 before considering the following questions.]

1. How, if at all, would the promulgation and publication of administrative rules to govern the behavior of police and prosecutor serve to subject criminal law enforcement to the rule of law?

2. Do you think such rules would facilitate or hinder the work of police? Prosecutors? Magistrates and trial judges? Appellate judges? Explain.

3. Might the very process of formulating such rules itself be a highly beneficial exercise tending to lessen the tension between the rule of law and the police duty to maintain order? Explain. What steps and what participants would you include in the rule-making process? Why?

SECTION 13. EUROPEAN CRIMINAL PROCEDURE PRIOR TO TRIAL: AN OUTLINE OF PRACTICE AND PROCEDURE IN FRANCE

[The following is taken from "DEVELOPMENTS IN THE LAW: CONFESSIONS," 79 Harvard Law Review 935, 1114–1119 (1966), an unsigned note prepared by student members of the Harvard Law Review staff.) Footnotes are omittted.]

The Civil Law View

Introduction.—Investigation and trial of crimes in civil law countries differ markedly from the common law pattern. Usually the accused may not be compelled to incriminate himself, but the police are granted extensive freedom to interrogate, and in judicial proceedings the accused may find it difficult in practice to assert his right to remain silent. There are, of course, significant differences among the civil law countries. For example, in Germany a suspect is free to consult his lawyer at any stage in the proceedings against him, while in France the suspect generally has no right to counsel until he is formally charged. In the Netherlands access to counsel may be suspended up to six days even after accusation if the magistrate in charge of the investigation feels that the defense attorney is frustrating his efforts to discover the truth. These differences, however, have less relevance for American problems than the underlying contrast between the common law and civil law conceptions of the proper role of police and courts. And this contrast can be best illustrated by a discussion of the civil law system as it operates in one country.

2. France.—When the police learn of a crime, they may detain on the scene anyone whose presence they deem necessary, or they may require anyone believed to have useful information to come to police headquarters and make a statement. After these preliminaries, investigation is theoretically subject to close judicial control. The police are required to report the crime to the prosecuting attorney (*procureur*), who in turn will petition a magistrate (*juge d'instruction*) to assume the investigation; the police are required to follow the magistrate's instructions. In practice, however, the magistrate will usually authorize a police officer to ascertain the facts with regard to the crime in question, and the relationship of the police to the magistrate will become one of "informal liaison."

The broad authorization from the magistrate, called a *commission rogatoire*, empowers the police to interrogate witnesses and to take their depositions under oath. Once suspicion focuses on a particular person, however, he is entitled to be warned of his right to remain silent and to be questioned only by the magistrate in the presence of counsel. To protect these rights, a 1955 case held that the police had no further power to question a suspect at this point and that any statements made could not be used as evidence. This rule was incorporated in article 105 of the 1958 Code of Penal Procedure, but in 1960 the section was amended to prohibit questioning of a prime suspect only when the police thereby intend to circumvent the rights of the defense. Protection for the accused is in practice even less than this limited safeguard would indicate, since the police can simply ask a suspect to waive his right to be brought before the magistrate, and frequently the suspect will consent in order not to seem guilty. Thus, in practice the police are probably free to take depositions under oath from the primary suspect as well as from other witnesses.

The police may also take a witness or suspect into custody for questioning, and the safeguards surrounding such interrogation seem limited. A person may be held for twenty-four hours without being brought before a magistrate, and this period may be extended for an additional twenty-four hours if there is substantial evidence justifying an accusation and if either the magistrate or the prosecuting attorney approves. It is assumed that the suspect may not be compelled to incriminate himself; apparently, the principle is considered so basic that it does not require specific statutory or constitutional recognition. The police are required to keep a record of the length of questioning periods, the rest periods between interrogations, and the time when custody started and ended, though it is not clear how persistent interrogation must be before judges will consider a confession illegally coerced. The code also attempts to guard against coercion by providing that after twenty-four hours a person in custody may demand a medical examination and that he must be advised of this right. Thus, the safeguards provided indicate by common law standards a rather narrow, physical conception of "coercion," although the French do recognize in principle that a confession may not be compelled.

By the end of the two-day interrogation period, the suspect must be brought before the examining magistrate and formally accused. Although the magistrate will, as in American procedure, determine whether further detention is warranted, his major function is to gather additional information concerning the crime. He will first inform the suspect of the charge and tell him that he may refuse to make a statement. However, the magistrate will also tell the suspect that he may make a statement if he wishes, and at this point the accused will often repeat a confession previously given to the police. The magistrate will then advise the accused that he may either choose counsel from among the members of the local bar or have counsel designated for him. Often the accused decides not to be represented by counsel, and in such a case further interrogation may take place immediately. Otherwise, further proceedings will ordinarily be postponed, but the magistrate may interrogate the accused or other witnesses at this time if there are urgent reasons for immediate questioning.

In the case of felonies, the magistrate must conduct additional hearings regardless of whether a confession has been obtained, and he, rather than the prosecutor, has the primary responsibility for taking "all acts of investigation that he deems useful to the manifestation of the truth." Similar hearings are usually held in cases involving lesser crimes, although the procedure is then only optional. The hearings are conducted in secrecy, apparently in order to protect the accused from publicity; each witness is heard out of the presence both of the accused and of other witnesses. A major step in this investigation process is the examination of the accused by the magistrate. Counsel must be present when the accused appears unless the right has been expressly waived, and counsel must be allowed to examine the *dossier*, which contains all the prosecution's evidence, at least twenty-four hours before the hearing. However, counsel for the accused may question his client or other witnesses only with the permission of the examining magistrate, and the accused may not confer with his lawyer prior to answering any particular question. In theory, the accused may refuse to answer all questions, but apparently such a refusal is rare since the magistrate would be certain to draw adverse inferences from it. Indeed, the suspect's opportunity to participate in the inquiry and to advance his version of the facts seems to be regarded as an important right, rather than as an interference with liberty or privacy.

When conflicts appear in the testimony received, the magistrate will frequently resort to *confrontation*; a witness whose testimony conflicts with that of the accused will be asked to repeat his statement in the presence of the accused, and the accused will then be asked to reconcile his version of the facts with that just given. This technique is undoubtedly of great help to the magistrate in presenting him with demeanor and other clues to the reliability of testimony. In addition, crucial admissions will often be made by the accused, and these become a part of the record along with other testimony. Another device often used to verify testimony is the *reconstitution:* the accused and the witnesses, along with the magistrate, prosecutor, and defense counsel, visit the scene of the crime, where each party re-enacts his role in the incident under investigation. Frequently, this procedure will provide a strong indication of the reliability of testimony, and again a record of the proceedings is included in the *dossier*.

Thus, the accused occupies a central position in the investigation process from beginning to end, and usually a confession is eventually obtained. Moreover, the investigation will produce an elaborate *dossier*, providing "a complete record of the events leading up to and constituting the crime, a portrait of the personalities involved in it, and a record of the judicial procedure which has followed upon it." It should be noted, however, that the record of a given proceeding can be included in the *dossier* only if the required safeguards have been provided. Failure to notify the accused of his right to remain silent and to have counsel, and failure to allow the accused's lawyer to examine the *dossier* prior to an examination, will render all subsequent proceedings void, and the record of proceedings thus nullified must be stricken from the *dossier*.

On the basis of the material in the *dossier*, the magistrate must determine whether to refer the case to an appropriate court for trial. Apparently much more than "probable cause" is required—the magistrate must conclude on the basis of the facts developed that the accused committed the crime, and this criterion seems to be interpreted to mean that doubts must be resolved in favor of the accused. Moreover, in the case of felonies, the magistrate's order alone is not sufficient. The case is automatically referred to an "indicting chamber" (*chambre d'accusation*), composed of three magistrates who review the *dossier*, hear argument by prosecution and defense attorneys, and determine whether the facts developed justify trial on a felony charge.

French trial procedure differs radically from that of the common law countries. There is a jury only in felony cases, and even then the jury deliberates with the three judges in reaching its verdict. The judges, the prosecuting attorney, and—in felony cases—the jurors all may question witnesses and the accused, but neither the accused nor his counsel has a right to question witnesses except through the presiding judge. Normally the trial begins with the presiding judge's questioning of the accused. The entire contents of the *dossier* are available to the court, and the judges base their questions on the facts revealed in it. Both favorable and unfavorable circumstances are discussed, and the testimony often ranges broadly over factors not directly relevant to the charge, such as the defendant's background and character. Thus, the trial appears to be more a cooperative investigation than an adversary proceeding.

The French trial also seems to have a purpose different from the one generally recognized in common law countries. Apparently the general feeling is that "the immensely careful preliminary investigations of the *juge d'instruction* make it unlikely that persons who in France are sent for trial are guiltless." It is of course recognized that consideration of the question of guilt in the trial court is desirable as "yet another device to minimize the risk of prejudice and error," and acquittals do occasionally occur. Nevertheless, it seems relatively rare even for the question of guilt to be disputed at trial, since often the defendant will have confessed on several occasions by that time. Although there have been a few celebrated cases of false confessions, usually the confession will also find full corroboration in other facts in the *dossier*.

Thus the decision about guilt or innocence is usually a formality at the trial stage, having been resolved for practical purposes at the pretrial examination. The major issue before the court is the determination of sentence—a decision made by judge and jury voting together, and in the context of such a process, the failure to insist upon an adversary proceeding with clearly defined issues is understandable even to the common law mind. However, just as extensive questioning and resolution of guilt prior to trial tend to make an open-ended trial procedure appropriate, so the United States Supreme Court has recently pointed out that in the American system, denial of the right to counsel prior to indictment "would make the trial no more than an appeal from the interrogation; and the 'right to use counsel at the formal trial [would be] a very hollow thing [if], for all practical purposes, the conviction is already assured by pretrial examination.' "

Notes and Questions

1.   Compare and contrast, point for point, the grand jury procedure in the federal courts and the French system of preliminary investigation and indictment by an examining magistrate.

2.   Do the differences in the two types of procedure appear to reflect differences in theories of, or attitudes toward, (a) crime, (b) law in general?

3.   Compare and contrast, point for point, the American system of procedure prior to trial in criminal cases with that in civil cases. What explanations can you suggest for the major differences?

4.   One commentator on European criminal procedure made the following observation regarding the role of the investigating magistrate:

"But there is a vice inherent in the nature of the investigation by the juge d'instruction which cannot be corrected by any reform.

The juge d'instruction is required to be at one and the same time an agent of the prosecution, counsel for the defense, and a judge. These are three incompatible roles. A judge may be impartial when he himself is not concerned in the dispute. But a juge d'instruction is himself in the thick of the fight. He does not wait for facts to be brought to him. He has a definite responsibility to collect them. The accused may seem to oppose him in the performance of his task. It is making great demands upon a man to require him to maintain impartiality under such circumstances. In questioning an accused in open court, in the presence of defense counsel who can object to unjust tactics, and in the presence of a judge who can suppress them, the American prosecutor is often unfair. One can imagine, then, the scene which may easily occur when a juge d'instruction, alone with a defendant, can question at will, with no time limit and no restriction upon the questions he can ask." [1]

Why is it "a vice inherent in the nature of the investigation by the juge d'instruction which cannot be corrected by any reform" that the same person "is required to be at one and the same time an agent of the prosecution, counsel for the defense and judge"?

––––––

American interest in European criminal procedure has quickened in recent years, prompted by the hope that the European approach might provide models for reform of American practice. Of chief interest is the possibility of adapting the European investigating magistracy as an element of the pre-trial process, and by so doing to substitute some effective pre-trial judicial supervision of police and prosecutor for the after the fact judicial supervision now characteristic of our system.

In 1977, two American scholars published the results of research aimed at testing the hypothesis that continental criminal procedure may provide a different and better model on which to base reform in American law.

[The following is taken from ABRAHAM S. GOLDSTEIN * and MARTIN MARCUS,** "THE MYTH OF JUDICIAL SUPERVISION IN THREE 'INQUISITORIAL SYSTEMS': FRANCE, ITALY, AND GERMANY," 87 Yale Law Journal 240, 279–283 (1977). Footnotes are omitted.]

* * *

In the United States, we are searching for new models with which to understand and manage our criminal justice system. The adversarial model, drawn primarily from the contested trial, seems almost irrelevant since more than ninety percent of those charged with crime plead guilty. At first glance, the inquisitorial model seems to be an attractive substitute.

1. Morris Ploscowe, "The Investigating Magistrate (Juge D'Instruction) In European Criminal Procedure," 33 Michigan Law Review 1010 (1935).

* Sterling Professor of Law, Yale University.

** Research Fellow, Yale Law School, 1975–1976, Member, New York Bar.

Based on a sophisticated analysis of criminal prosecution, it assumes that police and prosecutors are inevitably made partisan by the role they play in searching out the facts of crime. Only judges can be trusted to be "neutral and detached"—hence the insistence on "judicial" police, on "judicial" examination, on a principle of compulsory prosecution or controlled discretion, and on the rejection of guilty pleas in favor of full and judicially directed inquiry at the trial of every case.

Before we embrace the inquisitorial model, however, we must ask whether it describes these Continental systems any better than the adversarial model describes our own. Our study of Western European criminal procedure gives us a substantial basis for concluding that the usual portrait of "inquisitorial" systems is overdrawn. The findings that emerge most clearly have already been signalled. Even in France and Italy, which are most explicitly "inquisitorial," a judicial investigation rarely takes place before trial. It is the prosecutor who decides whether the case will receive a judicial examination, and, in most cases, he retains the file and conducts the examination himself. When a judicial examination does take place, as in the investigation of the most serious crimes, it is often little more than a limited superintendence of a police investigation. The dossier, on which the trial is based, is usually compiled by the police; only occasionally does the prosecutor or examining magistrate make an important contribution. And the contents of the dossier largely determine the charge, the course of the trial, and the sentence.

Claims that prosecutorial discretion has been eliminated, or is supervised closely, are exaggerated. Discretion is exercised in each of the systems for reasons similar to those supporting it in the United States. However much Continental writers describe their criminal statutes as narrowly drawn, the codes are sufficiently general to make it necessary for prosecutors to interpret fact and law. Fact situations lend themselves to diverse interpretations of the kind and number of offenses to charge. Compassion intrudes now and then, as do periodic law enforcement campaigns and disagreements with archaic or unpopular statutes. Decisions must be made, and when the Code—or the prevailing ideology—prevents them from being made openly, each system finds ways to mask them. French prosecutors can "correctionalize" * a case, or, if the victim does not complain, they may dismiss it altogether. Italian prosecutors can find the evidence in a case insufficient for trial, though their real concern may be a matter of policy. If German prosecutors are unwilling to manipulate rules or to use the discretion they have, they can achieve the requisite flexibility by accepting the judgments about investigation and charging already made by the police. Ironically, these systemic compromises are made necessary by the very principle that they contradict. The principle of compulsory prosecution, which formally permeates the German and Italian systems, and informally the French, demands the impossible: full enforcement of the law in a time of rising crime and fierce competition for resources. Inevitably, adjustments

---

* [Editor's note: In French law crimes are classified as *crimes*, i. e., major offenses/felonies, and *delits*, i. e., minor offenses/misdemeanors. When a case is presented to the prosecutor, he or she must decide whether the case is a *crime* or a *delit*. *Crimes* are referred to a *juge d'instruction* for further investigation; *delits* are sent to a criminal court, a *tribunel correctionnel*, for trial. The decision to classify a case as a *delit* is described as "correctionalizing" a case.]

must be made in the way in which the principle is to be applied; where formal law or ideology does not permit these adjustments, informal processes are created that do.

Even the view of Continental trials as aggressive inquiries by "inquisitorial" judges does not survive close analysis. Such trials rarely occur because most cases are not contested. The accused may have confessed and provided corroborating detail, or his crime may have been witnessed by others, or he may have been caught in the act. And these facts are known to the trial judge because they are recorded in the dossier that he reads before conducting the trial. Under such circumstances, the trial becomes little more than a ritual confirmation of the police report or the prosecutor's file. In Continental systems, as in ours, truth is pursued in most cases in much the same way: police gather facts, put them into a file, and through processes of acquiescence and consensus, the file and the prosecutor's characterization of it usually govern the result.

Given these findings, the role of the prosecutor takes on a new importance. By reviewing the contents of the dossier, and by determining which route the case will subsequently travel, the prosecutor is clearly more important than the judge in controlling the law enforcement process. His characterization of facts and law, the degree to which he pursues investigative leads or is content to accept what the police bring to him, the extent to which he recommends leniency for an accused who offers confession, cooperation, or contrition—these become the levers by which the rest of the process is moved. Though often characterized as a "judicial" figure in the inquisitorial tradition, the Continental prosecutor (like his American counterpart) is essentially an administrator who is relatively unsupervised by the courts.

Still, the myth of judicial control persists and has a distorting effect. By formally placing investigations in the hands of judges or prosecutors, who interpret their impartial role to be a reactive one, these Continental systems may succeed only in giving greater autonomy to the police. The very fact that the police may be free of the cumbersome regulations associated with judicial investigations encourages prosecutors to delay or omit formal examinations and examining magistrates to delegate most of their work to the police. Similarly, where the principle or practice of compulsory prosecution exists, it is inevitable that the police will exercise broad discretion in deciding which cases to begin and may deprive the prosecutor—overwhelmed by the caseload and the inflexibility of his own charging options—of the ability to monitor their decisions. Finally, in assuming that the pretrial process can effectively be put under judicial, or even prosecutorial, regulation, trial judges may place unwarranted reliance on the regularity and completeness of dossiers that are in the end no more than police files.

This attitude is reinforced by the view—common among officials as well as scholars—that "law" is exclusively concerned with formal statutory provisions and that the *administration* of law belongs to a lower and more flexible order of things. In the moral hierarchy of the legal order, judges do not take note of how prosecutors administer the law, and prosecutors take little interest in what the police do. These officials treat as virtually "taboo" what seems to Americans to be inevitable. The existence of any choices in charging beyond those provided by law is steadfastly denied.

There is a marked reluctance to concede an open texture even within the authorized areas of choice. Obvious patterns of evasion, designed to introduce free play into an otherwise rigid system, are described without noting the role they play in solving systemic problems.

The consequence of such attitudes is that judges and prosecutors in these Continental systems are in fact more passive and reactive than in the United States. Trial judges depend on prosecutors or examining magistrates to take initiatives in investigating and charging, and prosecutors, though not regarding themselves as truly "judicial," accept enough of the myth to prevent themselves from adopting what they see as the partisan stance of their American counterparts. Designating them as "judicial" figures seems only to reinforce their natural inclination to be reactive to police initiatives. Paradoxically, it seems to deprive them of the aggressive, yet impartial, posture that Americans associate with the European "inquisitorial" style. Overall, the result is that both judges and prosecutors deny the choices with which they are inevitably faced, leaving the police to emerge as the dominant force in the process.

A result of treating choice and discretion as exceptional or extra-legal is that charging decisions may receive even less reasoned consideration than in the United States, with less prospect that they will soon be brought out into the open. By persisting in describing their practice as if it accorded with their theory, most Continental commentators have not yet faced up to the critical distinction between full enforcement as a "regulating ideal" and full enforcement as an actual fact. In the United States we have tended, until recently, to the opposite extreme, accepting prosecutorial discretion as absolute, inevitable, and ungovernable, and abandoning full enforcement even as an ideal. But the same forces that have provoked interest in Continental procedure point towards greater efforts here to bring the law in action into line with the law on the books.

We do not yet know whether increasing judicial responsibility for investigations and trials will solve the critical problems of American criminal procedure, but we can say that it is a mistake to look uncritically to Europe for the answer. The emphasis placed by inquisitorial theory on the role of the judge, not only in supervising investigation and trial, but in carrying the ultimate responsibility for enforcing the rule of law, has great force and may even deserve emulation in the United States. But Continental experience counsels caution. There may be inherent limits to what judges can and will do. It is not true that in Western Europe judges really supervise any but the most major criminal investigations. Nor do they see to it that discretion is either abolished or tamed, that no one offers inducements that produce tacit plea bargains, or that everyone plays according to the legal rules. The problem there, as here, is how to keep police and prosecutors from escaping the legal constraints imposed upon them.

In the end, these Continental systems rely more on their ideology, and on the assumption that officials adhere to the ideology, than on detailed judicial supervision. Ideology may be a powerful force in making most officials observe the rules even when no one is watching or threatening. But ideology is by no means an inexorable force; its effect may be enhanced or defeated by myriad practical considerations—institutional, economic, and psychological. Each procedural system must search for the combination of devices that is appropriate to its situation. It may be that single-theory models—whether inquisitorial or adversarial—will not work because they are inevitably stretched beyond their capacity by the phenomena they are designed to control.

To the issues we now face in American criminal justice—the regulation of police investigation, prosecutorial discretion, and the guilty plea—the usual debate about whether an "adversarial" or "inquisitorial" system more fairly and accurately searches out the truth hardly seems relevant. That debate concerns only the relatively few cases into which each system chooses to place its full efforts. For the rest, the overwhelming number, each system of criminal justice is driven to compromise principles that are regularly vindicated only when the full process is applied. The critical questions, which have not yet been honestly faced by any of the systems, are how cases that will receive less than the full process should be chosen, and what combination of adversarial procedures and judicial initiative should constitute that summary process.

[The following is taken from JOHN H. LANGBEIN * and LLOYD L. WEINRIEB,** "CONTINENTAL CRIMINAL PROCEDURE: 'MYTH' AND REALITY," 87 Yale Law Journal 1549 (1978). Footnotes are omitted.]

In a recent issue of this *Journal*, Professor Abraham Goldstein and Research Fellow Martin Marcus discussed their observations about the criminal procedures of three European countries, France, Germany, and Italy, as representative of the "Continental" or "inquisitorial" model of investigation and prosecution. Their inquiry was prompted, they said, by a desire to probe claims that in those countries the extreme form of prosecutorial discretion that produces plea bargaining and pervasive reliance on guilty pleas in the United States is avoided by greater judicial control and supervision of the process. They were concerned also to find out to what extent judicial supervision of the investigation of crime obviates our after-the-fact efforts to deter official abuses by the exclusion of evidence unlawfully obtained. Their conclusions are summarized in the title of their article: "Judicial supervision" is a "myth." The claim that Continental systems of criminal procedure adhere to a rule of law more strictly than ours is based not on fact but on "ideology" and "the assumption that officials adhere to the ideology." The prosecutor and, in their sphere, the police are dominant in Europe as they are here; judicial responsibility is mostly "reactive" to the primary roles played by other officials. The authors advise that we Americans be skeptical and cautious about borrowing from the models they describe.

We believe that Goldstein and Marcus have misinterpreted the most important characteristics of the procedures they intended to describe and that their descriptions are substantially misleading. .   .   .

* * *

Goldstein and Marcus proceed by setting up a model of Continental criminal procedure to contrast with American "accusatorial" process; in their model, prosecutorial discretion is either eliminated entirely or "care-

---

* Professor of Law, The University of Chicago.   ** Professor of Law, Harvard University.

fully controlled," and "full judicial inquiry . . . [is] made into every offense formally charged." Most of their article describes findings in the countries they studied that conflict with the model. The model, however, portrays inaccurately both the theory and the practice in those countries. Indeed, there is not, as the authors suppose, a single "model" to which the procedures of the three countries conform; the differences among them are in many respects as important as the similarities. Having found that their model is false, they conclude that the reality must resemble practices in this country. Their conclusions, however, based mostly on conjecture about what "must be" the underlying reality, are as far afield as the model they replace.

France

Taking the investigation of a case and the preparation of formal charges by a *juge d'instruction* (the investigating magistrate) as the prototype of French procedure, Goldstein and Marcus found that in the majority of cases the reality is different. An *instruction* (magisterial investigation) is required only for the most serious category of offenses, *crimes*, and not for the much larger category of *délits*, which includes not only our misdemeanors but also most of the less serious felonies. Often the *procureur*, who is responsible for the decision to send a case to a *juge d'instruction*, ignores evidence that an offense should be prosecuted as a *crime* and qualifies it as a *délit*, which is then sent directly to the court (*tribunal correctionnel*) for trial and judgment. This practice of "correctionalization" reduces still further the number of cases prepared by an investigating magistrate.

Goldstein and Marcus regard the small proportion of cases submitted to a *juge d'instruction*, and the practice of "correctionalization" in particular, as a departure from the "model" of French criminal procedure; they strongly intimate that, at least at a theoretical level, the failure to conduct a judicial investigation in most if not all cases is improper and to be regretted. That view reflects their preoccupation with their own false model. An *instruction* is not prescribed even in theory if the charge is for one of the less serious offenses and further investigation does not appear to be necessary. While it is undoubtedly true that the *procureur* "correctionalizes" offenses in order not to burden the process with an *instruction* in too many cases, his decision to do so does not evade a required procedure. One may believe that charges and convictions in France are too lenient; whether that is so or not, persons charged with *délits* are not denied an investigation they ought to have had. Indeed, as Goldstein and Marcus note, when a case has been "correctionalized," the accused can challenge the jurisdiction of the *tribunal correctionnel* and urge that the case be examined by a *juge*, in which case it may be qualified as a *crime*.

One might use the distinction between *crimes* and *délits* and the procedures required for each to make a point quite different from what the authors suggest: when the responsible state official believes that the investigation of an offense is incomplete, and in all cases in which the state intends to prove a major offense, there *is* an investigation under the direction of a magistrate. The lesson that we might draw from the French experience is that we should be skeptical of any proposal for elaborate post-crime investigation in all cases, not that judicial investigation, limited to cases in which it is most likely to be valuable, is a myth. The false model of a judicial investigation in every case takes our attention away from the question we ought to ask: whether the procedure actually provided in France for the large number of *délits* is preferable to ours in comparable cases.

Most of the time, the authors observe, the *procureur* himself does little investigation even when a case is not submitted to a *juge d'instruction*. Like an American prosecutor, he usually relies on evidence gathered by the police and presented to him in the *dossier* of the case. So, they say, "the overwhelming proportion of *délits* is likely to proceed to trial with a dossier that is little more than a police report." Similarly, the *juge* relies heavily on the work of the police for investigation of a *crime* that is not especially serious or complex. The authors conclude that whether one speaks of *délits* or *crimes*, "[b]ehind the veil of the formal requirements of the Code, the French *dossier*, the manner in which it is compiled, and even its contents may not be as different from an American prosecutor's file as is commonly supposed."

In France, as in the United States, ordinary crimes are "solved" mostly on the basis of evidence that police gather routinely as part of their initial response at the scene of the crime. In such cases, it is a matter of course that investigation is largely completed before the case reaches the *procureur;* that he or the *juge d'instruction* ordinarily relies on the information provided by the police is likely to surprise only those who have taken judicial investigation as the invariable standard. French procedure prescribes nothing to the contrary. One who is familiar with American police work, however, will be misled by the statement that the French *dossier* is "little more than a police report." In this country, a "police report" is primarily an internal police document, the report of an incident that called for some response by the police and, if the incident was criminal and someone was arrested for the crime, a record of how it was cleared. The police are not expected to provide a legally competent basis for prosecution and conviction. The preparation of the report is subject to no prosecutorial requirements of form or content; it is used by the prosecutor, if at all, only as an unofficial document without evidentiary significance. The French *dossier*, on the other hand, is prepared and intended to be used as part of the evidentiary basis of the judgment. In their capacity as *police judiciaire*—which Goldstein and Marcus summarily dismiss as a fiction—French police are expected to prepare an investigative record that is complete and formally correct, available to the defense as well as the prosecution, and able to withstand a searching examination. If the *dossier* is inadequate to prove the commission of an offense, unless the case is dropped it must be turned over to a *juge d'instruction* for further investigation. Of course, a *dossier* is more easily compiled if the facts are uncomplicated and beyond dispute than if they are not. In the easy cases as well as the hard, the *dossier* of a French case, *crime* or *délit*, ordinarily provides a permanent record of both inculpatory and exculpatory evidence that is substantially superior to anything regularly available in this country short of a trial transcript.

Goldstein and Marcus' specific comments about the investigative responsibility of the French police do not concern the adequacy of the investigative record, but rather the lack of "judicial" oversight of police illegality. Again they observe that their model of judicial supervision of investigations has limited application—as it must unless police are to be accompanied by magistrates when they go to the scene of a crime. Beyond that, the authors are surprised by the lack of effective "review after the fact." The French *juge d'instruction* and the courts rarely inquire into the legality of police conduct; although they have authority to "nullify" an illegal act, they rarely do so in the manner of this country, by excluding illegally obtained evidence.

To a considerable extent, this simply makes the point that the exclusion of evidence is not applied as a remedy for police misconduct in France as it is here. Whether or not the exclusion of illegally obtained evidence is desirable, the late and faltering resort to that remedy in this country shows that it is not an essential characteristic of one process more than another. In England, where criminal procedure more closely resembles ours, the automatic application of an exclusionary rule has consistently been rejected. There are also differences between French and American law concerning what police practices are permissible, which have nothing to do one way or another with the choice of procedures for prosecution. A greater degree of force and, in our terms, abuse by the police is tolerated in France than is tolerated here, an aspect of the generally more authoritarian relationship between the state and the individual. The French code, for example, expressly authorizes under certain conditions the kind of custodial interrogation that, at least before *Miranda,* was carried out by police in this country without any authorization at all. We should not compare conduct that is lawful in France with conduct that is unlawful here and then conclude that, because it would be unlawful here, it is irregular and unsupervised in France.

For all their apparent disapproval of French police practices, Goldstein and Marcus say nothing to indicate whether or not French police are. generally responsive to the rules circumscribing their authority. Unaccountably, the authors do not mention that in the performance of criminal investigations, the French police are subject to the supervision and control of the magistracy (the *procureur* in particular). The *procureur* makes regular evaluations of the police officers subject to his supervision, which become part of the officers' official record. There is thus the framework for direct bureaucratic control of the police, for lack of which in this country we have had to depend on the dubious deterrent effect of exclusionary rules. That control is far from perfect and is much criticized by the French themselves; it is evidently less successful than the German bureaucratic structure that it somewhat resembles. But to ignore it altogether makes comparison worthless.

The concept of "judicial police" that Goldstein and Marcus dismiss as a fiction is not intended to suggest that the police are magistrates but that, however imperfectly, the investigative functions of the police are integrated into the criminal process and responsive to its demands, rather than to an entirely separate definition of their role. There is far more to be learned from the strengths and weaknesses alike of the institutional structure of the French police and its relationship to criminal prosecution than we are told simply by a comparison of exclusionary rules there and here.

The absence of direct judicial supervision of criminal investigation in France is not repaired, Goldstein and Marcus believe, by the trial. Although in theory the trial is "an active inquiry by the court into the defendant's guilt," for the "simpler and more routine cases," which are the majority, the Continental trial is, they assert, scarcely distinguishable from the entry of a guilty plea before a judge who conscientiously inquires into the basis of the plea before accepting it. The authors, however, say scarcely anything about the conduct of a French trial except to note that proceedings in the *tribunal correctionnel* may be swift, even "perfunctory," if the accused does not contest his guilt; in such cases, "the key to the sufficiency of the evidence and accuracy of the charge lies more in the dossier than in the trial itself."

Goldstein and Marcus do not suggest that a searching inquiry of contested facts is not available to an accused charged with a *crime* or a *délit*. Rather they claim that an accused is subject to pressure comparable to that of plea bargaining in this country not to contest the charges. Just as here, they say, dispositions are "plainly affected by what the prosecutor or judge may do for the accused, and what he may do for them." Most of their concrete observations about French practices, however, point the other way. They note that *procureurs* consistently deny that they engage in practices comparable to plea bargaining.

> "[*Procureurs*] insist that they do not reward confessions and co-operation with a favorable exercise of their discretion not to charge. They express suspicion of informers and hostility toward bargaining and profess to leave considerations of mercy to the courts. The system gives them the authority but not the inclination to drop the cases of helpful offenders; historic deference to the judge predisposes prosecutors to send cases on for trial and whatever amelioration the court may provide."

Nor does any of their information from other sources contradict the *procureurs'* description. The authors report that while there may be "conversations between prosecutor and defense counsel . . . there is little or no talk of 'trading' a confession for the reduction or 'correctionalization' of the charges." In sharp contrast with this country, where prosecutors and defense counsel acknowledge that they bargain and defense counsel in particular often assert their special ability to obtain a favorable bargain, in France plea bargaining is contrary to practice and to professional ethics alike.

How then do Goldstein and Marcus conclude that plea bargaining, or a close analogue, is a part of the French process? Aside from some general observations that in Europe, as here, a prosecuting official may have the power to deal leniently with an accused who cooperates, they rely entirely, despite what they were told, on the practice of "correctionalization": when the *procureur* "correctionalizes," "he is, in effect, offering an accused a lesser sentence for a *délit* in exchange for a waiver by the accused of the full process that he would have if he were charged with a *crime*."

This account of "correctionalization" as crypto-plea-bargaining would be unrecognizable to the persons who are supposed to engage in it. Starting once again from their own model, Goldstein and Marcus describe the situation of a French accused as if he were entitled to a judicial investigation, which he sacrifices in exchange for the certainty that this sentence will not exceed that prescribed for a *délit*. He is thus made to resemble the American defendant who gives up a trial for some benefit in sentencing. But it would startle all of those involved, the accused not least, to suggest that he has given up something when he does not insist on being prosecuted for a more serious offense. In France, unlike the United States, the seriousness of the accusation does have a bearing on the process of prosecution, and that has nothing to do with the accused's acceptance of a deal. The *procureur* makes the decision to "correctionalize" without discussing it with the accused or his lawyer. The accused ordinarily has no reason to suppose that the more elaborate proceeding for a *crime* would give him an advantage, lost if he pleads guilty, comparable to the American defendant's chance for an acquittal.

Unlike the American defendant who pleads guilty, a French accused who accepts "correctionalization" of the offense is not bound to accept the prosecution's evidence against him. No doubt an accused sometimes cooperates, in a sense unwillingly, because he hopes to benefit in some way. But his cooperation is not a condition of "correctionalization" explicitly or implicitly. The accused can, and often does, put the prosecution to its proof. He can claim his complete innocence of the charges, question the evidence against him, and present his own, without risking the loss of his side of the supposed bargain. In sharp contrast, the American defendant risks rejection of his guilty plea unless he corroborates the charges. Before the *tribunal correctionnel* as much as before the *Cour d'assises*, which judges *crimes*, conviction depends on the proof of guilt contained in the *dossier* and presented to the court.

Part of the explanation for Goldstein and Marcus' Americanized account of French criminal procedure is their overriding presupposition that investigative and prosecutorial functions are necessarily separate from judicial functions and cannot be performed with the attributes that we associate with the latter. So they assume that the "judicial responsibility" for which they were searching can only mean supervision by a judge of other officials, the police and prosecutors. The possibility that "judicial responsibility" might in some respects be provided by a redefinition of roles and integration of functions is ignored. Insistence that, in this context, a rose is a rose is a rose makes good sense if one has exclusively in mind the American criminal process. Not only are the prosecutorial and investigative functions separate from the judicial function in this country, but it is also a matter of principle that they be kept so. It is just that principle of separation, however, that has been rejected in France by long tradition. There are substantial links between prosecutorial and judicial functions unlike the alignment here, where district attorney and defense counsel share a common function as lawyers that is distinguished sharply from the role of a judge. Both the *procureurs* and the *juges d'instruction* are part of the magistracy, the former called *magistrats du parquet* and the latter *magistrats du siége*. *Magistrats* receive professional training in common, which includes the work of both branches of the magistracy and is distinct from the training of private attorneys. *Magistrats* of both types belong to common professional associations. Over the course of their careers, it is not uncommon for *magistrats* to change office from *magistrat du parquet* to *magistrat du siége*, and the reverse. Goldstein and Marcus disregard all of this, evidently because it is a "resort to fictions" to assert that the *procureur* is anything but an American prosecutor. We do not suggest that the combination of investigative or prosecutorial functions with judicial functions be approved or imitated uncritically. It is one thing, however, to conclude on the basis of close observation that such combination has been, or is likely to be, unsuccessful, quite another to label it a "fiction" and let it go at that.

* * *

As we have indicated, to a considerable extent Goldstein and Marcus are themselves captives of the myths they seek to explore. No practitioner or scholar in the countries they visited would assert that the procedures followed in the large majority of routine cases include the elaborate and extended investigative and adjudicative processes that characterize the most difficult and serious cases. If such a misconception can indeed be derived from some of the writings in English that Goldstein and Marcus exclusively quote, there is all the more reason not to rely only on such sources for descriptions of what actually occurs. We confess that we are baffled by an article in which the authors purport to describe the criminal procedures of three foreign countries, but refer to none of the literature of those countries and acknowledge that they have not even "reviewed" the foreign literature. They evidently made scant observations of their own in each of the countries and rely for their conclusions on interviews framed in advance on the basis of the literature in English, which they themselves say contains little except descriptions of the criminal codes. We wonder how seriously they would receive an article about American criminal procedure written in French by a Frenchman who had read none of the literature available in this country and whose personal observations were similarly limited.

Because we agree with Goldstein and Marcus that the time may be propitious for a critical assessment of criminal procedure in this country, we believe that the matters they discuss in their article are of considerable importance. We agree emphatically that the issues ought not be framed as a choice between "the adversarial model" and "the inquisitorial model," especially if the two models are presented as theoretical abstractions unrelated to the conditions in which they are or might be realized. The point made at the conclusion of their article—that any procedures that we devise must allow the relatively swift, summary disposition of most cases and must reserve painstaking and costly procedures for the few that are unusual, because of their seriousness or complexity or the inconclusiveness of readily available evidence—is correct, and it is fundamental to any effort to improve our criminal process. All of that is, indeed, borne out by the experience elsewhere.

On the other hand, we think there is far more to be learned from other countries' experience, particularly that of France and Germany which we know best, than Goldstein and Marcus allow. Summary procedures for determining guilt are not necessarily all alike just because they are the primary means of disposing of large numbers of cases. It is no less important to ask which system "more fairly and accurately searches out the truth" when we are comparing modes of simple, swift process than when we are comparing more painstaking procedures. We do not suppose that Goldstein and Marcus believe otherwise. Yet along with their dismissal of a comparison of unreal prototypes, they seem very nearly to dismiss a comparison of what actually takes place.

Much as we are encouraged by the effort to learn about criminal process elsewhere, we are also dismayed by the assumption that observations can be made accurately and interpreted without laying aside preconceptions engendered by the procedures we want to improve. It is simply pointless to study practices different from our own if one is guided by an *a priori* assumption that after all they cannot be very different. We do not ask for uncritical acceptance of foreign judgments that other procedures are preferable to ours. We do not assume that the social values and objectives that determine the criminal process abroad are in all respects the same as ours or that even when they are, what works elsewhere must work for us as well. We do believe that it is significant that dissatisfaction with criminal justice is greater and deeper at all levels, professional and public, in this country than it is in Western Europe; we believe that it is foolish and dangerous to suppose that the whole explanation for our dissatisfaction can be found in a greater commitment to the ideal of justice or a more acute perception of reality. If we look elsewhere expecting to find only what is familiar, our expectations will easily be confirmed. We shall, then, all too comfortably confuse the familiar with the necessary.

[The following is taken from ABRAHAM S. GOLDSTEIN and MARTIN MARCUS, "COMMENT ON CONTINENTAL CRIMINAL PROCEDURE," 87 Yale Law Journal 1570 (1978). Footnotes are omitted.]

In December 1977, we published in this *Journal* the results of a study we had made of Continental criminal procedure. We noted that in the face of a new concern in the United States for overly broad prosecutorial discretion, a growing mistrust of plea bargaining, and a continuing doubt of the effectiveness of exclusionary rules, American commentators had begun to turn to so-called "inquisitorial" systems for guidance. The literature then available in English described many of these systems as operating without prosecutorial discretion or with discretion carefully controlled, functioning without guilty pleas, and providing a full pretrial judicial (or quasi-judicial) investigation for serious cases. We were concerned that this literature might be misleading—that it might have described only how the codes of criminal procedure provided that these systems should operate, and not how they actually do. We decided to explore these issues by interviewing prosecutors, judges, defense attorneys, and scholars in France, Germany, and Italy. In reporting the results of those interviews, we hoped to stimulate the attitude of critical inquiry so crucial to any "borrowing" from the institutions of another country. We also wanted to encourage the development of a more detailed body of knowledge of the operation of these systems.

From our interviews, we concluded that judges in "inquisitorial" systems do not control or supervise the investigation, prosecution, or trial of most criminal cases much more closely than do judges in our own "adversarial" systems. We found that investigation was generally left to the police and that—despite statutory prohibitions to the contrary—charging discretion was exercised frequently and without significant supervision by both police and prosecutor. Although plea bargaining as such does not take place, we found analogous processes by which prosecutor and defendant made similar accommodations through "tacit understandings or patterns of reciprocal expectation."

In their response to our article, Professors Langbein and Weinreb regrettably seem to be more committed to presenting a formalistic view of European procedures than to communicating how such procedures work and the extent to which they may deviate from formal requirements. Their appraisal of French and German procedure reflects little of the skepticism about the relation between law on the books and law in action that they undoubtedly would bring to bear in discussing American criminal procedure. Seeing the seeds of domestic reform in practices abroad, they ignore elements that might call some of those reforms into question. In this respect, they may be even more bound to formalism than many European observers. As happens all too often, the acolytes may be more faithful than the priests.

Although Langbein and Weinreb assert that we have not fairly described the operation of the French and German systems, they do not challenge our central findings. For example, they concede that in France cases are "correctionalized"—treated as *délits* though chargeable as *crimes*—"in order not to burden the process" with unnecessary judicial investigations. They admit that "ordinary crimes" are routinely investigated in France only by the police and that the prosecutor usually relies on the evidence he receives from them. And they do not contest our view that most French trials are perfunctory proceedings in which " 'the key to the sufficiency of the evidence and accuracy of the charge lies more in the dossier than in the trial itself.' " Similarly, they do not challenge our contention that German criminal investigations are dominated by the police, that uncontested trials are shorter than contested ones, and that " '[i]f there is no apparent reason for the judge to question a witness closely and if there is no encouragement from counsel or the parties for him to do so, the result is a trial that is not especially probing and is unlikely to stray far from the dossier.' "

We were concerned that the failure of the American and English literature on Continental criminal procedure to describe when and what summary procedures were employed would mislead Americans into believing that on the Continent summary procedures were somehow not necessary. Langbein and Weinreb do not charge us so much with inaccurately describing these procedures as with mischaracterizing them. They are troubled, for example, when we analogize French "correctionalization" and the German penal order to American plea bargaining and when we find in uncontested Continental trials striking similarities to the taking of guilty pleas in the United States. They assert that we measure these summary procedures (along with comparable Italian devices) against an unrealistic yardstick of judicial supervision of the entire criminal process and that we unfairly suggest that these common-sense shortcuts are either unlawful or improper deviations from an "inquisitorial" norm.

Our point, however, was not to criticize summary procedures. Like Langbein and Weinreb, we realize that not all cases can or should receive a thorough judicial investigation and trial. Our purpose was to explain the ways in which Continental systems respond to problems like those we face in the United States and the extent to which their summary procedures may serve similar ends. Our critics resist this analysis. They admit that the French prosecutor "correctionalizes" cases to relieve the system of the obligation to conduct unnecessary judicial examinations, but, paradoxically, they claim that "his decision to do so does not evade a required procedure." They assume that because French prosecutors and defendants do not explicitly bargain over "correctionalization" or make other promises to exchange cooperation for leniency, the "seriousness of the accusation [in France] does have a bearing on the process of the prosecution," while in the United States it does not. This assertion errs in both directions: French "correctionalization" plainly allows factors other than the seriousness of the charge to affect the mode of prosecution; just as plainly, the seriousness of the charge in the United States is critically important to the scope of any bargaining that takes place about the plea or sentence.

* * *

The authors also maintain that we "dismiss as insignificant all the differences in the selection, training, and professional codes" of police and prosecutors, "as well as the institutional structure within which they work." We do not recognize, they say, that these officials can be fairly said to serve "judicial" functions, that *dossiers* prepared by the judicial police are something more than American police reports, and that judgments made by Continental prosecutors—even when made beyond the confines of the codes that regulate their conduct—are more evenhanded than comparable decisions by their American counterparts. With this criticism, the authors reveal that at bottom they do not rely on differences between "inquisitorial" and "adversarial" procedure but instead on the very point we affirm, that "[i]n the end these Continental systems rely more on their ideology, and on the assumption that officials adhere to the ideology, than on detailed judicial supervision." Our prosecutors, like those in Continental systems, are charged with the duty of uncovering exculpatory as well as inculpatory evidence. Our police, like theirs, are bound by law and face disciplinary proceedings and civil and criminal penalties when they violate it. Naked assertions that Continental officials are more committed ideologically or institutionally to the rule of law do not advance the debate on the merits of borrowing inquisitorial procedures.

We are not hostile to the redefinition of the judicial role in the American system. Indeed, one of us wrote earlier that in the United States

> "we are held captive by models built on the adversary trial. Yet it makes little sense to carry the idea of a reactive judge in an adversary trial to the quite different context of the judge who must supervise administrative processes. Adversary processes and accusatorial premises may be inapplicable to a system which has changed its shape and which increasingly casts the judge in a proactive role. We might better be served by practices drawn from inquisitorial systems, in which judges are routinely assigned tasks which are administrative and supervisory."

We looked to Continental criminal procedure precisely because it is there that a more active and effective judicial role is claimed. But our findings suggest the need to learn the limits of what judges and other officials can do and to assess the risk that judicial control may drive decisions into hiding in the inevitable cracks among the provisions of a code of criminal procedure. We reported our findings not to end an interesting and potentially important debate, but instead to develop it further by encouraging the analysis of issues and the production of empirical evidence that might separate myth from reality. The response by Professors Langbein and Weinreb suggests that the myths persist and continue to intrude in appraising the significance of European procedures for American criminal justice.

Chapter 4

THE TRIAL

It is the essence of legal procedure—and the quintessence of court procedure—that it is "staged," in the sense that it proceeds step by step. We have considered one stage in court procedure, the procedure prior to trial, and we have seen that this stage of litigation involves a series of steps in which (a) the plaintiff's (in criminal cases the prosecution's) charges are disclosed to the defendant, (b) the defendant's response is made known to the plaintiff or prosecutor, and (c) preparation by both sides ensues. This treatment of procedure prior to trial has thus emphasized the function of this stage of litigation as a preliminary or preparatory process which precedes a second stage of litigation, the trial. However, the judicial resolution of a dispute does not always require a trial. The pre-trial process may have, in addition to its preliminary and preparatory function, the function of finally resolving a dispute. For example, the relatively full disclosure of information which is possible under modern practice may lead to a settlement of a civil case by agreement of the parties. (Such agreements may be registered with the court and accorded the same effect as a judgment.) Furthermore, the pre-trial process may result in dismissal of the case by the court on the ground, for example, that the court does not have jurisdiction—in any of the various meanings of that word—or because the complaint fails to state a good cause of action (see *e. g.* Dioguardi v. Durning, *supra* p. 176), or because, in a criminal case, the indictment is defective. Moreover, the pre-trial phase may provide an opportunity for adjudication and judgment on the merits of a case. Thus, for example, in Poe v. Ullman (*supra* p. 92) the pleadings raised issues of law, constitutional law, which proved to be the crux of the dispute and which were resolved without trial. Note, however, that such disposition of a case in the pre-trial phase does not mean that there is no judicial hearing of the matter, but only that the case is resolved without that particular kind of hearing which is commonly called a trial.

What then is a trial and when is a trial necessary?

A trial is a judicial hearing in which (a) issues of fact that are still in dispute after the close of the pre-trial phase are finally resolved on the basis of information (evidence) from which findings of fact can be made, and (b) issues of law (that is, questions concerning the legal consequences of the facts proved) are decided, often after the hearing of argument by the opposing sides concerning the applicable law. This is essential for it is the ultimate function of the trial court to render judgment according to the facts as found and according to the applicable law. (Note that fact and law are not completely separable, for the facts in a case are not raw facts, but facts legally categorized. See Llewellyn, *supra* p. 167.)

A trial is necessary when the pre-trial stage ends in the preparation of a live case in which there are disputed—unresolved—questions of *fact*, for it is the unique and distinguishing characteristic of the trial that it provides the process for the authoritative resolution of issues of fact after the presentation of proof.

The trial stage, like the pre-trial stage, involves a series of steps through which the parties present evidence and argument as to fact and law.

The trial, in a civil case, commences customarily with the plaintiff's attorney's opening statement to the jury (or to the judge if the trial is without a jury), which explains the issues and what the plaintiff proposes to prove. Then the plaintiff's first witness is called to the stand. The examination of the witness by the plaintiff's lawyer— so-called direct examination—may be followed by examination of the same witness by the opposing lawyer—so-called cross-examination— and that in turn by re-direct and re-cross-examination. After both sides have finished questioning the first witness, the plaintiff's attorney may call a second, and so on. When the plaintiff's attorney completes the introduction of evidence, the plaintiff "rests". It is now the defendant's attorney's turn to make an opening statement and to call witnesses who are, in turn, subject to cross-examination by the plaintiff's attorney. Following presentation of the defendant's case, the plaintiff has the chance to offer rebuttal evidence, limited to evidence to meet new facts put in evidence by the defendant. After the rebuttal the defendant may present evidence in rejoinder, subject to the same limitation. And so on—until both parties rest.

When the presentation of proof is thus completed, each party is allowed to make a closing statement to sum up the case—particularly on the facts—for the benefit of judge or jury. In addition the parties may file written arguments on the applicable law for the consideration of the judge. In a trial conducted by a judge sitting without a jury, the case is submitted to the judge who makes findings of fact and law and announces the judgment based on these findings. In a jury trial, it is the judge's function to instruct the jury on the applicable law, and then to submit the case to the jury which retires from the courtroom to deliberate on the case. If the jury reaches a decision it announces a verdict—usually in the form, "We find for the plaintiff" or "we find for the defendant"—and the amount of damages, if any are awarded. The judgment of the court is then entered in accordance with the jury verdict—in most cases.

The materials in this chapter are concerned with aspects of the trial process, particularly the fact finding function in the trial court.

SECTION 14. THE SCIENCE AND THE ART OF PROOF

SECTION 14.1 WHAT ARE THE FACTS

[The following is taken from JEROME FRANK,* COURTS ON TRIAL (Princeton, 1949), pp. 14–16. Some footnotes omitted; others are renumbered.]

If you scrutinize a legal rule, you will see that it is a conditional statement referring to facts. Such a rule seems to say, in effect, "If such and such a fact exists, then this or that legal consequence should follow." It seems to say, for example, "If a trustee, for his own purposes, uses money he holds in trust, he must repay it." Or, "If a man, without provocation, kills another, the killer must be punished." In other words, a legal rule directs that (if properly asked to do so) a court should attach knowable consequences to certain facts, if and whenever there are such facts. That is what is meant by the conventional statement, used in describing the decisional process, that courts apply legal rules to the facts of law-suits.[1]

For convenience, let us symbolize a legal rule by the letter R, the facts of a case by the letter F, and the court's decision of that case by the letter D. We can then crudely schematize the conventional theory of how courts operate by saying

$$R \times F = D$$

In other words, according to the conventional theory, a decision is a product of an R and an F. If, as to any lawsuit, you know the R and the F, you should, then, know what the D will be.

* Judge Jerome Frank served on the U. S. Court of Appeals for the second circuit from 1941 until his death in 1957. Prior to that time he had held many public offices, having been General Counsel, Agricultural Adjustment Administration (1933–1935), and Commissioner—later Chairman—of the Securities and Exchange Commission (1937–1941). From 1946 to 1957 he was a lecturer at the Yale Law School. Judge Frank excelled as teacher, lawyer, administrator, and judge but he is perhaps best remembered as an insightful critic of the legal process. His major writings in addition to Courts on Trial are, Law and the Modern Mind (1930), If Men Were Angels (1942), and Not Guilty (1957).

1. I am here referring to so-called "substantive" rules, which state that certain sorts of out-of-court conduct, will, in court, yield certain consequences. There is another kind of rules, rules of "procedure," which relate to the way cases in court should be commenced and tried. I shall discuss those rules later. Suffice it to say here that upper courts, on appeals, deal not only with "substantive" rules, but also try to see that trial courts do not too widely depart from the "procedural" rules.

In a simple, stable, society, most of the R's are moderately well stabilized. Which legal rules that society will enforce it is not difficult for men— or at any rate, for the lawyer, the professional court-man—to know in advance of any trial. In such a society, the R—one of the two factors in the $R \times F = D$ formula—is usually fixed.

In our society, however, with the rapid changes brought about by modern life, many of the R's have become unstable. Accordingly, in our times, legal uncertainty—uncertainty about future decisions and therefore about legal rights—is generally ascribed to the indefiniteness of the R's. The increasing multiplicity of the rules, the conflicts between rules, and the flexibility of some of the rules, have arrested the attention of most legal thinkers. Those thinkers, perceiving the absence of rigidity in some rules, have assumed that the certainty or uncertainty of the D's, in the $R \times F = D$ equation, stems principally from the certainty or uncertainty of the R's.

That assumption leads to a grave miscomprehension of court-house government and to the neglect by most legal scholars of the more difficult part of the courts' undertaking. I refer to the courts' task with respect to the other factor in the $R \times F = D$ formula, the F. The courts, as we saw, are supposed to ascertain the facts in the disputes which become law-suits. That is, a court is supposed to determine the actual, objective acts of the parties, to find out just what they did or did not do, before the law-suit began, so far as those facts bear on the compliance with, or the violation of, some legal rule. If there is uncertainty as to whether the court will find the true relevant facts—if it is uncertain whether the court's F will match the real, objective F—then what? Then, since the decision, the D, is presumably the joint product of an R and an F, the D is bound to be uncertain. To put it differently: No matter how certain the legal rules may be, the decisions remain at the mercy of the courts' fact-finding. If there is doubt about what a court, in a law-suit, will find were the facts, then there is at least equal doubt about its decision.

* * *

What is the F? Is it what actually happened . . . ? Most emphatically not. At best, it is only what the trial court—the trial judge or jury— thinks happened? What the trial court thinks happened may, however, be hopelessly incorrect. But that does not matter—legally speaking. For court purposes, what the court thinks about the facts is all that matters. The actual events, the real objective acts and words . . . happened in the past. They do not walk into court. The court usually learns about these real, objective, past facts only through the oral testimony of fallible witnesses. Accordingly, the court, from hearing the testimony, must guess at the actual, past facts. Judicially, the facts consist of the reaction of the judge or jury to the testimony. The F is merely a guess about the actual facts. There can be no assurance that that F, that guess, will coincide with those actual, past facts.

To be sure, this difficulty becomes of no importance when the parties to the suit do not dispute about the facts, when their sole difference concerns the proper R. Then the R will settle the court fight. . . .

. . . With reference to that sort of law-suit, the trained lawyer, as a specialist in the R's, is frequently an excellent predicter of decisions. For often (although not always) the applicable R is fairly certain and knowable, or sufficiently so that a competent lawyer can foretell what the court will say it is.

But usually, when men "go to law," the facts are not admitted, and the testimony is oral and in conflict. For convenience, call such suits "contested" cases. It cannot be known in advance which cases will be "contested." To predict a decision in a suit not yet begun, about a dispute which has not yet occurred, requires then, the most extensive guessing. For whenever there is a question of the credibility of witnesses—of the believability, the reliability, of their testimony—then, unavoidably, the trial judge or jury must make a guess about the facts. The lawyer, accordingly, must make a guess about those guesses. The uncertainty of many "legal rights" corresponds to the correctness or incorrectness of such lawyer-guesses.

[Review the extract from KARL N. LLEWELLYN, THE BRAMBLE BUSH, p. 48 ff, reprinted *supra* at p. 167]

Question

Judge Frank and Professor Llewellyn both raise the question, "What are the facts?" Were they addressing themselves to the same aspects of that question?

SECTION 14.2   EVIDENCE

[The following is taken from JOHN H. WIGMORE,* A STUDENTS' TEXTBOOK OF THE LAW OF EVIDENCE (Chicago, 1935), p. 1 ff. Footnotes are omitted.]

Sec. 1. *History of the Jury-Trial Rules of Evidence.* (1) All down through the ages, in every region, clime, and people, comes the never-ending quest for Truth in Justice. "Evidence," said Jeremy Bentham, "is the basis of Justice." The Egyptian legislator-king Harmhab [Hammurabi], three thousand years ago, in one of his edicts tells us how earnestly he strove after this great end: "I have sailed and traveled throughout the land, seeking judges perfect in speech, upright in character, and skilled in penetrating the innermost thoughts of men. I have instructed them in the ways of justice." Wherever a community has reached a stage of organized justice, it is found devising and developing and relying upon some method, however crude, for searching out Truth, upon which Justice must ever be founded. Each culture, whatever its stage of advancement, has sought and found some method or system of its own,—a method congenial to the combined influences of climate, religion, social manners, temperament, economics, and government.

---

* John Henry Wigmore (1863–1943) was Professor of Law (1893–1943) and Dean of the Faculty of Law (1901–1929) at Northwestern University. He was, perhaps, the leading American authority on the law of evidence. His ten volume treatise on evidence is still the standard reference work on the subject.

The precocious Egyptian and Babylonian kings with their royal courts, —the Hindu rajah with his Brahman pundits,—the Hebrew people with their rabbi-judges,—the Islamic Arabs with their kadis and muftis, stand out in Oriental history. In the Occidental regions, the Greeks with their juries, and the Romans with their praetors, devised new expedients. Then came the Celts with their brehons, the Germanics with their ordeals and compurgation oaths, the Scandinavians with their law-men and law-speakers. Meanwhile the still primitive African tribes, according to varying degrees of intelligence, put faith in their fetishes, or their witch-doctors, or their palaver-assemblies. And through all these periods appears from time to time the ideal figure of the all-wise judge, who needs no formal system but pierces to the truth with his own native shrewdness and intuition,—a Daniel and a Solomon in the Hebrew annals, a Manu in the Buddhist, a Lan Lu-Chow in the Chinese, a Shotoku and an Oka in the Japanese.

And so at last the eternal quest develops two phases which have dominated and spread furthest in modern times,—the Ecclesiastical system and its successor the Romanesque system, with its bench of judges and few rules of evidence, and the English system, with its judge and lay jury and an elaborate network of evidence rules.

The English system has become the inheritance of our own country. But the Romanesque system (which today dominates in Continental Europe and in Latin America) had many points of contact with English judicial history, and its influence explains some of the rules that are to be considered later.

(2) The Romanesque system was developed originally by the Church courts, beginning about the 1200's. The Church (or Canon) system of justice was during that period far in advance of that of the royal and local baronial courts. The judge directed the gathering of evidence and was the sole arbiter of it; there was no jury of laymen. But judges were only human and they often lacked experience. Gradually a set of rules for obtaining and weighing evidence was built up. Ponderous volumes were written, embodying rules of guidance. There were many rules for (what we now call) circumstantial evidence or (as they called it) presumptive evidence, and many rules also for testimonial evidence.

But, as in many other legal systems, these rules later became overdeveloped. They began to be merely cramping rules—not guides, but self-sufficient formulas. For example, the simple principle that there must be two good witnesses for every main fact was developed into a network of artificial refinements, assigning the value of one-half (of a good witness) to certain relatives, and one-quarter to another kind of person, one-eighth to another, and so on; and allowing the judge to determine a fact by the mere arithmetical calculation of those fractions and integers.

This system had gone to seed by the end of the 1700's. When France, under Napoleon, framed its codes in the first decade of the 1800's, the system was abolished as being a mere hindrance. All the other continental nations, as well as the Latin American nations (in due time taking the French codes as their models), also abandoned this system. It had been known as the system of "legal evidence" (*preuves légales*). In its place there was now to be no system at all, i. e., the judge (and the jury) were to be free to hear and to weigh any evidence, without legal limitations. In France this principle is known as "natural proof" or "moral proof"; in Germany, as "free proof"; in Italy, as "rational persuasion."

In modern times, certain fixed rules have indeed again grown up, principally for the proof of documents. In very recent times, also, the art of investigation by scientific police methods, and the study of the psychology of testimony, have produced copious aids for the judge in using evidence. But (in contrast with our system) there is no analogous body of elaborate controlling rules of admissibility of evidence. A main reason is that the judge's discretion, even where the jury is used (in criminal trials), largely determines what evidence is to be used. The exclusionary rules are scanty.

(3) The contrasting features of the English system are due chiefly to use of the jury in all cases, criminal and civil (except chancery), but secondarily to a certain English spirit of fair play, or "true sport," in legal procedure generally. Moreover, the development of the system of evidence rules is fairly modern—scarcely two centuries old. In the United States, furthermore, its peculiarity is that the few score fundamental rules have been finespun into some thousands of refined discriminations, calling for a mastery that few lawyers or judges can claim to possess for ready use.

The way in which the jury influenced the development of these rules was as follows:

When the Norman judges organized the jury to assist them in their investigations, the jurors were at first left to their own discretion in the use of evidence (except for a few rules about documents). They might use their own impressions, obtained in the vicinage, and they might even go about among the neighbors asking for information out of court. In the earliest period, witnesses in court were not commonly heard—due chiefly to a scruple about "maintenance" (or officious intermeddling to influence the jury). But as this feature gradually disappeared, and witnesses in court became a usual means of information (say, in the later 1500's), the jury's own "knowledge" played a minor part. Finally, by the end of the 1600's, the jury were deemed and allowed to have no information except what was offered in court,—a complete reversal of function.

But this signified, to experienced judges, that the jurors, untrained in valuing evidence, must have guidance. Somewhat was given, to be sure, by the judge's comments, or "summing up." But more than guidance was needed; rules of restriction upon the mere admission of evidence were needed, to prevent the jurors from being misled by irrelevancies, or by biased or fraudulent testimony, or by their own emotions, sympathies, and prejudices. Accordingly the next two centuries (1600's and 1700's) saw the gradual growth of numerous exclusionary rules, keeping out various kinds of evidence. This growth had a rapid and complex expansion in the early 1800's. In short, the judges had developed a network of rules, like a sieve, which allowed only the rational and safe and valuable tidbits to get through to the jury.

Such is the basis, and such the spirit, of the Anglo-American system of jury-trial rules of evidence.

Thus it is *not* a pure *science* of logical proof. It is not rules for *weighing* evidence. It is a system of rules of *admissibility*. Without putting one's mind into this attitude one cannot well appreciate or use the rules. They are based on a long judicial experience with parties, witnesses, and jurors.

They aim to let the jury have only evidence that is as free as feasible from the known risks of irrelevancy, confusion, and fraud.

But it is important to remember that all of the fundamental rules have some *reason* underneath. They are not arbitrary. Their aim is to get at the truth by calm and careful reasoning. "The letter of the Law," once said old Serjeant Plowden, "is the body of the Law, but the sense and reason of it is the soul." Therefore to understand the reason of the rules is to be half way towards mastery of the rules deduced from those reasons. And in the following exposition of them the reason, or principle, will always be emphasized.

Sec. 2. *Definitions: Law and Fact; Argument and Evidence; Substantive Law and Evidence.* But, before proceeding to the rules themselves, some definitions must be premised, in order to have clearly in mind the scope of our subject.

(1) Law and Fact. In the first place, what part does the law of evidence play in the whole system of law?

Enforcement of the law requires, sooner or later, the application of the law to an individual person. When this is attempted, and is disputed, in a legal proceeding, the tribunal has before it two propositions for decision, in this form:

Major premise) (A) The law is that (for example) a person who has contracted to do an act X for a man P and has failed to do it, is liable to P for breach of contract;

(Minor premise) (B) Defendant D here has contracted to do act X for plaintiff P, and has failed to do it;

(Conclusion) (C) That D is liable to P for breach of contract.

Here the major premise, proposition (A), is one of law, not of fact.

Now the tribunal, in proceeding to satisfy itself as to proposition (B), the minor premise, may find that this proposition is a mixed one of law and fact, thus:

(B) (I) (Fact) D here has corresponded with P in certain telegrams and letters about doing act X, and has later refused to do act X;

(B) (II) (Law) This correspondence constitutes in law a binding contract, and also a breach thereof;

(C) (Conclusion) That D is liable to P for breach of contract.

Thus the conclusion and the intermediate proposition of law (B) (II) depend upon the proposition of fact (B) (I). The tribunal must therefore now satisfy itself as to this proposition of fact. For this purpose it must obtain or receive data that will enable it to reason and to reach a belief as to that proposition, one way or the other. Yes or No.

Are there any rules of law that control and assist the tribunal and the parties in the search and the use of those data?

There are such rules. They are known as the law of evidence.

Thus all enforcement of substantive law may depend ultimately on a use of the law of evidence.

(2) Argument and Evidence. Argument and evidence, taken together, represent the means by which the tribunal is sought to be persuaded as to some fact-in-issue.

A *fact* is any event or act or condition of things, assumed (for the moment) as happening or existing. A *fact-in-issue* is a fact as to the correctness of which the tribunal, under the law of the case, must be persuaded; the term "probandum" (thing to be proved) will here be used as the convenient single word. A *fact-in-evidence*, or, briefly, *evidence*, signifies any facts considered by the tribunal as data to persuade them to reach a reasoned belief upon a probandum. This process of thought by which the tribunal reasons from fact to probandum is termed *inference*. The remarks of counsel analyzing and pointing out or repudiating the desired inference, for the assistance of the tribunal, are termed *argument*.

Thus (as stated above) Evidence—the data presented—and Argument—comments offered—together form the means of persuading the tribunal.

Example

In an action against an express truck owner for misdelivery of a trunk to A instead of to B, witness M testifies to the signature of the driver on a receipt, and to an inscription of B's address on the trunk; witness N testifies to seeing the trunk afterwards at A's residence. The probanda are (1) the promise of the owner to deliver the trunk to B, and (2) the actual delivery to A. For the former probandum, the driver's receipt and the address on the trunk are evidence; for the latter probandum, the presence of the trunk in A's residence is evidence. Whether from each piece of evidence any inference ought to be drawn by the tribunal as to the probanda will be the subject of argument by counsel. Then the tribunal, considering all the aspects of inference, will decide whether they amount to proof of the two probanda.

. . .

(3) Substantive Law and Evidence. When you and your friend have met to dine at the restaurant, and the attentive waiter lays before each of you a copy of the menu, and the guest is concentrating upon the question "What to choose?", suppose that you, in your zeal for the horticultural topic just discussed with him, continue thus: "What proves that the Corona rose can be grown from cuttings in this climate is the testimony of four of my neighbors who did that very thing last winter!" Then might not your friend mildly protest, "I cannot listen to that testimony now, because the only issue before us is whether we are to consume a lamb chop or a porterhouse steak." Now your friend, in declining to listen to that testimony, is not invoking any rule of evidence. He is merely ruling that the probandum on which your testimony is offered, viz., rose-transplantation, is immaterial at the present moment, the immediate issue being the menu.

This situation is repeated daily in a thousand instances in trials. The judge refuses to hear (i. e., excludes) evidence, not because of any rule of evidence, but because under the substantive law and the pleadings the issue on which that evidence is offered is immaterial.

Examples

(1) In an action by A against D for battery, D offers a witness to insulting words uttered against D by A on the day before the battery. The court excludes this testimony, not

because of any rule of evidence, but because by the law of torts the insult is no excuse, and therefore not a probandum.

(2) In a prosecution of D for larceny by picking the pocket of J. S., a witness T is offered by D to prove that the suit of clothes worn by J. S. was made for him by T but is still unpaid for. The court excludes this, because J. S.'s failure to pay for his clothes is no excuse for the larceny under the criminal law, and therefore is not a probandum.

* * *

In all these cases it is plain enough that no rule of evidence (i. e., determining the persuasive effect of evidential data) is involved. Yet in all of them some rule of substantive law or of pleading was applied by refusing to receive evidence of the immaterial probandum. And so, in many of the older treatises on evidence, there used to be chapter after chapter on "evidence admissible or not admissible" in the various actions, listing them all alphabetically, "arson," "battery," "burglary," "contract," and so on. These chapters were really dealing with the substantive law, or pleading rules, for those actions. But the effect was to confuse completely the rules of evidence with the other parts of the law.

This confusion of treatment in law books has now almost entirely disappeared. It is found only here and there. But constant watchfulness is required, for the inexperienced, in reading a treatise or a judicial opinion, to avoid being misled by a ruling excluding "evidence of so-and-so." Such a ruling, on careful inspection, may be found to have nothing to do with a rule of evidence, i. e., the probative value of a piece of evidence.

Sec. 3. *Science of Proof Contrasted with the Jury-Trial Rules of Evidence.* But why should a body of rules of law be needed for this purpose? Are not the ordinary principles of reasoning, as known to us all, sufficient here as elsewhere? Is not the science of proof the same in court as in the scientist's laboratory?

(1) There is indeed a *science of proof*. It has been a subject of study for more than two thousand years, going back at least to the days of the Greek philosophers; for the process of proof is only one part of the general logical process that has occupied mankind's studies from the beginning days of systematic reflection. Logicians, rhetoricians, metaphysicians, and psychologists have all contributed something.

But these thinkers have rarely concerned themselves with the materials that are needed in litigation. They have dealt chiefly with mathematics and the natural and political sciences. E. g., to illustrate their principles the treatises of logic use such examples as "The sun is not seen at night; now the sun is not seen; therefore it is now night"; or, "All members of the Progressive Party believe in old-age insurance; you believe in old-age insurance; therefore you are a member of the Progressive Party."[1] Hence their books have been of little direct and practical service to guide the juristic investigator.

---

1. Is this a valid syllogism? See question 1, *infra* p. 544.

But there are several other reasons why the science of proof, as used by the solitary scientist, cannot be used in a court room without modifications:

(2) In forming the jury-trial rules of evidence, the following special considerations apply:

(a) In the first place, as above stated, the *materials* for inference are peculiar. In the scientist's laboratory, the phenomena of chemistry, biology, botany, physics, and the like, are the chief material. But in a law court the chief material consists of human conduct in its infinite varieties, and of everyday phenomena of streets, buildings, trucks, barrels, pistols, and the like, which have no interest usually for the scientist. Hence the principles of logic and psychology, that guide our reasoning, need to be applied to this distinctive but miscellaneous material.

(b) In the second place, the scientist is not much hampered, as a court is, by limitations of *time* and *place*. A scientist can wait till he finds the data he wants; and he can use past, present, and future data; and he can go anywhere to get them.

* * *

. . . But a judicial trial must be held at a fixed time and place, and the decision must be then made, once for all. Most of the data are distant, and in the past. Many can never be re-found or revived. These limitations seriously hamper the inquiry. The only compensating advantage is that a tribunal can compel the production of data, if available, from any citizen within the jurisdiction, while the scientist cannot do this.

(c) In the third place, the tribunal deals with data presented by *parties in dispute*. Thus, human nature being what it is, there is a constant risk of fraud and bias. This makes it specially difficult for the tribunal to obtain and to valuate the evidence. The search for truth in a judicial controversy is often a despairing task. When Pilate asked, "What is the truth?" he asked a question that thousands of judges have echoed. Some special rules of control or guidance are here needed. But the scientist in his laboratory is largely exempt from this limitation.

(d) In the fourth place, the judicial trial takes place under dramatic conditions of *emotional disturbance*. The disputant and defiant parties are present; their witnesses and other friends sense the antagonism. The spectators make it a public drama. Everyone is keyed up. Surprise, sympathy, contempt, ridicule, anger—all these emotions are latent. Even the most honest and disinterested witness feels the mental strain. Contrast this with the quiet and secluded laboratory of the scientist—the lifeless substances under his scrutiny—the routine matter-of-fact environment. He needs no special rules of control. But a judicial tribunal must have some, to meet this situation.

(e) And finally, the tribunal, whether judge alone or with a jury, consists of *laymen*. In a laboratory, the scientist, whatever his field, is trained in valuing the data of his special branch. But in a court room even the judge himself is not a specialist in the science of proof. The substantive law, and the law of procedure, from the main part of his equipment. And, under our system of frequent judicial change, the judge rarely has an opportunity to become a specialist in the valuing of evidence. Hence he needs the guidance of a certain set of conventional rules, based on the prior recorded experience of other judges.

If we add to this complex the *lay-jurors*, as deciders of facts, the need of guiding rules becomes even more obvious. The jury, in its pristine and unspoiled form, is an invaluable part of our system. But, even at its best, the members are untrained in the weighing of evidence. They are liable to be diverted by bias and emotion from calm reasoning. Here, again, is a need for some controlling rules of guidance.

That the jury element has been a chief influence in the shaping of our evidence system is obvious from the brief sketch of its history already given (ante, sec. 1).

Sec. 4. *The Jury-Trial Rules, to Be Supplemented by the Science and the Art*. We must not, however, make the error of assuming that a knowledge of the jury-trial rules of evidence is a sufficient equipment for practice in trials. The science and the art must be added to complete that equipment.

(1) Science of Proof. In the first place, the jury-trial rules of evidence are founded on the principles of the science of proof. Logic and psychology, each contributing its part, make up the science of proof, i. e., the science that describes the operations of the mind in reaching a belief from rational data. All belief, whether in court or out of court, follows certain processes, consciously or unconsciously; they cannot be evaded. Sometimes these processes reach a correct belief; sometimes they reach an incorrect belief. The science of proof analyzes these processes and tells us which are the ones that tend to reach a correct belief. The jury-trial rules of evidence utilize and rest upon some of these principles; hence, a self-training in them is so much gain in using those rules. Moreover, there are two other stages of litigation where the practitioner needs some acquaintance with the science of proof, viz., (a) the pre-trial gathering and analysis of his evidential data, and (b) the explanation of the probative force of those data in his argument to the jury. For these purposes he will need, sooner or later, something more than a knowledge of the jury-trial rules of admissibility applicable during the trial.

(2) Art of Using the Rules. In the second place, the art of presenting the evidence lucidly and effectively at the trial, and of using the rules promptly, tactfully, and accurately amidst the surprises and emergencies of a trial, requires something more than a correct knowledge of each single rule. It involves the *art of using them*—just as the mere knowledge of all the rules of a bridge game leaves one a long way from the skilful and successful use of the rules in a match.

Examples

(1) A witness for your opponent is on the stand. There are rules which permit or forbid certain unpleasant subjects to be asked for on cross-examination. But perhaps you will deem it prudent or tactful in this case not to ask for certain matters which would be allowable.

(2) Your witness is on the stand. He is asked a question which a rule of privilege would entitle him to refuse to answer. But you may deem it wiser for him not to claim the privilege.

(3) The party plaintiff, whom you represent, is asked by the opponent whether he has at one time written a letter on a certain subject. There are two or three rules that might stand in the way of this question. But at the moment you do not remember them exactly enough to make an effective objection. Thus you lose the benefit of them.

(4) Your case calls for the proof of an invoice. You have a copy of it, but the original is in the hands of the consignee, a third person. The opponent objects to your copy, as a rule entitles him to do. You have forgotten to notify the consignee to bring in the original, hence your proof fails.

Repeated experience, of course, leads to the acquirement of the art. But much can be done, before actual trial experience, to make a long start in avoiding errors and in laying the basis of the art. For this purpose, one should familiarize oneself with the annals of important trials that have been fully reported, and with the memoirs and experience records of eminent practitioners that are available for guidance.

. . .

Sec. 6. *The Jury-Trial Rules in Chancery, Ex parte Proceedings, Administrative Tribunals, etc.* The jury trial rules of evidence originated in jury trial, being peculiar to the historical control of the judge over the jury (ante, sec. 1). Hence they do not, in principle or in policy, apply as a matter of law to bind the judge or presiding officer in any other form of tribunal. But in the course of events they have come to have an important influence in the procedure of other tribunals. The chief reason was that the study and use of the jury-trial rules led them to be looked upon and venerated by the Bar as the systematic instrument for judicial ascertainment of truth, and that in almost all other tribunals the judges and the counsel were men in whose minds the rules had been indelibly ingrained.

A cursory survey of the other types of tribunals and proceedings must here suffice.

(1) In chancery the rules of evidence had originally been borrowed from the ecclesiastical procedure (ante, sec. 1). But as time went on, the maxim "Equity follows the Law" brought the Court of Chancery to concede that in chancery the jury-trial rules of admissibility would be followed, except where the chancery methods of procedure modified them. These differences were chiefly in the chancery mode of taking testimony (i. e., always by written deposition before the hearing), in the requirement of two witnesses to every material allegation . . ., and in the allowance of discovery from a party-opponent before trial. . . .

(2) In the trial of *crimes* before a common-law jury, the jury-trial rules of course applied. But there were several rules which were applicable only in criminal cases (e. g., proof of a bigamous marriage, an accused's character, etc.) and one or two which varied from the corresponding rule

in civil trials (e. g., burden of proof). Apart from this, the jury-trial rules were and are the same in civil and in criminal cases.

(3) In *ex parte* proceedings or *interlocutory* proceedings before a judge (e. g., habeas corpus applications) the jury-trial rules do not as matter of law apply (for example, affidavits are always used), though often their analogy is in practice followed. The same is true of *extradition* proceedings.

(4) In *grand jury* hearings the only purpose is to ascertain if there is probable cause for instituting an accusation, not to find a verdict of guilty; hence the jury-trial rules do not apply. But several States, moved by the occasional abuses of prosecutors, have by statute enacted that only "legal evidence" may be received.

(5) In *admiralty* courts, whose procedure was also founded on the ecclesiastical law and used no jury, the jury-trial rules do not apply as matter of law; "evidence of every kind and description" is admissible, said an eminent admiralty judge of the middle 1800's.

(6) In *military* courts (courts-martial), which are virtually criminal courts, the jury-trial rules have been adopted by presidential order.

(7) In *juvenile* courts the jury-trial rules do not apply as matter of law; but some of them are in practice occasionally invoked.

(8) In *conciliation* courts, the jury-trial rules do not apply.

(9) In *arbitration* proceedings some courts have required the arbitrator to observe the jury-trial rules; but this is unsound.

(10) In the federal court of *customs and patent appeals*, the court is empowered to make its own rules of procedure.

(11) In the federal *board of tax appeals* (which is really a court) the rules of evidence of the courts of equity in the District of Columbia (whatever those may be) are prescribed by statute.[2]

(12) In *administrative tribunals* the jury-trial rules are not binding. But in practice, since the members of the tribunal (or some of them) are usually members of the Bar or former judges, they are apt to enforce certain of the jury-trial rules when applicable. Whether such tribunals should free themselves from the technical shackles of those rules, whether it is feasible to preserve their fundamental principles of fairness and prudence and experience while rejecting their innate and obstructive and needless trivialities, is a large question, of which the future alone will see the solution. In some of these tribunals (e. g., the industrial accident boards) the jury-trial rules are usually found to be enforced with strictness; in others, not; the practice varies. . . .

(13) In a *legislative assembly*, when an impeachment trial takes place, the jury-trial rules cannot be said to be binding, though they have occasionally been invoked. In hearings before legislative committees there is no pretense to use them.

(14) In *international arbitral tribunals* there is no fixed practice; some of the rules are used (e. g., for the authentication of documents),

2. In 1942 the Board of Tax Appeals was renamed the Tax Court.

and some are not. Naturally, the Anglo-American rules cannot be insisted upon in a tribunal including members accustomed to some other legal system.

[The following is taken from RICHARD H. FIELD AND BENJAMIN KAPLAN,* MATERIALS FOR A BASIC COURSE IN CIVIL PROCEDURE (Brooklyn, N.Y., 1953), p. 88 ff. Footnotes are omitted.]

We now return to the point that the rules of evidence often prevent relevant evidence from being presented to the jury. As we examine these rules, you should ask yourself whether the claimed justification for them is valid. . . .

Competency of witnesses.—We have said that some persons are not permitted to testify at all—they are "incompetent." It is obvious enough that a person may be so lacking in mental capacity that he is unfit to be a witness. No court would listen, for example, to a two-year old child or a raving lunatic. But how about a four-year old, six-year old, or eight-year old child? How about an inmate of an insane asylum who although "of unsound mind" has sufficient mental capacity to observe an event and remember and narrate what he saw? Of what effect is lack of understanding of the nature and meaning of an oath? What about an atheist who says that the oath means nothing to him?

It is well to remember that although the judge has the first word on the competency of a witness, the jury will (if the judge allows him to testify) have the last. The judge may decide that a six-year old child has sufficient understanding so that he may testify; but the jury may give no credence to what he says. Does this suggest that in a doubtful case the judge should allow the testimony to come in and leave it to the jury to appraise the weight to be given it?

How does the judge go about determining whether a person is qualified to be a witness? In some instances, such as extreme infancy or idiocy, mere observation may be enough. In others, preliminary questioning of the prospective witness may satisfy the judge. Or perhaps it may be necessary to supplement these methods by calling other witnesses to testify as to qualifications. But suppose the incapacity is disclosed for the first time in the course of the direct examination or cross-examination of the witness? The judge may then strike out the testimony already given and tell the jury to disregard it. This raises for the first time a problem which will recur frequently: Is it realistic to assume that the jurors can or will obliterate from their minds testimony which they have heard, merely because the judge instructs them to do so?

Some jurisdictions still hold to an old common law rule rendering a person incompetent as a witness when he has been convicted of a serious crime. What is the theory behind this rule? Do you think the rule a sensible one? Suppose the crime was perjury? If there is no rule of exclusion, should the jury be informed of the fact of conviction?

* The authors are respectively, Story Professor of Law, and Royall Professor of Law at Harvard University.

Another type of incompetency demands a word, although only a slight vestige of it remains today. Until the middle of the nineteenth century the common law courts took the cynical view that a party to litigation was rendered so unreliable by his obvious interest in the outcome that he should not be allowed to testify. This frequently produced the bizarre result that those who knew the most about the controversy were silenced. Nowadays this disqualification is almost entirely abolished. Of course, juries are warned to take into account the interest of a witness when they come to judge the credibility of his testimony. . . .

Privilege.—There are various rules protecting particular matters from disclosure by given persons. To take a familiar example: L, a lawyer, is called as a witness and asked about what C, his client, had told him in the course of seeking legal advice. Assuming, as we shall see may be the case, that if C told the same things to a layman, the layman could testify to what C said, why is the lawyer dealt with differently? Confidential communications between husband and wife, patient and physician, penitent and priest, are commonly recognized as privileged. What are the reasons for and against each of these privileges? What would you say about confidential communications to an accountant? Would you compel a newspaper reporter to disclose the source of information given to him in confidence? How about a communication given to any person in confidence on a pledge of secrecy? These latter communications are commonly not privileged. Should they be?

In addition to privileged communications, there are topics privileged from disclosure. For example, the public interest may require that state secrets be privileged—an increasingly important question as much governmental activity is "classified." Within limits, too, trade secrets important to the existence of a particular business may be privileged. Here also falls the familiar privilege against self-incrimination. (Note that while a witness is privileged from revealing facts tending to incriminate himself, he is not privileged from revealing facts incriminating someone else.) This privilege can be claimed in all kinds of proceedings—criminal and civil actions, administrative hearings or legislative investigations.

The word "privilege" implies that the person for whose benefit it exists may waive it, and that a party to a case may not be able to control a privilege personal to anyone but himself. It is worth thinking about who should be able to claim each of the privileges mentioned. . . .

Hearsay.—We have already given one example of hearsay: In a suit on a promissory note, W testifies that X told W that he, X, saw B sign the note. This testimony is objectionable as hearsay. Why is it objectionable? Because W may be mistaken in his memory as to what X said? Suppose then that W produces in court a written statement, identifying it as having been prepared by X. The testimony is still objectionable. Is this because X was not under oath? Suppose then that W is a notary public and has taken X's oath that the statement is true. Even this does not cure the hearsay difficulty.

Why all this squeamishness about hearsay? Responsible persons daily make important decisions in their own lives in reliance upon patent hearsay; indeed, normal life could hardly go on if this were not so. Why should courts reject a type of evidence so commonly relied upon outside the courtroom? The heart of the objection to hearsay is the absence of an opportunity for cross-examination of the declarant (the person who made the out-of-court statement offered in evidence by the testimony of another). Cross-examination may bring out important matters omitted from the original statement; it may lay falsehood bare; it may expose errors in observation, memory, or narration; or it may at least raise doubts as to the weight the jury should give to the testimony. Often, of course, cross-examination fails of its purposes, and, particularly if it is unskillful, may serve only to solidify the original story. But the chance for cross-examination is regarded as such an essential check on the trustworthiness of testimony that the absence of it is ordinarily fatal to the admissibility of evidence.

Should this be so? Granting that there is a risk of falsehood or error that cross-examination might expose, does this risk so overcome the probative value of the testimony that the fact-finder should not be given the chance to hear and weigh it, making what he may think to be due allowance for its infirmity? Basic to the rule excluding hearsay and some other exclusionary rules is a distrust of the capacity of the jury to appraise the evidence properly. You will find that such rules are commonly not applied where the trier of fact is an expert administrative tribunal.

Question: What would you expect the situation to be when the trier of facts is a judge sitting in a non-jury case?

Do not fall into the error of assuming that repetition in court of the out-of-court statement of another person invariably raises a hearsay problem. Assume that A is suing B for slander, alleging that B called him a thief. W testifies that at the time and place in question he heard B say that A was a thief. In this case, although W is testifying to what he heard B say, W's testimony is admissible; no question of hearsay is involved.

What is the difference between this case and the one where W testified as to what X said about seeing B sign the note? There the purpose of the testimony was to prove that B signed the note, and the credibility of X's out-of-court statement was therefore important. In the present case, the purpose in offering W's testimony is simply to prove that B made the statement that W said he made. B's credibility is therefore unimportant. We can generalize and say that it is only when the statement of the declarant is offered to prove the truth of the statement—when, in effect, testimony by the declarant is being offered through the mouth of another—that a question of hearsay arises.

Question: P sued Dr. D for negligence in leaving a sponge in the incision after an operation on P. To establish liability it was necessary to prove (1) that a sponge was left in the incision and (2) that it was left there as the result of failure of Dr. D to exercise proper skill and care. P offered testimony by a witness W that someone in the operating room told Dr. D that the sponge count did not come out right. This testimony was excluded on the ground that it was hearsay. Testimony was admitted that it was a common practice for a sponge count to be taken for the purpose of preventing the loss of a sponge during an operation. There was a verdict for Dr. D, and P appealed. The question on appeal was the propriety of excluding the proffered testimony. What argument would you make for P and what do you think the decision should be? See Smedra v. Stanek, 187 F.2d 892 (10th Cir.1951).

Exceptions to the hearsay rule.—The rule excluding hearsay is riddled with exceptions. We shall not catalogue them all or probe the refinements of any of them. Were we to do so, you would quickly see that the pattern is haphazard rather than logical. Not only does the law vary greatly from State to State, but the law of any one State is likely to be shifting, uncertain, and abounding in logical inconsistencies. Rather we shall consider in a general way the reasons why the rejection of hearsay has not been complete and the conditions which must or ought to exist before an exception to the rule is made.

While an out-of-court utterance, free of the test of cross-examination, is a less desirable method of proof than the witness-testimony of the declarant, it is recognized that a rigorous exclusion of all hearsay would sometimes block all effective proof of an essential issue. Because of this practical reality, some types of hearsay have always been admitted. When, then, should an exception be made? If A is readily available to testify in court, there is no need to resort to the admittedly inferior method of letting B testify as to what A has previously said out of court (assuming, of course, as we do throughout the ensuing discussion, that the truth of A's statement, as distinguished from the fact that he made it, is the point in issue). This notion of necessity pervades the whole problem of exceptions to the hearsay rule. But commonly mere necessity is not enough. The courts do not say that whenever the declarant is unavailable (say because he is dead, insane, or absent from the jurisdiction), his out-of-court utterances may be proved through another witness. Usually there must be something which can be pointed to as a justification for the absence of the oath and cross-examination. In other words, the circumstances of the utterance must be such as to make it seem reasonably trustworthy. Absolute trustworthiness is not, of course, required; even the testimony of a witness subjected to cross-examination does not attain that ideal.

1. We take our first illustration from the criminal law. A is charged with the murder of B. Testimony of W is offered to the effect that B, knowing that death was immediately at hand, said, "A shot me," or, for that matter, "C shot me." W's testimony is clear hearsay, but the likelihood that B told the truth under the circumstances set forth is supposed to be so strong that W's account is held admissible. Of course, B may have lied to get revenge upon A, to protect someone else, or for some other reason, but these considerations will go to the weight to be given to the evidence. You may find it odd that in most States W's testimony of B's dying declaration, admissible in a murder trial with capital punishment involved, is not admissible in a civil action for wrongfully causing B's death. Indeed you may well ask how much scientific support there is for the supposition upon which the entire exception rests.

2. A, injured by a hit-and-run driver, sues B for the injuries he sustained. The identity of the driver is in dispute. B offers the testimony of W that C, now dead, said to W: "I ran over A and was lucky enough to get away." Should it be admitted? How is the requirement of trustworthiness satisfied? The theory is that a person is unlikely to make a statement against his own interest unless it is true. The "declaration against interest" exception to the hearsay rule is well recognized. It is, however, often narrowly limited. At common law the statement had to be against a *proprietary* or a *pecuniary* interest. Some courts say that a statement which would

subject the declarant to civil liability is not sufficiently against his pecuniary interest to be admissible. Such courts would therefore exclude the statement of the hit-and-run driver given above. (Is there any rational basis for this limitation?) Note, furthermore, that if the statement is admissible as against the declarant's interest, it may be accepted as evidence of a proposition in the statement which is not against interest. For instance, W testifies that A said, "I still owe the undertaker $300 for burying my wife." The statement, being against A's pecuniary interest, is admissible on the issue of the death of A's wife.

3. Admissions by a party form another exception. A is suing B for negligently inflicted injuries. He offers the testimony of W that B said, "I didn't see A until after I hit him"; or, "I had a half a dozen drinks before the accident"; or, "It was all my fault." Such testimony is admissible on the issue of B's negligence although B's statement was made out of court.

Questions: What is the justification for this exception? Should it make any difference whether the declarant is available?

4. Yet another exception deals with the admission in evidence of entries contemporaneously made in books and records in the regular course of business. The variations in its operation are substantial and confusing; the matter has sometimes been the subject of legislation.

* * *

5. Some other illustrative exceptions to the hearsay rule are: (a) The reported testimony at a previous trial of a witness now unavailable. This is an easy exception to justify when the parties to the former trial were the same. But suppose the testimony is offered against a person not a party before. Should the opportunity for cross-examination by someone else suffice as a voucher of trustworthiness? (b) Declarations concerning pedigree. If it were not for this exception, proof of matters of family history might be extremely difficult. What is the basis for holding such declarations trustworthy? (c) Ancient writings. A dispositive document, such as a deed, is sufficiently authenticated by its age alone to make it admissible if, according to the general rule, it is over thirty years old, is fair on its face, and comes from proper custody. (d) Official written statements by a public official made in the line of duty. . . .

The "best evidence" rule.—Suppose the contents of a written document are relevant to an issue in the case. As we know, the document may, upon sufficient authentication, be introduced in evidence. But may its contents be proved by a copy or by the oral testimony of a witness who has read it? Ordinarily not. The writing itself is said to be the "best evidence" of its contents. In order, therefore, to make admissible evidence of an inferior quality—a copy of the writing or oral testimony as to its contents—the absence of the original must be satisfactorily explained.

Remote and prejudicial evidence.—The fact that a piece of relevant evidence does not run afoul of any exclusionary rule does not necessarily mean that it will be admitted. The judge has discretion to exclude evidence of comparatively slight probative value when he believes that it is not worth the time it will take to hear it. A similar discretion exists when the value of the evidence is outweighed by the confusion or the prejudice that its admission would produce. For example, should the plaintiff in an automobile case be allowed to show that the defendant had had several previous accidents? Should the defendant be allowed to show a perfect safety record for thirty years of driving? Should the plaintiff be able to prove that the defendant is protected by liability insurance (as the basis for an inference that he had nothing to lose by his carelessness and hence was less likely to be careful)? In a suit for injuries allegedly due to a defective condition of the premises should evidence that the defendant made repairs after the accident be admissible as some proof of his negligence? Should the defendant's offer to make a compromise settlement be received?

Ways of combatting an opponent's evidence.—Let us assume that a party has called a witness whose direct testimony, if believed, will be damaging to the opponent. What may the opponent do to combat it? His first chance is in cross-examination. He may try in various ways to impeach (that is, discredit) the witness. This may be done by questions designed to bring out bias or prejudice, weakness of memory, faulty perception, prior inconsistent statements, or the like. Or the witness may be impeached by the testimony of other witnesses bringing out similar defects. Of course the story of the witness may be contradicted by other evidence. In line with the constant objective of keeping a trial within bounds, there are, however, limitations on the extent to which contradiction of "collateral" matters in a witness's testimony will be permitted.

Suppose a witness unexpectedly gives testimony damaging to the party who called him. Commonly a party is not allowed to "impeach his own witness," a witness he himself has called. But he may contradict him through other witnesses.

Scope and manner of cross-examination.—Beyond impeaching a witness, how far may the cross-examining party go in the course of the cross-examination in seeking to support his case out of the mouth of the witness? Not far, according to the so-called Federal rule; for under it a witness may be cross-examined only as to facts and circumstances connected with the matters covered in his direct examination. (Departures from this rule are permitted in the discretion of the trial judge.) On the other hand, in a large number of States the cross-examination may cover all aspects of the case, including matters on which the cross-examining party has the affirmative.

Where the scope of cross-examination is limited as under the so-called Federal rule, it may be necessary for the party who has cross-examined to recall the witness at a later stage in the trial. In doing so the party "makes the witness his own," thus commonly cutting off any opportunity to impeach on the matters elicited on recall and ordinarily subjecting the questioning on recall to the rules governing direct rather than cross-examination.

Question: What reasons can you advance for and against the so-called Federal rule on scope of cross-examination?

A conventional technique of cross-examination is to put "leading questions," such as "Isn't it a fact that . . . ?" or, "You did so-and-so, didn't you?" This type of questioning is improper on direct examination, although on routine matters of a preliminary nature it generally passes without objection.

Question: Why are leading questions objectionable on direct but permissible on cross-examination?

[The Federal Rules of Civil Procedure permit a] departure from the customary procedure when a party calls an *adverse party*, including an officer, director or managing agent of a corporate party, as a witness. (This is frequently good trial tactics and is occasionally essential if a party is to prove his case.) Such an adverse party may be asked leading questions and be impeached to the same extent as if he had been called by his own side. The Rule also makes it clear that leading questions may be put to any witness shown to be unwilling or hostile.

Objections to evidence [Rules 43(c), 46].—When evidence is offered which the opponent believes not to be admissible, he should object immediately. The objection has a two-fold purpose: (1) to keep the evidence out, and (2) to lay the foundation for a later appeal if it is admitted. Any evidence admitted without objection may be given such weight as the jury thinks it deserves, and any error in its admission is usually unavailable upon appeal. For instance, if testimony of the contents of a document is admitted without the objection that it is not the "best evidence," the jury may base a finding upon it. Similarly, a finding may be based upon hearsay evidence to which no objection is made. In either case, of course, the jury may discount or disregard the testimony because of the inherent weakness that gives rise to the exclusionary rule.

It will often happen that testimony is offered which is properly admissible for one purpose but inadmissible for another. The fact that the jury might improperly apply it to an inadmissible purpose does not ordinarily exclude it. But the party against whom it is offered may protect himself by asking the judge to instruct the jury as to the limited purpose for which it is admissible. If no such request is made, the jury may properly give the testimony its natural probative force for any purpose.

Question: If, in the case involving the statement that the sponge count did not come out right (p. 333, *supra*), the proffered testimony were admitted over objection, what should the objecting party then do?

A piece of evidence is often offered which will become relevant only after or in connection with other testimony not yet presented. Practical necessities prevent it from being excluded. A party must start somewhere, and the connecting evidence would very likely be subject to the same infirmity if presented first. The dilemma is resolved by admitting it conditionally on the assurance of counsel that it will be "connected up" later. If it turns out not to be, it will be stricken out on motion and the jury instructed to disregard it.

[Under] Rule 46 [of the Federal Rules of Civil Procedure] formal "exceptions" are not necessary, although the Rule indicates that "heretofore" they have been. This is a reference to the old requirement of such ritualistic words as "I except" or "Please note my exception" in order for the party against whom a ruling is made to have the right to rely upon it on appeal. By virtue of the Rule it is now necessary in the Federal courts only to make known the objection.

If a question is erroneously admitted over objection, the record is clear for purposes of appeal. If the objection is sustained and the question is excluded, the party against whom the ruling is made may make an "offer of proof"; that is, he may state, ordinarily out of the hearing of the jury, the answer he expected to get from the witness. . . . The purpose of this Rule is to enable the appellate court to appraise the seriousness of the error. . . .

SECTION 14.3   THE BURDEN OF GOING FORWARD WITH THE EVIDENCE AND THE BURDEN OF PROOF

We have seen that the dominant characteristic of the trial is its function as a process for adducing proof on disputed issues of fact. This process is directed by the attorneys and controlled by the judge according to the rules of relevance and admissibility of evidence. These rules determine, to some extent, the kind and the quality of evidence which may be presented in court, and in this manner they guide the attorney in the preparation and presentation of the case. However the evidentiary rules provide no guidelines regarding the selection of evidence which an attorney may make from that evidence which is available, relevant, and admissible. How do attorneys know how much evidence to produce and how do they know when they should "rest"? The answer lies, in part, in the phrases which head this section: "burden of going forward," and "burden of proof."

Since it is assumed that a court knows nothing about the truth of any proposition except as it is persuaded by the parties, no court may make a finding as to the truth of a contested proposition unless sufficient evidence is produced upon which a reasonable finding may be based. Furthermore, the adversary process imposes on the parties the responsibility to develop and produce this evidence. It follows from this that the court must allocate the responsibility for the introduction of evidence between the parties so that as to any contested proposition it can decide (a) which party must fail if no evidence is produced, and (b) which party must fail if, after evidence has been produced, the trier of fact (the judge or, in a jury trial, the jury) is not persuaded by the evidence. The party who will fail if no evidence is produced is said to bear "the burden of going forward with the evidence," and the party who will fail if the evidence is not persuasive is said to bear "the burden of proof."

These terms "burden of proof" and "burden of going forward with the evidence" are misleading insofar as they imply that the party who bears either burden is obligated to produce evidence. For example if the party who does not have the burden of going forward with evidence of a particular fact nevertheless introduces such evidence, it is not necessary for the other party also to introduce evidence of the fact. For that reason it is more accurate to speak of the risk of non-production of evidence, then to speak of the burden of going forward with evidence. Similarly if the party who does not have the burden of proof of a particular fact nevertheless introduces evidence which persuades the jury that the fact is true, the other party may have the benefit of this, and hence it is more accurate to speak of the risk of non-persuasion rather than the burden of proof.

As a general rule, the risk of non-production of evidence and the risk of non-persuasion as to any proposition rest on the party to whose case the allegation of fact is a necessary element. Thus in a civil suit in which the plaintiff charges the defendant with a breach of contract, the plaintiff will lose unless evidence is produced which shows that the contract was made and that it was broken. In a criminal case in which the charge is murder in the first degree, the prosecutor will lose unless evidence is produced that (a) the defendant committed the homicide, (b) intentionally, and (c) after some deliberation ("with malice aforethought"). Similarly the plaintiff, or the prosecutor, will lose even though evidence of these matters is produced if such evidence fails to persuade the trier of fact. However, the fact that the risk of not persuading the trier of fact is on the plaintiff, or the prosecution, as far as the charges as a whole are concerned, does not mean that the risk of non-persuasion is on the plaintiff as to every single fact in issue.

Suppose, for example, the plaintiff alleges that the defendant broke a contract, and the defendant pleads that he or she was a minor at the time alleged and hence not liable for breach of contract. In such a case the defendant bears the risk of failing to persuade the trier of the fact that he or she is a minor. If the defendant submits no evidence as to his or her age, or if the evidence is unpersuasive, the defendant loses as to that issue—though the risk of non-persuasion as to the issue of whether there was a contract and whether it was broken by the defendant remains on the plaintiff.

In general the party who bears the risk of non-production of evidence also bears the risk of not persuading the trier of fact. There are exceptions to this principle. For example, in a prosecution for murder the burden of persuading the jury that the defendant was sane at the time of the offense is sometimes put upon the prosecution. On the other hand, if no evidence is introduced tending to show that the defendant was insane, the defendant will be unable to successfully raise the insanity defense. In this example, the defendant has the risk of non-production of evidence; and the prosecution has the risk of non-persuasion—the "burden of proof."

"It has been suggested," write Scott and Simpson, "that the allocation of the burden of persuasion can be determined by the application of *a priori* rules. . . . The truth is, and the better courts are now explicitly saying, that the fixing of the burden calls for the same sort of considerations that are applicable in determining the content of a rule of substantive law, namely, considerations of fairness and policy based on previous judicial experience and practice. If an *a priori* rule of thumb were applicable, there would be no conflict, for example, as to whether in a negligence case plaintiff has the burden of proving due care or defendant the burden of proving contributory negligence; or whether in an action on a promissory note, the plaintiff had the burden of persuading the trier that the note had not been altered, or the defendant the burden of showing alteration." [1]

What are these "considerations of fairness and policy based on previous judicial experience and practice?" They are very diverse and not easy to state. To take one example: Those jurisdictions which impose on the defendant the burden of proof of the plaintiff's contributory fault in negligence cases do so, one may assume, in order to be "fair" to the plaintiff. Thus in the case of a collision between two automobiles, it might be asking too much of the plaintiff to prove, in addition to the facts constituting the defendant's lack of due care for the safety of others, the facts constituting due care for the plaintiff's own safety—the fact that the plaintiff gave the proper hand signal, that he or she was looking straight ahead, and so forth. It might well be thought fairer to put the burden on the defendant to allege and prove exactly what careless acts the plaintiff committed, if any, that should bar the defendant's liability. On the other hand, those jurisdictions which impose on the plaintiff the burden of proving lack of contributory fault may take the view that the proof of defendant's fault is so bound up with proof of plaintiff's lack of fault that the burden of one rightly involves the burden of the other, and that in addition such a rule helps to equalize the position of the parties since the jury (it is thought) generally assumes the defendant is insured and can hence more easily bear the loss. More specifically, the rule which casts the burden of proving lack of contributory fault on the plaintiff enables the court to direct a verdict on the ground that that burden has not been satisfied in cases which, under the opposite rule, might go to a jury whose sympathies are not wholly trusted.

Yet this analysis by no means does justice to the complexity of the question. For the rule with respect to burden of proof of contributory negligence must be weighed together with many other rules with respect to burden of proof, and all those rules must be weighed together with many other rules respecting other aspects of the trial procedure.

There is one more issue regarding the burden of proof which should be mentioned, namely: "To what extent must the trier of fact be persuaded?" Here Anglo-American legal tradition makes a sharp distinction between civil and criminal cases. In most civil suits the burden of persuasion is measured by a "preponderance of the evidence," that is, by the fact that the evidence in support of the proposition outweighs the evidence against it, no matter how slightly. It is often said that the burden consists in showing that it is "more likely than not" that the proposition is true. If the mind

1. A. W. Scott and S. P. Simpson, Cases and Materials on Civil Procedure (Boston, 1950), pp. 603–604.

of the trier is in equilibrium, the party having the burden of proof is in the same position as if the trier were persuaded the proposition is untrue. In exceptional civil cases, as, for example, where fraud is alleged, the proof is required to be by "clear and convincing evidence;" that is, the party who has the burden of proof must persuade the trier not only that the proposition is more probable than not but that it is much more probable than not.

In criminal cases the prosecution has a still heavier burden of persuasion, called proof "beyond a reasonable doubt." The trier must be entirely convinced, that is, must have no substantial doubt, that the defendant committed the act, was sane at the time, was not acting in self-defense, and so forth.

The difference in standards of proof in civil and criminal cases in Anglo-American law makes it impossible for our courts to follow the European practice of trying the civil and criminal actions together where a single act gives rise to both types of liability. In European countries there are no legal degrees of persuasion; the court is either persuaded or it is not persuaded. If the court is convinced that the defendant beat and wounded the plaintiff it can sentence the defendant to jail and, in the same case, award damages to the aggrieved party—the "civil complainant". In our procedure the two actions are entirely separate and evidence of a conviction in the criminal case is not admissible in the civil case for fear the jury might be prejudiced thereby.[2] What advantages and disadvantages do you see in each of the two practices?

SECTION 15. TRIAL BY JURY

SECTION 15.1 THE RIGHT TO A JURY TRIAL

UNITED STATES CONSTITUTION
AMENDMENTS V, VI, VII, XIV

AMENDMENT V. . . . nor [shall any person] be deprived of life, liberty, or property, without due process of law . . .

AMENDMENT VI. In all criminal prosecutions, the accused shall enjoy the right to a speedy and public trial, by an impartial jury of the State and district wherein the crime shall have been committed . . .

AMENDMENT VII. In Suits at common law, where the value in controversy shall exceed twenty dollars, the right of trial by

2. One notable exception to this general rule occurs in treble damage actions under the Sherman Antitrust Act (*supra* p. 135). If the defendant in the treble damage case (a civil action) has been convicted, on the same facts, in a criminal case, then the conviction may be admitted in evidence to establish the facts alleged by the plaintiff as the basis for his suit.

jury shall be preserved, and no fact tried by a jury, shall be otherwise reexamined in any Court of the United States, than according to the rules of the common law.

AMENDMENT XIV. *Section 1.* . . . nor shall any State deprive any person of life, liberty, or property, without due process of law . . .

MASSACHUSETTS CONSTITUTION ARTICLE XV

In all controversies concerning property, and in all suits between two or more persons, except in cases in which it has heretofore been otherways used and practised, the parties have a right to a trial by jury; and this method of procedure shall be held sacred, unless, in causes arising on the high seas, and such as relate to mariners' wages, the legislature shall hereafter find it necessary to alter it.

NEW YORK CONSTITUTION ARTICLE I, SECTION 2

The trial by jury in all cases in which it has heretofore been guaranteed by constitutional provision shall remain inviolate forever; but a jury trial may be waived by the parties in all civil cases in the manner to be prescribed by law. The legislature may provide, however, by law, that a verdict may be rendered by not less than five-sixths of the jury in any civil case.

The Right to Jury Trial in Civil Cases in England

Administration of Justice (Miscellaneous Provisions) Act, 23 & 24 Geo. V, c. 36 (1933)

6. (1) Subject as hereinafter provided, if, on the application of any party to an action to be tried in the King's Bench Division of the High Court made not later than such time before the trial as may be limited by rules of court, the Court or a judge is satisfied that—

(a) a charge of fraud against that party; or

(b) a claim in respect of libel, slander, malicious prosecution, false imprisonment, seduction or breach of promise of marriage, is in issue, the action shall be ordered to be tried with a jury unless the Court or judge is of opinion that the trial thereof requires any prolonged examination of documents or accounts or any scientific or local investigation which cannot conveniently be made with a jury; but, save as aforesaid, any action to be tried in that Division may, in the discretion of the Court or a judge, be ordered to be tried either with or without a jury:

Provided that the provisions of this section shall be without prejudice to the power of the Court or a judge to order, in accordance with rules of court, that different questions of fact arising in any action be tried by different modes of trial, and where any such order is made the provision of this section requiring trial with a jury in certain cases shall have effect only as respects questions relating to any such charge or claim as aforesaid.

Questions

What answers would you give to the following questions of interpretation of the Constitutional provisions reproduced in the preceding pages? The answers which the courts have given are presented below. See in how many instances you agree with the courts— (a) before you have read their answers, and (b) after.

1. Do the Constitutions of the United States, Massachusetts and New York require trial by jury in criminal cases? in civil cases?

2. Does the United States Constitution require a jury verdict to be unanimous in federal criminal cases? in federal civil cases?

3. Does the due process clause of the Fourteenth Amendment of the United States Constitution impose on the states the federal standards of twelve person juries, and unanimous jury verdicts in criminal cases? in civil cases?

4. Are the requirements of the Seventh Amendment applicable to proceedings in state courts in which rights under a federal statute are asserted?

5. Since the Seventh Amendment (and analogous provisions of many state constitutions) leaves cases in courts of equity to be tried, as they had been traditionally, without a jury, and since in practically all American jurisdictions the distinction between courts of law and courts of equity has now been eliminated, how is the constitutional right to trial by jury preserved in an action in which the plaintiff seeks both damages for breach of contract (a remedy "at law") and an injunction (a remedy "in equity")?

Answers

1. The United States Constitution, like the various state constitutions does not require trial by jury in any case. It provides a *right* to trial by jury in all criminal cases and in certain types of civil cases, but that right may be waived; that is, the parties may agree to have the case tried by a judge without a jury, or a statute may constitutionally provide that unless a party demands a jury trial at a proper stage in the proceedings he shall be held to have waived his right to it.

2. "Trial by jury" in the United States Constitution (and in most but not all state constitutions) means trial by a jury of twelve in both civil and criminal cases, and the verdict of the twelve is not valid unless it is unanimous—since this was the rule in force under English and American law when the Constitution was adopted. As

statutes may constitutionally provide that jury trial may be waived by consent of both parties, however, so·they may also provide that the parties may stipulate that the jury shall consist of less than twelve or that a verdict of a stated majority shall be taken as the verdict of the jury as a whole.

3. Although the Sixth Amendment guarantee of jury trial is part of the due process of law required by the Fourteenth Amendment, the states are not required to conform exactly to the standards applied in federal courts in order to comply with that mandate. Juries of only six persons have been held to satisfy the due process mandate in state criminal cases,´see Williams v. Florida, 399 U.S. 78, 90 S.Ct. 1893 (1970); less than unanimous jury verdicts have also been held to satisfy due process requirements, see Apodaca v. Oregon, 406 U.S. 404, 92 S.Ct. 628 (1972). The Supreme Court has also held that six person juries are permissible in state civil actions. See Colgrove v. Battin, 413 U.S. 149, 93 S.Ct. 2448 (1973).

4. No. The Seventh Amendment, like the rest of the Bill of Rights, is directly applicable to cases in the federal courts and not to cases in state courts. Since under our dual constitutional system of government rights—whether arising under state or under national law—are generally subject to enforcement concurrently in both state and federal courts, it would defeat the power of the states to regulate the mode of trial in state courts if the Seventh Amendment were made applicable on the ground the rights asserted in the case arose under national law. See Minneapolis & St. Louis Railroad Co. v. Bombolis, 241 U.S. 211, 36 S.Ct. 595 (1916).

5. With the merger of courts of law and courts of equity, the constitutional right to trial by jury in suits at common law is preserved by determining whether in the particular action the parties would have been entitled to trial by jury prior to the merger. Where there are two separate issues, one of which would have been triable by a jury prior to the merger and the other not, the parties are normally entitled to a jury verdict on the first (in the instant case, the issue of damages for breach of contract) but the second (in the instant case, the injunction) would be for the judge to decide.

SECTION 15.2   TRIAL BY JURY: TWO VIEWS

[The following is taken from JEROME FRANK, COURTS ON TRIAL (cited above in Section 14.1), pp. 110–111, 114–117, 126–128, 135–137, 139–145. Footnotes are omitted.]

In most jury trials, the jury renders what is called a "general verdict." Suppose that Williams sues Allen claiming (1) that Allen falsely told him there was oil on some land Williams bought from Allen, but (2) that in fact there was no oil there, so that Williams was defrauded. The jury listens to the witnesses. Then the judge tells the jurors, "If you find Allen lied, and Williams relied on that lie, a legal rule requires that you hold for the plaintiff Williams, and you must compute the damages according to another rule," which the judge explains. "But if you find that Allen did not lie, then the legal rule requires you to hold for the defendant Allen." The jury deliberately deliberates in the jury-room and reports either, "We find for the plaintiff in the sum of $5,000," or "We find for the defendant." In other words, the jury does not report what facts it found. Such an undetailed, unexplained, jury report is called a "general verdict."

There are three theories of the jury's function:

(1) The naive theory is that the jury merely finds the facts; that it must not, and does not concern itself with the legal rules, but faithfully accepts the rules as stated to them by the trial judge.

(2) A more sophisticated theory has it that the jury not only finds the facts but, in its deliberation in the juryroom, uses legal reasoning to apply to those facts the legal rules it learned from the judge. A much respected judge said in 1944 that a jury's verdict should be regarded as "the reasoned and logical result of the concrete application of the law [i. e., the rules] to the facts."

On the basis of this sophisticated theory, the jury system has been criticized. It is said that juries often do not find the facts in accordance with the evidence, but distort—or "fudge"—the facts, and find them in such a manner that (by applying the legal rules laid down by the judge to the facts thus deliberately misfound) the jury is able to produce the result which it desires, in favor of one party or the other. "The facts," we are told, "are found in order to reach the result."

This theory ascribes to jurors a serpentine wisdom. It assumes that they thoroughly understand what the judge tells them about the rules, and that they circumvent the rules by falsely contriving—with consummate skill and cunning—the exact findings of fact which, correlated with those rules, will logically compel the result they desire.

(3) We come now to a third theory which may be called the "realistic" theory. It is based on what anyone can discover by questioning the average person who has served as a juror—namely that often the jury are neither able to, nor do they attempt to, apply the instructions of the court. The jury are more brutally direct. They determine that they want Jones to collect $5,000 from the railroad company, or that they don't want pretty Nellie Brown to go to jail for killing her husband; and they bring in their general verdict accordingly. Often, to all practical intents and purposes, the judge's statement of the legal rules might just as well never have been expressed. "Nor can we," writes Clementson, "cut away the mantle of mystery in which the general verdict is enveloped, to see how the principal facts were determined, and whether the law was applied under the judge's instructions. . . . It is a matter of common knowledge that the general verdict may be the result of anything but the calm deliberation, exchange of impressions and opinions, resolution of doubts, and final intelligent concurrence which, theoretically, produced it. It comes into court unexplained and impenetrable."

The "realistic" theory, then, is that, in many cases, the jury, often without heeding the legal rules, determine, not the "facts," but the respective legal rights and duties of the parties to the suit. For the judgment of the court usually follows the general verdict of the jury, so that the verdict results in a decision which determines those rights and duties. . . .

Now what does bring about verdicts? Longenecker, in a book written by a practical trial lawyer for practical trial lawyers, says: "In talking to a man who had recently served for two weeks on juries, he stated that in one case after they had retired to consider the verdict, the foreman made a speech to them somewhat like this: 'Now boys, you know there was lying on both sides. Which one did the most lying? The plaintiff is a poor man and the defendant is rich and can afford to pay the plaintiff something. Of course the dog did not hurt the plaintiff much, but I think we ought to give him something, don't you?' There were several 'sures'; we thought the plaintiff might have to split with his lawyers, so we gave him a big verdict." A case is reported in which the jurors explained their verdict thus: "We couldn't make head or tail of the case, or follow all the messing around the lawyers did. None of us believed the witnesses on either side, anyway, so we made up our minds to disregard the evidence on both sides and decide the case on its merits." "Competent observers," says Judge Rossman, "who have interviewed the jurors in scores of jury trials, declare that in many cases . . . principal issues received no consideration from the jury." Bear that in mind, when considering these remarks by Ram: "And to what a fearful extent may a verdict affect a person! It may pronounce a man sane or insane; it may establish character, or take it away; it may give liberty to the captive, or turn liberty into slavery; it may continue life to a prisoner, or consign him to death."

Again and again, it has been disclosed that juries have arrived at their verdicts by one of the following methods: (1) Each juror, in a civil case, writes down the amount he wants to award; the total is added and the average taken as the verdict. (2) The jurors, by agreement decide for one side or the other according to the flip of a coin. (3) A related method, reported in a case where a man was convicted of manslaughter and sentenced to life imprisonment, is as follows: The "jury at first stood six for assault and battery, and, as a compromise, the six agreed to vote for manslaughter, and the vote then stood six for manslaughter, and six for murder in the second degree; it was then agreed to prepare 24 ballots—12 for manslaughter and 12 for murder in the second degree—place all of them in a hat, and each juror draw one ballot therefrom, and render a verdict either for manslaughter or murder in the second degree, as the majority should appear; the first drawing was a tie, but the second one resulted in eight ballots for murder in the second degree and four for manslaughter, and thereupon, according to the agreement, a verdict was rendered for murder in the second degree."

How do the courts react to such a disclosure? When it is made known before the jury is discharged, a court will usually reject the verdict. But, frequently, the revelation occurs after the jury's discharge. In most states, and in the federal system, the courts then refuse to disturb the verdict. They say that any other result would mean that jurors would be subjected to pressures, after a case is over, to induce them to falsify what had occurred in the jury-room, so that all verdicts would be imperilled.

One may doubt whether there is much danger of such falsifications. I surmise that the underlying reason for that judicial attitude is this: The judges feel that, were they obliged to learn the methods used by jurors, the actual workings of the jury-system would be shown up, devastatingly. From my point of view, such a consequence would be desirable: The public would soon discover this skeleton in the judicial closet. . . .

Are jurors to blame when they decide cases in the ways I've described? I think not. In the first place, often they cannot understand what the judge tells them about the legal rules. To comprehend the meaning of many a legal rule requires special training. It is inconceivable that a body of twelve ordinary men, casually gathered together for a few days, could, merely from listening to the instructions of the judge, gain the knowledge necessary to grasp the true import of the judge's words. For these words have often acquired their meaning as the result of hundreds of years of professional disputation in the courts. The jurors usually are as unlikely to get the meaning of those words as if they were spoken in Chinese, Sanskrit, or Choctaw. "Can anything be more fatuous," queries Sunderland, "than the expectation that the law which the judge so carefully, learnedly and laboriously expounds to the laymen in the jury box becomes operative in their minds in true form?" Judge Rossman pointedly asks whether it "is right to demand that a juror swear that he will obey the instructions (which the lawyers frequently say they are not sure of until they have been transcribed) and return a general verdict in obedience thereto." Judge Bok says that "juries have the disadvantage . . . of being treated like children while the testimony is going on, but then being doused with a kettleful of law, during the charge, that would make a third-year law student blanch."

Under our system, however, the courts are obligated to make the unrealistic assumption that the often incomprehensible words, uttered in the physical presence of the jurors, have some real effect on their thought processes. As a logical deduction from that unfounded assumption, the trial judge is required to state the applicable rule to the jury with such nicety that some lawyers do not thoroughly comprehend it. If the judge omits any of those niceties, the upper court will reverse a judgment based on the jury's verdict. . . .

Let us, now, consider the arguments of those who defend the jury system.

(1) *Juries said to be better at fact-finding than judges.* The first defense is that juries are better fact-finders than judges. Judge Cooley said: "The law has established this tribunal because it is believed that, from its numbers, the mode of their selection and the fact that the jurors come from all classes of society, they are better calculated to judge the motives," and "weigh the possibilities . . . than a single man, however . . . wise . . . he may be."

Is that a correct appraisal? Would any sensible business organization reach a decision, as to the competence and honesty of a prospective executive, by seeking, on that question of fact, the judgment of twelve men or women gathered together at random—and after first weeding out all those men or women who might have any special qualifications for answering the questions? Would an historian thus decide a question of fact?

If juries are better than judges as fact-finders, then, were we sensible, we would allow no cases to be decided by a judge without a jury. But that is not our practice. Ordinarily if you sue a man for breach of a contract, you may have a jury trial; but not if you sue to have that same contract set aside for fraud, or if that man died or went into bankruptcy before you sued. If jurors were superior in fact-finding, such distinctions would be intolerable, as would also be the denial of trial by jury in thousands of admiralty and almost all "equity" cases, cases which affect legal rights fully as important as those involved in most jury trials. Yet I know of no one who proposes that all those cases shall be jury cases. . . .

(2) *Jurors as legislators.* I now come to the argument for the jury system most frequently advanced. It is contended that the legal rules (made by the legislatures or formulated by the judges) often work injustice, and that juries, through their general verdicts, wisely nullify those rules. This argument, strangely enough, is put forward by many of the same lawyers who insist that substantial adherence by the judges to those rules constitute an essential of a sound civilization, since, they say, without such adherence men could not know their legal rights or intelligently handle their affairs.

Hear, for instance, Dean Roscoe Pound. In an article, published in 1910, describing jury nullification of the legal rules as "jury lawlessness," he pronounces it "the great corrective of law in its actual administration." He says that the purpose of "jury lawlessness" is, "in largest part, to keep the letter of the law in the books, while allowing the jury free rein to apply different rules or extra-legal considerations in the actual decision of causes . . . ." Because "popular thought and popular action are at variance with many of the doctrines and rules in the books," the function of the jury is to preserve the appearance that the rules are being applied while the popular attitudes, inconsistent with the rules, are actually followed. "If," said Pound, "the ritual of charging the jury on the law with exactness is preserved, the record will show that the case was decided according to law, and the fact that the jury dealt with it according to extra-legal notions of conformity to the views of the community, is covered up."

In 1929, Wigmore wrote: "Law and Justice are from time to time inevitably in conflict. That is because law is a general rule (even the stated exceptions to the rules are general exceptions); while justice is the fairness of this precise case under *all* its circumstances. And as a rule of law only takes account of broadly typical conditions, and is aimed at average results, law and justice every so often do not coincide. Everyone knows this, and can supply instances. But the trouble is that Law cannot concede it: Law —the rule—must be enforced—the exact terms of the rule, justice or no justice. 'All Persons Are Equal before the Law'; this solemn injunction, in large letters, is painted on the wall over the judge's bench in every Italian court. So that the judge must apply the law as he finds it alike for all. And not even the general exceptions that the law itself may concede will enable the judge to get down to the justice of the particular case, in extreme instances. The whole basis of our general confidence in the judge rests on our experience that we can rely on him for the law as it is. But, this being so, the repeated instances of hardship and injustice that are bound to occur in the judge's rulings will in the long run injure that same public confidence in justice, and bring odium on the law. We want justice, and we think we are going to get it through 'the law,' and when we do not, we blame 'the law.' Now this is where the jury comes in. The jury, in the privacy of its retirement, adjusts the general rule of law to the justice of the particular case. Thus the odium of inflexible rules of law is avoided, and popular satisfaction is preserved. . . . That is what jury trial does. It supplies that flexibility of legal rules which is essential to justice and popular contentment. And that flexibility could never be given by judge trial. The judge (as in a chancery case) must write out his opinion, declaring the law and the findings of fact. He cannot in this public record deviate one jot from those requirements. The jury, and the secrecy of the jury room, are the indispensable elements in popular justice."

Mr. Justice Chalmers, an English judge, stated this position thus: "Again there is an old saying that hard cases make bad law. So they do when there is no jury. The Judge is anxious to do justice to the particular parties before him. To meet a particular hard case he is tempted to qualify or engraft an exception upon a sound general principle. When a judge once leaves the straight and narrow path of law, and wanders into the wide fields of substantial justice, he is soon irretrievably lost. . . . But hard cases tried with a jury do not make bad law, for they make no law at all, as far as the findings of the jury are concerned. The principle is kept intact while the jury do justice in the particular case by not applying it." . . .

(3) *The jury as an escape from corrupt or incompetent trial judges.* A third defense of the jury is seldom published: In a local community where some trial judges are corrupt, or subject to dictation by political bosses, or where some judges are rigid bigots or otherwise incompetent, lawyers prefer to take their chances with juries.

No one can deny that there is some force to that argument. It points to a fact I shall discuss later—that the electorate pays too little attention to the immense significance of trial courts. But unless honest, competent trial judges can be and are procured, the resort to juries is a feeble device. For, remember that, in many types of law-suits, the litigant cannot have a jury trial, must try his case before a judge without a jury.

(4) *The jury as alleged educator and creator of confidence in government.* Another argument for the jury system is that it helps to educate citizens in government, gives them added confidence in democracy. Can that contention be proved? Do not many jurors become cynical about the court-house aspects of government? And should education in government be obtained at the expense of litigants?

(5) *Citizens said to demand this participation in government.* Closely related to the previous argument is the contention that citizens demand participation in government through acting on juries. One wonders. If so, why do so many citizens seek to be excused from jury service?

Nevertheless, the need for popular participation in the administration of justice is the argument most frequently advanced in defense of the jury system. If we take that argument seriously—as something more than a rationalization of an irrational adherence to tradition—then we face a clash of social policies: (1) the policy favoring such popular participation undermines (2) the policy of obtaining that adequate fact-finding which is indispensable to the doing of justice. Which policy should yield? Is it less important to do justice to litigants than to have citizens serve on juries?

(6) *Jury trial as popular entertainment.* Doubtless, at one time, jury trials supplied cheap popular dramatic entertainment. This was true when the theater, the motion-picture and the automobile were not at hand. But now that these substitutes are available, now that we have Hollywood and television, surely the lives and fortunes of litigants need no longer be risked to provide such entertainment.

(7) *The jury in criminal litigation.* Especially in criminal cases is the jury highly regarded as a means of necessary humane individualization. Not easily would our people relinquish to the judges the power to pass on the guilt or innocence one accused of crime, if he prefers a jury trial. For the jury is assumed to be more merciful to the alleged criminal, more responsive to unique extenuating circumstances. Yet it may be doubted whether the popular estimate of the benevolent character of jurors in criminal cases is invariably correct. "Parties charged with crime," it has been wisely said, "need protection . . . against unjust convictions quite as often as the public needs it against groundless acquittals."

Recall Borchard's *Convicting the Innocent.* Did the juries in the cases reported by Borchard adequately protect the innocent defendants? Would not honest competent judges, sitting without juries, probably have done better?

(8) *"Passing the Buck" to juries.* Juries, it is argued, provide buffers to judges against popular indignation aroused by unpopular decisions. That is, the jury is an insulator for the judge, a buck-passing device. As a rational argument for the jury this seems indeed questionable. Men fit to be trial judges should be able and willing to accept public criticism. Moreover, they are obliged to do so in the many cases they must try without juries. Probably this argument is but an ingenious rationalization. . . .

It is extremely doubtful whether, if we did not now have the jury system, we could today be persuaded to adopt it. The chances are that most conservative lawyers would oppose such a "reform"; they would refer us to Scotland, an "Anglo-Saxon" country, where the jury has never played an important role. They would call attention to the marked decline of the jury's popularity in England. They would denounce trial by jury as an absurd New Dealish idea.

The point is that the jury, once popular thanks to its efficacy as a protection against oppression, has become embedded in our customs, our traditions. And matters traditional are likely to be regarded as inherently right. Men invoke all sorts of rationalizations to justify their accustomed ways. "No man," writes Ruth Benedict, "ever looks at the world with pristine eyes. He sees it edited by a definite set of customs and institutions and ways of thinking. . . . The observer will see the bizarre developments of behavior only in alien cultures, not in his own." The "importance of an institution in a culture gives no direct indication of its usefulness or its inevitability. . . . In a certain island in Oceana, fish-hooks are currency and to have large fish-hooks came gradually to be outward sign of wealth. Fish-hooks are therefore very nearly as large as a man. They will no longer catch fish, of course. In proportion as they have lost their usefulness, they are supremely coveted." . . .

Only thus, I think, can one explain why, in these United States, the jury still has its passionate defenders, its sincere admirers, and why, on the whole, the public finds no fault with it. . . .

Nevertheless, we are saddled with the jury. For our federal and state constitutions require trial by jury in most criminal and many kinds of civil cases. In most jurisdictions, the defendant in a criminal action may waive a jury and go to trial by judge alone; both parties in a civil suit may give such waivers. The number of those jury-waived cases seems to be on the increase, but the number of jury cases still remains very considerable. As it will almost surely be impossible, in the reasonably near future, to repeal the constitutional provisions concerning the jury, we must, then, face the fact that, for many years to come, the jury will be with us. Accordingly, to meet the difficulties caused by the jury system, we can today look only to palliating reforms which aim at making jurors somewhat better fact-finders. Let us now consider some proposed reforms.

1. *Special (or Fact) Verdicts*

As we saw, usually juries return general verdicts. There is, however, another type of verdict—a "special verdict" (or "fact verdict"): the trial judge tells the jury to report its beliefs, its findings, about specified issues of fact raised at the trial. The jury reports that Henry did or did not promise to deliver so many tons of coal to Williams on a particular day; or at what speed Jenkins was driving when he hit Olsen; or whether or not Adolf Brown and Helen Holt were present when John Gotrox signed his will. To those facts, thus "found" by the jury, the trial judge applies the appropriate legal rule.

A special verdict would seem to do away with some of the most objectionable features of trial by jury. The division of functions between jury and judge is apparently assured, the one attending to the facts alone, the other to the legal rules alone. The jury seems, by this device, to be shorn of its power to ignore the rules or to make rules to suit itself. As one court said, special verdicts "dispel . . . the darkness visible of general verdicts." The finding of facts, says Sunderland, "is much better done by means of the special verdict. Every advantage which the jury is popularly supposed to have over the [judge] as a trier of facts is retained, with the very great additional advantage that the analysis and separation of the facts in the case which the court and the attorney must necessarily effect in employing the special verdict, materially reduce the chance of error. It is easy to make mistakes in dealing at large with aggregates of facts. The special verdict compels detailed consideration. But above all it enables the public, the parties and the court to see what the jury has really done. . . . The morale of the jury also is aided by throwing off the cloak of secrecy for only through publicity is there developed the proper feeling of responsibility in public servants. So far, then, as the facts go, they can be much more effectively, conveniently, and usefully tried by abandoning the general verdict . . . The special verdict is devised for the express purpose of escaping the sham of false appearances."

In some jurisdictions, the judge, when using a special verdict, need not— should not—give any charge about the substantive legal rules beyond what is reasonably necessary to enable the jury to answer intelligently the questions put to them. As, accordingly, the jury is less able to know whether its findings will favor one side or the other, the appeal to the jurors' cruder prejudices will frequently be less effective. "A perverse verdict," it is said, "may still be returned, granted a jury clever enough to appreciate the effect of its answers, and to shape them to harmonize with its general conclusions. But it is much more difficult   .   .   ., and by requiring the jury to return the naked facts only we may fairly expect to escape the results of sympathy, prejudice and passion." That may be too sanguine a hope; but the fact verdict may often reduce the sway of the more undesirable emotions. It is suggested, too, that a special verdict "searches the conscience of the individual juror, as a general verdict does not," because "such are the contradictions in human nature that many a man who will unite in a general verdict for a large and unwarranted sum of money will shrink from a specific finding against his judgment of right and wrong."

A related device is to retain the general verdict but to accompany it with written answers by the jury to special "interrogatories" concerning specific facts. This enables the trial judge to learn something about the jurors' reasons for their general verdict. "The submission of interrogatories .   .   . is," says Clementson, "a sort of 'exploratory opening into the abdominal cavity of the general verdict'   .   .   . by which the court determines whether the organs are sound and in place, and the proper treatment to be pursued."

The special verdict is nothing new. It was used in England centuries ago, and was early imported into this country. But it was used here in most states in so complicated a way that it fell into disrepute. However, in a few states, those complications seem to have been largely avoided. A streamlined form of special verdict and of special interrogatories was authorized in the federal courts in 1938. In those courts, as in the courts of some states, it is optional with the trial judge in each civil jury case to employ either or neither of these methods, and the judges seldom use either of them. I think that one or the other should be made compulsory in most civil suits.

Such a reform will not overcome all the objections to the jury system. Aside from the fact, already noted, that in a relatively simple case a jury will still be able to circumvent the rules by disingenuous answers to the questions, the special verdict does not eliminate the grave difficulty that most jurors are not adequately equipped to find facts, are less competent to perform that task than a well-trained trial judge.

2. *Special Juries*

At one time, in England, it was not unusual, when a case related to a particular trade, to have a jury consisting of men engaged in that trade. Such jurors could more informedly consider the matters in dispute. Unfortunately, that practice was discontinued, and it has not been adopted in this country. It might be well to do so now, although I will not guarantee the constitutionality of such a mode of jury selection. If juries of that sort had been in use, perhaps the remarkable recent growth of administrative agencies might not have occurred, and business arbitrations might not have become popular.

In many kinds of cases, where jury trial is not required, a trial judge has the power to call in an "advisory jury" whose verdict does not bind him. If advisory juries were made up of "special" jurors of the kind I have just described, they could be of considerable value.

3. *Intermediate Fact-Finders*

Where some of the facts of a civil jury suit are complex, the trial judge in some jurisdictions may refer those facts to an expert; the expert's report on those facts, together with the evidence on which he based it, are both presented to the jury, which, however, is not obligated to accept the report. This helpful technique is too little employed.

4. *Revision of the Exclusionary Rules*

Judge Learned Hand, speaking of the exclusionary evidence rules, said that "it is entirely inconsistent to trust them [the jurors] as reverently as we do, and still surround them with restrictions which . . . depend upon distrust." More emphatically, Boston remarked that "our law requires that all matters for the consideration of the jury shall be, as it were, pre-digested food for mental invalids, and so it strains this food through the most highly developed rules of evidence . . . In short, we recognize in every imaginable way that the jury is the weakest element in our judicial system, and yet we ponder it as a sacred institution. We . . . regard it, in all ways in which our regard can be measured, as wholly incompetent for the purpose for which we establish it." In other words, if we have to have the jury, let us abolish, or modify, most (not all) of the exclusionary rules, since they often shut out important evidence without which the actual past facts cannot be approximated.

5. *Recording Jury-room Deliberations*

Judge Galston suggests that a stenographic record be made of the jurors' discussions while they are deliberating in the jury-room; the trial judge, with such a record before him, could learn, to some extent, whether the verdict was reached by improper means; if so, he would set aside the verdict. That suggestion deserves consideration.

6. *Training For Jury Service*

The late Judge Merle Otis asserted that jurors should be men and women who have the "capacity quickly to comprehend the applicable law and intelligently to apply it." Judge Knox has said that, "to accomplish justice," we must have jurors "with intelligence" and "sound judgment" which will "enable them to decide intricate questions of fact." Each of those judges proposed to reach that highly desirable result by the quite simple means of providing, in very general terms, higher standards for jurors and of using more care (in part through better personnel) in the mode of selecting persons eligible to serve on juries. Such a reform seems to me incapable of doing the trick. It will not, I think, restrict jurors to those singularly few laymen who, without special training, can "quickly comprehend and intelligently apply" legal rules which lawyers must study to understand, or who are able "to decide intricate questions of fact" as they are presented in the course of a trial. Doubtless the impossibility of obtaining jurors of that caliber accounts for the virtual elimination of the civil jury in England and Scotland.

Nor can we expect much from the practice of distributing to prospective jurors handbooks briefly describing the duties of jurors, or from short talks on that subject delivered by judges to jury panels. A practice established in Los Angeles has more merit: There a prospective juror must pass a written and oral test showing his aptitude for the job. But even that scheme, I think, falls far short of the bull's-eye.

A more helpful proposal is this: Let us, in the public schools and in adult education classes, give courses in which the students will be taught, in some detail, the function of the jury and the nature of trial-court fact-finding; require all citizens to attend such a course; bar from jury service any person who has not taken such a course and successfully passed an examination. Some such plan has been urged by Judge Galston and former Judge William Clark. I heartily favor it. Again, I give no guaranty of constitutionality.

Were all those reforms adopted, trials by jury would be less dangerous to litigants than they now are; but I think they would still be far less desirable than jury-less trials before well trained honest trial judges.

I must add that, despite my views about the undesirability of the jury (except perhaps in criminal trials), I have, as a judge, felt a strong obligation to see that, in cases which came before our court, trials by jury have been conducted in accordance with the rules supposed to govern such proceedings. As I said in an opinion: "It has been suggested that a judge (like me) who shares the doubts about the wisdom of the jury system is inconsistent if he urges that the courts be vigilant in preserving the jury's function. I do not understand that criticism. It is the sworn duty of judges to enforce many statutes they may deem unwise. And so, when on the bench, our private views concerning the desirability of the jury system are as irrelevant as our attitudes towards bimetallism or transmigration of souls. Consequently, as long as jury trials are guaranteed by constitutional or statutory provisions, it is the obligation of every judge, no matter what he thinks of such trials, to see that they are fairly conducted and that the jury's province is not invaded. That does not mean that a judge may not freely express his skepticism about the system, may not seek to bring about constitutional and statutory changes which will avoid or reduce what he considers its unfortunate results as it now operates."

[The following is taken from HARRY KALVEN, JR.,* "THE DIGNITY OF THE CIVIL JURY," 50 University of Virginia Law Review 1055, 1056, 1065–1075 (1964). Some footnotes omitted; others are renumbered.]

A few years ago I had occasion to write a paragraph about the jury which seems so apt for the purpose of introducing the present discussion that, rather than attempt a paraphrase, I risk the gracelessness of opening with a direct quotation from myself.

The judge and jury are two remarkably different institutions for reaching the same objective—fair, impersonal adjudication of controversies. The judge represents tradition, discipline, professional

* Mr. Kalven is Professor of Law at the University of Chicago.

competence and repeated experience with the matter. This is undoubtedly a good formula. But the endless fascination of the jury is to see whether something quite different—the layman amateur drawn from a wide public, disciplined only by the trial process, and by an obligation to reach a group verdict—can somehow work as well or perhaps better.

The passage suggests what I hope is the proper stance for discussing the merits of the jury system. The jury is almost by definition an exciting and gallant experiment in the conduct of serious human affairs; it is not surprising that virtually since its inception it has been embroiled in controversy, attracting at once the most extravagant praise and the harshest criticism.[1] Nor is it surprising that the issue cannot be narrowly focussed or definitively put to rest.

For the past several years at the University of Chicago Law School we have been engaged in a major empirical research project dedicated to discovering facts about contemporary jury behavior.[2] The materials are rich and complex and furnish ammunition for both sides of the argument; and ideally we should let the systematic reporting of the research speak for itself in appropriate and balanced detail. Unfortunately, as seems to be the case with most large-scale research projects, it is taking longer than anticipated to put the results into publishable book form, and the data most relevant to the civil jury have not as yet been reported.

I shall therefore attempt no more in the present essay than to offer certain reflections of my own on the jury and the debate which surrounds it, documented by a selective sampling of the project materials.

1. The basic contemporary American criticism is Frank, Courts on Trial (1949); careful assessments of the argument by English lawyers, who draw somewhat different conclusions, are Devlin, Trial by Jury (1956), and G. Williams, The Proof of Guilt 218–304 (2d ed. 1958). Useful bibliographies are found in Joiner, Civil Justice and the Jury (1962); Broeder, The Functions of the Jury—Facts or Fictions? 21 U.Chi.L.Rev. 386 (1954); Green, Juries and Justice—The Jury's Role in Personal Injury Cases, 1962 U.Ill. L.F. 152. The most recent criticism has come from two distinguished New York judges. See Desmond, Should It Take 34 Months for a Trial?, N.Y. Times, Dec. 8, 1963, § 6 (Magazine), p. 29; Peck, Do Juries Delay Justice?, 18 F.R.D. 455 (1956).

Another distinguished New York jurist, Judge Hart, has recently joined the debate on the side of the jury. See Hart, Long Live the American Jury (1964).

2. For various publications to date from the project see Zeisel, Kalven & Buch-

holz, Delay in the Court (1959); Kalven, Report on the Jury Project of the University of Chicago Law School, in Conference on Aims and Methods of Legal Research 155 (U.Mich.Law School 1957); Strodtbeck, Social Process, The Law and Jury Functioning, in Law and Sociology 144 (Evan ed. 1962); Zeisel, Social Research on the Law: The Ideal and the Practical, in Law and Sociology 124 (Evan ed. 1962); Broeder, The University of Chicago Jury Project, 38 Neb.L.Rev. 744 (1959); Kalven, The Jury, The Law, and The Personal Injury Damage Award, 19 Ohio St.L.J. 158 (1958); Kalven, A Report on the Jury Project of the University of Chicago Law School, 24 Ins.Counsel J. 368 (1957). Two further books, Zeisel & Kalven, The Jury, the Judge, and the Criminal Law and Simon, The Jury and the Defense of Insanity, will be published soon. The manuscript for the fourth of the project books, Zeisel, Kalven, & Callahan, The Jury, the Judge, and the Civil Case is in process of completion.

* * *

As we come to the merits of the institution, it may be useful to sketch three main heads under which criticism and defense of the jury have fallen.

First, there is a series of collateral advantages and disadvantages such as the fact that the jury provides an important civic experience for the citizen; that, because of popular participation the jury makes tolerable the stringency of certain decisions; or that because of its transient personnel the jury acts as a lightning rod for animosity and suspicion which might otherwise center on the more exposed judge; or that the jury is a guarantor of integrity since it is said to be more difficult to reach twelve men than one. On the negative side it is urged that jury fees are an added expense to the administration of justice; that jury service often imposes an unfair economic and social burden on those forced to serve; and that exposure to jury service disenchants the citizen and leads him to lose confidence in the administration of justice.

Although many of these considerations loom large in the tradition of jury debate, they are unamenable to research and will not concern us here. We have, however, collected considerable data bearing on the reaction of jurors to service. It will suffice for present purposes simply to state that there is much evidence that most people, once actually serving in a trial, become highly serious and responsible toward their task and toward the joint effort to deliberate through to a verdict. Whether they are good at the job may be open to question, but that they are serious about it and give it a real try is abundantly documentable. Anecdotes about jury frivolity and irresponsibility are almost always false. Further, we can document that jury service does not disenchant, but actually increases the public's preference for trial by jury. A distinction must be made between the attitude of those who have never served and seek to avoid service and the response of the juror once he has been "drafted," so to speak. Finally, the things jurors do not like about the system are quite extrinsic housekeeping defects which can and should be corrected, such as the waiting, the loss of income due to serving, and the often miserable quarters in which they are kept. The heart of the matter, the trial itself and the deliberation, is very often a major and moving experience in the life of the citizen-juror.

The second cluster of issues goes to the competence of the jury. Can it follow and remember the presentation of the facts and weigh the conflicting evidence? Can it follow and remember the law? Can it deliberate effectively?

The third cluster of issues goes to the adherence of the jury to the law, to what its admirers call its sense of equity and what its detractors view as its taste for anarchy.

The latter two issues go to the heart of the debate and have long been the occasion for a heated exchange of proverbs. Further, they may seem so heavily enmeshed in difficult value judgments as to make further discussion unpromising. Yet it is precisely here that our empirical studies can offer some insight, although they too cannot dispose fully of the issues.

When one asserts that jury adjudication is of low quality, he must be asserting that jury decisions vary in some significant degree from those a judge would have made in the same cases. If he denies this and wishes to include the judge, he has lost any baseline, and with it any force, for his criticism. While it is possible to say that even those juries whose decision patterns coincide with those of judges are nevertheless given to caprice, lack of understanding, and sheer anarchic disobedience to law, it is not likely that the critic means to go this far. If he does, he may have an interesting point to make about the legal order as a whole, but he has lost any distinctive point about the jury as a mode of trial. Further, trial by judge is the relevant and obvious alternative to trial by jury. To argue against jury trial is, therefore, to argue for bench trial.

Can one say anything, then, about how often judge and jury decisions agree and how often they differ? We can. One of our major research ventures has been a massive survey of trial judges on a nation-wide basis. With their cooperation we were able to obtain reports on actual cases tried to a jury before them, to get the jury's verdict in each case, and to get from the judge a statement of how he would have decided the case had it been tried to him alone. Finally, the trial judge gave us his explanation of any instance of disagreement. We have, in this fashion, collected from some 600 judges, reports on some 8,000 jury trials throughout the United States for each of which we have an actual jury verdict and a hypothetical verdict from the bench. We are just completing a full, book-length, analysis of the picture thus obtained for criminal cases and plan in the ensuing year to complete the companion book reporting on the civil cases. The methodological details about the sample, about the reality and accuracy of the judges' responses, and about the logic by which we infer explanations for the disagreements must be left to the book presentation. We are satisfied that the methods were sound and that we have developed an effective tool for studying the nature of the jury's performance.

While there are rich nuances in the patterns of jury disagreement that cannot be detailed here, we can report the main findings and place the jury system against the baseline of the bench trial system, thus giving an empirical measure of the quality of the jury performance. We shall do so first for criminal cases and then for civil cases; the contrast may help to put the performance of the civil jury in perspective.

It is evident that the matching of verdicts in criminal cases yields four possible combinations: cases where judge and jury agree to convict, where they agree to acquit, where the judge would acquit the jury convict, and where the jury would acquit and the judge convict. Hence, the quantitative results can be readily summarized in a fourfold table. Table 1 gives the data on the criminal cases.

Table 1

Judge and Jury Agreement and Disagreement
on Guilt in Criminal Cases

Judge Would Have found:	Jury Found:		
	For Defendant	Against Defendant	Total Judge
For Defendant	13	2	15
Against Defendant	18	67	85
Total Jury	31	69	100

The table contains two main conclusions. First, the jury and judge agree in the large majority of cases; to be exact in 13 per cent plus 67 per cent or 80 per cent in all. Second, in the remaining 20 per cent of the cases, in which they disagree, the disagreement is generally due to the jury's being more lenient toward the criminal defendant. In summary, the overall performance of the jury is such as to produce a high degree of conformity to that of the judge, but with elbow room left for the jury to perform a distinctive function. Or, as we have put it on other occasions, the jury agrees with the judge often enough to be reassuring, yet disagrees often enough to keep it interesting.

Table 2 gives the companion figures for personal injury cases.

Table 2

Judge and Jury Agreement on Liability in Personal Injury Cases

Judge Would Have Found:	Jury Found:		
	For Plaintiff	For Defendant	Total Judge
For Plaintiff	44	10	54
For Defendant	11	35	46
Total Jury	55	45	100

Again we see that there is massive agreement; in the personal injury cases it runs 44 per cent plus 35 per cent or 79 per cent, almost exactly the same as for the criminal cases. Here, however, the pattern of disagreement is much more evenly balanced. The judge disagrees with the jury because he is more pro-plaintiff about as often as the jury disagrees with him because it is more pro-plaintiff. Whereas the greater leniency of the jury toward the criminal defendant is congruent with popular expectations, the equality of pro-plaintiff response between judge and jury in civil cases is in sharp contrast to popular expectations.

It must be added that Table 2 does not present quite the whole picture. If we look for the moment simply at the 44 per cent of the cases where both decide for the plaintiff, we find considerable disagreement on the level of damages. In roughly 23 per cent the jury gives the higher award, in 17 per cent the judge gives the higher award and in the remaining 4 per cent they are in approximate agreement. More important, however, is the fact that the jury awards average 20 per cent higher than those of the judge.

The two tables considered together imply that the jury's disagreement with the judge is not a random matter; they indicate something more interesting about the nature both of judge and jury as decision makers. The precise quality of that something cannot be properly sketched here. We have had considerable success in finding explanations for the instances of disagreement and thus in reconstructing a full and rounded rationale. Our thesis is that it is the jury's sense of equity, and not its relative competence, that is producing most of the disagreement. Thus, debate over the merits of the jury system is in the end debate over the jury as a means of introducing flexibility and equity into the legal process.

There are, however, some further observations about the issue of jury competence. We have been told often enough that the jury trial is a process whereby twelve inexperienced laymen, who are probably strangers to each other, are invited to apply law which they will not understand to facts which they will not get straight and by secret deliberation arrive at a group decision. We are told also that heroic feats of learning law, remembering facts, and running an orderly discussion as a group are called for in every jury trial. In the forum of armchair speculation, a forum which on this topic has enrolled some of the most able and distinguished names in law, the jury often loses the day.

The two basic tables giving the architectural statistics of the jury's performance vis-à-vis the judge's performance have already indicated that the armchair indictment of the jury must go awry somewhere. We can, however, in a variety of ways document more securely our assertion that intellectual incompetence or sheer misunderstanding of the case is not a problem with the jury.

In the judge-jury survey the trial judge, among other things, classified each case as to whether it was "difficult to understand" or "easy." We can therefore spell out the following hypothesis to test against the judge-jury data. If the jury has a propensity not to understand, that propensity should be more evident in the cases rated by the judges as difficult than in those rated as easy. Further, disagreement should be higher in cases which the jury does not understand than in cases which they do understand since, where the jury misunderstands the case, it must be deciding on a different basis than the judge. We reach, then, the decisive hypothesis to test, namely, that the jury should disagree more often with the judge in difficult cases than in easy ones. However, when we compare the decision patterns in easy cases with those in difficult cases we find that the level of disagreement remains the same.

This rather intricate proof is corroborated by the fact that although the trial judges polled gave a wide variety of explanations for the cases in which there was disagreement, they virtually never offered the jury's inability to understand the case as a reason.

Any mystery as to why the plausible *a priori* surmises of jury incompetence should prove so wrong is considerably reduced when we take a closer look at the dynamics of the jury process, a look we have been able to take as a result of intensive and extensive post-trial juror interviews in actual cases and as a result of complete observation of jury deliberations in mock experimental cases, a technique used widely in the project. We observed that the trial had structured the communication to the jury far more than the usual comment recognizes and had made certain points quite salient. A more important point is that the jury can operate by *collective* recall. Different jurors remember, and make available to all, different items of the trial so that the jury as a group remembers far more than most of its members could as individuals. It tends, in this connection, to be as strong as its strongest link. The conclusion, therefore, is that the jury understands well enough for its purposes and that its intellectual incompetence has been vastly exaggerated.

Often in the debate over the jury the capacity of *one* layman is compared to the capacity of one judge, as though this were the issue. The distinctive strength and safeguard of the jury system is that the jury operates as a group. Whether twelve lay heads are better than one judicial head is still open to argument, but it should be recognized that twelve lay heads are very probably better than one.

It has been a major characteristic of debate over the jury that its critics are quick to announce at the outset that they are talking only of civil juries—their argument is not meant to impeach juries in criminal cases. The view I have been developing in this paper sees the jury as an adjudicating institution with certain basic characteristics and qualities which would be relatively constant as its business moves from civil to criminal cases. The question I wish to explore for a moment is the logic by which one would abolish the civil jury and cherish the criminal jury. I recognize, of course, that as a practical matter there are great differences here in terms of both constitutional requirements and popular reaction. I wish, however, to look theoretically at this matter. If the jury operates in a civil case as its critics say, can one justify retaining such an archaic and incompetent institution in criminal cases?

Dean Griswold, for example, has recently observed:

> But jury trial, at best, is the apotheosis of the amateur. Why should anyone think that twelve persons brought in from the street, selected in various ways, for their lack of general ability, should have any special capacity for deciding controversies between persons?

Dean Griswold was arguing for the abolition of the jury in civil cases. Is there not an obligation to try this biting premise on the criminal jury as well? For these grave and important controversies the jury should not be any abler; it must still be "the apotheosis of the amateur" and the twelve men must still be "selected in various ways for their lack of general ability."

The answer to all this, of course, is likely to be that we favor the jury in criminal cases as a safeguard for the accused, and that we need no corresponding safeguard in the civil case. There are two things to note about this line of reasoning, however. First, it would seem to be waiving any objections about the jury's incompetence and resting the case on the jury's sense of equity. Second, since it recognizes that introducing equity into the legal scheme is a characteristic of the jury, is there sufficient basis for applauding the jury's brand of equity in criminal cases while being critical of it in civil cases?

III

The discussion thus far has been regrettably general and colorless and removed from the particular issue or the particular case. I should like to try to compensate a bit for this abstractness by pausing to explore one pocket of "jury law" as an example of the human flavor of the jury process and of the ambivalence of the legal system toward the jury's precise function. The topic is the jury's handling of counsel fees in the personal injury case.

I begin with an anecdote that comes, not from our study, but from a bar meeting I attended a few years ago. It seems a lawyer chanced to overhear a jury deliberating in a personal injury case. They had agreed on liability and were moving to the issue of damages. Their first step was to agree on a fee for the plaintiff's lawyer. They then proceeded to multiply it by three to get the damages!

What do the materials from our study do to the picture of the jury suggested by this story? To begin with we might note some points about the law within this area. Under American law counsel fees are not to be awarded as part of the plaintiff's damages. This rule, although clear, embodies a controversial policy which is not uniformly followed in other legal systems. Second, the jury normally is not instructed about fees; that is, they are not told they are not to award them. The theory is that it is enough to explain the heads under which damages are to be awarded and that it would be dangerous to mention the fee problem for fear that the negative instruction might boomerang. Fees along with taxes and interest are therefore instances of what may be called "silent" instructions.

What then does the jury do about fees? It is curiously difficult to come to a firm conclusion, but the data run about as follows. The jurors often discuss fees in the course of deliberations and see no impropriety in so doing. They are frequently but not invariably well informed about the one-third contingent fee contract. Do they then add the fee? We are inclined to conclude not. It is more that fees provide a useful talking point in the deliberations over damages, functioning as a device in argument to facilitate agreement. And the salience of fees in the discussion appears to vary inversely with the clarity of the damage measurement. Thus, in a series of property damage cases where the damages had objective referents, the jury did not discuss fees. Furthermore, we never found a jury determining the damage total and then as a group deciding on the fee and adding it.

I shall conclude this brief sketch with an anecdote that does come from our own files. In one of the experimental jury deliberations there was a sharp split in the jury over the damages. The majority faction favored 35,000 dollars and the minority 25,000 dollars and after considerable discussion the impasse seemed firm. Finally, one of the majority raised the fee issue for the first time and reminded the holdouts that the plaintiff would have to pay his lawyer. The holdouts agreed that this was a point they had not previously considered and yielded rather rapidly. An overly logical member of the majority then raised the point that in reaching their figure of 35,000 dollars they had not considered fees either. He was summarily silenced by the other majority jurors, and a verdict of 35,000 dollars was unanimously agreed upon!

The anecdote has echoes at the appellate court level. In Renuart Lumber Yards, Inc. v. Levine, a relatively recent Florida case, the court found an award of 75,000 dollars excessive, estimated that some 30,000 dollars must have been for pain and suffering, and ordered a remittitur. Judge Hobson in dissent argued that for this purpose the court should consider the facts of life as to fees. He said:

> Moreover, although there is no legal basis for the inclusion of an attorney's fee in the judgment it is a matter of common knowl-

edge that in personal injury actions lawyers do not customarily perform services for the plaintiff gratuitously. As a practical proposition it is indeed probable that after paying for the services of his
attorney appellee would have little, if any, of the $30,000 left.
. . . . Such circumstances cannot be ignored by the writer in performing his part of this Appellate Court's duty to determine whether the judgment is so grossly excessive as to shock the judicial conscience.

Presumably Judge Hobson would have held it error for the jury to be
instructed to consider fees. Yet he feels it appropriate to consider them
himself for the special purpose of resolving the issue before him. We are
tempted to say that the jury, insofar as we can tell, treats fees much the
same as the judge did—not as simply additive but as an acceptable reason
for not rejecting a given award as excessive.

Finally, I suspect the law likes the fee rule the way it is. The fee question as an explicit issue of policy is difficult to resolve. Since we cannot
decide what we want to do about fees as damages, we are happy to let the
whole troublesome issue go to the jury. The jury's performance with respect to counsel fees can be read as furnishing both an argument for the
civil jury and an argument against it. My immediate point in reviewing it
was not so much to sharpen the debate as to give some indication of how complex jury decision-making behavior is.

It has been a traditional point of argument against the jury that it
ameliorated the harsh rules of law just enough to dampen any enthusiasm
or momentum toward proper reform. And the fee example may support this.
It is easy to say that a rule of law is either sound or unsound. If it is sound
it should be enforced as written; if it is unsound it should be changed by
proper process. This logical scheme, however, seems to me too rigid. Reform of private law is notoriously hard to effectuate, and in the long interim there is room for the jury's touch. Further, there is not inconsiderable evidence that jury resistance to a rule is often a catalyst of change.
Finally, and perhaps most important, we have a sense that many of the
jury's most interesting deviations would be exceedingly hard to codify and
incorporate by rule.

The content of jury equity in civil cases is obviously a topic of high interest, and we have not yet documented it fully in our studies. There are,
however, three or four major points to be at least noted here. First, as has
been long recognized, in certain areas of law jury equity is fully legitimated
by the system. Here, it is not what we suspect the jury may do in bending
the law; it is what the jury is instructed to do according to the official
view. For example, in defamation it is the jury's official task to define the
content of the defamatory standard, and in negligence cases its task is to
define negligence for the particular conduct involved. Although I realize
that history and comparative law are against the notion, I cannot but wonder whether a negligence criterion would have developed without the jury—
and whether it can make any real sense without a jury.

Second, there are three big points of jury equity on which our research
may alter the popular view. The jury does not simply ignore the contributory negligence rule and apply a comparative negligence formula of its own;
this view, popular among torts professors, is at most a half-truth, and the
less interesting half at that.

Again, it is perhaps evident from Table 2 that the jury has not, in keeping with the mood of the day, silently revolutionized the basis of liability so that today we have in effect a strict liability system.

Finally, the jury in personal injury cases has perhaps radically altered the official doctrine on computing damages; it tends to price the injury as a whole in a fashion analogous to the use of general damages in defamation.

And as a final teaser it should be recalled that the jury, as Table 2 warns, is not monolithically pro-plaintiff in personal injury cases. The thesis here is complex and centers on the distribution of the equities vis-à-vis the existing legal rules. The jury tends to follow the equities, in a very loose and rough sense, and the law has not uniformly deprived the plaintiff of them. The jury's response to collateral benefits, to imputed negligence, and, on occasion, to the use of criminal statutes to establish negligence may be quickly cited as instances of what we have in mind here.

In the end, then, debate about the merits of the jury system should center far more on the value and propriety of the jury's sense of equity, of its modest war with the law, than on its sheer competence. Criticism of the jury raises a deep, durable, and perplexing jurisprudential issue, and not a simple one of the professional engineer versus the amateur.

IV

On most issues of policy one may question the relevance of an opinion poll as an aid to forming his own opinion. In the case of the jury, however, an opinion poll may have extra force. In any event, the final item of data I wish to report is a survey we conducted among a national sample of trial judges as to their opinions of, and attitudes toward, the jury system. The trial judge's views as to the value of the jury are especially entitled to respectful hearing: he is the daily observer of the jury system in action, its daily partner in the administration of justice, and the one who would be most affected if the civil jury were abolished.

The questionnaire was elaborate and reflected a series of specific points about which we had become concerned during the life of the project. When reported in full, it should yield a rounded profile of contemporary judicial attitudes toward the jury and toward specific reforms that might increase its usefulness. At the moment we shall rest with reporting two basic tables. The judges were asked to choose among three positions on the jury for criminal, and then for civil trials:

(1) On balance the jury system is thoroughly satisfactory.

(2) The jury system has serious disadvantages which could be corrected and should be corrected if the system is to remain useful.

(3) The disadvantages of the jury system outweigh its advantages so much that its use should be sharply curtailed.

There were some 1,060 trial judges in the national sample. Table 3 gives the results for criminal cases and Table 4 for civil cases.

Table 3

Trial Judges' Opinions of Jury—Criminal Cases

	Number	Per Cent
(1) Thoroughly Satisfactory	791	77
(2) Satisfactory if Certain Changes..............	210	20
(3) Unsatisfactory	29	3
	1,030	100

Table 4

Trial Judges' Opinions of Jury—Civil Cases

	Number	Per Cent
(1) Thoroughly Satisfactory	661	64
(2) Satisfactory if Certain Changes	280	27
(3) Unsatisfactory	97	9
	1,038	100

The tables require little comment. It is evident that the trial judges are overwhelmingly against sharp curtailment of the jury; that a substantial majority find the jury thoroughly satisfactory; and that this support for the jury does not decline appreciably as we shift from criminal to civil cases.

V

As the second alternative offered the judges in our opinion poll suggests, it has been a strong tradition in the jury debate for one group of its supporters to specify certain reforms of the jury which would then make it a satisfactory institution. I have said nothing thus far about reforms and deliberately elect not to do so. It is not that the jury system could not conceivably be improved; nor is it that all of the specific reforms suggested are unsound. It is, rather, that the debate is over the basic architecture of a jury trial system and the basic architecture of a bench trial system.

I am therefore not discussing such matters as: improving the administration of jury selection systems; having the judge do the *voir dire* questioning; standardizing jury instructions; summation of the evidence by the judge; comment on the evidence by the judge; use of vigorous pretrial procedures to narrow issues; whether the jury is instructed before or after the closing arguments; written versus oral instructions; special verdicts; impartial medical experts; reducing the size of the jury; eliminating the unanimity requirement; or permitting the jurors to take notes. These measures have a considerable literature in their own right and appear to constitute a good part of what is currently called judicial administration. In varying degrees our studies have given us data and views on virtually all of these measures. Some of the measures are ill-advised, in my view, some are trivial, and some would be definite improvements. But the case for the civil jury does not, I think, stand or fall on the adoption of any one or any combination of them.

Sometimes I suspect that the jury issue will go to whichever side does not have the burden of proof. And in the forum of policy debate the assignment of the burden of proof tends to be a debater's strategy rather than an accepted convention. Does the argument stand differently if, on the one hand, the issue is put in terms of introducing the civil jury into a system that does not have it or perhaps extending it to areas where we do not have it today, such as the Federal Tort Claims Act, than it does if, on the other hand, the issue is whether we should abolish the jury in areas where we do now have it? I think it does, and I incline toward the view that old institutions should not be changed lightly. We lack, I feel, fresh arguments against the civil jury, apart perhaps from delay. I cannot resist observing that we need to hear a fresher point than that the civil jury consists of twelve laymen.

Inevitably, debate over an institution as complex and long standing as the jury will continue to be inviting and will continue to be inconclusive. It should be stressed that it was not the primary purpose of our project to appraise the jury, but simply to study it. In the course of the many years of that study it should be clear that I, personally, have become increasingly impressed with the humanity, strength, sanity, and responsibility of the jury. I suspect that that is not a proper argument for it, and I profoundly agree that it would be far better to have our careful studies ready to speak for themselves and give the rounded picture.

Questions

1. What reasons can be offered for the practice prevailing in all the countries of Western Europe except England of confining jury trial to criminal cases only?

2. What reasons can be offered for the English practice of extending jury trials to certain classes of civil cases (set forth *supra*, p. 384) but not others?

3. Can you see any advantages in the Soviet system, adopted also in other Eastern European countries, of trial before a court consisting of one permanent professional judge and two laymen elected for ten-day periods, all three sitting as co-judges with equal powers and equal votes?

4. As between a jury, single judge sitting with a jury, and a three-judge court sitting without a jury, which would you prefer if you were charged with murder? Consider in this connection the rule in Connecticut that the defendant accused of a capital crime may elect to be tried by a three-judge court instead of a jury.

5. Judge Frank makes much of the difficulty a jury may have in absorbing and understanding the law delivered in the judge's charge at the end of the case? Is that the first contact the jury has with the law of the particular case? Isn't much of the law of the case implicit in the evidence presented during the trial?

6. What is the standard or benchmark against which Judge Frank measures the performance of the jury? What standard does Professor Kalven use?

7. Do Judge Frank and Professor Kalven agree as to what juries do in fact? Do they agree as to what juries ought to do?

8. Does Professor Kalven supply a satisfactory defense to the various criticisms of jury trial voiced by Judge Frank?

Note

Directed verdicts; judgments notwithstanding the verdict. It is not always necessary to submit a case to the jury, after a jury trial. For a variety of reasons a trial may never reach the point where it is necessary to submit the case to the jury. The parties in a civil case may reach agreement and settle the case during the trial stage; or in a criminal case the defendant may decide to plead guilty; or the judge may find that the court does not have jurisdiction; or when the plaintiff—or in a criminal case the prosecution—rests, the case may be dismissed if the judge finds that the proof adduced by the plaintiff—or the prosecutor—is not sufficient to satisfy the burden of going forward with evidence or the burden of proof. These are but a few of the grounds on which a case may be terminated short of completion.

There are also instances where a jury trial may be completed and yet the jury not be allowed to reach an independent verdict. The traditional formulation of the jury's function is that *the jury resolves disputed issues of fact in cases where reasonable persons could differ regarding the inferences which can be drawn from the evidence presented.* If the evidence presented in a *civil* case is such that reasonable people could reach only one conclusion as to the facts, then there is no need to submit the case to the jury. In such a case it is said that, as a matter of law, there is no real dispute over the facts and therefore the judge may resolve the case on the application of law to the "undisputed" facts which must be inferred from the evidence. When such a judicial finding is made, the jury is said to be directed to return a verdict in accordance with the judge's conclusions. (On a directed verdict in a federal court the clerk enters the verdict according to the judge's instruction and the jury is discharged without deliberating the case.) There are also instances where a *civil* case may be submitted to the jury, the jury may deliberate and return a verdict, and yet the judge may decide not to enter judgment in accordance with the jury verdict. For example, after the jury verdict is received the judge may grant a motion for a new trial (assuming of course, that one or both of the parties demonstrates a valid reason for a new trial); or the judge may enter a judgment "notwithstanding the verdict" on a finding that the jury's verdict is not consistent with the evidence presented in the courtroom. The latter type of judgment is much like a judgment entered after a directed verdict. The only difference is that the judge reserves the decision as to whether or not reasonable people could differ as to the conclusions to be drawn from the evidence until the jury has had an opportunity to decide the case.

In criminal cases, the judge may direct a verdict of acquittal or set aside a jury verdict that the defendant is guilty; however, the judge may not direct a verdict of guilty nor set aside a jury verdict that the defendant is innocent, since this is considered to violate the constitutional rule against *double jeopardy.* (See p. 211 *supra.*)

The preceding is but a cursory examination of some of the situations where a jury may be effectively, and lawfully, removed from the deliberation of a case. The important point to note here is that these, and other procedural techniques, provide the parties and the judges some opportunity to control the jury and to prevent gross abuses by the jury of its restricted though crucial role in the trial process.

SECTION 16. THE TRIAL JUDGE

SECTION 16.1 THE ROLE OF THE TRIAL JUDGE

[The following is taken from CHARLES E. WYZANSKI, JR.,* "A TRIAL JUDGE'S FREEDOM AND RESPONSIBILITY," 65 Harvard Law Review 1281 (1952). Some footnotes omitted; others are renumbered.]

I. Judge and Jury

The trial judge's first problem is his relationship to the jury. Much of the debate about the jury system rests on political premises as old as the eighteenth century. Montesquieu, Blackstone and their followers contended that lay tribunals with a plurality of members were the safeguard of liberty. Bentham and more modern reformers replied that when the rule of law itself is sound, its integrity requires that its application be entrusted to magistrates acting alone. In their view responsibility is the secret of integrity, and a reasoned choice is the secret of responsibility.

Experience will not give a sovereign answer to these warring contentions. Yet the disagreement can be narrowed if the question of the jury's utility is subdivided with specific emphasis on separate types of suits.

The importance of this subdivision may be concealed by the striking phrase that a federal judge is the "governor of the trial." [1] Some regard this

---

* Judge Wyzanski was appointed to the federal bench in 1942. He is a U. S. District Judge for the District of Massachusetts.

1. The phrase comes from several Supreme Court opinions, the most notable being that of Hughes, C. J., in Quercia v. United States, 289 U.S. 466, 469, 53 S.Ct. 698, 699 (1933).

as an implied acceptance of the practice of English courts.[2]   And others construe it as a broad invitation to exercise in all types of cases a right to comment upon the evidence, provided of course that the judge always reminds the jury in his charge that they are not bound to follow the court's view of the facts or the credibility of the witnesses.   But such boldness is not the surest way to end disputes in all types of cases.

A. Tort Cases

The trial judge's comments upon evidence are particularly unwelcome in defamation cases.   In 1944 a discharged OPA official brought a libel suit against the radio commentator, Fulton Lewis, Jr.[3]   At one stage in the examination I suggested that Mr. Lewis' counsel was throwing pepper in the eyes of the jury; and at the final summation I indicated plainly enough that, although the jury was free to reject my opinion, I thought Mr. Lewis had been reckless in his calumnious charges against the ex-OPA official.   It makes no difference whether what I said was true;   I should not have said it, as the reaction of the bar and public reminded me.   A political libel suit is the modern substitute for ordeal by battle.   It is the means which society has chosen to induce bitter partisans to wager money instead of exchanging bloody noses.   And in such a contest the prudent and the second-thinking judge will stand severely aside, acting merely as a referee applying the Marquis of Queensberry rules.   In a later trial of a libel suit brought by James Michael Curley the gravamen of the complaint was that the Saturday Evening Post had said that Mr. Curley was a Catholic of whom His Eminence, Cardinal O'Connell would have no part.[4]   Who knew better than the Cardinal whether that charge was true?   Mr. Curley, the plaintiff, did not call the Cardinal to the stand.   The defendant's distinguished counsel did not desire to find out what would be the effect upon a Greater Boston jury if a Protestant lawyer should call a Catholic prelate to the witness stand.   Should the court have intervened and summoned the Cardinal on its own initiative?   The Fulton Lewis case gave the answer.   In a political [5] libel suit the judge is not the commander but merely the umpire.

Those tort cases which involve sordid family disputes also are better left to the jury without too explicit instructions.   Plato implied [6] and Holmes explicitly stated [7] that judges are apt to be naïve men.   If judges seem to comment on the morality of conduct or the extent of damages, they may discover that the jurors entirely disregard the comment because they believe that their own knowledge of such matters is more extensive than the judges'.

2.   Yet no federal judge would be likely to give as detailed, as long or as leading a charge as say Lord Wright's admirable summing up in The Royal Mail Case, see Notable British Trials, The Royal Mail Case 222–62 (Brooks ed. 1933); or Lord Chief Justice Goddard's summing up in The Laski Libel Action, see the Laski Libel Action 367–98 (1947).   Lord Wright's charge must have lasted at least four hours and Lord Goddard's two.

3.   Balsam v. Lewis, Civil No. 2259, D.C. Mass., Jan. 27, 1944.

4.   Curley v. Curtis Publishing Company, Civil No. 1872, D.C.Mass., Feb. 25, 1944.

5.   In a libel suit where political and like emotional elements are absent, a judge may do as well as a jury.   Cf. Kelly v. Loew's, Inc., 76 F.Supp. 473 (D.C.Mass.1948).

6.   Plato, The Republic III.

7.   Holmes, Law and the Court in Collected Legal Papers 291, 295 (1920).

At any rate when brother sues brother,[8] or when spouse sues paramour,[9] the very anonymity of the jury's judgment often does more to still the controversy than the most clearly reasoned opinion or charge of an identified judge could have done.

What of the trial judge's role in accident cases? How far should he go in requiring available evidence to be produced,[10] in commenting on the testimony, and in using special verdicts [11] and like devices to seek to keep the jury within the precise bounds laid down by the appellate courts? There are some who would say that the trial judge has not fulfilled his moral obligation if he merely states clearly the law regarding negligence, causation, contributory fault and types of recoverable damage. In their opinion it is his duty to analyze the evidence and demonstrate where the evidence seems strong or thin and where it appears reliable or untrustworthy. But most federal judges do not make such analyses. They are not deterred through laziness, a sentimental regard for the afflatus of the Seventh Amendment or even a fear of reversal. They are mindful that the community no longer accepts as completely valid legal principles basing liability upon fault. They perceive a general recognition of the inevitability of numerous accidents in modern life, which has made insurance widely available and widely used. Workmen's compensation acts and other social and economic legislation have revealed a trend that did not exist when the common law doctrines of tort were formulated. And the judges sense a new climate of public opinion which rates security as one of the chief goals of men.

Trial judges cannot, without violating their oaths, bow directly to this altered policy.[12] In instructions of law they must repeat the doctrines which judges of superior courts formulated and which only they or the legislatures can change. But trial judges are not giving "rein to the passional element of

---

8. Hegarty v. Hegarty, 52 F.Supp. 296 (D.C.Mass.1943).

9. Gordon v. Parker, 83 F.Supp. 40, 43, 45 (D.C.Mass.), affirmed 178 F.2d 888 (1st Cir. 1949). It may be said that divorce cases are contrary to my thesis. But is it not true that most divorce cases involve either no contest or an attempt by the judge to act as conciliator? Where there is a bitter contest, many divorce court judges, I believe, would rather have the issue put to a jury, if that were possible.

10. See the suggestion of Frankfurter, J., dissenting in Johnson v. United States, 333 U.S. 46, 54–55, 68 S.Ct. 391, 395–396 (1948).

11. A special verdict in a tort case, by minimizing the emotional considerations, is more likely than a general verdict to produce a judgment for defendant. Mills v. Eastern Steamship Lines, Inc., Civil No. 7366, D.C.Mass., Dec. 3, 1948. Perhaps this considera-

tion was not absent in the different approaches disclosed in the opinions of Judge Clark and Judge Frank in Morris v. Pennsylvania R. R., 187 F.2d 837, 840–41, 843 (2d Cir. 1951). See also Skidmore v. Baltimore & Ohio R. R., 167 F.2d 54, 65–67, 70 (2d Cir. 1948).

12. There are some judges who take this altered policy into account in inducing parties to settle. No study of the living law of torts can properly neglect the importance of these settlements. They have increased at a rapid rate as a consequence of congested dockets and the wider use of pre-trial techniques encouraged by Rule 16 of the Federal Rules of Civil Procedure. They are popular with the bar and many clients. They ease the otherwise insupportable load on the judicial system. And they make even the judge who does not approve of the degree to which other judges induce settlements unwilling to take strong measures to lead a jury in directions contrary to those upon which settlements have been and will be reached.

our nature" [13] nor forswearing themselves by following Lord Coke's maxim that "the jurors are chancellors." [14] Traditionally juries are the device by which the rigor of the law is modified pending the enactment of new statutes.

Some will say that this abdication is not merely cowardly but ignores the "French saying about small reforms being the worst enemies of great reforms." [15] To them the proper course would be to apply the ancient rules with full rigidity in the anticipation of adverse reactions leading to a complete resurvey of accident law; to a scrutiny of the costs, delays and burdens of present litigation; to a comparative study of what injured persons actually get in cash as a result of lawsuits, settlements out of court, administrative compensation proceedings and other types of insurance plans; and ultimately to a new codification. To this one answer is that in Anglo-American legal history reform has rarely come as a result of prompt, comprehensive investigation and legislation. The usual course has been by resort to juries,[16] to fictions, to compromises with logic. Only at the last stages are outright changes in the formal rules announced by the legislators or the appellate judges. This is consistent with Burke's principle that "reform is impracticable in the sense of an abrupt reconstruction of society, and can only be understood as the gradual modification of a complex structure." [17]

Parenthetically, let me say that I am not at all clear that it would be a desirable reform in tort cases to substitute trial by judges for trial by juries. Just such a substitution has been made in the Federal Tort Claims Act. And experience under that statute does not prove that in this type of case a single professional is as satisfactory a tribunal as a group of laymen of mixed backgrounds. In estimating how a reasonable and prudent man would act, judges' court experience counts for no more than juries' out-of-court experience. In determining the credibility of that type of witness who appears in accident cases an expert tribunal is somewhat too ready to see a familiar pattern. Shrewdness founded on skepticism and sophistication has its place in scrutinizing the stories of witnesses. But there is a danger that the professional trier of fact will expect people of varied callings and cultures to reach levels of observation and narration which would not be expected by men of the witness' own background. Moreover, when it comes to a calcula-

---

13. L. Hand, J., in Skidmore v. Baltimore & Ohio R. R., 167 F.2d 54, 70 (2d Cir. 1948).

14. Quoted from Pound, An Introduction to the Philosophy of Law 133 (1922).

15. Morley, On Compromise 185 (rev. ed. 1877).

16. In Chapters VIII and IX of Courts on Trial (1949), Judge Frank, while admitting that some reforms are attributable to jury lawlessness, in general distrusts such methods. He suggests that certainty and equality are impossible because one jury differs so much from another. This difference he says is recognized by the bar which gives great attention to the selection of jurors (pp. 120–21). This argument may be overstated. In the Massachusetts District there are rarely more than two or three challenges to jurors in any but criminal cases. It ordinarily takes less than five minutes and in the last decade has never taken more than half an hour to select a jury. And these juries tend to act so uniformly that the court officers and attendants who have sat with hundreds of juries can make a substantially accurate prediction of how any given jury will act. Indeed, their prediction of jury action is much closer to the ultimate result than their prediction of judicial actions.

17. Quoted in 2 L. Stephen, A History of English Thought in the Eighteenth Century 230 (1881).

tion of damages under the flexible rules of tort law the estimate of what loss the plaintiff suffered can best be made by men who know different standards of working and living in our society. Indeed I have heard federal judges confess that in a Federal Tort Claims Act case they try to make their judgments correspond with what they believe a jury would do in a private case. And not a few judges would prefer to have such cases tried by juries.

B. Commercial Litigation

In commercial cases and those arising under regulatory statutes there is reason to hold a jury by a much tighter rein than in tort cases. This is not because the rules of law are more consonant with prevailing notions of justice. In these controversies judges have a specialized knowledge. Parties have usually acted with specific reference to their legal rights,[18] and departures from the declared standard would undermine the legislative declaration and would be likely to produce confusion and further litigation rather than reform. An extreme example will serve as an illustration. In a tax case tried before a jury at the suit of one holder of International Match Company preference stock, the issue was whether for tax purposes those certificates had become worthless in the year 1936. In another taxpayer's case the Second Circuit Court of Appeals had affirmed a ruling of the Board of Tax Appeals that similar stock had become valueless in the year 1932. Technically this adjudication did not bind the jury, though the evidence before it was substantially the same as that in the earlier case. To preserve uniformity on a factual tax problem of general application I had no hesitation in strongly intimating to the jury that they should reach the same result as the Second Circuit.

In sales cases, moreover, something close to a scientific appraisal of the facts is possible. There are strong mercantile interests favoring certainty and future litigation can be reduced by strict adherence to carefully prescribed statutory standards. These considerations sometimes warrant giving juries written instructions or summaries and often warrant the use of special verdicts. Either method makes jurors focus precisely on the formalities of the contract, the warranties alleged to have been broken, the types of damage alleged to have been sustained, and the allowable formulae for calculating those damages. Indeed, except for tort cases, I find myself in agreement with Judge Frank that the trial judge ought to use special verdicts to a much larger extent, though it is more difficult than may at first be realized to frame questions to the satisfaction of counsel and to the comprehension of juries. Once when I used what I thought simple questions, a fellow judge, half in jest, accused me of trying to promote a disagreement of the jury and thus to force a settlement.

The arguments supporting special verdicts in commercial or statutory cases also support a trial judge in giving in such cases a more detailed charge and more specific guidance in estimating the testimony. In compli-

---

18. Although there are some exceptions, usually parties to an accident case have acted without reference to the law, whereas the law has been one of the considerations in contemplation when parties to a commercial transaction took their action. The chief exceptions are where the tort defendant failed to take out insurance because he supposed there was no risk of liability save for misconduct, and the rare case where a contract defendant made or broke his promise without attention to the written rules of law.

cated cases or those in fields where the experience of the average juror is much less than that of the average judge, there is a substantial risk of a miscarriage of justice unless the judge points rather plainly to the "knots" in the evidence and suggests how they can be unravelled. The only time I have ever entered judgment notwithstanding a verdict was in a private antitrust suit. The jury had awarded damages of over one million dollars due, I believe, to the generality of my instructions. I should have spent as much time on my charge in helping them understand the testimony as I later spent on the memorandum in which I analyzed the evidence for an appellate court. And one of the few totally irrational awards that I have seen a jury make came in a compromise verdict in a breach of contract case brought by a plaintiff of foreign birth against a defendant who came from the dominant local group. The charge had stopped with broad, though probably correct, statements of the substantive law. The jury should have been told that their choice lay between only two alternatives—either to find for the plaintiff for the full amount claimed or to find for the defendant. Any intermediate sum could be attributable only to a discount for prejudice or a bounty for sympathy.

C.   Criminal Prosecutions

At the trial of criminal cases the judge's role more closely resembles his role in tort cases than in commercial litigation. About ninety percent of all defendants in the federal courts plead guilty. In those federal cases which come to trial the crime charged frequently concerns economic facts, and generally, though not invariably, the preliminary investigation by the FBI and other agencies of detection has reduced to a small compass the area of doubt. Often the only remaining substantive issue of significance is whether the defendant acted "knowingly." Indeed, the usual federal criminal trial is as apt to turn on whether the prosecution has procured its evidence in accordance with law and is presenting it fairly, as on whether the defendant is guilty as charged. All these factors combine to concentrate the judge's attention upon the avoidance of prejudicial inquiries, confusion of proof [19] and inflammatory arguments. Counsel can aid the judge to maintain the proper atmosphere by stipulation,[20] by refraining from putting doubtful questions until the judge has ruled at the bench, and by other cooperative efforts. But if cooperation is not forthcoming, the judge should hesitate to fill the gap by becoming himself a participant in the interrogation or to indicate any view of the evidence. For the criminal trial is as much a ceremony as an investigation. Dignity and forbearance are almost the chief desiderata.

---

19. As is well recognized, risk of confusion and hence judicial responsibility is greatest in conspiracy cases. See the opinion of Jackson, J., in Krulewitch v. United States, 336 U.S. 440, 453, 69 S.Ct. 716, 723 (1949).

20. Although there is no provision in the federal *criminal* rules for pre-trial, my own experience is that counsel in complicated cases often welcome pre-trial stipulations. In the scores of separate prosecutions for conspiracy to defraud the United States by false time-slips at the Bethlehem-Hingham yard which followed McGunnigal v. United States, 151 F.2d 162 (1st Cir.), cert. denied 326 U.S. 776, 66 S.Ct. 267 (1945), each defendant, who was tried separately, agreed to stipulate every underlying fact except his personal participation. This reduced the time of trial from over a week to less than half a day. And some of the defendants were, in my opinion, justifiably acquitted. Similar stipulations have been successful in Dyer Act conspiracies and conspiracies to violate the alcohol tax laws.

But as Mr. Justice McCardie said, "Anyone can try a criminal case. The real problem arises when the judge has to decide what punishment to award." [21] On the sentencing problem [22] three observations may be worth making:

(1) Despite the latitude permitted by the Due Process Clause, it seems to me that a judge in considering his sentence, just as in trying a defendant, should never take into account any evidence, report or other fact which is not brought to the attention of defendant's counsel with opportunity to rebut it. *Audi alteram partem*, if it is not a universal principle of democratic justice, is at any rate sufficiently well-founded not to be departed from by a trial judge when he is performing his most important function. In those situations where a wife, a minister, a doctor or other person is willing to give confidential information to the judge provided that the defendant does not hear it, this information ought to be revealed to the defendant's counsel for scrutiny and reply. This in no sense implies "a requirement of rigid adherence to restrictive rules of evidence properly applicable to the trial" [23] or "open court testimony with cross-examination." [24] Other methods will avoid those grave errors which sometimes follow from acting on undisclosed rumor and prejudice.

(2) Another nearly universal principle applicable to criminal sentences is equality of treatment. Despite the "prevalent modern philosophy of penology that the punishment should fit the offender and not merely the crime," [25] the sentencing judge is not the precise equivalent of a doctor giving an individual a medical prescription appropriate to a unique personality. Offenders of the same general type should be treated alike at least in the same community.[26] One reason is grounded on a strictly scientific consideration emphasized by Morris R. Cohen: "We are apt to have more reliable knowledge about classes than about individuals." [27] But a deeper ethical consideration is embedded in an Alexandrian metaphor, "equality is the mother of justice." [28] With this test in mind, I submit that if in the district in which a judge sits his fellow judges have established and insist on following a pattern for dealing with offenders of a particular type, it is his responsibility either to get them to change or to come close to their standard.

---

21. Goodhart, English Contributions to the Philosophy of Law 14 (1949).

22. Judge Lummus has given illuminating criteria for sentencing. Lummus, The Trial Judge 46, 54–55 (1937). See also, Ulman, A Judge Takes the Stand 234–59 (1933); Wortley, The English Law of Punishment in The Modern Approach to Criminal Law, IV English Studies in Criminal Science 50 (1945), and Radzinowicz, The Assessment of Punishments by English Courts in *id.* at 110.

23. Williams v. New York, 337 U.S. 241, 247, 69 S.Ct. 1079, 1083 (1949).

24. *Id.*, at 250.

25. *Id.*, at 247.

26. A problem inherent in the federal system is whether there should be national equality of treatment. Those who sponsored the revised Federal Corrections Bill were mindful of the significance of a sentence in the area where the court sits as well as in the area where the defendant is imprisoned. See Report of Committee on Punishment for Crime, Rep. Att'y Gen. 25, 26 (1942).

27. Cohen, Reason and Law 56 (1950).

28. Quotation of Philo in letter from Burke to Burgh cited in 2 L. Stephen, A History of English Thought in the Eighteenth Century 226 (1881).

(3) My third observation relates to whether a judge should give the reasons for his sentence. Eminent and wise judges have warned me against this. Our judgment, they say, is better than our reasons. And it is vain to attempt to explain the exact proportions attributable to our interest in punishment, retribution, reform, deterrence, even vengeance. But are these arguments valid? For there is grave danger that a sentencing judge will allow his emotion or other transient factors to sway him. The strongest safeguard is for him to act only after formulating a statement of the considerations which he allows himself to take into account. Moreover, the explicit utterance of relevant criteria serves as a guide for future dispositions both by him and other judges.[29]

II. Nonjury Trials

A. Handling of Evidence and Extra-judicial Material

In nonjury as in jury cases, a substantial part of the bar prefers to have the judge sit patiently while the evidence comes in and then at the end of the trial summarize the testimony which he believes. This seems the sounder practice in the great bulk of trials. But in cases of public significance, Edmund Burke admonished us: "It is the duty of the Judge to receive every offer of evidence, apparently material, suggested to him, though the parties themselves through negligence, ignorance, or corrupt collusion, should not bring it forward. A judge is not placed in that high situation merely as a passive instrument of parties. He has a duty of his own, independent of them, and that duty is to investigate the truth." [30]

Let me give some examples of when I believe the judge has a duty to elicit facts in addition to those that are offered by the parties. The plaintiff, an owner of a multiple dwelling, brought suit for a declaratory judgment seeking to have the premises declared a "hotel" and thus exempt from the rent regulations of the OPA.[31] Only one of the numerous tenants was named as defendant. In the trial the plaintiff offered evidence that the building was a hotel and not an apartment. Due to lack of funds or due to lack of forensic skill, the tenant's counsel failed to shake the stories of the plaintiff's witnesses or to offer adequate testimony to the contrary. Yet if the trial judge had called specialists and others familiar with the community and the property, the evidence would have demonstrated that in truth the building was a mere apartment house. I took no step myself to call witnesses or to interrogate those who did testify but, relying exclusively on what the parties offered, entered a judgment declaring the premises a "hotel" and thus exempt. Since this declaration of status became in effect, though not in law, a general rule practically, though not theoretically, binding on scores of persons not actually represented in the proceedings, would it not have been

29. It may be contended that the grounds for administrative action need be explicitly set forth only when judicial review is permissible, and as an aid to such review, and that since the federal trial judge's sentencing discretion is unreviewable no grounds need be asserted. This is not a complete answer, for the trial judge's sentencing discretion is in effect reviewable by pardoning and commutation authorities.

30. Quoted in 3 Wigmore, Evidence 151 (3d ed. 1940).

31. Riverside Apt. Hotel, Inc. v. Rudnick, Civil No. 7823, D.C.Mass., Nov. 15, 1948.

sounder for the court to take a larger initiative in seeing that the record corresponded with reality?

A later controversy of even greater public importance posed a similar problem. In a case still undecided, the United States sued the United Shoe Machinery Corporation for violation of the antitrust laws.[32] Among the issues presented was what was the effect of the corporation's acts upon its customers and upon its competitors. The Government in its case in chief relied exclusively on the corporation's documents and officers. The corporation planned to call some customers, though the method by which they were drawn was not disclosed to the court. This seemed an inadequate survey. So the court asked the parties to take depositions from forty-five customers, selected from a standard directory by taking the first fifteen names under the first, eleventh and twenty-first letters of the alphabet; and the court itself called to the stand the officers of the principal competitor. In the summons the court listed topics appropriate for the questioning of the officers. The actual examination was conducted in turn by the competitor's counsel and the defendant's counsel. Both these types of testimony resulted in giving a much clearer understanding of the total picture of the industries that will be affected by any ultimate decision.

Another problem in the United Shoe case has been to determine what have been the usual methods followed by the defendant in setting prices, in supplying services, and in suing competitors. An adequately grounded conclusion can hardly be based entirely on the plaintiff's selection of a few dramatic incidents and on the defendant's testimony of the general attitude of its officers. The critical point in determining liability and, even more probably, the form of relief, if any, may turn on what has been the typical pattern of the defendant's conduct and the typical effect of that conduct on outsiders. •Here the judge can perform a useful function if he, through pre-trial conferences or at a later stage of the litigation when he is more aware of its dimensions, provides for appropriate samplings of the conduct and the effects. If the judge is fortunate, the parties may agree on the sampling. But where they do not, it seems to me to be the judge's responsibility first to elicit from witnesses on the stand the criteria necessary to determine what are fair samples and then to direct the parties to prepare such samples for examination and cross-examination. Sampling will make for not merely a more informative but a shorter record—an object to which both bench and bar must give more attention if the judicial process is to survive in anti-trust cases.

The question as to what has been the custom of the market and what would be the consequence of a judicial decree altering those practices arises not only in antitrust cases but also when the judge is faced with the problem of determining either the appropriate standard of fair competition in trademarks or the appropriate standard for fiduciaries. Usually, to be sure, diligent counsel offer in evidence enough relevant material. But where this has not been done, there have been times when a judge has tended to reach his result partly on the basis of general information and partly on the basis

---

32. United States v. United Shoe Machinery Corp., Civil No. 7198, D.C. Mass., complaint filed Dec. 15, 1947.

of his studies in a library. This tendency of a court to inform itself has increased in recent years following the lead of the Supreme Court of the United States. Not merely in constitutional controversies and in statutory interpretation but also in formulation of judge-made rules of law, the justices have resorted, in footnotes and elsewhere, to references drawn from legislative hearings, studies by executive departments, and scholarly monographs. Such resort is sometimes defended as an extension of Mr. Brandeis' technique as counsel for the state in Muller v. Oregon.[33] In Muller's case, however, Mr. Brandeis' object was to demonstrate that there was a body of informed public opinion which supported the reasonableness of the *legislative* rule of law. But in the cases of which I am speaking these extra-judicial studies are drawn upon to determine what would be a reasonable *judicial* rule of law.[34] Thus the focus of the inquiry becomes not what judgment is permissible, but what judgment is sound. And here it seems to me that the judge, before deriving any conclusions from any such extra-judicial document or information, should lay it before the parties for their criticism.

How this criticism should be offered is itself a problem not free from difficulty. In some situations, the better course may be to submit the material for examination, cross-examination and rebuttal evidence. In others, where expert criticism has primarily an argumentative character, it can be received better from the counsel table and from briefs than from the witness box. The important point is that before a judge acts upon a consideration of any kind, he ought to give the parties a chance to meet it. This opportunity is owed as a matter of fairness and also to prevent egregious error. As Professor Lon Fuller has observed, the "moral force of a judgment is at maximum if a judge decides solely on the basis of arguments presented to him. Because if he goes beyond these he will lack guidance and may not understand interests that are affected by a decision outside the framework." [35]

The duty of the judge to act only upon the basis of material debated in public in no sense implies that the judge's findings should be in the precise terms offered by counsel. Nor does Rule 52(a) of the Federal Rules of Civil Procedure require the judge always to recite all relevant evidence and to rely for persuasive effect exclusively upon mass and orderly arrangement. Yet in corporate cases or other litigation where the issues turn on documentary construction and precise analysis of business details, and where ap-

---

33. 208 U.S. 412, 28 S.Ct. 324 (1908).

34. It may be needless to emphasize that the problem with which I am concerned is the formulation of a rule of law. Where a court is formulating a finding of fact it, of course, cannot rely on knowledge gained dehors the record, except in so far as it comes within the narrow ambit of the doctrine of judicial notice. *Cf.* West Ohio Gas Co. v. PUC, 294 U.S. 79, 55 S.Ct. 324 (1935).

35. Fuller, The Problems of Jurisprudence 707 (temp. ed. 1949). [This is a greatly condensed version of Professor Fuller's statement, which is quoted in full at p. 101, *supra.*] This reasoning may well apply to the appropriate treatment of novel arguments presented to a judge by his law clerk. It may be the responsibility of the judge to present those arguments to counsel for examination. *Cf.* Experts As Consultants to Courts, 74 N. J.L.J. 52 (1951). This is especially important because of the often unrecognized importance of those who are associates of the judge in his work. On this point consider the perceptive remark made by Bracton in Concerning the Laws and Customs of England, bk. II, c. 16, f. 34 (1569), "qui habet socium, habet magistrum . . . ."

peal is almost certain to be taken, the trial judge may perform the greatest service by acting almost as a master summarizing evidence for a higher tribunal.

On the other hand, if a judge sitting alone hears a simple tort or contract case falling within a familiar framework and analogous to jury litigation, it is perhaps the best practice for him to state his findings of fact from the bench in those pungent colloquial terms with which the traditional English judge addresses the average man of common sense. When credibility of witnesses is the essence of the controversy, the parties and the lawyers like to have judges act as promptly as juries and, like them, on the basis of fresh impressions.   .   .   .

SECTION 16.2   A JUDGE'S DELIBERATION OF A CASE

[The following is taken from JOSEPH N. ULMAN,* A JUDGE TAKES THE STAND (New York, 1933), pp. 52–66.]

Saturday, June 4, 1932. It happens that the question I want to discuss at this point is illustrated by a case the trial of which began yesterday morning. When court adjourned in the afternoon, to convene again on Monday, the trial had progressed to a stage which makes my judicial task at this moment the consideration of the very matter about which I want to write in this chapter. Therefore I can write about it today before it is decided. On Monday I shall be able to announce my decision in court and also to tell about it in this book. By following this plan, I shall at the same time furnish a personal, and therefore only partial, answer to the question asked by Mr. Jerome Frank, and other recent writers for the technical journals of the law: How do judges think?

The case is that of Paul Lacotti vs. The Pennsylvania Railroad Company. Lacotti owns a little truck farm a few miles from Baltimore. He is sixty-eight years old, and though he has been in America nearly twenty-five years, he knows practically no English. That makes it necessary to conduct his examination through an interpreter, which, of course, slows up the case. But nobody minds very much because this old man has a magnetic personality, which breaks through the tedium of the procedure just as his frequent smiles and his eloquent gestures break through the barriers which his lack of English would otherwise set up.

The work done by a court interpreter is always interesting. Our official interpreter in Baltimore knows eight or nine languages. More than that, though, he seems to know eight or nine foreign temperaments. Unfortunately Lacotti is an Italian from Sicily, so he doesn't speak Italian. The Sicilian dialect which he does speak, happens to be one language which our official interpreter does not know. Therefore it has been necessary to swear in a young law student as a special interpreter for this case. He knows Sicilian and he knows English perfectly but he lacks the professional touch of our skilled court officer.

---

* Judge Ulman served on the Supreme Bench of Baltimore, Maryland from 1924 until his death in 1943. He was also a member of the law faculty at the University of Maryland from 1908 to 1928.

For example, one of the introductory questions asked of the plaintiff is a very simple question which can be answered by an obvious "yes" or "no." When Lacotti hears it he frowns. Then he smiles. Then he launches into a long speech with many gestures. He becomes so excited that he gets up from the witness chair and sits down again three times before he finishes his answer. I am tempted at this point to suggest that perhaps the witness has said either "yes" or "no," and that the interpreter shall confine his rendition of the answer to one or the other of those words. But I am glad that I restrain myself; for the interpreter looks at me and reports, "He says he does not understand the question." So it has to be asked and answered all over again.

The suit grows out of a collision between a fast passenger train and a wagon loaded with manure and driven by the plaintiff. One of the early questions put to the plaintiff is, "What part of your wagon was struck?" Again a long and excited answer, and again the interpreter tells me the witness does not understand the question. When the question is repeated, I catch two words of it. The question was, "What part of your wagon was struck?" The young interpreter, in a perfectly honest effort to make the witness understand, adds, "the right side or the left side?" That particular addition did not do a bit of harm. It was perfectly obvious that it was the right side which must have been struck; and the purpose of the question was to bring out the fact that the right rear wheel was the point of impact. Finally the witness catches the point and gives the desired information.

This incident, however, affords me an opportunity to assure myself that the interpreter will do his work as it ought to be done. I call him and counsel up to the bench, so that I may speak to them out of the jury's hearing. I tell them that I have observed that the interpreter has added something to the question. I explain to him, very firmly, that as interpreter he must confine himself to interpreting; and that he has no right to add anything either to questions or to answers. But I do not tell him that the words "right" and "left" are the only Italian words I have understood all morning and that I am not likely to understand another.

By yesterday afternoon the plaintiff's witnesses had all testified and had developed the following facts. The plaintiff, driving his wagon loaded with manure, came to a point where the road crossed the railroad tracks. It was a grade crossing without safety gates or watchman, but it was guarded by the usual prominent "Stop, Look, and Listen" signs, and by blinker-lights. These are large red lights, automatically operated by electric current, and so devised that they burn alternately and conspicuously while a train is within the block approaching the crossing either from the north or from the south. The plaintiff said the lights were blinking when he approached the crossing, so he drew up his horse and waited. While he was waiting, an automobile pulled up beside him. After a few moments a train approached and passed from the north, running on the south-bound track, which was the track nearer to which the plaintiff was standing. After this train passed, the lights stopped blinking. The automobile started off, crossed the tracks in safety, and was about one hundred yards down the road before anything happened. The plaintiff could not get under way so quickly, because his loaded wagon was heavy for the one horse which was drawing it. However, he did get started; and as he passed beneath the blinker-lights, he looked up and saw that they were not blinking. They are very close to the tracks, and the plaintiff went on. When his horse's feet were between the rails of the second, or north-bound, track he looked to his right, and there was a train coming. "How far away was the train when you first saw it? How many feet away?" "It was close. So close the locomotive looked to me big like a mountain." The interpreter did not spoil that graphic touch.

In this emergency the plaintiff whipped his horse, and all but the last foot or two of his wagon cleared the track. The wagon was demolished, the manure fertilized the wrong field, and the plaintiff was toppled to the ground. When he got up, he had a badly injured knee. His doctor testified that his injuries are permanent. He himself testified that he has not been able to work at all since the accident whereas before he had worked his little farm practically without assistance and had made about five hundred dollars a year net profit. His expectation of life, as shown by life insurance tables, is about nine years. Therefore, if he wins his case, he may get four or five thousand dollars, perhaps even more.

What concerns me today, however, is not any question of the amount of verdict. It is something very much more serious than that, serious both to the plaintiff and to me. It is whether or not I, as judge, shall allow the case to go on and permit the plaintiff to ask the jury for any verdict at all. In other words, shall I, or shall I not, "take the case from the jury"? If you do not know anything about the law and court proceedings, and I am assuming that you do not, I shall not blame you if at this point you feel both puzzled and indignant. Have I not said in the earlier chapter that the jury's job is to pass on the facts, and the judge's to pass on the law? By what right then, you may ask, do I as judge propose to brush aside the jury in this case and to decide it myself in favor of the defendant? If I do that, what becomes of the vaunted right to trial by jury?

Nevertheless, that is precisely what I may decide to do. I won't know until Monday morning. So you must be patient for a few pages while I try to tell you and Mr. Jerome Frank how a judge thinks and what he has to think about in a situation of this kind.

As far back as the 15th century, English judges had begun to control cases in a manner quite similar to that which I am now contemplating. The legal form was different, but it amounted to the same thing. In modern times, when we talk about a judge taking a case from the jury, what we really mean is that the judge, at the request of the defendant, grants a binding instruction, telling the jury that it *must*, upon the evidence, find a verdict in favor of the defendant. He doesn't take the case away from the jury so much as he takes the jury away from the case. He takes away from the case the privilege of the jury to exercise any independent judgment upon it and tells the jury what verdict it must hand down. There is a record of an early English case in which the judge did this, but the jury rebelled. Directed to find a verdict for the defendant, the jury nevertheless found for the plaintiff. They were admonished by the judge and sent back to reconsider and bring in a proper verdict in accordance with the judge's instructions. A second time the jury took the bit in its teeth and announced that it had decided the case in favor of the plaintiff. This time the judge asserted his authority. He sent for the sheriff, directed him to load the members of the jury into a cart, drive them into the country, and dump them into the nearest ditch.

I have never had to do anything like that. But I have seen jurors look at me, when I directed them to find a verdict, as though they wished they had the right to express their disapproval of me in some such vigorous and direct manner.

What, then, is the legal theory behind this ancient practice? Why does a judge sometimes direct a certain verdict? Why is it, under some circumstances, his legal duty to do so? Let me try to answer that question by a very simple illustration. Plaintiff sues Defendant on a promissory note. He produces the note in court and swears that Defendant signed it and gave it to him in exchange for a loan of $100. Plaintiff is then cross-examined by Defendant's lawyer. He breaks down and admits that he never lent Defendant $100 nor any other sum of money and that Defendant never gave him the note sued on. Pressed still harder, he admits that he himself wrote the note, signed Defendant's name to it, and that it is a forgery.

Obviously, that ought to be the end of Plaintiff's case. There is no reason to put Defendant to the trouble of offering any evidence. The legal proposition is as simple as are the facts of the case. Defendant is not liable, as a matter of law, upon a piece of paper that looks as though it might be his promissory note but actually is merely a piece of paper on which somebody else has forged his name. That is the law of the case, to be decided by the judge. The facts of the case are to be decided, under our system, by the jury. But there is no room for any question about the facts. Plaintiff has admitted enough to force the jury to decide the facts against him. There is only one rational conclusion which the jury can reach, and that is a conclusion against Plaintiff. Therefore, the judge will grant a binding instruction, directing the jury that under the evidence it *must* find a verdict in favor of the Defendant. The rendition of the verdict by the jury becomes a mere form, necessary only in order to complete the ceremonial record of the case.

An extreme case like that does not call for any further explanation. Nobody is likely to object very seriously to what the judge has done. Plaintiff has tried to perpetrate a gross fraud. He ought to be thrown out of court, and nobody cares whether he is thrown out of the front door, the back door, or through the window. In fact he should be prosecuted for his crime, in addition to being thrown out of the civil court. The form of his ejection is by means of a directed verdict in favor of the defendant. The substance of it is a judicial declaration that he has no legal right to recover on the strength of the evidence as presented. Bound up in that judicial declaration is the assertion that there is only one rational view to take of the evidence. And, in this simple case, it is perfectly plain that this is so.

Now come back to my problem with the Lacotti case. What is the law of that case? I shall state it as simply as I can. Lacotti was injured at a railroad crossing. I have said before that, at each side of the crossing, were the familiar "Stop, Look and Listen" signs. Probably comparatively few travellers know why those particular words are on these signs. They are there, because, in this instance, a rule of judge-made-law has become a tradition not only for lawyers and judges, but for railroad presidents as well. In a case decided many years ago when railroads were in their infancy, a judge said that it was dangerous to cross a railroad track and that a prudent man would "stop, look, and listen" before he did so. That was good, snappy

English. It didn't take long for other judges to begin repeating it. Soon it was generally recognized rule of law; and it followed that if a man went on the tracks without stopping, looking, and listening, he was not a prudent man. Then, if he got hurt, it was his own fault, and the railroad did not have to pay him anything. In other words, he was guilty of contributory negligence; and the verdict of the jury, according to the law-in-the-law-books, *had to be* a verdict for the defendant. Railroad presidents like this rule of law; and for many years they have been painting it in large black letters on white sign-boards at every grade-crossing. It has become so common that if it weren't there, you probably would not believe that the tracks you see are real tracks for real trains to run on.

Like many rules of law, however, this one started out very simply and then became more complicated as cases arose the facts of which did not fit exactly into the pattern. Take my Lacotti case, for example. The Pennsylvania Railroad Company, at this particular crossing, made a definite effort to protect persons travelling on the highway. It did not station a watchman there nor put up safety-gates. The crossing was not used enough to make that seem worth while. But it did put up those conspicuous red blinker-lights. When they worked as they are supposed to work, they were a great help. People got used to looking for the blink. If the lights were blinking, it would be a very careless man indeed who deliberately went on the tracks, fully expecting a train to rush down on him at any moment.

But suppose the blinkers should fail to blink when they ought to blink. Lacotti said that is exactly what happened when he started across the track. Therefore, said his lawyer, this elaborate electrical device, installed to protect the traveller on the highway, had become an actual source of additional danger. A blinker-light that fails to blink is a lure and a trap. Surely Lacotti ought to win his case.

Now I have sketched in only the very high spots of the evidence; and I shall, for purposes of simplicity, add as few details as possible. A plat made by a competent surveyor has been offered in evidence. It shows the slight curvature of the railroad track, the near-by railroad station, the location of the blinker-lights, and of every tree and every telegraph pole and every road and house for several hundred feet on each side of the crossing. Photographs have been introduced, showing the view up and down the tracks from several accurately marked points on the highway. The plaintiff's son has testified to measurements he has made showing precisely how far down the track he could see as he stood at various points beginning twenty-five feet away from the track and then moving up by five-foot intervals and measuring again. From all this evidence and more of like nature, I have discovered that the view down the track in the direction from which the train came is obscured from certain points by the little railroad station. When I look at the surveyor's plat, I observe that the plaintiff's son seems to have made fairly accurate measurements, but they do not appear to be perfect. The testimony has also informed me that the train was running at sixty miles an hour and that the blinker-lights were supposed to be set in operation automatically when it passed a point a little over three thousand feet from the crossing. Therefore, they should have been blinking for a full half minute before the train arrived at the crossing. Yet the plaintiff has testified that they were not blinking when he passed beneath them, about fifty feet away from the point which he had reached when his right rear wheel was struck by the locomotive. How long did it take the plaintiff to travel those fifty feet? If he was going at the rate of three miles per hour, it took him about eleven seconds. Well then, he certainly was trapped. The lights ought to have blinked for over thirty seconds; they did not blink for even eleven seconds. Another witness has testified that the lights were not blinking properly three days before the accident. Therefore the company ought to have known they were out of order.

But yesterday afternoon, the defendant's lawyers referred me to a number of important precedents. They gave me a list of cases decided by the Maryland Court of Appeals and by other courts, in which the law of railroad crossing accidents has been applied and developed. After court adjourned, I read a considerable number of these cases. In a general way, perhaps, I was familiar with them before; but yesterday I read them carefully and with special reference to the facts of the Lacotti case. And I find that I am faced with a real problem. I find that our Court of Appeals holds very strongly to the stop, look, and listen rule. I find there are cases in which it has decided that a person is not relieved of his obligation to stop, look, and listen, merely because the railroad company has installed safety devices for his protection. It appears that he must still make use of his senses for his own protection, even though a safety device out of order has given him a sense of false security. In one of the cases cited, an automatic bell failed to ring; in another a watchman did not put down the safety-gates. In both these cases the Court of Appeals has said that the traveller was nevertheless guilty of contributory negligence if he did not look before he left a place of safety. It has also said in many cases, that if a man says he looked and did not see a dangerous object which was there, he is bound just as though he admits that he did not look at all.

I find this very puzzling. That is one of the troubles about judge-made law. In each case the judge who wrote the opinion used general language, expressing general rules and principles, in words that might apply to any case. But when you want to find out exactly what he meant and just how far his decision is an authority which it is your duty to follow, you have to study the facts of the particular case in which his opinion was written and to try to determine whether the facts of the case with which you are wrestling are sufficiently similar to make the reasons and principles of his opinion applicable to your case.

I shall assume that you will not be interested in many more details of my legal puzzle. Let it suffice to say that yesterday, while studying the authorities, I had what Joseph C. Hutcheson, a great judge and learned writer upon the law, has called a hunch. I suddenly made up my mind that my decision in this case was going to hinge upon the question of how far down the track Mr. Lacotti could see when he was twelve feet away from the nearest rail. I selected that point as being approximately where he was just before his horse's nose reached the tracks. At that moment, Lacotti was still in a place of absolute safety. If, looking southward from that point, he could have seen far enough to observe a train, coming at the rate of sixty miles an hour, that would reach the crossing before he got over it, then he ought to have stopped and let the train pass. In reaching that decision, I have given Lacotti a considerable advantage growing out of his being deceived by the bad blinker-lights. For the Court of Appeals has decided also that a man does not comply with the stop, look, and listen rule by looking before he gets on either track. He has to keep on looking as he proceeds across the tracks; and there is no doubt that Lacotti had a clear view down the north-bound track to the south for several thousand feet when he had reached the south-bound track.

So that was my hunch. How far down the track could Lacotti see when he was twelve feet from the very first rail? I looked over my notes, and found that his son had testified that, from that point, the track on which the train came was visible for only about three hundred feet. If that was accurate, the mile-a-minute train, moving eighty-eight feet per second, was visible from that point for only four seconds before it reached the crossing. But I was by no means satisfied with the accuracy of young Lacotti's measurements. He was not an engineer. Therefore, I examined the plat and the photographs which were in evidence. I grew more dissatisfied. Counting telegraph poles on one of the photographs, a photograph taken from the very spot twelve feet from the track which was my hunch spot, seemed to indicate visibility of the north-bound track for about a thousand feet. But I do not trust photographs for that kind of information—I've seen too many mistakes made that way. So I took the surveyor's plat and tried to measure it off on that. Then I got stuck. I did not have a ruler long enough to enable me to mark off the line I needed to draw, without shifting the ruler. When I tried to shift it, I found that the slightest inaccuracy made a difference of two or three hundred feet in my apparent results. At that point I became discouraged and went home to dinner.

This morning I sent for the lawyers for plaintiff and defendant and told them what I want to know. They have promised to have their expert engineers make accurate measurements on the plat and report to me on Monday morning. I did not tell the lawyers why I wanted to know this measurement nor what effect it would have on my decision. Thus I have left the way open to change my mind if I should get a new hunch between now and Monday. Now, having brought this "true confession" down to date, I'm going to read some more authorities on the case and then go for a swim.

Monday, June 6, 1932. The engineers reported this morning—one for the plaintiff, one for the defendant. They agreed almost exactly. From my twelve-foot point, the north-bound track is visible for about seven hundred feet. Incidentally, one of the lawyers told me how to avoid the trouble I had with a shifting ruler. His engineer had told him you put a pin in the plat at the point from which you want to measure, tie a piece of thread to the pin, and then stretch the thread along the line which you want to locate. Next time I'll know how to do that myself.

Very well, then. The mile-a-minute train was about eight seconds away when it first came into the sight of a person at my hunch point. I had calculated that the distance from that point to the first rail of the north-bound track is twenty-seven feet. At three miles an hour, it would take Lacotti about six seconds to cover those twenty-seven feet. Therefore it looked very much as though Lacotti had already passed my hunch point before the train came into sight from that point. If so, Lacotti has the edge.

But at the last moment, I hesitate. I recall that nobody has testified that Lacotti crossed the tracks at three miles an hour. That was just an assumption on my part. I know that when I walk at three and a half miles an hour, I go slightly faster than a cart-load of manure. I've done it often. Have I a right, though, to allow this assumption based on my own experience, to take the place of testimony?

These are some of the thoughts that are passing through my mind while counsel make their last minute arguments before me in chambers, out of the presence of the jury. If I am not paying very close attention to what they say, at all events I am thinking about the case; so my conscience is clear. Besides, I have already read and re-read the cases which counsel are citing and have made up my mind just what they mean. Therefore I go on in the mental pursuit of my hunch and say nothing until they get through talking. Just as counsel are about to conclude, I drive my hunch into a corner; or it drives me into a corner, I don't know which. All at once, I find that I have decided; and, from that moment, I wonder, why I ever was in the slightest doubt.

My decision was, to let the case go to the jury. That is, to refuse to grant an instruction directing the jury that its decision *must* be for the defendant. Therefore the defendant has had to go on with the presentation of its defense. Today we have been listening to the defendant's witnesses. They finished at adjournment time. Tomorrow morning the case will be argued, and the jury will decide it. Meanwhile, let me try to explain finally why I did not take it from the jury.

Can you recall what I said in connection with my very simple illustration, a few pages back, of the case of the suit on a promissory note that turned out to be a forgery? I said when the judge took the case from the jury, there was bound up in his judicial declaration the assertion that there was only one rational view to take of the evidence. In that case it was perfectly obvious that there was only one rational conclusion the jury could reach, and that was a conclusion against the plaintiff. Therefore, as a matter of law, the judge directed a verdict for the defendant.

Now, according to the law-in-the-law-books that is always the basis for a directed verdict. Whenever a judge takes a case from the jury, he does it because, in his opinion as a lawyer (or better, as a law-knower) the jury would be doing something absurd, unreasonable, and irrational, if it decided for the plaintiff. Apply that test to the Lacotti case. If the evidence showed that before his horse got on the first track, Lacotti was in a position from which he could have seen the on-coming train, then he certainly ought to have stopped and let the train pass. If he did not look, and if he did not stop, he was not merely negligent, he was reckless. If he was reckless, then there was only one rational conclusion which the jury could reach. If that were so, then there was no need for the defendant to go on with its side of the case. The whole matter should be settled by an instruction from the judge that the jury *must* decide for the defendant. In short, it was a perfectly clear case exactly like the case of the forged promissory note.

On the other hand, if the evidence showed that Lacotti could not see the on-coming train from that point, or that it was doubtful whether he could or not, then maybe he was careless and maybe he wasn't. It became a matter of judgment. There was more than one reasonable way to look at it. It was precisely the kind of question, a doubtful question of fact, that juries are supposed to deal with and to decide.

Perhaps now you will see the hunch that I had, and why I call the point twelve feet from the first rail my hunch point. I wanted to know definitely what was visible from that point because, as I reasoned upon the law, that would enable me to decide whether there was only one, or more than one rational, and at the same time legal, conclusion to be drawn from the evidence. When I got that bit of information precisely, I concluded that there was more than one rational way of deciding the case. Instead of a dead open and shut question, it was an open question, with a plausible and quite rational argument to be made on either side. Therefore I have let the case go to the jury. Tomorrow we shall see what the jury does with it.

Tuesday, June 7, 1932. 11:30 a. m. The argument of the Lacotti case had been finished. The jury has retired. I have made this entry in my note book, at the end of my notes of the case.

My Verdict	*Jury*
Defendant	?

N.B.—In this case, the evidence of contributory negligence is so strong that I nearly took it from the jury. Moreover there ought to be a verdict for defendant on other grounds. Defendant's witnesses have convinced me that the blinker-light never was out of order and that Lacotti probably did not look at it when he passed beneath it. Plaintiff's injuries would entitle him to a verdict of at least $5000. I anticipate a verdict in his favor for much less than that. It is a case in which the jury probably will apply the jury-made-law-of-contributory-negligence, and, by a small verdict, will apportion the blame.

I also anticipate that my decision may be reversed by the Court of Appeals if there is an appeal. I am sure of the soundness of it; but the point is a close one.

Tuesday, June 7, 1932. 1:00 p. m. The jury is in with a verdict for the plaintiff for $1200. . . .

A few words more about taking cases from the jury. I wonder whether you have caught the grim humor of the practice. A judge takes a case from the jury, that is, he grants a binding instruction which compels the jury to decide for the defendant because that is the only *rational* decision that can be made. The lawyers for the defendant work like Turks to convince the judge that he ought to take the case from the jury because they anticipate that if the jury gets the case, it will decide for the plaintiff. In fact, not only the defendant's lawyers, but the plaintiff's lawyers, the clerk of the court, the bailiffs, and the judge himself all seem to believe that such will be the result.

In other words, everybody in the court room seems to believe that the jury is not rational! Is that what they actually believe? Well, I for one, do not. . . .

The second printing of A Judge Takes the Stand, appearing in 1936, contains Judge Ulman's comment on the appeal in the Lacotti case:

March 2, 1933. What might have been a joke on me has been narrowly averted. I wrote about this case while the trial was in progress, and the above account of my uncertainties was not exaggerated. But when I wrote as I did I was cheating just a little, for I had no idea the case would be appealed. When I discovered that an appeal had been taken I was much disturbed. Ninety-nine times out of a hundred an appellate court disposes of a case of this kind as though it was really quite simple. The higher court skeletonizes the facts, applies the rules of law, and files an opinion that make its decision seem inevitable. Therefore I stood to be put in the position of having created imaginary difficulties in order to make a good story.

This case was argued in the Court of Appeals on December 2, 1932, and was held under advisement until yesterday. Eight judges heard the argument. They finally agreed to disagree, by a four to four vote. Therefore my decision was affirmed, but only because no five judges were able to agree that I was wrong.

In over thirty years at the bar and on the bench this is the first case in which I have been concerned where there was an entirely divided appellate bench. The event is of rare occurrence; during the past five years there have been only eight cases in which the Maryland Court of Appeals has divided evenly.

Questions

1. Suppose there were no judicial process or other legal means of resolution of disputes, what steps might Lacotti have taken after his wagon was hit by the railroad train? In this connection consider the following sentence by an English psychiatrist: "We ought to be able to regard the law as controlling for us those qualities in us which we never really master ourselves." (Ranyard West, Conscience and Society: A Study of the Psychological Prerequisites of Law and Order, pp. 166–167.)

2. Apart from the social function of this lawsuit in achieving a peaceful resolution of the dispute over who should bear the cost of the collision, what social function does it serve with respect to the railroad's calculation of the consequences of its methods of conducting its operations?

3. Does this lawsuit serve any social functions with respect to the attitudes of the parties and of the public generally toward (a) carefulness, (b) respect for others, (c) sense of responsibility to the society as a whole?

4. How does the division of responsibility between judge and jury affect the various social functions of this lawsuit?

———

SECTION 17. THE RESPONSIBILITY OF THE LAWYER TO THE COURT AND TO THE CLIENT

[The following is taken from "PROFESSIONAL RESPONSIBILITY: REPORT OF THE JOINT CONFERENCE." 44 American Bar Association Journal 1159, 1159–1160 (1958).]

The Lawyer's Role as Advocate in Open Court

The lawyer appearing as an advocate before a tribunal presents, as persuasively as he can, the facts and the law of the case as seen from the standpoint of his client's interest. It is essential that both the lawyer and the public understand clearly the nature of the role thus discharged. Such an understanding is required not only to appreciate the need for an adversary presentation of issues, but also in order to perceive truly the limits partisan advocacy must impose on itself if it is to remain wholesome and useful.

In a very real sense it may be said that the integrity of the adjudicative process itself depends upon the participation of the advocate. This becomes apparent when we contemplate the nature of the task assumed by any arbiter who attempts to decide a dispute without the aid of partisan advocacy.

Such an arbiter must undertake, not only the role of judge, but that of representative for both of the litigants. Each of these roles must be played to the full without being muted by qualifications derived from the others. When he is developing for each side the most effective statement of its case, the arbiter must put aside his neutrality and permit himself to be moved by a sympathetic identification sufficiently intense to draw from his mind all that it is capable of giving,—in analysis, patience and creative power. When he resumes his neutral position, he must be able to view with distrust the fruits of this identification and be ready to reject the products of his own best mental efforts. The difficulties of this undertaking are obvious. If it is true that a man in his time must play many parts, it is scarcely given to him to play them all at once.

It is small wonder, then, that failure generally attends the attempt to dispense with the distinct roles traditionally implied in adjudication. What generally occurs in practice is that at some early point a familiar pattern will seem to emerge from the evidence; an accustomed label is waiting for the case and, without awaiting further proofs, this label is promptly assigned to it. It is a mistake to suppose that this premature cataloguing must necessarily result from impatience, prejudice or mental sloth. Often it proceeds from a very understandable desire to bring the hearing into some order and coherence, for without some tentative theory of the case there is no standard of relevance by which testimony may be measured. But what starts as a preliminary diagnosis designed to direct the inquiry tends, quickly and imperceptibly to become a fixed conclusion, as all that confirms the diagnosis makes a strong imprint on the mind, while all that runs counter to it is received with diverted attention.

An adversary presentation seems the only effective means for combatting this natural human tendency to judge too swiftly in terms of the familiar that which is not yet fully known. The arguments of counsel hold the case, as it were, in suspension between two opposing interpretations of it. While the proper classification of the case is thus kept unresolved, there is time to explore all of its peculiarities and nuances.

These are the contributions made by partisan advocacy during the public hearing of the cause. When we take into account the preparations that must precede the hearing, the essential quality of the advocate's contribution becomes even more apparent. Preceding the hearing, inquiries must be instituted to determine what facts can be proved or seem sufficiently established to warrant a formal test of their truth during the hearing. There must also be a preliminary analysis of the issues, so that the hearing may have form and direction. These preparatory measures are indispensable whether or not the parties involved in the controversy are represented by advocates.

Where that representation is present there is an obvious advantage in the fact that the area of dispute may be greatly reduced by an exchange of written pleadings or by stipulation of counsel. Without the participation of someone who can act responsibly for each of the parties, this essential narrowing of the issues becomes impossible. But here again the true significance of partisan advocacy lies deeper, touching once more the integrity of the adjudicative process itself. It is only through the advocate's participation that the hearing may remain in fact what it purports to be in theory: a public trial of the facts and issues. Each advocate comes to the hearing prepared to present his proofs and arguments, knowing at the same time that his arguments may fail to persuade and that his proofs may be rejected as inadequate. It is a part of his role to absorb these possible disappointments. The deciding tribunal, on the other hand, comes to the hearing uncommitted. It has not represented to the public that any fact can be proved, that any argument is sound, or that any particular way of stating a litigant's case is the most effective expression of its merits.

The matter assumes a very different aspect when the deciding tribunal is compelled to take into its own hands the preparations that must precede the public hearing. In such a case the tribunal cannot truly be said to come to the hearing uncommitted, for it has itself appointed the channels along which the public inquiry is to run. If an unexpected turn in the testimony reveals a miscalculation in the design of these channels, there is no advocate to absorb the blame. The deciding tribunal is under a strong temptation to keep the hearing moving within the boundaries originally set for it. The result may be that the hearing loses its character as an open trial of the facts and issues, and becomes instead a ritual designed to provide public confirmation for what the tribunal considers it has already established in private. When this occurs adjudication acquires the taint affecting all institutions that become subject to manipulation, presenting one aspect to the public, another to knowing participants.

These, then, are the reasons for believing that partisan advocacy plays a vital and essential role in one of the most fundamental procedures of a democratic society. But if we were to put all of these detailed considerations to one side, we should still be confronted by the fact that, in whatever form adjudication may appear, the experienced judge or arbitrator desires and actively seeks to obtain an adversary presentation of the issues. Only when he has had the benefit of intelligent and vigorous advocacy on both sides can he feel fully confident of his decision.

Viewed in this light, the role of the lawyer as a partisan advocate appears not as a regrettable necessity, but as an indispensable part of a larger ordering of affairs. The institution of advocacy is not a concession to the frailties of human nature, but an expression of human insight in the design of a social framework within which man's capacity for impartial judgment can attain its fullest realization.

When advocacy is thus viewed, it becomes clear by what principle limits must be set to partisanship. The advocate plays his roll well when zeal for his client's cause promotes a wise and informed decision of the case. He plays his role badly, and trespasses against the obligations of professional responsibility, when his desire to win leads him to muddy the headwaters of decision, when, instead of lending a needed perspective to the controversy, he distorts and obscures its true nature.

SECTION 17.1 ENGLISH AND AMERICAN VIEWS OF THE ADVOCATE'S ROLE IN THE ADVERSARY PROCESS

[The following is taken from SIR HARTLEY W. SHAWCROSS,* "THE FUNCTIONS AND RESPONSIBILITIES OF AN ADVO-CATE" (17th annual Benjamin N. Cardozo lecture, delivered before the Association of the Bar of the City of New York, May 28, 1958), pp. 10–21, 25–28.]

One may start, may one not, with the proposition that no one denies the necessity for having lawyers. When in Henry VI Shakespeare put into the mouth of Dick the Butcher the exhortation "Let's kill all the lawyers," it was not because of any philosophic conviction that lawyers were unnecessary in an ideal society: it was because it was felt that they had abused their privileged position. It has always been accepted in all countries, at all stages of development ever since the State has assumed to administer justice between man and man that those who may have recourse to the Courts ought to be entitled, if they wish, to have the services of an advocate to represent them. And why so? The law is not an exact science. To appreciate its content requires special training and knowledge. And the application of the law to particular facts—the ascertainment of justice in the particular case— is a matter of infinite complexity. There is hardly a case comes before the Courts but the opposing lawyers have at some stage, honestly but with the matter illuminated for each of them only from his particular side, advised their respective clients that they were in the right. And at the end of the day, when the law has been ascertained, it is often very hard to say how, in its application to the facts, absolute justice would decide. Indeed absolute justice, like absolute truth, is probably incapable of ascertainment. In our common law system the most we seek is objective truth within the limits of the admissible evidence. But the application of even objective justice requires technical skill in knowledge of the law, dialectical skill in its presentation and argument. The ordinary citizen, often overawed and tongue-tied by his unfamiliar surroundings, must have a spokesman to argue for him. As Lord Macmillan put it in one of those charming Essays of his, the lawyer is there to assist justice: "It is his business to present to the Court all that his client would have said for himself had he possessed the requisite skill and knowledge."

.   .   .   The importance of argument in contributing to sound conclusion cannot be overrated. Some there are, of course, who subscribe to the fallacy that a lawyer's argument cannot be of value because the lawyer is

---

* Hartley W. Shawcross, now Baron Shawcross of Friston, was called to the bar in 1925. He practiced law and held many public offices, and served as Attorney General of Great Britain from 1945 to 1951. He was chief prosecutor for the U. K. at the Nuremburg war crimes trials.

paid to deliver it. The great Dr. Johnson is recorded as having been told by a Member of Parliament that "he paid no regard to the arguments of counsel at the Bar, because they were paid for speaking."

> Johnson: "Nay, Sir. Argument is argument. You cannot help paying regard to their arguments if they are good. If it were testimony you might disregard it, if you knew that it were purchased. There is a beautiful image in Bacon upon this subject: testimony is like an arrow shot from a long bow: the force of it depends on the strength of the hand that draws it. Argument is like an arrow from a cross bow which has equal force though shot by a child."

Sound arguments—the question of sincerity does not arise here: the question is their logic, their cogency—produce sound judgments. That is why it is often said, and indeed it is a matter of the greatest truth, that a strong Bar begets a strong Bench. I need not take up more time, in pointing to the ethical justification and practical necessity for advocates as a professional class. The criticism against us, partly arising from a misconception of our function, but partly contributed to by our own failure sometimes to live up to the high principles which justify our calling, is that we abuse our position. Not by material dishonesty. It is not that people think we are corrupt. . . . The lawyer nowadays is not suspected of financial dishonesty. What is suspect is his intellectual sincerity. The doctor is regarded, and rightly, as the servant of humanity, but the lawyer is too often looked upon as a parasitical and hypocritical person who makes money out of the misfortunes of others by prostituting his intellectual capacities. That he seeks to make the worse appear the better cause.

*   *   *

Let it be said that the lawyer who regards his function as making the worse appear the better cause, who devotes his skill to elaborating schemes for frustrating and deceiving the law or the Courts, who deliberately pits his wits against the legislature and against the Judges is unworthy of his gown. These are not the high tasks of the lawyers in the common law countries.

*   *   *

It is true that you may find in the books earlier expressions of opinion which seem inconsistent with this conception of the duty of the advocate. Thus Lord Brougham, in his well known defence of Queen Caroline before the House of Lords:

> "I once before took occasion to remind your Lordships, which was unnecessary but there are many whom it may be needful to remind, that an advocate by the sacred duty which he owes to his client knows in the discharge of that office but one person in the world— that client and none other. To save that client by all expedient means, to protect that client at all hazards and costs to all others, and among others to himself, is the highest and most unquestioned of his duties; and he must not regard the alarm, the suffering, the torment, the destruction which he may bring upon any other. Nay separating even the duties of a patriot from those of an advocate, and casting them if need be to the wind, he must go on reckless of the consequences if his fate it should be unhappily to involve his country in confusion for his client's protection."

Lord Brougham perhaps allowed himself to be carried away; that would certainly not be regarded now as the advocate's position. . . . But later years brought greater wisdom. When Brougham had reached the ripe old age of 86, in 1864, the English Bar entertained a distinguished French advocate at one of those dinners at the Inns of Court at which we have had the honour of entertaining many of you. Lord Brougham made a speech and then Lord Chief Justice Cockburn spoke, in reply to the toast of the Judges. He explained the position, as he said, "feeling that our guest might leave us with a false impression of our ideals." What he said has often been quoted:

> "My noble and learned friend Lord Brougham, whose words are the words of wisdom, said an advocate should be fearless in carrying out the interests of his client; but I couple that with this qualification and this restriction: that the arms which he wields are to be the arms of the warrior and not of the assassin. It is his duty to strive to accomplish the interests of his client—*per fas*, but not *per nefas*. It is his duty, to the utmost of his power, to seek to reconcile the interests he is bound to maintain and the duty it is incumbent upon him to discharge with the eternal and immutable interests of truth and justice."

And history records that Lord Brougham nodded his head in agreement.

* * *

Sometimes there may seem to be a nice conflict between the duty to the Court and a duty to the client . . . But our supreme loyalty always is to our profession and to the cause of justice; our overriding duty to the Court. . . . We are entitled to put our client's case—we are his representative—with courage and with vigour. We have no right to invent a case for him. A clear distinction has to be drawn between suggesting the facts which it would be desirable to prove in order to establish some particular case, which is something we may never do, and indicating what is the proper line of defence or claim available on the facts as we are told them by our clients. We can point out the nature of the evidence which is required to establish the facts as the client states them to be, but it is manifestly not for us to concoct a case. It is axiomatic that the advocate must never knowingly mislead the Court. Whether in a criminal or a civil case, subject to rules as to onus, the duty is to present to the Court the whole truth. . . . And just as with the facts, so with the law. It sometimes happens that one's researches lead to the discovery of some authority adverse to the case for which one is contending—but that neither opposing counsel nor the Judge is aware of it. Or occasionally a barrister will hear the Court misdirecting itself on some point of law. It is always the duty of the advocate to assist the Court and bring all cases to the notice of the Court.

* * *

Abraham Lincoln, . . . gave, as one might expect, a good example of that intellectual honesty and at the same time of effectively disarming advocacy: always put all the points against yourself before they are taken by the other side—and answer them in advance.

.   .   .   The first time Lincoln appeared in the Supreme Court of
Illinois, he is recorded as saying:

> "This is the first case I have ever had in this Court and I have there-
> fore examined it with great care.   As the Court will perceive by
> looking at the abstract of the record the only question in the case is
> one of authority.   I have not been able to find any authority to
> sustain my side of the case.   But I have found several Cases directly
> in point on the other side.   I will now give these authorities to the
> Court and then submit the case."

The position of the Bar possessing an exclusive right of audience in the
Courts is one which carries with it very great responsibilities.   Certainly we
can do irreparable harm if we abuse our privileges.   For instance, it is axiomatic that an advocate must never yield to the pressure of his client in
pleading an improper case—in alleging fraud, for instance in the Statement
of Claim, or other improper conduct.   An advocate must never do that unless he is convinced that the available evidence establishes the proof of what
the client alleges and *also* that it is *necessary and just* to allege it.   .   .   .
It is no part of our duty as advocates to damage the reputation of the other
party to a case, still less the reputation of a witness or a stranger, unless the
matter is one which really goes to the issues in the case itself and only then
if the facts justify it.   It is all well summed up in an often quoted passage
in the opinion of an Irish Judge, Mr. Justice Crampton, in the famous case
of O'Connell.   Talking of the duty of the Advocate, he said:

> "He gives to his client the benefit of his learning, his talents, and
> his judgment; but all through he never forgets what he owes to
> himself and to others.   He will not knowingly misstate the law—he
> will not wilfully misstate the facts, though it be to gain the cause
> for his client.   He will ever bear in mind that if he be the Advocate
> of an individual, and *retained* and remunerated (often inadequate-
> ly) for his valuable services, yet he has a prior and perpetual *retain-
> er* on behalf of truth and justice; and there is no Crown or other
> license which in any case, or for any party or purpose, can discharge
> him from that primary and paramount retainer."   [1844, 7 I.R.
> 261]

But, the critic will say, how is all this high sounding language about
the cause of truth, this analogy between the lawyer and a Minister of Justice,
to be reconciled with the advocate's support of some odious case—perhaps
some case against the State, perhaps the defence of some disreputable criminal.   The answer, of course, lies in the fact that the advocate is not to be
identified with his client.   He is the representative but not the alter ego.
And he must preserve his objectivity and detachment.   At the English Bar,
we have a rule—I do not know whether you do here—which may seem trivial
in itself but which I believe is important.   Counsel in England never says
"I think."   He says "I submit" or, "I suggest," or, to the Judge or Jury,
"You may think."   But what Counsel thinks is as a rule irrelevant.   To say—
"I think my client is innocent" or "I think the correct view of the facts in
evidence is this" is to make the personal judgment and reliability of Counsel
an issue for the Court.   And if of one Counsel, then of both.   That is manifestly most undesirable.   The rule therefore rests upon a very practical, as
well as upon an ethical foundation.   If an honest Counsel were allowed to
pledge his personal beliefs in the justice of his case, either the other side

would be without Counsel at all or dishonest barristers would appear to pledge a conviction they did not sincerely hold. The importance of detachment, of not being identified with a client's case is really of very great significance. It is, indeed, an essential aspect of the Advocate's independence. Lord Eldon well expressed the position when he said of Counsel: "He lends his exertions to all, himself to none. It is for him to argue. He is merely an officer assisting in the administration of justice."

That position being recognised—or I would say, rather, that being the true position, for very often it is not recognised by our critics and sometimes not even by ourselves, the duty of the lawyer in regard to the odious case, the unpopular cause, the case which involves a conflict with the State, and so on, is the more obvious. And let there be no doubt about it. The failure to recognise it is one of the main reasons why people sometimes look askance at the Criminal Bar. The general nature of a case may appear odious, unpopular, politically embarrassing. The extent to which these epithets can be applied to particular parties in the case will only appear in the judgment of the Court. We as advocates must not make that judgment. If we do, persons involved (whether rightly or wrongly) in odious, unpopular or politically embarrassing cases may be unable to secure advocates to represent them and, since it is agreed that the assistance of advocates is necessary to the administration of justice, they will be denied justice. Baron Bramwell put the point succinctly when he said: "A client is entitled to say to his Counsel, 'I want your advocacy, not your judgment. I prefer that of the Court.'" (Johnson v. Emerson, 1871, 6 Ex., 367). . . .

This duty to act as an advocate, not indeed to obstruct the course of justice but to help in bringing out all of the truth is, of course, the answer to those who ask—and this is the very basis of the disfavour with which lawyers are often regarded—how can any honest lawyer appear for one whom perhaps he knows to be guilty or who is at least involved in some odious offence? But what has become almost the locus classicus for the statement of the true position is of course Boswell's life of Dr. Johnson.

* * *

Boswell wrote . . . We talked of the practice of the Law. Sir William Forbes said, he thought an honest lawyer should never undertake a cause which he was satisfied was not a just one. Sir (said Dr. Johnson) a lawyer has no business with the justice or injustice of the cause which he undertakes, unless his client asks his opinion, and then he is bound to give it honestly. The justice or injustice of the cause is to be decided by the judge. Consider, sir; what is the purpose of courts of justice? It is that every man may have his cause fairly tried, by men appointed to try causes. A lawyer is not to tell what he knows to be a lie: he is not to produce what he knows to be a false deed; but he is not to usurp the province of the jury and of the judge, and determine what shall be the effect of evidence—what shall be the result of legal argument. As it rarely happens that a man is fit to plead his own cause, lawyers are a class of the community, who, by study and experience, have acquired the art and power of arranging evidence, and of applying to the points at issue what the law has settled. A lawyer is to do for his client all that his client might fairly do for himself, if he could. If lawyers were to undertake no causes till they were sure they were just, a man might be precluded altogether from a trial of his claim, though, were it judicially examined, it

I have myself always found it best to avoid forming any personal opinion on the merits of cases I have dealt with. Eventually that becomes rather a habit of mind. Of course, that may mean that one lacks the enthusiasm of an advocate firmly convinced that his cause is just: it also protects one from despair or hypocrisy when we feel the opposite. There is an account in the life of Marshall Hall of a case in which a client, who wished him to act, had given him an account of the matter which he did not believe. . . . He was minded, accordingly, to refuse the brief. But he asked the advice of the Attorney General, afterwards Lord Alverston. "If you were a doctor," said Sir Richard Webster, "would you refuse your aid to a poor Magdalen dying of a horrible disease?" Hall, thus advised, did the case and as the evidence developed he realised that his first impression was wrong and became convinced of his client's innocence, as was the Jury. "That taught me a lesson," observed Marshall Hall, "which I shall never forget."

* * *

. . . Of course, sometimes we know that a client who desires to plead not guilty is in fact guilty, perhaps because he has admitted it to us (although this never once happened to me as an English trial lawyer) or because of other incontrovertible facts. If that happens before we have embarked upon the case, the rules of the English Bar permit Counsel to withdraw to avoid embarrassment—some other Counsel may proceed unencumbered by similar knowledge. But if it occurs in the course of a case, the position is different. To withdraw then would gravely prejudice the client. But very strict limitations are then laid upon the conduct of the defence. . . . in such a case Counsel must not lend himself to any deception. He must not say his client is innocent—he knows he is not. He must not call him as a witness—for he would be a perjured witness. He must not suggest that some third person is guilty, for he knows his client is the guilty man. For the same reason he must not imply that the witnesses for the prosecution are lying. All he can do is to insist that the prosecution discharge the onus of proof. . . .

[The following is taken from CHARLES P. CURTIS,* IT'S YOUR LAW (Cambridge, Mass., 1954), pp. 4–8, 17, 19–21, 25, 28. Footnotes are omitted.]

The Adversary Process

Justice is a chilly virtue. It is of high importance that we be introduced into the inhospitable halls of justice by a friend. I think we neglect the fact that the first function of the lawyer, and the first great purpose of the devotion which a lawyer owes to his client, is the overcoming of this feeling of unfriendliness. The first duty of the bar is to make sure that everyone who feels the need of a friend in court shall have one, . . . But if the devotion a lawyer owes to his client were no more than friendliness, if it were simply to serve the purpose of taking the chill off justice, there would be no more to say. We make greater demands upon our lawyers than that.

---

* Charles P. Curtis (1891–1959) was a member of the Massachusetts bar. He practiced law in Boston for many years, but still found time to lecture at Harvard University—government and sociology—and to write several articles and books.

They must be not only our friends. They must be our champions. For the way we administer justice is by an adversary proceeding, which is as much as to say, we set the parties fighting. . . .

There are some subjects of litigation in which the adversary proceeding is an admirable way of administering justice. One wise judge implied as much when Charles E. Wyzanski said, "A political libel suit is the modern substitute for ordeal by battle. It is the means which society has chosen to induce bitter partisans to wager money instead of exchanging bloody noses." But litigation by an adversary proceeding is the way we cut the knot of many disputes in which it is disastrously inappropriate. Divorces, the custody of children, will contests, almost any kind of dispute which springs from family or equally intimate dissension—there a broken bone is more easily mendable. And it is intolerably too often true that a criminal trial turns into an adversary proceeding. "Criminal justice is concerned with the pathology of the body politic. In administering the criminal law, judges wield the most awesome surgical instruments of society. A criminal trial, it has been well said, should have the atmosphere of the operating room. The presiding judge determines the atmosphere. He is not an umpire who enforces the rules of a game, or merely a moderator between contestants. If he is adequate to his functions, the moral authority which he radiates will impose the indispensable standards of dignity and austerity upon all those who participate in a criminal trial."

What, then, is the justification for this approach to justice, other than the fact we are several centuries used to it and aside from the fact that spectators in small communities and newspaper readers in cities enjoy the spectacle? It seems to me that the justification of the adversary proceeding is the satisfaction of the parties, and not our satisfaction, except as we too are prospective litigants. This is a rational justification of the adversary approach to justice. Along this line, what the law is trying to do is give the algebraic maximum of satisfaction to both parties. This is a crude, but indeed it is not a bad, definition of the justice which the adversary proceeding provides. The law is trying to do justice between the parties for the parties rather than for us, trying to give them their own justice so far as possible and so far as compatible with what may be distinguished as our justice.

It is necessary, to be sure, to apply the general terms of what we regard as justice to their particular case. For we too must be satisfied. We are prospective customers. But the difference is not great. They are some of us, and they are much influenced by what we regard as just. The law pays more attention to the satisfaction of the needs of the parties in the particular case than it does to our ideas about justice in general. The law takes the position that we ought to be satisfied if the parties are; and it believes that the best way to get that done is to encourage them to fight it out, and dissolve their differences in dissension. We are still a combative people, not yet so civilized and sophisticated as to forget that combat is one way to justice. . . .

The devotion and the fidelity which a lawyer owes to his client is great enough to strew quandaries and perplexities in the way of his relations with his clients which seem to me to be peculiar to his profession. At any rate, these perplexities offer us by far the best, indeed so far as I know, the only approach to some understanding of the chief function of the lawyer in the

law, which is advocacy.   And the heart of advocacy, as with other things of
the spirit, lies in its ethics.

A Lawyer's Loyalties

I want first of all to put advocacy in its proper setting.   It is a special
case of vicarious conduct.   A lawyer devotes his life and career to acting for
other people.   So too do the parson and the priest, and, in another way, the
banker.   The banker handles other people's money.   The parson and the
priest handle other people's spiritual aspirations.   A lawyer handles other
people's troubles.

But there is a difference.   The loyalty of a clergyman runs, not to the
particular parishioner whose joys or troubles he is busy with, but to his
church; and the banker looks to his bank.   It is the church or the bank on
whose behalf they are acting, which serves the communicant or the borrower.   Thus their loyalties run in a different direction from a lawyer's.

Not so the lawyer in private practice.   His loyalty runs to his client.
Not the court? you ask.   Does not the court take the same position as the
church or the bank?   Is not the lawyer an officer of the court?   Why doesn't
the court have first claim on his loyalty?   No, in a paradoxical way.   The
lawyer's official duty, required of him indeed by the court, is to devote himself to the client.   He has two masters, and it is sometimes hard to say which
comes first.   There are occasions when our system of justice seems to give
the nod to the client.

* * *

The person for whom you are acting very reasonably expects you to
treat him better than you do other people, which is just another way of saying that you owe him a higher standard of conduct than you owe to others.
This goes back a long way.   It is the pre-platonic ethics which Socrates disposed of at the very outset of the Republic; that is, that justice consists of
doing good to your friends and harms to your enemies.   A lawyer, therefore,
insensibly finds himself treating his client better than others; and therefore others worse than his client.   A lawyer, or a trustee, or anyone acting
for another, has lower standards of conduct toward outsiders than he has
toward his clients or his beneficiaries against the outsiders.   He is required
to treat outsiders as if they were barbarians and enemies.   The more
devotion and zeal the lawyer owes to his client, the less he owes to others
when he is acting for his client.   It is as if a man had only so much virtue,
and the more he gives to one, the less he has available for anyone else.   The
upshot is that a man whose business it is to act for others finds himself, in
his dealings on his client's behalf with outsiders, acting on a lower standard
than he would if he were acting for himself, lower than any standard his
client himself would be willing to act on, lower in fact than anyone on his
own.

* * *

I have said that a lawyer may not lie to the court.   But it may be a
lawyer's duty not to speak.   Let me give you a case from the autobiography
of one of the most distinguished and conscientious lawyers I or any man
have ever known.   Samuel Williston.   In his autobiography, he tells of one
of his early cases.   His client was sued in some financial matter.   The details of the claim are not important.   Mr. Williston, of course, at once got his
client's letter file and went through it painstakingly, sorting, arranging,

and collating it. The letters, we may well believe, told the whole story, as they usually do in such a case. Trial approached, but the plaintiff's lawyers did not ask for the file or that the letters be produced. "They did not demand their production and we did not feel bound to disclose them." At the close of the trial, "In the course of his remarks the Chief Justice stated as one reason for his decision a supposed fact which I knew to be unfounded. I had in front of me a letter that showed his error. Though I have no doubt of the propriety of my behavior in keeping silent, I was somewhat uncomfortable at the time."

You will note that Williston was the attorney for the defendant in the case. The other attorney, who was trying to make a case for the plaintiff, had the burden of proof. If he had found a damaging letter in his client's file, or if Williston's client had been bringing instead of defending the suit, what then? Quite a different situation would be presented, such is our adversary system of justice. If the ugly fact belongs to the plaintiff's case, it must go in with it; and if it is so ugly that it spoils the case, then either the plaintiff must withdraw his case or his lawyer must withdraw from it. The point is, that the reason for this difference between the claim and the defense is, simply that, unless a lawyer presents all the available relevant facts, he would be presenting a different case to the court than the one which his client brought to him.

* * *

Here is what Williston went on to say in his autobiography.

"One of the troublesome ethical questions which a young trial lawyer is confronted with is the extent to which he is bound to disclose to the court facts which are injurious to his client's case. The answer is not doubtful. The lawyer must decide when he takes a case whether it is a suitable one for him to undertake and after this decision is made, he is not justified in turning against his client by exposing injurious evidence entrusted to him. If that evidence was unknown to him when he took the case, he may sometimes withdraw from it, but while he is engaged as counsel he is not only not obliged to disclose unfavorable evidence, but it is a violation of his duty to his client if he does so."

And Williston concluded

". . . doing something intrinsically regrettable, because the only alternative involves worse consequences, is a necessity in every profession."

* * *

"I must be cruel, only to be kind," said Hamlet, on his way to his mother. And so likewise a lawyer has to tell himself strange things on his way to court. But they are strange only to those who do not distinguish between truth and justice. Justice is something larger and more intimate than truth. Truth is only one of the ingredients of justice. Its whole is the satisfaction of those concerned. It is to that end that each attorney must say the best, and only the best, of his own case.

The problem presented to a lawyer when he defends a man he knows is guilty or takes a case he knows is bad is perplexing only to laymen. Brandeis said, "As a practical matter, I think the lawyer is not often harassed by this problem, partly because he is apt to believe at the time in most of the cases that he actually tries, and partly because he either abandons or settles a large number of those he does not believe in."

It is profoundly true that the first person a lawyer persuades is himself. A practicing lawyer will soon detect in himself a perfectly astonishing amount of sincerity. By the time he has even sketched out his brief, however skeptically he started, he finds himself believing more and more in what it says, until later, when he starts arguing the case before the court, his belief is total; and he is quite sincere about it. You cannot very well keep your tongue in your cheek while you are talking. He believes what he is saying in a way that will later astonish himself as much as now it does others.

* * *

Not that he cares how much we are astonished. What he does care about is whether we are persuaded, and he is aware that an unsound argument can do much worse than fall flat. For it may carry the implication that he has no better one. He will not want to make it unless he really has no better.

* * *

This sort of self-sown sincerity, however, is not deep-rooted; and it had better not be, if what Justice Darling said was true. "I think," he said, "that most Counsel would be better advocates did they content themselves with simulating the belief instead of actually embracing it. The manifest appearance of a believer is all that is wanted; and this can well be acted after a little study, and will not interfere with that calmness of judgment which it is well to preserve in the midst of uncertainties, and which does not appear to be consistent with much faith." "Better advocates," Justice Darling says, not better men. I trust you understand that I am drawing a distinction which I have no doubt Justice Darling would draw too, and equally emphatically. I am talking about cases, not about causes. I am not talking about the integrity and righteousness on which our best hopes hang. This is vicarious zeal and enthusiasm, not one's own belief. To be truly honest, you've got to be honest, not only with yourself, but also for yourself. At some time or other, you stand alone. We are bipeds, which means we must stand on our own two feet, not on the four feet we may make with another.

This is more than a domestic problem. It strikes close to the best the bar can do for the community, as the bar very well knows. The trouble is, there is also the right of a lawyer to take only the cases he wants to take. It is the same problem of reconciling two confronting rights which festers in racial discrimination. There is the right to choose whom you prefer to employ confronting the right to a job on something better than the color of your skin. Likewise a lawyer's right to choose his clients confronts a free man's right to counsel. The bar, as I say, is wholly aware of this. Just this year, the foremost bar association we have, the Association of the Bar of the City of New York, made this matter clear. Its Committee on the Bill of Rights, whose chairman is George S. Leisure, said this,

"A principal duty of the bar is to see that no accused lacks counsel because his person is infamous or his cause detested. When a member of the bar defends a client who is publicly abhorred, the bar expects that representation none the less to be vigorous, competent and responsible in every way.

The bar regards that lawyer as fundamentally independent of his client and therefore holds him accountable to it for guiding his client's cause by its standards of professional conduct. Public misapprehension of the duty threatens its performance. The prevalence of the error, too often reflected in our local press, which confuses professional obligation with personal belief, will deter lawyers from representing unpopular clients. The organized bar should act to dispel such misunderstanding, and should support against criticism arising from it those lawyers who, guided by the profession's standards, follow its most honored tradition and help discharge its most essential responsibility."

The classical solution to a lawyer taking a case he knows is bad is Dr. Johnson's. It is perfectly simple and quite specious. Boswell asked Johnson whether as a moralist Johnson did not think that the practice of the law, in some degree, hurt the nice feeling of honesty.

"What do you think," said Boswell, "of supporting a cause which you know to be bad?"

Johnson answered, "Sir, you do not know it to be good or bad till the Judge determines it. I have said that you are to state facts fairly; so that your thinking, or what you call knowing, a cause to be bad, must be from reasoning, must be from your supposing your arguments to be weak and inconclusive. But, Sir, that is not enough. An argument which does not convince yourself, may convince the Judge to whom you urge it: and if it does convince him, why, then, Sir, you are wrong, and he is right."

Dr. Johnson ignored the fact that it is the lawyer's job to know how good or how bad his case is. It is his peculiar function to find out, for otherwise he can't make it look better. Dr. Johnson's answer is sound only in cases where the problem does not arise. It is not the lawyer, but the law, that does not know whether his case is good or bad. The law is trying to find out, and so wants everyone defended and every debatable case tried. To this end, the law tries to make it easy for a lawyer to take a bad case, whether it's bad in the relevant sense of looking hopeless, or bad in the irrelevant sense of being unpopular, perhaps even deliberately made offensive by the capering of some Congressional Committee.

In England, the law goes so far as to make it the duty of a barrister to take the case of any client who properly and adequately retains him. In this country we lay that duty upon the bar as a whole, and so we don't try to do more than make it as easy as we can for a lawyer to take a bad case. One of the ways the bar helps itself to perform this duty is the Canon of Ethics which says, "It is improper for a lawyer to assert in argument his personal belief in his client's innocence or in the justice of his cause." It is called improper just so that the lawyer may feel that he does not have to. This, I think, must be its only purpose, for it is honored in no other way, as you will agree if you have ever heard a lawyer argue a case which he has chosen to turn into a cause. How else would you have your lawyer argue any case to a jury or a constitutional case to the Supreme Court?

Listen to George Wharton Pepper's peroration to his argument to the Supreme Court on a constitutional question. Having argued in the most precise terms that the AAA is unconstitutional, he proceeds most eloquently to express his own personal belief in the justice of his cause. "My time is fleeting and I must not pause to sum up the argument I have made. . .

But I do want to say just one final and somewhat personal word. I have tried very hard to argue this case calmly and dispassionately, and without vehement attack upon things which I cannot approve, and I have done it thus because it seems to me that this is the best way in which an advocate can discharge his duty to this Court. But I do not want your Honors to think that my feelings are not involved, and that my emotions are not deeply stirred. Indeed, may it please Your Honors, I believe I am standing here today to plead the cause of the America I have loved; and I pray Almighty God that not in my time may 'the land of the regimented' be accepted as a worthy substitute for 'the land of the free.' "

Questions

1. Are there differences between the Shawcross and Curtis views of the advocate's role? What are they? Which view do you prefer? Why?

2. Are you satisfied with the Shawcross rationale for the guilty client problem? Does Curtis meet this problem in a more satisfactory way?

3. Compare the Shawcross anecdote about Abraham Lincoln with the Curtis anecdote about Professor Williston. Why didn't Lincoln sit on his precedents the way Williston sat on his facts?

4. Does the Williston anecdote and the ensuing comments from his autobiography—*supra* pp. 438 ff.—suggest that a lawyer may have different standards of conduct as an advocate than he has as an advisor? Consider the following:

"*The Lawyer's Role as Counselor*

"Vital as is the lawyer's role in adjudication, it should not be thought that it is only as an advocate pleading in open court that he contributes to the administration of the law. The most effective realization of the law's aims often takes place in the attorney's office, where litigation is forestalled by anticipating its outcome, where the lawyer's quiet counsel takes the place of public force. Contrary to popular belief, the compliance with the law thus brought about is not generally lip-serving and narrow, for by reminding him of its long-run costs the lawyer often deters his client from a course of conduct technically permissible under existing law, though inconsistent with its underlying spirit and purpose.

"Although the lawyer serves the administration of justice indispensably both as advocate and as office counselor, the demands imposed on him by these two roles must be sharply distinguished. The man who has been called into court to answer for his own actions is entitled to a fair hearing. Partisan advocacy plays its essential part in such a hearing, and the lawyer pleading his client's case may properly present it in the most favorable light. A similar resolution of doubts in one direction becomes inappropriate when the lawyer acts as counselor. The reasons that justify and even require partisan advocacy in the trial of a cause do not grant any license to the lawyer to participate as legal adviser in a line of conduct that is immoral, unfair, or of doubtful legality. In saving himself from this unworthy involvement, the lawyer cannot be guided solely by an unreflective inner sense of good faith; he must be at pains to preserve a sufficient detachment from his client's interests so that he remains capable of a sound and objective appraisal of the propriety of what his client proposes to do." ["Professional Responsibility: Report of the Joint Conference," 44 American Bar Association Journal 1159, 1161 (1958).]

SECTION 17.2   THE ETHICAL DILEMMAS OF THE ADVOCATE IN AN ADVERSARY PROCESS

The American Bar Association and affiliated State Bar Associations perform, among other functions, the role of promulgating norms to guide lawyers in the ethics of law practice. The formal means for the performance of this function includes the publication of a Code of Professional Responsibility, expositary commentary and disciplinary rules which expand on the general precepts of the Code, and advisory opinions on the application of the Code to specific situations posed to the ABA or State Bar Committees charged with the duty to administer the Code. Excerpts from the ABA Code of Professional Responsibility, and associated Commentary and Disciplinary Rules are reprinted below.

CANON 1

A Lawyer Should Assist in Maintaining the Integrity and Competence of the Legal Profession

ETHICAL CONSIDERATIONS

EC 1–5 A lawyer should maintain high standards of professional conduct and should encourage fellow lawyers to do likewise. He should be temperate and dignified, and he should refrain from all illegal and morally reprehensible conduct. Because of his position in society, even minor violations of law by a lawyer may tend to lessen public confidence in the legal profession. Obedience to law exemplifies respect for law. To lawyers especially, respect for the law should be more than a platitude.

DISCIPLINARY RULES

DR 1–102 Misconduct.

(A) A lawyer shall not:

   (1) Violate a Disciplinary Rule.

   (2) Circumvent a Disciplinary Rule through actions of another.

   (3) Engage in illegal conduct involving moral turpitude.

   (4) Engage in conduct involving dishonesty, fraud, deceit, or misrepresentation.

   (5) Engage in conduct that is prejudicial to the administration of justice.

(6) Engage in any other conduct that adversely reflects on his fitness to practice law.

DR 1–103 Disclosure of Information to Authorities.

(A) A lawyer possessing unprivileged knowledge of a violation of DR 1–102 shall report such knowledge to a tribunal or other authority empowered to investigate or act upon such violation.

(B) A lawyer possessing unprivileged knowledge or evidence concerning another lawyer or a judge shall reveal fully such knowledge or evidence upon proper request of a tribunal or other authority empowered to investigate or act upon the conduct of lawyers or judges.

CANON 4

A Lawyer Should Preserve the Confidences and Secrets of a Client

ETHICAL CONSIDERATIONS

EC 4–1 Both the fiduciary relationship existing between lawyer and client and the proper functioning of the legal system require the preservation by the lawyer of confidences and secrets of one who has employed or sought to employ him. A client must feel free to discuss whatever he wishes with his lawyer and a lawyer must be equally free to obtain information beyond that volunteered by his client. A lawyer should be fully informed of all the facts of the matter he is handling in order for his client to obtain the full advantage of our legal system. It is for the lawyer in the exercise of his independent professional judgment to separate the relevant and important from the irrelevant and unimportant. The observance of the ethical obligation of a lawyer to hold inviolate the confidences and secrets of his client not only facilitates the full development of facts essential to proper representation of the client but also encourages laymen to seek early legal assistance.

DISCIPLINARY RULES

DR–4–101 Preservation of Confidences and Secrets of a Client.

(A) "Confidence" refers to information protected by the attorney-client privilege under applicable law, and "secret" refers to other information gained in the professional relationship that the client has requested be held inviolate or the disclosure of which would be embarrassing or would be likely to be detrimental to the client.

(B) Except when permitted under DR 4–101(C), a lawyer shall not knowingly:

(1) Reveal a confidence or secret of his client.

(2) Use a confidence or secret of his client to the disadvantage of the client.

(3) Use a confidence or secret of his client for the advantage of himself or of a third person, unless the client consents after full disclosure.

(C) A lawyer may reveal:

(1) Confidences or secrets with the consent of the client or clients affected, but only after a full disclosure to them.

(2) Confidences or secrets when permitted under Disciplinary Rules or required by law or court order.

(3) The intention of his client to commit a crime and the information necessary to prevent the crime.

(4) Confidences or secrets necessary to establish or collect his fee or to defend himself or his employees or associates against an accusation of wrongful conduct.

(D) A lawyer shall exercise reasonable care to prevent his employees, associates, and others whose services are utilized by him from disclosing or using confidences or secrets of a client, except that a lawyer may reveal the information allowed by DR 4–101(C) through an employee.

CANON 7

A Lawyer Should Represent a Client Zealously Within the Bounds of the Law

ETHICAL CONSIDERATIONS

EC 7–1 The duty of a lawyer, both to his client and to the legal system, is to represent his client zealously within the bounds of the law, which includes Disciplinary Rules and enforceable professional regulations. The professional responsibility of a lawyer derives from his membership in a profession which has the duty of assisting members of the public to secure and protect available legal rights and benefits. In our government of laws and not of men, each member of our society is entitled to have his conduct judged and regulated in accordance with the law; to seek any lawful objective through legally permissible means; and to present for adjudication any lawful claim, issue, or defense.

* * *

EC 7–3 Where the bounds of law are uncertain, the action of a lawyer may depend on whether he is serving as advocate or adviser. A lawyer may serve simultaneously as both advocate and adviser, but the two roles are essentially different. In asserting a position on behalf of his client, an advocate for the most part deals with past conduct and must take the facts as he finds them. By contrast, a lawyer serving as adviser primarily assists his client in determining the course of future conduct and relationships. While serving as advocate, a lawyer should resolve in favor of his client doubts as to the bounds of the law. In serving a client as adviser, a lawyer in appropriate circumstances should give his professional opinion as to what the ultimate decisions of the courts would likely be as to the applicable law.

Duty of the Lawyer to a Client

EC 7–4 The advocate may urge any permissible construction of the law favorable to his client, without regard to his professional opinion as to the likelihood that the construction will ultimately prevail. His conduct is within the bounds of the law, and therefore permissible, if the position taken is supported by the law or is supportable by a good faith argument for an extension, modification, or reversal of the law. However, a lawyer is not justified in asserting a position in litigation that is frivolous.

EC 7–5 A lawyer as adviser furthers the interest of his client by giving his professional opinion as to what he believes would likely be the ultimate decision of the courts on the matter at hand and by informing his client of the practical effect of such decision. He may continue in the representation of his client even though his client has elected to pursue a course of conduct contrary to the advice of the lawyer so long as he does not thereby knowingly assist the client to engage in illegal conduct or to take a frivolous legal position. A lawyer should never encourage or aid his client to commit criminal acts or counsel his client on how to violate the law and avoid punishment therefor.

EC 7–6 Whether the proposed action of a lawyer is within the bounds of the law may be a perplexing question when his client is contemplating a course of conduct having legal consequences that vary according to the client's intent, motive, or desires at the time of the action. Often a lawyer is asked to assist his client in developing evidence relevant to the state of mind of the client at a particular time. He may properly assist his client in the development and preservation of evidence of existing motive, intent, or desire; obviously, he may not do anything furthering the creation of preservation of false evidence. In many cases a lawyer may not be certain as to the state of mind of his client, and in those situations he should resolve reasonable doubts in favor of his client.

* * *

EC 7–10 The duty of a lawyer to represent his client with zeal does not militate against his concurrent obligation to treat with consideration all persons involved in the legal process and to avoid the infliction of needless harm.

* * *

Duty of the Lawyer to the Adversary System of Justice

EC 7–19 Our legal system provides for the adjudication of disputes governed by the rules of substantive, evidentiary, and procedural law. An adversary presentation counters the natural human tendency to judge too swiftly in terms of the familiar that which is not yet fully known; the advocate, by his zealous preparation and presentation of facts and law, enables the tribunal to come to the hearing with an open and neutral mind and to render impartial judgments. The duty of a lawyer to his client and his duty to the legal system are the same: to represent his client zealously within the bounds of the law.

* * *

EC 7–23 The complexity of law often makes it difficult for a tribunal to be fully informed unless the pertinent law is presented by the lawyers in the cause. A tribunal that is fully informed on the applicable law is better able to make a fair and accurate determination of the matter before it. The adversary system contemplates that each lawyer will present and argue the existing law in the light most favorable to his client. Where a lawyer knows of legal authority in the controlling jurisdiction directly adverse to the position of his client, he should inform the tribunal of its existence unless his adversary has done so; but, having made such disclosure, he may challenge its soundness in whole or in part.

* * *

EC 7–26 The law and Disciplinary Rules prohibit the use of fraudulent, false, or perjured testimony or evidence. A lawyer who knowingly participates in introduction of such testimony or evidence is subject to discipline. A lawyer should, however, present any admissible evidence his client desires to have presented unless he knows, or from facts within his knowledge should know, that such testimony or evidence is false, fraudulent, or perjured.

DISCIPLINARY RULES

DR 7–101 Representing a Client Zealously.

(A) A lawyer shall not intentionally:

    (1) Fail to seek the lawful objectives of his client through reasonably available means permitted by law and the Disciplinary Rules, except as provided by DR 7–101(b). A lawyer does not violate this Disciplinary Rule, however, by acceding to reasonable requests of opposing counsel which do not prejudice the rights of his client, by being punctual in fulfilling all professional commitments, by avoiding offensive tactics, or by treating with courtesy and consideration all persons involved in the legal process.

    (2) Fail to carry out a contract of employment entered into with a client for professional services, but he may withdraw as permitted under DR 2–110, DR 5–102, and DR 5–105.

    (3) Prejudice or damage his client during the course of the professional relationship, except as required under DR 7–102(B).

(B) In his representation of a client, a lawyer may:

    (1) Where permissible, exercise his professional judgment to waive or fail to assert a right or position of his client.

    (2) Refuse to aid or participate in conduct that he believes to be unlawful, even though there is some support for an argument that the conduct is legal.

DR 7–102 Representing a Client Within the Bounds of the Law.

(A) In his representation of a client, a lawyer shall not:

    (1) File a suit, assert a position, conduct a defense, delay a trial, or take other action on behalf of his client when he knows or when it is obvious that such action would serve merely to harass or maliciously injure another.

    (2) Knowingly advance a claim or defense that is unwarranted under existing law, except that he may advance such claim or defense if it can be supported by good faith argument for an extension, modification, or reversal of existing law.

    (3) Conceal or knowingly fail to disclose that which he is required by law to reveal.

    (4) Knowingly use perjured testimony or false evidence.

    (5) Knowingly make a false statement of law or fact.

    (6) Participate in the creation or preservation of evidence when he knows or it is obvious that the evidence is false.

    (7) Counsel or assist his client in conduct that the lawyer knows to be illegal or fraudulent.

    (8) Knowingly engage in other illegal conduct or conduct contrary to a Disciplinary Rule.

(B) A lawyer who receives information clearly establishing that:

    (1) His client has, in the course of the representation, perpetrated a fraud upon a person or tribunal shall promptly call upon his client to rectify the same, and if his client refuses or is unable to do so, he shall reveal the fraud to the affected person or tribunal.

    (2) A person other than his client has perpetrated a fraud upon a tribunal shall promptly reveal the fraud to the tribunal.

* * *

DR 7–106   Trial Conduct.

(A) A lawyer shall not disregard or advise his client to disregard a standing rule of a tribunal or a ruling of a tribunal made in the course of a proceeding, but he may take appropriate steps in good faith to test the validity of such rule or ruling.

(B) In presenting a matter to a tribunal, a lawyer shall disclose:

    (1) Legal authority in the controlling jurisdiction known to him to be directly adverse to the position of his client and which is not disclosed by opposing counsel.

    (2) Unless privileged or irrelevant, the identities of the clients he represents and of the persons who employed him.

(C) In appearing in his professional capacity before a tribunal, a lawyer shall not:

    (1) State or allude to any matter that he has no reasonable basis to believe is relevant to the case or that will not be supported by admissible evidence.

    (2) Ask any question that he has no reasonable basis to believe is relevant to the case and that is intended to degrade a witness or other person.

    (3) Assert his personal knowledge of the facts in issue, except when testifying as a witness.

    (4) Assert his personal opinion as to the justness of a cause, as to the credibility of a witness, as to the culpability of a civil litigant, or as to the guilt or innocence of an accused; but he may argue, on his analysis of the evidence, for any position or conclusion with respect to the matters stated herein.

    (5) Fail to comply with known local customs of courtesy or practice of the bar or a particular tribunal without giving to opposing counsel timely notice of his intent not to comply.

    (6) Engage in undignified or discourteous conduct which is degrading to a tribunal.

    (7) Intentionally or habitually violate any established rule of procedure or of evidence.

Problem

A few years ago the citizens of Lake Pleasant, New York, were disturbed and concerned by the mysterious disappearance of a young man and woman in the vicinity of Lake Pleasant. The disappearance was reported to the local police and accounts of the report and police investigation were published in local newspapers. Some weeks after this event, two lawyers undertook the defense of a man charged with a murder in another case. In the course of interviewing their client regarding that charge, the client revealed to them that he had murdered the missing young man and woman, and he disclosed the place where he had hidden their bodies. The attorneys went to the place described by their client, and found the bodies of the young man and woman.

Questions

1. What should the attorneys have done in response to this discovery?

2. Do the Canons, Ethical Considerations, and Disciplinary Rules reprinted above give clear guidance on this issue?

3. What ethical considerations and professional obligations did the attorneys have to reconcile in deciding what to do next?

4. Do the excerpts from Shawcross and Curtis suggest answers to this ethical dilemma? What are they?

Ethical problems of advocacy, particularly in criminal cases, have been addressed in a most challenging way in the writings of Professor Monroe H. Freedman.* His views are more nearly compatible with the Curtis view of total advocacy, and somewhat unsettling to lawyers, judges and others who might take comfort from the more genteel position expressed in the excerpt from Sir Hartley Shawcross. An example of Professor Freedman's views, and a response to them, are set out in the following pages.

[The following is taken from MONROE H. FREEDMAN, "WHERE THE BODIES ARE BURIED: THE ADVERSARY SYSTEM AND THE OBLIGATION OF CONFIDENTIALITY," 10 Criminal Law Bulletin 979 (1974). Footnotes are omitted.] †

There were interesting reactions to that dramatic event. Members of the public were shocked at the apparent callousness of these lawyers, whose conduct was seen as typifying the unhealthy lack of concern of most lawyers with the public interest and with simple decency. That attitude was encouraged by the public statements of the local prosecutor, who sought to indict the lawyers for failing to reveal knowledge of a crime and for failing to see that dead bodies were properly buried. In addition, when questioned by the press, lawyers and law professors gave ambivalent and confused responses, indicating that few members of the legal profession had given serious thought to the fundamental questions of administration of justice and of professional responsibility that were raised by the case.

---

* Monroe Freedman is Professor of Law at Hofstra University Law School. He has been an active participant in civil rights and civil liberties cases. He has served on committees concerned with legal ethics and professional responsibility, and has written many articles and a leading book in this field, Lawyers' Ethics in an Adversary System (1975).

† The reference is to the Lake Pleasant case described in the preceding problem. In that case the lawyers did not disclose their macabre discovery to the authorities.

One can certainly understand the sense of moral compulsion to assist the parents and to accord the victims the dignity of proper burial. What seems to be less readily understood—but which, to my mind, throws the moral balance in the other direction—is the obligation of the lawyers to their client and, in a larger sense, to a system of administering justice which is itself essential to maintaining human dignity. In short, not only did the two lawyers behave properly, but they would have committed a serious breach of professional responsibility if they had divulged information that was contrary to their client's interest. The explanation to that answer takes us to the very nature of our system of criminal justice and, indeed, to the fundamentals of our system of government.

Role of Defense Attorney Under Adversary System

Let us begin, by way of contrast, with an understanding of the role of a criminal defense attorney in a totalitarian state. As expressed by law professors at the University of Havana, "the first job of a revolutionary lawyer is not to argue that his client is innocent, but rather to determine if his client is guilty and, if so, to seek the sanction which will best rehabilitate him."

Similarly, a Bulgarian attorney began his defense in a treason trial by noting that, "in a Socialist state there is no division of duty between the judge, prosecutor, and defense counsel. . . . The defense must assist the prosecution to find the objective truth in a case." In that case, the defense attorney ridiculed his client's defense, and the client was convicted and executed. Some time later the verdict was found to have been erroneous, and the defendant was "rehabilitated."

The emphasis in a free society is, of course, sharply different. Under our adversary system, the interests of the state are not absolute, or even paramount. The dignity of the individual is respected to the point that even when the citizen is known by the state to have committed a heinous offense, the individual is nevertheless accorded such rights as counsel, trial by jury, due process, and the privilege against self-incrimination.

Constitutional Rights v. Truth Seeking

A trial is, in part, a search for truth. Accordingly, those basic rights are most often characterized as procedural safeguards against error in the search for truth. Actually, however, a trial is far more than a search for truth, and the constitutional rights that are provided by our system of justice may outweigh the truth-seeking value—a fact which is manifest when we consider that those rights and others guaranteed by the Constitution may well impede the search for truth rather than further it. For example, what more effective way is there to expose a defendant's guilt than to require self-incrimination, at least to the extent of compelling the defendant to take the stand and respond to interrogation before the jury? The defendant, however, is presumed innocent, the burden is on the prosecution to prove guilt beyond a reasonable doubt, and even the guilty accused has an "absolute constitutional right" to remain silent and to put the government to its proof.

Thus, the defense lawyer's professional obligation may well be to advise the client to withhold the truth. As Justice Jackson said, "Any lawyer

worth his salt will tell the suspect in no uncertain terms to make no statement to police under any circumstances." Similarly, the defense lawyer is
obligated to prevent the introduction of evidence that may be wholly reliable, such as a murder weapon seized in violation of the Fourth Amendment,
or a truthful but involuntary confession. Justice White has observed that
although law enforcement officials must be dedicated to using only truthful
evidence, "defense counsel has no comparable obligation to ascertain or
present the truth. Our system assigns him a different mission. . . .
We . . . insist that he defend his client whether he is innocent or
guilty."

Such conduct by defense counsel does not constitute obstruction of justice. On the contrary, it is "part of the duty imposed on the most honorable defense counsel," from whom "we countenance or require conduct which
in many instances has little, if any, relation to the search for truth." The
same observation has been made by Justice Harlan, who noted that "in fulfilling his professional responsibilities," the lawyer "of necessity may become an obstacle to truth finding." Chief Justice Warren, too, has recognized that when the criminal defense attorney successfully obstructs efforts
by the government to elicit truthful evidence in ways that violate constitutional rights, the attorney is "merely exercising . . . good professional judgment," and "carrying out what he is sworn to do under his oath—to
protect to the extent of his ability the rights of his client." Chief Justice
Warren concluded, "In fulfilling this responsibility the attorney plays a vital role in the administration of criminal justice under our Constitution."

Obviously, such eminent jurists would not arrive lightly at the conclusion that an officer of the court has a professional obligation to place obstacles in the path of truth. Their reasons, again, go back to the nature of
our system of criminal justice and to the fundamentals of our system of
government. Before we will permit the state to deprive any person of life,
liberty, or property, we require that certain processes be duly followed
which ensure regard for the dignity of the individual, irrespective of the
impact of those processes upon the determination of truth.

By emphasizing that the adversary process has its foundations in respect for human dignity, even at the expense of the search for truth, I do
not mean to deprecate the search for truth or to suggest that the adversary
system is not concerned with it. On the contrary, truth is a basic value,
and the adversary system is one of the most efficient and the fairest method for determining it. That system proceeds on the assumption that the
best way to ascertain the truth is to present to an impartial judge or jury a
confrontation between the proponents of conflicting views, assigning to
each the task of marshalling and presenting the evidence in as thorough and
persuasive a way as possible. The truth-seeking techniques used by the advocates on each side include investigation, pretrial discovery, cross-examination of opposing witnesses, and a marshalling of the evidence in summation.
Thus, the judge or jury is given the strongest possible view of each side
and is put in the best possible position to make an accurate and fair judgment. Nevertheless, the point here emphasized is that in a society that
honors the dignity of the individual, the high value assigned to truth seeking is not absolute and may on occasion be subordinated to even higher values.

Concept of Right to Counsel

The concept of a right to counsel is one of the most significant manifestations of our regard for the dignity of the individual. No person is required to stand alone against the awesome power of the People of New York or the Government of the United States of America. Rather, every criminal defendant is guaranteed an advocate—a "champion" against a "hostile world," the "single voice on which he must rely with confidence that his interests will be protected to the fullest extent consistent with the rules of procedure and the standards of professional conduct." In addition, the attorney serves, in significant part, to assure equality before the law. Thus, the lawyer has been referred to as "the equalizer," who "places each litigant as nearly as possible on an equal footing under the substantive and procedural law under which he is tried."

The lawyer can serve effectively as advocate, however, "only if he knows all that his client knows" concerning the facts of the case. Nor is the client competent to evaluate the relevance or significance of particular facts. What may seem incriminating to the client, may actually be exculpatory. For example, one client was reluctant to tell her lawyer that her husband had attacked her with a knife, because it tended to confirm that she had, in fact, shot him (contrary to what she had at first maintained). Having been persuaded by her attorney's insistence on "complete and candid disclosure," she finally "confessed all"—which permitted the lawyer to defend her properly and successfully on grounds of self-defense.

Rule of Confidentiality

Obviously, however, the client cannot be expected to reveal to the lawyer all information that is potentially relevant, including that which may well be incriminating, unless the client can be assured that the lawyer will maintain all such information in the strictest confidence. "The purposes and necessities of the relation between a client and his attorney" require "the fullest and freest disclosures" of the client's "objects, motives and acts." If the attorney were permitted to reveal such disclosures, it would be "not only a gross violation of a sacred trust upon his part," but it would "utterly destroy and prevent the usefulness and benefits to be derived from professional assistance." That "sacred trust" of confidentiality must "upon all occasions be inviolable," or else the client could not feel free "to repose [confidence] in the attorney to whom he resorts for legal advice and assistance." Destroy that confidence, and "a man would not venture to consult any skillful person, or would only dare to tell his counselor half his case." The result would be impairment of the "perfect freedom of consultation by client with attorney," which is "essential to the administration of justice." Accordingly, the new Code of Professional Responsibility provides that a lawyer shall not knowingly reveal a confidence or secret of the client, nor use a confidence or secret to the disadvantage of the client, or to the advantage of a third person, without the client's consent.

Scope of Confidentiality

It must be obvious at this point that the adversary system, within which the lawyer functions, contemplates that the lawyer frequently will learn from the client information that is highly incriminating and may even learn, as in the Lake Pleasant case, that the client has, in fact, committed serious crimes. In such a case, if the attorney were required to divulge that information, the obligation of confidentiality would be destroyed, and with it, the adversary system itself. Even so, it is occasionally suggested that a lawyer who does not divulge a client's self-incriminatory information, would be guilty of such crimes as obstruction of justice, misprision of a felony, or becoming an accomplice after the fact. Such statutes, however, cannot be understood as applying to lawyers who have learned incriminating information after the crime has already been committed. First, criminal statutes should be strictly construed to avoid applying them more broadly than the legislature intended or to those who may not have been adequately on notice that their conduct was unlawful. Second, a statute should be strictly construed to avoid unnecessarily raising constitutional issues, particularly when there is likelihood that the statute would have to be found constitutionally invalid. Finally, to construe an ordinary obstruction-of-justice statute or other criminal law in a way that would destroy the traditional lawyer-client relationship would violate the constitutional rights to counsel, trial by jury, due process, and the privilege against self-incrimination.

That is not to say, of course, that the attorney is privileged to go beyond the needs of confidentiality imposed by the adversary system, and actively participate in the concealment of evidence or the obstruction of justice. For example, in the *Ryder* case, which arose in Virginia several years ago, the attorney removed a sawed-off shotgun and the money from a bank robbery from his client's safe deposit box and put it, for greater safety, into the lawyer's own safe deposit box. The attorney, quite properly, was suspended from practice for 18 months. (The penalty might well have been heavier, except for the fact that Ryder sought advice from senior members of the bench and bar, and apparently acted more in ignorance than in venality.) The important difference between the *Ryder* case and the one in Lake Pleasant lies in the active role played by the attorney in *Ryder* to conceal evidence. There is no indication, for example, that the attorneys in Lake Pleasant attempted to hide the bodies more effectively. If they had done so, they would have gone beyond maintaining confidentiality and into active participation in the concealment of evidence.

Exception—Future Crimes

The distinction should also be noted between the attorney's knowledge of a past crime (which is what we have been discussing so far) and knowledge of a crime to be committed in the future. Thus, a major exception to the strict rule of confidentiality is the "intention of his client to commit a crime, and information necessary to prevent the crime." Significantly, however, even in that exceptional circumstance, disclosure of the confidence is only permissive, not mandatory. Moreover, a footnote in the Code suggests that the exception is applicable only when the attorney knows "beyond a reasonable doubt" that a crime will be committed. There is little guidance as to how the lawyer is to exercise the discretion to report future crimes. At one extreme, it seems clear that the lawyer should reveal information necessary to save a life. On the other hand, the lawyer should not reveal the intention of a client in a criminal case to commit perjury in his or her own defense.

Plea Bargaining

The suggestion has also been made with respect to the Lake Pleasant case that the obligation of confidentiality was destroyed because the defendant had authorized disclosure to the prosecutor insofar as it might be helpful in plea bargaining. Plea bargaining is, unfortunately, an integral part of the criminal justice system. Therefore, a defendant would be deprived of basic rights if disclosure could not be authorized for that limited but crucial purpose, without forfeiting confidentiality in general.

Unrelated Crimes

Another suggestion is that the two bodies in the Lake Pleasant case were not related to the crime for which the defendant was being prosecuted, and that therefore that knowledge was outside the scope of confidentiality. That point lacks merit for three reasons. First, as suggested above, an unsophisticated lay person should not be required to anticipate which disclosure falls outside the scope of confidentiality because of insufficient relevance. Second, the information in question might have been highly relevant to a defense of insanity. Third, a lawyer has an obligation to merge other, unrelated crimes in the plea bargaining process, if it is possible to do so. Therefore, even if the client had not volunteered the information about the other murders, the lawyers should have asked about other crimes that the defendant might have committed.

Forfeiture

A significantly different situation was presented in the case of a lawyer representing a figure in the Watergate investigations. There, the lawyer had been authorized by the client to sell to a newspaper columnist the information that had been communicated to the lawyer by the client. Since the authorized disclosure in that case went beyond the needs of effective representation in the judicial proceeding, the client forfeited the right to confidentiality, and the attorney was properly directed to testify before a grand jury. Similarly, if the attorneys in the Lake Pleasant case had been authorized to inform the victims' parents, confidentiality would have been jeopardized.

Investigation

It has also been suggested that the attorneys in Lake Pleasant were not bound by confidentiality once they had undertaken to corroborate the client's information through their own investigation. It is the duty of the lawyer, however, to conduct a thorough investigation of all aspects of the case, and that duty "exists regardless of the accused's admissions or statements to the lawyer of facts constituting guilt." For example, upon investigation, the attorneys in the Lake Pleasant case might have discovered that the client's belief that he had killed other people was false, which would have had important bearing on an insanity defense.

Conclusion

The Constitution has committed us to an adversary system for the administration of criminal justice. The essentially humanitarian reason for such a system is that it preserves the dignity of the individual, even though that may occasionally require significant frustration of the search for truth and the will of the state. An essential element of that system is the right to counsel, a right that would be meaningless if the defendant were not able to communicate freely and fully with the attorney.

In order to project that communication—and, ultimately, the adversary system itself—we impose upon attorneys what has been called the "sacred trust" of confidentiality. It was pursuant to that high trust that the lawyers acted in Lake Pleasant, New York, when they refrained from divulging their knowledge of where the bodies were hidden.

[The following is taken from ELGIN EDWARDS, "HARD ANSWERS FOR HARD QUESTIONS: DISSENTING IN PART FROM DEAN FREEDMAN'S VIEWS ON THE ATTORNEY CLIENT PRIVILEGE," 11 Criminal Law Bulletin 478, 478–485 (1975). Footnotes are omitted.]

Dean Freedman has concisely defended the conduct of lawyers in a murder case whose client confessed to them that he had committed additional murders. The client also told his lawyers where the victims' bodies were hidden. The lawyers went and photographed the bodies but did not disclose the information until the client confessed months later.

The result Dean Freedman reaches, justifying the lawyers' silence, is probably correct, but his reasoning would be misleading in other fact situations.

* * *

The Dean justifies the refusal of one of the lawyers to give any information, even to the parents of one of the murder victims "who came to see him in the course of seeking their missing daughter," as follows:

> "One can certainly understand the sense of moral compulsion to assist the parents. . . . What seems to be less readily understood—but which, to my mind, throws the moral balance in the other direction—is the obligation of the lawyers to their client and, in a larger sense, to a system of administering justice which is itself essential to maintaining human dignity."

Regrettably, this concession that "moral balance" is the sine qua non of the decision-making process is thereafter ignored as the article takes a nearly absolutist position on the inviolability of the attorney-client privilege. . . .

* * *

Obviously, if the lawyers who took pictures of the murder victims recognized the bodies to be infected with a contagious disease and the fleas or bugs (or whatever transmits those diseases to humans) were swarming, they would not have hesitated to call the authorities to prevent disaster. Nor could the lawyers hesitate if they found one of the victims still alive. They would hastily call for medical aid, even while recognizing that the victim, upon recovery, would identify their client as the attacker, as well as the murderer of the other victim. It would surely foster free disclosure between attorney and client if the client believed that even in these situations, the attorney would preserve his confidences. The simple fact, however, is that the benefits inherent in the attorney-client privilege are outweighed by other values.

Dean Freedman, I trust, would concede that where human lives are at stake, the lawyer must act. Would the lawyer feel obligated to first consult his client to beg for release from the restraints of the attorney-client privilege? Clearly not, since even if the client refused, the attorney would ignore confidentiality and act to save lives.

It might be argued that by saving lives, the attorney is merely keeping the client from committing "future crimes" and that such conduct is not prohibited by the lawyer's Code of Ethics; but this kind of argument begs the question. Whether you call it "construing the scope" of the attorney-client privilege or "ignoring" the privilege, the consequence is the same and the reason is clear: Other factors outweigh the values associated with the privilege.

Other examples are equally obvious: What if the attorney went to the scene to photograph the bodies and was arrested for the murders himself? Alternatively, what if he knew that another person had been convicted of the murder and, taking an extreme case, was about to be executed? Even if it were a *crime* to disclose information covered by the attorney-client privilege, the fact that a lawyer acted to save his own life or that of another person would obviously be a complete defense. If conduct that would otherwise be criminal is excusable because of circumstances, no sufficient reason is apparent why a noncriminal breach of confidentiality should not also be excusable. Indeed, such conduct under the circumstances would be more than excusable; it would be desirable.

. . . Surprisingly, Dean Freedman does not quarrel with the "future crimes" exception to the rule; yet he opposes other exceptions on the ground that "an unsophisticated lay person should not be required to anticipate which disclosure falls outside the scope of confidentiality. . . ." Yet even to lawyers and judges, it is not always clear when a crime is completed or when it is anticipated to occur or continue into the future. Nevertheless, if the client speaks, he assumes the risk, whether he knows it or not, that the attorney will be required to disclose the conversation.

Similarly, a client would hardly expect that if he and a friend came to an attorney and disclosed information, the client might later be found to have not intended the communication to be privileged because of the presence of the third party. Yet precisely that consequence might result from his conduct. Even more difficult decisions are expected of the unwary client: He must be sure that he is consulting the attorney in *that capacity* before he speaks. Thus, if the attorney acts both as lawyer and "negotiator," communications relating to his function as a negotiator are not privileged. The client takes similar risks when he consults the lawyer not as an attorney but as a friend, or business adviser, or banker, or accountant, or as a mere scrivener, or executor, or agent.

It seems clear that our adversary system was never meant to be absolute to the exclusion of all other considerations. Nor could the Constitution's draftsmen have contemplated that the right to counsel would be construed to require a lawyer to be "absolutely adversary." In fact, attorneys unduly flatter themselves if they believe the profession was held in such esteem at the time as to warrant such elevation of the attorney's status in the constitutional scheme of individual rights.

If the attorney has no easy guidelines of absolutism, how, then, is he to know how to conduct himself? The answer, of course, is that he must make decisions relating to the attorney-client privilege the same way he makes decisions about any other moral action. At the extremes, decisions are easy; elsewhere, they are not.

As already noted, when human life is at stake, the privilege is outweighed, with the "moral balance" tipped toward disclosure. Similarly, if the client was granted immunity from prosecution but still refused to confess, it would be folly to suggest that the attorney-client privilege should prohibit disclosure when significant reasons existed to require revelation. Likewise, if the possible consequence was merely a civil tort action against the client, rather than criminal prosecution, it would be absurd for the attorney to be required or even permitted to stand mute where other values were at stake—for example, where a whole herd of cattle or a forest (not to mention human lives) might be destroyed as a result of the client's prior negligence if a warning were not given.

Nor does the attorney's decision-making duty end when he decides he is compelled to divulge the information obtained from his client. Simply deciding that the moral balance is tipped toward disclosure should not mean that the client's interests or wishes are to be ignored. To the contrary, the attorney must then make decisions about the mode of disclosure. The Dean scoffs at the suggestion that attorneys might reveal confidential information to the authorities through an anonymous phone call, rather than confronting them directly. However, the suggestion is not without merit. Indeed, it involves precisely that balancing of values and risks essential to proper conduct in all moral actions—unless one is insistent upon taking an absolutist position.

Dean Freedman also appears critical of scholars who suggest that when confronted with inconsistent demands to disclose and to maintain confidences, an attorney's dilemma presents "touchy and interesting" problems. But why shouldn't attorneys have to deal with hard questions? Everyone else does. Yet it appears that the Dean's real objection to requiring disclosure in some cases is that it would present attorneys and their clients with difficult dilemmas that would chill and weaken the attorney-client relationship. As already shown, however, that relationship is not absolute, nor should it be.

* * *

Questions

1. You were asked to answer some questions about the problem discussed in Professor Freedman's article (see questions 1–3 *supra* p. 449). Did Professor Freedman's arguments cause you to reconsider and then change your answers to those questions? If so, why? If not, why not?

2. What is the gist of Professor Edwards' critique of the Freedman view? Does his analysis help you to resolve the dilemma posed to the lawyers in the Mount Pleasant case?

3. How would Professor Freedman respond to Professor Edwards? See Monroe H. Freedman, "Reply to Professor Edwards," 11 Criminal Law Bulletin 486 (1975).

————

The events leading up to the resignation of the 37th President of the United States—the so-called Watergate scandals—were widely chronicled in the press and broadcast media. Throughout that era, the public was treated to a spectacle in which lawyers were much in evidence, both among the perpetrators and the investigators and prosecutors of the Watergate scandals.

Lawyers who were forced to resign from office, and/or indicted and convicted of crimes associated with their public service included a President, Vice-President, Attorney General, and numerous lesser but high ranking officials. That traumatic sequence of events contributed a good deal to a heightened interest in legal ethics, and the relationship of the adversary system of the common law to the ethical standards of lawyers both in and out of court. Suggestions for changes in the way lawyers are taught and in the way they practice have been advanced from many quarters. In the following pages, a distinguished Federal Judge grapples with problems posed by the adversary system, and suggests one means to deal with some of these problems.

[The following is taken from MARVIN FRANKEL, "THE SEARCH FOR TRUTH: AN UMPIREAL VIEW," 123 University of Pennsylvania Law Review 1031, 1031–1034, 1035–1038, 1039, 1040–1041, 1052–1054, 1055–1059 (1975). Some footnotes omitted; others are renumbered.]

I. The Judicial Perspective

My theme, to be elaborated at some length, is that our adversary system rates truth too low among the values that institutions of justice are meant to serve. Having worked for nine years at judging, and having evolved in that job the doubts and questions to be shared with you, I find it convenient to move into the subject with some initial reminders about our judges: who they are, how they come to be, and how their arena looks to them.

Except when we rely upon credentials even more questionable, we tend to select our trial judges from among people with substantial experience as trial lawyers. Most of us have had occasion to think of the analogy to the selection of former athletes as umpires for athletic contests. It may not press the comparison too hard to say it serves as a reminder that the "sporting theory" continues to infuse much of the business of our trial courts. Reflective people have suggested from time to time that qualities of detachment and calm neutrality are not necessarily cultivated by long years of partisan combat. Merely in passing, because it is not central to my theme, I question whether we are wise to have rejected totally the widespread practice in civil law countries of having career magistrates, selected when relatively young to function in the role of impartial adjudicators. Reserving a fuller effort for another time, I wonder now whether we might benefit from some admixture of such magistrates to leaven or test our trial benches of elderly lawyers.

In any event, our more or less typical lawyer selected as a trial judge experiences a dramatic change in perspective as he moves to the other side of the bench. It is said, commonly by judges, that "[t]he basic purpose of a trial is the determination of truth . . . ." Justice David W. Peck identified "truth and . . . the right result" as not merely "basic" but "the sole objective of the judge . . . ."

These are not questionable propositions as a matter of doctrine or logic. Trials occur because there are questions of fact. In principle, the paramount objective is the truth. Nevertheless, for the advocate turned judge this objective marks a sharp break with settled habits of partisanship. The novelty is quickly accepted because it has been seen for so long from the other side. But the novelty is palpable, and the change of role may be unsettling. . . .

However the trial judge reacts, in general or from time to time, the bench affords a changed and broadened view of the adversary process. "Many things look different from the bench. Being a judge is a different profession from being a lawyer." In the strictest sense I can speak only for myself, but I believe many other trial judges would affirm that the different perspective helps to arouse doubts about a process that there had been neither time nor impetus to question in the years at the bar. It becomes evident that the search for truth fails too much of the time. The rules and devices accounting for the failures come to seem less agreeable and less clearly worthy than they once did. The skills of the advocate seem less noble, and the place of the judge, which once looked so high, is lowered in consequence. There is, despite the years of professional weathering that went before the assumption of the judicial office, a measure of disillusionment.

* * *

Having argued that we are too much committed to contentiousness as a good in itself and too little devoted to truth, I proceed to some prescriptions of a general nature for remedying these flaws. Simply stated, these prescriptions are that we should:

(1) modify (not abandon) the adversary ideal,

(2) make truth a paramount objective, and

(3) impose upon the contestants a duty to pursue that objective.

A. *Modifying the Adversary Ideal*

We should begin, as a concerted professional task, to question the premise that adversariness is ultimately and invariably good. For most of us trained in American law, the superiority of the adversary process over any other is too plain to doubt or examine. The certainty is shared by people who are in other respects widely separated on the ideological spectrum. The august Code of Professional Responsibility, as has been mentioned, proclaims, in order, the "Duty of the Lawyer to a Client," then the "Duty of the Lawyer to the Adversary System of Justice." There is no announced "Duty to the Truth" or "Duty to the Community." Public interest lawyers, while they otherwise test the law's bounds, profess a basic commitment "to the adversary system itself" as the means of giving "everyone affected by corporate and bureaucratic decisions . . . a voice in those decisions . . . ." [1] We may note similarly the earnest and idealistic scholar who brought the fury of the (not necessarily consistent) establishment upon himself when he wrote, reflecting upon experience as devoted defense counsel for poor people, that as an advocate you must (a) try to destroy a witness "whom you know to be telling the truth," (b) "put a witness on the stand when you know he will commit perjury," and (c) "give your client legal advice when you have reason to believe that the knowledge you give him will tempt him to commit perjury." [2] The "policies" he found to justify these views, included, as the first and most fundamental, the maintenance of "an adversary system based upon the presupposition that the most effective means of determining truth is to present to a judge and jury a clash between proponents of conflicting views." [3]

Our commitment to the adversary or "accusatorial" mode is buttressed by a corollary certainty that other, alien systems are inferior. We contrast our form of criminal procedure with the "inquisitorial" system, conjuring up visions of torture, secrecy, and dictatorial government. Confident of our superiority, we do not bother to find out how others work. It is not common knowledge among us that purely inquisitorial systems exist scarcely anywhere; the elements of our adversary approach exist probably everywhere; and that the evolving procedures of criminal justice, in Europe and elsewhere, are better described as "mixed" than as strictly accusatorial or strictly inquisitorial.[4]

In considering the possbility of change, we must open our minds to the variants and alternatives employed by other communities that also aspire to civilization. Without voting firmly, I raise the question whether the virginally ignorant judge is always to be preferred to one with an investigative file. We should be prepared to inquire whether our arts of examining and cross-examining, often geared to preventing excessive outpourings of facts, are inescapably preferable to safeguarded interrogation by an informed judicial officer. It is permissible to keep asking, because nobody has satisfactorily answered, why our present system of confessions in the police station versus no confessions at all is better than an open and orderly procedure of having a judicial official question suspects.[5]

If the mention of such a question has not exhausted your tolerance, consider whether our study of foreign alternatives might suggest means for easing the unending tension surrounding the privilege against self-incrimination as it frequently operates in criminal trials. It would be prudent at least to study closely whether our criminal defendant, privileged to stay sus-

1. Halpern & Cunningham, Reflections on the New Public Interest Law, 59 Geo.L.J. 1095, 1109 (1971).

2. Freedman, Professional Responsibility of the Criminal Defense Lawyer: The Three Hardest Questions, 64 Mich. L.Rev. 1469 (1966).

3. *Id.* 1470. *See also id.* 1471, 1477–78, 1482.

4. W. Schaefer, The Suspect and Society 71 (1967); Damaska, Evidentiary Barriers to Conviction and Two Models of Criminal Procedure: A Comparative Study, 121 U.Pa.L.Rev. 506, 557–61, 569–70 (1973).

5. *See* W. Schaefer, *supra* note 60; *cf.* Friendly, The Fifth Amendment Tomorrow: The Case for Constitutional Change, 37 U.Cin.L.Rev. 671, 685, 700–01, 713–16 (1968).

piciously absent from the stand or to testify subject to a perjury prosecution or "impeachment" by prior crimes, is surely better off than the European defendant who cannot escape questioning both before and at trial, though he may refuse to answer, but is free to tell his story without either the oath or the impeachment pretext for using his criminal record against him. Whether or not the defendant is better off, the question remains open whether the balance we have struck is the best possible.

To propose only one other topic for illustration, we need to study whether our elaborate struggles over discovery, especially in criminal cases, may be incurable symptoms of pathology inherent in our rigid insistence that the parties control the evidence until it is all "prepared" and packaged for competitive manipulation at the eventual continuous trial. Central in the debates on discovery is the concern of the ungenerous that the evidence may be tainted or alchemized between the time it is discovered and the time it is produced or countered at the trial. The concern, though the debaters report it in differing degrees, is well founded. It is significant enough to warrant our exploring alternative arrangements abroad where investigation "freezes" the evidence (that is, preserves usable depositions and other forms of relatively contemporaneous evidence) for use at trial, thus serving both to inhibit spoilage and to avoid pitfalls and surprises that may defeat justice.[6]

*   *   *

B. *Making Truth the Paramount Objective*

We should consider whether the paramount commitment of counsel concerning matters of fact should be to the discovery of truth rather than to the advancement of the client's interest. This topic heading contains for me the most debatable and the least thoroughly considered of the thoughts offered here. It is a brief suggestion for a revolution, but with no apparatus of doctrine or program.

We should face the fact that the quality of "hired gun" is close to the heart and substance of the litigating lawyer's role. As is true always of the mercenary warrior, the litigator has not won the highest esteem for his scars and his service. Apart from our image, we have had to reckon for ourselves in the dark hours with the knowledge that "selling" our stories rather than striving for the truth cannot always seem, because it is not,

---

6. In the depths of the cold war, Mr. Justice Jackson reported a comparison that should be no more offensive in a time of even tremulous détente:

[T]he Soviet Delegation objected to our practice on the ground that it is not fair to defendants. Under the Soviet System when an indictment is filed every document and the statement of every witness which is expected to be used against the defendant must be filed with the court and made known to the defense. It was objected that under our system the accused does not know the statements of accusing witnesses nor the documents that may be used against him, that such evidence is first made known to him at the trial too late to prepare a defense, and that this tends to make the trial something of a game instead of a real inquest into guilt. It must be admitted that there is a great deal of truth in this criticism. We reached a compromise by which the Nurnberg indictment was more informative than in English or American practice but less so than in Soviet and French practice.

Bull, Nurnberg Trial, 7 F.R.D. 175, 178 (n.d.) (quoting Justice Jackson, source not indicated).

such noble work as befits the practitioner of a learned profession. The struggle to win, with its powerful pressures to subordinate the love of truth, is often only incidentally, or coincidentally, if at all, a service to the public interest.

We have been bemused through the ages by the hardy (and somewhat appealing) notion that we are to serve rather than judge the client. Among the implications of this theme is the idea that lawyers are not to place themselves above others and that the client must be equipped to decide for himself whether or not he will follow the path of truth and justice. This means quite specifically, whether in Anatomy of a Murder [7] or in Dean Freedman's altruistic sense of commitment,[8] that the client must be armed for effective perjury as well as he would be if he were himself legally trained. To offer anything less is arrogant, elitist, and undemocratic.

It is impossible to guess closely how prevalent this view may be as a practical matter. Nor am I clear to what degree, if any, received canons of legal ethics give it sanction. My submission is in any case that it is a crass and pernicious idea, unworthy of a public profession. It is true that legal training is a source of power, for evil as well as good, and that a wicked lawyer is capable of specially skilled wrongdoing. It is likewise true that a physician or pharmacist knows homicidal devices hidden from the rest of us. Our goals must include means for limiting the numbers of crooked and malevolent people trained in the vital professions. We may be certain, notwithstanding our best efforts, that some lawyers and judges will abuse their trust. But this is no reason to encourage or facilitate wrongdoing by everyone.

Professional standards that placed truth above the client's interests would raise more perplexing questions. The privilege for client's confidences might come in for reexamination and possible modification. We have all been trained to know without question that the privilege is indispensable for effective representation. The client must know his confidences are safe so that he can tell all and thus have fully knowledgeable advice. We may want to ask, nevertheless, whether it would be an excessive price for the client to be stuck with the truth rather than having counsel allied with him for concealment and distortion. The full development of this thought is beyond my studies to date. Its implications may be unacceptable. I urge only that it is among the premises in need of examination.

If the lawyer is to be more truth-seeker than combatant, troublesome questions of economics and professional organization may demand early confrontation. How and why should the client pay for loyalties divided be-

---

7. R. Traver, Anatomy of a Murder (1958). For those who did not read or have forgotten it, the novel, by a state supreme court justice, involved an eventually successful homicide defense of impaired mental capacity with the defendant supplying the requisite "facts" after having been told in advance by counsel what type of facts would constitute the defense.

8. *See* text accompanying note 2 *supra.* In M. Freedman, Lawyers' Ethics in an Adversary System, ch. 6 (forthcoming), Dean Freedman reports a changed view on this last of his "three hardest questions." He would under some circumstances (including the case in Anatomy of a Murder) condemn the lawyer's supplying of the legal knowledge to promote perjury. Exploring whether the Dean's new position is workable would transcend even the wide leeway I arrogate in footnotes.

tween himself and the truth? Will we not stultify the energies and resources of the advocate by demanding that he judge the honesty of his
cause along the way? Can we preserve the heroic lawyer shielding his client against all the world—and not least against the State—while demanding
that he honor a paramount commitment to the elusive and ambiguous truth?
It is strongly arguable, in short, that a simplistic preference for the truth
may not comport with more fundamental ideals—including notably the ideal
that generally values individual freedom and dignity above order and efficiency in government.[9] Having stated such issues too broadly, I leave them
in the hope that their refinement and study may seem worthy endeavors for
the future.

C. *A Duty to Pursue the Truth*

The rules of professional responsibility should compel disclosures of
material facts and forbid material omissions rather than merely proscribe
positive frauds. This final suggestion is meant to implement the broad and
general proposition that precedes it. In an effort to be still more specific, I
submit a draft of a new disciplinary rule that would supplement or in large
measure displace existing disciplinary rule 7–102 of the Code of Professional Responsibility. The draft says:

(1) In his representation of a client, unless prevented from doing
so by a privilege reasonably believed to apply, a lawyer shall:

(a) Report to the court and opposing counsel the existence of relevant evidence or witnesses where the lawyer does not intend to
offer such evidence or witnesses.

(b) Prevent, or when prevention has proved unsuccessful, report
to the court and opposing counsel the making of any untrue
statement by client or witness or any omission to state a material fact necessary in order to make statements made, in the
light of the circumstances under which they were made, not
misleading.

(c) Question witnesses with a purpose and design to elicit the
whole truth, including particularly supplementary and qualifying matters that render evidence already given more accurate,
intelligible, or fair than it otherwise would be.

(2) In the construction and application of the rules in subdivision
(1), a lawyer will be held to possess knowledge he actually has or, in
the exercise of reasonable diligence, should have.

Key words in the draft, namely, in (1)(b), have been plagiarized, of
course, from the Securities and Exchange Commission's rule 10b–5. That
should serve not only for respectability; it should also answer, at least to
some extent, the complaint that the draft would impose impossibly stringent

9. Two previous Cardozo Lecturers
have been among the line of careful
thinkers cautioning against too single-
minded a concern for truth. "While
our adversary system of litigation may
not prove to be the best means of ascertaining truth, its emphasis upon
respect for human dignity at every
step is not to be undermined lightly
in a democratic state." Botein, The
Future of the Judicial Process, 15
Record of N.Y.C.B.A. 152, 166 (1960).
See also Shawcross, The Functions
and Responsibilities of an Advocate,
13 Record of N.Y.C.B.A. 483, 498, 500
(1958).

standards.   The morals we have evolved for business clients cannot be deemed unattainable by the legal profession.

Harder questions suggest themselves.   The draft provision for wholesale disclosure of evidence in litigation may be visionary or outrageous, or both.   It certainly stretches out of existing shape our conception of the advocate retained to be partisan.   As against the yielding up of everything, we are accustomed to strenuous debates about giving a supposedly laggard or less energetic party a share in his adversary's litigation property safeguarded as "work product."   A lawyer must now surmount partisan loyalty and disclose "information clearly establishing" frauds by his client or others.[10]   But that is a far remove from any duty to turn over all the fruits of factual investigation,[11] as the draft proffered here would direct.   It has lately come to be required that some approach to helpful disclosures be made by prosecutors in criminal cases; "the suppression by the prosecution of evidence favorable to an accused upon request violates due process where the evidence is material either to guilt or to punishment, irrespective of the good faith or bad faith of the prosecution."   One may be permitted as a respectful subordinate to note the awkward placement in the quoted passage of the words "upon request," and to imagine their careful insertion to keep the duty of disclosure within narrow bounds.   But even that restricted rule is for the *public* lawyer.   Can we, should we, adopt a far broader rule as a command to the bar generally?

That question touches once again the most sensitive nerve of all.   A bar too tightly regulated, too conformist, too "governmental," is not acceptable to any of us.   We speak often of lawyers as "officers of the court" and as "public" people.   Yet our basic conception of the office is of one essentially private—private in political, economic, and ideological terms—congruent with a system of private ownership, enterprise, and competition, however modified the system has come to be.   It is not necessary to recount here the contributions of a legal profession thus conceived to the creation and maintenance of a relatively free society.   It *is* necessary to acknowledge those contributions and to consider squarely whether, or how much, they are endangered by proposed reforms.

If we must choose between truth and liberty, the decision is not in doubt.   If the choice seemed to me that clear and that stark, this essay would never have reached even the tentative form of its present submission.   But I think the picture is quite unclear.   I lean to the view that we can hope to preserve the benefits of a free, skeptical, contentious bar while paying a lesser price in trickery and obfuscation.

Questions

1.   What, if any, ethical dilemmas are posed by Judge Frankel's proposed revision of the Canons of Ethics?   Does that revision tend to lessen internal conflicts in the Canons of Ethics?

10.   ABA Code of Professional Responsibility, DR 7–102(B).

11.   Cf. American College of Trial Lawyers, Code of Trial Conduct R. 15(b): A lawyer should not suppress any evidence that he or his client has a legal obligation to reveal or produce.   He should not advise or cause a person to secrete himself or to leave the jurisdiction of a tribunal for the purpose of making himself unavailable as a witness therein.   However, except when legally required, it is not his duty to disclose any evidence or the identity of any witness.

2. What response do you suppose Professor Freedman might make to Judge Frankel's views? See Monroe H. Freedman, "Judge Frankel's Search for Truth," 123 University of Pennsylvania Law Review 1060 (1975).

SECTION 18.   CIVIL PROCEDURE IN GERMANY

[The following is taken from BENJAMIN KAPLAN, "CIVIL PROCEDURE—REFLECTIONS ON THE COMPARISON OF SYSTEMS," 9 University of Buffalo Law Review 409, 409–421 (1960). Footnotes are omitted.]

I.

To begin, the rules governing civil procedure in Germany today are laid down by legislative enactment stemming from the famous code of 1877; judicial rule-making plays virtually no part. There is no jury. The courts, at least those concerned in the regular proceedings for cases of consequence, are collegial in structure, acting through benches of three or—in the court of final review—five judges. To some extent, however, the plural bench may use a single judge as a representative or helper.

One of the leitmotifs of the German process is sounded by the Siegfried horn of the summons in the action. This invites appearance at a *Termin zur mündlichen Verhandlung,* a court-session for oral-argument, or rather for conference, since the ideal style of proceeding is less that of a contentious confrontation than a cooperative discussion. The conference is set perhaps three to four weeks after initial service of the papers—which by the way is usually accomplished by mail—and it is commonly attended by the parties as well as counsel. Now the point to be made is that the whole procedure up to judgment may be viewed as being essentially a series of such conferences, the rest of the process having a sort of dependent status. Prooftaking occurs to the extent necessary in the spaces, as it were, between conferences. Intermediate decisions are made along the way. But the conferences are the heart of the matter. Very promptly, then, the litigants are brought under the eye of the court and the case begins to be shaped; and this treatment is applied to the action at intervals until it is fully opened and finally broken. "Conference" betokens informality and this characterizes the entire German procedure. "Conference" also suggests what is the fact, that possibilities of settlement are openly, vigorously, and continually exploited.

I must relate German pleadings to the conference method—I shall use the word "pleadings" although these writings are quite different from the American variety. The action starts with a complaint served together with the summons, but beyond this there is no prescribed number or sequence of pleadings. Pleadings are to be put in in such numbers and at such times as to prepare for, strengthen, and expedite the conferences and thereby the general movement of the case. They have no position independent of the conferences. Indeed the framers of the code of 1877 looked to a free, oral restatement of the pleadings at conference. Such oral recapitulation no longer occurs: the court reads the pleadings in advance and the lawyers are assumed to adopt the pleadings except as they speak up to the contrary. Still no question arises as to the sufficiency of the pleadings as such, nor is there any motion practice directed to the pleadings themselves. In short, pleadings merge into, are an ingredient of the conferences. What is wanted from the pleadings as adopted and perhaps revised at conference is a narrative of the facts as the parties see them at the time, with offers of proof —mainly designated witnesses and documents—and demands for relief. There is no insistence on niceties of form, and legal argumentation, though strictly out of place, is common in today's pleadings. Amendments, even drastic amendments, of the statements can be made until the end of the case, normally without any penalty for late change. This malleability of the pleadings flows from the realization and expectation that a case may change its content and color as it is repeatedly discussed and as proof is from time to time adduced.

Returning to the conduct of the conferences, we find the presiding judge highly vocal and dominant, the parties themselves often voluble, the lawyers relatively subdued. To understand the judicial attitude and contribution at conference, we must take account of two related concepts. First, there is the principle jura novit curia, the court knows and applies the law without relying on the parties to bring it forward. Second, article 139 of the code, as strengthened in recent years, imposes a duty on all courts to clarify the cause and lead the parties toward full development of their respective positions. Thus with awareness of the law implicit in the case, the court is obliged to discuss it freely with the litigants, and in that light to indicate what will be material to decision. By discussion with counsel and the parties the court completes the picture of the controversy as presented by the litigants, throwing light upon obscurities, correcting misunderstandings, marking out areas of agreement and disagreement. It spurs and guides the parties to any necessary further exploration of facts and theories, and may suggest appropriate allegations, proof offers, and demands. The court, however, is not bound to take over and commandeer the litigation, nor does it have the power to do so in an ultimate sense. To some degree—the power is greater in "family" matters than in ordinary cases—the court may call up evidence and background information and disregard parties' admissions. The calling of experts is basically a matter for the court. But, in general, allegations, proof offers, and demands can be made only by the parties and so in the last analysis major control of the cause-materials remains with them. Nevertheless, as the parties are likely to follow the court's suggestions, we have here a significant potential in the court which imparts a special quality to the procedure; and this is so despite the fact that clarification and leading are hardly noticeable in simpler cases where the lawyers seem to be providing competent representation. The role of the court not only at conference but throughout the proceedings is envisioned as being both directive and protective. The court as vigorous chairman is to move the case along at a good pace, stirring the parties to action on their own behalf, exercising its limited sua sponte powers where necessary, conscious of a duty to strive for the right solution of the controversy regardless of faults of advocacy.

Conferences propel the lawsuit. Most dates are set by the court in open session. It acts in discretion with due regard to the convenience of the parties: few "iron" time provisions are laid down in the code, and the parties cannot control the pace by stipulation. When discussions disclose ripe questions of law, a time will be set for decision. If they show up disputed issues of fact, there will be an order and a time set for prooftaking.

To understand German prooftaking, we have first to ask what investigation of the facts a German lawyer customarily makes. He consults his client and his client's papers. But he has substantially no coercive means of "discovering" material for the purpose of preparing his proof offers or readying himself for prooftaking. Moreover he is by no means at liberty to go out and talk informally with prospective witnesses. He is hobbled by the principle that he is to avoid all suspicion of influencing those who may be later called to give evidence in court. I shall not attempt to mark the exact boundaries of this inhibition or to dredge up the possible evasive contrivances. I shall simply say that German lawyers are not prime movers with respect to the facts. The régime just described does make for unrehearsed witnesses. It begins to explain why a party in German litigation is not charged with any "proprietorship" over the witnesses whom he has nominated and neither "vouches" for them nor is "bound" by their testimony.

The court draws up the order for prooftaking, the *Beweisbeschluss*, from the nominations set out in the pleadings as they may have been revised at conference. Prooftaking need not be concentrated at a single session, and is in fact not often so concentrated. Accordingly the court may pick and choose what it wants to hear at particular sessions. It can take proof in any order— evidence on a defense ahead of evidence on the main case, even evidence on the negative of an issue ahead of the affirmative.

Witnesses are sequestered, kept out of the courtroom until called. The court asks the witness to state what he knows about the proof theme on which he has been summoned. When the witness has done that in narrative without undue interruption, the court interrogates him, and this is the principal interrogation. Counsel put supplemental questions. Lawyers' participation is likely to be meager. If a lawyer puts too many questions he is implying that the court does not know its business, and that is a dubious tactic. A full stenographic transcript is not kept. Instead the court dictates a summary of the witness' testimony for the minutes which is then read back and perhaps corrected.

German law has few rules excluding relevant evidence. In general relevant evidence is admissible and when admitted is freely evaluated: thus there is no bar to the admission of hearsay. But a few qualifications must be made. German law recognizes a series of privileges. It is somewhat irresolute in compelling production in court of various kinds of documentary proof. Testimony will be received from the parties themselves only in particular circumstances defined by law, and in no event may a party be compelled to testify. Party-testimony is viewed as a kind of last resort. This raises a quiddity, for parties are regularly heard in conference, nominally for purposes of clarification, not proof. I say "nominally" because German law tends to blur the line between evidence stricto sensu and other happenings in the courtroom.

Prooftaking is succeeded by conference, conference by prooftaking, and so on to the end of the regular proceedings in the first-instance court; and now we naturally ask, are there any shortcuts, any special devices for closing a case out promptly when it appears that there is overwhelming strength on one side and corresponding weakness on the other? The answer is no.

The German system relies on the succession of conferences and prooftakings to show up strength or weakness with reasonable dispatch. Nor is there much in the way of stage-preclusion, that is, rules intended to discourage delaying afterthoughts by requiring that particular offers or objections be made at fixed points in the proceeding on pain of being otherwise lost to the party. The German action is not segmented into clear-cut stages—recall how pleadings may be thrown in late in the day—and it has in general a quality of "wholeness" or unity. But we do need to say here that the German system makes interestingly brisk provision for handling defaults; and we should also call attention to certain special speed-up devices: "dunning" proceedings, *Mahnverfahren,* available for "collection" cases and carried on regardless of amount in the inferior one-judge court; and "documentary-process," *Urkundenprozess,* used chiefly in suits on commercial paper, with proof initially limited to documents and party-testimony.

We come now to appellate review. The most notable fact about it is that on appeal to the court of second instance from final judgment, or from the important type of intermediate judgment which determines liability but leaves damages to be ascertained, the parties are entitled to a redoing of the case. The record made below, so far as it is thought to be free of error, stands as part of the proceedings, but the parties may add new proofs and invoke new legal theories, and the conduct of the cause is quite similar to that in the court below. Remember that article 139 on clarification and leading, with related duties and powers, continues to apply. The final court of review hears "revisions" on questions of law. As to matters of substance as distinguished from procedure, the court is not confined to the grounds urged by counsel. It seems a mark of the reality of the principle jura novit curia that this national court, dealing with a very large number of revisions coming up from the lower courts adminstered by the states, the *Länder,* is served by a bar limited by law to less than a score of lawyers.

The German court system is manned by a quite sizeable number of judges. They are career men, appointed on the basis of government examinations, modestly paid, of good but not exalted social prestige, looking primarily to ministerial departments of justice for advancement. In normal times men customarily enter into judicial service at an early age, generally without substantial experience in practice. Judges have traditionally been chided for *Lebensfremdheit,* undue detachment from the rough-and-tumble of life. We have caught a hint of their paternalistic role in the court procedure. This is not far distant from, indeed it comprises, an element of the bureaucratic. Working, many of them, in collegial courts whose judgments, stiffly authoritative in style, disclose neither individual authorship nor individual dissent, German judges live rather anonymous lives. And they are deskbound through a large part of their working time, for files must be read in preparation for court sessions, and most decisions in actions large and small must be compendiously written up.

As to the German lawyers, I must avoid leaving the impression that their contribution to litigation is unimportant, or that their attitude is flaccid. Despite the court's capacity for active interposition, the frame of the case is made by the lawyers and there is room for contentious striving. Still the procedural system we have outlined does not make for notably vigorous performance by counsel. Moreover the education of lawyers tends against their full identification with clients as combatants: a significant part of their post-University required training is as apprentice-judges. Most important, we must notice some economic facts. Lawyers' fees for litigation, generally corresponding with statutory scales fixed in relation to the amount in controversy, are low.

Court costs are also fixed by statute in relation to the amount in suit, so that a litigant is on the one hand prompted to moderate his demand for judgment, and can on the other hand make a reasonably accurate advance estimate of the expense of litigation. Taking all elements of expense into consideration, German litigation is cheap by comparison with the American brand. But on the threshold a German litigant must conjure with the fact that if as plaintiff or defendant he turns out loser in the lawsuit, he will have to reimburse his opponent's expenses—counsel fees and court costs at the statutory rates together with ordinary disbursements. Let us note here that contingent-fee arrangements—agreements for quota litis—are proscribed in German practice. A comprehensive system of state-provided legal aid aims to enable not only downright paupers but any citizens of insufficient means to prosecute or defend civil cases upon a plausible showing of a prospect of success.

Lastly I must respond to the nervous question which any American lawyer would surely want to ask: Does the German system get over its court business without undue delay? German court statistics—at least those publicly available and not held in subterranean tunnels by the ministries— are curiously sparse; but these figures combine with the opinion of German lawyers familiar with the scene to indicate that the courts, although handling a very considerable volume of cases, are disposing of their calendars with fair speed. However, the court of final review—the *Bundesgerichtshof* sitting in Karlsruhe, successor to the famous *Reichsgericht* which used to reside in Leipzig—has had a hard time in recent years overcoming a serious backlog.

II.

The nutshell is now fully packed. To vary the figure of speech, I have sought to do a rough charcoal sketch of the German process which might prepare for a modulated painting in oil. I have had to omit many necessary qualifications. At some points I have perhaps let the ideal overweigh the real; I have not stopped to say that in Germany as with us procedural forms are in practice sometimes utterly debased. I am no doubt led by prior aquaintance with American procedure to some distorted or false ideas about the German. As Holmes remarked about a foreign legal system, "When we contemplate such a system from the outside it seems like a wall of stone, every part even with all the others. . . . But to one brought up within it, varying emphasis, tacit assumptions, unwritten practices, a thousand influences gained only from life, may give to the different parts wholly new values that logic and grammar never could have got from the books." Yet I think one observation can be made with confidence about the German process: it differs materially from the American, differs not merely in particulars but in general features. Let your mind range backward over my account of German procedure and contrast for the two systems the modes of determining and allocating expenses of litigation; the character and functions of the lawyers and of the judges; the concept of appeal; the approach to facts and proof; the pleadings; the central motor power of the process as a whole. Our short journey through the German system may well make us wary of joining hands with those amiable scholars who like to conclude, even over great apparent odds, that legal institutions in the Western world are in essence really the same.

We can agree that if analysis is carried on at a sufficiently high level of abstraction, all processes for rational decisions of disputes by governmental authority will be seen to have certain broad similarities. The logic and fundamental decencies of controversy tend to impose uniformities. We must grant, too, that the professed ultimate aims of most if not all modern procedural systems are much alike. Surely the German jurist would say that his system aims at careful consideration of law and fact, resoluteness, speed, economy, and impartiality in handling cases: aims shortly stated in the American Federal Rules, as well as in the legislation proposed for New York, as "the just, speedy, and inexpensive determination" of every action. It will indeed be one of the fascinating tasks of comparative scholarship to show how procedural systems announcing similar goals came to develop their divergent procedural institutions.

"Very deep is the well of the past," said Thomas Mann; and he asked, "Should we not call it bottomless?" Let Mann's riddling question stand, and consider the course of the intertwined English and American procedural history since the turn of the nineteenth century. Recall the scene upon which Jeremy Bentham and Lord Brougham erupted; the issues to which David Dudley Field's New York Code of 1848 and the English legislation of the 1870's responded; in recent memory, the challenges presented to Charles E. Clark and his colleagues when they set about formulating the Federal Civil Rules of 1938. Examining German procedural history, the must-do's, can't-do's, and lesser compulsions and inhibitions which have channelled the development of German procedural institutions, we shall find few real counterparts to the Anglo-American story.

German scholarship has provided us only with bits and pieces of the political, social, and intellectual forces that produced the modern code. It is, however, plain that the men who met in the 1870's under the leadership of the astute Hannoverian lawyer, Adolf Leonhardt, to frame a uniform procedural code for all of Germany, were executors of the half-formed designs of the liberals of 1848, and were responding to battle cries and slogans of that and indeed of a previous era which in the course of time had become irreducible popular demands.

The Emperor Napoleon had brought to conquered German states and principalities a new system for the administration of justice fathered by French revolutionary thought. After the final departure of Napoleon, the movement for *deutsche Rechtseinheit*, German legal unity, a phase of larger pressures for German political unification, took up standards in one way or another associated with the French incursion. Thus we hear great outcries for equality of citizens in the legal process, which meant the abolition of patrimonial jurisdiction and of special access of favored classes to particular courts. We hear demands for independence of the courts in the double sense of separation of the judicial function from the executive and of protection of judges from arbitrary interference with status and tenure. There is widespread agitation for a jury in criminal cases. Finally the slogans of "orality" and "publicity" are set loose in the land.

By contrast with the so-called "common" procedure then prevailing in German territory, a secretive, written, stiff procedure, the French system, the code de procédure civile of 1806, had proclaimed itself as open, oral, flexible, informal. The French mode introduced in the Prussian Rhineland held on for well over a half-century: resistance of this province to the Prussianization of its law is a long tale of odd surprises involving some of the great names of German legal science, including Savigny. French procedure caught the liberal imagination and brought forth a rationalizing German literature centering upon the idea that the parties in litigation should confront each other in free debate in the sight and hearing of the court, and the further idea that the court process should be open to the view of the parties and the public. The important writings of Anselm von Feuerbach, although seeking to avoid reproaches of Francophilism, elevated these notions almost to the rank of natural rights. Over a long period of time German liberals could point to the Rhineland as proof that French transplants could survive on native soil. Emotive power was added to the reform program for civil procedure by linkage with forces urging vital changes in criminal procedure, and all these demands took on messianic coloring as part and parcel of the revolutionary struggle of 1848. In 1849 the abortive constitution written by the National Assembly in the Paulskirche at Frankfurt adopted orality and publicity as central features of court process. In the same year an attempt to pacify opinion in Hannover by a somewhat liberalized code on the lines of the "common" procedure collapsed entirely. In 1850 Hannover adopted a code of civil procedure blending French ideas— some of them as transformed in a Swiss cantonal code for Geneva—with the older German, but essentially preferring the French. This Hannoverian reform proved an immediate success, and from this point onwards the programmatic demands of the liberals could not be gainsaid despite the temporary general failure of the 1848 movement. The complicated deliberations of the 1860's and 1870's leading to the code of 1877 could hardly move outside the limits fixed by public acceptance of erstwhile liberal dogmas. In a large sense it was true that France, defeated on the battlefields, had conquered in the law books. Bismarck implicitly referred to the same phenomenon when he said that the code was Hannover's revenge for its defeat and amalgamation by Prussia in 1866, for it was Leonhardt who had written the Frenchified Hannoverian code of 1850, became Prussian minister of justice after the absorption of Hannover, and survived to influence the new all-German code.

This is part of the background of the *Mündlichkeit,* the orality of German procedure exemplified by the conference method, and serves to explain the strong, one may say the emotional, attachment of the German system to this basic idea. The code-makers, however, had to translate the sloganeers' old appeal for an oral procedure into precise and viable modes, and this they did by careful ratiocination, by a variety of compromises, by blending practices drawn from the several parts of Germany with the French model as that had itself been altered in German hands.

The enthusiasts of 1848 would perhaps have been not entirely satisfied with the code of 1877 and might be less so with the present procedure. Thus the place accorded in the code to written statements of position might have disappointed at least the more extreme champions of orality, and we have seen that the conference no longer comprises free recapitulation of positions.

In the vision of the 1848 reformers, the oral, open clash of the litigants pursuing their competing self-interests was relied on both to propel and shape the proceedings. The reformers accepted that the court would have some duty of elucidation, but they were against state tutelage in the form of the paternalistic judge. Experience since 1877, however, showed that the parties themselves would not give proper propulsion to the lawsuit, and control in this respect has gradually passed to the judge. The directive-protective role of the judge at conference as well as in other phases of the procedure, the bureaucratic tinge of the lawsuit, result from a cumulation of forces, some of them going back to the early days of the Hohenzollern dynasty. Under Frederick William I and Frederick the Great, the minister Samuel von Cocceji improved the quality of the Prussian judiciary but at the cost of leading the judges into the bureaucratic hierarchy. German judges have never since escaped bureaucratic involvement. As the late Piero Calamandrei said of the Italian judge, "Two qualities that appear incompatible are thus united in the same person—the constitutional independence of the function and the administrative dependence of the functionary." It is indeed a major concern of German procedural reform today to cure the dilemma by removing judges from the general class of administrative officialdom. The administration of justice was seen by the Prussians as only another state social service; this view combined with royal distrust of the attorney class to give Prussia in 1793 and for about a half-century thereafter a procedural code which sought, although in the end vainly, to go almost the whole way in committing the management of the civil lawsuit to the judges as civil servants, and correspondingly to eliminate the attorneys as champions of the parties. Although German scholars have sometimes discounted the importance of this Prussian development, it has, I think, left its mark on German procedure. In the latter part of the nineteenth and in the early years of the twentieth century, a stream of thought emanating from Austria, more specifically from the great Austrian proceduralist Franz Klein, gave measured justification for the proposition that the state should strive to equalize opportunity in court proceedings, which were to be viewed as a *Massenerscheinung*, a mass-phenomenon, having important social purposes and consequences. Playing upon the German background, these ideas led to the strengthening of article 139 and to other vital alterations of the German code.

So we can see that large historical forces including the movement of general ideas in a given society may determine some of the main themes of a procedural system. Scholars who accept this proposition as applied to the substantive law have sometimes been prone to ignore or minimize it in the procedural field, have confined attention too closely to particular contemporaneous dissatisfactions as the determinants of specific procedural changes. But if large historical pressures may be significant for procedural development, it is also true that certain elections made by a system under no such grand impulsions—even elections of a technical character made more or less unwittingly—may have almost equally decisive effect by setting up pervasive, interlocking, interdependent relationships throughout the process.

Obedience to the master idea of orality did not necessarily call for an unsegmented system. On the contrary Leonhardt himself seems to have believed that an open, oral procedure would become diffuse unless accompanied and controlled by some sharp stage division. The issue was not foreclosed by political battlecries old or new. It seems rather to have been viewed as a technical and prudential matter. Thus scholars debated the pros and cons of the *Beweisinterlokut,* an order which would definitely separate a pleading stage from a proof stage and provide a clear pattern for the balance of the proceeding. In the end this device was rejected. Among the considerations was this, that so important an order would deserve to be subject to immediate review, but so rampant an opportunity for interlocutory appeal would threaten delay. As the system has worked out, there is a minimum of stage division or preclusion, and prooftaking occurs on the installment plan interwoven with conferences.

Now see how this feature determines and intermeshes with others. Staggered prooftaking, which allows for afterthoughts, relieves the pressure to articulate fixed and precise issues in advance of receiving proof in order to prevent "surprise." There is little anxiety about the pleadings and small room for devices to trim and correct them. So also "discovery" mechanisms ahead of the display of proof in court, again directed to preventing surprise, can hardly be felt as an urgent need in the German system. Lawyers can get along with limited informal access to prospective witnesses. Incidentally, expense of investigation is not a large figure on the litigation budget. These are a few obvious examples of how episodic prooftaking ramifies its effects further and still further through the German procedure.

With us in this country jury trial must be carried out as a single continuous drama, for a jury cannot be assembled, dismissed and reconvened over a period of time. We tend toward concentrated trial even when the judge sits alone, perhaps by magnetic attraction to jury trial as the historic centerpiece of civil procedure, perhaps because the system puts a high value on the trier's fresh impression of live proof, perhaps for other reasons. Hence the opposing sides must appear in court knowing the precise issues and fully armed and prepared to meet them. To these ends we have our pleadings and amendments and motions, our discovery devices, our pretrial conference. Concentrated trial forces accommodations in many rules and practices and has no doubt profoundly affected the character and role of the American lawyer and judge.

Decisive elections within a system bring on their characteristic dilemmas and problems. To speak again of episodic as against concentrated prooftaking, the former raises the specter of undue protraction of the case and this insistent problem has prompted a series of German experiments with sanctions for delay, stronger motor power in the court, use of single-judge proceedings to prepare the case so that it can then be brought to a conclusion in one or a few sessions before the full bench. But single-judge proceedings work against true "collegiality" (itself curiously connected in German thought with orality); they also offend against the principle of "immediacy," the notion that judges who have power of final decision should get a direct rather than a second-hand impression of the cause-materials. With us, in actions at law the pleadings were early relied on almost exclusively for defining issues, and this they did very imperfectly. Facilities for discovery were meager. Yet jury trial must be carried off without interruption. Bentham rightly said that trial in these circumstances must intrinsically lead to unjust decision, for upon trial the case would often shape up differently than had been anticipated—yet there would be no opportunity to search out additional facts or examine the implications of theories now newly found relevant. With diminished faith in pleadings and corrective motions, rights to discovery have been enlarged. The pretrial conference has been added. American code-makers have combined these devices in varying ways in an effort to attain just the right mixture; recently they have begun to flirt with the idea of using masters to energize the whole pretrial process. The current New York proposal attempts its own adjustment of the basic elements, pleadings, discovery, and pretrial conference: it puts somewhat greater stress on pleadings than has been lately fashionable, and makes a carefully calculated effort after much historic failure to elicit informing and helpful initial statements of position from the parties. Elaborate mechanisms for perfecting definition of issues and laying bare the facts to prepare for trial create dangers of excessive delay and expense, although concomitantly opening up chances for disposition without trial; and we retain devices to avoid trial where possible. It is in all events made doubly clear as we compare episodic with concentrated prooftaking that adherence to one or the other mode affects the code-maker's range of maneuver.

Probing further into attitudes toward facts and proof, do we not find on the American side a striking concern with exhausting sources of evidence and squeezing the last drop of advantage out of the pulp of multitudinous details? Facts are today often thrice canvassed at heavy expense: by informal methods, again by official discovery devices, and again at the trial proper. Pretrial sifting of the facts may improve the chance for settlement or other disposition without trial; it minimizes surprise at some risk of taking the fresh bloom off the testimony if the matter should reach trial. Although pretrial investigation is loose and far-ranging, the trial itself, faithful to its tough adversary spirit, perhaps responsive to the supposed needs of the jury as inexperienced, once-in-a-life-time triers, proceeds according to a code duello of exclusionary rules of evidence, with litigants "bound" by "their" witnesses. Examination and cross-examination, minutely recorded, pursue detail and test credibility with relentless assiduity.

In many respects German practice turns the tables. Prooftaking in court is notably untrammeled by tight rules of evidence: the triers are professionals, the adversary spirit is muffled. To be sure a restrictive attitude persists toward party-testimony. On a superficial view this attitude seems to be traceable to a cynical estimate of the amount of truthtelling that can be expected from those interested in the stakes. Continental writers sometimes relate it to a desire to preserve the individual's dignity. As we have seen, the restriction is in practice substantially overcome by interrogation of parties at conference and I should perhaps add that it does not go so far as to prevent blood tests of the parties. The rules as to party-testimony thus hardly confound the generalization that prooftaking is "free." On the other hand the search for facts is neither broad nor vigorous. We have spoken of the limited access of lawyers to prospective witnesses out-of-court. It is true that the episodic movement of the case affords opportunity to the litigant—led by the court or stirred by hints in the testimony—to search for and offer additional proof whose existence or pertinence was unknown to him at the start; and there is still a further chance to enlarge the proofs on appeal. But episodic prooftaking, while providing room for something on the order of American discovery, is not thought of in that way. So the tendency is to bar "fishing" exercises at prooftakings, that is, to disallow questions to witnesses designed merely to uncover possible sources of proof. We may surely conclude that fact investigation in the German system does not in practice attain anywhere near the strength of the American.

The German method of taking testimony itself strikes an American lawyer as lamentably imprecise. Remember that the initial and principal interrogation of witnesses is conducted by the court which at least in the early stages of litigation will not have a comprehensive idea of the facts. Recording testimony in paraphrase is well calculated to bleach out color and blur detail. Some evidence may be received by the deciding plural bench only at relay from the single-judge acting as representative of the court. Impressions of the evidence are dulled by the very process of receiving it in installments over a period of time.

If the Germans are more casual than we are about the facts, if they are content to get a kind of generalized or synoptic rather than meticulous perception of the events in suit, if, as I believe, prooftaking as a whole has a subsidiary place in the German system, then we are led to speculations about the relation of procedural forms to the style of the substantive law. Is a fully codified substantive-law system of the civil-law type congenial to a pattern of fact-finding which would be felt to be inadequate to the needs of a common-law system? Is it significant for procedural development that primary reference in the one system is to the generalizations of the substantive code, not the case decisions, while the other system grows by matching case with case? Or are we in this country simply paying too much in time, effort, and money to pursue the finer lineaments of truth which must in any event elude us? I pass over specific attitudes toward problems of forensic psychology, such as the question of the value attached to oral as against documentary evidence, and I stop short of the pons asinorum of "national character."

To sum up: I have touched upon certain of the forces which have bent the German system of civil procedure into its characteristic patterns and forms and I have posed some comparisons between the German and American procedure. Historical exegesis has a natural place in the comparative inquiry if only because one cannot meaningfully juxtapose systems which one does not reasonably well understand; it gives us, besides, a sense of the grip of particular institutions upon a society and so of their susceptibility to change. Side-by-side examination of systems puts in clearer light the crucial elections which they have severally made. Again comparison invites thought about the interactions of procedure with the rest of the legal cosmos, and frames cogent questions of ultimate purpose and value.

Questions

1. Compare and contrast American civil procedure with the West German procedure described by Professor Kaplan. Which system do you prefer? Why?

2. Professor Kaplan suggests that West German civil procedure has been shaped by powerful forces—political, social, and intellectual. Can you identify forces—political, social, intellectual—which have shaped American civil procedure?

Part Two

LAW AS A PROCESS OF MAINTAINING HISTORICAL CONTINUITY AND DOCTRINAL CONSISTENCY: ILLUSTRATIONS FROM MANUFACTURERS' LIABILITY IN TORT

Chapter 5

REASONING BY ANALOGY OF PRECEDENT

SECTION 19. LEGAL REASONING

Legal reasoning often appears to the layman to be a mysterious science, and lawyers have often been guilty of contributing to the misconception that legal methods of thinking are somehow essentially different from the mental processes of persons engaged in other human and social activities. It is true, of course, that insofar as the subject matter of law is different from, say, the subject matter of mathematics, or that of economics, the method of reaching legal conclusions will not coincide with the method of reaching conclusions in mathematics or economics. It has been truly said that there is no one scientific method, but that each science must use a method appropriate to its subject matter. Yet all sciences, including legal science, have something in common as well, and law is no less "logical," in the broadest sense of that term, than other disciplines.

What distinguishes legal reasoning from other kinds of reasoning is its focus upon characteristic legal activities. In the United States and England, where legal scholars have been especially concerned with adjudication, legal reasoning is often identified by them with the intellectual processes by which judges reach conclusions in deciding cases. In France and Germany, on the other hand, where thought about law has focused primarily on the creation of a complex and harmonious body of rules, expressed especially in codes, legal reasoning is often identified with the intellectual processes by which the consistency and rationality of legal doctrines are maintained and justified. However, these two types of reasoning are in fact closely related to each other, and both should be included in any definition of legal reasoning; indeed, we would propose to broaden the definition still further to include the types of reasoning used in other kinds of legal activities as well, such as the making of laws, the administration of law, the trial (and not only the decision) of cases in court, the drafting of legal documents, and the negotiation of legal transactions.

Conceived in these broader terms, legal reasoning involves not only, and not primarily, the application of rules of formal logic but also other methods of exposition. To reason, according to dictionary definitions, may mean to give grounds (reasons) for one's statements, to argue persuasively, or to engage in discourse. Law, insofar as it has a distinctive subject matter and is founded on distinctive principles and purposes, has not only its own kinds of logic, but also its own kinds of rhetoric, and its own kinds of discourse, which are, of course, similar to but distinct from the logic, rhetoric, and discourse of other social institutions and scholarly disciplines, such as religion, politics, social science, or economic activities.

It must be kept in mind, in seeking to identify these distinctive characteristics, that legal reasoning is not identical in all societies, and that in addition the degree of its distinctiveness is not identical in all societies. In a theocracy, for example, there may be a close relationship between sacerdotal reasoning and legal reasoning; at one time the high priests of Israel found the law by consulting the breastplates which they wore (the Urim and Thummim)—that is, their legal decisions were justified in terms of divine revelation. In many primitive societies, law is characterized less by developed concepts than by symbolic acts, such as solemnly repeated ceremonies and formulae, and many such symbolic acts still survive in modern law. On the other hand, in a society that is undergoing a political revolution, such as the Soviet Union in the first years after 1917, or France in the first years after 1789, legal reasoning may dissolve into the reasoning of politics and class struggle, as traditional concepts and symbols become subordinate to the sudden creation of a whole new social order. These variations strongly suggest that in any society there is an intimate connection between the logic, rhetoric, and discourse of law and the dominant beliefs of the society concerning religion, politics, and other aspects of social life, including its beliefs about the nature of reasoning itself.

In those societies that have experienced the emergence of a special professional class of law-men, with its own special professional traditions and institutional values, legal reasoning acquires distinguishing features; here special modes of logic, rhetoric, and discourse have as part of their functions the preservation and further development of the legal profession's traditions and values, although even in such societies the intimate connections between legal reasoning and other types of reasoning must be maintained, if the legal profession is to retain the respect of the community as a whole.

Legal logic. Especially in the 18th and 19th centuries, many Western jurists sought to make legal reasoning conform to syllogistic logic. The rules of law declared by legislatures, courts, and legal scholars were viewed as major premises, and the fact situations of particular cases or the terms of particular legal problems were viewed as minor premises. The decision of a case, or the resolution of a legal problem, was thought to follow inevitably from a proper juxtaposition of the major and minor premises. Given a doctrine or rule defining contract, or burglary, or some other basis of legal duty, it was thought legal responsibility could be attached to a particular act by stating whether or not it falls within the definition. It was supposed by many that if the entire body of law could be summarized in a set of rules, the sole remaining task of law would be to classify particular facts under one rule or another.

This mechanical model of the application of rules to facts did not go unchallenged even in its heyday. In Germany, Rudolf von Jhering (1818–1892) ridiculed a "jurisprudence of concepts" (*Begriffsjurisprudenz*) and called for a conscious legal policy of evaluating the social and personal interests involved in the legal resolution of conflicts (*Interessenjurisprudenz*). Similarly, in the United States, Oliver Wendell Holmes, Jr., in some of his writings, viewed the logical form in which judges announced their conclusions as a veil covering their views of public policy. "The life of the law has not been logic; it has been experience," Holmes wrote in 1881. By "logic," Holmes indicated, he meant "the syllogism," and "the axioms and corollaries of a book of mathematics"; by "experience" he meant "considerations of what is socially expedient."

Syllogistic logic may be useful in testing the validity of conclusions drawn from given premises, but it is clearly inadequate as a method of reasoning in a practical science such as law, where the premises are not given but must be created. Legal rules, viewed as major premises, have to be susceptible to qualification in the light of particular circumstances; it is a rule of English and American law, for example, that a person who intentionally strikes another is civilly liable for battery, but in legal practice such a rule is subject to infinite modification in the light of possible defenses (*e.g.*, self-defense, defense of property, parental privilege, immunity from suit, lack of jurisdiction, insufficiency of evidence, *etc.*). In addition life continually presents new situations to which no existing rule is applicable; we simply do not know the legal limits of freedom of speech, for example, since the social context in which words are spoken is continually changing. This does not mean that it is always difficult to predict the outcome of a legal dispute; there are many cases where it is easy to apply the rule to the given state of facts. Indeed, legal scholars, being inclined to deal with borderline cases, are sometimes charged with giving the impression that the entire body of law is uncertain. The fact, however, that many legal questions are easy to answer should not obscure the more fundamental truth that all legal rules are continually being made and re-made, as the circumstances of life themselves continually change.

Also the "minor premises"—the facts of particular cases or the terms of particular legal problems—are not simply "there" but must be perceived and characterized, and this, too, requires interpretation and evaluation. Indeed, the legal facts of a case are not raw data but rather those facts that have been selected and classified in terms of legal categories.

Finally, the conclusion, that is, the application of the rule to the particular case or problem, since it is a responsible decision directly affecting particular people in particular situations, is never mathematically inevitable, but always contingent upon the exercise of judgment. In the telling words of Immanuel Kant, "there is no rule for applying a rule"; that is, there are no rules that can tell us in advance, with certainty, how a particular judge (legislator, administrator, *etc.*) ought to resolve a concrete case or problem that is before him or her—and this would be true even though we were able to say in advance what rules are relevant to such a resolution. Once a legal conclusion is reached, it may often be stated in syllogistic form; but in the process of reaching it, the determination of the major and minor premises may have come last.

However, in saying that legal reasoning cannot be reduced to the classical rules of formal logic is not to deny that it has logical qualities. Legal reasoning has three basic characteristics which impose upon it certain logical requirements. In the first place, it is characteristic of legal reasoning that it strives toward consistency both of legal rules and of legal judgments; such a striving for consistency is implicit in the belief that law should apply equally to all who are subject to it and that like cases should be decided in a like manner. Even the judgments of the ancient Greek oracles were believed to reflect a hidden consistency. Secondly, it is characteristic of legal reasoning that it strives toward continuity in time; it looks to the authority of the past, embodied in previously declared rules and decisions, and it attempts to regulate social relations in such a way as to preserve stability. Finally, legal reasoning is dialectical reasoning; it is characteristically concerned with the weighing of opposing claims, whether expressed in legislative debate, in forensic argument, or the like.

The most pervasive form of legal logic is that of analogy, in the broad sense of the comparison and contrast of similar and dissimilar examples. Analogical reasoning is implicit in the striving for consistency; the striving for continuity (that is, historical consistency) also involves analogical reasoning, the analogies being found in past experience; similarly, the dialectical quality of legal reasoning involves comparison and contrast between the examples put forward by the opposing sides.

It should be noted that most legal writers define the term "analogy" more narrowly, giving it a technical meaning signifying the extension of a legal category to a situation which is "similar to," but not "the same as" those situations which the category "logically" includes; in contrast, we use the term "analogy" here more broadly, and include under it the process by which it is determined that one situation is "the same as" another.

In a legal system which attaches primary importance to the authority of past judicial decisions (precedents), as in England and the United States, analogical reasoning in adjudication characteristically takes the form of (a) the search for a fact situation in a previously decided case comparable to the fact situation of the case before the court, (b) extraction from the previously decided comparable case of the principle upon which that case was decided, and (c) application of that principle to the case at hand. Each of these three steps is generally recognized to be dependent upon the other two. Moreover, the second step—the extraction of the principle of the previous case— is complicated by the fact that the principle expressly relied on by the court in deciding the previous case is not necessarily binding upon future courts. Under a strict doctrine of precedents, at least as understood in the United States, a court is bound by the decisions in previous cases, but it may reject the reasons previously given for those decisions—for example in instances where much broader reasons were given than were required. In technical terms, the court is not bound by (may treat as mere dictum) any statement made in a previous comparable case which was not necessary in reaching the decision in that case, and if the later court considers that the same decision could have been reached on other (better) grounds, it may even treat as dictum a reason stated by the previous court as the necessary ground for its decision. Thus what is binding on future courts—the "holding" of the case—is determined in part by its subsequent application to similar fact situations.

Reasoning from case to case has been called by one writer "the basic pattern of legal reasoning." However, it is also a characteristic method of legal reasoning—especially (but not exclusively) in legal systems that do not recognize the binding force of precedents— to decide cases, or resolve particular legal problems, also by analogy of doctrines expressed in statutes and in other forms of legal rules. To give an American example: in the latter part of the 19th century, most states enacted statutes giving to married women the right to own their separate property, to make contracts, and to sue and be sued. Using the authority of such Married Women's Acts, many courts overruled various earlier precedents which made a wife and husband incompetent to testify for or against each other, which made a husband liable for his wife's torts, which made one spouse not liable to conviction for stealing from the other, *etc.* These matters, although not dealt with in terms by the Married Women's Acts, were sufficiently similar to the matters with which the Married Women's Acts did deal, that the policy of those Acts was considered to be applicable. Such use of analogy of statute (or of legal doctrine) is especially prevalent in those countries of Europe in which the law is largely found in codes and in which the writings of leading legal scholars in interpreting the codes have more authority than judicial decisions.

It is sometimes said that analogical reasoning, and especially reasoning from analogy of decided cases, is "inductive" reasoning, while reasoning from legal rules is "deductive." Such a characterization presupposes that the facts of cases are first analyzed and then legal principles are "inferred" from such facts. However, the distinction between the facts of a legal case and the legal principle governing those facts is not the same as the distinction sometimes drawn between the facts of a laboratory experiment and the hypothesis offered by the scientist to explain the facts. The facts of a legal case do not have an existence independent of the theory of liability applied to them. A collision between X and Y may be a "fact" which natural science can "explain;" but in reaching a decision as to whether or not X should be legally liable to Y, or Y to X, it must first be determined whether or not X or Y was "negligent," or was carrying on an "extrahazardous activity," or was otherwise engaged in liability-creating conduct. Thus, as suggested earlier, the same kind of judgment that is required to determine the applicable legal principle (liability for harm caused by negligence, liability for harm caused by extrahazardous activity) is also required in characterizing the legally operative facts (X drove negligently, X was engaged in an extrahazardous activity). To contend that since liability is imposed in situation A (*e.g.*, harm caused by collision of aircraft with ground structures, regardless of fault, air travel being considered an extrahazardous activity), and since situation B (*e.g.*, harm caused by automobile travel) is (or is not) comparable to situation A, therefore liability should (or should not) be imposed in situation B—is an example neither of deductive nor of inductive reasoning, though it contains elements of each. It is an example of reasoning applied to reach decisions for action, and, like the reasoning of a physician or an engineer or a politician, it is based on the consideration of a wide range of factors, many of which cannot be fully articulated.

In emphasizing reasoning by analogy as the primary form of legal logic, we do not mean that the use of such reasoning is sufficient in itself to compel particular legal results. In all analogical reasoning there is in fact a large area of indeterminacy, since the criteria for selecting similarities and differences are not definitively laid down but are open to debate. A rigid definition confining the term "logic" to those propositions that necessarily follow from given premises might therefore exclude analogy altogether. According to an old proverb, " 'For example' is not proof." Yet despite its flexibility, analogical reasoning does impose limits upon legal results even if it does not in itself compel them. In each society, there are some similarities and differences so strongly felt that they cannot be denied. Moreover, the range within which analogies may be found is often restricted by particular legal doctrines. Thus, as we have seen earlier, most modern legal systems require that a criminal statute be interpreted much more "strictly" than a statute imposing only civil obligations; similarly courts are generally more reluctant to extend analogies under rules of commercial law than under rules of personal injury law, since commercial rules are relied on in business transactions where a high degree of stability and predictability is desired. In addition, each legal system establishes procedures and methods for drawing analogies—such as adversary and investigative procedures or the method of precedent and the method of codification—and these procedures and methods are designed to prevent analogical reasoning from becoming arbitrary.

Analogical reasoning is, of course, a universal mode of reasoning and by no means unique to law. What is distinctive about law, in this respect, is the degree of emphasis placed upon the use of analogy and the development of special legal rules, procedures, and methods for drawing analogies. In law, the method of analogy has the special virtue—as compared with syllogistic reasoning—of exposing the examples by which consistency, continuity, and the weighing of opposing claims and defenses are tested.

Legal rhetoric. Traditionally, the "active" side of legal language, the relationship of legal words to the contexts in which they are uttered, has been studied under the heading of legal rhetoric. Rhetoric itself, however, under the influence of Aristotle, has traditionally been separated from logic, ethics, and politics (as, indeed, each of those three has been separated from the others); moreover, rhetoric itself has been reduced to a study of the art of persuasion through appeals to emotions, whereas the original Aristotelian conception of it also embraced the art of public deliberation through appeals to reason. Thus rhetoric in its original meaning involves much more than the tricks of argumentation; it is also a mode of reasoning. At the same time rhetoric is distinguished from logic (in the formal Aristotelian sense), since logic is concerned with declarative (indicative) statements that are considered to be either true or false ("propositions"), whereas rhetoric is concerned with subjunctive, normative, and imperative statements, uttered in order to influence thought or action. The classical formula of logic: All men are mortal, Socrates is a man, therefore Socrates is mortal—might be rendered in rhetorical form as: If you would be a man, O Socrates, you must prepare yourself for death!

Since legal rules are usually stated in the indicative mood, they give the deceptive appearance of being only logical propositions; yet on closer analysis, it is apparent that they have a rhetorical significance at least equally as great as their logical significance. The statement, for example, that the intentional premeditated killing of a person with malice aforethought constitutes the crime of murder in the first degree and is punishable by life imprisonment or death, is not only a "true proposition" concerning what *is* murder (assuming it has been authoritatively declared) ; it is also a warning to potential murderers, an assurance to potential victims, a mandate to law enforcement officials, and, in general, an expression of the desires and beliefs of the political community. Legal reasoning with respect to the crime of murder consists, therefore, not only in the logical analysis of its definition, involving the comparison of various kinds of homicide (*e. g.*, homicide committed from motives of mercy, in self-defense, in the heat of passion, negligently, *etc.*) ; it also consists in both legislative and forensic rhetoric ("The death penalty should be abolished," "The defendant is not a murderer") as well as in other less formal types of argumentative speech (*e. g.*, "A person should certainly not escape responsibility for murder just because he believed his act would benefit society").

As the logical aspect of legal reasoning focuses attention on legal rules and on the principles to be derived from decisions in analogous cases, so the rhetorical aspect of legal reasoning focuses attention on legal activities. Law itself, as many writers have emphasized, is not simply, or primarily, a body of rules but an activity, an enterprise. As Lon L. Fuller has stressed, a principal purpose of this enterprise is to subject human conduct to the governance of rules; but to achieve that purpose rules must be drafted, debated, voted, published, interpreted, obeyed, applied, enforced—all of which legal activities involve the use not only of logic but also of rhetoric. Moreover, it is also a purpose of the legal enterprise, apart from activities connected with rule-making, to render decisions, which may be done by the casting of votes, the issuance of orders, the handing down of judgments; and the rendering of such decisions, like the making of legal rules, is both a product and an expression of rhetorical utterance. In addition, legal reasoning is directed to the negotiation of legal transactions, the making of petitions or recommendations, the writing of legal opinions, the issuance of legal documents, and a variety of other types of legal activities, all of which involve the use of language to induce a response in those to whom the language is addressed.

As the use of analogy is a characteristic and pervasive form of legal logic, so the appeal to authority is a characteristic and pervasive form of legal rhetoric. The nature of the authority to which appeal is made differs in different legal systems. It is said, for example, that in traditional Moslem law, the authority of the Koran is decisive, and that only a literal interpretation of its provisions is permissible. In Judaic law, on the other hand, with the development of the Talmud, there emerged the authority of leading rabbis who interpreted the Torah. In Roman law a similar authority was vested in leading jurists. Thus the fifth century Roman Law of Citations named five great jurists whose writings should be authoritative, and stated that in case of a difference among the five on a particular point, the view of the majority should prevail, unless there was an even split among those of the five who expressed an opinion, in which case the view of Papinian was to prevail. We have already referred to the authority of judicial precedents in English and American law, and of codes in modern Continental European law. Probably the highest authority governing judicial decisions in most contemporary legal systems is that of statutes enacted by the legislature, although in the United States and some other countries the authority even of statutes must yield to that of constitutional provisions.

The rhetorical appeal to authority, in legal reasoning, is not necessarily limited, however, to an appeal to legislation (whether embodied in statutes, codes, an authoritative book, or a constitution) or to judicial precedents, or to juristic commentaries on such legislation or precedents. In many legal systems, and perhaps in all, some room, at least, is left for appeal also to custom (that is, what is commonly done, and what is commonly believed ought to be done) and to a sense of justice. Thus it is often said that there are four sources of law: legislation (including rules made by administrative authorities), precedent, custom, and equity. These four sources may also be viewed as four dimensions of law—legislation (and administrative rules) being directed to what should be done in the future, precedent being directed to what has been done in the past, custom being directed to outer social patterns and norms of behavior, and equity being directed to the inner sense of justice or fairness. Different legal systems, and different branches within a particular legal system, emphasize one or another of these four dimensions or sources or types of authority, and hence legal rhetoric is not uniform as between different legal systems or even within a single system. In American law, for example, the legislation-based rhetoric of a traffic regulation ("Parked cars will be towed away") differs from the precedent-based rhetoric of a judicial decision ("This court has consistently held that the manufacturer is not liable to retail purchasers unless he is shown to have been negligent"); and both of these differ from the custom-based rhetoric of a negotiable instrument ("Pay to the order of John Jones $1000"), or the equity-based rhetoric of a divorce decree ("The father may have the child visit him four times a year for a week at a time").

Legal discourse. Just as legal logic is itself a form of legal rhetoric, so legal rhetoric, in turn, is a form of legal discourse, whose functions go beyond that of influencing immediate thought and action and include the preservation and development of the legal traditions and values of the entire political-legal community as well as the traditions and values of the legal profession itself in societies where a legal profession exists.

Legal discourse has gained its distinctive characteristics principally from the institution of *the hearing,* which has provided the basis from which all legal activities have developed, including not only adjudication but also legislation, administration, negotiation of legal transactions, and other legal activities. It is the opportunity of both sides to be heard that principally distinguishes adjudication from vengeance. Similarly, it is, above all, the opportunity to debate pending enactments that distinguishes legislation from mere commands, and the opportunity to petition for relief that distinguishes lawful administration from bureaucratic fiat. Even a unilateral legal act such as the writing of a will requires the draftsman to put himself in the position of third persons who might be called upon to interpret the will in the light of a dispute over its validity or its meaning.

Two qualities of discourse are involved in a legal hearing that are not necessarily present in non-legal procedures of listening and speaking. The first quality may be described as formality, that is, the use of a deliberate and ceremonial form of discourse, which usually is reflected in a formal presentation of claims and defenses, formal deliberation of the court or other tribunal, and the formal rendering of a decision. The formalities of the hearing help to secure its objectivity, that is, its impartiality, internal consistency, restraint, and authority.

A second distinctive quality of discourse characteristic of a legal hearing is the tendency to categorize the persons and events that are involved. The specific, unique qualities of the dispute are named in general terms. John Jones is called "the plaintiff"; Sam Smith is called "the defendant"; the defendant is alleged, for example, to have broken a "lease" by causing certain "damage" to the leased "premises." These are the "legally operative facts." The "real" facts—Smith's obnoxious personal habits, the neighbors' gossip, the family feud, *etc.*—are excluded unless they can be brought into relevant legal categories. This helps to secure the generality of the hearing. For the issue is not whether John Jones or Sam Smith is the better man but rather whether the rights of a lessor, rights established by the law of the community, have been violated by a lessee.

The formulation of the dispute or problem in terms of general categories and thus the viewing of the concrete facts *sub specie communitatis,* is organically derived from the hearing, though it is logically distinct from it. The dispute or the problem has challenged the existing legal rules; the parties have invoked a re-formulation of them in the light of the concrete facts; and the court (if it is a judicial proceeding) or legislature (if it is a proposed statute) or administrative agency (if it is a new regulation that is sought) or lawyer (if it is a contract that is being negotiated or a will that is being drawn) is asked to re-interpret the existing rules, or to create new rules, in the light of the new dispute or new problem. Categorization of the specific, unique facts, carried out in the context of a deliberate and ceremonial presentation of claims and defenses with a formal procedure for interrogation, argument, and decision, helps to secure the generality and objectivity not only of the hearing but also of the re-interpreted or newly created rules, and hence their acceptance by the community. Another outcome of this process is the emergence of specialized legal vocabulary and techniques that provide a professional shorthand or jargon designed to contribute to the efficiency of legal procedures or to the fraternity of the legal profession, or to both; unfortunately, however, the specialized language of law often has the effect of making both law and lawyers seem alien to the society that has produced them.

The circularity of legal reasoning. If law is seen, in the first instance, not as rules but as the enterprise of hearing, judging, prescribing, ordering, negotiating, declaring, *etc.*, then it becomes possible to give a satisfactory explanation of what Jeremy Bentham called the tautology and circuity of legal terms, and what H. L. A. Hart calls the "great anomaly of legal language—our inability to define its crucial words in terms of ordinary factual counterparts." It is, indeed, true that legal reasoning characteristically appears to be circular. When it is said, for example, that a man has a "right" to something because someone has an "obligation" to transfer it to him, the "right" of the one and the "obligation" of the other seem to be merely two different terms for the same thing. Similarly, the word "crime" and the word "law" itself seem to be only alternative ways of saying "right," "obligation," *etc.* "Each of these words may be substituted one for the other," wrote Bentham. "The law directs me to support you—it imposes upon me the *obligation* of supporting you—it grants you the *right* of being supported by me—it converts into an *offence* the negative act by which I omit to support you—it obliges me to render you the *service* of supporting you . . . This then is the connexion between these legal entities: they are only the law considered under different aspects; they exist as long as it exists; they are born and they die with it . . ." The legal terms seem to have no "empirical referents"—no "things" to which they "correspond."

The proliferation of interdependent legal terms that may all be used to refer to the same thing is due to the fact that the terms are not supposed to "refer" to "things" but instead to regulate a complex interrelationship of people engaged, actually or potentially, in legal activities of various kinds. From the standpoint of the child, support is a "right;" from the standpoint of the parent, it is an "obligation;" from the standpoint of the prosecutor, failure to fulfill the obligation may be a "crime." It is true that if there were no right there would be no obligation and no crime, and if there were no crime there would be no obligation and no right (or at least a different kind of obligation and right). But these (and many other) terms are needed to identify the complexity of the relationship between the child, the parent, and the state; they are needed especially when the relationship is described in abstract terms. The decision of the court may be simple enough: "Pay $25 a week for support of the child or go to jail."

It may seem fallacious for courts or writers to reason (as they sometimes do) from right to obligation to penalty as if in a logical sequence. Yet what may be fallacious as a logical proposition may be sensible as a means of identifying the parties to a dispute and the nature of the disputed issue. To attack legal rules as question-begging is itself to beg the question of their function. Indeed, in some cases it is the function of judicial tautology and circularity to avoid giving a reason for a decision in a situation in which it is better to give no reason than to give the real reason. This is apt to be especially true of legal fictions, which are legal doctrines that state a legal result in terms of assumed facts that are known to be non-existent. Here what are understood to be only analogies are consciously treated as identities, in order to preserve consistency of doctrine in the face of an unexplained inconsistent result. For example, a battery is traditionally defined as an unpermitted blow which the defendant intended to inflict on the plaintiff, but the courts nevertheless give a recovery to a person whom the defendant struck unintentionally while intending to strike another, applying the fiction that the defendant's intent to strike the third person is "transferred" to the person whom he in fact struck. Thus the original definition is preserved in form but its consequences are changed. In most cases, however, legal tautologies and circularities are not intended to change the consequences of legal rules but are primarily a means of specifying and categorizing the various aspects of legal relationships, often for procedural reasons. In any event, not only circular but also other "unscientific" qualities of law may often be understood if they are seen as part of the logic of analogy, the rhetoric of appeals to authority, and the discourse of formality and categorization, which together make up the distinguishing characteristics of legal reasoning.

SECTION 20. CASE ANALYSIS

[The following is taken from KARL N. LLEWELLYN, THE BRAMBLE BUSH (New York, 1951), pp. 42–53.]

. . . all our cases are decided, all our opinions are written, all our predictions, all our arguments are made, on certain four assumptions. . . .

1) *The court must decide the dispute that is before it.* It cannot refuse because the job is hard, or dubious, or dangerous.

2) *The court can decide only the particular dispute which is before it.* When it speaks to that question it speaks ex cathedra, with authority, with finality, with an almost magic power. When it speaks to the question before it, it announces *law*, and if what it announces is new, it legislates, it *makes* the law. But when it speaks to any other question at all, it says mere

words, which no man needs to follow. Are such words worthless? They
are not. We know them as judicial *dicta*; when they are wholly off the point
at issue we call them *obiter dicta*—words dropped along the road, wayside
remarks. Yet even wayside remarks shed light on the remarker. They may
be very useful in the future to him, or to us. But he will not feel bound to
them, as to his ex cathedra utterance. They came not hallowed by a Delphic
frenzy. He may be slow to change them; but not slow as in the other
case.

3) *The court can decide the particular dispute only according to
a general rule which covers a whole class of like disputes.* Our legal
theory does not admit of single decisions standing on their own. If
judges are free, are indeed forced, to decide new cases for which there
is no rule, they must at least make a new rule as they decide. So far,
good. But how wide, or how narrow, is the general rule in this particular case? That is a troublesome matter. The practice of our case law, however, is I think fairly stated thus: it pays to be suspicious of general rules
which look too wide; it pays to go slow in feeling *certain* that a wide
rule has been laid down at all, or that, if seemingly laid down, it will be
followed. For there is a fourth accepted canon:

4) *Everything, everything, everything, big or small, a judge may
say in an opinion, is to be read with primary reference to the particular
dispute, the particular question before him.* You are not to think that
the words mean what they might if they stood alone. You are to have
your eye on the case in hand, and to learn how to interpret all that has
been said *merely* as a reason for deciding *that* case *that* way. . . .

Now why these canons? The first, I take it, goes back to the primary purpose of law. If the job is in first instance to settle disputes
which do not otherwise get settled, then the only way to do it is to do it.
And it will not matter so much *how* it is done, in a baffling instance, so
long as it is done at all.

The third, that cases must be decided according to a general rule,
goes back in origin less to purpose than to superstition.* As long as
law was felt as something ordained of God, or even as something inherently right in the order of nature, the judge was to be regarded as a mouthpiece, not as a creator; and a mouthpiece of the general, who but made
clear an application to the particular. Else he broke faith, else he was
arbitrary, and either biased or corrupt. Moreover, justice demands, wherever that concept is found, that like men be treated alike in like conditions. Why, I do not know; the fact is given. That calls for general rules,
and for their even application. So, too, the "separation of powers" comes in
powerfully to urge that general rules are made by the Legislature or the
system, not the judges, and that the judge has but to act *according* to the
general rules there are. Finally, a philosophy even of expediency will urge
the same. Whatever may be the need of shaping decision to individual cases
in the juvenile court, or in the court of domestic relations, or in a business
man's tribunal for commercial cases—still, when the supreme court of a
state speaks, it speaks first to clear up a point of general interest. And the

* Is this statement consistent with the passage from the same book, reprinted *supra* p. 167, in which Prof. Llewel- lyn states that the facts of a case can
only be dealt with in categories which are deemed to be significant?

responsibility for formulating general policy forces a wider survey, a more thorough study of the policies involved. So, too, we gain an added guarantee against either sentimentalism or influence in individual cases. And, what is not to be disregarded, we fit with the common notion of what justice calls for. . . .

Back, if I may now, to the why of the two canons I have left: that the court *can* decide only the particular dispute before it; that all that is said is to be read with eyes on that dispute. Why these? I do believe, gentlemen, that here we have as fine a deposit of slow-growing wisdom as ever has been laid down through the centuries by the unthinking social sea. Here, hardened into institutions, carved out and given line by rationale. What is this wisdom? Look to your own discussion, look to any argument. You know where you would go. You reach, at random if hurried, more carefully if not, for a foundation, for a major premise. But never for itself. Its interest lies in leading to the conclusion you are headed for. You shape its words, its content, to an end decreed. More, with your mind upon your object you use words, you bring in illustrations, you deploy and advance and concentrate again. When you have done, you have said much you did not mean. You did not mean, that is, *except* in reference to your point. You have brought generalization after generalization up, and discharged it at your goal; all, in the heat of argument, were over-stated. None would you stand to, if your opponent should urge them to *another* issue.

So with the judge. Nay, more so with the judge. He is not merely human, as are you. He is, as well, a lawyer; which you, yet, are not. A lawyer, and as such skilled in manipulating the resources of persuasion at his hand. A lawyer, and as such prone without thought to twist analogies, and rules, and instances, to his conclusion. A lawyer, and as such peculiarly prone to disregard the implications which do not bear directly on his case.

More, as a practiced exponent of the art of exposition, he has learned that one must prepare the way for argument. You set the mood, the tone, you lay the intellectual foundation—all with the case in mind, with the conclusion—all, because those who hear you also have the case in mind, without the niggling criticism which may later follow. You wind up, as a pitcher will wind up—and as in the pitcher's case, the wind-up often is superfluous. As in the pitcher's case, it has been known to be intentionally misleading.

With this it should be clear, then, why our canons thunder. Why we create a class of dicta, of unnecessary words, which later readers, their minds now on quite other cases, can mark off as not quite essential to the argument. Why we create a class of *obiter dicta*, the wilder flailings of the pitcher's arms, the wilder motions of his gum-ruminant jaws. Why we set about, as our job, to crack the kernel from the nut, to find the true rule the case in fact decides: the *rule of the case*.

Now for a while I am going to risk confusion for the sake of talking simply. I am going to treat as the rule of the case the *ratio decidendi*, the rule *the court tells you* is the rule of the case, the ground, as the phrase goes, upon which the court itself has rested its decision. For there is where you must begin, and such refinements as are needed may come after.

The court, I will assume, has talked for five pages, only one of which portrayed the facts assumed. The rest has been discussion. And judgment has been given for the party who won below: judgment affirmed. We seek the rule.

The first thing to note is this: *no rule can be the ratio decidendi from which* the *actual judgment* (here: affirmance) *does not follow*. Unless affirmance follows from a rule, it *cannot* be the rule which produced an actual holding of affirmance. But that holding is the decision, and the court speaks ex cathedra only as to the dispute decided, and only as to the decision it has made. At this point, too, I think you begin to see the bearing of the *procedural* issue. There *can* be a decision (and so an ex cathedra ratio) *only* as to a point which is before the court. But points come before a court of review by way of specific complaint about specific action of the court below, and in no other way. Hence nothing can be *held* which is not thus brought up.

You will have noted that these two statements are not quite the same. For the losing party may have complained of five, or fourteen, different rulings by the court below, but the final judgment below is affirmed or reversed but once. If you see what is ahead you will see that—on my argument to date—I am about to be driven either into inconsistency or into an affront to common sense. For obviously the court will in many or most instances take up the objections made before it, one by one. Now in that event we shall meet either of two phenomena, and very likely both at once. I shall assume this time, to set my picture more neatly, that the court *reverses* the judgment below. Then *either* it will say that the court below was wrong *on all five points*, or it will say that although on less than all, it was nonetheless wrong on *at least one*. Suppose, first, it says: wrong on all. It is clear that *any one* would be sufficient for reversal. It is more than likely that the court will not rest peculiarly on any of the five. Any one of the five rulings would then be enough to justify a reversal, and four of them are by consequence wholly unnecessary. Which, now, are which? Further, under the canon I so proudly wheeled before you, the court *can* decide only the particular dispute before it. Which was that particular dispute?

Again, take a case where the court rules on four points in favor of a man who won below, but reverses, for all that, on the fifth point. Of the four rulings, not a single one *can* be a premise for the actual holding. They are, then dicta, merely?

Here, I say, common sense and my canons seem to be at odds. The fact is, that they are both right, and yet both wrong. To that, as a phase of the doctrine of precedent, I shall return. Here merely the solution. One of the reasons, of the sound ones, often given for weighing dicta lightly, is that the background and consequences of the statement have not been illumined by the argument of counsel, have not received, as being matters to be weighed with brows-a-wrinkle, the full consideration of the court. In the case put the first reason does not fit; the second, if it is to be put on at all, hangs loose and flaps. No one point being the only crucial point, and the points decided which do not lead to judgment not being absolutely necessary to decide, it may be the court has not sweated over them as it would had each stood alone. But sweated some, it has; and with due antecedent argument. Hence we have, in what we may call *the multi-*

point decision, an intermediate type of authority. If a decision stands on two, or three, or five legs, any one of them is much more subject to challenge than it would be if the decision stood on it alone. Yet prima facie there remains "a decision" on each one of the points concerned. It is, as Morgan well says, within the province of a court to instruct the trial court how to act on points disputed and argued in the case in hand. The same reasoning in form, yet with distinctly lesser cogency in fact, applies to the multi-points ruled in favor of the party which ultimately loses the appeal. Authorities of a third water, these; and getting watery.

But our troubles with the ratio decidendi are not over. We meet forthwith a further formal one. Our judge states his facts, he argues his position, he announces his rule. And lo, he seems but to have begun. Once clean across the plate. But he begins again, winds up again and again he delivers his ratio—this time, to our puzzlement, the words are not the same. At this point it is broader than it was before, there it is narrower. And like as not he will warm up another time, and do the same job over— differently again. I have never made out quite why this happens. A little, it may be due to a lawyer's tendency to clinch an argument by summarizing its course, when he is through. A little, it may be due to mere sloppiness of composition, to the lack, typical of our law and all its work, of a developed sense for form, juristic or esthetic, for what the Romans knew as *elegantia.* Sometimes, I get a wry suspicion that the judge repeats because he is uneasy on his ground, that he lifts up his voice, prays his conclusion over loud and louder to gain and make conviction, much like an advertiser bare of arguments except his slogan. At other times I feel as I read opinions the thrill of adventure in an undiscovered country; the first and second statements of the ratio, with all that has led up to them, are like first and second reconnoiterings of strange hills; like first and second chartings of what has been found and what surmised—knowledge and insight growing as the opinion builds to its conclusion. But whatever the reason, recurrent almost-repetition faces us; also the worry that the repetition seldom is exact. Which phrasing are we then to tie to?

Perhaps in this, as in judging how far to trust a broadly stated rule, we may find guidance in the facts the court assumes. Surely this much is certain. The actual dispute before the court is limited as straitly by the facts as by the form which the procedural issue has assumed. What is not in the facts cannot be present for decision. Rules which proceed an inch beyond the facts must be suspect.   .   .   .

This brings us at last to the case system. For the truth of the matter is a truth so obvious and trite that it is somewhat regularly overlooked by students. *That no case can have a meaning by itself!* Standing alone it gives you no guidance. It can give you no guidance as to how far it carries, as to how much of its language will hold water later. What counts, what gives you leads, what gives you sureness, *that is the background of the other cases* in relation to which you must read the one. They color the language, the technical terms, used in the opinion. But above all they give you the wherewithal to find which of the facts are significant, and in what aspect they are significant, and how far the rules laid down are to be trusted.

Here, I say, is the foundation of the case system. For what, in a case class, do we do? We have set before you, at either the editor's selection or our own, a *series* of opinions which in some manner are related. They may or may not be exactly alike in their outcome. They are always supposedly somewhat similar on their legally relevant facts. Indeed, it is *the aspects in which their facts are similar* which give you your first guidance as to what *classes* of fact will be found legally relevant, that is, will be found *to operate alike*, or to operate *at all*, upon the court. On the other hand, the states of fact are rarely, if ever, quite alike. And one of the most striking problems before you is: when you find two cases side by side which show a difference in result, then to determine *what* difference in their facts, or *what* difference in the procedural set-up, has produced that difference in result. Those are the two problems which must be in your mind as you examine the language of the opinions. I repeat them. First, what *are* the significant categories of facts, and what is their significance to the court? Second, what *differences* in facts or in procedural set-up produce differences in the court's action when the situations are otherwise alike?

This, then, is the case system game, the game of matching cases. We proceed by a rough application of the logical method of comparison and difference.

And here there are three things that need saying. The first is that by this matching of facts and issues in the different cases we get, to come back to where we started, some indication of when the court in a given case has over-generalized; of when, on the other hand, it has meant all the ratio decidendi that it said. "The Supreme Court of the United States," remarks the sage Professor T. R. Powell, "are by no means such fools as they talk, or as the people are who think them so." We go into the matter expecting a certain amount of inconsistency in the broader language of the cases. We go into the matter set in advance to find distinctions by means of which we can reconcile and harmonize the outcomes of the cases, even though the rules that the courts seem to lay down in their deciding may be inconsistent. We are prepared to whittle down the categories of the facts, to limit the rule of one case to its new whittled narrow category, to limit the rule of the other to its new other narrow category—and thus to make two cases stand together. The first case involves a man who makes an offer and gets in his revocation before his offer is accepted. The court decides that he cannot be sued upon his promise, and says that no contract can be made unless the minds of both parties are at one at once. The second case involves a man who has made a similar offer and has mailed a revocation, but to whom a letter of acceptance has been sent before his revocation was received. The court holds that he can be sued upon his promise, and says that his offer was being repeated every moment from the time that it arrived until the letter of acceptance was duly mailed. Here are two rules which are a little difficult to put together, and to square with sense, and which are, too, a little hard to square with the two holdings in the cases. We set to work to seek a way out which will do justice to the holdings. We arrive perhaps at this, that it is not necessary for the two minds to be at one at once, if the person who has received an offer thinks, and thinks reasonably, as he takes the last step of acceptance, that the offeror is standing by the offer. And to test the rule laid down in either case, as also to test our tentative formulation which we have built to cover both, we do two things. First and easiest, is to play variations on the facts, making the case gradually more and more extreme until we find the place beyond which it does not seem sense to go. Suppose, for example, our man does think the offeror still stands to his offer, and thinks it reasonably, on all his information; but yet a revocation has arrived, which his own clerk has failed to bring to his attention? We may find the stopping-place much sooner than we had expected, and thus be forced to recast and narrow the generalization we have made, or to recast it even on wholly different lines. The second and more difficult way of testing is to go to the books and find further cases in which variations on the facts occur, and in which the importance of such variations has been put to the proof. The first way is the intuitional correction of hypothesis; the second way is the experimental test of whether an hypothesis is sound. Both are needed. The first, to save time. The second, to make sure.   .   .   .

In all of this I have been proceeding upon the assumption—and this is the second further point about case method that I had in mind—that all the cases everywhere can stand together. It is unquestionably the assumption you must also make, at first. If they can be brought together you must bring them. At the same time you must not overlook that our law is built up statewise. It is not built up in one piece. With forty-eight supreme courts plus the federal courts at work, it is inevitable that from time to time conflicting rules emerge. The startling thing is that they have been so few. And where a given state, say Pennsylvania, has laid down one rule, but another state, New York, say, has laid down another, the mere fact that fifteen further states go with New York is unlikely in the extreme to change the Pennsylvania point of view. A *common* law in one sense is therefore non-existent on that point. What we have is fifteen states deciding one way, one state deciding another way *and thirty states whose law is still uncertain.* Yet in these circumstances we do speak of "common law", and for this reason: True though it is that each state sticks, in the main, to its own authorities, when it has them, yet common to all the states is a large fundamental body of institutions which show at least a brother and sister type of likeness, which, to a surprising extent, as I have indicated, can even fairly be called identical. Furthermore, the *manner* of dealing with the legal authorities, the *way* of thinking, the *way* of working, the *way* of reading cases, the reasoning from them—or from statutes—these *common law techniques* are in all our courts in all our states substantially alike. And finally, if in a given state a point has not been settled, the court will turn to the decisions of the country as a whole as to a common reservoir of law. If there is but a single line of decision that court, although it never decided on the point before, is likely to lead off its argument: "It is well settled". If the decisions are divided on the point, the court is more likely than not to go with any substantial majority which may exist. But whether it goes with the majority or with the minority or picks a third variant of its own, its works with the materials from the other states almost as if they were its own, save that there is rarely any one of them which carries the sanction of transcendent authority.

Hence, in your matching of cases, you may, as a last resort when unable to make the cases fit together, fall back upon the answer: here is a conflict; these cases represent two different points of view.

You must, however, before you do that, make sure that they come from different jurisdictions, else one will have to be regarded as flatly overruling the other. Which brings me to the point of dates. Not the least important feature in the cases you are comparing will be their dates. For you must assume that the law, like any other human institution, has undergone, still undergoes development, clarification, change, as time goes on, as experience accumulates, as conditions vary.   The earlier cases in a series, therefore, while they *may* stand unchanged today, are yet more likely to be forerunners, to be indications of the first gropings with a problem, rather than to present its final solution even in the state from which they come.   That holds particularly for cases prior to 1800.   It holds in many fields of law for cases of much more recent date.   But in any event you will be concerned to place the case in time as well as in space, if putting it together with the others makes for difficulty.

The third thing that needs saying as you set to matching cases, is that on your materials, often indeed on all the materials that there are, a perfect working out of comparison and difference cannot be had.   In the first case you have facts a and b and c, procedural set-up m, and outcome x.   In the second case you have, *if* you are lucky, procedural set-up m again, but this time with facts a and b and d, and outcome y.   How, now, are you to know with any certainty whether the changed result is due in the second instance to the absence of fact c or the presence of the new fact d?   The court may tell you.   But I repeat: your object is to *test* the telling of the court.   You turn to your third case.   Here once more is the outcome x, and the facts are b and c and e; but fact a is missing, and the procedural set-up this time is not m but n.   This strengthens somewhat your suspicion that fact c is the lad who works the changed result.   But an experimentum crucis still is lacking. Cases in life are not made to our hand.   A scientific *approach* to prediction we may have, and we may use it as far as our materials will permit.   An exact science *in result* we have not now.   Carry this in your minds: a scientific approach, no more.   Onto the green, with luck, your science takes you. But when it comes to putting you will work by art and hunch.

Where are we now?   We have seen the background of the cases.   We have seen what they consist of.   We have seen that they must be read and analyzed for their facts, for their procedural issue and for their decision. We have seen that they are to be matched together to see which are the facts which have the legal consequences, and in what catgories we must class the facts with that in view.   And out of this same matching process we can reach a judgment as to how much of the language, even in the ratio decidendi, the court has really meant.

But if you arrive at the conclusion that a given court did not mean all it said in the express ratio decidendi it laid down, that the case must really be confined to facts narrower than the court itself assumed to be its measure, then you are ready for the distinction that I hinted at earlier in this lecture, the distinction between the ratio decidendi, the court's own version of the rule of the case, and the *true* rule of the case, to wit, what *it will be made to stand for by another later court*.   For one of the vital elements of our doctrine of precedent is this: that any later court can always reexamine a prior case, and under the principle that the court could decide only what was before it, and that the older case must now be read with that in view, can arrive at the conclusion that the dispute before the earlier court was much narrower than that court thought it was, called therefore for the application of a much narrower rule.   Indeed, the argument goes further.   It goes on to state that no broader rule *could* have been laid down ex-cathedra, because to do that would transcend the powers of the earlier court.

You have seen further that out of the matching of a number of related cases it is your job to formulate a rule that covers them all in harmony, if that can be done, and to test your formulation against possible variants on the facts.   .   .   .

SECTION 21. DEVELOPMENT OF THE DOCTRINE OF MANUFACTURERS' LIABILITY FOR NEGLIGENCE

The cases which follow consist of reports of the resolution of a series of lawsuits in the Court of Appeals of the state of New York. In each of these cases the court was required to make a decision as to the extent of a manufacturer's liability for damage caused by defective products. In each case the court was asked to find the defendant civilly liable for an injury to another and to award compensation to the plaintiff. Two great legal theories regarding civil liability are germane to an understanding of this material. These theories are designated by the terms "tort" and "contract."

Although it is impossible in a few paragraphs to adequately define tort and contract, it may be useful to indicate, briefly, their relationship to each other and main distinctions between them in order to help the reader to understand the materials that follow.

The term "tort" refers to conduct which causes injury to persons or property and which is in violation of a duty or duties owed by the tortfeasor to the injured person. The commission of a tort is said to be a civil wrong because the remedies provided are civil remedies, *i.e.*, damages or an injunction.

The law of torts is divisible into several categories. One of these is concerned with the intentional infliction of injury upon another. Beating a person—battery—is an intentional tort. A second category of torts consists of unintentional but negligent infliction of harm. We may define negligence as acting without due care and thereby inadvertently exposing others to an unreasonable risk of harm. If such conduct actually causes harm to another a tort has been committed and an action to recover for the injury would proceed on a negligence theory. This theory is based on the principle of fault. Negligent conduct is faulty conduct in that it falls below the standard of care which reasonable men expect of themselves and others. In this sense the idea of negligence embodies some notion of moral sanction. A third category of tort law is concerned with the imposition of liability for injuries resulting from conduct which is neither intentionally wrongful nor negligent. This is the so-called "strict liability" or liability without fault. An example is the liability which is imposed for injuries which result from ultra-hazardous activities, such as storing explosives, or blasting.

The term "contract" refers to rights and obligations which arise out of the making or breaking of agreements. For example if A agrees to sell a widget to B, and B agrees to buy the widget at a stipulated price, a relation has been established which may give rise to civil liability. Should A then refuse to sell, or B refuse to buy, the parties might have recourse to the courts for a remedy. The validity of the claim, and the nature and availability of a remedy would be determined according to the law of contract. The rights and duties of the parties, their respective liabilities, are contractual. If it is found that A and B have made a contract, and that one or the other has broken the contract by refusing to perform as promised, a civil wrong has been committed and the law will afford a civil remedy.

A breach of contract may also result from faulty conduct by one of the parties to the contract. For example, A may promise B to deliver a package to C. If as a result of A's faulty conduct the package is lost or destroyed, A may be liable in tort for his negligence. But A may also be liable in contract because of his failure to perform as promised. The recovery in the contract action would not be based on a fault theory, but would turn on the policy of the law that some kinds of promises should be made good, either by performance or by the payment of damages. It may be noted that the tort liability for negligence by failing to deliver the package arises out of relations between A, B, and C which were established by a contract. That relationship—sometimes referred to as "privity of contract"—provides the foundation for a recovery by B or C against A, and it may also set a limit on A's liability to other persons damaged by A's neglect. For example, D, as an outsider to this agreement—D is not in "privity of contract" with A—could not recover *in contract* for damages occasioned by A's breach. Furthermore, D's remoteness from the agreement may be viewed by the courts as a reason to bar D from a *tort* recovery against A.

THOMAS and WIFE v. WINCHESTER

Court of Appeals of New York, 1852.
6 N.Y. 397.

Action in the supreme court, commenced in August, 1849, against Winchester and Gilbert, for injuries sustained by Mrs. Thomas, from the effects of a quantity of extract of belladonna, administered to her by mistake as extract of dandelion.

In the complaint it was alleged, that the defendants from the year 1843, to the first of January, 1849, were engaged in putting up and vending certain vegetable extracts, at a store in the city of New York, designated as "108 John-street," and that the defendant Gilbert had for a long time previous thereto been so engaged, at the same place. That among the extracts so prepared and sold by them, were those respectively known as the "extract of dandelion," and the "extract of belladonna", the former a mild and harmless medicine, and the latter a vegetable poison, which if taken as a medicine in such quantity as might be safely administered of the former, would destroy the life, or seriously impair the health of the person to whom the same might be administered. That at some time between the periods above mentioned, the defendants put up and sold to James S. Aspinwall, a druggist in the city of New York, a jar of the extract of belladonna, which had been labeled by them as the extract of dandelion, and was purchased of them as such by said Aspinwall. That said Aspinwall afterwards, and on the 10th day of May, 1845, relying upon the label so affixed by the defendants, sold the said jar of belladonna to Alvin Foord, a druggist of Cazenovia, in the county of Madison, as the extract of dandelion. That afterwards, and on the 27th of March, 1849, the plaintiff Mrs. Thomas, being sick, a portion of the extract of dandelion was prescribed for her by her physician, and the said Alvin Foord, relying upon the label affixed by the defendants to said jar of belladonna, and believing the same to be the extract of dandelion, did on the application of the plaintiff, Samuel Thomas, sell and deliver to him from the said jar of belladonna, a portion of its contents, which was administered to the plaintiff, Mrs. Thomas, under the belief that it was the extract of dandelion; by which she was greatly injured, so that her life was despaired of, etc. The plaintiffs also alleged that the whole injury was occasioned by the negligence and unskillfulness of the defendants in putting up and falsely labeling the jar of belladonna as the extract of dandelion, whereby the plaintiffs, as well as the druggists and all other persons through whose hands it passed before being administered as aforesaid, were induced to believe, and did believe that it contained the extract of dandelion. Wherefore, etc.

The defendants in their answers, severally denied the allegations of the complaint, and insisted that they were not liable for the medicines sold by Aspinwall and Foord.

The cause was tried at the Madison circuit, in December 1849, before Mason, J.[1] The defendant Gilbert was acquitted by the jury under the direction of the court, and a verdict was rendered against Winchester, for eight hundred dollars. A motion for a new trial, made upon a bill of exceptions[2] taken at the trial, having been denied at a general term[3] in the sixth district, the defendant Winchester, brought this appeal. The facts which appeared on the trial are sufficiently stated in the opinion of RUGGLES, CH. J.

. . .

1. This refers to the older practice of trial judges to "go on circuit," holding court in various towns, at a time when the population was more widely scattered.

2. At the trial of the action the defendant's attorney took exception to rulings made by the trial judge during the course of the trial. Defendant's motion for a new trial was based on a claim that the trial judge had erred in making these rulings, and that this error was prejudicial to defendant's case. The bill of exceptions is a written statement listing the various rulings of the trial judge to which the defendant's attorney had excepted, and upon which the request for a new trial was based.

3. "General term" is a phrase used in some jurisdictions to denote the ordinary session of a court, as distinguished from a "special term" for hearing motions and the like or for trial of special classes of cases.

RUGGLES, CH. J. delivered the opinion of the court. This is an action brought to recover damages from the defendant for negligently putting up, labeling and selling as and for the extract of *dandelion*, which is a simple and harmless medicine, a jar of the extract of *belladonna*, which is a deadly poison; by means of which the plaintiff Mary Ann Thomas, to whom, being sick, a dose of dandelion was prescribed by a physician, and a portion of the contents of the jar, was administered as and for the extract of dandelion, was greatly injured, etc.

The facts proved were briefly these: Mrs. Thomas being in ill health, her physician prescribed for her a dose of dandelion. Her husband purchased what was believed to be the medicine prescribed, at the store of Dr. Foord, a physician and druggist in Cazenovia, Madison county, where the plaintiffs reside.

A small quantity of the medicine thus purchased was administered to Mrs. Thomas on whom it produced very alarming effects; such as coldness of the surface and extremities, feebleness of circulation, spasms of the muscles, giddiness of the head, dilation of the pupils of the eyes, and derangement of the mind. She recovered, however, after some time, from its effects, although for a short time her life was thought to be in great danger. The medicine administered was *belladonna, and not dandelion*. The jar from which it was taken was labeled "½ *lb. dandelion, prepared by A. Gilbert, No. 108 John-street, N. Y. Jar 8 oz."* It was sold for and believed by Dr. Foord to be the extract of dandelion as labeled. Dr. Foord purchased the article as the extract of dandelion from Jas. A. Aspinwall, a druggist at New York. Aspinwall bought it of the defendant as extract of dandelion, believing it to be such. The defendant was engaged at No. 108 John-street, New York, in the manufacture and sale of certain vegetable extracts for medicinal purposes, and in the purchase and sale of others. The extracts manufactured by him were put up in jars for sale, and those which he purchased were put up by him in like manner. The jars containing extracts manufactured by himself and those containing extracts purchased by him from others, were labeled alike. Both were labeled like the jar in question, as "prepared by A. Gilbert." Gilbert was a person employed by the defendant at a salary, as an assistant in his business. The jars were labeled in Gilbert's name because he had been previously engaged in the same business on his own account at No. 108 John-street, and probably because Gilbert's labels rendered the articles more salable. The extract contained in the jar sold to Aspinwall, and by him to Foord, was not manufactured by the defendant, but was purchased by him from another manufacturer or dealer. The extract of dandelion and the extract of belladonna resemble each other in color, consistence, smell and taste; but may on careful examination be distinguished the one from the other by those who are well acquainted with these articles. Gilbert's labels were paid for by Winchester and used in his business with his knowledge and assent.

The defendant's counsel moved for a nonsuit [4] on the following grounds:

1. That the action could not be sustained, as the defendant was the remote vendor of the article in question; and there was no connection, transaction or privity between him and the plaintiffs, or either of them.

---

4. To move for a nonsuit is to move to dismiss the case on the ground that there is no evidence on which a jury could reasonably decide for the plaintiff.

2. That this action sought to charge the defendant with the consequences of the negligence of Aspinwall and Foord.

3. That the plaintiffs were liable to, and chargeable with the negligence of Aspinwall and Foord, and therefore could not maintain this action.

4. That according to the testimony Foord was chargeable with negligence, and that the plaintiffs therefore could not sustain this suit against the defendant; if they could sustain a suit at all it would be against Foord only.

5. [Omitted.]

6. That there was not sufficient evidence of negligence in the defendant to go to the jury.

The judge overruled the motion for a nonsuit, and the defendant's counsel excepted.[5]

The judge among other things charged the jury, that if they should find from the evidence that either Aspinwall or Foord was guilty of negligence in vending as and for dandelion the extract taken by Mrs. Thomas, or that the plaintiff Thomas, or those who administered it to Mrs. Thomas were chargeable with negligence in administering it, the plaintiffs were not entitled to recover; but if they were free from negligence, and if the defendant Winchester was guilty of negligence in putting up and vending the extracts in question, the plaintiffs were entitled to recover, provided the extract administered to Mrs. Thomas was the same which was put up by the defendant and sold by him to Aspinwall and by Aspinwall to Foord. . . .

The case depends on the first point taken by the defendant on his motion for a nonsuit; and the question is, whether the defendant, being a remote vendor of the medicine, and there being no privity or connection between him and the plaintiffs, the action can be maintained.

If, in labeling a poisonous drug with the name of a harmless medicine, for public market, no duty was violated by the defendant, excepting that which he owed to Aspinwall, his immediate vendee, in virtue of his contract of sale, this action cannot be maintained. If A. build a wagon and sell it to B., who sells it to C., and C. hires it to D., who in consequence of the gross negligence of A. in building the wagon is overturned and injured, D. cannot recover damages against A., the builder. A.'s obligation to build the wagon faithfully, arises solely out of his contract with B. The public have nothing to do with it. Misfortune to third persons, not parties to the contract, would not be a natural and necessary consequence of the builder's negligence; and such negligence is not an act imminently dangerous to human life.

So, for the same reason, if a horse be defectively shod by a smith, and a person hiring the horse from the owner is thrown and injured in consequence of the smith's negligence in shoeing; the smith is not liable for the injury. The smith's duty in such case grows exclusively out of his contract with the owner of the horse; it was a duty which the smith owed to him alone, and to no one else. And although the injury to the rider may have happened in consequence of the negligence of the smith, the latter was not bound, either by his contract or by any considerations of public policy of

---

5. See note 2 *supra*.

safety, to respond for his breach of duty to any one except the person he contracted with.

This was the ground on which the case of Winterbottom v. Wright, (10 Mees. & Welsb. 109) was decided. A. contracted with the postmaster general to provide a coach to convey the mail bags along a certain line of road, and B. and others also contracted to horse the coach along the same line. B. and his co-contractors hired C., who was the plaintiff, to drive the coach. The coach, in consequence of some latent defect, broke down; the plaintiff was thrown from his seat and lamed. It was held that C. could not maintain an action against A. for the injury thus sustained. The reason of the decision is best stated by Baron Rolfe. A.'s duty to keep the coach in good condition, was a duty to the postmaster general, with whom he made his contract and not a duty to the driver employed by the owners of the horses.

But the case in hand stands on a different ground. The defendant was a dealer in poisonous drugs. Gilbert was his agent in preparing them for market. The death or great bodily harm of some person was the natural and almost inevitable consequence of the sale of belladonna by means of the false label.

Gilbert, the defendant's agent, would have been punishable for man-slaughter if Mrs. Thomas had died in consequence of taking the falsely la-beled medicine. Every man who, by his culpable negligence, causes the death of another, although without intent to kill, is guilty of manslaughter. 2 R.S. 662 § 19. A chemist who negligently sells laudanum in a phial labeled as peragoric, and thereby causes the death of a person to whom it is admin-istered, is guilty of manslaughter. Tessymond's case, 1 Lewin's Crown Cases, 169. "So highly does the law value human life that it admits of no justification wherever life has been lost and the carelessness or negligence of one person has contributed to the death of another." Regina v. Swindall, 2 Car. & Kir. 232–3. And this rule applies not only where the death of one is occasioned by the negligent act of another, but where it is caused by the negligent omission of a duty of that other. 2 Car. & Kir. 368, 371. Al-though the defendant Winchester may not be answerable criminally for the negligence of his agent, there can be no doubt of his liability in a civil action, in which the act of the agent is to be regarded as the act of the principal.

In respect to the wrongful and criminal character of the negligence com-plained of this case differs widely from those put by the defendant's counsel. No such imminent danger existed in those cases. In the present case the sale of the poisonous article was made to a dealer in drugs, and not to a con-sumer. The injury therefore was not likely to fall on him, or on his vendee who was also a dealer; but much more likely to be visited on a remote pur-chaser as actually happened. The defendant's negligence put human life in imminent danger. Can it be said that there was no duty on the part of the defendant, to avoid the creation of that danger by the exercise of greater caution? or that the exercise of that caution was a duty only to his immediate vendee, whose life was not endangered? The defendant's duty arose out of the nature of his business and the danger to others incident to its mis-management. Nothing but mischief like that which actually happened could have been expected from sending the poison falsely labeled into the market; and the defendant is justly responsible for the probable consequence of the act. The duty of exercising caution in this respect did not arise out of the defendant's contract of sale to Aspinwall. The wrong done by the defendant was in putting the poison, mislabeled, into the hands of Aspinwall as an article of merchandise to be sold and afterwards used as the extract of dandelion, by some person then unknown. The owner of a horse and cart who leaves them unattended in the street is liable for any damage which may result from his negligence. Lynch v. Nurdin, 1 Ad. & Ellis, N.S. 29; Illidge v. Goodwin, 5 Car. & Payne, 190. The owner of a loaded gun who puts it into the hands of a child by whose indiscretion it is discharged, is liable for the damage occasioned by the discharge. Dixon v. Bell, 5 Maule & Sel. 198. The defendant's contract of sale to Aspinwall does not excuse the wrong done to the plaintiffs. It was a part of the means by which the wrong was effect-ed. The plaintiffs' injury and their remedy would have stood on the same principle, if the defendant had given the belladonna to Dr. Foord without price, or if he had put it in his shop without his knowledge, which would probably have led to its sale on the faith of the label.

In Longmeid v. Holliday, 6 Law and Eq.Rep. 562, the distinction is rec-ognized between an act of negligence imminently dangerous to the lives of others, and one that is not so. In the former case, the party guilty of the negligence is liable to the party injured, whether there be a contract be-tween them or not; in the latter, the negligent party is liable only to the party with whom he contracted, and on the ground that negligence is a breach of the contract.

The defendant, on the trial, insisted that Aspinwall and Foord were guilty of negligence in selling the article in question for what it was repre-sented to be in the label; and that the suit, if it could be sustained at all, should have been brought against Foord. The judge charged the jury that if they, or either of them were guilty of negligence in selling the belladonna for dandelion, the verdict must be for the defendant; and left the question of their negligence to the jury, who found on that point for the plaintiff. If the case really depended on the point thus raised, the question was properly left to the jury. But I think it did not. The defendant, by affixing the label to the jar, represented its contents to be dandelion; and to have been "prepared" by his agent Gilbert. The word "prepared" on the label, must be understood to mean that the article was manufactured by him, or that it had passed through some process under his hands, which would give him personal knowledge of its true name and quality. Whether Foord was justi-fied in selling the article upon the faith of the defendant's label, would have been an open question in an action by the plaintiffs against him, and I wish to be understood as giving no opinion on that point. But it seems to me to be clear that the defendant cannot, in this case, set up as a defense, that Foord sold the contents of the jar as and for what the defendant repre-sented it to be. The label conveyed the idea distinctly to Foord that the contents of the jar was the extract of dandelion; and that the defendant knew it to be such. So far as the defendant is concerned, Foord was under no obligation to test the truth of the representation. The charge of the judge in submitting to the jury the question in relation to the negligence of Foord and Aspinwall, cannot be complained of by the defendant.

GARDNER, J., concurred in affirming the judgment, on the ground that selling the belladonna without a label indicating that it was a *poison* was de-clared a misdemeanor by statute; (2 R.S. 694, § 23;), but expressed no opinion upon the question whether, independent of the statute, the defendant would have been liable to these plaintiffs.

GRIDLEY, J. was not present when the cause was decided. All the other members of the court concurred in the opinion delivered by CH. J. RUGGLES.

Judgment affirmed.

Questions

1. Who is suing whom? What actions have the respective parties asked the courts to take: a) at the trial, b) on appeal?

2. Write a short statement of the case giving a) the important facts, b) the procedural development of the case, c) the judgment of the Court of Appeals.

3. What is the wrong complained of by the plaintiffs? Is it a breach of contract or a tort?

4. Which of the issues raised by the attorney for the defendant is the main issue before the Court of Appeals?

5. What rule does the defendant invoke as decisive of the case? What precedent is cited by Chief Judge Ruggles as establishing the existence of that rule?

6. The Court of Appeals formulates an alternative rule which may be applicable to this case. What is the alternative rule? What precedents are cited by Chief Judge Ruggles as establishing the existence of this rule?

7. Which of the alternative rules does the Court find applicable in this case? What reasons does the Court advance in support of this decision?

8. Why should the question of Foord's obligation to test the accuracy of the label be treated as irrelevant to Winchester's liability?

9. Of the various analogies which the court uses in reaching its decision, which seem to you convincing?

10. Of the various precedents which the court cites in reaching its decision, do any compel that decision?

LOOP v. LITCHFIELD

Court of Appeals of New York, 1870.
42 N.Y. 351.

HUNT, J. A piece of machinery already made and on hand, having defects which weaken it, is sold by the manufacturer to one who buys it for his own use. The defects are pointed out to the purchaser and are fully understood by him. This piece of machinery is used by the buyer for five years, and is then taken into the possession of a neighbor, who uses it for his own purposes. While so in use, it flies apart by reason of its original defects, and the person using it is killed. Is the seller, upon this state of facts, liable to the representatives of the deceased party? I omit at this stage of the inquiry the elements, that the deceased had no authority to use the machine; that he knew of the defects and that he did not exercise proper care in the management of the machine. Under the circumstances I have stated, does a liability exist, supposing that the use was careful, and that it was by permission of the owner of the machine?

To maintain this liability, the appellants rely upon the case of Thomas v. Winchester (6 N.Y., 2 Seld., 397). In that case, the defendant was engaged in the manufacture and sale of vegetable extracts for medicinal purposes. The extracts were put up in jars with appropriate labels. The defendant sold the articles to Mr. Aspinwall, a druggist of New York. Aspinwall sold to Dr. Ford, a physician and druggist of Cazenovia, where the plaintiff resided. Mrs. Thomas, one of the plaintiffs, being ill, her physician prescribed for her a dose of the extract of dandelion, which is a simple and harmless medicine. The article furnished by Dr. Ford in response to this prescription was the extract of belladonna, a deadly poison. The jar from which this medicine was taken was labeled "*½ lb. dandelion, prepared by A. Gilbert, 108 John St., N. Y., Jar 8 oz.,*" and thus labeled was sold to Dr. Ford. He relied upon the label, believed the medicine to be dandelion, and sold and delivered it to the plaintiffs as such. Mrs. Thomas suffered a severe illness by reason of this mistake. It was conceded by the counsel in that case and held by the court, that there was no privity of contract between Winchester and Thomas, and that there could be no recovery upon that ground. The court illustrate the argument by the case of a wagon built by A, who sells it to B, who hires it to C, who, in consequence of negligence in the building, is overturned and injured. C cannot recover against A, the builder. It is added: "Misfortune to third persons, not parties to the contract, would not be a natural and necessary consequence of the builder's negligence, and such negligence is not an act imminently dangerous to human life." So, if a horse, defectively shod, is hired to another, and by reason of the negligent shoeing, the horse stumbles, the rider is thrown and injured, no action lies against the smith. In these and numerous other cases put in the books, the answer to the action is, that there is no contract with the party injured, and no duty arising to him by the party guilty of negligence. "But," the learned judge says "the case in hand stands on a different ground. The defendant was a dealer in poisonous drugs. Gilbert was his agent in preparing them for market. The death or great bodily harm of some person was the natural and almost inevitable consequence of the sale of belladonna by means of the false label." "The defendant's neglect puts human life in imminent danger. Can it be said that there was no duty on the part of the defendant to avoid the creation of that danger by the exercise of greater caution?"

The appellants recognize the principle of this decision, and seek to bring their case within it, by asserting that the fly wheel in question was a dangerous instrument. Poison is a dangerous subject. Gunpowder is the same. A torpedo is a dangerous instrument, as is a spring gun, a loaded rifle or the like. They are instruments and articles in their nature calculated to do injury to mankind, and generally intended to accomplish that purpose. They are essentially, and in their elements, instruments of danger. Not so, however, an iron wheel, a few feet in diameter and a few inches in thickness although one part may be weaker than another. If the article is abused by too long use, or by applying too much weight or speed, an injury may occur, as it may from an ordinary carriage wheel, a wagon axle, or the common chair in which we sit. There is scarcely an object in art or nature, from which an injury may not occur under such circumstances. Yet they are not in their nature sources of danger, nor can they, with any regard to the accurate use of language, be called dangerous instruments. That an injury actually occurred by the breaking of a carriage axle, the failure of the carriage body, the falling to pieces of a chair or sofa, or the bursting of a fly wheel, does not in the least alter its character.

It is suggested that it is no more dangerous or illegal to label a deadly poison as a harmless medicine than to conceal a defect in a machine and paint it over so that it will appear sound. Waiving the point that there was no concealment, but the defect was fully explained to the purchaser, I answer, that the decision in Thomas v. Winchester was based upon the idea that the negligent sale of poisons is both at common law and by statute an indictable offence. If the act in that case had been done by the defendant instead of his agent, and the death of Mrs. Thomas had ensued, the defendant would have been guilty of manslaughter, as held by the court. The injury in that case was a natural result of the act. It was just what was to have been expected from putting falsely labeled poisons in the market, to be used by whomever should need the true articles. It was in its nature an act imminently dangerous to the lives of others. Not so here. The bursting of the wheel and the injury to human life was not the natural result or the expected consequence of the manufacture and sale of the wheel. Every use of the counterfeit medicines would be necessarily injurious, while this wheel was in fact used with safety for five years.

It is said that the verdict of the jury established the fact that this wheel was a dangerous instrument. I do not see how this can be, when there is no such allegation in the complaint, and no such question was submitted to the jury. "The court stated to the counsel that the only question on which they would go to the jury would be that of negligence. Whether in the manufacture and sale of this article, the defendants are guilty of negligence, which negligence produced the injury complained of." If the action had been for negligence in constructing a carriage, sold by the defendants to Collister, by him lent to the deceased, which had been broken down, through the negligence of its construction, it might have been contended with the same propriety, that the finding of those facts by the jury established that a carriage was a dangerous instrument, and thereby the liability of the defendants became fixed. The jury found simply that there was negligence in the construction of the wheel, and that the injury resulted therefrom. It is quite illogical to deduce from this, the conclusion that the wheel was itself a dangerous instrument.

Upon the facts as stated, assuming that the deceased had no knowledge of the defects complained of, and assuming that he was in the rightful and lawful use of the machine, I am of the opinion that the verdict cannot be sustained. The facts constitute no cause of action.

The case contains the element, that the deceased was himself personally aware of the defects complained of. Collister testifies that he pointed them out to him, and conferred with him in relation to their effect. Instead of submitting this question of knowledge to the jury, the judge charged, "that if they find from the evidence, that the defendants made this defective wheel for use, and that it broke by reason of the defect, the defendants are liable for the defect to whoever used it." To which the defendants excepted.

The question is also presented of the effect of the circumstance, that the deceased was engaged in the use of the machine, without the permission of the owner. Having reached the conclusion, that there can be no recovery independent of these difficulties, it would not be profitable to spend time in their discussion. It is only necessary to say, that in my judgment, they are very important elements, and that, were the plaintiffs otherwise entitled to recover, they would merit the gravest consideration.

I cannot say that there was error in the charge, on the subject of negligence. It was not submitted with clearness, certainly, nor in the most appreciable form. The question is rather, what care the deceased was bound to exercise, than what negligence would be excused. The charge stated, that the "defendants were not exonerated by slight negligence on the part of the deceased, although if he had used the utmost possible care, the accident would not have happened." This is equivalent to a charge, that the deceased was not bound to use the utmost possible care and was free from objection. The deceased was bound to exercise that care and attention in and about the business he was engaged in, that prudent, discreet, and sensible men are accustomed to bestow under like circumstances. The utmost possible care is not required. Indeed, its exercise would require an extent of time and caution that would terminate half the business of the world. (Sheridan v. Brooklyn, 36 N.Y. 43; Wells v. Long Island, 32 Barb. 398, aff'd, 34 N.Y. 670; Button v. Hudson River Co., 28 N.Y. 258; Curran v. Warren Co., 36 N.Y. 153; Milton v. Hudson S. B. Co., 37 N.Y. 212; Owen v. Hudson River Co., 35, 516.)

The order of the General Term should be affirmed, and judgment absolute given for the defendants.

All concur. Judgment affirmed, and judgment absolute ordered for the defendants.

Questions

1. What are the facts upon which the court based its decision? How are these facts similar to the facts in Thomas v. Winchester? How are they different from the facts in Thomas v. Winchester?

2. The court apparently considers that it is bound not to depart from the decision in Thomas v. Winchester. By what, in that decision, does it consider itself bound?

3. According to the court in this case, what is the principle in Thomas v. Winchester?

4. a) Do you agree with the statement that "the decision in Thomas v. Winchester was based on the idea that the negligent sale of poisons is both at common law and statute an indictable offense"?

b) What line of argument was Judge Hunt countering with this statement?

c) Should you reconsider your answer to part a) in light of your answer to part b)?

5.   What criteria does Judge Hunt use to determine what is a dangerous instrumentality?

6.   After the decision in this case, how should a lawyer advise a client concerning what constitutes a dangerous instrumentality?

7.   After stating the facts and discussing the meaning and application of the principle of Thomas v. Winchester in this case Judge Hunt said: "Upon the facts as stated, assuming that the deceased had no knowledge of the defects complained of, and assuming that he was in the lawful and rightful use of the machine, I am of the opinion that the verdict cannot be sustained. The facts constitute no cause of action."

What does the last sentence above mean?

8.   Was it necessary for Judge Hunt to discuss: a) the deceased's knowledge of the defect; b) the question of whether the deceased was using the machine without permission; c) the adequacy of the charge to the jury on the issue of the defendant's negligence? Can you think of any reason why the judge considered these matters in his opinion? Does anything he had to say on these points have any value as precedent?

LOSEE v. CLUTE

Commission of Appeals of New York,[1] 1873.
51 N.Y. 494.

Appeal from judgment of the General Term of the Supreme Court in the fourth judicial district, affirming a judgment entered upon an order dismissing plaintiff's complaint on the trial.

The action was brought to recover damages caused to the property of the plaintiff by the explosion of a steam boiler while the same was owned and being used by the Saratoga Paper Company at their mill situated in the village of Schuylerville, Saratoga County and State of New York, on the thirteenth day of February, 1864, by means whereof the boiler was thrown on to the plaintiff's premises and through several of his buildings, thereby injuring and damaging the same.

The defendants, Clute, were made parties defendants to the action with the Saratoga Paper Company and Coe S. Buchanan and Daniel A. Bullard, trustees and agents of said company, on the ground that they were the manufacturers of the boiler, and made the same out of poor and brittle iron and in a negligent and defective manner, in consequence of which negligence said explosion occurred.

At the close of the evidence the complaint was dismissed as to the defendants Clute.

The facts, so far as they are material to the decision in this court, are sufficiently stated in the opinion. . . .

1. Commissions on Appeals were established at one time in a considerable number of states to help relieve the highest state courts of some of the burden imposed by an excessive caseload.

LOTT, CH. C. It appears by the case that the defendants Clute manufactured the boiler in question for the Saratoga Paper Company, in which they were stockholders, for the purposes and uses to which it was subsequently applied by it; and the testimony tended to show that it was constructed improperly and of poor iron, that the said defendants knew at the time that it was to be used in the immediate vicinity of and adjacent to dwelling-houses and stores in a village, so that, in case of an explosion while in use, it would be likely to be destructive to human life and adjacent property, and that, in consequence of the negligence of the said defendants in the improper construction of the boiler, the explosion that took place occurred and damaged the plaintiff's property. The evidence also tended to show that the boiler was tested by the company to its satisfaction, and then accepted, and was thereafter used by it for about three months prior to the explosion, and that after such test and acceptance the said defendants had nothing whatever to do with the boiler, and had no care or management of it at the time of the explosion, but that the company had the sole and exclusive ownership, management and conduct of it.

In determining whether the complaint was properly dismissed, we must assume all the facts which the evidence tended to show as established, and the question is thereby presented whether the defendants have incurred any liability to the plaintiff. They contracted with the company, and did what was done by them for it and to its satisfaction, and when the boiler was accepted they ceased to have any further control over it or its management, and all responsibility for what was subsequently done with it devolved upon the company and those having charge of it, and the case falls within the principle decided by the Court of Appeals in The Mayor, etc., of Albany v. Cunliff (2 Comst. 165), which is, that at the most an architect or builder of a work is answerable only to his employees for any want of care or skill in the execution thereof, and he is not liable for accidents or injuries which may occur after the execution of the work; and the opinions published in that case clearly show that there is no ground of liability by the defendants to the plaintiff in this action. They owed *him* no *duty* whatever at the time of the explosion either growing out of contract or imposed by law.

It may be proper to refer to the case of Thomas v. Winchester (2 Selden, 397), cited by the appellant's counsel, and I deem it sufficient to say that the opinion of Hunt, J., in Loop v. Litchfield (42 N.Y. 351) clearly shows that the principle decided in that case has no application to this.

It appears from these considerations that the complaint was properly dismissed, and it follows that there was no case made for the consideration of the jury, and, consequently, there was no error in the refusal to submit it to them.

There was an exception taken to the exclusion of evidence to show that two persons were killed by this boiler in passing through a dwelling-house in its course, but as it is not urged on this appeal, it is, I presume, abandoned; but if not, it was matter, as the judge held at the trial, wholly immaterial to the issue between the parties in this action.

There is, for the reasons stated, no ground for the reversal of the judgment. It must, therefore, be affirmed, with costs.

All concur.

Judgment affirmed.

Questions

1. Who is suing whom?

2. Write a short statement of the case giving, a) the facts upon which the decision is based, b) the procedural development of the case, c) the judgment of the court.

3. What is the holding of the case?

4. Is this decision consistent with the decisions in Thomas v. Winchester and Loop v. Litchfield?

5. Should the fact that the paper company subjected the boiler to tests have any bearing upon the liability of the defendant manufacturer? Compare the court's treatment of this issue with the treatment of the responsibility of Foord and Aspinwall in the Thomas case.

6. The court in Thomas v. Winchester, in discussing the hypothetical case of a horse defectively shod by a smith, states that the smith would not be liable for harmful consequences to a rider, not the owner, since the smith "was not bound, either by his contract or by any considerations of public policy of safety, to respond for his breach of duty to any one except the person he contracted with." In the present case, the court says that the defendants owed the plaintiff no duty "either growing out of contract or imposed by law." Why do not "considerations of public policy of safety" give rise here to a duty "imposed by law"?

DEVLIN v. SMITH

Court of Appeals of New York, 1882.
89 N.Y. 470.

Appeal from judgment of the General Term of the Supreme Court, in the second judicial department, entered upon an order made December 12, 1881, which affirmed a judgment entered upon an order dismissing plaintiff's complaint on trial. . . .

This action was brought to recover damages for alleged negligence, causing the death of Hugh Devlin, plaintiff's intestate.

Defendant Smith entered into a contract with the supervisors of the county of Kings, by which he agreed to paint the inside of the dome of the court-house in that county. Smith was not a scaffold-builder, and knew nothing of that business. He entered into a contract with defendant Stevenson, who was an experienced scaffold-builder, and had been previously employed by Smith, to build the necessary scaffold. This was to be of the best of materials, and first-class in every way. Stevenson built the scaffold of poles, in sections. To the poles used for uprights, horizontal poles were lashed with ropes; these were called ledgers. Upon these ledgers, planks were placed, and upon the top of each section so constructed, was placed another similarly constructed. When the scaffolding reached the curve of the dome, it was necessary to lessen the width of the upper section. For this purpose a strip of plank was used as an upright to support the end of the shorter ledger. This upright was called a cripple; but instead of fastening the ledger to it by lashing it was fastened by nailing. The scaffold was ninety feet in height.

Devlin was a workman in Smith's employ. He was working on the curve of the dome, and sitting on a plank laid upon a ledger which was nailed to an upright or cripple, as above described, when the ledger gave way and broke. He was precipitated to the floor below and so injured that he died soon after. . . .

RAPALLO, J. Upon a careful review of all the testimony in this case, we are of opinion that there was sufficient evidence to require the submission to the jury of the question, whether the breaking down of the scaffold was attributable to negligence in its construction. It appears that the ledger which supported the plank upon which the deceased was sitting broke down without any excessive weight being put upon it, and without any apparent cause sufficient to break a well-constructed scaffold. One witness on the part of the plaintiff, accustomed to work on scaffolds and to see them built, testified that the upright which supported the end of the ledger should have been fastened to it by lashing with ropes, instead of by nailing, and that lashing would have made it stronger, giving as reasons for this opinion, that the springing of the planks when walked upon was liable to break nails or push them out, whereas lashings would only become tighter, and the witness testified that the kind of scaffold in question was generally fastened by lashing, and that it was not the proper way to support the end of the ledger which broke, with an upright nailed to the ledger, and that the ledger in question was fastened by nailing.

Another, a carpenter and builder, testified, that when, on account of the curving of a dome, it became necessary to put in a cripple, the cripple as well as the main uprights should be tied to the ledgers with rope; that the springing of the scaffold will break nails.

The appearances after the breakage were described to the jury, and a model of the scaffold was exhibited to them. Testimony touching the same points was submitted on the part of the defendants, and we think that on the whole evidence it was a question of fact for the jury, and not of law for the court, whether or not the injury was the result of the negligent construction of the scaffold.

The question of contributory negligence on the part of the deceased was also one for the jury.[1] They had before them the circumstances of the

1. Contributory negligence, that is, failure by the plaintiff to take due care for his own safety, is in almost all states of the United States a bar to recovery in an ordinary action for negligence provided that the plaintiff's own lack of care was a contributing cause of the injury and provided also (in most states) that the negligent defendant did not have a "last clear chance" to avoid the injury in spite of the plaintiff's own lack of care. In a few states, and in most foreign countries, the courts are permitted to compare the fault of the defendant and that of the plaintiff and to award damages based upon the difference. Thus in Wisconsin, for example, if the defendant's fault is found to be twice as great as that of the plaintiff, the latter will recover two-thirds of his damages, and himself bear the remaining loss. Similarly, the Federal Employers' Liability Act, the Merchant Marine Act, and the state railway labor acts all provide that the contribu-

accident. It appeared that the deceased was sitting on a plank, performing the work for which the scaffold had been erected. He was washing the interior wall of the dome, preparatory to its being painted. There was nothing to indicate that he was in an improper place, or that he unnecessarily exposed himself to danger, or did any act to contribute to the accident. It is suggested that he, or some of his fellow-servants, may have kicked against the upright or brace which supported the end of the ledger, and thus thrown it out of place, but there was no evidence which would entitle the court to assume that the accident occurred from any such cause. The case was, therefore, one in which the jury might have found from the evidence that the death was caused by the improper or negligent construction of the scaffold, and without any fault on the part of the deceased, and the remaining question is, whether, if those facts should be found, the defendants, or either of them, should be held liable in this action.

The defendant Smith claims that no negligence on his part was shown. He was a painter who had made a contract with the supervisors of Kings county to paint the interior of the dome of the county court-house, and the deceased was a workman employed by him upon that work. As between Smith and the county, he was bound to furnish the necessary scaffolding; but he was not a scaffold-builder, nor had he any knowledge of the business of building scaffolds, or any experience therein. He did not undertake to build the scaffold in question himself, or by means of servants or workmen under his direction, but made a contract with the defendant Stevenson to erect the structure for a gross sum, and the work was done under that contract, by Stevenson, who employed his own workmen and superintended the job himself. Mr. Stevenson had been known to Smith as a scaffold-builder since 1844. His experience had been very large, and Smith had employed him before, and on this occasion the contract with him was for a first-class scaffold. There is no evidence upon which to base any allegation of incompetency on the part of Stevenson, nor any charge of negligence on the part of Smith in selecting him as a contractor, nor is there any evidence that Smith knew, or had reason to know, of any defect in the scaffold.

An employer does not undertake absolutely with his employees for the sufficiency or safety of the implements and facilities furnished for their work, but only for the exercise of reasonable care in that respect, and where injury to an employee results from a defect in the implements furnished, knowledge of the defect must be brought home to the employer, or proof given that he omitted the exercise of proper care to discover it. Personal negligence is the gist of the action. [Citations omitted.]

Under the recent decisions in this State, it may be that if Smith had undertaken to erect the scaffold through agents, or workmen acting under his direction, he would have been liable for negligence on their part in doing the work, . . . But in this case he did not so undertake. Stevenson was not the agent or servant of Smith, but an independent contractor for whose acts or omissions Smith was not liable. [Citation omitted.] Smith received the scaffold from him as a completed work, and we do not think that it was negligence to rely upon its sufficiency and permit his employees to go upon it for the purpose of performing their work. Stevenson

tory negligence of an injured workman shall not bar his recovery, but his damages shall be reduced in proportion to his negligence.

was, as appears from the evidence, much more competent than Smith to judge of its sufficiency. He had undertaken to construct a first-class scaffold, and had delivered it to Smith in performance of this contract, and we do not think that Smith is chargeable with negligence for accepting it without further examination. All that such an examination would have disclosed would have been that the upright was nailed to the ledger, and Smith, not being an expert, would have been justified in relying upon the judgment of Stevenson as to the propriety of that mode of fastening. The defect was not such as to admonish Smith of danger.

If any person was at fault in the matter it was the defendant Stevenson. It is contended, however, that even if through his negligence the scaffold was defective, he is not liable in this action because there was no privity between him and the deceased, and he owed no duty to the deceased, his obligation and duty being only to Smith, with whom he contracted.

As a general rule the builder of a structure for another party, under a contract with him, or one who sells an article of his own manufacture, is not liable to an action by a third party who uses the same with the consent of the owner or purchaser, for injuries resulting from a defect therein, caused by negligence. The liability of the builder or manufacturer for such defects is, in general, only to the person with whom he contracted. But, notwithstanding this rule, liability to third parties has been held to exist when the defect is such as to render the article in itself imminently dangerous, and serious injury to any person using it is a natural and probable consequence of its use. As where a dealer in drugs carelessly labeled a deadly poison as a harmless medicine, it was held that he was liable not merely to the person to whom he sold it, but to the person who ultimately used it, though it had passed through many hands. This liability was held to rest, not upon any contract or direct privity between him and the party injured, but upon the duty which the law imposes on every one to avoid acts in their nature dangerous to the lives of others. (Thomas v. Winchester, 6 N.Y. 397.) In that case Mayor, etc., v. Cunliff (2 N.Y. 165) was cited as an authority for the position that a builder is liable only to the party for whom he builds. Some of the examples there put by way of illustration were commented upon, and among others the case of one who builds a carriage carelessly and of defective materials, and sells it, and the purchaser lends it to a friend, and the carriage, by reason of its original defect, breaks down and the friend is injured, and the question is put, can he recover against the maker? The comments of Ruggles, Ch. J., upon this supposititious case, in Thomas v. Winchester, and the ground upon which he answers the question in the negative, show clearly the distinction between the two classes of cases. He says that in the case supposed, the obligation of the maker to build faithfully arises only out of his contract with the purchaser. The public have nothing to do with it. Misfortune to third persons, not parties to the contract, would not be a natural and necessary consequence of the builder's negligence, and such negligence is not an act imminently dangerous to human life.

Applying these tests to the question now before us, the solution is not difficult. Stevenson undertook to build a scaffold ninety feet in height, for the express purpose of enabling the workmen of Smith to stand upon it to paint the interior of the dome. Any defect or negligence in its construction, which should cause it to give way, would naturally result in these men being precipitated from that great height. A stronger case where misfortune to third persons not parties to the contract would be a natural and necessary consequence of the builder's negligence, can hardly be supposed, nor is it easy to imagine a more apt illustration of a case where such negligence would be an act imminently dangerous to human life. These circumstances seem to us to bring the case fairly within the principle of Thomas v. Winchester.

The same principle was recognized in Coughtry v. The Globe Woolen Co. (56 N.Y. 124,) and applied to the case of a scaffold. It is true there was in that case the additional fact that the scaffold was erected by the defendant upon its own premises, but the case did not depend wholly upon that point. The scaffold was erected under a contract between the defendant and the employers of the person killed. The deceased was not a party to that contract, and the same argument was made as is urged here on the part of the defendant, that the latter owed no duty to the deceased; but this court held that in view of the facts that the scaffold was upwards of fifty feet from the ground, and unless properly constructed was a most dangerous trap, imperiling the life of any person who might go upon it, and that it was erected for the very purpose of accommodating the workmen, of whom the person killed was one, there was a duty toward them resting upon the defendant, independent of the contract under which the structure was built, to use proper diligence in its construction. The additional fact that the structure was on the premises of the defendant was relied upon, but we think that, even in the absence of that feature, the liability can rest upon the principle of Thomas v. Winchester.

Loop v. Litchfield (42 N.Y. 351, 1 Am.Rep. 543) was decided upon the ground that the wheel which caused the injury was not in itself a dangerous instrument, and that the injury was not a natural consequence of the defect, or one reasonably to be anticipated. Losee v. Clute (51 N.Y. 494, 10 Am.Rep. 638) was distinguished from Thomas v. Winchester, upon the authority of Loop v. Litchfield.

We think there should be a new trial as to the defendant Stevenson, and that it will be for the jury to determine whether the death of the plaintiff's intestate was caused by negligence on the part of Stevenson in the construction of the scaffold.

The judgment should be affirmed, with costs, as to the defendant Smith, and reversed as to the defendant Stevenson, and a new trial ordered as to him, costs to abide the event.

ANDREWS, CH. J., DANFORTH and FINCH, JJ., concur; EARL, J., concurs as to defendant Smith and dissents as to defendant Stevenson. MILLER, J., absent; TRACY, J., not sitting.

Judgment accordingly.

Questions

1. Who is suing whom?

2. Write a short statement of the case giving: a) the facts on which the decision is based; b) the procedural development of the case; c) the judgment of the court.

3. How does Judge Rapallo formulate the rule of Thomas v. Winchester? Do you agree with that formulation? Is it consistent

with the decisions in Loop v. Litchfield and Losee v. Clute? How does Judge Rapallo distinguish those decisions from the case at hand? According to Judge Rapallo, what is the general rule regarding a builder's liability in cases similar to this?

4. Would a scaffold constructed as this one was but only 8 feet high be a dangerous instrumentality within the terms of the doctrine developed in these cases?

5. After this decision would a lawyer be better able to advise a client as to what constitutes a dangerous instrumentality?

6. Does the case extend the principle of Thomas v. Winchester?

7. If Stevenson had introduced evidence tending to prove that Smith had inspected the scaffold and accepted it, do you think the court would have reached a different result? Compare the Court's discussion of Smith's responsibility with the responsibilities of the Saratoga Paper Co. (Losee v. Clute) and Foord and Aspinwall (Thomas v. Winchester)? Why was Winchester liable for the negligence of an employee while Smith is not held liable for Stevenson's negligence?

TORGESEN v. SCHULTZ

Court of Appeals of New York, 1908.
192 N.Y. 156, 84 N.E. 956.

Appeal from a judgment of the Appellate Division of the Supreme Court in the first judicial department, entered April 12, 1906, affirming a judgment in favor of defendant entered upon a dismissal of the complaint by the court at a Trial Term.

The nature of the action and the facts, so far as material, are stated in the opinion. . . .

WILLARD BARTLETT, J. The plaintiff has suffered the loss of an eye by reason of the explosion of a siphon bottle of aerated water filled and put upon the market by the defendant corporation. The siphon had been charged at a pressure of 125 pounds to the square inch. The plaintiff was a domestic servant and on July 1, 1901, between one and two o'clock in the afternoon she received at the door of her employer's house in the city of New York two siphons which had been filled with water by the defendant and which had been purchased from a druggist who had obtained them from the defendant. The day was very hot, the registered temperature at the weather bureau being as follows: 1 P.M., 95 degrees; 2 P.M., 96 degrees; 3 P.M., 96 degrees; 4 P.M., 96 degrees; 5 P.M., 96 degrees; 6 P.M., 97 degrees; 7 P.M., 96 degrees, and 8 P.M., 93 degrees. Upon receiving the siphons the plaintiff took them to a room in the third story, where they remained until between 7 and 8 o'clock in the evening when she carried them down stairs and placed them in a standing position in a pan containing ice, so that one side of each bottle was against the ice. As she turned away one of the siphons exploded with the result stated.

To show the necessity of taking precautions to prevent such explosions, and also to show the extent of the precautions actually taken by the defendant to that end, plaintiff's counsel read in evidence certain extracts from a printed circular of the defendant and counsel for the defendant also read certain other extracts, all of which taken together are as follows:

"We take all possible precautions to guard against accidents by not allowing any siphons or bottles to leave our premises without first being thoroughly tested. On account of the sudden change of temperature any defect in the glass will at once cause the siphon bottle to break. The accompanying cut shows our siphon testing department. All siphon bottles are imported direct from Austria and are received in large casks. They are unpacked and filled with water at a temperature of from 98 to 100 F. They are then put in cages and subjected to a hydrostatic pressure of 350 lbs. to the square inch. This pressure is allowed to remain for about 30 seconds. Then it is reduced to a pressure of 100 lbs. to the square inch, and the entire cage containing five siphons is then submerged in a tank containing cracked ice and water. On account of the sudden change of temperature any defect in the glass will at once cause the siphon bottle to break. The second step in our test is the only definite method to discover flaws in the anneal of the glass, and is by far severer than any condition a siphon is ever subjected to in the ordinary run of our business."

The plaintiff also called as an expert witness an instructor in physics at Columbia University, who described a series of experimental tests which he had made upon a number of siphon bottles of aerated water sold by the defendant. These experiments were conducted by subjecting the siphons to conditions designed to reproduce approximately those which existed at the time when the explosion occurred by which the plaintiff was injured. Out of seventy-one bottles which were thus tested five exploded, and all of the explosions occurred within half a minute after the bottles were placed in contact with ice. It furthermore appeared that when the siphons came back to the defendant, after having once been distributed to its customers, they were not tested again, and that the defendant had no means of determining how many times the bottles were sent out after they had been filled and after they were returned for filling, although they were probably sent out a large number of times.

It is manifest that there was no contract relation between the plaintiff and the defendant, but the defendant is sought to be held liable under the doctrine of Thomas v. Winchester (6 N.Y. 397), and similar cases based upon the duty of the vendor of an article dangerous in its nature, or likely to become so in the course of the ordinary usage to be contemplated by the vendor, either to exercise due care to warn user of the danger or to take reasonable care to prevent the article sold from proving dangerous when subjected only to customary usage. The principle of law invoked is that which was well stated by Lord Justice Cotton in Heaven v. Pender (L.R. [11 Q.B.D.] 503), as follows: "Any one who leaves a dangerous instrument, as a gun, in such a way as to cause danger, or who without due warning supplies to others for use an instrument or thing which to his knowledge, from its construction or otherwise is in such a condition as to cause danger, not necessarily incident to the use of such an instrument or thing, is liable for injury caused to others by reason of his negligent act."

A case in which the accident closely resembled that which happened to the plaintiff in the present action is O'Neill v. James (138 Mich. 567, 101 N.W. 828). The plaintiff there was a bartender employed by his brother.

The defendant was a bottler of champagne cider charged with carbonic acid gas at a pressure of sixty pounds or less to the square inch. The defendant sold to the plaintiff's employer a quantity of this cider, which was placed in an ice box, and while the plaintiff was taking a bottle of the cider out of the ice box it exploded and a piece of the glass destroyed one of his eyes. He recovered a verdict, but the judgment thereon was reversed on the ground that there was no evidence in the case from which the inference could be drawn that the defendant had any knowledge of the dangerous character of the thing sold, inasmuch as the testimony of both sides showed that champagne cider bottled at a pressure of sixty pounds or under was "a harmless, ordinary article of commerce, usually kept for sale where soft drinks are sold." The court held, however, that if the testimony for the plaintiff had tended to show that the explosion could not have occurred if the bottle had been charged in the usual way, and the testimony of the defendant that it was so charged and that the explosion might have been otherwise caused, then the issue of the defendant's negligence would have been a question for the jury. The decision reversing the judgment, therefore, was merely a recognition of the doctrine that there must be knowledge of the dangerous character before the defendant can be held liable.

Without questioning in the least the applicability of this doctrine to the case at bar, I think there was sufficient evidence of the defendant's knowledge in this respect to require a submission of the issues to a jury. The language of the defendant's circular tends to show that it was well aware that siphons charged under a pressure of 125 pounds to the square inch were liable to explode unless the bottles had been first subjected to an adequate test. This is plainly inferable from the statement: "We take all possible precautions to guard against accidents." There could be no possible occasion for this assertion unless accidents were likely to happen in the absence of proper precaution to avert them. The testimony of the expert witness to which we have referred tended to show, although, of course, it did not necessarily establish the fact, that the test described in the defendant's circular (which, it may fairly be assumed, was the severest test applied to the siphons) was insufficient to establish that the bottles would not explode when used as customers might be expected to use them. The defendant might reasonably be held chargeable with knowledge that it was customary, especially in hot weather, to place siphons charged with aerated water in contact with ice, and in view of this fact a jury might well find that the tests applied to such bottles should be such as to render it tolerably certain that they would not explode when thus used. As has already been suggested, the expert testimony indicated that the test actually employed by the defendant was not adequate to justify such a conclusion.

It may very well be that the defendant, if put to its proof on the subject, may establish the adequacy of its test and that nothing further can reasonably be required to be done to assure the safety of those making use of their charged siphons as against explosions of the character which injured the plaintiff, but upon the evidence as it stood at the close of her case I think there was enough to entitle the plaintiff to have the question of the defendant's negligence submitted to the jury.

The judgment should be reversed and a new trial granted, costs to abide the event.

CULLEN, CH. J., GRAY, HAIGHT, VANN, HISCOCK and CHASE, JJ., concur.

Judgment reversed, etc.

Questions

1. On what ground do you suppose the trial court had dismissed the complaint?

2. What is Judge Bartlett's formulation of the principle of Thomas v. Winchester? Do you agree with that formulation? Is it consistent with the decision in Loop v. Litchfield and Devlin v. Smith?

3. Is the decision in Losee v. Clute particularly relevant to this case? How would you distinguish the two cases?

4. Do you believe there is a significant difference between the case of the explosion of a bottle of champagne cider charged at 60 pounds to the square inch and the case of the explosion of a bottle of aerated water charged at 125 pounds to the square inch?

MacPHERSON v. BUICK MOTOR CO.

Court of Appeals of New York, 1916.
217 N.Y. 382, 111 N.E. 1050.

Appeal, by permission, from a judgment of the Appellate Division of the Supreme Court in the third judicial department, entered January 8, 1914, affirming a judgment in favor of plaintiff entered upon a verdict.

The nature of the action and the facts, so far as material, are stated in the opinion. . . .

CARDOZO, J. The defendant is a manufacturer of automobiles. It sold an automobile to a retail dealer. The retail dealer resold to the plaintiff. While the plaintiff was in the car, it suddenly collapsed. He was thrown out and injured. One of the wheels was made of defective wood, and its spokes crumbled into fragments. The wheel was not made by the defendant; it was bought from another manufacturer. There is evidence, however, that its defects could have been discovered by reasonable inspection, and that inspection was omitted. There is no claim that the defendant knew of the defect and wilfully concealed it. The case, in other words, is not brought within the rule of Kuelling v. Lean Mfg. Co. (183 N.Y. 78, 75 N.E. 1098). The charge is one, not of fraud, but of negligence. The question to be determined is whether the defendant owed a duty of care and vigilance to any one but the immediate purchaser.

The foundations of this branch of the law, at least in this state, were laid in Thomas v. Winchester (6 N.Y. 397). A poison was falsely labeled. The sale was made to a druggist, who in turn sold to a customer. The customer recovered damages from the seller who affixed the label. "The defendant's negligence," it was said, "put human life in imminent danger." A poison falsely labeled is likely to injure any one who gets it. Because the danger is to be foreseen, there is a duty to avoid the injury. Cases were cited by way of illustration in which manufacturers were not subject to any duty irrespective of contract. The distinction was said to be that their conduct, though negligent, was not likely to result in injury to any one except the purchaser. We are not required to say whether the chance of injury was always as remote as the distinction assumes. Some of the illustrations might be rejected today. The *principle* of the distinction is for present purposes the important thing.

Thomas v. Winchester became quickly a landmark of the law. In the application of its principle there may at times have been uncertainty or even error. There has never in this state been doubt or disavowal of the principle itself. The chief cases are well known, yet to recall some of them will be helpful. Loop v. Litchfield (42 N.Y. 351) is the earliest. It was the case of a defect in a small balance wheel used on a circular saw. The manufacturer pointed out the defect to the buyer, who wished a cheap article and was ready to assume the risk. The risk can hardly have been an imminent one, for the wheel lasted five years before it broke. In the meanwhile the buyer had made a lease of the machinery. It was held that the manufacturer was not answerable to the lessee. Loop v. Litchfield was followed in Losee v. Clute (51 N.Y. 494), the case of the explosion of a steam boiler. That decision has been criticized (Thompson on Negligence, 233; Shearman & Redfield on Negligence [6th ed.], § 117), but it must be confined to its special facts. It was put upon the ground that the risk of injury was too remote. The buyer in that case had not only accepted the boiler, but had tested it. The manufacturer knew that his own test was not the final one. The finality of the test has a bearing on the measure of diligence owing to persons other than the purchaser (Bevin, Negligence [3d ed.], pp. 50, 51, 54; Wharton, Negligence [2d ed.], § 134).

These early cases suggest a narrow construction of the rule. Later cases, however, evince a more liberal spirit. First in importance is Devlin v. Smith (89 N.Y. 470). The defendant, a contractor, built a scaffold for a painter. The painter's servants were injured. The contractor was held liable. He knew that the scaffold, if improperly constructed, was a most dangerous trap. He knew that it was to be used by the workmen. He was building it for that very purpose. Building it for their use, he owed them a duty, irrespective of his contract with their master, to build it with care.

From Devlin v. Smith we pass over intermediate cases and turn to the latest case in this court in which Thomas v. Winchester was followed. That case is Statler v. Ray Mfg. Co. (195 N.Y. 478, 480, 88 N.E. 1063). The defendant manufactured a large coffee urn. It was installed in a restaurant. When heated, the urn exploded and injured the plaintiff. We held that the manufacturer was liable. We said that the urn "was of such a character inherently that, when applied to the purposes for which it was designed, it was liable to become a source of great danger to many people if not carefully and properly constructed."

It may be that Devlin v. Smith and Statler v. Ray Mfg. Co. have extended the rule of Thomas v. Winchester. If so, this court is committed to the extension. The defendant argues that things imminently dangerous to life are poisons, explosives, deadly weapons—things whose normal function is to injure or destroy. But whatever the rule in Thomas v. Winchester may once have been, it has no longer that restricted meaning. A scaffold (Devlin v. Smith, *supra*) is not inherently a destructive instrument. It becomes destructive only if imperfectly constructed. A large coffee urn (Statler v. Ray Mfg. Co., *supra*) may have within itself, if negligently made, the potency of danger, yet no one thinks of it as an implement whose normal function is destruction. What is true of the coffee urn is equally true of bottles of aerated water (Torgeson v. Schultz, 192 N.Y. 156, 84 N.E. 956). We have mentioned only cases in this court. But the rule has received a like extension in our courts of intermediate appeal. In Burke v. Ireland (26 App.Div. 487, 50 N.Y.S. 369), in an opinion by Cullen, J., it was applied to a builder who constructed a defective building; in Kahner v. Otis Elevator Co. (96 App.Div. 169, 89 N.Y.S. 185) to the manufacturer of an elevator; in Davies v. Pelham Hod Elevating Co. (65 Hun, 573, 20 N.Y.S. 523; affirmed in this court without opinion, 146 N.Y. 363) to a contractor who furnished a defective rope with knowledge of the purpose for which the rope was to be used. We are not required at this time either to approve or to disapprove the application of the rule that was made in these cases. It is enough that they help to characterize the trend of judicial thought.

Devlin v. Smith was decided in 1882. A year later a very similar case came before the Court of Appeal in England (Heaven v. Pender, L.R. [11 Q.B.D.] 503). We find in the opinion of Brett, M. R., afterwards Lord Esher (p. 510), the same conception of a duty, irrespective of contract, imposed upon the manufacturer by the law itself: "Whenever one person supplies goods, or machinery, or the like, for the purpose of their being used by another person under such circumstances that every one of ordinary sense would, if he thought, recognize at once that unless he used ordinary care and skill with regard to the condition of the thing supplied or the mode of supplying it, there will be danger of injury to the person or property of him for whose use the thing is supplied, and who is to use it, a duty arises to use ordinary care and skill as to the condition or manner of supplying such thing." He then points out that for a neglect of such ordinary care or skill whereby injury happens, the appropriate remedy is an action for negligence. The right to enforce this liability is not to be confined to the immediate buyer. The right, he says, extends to the persons or class of persons for whose use the thing is supplied. It is enough that the goods "would in all probability be used at once * * * before a reasonable opportunity for discovering any defect which might exist," and that the thing supplied is of such a nature "that a neglect of ordinary care or skill as to its condition or the manner of supplying it would probably cause danger to the person or property of the person for whose use it was supplied, and who was about to use it." On the other hand, he would exclude a case "in which the goods are supplied under circumstances in which it would be a chance by whom they would be used or whether they would be used or not, or whether they would be used before there would probably be means of observing any defect," or where the goods are of such a nature that "a want of care or skill as to their condition or the manner of supplying them would not probably produce danger of injury to person or property." What was said by Lord Esher in that case did not command the full assent of his associates. His opinion has been criticized "as requiring every man to take affirmative precautions to protect his neighbors as well as to refrain from injuring them" (Bohlen, Affirmative Obligations in the Law of Torts, 44 Am.Law Reg. [N.S.] 341). It may not be an accurate exposition of the law of England. Perhaps it may need some qualification even in our own state. Like most attempts at comprehensive definition, it may involve errors of inclusion and of exclusion. But its tests and standards, at least in their underlying principles, with whatever qualifications may be called for as they are applied to varying conditions, are the tests and standards of our law.

We hold, then, that the principle of Thomas v. Winchester is not limited to poisons, explosives, and things of like nature, to things which in their normal operation are implements of destruction. If the nature of a thing is such that it is reasonably certain to place life and limb in peril when negligently made, it is then a thing of danger. Its nature gives warning of the consequences to be expected. If to the element of danger there is added knowledge that the thing will be used by persons other than the purchaser, and used without new tests, then, irrespective of contract, the manufacturer of this thing of danger is under a duty to make it carefully. That is as far as we are required to go for the decision of this case. There must be knowledge of a danger, not merely possible, but probable. It is *possible* to use almost anything in a way that will make it dangerous if defective. That is not enough to charge the manufacturer with a duty independent of his contract. Whether a given thing is dangerous may be sometimes a question for the court and sometimes a question for the jury. There must also be knowledge that in the usual course of events the danger will be shared by others than the buyer. Such knowledge may often be inferred from the nature of the transaction. But it is possible that even knowledge of the danger and of the use will not always be enough. The proximity or remoteness of the relation is a factor to be considered. We are dealing now with the liability of the manufacturer of the finished product, who puts it on the market to be used without inspection by his customers. If he is negligent, where danger is to be foreseen, a liability will follow. We are not required at this time to say that it is legitimate to go back of the manufacturer of the finished product and hold the manufacturers of the component parts. To make their negligence a cause of imminent danger, an independent cause must often intervene; the manufacturer of the finished product must also fail in *his* duty of inspection. It may be that in those circumstances the negligence of the earlier members of the series is too remote to constitute, as to the ultimate user, an actionable wrong (Beven on Negligence [3d ed.], 50, 51, 54; Wharton on Negligence [2d ed.], § 134; Leeds v. N. Y. Tel. Co., 178 N.Y. 118, 70 N.E. 219; Sweet v. Perkins, 196 N.Y. 482, 90 N.E. 50; Hayes v. Hyde Park, 153 Mass. 514, 516, 27 N.E. 522). We leave that question open. We shall have to deal with it when it arises. The difficulty which it suggests is not present in this case. There is here no break in the chain of cause and effect. In such circumstances, the presence of a known danger, attendant upon a known use, makes vigilance a duty. We have put aside the notion that the duty to safeguard life and limb, when the consequences of negligence may be foreseen, grows out of contract and nothing else. We have put the source of the obligation where it ought to be. We have put its source in law.

From this survey of the decisions, there thus emerges a definition of the duty of a manufacturer which enables us to measure this defendant's liability. Beyond all question, the nature of an automobile gives warning of probable danger if its construction is defective. This automobile was designed to go fifty miles an hour. Unless its wheels were sound and strong, injury was almost certain. It was as much a thing of danger as a defective engine for a railroad. The defendant knew the danger. It knew also that the car would be used by persons other than the buyer. This was apparent from its size; there were seats for three persons. It was apparent also from the fact that the buyer was a dealer in cars, who bought to resell. The maker of this car supplied it for the use of purchasers from the dealer just as plainly as the contractor in Devlin v. Smith supplied the scaffold for use by the servants of the owner. The dealer was indeed the one person of whom it might be said with some approach to certainty that by him the car would not be used. Yet the defendant would have us say that he was the one person whom it was under a legal duty to protect. The law does not lead us to so inconsequent a conclusion. Precedents drawn from the days of travel by stage coach do not fit the conditions of travel today. The principle that the danger must be imminent does not change, but the things subject to the principle do change. They are whatever the needs of life in a developing civilization require them to be.

In reaching this conclusion, we do not ignore the decisions to the contrary in other jurisdictions. It was held in Cadillac M. C. Co. v. Johnson (221 F. 801) that an automobile is not within the rule of Thomas v. Winchester. There was, however, a vigorous dissent. Opposed to that decision is one of the Court of Appeals of Kentucky (Olds Motor Works v. Shaffer, 145 Ky. 616, 140 S.W. 1047). The earlier cases are summarized by Judge Sanborn in Huset v. J. I. Case Threshing Machine Co. (120 F. 865). Some of them, at first sight inconsistent with our conclusion, may be reconciled upon the ground that the negligence was too remote, and that another cause had intervened. But even when they cannot be reconciled, the difference is rather in the application of the principle than in the principle itself. Judge Sanborn says, for example, that the contractor who builds a bridge, or the manufacturer who builds a car, cannot ordinarily foresee injury to other persons than the owner as the probable result. (120 F. 865, at p. 867). We take a different view. We think that injury to others is to be foreseen not merely as a possibility, but as an almost inevitable result. (See the trenchant criticism in Bohlen, *supra*, at p. 351). Indeed, Judge Sanborn concedes that his view is not to be reconciled with our decision in Devlin v. Smith (*supra*). The doctrine of that decision has now become the settled law of this state, and we have no desire to depart from it.

In England the limits of the rule are still unsettled. Winterbottom v. Wright (10 M. & W. 109) is often cited. The defendant undertook to provide a mail coach to carry the mail bags. The coach broke down from latent defects in its construction. The defendant, however, was not the manufacturer. The court held that he was not liable for injuries to a passenger. The case was decided on a demurrer to the declaration. Lord Esher points out in Heaven v. Pender (*supra*, at p. 513) that the form of the declaration was subject to criticism. It did not fairly suggest the existence of a duty aside from the special contract which was the plaintiff's main reliance. (See the criticism of Winterbottom v. Wright, in Bohlen, *supra*, at pp. 281, 283). At all events, in Heaven v. Pender (*supra*) the defendant, a dock owner, who put up a staging outside a ship, was held liable to the servants of the shipowner. In Elliott v. Hall (15 Q.B.D. 315) the defendant sent out a defective truck laden with goods which he had sold. The buyer's servants unloaded it, and were injured because of the defects. It was held that the defendant was under a duty "not to be guilty of negligence with regard to the state and condition of the truck." There seems to have been a return to the doctrine of Winterbottom v. Wright in Earl v. Lubbock (L.R. [1905] 1 K.B. 253). In that case, however, as in the earlier one, the defendant was not the manufacturer. He had merely made a contract to keep the van in repair. A later case (White v. Steadman, L.R. [1913], 3 K.B. 340,

348) emphasizes that element. A livery stable keeper who sent out a vicious horse was held liable not merely to his customer but also to another occupant of the carriage, and Thomas v. Winchester was cited and followed (White v. Steadman, *supra*, at pp. 348, 349). It was again cited and followed in Dominion Natural Gas Co. v. Collins (L.R. [1909] A.C. 640, 646). From these cases a consistent principle is with difficulty extracted. The English courts, however, agree with ours in holding that one who invites another to make use of an appliance is bound to the exercise of reasonable care (Caledonian Ry. Co. v. Mulholland, L.R. [1898] A.C. 216, 227; Indermaur v. Dames, L. R. [1 C.P.] 274). That at bottom is the underlying principle of Devlin v. Smith. The contractor who builds the scaffold invites the owner's workmen to use it. The manufacturer who sells the automobile to the retail dealer invites the dealer's customers to use it. The invitation is addressed in the one case to determinate persons and in the other to an indeterminate class, but in each case it is equally plain, and in each its consequences must be the same.

There is nothing anomalous in a rule which imposes upon A, who has contracted with B, a duty to C and D and others according as he knows or does not know that the subject-matter of the contract is intended for their use. We may find an analogy in the law which measures the liability of landlords. If A leases to B a tumble-down house he is not liable in the absence of fraud, to B's guests who enter it and are injured. This is because B is then under the duty to repair it, the lessor has the right to suppose that he will fulfill that duty, and if he omits to do so, his guests must look to him (Bohlen, *supra*, at p. 276). But if A leases a building to be used by the lessee at once as a place of public entertainment, the rule is different. There injury to persons other than the lessee is to be foreseen, and foresight of the consequences involves the creation of a duty (Junkermann v. Tilyou R. Co., 213 N.Y. 404, 108 N.E. 190, and cases there cited).

In this view of the defendant's liability there is nothing inconsistent with the theory of liability on which the case was tried. It is true that the court told the jury that "an automobile is not an inherently dangerous vehicle." The meaning, however, is made plain by the context. The meaning is that danger is not to be expected when the vehicle is well constructed. The court left it to the jury to say whether the defendant ought to have foreseen that the car, if negligently constructed, would become "imminently dangerous." Subtle distinctions are drawn by the defendant between things inherently dangerous and things imminently dangerous, but the case does not turn upon these verbal niceties. If danger was to be expected as reasonably certain, there was a duty of vigilance, and this whether you call the danger inherent or imminent. In varying forms that thought was put before the jury. We do not say that the court would not have been justified in ruling as a matter of law that the car was a dangerous thing. If there was any error, it was none of which the defendant can complain.

We think the defendant was not absolved from a duty of inspection because it bought the wheels from a reputable manufacturer. It was not merely a dealer in automobiles. It was a manufacturer of automobiles. It was responsible for the finished product. It was not at liberty to put the finished product on the market without subjecting the component parts to ordinary and simple tests (Richmond & Danville R. R. Co. v. Elliott, 149 U.S. 266, 272, 13 S.Ct. 837). Under the charge of the trial judge nothing more was required of it. The obligation to inspect must vary with the nature of the thing to be inspected. The more probable the danger, the greater the need of caution. There is little analogy between this case and Carlson v. Phoenix Bridge Co. (132 N.Y. 273, 30 N.E. 750), where the defendant bought a tool for a servant's use. The making of tools was not the business in which the master was engaged. Reliance on the skill of the manufacturer was proper and almost inevitable. But that is not the defendant's situation. Both by its relation to the work and by the nature of its business, it is charged with a stricter duty.

Other rulings complained of have been considered, but no error has been found in them.

The judgment should be affirmed with costs.

WILLARD BARTLETT, CH. J. (dissenting). The plaintiff was injured in consequence of the collapse of a wheel of an automobile manufactured by the defendant corporation which sold it to a firm of automobile dealers in Schenectady, who in turn sold the car to the plaintiff. The wheel was purchased by the Buick Motor Company, ready made, from the Imperial Wheel Company of Flint, Michigan, a reputable manufacturer of automobile wheels which had furnished the defendant with eighty thousand wheels, none of which had proved to be made of defective wood prior to the accident in the present case. The defendant relied upon the wheel manufacturer to make all necessary tests as to the strength of the material therein and made no such tests itself. The present suit is an action for negligence brought by the subvendee of the motor car against the manufacturer as the original vendor. The evidence warranted a finding by the jury that the wheel which collapsed was defective when it left the hands of the defendant. The automobile was being prudently operated at the time of the accident and was moving at a speed of only eight miles an hour. There was no allegation of proof of any actual knowledge of the defect on the part of the defendant or any suggestion that any element of fraud or deceit or misrepresentation entered into the sale.

The theory upon which the case was submitted to the jury by the learned judge who presided at the trial was that, although an automobile is not an inherently dangerous vehicle, it may become such if equipped with a weak wheel; and that if the motor car in question, when it was put upon the market was in itself inherently dangerous by reason of its being equipped with a weak wheel, the defendant was chargeable with a knowledge of the defect so far as it might be discovered by a reasonable inspection and the application of reasonable tests. This liability, it was further held, was not limited to the original vendee, but extended to a subvendee like the plaintiff, who was not a party to the original contract of sale.

I think that these rulings, which have been approved by the Appellate Division, extend the liability of the vendor of a manufactured article further than any case which has yet received sanction of this court. It has heretofore been held in this state that the liability of the vendor of a manufactured article for negligence arising out of the existence of defects therein does not extend to strangers injured in consequence of such defects but is confined to the immediate vendee. The exceptions to this general rule which have thus far been recognized in New York are cases in which the article sold was of such character that danger to life or limb was involved in the ordinary use thereof; in other words, where the article sold was inherently dangerous. As has already been pointed out, the learned trial judge instructed the jury that an automobile is not an inherently dangerous vehicle.

The late Chief Justice Cooley of Michigan, one of the most learned and accurate of American law writers, states the general rule thus: "The general rule is that a contractor, manufacturer, vendor, or furnisher of an article is not liable to third parties who have no contractual relations with him for negligence in the construction, manufacturing, or sale of such article." (2 Cooley on Torts [3d ed.], 1486.)

The leading English authority in support of this rule, to which all the later cases on the same subject refer, is Winterbottom v. Wright (10 Meeson & Welsby, 109), which was an action by the driver of a stage coach against a contractor who had agreed with the postmaster-general to provide and keep the vehicle in repair for the purpose of conveying the royal mail over a prescribed route. The coach broke down and upset, injuring the driver, who sought to recover against the contractor on account of its defective construction. The Court of Exchequer denied him any right of recovery on the ground that there was no privity of contract between the parties, the agreement having been made with the postmaster-general alone. "If the plaintiff can sue," said Lord Abinger, the Chief Baron, "every passenger or even any person passing along the road, who was injured by the upsetting of the coach, might bring a similar action. Unless we confine the operation of such contracts as this to the parties who enter into them, the most absurd and outrageous consequences, to which I can see no limit, would ensue."

The doctrine of that decision was recognized as the law of this state by the leading New York case of Thomas v. Winchester (6 N.Y. 397, 408), which, however, involved an exception to the general rule. There the defendant, who was a dealer in medicines, sold to a druggist a quantity of belladonna, which is a deadly poison, negligently labeled as extract of dandelion. The druggist in good faith used the poison in filling a prescription calling for the harmless dandelion extract and the plaintiff for whom the prescription was put up was poisoned by the belladonna. This court held that the original vendor was liable for the injuries suffered by the patient. Chief Judge Ruggles, who delivered the opinion of the court, distinguished between an act of negligence imminently dangerous to the lives of others and one that is not so, saying: "If A. build a wagon and sell it to B., who sells it to C. and C. hires it to D., who in consequence of the gross negligence of A. in building the wagon is overturned and injured, D. cannot recover damages against A., the builder. A.'s obligation to build the wagon faithfully, arises solely out of his contract with B. The public have nothing to do with it. . . . So, for the same reason, if a horse be defectively shod by a smith, and a person hiring the horse from the owner is thrown and injured in consequence of the smith's negligence in shoeing; the smith is not liable for the injury."

In Torgeson v. Schultz (192 N.Y. 156, 159, 84 N.E. 956) the defendant was the vendor of bottles of aerated water which were charged under high pressure and likely to explode unless used with precaution when exposed to sudden changes of temperature. The plaintiff, who was a servant of the purchaser, was injured by the explosion of one of these bottles. There was evidence tending to show that it had not been properly tested in order to insure users against such accidents. We held that the defendant corporation was liable notwithstanding the absence of any contract relation between it and the plaintiff "under the doctrine of Thomas v. Winchester (*supra*), and similar cases based upon the duty of the vendor of an article dangerous in its nature, or likely to become so in the course of the ordinary usage to be contemplated by the vendor, either to exercise due care to warn users of the danger or to take reasonable care to prevent the article sold from proving dangerous when subjected only to customary usage." The character of the exception to the general rule limiting liability for negligence to the original parties to the contract of sale, was still more clearly stated by Judge Hiscock, writing for the court in Statler v. Ray Manufacturing Co. (195 N.Y. 478, 482, 88 N.E. 1063), where he said that "in the case of an article of an inherently dangerous nature, a manufacturer may become liable for a negligent construction which, when added to the inherent character of the appliance, makes it immediately dangerous, and causes or contributes to a resulting injury not necessarily incident to the use of such an article if properly constructed, but naturally following from a defective construction." In that case the injuries were inflicted by the explosion of a battery of steam-driven coffee urns, constituting an appliance liable to become dangerous in the course of ordinary usage.

The case of Devlin v. Smith (89 N.Y. 470) is cited as an authority in conflict with the view that the liability of the manufacturer and vendor extends to third parties only when the article manufactured and sold is inherently dangerous. In that case the builder of a scaffold ninety feet high which was erected for the purpose of enabling painters to stand upon it, was held to be liable to the administratrix of a painter who fell therefrom and was killed, being at the time in the employ of the person for whom the scaffold was built. It is said that the scaffold if properly constructed was not inherently dangerous; and hence that this decision affirms the existence of liability in the case of an article not dangerous in itself but made so only in consequence of negligent construction. Whatever logical force there may be in this view it seems to me clear from the language of Judge Rapallo, who wrote the opinion of the court, that the scaffold was deemed to be an inherently dangerous structure; and that the case was decided as it was because the court entertained that view. Otherwise he would hardly have said, as he did, that the circumstances seemed to bring the case fairly within the principle of Thomas v. Winchester.

I do not see how we can uphold the judgment in the present case without overruling what has been so often said by this court and other courts of like authority in reference to the absence of any liability for negligence on the part of the original vendor of an ordinary carriage to any one except his immediate vendee. The absence of such liability was the very point actually decided in the English case of Winterbottom v. Wright (*supra*), and the illustration quoted from the opinion of Chief Judge Ruggles in Thomas v. Winchester (*supra*) assumes that the law on the subject was so plain that the statement would be accepted almost as a matter of course. In the case at bar the defective wheel on an automobile moving only eight miles an hour was not any more dangerous to the occupants of the car than a similarly defective wheel would be to the occupants of a carriage drawn by a horse at the same speed; and yet unless the courts have been all wrong on this question up to the present time there would be no liability to strangers to the original sale in the case of the horse-drawn carriage.

The rule upon which, in my judgment, the determination of this case depends, and the recognized exceptions thereto, were discussed by Circuit Judge Sanborn of the United States Circuit Court of Appeals in the Eighth Circuit in Huset v. J. I. Case Threshing Machine Co. (120 F. 865) in an opinion which reviews all the leading American and English decisions on the subject up to the time when it was rendered (1903). I have already discussed the leading New York cases, but as to the rest I feel that I can add nothing to the learning of that opinion or the cogency of its reasoning. I have examined the cases to which Judge Sanborn refers, but if I were to discuss them at length I should be forced merely to paraphrase his language, as a study of the authorities he cites has led me to the same conclusion; and the repetition of what has already been so well said would contribute nothing to the advantage of the bench, the bar or the individual litigants whose case is before us.

A few cases decided since his opinion was written, however, may be noticed. In Earl v. Lubbock (L.R.1905 [1 K.B.Div.] 253) the Court of Appeal in 1904 considered and approved the propositions of law laid down by the Court of Exchequer in Winterbottom v. Wright (*supra*), declaring that the decision in that case, since the year 1842, had stood the test of repeated discussion. The master of the rolls approved the principles laid down by Lord Abinger as based upon sound reasoning; and all the members of the court agreed that his decision was a controlling authority which must be followed. That the Federal courts still adhere to the general rule, as I have stated it, appears by the decision of the Circuit Court of Appeals in the Second Circuit, in March, 1915, in the case of Cadillac Motor Car Co. v. Johnson (221 F. 801). That case, like this, was an action by a subvendee against a manufacturer of automobiles for negligence in failing to discover that one of its wheels was defective, the court holding that such an action could not be maintained. It is true there was a dissenting opinion in that case, but it was based chiefly on the proposition that rules applicable to stage coaches are archaic when applied to automobiles and that if the law did not afford a remedy to strangers to the contract the law should be changed. If this be true, the change should be effected by the legislature and not by the courts. A perusal of the opinion in that case and in the Huset case will disclose how uniformly the courts throughout this country have adhered to the rule and how consistently they have refused to broaden the scope of the exceptions. I think we should adhere to it in the case at bar and, therefore, I vote for a reversal of this judgment.

HISCOCK, CHASE, and CUDDEBACK, JJ., concur with CARDOZO, J., and HOGAN, J., concurs in result; WILLARD BARTLETT, CH. J., reads dissenting opinion; POUND, J., not voting.

Judgment affirmed.

Questions

1. What is the holding of the majority opinion?

2. Do you agree with the majority opinion or with the dissent? What purpose is served by writing a dissenting opinion?

3. In his reasoning Judge Cardozo relies on the authority of several cases which you have read. Do you agree with his analysis of these cases and the meaning which he attributes to them?

4. Does the principle upon which the MacPherson case was decided differ from that upon which Thomas v. Winchester was decided? Torgesen v. Schultz?

5. What answer can you give, if any, to Chief Judge Bartlett's reasoning that since Devlin v. Smith was expressly decided on the principle of Thomas v. Winchester, as an exception to the rule of Winterbottom v. Wright, it is now improper for the court to say that Devlin v. Smith extended Thomas v. Winchester and in effect overruled Winterbottom?

6. Bartlett intimates that the majority opinion has changed the law of manufacturers' liability. He argues that such a change "should be affected by the legislature and not by the courts." Is this decision an example of judicial legislation? Was the decision in Thomas v. Winchester an example of judicial legislation?

7. Why does not Cardozo state the law applicable to the liability of manufacturers of component parts and liability of distributors?

8. Would it have been more honest if the court had simply overruled all earlier decisions holding that the manufacturer is not liable in tort to remote purchasers for harm caused by defective products?

SECTION 22.   REASONING FROM CASE TO CASE

[The following is taken from EDWARD H. LEVI,* AN INTRODUCTION TO LEGAL REASONING (Chicago, 1949), pp. 1–19, 72–74. Some footnotes omitted; others are renumbered.]

I

This is an attempt to describe generally the process of legal reasoning in the field of case law and in the interpretation of statutes and of the Constitution. It is important that the mechanism of legal reasoning should not be concealed by its pretense. The pretense is that the law is a system of known rules applied by a judge; the pretense has long been under attack.[1] In an important sense legal rules are never clear, and, if a rule had to be clear before it could be imposed, society would be impossible. The mechanism accepts the differences of view and ambiguities of words. It provides for the participation of the community in resolving the ambiguity by providing a forum for the discussion of policy in the gap of ambiguity. On serious controversial questions, it makes it possible to take the first step in the direc-

---

* Mr. Levi was Professor of Law at the University of Chicago at the time he authored this work. Since then he has served as President of the University of Chicago, and Attorney General of the United States.

1. The controlling book is Frank, Law and the Modern Mind (1930).

tion of what otherwise would be forbidden ends.   The mechansim is indispensable to peace in a community.

The basic pattern of legal reasoning is reasoning by example.[2] It is reasoning from case to case.   It is a three-step process described by the doctrine of precedent in which a proposition descriptive of the first case is made into a rule of law and then applied to a next similar situation.   The steps are these: similarity is seen between cases; next the rule of law inherent in the first case is announced; then the rule of law is made applicable to the second case.   This is a method of reasoning necessary for the law, but it has characteristics which under other circumstances might be considered imperfections.

These characteristics become evident if the legal process is approached as though it were a method of applying general rules of law to diverse facts— in short, as though the doctrine of precedent meant that general rules, once properly determined, remained unchanged, and then were applied, albeit imperfectly, in later cases.   If this were the doctrine, it would be disturbing to find that the rules change from case to case and are remade with each case. Yet this change in the rules is the indispensable dynamic quality of law.   It occurs because the scope of a rule of law, and therefore its meaning, depends upon a determination of what facts will be considered similar to those present when the rule was first announced.   The finding of similarity or difference is the key step in the legal process.

The determination of similarity or difference is the function of each judge.   Where case law is considered, and there is no statute, he is not bound by the statement of the rule of law made by the prior judge even in the controlling case.   The statement is mere dictum, and this means the judge in the present case may find irrelevant the existence or absence of facts which prior judges thought important.[3] It is not what the prior judge intended that is of any importance; rather it is what the present judge, attempting to see the law as a fairly consistent whole, thinks should be the determining classification.   In arriving at his result he will ignore what the past thought important; he will emphasize facts which prior judges would have thought made no difference.   It is not alone that he could not see the law through the eyes of another, for he could at least try to do so.   It is rather that the doctrine of dictum forces him to make his own decision.[4]

Thus it cannot be said that the legal process is the application of known rules to diverse facts.   Yet it is a system of rules; the rules are discovered in the process of determining similarity or difference.   But if attention is directed toward the finding of similarity or difference, other peculiarities appear.   The problem for the law is: When will it be just to treat different

2. "Clearly then to argue by example is neither like reasoning from part to whole, nor like reasoning from whole to part, but rather reasoning from part to part, when both particulars are subordinate to the same term and one of them is known.   It differs from induction, because induction starting from all the particular cases proves . . . that the major term belongs to the middle and does not apply the syllogistic conclusion to the minor term, whereas argument by example does make this application and does not draw its proof from all the particular cases."   Aristotle, Analytica Priora 69a (McKeon ed., 1941).

3. But *cf.* Goodhart, "Determining the Ratio Decidendi of a Case," 40 Yale L. J. 161 (1930).

4. *Cf.* Mead, The Philosophy of the Act 81, 92–102 (1938).

cases as though they were the same? A working legal system must therefore be willing to pick out key similarities and to reason from them to the justice of applying a common classification. The existence of some facts in common brings into play the general rule. If this is really reasoning, then by common standards, thought of in terms of closed systems, it is imperfect unless some over-all rule has announced that this common and ascertainable similarity is to be decisive. But no such fixed prior rule exists. It could be suggested that reasoning is not involved at all; that is, that no new insight is arrived at through a comparison of cases. But reasoning appears to be involved; the conclusion is arrived at through a process and was not immediately apparent. It seems better to say that there is reasoning, but it is imperfect.[5]

Therefore it appears that the kind of reasoning involved in the legal process is one in which the classification changes as the classification is made. The rules change as the rules are applied. More important, the rules arise out of a process which, while comparing fact situations, creates the rules and then applies them. But this kind of reasoning is open to the charge that it is classifying things as equal when they are somewhat different, justifying the classification by rules made up as the reasoning or classification proceeds. In a sense all reasoning is of this type,[6] but there is an additional requirement which compels the legal process to be this way. Not only do new situations arise, but in addition peoples' wants change. The categories used in the legal process must be left ambiguous in order to permit the infusion of new ideas. And this is true even where legislation or a constitution is involved. The words used by the legislature or the constitutional convention must come to have new meanings. Furthermore, agreement on any other basis would be impossible. In this manner the laws come to express the ideas of the community and even when written in general terms, in statute or constitution, are molded for the specific case.

But attention must be paid to the process. A controversy as to whether the law is certain, unchanging, and expressed in rules, or uncertain, changing, and only a technique for deciding specific cases misses the point. It is both. Nor is it helpful to dispose of the process as a wonderful mystery possibly reflecting a higher law, by which the law can remain the same and yet change. The law forum is the most explicit demonstration of the mechanism required for a moving classification system. The folklore of law may choose to ignore the imperfections in legal reasoning,[7] but the law forum itself has taken care of them.

What does the law forum require? It requires the presentation of competing examples. The forum protects the parties and the community by making sure that the competing analogies are before the court. The rule

---

5. The logical fallacy is the fallacy of the undistributed middle or the fallacy of assuming the antecedent is true because the consequent has been affirmed.

6. Dewey, Logic, The Theory of Inquiry, Ch. 6 (1938); *cf.* Pareto, The Mind and Society sec. 894 (1935); Arnold, The Folklore of Capitalism, Ch. 7 (1937).

7. "That the law can be obeyed even when it grows is often more than the legal profession itself can grasp." Cohen and Nagel, An Introduction to Logic and Scientific Method 371 (1934); see Stone, The Province and Function of Law 140–206 (1946).

which will be created arises out of a process in which if different things are to be treated as similar, at least the differences have been urged.[8] In this sense the parties as well as the court participate in the law making. In this sense, also, lawyers represent more than the litigants.

Reasoning by example in the law is a key to many things. It indicates in part the hold which the law process has over the litigants. They have participated in the law making. They are bound by something they helped to make. Moreover, the examples or analogies urged by the parties bring into the law the common ideas of the society. The ideas have their day in court, and they will have their day again. This is what makes the hearing fair, rather than any idea that the judge is completely impartial, for of course he cannot be completely so. Moreover, the hearing in a sense compels at least vicarious participation by all the citizens, for the rule which is made, even though ambiguous, will be law as to them.

Reasoning by example shows the decisive role which the common ideas of the society and the distinctions made by experts can have in shaping the law. The movement of common or expert concepts into the law may be followed. The concept is suggested in arguing difference or similarity in a brief, but it wins no approval from the court. The idea achieves standing in the society. It is suggested again to a court. The court this time reinterprets the prior case and in doing so adopts the rejected idea. In subsequent cases, the idea is given further definition and is tied to other ideas which have been accepted by courts. It is now no longer the idea which was commonly held in the society. It becomes modified in subsequent cases. Ideas first rejected but which gradually have won acceptance now push what has become a legal category out of the system or convert it into something which may be its opposite. The process is one in which the ideas of the community and of the social sciences, whether correct or not, as they win acceptance in the community, control legal decisions. Erroneous ideas, of course, have played an enormous part in shaping the law. An idea, adopted by a court, is in a superior position to influence conduct and opinion in the community; judges, after all, are rulers. And the adoption of an idea by a court reflects the power structure in the community. But reasoning by example will operate to change the idea after it has been adopted.

Moreover, reasoning by example brings into focus important similarity and difference in the interpretation of case law, statutes, and the constitution of a nation. There is a striking similarity. It is only folklore which holds that a statute if clearly written can be completely unambiguous and applied as intended to a specific case. Fortunately or otherwise, ambiguity is inevitable in both statute and constitution as well as with case law. Hence reasoning by example operates with all three. But there are important differences. What a court says is dictum, but what a legislature says is a statute. The reference of the reasoning changes. Interpretation of intention when dealing with a statute is the way of describing the attempt to compare cases on the basis of the standard thought to be common at the time the legisla-

8. The reasoning may take this form: A falls more appropriately in B than in C. It does so because A is more like D which is of B than it is like E which is of C. Since A is in B and B is in G (legal concept), then A is in G. But perhaps C is in G also. If so, then B is in a decisively different segment of G, because B is like H which is in G and has a different result than C.

tion was passed. While this is the attempt, it may not initially accomplish any different result than if the standard of the judge had been explicitly used. Nevertheless, the remarks of the judge are directed toward describing a category set up by the legislature. These remarks are different from ordinary dicta. They set the course of the statute, and later reasoning in subsequent cases is tied to them. As a consequence, courts are less free in applying a statute than in dealing with case law. The current rationale for this is the notion that the legislature has acquiesced by legislative silence in the prior, even though erroneous, interpretation of the court. But the change in reasoning where legislation is concerned seems an inevitable consequence of the division of function between court and legislature, and, paradoxically, a recognition also of the impossibility of determining legislative intent. The impairment of a court's freedom in interpreting legislation is reflected in frequent appeals to the constitution as a necessary justification for overruling cases even though these cases are thought to have interpreted the legislation erroneously.

Under the United States experience, contrary to what has sometimes been believed when a written constitution of a nation is involved, the court has greater freedom than it has with the application of a statute or case law. In case law, when a judge determines what the controlling similarity between the present and prior case is, the case is decided. The judge does not feel free to ignore the results of a great number of cases which he cannot explain under a remade rule. And in interpreting legislation, when the prior interpretation, even though erroneous, is determined after a comparison of facts to cover the case, the case is decided. But this is not true with a constitution. The constitution sets up the conflicting ideals of the community in certain ambiguous categories.[9] These categories bring along with them satellite concepts covering the areas of ambiguity. It is with a set of these satellite concepts that reasoning by example must work. But no satellite concept, no matter how well developed, can prevent the court from shifting its course, not only by realigning cases which impose certain restrictions, but by going beyond realignment back to the overall ambiguous category written into the document. The constitution, in other words, permits the court to be inconsistent. The freedom is concealed either as a search for the intention of the framers or as a proper understanding of a living instrument, and sometimes as both. But this does not mean that reasoning by example has any less validity in this field.

II

It may be objected that this analysis of legal reasoning places too much emphasis on the comparison of cases and too little on the legal concepts which are created. It is true that similarity is seen in terms of a word, and inability to find a ready word to express similarity or difference may prevent change in the law. The words which have been found in the past are much spoken of, have acquired a dignity of their own, and to a considerable measure control results. As Judge Cardozo suggested in speaking of metaphors, the word starts out to free thought and ends by enslaving it.[10] The movement of concepts into and out of the law makes the point. If the society

9. Compare Myrdal, An American Dilemma, Ch. I (1944); Dicey, Law of the Constitution 126, 146 (9th ed., 1939).

10. Berkey v. Third Ave. Ry. Co., 244 N.Y. 84, 94, 155 N.E. 58, 61 (1926).

has begun to see certain significant similarities or differences, the comparison emerges with a word. When the word is finally accepted, it becomes a legal concept. Its meaning continues to change. But the comparison is not only between the instances which have been included under it and the actual case at hand, but also in terms of hypothetical instances which the word by itself suggests. Thus the connotation of the word for a time has a limiting influence—so much so that the reasoning may even appear to be simply deductive.

But it is not simply deductive. In the long run a circular motion can be seen. The first stage is the creation of the legal concept which is built up as cases are compared. The period is one in which the court fumbles for a phrase. Several phrases may be tried out; the misuse or misunderstanding of words itself may have an effect. The concept sounds like another, and the jump to the second is made. The second stage is the period when the concept is more or less fixed, although reasoning by example continues to classify items inside and out of the concept. The third stage is the break-down of the concept, as reasoning by example has moved so far ahead as to make it clear that the suggestive influence of the word is no longer desired.

The process is likely to make judges and lawyers uncomfortable. It runs contrary to the pretense of the system. It seems inevitable, therefore, that as matters of kind vanish into matters of degree and then entirely new meanings turn up, there will be the attempt to escape to some overall rule which can be said to have always operated and which will make the reasoning look deductive. The rule will be useless. It will have to operate on a level where it has no meaning.[11] Even when lip service is paid to it, care will be taken to say that it may be too wide or too narrow but that nevertheless it is a good rule. The statement of the rule is roughly analogous to the appeal to the meaning of a statute or of a constitution, but it has less of a function to perform. It is window dressing. Yet it can be very misleading. Particularly when a concept has broken down and reasoning by example is about to build another, textbook writers, well aware of the unreal aspect of old rules, will announce new ones, equally ambiguous and meaningless, forgetting that the legal process does not work with the rule but on a much lower level.

The movement of legal concepts in case law has frequently been shown by pointing to the breakdown of the so-called "inherently dangerous" rule.[12] It is easy to do this because the opinion in MacPherson v. Buick Motor Co.[13] is the work of a judge acutely conscious of the legal process and articulate about it. But MacPherson v. Buick was only a part of a cyclical movement

---

11. See 3 Mill, A System of Logic, Ch. I, sec. 2 (1887).

12. The concept has been used for the precise demonstration intended here: Radin, "Case Law and Stare Decisis: Concerning Prajudizienrecht in Amerika," 33 Col.L.Rev. 199 (1933); Llewellyn, "The Status of the Rule of Judicial Precedent," 14 U. of Cin.L.Rev. 208 (1940); cf. Pound, "What of Stare Decisis?" 10 Fordham L.Rev. 1 (1941). In connection with the general problem, see also Fuller, "Reason and Fiat in Case Law," 59 Harv.L.Rev. 376 (1946); Llewellyn, "The Rule of Law in Our Case Law of Contract," 47 Yale L.J. 1243 (1938); Llewellyn, "On Our Case Law of Contract: Offer and Acceptance, I," 48 Yale L.J. 1 (1938); Lobingier, "Precedent in Past and Present Legal Systems," 44 Mich.L. Rev. 955 (1946); Rheinstein, "The Place of Wrong: A Study in the Method of Case Law," 19 Tulane L. Rev. 4 (1944); cf. Republic of Mexico v. Hoffman, 324 U.S. 30 (1945).

13. 217 N.Y. 382, 111 N.E. 1050 (1916); see Parker, Attorneys at Law, Ch. 8 (1942).

in which differences and similarities first rejected are then adopted and later cast aside. The description of the movement can serve as an example of case law. Roughly the problem has become: the potential liability of a seller of an article which causes injury to a person who did not buy the article from the seller. In recent times the three phases in the movement of the concepts used in handling this problem can be traced.

The first of these begins in 1816 and carries us to 1851. It begins with a loaded gun and ends with an exploding lamp. The loaded gun brought liability to its owner in the case Dixon v. Bell.[14] He had sent his thirteen-or-fourteen-year old servant girl to get the gun; in playing with the gun she had shot if off into the face of the plaintiff's son, who lost his right eye and two teeth. In holding that the plaintiff might recover, Lord Ellenborough attempted no classification of dangerous articles. He was content to describe the gun "as by this want of care . . . left in a state capable of doing mischief." [15] Thus the pattern begins with commodities mischievous through want of care.

The pattern becomes complicated in 1837 in the case of Langridge v. Levy,[16] where a plaintiff complained that the defendant had sold his father a defective gun for the use of himself and his sons. The gun had blown up in the plaintiff's hand. The court allowed recovery, apparently on the theory that the seller had falsely declared that the gun was safe when he knew it was defective and had sold the gun to the father knowing it was to be used by the plaintiff. It was therefore both a case of fraud, and, in some sense, one of direct dealing between the seller and the plaintiff. The example used by the court was the case of a direct sale to the plaintiff, or where the instrument had been "placed in the hands of a third person for the purpose of being delivered to and then used by the plaintiff." [17] The direct dealing point is also emphasized by the statement of one of the judges during the argument to the effect that it would have helped the plaintiff's case if he had alleged that his father "was an unconscious agent in the transaction" because "the act of an unconscious agent is the act of the party who sets him in motion." [18]

In the argument of Langridge v. Levy, counsel for the defendant had pointed to a distinction between things "immediately dangerous or mischievous by the act of the defendant" and "such as may become so by some further act to be done to it." [19] They had urged what might be considered the pattern suggested by Dixon v. Bell. But the court rejected the use of any such distinction, although it remarked in passing that the gun was not "of itself dangerous, but . . . requires an act to be done, that is to be loaded, in order to make it so." It rejected not only the distinction but any category of dangerous articles, because it "should pause before we made a precedent by our decision which would be an authority for an action against

14. 5 Maule & Selwyn 198 (1816).

15. Ibid., at 199.

16. 2 Meeson & Welsby 519 (1837).

17. Ibid., at 531.

18. Alderson, B., ibid., at 525.

19. Ibid., at 528; note also the hypothetical case set forth by counsel for the plaintiff in Langridge v. Levy reported in 6 L.J.(N.S.) Ex. 137, 138 (1837). "A case might be put of a wrong medicine sent from a chemist, which is received by a person, and placed by him in a cupboard, and afterwards taken by a third person, who, in consequence receives an injury; can it be said that he has no remedy against the chemists?"

the vendors, even of such instruments and articles as are dangerous in themselves, at the suit of *any person* whomsoever into whose hands they might happen to pass and who should be injured thereby." [20]

Nevertheless the category of dangerous articles and the distinction between things of a dangerous nature and those which become so if improperly constructed (which need not be the same as requiring a further act to be done to make it dangerous) were again urged before the court five years later in Winterbottom v. Wright.[21] The court refused to permit a coach man to recover against the defendant who had provided a defective coach under contract with the Postmaster General. The plaintiff had been driving the coach from Hartford to Holyhead when it broke down due to some latent defect; the plaintiff was thrown from his seat and lamed for life. He could not recover because to extend liability this far would lead to "absurd and outrageous consequences." The court refused to discuss whether the defective coach was a weapon of a dangerous nature, even though defendant's counsel seemed to be willing to acknowledge the existence of a special rule of liability for that category. And as for the application of Langridge v. Levy, in that case there was a "distinct fraud" and the plaintiff "was really and substantially the party contracting." The court refused to find similarity under the fraud concept in the fact that the defendant had sold a coach as safe when he did not know it to be in good condition, or under the direct dealing concept in Langridge v. Levy, in that "there was nothing to show that the defendant was aware even of the existence of the particular son who was injured" whereas here the coach "was necessarily to be driven by a coachman." [22] The further argument that the plaintiff had no opportunity of seeing that the coach was sound and secure was insufficient to bring liability.

But in 1851, in Longmeid v. Holliday,[23] the concept of things dangerous in themselves, twice urged before the court and rejected, finally won out. Longmeid had bought a lamp for the use of himself and his wife from Holliday, the defendant storekeeper, who called the lamp "Holliday's Patent Lamp" and had it put together by other persons from parts which he had purchased. When Eliza Longmeid, the wife and plaintiff, tried to light the lamp, it exploded; the naphtha ran over her and scorched and burned her. She was not permitted to collect from the storekeeper. It had not been shown that the defendant knew the lamp was unfit and warrant it to be sound. And the lamp was not in its nature dangerous. In discussing those cases where a third person, not a party to a contract, might recover damages, the court said:

"And it may be the same when any one delivers to another without notice an instrument in its nature dangerous, or under particular circumstances, as a loaded gun which he himself loaded, and that other person to whom it is delivered is injured thereby, or if he places it in a situation easily accessible to a third person, who sustains damage from it. A very strong case to that effect is Dixon v. Bell. But it would be going much too far to say that so much care is required in the ordinary intercourse of life between one individual and another, that, if a machine not in its nature dangerous,—a carriage

20. *Ibid.*, at 530.

21. 10 Meeson & Welsby 109 (1842).

22. *Ibid.*, at 112.

23. 155 Eng.Rep. 752 (1851).

for instance,—but which might become so by a latent defect entirely un-known, although discoverable by the exercise of ordinary care, should be lent or given by one person, even by the person who manufactured it, to another, the former should be answerable to the latter for a subsequent damage ac-cruing by the use of it." [24]

Thus the doctrine of the distinction between things in their nature dan-gerous and those which become so by an unknown latent defect is announced as a way of explaining the difference between a loaded gun (which under the rule however, is explained as a particular circumstance) and a defective lamp. As applied in the case, the doctrine describes the classification of the lamp as dangerous only through a latent defect and results in no liability. But a court could have found as much direct dealing in the purchase of a lamp for the use of the purchaser and his wife as in the case of the purchase of a gun for the use of the purchaser and his sons. Under the rule as stated a carriage is not in its nature dangerous.

The second phase of the development of the doctrine of dangerous arti-cles is the period during which the rule as announced in the Longmeid case is applied. The phase begins with mislabeled poison and ends with a defec-tive automobile. During this time also there is the inevitable attempt to soar above the cases and to find some great overall rule which can classify the cases as though the pattern were really not a changing one.

It was the purchase of belladonna, erroneously marked as extract of dandelion, which in Thomas v. Winchester [25] in 1852, produced the first ap-plication and restatement of the rule announced in the Longmeid case. The poison had been bought at the store of Dr. Foord, but it had been put into its jar and incorrectly labeled in the shop of the defendant Winchester—prob-ably through the negligence of his employee. Mrs. Thomas, who used what she thought was extract of dandelion, reacted by having "coldness of the sur-face and extremities, feebleness of circulation, spasms of the muscles, giddi-ness of the head, dilation of the pupils of the eye and derangement of mind." She was allowed to recover against Winchester. The defendant's negligence had "put human life in imminent danger." No such imminent danger had existed in the Winterbottom case, the Court explained. This was more like the case of the loaded gun in Dixon v. Bell. The imminent danger category would not include a defective wagon but it did include poison.

Looking back, one might say today that the category of things by their nature dangerous or imminently dangerous soon came to include a defective hair wash. At least in George v. Skivington [26] in 1869, a chemist who com-pounded a secret hair wash was liable to the wife of the purchaser for in-juries caused by the wash. But the court went about its business without explicit regard for the imminently dangerous category. It thought that the imperfect hair wash was like the imperfect gun in the Langridge case. It chose to ignore the emphasis in the Langridge case on the purported fact that the seller there knew the gun was defective and lied. It said, "substitute the word 'negligence' for fraud and the analogy between Langridge v. Levy and this case is complete." And as for the case of the defective lamp where there was no liability, that was different because negligence had not been

24. *Ibid.*, at 755. The opinion was by   25. 6 N.Y. 397 (1852).
Parke, B.

26. 5 L.R.Ex. 1 (1869).

found. In constructing a pattern for the cases, it appears that loaded guns, defective guns, poison, and now hair wash were in the imminently dangerous category. Defective wagons and lamps were outside.

The next year it became known that a defective balance wheel for a circular saw was not imminently dangerous. The New York court stated: "Poison is a dangerous subject. Gunpowder is the same. A torpedo is a dangerous instrument, as is a spring gun, a loaded rifle or the like. . . . Not so, however, an iron wheel, a few feet in diameter and a few inches in thickness although one part may be weaker than another. If the article is abused by too long use, or by applying too much weight or speed, an injury may occur, as it may from an ordinary carriage wheel, a wagon axle, or the common chair in which we sit." [27] While applying the imminently dangerous category to defeat liability, the New York court took occasion to give a somewhat new emphasis to Thomas v. Winchester. It found that "the decision in Thomas v. Winchester was based upon the idea that the negligent sale of poisons is both at common law and by statute an indictable offense." And certainly that could be argued. At any rate, three years later the New York court said its opinion in the balance-wheel case showed that Thomas v. Winchester would not result in liability in a case where a boiler blew up.[28] But the imminently dangerous category received a new member in 1882 when the builder of a ninety-foot scaffold to be used in painting the dome of the courthouse was held liable to the estate of an employee-painter who was killed when the ledger gave way.[29] Yet if a defective scaffold was in, the court followed tradition in announcing that a defective carriage would be out.

In England, a defective scaffold was also put in the category. The plaintiff in Heaven v. Pender [30] was a ship painter who was injured, while engaged in his work, due to the breaking of defective ropes which held his support outside the ship. He was allowed to recover against the dock owner who had supplied the support and ropes. But the majority of the judges decided the case on the rather narrow point that the necessary workmen were in effect invited by the dock owner to use the dock and appliances. That could have been the explanation also for the American scaffold case. The most noteworthy feature of Heaven v. Pender, however, was the flight of one of the judges, Lord Esher, at that time Brett, toward a rule above the legal categories which would classify the cases.

Brett thought recovery should be allowed because:

"Whenever one person supplies goods or machinery, or the like for the purpose of their being used by another person under such circumstances that everyone of ordinary sense would, if he thought, recognize at once that unless he used ordinary care and skill with regard to the condition of the thing supplied or the mode of supplying it, there will be danger of injury to the person or property of him for whose use the thing is supplied, and who is to use it, a duty arises to use ordinary care and skill as to the condition or manner of supplying such thing." [31]

This statement was concocted by Brett from two types of cases: first, the case where two drivers or two ships are approaching each other and due

27. Loop v. Litchfield, 42 N.Y. 351, 359 (1870).

28. Losee v. Clute, 51 N.Y. 494 (1873).

29. Devlin v. Smith, 89 N.Y. 470 (1882).

30. 11 L.R.Q.B. 503 (1883).

31. *Ibid.*, at 510; see also rule as stated at 509.

care is required toward each other, and second, where a man is invited into a shop or warehouse and the owner must use reasonable care "to keep his house or warehouse that it may not endanger the person or property of the person invited." Since these two different situations resulted in the same legal rule, or stated differently, since two general principles when applied resulted in the same legal rule, Brett thought there must be "some larger proposition which involves and covers both set of circumstances." This was because "the logic of inductive reasoning requires that where two propositions lead to exactly similar premises there must be a more remote and larger premise which embraces both of the major propositions." Brett's rule of ordinary care ran into some difficulty in looking back at the Langridge case and its insistence on both fraud and direct dealing. But Brett said of the Langridge case, "It is not, it cannot be accurately reported," and in any event the fact that recovery was allowed on the basis of fraud "in no way negatives the proposition that the action might have been supported on the ground of negligence without fraud."

The majority opinion in Heaven v. Pender, while proceeding on the invitee point, and while refusing to follow Brett in his flight, agrees that liability for negligence follows when the instrument is dangerous "as a gun" or when the instrument is in such a condition as to cause danger "not necessarily incident to the use of such an instrument" and no due warning is given. Approving this statement, the New York court in 1908 held that the question of a manufacturer's negligence could be left to a jury where the plaintiff lost an eye due to explosion of a bottle of aerated water.[32] The next year a defective coffee urn or boiler which blew up and killed a man was permitted to join the aerated bottle in the danger concept.[33] The coffee-urn case provided the occasion for explaining two of the names given the dangerous category. Given an "inherently dangerous" article, the court explained, a manufacturer becomes liable for negligent construction which, when added to its inherent characteristics, makes it "imminently dangerous."

The categories by now were fairly well occupied. The dangerous concept had in it a loaded gun, possibly a defective gun, mislabeled poison, defective hair wash, scaffolds, a defective coffee urn, and a defective aerated bottle. The not-dangerous category, once referred to as only latently dangerous, had in it a defective carriage, a bursting lamp, a defective balance wheel for a circular saw, and defective boiler. Perhaps it is not too surprising, to find a defective soldering lamp in Blacker v. Lake [34] joining the not-dangerous class. But the English court, in the opinions of its two judges, experienced some difficulty. For the first judge there appears to have been no difficulty in classifying the soldering lamp as not dangerous. Yet the Skivington case caused trouble because it appeared to suggest that negligence could be substituted for fraud and perhaps liability would follow even though the article was not dangerous. But in that event the Skivington case should not be followed because it was in conflict with Winterbottom v. Wright. Accordingly, the soldering lamp not being dangerous, it was error to leave the question of negligence to the jury. The second judge suggested a more surprising realignment of the cases which threatened the whole danger category.

---

32. Torgesen v. Schultz, 192 N.Y. 156, 84 N.E. 956 (1908).

33. Statler v. George A. Ray Mfg. Co., 195 N.Y. 478, 88 N.E. 1063 (1909).

34. 106 L.T. 533 (1912).

He suggested that no recovery should be permitted even though the lamp fell into the class of things dangerous in themselves. The duty of the vendor in such a case, he pointed out, would be a duty to warn, but that duty is discharged if the nature of the article is obvious or known, as was true in this case. Indeed, the Skivington and Thomas v. Winchester cases were explainable on the very ground that the articles appeared harmless and their contents were unknown. One might almost say that recovery was permitted in those cases because the danger was only latent.

The period of the application of the doctrine of dangerous articles as set forth in the Longmeid case and adopted in Thomas v. Winchester may be thought to come to an end in 1915 with its application by a federal court—the Circuit Court of Appeals for the Second Circuit. This was the way the law looked to the court. "One who manufactures articles inherently dangerous, e. g. poisons, dynamite, gunpowder, torpedoes, bottles of water under gas pressure, is liable in tort to third parties which they injure, unless he has exercised reasonable care with reference to the articles manufactured. . . On the other hand, one who manufactures articles dangerous only if defectively made, or installed, e. g., tables, chairs, pictures or mirrors hung on the walls, carriages, automobiles, and so on is not liable to third parties for injuries caused by them, except in cases of willful injury or fraud." [35] Accordingly, the court denied recovery in a suit by the purchaser of a car from a dealer against the manufacturer when the front right wheel broke and the car turned over.

MacPherson v. Buick [36] begins the third phase of the life of the dangerous instrument concept. The New York Court of Appeals in 1916 had before it almost a repetition of the automobile case passed upon by the federal court the previous year. The plaintiff was driving his car, carrying a friend to the hospital, when the car suddenly collapsed due to a defective wheel. The plaintiff was seriously injured. The Buick Motor Company, the defendant, had sold the car to a retail dealer who in turn had sold it to the plaintiff. The defective wheel had been sold to the Buick Company by the Imperial Wheel Company.

As was to be expected, counsel for the plaintiff urged that an automobile was "dangerous to a high degree." [37] It was, in fact, similar to a locomotive. It was much more like a locomotive than like a wagon. "The machine is a fair rival for the Empire Express," he said. "This is evidenced further by the fact that the person running an automobile must have a license of competency, equally with the locomotive engineer and by the legal restrictions imposed by law in the use of the automobile." It was "almost childish to say that an automobile at rest is not dangerous. Neither is a locomotive with the fire drawn" nor a battery of coffee boilers nor a 42-centimeter gun. The automobile, propelled by explosive gases, was "inherently dangerous." The trial judge had charged the jury that "an automobile is not an inherently dangerous vehicle" but had said that they might find it "imminently dangerous if defective." [38] As to the difference between the two phrases, counsel

35. Cadillac Motor Car Co. v. Johnson, 221 F. 801, 803 (C.C.A.2d, 1915).

36. 217 N.Y. 382, 111 N.E. 1050 (1916); See Bohlen, "Liability of Manufacturers to Persons Other Than Their Immediate Vendors," 45 L.Q.Rev. 343 (1929).

37. Brief for the Plaintiff 16, 17, 18.

38. 217 N.Y. 382, 396, 111 N.E. 1050, 1055 (1916).

said there was no point "juggling over definitions. 'Inherently' means 'inseparably.' 'Imminently' means 'threateningly.' " He did not comment on the request of the defendant that the judge charge the jury that recovery depended on the car being "eminently dangerous." [39]

Counsel did write, however, that he "was powerfully impressed with a remark of Lord Chief Justice Isaacs, on his recent visit to this country, to the effect that in England they were getting away from merely abstract forms and were seeking to administer justice in each individual case." [40]

The New York Court of Appeals allowed recovery. Judge Cardozo recognized that "the foundations of this branch of the law . . . were laid in Thomas v. Winchester." He said that some of the illustrations used in Thomas v. Winchester might be rejected today (having in mind no doubt the example of the defective carriage), but the principle of the case was the important thing. "There never has in this state been doubt or disavowal of the principle itself." Even while remarking that "precedents drawn from the days of travel by stagecoach do not fit the conditions of travel today," he was quick to add the explanation: "The principle that the danger must be imminent does not change, but the things subject to the principle do change." And in addition there were underlying principles. They were stated, more or less, Cardozo said, by Brett in Heaven v. Pender.

To be sure, Cardozo was not certain that this statement of underlying principles was an accurate exposition of the law of England. He thought "it may need some qualification even in our own state. Like most attempts at comprehensive definition, it may involve errors of inclusion and exclusion." He thought, however, that "its tests and standards, at least in their underlying principles, with whatever qualifications may be called for as they are applied to varying conditions, are the tests and standards of our law." He did not comment on the statement of Brett concerning Thomas v. Winchester that it "goes a very long way. I doubt whether it does not go too far."

As to the cases, Cardozo recognized that the early ones "suggest a narrow construction of the rule." He had reference to the boiler and balance-wheel cases. But the way to set them aside had already been shown. They could be distinguished because there the manufacturer had either pointed out the defect or had known that his test was not the final one. The distinction was based upon a point unsuccessfully advanced by losing counsel in Winterbottom v. Wright. Other cases showed that it was not necessary to be destructive in order to be dangerous. "A large coffee urn . . . may have within itself, if negligently made, the potency of danger, yet no one thinks of it as an implement whose normal function is destruction." And "what is true of the coffee urn is equally true of bottles of aerated water." Devlin v. Smith was important too. "A scaffold," Cardozo pointed out, "is not inherently a dangerous instrument." He admitted that the scaffold and the coffee-urn cases may "have extended the rule of Thomas v. Winchester," but "If so, this court is committed to the extension. The defendant argues that things inherently dangerous to life are poisons, explosives, deadly weapons, things whose normal function is to injure or destroy. But whatever the rule in Thomas v. Winchester may once have been, it has no longer that restricted meaning."

He showed a certain impatience for what he called "verbal niceties." He complained that "subtle distinctions are drawn by the defendant between

---

39. *Ibid.*, at 399, 1056.   **40.** Brief for the Plaintiff 23.

things inherently dangerous and things imminently dangerous." As to this it was sufficient to say, "If danger was to be expected as reasonably certain, there was a duty of vigilance, and this whether you call the danger inherent or imminent." The rule was: "If the nature of a thing is such that it is reasonably certain to place life and limb in peril, when negligently made, it is then a thing of danger." But "there must be a knowledge of a danger not merely possible but probable." Thus what was only latently dangerous in Thomas v. Winchester now became imminently dangerous or inherently dangerous, or, if verbal niceties are to be disregarded, just plain or probably dangerous.

Elsewhere in commenting on the case, Cardozo seems to make somewhat less of the matter of principles. He wrote: "What, however, was the posture of affairs before the Buick case had been determined? Was there any law on the subject? A mass of judgments, more or less relevant, had been rendered by the same and other courts. A body of particulars existed in which an hypothesis might be reared. None the less, their implications were equivocal. . . . The things classified as dangerous have been steadily extended with a corresponding extension of the application of the remedy. . . . They have widened till they include a scaffold or an automobile or even pies and cakes when nails and other foreign substances have supplied ingredients not mentioned in the recipes of cook books." Cardozo described the legal process in connection with these cases as one in which "logic and utility still struggle for the mastery." [41] One can forgive Judge Cardozo for this language. It is traditional to think of logic as fighting with something. Sometimes it is thought of as fighting with history and experience.

In a reversal of itself, not so striking because the membership of the court was different, the same federal court hearing another appeal in the same case in which it had been decided that a defective automobile was not inherently dangerous now stated with new wisdom: "We cannot believe that the liability of a manufacturer of an automobile has any analogy to the liability of a manufacturer of 'tables, chairs, pictures or mirrors hung on walls.' The analogy is rather that of a manufacturer of unwholesome food or of a poisonous drug." [42]

MacPherson v. Buick renamed and enlarged the danger category. It is usually thought to have brought the law into line with "social considerations." [43] But it did not remove the necessity for deciding cases. Later the New York courts were able to put into the category of things of danger or probably dangerous a defective bottle [44] and another coffee urn,[45] although one less terrifying than the coffee boiler of 1909. But for some reason or other, admission was denied to a defective automobile when the defect was a door handle which gave way, causing one of the doors to open with the result that the plaintiff was thrown through the door and under the car. The defective handle did not make the car a "thing of danger." [46] And if one is

41. Cardozo, The Growth of the Law 40–41, 76–78 (1924).

42. Johnson v. Cadillac Motor Car Co., 261 F. 878, 886 (C.C.A.2d, 1919).

43. See "Torts: Liability of Manufacturer to Consumer for Article Dangerous Because of Defective Construction," 9 Corn.L.Q. 494 (1924).

44. Smith v. Peerless Glass Co., 259 N. Y. 292, 181 N.E. 576 (1932); *cf.* Bates v. Batey & Co., [1913] 3 K.B. 351.

45. Hoenig v. Central Stamping Co., 273 N.Y. 485, 6 N.E.2d 415 (1936).

46. Cohen v. Brockway Motor Corp., 240 App.Div. 18, 268 N.Y.S. 545 (1934).

comparing cases and examples, it has to be admitted that a door handle is less closely connected with those things which make a car like a locomotive than is the wheel on which it runs.

Nevertheless, a new freedom follows from MacPherson v. Buick. Under it, as the Massachusetts court has said, the exception in favor of liability for negligence where the instrument is probably dangerous has swallowed up the purported rule that "a manufacturer or supplier is never liable for negligence to a remote vendee." [47] The exception now seems to have the same certainty the rule once had. The exception is now a general principle of liability which can be stated nicely in the Restatement, and text writers can criticize courts for not applying what is now an obvious rule of liability.[48]

A somewhat similar development has occurred in England. In Donoghue v. Stevenson [49] in 1932, the manufacturer of a bottle of ginger beer was held liable to the plaintiff who had purchased the bottle through a friend at a café. The bottle contained the decomposed remains of a snail. The opinions of the majority judges stressed the close and almost direct relationship between the manufacturer and the remote vendee. The control of the manufacturer of this type of article was thought to be "effective until the article reaches the consumer. . . . A manufacturer puts up an article of food in containers which he knows will be opened by the actual consumer. There can be no inspection by any purchaser and no reasonable preliminary inspection by the consumer." Lord Atkin, while stating that Brett's rule in Heaven v. Pender was too broad, found that the moral rule requiring the lover of one's neighbor in law was translated into the injunction "you must not injure your neighbor." The question then was: "Who is my neighbor?" The practical rule evolved was of persons "closely and directly affected" and as to acts "which you can reasonably foresee would be likely to injure your neighbor." The emphasis on control and proximity revives the notion of the unconscious agent in Langridge v. Levy, as well as the inability to inspect, unsuccessfully urged in Winterbottom v. Wright and apparently implicit in the Skivington case.

As for other prior cases it was now said that the distinction between things dangerous and those dangerous in themselves was "an unnatural one" and anyway the fact that there might be a special duty for one category no longer meant that a duty might not exist for others. Winterbottom and Longmeid were no longer controlling because negligence had not been alleged and proved in those cases. And as for the Blacker case, Lord Atkin had read and re-read it but had difficulty "in formulating the precise grounds upon which the judgment was given." Thus prior cases were realigned out of the way despite the protest of dissenting judges who adhered to the view of the exception only for dangerous articles in the more traditional sense.

While the emphasis was on continuing control in the Donoghue case, and counsel urged that the Donoghue case applied only to articles intended for internal consumption, its rule was applied in Grant v. Australian Knitting Mills [50] in 1936 to underpants defective due to the presence of an irritating chemical. Here the emphasis could be more on the point that the defect

---

47. Carter v. Yardley & Co., 319 Mass. 92, 64 N.E.2d 693 (1946).

48. See Harper, Law of Torts, sec. 106 (1933).

49. [1932] A.C. 562. Note the reference to trade names and patents at 583.

50. [1936] A.C. 85.

was hidden. While the Blacker case was in a sense disregarded, the point made by one of its judges was in fact accepted. Reasoning in a manner not unlike Skivington, which substituted negligence for fraud, the court put secrecy in the place of control. Donoghue's case was now seen not to "depend on the bottle being stopped and sealed; the essential point in this regard was that the article should reach the consumer or user subject to the same defect as it had when it left the manufacturer." The court realized that in applying its test of directness, control, proximity and hidden defect, "many difficult problems will arise. . . . Many qualifying conditions and many complications of fact may in the future come before the Courts for decision." But "in their Lordships' opinion it is enough for them to decide this case on its actual facts."

With the breakdown of the inherently dangerous rule, the cycle from Dixon v. Bell was complete. But it would be a mistake to believe that the breakdown makes possible a general rule, such as the rule of negligence, which now can be applied. A rule so stated would be equivalent to the flight of Brett. Negligence itself must be given meaning by the examples to be included under it. Unlimited liability is not intended. As the comparison of cases proceeds, new categories will be stressed. Perhaps, for example, there will be a category for trademarked, patented, advertised, or monopolized articles. The basis for such a category exists. The process of reasoning by example will decide. . . .

* * *

V

. . . The history of the gradual growth of the inherently dangerous . . . category is a history of expansion through reasoning by example until previously innocuous items are included. The growth is a reflection of a period in which increasing governmental control and responsibility for the individual were thought to be proper. No one economic or social theory was responsible, although as changes came about in the manner of living, the social theory moved ahead to explain and persuade. The social theory then became useful in explaining connections. The point of view of the society changed. It could not have been planned; it happened.

The legal theories were not an exact reflection of social theories. The liability of a seller of a previously innocuous article was not enlarged because some economic theory said this would be appropriate. Rather the growth of inventions made it hard to distinguish, when reasoning by example was used, between steam engines thought unusual and dangerous in an early day, and engines that moved and were now commonplace. A change in the method of selling and in social life made it hard to distinguish between what had once been the small known group around a seller and the vast outside world. Since the difference could no longer be felt, it fell away. . . .

The emphasis should be on the process. The contrast between logic and the actual legal method is a disservice to both. Legal reasoning has a logic of its own. Its structure fits it to give meaning to ambiguity and to test constantly whether the society has come to see new differences or similarities. Social theories and other changes in society will be relevant when the ambiguity has to be resolved for a particular case. Nor can it be said that the result of such a method is too uncertain to compel. The compulsion of the law is clear; the explanation is that the area of doubt is constantly set forth. The probable area of expansion or contraction is foreshadowed as the system works. This is the only kind of system which will work when people do not agree completely. The loyalty of the community is directed toward the institution in which it participates. The words change to receive the content which the community gives to them. The effort to find complete agreement before the institution goes to work is meaningless. It is to forget the very purpose for which the institution of legal reasoning has been fashioned. This should be remembered as a world community suffers in the absence of law.

Questions

1. Apply the three-step process of legal reasoning described by Levi, *supra* p. 527 ff, in constructing an argument in behalf of the defendant in MacPherson v. Buick Motor Co.

2. In Carter v. Yardley, discussed *supra* p. 540, the Supreme Judicial Court of Massachusetts held that one who negligently manufactured facial cream was liable to a remote purchaser whose skin was injured as a result. The Massachusetts court did not attempt to reconcile this holding with previous decisions which exempted a manufacturer from liability, absent privity of contract, except when the manufactured product was "inherently dangerous," but simply overruled those decisions, stating that the reasoning of the New York court in the MacPherson case makes it obvious that the exception has swallowed up the rule. It is characteristic of the Massachusetts court in recent history that it tends squarely to overrule previous decisions which it finds no longer make sense, whereas it is characteristic of the New York Court of Appeals, especially since Cardozo's tenure (1914–. 1932), that it tends to "distinguish away" previous decisions which it finds no longer make sense. What are the advantages and disadvantages of each method?

3. Levi speaks of "the process of legal reasoning," and gives as an example the synthesis of decisions affecting manufacturers' liability in tort. Is reasoning by analogy of previous decisions the only process of legal reasoning used in Lord v. Veazie, *supra* p. 56; in McBoyle v. U. S., *supra* p. 125; in Miranda v. Arizona, *supra* p. 273?

4. In a famous passage, Humpty Dumpty said to Alice, "When I use a word it means what I want it to mean, neither more nor less." "The question is," said Alice, "whether one word *can* mean so many things." "The question is," said Humpty Dumpty, "who is to be master." What is the difference between Humpty Dumpty's view and Levi's statement, "The words change to receive the content which the community gives to them"?

[Compare the extract from Levi with the following, taken from JEROME FRANK, LAW AND THE MODERN MIND (New York, 1963) pp. 70–72. Footnotes are omitted.]

The school board of Seattle is reported to have insisted that all teachers, as a condition of procuring employment in the Seattle schools, should sign a contract by which they would agree not to join a teachers' union. Suppose that a suit were brought to compel the school board to hire teachers without imposing this condition. If a court were to decide such a suit in favor of the school board, an analysis of its opinion would show that its reasoning was apparently based upon a "fundamental principle." The court would argue that one who is under no duty to enter into a contract with another may stipulate any condition he pleases as a condition to entering into a contract. This principle the court would take as its major premise. It would then state, as a minor premise, that the school board is under no duty to enter into a contract with any particular teachers. The court would then reason syllogistically—that is, it would apply its major premise to its minor premise—and thus reach the conclusion that the school board has a right, as a condition to entering into contracts with teachers, to impose any terms which it pleases, including the stipulation that teachers are not to become members of the teachers' union.

The court would find its major premise in one of two ways. It might state that this liberty of contract was an "abiding and eternal principle of justice,"—a method of finding major premises which many courts employ. Or the court might refer to prior decisions not involving teachers or contracts with governmental officials, and purport to derive this principle "indirectly" from such decisions.

But however the principle is derived, this method of syllogistic reasoning, which is that of formal logic, is the method used by the courts today. Because of its use, the courts' conclusions appear inescapable and inevitable. This seeming machine-like certainty, however, is artificial and conceals a fatal weakness. For a decision against the school board might have been rendered and, if so, could have been justified, with reasoning which would have seemed similarly inevitable. The court could have argued thus: Officials administering the trust of public office may not unreasonably discriminate between applicants for employment. That is an eternal principle of justice or a principle to be found in numerous earlier cases. (There is your major premise.) To deny employment to a teacher because he refuses to agree not to join an organization of teachers is an unreasonable discrimination. (And there is your minor premise.) The ineluctable conclusion is that the school board cannot rightfully refuse to hire a teacher because of his refusal to sign a contract by which he agrees not to become a member of the teachers' union.

The weakness of the use of formal logic is now exposed. The court can decide one way or the other and in either case can make its reasoning appear equally flawless. Formal logic is what its name indicates; it deals with form and not with substance. The syllogism will not supply either the major premise or the minor premise. The "joker" is to be found in the selection of these premises. In the great run of cases which come before the courts, the selection of principles, and the determination of whether the facts are to be stated in terms of one or another minor premise, are the chief tasks to be performed. These are difficult tasks, full of hazards and uncertainties, but the hazards and uncertainties are ordinarily concealed by the glib use of formal logic.

Questions

1. A syllogism is a formal logical analysis of an argument, consisting of a major premise, minor premise, and conclusion. Example:

Major premise: All men have two eyes.

Minor premise: Socrates is a man.

Conclusion: Socrates has two eyes.

Construct a syllogism which summarizes Cardozo's opinion in the MacPherson case. Construct a syllogism which summarizes Bartlett's dissent in MacPherson.

2. Is this *form* of reasoning the same as the three-step process of legal reasoning described in Levi, *supra* p. 527 ff?

3. What is the "fatal weakness" alluded to by Judge Frank? Is it a weakness in syllogistic reasoning, or is it a weakness in legal reasoning as applied in the decision of cases?

4. Do you agree with any of the assertions made by Judge Frank in the last full paragraph of the extract reprinted above? Has Judge Frank, in contrasting logic and the actual legal method, done "a disservice to both"?

5. Is there a difference between reasoning by example, in Levi's sense, and reasoning from precedent?

Chapter 6

REASONING BY ANALOGY OF DOCTRINE AND STATUTE

SECTION 23. THE DEVELOPMENT OF DOCTRINES OF MANUFACTURERS' LIABILITY WITHOUT FAULT

In the cases considered in the preceding chapter, the courts predicated liability on the negligence of the manufacturer. In other words, it was assumed that the manufacturer would be liable neither to the person to whom the product was sold, nor to any sub-purchaser, nor to anyone else, for harm caused by a defect in the product, unless it could be shown that the defect was due to some act of carelessness in manufacture. It was an employee's lack of due care in inspecting the wheel which rendered the Buick Motor Co. liable in the MacPherson case. In Devlin v. Smith the person who was at fault in building the scaffold was held liable, and the contractor who supplied the scaffold to the injured plaintiff was absolved from liability on the ground that he had done nothing careless. Negligence, lack of due care, fault, is the traditional key to liability in tort actions for bodily injury; indeed the very word tort, derived from the Law French of the Norman-English period of our legal history, means "wrong," and there is a widespread sentiment that a person should not be obliged to compensate for a harm caused to another unless the act causing the harm was a "wrongful" act. This sentiment found expression in the 19th century, throughout Europe as well as in England and America, in the maxim "No liability without fault."

The maxim never entirely corresponded with reality, however. There have always been situations in which a person is liable for injury to another though he has acted with utmost care not to cause the injury. A person who keeps a dangerous animal—a zookeeper, for example—has traditionally been held liable for harm caused by its escape, even though the keeper took every precaution to prevent such escape. One who arrests another, having every reason to believe the arrested person is an escaping felon, is civilly liable for wrongful arrest even though the arrest is an innocent mistake—if the person arrested, for example, is the escaping felon's twin brother. More important, the employer is responsible for the torts of employees—no matter how careful he or she is in selecting employees, and no matter how carefully he or she instructs them—if they are acting "in the course of their employment." In other words, a truck driver who damages the person or property of another, while in the course of employment as truck driver, is generally liable only if he or she was negligent;

545

if the driver is liable, the employer is also liable—though the employer was in no way negligent—on the principle that the master should answer for the acts of the servant (*respondeat superior*). Thus the injured person can recover either from the employee or the employer; if he or she chooses the employer, the latter, having paid, has a right of indemnity against the employee—a right which in most cases today is useless, however, since the employee is apt to be "judgment-proof", *i.e.*, too poor to pay.

In addition to these traditional forms of liability without fault (sometimes loosely called "strict" liability, or "absolute" liability), there has developed within the last 100 years a liability for damage innocently caused by activities considered extra-hazardous, or, in some special cases, simply unusual. Thus one who stores dynamite, however carefully, is in many American jurisdictions liable for injuries caused by its explosion. Similarly, in many jurisdictions the owner of an airplane is liable for damage caused by its fall though the accident was due to causes beyond the owner's control. In some European countries a strict liability is imposed upon the driver of an automobile who causes harm to another; thus in France it has been held that if two automobiles collide head-on, each driver is liable for the injuries which he or she causes the other, even though neither was at fault.

In modern times liability without fault has been imposed in many types of situations by statute. Among the most important are the workmen's compensation acts, which generally require the employer to contribute to an insurance fund out of which injured workmen are paid even though the injury was the workman's own fault and not that of the employer. Also pure food and drug laws generally impose a civil (as well as a criminal) responsibility upon persons who sell adulterated food products even though they had every reason to believe the food was pure. Again, statutes in many states make the seller of intoxicating liquor liable for harm caused by a purchaser without proof that the seller knew or should have known that the purchaser was likely to cause harm. A fourth example are the statutes of several states which make the owner of a car liable for the harm caused by the negligence of any person who is driving it with the owner's consent.

Question: What are the various policies underlying these four examples of liability without fault imposed by statute? What policies underlie the examples of judge-made liability without fault given in the preceding two paragraphs?

In most cases, however, liability for bodily harm must rest upon negligence, and it is this rule which is applied generally in case of harm caused by defective manufactured products. To recover damages from the manufacturer the injured person must prove that the injury was caused by the manufacturer's failure to live up to a standard of care—a standard usually defined in terms of "reasonableness under the circumstances."

The preceding discussion has presupposed that the injured party is seeking compensation on the ground that the defendant has committed a *tort*. Where the plaintiff sues for breach of *contract*, however, the idea of "no liability without fault" is not so significant. Liability for breach of contract is normally imposed regardless of whether or not the breach was due to the promisor's faulty conduct; it is enough that the promisor failed to keep the promise. Thus if a supplier of goods has *promised* that the goods are not defective, or has *agreed* to pay for any harm that they cause, a "strict" liability might arise which is independent of tort. Such a promise, or agreement, often takes the form of a *warranty* ("guarantee"), obligating the seller to protect the buyer against losses stemming from defects in the quality or character of the goods sold. The seller's warranty may be express (a promise explicitly made, either orally or in writing) or it may be implied from the conduct of the seller ("implied in fact"). It may also, however, be "implied in law"—that is, it may be imposed upon the seller by statute or by judicial decision, as a result of public policy. In the latter instance the promise on which such liability is based is clearly a legal fiction.

Thus in certain types of cases a person injured by a defective product may recover damages from the person who sold the product—whether or not the seller is the manufacturer—on a fictitious theory of breach of contract. Under this theory the seller is said to have guaranteed to the buyer that the product was fit for the purpose for which it was sold. Or to put it another way, regardless of whether the seller in fact guaranteed the fitness of the product, the seller is held liable as though he or she had made such a guarantee. The damages awarded on such a finding of liability will cover financial losses—return of the purchase price, business losses due to the defect, *etc.*—and in some cases losses due to bodily harms caused by the defective product. Thus in a New York case a purchaser of a loaf of bread was allowed to recover, from the grocer who sold it to her, damages for bodily harm caused by a small pin in the loaf.[1] In such a situation, on the same theory of implied warranty, the grocer may recover the losses from the wholesaler who sold the loaf to the grocer, and the wholesaler may recover in turn from the manufacturer.

Many of the cases in which the seller has been held liable for bodily injuries occasioned by a breach of implied warranty have involved defective food products. Many jurisdictions have extended this liability to other kinds of products. Also it has been held in some cases that the injured person is not confined to a suit for breach of

1. Ryan v. Progressive Grocery Stores, 255 N.Y. 388, 175 N.E. 105 (1931).

implied warranty against the immediate seller, who would then have a right to reimbursement against the manufacturer, but that the plaintiff may go directly against the manufacturer; the warranty is said to "run with" the product, or else the intermediate seller is said to "assign his cause of action" to the plaintiff, or else the plaintiff is said to be a "third party beneficiary" of the contract between the manufacturer and the intermediate seller and hence to have a right to sue for its breach. Thus one fiction is placed on top of another in order to allow the purchaser of a defective product, in a restricted class of cases, to recover from the manufacturer without proof of negligence.

Note that these fictions usually confine the remedy to the purchaser. Is this limitation justified? If it is, does it provide a possible justification for the use of the fictions?

One other development in the direction of the strict liability of manufacturers for harm caused by defective products deserves mention here. In an English case in 1863, in which the plaintiff proved that a barrel fell out of the defendant's warehouse onto the plaintiff's head, the court held that this evidence standing alone was sufficient to support a jury finding of negligence. *Res ipsa loquitur*—"the thing speaks for itself"—said one of the judges. In the course of years this Latin phrase has in many courts developed into a doctrine which shifts the burden of explanation, and in some jurisdictions the burden of proof, to the defendant in cases in which the defendant has "control" of the evidence—that is, has greater access to the facts than the plaintiff. Thus if a waitress shows that she was injured by an exploding Coca-Cola bottle she has established—in most jurisdictions— a prima facie case of negligence on the part of the bottler; if the bottler then produces evidence tending to rebut the inference of negligence (by showing, for example, proper methods of inspection plus the fact that the bottle in question was subsequently struck or exposed to heat by someone else), the doctrine of *res ipsa loquitur* might still be invoked to permit the case to go to the jury on the issue of negligence. It is widely believed that juries often give verdicts to plaintiffs in such cases simply because they consider the defendant to be in a better position to bear the loss.

When we speak, therefore, of the doctrine of a manufacturer's liability for harm caused by defective products, we must have in mind two developments. The first is the adoption, in one state after another, of the rule of MacPherson v. Buick, which withdraws the immunity that formerly protected a *negligent* manufacturer against an action by a sub-purchaser. The second is the gradual extension of the liability of a *non-negligent* manufacturer—in some classes of cases to purchasers, in some classes of cases to any user; in some classes of cases explicitly, in some by indirect and in part fictitious means.

The question arises whether another Cardozo might extract from the various cases in which a strict liability has been imposed on manufacturers—on the basis of extra-hazardous activity, for so-called breach of implied warranty, or under a theory of *res ipsa loquitur*—a new general principle. Can such a principle "emerge" *not* from the holdings of the cases but from the doctrines and statutes which impose strict liability in restricted situations?

ESCOLA v. COCA COLA BOTTLING CO. OF FRESNO

Supreme Court of California, 1944.
24 Cal.2d 453, 150 P.2d 436.

[Plaintiff, a waitress in a restaurant, was injured when a bottle of Coca Cola exploded in her hand. Plaintiff did not allege any specific act of negligence on the part of defendant, but merely showed that defendant was a bottler who sold and delivered the bottles to the restaurant. Defendant presented evidence that approved methods of inspection had been used. The trial judge let the case go to the jury, which found for plaintiff. Gibson, C. J., speaking for the majority of the Supreme Court, held that under the rule of *res ipsa loquitur* there was sufficient evidence of negligence to enable the jury to find for plaintiff. Edmonds, J., dissented.]

TRAYNOR, J. I concur in the judgment, but I believe the manufacturer's negligence should no longer be singled out as the basis of a plaintiff's right to recover in cases like the present one. In my opinion it should now be recognized that a manufacturer incurs an absolute liability when an article that he has placed on the market, knowing that it is to be used without inspection, proves to have a defect that causes injury to human beings. MacPherson v. Buick Motor Co., 217 N.Y. 382, 111 N.E. 1050 . . . established the principle, recognized by this court, that irrespective of privity of contract, the manufacturer is responsible for an injury caused by such an article to any person who comes in lawful contact with it. [Citations omitted.] In these cases the source of the manufacturer's liability was his negligence in the manufacturing process or in the inspection of component parts supplied by others. Even if there is no negligence, however, public policy demands that responsibility be fixed wherever it will most effectively reduce the hazards of life and health inherent in defective products that reach the market. It is evident that the manufacturer can anticipate some hazards and guard against the recurrence of others, as the public cannot. Those who suffer injury from defective products are unprepared to meet its consequences.

The cost of injury and the loss of time or health may be an overwhelming misfortune to the person injured, and a needless one, for the risk of injury can be insured by the manufacturer and distributed among the public as the cost of doing business. It is to the public interest to discourage the marketing of products having defects that are a menace to the public. If such products nevertheless find their way into the market it is to the public interest to place the responsibility for whatever injury they may cause upon the manufacturer, who, even if he is not negligent in the manufacture of the product, is responsible for its reaching the market. However intermittently such injuries may occur and however haphazardly they may strike, the risk of their occurrence is a constant risk and a general one. Against such a risk there should be general and constant protection and the manufacturer is best situated to afford such protection.

The injury from a defective product does not become a matter of indifference because the defect arises from causes other than the negligence of the manufacturer, such as negligence of a submanufacturer of a component part whose defects could not be revealed by inspection, [citations omitted] or unknown causes that even by the device of res ipsa loquitur cannot be classified as negligence of the manufacturer. The inference of negligence may be dispelled by an affirmative showing of proper care. If the evidence against the fact inferred is "clear, positive, uncontradicted, and of such a nature that it cannot rationally be disbelieved, the court must instruct the jury that the nonexistence of the fact has been established as a matter of law." Blank v. Coffin, 20 Cal.2d 457, 461, 126 P.2d 868, 870. An injured person, however, is not ordinarily in a position to refute such evidence or identify the cause of the defect, for he can hardly be familiar with the manufacturing process as the manufacturer himself is. In leaving it to the jury to decide whether the inference has been dispelled, regardless of the evidence against it, the negligence rule approaches the rule of strict liability. It is needlessly circuitous to make negligence the basis of recovery and impose what is in reality liability without negligence. If public policy demands that a manufacturer of goods be responsible for their quality regardless of negligence there is no reason not to fix that responsibility openly. . . .

[The judge here calls attention to a statute which imposes criminal liability for the manufacture or disposition of unwholesome food, irrespective of negligence.]

The statute may well be applicable to a bottle whose defects cause it to explode. In any event it is significant that the statute imposes criminal liability without fault, reflecting the public policy of protecting the public from dangerous products placed on the markets, irrespective of negligence in their manufacture. While the Legislature imposes criminal liability only with regard to food products and their containers, there are many other sources of danger. It is to the public interest to prevent injury to the public from any defective goods by the imposition of civil liability generally.

The retailer, even though not equipped to test a product, is under an absolute liability to his customer, for the implied warranties of fitness for proposed use and merchantable quality include a warranty of safety of the product. [Citations omitted.] This warranty is not necessarily a contractual one [citations omitted], for public policy requires that the buyer be insured at the seller's expense against injury. [Citations omitted.] See Prosser, The Implied Warranty of Merchantable Quality, 27 Minn.L.Rev. 117, 124; Brown, The Liability of Retail Dealers for Defective Food Products, 23 Minn.L.Rev. 585. The courts recognize, however, that the retailer cannot bear the burden of this warranty, and allow him to recoup any losses by means of the warranty of safety attending the wholesaler's or manufacturer's sale to him. [Citation omitted.] See Waite, Retail Responsibility and Judicial Law Making, 34 Mich.L.Rev. 494, 509. Such a procedure, however, is needlessly circuitous and engenders wasteful litigation. Much would be gained if the injured person could base his action directly on the manufacturer's warranty.

The liability of the manufacturer to an immediate buyer injured by a defective product follows without proof of negligence from the implied warranty of safety attending the sale. Ordinarily, however, the immediate buyer is a dealer who does not intend to use the product himself, and if the warranty of safety is to serve the purpose of protecting health and safety it must give rights to others than the dealer. In the words of Judge Cardozo in the MacPherson case: "The dealer was indeed the one person of whom it might be said with some approach to certainty that by him the car would not be used. Yet the defendant would have us say that he was the one person whom it was under a legal duty to protect. The law does not lead us to so inconsequent a solution." While the defendant's negligence in the MacPherson case made it unnecessary for the court to base liability on warranty, Judge Cardozo's reasoning recognized the injured person as the real party in interest and effectively disposed of the theory that the liability of the manufacturer incurred by his warranty should apply only to the immediate purchaser. It thus paves the way for a standard of liability that would make the manufacturer guarantee the safety of his product even when there is no negligence.

This court and many others have extended protection according to such a standard to consumers of food products, taking the view that the right of a consumer injured by unwholesome food does not depend "upon the intricacies of the law of sales" and that the warranty of the manufacturer to the consumer in absence of privity of contract rests on public policy. [Citations omitted.] See Perkins, Unwholesome Food as a Source of Liability, 5 Iowa L.Bull. 6, 86. Dangers to life and health inhere in other consumers' goods that are defective and there is no reason to differentiate them from the dangers of defective food products. See Bohlen, Studies in Torts, Basis of Affirmative Obligations, American Cases upon the Liability of Manufacturers and Vendors of Personal Property, 109, 135; Llewellyn, On Warranty of Quality and Society, 36 Col.L.Rev. 699, 704, note 14; Prosser, Torts, p. 692.

In the food products cases the courts have resorted to various fictions to rationalize the extension of the manufacturer's warranty to the consumer: that a warranty runs with the chattel; that the cause of action of the dealer is assigned to the consumer; that the consumer is a third party beneficiary of the manufacturer's contract with the dealer. They have also held the manufacturer liable on a mere fiction of negligence: "Practically he must know it [the product] is fit, or bear the consequences, if it proves destructive." Parks v. C. C. Yost Pie Co., 93 Kan. 334, 144 P. 202, L.R.A.1915C, 179; see Jeanblanc, Manufacturer's Liability to Persons Other than Their Immediate Vendees, 24 Va.L.Rev. 134. Such fictions are not necessary to fix the manufacturer's liability under a warranty if the warranty is severed from the contract of sale between the dealer and the consumer and based on the law of torts as a strict liability. [Citation omitted.] See Prosser, Nuisance Without Fault, 20 Tex.L.Rev. 399, 403; Feezer, Capacity To Bear The Loss As A Factor In The Decison Of Certain Types of Tort Cases, 78 U. of Pa.L.Rev. 805, 79 U. of Pa.L.Rev. 742; Carpenter, The Doctrine of Green v. General Petroleum Corp., 5 So.Cal.L.Rev. 263, 271; Pound, The End of Law As Developed In Legal Rules and Doctrines, 27 Harv.L.Rev. 195, 233. Warranties are not necessarily rights arising under a contract. An action on a warranty "was, in its origin, a pure action of tort," and only late in the historical development of warranties was an action in assumpsit allowed. Ames, The History of Assumpsit, 2 Harv.L.Rev. 1, 8; 4 Williston on Contracts (1936)

§ 970. "And it is still generally possible where a distinction of procedure is observed between actions of tort and of contract to frame the declaration for breach of warranty in tort." Williston, *loc. cit.*; see Prosser, Warranty on Merchantable Quality, 27 Minn.L.Rev. 117, 118. On the basis of the tort character of an action on a warranty, recovery has been allowed for wrongful death as it could not be in an action for breach of contract. [Citations omitted.] Even a seller's express warranty can arise from a noncontractual affirmation inducing a person to purchase the goods. Chamberlain Co. v. Allis-Chalmers, etc., Co., 51 Cal.App.2d 520, 125 P.2d 113. "As an actual agreement to contract is not essential, the obligation of a seller in such a case is one imposed by law as distinguished from one voluntarily assumed. It may be called an obligation either on a quasi-contract or quasi-tort, because remedies appropriate to contract and also to tort are applicable." 1 Williston on Sales, 2d Ed. § 197; see Ballantine, Classification of Obligations, 15 Ill.L. Rev. 310, 325.

As handicrafts have been replaced by mass production with its great markets and transportation facilities, the close relationship between the producer and consumer of a product has been altered. Manufacturing processes, frequently valuable secrets, are ordinarily either inaccessible to or beyond the ken of the general public. The consumer no longer has means or skill enough to investigate for himself the soundness of a product, even when it is not contained in a sealed package, and his erstwhile vigilance has been lulled by the steady efforts of manufacturers to build up confidence by advertising and marketing devices such as trademarks. [Citations omitted.] See Handler, False and Misleading Advertising, 39 Yale L.J. 22; Rogers, Good Will, Trade Marks and Unfair Trading (1914) ch. VI, A Study of the Consumer, p. 65 et seq.; Williston, Liability for Honest Misrepresentations as Deceit, Negligence or Warranty, 42 Harv.L.Rev. 733; 18 Cornell L.Q. 445. Consumers no longer approach products warily but accept them on faith, relying on the reputation of the manufacturer or the trade mark. [Citations omitted.] See Schechter, The Rational Basis for Trade Mark Protection, 40 Harv.L.Rev. 813, 818. Manufacturers have sought to justify that faith by increasingly high standards of inspection and a readiness to make good on defective products by way of replacements and refunds. See Bogert and Fink, Business Practices, Regarding Warranties In the Sale of Goods, 25 Ill.L.Rev. 400. The manufacturer's obligation to the consumer must keep pace with the changing relationship between them; it cannot be escaped because the marketing of a product has become so complicated as to require one or more intermediaries. Certainly there is greater reason to impose liability on the manufacturer than on the retailer who is but a conduit of a product that he is not himself able to test. See Soule, Consumer Protection, 4 Encyclopedia of the Social Sciences, 282; Feezer, Manufacturer's Liability for Injuries Caused by His Products: Defective Automobiles, 37 Mich.L.Rev. 1; Llewellyn, Cases and Materials on Sales, 340 et seq.

The manufacturer's liability should, of course, be defined in terms of the safety of the product in normal and proper use, and should not extend to injuries that cannot be traced to the product as it reached the market.

Questions

1. What is the rule which Judge Traynor, in his concurring opinion, would apply in cases such as this? Is his proposed rule in conflict with the MacPherson rule?

2. What are the moral and social considerations underlying extension of liability, under the proposed Traynor rule, to cases in which the manufacturer is not negligent?

3. How would the widespread adoption of the rule proposed by Judge Traynor affect (a) the price of manufactured goods? (b) the amount of care used to prevent dangerous defects in manufactured goods?

4. Suppose it can be shown from examination of the broken bottle that it was a normal bottle, in no way defective, and suppose further it can be shown that it was subjected to abnormally rough handling by delivery men and that this was probably the cause of its breaking. Should the bottler nevertheless be liable under Judge Traynor's reasoning?

5. Suppose the only evidence introduced by the plaintiff is that the bottle broke and put out her eye, and the only evidence introduced by the defendant is that forty-five per cent of all bottles which break do so because the internal surface is damaged, fifty per cent break because of being struck an abnormally hard blow, three per cent are cracked by the machine that places the cap on them and break when the cap is later removed, and two per cent break because of manufacturing defects in the glass which the manufacturer's inspectors failed to catch and which it would be prohibitively expensive for the bottler to test for. Should the case go to the jury under the doctrine of *res ipsa loquitur?* Should the bottler nevertheless be liable under Traynor's reasoning? See in this connection Andrew Dingwall, "Exploding Bottles," NAACA Law Journal, Vol. 11, p. 158 (1953).

6. If the plaintiff had sued the manufacturer of the bottle, instead of the bottler, could she have won on the same facts? As between the manufacturer and the bottler, which should ultimately bear the loss?

7. Examine the various authorities cited by Judge Traynor to support his argument. Are there significant differences between the type of material cited by Judge Traynor and, for example, the type of material cited by Judge Cardozo in the MacPherson case? Is Judge Traynor's process of reasoning the same as that described by Professor Levi, *supra* p. 527, as "the" process of legal reasoning? What makes it a process of legal reasoning at all?

8. If courts were to follow the suggestions of Judge Traynor in Escola, and apply a strict liability doctrine in such cases, would this constitute judicial legislation?

Note

Legal fictions. In his concurring opinion in Escola (*supra* p. 549), Judge Traynor displays some impatience at judicial use of "fictions." However, the use of legal fictions has been, and still is, a significant aspect of legal reasoning.

A legal fiction is not a lie; it is not intended to deceive. To that extent, at least, the term "fiction" is very apt, for it applies equally well to literature and to law. In writing *The Brothers Karamazov*, Dostoevsky did not intend to make his readers believe that at a certain time and place a man named Smerdyakov killed his natural father Fyodor Karamazov. The reader is asked, rather, to *imagine* that this happened. We call such novels or stories "fiction" to indicate that they are not meant to be taken as true. Similarly a legal fiction is a legal proposition that is not meant to be taken as true.

The term "fiction" derives from the Roman law of procedure, under which certain untrue pleadings could not be challenged. A famous Roman *fictio* was the civil action brought by a foreigner. The older rule had been that only a Roman citizen could bring an action under the Roman civil law—indeed in Latin "civil" law literally meant "citizens'" law; foreigners were governed by the *ius gentium*, the law of (foreign) peoples, of the clans or "nations." In time, however, the foreigner was permitted to bring a "civil" action, but only by alleging that he was (or might have been) a citizen, an allegation which the defendant was forbidden to deny. Thus the wording of the rule—that only a citizen could bring a civil (citizen's) action—was maintained, although the meaning of the words was substantially altered.

Another famous fiction from ancient times is that of adoption. In ancient Rome, as in some contemporary primitive societies, adoption was effectuated by a ceremonious simulation of childbirth; that is, the adoptive mother pretended to be in labor and to give birth to the adopted child, who was brought out from her skirts. This ritual enabled family ties to be created despite the absence of blood relationship, while preserving the form of the older tribal rule to the contrary. In the words of Sir Henry Maine, without the fiction of adoption "it is difficult to understand how society would ever have escaped from its swaddling clothes and taken its first steps toward civilization."

Although we say that the adoptive mother "pretended" to give birth to the adopted child, it is obvious that the pretense was not intended to conceal the fact that the child was not the biological offspring of the mother. The simulation of childbirth did, however, pay formal respect to the older rule that only blood relationship could create family ties. The change in the meaning of that rule was clothed in a ritual designed to reconcile the new with the old and to give to the new the authority of the old.

Where continuity in legal development is highly prized, as in the English common law, legal fictions tend to be favored. Instead of openly making new rules, English and American courts have often adapted old rules to new uses by accepting allegations of fact that are clearly untrue. Thus where the old rule required delivery, and such a requirement no longer made sense, the court spoke of "constructive delivery"—something which was *not* delivery was "deemed to be" delivery. Similarly, the courts have developed doctrines of "constructive notice," "constructive intent," and the like—to avoid the consequences of older rules requiring notice or intent without openly rejecting those rules. In addition, judges may resort to "conclusive presumptions" which have the effect of excluding from consideration matters that were once required to be proved, or that might be required to be proved, by a literal interpretation of existing doctrine: thus according to existing doctrine, a gift must be accepted in order to take effect, but it is "conclusively presumed" that property delivered by a donor out of the donee's presence is accepted by the donee—hence no proof of acceptance is required and no evidence of non-acceptance will be considered. In Wigmore's words, a "conclusive presumption" is a rule of substantive law masquerading as a rule of procedure.

One of the most notorious fictions of English law was the adaptation of the action of trover to enable it to be used to try the question of title to goods. The action had developed in the late middle ages as a means of recovering goods from one who had found them and refused to return them to their owner. In the 17th century, the mere allegation of a finding came to be treated as irrebuttable. The defendant might in fact have taken the goods by force; or he might have honestly believed that they were his as a matter of right. Nevertheless, it was sufficient for the plaintiff to allege that the defendant had found the goods in order to raise the question of which of the two owned them. A similar development took place with respect to the action of ejectment. In order to escape from the rigidities of procedural distinctions rooted in the feudal system of medieval English law, without appearing to reject the authority of the older law, English courts ingeniously devised new forms and new concepts framed in the older language.

It is sometimes assumed that legal fictions no longer have a positive role to play in the development of modern law, that they are a thing of the past. Yet as Lon Fuller wrote in 1931, "the age of the legal fiction is not over." He pointed to two important fictions of contemporary law: the fiction that a child who enters without permission upon land and is injured—for example, is electrocuted by an exposed wire—is not a trespasser but an invitee, who has been "attracted" by the dangerous condition of the premises, with the consequence that the landowner is liable to the child as if the child was one of his guests; and the fiction that an out-of-state driver of an automobile "shall be deemed" to appoint the state registrar of motor vehicles as his or her agent to accept service of a summons, thus enabling the state prosecutor or a resident of the state to initiate a criminal or civil action against the driver within the state. Many other such contemporary fictions could be mentioned, both judicial and statutory in origin. The "implied warranty," for example, is a concept that has great vitality in American courts today, and is the source of a great deal of commercial law and tort law; a warranty "implied in law" presupposes a fictitious promise by the seller of goods to be liable for losses resulting from defects in the goods, and in certain matters the legal implication cannot be defeated even by an express disclaimer by the seller.

We have suggested that a major function of legal fictions is to give to new law the authority of the older law. This means more than many writers have assumed. It means more than merely paying lip-service to the old while in fact rejecting it. It may be true, as Maine and others have stressed, that a legal fiction "conceals, or affects to conceal, the fact that a rule of law has undergone alteration." But that is not the main point. What the fiction accomplishes is to attach the authority of the older words to the altered rule. This was put brilliantly by the great German jurist Savigny, who wrote:

"When a new judicial form arises it is joined directly on to an old and existing institution and in this way the certainty and development of the old is procured for the new. This is the notion of the Fiction, which was of the greatest importance in the development of the Roman law and which has often been laughably misunderstood by moderns . . ."

It is not enough to say that fictions are a useful way of obscuring the fact that the law is changing, and thus of making change palatable to those who would oppose it if it were openly proclaimed. Nor is it enough to attribute fictions to our inability to grasp the full implications of new developments—a "first step toward the mastery of a new thought" (as the German jurist von Jhering put it) or a means of making "a new situation 'thinkable' by converting it into familiar terms" (as Fuller put it). These justifications of fictions are valid, but they do not exhaust their true nature. Fictions are much more than a convenient necessity when a reform of law cannot easily be stated in nonfictitious terms. They have, in addition the positive virtue, in many instances, of procuring for the reform, as Savigny stated, "the certainty and development of the old."

We may better appreciate what fictions may accomplish if we compare them with their nearest relative, the so-called "exception to the rule." Any legal fiction can be restated as an exception to the rule, just as it can be restated as a change in the rule (and just as an exception can be restated as a change in the rule). Given, for example, a rule that only persons can sue and be sued, we can change the rule by saying (a) that a corporation is a (fictitious) person, or (b) that the power of corporations to sue and be sued is an exception to the rule, or (c) that the rule is changed—not only persons but also corporations can sue and be sued. None of these linguistic forms is inherently more odious or less odious than the others. Each has its virtues and its vices.

Both the fiction and the exception pay respect to the older rule. However, the exception does more violence to the rule than the fiction. The exception raises more sharply the question whether there may not be other situations which also call for exceptional treatment. The justification and the limits of the exception require definition. The third alternative—a reformulation of the rule—goes still farther in opening up new possibilities. May corporations sue and be sued because they are associations of persons? May all types of associations sue and be sued? Should different rules be adopted with respect to the procedural powers and liabilities of corporations from those which are applied to the procedural powers and liabilities of persons? Such questions are avoided when the certainty and development of the rules concerning a natural person are procured for an artificial person— by calling them both persons. Indeed, when the term "legal person" was first used in Roman law, the word "person"—*persona*—did not refer to natural persons as such but to the facial masks worn on the stage by actors representing heroes, mythological figures, and gods.

Over a century ago, Maine advanced the brilliant hypothesis that where social necessities and social opinion are in advance of law, there are three instrumentalities "by which law may be brought into harmony with society .   .   . Legal Fictions, Equity, and Legislation." "Their historical order," he wrote, "is that in which I have placed them. Sometimes two of them will be seen operating together, and there are legal systems which have escaped the influence of one or other of them. But I know of no instances in which the order of their appearance has been changed or inverted."

"It is not difficult to understand why fictions in all their forms are particularly congenial to the infancy of society," Maine wrote. "They satisfy the desire for improvement, which is not quite wanting, at the same time that they do not offend the superstitious disrelish for change which is always present. At a particular stage of social progress they are invaluable expedients for overcoming the rigidity of law .   .   ."

At a later stage of historical development, Maine continued, there emerges a new instrumentality for reform of law, Equity, which he defined as "that body of rules existing by the side of the original civil law, founded on distinct principles and claiming incidentally to supersede the civil law in virtue of a superior sanctity inherent in those principles."

"The Equity whether of the Roman Praetors or of the English Chancellors, differs from the Fictions which in each case preceded it, in that the interference with law is open and avowed. On the other hand, it differs from Legislation, the agent of legal improvement which comes after it, in that its claim to authority is grounded not on the prerogative of any external person or body, not even on that of the magistrate who enunciates it, but on the special nature of its principles, to which it is alleged that all law ought to conform. The very conception of a set of principles, invested with a higher sacredness than those of the original law and demanding application independently of the consent of any external body, belongs to a much more advanced stage of thought than that to which legal fictions originally suggested themselves.

"Legislation, the enactments of a legislature which, whether it take the form of an autocratic prince or of a parliamentary assembly, is the assumed organ of the entire society, is the last of the ameliorating instrumentalities. It differs from Legal Fictions just as Equity differs from them, and it is also distinguished from Equity, as deriving its authority from an external body or person. Its obligatory force is independent of its principles. The legislature, what ever be the actual restraints imposed on it by public opinion, is in theory empowered to impose what obligations it pleases on the members of the community. There is nothing to prevent its legislating in the wantonness of caprice. Legislation may be dictated by equity, if that last word be used to indicate some standard of right and wrong to which its enactments happen to be adjusted; but then these enactments are indebted for their binding force to the authority of the legislature, and not to that of the principles on which the legislature acted; and thus they differ from rules of Equity, in the technical sense of the word, which pretend to a paramount sacredness entitling them at once to the recognition of the courts even without the concurrence of prince or parliamentary assembly. It is the more necessary to note these differences because a student of Bentham would be apt to confound Fictions, Equity, and Statute law under the single head of legislation. They all, he would say, involve *law-making;* they differ only in respect of the machinery by which the new law is produced. That is perfectly true, and we must never forget it; but it furnishes no reason why we should deprive ourselves of so convenient a term as Legislation in the special sense. Legislation and Equity are disjoined in the popular mind and in the minds of most lawyers; and it will never do to neglect the distinction between them however conventional, when important practical consequences follow from it."

We have reproduced at some length this famous passage from Maine not for its historical accuracy, which in some respects is doubtful, but because it sheds much light on the process by which the language of law develops—not only the process by which it has developed in past centuries but also the process by which it develops today. Wherever necessary social change is impeded by the rigidity of existing law, and pressure is generated for legal reform three alternatives are presented: to re-define the existing law, giving the old words meaning that they did not formerly have (fiction), to apply the moral principles and ideals which underlie all law and to which the existing law should be subordinated in exceptional cases (equity), or to overthrow the existing law and introduce a new law (legislation).

We have already discussed equity and legislation as two sources and dimensions of law, and two types of legal utterance, placing them in juxtaposition with precedent and custom. Precedent, as Maine himself perceived, is closely related to fiction: when applied in its strict form, it presupposes that the old rule has not changed when it is applied to a new case. Maine's insight that fiction (precedent) precedes equity, and equity precedes legislation, permits us to add a historical dimension to our previous discussion. The balancing of precedent, equity, and legislation tends to proceed in a historical sequence. The pressure of change upon custom—the "is" of the external environment—is met initially by the attempt to find a solution in terms of precedent, what "was." The custom is restated to respond to the pressure of change without conceding that the older rule has been abandoned. At a later stage, a second response is available: to apply a subsidiary law of equity, what "ought to be," envisioned as governing exceptional cases when the ordinary legal remedies are inadequate. Here custom and precedent—what "is" and "was"—are bypassed by what "ought to be." When the time is ripe to embark upon a wholly new course, a third kind of response—legislation—may discard the old rule and restate what henceforth "shall be."

Maine's optimism concerning the time in which he lived, coupled with his interest in large-scale legal development viewed in the perspective of centuries, led him to neglect the fact that the sequence which he discovered is applicable not only to the past but also to current history. Not only "ancient" law but also newly developing law within a "modern" legal system tends to grow through fictions, equity, and legislation, in that sequence. Nor is this accidental, since the human mind—language itself—proceeds in the same way. We start with the old words, the words we have been taught, the speech that has made us what we are. This is the sacred language. These are the names that create the times and spaces in which we live. When our ideas are challenged by new events, we can only respond—at first—by investing the new in the language of the old. The familiar names take on new meaning. But later something more may be needed, and may become possible: a bigger, more general name, drawn from outside the existing legal rules. The allegation that the foreigner is, or might be, a citizen, or that the adopted child is "really" the offspring of the adoptive parent, or that the landowner "attracted" the child onto the land by building an electrified wire fence around it—may fail to satisfy. These now appear as exceptional instances. Equity, fairness, mercy, require that the usual rule be waived. But how to explain the exception? Ultimately, the time may come when a new name is suggested—or shouted: not blood relationship but the sacrament of marriage creates the family; the outsider is "naturalized;" landowners are charged with liability not only to children but also to other innocent persons injured by conditions on their premises, because they can insure against such liability and thus spread the risk among many at low cost. The exception, we now say, has swallowed up the rule, and a new rule is ready to be formulated. New names emerge out of the dialectic of "was," "ought," and "shall be."

HENNINGSEN v. BLOOMFIELD MOTORS, INC., and CHRYSLER CORPORATION

Supreme Court of New Jersey, 1960.
32 N.J. 358, 161 A.2d 69.

FRANCIS, J. Plaintiff Claus H. Henningsen purchased a Plymouth automobile, manufactured by defendant Chrysler Corporation, from defendant Bloomfield Motors, Inc. His wife, plaintiff Helen Henningsen, was injured while driving it and instituted suit against both defendants to recover damages on account of her injuries. Her husband joined in the action seeking compensation for his consequential losses. The complaint was predicated upon breach of express and implied warranties and upon negligence. At the trial the negligence counts were dismissed by the court and the cause was submitted to the jury for determination solely on the issues of implied warranty of merchantability. Verdicts were returned against both defendants and in favor of the plaintiffs. Defendants appealed and plaintiffs cross-appealed from the dismissal of their negligence claim. The matter was certified by this court prior to consideration in the Appellate Division.

The facts are not complicated, but a general outline of them is necessary to an understanding of the case.

On May 7, 1955 Mr. and Mrs. Henningsen visited the place of business of Bloomfield Motors, Inc., an authorized De Soto and Plymouth dealer, to look at a Plymouth. They wanted to buy a car and were considering a Ford or a Chevrolet as well as a Plymouth. They were shown a Plymouth which appealed to them and the purchase followed. The record indicates that Mr. Henningsen intended the car as a Mother's Day gift to his wife. He said the intention was communicated to the dealer. When the purchase order or contract was prepared and presented, the husband executed it alone. His wife did not join as a party.

* * *

The new Plymouth was turned over to the Henningsens on May 9, 1955. No proof was adduced by the dealer to show precisely what was done in the way of mechanical or road testing beyond testimony that the manufacturer's instructions were probably followed. Mr. Henningsen drove it from the dealer's place of business in Bloomfield to their home in Keansburg. On the trip nothing unusual appeared in the way in which it operated. Thereafter, it was used for short trips on paved streets about the town. It had no servicing and no mishaps of any kind before the event of May 19. That day, Mrs. Henningsen drove to Asbury Park. On the way down and in returning the car performed in normal fashion until the accident occurred. She was proceeding north on Route 36 in Highlands, New Jersey, at 20–22 miles per hour. The highway was paved and smooth, and contained two lanes for northbound travel. She was riding in the right-hand lane. Suddenly she heard a loud noise "from the bottom, by the hood." It "felt as if something cracked." The steering wheel spun in her hands; the car veered sharply to the right and crashed into a highway sign and a brick wall. No other vehicle was in any way involved. A bus operator driving in the left-hand lane testified that he observed plaintiffs' car approaching in normal fashion in the opposite direction; "all of a sudden [it] veered at 90 degrees . . . and right into this wall." As a result of the impact, the front of the car was so badly damaged that it was impossible to determine if any of the parts of the steering wheel mechanism or workmanship or assembly were defective or improper prior to the accident. The condition was such that the collision insurance carrier, after inspection, declared the vehicle a total loss. It had 468 miles on the speedometer at the time.

The insurance carrier's inspector and appraiser of damaged cars, with 11 years of experience, advanced the opinion, based on the history and his examination, that something definitely went "wrong from the steering wheel down to the front wheels" and that the untoward happening must have been due to mechanical defect or failure; "something down there had to drop off or break loose to cause the car" to act in the manner described.

As has been indicated, the trial court felt that the proof was not sufficient to make out a *prima facie* case as to the negligence of either the manufacturer or the dealer. The case was given to the jury, therefore, solely on the warranty theory, with results favorable to the plaintiffs against both defendants.

* * *

I.

The Claim of Implied Warranty against the Manufacturer.

In the ordinary case of sale of goods by description an implied warranty of merchantability is an integral part of the transaction. R.S. 46:30–20, N.J.S.A. If the buyer, expressly or by implication, makes known to the seller the particular purpose for which the article is required and it appears that he has relied on the seller's skill or judgment, an implied warranty arises of reasonable fitness for that purpose. R.S. 46:30–21(1), N.J.S.A. The former type of warranty simply means that the thing sold is reasonably fit for the general purpose for which it is manufactured and sold. . . .

Of course such sales, whether oral or written, may be accompanied by an express warranty. Under the broad terms of the Uniform Sale of Goods Law any affirmation of fact relating to the goods is an express warranty if the natural tendency of the statement is to induce the buyer to make the purchase. R.S. 46:30–18, N.J.S.A. And over the years since the almost universal adoption of the act, a growing awareness of the tremendous development of modern business methods has prompted the courts to administer that provision with a liberal hand. Vold, Law of Sales, § 86, p. 429 (2d ed. 1959). Solicitude toward the buyer plainly harmonizes with the intention of the Legislature. That fact is manifested further by the later section of the act which preserves and continues any permissible implied warranty, despite an express warranty, unless the two are inconsistent. R.S. 46:30–21 (6), N.J.S.A.

The uniform act codified, extended and liberalized the common law of sales. The motivation in part was to ameliorate the harsh doctrine of *caveat emptor,* and in some measure to impose a reciprocal obligation on the seller to beware. The transcendent value of the legislation, particularly with respect to implied warranties, rests in the fact that obligations on the part of the seller were imposed by operation of law, and did not depend for their existence upon express agreement of the parties. And of tremendous significance in a rapidly expanding commercial society was the recognition of the right to recover damages on account of personal injuries arising from a breach of warranty. . . .

The particular importance of this advance resides in the fact that under such circumstances strict liability is imposed upon the maker or seller of the product. Recovery of damages does not depend upon proof of negligence or knowledge of the defect. . . .

As the Sales Act and its liberal interpretation by the courts threw this protective cloak about the buyer, the decisions in various jurisdictions revealed beyond doubt that many manufacturers took steps to avoid these ever increasing warranty obligations. Realizing that the act governed the relationship of buyer and seller, they undertook to withdraw from actual and direct contractual contact with the buyer. They ceased selling products to the consuming public through their own employees and making contracts of sale in their own names. Instead, a system of independent dealers was established; their products were sold to dealers who in turn dealt with the buying public, ostensibly solely in their own personal capacity as sellers. In the past in many instances, manufacturers were able to transfer to the dealers burdens imposed by the act and thus achieved a large measure of immunity for themselves. But, as will be noted in more detail hereafter, such marketing practices, coupled with the advent of large scale advertising by manufacturers to promote the purchase of these goods from dealers by members of the public, provided a basis upon which the existence of express or implied warranties was predicated, even though the manufacturer was not a party to the contract of sale.

. . . [A] question of first importance to be decided is whether an implied warranty of merchantability by Chrysler Corporation accompanied the sale of the automobile to Claus Henningsen.

* * *

Chrysler points out that an implied warranty of merchantability is an incident of a contract of sale. It concedes, of course, the making of the original sale to Bloomfield Motors, Inc., but maintains that this transaction marked the terminal point of its contractual connection with the car. Then Chrysler urges that since it was not a party to the sale by the dealer to Henningsen, there is no privity of contract between it and the plaintiffs, and the absence of this privity eliminates any such implied warranty.

There is no doubt that under early common-law concepts of contractual liability only those persons who were parties to the bargain could sue for a breach of it. In more recent times a noticeable disposition has appeared in a number of jurisdictions to break through the narrow barrier of privity when dealing with sales of goods in order to give realistic recognition to a universally accepted fact. The fact is that the dealer and the ordinary buyer do not, and are not expected to, buy goods, whether they be foodstuffs or automobiles, exclusively for their own consumption or use. Makers and manufacturers know this and advertise and market their products on that assumption; witness, the "family" car, the baby foods, etc. The limitations of privity in contracts for the sale of goods developed their place in the law when marketing conditions were simple, when maker and buyer frequently met face to face on an equal bargaining plane and when many of the products were relatively uncomplicated and conducive to inspection by a buyer competent to evaluate their quality. See, Feezer, "Manufacturer's Liability for Injuries Caused by His Products," 37 Mich.L.Rev. 1 (1938). With the advent of mass marketing, the manufacturer became remote from the purchaser, sales were accomplished through intermediaries, and the demand for the product was created by advertising media. In such an economy it became obvious that the consumer was the person being cultivated. Manifestly, the connotation of "consumer" was broader than that of "buyer." He signified such a person who, in the reasonable contemplation of the parties to the sale, might be expected to use the product. Thus, where the commodities sold are such that if defectively manufactured they will be dangerous to life or limb, then society's interests can only be protected by eliminating the requirement of privity between the maker and his dealers and the reasonably expected ultimate consumer. In that way the burden of losses consequent upon use of defective articles is borne by those who are in a position to either control the danger or make an equitable distribution of the losses when they do occur. As Harper & James put it, "The interest in consumer protection calls for warranties by the maker that *do* run with the goods, to reach all who are likely to be hurt by the use of the unfit commodity for a purpose ordinarily to be expected." 2 Harper & James, supra 1571, 1572; also see, 1535; Prosser, supra, 506–511. As far back as 1932, in the well known case of Baxter v. Ford Motor Co., 168 Wash. 456, 12 P.2d 409 (Sup.Ct.1932), affirmed 15 P.2d 1118, 88 A.L.R. 521 (Sup.Ct.1932), the Supreme Court of Washington gave recognition to the impact of then existing commercial practices on the strait jacket of privity, saying:

"It would be unjust to recognize a rule that would permit manufacturers of goods to create a demand for their products by representing that they possess qualities which they, in fact, do not possess, and then, because there is no privity of contract existing between the consumer and the manufacturer, deny the consumer the right to recover if damages result from the absence of those qualities, when such absence is not readily noticeable." 12 P.2d at page 412.

* * *

Although only a minority of jurisdictions have thus far departed from the requirement of privity, the movement in that direction is most certainly gathering momentum. Liability to the ultimate consumer in the absence of direct contractual connection has been predicated upon a variety of theories. Some courts hold that the warranty runs with the article like a covenant running with land; others recognize a third-party beneficiary thesis; still others rest their decision on the ground that public policy requires recognition of a warranty made directly to the consumer.

* * *

Most of the cases where lack of privity has not been permitted to interfere with recovery have involved food and drugs. [Citations omitted] In fact, the rule as to such products has been characterized as an exception to the general doctrine. But more recently courts, sensing the inequity of such limitation, have moved into broader fields. . . .

We see no rational doctrinal basis for differentiating between a fly in a bottle of beverage and a defective automobile. The unwholesome beverage may bring illness to one person, the defective car, with its great potentiality for harm to the driver, occupants, and others, demands even less adherence to the narrow barrier of privity.

Under modern conditions the ordinary layman, on responding to the importuning of colorful advertising, has neither the opportunity nor the capacity to inspect or to determine the fitness of an automobile for use; he must rely on the manufacturer who has control of its construction, and to some degree on the dealer who, to the limited extent called for by the manufacturer's instructions, inspects and services it before delivery. In such a marketing milieu his remedies and those of persons who properly claim through him should not depend "upon the intricacies of the law of sales. The obligation of the manufacturer should not be based alone on privity of contract. It should rest, as was once said, upon 'the demands of social justice.'" Mazetti v. Armour & Co., 75 Wash. 622, 135 P. 633, 635, 48 L.R.A., N.S., 213 (Sup.Ct.1913). "If privity of contract is required," then, under the circumstances of modern merchandising, "privity of contract exists in the consciousness and understanding of all right-thinking persons." Madouros v. Kansas City Coca-Cola Bottling Co., supra, 90 S.W.2d at page 450.

Accordingly, we hold that under modern marketing conditions, when a manufacturer puts a new automobile in the stream of trade and promotes its purchase by the public, an implied warranty that it is reasonably suitable for use as such accompanies it into the hands of the ultimate purchaser. Absence of agency between the manufacturer and the dealer who makes the ultimate sale is immaterial.

Questions

1. Do you agree with the decision in Henningsen v. Chrysler? Why?

2. Would it be proper to say that the Uniform Sales Act served as a precedent for the decision in Henningsen v. Chrysler?

3. Review section 3.3, *supra* p. 128. Is the opinion in Henningsen v. Chrysler an example of the application of the doctrine of analogy in a civil case?

Note

The Henningsen case is but one of many state court decisions in which manufacturers' liability is predicated on a warranty or strict liability theory. Compare and contrast the reasoning and the judicial styles displayed in two of these cases which are summarized below.

1. In Greenman v. Yuba Power Products Inc., 59 Cal.2d 57, 27 Cal.Rptr. 697, 377 P.2d 897 (1963), plaintiff sued to recover damages for personal injuries caused by a defective power tool. The defendants were the manufacturer of the tool and the retailer who had sold it to the plaintiff.

The case against the retailer was submitted to the jury on a theory of breach of implied warranty. The case against the manufacturer went to the jury on alternative theories of negligence in manufacture, and breach of express warranties. (Plaintiff had alleged that express warranties were made in a manufacturer's brochure which accompanied the tool.) The trial judge dismissed that part of the plaintiff's complaint which alleged breach of implied warranty by the manufacturer. The jury returned a verdict in favor of the defendant retailer but found the manufacturer liable in the amount of $65,000. An appeal from that verdict and the judgment of the trial court was taken to the Supreme Court of California.

On appeal the manufacturer made several assignments of error which challenged the sufficiency of that part of the plaintiff's case which was based on breach of express warranty. The Supreme Court of California found no merit in those assignments of error and affirmed the judgment in a unanimous opinion delivered by Judge Traynor, author of the concurring opinion in Escola v. Coca Cola Bottling Co., reprinted *supra* at p. 549. After discussing the propriety of plaintiff's express warranty theory, and apparently holding that the plaintiff could succeed on that theory, Judge Traynor found a broader ground for affirming the trial court decision.

> ". . . [T]o impose strict liability on the manufacturer under the circumstances of this case, it was not necessary for plaintiff to establish an express warranty . . . A manufacturer is strictly liable in tort when an article he places on the market knowing that it is to be used without inspection for defects, proves to have a defect that causes injury to a human being. Recognized first in the case of unwholesome food products, such liability has now been extended to a variety of other products that create as great or greater hazards if defective. [Citations omitted.]
>
> "Although in these cases strict liability has usually been based on the theory of an express or implied warranty running from the manufacturer to the plaintiff, the abandonment of the requirement of a contract between them, the recognition that the liability is not assumed by agreement but imposed by law . . . [citations omitted], and the refusal to permit the manufacturer to define the scope of its own responsibility for defective products . . . [citations omitted], make clear that the liability is not one governed by the law of contract warranties but by the law of strict liability in tort. . . .
>
> "We need not recanvass the reasons for imposing strict liability on the manufacturer. They have been fully articulated in the cases cited above. (See also . . . Escola v. Coca Cola Bottling Co., 24 Cal.2d 453, 461 [150 P.2d 436], concurring opinion.) The purpose of such liability is to insure that the costs of injuries resulting from defective products are borne by the manufacturers that put such products on the market rather than by the injured persons who are powerless to protect themselves. . . . To establish the manufacturer's liability it was sufficient that plaintiff proved that he was injured while using the [tool] in a way it was intended to be used as a result of a defect in design and manufacture of which plaintiff was not aware that made the [tool] unsafe for its intended use."

2.   In Goldberg v. Kollsman Instrument Corp., 12 N.Y.2d 432, 240 N.Y.S.2d 592, 191 N.E.2d 81 (1963), plaintiff, as administratrix of her daughter's estate, sued to recover damages.   The daughter had succumbed to injuries suffered in the crash of a commercial airliner. Defendants were American Airlines Inc., the owner and operator of the plane, Lockheed Aircraft Inc., the designer and builder of the plane, and Kollsman Instrument Corporation, the manufacturer of the plane's altimeter.   Plaintiff alleged that the crash was caused by defects in the altimeter.

The trial judge dismissed the causes of action in which plaintiff sought to recover against Lockheed and Kollsman on a theory of breach of implied warranty.   On appeal the Court of Appeals of New York reversed the decision as to Lockheed and affirmed the decision as to Kollsman.   The majority (four judges) opinion alluded to, but did not adopt, the "strict liability in tort" theory advanced by Judge Traynor in the Greenman case, *supra*.   Instead the majority held against Lockheed on an implied warranty theory which, however, it treated as a remedy in tort rather than in contract.   The majority opinion stated:

" . . .   A breach of warranty, it is now clear, is not only a violation of the sales contract out of which the warranty arises but is a tortious wrong suable by a non-contracting party whose use of the warranted article is within the reasonable contemplation of the vendor or manufacturer.   As to foodstuffs we definitely ruled in Greenberg v. Forenz, (9 N.Y.2d 1950 . . .) that persons thus protected . . .   include the purchaser's family.   We went no further in that case because the facts required no farther reach of the rule.

"The concept that as to 'things of danger,' the manufacturer must answer to intended users for faulty design or manufacture is an old one in this state.   The most famous decision is MacPherson v. Buick Motor Co., (217 N.Y. 382) holding the manufacturer liable in negligence to one who purchased a faulty Buick automobile from a dealer . . .   But the MacPherson opinion cites much older cases such as Devlin v. Smith, (89 N.Y. 470 [1882]) . . .   MacPherson and its successors dispelled the idea that a manufacturer was immune from liability in tort for violation of his duty to make his manufactures fit and safe.   Today we know . . .   that, at least where an article is of such character that when used for the purpose for which it is made it is likely to be a source of danger to several or many people if not properly designed and fashioned, the manufacturer as well as the vendor is liable, for breach of law-implied warranties, to the persons whose use is contemplated.   The MacPherson holding was an 'extension' of existing court-made liability law.   In a sense, Greenberg v. Forenz . . .   [was an extension] in favor of noncontracting consumers.   But it is no extension at all to include airplanes and the passengers for whose use they are built—and, indeed, decisions are at hand which have upheld complaints, sounding in breach of warranty, against manufacturers of aircraft where passengers lost their lives when the planes crashed [citations omitted].

> ". . . However, for the present at least we do not think it is necessary so to extend this rule as to hold liable the manufacturer (defendant Kollsman) of a component part. Adequate protection is provided for the passengers by casting in liability the airplane manufacturer which put into the market the completed aircraft."

Three judges dissented in this case. They argued that there were numerous deficiencies in the approach taken by the majority. Their chief objections were: that the plane in question had been inspected and certified for use by a government agency, the Federal Aviation Agency, and this should have some bearing on the scope of the defendant's liability to the public; that it is anomalous to hold the airframe manufacturer strictly liable and excuse the manufacturer of the part which ostensibly caused the crash; that it is equally anomalous to hold the airframe manufacturer strictly liable while the prevailing view in New York is that the airline could only be held liable for actual negligence (thus the airline would be excused if the crash was caused by a non-negligent failure in maintenance of the altimeter); and that the majority, while purporting to enforce an implied warranty, was in fact imposing strict liability in tort. The dissenters were especially concerned about this last point. They argued that a decision to impose strict liability in tort should be based on a finding that the party held strictly liable is in the best position to bear the loss and distribute the risk of such losses. The dissenters argued that of the three defendants in this case, the airline was in the best position to assume this liability. But they argued further that as between the airline and its passengers there was no reason to impose strict liability. First, because insurance is available to airline passengers at reasonable rates, and the passengers should be presumed to be aware of the hazards of air travel. Second, because the passengers' interest in air safety is protected by the work of the FAA, thus they do not stand on the same footing as consumers in other markets where there is little or no governmental supervision of product quality.

Questions: If you were a judge faced with the task of articulating a rationale for the imposition of liability on the non-negligent manufacturer of a defective product, would you prefer Judge Traynor's approach in Greenman to the approach taken by the majority of the New York court in Goldberg?

Is the MacPherson case in any sense a precedent for the decision in any of the cases presented in this section (Escola, Henningsen, Greenman, Goldberg)? Or has the MacPherson *doctrine* become simply one of the doctrines (like *res ipsa loquitur*) considered by the courts as providing an analogy to the new doctrine being enunciated?

SECTION 24. THE "PRECEDENT" OF A STATUTE

[The following is taken from WALTER V. SCHAEFER, PRE-
CEDENT AND POLICY, an address given by the Chief Justice of the
Supreme Court of Illinois at the University of Chicago Law School,
April 21, 1955, and published by the University of Chicago Press in
1956. Footnotes are renumbered.]

In what I have said I have used the term "precedent" to refer only to
judicial decisions. That is the way in which working lawyers use it. And
even writers who deal with the problems and the resources of the judge
who is working on the frontiers of the law do not often speak of statutes.
That is because the common law has drawn the principle which decides the
future case from the facts and the decision of the past case. Common-law
courts have had an uneasy way with statutes. Legislation is grudgingly
given its letter, but no more. The common-law attitude, says Sir Frederick
Pollock, "cannot well be accounted for except upon the theory that Parliament generally changes the law for the worse, and that the business of the
judge is to keep the mischief of its interference within the narrowest possible bounds." [1]

Writing in 1908, however, Dean Pound suggested that the trend of the
common law was toward a view more like that of the civil law, which finds
its rules for decision in statutes. He predicted that common-law courts
would one day receive a statute "fully into the body of the law to be reasoned from by analogy the same as any other rule of law, regarding it . . .
as of equal or coordinate authority in this respect with judge-made rules
upon the same general subject." [2] Such an attitude indeed prevailed in England in early days under the doctrine of "the equity of the statute." But
Blackstone's view of the common law as a completed, fully rounded system
left no room for that doctrine. And so we find English judges saying in
1785: "We are bound to take the act of Parliament as they have made it;
a *casus omissus* can in no way be supplied by a court of law for that would
be to make law." [3] And in this country, in 1797, we find: "The Act . . .
being in derogation of the common law is to be taken strictly." [4]

Chief Justice Stone, surveying the future of the common law in 1936,
regretted that statutes were regarded as "in, but not of, the law." "Notwithstanding their genius for the generation of new law from that already
established," he said, "the common-law courts have given little recognition
to statutes as starting points for judicial law-making comparable to judicial
decisions." [5] He looked forward to a day when statutes, like judicial de-

---

1. Sir Frederick Pollock, Essays in Jurisprudence and Ethics (London, 1882),
p. 85.

2. Roscoe Pound, "Common Law and
Legislation," Harvard Law Review,
Vol. 21, pp. 385–386 (1908).

3. See James L. Landis, "Statutes and
the Sources of Law," Harvard Legal

Essays (Cambridge, Mass., 1934), p.
235.

4. Brown v. Barry, 3 Dall. (U.S.) 365,
367.

5. Harlan F. Stone, "The Common Law
in the United States," Harvard Law
Review, Vol. 50, p. 14 (1936).

cisions, would be used as social data, or as points of departure, in the common-law technique of reasoning by analogy. And he spoke of "the ideal of a unified system of judge-made and statutory law woven into a seamless whole by the processes of adjudication." "On occasion," he said, "legislatures have made so bold as to direct that a statute shall be extended to cases plainly within its reason and spirit though not within the strict letter, a practice which if skillfully employed may yet restore to the courts a privilege which they renounced only because they have mistakenly regarded statutory enactments in some degree less a part of the law than their own decisions." [6] I should like to explore the extent to which these prophecies are materializing.

The contrast between the impact of a statute and that of a common-law decision upon the body of the law is graphically shown in Dean Landis' description of the effect of Rylands v. Fletcher [7] upon Anglo-American law. There the House of Lords decided that one who artificially accumulated water upon his land was absolutely liable for damage caused by its escape. The decision was based upon the analogy drawn from earlier cases which had dealt with the liability of the man who kept wild animals upon his land. The doctrine of Rylands v. Fletcher has been important in our law since 1868, and the rule there announced has been applied in many situations. Dean Landis says:

> Had Parliament in 1868 adopted a similar rule, no such permeating results to the general body of Anglo-American law would have ensued. And this would be true, though the act had been preceded by a thorough and patient inquiry by a Royal Commission into the business of storing large volumes of water and its concommitant risks, and even though the same Lords who approved Mr. Fletcher's claim had in voting 'aye' upon the measure given reasons identical with those contained in their judgments. Such a statute would have caused no ripple in the processes of adjudication either in England or on the other side of the Atlantic, and the judicial mind would have failed to discern the essential similarity between water stored in reservoirs, crude petroleum stored in tanks, and gas and electricity confined and maintained upon the premises.[8]

There has not been complete agreement as to precisely what is meant by the use of statutes by analogy. Ernest Freund had his view on this ques-

---

6. *Ibid.*, at 12, 15–16.

7. 1866, L.R. 1 Ex. 265, aff'd 1868, L.R. 3 H.L. 330. [The defendants (Rylands and his associates) built a dam to accumulate water for their mill. The reservoir site had formerly been used for coal mining. There were several old shafts on the site, all of which were filled with earth and debris so that they were not visible from the surface. As the water accumulated in the reservoir it percolated into one of the old shafts and burst through the earth fill. The water then flowed under the property adjacent to the mill

site and flooded a mine which was being worked by the plaintiffs (Fletcher and his associates). The flooding prevented further work in that mine and it had to be abandoned. Fletcher sued for damages and Rylands pleaded in defense that there had been no negligence in the construction of the reservoir. The House of Lords decision for Fletcher is often cited as the leading case on strict liability—liability without fault—in Anglo-American tort law.]

8. Landis, *op. cit.* p. 221.

tion,[9] and more recent writers have used their own shadings of meaning. Because my present concern is with the materials available to a judge in deciding a case, I want to look broadly at the ways in which judges apply statutes beyond the letter of their terms, without concern for refinements of definition.

Some of the doctrines of the common law have been so long accepted that we tend to forget that their origin is statutory. The prescriptive period of twenty years of adverse possession came into the common law from an early statute of limitations. It appeared first unobtrusively, the lapse of time giving rise to a presumption of a lost deed, and over the years was converted into a rule of law. So with the presumption of death arising from seven years' unexplained absence, which was drawn from statutes dealing with remarriage when husband or wife had been absent for seven years, and with succession to property in the case of the vanished life-tenant.[10]

There are other illustrations. Congress specifies a form of bill of lading to govern shipments by rail, and by analogy the requirements of that statute are read into bills of lading governing shipments by boat.[11] In the Coronado Coal case it is held that an unincorporated labor union may be sued in its own name, because it has so many of the attributes of a corporation, which of course is suable by statute.[12] And in the Hutcheson case a policy drawn from a statute regulating injunctions in labor disputes governs decisions as to the legality of union conduct.[13] In the United Mine Workers case [14] four dissenting justices would have found in the maximum penalty provision of the War Labor Disputes Act a limitation upon the penalty to be imposed for violation of an injunction, although the statute did not directly bear upon the problem before the court. Statutes which prohibit strikes against public utilities motivate decisions enjoining strikes against hospitals, although the statutes are silent as to hospitals.[15]

These are scattered instances. Let us turn to a field where the cases come in clusters. After the middle of the last century the Married Women's Acts gave to married women the right to own their separate property, to contract, and to sue and be sued. Almost a hundred years have passed, and areas of the law which were not directly mentioned in those acts are still responding in lively fashion to their impact. Can one spouse be guilty of stealing from the other? Can they conspire together to violate the law? Is the crime committed by the wife in her husband's presence presumed to have been coerced by him? So with the law of evidence. Are husband and wife still incompetent to testify for or against each other, as they were at common law? And, in the law of torts, can one spouse sue the other for

9. Ernest Freund, "The Interpretation of Statutes," Univ. of Pennsylvania Law Review, Vol. 65, p. 207 (1917).

10. See James B. Thayer, A Preliminary Treatise on Evidence (Boston, 1898), p. 319 ff.

11. South & Central American Commercial Co., Inc. v. Panama R. R. Co., 237 N.Y. 287, 142 N.E. 666 (1923).

12. United Mine Workers of America v. Coronado Coal Co., 259 U.S. 344, 42 S. Ct. 570 (1922).

13. United States v. Hutcheson, 312 U. S. 219, 61 S.Ct. 463 (1941).

14. United States v. United Mine Workers of America, 330 U.S. 258, 67 S.Ct. 677 (1947).

15. See Jewish Hospital of Brooklyn v. "John Doe" and "Richard Roe," 252 App.Div. 581, 300 N.Y.S. 1111 (1937).

negligent or wilful injury, or does the common-law barrier still exist? Is the husband liable for his wife's torts, as he was at common law? Has the common-law immunity of one spouse from an action by the other sufficient vitality today to justify its importation into a wrongful death statute? Is the husband's common-law immunity available to his employer when the wife's injury has been caused by her husband's negligence during the course of his employment?

These, and many more, are live questions in the law today. Different answers are given by different courts. But, whatever answer is given, it rests upon an appraisal of the effect of the Married Women's Acts. The radiations from those statutes cover a breadth not even suggested in their language.

Another use of statutes to govern conduct beyond their letter is so commonplace as to go almost without notice. A statute prohibits certain conduct and provides a penalty by way of fine or imprisonment for its violation. It contains no suggestion as to civil liability. Yet everywhere the breach of such a statute which causes harm to another can give rise to civil liability. Dispute will center upon whether or not a particular statute should be so applied, but the propriety of the technique which extends the statute beyond its words goes unchallenged.

The new way with a statute which Dean Pound predicted is not yet here. But it is clear, I think, that the common law's insulation from statutes is thinner than it was. The shift has not been pronounced; the instances are still sporadic. But such a shift in attitude can be measured accurately only from a perspective more remote than ours. I should guess that the pace will accelerate as advocates become alert to the possibility that decisions in common-law cases can be influenced by principles drawn from statutes.

SECTION 25. REASONING FROM DOCTRINE AND PRECEDENT: A COMPARATIVE AND HISTORICAL ANALYSIS

SECTION 25.1 "COMMON LAW" AND "CIVIL LAW"

Scholars have classified the legal systems of the West into two main types, the so-called common law system and the so-called civil law system. The common law system is derived from the law of England and prevails in Great Britain (except Scotland), the United States (except the state of Louisiana), Canada (except the province of Quebec), Australia, New Zealand, Ireland, the Philippines, India, Israel, Egypt, and other countries which have been subject to English influence. The civil law system is derived, in part, from Roman law and prevails in France, Germany, Italy, Spain, Switzerland, some other countries of Continental Europe (but not the Scandanavian countries), and in some non-European countries—notably Japan, Turkey, and the countries of Latin America.

The main distinctions between these two types of legal systems lie in differences regarding the kinds of authoritative materials upon which decisions are based. In "common law" countries judicial opinions are a primary source of law and prior judicial decisions are binding precedents in subsequent cases. In "civil law" countries, on the other hand, the primary source of law is legislation and courts are bound not by precedents but by provisions of comprehensive *codes* of criminal law, civil law, and procedure. Such codes do not generally exist in "common law" countries. Statutory law is, to be sure, an important part of the common law system, but it usually consists of a large body of separate enactments, each of which deals with some particular type of problem. The codes, on the other hand, are unified bodies of statutory law which are intended to be systematic, comprehensive, and internally consistent. They provide a broad doctrinal base for deciding cases. Accordingly they tend to be more general and abstract than statutes in "common law" countries.[1]

Derived from the distinction between the kinds of authoritative materials upon which decisions are based in the two systems is a further distinction between methods of judicial reasoning. In "common law" countries the starting point for judicial reasoning is said to lie in past decisions. (This is so even in cases where a statute is applied, for a prior judicial interpretation of the statute has force as precedent.) In "civil law" countries, on the other hand, the starting point for judicial reasoning is said to lie in principles and concepts laid down in the codes—or in statutes. Thus "common law" judicial reasoning is said to be more empirical, "civil law" judicial reasoning more abstract.

SECTION 25.2   THE COMMON FOUNDATIONS OF WESTERN LEGAL SCIENCE

These distinctions between the "common law" and "civil law" systems are overdrawn. In fact, as Edmund Burke said almost two hundred years ago, "the law of every country of Europe is derived from the same sources."

The legal tradition of all the nations of Western Europe, and hence of all nations which have inherited or adopted that tradition, dates from the 11th and 12th centuries. To understand the legal transformation that took place at that time, it is necessary to start by depicting the kind of law which existed in the Frankish Empire and in Anglo-Saxon England from the 6th to the 10th centuries.

Frankish (and Anglo-Saxon) law was, on the one hand, *folklaw*, tribal and local in character, and, on the other hand, *official law*, im-

---

1. For a general survey of the con-   Mehren, The Civil Law System, (Engle-
   tinental codes, see Arthur T. Von   wood, Cliffs, N. J., 1957), Ch. 2.

perial and feudal in character.[1] The folklaw was based primarily on the family unit, and most of the rules found in the codes occasionally promulgated (the so-called *leges barbarorum*—the Salic law, the Laws of Alfred, and others) were rules of the blood-feud, largely concerning negotiations between the family of a victim and that of the assailant, payment of tariffs to the injured person or his or her kin or perhaps to a local official (so much for the loss of a leg, so much for an eye, so much if the victim was a free man, so much if a slave, and the like).

Local courts existed to decide disputes; jurisdiction was voluntary, however, and even if the parties accepted its jurisdiction the court could not compel them to submit to its decision. In Anglo-Saxon England the hundred court met every four weeks and the shire court twice a year;[2] the system on the Continent was similar. The freemen of the hundred were in duty bound to attend the court as "doomsmen"—to declare the law and make the dooms.[3] These early People's Courts administered formal law, that is, law based on form and formality. Proof was by oath and by ordeal: in oath procedure, the right words had to be said without slip or trip, and the right ceremonial acts had to be performed punctiliously; in the ordeals, if the defendant sank in the water he or she was innocent, if not he or she was guilty, or if his hand blistered from the hot iron he or she was guilty, if not, innocent.

The formality of proof was connected with the fact that the law was almost entirely unwritten. "So long as law is unwritten," says Maitland, "it must be dramatized and acted. Justice must assume a picturesque garb, or she will not be seen."[4] Occasional written documents issued by kings indicated laws which were recently enacted or difficult to enforce or which for some other special reason had to be in writing.

The king took little initiative in the making of folklaw. It was not administered in his name or under his supervision. Further, the local authorities who carried on administration did not do so as the king's delegates. There was no royal law of contract, or of inheritance, or of marriage, or of landlord and tenant. When the king promulgated written laws they were more in the nature of exhortations to keep the peace and desist from crime; he had to beg and pray, as Maitland says,

1. *Cf.* Rudolf Sohm, Fränkisches Recht und römisches Recht (Weimar, 1880); Munroe Smith, The Development of European Law (New York, 1928), p. 155ff.

2. The hundred and the shire were administrative units organized largely for purposes of taxation and law enforcement. The hundred was smaller than the shire, the relationship between them being something on the order of the relationship between a town and a county.

3. The dooms were the judgments of these courts, usually assessments of money.

4. *Cf.* F. W. Maitland, The Constitutional History of England (Cambridge, 1913), p. 4 ff. "Justice must not only be done, it must also be seen to be done," is an often quoted aphorism of a modern English judge.

for he could not command and punish. Indeed, Anglo-Saxon laws contain provisions stating that when a person exhausted his opportunities in the local courts, he should *not* go to the king for a remedy.

The pagan folklaw of the tribal people of the West was essentially static. There were few, if any, built-in forces for progress. The kingship, however, exerted strong pressures for change, especially after the introduction of Christianity. The king was the military and religious head of the peoples under him. Thus Charlemagne, for example, was able to mobilize the various peoples into a unified military power in wars against the Arabs, the Norse, and the Slavs, just as across the Channel a century later Alfred the Great was able to establish military unity among the Angles, Saxons and other tribes. Moreover, both Charlemagne and Alfred were also the spiritual heads of their respective empires. They called church councils and promulgated Canon Law. They appointed bishops and archbishops. Moving about through the localities of their realm—and the king's court was continually moving, for otherwise there were few means of communication—they heard cases for mercy's sake: cases of widows or orphans or men who had no families to protect them, or no lords; cases of the very worst crimes for which no money payment could be satisfaction. This was part of their jurisdiction as patriarchs of their people.

The king was outside the folklaw. He governed his large and important household by his own law, official law. His household officers—treasurer, secretary, and the like—gradually became institutionalized; the count of the stable became the constable, the secretary became the chancellor, the chamberlain and butler and other household servants in time became high officials of the realm. The king granted lands to the members of his household, and especially to churchmen. These lands were given immunity from local tribal law and placed directly under the household law of the king. Further, the guardianship which the king exercised over his household, as well as over widows, orphans, and the like, was transferred by him to his officials dispersed on the lands which they held of him. In this way feudalism developed. Bishops and great men parcelled out the lands thus given them by the king, and in turn received the official allegiance and subordination of the lords to whom they made these grants. This process, which developed rapidly in the 9th and 10th centuries on the Continent, does not seem to have made headway until the 11th century in Anglo-Saxon England, and then only slightly. Therefore it has been said that when the Normans, who succeeded to the Western part of the Frankish Empire in the 10th and 11th centuries, came to England they saw there a law which was the image of that of their own childhood. England was still largely in a folklaw stage while among the Normans folklaw had been largely covered over with feudalism.

But Frankish official law, despite its central origins, tended to become local; its force was centrifugal, and by the time power had been distributed to lords and underlords and under-underlords there was little left at the center.   The king as Chief Baron had remarkably little strength in a society whose economy was so completely decentralized.   Thus if we look at Norman England from the Conquest to the accession of Henry II in 1154 we see the substitution of feudal legal institutions for tribal without any real change in the substance of the folklaw or in its local character.   What happened was that the hundred courts began to fall into the hands of the feudal lords and the task of judging in these courts ceased to be the personal duty of the freemen in the hundreds; instead this power became one of the incidents of land tenure, and the lord assumed the duties formerly performed by his tenants in the hundred courts.   In addition there were other changes in the structure of the local court system, changes which also resulted from the introduction of feudalism into England.   However, this restructuring of the local courts did not result in any fundamental changes in substantive law.   For more than one hundred years after the Norman Conquest there was no important modification of contract law, real property law, or any other field of private law, and not a single important piece of legislation.   The change that occurred was administrative—and the strength of the Normans was in administration: the king extended his household system, his feudal system, into the fabric of local and tribal life.   But if we study the king's court in the early 1100s, under Henry I, we find it still a court for "great men and great causes"; a court not in permanent session; a court held only three times a year; a court which rendered only extraordinary justice.

The first mention in English history of a central law-court in the modern sense was in the year 1178.   By a central law-court in the modern sense is meant (a) a permanent tribunal, (b) which exists solely to hear and decide cases, (c) exercising general jurisdiction (that is, hearing cases more or less of all kinds), (d) in the name of the king as head of the English realm.

In 1178 Henry II appointed five members of his household (*de sua familia*)—two clergy and three laymen—to "remain in his court" to hear the claims of the people.   This was a body separate from the rest of the household, separate from what had for some time been called the King's Court (*Curia Regis*), though it was expressly stated that the new body was not to depart from the Curia Regis as that court made its travels, with the king, throughout the realm.   Moreover, it was also stated that the newly appointed five-man tribunal was to leave more important and more difficult cases to the *sapientiores*, the wiser men, of the Curia Regis.   Thus the Curia Regis was divided into a law-court of five men—called justiciars (*justiciares*)—and the *sapientiores*, who are usually thought to have been the emerging King's Council.   The justiciars were in effect delegates of the Curia Regis.   Apart from the ecclesiastical judges, of whom we shall speak in more detail shortly, they were the first professional judges in English history.

By 1180 the justices who made up the newly established court were no longer traveling about with the king and his whole *familia*, his whole Curia, but residing at Westminster. And from 1194 there are continuous records of the pleas held before this court of Westminster, then called "the bench," subsequently called the Court of Common Pleas.

The king also continued to administer justice in his own person, in his travels around the country. Gradually the task of judging before the king (*coram rege*) was allocated to professional judges. At first the court *coram rege*, or Court of King's Bench as it later came to be called, handled exactly the same kinds of cases as the Court of Common Pleas, but during the 1200s the functions of the two courts became more clearly differentiated. The court *coram rege* began to restrict its jurisdiction to cases affecting the royal person and to crimes, while "common pleas"—that is, ordinary civil disputes between ordinary freemen—were left to the Court of Common Pleas. By the late 1200s it was possible to say that common pleas were tried at Westminster and pleas of the crown before the king (wherever he might be). (Note that crown pleas included criminal causes, since the keeping of the peace was considered a special royal interest; hence the division of criminal and civil jurisdictions between two separate courts is the beginning of the strict separation of the two jurisdictions which is still characteristic of Anglo-American law.) [5]

Thus by the 13th century central law-courts in the modern sense had been established in England for the adjudication of private disputes. In addition, by that time two treatises on English law had been published—Glanvill's in 1187 and Bracton's in 1255. A legal profession had grown up. Royal officers called sheriffs existed to execute writs issued by the Chancellor. Thus Henry II (1154–1189) founded a system of law which in some respects was to bear greater resemblance to American law of the 20th century than it did to the law of his grandfather Henry I.

To understand this, it is necessary to consider what was happening throughout Europe in the same period. This was the age of the emergence of a new theology based on Aristotle and a new science of law based on Justinian. It was the age of Gothic architecture and of scholasticism, the age of the founding of the European universities.

5. Mention should also be made of a third great common law court, the Court of Exchequer, whose beginnings antedate the Court of Common Pleas. This court developed out of proceedings in which officers of the crown administered matters affecting the royal treasury. These proceedings became judicialized in time and the jurisdiction of this court, which at the outset was limited to fiscal matters, was expanded so that it too could handle many of the cases which were subject to the jurisdiction of the Common Pleas and the King's Bench.

It was the age of the separation of the Church from the secular authorities and of the establishment of an ecclesiastical hierarchy legally subordinate to the Pope.

In the Frankish Empire, as in the Anglo-Saxon kingdoms, bishops were appointed by the leading laymen and sat in the local governing bodies; diocesan synods were composed not only of clergy but of laity; secular assemblies issued ecclesiastical regulations and ecclesiastical assemblies issued police regulations. Charlemagne himself promulgated new canons of the Church at the Council of Frankfurt in 794—six years before he was crowned Emperor by the Bishop of Rome! In the 9th and 10th centuries, with the disintegration of the Carolingian Empire and the rise of feudatory warring lords, who often appointed their relatives to bishoprics for the sake of the financial returns involved, Church reformers struggled to strengthen the hand of the German emperors against the local lords. But in 1075 Pope Gregory VII declared the independence of the Church from the Emperor; kings, he declared in his famous *dictatus papae* of that year, must kiss the feet of the Bishop of Rome. At the same time Gregory VII decreed that decisions of the bishops' courts could be appealed to the court of the Bishop of Rome. The establishment of the appellate jurisdiction of the papal curia reflects the establishment of a hierarchy of courts and the creation of a body of law governing the distribution of functions within the Church—a systematic body of Canon Law which was not centered around liturgy and the sacraments, as it had been previously, but was centered around the structure of the visible hierarchical Church and its relations with the secular authorities.

Between 1050 and 1150 there emerged in Western Europe, for the first time, a class of professional lawyers, law schools, law treatises, hierarchies of courts, and a rational science of law. European jurists, working on the primitive tribal customs of the various peoples, on the liturgy and sacraments of the Church, and on Justinian's Digest, which was rediscovered in about 1100 after some five centuries of oblivion, read into these materials certain principles which were new to the history of law.

The key to the new legal science was the dialectical method which was first developed in theology by Abelard. The essence of this method was the attempt to reconcile opposites. In law, this took the form of analyzing and synthesizing the conflicting customs, statutes, cases and doctrines. Such analysis and synthesis presupposed the existence of rational criteria for judging which rules were universal and which were of only relative validity. Thus the canonists, for example, developed doctrines to test the validity of a custom: its duration, its universality, its reasonableness, and so forth. At the end of the 11th century they developed "a new method of interpretation," whereby they "marked off from principles of eternal validity the variable elements of the law, which had been suggested by particular circumstances, whether of time, place, or persons, and enforcement of which other conditions might render unseasonable. This amounted to the recognition of the relativity of rules and provided a technical method of harmonizing contradictions." [6]

The earlier Roman Law of Justinian's time (565 A.D.) and before had proceeded from the premise that texts were to be applied on the basis of their authority, more authoritative statements having more weight than less authoritative. Using this method, the older jurists had been able to distinguish and analogize rules of law, but not to develop basic abstract concepts. The medieval dialectic made it possible to go behind the rules to the abstract concepts which they reflected—to analyze "ownership," for example, and to show its independence of "possession," or to view "the intention" of a person as something apart from the specific words uttered or acts done. The older Roman Law was more empirical in character, stating the particular legal consequences which flowed from particular acts; the medieval law, whether Roman or Canon or national, related the rules to a system of concepts.

Thus Gratian, in his famous Concordance of Discordant Canons of 1140, the first systematic legal treatise of Western history, organized into one coherent body of legal doctrine the whole mass of collections of canons, decrees, and fragments of writings of Church councils, bishops, and Church Fathers, which had been handed down in entirely unsystematic form in the preceding thousand years. "On each question he proposed the tests *pro et contra*, as in two pleadings, and sought for an explanation of the divergence by careful definitions of the meaning of the words and of the precise applicability of the rules." [7] The same technique was used by the Glossators working on the Roman Law at Bologna, Paris, and other schools; the same technique was used subsequently by Glanvill and Bracton working on the newly developing English law. Indeed, the same basic technique underlies a great deal of legal scholarship throughout the world today.

It should be stressed that Roman Law in the 11th and 12th centuries was largely "dead" law, existing only in books; with a few exceptions people were not governed by Roman Law and courts were not bound by it. Indeed, the rules of Justinian's Digest bore little relationship to the actual situation in which Europe found itself. But the jurists of the universities literally revived Roman Law, breathed new life into it, so that gradually it came to have an impact upon the law both of the Church and of the secular states. The law of the Church —Canon Law—was, of course, a living law applied in the ecclesiastical courts. The living secular law was the folklaw and official law of

6. Gabriel Le Bras, "Canon Law," in C. G. Crump and E. F. Jacob, editors, The Legacy of the Middle Ages (Oxford, 1926) pp. 321, 325–6.

7. *Ibid.*

the local, tribal, feudal, imperial polity which we have described. But the emerging monarchies of the later Middle Ages were strongly influenced by Roman and Canon Law, in developing their national legal systems. In England the impact of both Roman and Canon Law was felt quite strongly in the creation of the English legal system under Henry II and in its subsequent development in the 13th century, although by the 14th and 15th centuries English law had developed its own unique character and its own independent principles of growth.

Thus the English system of initiating court proceedings by writs issued by the Chancellor, upon application by the plaintiff, ordering the sheriff to have the defendant present before the court to answer such-and-such a charge, differed from the writ system of the ecclesiastical courts. Or, to take another example, the English action called novel disseisin, which introduced into English law the principle that a person unjustly dispossessed of land was not entitled to repossess it by self-help but must prove in court both prior possession and wrongful eviction, was probably inspired by a similar Canon Law action (*actio spolii*) used in the ecclesiastical courts, yet it had its own history, giving birth to various forms of tort actions characteristic of English legal development. There was no thought that English law, or the more slowly developing French law, or the still more slowly developing law of the various parts of what later became Germany, should "take over" or "copy" the Canon Law of the Church or the Roman Law of the universities.

Still, the men who were making English, French and German law could not help but be influenced by the new Romano-Canonical system, and it was undoubtedly this influence which produced the common features of all the European legal systems in the 12th and 13th centuries. All were based on what might be called a principle of Reason, that is, a principle that law was not a system of magic, or of arbitrary force, but rather a coherent and rational system of rights and remedies. Thus the judge was not to decide on the basis of oaths and ordeals (indeed, the Fourth Lateran Council in 1215 brought about the abolition of ordeals throughout the West by prohibiting priests from participating in them), but rather on the basis of rational evaluation of the evidence and rational application of the law. Moreover, as the medieval theologians asserted that Reason governs the universe, so medieval jurists said that Law governs the universe, including all human relations, even the relation of the sovereign to his subjects. Thus from the principle that Law is Reason came the idea that Law is complete, covering all situations, as well as the idea that Law is supreme, governing all men.

All legal systems of the West were based also on what might be called a principle of Conscience, namely that the judge must find the law not merely in books or reason but also, somehow, in his own sense of justice. A new science of pleading and procedure was created "to inform the conscience of the judge." The written complaint, written summons by the court, and written records of proceedings were introduced for the first time. Direct legal representation by professional lawyers replaced the older system whereby the representative, if any, really substituted himself as the party. Interrogation by the judge was also introduced—a symbol of the great increase in judicial powers. Out of the idea of the conscience of the judge was elaborated the concept of judicial discretion. As Reason was associated with the idea of the supremacy and completeness of law, so Conscience was associated with the idea of the equality of the law, since in Conscience all litigants are equal; and from the idea of equality, or equity, came the systematic protection of the poor and helpless, the enforcement of relationships of trust and confidence, and the granting of personal remedies such as specific performance and injunctions. In time equity came to be treated in English law as a distinct system administered by the Chancellor's court, but in the formative period of English legal history in the 12th and 13th centuries equity was administered by all the English courts including the King's Bench and Common Pleas,[8] as it was administered in various courts in other Western countries. Thus it may be said that equity in a broad sense is a common feature of all Western law, though in different countries its institutionalization has taken different forms.

Finally, it has been a common feature of all Western legal systems since the 11th and 12th centuries that the law is considered to be a unified body of doctrine and practice, with capacity for organic growth. In all legal systems of the West from that time there developed a system of a hierarchy of courts, with appeals from lower to higher tribunals; a system of records and reports; a system of similar remedies for similar cases; and a system of interdependence of legislation and judicial decisions. Thus the means were created for law to develop on the basis of historical continuity; each judicial decision, each piece of legislation, is seen as related both to what has gone before and to what will come after. Thus the law moves from the past into the future; it is neither static nor revolutionary. This principle of Growth is common to both English and continental law. It is by no means inherent in all legal systems; indeed, it is probably a unique principle of Western law.

SECTION 25.3 THE EMERGENCE OF THE MODERN DISTINCTION BETWEEN "CIVIL LAW" AND "COMMON LAW" METHODS OF REASONING

Legal historians speak of the "Revival" or the "Renovation" of Roman Law in the 11th and 12 centuries. They speak also of the "Reception" of Roman Law in the 16th century. The second cannot

---

8. *Cf.* Harold D. Hazeltine, "The Early History of English Equity," in Essays in Legal History (Vinogradoff ed., London, 1913), p. 261.

be understood without the first. The first was connected, as we have seen, with the creation of a new type of Canon Law in the Church and with the emergence of secular law as an instrument of royal or imperial control in the medieval monarchies which succeeded the Frankish Empire. English law was the most advanced of the secular systems of the Middle Ages. The 14th and 15th centuries in England saw the development of a secular legal profession centered in the Inns of Court and a unified body of law administered by the centralized royal courts. The other countries of Europe had not experienced so complete a development of secular law or so perfected a unity of royal power. In Germany, especially, and to a lesser extent France, it was not until the 16th century that a unified body of secular royal law was created, and the return to earlier Roman Law texts played an important part, once again, in this creation.

Faced with a multiplicity of local laws, with the absence of a secular legal profession possessed of strong vocational traditions, and with the absence of a strong central judiciary, the 16th century princes of Germany and neighboring countries of Western Europe drew upon the university law professors and the university-trained jurists (a) to help constitute a new secular civil service, and (b) to provide a systematic body of legal concepts and doctrines to meet the new political, economic, and social conditions. The concepts and doctrines were derived by the jurists from their study of the Roman Law as it had been developed in the medieval universities and from their adaption of it to the new economic and political circumstances of the time.

If one asks, Why did the new national states turn to Roman Law instead of fashioning a new German or French or Dutch law, the answer is that they did in fact fashion a new German or French or Dutch law, but the *old* "national" law, insofar as it survived, was Frankish law, too primitive for modern purposes, and so Roman Law was once again *adapted* to a new purpose.

In England, on the other hand, despite some pressure for a Reception of Roman Law under the Tudors, the system of common law and equity had become well enough established as a national law in the 12th to 15th centuries, the secular legal profession centered in the Inns of Court in Westminster was strong enough, the secular judiciary of the King's Bench, the Common Pleas, the Exchequer, and other courts were sufficiently able and powerful, and the system of procedure and substantive law applied in the courts was rational enough and flexible enough, so that the administrative and legal problems of the Tudor national state could be handled without a Reception of Roman Law.

When the battle for Parliamentary supremacy developed in the 17th century, the judiciary and the legal profession were in general on the side of the Parliament and the landed gentry. They were able to preserve the traditional legal structure and technique, amidst all the changes of that time. Moreover, it was just at that time, as part of the Puritan and Parliamentary Revolution, that the constitutional and legal history of the pre-Tudor period was rewritten to show that the independence of Parliament and the judiciary was rooted in the medieval past. To the legal craftsman's vested professional interest in his traditional technique was added a political fiction of historical continuity in the English system of government from the time of the Norman Conquest and even from Anglo-Saxon times.

Thus there grew up the English conception of historical continuity, as contrasted with the German conception of doctrinal consistency, as the basis of legal rationality. The significance of this difference and the reasons for the development of these different conceptions are explored in the following pages.

———

[The following is taken from OTTO KAHN-FREUND,* INTRODUCTION TO KARL RENNER, THE INSTITUTIONS OF PRIVATE LAW AND THEIR SOCIAL FUNCTIONS (London, 1949), p. 8 ff. Footnotes are omitted.]

Every legal system requires an element of ideological unity. However much one may be aware that the application of the legal norm is, in many cases, a policy-making process, one cannot dispense with a principle which links one decision with another, which raises the judicial act beyond the level of the realm of sheer expediency. Without such a principle the practical lawyer cannot operate, without it the law cannot command the respect of the public. . . .

In a systematised legal structure such as [that of] the modern Continental Codes, legal institutions such as ownership, sale, marriage, appear as part and parcel of a self-contained logical entity, of an intricate network of major and minor premises. It is the task of the jurist, of the legal scholar, to analyse and re-analyse the normative content of the law, to make the logical network more and more refined and pliable. It is the function of the judge to find his decision with the help of the intellectual tools which the "science of law" has put at his disposal. Every new factual situation must somehow be fitted into the existing system. That system is comprehensive and without "gaps". It stands firm like a rock, be it even in the midst of a turbulent sea of social change.

The conceptualist school of thought was, on the Continent, the dominant variety of positivism in the 19th century. It postulated the logical consistency of the legal system as a whole. The judicial process, it insisted, is of a strictly deductive nature. The norm which the judge applies is, in its view, incapable of being transformed by the process of application. Hence, the judicial decision itself can in no sense be considered as a source

* Otto Kahn-Freund is Professor of Comparative Law at Oxford University. Prior to 1964 he was Professor of Law at the University of London.

of law. It must justify itself exclusively by the process of deduction from abstract premises on which it is based.

Although this conceptualist doctrine has for many decades been discarded by the majority of continental scholars, it has left as its legacy the fiction of systematic consistency as the primary element of ideological unity in the law.

In this country [England] and in the whole common-law world, the place of the systematic fiction is taken to a considerable extent by the fiction of historical continuity. Every decision appears in the cloak of a mere application or adaptation of pre-existing "principles" laid down in earlier judicial pronouncements. Where historical continuity and systematic consistency are in conflict, it is the former which prevails, and it prevails even where the question at stake is the interpretation of a statute. If law can be called a science, it is, in this country, an empirical not a speculative science. It is an answer—primarily—to the question: "what was done previously?", not a logical process untrammelled by previous attempts to grapple with a similar situation. The positivist utopia has its place in a systematic as well as in a casuistic legal structure, but, in the latter, the logical fiction will be pushed into the background by the historical fiction.
. . .

It is not, as is sometimes argued, the codification of the law which gives rise to the idea of systematic consistency. Germany before 1900 was the Mecca of "legal science." It paved the way for the Code which came into force that year, the Code was its fruit, not its root. On the other hand, large parts of Land Law, of Commercial Law, of Administrative Law, and of Criminal Law have been codified in England, but the "principle of precedent" continues to dominate these branches of law to such an extent that the highest Court had occasion to remind the lower instances that there was— after all—a codification. Codification does not necessarily engender "scientific" legal thought (as Bentham erroneously assumed), a code can be survived by the fiction of historical continuity. . . .

Systematic positivism is, in this country, sometimes associated with the influence of Roman Law. To some extent this too is a misunderstanding. It is quite true that the systematic grouping of positive norms as "legal institutions" and the definition of these institutions (ownership, obligation, sale, hire, pledge, etc.) was one of the great contributions of the Roman mind to human civilization. It is equally true that, as Ihering has formulated it, it was the Romans who succeeded in "precipitating" legal concepts out of the multitude of legal norms, and in building up an "alphabet" of legal concepts which is the precondition and indispensable tool of scientific legal thought. Nevertheless, no one who has endeavoured to compare the method of the common lawyer with that of the Roman jurist and of the 19th century continental legal scholar can fail to agree with Buckland and McNair "that there is more affinity between the Roman jurist and the common lawyer than there is between the Roman jurist and his modern civilian successor". "Both the common lawyer and the Roman jurist avoid generalisations and, so far as possible, definitions. Their method is intensely casuistic. . . . That is not the method of the Pandectist. For him the law is a set of rules to be deduced from a group of primary principles, the statement of which constitutes the *Allgemeiner Teil* of his structure." The conceptual method which implies the "purity" of the norm and which claims to be capable of establishing and enforcing a *judicium finium regundorum* between "norm" and "substratum" is not inherent in Roman Law. It is the heritage of the *Usus Modernus Pandectarum*, of the "Roman common law" influenced by natural law concepts and by Germanic customs and developed on the Continent since the Middle Ages.

Neither codification nor the influence of Roman Law can account for the difference between the Continental and the Anglo-Saxon types of positivism. The axiom that the law is a logical system, self-sufficient, comprehensive, without "gaps", arose on the Continent as a response to the needs of the growing civil service state. Max Weber has demonstrated how the continental monarchies from the 16th to the 19th centuries availed themselves of the systematised structure of legal conceptions built up by the scholarly expositors of the Roman Law. The rigid framework of positive legal concepts made for unity of administration, it also facilitated the smooth operation and the supervision of the administration of the law by a judicial and administrative civil service, a civil service which was scattered over wide areas, but subject to a centralised control. It is not, of course, suggested that the growth of systematic positivism on the Continent can be entirely explained by a simple formula like this. Many factors, the influence of natural law not being the least of them, have contributed to the development of this particular type of what Weber calls the "formal rationality" of the law. It cannot, however, be denied that the social structure of the legal profession on the Continent and, above all, the political structure of the absolute monarchies were the "prime movers" in the creation of this unique phenomenon of a "logical utopia" in the law.

None of the sociological and political factors which, on the Continent, made for systematisation and for the restriction of judicial discretion to a minimum was present in this country, not, at any rate, since the middle of the 17th century.

In this country the unification of the law had been the work of the medieval monarchy operating largely through the common law courts. It is impossible to over-emphasise the historical importance of this fact. What was a problem still to be solved on the Continent at the inception of the capitalist era—the creation of a uniform law—was, in England, an accomplished achievement. Systematisation was very largely unnecessary, because it was not required in order to overcome the chaos of local laws and customs. Of all the important jurisdictions of Europe, England was the only one to emerge from the Middle Ages with a *"common* law". The heritage of feudalism in this country was a unified body of institutions and rules which, while lacking in logic, were nevertheless capable of being intellectually absorbed and—above all—capable of being applied throughout the country. The lawyer did not need the Ariadne thread of systematic thought to help him to grope his way through a labyrinth of *"Stadtrechte"*, of *"coutumes"*, etc.

Moreover—and Max Weber's sociological analysis has made this convincingly clear—the thought-processes of the common law can and should be understood as the outcome of the needs and habits of a legal profession organised in guilds and preserving the structure and the power of a medieval vocational body. The modern continental systems were developed in the universities by legal scholars for the use of officials. English law evolved as a series of guilds rules for the use and guidance of the members and apprentices of the Inns of Court. It was due to political factors, to the failure of the absolute monarchy in England, to the aristocratic structure of the body politic in the 18th century, that the administration of the law remained in the hands of the lawyers' guilds. With some exaggeration one might say that it was the Revolution of 1688, not the refusal to "receive" Roman Law that, in this country, sealed the fate of systematic legal science in the continental sense.

The common law was developed by that branch of the legal profession whose main interest lies in litigation. It was, until well into the 19th century (and, to a degree, it still is), a series of rules of conduct for practising advocates, a comprehensive answer to the question: "how do I behave in court?" It was a body of practical and technical craft-rules, handed down from master to apprentice, and designed to instruct the advocate in the art of raising and defending claims. This largely accounts for its "empirical", for its casuistic as opposed to the continental logical and systematic method. The craftsman asks: "how has this—or a similar—case been handled before?" He is not very much concerned with the question, whether the answer is capable of being fitted into an abstract system. It is, of course, easy to over-emphasise the contrast between the two methods. Logical deduction was never absent from the thought-processes of English judges and advocates, and precedents have played and are playing an important and rapidly increasing rôle on the Continent. We are merely concerned with a basic difference in outlook and with the historical factors which account for this difference.

The contrast between the methods of thought of university trained and guild trained lawyers may also serve as an explanation for the essentially "remedial" or "procedural" structure of English legal ideas. English law does not pose and answer the question: "what are the legal guarantees for the freedom of the individual from arbitrary arrest?" It is content to ask: "in what circumstances will you, the barrister, be able to obtain for your client a writ of *habeas corpus* or a judgment for damages on the ground of false imprisonment?" From a practical point of view there is no difference between these two types of questions. Nevertheless the contrast between the two formulations reveals the gulf between thought processes influenced by natural law and orientated towards a systematic structure of rights and duties, and a method of argument whose primary pre-occupation is with remedies, not with rights, with procedural form, not with juridical substance. It will be seen that the difference in approach to the law of property can and must be explained as a similar divergence in method rather than in practical results. It is not so much in the practical operation of legal institutions as in the intellectual machinery which promotes that operation that systematic and historical positivism, the continental and the Anglo-Saxon methods, are divided. . . .

The consequences of the differences between Anglo-American and Continental legal thought may be negligible in terms of the solution of a particular legal problem. From the standpoint of the interests affected, it may make no difference whatsoever that the court relies on a precedent instead of on a provision of a code.   Indeed, *a priori* there is as much or as little predictability of judicial decisions to be obtained from a system which relies on analogy of precedent as from a system which relies on analogy of doctrine.   One kind of technique is just as rational, just as flexible or inflexible, as the other—in and of itself.   Differences which exist between English or American law on the one hand, and French or German on the other, with respect to the quality of adjudication, predictability of decisions, and the degree to which judges exercise creative imagination in the decision of cases and the adaptation of the law to changing circumstances, are *not* significantly attributable to differences in the respective techniques of legal reasoning.   They are attributable to differences in the political and social role of the judiciary, differences in constitutional structure, and differences in basic attitudes toward law, far more than to differences in techniques of legal reasoning.

This is not to say that a judge striving for historical consistency will always reach the same result as a judge striving for doctrinal consistency, other things being equal.   On the contrary, often the two techniques will produce different results.   It is possible, for example, that doctrinal consistency is more workable in contracts, historical consistency more workable in torts.[9]

Yet here it should be added that the two kinds of consistency are by no means mutually exclusive, and that both are factors in every Western system of law.   The differences are in emphasis.   There are, in fact, areas of law in the French or German or Swiss systems in which the code provisions are so few and so broad that the courts have worked out their own doctrines on the basis of a series of decisions, to which persuasive authority is attached; just as there are areas of English or American law where reasoning from code provisions and from statute predominates over "case law" as such.   Indeed in every case an American judge should be mindful both of precedent and of doctrine, and so should a European judge, though the proportions in which the two elements are mixed may differ.

Question: Kahn-Freund speaks of the "fiction" of historical continuity and of the "fiction" of doctrinal consistency.   Are these necessarily fictions?

25.4   THE HISTORICAL DEVELOPMENT OF THE DOCTRINE OF PRECEDENT

If we go back to the early history of modern English law, we find that by the end of the 12th century, virtually as soon as records of court proceedings were kept, there developed an interest in judicial

---

9.   *Cf*. Roscoe Pound, "Contract," in
Encyclopaedia of the Social Sciences
(1930 ed.), Vol. 4, p. 329.

decisions as guides to what the law is. Bracton in his treatise on English law, written in the middle of the 13th century, referred to about 500 decided cases; he also wrote a Notebook containing digests of 2000 cases. The word "precedent," however, is entirely absent from Bracton's vocabulary; cases for him and for his contemporaries were not binding authorities but merely illustrations of legal principles.

In the 14th, 15th and early 16th centuries law students kept notes of oral arguments in court cases. These notes, preserved in the so-called Yearbooks, show that not only the students but also the courts were concerned with analogizing and distinguishing cases. Again, however, the decisions were not treated as authorities in any sense, and if a judge did not approve of a decision he would just say it was wrong.

In the 16th and 17th centuries we get the first systematic reports of cases and the first mention of precedent. Judges then began to say that they are bound by precedents in matters of procedure, and especially in matters of pleading, and the practice of citing previous cases became firmly established. It is interesting to note, however, that in the first known use of the word precedent, in 1557, it is stated that a decision was given "notwithstanding two presidents." Indeed, the doctrine of precedent which developed in those centuries did not provide that a single decision was binding but rather that a line of decisions would not be overturned. Lord Mansfield could still say, in the latter part of the 18th century, "The reason and spirit of cases make law; not the letter of particular precedents."

Nevertheless, with the development in the 17th century of the distinction between dictum and holding, the way was paved for the modern doctrine. It should be noted that the 17th century in England was a time when analogical reasoning also became prevalent in fields other than law.

In the later 19th century for the first time there developed the rule that a holding by a court in a previous case is binding on the same court (or on an inferior court) in a similar case. The doctrine was called *stare decisis*—"to stand by the decisions." It was never absolute. The court is only bound "in the absence of weighty reasons." There is always the possibility of over-ruling the previous holding.

Not only is *stare decisis* not absolute but it also has no clear meaning. As is seen from the cases on manufacturers' liability, the ratio decidendi of a case is never certain. Moreover, the doctrine of precedent has different values in different fields of law. In dealing with questions of property law or commercial law a court is reluctant to overturn the holdings of previous cases since the community relies upon the stability of court decisions in making property or business transactions; indeed the expression "rule of property" is sometimes used with reference to a doctrine laid down in previous decisions which the court will not overturn because business people rely upon it (whether or not the doctrine relates to property law as such). In dealing with questions of tort law, on the other hand, courts have less reason to be reluctant to overrule precedent or to "distinguish away" past cases; presumably if a driver of a car proceeds carelessly through an intersection when another careless driver is approaching from the opposite direction, he or she does not do so in reliance upon the rule that the contributory negligence of the other driver will bar the latter's recovery. Nevertheless, predictability of judicial decision is a factor to be considered in tort cases as in any other, if only for the reason that the lawyers for the parties rely on past decisions in bringing suit or in defending.

In matters of constitutional law—to take a third example—the doctrine of precedent has still less value than in matters of tort law, since it is a function of the courts under our system of law to adapt the provisions of the Constitution to the changing needs of society. This does not mean that the Constitution has no fixed meaning and that the courts will overturn previous constitutional decisions whenever they disapprove of them; on the contrary, the Constitution has an extraordinary stability as a framework of our social, economic and political life over the centuries, and the Supreme Court of the United States, in interpreting it, is strongly influenced by its own past decisions. But the interpretation of the Constitution is bound to be more flexible than the interpretation, say, of a contract.

Finally, *stare decisis* is often given a rather different value in matters of statutory interpretation because of a theory that a prior judicial decision interpreting a statute is presumed to have the approval of the legislature unless the legislature has overruled the decision by amending the statute. Thus a kind of legislative "rule of property", so to speak, is sometimes introduced into the field of statutory interpretation.

In the heyday of the doctrine of *stare decisis*, that is, in the last quarter of the 19th and the first quarter of the 20th century, belief was prevalent that certainty in law could be obtained by a scientific use of precedent. The legislature alone was thought to have the function of changing the law; the court's function was "merely" to apply the law, and to apply it in accordance with the holdings of previous decisions. The common law as an organically growing body of experience and doctrine was supposed, in effect, to have been superseded by a body of fixed rules which could be mechanically applied.

The idea that the common law is a body of fixed rules vanished in the second quarter of the 20th century, and perhaps earlier, in the face of overwhelming changes in social, economic and political life. The mathematical or mechanical jurisprudence of the late 19th century which denied that there is an ethical element in the analogizing and distinguishing of cases can seldom be found today among leaders of legal thought, at least in the United States. This does not mean, however, that the doctrine of precedent has been repudiated. It means, rather, that there has been a return to an older concept of precedent. Precedent is seen as a means of marshalling past experience, of providing a historical context, for making the choice at hand. While condemning the hocus-pocus aspects of the strict 19th century doctrine, many American thinkers about law would agree with Lord Mansfield that "the common law works itself pure."

Note

Sources of Law

Although judicial precedents, statutes, and written constitutions are the primary sources of law in the United States, others deserve mention.

1. The President of the United States and the governors of the several states have authority, within limits, to promulgate executive orders which have the force of law. Moreover, various agencies within the executive departments—state and federal—have the power to promulgate rules and regulations governing both the internal functions of the departments and also the activities of persons subject to the jurisdiction of these departments. For example, the Internal Revenue Service, a bureau of the United States Treasury Department, has promulgated an extensive body of regulations which supplement the federal internal revenue laws.

2. There are numerous regulatory boards, commissions, and agencies, at both the state and federal levels, which also have the power to promulgate rules and regulations. (We will consider some aspects of this subject in Part Four of the book.)

3. There has been some codification of law. During the 19th century some states codified their procedural law as part of the movement for reform in civil procedure—see *supra* p. 170 ff. California went further and enacted a comprehensive code patterned after the continental codes. (In spite of this California is essentially a "common law" jurisdiction. See the Escola case *supra* p. 549 and the note on p. 564.) The state of Louisiana is also a code state, having retained the French tradition introduced prior to the Louisiana Purchase.

More typically, codification has been undertaken in some limited field of the law. Perhaps the best example of this type of codification is the Uniform Commercial Code, which has been adopted in 49 states. Some states have also codified their criminal law.

4. There are certain non-official but, in a sense, authoritative sources of law. The work of legal scholars and commentators which appears in articles, books, treatises, and encyclopedias is one such source. Another non-official source of law is the work of various

organizations which devote their efforts to law reform and the systematization of law. For example, the American Law Institute has harnessed the efforts of numerous teachers and practitioners to the task of "restating" the law in various substantive fields. Typically these restatements of law are based on an assimilation of a great body of judicial opinions from which is drawn a unified, systematic, comprehensive, and (ideally) internally consistent statement of the doctrines and principles formulated by the courts. In a sense, the restatements are similar to the work of codifiers in the Roman and Continental traditions. (To date, restatements have been published in the following fields: agency, conflicts of law, contracts, evidence, property, restitution, security, torts, and trusts.)

Of course the work of scholars, commentators, "restaters," *etc.* is not in itself a source of law, in the technical legal sense of the term "source". Such writings do not have binding authority. Yet they influence judges and legislators and increasingly permeate the official law announced in judicial decisions and statutes.

Questions

[Review Section 19 *supra* before answering these questions.]

1. Is the maintenance of historical continuity a desirable function of law?

2. In what ways, if any, does reasoning by analogy of precedent contribute to the maintenance of historical continuity?

3. In what ways, if any, does the use of legal fictions contribute to the maintenance of historical continuity?

4. In what ways, if any, does the recognition of exceptions to rules contribute to the maintenance of historical continuity?

5. Is reasoning by analogy of precedent essential to a rational resolution of disputes through a legal process?

6. Is reasoning by analogy of doctrine essential to a rational resolution of disputes through a legal process?

7. Is reasoning by analogy essential to a rational resolution of disputes through a legal process?

LAW AS A PROCESS OF PROTECTING AND FACILITATING VOLUNTARY ARRANGEMENTS: ILLUSTRATIONS FROM THE LAW OF CONTRACT

In the preceding parts of this book we have considered law primarily in terms of two of its basic social functions: that of providing procedures for the peaceful resolution of disputes, and that of maintaining historical continuity and doctrinal consistency in the elaboration of norms for the regulation of social life. We turn now to a third basic function of law, that of protecting and facilitating voluntary arrangements.

To analyze the first function of law we focused attention on legal procedure, and especially on court procedure as an archetype, or model, of legal procedure. By a series of deliberate steps taken by the parties in relation to each other—almost like negotiations, but under the strict control of the courts—disputants who are unwilling or unable to settle their differences either amicably or by force find a solution which, by redramatizing the events that gave rise to the dispute, provides a catharsis, and at the same time, by its impartiality and authoritativeness, has the quality of objectivity. The judicial duel is fought by the disputants, but the decision is in the hands of the court. The combination of individual and social elements is designed to provide satisfaction both to the parties and to the community.

To understand the second function of law we dealt particularly with methods of legal reasoning, and especially reasoning by analogy of precedents and by analogy of doctrine or statute. Adjudication —like other legal processes of which it is an archetype, or model— involves not merely pacification of the parties and of the community, but also the continual creation and re-creation of general standards (precepts, norms, rules) which not only guide the decision of the case at hand but also strengthen and develop the normative patterns of social life. Whether the consistency which law thus serves and fosters is primarily a historical consistency, as in the Anglo-American tradition, or primarily doctrinal, as in the "Roman" tradition of many Continental European countries, it is of necessity dynamic rather than static, for new situations continually press against the old rules. Indeed, a static consistency is, in a dynamic society, a contradiction in terms. To apply a precedent or a doctrine in a mechanical fashion to a new situation, ignoring the difference between the new situation and the old one to which the precedent or doctrine was formerly applied, itself alters the precedent or doctrine. We can speak intelligently of legal decision-making as the "application" of "rules" to "facts" only if we recognize that in each application to new facts the rule changes—and that it is by this subtle and gradual process of change that true consistency is maintained.

To approach our third basic function of law—that of protecting and facilitating voluntary arrangements—we single out contract in order, as in other parts of our study, to have a focus small enough to avoid overexposure. It should be understood, however, that the function of law with which we are here concerned extends far beyond contract in the technical sense. Examples could also be chosen from property, corporations, labor relations, and many other fields. Nevertheless, contract is perhaps the "pure type" of voluntary legal arrangement.

Chapter 7

CONTRACT LAW AS A PROCESS OF PROTECTING VOLUNTARY ARRANGEMENTS

This Chapter presents an introduction to a body of law, contract law, which provides a framework within which voluntary arrangements are planned, and within which disputes arising out of those arrangements are resolved. Central to this introduction is an attempt to make explicit both functions and limits of contract law. We will ask, "What kinds of relationships are proper subjects for establishment and regulation through contract?" and "What means should the law employ to decide whether or not to afford contract protection to a voluntary relationship?" and "What protections should the law extend to a contract relationship?" The materials and cases in this Chapter provide a basis for formulating some answers to these questions.

SECTION 26. WHAT KINDS OF VOLUNTARY ARRANGEMENTS ARE ENFORCEABLE AS CONTRACTS?

This section of our materials deals with the question "What kinds of promissory arrangements will the law recognize as creating duties for breach of which the law will afford a contract remedy?" That implies, of course, that there are some kinds of voluntary promissory arrangements which are not entitled to be included within the legal regime of contracts. The following contract cases, well-known to first year law students, and beloved by contracts teachers, afford a basis for formulating at least preliminary answers to this fundamental issue.

SECTION 26.1 BARGAIN AND EXCHANGE AS AN ESSENTIAL ELEMENT OF CONTRACT

BALFOUR v. BALFOUR

Court of Appeal.
[1919] 2 K.B. 271.

The plaintiff sued the defendant (her husband) for money which she claimed to be due in respect of an agreed allowance of 30£ a month. The alleged agreement was entered into under the following circumstances. The parties were married in August, 1900. The husband, a civil engineer, had a post under the Government of Ceylon as Director of Irrigation, and

593

after the marriage he and his wife went to Ceylon, and lived there together until the year 1915, except that in 1906 they paid a short visit to this country, and in 1908 the wife came to England in order to undergo an operation, after which she returned to Ceylon. In November, 1915, she came to this country with her husband, who was on leave. They remained in England until August, 1916, when the husband's leave was up and he had to return. The wife however on the doctor's advice remained in England. On August 8, 1916, the husband being about to sail, the alleged parol agreement sued upon was made. The plaintiff, as appeared from the judge's note, gave the following evidence of what took place: "In August, 1916, defendant's leave was up. I was suffering from rheumatic arthritis. The doctor advised my staying in England for some months, not to go out till November 4. On August 8 my husband sailed. He gave me a cheque from 8th to 31st for 24£, and promised to give me 30£ per month till I returned." Later on she said: "My husband and I wrote the figures together on August 8; 34£ shown. Afterwards he said 30£." In cross-examination she said that they had not agreed to live apart until subsequent differences arose between them, and that the agreement of August, 1916, was one which might be made by a couple in amity. Her husband in consultation with her assessed her needs, and said he would send 30£ per month for her maintenance. She further said that she then understood that the defendant would be returning to England in a few months, but that he afterwards wrote to her suggesting that they had better remain apart. In March, 1918, she commenced proceedings for restitution of conjugal rights, and on July 30 she obtained a decree *nisi*. On December 16, 1918, she obtained an order for alimony.

Sargant J. held that the husband was under an obligation to support his wife, and the parties had contracted that the extent of that obligation should be defined in terms of so much a month. The consent of the wife to that arrangement was a sufficient consideration to constitute a contract which could be sued upon.

He accordingly gave judgment for the plaintiff.

The husband appealed.

* * *

WARRINGTON, L. J. [after stating the facts]. Those being the facts we have to say whether there is a legal contract between the parties, in other words, whether what took place between them was in the domain of a contract or whether it was merely a domestic arrangement such as may be made every day between a husband and wife who are living together in friendly intercourse. It may be, and I do not for a moment say that it is not, possible for such a contract as is alleged in the present case to be made between husband and wife. The question is whether such a contract was made. That can only be determined either by proving that it was made in express terms, or that there is a necessary implication from the circumstances of the parties, and the transaction generally, that such a contract was made. It is quite plain that no such contract was made in express terms, and there was no bargain on the part of the wife at all. All that took place was this: The husband and wife met in a friendly way and discussed what would be necessary for her support while she was detained in England, the husband being in Ceylon, and they came to the conclusion that 30£ a month would be about right, but there is no evidence of any express bargain by the wife that she would in all the circumstances treat that as in satisfaction of the obligation of the husband to maintain her. Can we find a contract from the position of the parties? It seems to me it is quite impossible. If we were to imply such a contract in this case we should be implying on the part of the wife that whatever happened and whatever might be the change of circumstances while the husband was away she should be content with this 30£ a month, and bind herself by an obligation in law not to require him to pay anything more; and on the other hand we should be implying on the part of the husband a bargain to pay 30£ a month for some indefinite period whatever might be his circumstances. Then again it seems to me that it would be impossible to make any such implication, The matter really reduces itself to an absurdity when one considers it, because if we were to hold that there was a contract in this case we should have to hold that with regard to all the more or less trivial concerns of life where a wife, at the request of her husband, makes a promise to him that is a promise which can be enforced in law. All I can say is that there is no such contract here. These two people never intended to make a bargain which could be enforced in law. The husband expressed his intention to make this payment, and he promised to make it, and was bound in honour to continue it so long as he was in a position to do so. The wife on the other hand, so far as I can see, made no bargain at all. That is in my opinion sufficient to dispose of the case.

It is unnecessary to consider whether if the husband failed to make the payments the wife could pledge his credit or whether if he failed to make the payments she could have made some other arrangements. The only question we have to consider is whether the wife has made out a contract which she has set out to do. In my opinion she has not.

I think the judgment of Sargant J. cannot stand, the appeal ought to be allowed and judgment ought to be entered for the defendant.

Duke, L. J. I agree. This is in some respects an important case, and as we differ from the judgment of the Court below I propose to state concisely my views and the grounds which have led me to the conclusion at which I have arrived. Substantially the question is whether the promise of the husband to the wife that while she is living absent from him he will make her a periodical allowance involves in law a consideration on the part of the wife sufficient to convert that promise into a binding agreement. In my opinion it does not. I do not dissent, as at present advised, from the proposition that the spouses in this case might have made an agreement which would have given the plaintiff a cause of action, and I am inclined to think that the promise of the wife in respect of her separate estate could have founded an action in contract within the principles of the Married Women's Property Act, 1882. But we have to see whether there is evidence of any such exchange of promises as would make the promise of the husband the basis of an agreement. It was strongly urged by Mr. Hawke that the promise being absolute in form ought to be construed as one of the mutual promises which make an agreement. It was said that a promise and an implied undertaking between strangers such as the promise and implied undertaking alleged in this case would have founded an action on contract. That may be so, but it is impossible to disregard in this case what was the basis of the whole communications between the parties under which the alleged contract is said to have been formed. The basis of their communications was their relationship of husband and wife, a relationship which creates certain obligations, but not that which is here put in suit. There was a discussion between the parties while they were absent from one another, whether they should agree upon a separation. In the Court below the plaintiff conceded that down to the time of her suing in the Divorce Division there was no separation, and that the period of absence was a period of absence as between husband and wife living in amity. An agreement for separation when it is established does involve mutual considerations.

ATKIN, L. J. The defence to this action on the alleged contract is that the defendant, the husband, entered into no contract with his wife, and for the determination of that it is necessary to remember that there are agreements between parties which do not result in contracts within the meaning of that term in our law. The ordinary example is where two parties agree to take a walk together, or where there is an offer and an acceptance of hospitality. Nobody would suggest in ordinary circumstances that those agreements result in what we know as a contract, and one of the most usual forms of agreement which does not constitute a contract appears to me to be the arrangements which are made between husband and wife. It is quite common, and it is the natural and inevitable result of the relationship of husband and wife, that the two spouses should make arrangements between themselves—agreements such as are in dispute in this action —agreements for allowances, by which the husband agrees that he will pay to his wife a certain sum of money, per week, or per month, or per year, to cover either her own expenses or the necessary expenses of the household and of the children of the marriage, and in which the wife promises either expressly or impliedly to apply the allowance for the purpose for which it is given. To my mind those agreements, or many of them, do not result in contracts at all, and they do not result in contracts even though there may be what as between other parties would constitute consideration for the agreement. The consideration, as we know, may consist either in some right, interest, profit or benefit accruing to one party, or some forbearance, detriment, loss or responsibility given, suffered or undertaken by the other. That is a well-known definition, and it constantly happens, I think, that such arrangements made between husband and wife are arrangements in which there are mutual promises, or in which there is consideration in form within the definition that I have mentioned. Nevertheless they are not contracts, and they are not contracts because the parties did not intend that they should be attended by legal consequences. To my mind it would be of the worst possible example to hold that agreements such as this resulted in legal obligations which could be enforced in the Courts. It would mean this, that when the husband makes his wife a promise to give her an allowance of 30s. or 2£ a week, whatever he can afford to give her, for the maintenance of the household and children, and she promises so to apply it, not only could she sue him for his failure in any week to supply the allowance, but he could sue her for non-performance of the obligation, express or implied, which she had undertaken upon her part. All I can say is that the small Courts of this country would have to be multiplied one hundredfold if these arrangements were held to result in legal obligations. They are not sued upon, not because the parties are reluctant to enforce their legal rights when the agreement is broken, but because the parties, in the inception of the arrangement, never intended that they should be sued upon. Agreements such as these are outside the realm of contracts altogether. The common law does not regulate the form of agreements between spouses. Their promises are not sealed with seals and sealing wax. The consideration that really obtains for them is that natural love and affection which counts for so little in these cold Courts. The terms may be repudiated, varied or renewed as performance proceeds or as disagreements develop, and the principles of the common law as to exoneration and discharge and accord and satisfaction are such as find no place in the domestic code. The parties themselves are advocates, judges, Courts, sheriff's officer and reporter. In respect of these promises each house is a domain into which the King's writ does not seek to run, and to which his officers do not seek to be admitted. The only question in this case is whether or not this promise was of such a class or not. For the reasons given by my brethren it appears to me to be plainly established that the promise here was not intended by either party to be attended by legal consequences. I think the onus was upon the plaintiff, and the plaintiff has not established any contract. The parties were living together, the wife intending to return. The suggestion is that the husband bound himself to pay 30£ a month under all circumstances, and she bound herself to be satisfied with that sum under all circumstances, and, although she was in ill-health and alone in this country, that out of that sum she undertook to defray the whole of the medical expenses that might fall upon her, whatever might be the development of her illness, and in whatever expenses it might involve her. To my mind neither party contemplated such a result. I think that the parol evidence upon which the case turns does not establish a contract. I think that the letters do not evidence such a contract, or amplify the oral evidence which was given by the wife, which is not in dispute. For these reasons I think the judgment of the Court below was wrong and that this appeal should be allowed.

Appeal allowed.

Questions

1. Why isn't Mrs. Balfour's agreement with her husband a contract? Is it because there was no promise made to her by the husband? Is it because "there was no bargain on the part of the wife"? (See opinion of Warrington, J. at p. 594 *supra.*) What does that mean?

2. Why should the decision whether or not to enforce this agreement rest, in whole or in part, on a finding that "there was no bargain on the part of the wife"?

— — —   —

3. Does the court hold that the promise is not enforceable because the parties did not spell out the terms of the "contract" in clear and unequivocal terms? Should that be a prerequisite to enforcement of a promise?

4.   Is this promise unenforceable because the parties did not intend to make "a bargain which could be enforced in law"? How would you determine whether such an intention existed?

5.   Does the court start from the premise that an amicable agreement between husband and wife should not be treated as a contract? Why does it make a distinction between this case and the case of a separation agreement?

6.   Do you think it likely that "the small Courts . . . would have to be multiplied one hundredfold if [such] arrangements were held to result in legal obligations"? Should that be taken into consideration in the resolution of this case?

7.   Is there anything inherently wrong with enforcing an unconditional promise to pay a specified sum monthly regardless of "whatever might be the change in circumstances"? Should the enforceability of such a promise depend on the nature of the particular change in circumstances that has occurred?

8.   Do you think that the husband's agreement should be enforced as a contract? Why? If you do not think it should be enforced as a contract, what other legal significance might be attached to it? Who should decide how much, if anything, a divorced spouse receives as support from the other spouse? Why?

[The following is taken from RESTATEMENT OF THE LAW SECOND: CONTRACTS. (The American Law Institute, 1974).]

§ 1. CONTRACT DEFINED

A contract is a promise or a set of promises for the breach of which the law gives a remedy, or the performance of which the law in some way recognizes as a duty.

§ 2. PROMISE; PROMISOR; PROMISEE; BENEFICIARY

(1) A promise is a manifestation of intention to act or refrain from acting in a specified way, so made as to justify a promisee in understanding that a commitment has been made.

(2) The person manifesting the intention is the promisor.

(3) The person to whom the manifestation is addressed is the promisee.

(4) Where performance will benefit a person other than the promisee, that person is a beneficiary.

* * *

§ 4. BARGAIN DEFINED

A bargain is an agreement to exchange promises or to exchange a promise for a performance or to exchange performances.

* * *

§ 19. REQUIREMENT OF A BARGAIN

(1) Except as stated in subsection (2), the formation of a contract requires a bargain in which there is a manifestation of mutual assent to the exchange and a consideration.

(2) Whether or not there is a bargain a contract may be formed under special rules applicable to formal contracts or under the rules stated in §§ 86–94 and § 535.*

These first sections of the American Law Institute's second Restatement of the law of contracts assert fundamentally true propositions. These true statements are, however, a highly simplified introduction to a complex body of law which has been the subject of an extraordinary intellectual enterprise spanning the better part of the last two centuries of the development of the Anglo-American legal system. Contract and property were the central preoccupations of the jurists who built the common law system from its infancy in the Middle Ages to its maturity in the late 19th and early 20th centuries. This juridical history is a fascinating subject of inquiry. It has played a preeminent role in American legal education. The fundamental law school teaching method, the case method of study, was first developed in Christopher Columbus Langdell's classes in Contracts offered in the Harvard Law School a century ago. Since that time generations of lawyers have been initiated into their profession in a first year of law study in which the historical materials of contract have been a major focus. That historical material is still used to introduce law students to the origins of commercial law. The materials in this and the ensuing sections of this chapter draw heavily on that history; not only to raise questions as to the nature and limits of contract, but also to expose the reader to some classic examples of the materials used to induce students to begin "thinking like a lawyer".

Sections 4 and 19 of the Restatement suggest that a fundamental element of most contracts is a bargain—an exchange relationship—between the two parties. As we saw in Balfour v. Balfour, one reason advanced to explain the result in that case was the alleged failure of the wife to make a bargain with her husband by offering him something in exchange for his promise of support. The bargain requirement has been developed most extensively in contract doctrine through the concept of consideration. The following materials will elucidate this idea

---

* Formal contracts are agreements, evidenced in writing, which satisfy certain formal legal requirements, *e.g.*, sealed instruments (at one time literally bearing a wax seal), and negotiable instruments such as personal or banks checks. Sealed instruments are largely obsolete; negotiable instruments are still highly significant in commerce and personal finance.

These examples of contracts valid without satisfaction of the bargain requirement were, at one time, the only kinds of agreements enforceable in common law courts. The development of modern common law of contract from the 17th through early 20th centuries was largely a process of extending legal protection to informal agreements. In that process legal theorists developed the bargain requirement as a test for deciding which informal agreements should be given treatment as contracts. As we shall see, exceptions to the bargain theory have been developed in this century so that bargain is not quite so general a requirement for contract enforcement as Restatement § 19(1) suggests.

and also something of its limits and its relation to social and economic theory underlying contract doctrine.

———

SCHNELL v. NELL

Supreme Court of Indiana, 1861.
17 Ind. 29, 79 Am.Dec. 453.

PERKINS, J.   Action by J. B. Nell against Zacharias Schnell upon the following instrument:

"This agreement, entered into this 13th day of February, 1856, between Zach. Schnell, of Indianapolis, Marion county, state of Indiana, as party of the first part, and J. B. Nell, of the same place, Wendelin Lorenz, of Stilesville, Hendricks county, state of Indiana, and Donata Lorenz, of Frickinger, Grand Duchy of Baden, Germany, as parties of the second part, witnesseth: The said Zacharias Schnell agrees as follows: Whereas his wife, Theresa Schnell, now deceased, has made a last will and testament, in which among other provisions, it was ordained that every one of the above named second parties, should receive the sum of $200; and whereas the said provisions of the will must remain a nullity, for the reason that no property, real or personal, was in the possession of the said Theresa Schnell, deceased, in her own name, at the time of her death, and all property held by Zacharias and Theresa Schnell jointly, therefore reverts to her husband; and whereas the said Theresa Schnell has also been a dutiful and loving wife to the said Zach. Schnell, and has materially aided him in the acquisition of all property, real and personal, now possessed by him; for, and in consideration of all this, and the love and respect he bears to his wife; and, furthermore, in consideration of one cent, received by him of the second parties, he, the said Zach. Schnell, agrees to pay the above named sums of money to the parties of the second part, to wit: $200 to the said J. B. Nell; $200 to the said Wendelin Lorenz; and $200 to the said Donata Lorenz, in the following installments, viz., $200 in one year from the date of these presents; $200 in two years, and $200 in three years; to be divided between the parties in equal portions of $66⅔ each year, or as they may agree, till each one has received his full sum of $200.

"And the said parties of the second part, for, and in consideration of this, agree to pay the above named sum of money (one cent), and to deliver up to said Schnell, and abstain from collecting any real or supposed claims upon him or his estate, arising from the said last will and testament of the said Theresa Schnell, deceased.   In witness whereof, the said parties have, on this 13th day of February, 1856, set hereunto their hands and seals.

"Zacharias Schnell.   [Seal.]

"J. B. Nell.   [Seal.]

"Wen. Lorenz.   [Seal]." *

---

* Under Indiana law prevailing at the time this case was decided, sealing an instrument was not sufficient to make the instrument enforceable.

The complaint contained no averment of a consideration for the instrument, outside of those expressed in it; and did not aver that the one cent agreed to be paid, had been paid or tendered.

A demurrer to the complaint was overruled.

The defendant answered, that the instrument sued on was given for no consideration whatever.

He further answered, that it was given for no consideration, because his said wife, Theresa, at the time she made the will mentioned, and at the time of her death, owned, neither separately, nor jointly with her husband, or any one else (except so far as the law gave her an interest in her husband's property), any property, real or personal, &c.

The will is copied into the record, but need not be into this opinion.

The court sustained a demurrer to these answers, evidently on the ground that they were regarded as contradicting the instrument sued on, which particularly set out the considerations upon which it was executed. But the instrument is latently ambiguous on this point. See Ind.Dig., p. 110.

The case turned below, and must turn here, upon the question whether the instrument sued on does express a consideration sufficient to give it legal obligation, as against Zacharias Schnell. It specifies three distinct considerations for his promise to pay $600:

(1) A promise, on the part of the plaintiffs, to pay him one cent.

(2) The love and affection he bore his deceased wife, and the fact that she had done her part, as his wife, in the acquisition of the property.

(3) The fact that she had expressed her desire, in the form of an inoperative will, that the persons named therein should have the sums of money specified.

The consideration of one cent will not support the promise of Schnell. It is true, that as a general proposition, inadequacy of consideration will not vitiate an agreement. Baker v. Roberts, 14 Ind. 552. But this doctrine does not apply to a mere exchange of sums of money, of coin, whose value is exactly fixed, but to the exchange of something of, in itself, indeterminate value, for money, or, perhaps, for other thing of indeterminate value. In this case, had the one cent mentioned, been some particular one cent, a family piece, or ancient, remarkable coin, possessing an indeterminate value, extrinsic from its simple money value, a different view might be taken. As it is, the mere promise to pay six hundred dollars for one cent, even had the portion of that cent due from the plaintiff been tendered, is an unconscionable contract, void, at first blush, upon its face, if it be regarded as an earnest one. Hardesty v. Smith, 3 Ind. 39. The consideration of one cent is, plainly, in this case, merely nominal, and intended to be so. As the will and testament of Schnell's wife imposed no legal obligation upon him to discharge her bequests out of his property, and as she had none of her own, his promise to discharge them was not legally binding upon him, on that ground. A moral consideration, only, will not support a promise. Ind.Dig., p. 13. And for the same reason, a valid consideration for his promise cannot be found in the fact of a compromise of a disputed claim; for where such claim is legally groundless, a promise upon a compromise of it, or of a suit upon it, is not legally binding. Spahr v. Hollingshead, 8 Blackf. 415.

There was no mistake of law or fact in this case, as the agreement admits the will inoperative and void. The promise was simply one to make a gift. The past services of his wife, and the love and affection he had borne her, are objectionable as legal considerations for Schnell's promise, on two grounds: (1) They are past considerations. Ind.Dig., p. 13. (2) The fact that Schnell loved his wife, and that she had been industrious, constituted no consideration for his promise to pay J. B. Nell, and the Lorenzes, a sum of money. Whether, if his wife, in her lifetime, had made a bargain with Schnell, that, in consideration of his promising to pay, after her death, to the persons named, a sum of money, she would be industrious, and worthy of his affection, such a promise would have been valid and consistent with public policy, we need not decide. Nor is the fact that Schnell now venerates the memory of his deceased wife, a legal consideration for a promise to pay any third person money.

The instrument sued on, interpreted in the light of the facts alleged in the second paragraph of the answer, will not support an action. The demurrer to the answer should have been overruled. See Stevenson v. Druley, 4 Ind. 519.

PER CURIAM.—The judgment is reversed, with costs.

Notes and Questions

1. The terms of the agreement between Schnell and Nell et al. suggest that Mrs. Schnell owned property at the time her will was drafted, and so thought she could make effective bequests. It also appears, however, that she held that property with her husband in one of the forms of concurrent ownership through which the surviving joint owner takes full ownership upon the death or his or her co-tenant. Accordingly, when Mrs. Schnell died her ownership interest expired with her and she left nothing to support her bequests. Her husband assumed full ownership of the jointly owned property subject only to a debt of conscience regarding his wife's bequests.

2. Does it appear to you from the instrument of agreement that Zacharias Schnell thought that his wife's will imposed no obligation on him to pay the sums specified in her will? Does it appear to you that he thought that her will imposed no valid claim against the property he had owned jointly with his wife? Does it appear to you that he nevertheless intended to honor his wife's purpose and fulfill the bequests in her will? Does it appear to you that Nell et al. would have been justified in concluding that a promise—a commitment—to pay them money had been made by Schnell?

3. Does it appear to you that when Schnell entered the agreement he intended to be bound by it? If so, why do you reach that result?

4. Does it appear to you that the person who drafted the agreement intended to make it effective and enforceable?

5. Why is one cent not a sufficient consideration for Schnell's promise to pay? Would one dollar be a sufficient consideration? Ten dollars? One hundred dollars?

6. Why is the wife's contribution to earning the jointly owned property not consideration for Schnell's promise to Nell?

7. Why isn't the discharge by Schnell of his wife's bequests a consideration for his promise?

8. Does a careful reading of the instrument suggest to you that there may in fact have been a sufficient consideration for Schnell's promise? Could the draftsman have so drafted the instrument as to make this consideration clear and convincing, and the instrument clearly enforceable?

9. Is the case for enforcement of the Schnell/Nell agreement weaker or stronger than the case for enforcement of the agreement in Balfour v. Balfour (*supra* p. 593)?

10. As best you can determine from Balfour v. Balfour and Schnell v. Nell, what is consideration and what purposes does the consideration doctrine serve?

Problems

1. Is the following agreement enforceable? Is there consideration for the option promise?

"April 18th, 1928.

"Real Estate Company of Pittsburgh,

    "Wood and Fourth,

    "Pittsburgh, Pennsylvania.

"Gentlemen:

"In consideration of One ($1.00) Dollar in hand paid, I hereby give you the option to purchase my property situate 1628 Penn Ave., at the price of $15,000.00. This option to expire at 12 o'clock noon, April 24th, 1928.

"If this option is accepted by you and transaction closed, I agree to pay you a commission of 3% on the sale price. It is understood that the property is free and clear of encumbrances excepting a mortgage in the amount of $6,000.00.

    "Very truly yours,

"J. A. Rudolph."

See Real Estate Co. of Pittsburgh v. Rudolph, 301 Pa. 502, 153 A. 438 (1930).

2. How would you decide the following case.

"On the 3d day of August, 1925, appellant while in the employ of the W. T. Smith Lumber Company, a corporation, and acting within the scope of his employment, was engaged in clearing the upper floor of mill No. 2 of the company. While so engaged he was in the act of dropping a pine block from the upper floor of the mill to the ground below; this being the usual and ordinary way of clearing the floor, and it being the duty of the plaintiff in the course of his employment to so drop it. The block weighed about 75 pounds.

"As appellant was in the act of dropping the block to the ground below, he was on the edge of the upper floor of the mill. As he started to turn the block loose so that it would drop to the ground, he saw J. Greeley McGowin, testator of the defendants, on the ground below and directly under where the block would have fallen had appellant turned it loose. Had he turned it loose it would have struck McGowin with such force as to have caused him serious bodily harm or death. Appellant could have remained safely on the upper floor of the mill by turning the block loose and allowing it to drop, but had he done this the block would have fallen on McGowin and caused him serious injuries or death. The only safe and reasonable way to prevent this was for appellant to hold to the block and divert its direction in falling from the place where McGowin was standing and the only safe way to divert it so as to prevent its coming into contact with McGowin was for appellant to fall with it to the ground below. Appellant did this, and by holding to the block and falling with it to the ground below, he diverted the course of its fall in such way that McGowin was not injured. In thus preventing the injuries to McGowin appellant himself received serious bodily injuries, resulting in his right leg being broken, the heel of his right foot torn off and his right arm broken. He was badly crippled for life and rendered unable to do physical or mental labor.

"On September 1, 1925, in consideration of appellant having prevented him from sustaining death or serious bodily harm and in consideration of the injuries appellant had received, McGowin agreed with him to care for and maintain him for the remainder of appellant's life at the rate of $15 every two weeks from the time he sustained his injuries to and during the remainder of appellant's life; it being agreed that McGowin would pay this sum to appellant for his maintenance. Under the agreement McGowin paid or caused to be paid to appellant the sum so agreed on up until McGowin's death on January 1, 1934. After his death the payments were continued to and including January 27, 1934, at which time they were discontinued. Thereupon plaintiff brought suit to recover the unpaid installments accruing up to the time of the bringing of the suit.

See Webb v. McGowin, 27 Ala.App. 82, 168 So. 196 (1935).

Was there consideration sufficient to make McGowin's promise a contract? If you decide for Webb, how can you reconcile that decision with Schnell v. Nell and Balfour v. Balfour?

HAMER v. SIDWAY

Court of Appeals of New York, 1891.
124 N.Y. 538, 27 N.E. 256.

Appeal from order of the General Term of the Supreme Court in the fourth judicial department, made July 1, 1890, which reversed a judgment in favor of plaintiff entered upon a decision of the court on trial at Special Term and granted a new trial.

This action was brought upon an alleged contract.

The plaintiff presented a claim to the executor of William E. Story, Sr., for $5,000 and interest from the 6th day of February, 1875. She acquired it through several mesne assignments from William E. Story, 2d.

The claim being rejected by the executor, this action was brought. It appears that William E. Story, Sr., was the uncle of William E. Story, 2d; that at the celebration of the golden wedding of Samuel Story and wife, father and mother of William E. Story, Sr., on the 20th day of March, 1869, in the presence of the family and invited guests he promised his nephew that if he would refrain from drinking, using tobacco, swearing and playing cards or billiards for money until he became twenty-one years of age he would pay him a sum of $5,000. The nephew assented thereto and fully performed the conditions inducing the promise. When the nephew arrived at the age of twenty-one years and on the 31st day of January, 1875, he wrote to his uncle informing him that he had performed his part of the agreement and had thereby become entitled to the sum of $5,000. The uncle received the letter and a few days later and on the sixth of February, he wrote and mailed to his nephew the following letter:

"Buffalo, Feb. 6, 1875.

"W. E. Story, Jr.:

"Dear Nephew—Your letter of the 31st ult. came to hand all right, saying that you had lived up to the promise made to me several years ago. I have no doubt but you have, for which you shall have five thousand dollars as I promised you. I had the money in the bank the day you was 21 years old that I intend for you, and you shall have the money certain. Now, Willie, I do not intend to interfere with this money in any way till I think you are capable of taking care of it and the sooner that time comes the better it will please me. I would hate very much to have you start out in some adventure that you thought all right and lose this money in one year. The first five thousand dollars that I got together cost me a heap of hard work. You would hardly believe me when I tell you that to obtain this I shoved a jackplane many a day, butchered three or four years, then came to this city, and after three months' perseverence I obtained a situation in a grocery store. I opened this store early, closed late, slept in the fourth story of the building in a room 30 by 40 feet and not a human being in the building but myself. All this I done to live as cheap as I could to save something. I don't want you to take up with this kind of fare. I was here in the cholera season '49 and '52 and the deaths averaged 80 to 125 daily and plenty of smallpox. I wanted to go home, but Mr. Fisk, the gentleman I was working for, told me if I left then, after it got healthy he probably would not want me. I stayed. All the money I have saved I know just how I got it. It did not come to me in any mysterious way, and the reason I speak of this is that money got in this way stops longer with a fellow that gets it with hard knocks than it does when he find it. Willie, you are 21 and you have many a thing to learn yet. This money you have earned much easier than I did besides acquiring good habits at the same time and you are quite welcome to the money; hope you will make good use of it. I was ten long years getting this together after I was your age. Now, hoping this will be satisfactory, I stop.   *   *   *

Truly Yours,
"W. E. Story.

"P.S.—You can consider this money on interest."

The nephew received the letter and thereafter consented that the money should remain with his uncle in accordance with the terms and conditions of the letters. The uncle died on the 29th day of January, 1887, without having paid over to his nephew any portion of the said $5,000 and interest.

PARKER, J. The question which provoked the most discussion by counsel on this appeal, and which lies at the foundation of plaintiff's asserted right of recovery, is whether by virtue of a contract defendant's testator William E. Story became indebted to his nephew William E. Story, 2d, on his twenty-first birthday in the sum of five thousand dollars. The trial court found as a fact that "on the 20th day of March, 1869, * * * William E. Story agreed to and with William E. Story, 2d, that if he would refrain from drinking liquor, using tobacco, swearing, and playing cards or billiards for money until he should become 21 years of age then he, the said William E. Story, would at that time pay him, the said William E. Story, 2d, the sum of $5,000 for such refraining, to which the said William E. Story, 2d, agreed," and that he "in all things fully performed his part of said agreement."

The defendant contends that the contract was without consideration to support it, and, therefore, invalid. He asserts that the promisee by refraining from the use of liquor and tobacco was not harmed but benefited; that that which he did was best for him to do independently of his uncle's promise, and insists that it follows that unless the promisor was benefited, the contract was without consideration. A contention, which if well founded, would seem to leave open for controversy in many cases whether that which the promisee did or omitted to do was, in fact, of such benefit to him as to leave no consideration to support the enforcement of the promisor's agreement. Such a rule could not be tolerated, and is without foundation in the law. The Exchequer Chamber, in 1875, defined consideration as follows: "A valuable consideration in the sense of the law may consist either in some right, interest, profit or benefit accruing to the one party, or some forbearance, detriment, loss or responsibility given, suffered or undertaken by the other." Courts "will not ask whether the thing which forms the consideration does in fact benefit the promisee or a third party, or is of any substantial value to anyone. It is enough that something is promised, done, forborne or suffered by the party to whom the promise is made as consideration for the promise made to him." (Anson's Prin. of Con. 63.)

"In general a waiver of any legal right at the request of another party is a sufficient consideration for a promise." (Parsons on Contracts, 444.)

"Any damage, or suspension, or forbearance of a right will be sufficient to sustain a promise." (Kent, vol. 2, 465, 12th ed.)

Pollock, in his work on contracts, page 166, after citing the definition given by the Exchequer Chamber already quoted, says: "The second branch of this judicial description is really the most important one. Consideration means not so much that one party is profiting as that the other abandons some legal right in the present or limits his legal freedom of action in the future as an inducement for the promise of the first."

Now, applying this rule to the facts before us, the promisee used tobacco, occasionally drank liquor, and he had a legal right to do so. That right he abandoned for a period of years upon the strength of the promise of the testator that for such forbearance he would give him $5,000. We need not speculate on the effort which they have been required to give up the use of those stimulants. It is sufficient that he restricted his lawful freedom of action within certain prescribed limits upon the faith of his uncle's agreement, and now having fully performed the conditions imposed, it is of no moment whether such performance actually proved a benefit to the promisor, and the court will not inquire into it, but were it a proper subject of inquiry, we see nothing in this record that would permit a determination that the uncle was not benefited in a legal sense. . . .

The order appealed from should be reversed and the judgment of the Special Term affirmed, with costs payable out of the estate.

All concur.

Questions

1.   What precisely is the consideration for Story's promise to his namesake nephew?

2.   If forbearance as to some right or action can be consideration, was there some ground for finding consideration in Balfour v. Balfour? In Schnell v. Nell?

3.   Can you offer an alternative to the consideration doctrine to explain why the promise in this case should be enforced? Consider the following formulation.

RESTATEMENT OF THE LAW SECOND: CONTRACTS

§ 90. PROMISE REASONABLY INDUCING ACTION OR FORBEARANCE.

A promise which the promisor should reasonably expect to induce action or forbearance on the part of the promisee or a third person and which does induce such action or forbearance is binding if injustice can be avoided only by enforcement of the promise. The remedy granted for breach may be limited as justice requires.

Comment:

  a. Relation to other rules. Obligations and remedies based on reliance are not peculiar to the law of contracts. This Section is often referred to in terms of "promissory estoppel," a phrase suggesting an extension of the doctrine of estoppel. Estoppel prevents a person from showing the truth contrary to a representation of fact made by him after another has relied on the representation. See Restatement, Second, Agency § 8B; Restatement, Second, Torts §§ 872, 894. Reliance is also a significant feature of numerous rules in the law of negligence, deceit and restitution. See, e. g., Restatement, Second, Agency §§ 354, 378; Restatement, Second, Torts §§ 325, 537; Restatement of Restitution § 55. In some cases those rules and this Section overlap; in others they provide analogies useful in determining the extent to which enforcement is necessary to avoid injustice.

* * *

SECTION 26.2   AGREEMENTS WITH OPEN TERMS: ARBITRATION AGREEMENTS; AGREEMENTS "AGAINST PUBLIC POLICY"

ROSE AND FRANK CO. v. J. R. CROMPTON AND BROTHERS, LD.

Court of Appeal.
[1923] 2 K.B. 261.

[The opinion of Bailhache J. in the King's Bench Division, the arguments of counsel, footnotes of the Court, and parts of the opinions of Bankes, L. J., Scrutton, L. J., and Atkin, L. J., dealing with an alternative claim of the plaintiffs, are omitted. With respect to the alternative claim, Atkin, L. J., dissented from the opinion of the other members of the Court.]

Appeal from the judgment of Bailhache J. in an action tried before the learned judge without a jury.

The action was for breach of an alleged contract in writing signed by the defendants respectively on July 11 and July 8, 1913, a counterpart of which was signed by the plaintiffs on August 12, 1913.

The plaintiffs were an American company carrying on business in New York. The defendants J. R. Crompton & Brothers, Ld., and Brittains, Ld., carried on business at Bury in Lancashire and at Cheddleton in Staffordshire respectively.

The facts were as follows: J. R. Crompton & Brothers, Ld., were manufacturers of carbonizing tissue paper. Messrs. Rose & Frank, who were later incorporated as the Rose & Frank Company, were merchants who dealt in this paper. Business relations between these two firms began in 1905. . . .

The learned judge at the trial held that these arrangements were binding contracts, the effect of which was that Rose & Frank had the sole agency, not confined to the United States and Canada, of the blue carbonizing paper, subject to a twelve months' notice on either side, the sole agency of the 7 lbs. substance in the United States and Canada, subject to a similar notice, and the sole agency of all other carbonizing tissues in the United States only (with an exception in favour of one customer in Boston).

During the continuance of these relations, which were renewed from time to time and resulted in a profitable business to both parties, J. R. Crompton & Brothers, Ld., were in close commercial relations with Brittains, Ld., who produced paper tissues differing in quality from those of J. R. Crompton & Brothers, Ld., and a considerable quantity of the tissues supplied by J. R. Crompton & Brothers, Ld., to Rose & Frank, and to the Rose & Frank Company after its incorporation in March, 1911, were in fact manufactured by Brittains, Ld.; but there were so far no direct dealings between Brittains, Ld., and Rose & Frank or the Rose & Frank Company.

These relations continued until the end of 1912. Then the Rose & Frank Company, in order to give more permanence and stability to their business, proposed that an agreement should be drawn up between themselves, J. R. Crompton & Brothers, Ld., and Brittains, Ld., whereby the last named company should come into direct contractual relations with the Rose & Frank Company for a period of three years and thereafter for a further period of three years unless notice to the contrary were given by any of the parties to the others. An agreement to this effect dated January 1, 1913, was actually drafted but was never executed.

Instead of that agreement the following document was drawn up. It was signed by Brittains, Ld., on July 8, and by J. R. Crompton & Brothers, Ld., on July 11, and a counterpart thereof was signed by the Rose & Frank Company on August 12, 1913. It was in these terms:—

"As the business in carbonizing tissues which is now being done between Messrs. Rose & Frank Co. of New York as purchasers and Messrs. J. R. Crompton & Brothers Ld. of Bury, Lancashire, and Messrs. Brittains Ld. Cheddleton, Staffordshire, as manufacturers, has attained to a considerable volume, and Messrs. Rose & Frank Co. are of opinion that in the interests of the traders they represent assured arrangements for the supply of these papers should be made for some considerable period ahead, Messrs. J. R. Crompton & Brothers Ld. and Messrs. Brittains Ld. hereby express their willingness that the present arrangements with Messrs. Rose & Frank Co. for the sale of these papers, which are now for one year only, shall be continued on the same lines as at present for a period of three years, say until March 31, 1916, with the understanding that if it is desired by any of the three parties to alter or abrogate this arrangement at the expiration of that period six months' notice shall be given before that date. If no notice be given by either party the arrangement shall be regarded as continuing for a second period of three years subject to the same six months' notice for alteration or abrogation as in the first period of three years.

". . . [There followed here provisions as to the extent of the exclusiveness of plaintiffs' distributorship of defendants' products, plaintiffs' undertakings with respect to the purchase of defendants' products, and defendants' undertakings as to deliveries.]

"This arrangement is not entered into, nor is this memorandum written, as a formal or legal agreement, and shall not be subject to legal jurisdiction in the Law Courts either of the United States or England, but it is only a definite expression and record of the purpose and intention of the three parties concerned to which they each honourably pledge themselves with the fullest confidence, based on past business with each other, that it will be carried through by each of the three parties with mutual loyalty and friendly co-operation.

". . . [There followed here provisions as to the prices to be charged plaintiffs for defendants' products.]"

The arrangement contained in this document was extended to March 30, 1920. In May, 1919, the defendants J. R. Crompton & Brothers, Ld., and Brittains, Ld., became discontented with the way in which the plaintiffs, the Rose & Frank Company, were conducting their business in America. In the defendants' view the plaintiffs were demanding prices for their goods which encouraged competition and was injuring the business of the defendants. They sent a telegram inviting a representative of the plaintiffs to come over to England, but the invitation was not accepted. On May 7, 1919, the defendants definitely determined the arrangement between the parties.

The plaintiffs then brought this action. . . .

[The statement of claim alleged] (para. 13) that by cables on May 5 and 9, and by letter of May 10, 1919, the defendants refused to make any further deliveries to the plaintiffs and wrongfully repudiated the alleged agreement of July, 1913; (para. 14) that between March 31, 1919, and March 30, 1920, the plaintiffs would have required 200 cases of paper from the defendants J. R. Crompton & Brothers, Ld., and 800 cases from the defendants Brittains, Ld., and that their estimated loss on the non-delivery of these goods was 10,146£ on the 200 cases and 112,977£ on the 800 cases.

. . .

The formal judgment of the learned judge was drawn up as follows:—

(a) It was adjudged and declared that the agreement of July, 1913, mentioned in para. 8 of the statement of claim was a legally binding agreement against both defendants . . .

* * *

BANKES, L. J. This is a curious case. . . . The plaintiffs allege that the document is a contract in the strict sense of the word, involving each of the parties to it in a legal obligation to perform it. The defendants, on the other hand, say that the document is nothing of the kind, because it expressly provides that it shall not involve any of the parties in any legal obligation to perform any of its terms. There is, I think, no doubt that it is essential to the creation of a contract, using that word in its legal sense, that the parties to an agreement shall not only be ad idem as to the terms of their agreement, but that they shall have intended that it shall have legal consequences and be legally enforceable. In the case of agreements regulating business relations it follows almost as a matter of course that the parties intend legal consequences to follow. In the case of agreements regulating social engagements it equally follows almost as a matter of course that the parties do not intend legal consequences to follow. In some cases, such as Balfour v. Balfour, the law will, from the circumstances of the case, imply that the parties did not intend that their agreement should be attended by legal consequences. It no doubt sounds in the highest degree improbable that two firms in this country, arranging with a firm in the United States the terms upon which a very considerable business should be carried on between them over a term of years, should not have intended that their agreement as to those terms should be attended by legal consequences. It cannot however be denied that there is no reason in law why they should not so provide, if they desire to do so. The question therefore in the present case resolves itself into a question of construction. I see nothing in the surrounding circumstances which could justify an interpretation of the language used by the parties in the document of July, 1913, in any other than its ordinary meaning. The document itself is a curious one from a drafting point of view. A skilled draftsman could easily have rendered the discussion which has taken place in the Court below and in this Court impossible. As it is, the draftsman appears at times to have remembered, and at times to have lost sight of, the object he is alleged to have had in view. For instance, the document opens with a clause apparently studiously worded to avoid the usual appearance of a contract. The draftsman then adopts language which at times is strongly suggestive of a contract, and at times indicates something other than a contract. Then follows what is said to be the governing clause, and the document concludes with language suggestive of a contract. What I have called the governing clause is not couched in legal phraseology. A great deal more is said than need have been said in order to record the intention of the parties. I read it as a genuine attempt by some one not a skilled draftsman to go much further than merely providing a means for ousting the jurisdiction of the Courts of law. There is no ground for suggesting that the language used in the clause is not a bona fide expression of the intention of the parties. If so, it appears to me to admit of but one construction, which applies to and dominates the entire agreement. The intention clearly expressed is that the arrangement set out in the document is only an honourable pledge, and that all legal consequences and remedies are excluded from it. If this is the true construction of the clause, it must govern the entire arrangement, and there is consequently no room for the principle upon which the learned judge decided this part of the case. It would no doubt have simplified matters if the clause in question had been inserted at the head of the document, or even at the end, rather than in the position it occupies. I attribute its position to the want of that skill in drafting of which the document affords plenty of evidence, rather than to any want of bona fides in the language used. Once it is established that the language of the clause is the bona fide expression of the intention of the parties, the matter is in my opinion concluded, and it becomes manifest that no action can be maintained upon the agreement contained in the document of 1913.

* * *

For the reasons I have given, I think that this case fails. . . . the judgment of Bailhache J. must be varied by making the declaration contained in the first paragraph of the formal judgment in the negative instead of in the affirmative . . . .

SCRUTTON, L. J. The facts giving rise to the present dispute are clearly stated by Bailhache J., and I do not repeat them. Down to 1913 there were agreements between Messrs. Rose & Frank Co. in the United States and Messrs. Crompton in England which in my opinion gave rise to legal relations, though owing to the vagueness of the language used there might be considerable difficulty in ascertaining with exactitude what those legal relations were. In 1913 the parties concurred in signing a document which gives rise to the present dispute. I agree that if the clause beginning "This arrangement" were omitted, the Courts would treat the rest of the agreement as giving rise to legal relations, though again of great vagueness. An agreement that Messrs. Brittain & Crompton "will subject to unforeseen circumstances and contingencies do their best, as in the past, to respond efficiently and satisfactorily to the calls of Messrs. Rose & Frank Co. for deliveries both in quantity and quality," is not very helpful or precise. But the clause in question beginning "This arrangement" is not omitted and reads as follows: "This arrangement is not entered into, nor is this memorandum written, as a formal or legal agreement, and shall not be subject to legal jurisdiction in the Law Courts either of the United States or England, but it is only a definite expression and record of the purpose and intention of the three parties concerned to which they each honourably pledge themselves with the fullest confidence, based upon past business with each other, that it will be carried through by each of the three parties with mutual loyalty and friendly co-operation." The judge below thinks that by itself this clause "plain as it is" means that the parties shall not be under any legal obligation to each other at all. But coming to the conclusion that without this clause the agreement would create legal obligations, he takes the view that the clause must be rejected as repugnant to the rest of the agreement. He also holds that if the clause merely means to exclude recourse to the Law Courts as a means of settling disputes, it is contrary to public policy as ousting the jurisdiction of the King's Courts.

In my view the learned judge adopts a wrong canon of construction. He should not seek the intention of the parties as shown by the language they use in part of the language only, but in the whole of that language. It is true that in deeds and wills where it is impossible from the whole of the contradictory language used to ascertain the true intention of the framers, resort may be had, but only as a last expedient, to what Jessel M. R. called "the rule of thumb" in In re Bywater of rejecting clauses as repugnant according to their place in the document, the later clause being rejected in deeds and the earlier in wills. But before this heroic method is adopted of finding out what the parties meant by assuming that they did not mean part of what they have said, it must be clearly impossible to harmonize the whole of the language they have used.

Now it is quite possible for parties to come to an agreement by accepting a proposal with the result that the agreement concluded does not give rise to legal relations. The reason of this is that the parties do not intend that their agreement shall give rise to legal relations. This intention may be implied from the subject matter of the agreement, but it may also be expressed by the parties. In social and family relations such an intention is readily implied, while in business matters the opposite result would ordinarily follow. But I can see no reason why, even in business matters, the parties should not intend to rely on each other's good faith and honour, and to exclude all idea of settling disputes by any outside intervention, with the accompanying necessity of expressing themselves so precisely that outsiders may have no difficulty in understanding what they mean. If they clearly express such an intention I can see no reason in public policy why effect should not be given to their intention.

Both legal decisions and the opinions of standard text writers support this view. In Balfour v. Balfour the Court declined to recognize relations of contract as flowing from an agreement between husband and wife that he should send her 30£ a month for her maintenance. Atkin L. J., speaking of agreements or arrangements between husband and wife involving mutual promises and consideration in form, said "They are not contracts because the parties did not intend that they should be attended by legal consequences." In the early years of the war, when a member of a club brought an action against the committee to enforce his supposed rights in a club golf competition, I non-suited him for the same reason, that from the nature of the domestic and social relations, I drew the inference that the parties did not intend legal consequences to follow from them: Lens v. Devonshire Club. Mr. Leake says that "an agreement as the source of a legal contract imports that the one party shall be bound to some performance, which the latter (sic) shall have a legal right to enforce." In Sir Frederick Pollock's language an agreement to become enforceable at law must "be concerned with duties and rights which can be dealt with by a court of justice. And it must be the intention of the parties that the matter in hand shall, if necessary, be so dealt with, or at least they must not have the contrary intention." Sir William Anson requires in contract "a common intention to affect" the legal relations of the parties.

Judged by this test, I come to the same conclusion as the learned judge, that the particular clause in question shows a clear intention by the parties that the rest of their arrangement or agreement shall not affect their legal relations, or be enforceable in a Court of law, but in the words of the clause, shall be "only a definite expression and record of the purpose and intention of the three parties concerned to which they each honourably pledge themselves," "and shall not be subject to legal jurisdiction." If the clause stood first in the document, the intention of the parties would be exceedingly plain.

*   *   *

In my view, therefore, the judgment of Bailhache J. ordering that the issue of liability for damages under the "legally binding agreement" of 1913 . . . shall be tried by himself, should be reversed.

*   *   *

ATKIN, L. J. The first question in this case is whether the document signed by the defendants on July 11, 1913, with a counterpart signed by the plaintiffs on August 12, 1913, constituted a contract between the parties. To create a contract there must be a common intention of the parties to enter into legal obligations, mutually communicated expressly or impliedly. Such an intention ordinarily will be inferred when parties enter into an agreement which in other respects conforms to the rules of law as to the formation of contracts. It may be negatived impliedly by the nature of the agreed promise or promises, as in the case of offer and acceptance of hospitality, or of some agreements made in the course of family life between members of a family as in Balfour v. Balfour. If the intention may be negatived impliedly it may be negatived expressly. In this document, construed as a whole, I find myself driven to the conclusion that the clause in question expresses in clear terms the mutual intention of the parties not to enter into legal obligations in respect to the matters upon which they are recording their agreement. I have never seen such a clause before, but I see nothing necessarily absurd in business men seeking to regulate their business relations by mutual promises which fall short of legal obligations, and rest on obligations of either honour or self-interest, or perhaps both. In this agreement I consider the clause a dominant clause, and not to be rejected, as the learned judge thought, on the ground of repugnancy.

. . . On this, the main question, I agree with the judgments of the other members of the Court.

Questions

1. Is the meaning of the clause in question unclear to you? Would you say that it expresses a clear intention that the agreement between them should not be treated as a promise or set of promises which would be recognized as creating a legal duty or for breach of which the law should afford a remedy? If so, what purpose was served by negotiating the agreement, and memorializing it in a written instrument?

Suppose that at some time prior to the termination of the agreement, Rose and Frank had ordered 200 cases of carbon paper, Brittains or Crompton Brothers had shipped the order, and then Rose and Frank refused to accept delivery or pay for the 200 cases. Would the clause in question have protected Rose and Frank from liability to the shipper?

2.   If you were an attorney representing either of the parties to the transaction at the time the document was drafted, would you have cautioned them against entering into a legally enforceable agreement?

3.   Why do you suppose the trial judge reached the result that he did?

4.   What is "ousting the jurisdiction of the King's Courts", and why should it be contrary to public policy?

5.   What is so "curious" about this case? Does it seem "curious" to you that this case should be so difficult for the judges to decide?

6.   Does the court seem to start from the premise that a commercial bargain should be treated as a contract? Why might a promise made in a commercial setting be treated differently than a promise made in the context of a marital relationship (see Balfour v. Balfour, *supra*)?

––––––––

Rose and Frank involves an attempt by "commercial men" to work out a loose framework for an ongoing relationship between manufacturers of goods (Crompton and Brothers, Ltd., and Brittains, Ltd.) and a middleman (Rose and Frank) whose business was selling those goods to retailers and ultimate consumers. Such an arrangement makes economic good sense. The manufacturer is freed to use capital, labor and entrepreneurial skill to concentrate on the business of manufacturing its product, leaving the direct marketing function to a commercial middleman. This practical application of the economic principles of division of labor and specialization of function was no doubt mutually beneficial to both parties. The manufacturers could rely on the middleman to sell the product and expand the trade; the middleman could rely on the manufacturers to provide a steady flow of quality product. The exchange relationship between the two sides is essentially a cooperative enterprise looking towards mostly common goals. That such relationships can be effective and beneficial is evidenced by the extent to which they were and are used in our society. Anyone who has bought gasoline from a service station, a car from an automobile dealer, or a "Big Mac" under the golden arches, has probably made a purchase from an independent business which is tied by contract to a long term arrangement with the producer or franchiser whose brand name appears on the product. Ideally, this system of contractual integration from manufacturer to retailer will rest on confidence, good faith, and mutual undertakings. In Rose and Frank the parties fairly clearly intended that their long term undertaking would rest solely on those principles without benefit of legal remedy should either party breach. It is more common practice, however, for the parties to long term arrangements to attempt to introduce the power of the law into their arrangement by negotiating their agreements as contracts. The case which follows is an example of one such an attempt, and judicial responses to it.

OSCAR SCHLEGEL MFG. CO. v. PETER COOPER'S GLUE FACTORY

Court of Appeals of New York, 1921.
231 N.Y. 459, 132 N.E. 148.

McLAUGHLIN, J. Action to recover damages for alleged breach of contract. The complaint alleged that on or about December 9, 1915, the parties entered into a written agreement by which the defendant agreed to sell and deliver to the plaintiff, and the plaintiff agreed to purchase from the defendant, all its "requirements" of special BB glue for the year 1916, at the price of nine cents per pound. It also alleged the terms of payment, the manner in which the glue was to be packed, the place of delivery, the neglect and refusal of defendant to make certain deliveries, and the damages sustained, for which judgment was demanded. The answer put in issue the material allegations of the complaint. At the trial a jury was waived and the trial proceeded before the trial justice. At its conclusion he rendered a decision awarding the plaintiff a substantial amount. Judgment was entered upon the decision, from which an appeal was taken to the Appellate Division, first department, where the same was affirmed, two of the justices dissenting. The appeal to this court followed.

I am of the opinion that the judgment appealed from should be reversed, upon the ground that the alleged contract, for the breach of which a recovery was had, was invalid since it lacked mutuality. It consisted solely of a letter written by defendant to plaintiff, the material part of which is as follows:

"GENTLEMEN.—We are instructed by our Mr. Von Schuckmann to enter your contract for your requirements of 'Special BB' glue for the year 1916, price to be 9¢ per lb., terms 2% 20th to 30th of month following purchase. Deliveries, to be made to you as per your orders during the year and quality same as heretofore. Glue to be packed in 500 lb. or 350 lb. barrels and 100 lb. kegs, and your special Label to be carefully pasted on top, bottom and side of each barrel or keg. *   *   *

"PETER COOPER'S GLUE FACTORY,
"W. D. Donaldson,
"Sales Manager."

At the bottom of the letter the president of the plaintiff wrote: "Accepted, Oscar Schlegel Manufacturing Company," and returned it to the defendant.

The plaintiff, at the time, was engaged in no manufacturing business in which glue was used or required, nor was it then under contract to deliver glue to any third parties at a fixed price or otherwise. It was simply a jobber, selling, among other things, glue to such customers as might be obtained by sending out salesmen to solicit orders therefor. The contract was invalid since a consideration was lacking. Mutual promises or obligations of parties to a contract, either express or necessarily implied, may furnish the requisite consideration. The defect in the alleged contract here under consideration is that it contains no express consideration, nor are there any mutual promises of the parties to it from which such consideration can be fairly inferred. The plaintiff, it will be observed, did not agree to do or refrain from doing anything. It was not obligated to sell a pound of defendant's glue or to make any effort in that direction. It did not agree not to sell other glue in competition with defendant's. The only obligation assumed by it was to pay nine cents a pound for such glue as it might order. Whether it should order any at all rested entirely with it. If it did not order any glue, then nothing was to be paid. The agreement was not under seal, and, therefore, fell within the rule that a promise not under seal made by one party, with none by the other, is void. Unless both parties to a contract are bound, so that either can sue the other for a breach, neither is bound. [Citations omitted.] Had the plaintiff neglected or refused to order any glue during the year 1916, defendant could not have maintained an action to recover damages against it, because there would have been no breach of the contract. In order to recover damages, a breach had to be shown, and this could not have been established by a mere failure on the part of the plaintiff to order glue, since it had not promised to give such orders.

There are certain contracts in which mutual promises are implied: Thus, where the purchaser, to the knowledge of the seller, has entered into a contract for the resale of the article purchased (Shipman v. Straitsville Central Mining Co., 158 U.S. 356, 15 S.Ct. 886); where the purchaser contracts for his requirements of an article necessary to be used in the business carried on by him (Wells v. Alexandre, 130 N.Y. 642, 29 N.E. 142); or for all the cans needed in a canning factory (Daily Co. v. Clark Can Co., 128 Mich. 591, 87 N.W. 761); all the lubricating oil for party's own use (Manhattan Oil Co. v. Richardson Lubricating Co., 113 Fed.Rep. 923); all the coal needed for a foundry during a specified time (Minnesota Lumber Co. v. Whitebreast Coal Co. (160 Ill. 85, 43 N.E. 774); all the iron required during a certain period in a furnace (National Furnace Co. v. Keystone Mfg. Co., 110 Ill. 427); and all the ice required in a hotel during a certain season (G. N. Railway Co. v. Witham, L.R. 9 C.P. 16). In cases of this character, while the quantity of the article contracted to be sold is indefinite, nevertheless there is a certain standard mentioned in the agreement by which such quantity can be determined by an approximately accurate forecast. In the contract here under consideration there is no standard mentioned by which the quantity of glue to be furnished can be determined with any approximate degree of accuracy.

The view above expressed is not in conflict with the authorities cited by the respondent. Thus, in N. Y. C. Iron Works Co. v. U. S. Radiator Co. (174 N.Y. 331, 66 N.E. 967), principally relied upon and cited in the prevailing opinion at the Appellate Division, "the defendant bound the plaintiff to deal exclusively in goods to be ordered from it under the contract, and to enlarge and develop the market for the defendant's wares so far as possible."

In Fuller & Co. v. Schrenk (58 App.Div. 222, 68 N.Y.S. 781; affd. 171 N.Y. 671, 64 N.E. 1126) the contract provided: "It is hereby agreed that in consideration of W. P. Fuller & Co. buying *all* their supply of German Mirror Plates from the United Bavarian Looking Glass Works, for a period of six months from this date, the said United Bavarian Looking Glass Works" agrees to sell certain mirrors at specified prices.

In Wood v. Duff-Gordon (222 N.Y. 88, 118 N.E. 214) the plaintiff was to have, for the term of one year, the exclusive right to place defendant's indorsement on certain designs, in return for which she was to have one-half of all the profits and revenue derived from any contracts he might make. The point was there made, as here, that plaintiff did not promise that he would use reasonable efforts to place defendant's indorsement and market her designs, but this court held that such a promise was fairly to be implied; that when defendant gave to the plaintiff an exclusive privilege for a period of one year, during which time she could not place her own indorsements, or market her own designs, except through the agency of the plaintiff, that the acceptance of such an exclusive agency carried with it an assumption of its duties.

In Ehrenworth v. Stuhmer & Co. (229 N.Y. 210, 128 N.E. 108) defendant and its predecessor were desirous of obtaining a market for a particular kind of bread which it manufactured. In order to accomplish this purpose it was agreed that plaintiff should purchase and defendant sell *all* the bread of the kind specified which plaintiff required in a certain locality and pay therefor a price specified in the agreement. The plaintiff also agreed he would not sell any other bread of that kind on that route during the life of the contract, which was to continue so long as the parties remained in business. This contract, it will be noticed, specified the articles to be sold, the price to be paid, the quantity to be furnished, and the term of the contract, during which time plaintiff agreed not to sell any other bread of the kind named in that territory.

In the instant case, as we have already seen, there was no obligation on the part of the plaintiff to sell any of the defendant's glue, to make any effort towards bringing about such sale, or not to sell other glues in competition with it. There is not in the letter a single obligation from which it can fairly be inferred that the plaintiff was to do or refrain from doing anything whatever.

The price of glue having risen during the year 1916 from nine to twenty-four cents per pound, it is quite obvious why orders for glue increased correspondingly. Had the price dropped below nine cents it may fairly be inferred such orders would not have been given. In that case, if the interpretation put upon the agreement be the correct one, plaintiff would not have been liable to the defendant for damages for a breach, since he had not agreed to sell any glue.

The judgments of the Appellate Division and trial court should be reversed and the complaint dismissed, with costs in all courts.

HISCOCK, Ch. J., HOGAN, POUND, CRANE and ANDREWS, JJ., concur; CHASE, J., deceased.

Judgments reversed, etc.

The intermediate appellate court and the trial court had both found for the plaintiff. Their reasons for so doing, and the lower appellate court's view of the facts in the case are set out in the following excerpt from that court's majority opinion.

OSCAR SCHLEGEL MFG. CO. v. PETER COOPER'S GLUE FACTORY

Appellate Division of the Supreme Court of New York, 1919.
189 App.Div. 843, 179 N.Y.S. 271.

DOWLING, J.: . . . The parties entered upon [performance of the requirements contract] and deliveries were made from time to time amounting in the aggregate to 169,800 pounds or 340 barrels. For the first nine months of 1916, from January to September inclusive, plaintiff received and paid for 87½ barrels or 43,700 pounds. The average for these months was a little less than 5,000 pounds. In October, November and December, however, the plaintiff ordered an aggregate of 126,100 pounds. Between October 30, 1916, and December 26, 1916, plaintiff ordered the delivery pursuant to the contract of 79,891 pounds of glue which plaintiff needed to meet its requirements and the defendant did not deliver the same. Plaintiff in anticipation of the performance of the contract had sold 42,000 pounds of this glue and as it could no longer be bought in the open market it lost its profits on such sales. The other damage sustained by plaintiff pursuant to defendant's failure to deliver the balance of the amount ordered brought the plaintiff's damages up to a total of $6,431.28 for which it has recovered judgment.

The plaintiff was a jobber exclusively, handling glues, shellacs, paints and chemicals. It bought only for retailing to the trade and did not manufacture or use any of these articles in its own business. It sent out salesmen to solicit orders and when "BB Special Glue" was ordered by a customer a requisition covering the same would be sent to defendant who would fill the order. The plaintiff dealt in none of the glue from its own stock but filled the orders of its customers as it received them by calling upon defendant to deliver the goods under the contract between the plaintiff and defendant. Therefore, the plaintiff's requirements of Special BB Glue for the year 1916 were the amounts of orders received therefor from its customers to whom its salesmen had sold such goods. This method of doing business, and the meaning of the term "requirements" as used in the contract, were concededly well known to defendant, which had theretofore done business under the same system with the plaintiff, to which it had sold goods as far back as 1910. The contract in question is similar in general terms to the contract between the parties for the year 1915 which also was for plaintiff's "requirements" of special bookbinders' glue, for the balance of the year from March 3, 1915, at a fixed price quoted. No question arose between the parties as to the meaning of such a contract during the year 1915 and plaintiff's requirements, evidenced by orders from its customers, were filled without question during that year. Nor did any question arise as to the meaning or validity of the contract for the year 1916, until the price for this special glue rose so high that the contract became very valuable to the plaintiff and entailed a corresponding loss of profit to the defendant which it could have made by selling the goods elsewhere. The contract price was nine cents per pound and by December, 1916, prices were quoted as high as twenty-one to twenty-five cents, and plaintiff itself had sold at the price of fifteen cents and twenty-four cents goods which it was unable to buy in the open market in order to fill its sales. For such goods as plaintiff did obtain in the open market it paid seventeen cents a pound in December, 1916, and then the quality was lower than that which defendant was to supply. Furthermore, in the month of December, 1916, no quotations whatever were available for 1917 deliveries.

Under these conditions plaintiff not unnaturally sought to reap a legitimate advantage from its contract and by soliciting the trade received orders for the last three months of 1916 which, as has been said, aggregated 126,100 pounds. In the meantime the defendant was furnished by plaintiff with requisitions for orders for 79,891 pounds of glue which it has failed to deliver under the contract, and upon the trial these requisitions were produced by the defendant upon notice and received in evidence. At no time during the receipt of these orders did the defendant repudiate the contract or disavow the same, nor did it object to, or question, the good faith of the orders. Plaintiff repeatedly demanded performance of the contract and defendant's representative with whom the original contract was made promised repeatedly as late as the month of December, 1916, to ship glue to cover the requisitions and said that the glue was on the way. Instead of repudiating the contract, the defendant undertook to place an arbitrary limitation upon the same, by saying it would give the plaintiff as a jobber ten per cent more than it had purchased during the year 1915 or about 40,000 pounds. But despite this the defendant never notified plaintiff to cease taking orders from its customers for delivery of this glue, nor did it ever notify plaintiff while the orders in question were being taken that it would not live up to its contract.

The defendant now claims that this contract lacked mutuality and, therefore, was unenforcible. I do not think this contention can be sustained. Both parties were dealing with full knowledge that the plaintiff required no glue for use in any manufacturing business of its own, but desired and agreed only to purchase such glue as it might be able to sell through its salesmen to customers. The course of dealing between plaintiff and defendant kept defendant constantly advised of this fact and it knew that the plaintiff kept no stock of goods, but as soon as it received an order for glue it notified the defendant thereof and had the order filled by the defendant. In other words, plaintiff's requirements which, under the contract, defendant was to supply for the year 1916, were its requirements for the amount of glue which during that time it might be able to sell to customers. The recovery herein is based upon the loss which plaintiff sustained by reason of defendant's failure to fill orders which plaintiff had so obtained from customers and of which the defendant had been promptly notified. The defendant had not protected itself against any abnormal variation in price during the year nor had it fixed any limitation upon the amount of glue which it would furnish the plaintiff, if it received orders from its customers therefor. The only proviso in the contract which the defendant cared to insert was that the contract was contingent upon fires, strikes, accidents and other causes beyond the control of the parties. A rising market could have been guarded against by the defendant by inserting in the contract a clause fixing the maximum amount which the plaintiff might be entitled to receive thereunder; but instead the defendant made an absolute contract at a fixed price for the entire year to deliver as much glue as plaintiff might be able to sell to customers during that period. If the plaintiff had taken orders for this quality of glue and had failed to buy the amount to fill such orders from the defendant, the defendant could have held the plaintiff under the contract and recovered the damages which it sustained by reason of plaintiff's failure to order such glue from the defendant. And this it could have done no matter how low the market price might have fallen during the year. Both parties acted with full knowledge of their respective methods of doing business and of the uncertain and fluctuating demand for glue which might come from plaintiff's customers and which must naturally to some extent be dependent upon the market price. They entered upon this contract with their eyes open to all the conditions then existing, or which might possibly arise, and with the intention of being mutually bound thereby. I believe that under the contract the plaintiff was bound to order from the defendant every pound of this quality of glue which it sold to its customers and that in like manner defendant was bound to supply every pound of this quality of glue which plaintiff sold to customers and called upon the defendant to furnish. The mere uncertainty as to the amount which might be required to be furnished under the contract is no reason why it was not a mutual one nor does it make the contract unenforcible.

The court has found that the orders in question were received by plaintiff and transmitted to defendant under the contract. The plaintiff's good faith in soliciting these orders and their validity have not been successfully attacked. Having a valid and enforcible contract with the defendant, obtained without any unfair dealing on its part, but as the result of the deliberate judgment of both parties thereto, the plaintiff had a right in the absence of any notification from the defendant that it could not or would not fill all its orders to proceed legitimately in good faith to solicit orders from the trade for this quality of glue and to expect the filling of these orders by the defendant. The defendant had no right to arbitrarily limit the amount which plaintiff should receive under the contract, and it was, therefore, properly held liable for the damages which the plaintiff sustained.

The situation presented by this case is similar to that which was before the Court of Appeals in New York Central Iron Works Co. v. U. S. Radiator Co. (174 N.Y. 331, 66 N.E. 967). There also the parties had left the contract open and indefinite as to the quantity of the goods that plaintiff might order from time to time. Defendant had there sought to have the contract reformed so as to call for only the usual amount of goods sold in the preceding year, as an answer to the vendee's action for damages sustained by reason of the vendor's refusal to furnish the goods called for under its orders for the second year. Judge O'BRIEN said (p. 334): "It is quite probable that this controversy originated in a circumstance which the defendant, at least, had not anticipated or provided for. After the execution of the contract there was a large advance in the market price of iron and the manufactured products of iron, and, consequently, the value and selling price of the goods covered by this contract advanced in the same or possibly in a greater proportion. The *needs* of the plaintiff could be indefinitely enlarged when the market was in such a condition as to enable it to undersell its competitors in the same business in consequence of a favorable contract with the manufacturer of the goods. If a party contracts for goods upon a rising market he is ordinarily entitled to such profits as may accrue to him by reason of a prudent or favorable contract. We cannot perceive that there is any error of law in this judgment, although the plaintiff has recovered a considerable sum in damages for the breach. The case in its general features is the same as another case which was recently before this court, where there was a similar recovery that was sustained. (Fuller & Co. v. Schrenk, 58 App.Div. 222, 68 N.Y.S. 781, affirmed, 171 N.Y. 671, 64 N.E. 1126.)"

The judgment appealed from should be affirmed, with costs.

MERRELL and PHILBIN, JJ., concurred; CLARKE, P. J., and PAGE, J., dissented. [Dissenting opinion omitted.]

Questions

1. Look carefully at the lower court opinion and see precisely what the plaintiff alleged as the amount of damages, and how that amount was determined. Does that give some clue as to why the lower court could find for the defendant? Does Section 90 of the Restatement (*supra* p. 607) afford a doctrinal ground supporting the lower court opinion?

2. Does the lower court consider issues of fairness and good faith between the parties? Does it suggest that Peter Cooper failed to act fairly and in good faith? Does it hint that Peter Cooper might have taken steps to avoid the loss itself and to avoid losses incurred by Oscar Schlegel?

3. Does the lower court opinion suggest that there were some objective measures of the scope of the contract which Peter Cooper might have invoked to put a limit on the amount of glue it could be required to supply at the contract price? If the court were to read such implicit terms into a contract, would that impinge on the parties freedom to contract?

4. Does the fact that Oscar Schlegel is a broker—a middleman— have some bearing on the Court of Appeals' decision not to enforce the agreement? What problem does Schlegel's middleman status pose regarding the scope and limits of Peter Cooper's undertaking and potential liability?

5. The Court of Appeals rests its determination of the case on one of the extensions of the consideration doctrine, namely lack of mutuality of obligation between the parties. What precisely is the basis for finding that there was no commitment or undertaking on the part of Oscar Schlegel? Is it because there was no written evidence of any promise or commitment by Oscar Schlegel? Could some commitment or promise by Oscar Schlegel have been inferred from the circumstances surrounding the agreement? If so, what? Put another way, can you think of any circumstances which could have afforded Peter Cooper a remedy against Oscar Schlegel for not ordering glue? Sup-

pose, for example, the retail price of glue had remained constant, and a competing glue manufacturer had offered to supply Oscar Schlegel's requirements for glue at 8½ cents per pound? Should Peter Cooper have had a remedy if Oscar Schlegel filled its requirements from the competitor rather than from Peter Cooper?

6. In Wood v. Duff-Gordon (discussed in the Court of Appeals opinion, *supra* p. 617), the Court of Appeals inferred mutuality of obligation in a case similar to Oscar Schlegel. How did the Court distinguish the two cases? Is that distinction persuasive to you? Why? Why Not?

Oscar Schlegel presents a somewhat antiquated view of the proper treatment of requirements and other open term contracts. A more contemporary approach to this problem is shown in the following excerpts.

UNIFORM COMMERCIAL CODE
ARTICLE TWO

§ 2—305. Open Price Term

(1) The parties if they so intend can conclude a contract for sale even though the price is not settled. In such a case the price is a reasonable price at the time for delivery if

    (a) nothing is said as to price; or

    (b) the price is left to be agreed by the parties and they fail to agree; or

    (c) the price is to be fixed in terms of some agreed market or other standard as set or recorded by a third person or agency and it is not so set or recorded.

(2) A price to be fixed by the seller or by the buyer means a price for him to fix in good faith.

(3) When a price left to be fixed otherwise than by agreement of the parties fails to be fixed through fault of one party the other may at his option treat the contract as cancelled or himself fix a reasonable price.

(4) Where, however, the parties intend not to be bound unless the price be fixed or agreed and it is not fixed or agreed there is no contract. In such a case the buyer must return any goods already received or if unable so to do must pay their reasonable value at the time of delivery and the seller must return any portion of the price paid on account.

Official Comment

1. This section applies when the price term is left open on the making of an agreement which is nevertheless intended by the parties to be a binding agreement. This Article rejects in these instances the formula that "an agreement to agree is unenforceable" if the case falls within subsection (1) of this section, and rejects also defeating such agreements on the ground of "indefiniteness". Instead this Article recognizes the dominant intention of

the parties to have the deal continue to be binding upon both. As to future performance, since this Article recognizes remedies such as cover (Section 2–712), resale (Section 2–706) and specific performance (Section 2–716) which go beyond any mere arithmetic as between contract price and market price, there is usually a "reasonably certain basis for granting an appropriate remedy for breach" so that the contract need not fail for indefiniteness.

2. Under some circumstances the postponement of agreement on price will mean that no deal has really been concluded, and this is made express in the preamble of subsection (1) ("The parties *if they so intend*") and in subsection (4). Whether or not this is so is, in most cases, a question to be determined by the trier of fact.

3. Subsection (2), dealing with the situation where the price is to be fixed by one party rejects the uncommercial idea that an agreement that the seller may fix the price means that he may fix any price he may wish by the express qualification that the price so fixed must be fixed in good faith. Good faith includes observance of reasonable commercial standards of fair dealing in the trade if the party is a merchant. (Section 2–103). But in the normal case a "posted price" or a future seller's or buyer's "given price," "price in effect," "market price," or the like satisfies the good faith requirement.

4. The section recognizes that there may be cases in which a particular person's judgment is not chosen merely as a barometer or index of a fair price but is an essential condition to the parties' intent to make any contract at all. For example, the case where a known and trusted expert is to "value" a particular painting for which there is no market standard differs sharply from the situation where a named expert is to determine the grade of cotton, and the difference would support a finding that in the one the parties did not intend to make a binding agreement if that expert were unavailable whereas in the other they did so intend. Other circumstances would of course affect the validity of such a finding.

5. Under subsection (3), wrongful interference by one party with any agreed machinery for price fixing in the contract may be treated by the other party as a repudiation justifying cancellation, or merely as a failure to take cooperative action thus shifting to the aggrieved party the reasonable leeway in fixing the price.

6. Throughout the entire section, the purpose is to give effect to the agreement which has been made. That effect, however, is always conditioned by the requirement of good faith action which is made an inherent part of all contracts within this Act. (Section 1–203).

§ 2—306. Output, Requirements and Exclusive Dealings

(1) A term which measures the quantity by the output of the seller or the requirements of the buyer means such actual output or requirements as may occur in good faith, except that no quantity unreasonably disproportionate to any stated estimate or in the absence of a stated estimate to any normal or otherwise comparable prior output or requirements may be tendered or demanded.

(2) A lawful agreement by either the seller or the buyer for exclusive dealing in the kind of goods concerned imposes unless otherwise agreed an obligation by the seller to use best efforts to supply the goods and by the buyer to use best efforts to promote their sale.

Official Comment

Purposes:

1. Subsection (1) of this section, in regard to output and requirements, applies to this specific problem the general approach of this Act which requires the reading of commercial background and intent into the language of any agreement and demands good faith in the performance of that agreement. It applies to such contracts of nonproducing establishments such as dealers or distributors as well as to manufacturing concerns.

2. Under this Article, a contract for output or requirements is not too indefinite since it is held to mean the actual good faith output or requirements of the particular party. Nor does such a contract lack mutuality of obligation since, under this section, the party who will determine quantity is required to operate his plant or conduct his business in good faith and according to commercial standards of fair dealing in the trade so that his output or requirements will approximate a reasonably foreseeable figure. Reasonable elasticity in the requirements is expressly envisaged by this section and good faith variations from prior requirements are permitted even when the variation may be such as to result in discontinuance. A shutdown by a requirements buyer for lack of orders might be permissible when a shutdown merely to curtail losses would not. The essential test is whether the party is acting in good faith. Similarly, a sudden expansion of the plant by which requirements are to be measured would not be included within the scope of the contract as made but normal expansion undertaken in good faith would be within the scope of this section. One of the factors in an expansion situation would be whether the market price had risen greatly in a case in which the requirements contract contained a fixed price. Reasonable variation of an extreme sort is exemplified in Southwest Natural Gas Co. v. Oklahoma Portland Cement Co., 102 F.2d 630 (C.C.A. 10, 1939). This Article takes no position as to whether a requirements contract is a provable claim in bankruptcy.

3. If an estimate of output or requirements is included in the agreement, no quantity unreasonably disproportionate to it may be tendered or demanded. Any minimum or maximum set by the agreement shows a clear limit on the intended elasticity. In similar fashion, the agreed estimate is to be regarded as a center around which the parties intend the variation to occur.

4. When an enterprise is sold, the question may arise whether the buyer is bound by an existing output or requirements contract. That question is outside the scope of this Article, and is to be determined on other principles of law. Assuming that the contract continues, the output or requirements in the hands of the new owner continue to be measured by the actual good faith output or requirements under the normal operation of the enterprise prior to sale. The sale itself is not grounds for sudden expansion or decrease.

5. Subsection (2), on exclusive dealing, makes explicit the commercial rule embodied in this Act under which the parties to such contracts are held to have impliedly, even when not expressly, bound themselves to use reasonable diligence as well as good faith in their performance of the contract. Under such contracts the exclusive agent is required, although no express

commitment has been made, to use reasonable effort and due diligence in the expansion of the market or the promotion of the product, as the case may be. The principal is expected under such a contract to refrain from supplying any other dealer or agent within the exclusive territory. An exclusive dealing agreement brings into play all of the good faith aspects of the output and requirement problems of subsection (1). It also raises questions of insecurity and right to adequate assurance under this Article.

Questions

1. Do the official comments regarding UCC 2–305 and 2–306 suggest some of the practical reasons why judges might be hostile to treating open term arrangements as contracts?

2. If you were a trial judge would you prefer contract doctrine which would deny contract treatment to open term agreements, or would you prefer the UCC approach regarding open terms? Why? Which approach poses greater problems as to the proof required to show (a) that an agreement has been made, and (b) that an agreement has been breached? How are these problems to be resolved under the UCC approach? Does that approach require that the lawyers who try and the judges and juries who decide cases become reasonably well informed regarding the commercial context within which open term agreements are made?

3. Did either of the Oscar Schlegel courts demonstrate any inclination to draw inferences from and rely upon the commercial context of the Cooper/Schlegel bargain in order to resolve that dispute? Are courts particularly well suited to perform that task? Can you think of persons or institutions who might be better suited to perform that task?

4. Comparing the UCC and Oscar Schlegel approaches to open terms, which would you say is more likely to facilitate the making of long term arrangements? Which is more likely to require more careful and elaborate planning for long term arrangements?

5. UCC Article 2 deals with sales of personal property, e. g., glue, carbon paper, and other movable goods. Do you think that the UCC methods and approaches for dealing with such goods are equally valid with respect to real property transactions? To family transactions such as Balfour v. Balfour, Schnell v. Nell, and Hamer v. Sidway?

6. Does Section 90 of the Restatement (*supra* p. 607) call for judges to define and impose contract obligations in terms similar to UCC 2–305 and 2–306 and the associated official commentary?

In earlier materials we paid some attention, at least briefly, to the idea of codes and the codification of bodies of legal doctrine (see Ch. 6, at pp. 582–585, and p. 585, Note 3). The Uniform Commercial Code is a very special and significant example of a modern American code.

The following excerpts give a brief description of origins and aspects of the Uniform Commercial Code.

[The following is taken from RICHARD E. SPEIDEL, ROBERT S. SUMMERS, and JAMES J. WHITE, COMMERCIAL AND CONSUMER LAW, 2d ed. (St. Paul, Minn., 1974), pp. 18–24.]

In the 1890's the National Conference of Commissioners on Uniform State Laws had been formed, with representatives from each state many of whom were dedicated to the cause of uniform codification. In 1896, the Conference promulgated the Negotiable Instruments Law, a Code governing the rights and liabilities of parties to checks, promissory notes, and other kinds of commercial paper. Ultimately, the "NIL" was adopted by all state legislatures. In 1906, the Conference presented the Uniform Sales Act for adoption and more than two-thirds of the states enacted it. With this Act, American law professors entered the codification arena, and have been central figures there ever since. Professor Samuel Williston of the Harvard Law School drafted the Uniform Sales Act on behalf of the Conference, and also the Uniform Warehouse Receipts Act, promulgated in 1906, and the Uniform Bills of Lading Act promulgated in 1909 both of which became law in all states. Later, Professor Karl Llewellyn of the Columbia Law School drafted the Uniform Trust Receipts Act, which the Conference promulgated in 1933. Thirty-two states adopted it. Another uniform commercial act, dealing with "conditional" sales, was drafted by Professor Bogert, but it met with success in only ten state legislatures.

In 1940, the idea of a single comprehensive commercial code covering all the foregoing branches of commercial law was conceived and proposed to the Conference of Commissioners on Uniform State Laws. The foregoing uniform acts had become outdated in two ways: changes had occurred in the patterns of commercial activity extant when these laws were enacted, and wholly new patterns had emerged giving rise to new kinds of legal needs. Moreover, even with the Uniform Acts most widely enacted, uniformity no longer existed, for the various state legislatures and judiciaries had added their own distinctive amendments and glosses.

The American Law Institute joined with the National Conference of Commissioners to co-sponsor the "Uniform Commercial Code" project. Professor Karl Llewellyn, then still at Columbia Law School, became chief architect, and his wife, Miss Soia Mentschikoff, his principal assistant (designated, respectively, "Chief Reporter" and "Associate Chief Reporter"). Miss Mentschikoff has described the drafting process, in Mentschikoff, The Uniform Commercial Code: An Experiment In Democracy In Drafting, 36 A.B.A.J. 419 (1950).

In 1951, the sponsors promulgated the Uniform Commercial Code, and, with minor revisions, it was enacted in Pennsylvania in 1953, effective July 1, 1954. Between 1953 and 1955, the New York Law Revision Commission dropped all other work and made a thorough study of the Code, recommending many changes in the official text. During the hearings there were, from time to time, rather sharp conflicts between academicians defending the Code and practitioners attacking it.

In 1956, the Editorial Board of the Code made recommendations for revision of the 1952 official text, many of which were based on criticisms made at the New York Law Revision Commission Hearings. In 1957 a revised Official Text was promulgated incorporating recommended changes. Further Official Texts, with minor changes, were promulgated in 1958 and 1962.

By 1968, the Uniform Commercial Code had been enacted by all but one state in the United States. A "Permanent Editorial Board" was established by the sponsoring organizations primarily to consider the wisdom of proposed amendments to the Code. . . .

The Code is divided into ten articles. The first is a general article bearing on various aspects of the entire Code. Article ten consists of provisions on repeal and effective date. The remaining eight articles are "substantive" in nature, and are broken down first into "Parts" and the "Parts" are in turn subdivided into sections. Some brief remarks on each article are in order:

Article 2: Sale of Goods

Article 2 applies to "transactions in goods" and supersedes the Uniform Sales Act. Major innovations in Article 2 include de-emphasis of the title concept in settling sales controversies, several novel provisions governing formation of the sales contract, and different standards of conduct applicable to merchants and to nonmerchants in discharging their contract obligations.

Article 3: Commercial Paper

Article 3 is a revision of the Uniform Negotiable Instruments Law. It includes fewer innovations than any other major Article of the Code. Unlike the Uniform Negotiable Instruments Law, Article 3 does not apply to bank deposits and collections (but see UCC 3–104, Comment (2)), letters of credit, or corporate securities. Articles 4, 5, and 8, respectively, deal with these subjects.

Consolidation was a chief aim of the draftsmen of Article 3. While the Uniform Negotiable Instruments Law had 198 provisions, Article 3 has only 80. The most dramatic instance of consolidation in the entire Code appears in Article 3: The Code takes only 11 sections to deal with presentment, notice of dishonor, and protest, while the Uniform Negotiable Instruments Law took 67 sections to deal with these subjects.

Article 4: Bank Deposits and Collections

Article 4 replaces statutes governing bank deposits and collections. There was no prior uniform act in this field. Article 4 therefore fills an important void. Article 4 includes basic provisions settling such old questions as: When does a depository bank buy an item rather than take it for collection only? UCC 4–201, 4–213. And, as of what point in time does a bank pay an item? UCC 4–213. Among the novel provisions of Article 4 are those requiring depositors to exercise due care in discovering forgeries, UCC 4–406(1), and a provision granting bank and depositor full freedom to govern their relations by contract, "except that no agreement can disclaim a bank's responsibility for its own lack of good faith or failure to exercise ordinary care . . . ." UCC 4–103(1).

Article 5: Letters of Credit

Article 5 governs a subject that in most states has been governed almost entirely by case law. In the typical letter of credit transaction, a bank, at the buyer's request, issues a "letter" to the seller, providing that the bank will, under certain conditions, honor drafts drawn by the seller on the buyer for payment of the purchase price of goods.

Article 6: Bulk Transfers

Article 6 deals with bulk transfers and, as such, emphasizes protection of the transferor's creditors.

Article 7: Documents of Title

Article 7 applies both to warehouse receipts and to bills of lading, two types of documents of title formerly governed separately by the Uniform Warehouse Receipts Act and the Uniform Bills of Lading Act.

Article 8: Investment Securities

Article 8 replaces the Uniform Stock Transfer Act and related statutes, including several provisions of the Uniform Negotiable Instruments Law. Article 8 is often called a "negotiable instruments" law for investment securities. It endows certain bonds, stocks, and other securities with attributes of negotiability and defines the rights and liabilities of issuers, transferors, and transferees. Article 8 does not supersede regulatory laws governing issuance of securities.

Article 9: Secured Transactions

Article 9 is the most novel division in the Code. It is designed to provide a simple and unified structure within which the immense variety of present-day secured financing transactions can be effected with less cost and greater certainty. The most radical innovation in Article 9 is its substitution of a unitary security device for the plethora of security devices previously in use. Terms such as "mortgagee," "pledgee," "conditional sale," and "trust receipt" do not appear in Article 9. Instead, its unitary security device is formulated in terms of four basic concepts: "Secured party," "debtor," "collateral," and "security interest."

The foregoing, then, represents the general structure of the Code and demonstrates that its scope is broad. Chronologically, the Code applies to transactions "entered into" after its effective date. See UCC 10–102(2). In terms of territorial application, it applies to transactions "bearing an appropriate relation" to the enacting state. In terms of subject-matter, it applies to a wide range of transactions. . . .

* * *

While many of the articles of the Code can, in relation to some kinds of transactions, apply separately and alone, frequently provisions from more than one article will be applicable to the transaction at hand.

The Code recognizes the possibilities of conflict between Articles, and includes provisions governing such possibilities. See, e. g., UCC 2–102, 9–113, 3–103, 4–102(1), 8–102(1)(b), and 9–102.

* * *

One of the Code draftsmen has had this to say [regarding the nature of the Code.]

GILMORE, ARTICLE 9: WHAT IT DOES FOR THE PAST, 26 La. L.Rev. 285, 286 (1966).

"Surely the principal function of a Code is to abolish the past. At least a common lawyer assumes that that was the theory on which the great civil law codes were based. From the date of the Code's enactment, the pre-Code law is no longer available as a source of law. The gaps, the ambiguities, the unforeseen situations cannot be referred for decision to the accumulated wisdom of the past. There is a fresh start, a new universe of legal discourse, in which the only permissible way of solving a problem is to find (or pretend to find) the answer in the undefiled, the unconstrued, the uncontaminated text of the Code itself. How well the theory worked in practice, or whether it worked at all, you, as civilians, are much better equipped to say than I.

"The Uniform Commercial Code, so-called, is not that sort of Code— even in theory. It derives from the common law, not the civil law, tradition. We shall do better to think of it as a big statute—or a collection of statutes bound together in the same book—which goes as far as it goes and no further. It assumes the continuing existence of a large body of pre-Code and non-Code law on which it rests for support, which it displaces to the least possible extent, and without which it could not survive. The solid stuff of pre-Code law will furnish the rationale of decision quite as often as the Code's own gossamer substance."

*　*　*

Despite its seemingly wide sweep, the Code is far from comprehensive. There are some transactions it does not govern at all, and there are many aspects of many transactions to which its provisions might apply but will not, for various reasons.

First and at the fore, the parties can generally make their own "law." As one authority has put it, "We are within that area of law where—to use an old-fashioned, pre-positivistic phrase—businessmen are free to make their own law. They do so expressly through contract, implicitly through a course of dealing, collectively through custom and resultant business understanding." By agreement, then, the parties to a commercial deal can vary most of the provisions of the Code.

Second, the Code itself, by its own terms, does not purport to control many important types of transactions that can fairly be called commercial. For example, it does not apply to sales of commercial realty nor to security interests therein. It does not apply to the formation, performance, and enforcement of insurance contracts. It does not apply to suretyship transactions (except where a surety is a party to a negotiable instrument). It does not encompass the law of bankruptcy. It does not govern legal tender.

Third, the Code does not even purport to govern exhaustively all aspects of all transactions to which its provisions do apply. Many of its provisions obviously can come into play only by virtue of some key event, e. g., "default," which may be defined by the terms of the agreement between the parties. See, e. g., UCC 9–501(1). Furthermore, resort to supplemental principles of law outside the Code will sometimes be necessary. See generally, UCC 1–103. Consider the following three examples. To apply the provisions on authorized and unauthorized signatures in Article 3 (UCC 3–403 and 3–404), local agency principles must be considered. To determine what title a "transferor" has under UCC 2–403, it is essential to refer to non-Code law. The "grounds" of impossibility and frustration as a defense to the breach of a contract of sale are not exhaustively stated in the Code. See UCC 2–613, 2–614, and 2–615. Presumably additional grounds recognized in "general contract law" can be invoked. In addition, the Code has its own "gaps"—situations arising within the framework of the Code on specific aspects of which the Code is altogether silent.

Fourth, there are state statutes, most of which are regulatory in nature, which either supplement or supersede Code provisions altogether. See, e. g., UCC 2–102, 9–201, and 9–203(2) for references to the possible existence of such statutes. Usury laws and so-called "Retail Installment Sales Acts" are outstanding examples. It is appropriate at this point to emphasize that the Code does *not*, in terms, concern itself with the general problems of the *consumer* as consumer.

Fifth, the Uniform Commercial Code is *state* law. This means that any valid and conflicting federal commercial law supersedes it. For example, the Federal Bills of Lading Act (sometimes called the Pomerene Act) 49 U.S.C. §§ 89–124 (1964), rather than Article 7 of the Code, applies to all interstate bills of lading transactions.

Sixth, there is a growing body of federal regulatory law that supplements commercial law at many points. For example, the federal Food and Drug Act imposes controls on the quality of goods sold and on the ways they are marketed. The Robinson-Patman Act operates to regulate the price of some goods. Federal statutes govern the creation of security interests in some types of collateral. See, e. g., the Ship Mortgage Act, 1920, referred to in UCC 9–104(a).

Seventh, this survey of non-Code sources of commercial law would not be complete without some reference to procedural law. Generally, commercial claims are litigated in accordance with the procedures applicable in any ordinary case. There are, however, a few procedural doctrines that have a distinctively commercial flavor. Some of these are incorporated in the Code, although it generally does not purport to cover procedural law. See, e. g., the "vouching in" provisions of UCC 2–607(5).

Finally, there are practices and attitudes of legal officials and of men of commerce which cannot really be captured in the language of any Code but which, nonetheless, have an inevitable impact on legal evolution. Professor Edwin W. Patterson has said of these that they seem "to be a part of the societal matrix, a kind of semantic and narrative substratum of law and other articulate forms of social control." 1 N.Y.Law Revision Commission Report 56(1955).

UNITED STATES ASPHALT REFINING CO. v. TRINIDAD LAKE PETROLEUM CO. Limited

District Court, S.D. New York, 1915.
222 Fed. 1006.

HOUGH, DISTRICT JUDGE. One of these actions is brought for the alleged breach of the charter party of the steamship Russian Prince, and the other for a similar breach of a like charter party relating to the steamship Roumanian Prince. Libelant is a corporation of South Dakota. Respondent was the chartered owner of the steamships above named. It is a British corporation, and the vessels are of British registry.

The charter parties by which libelant took the steamers from respondent were made in London, and granted libelant the right to use the vessels in any lawful traffic in most parts of the world. As matter of fact the steamers were employed between Trinidad and United States ports until the outbreak of war in August, 1914, when it is alleged that the vessels were wrongfully withdrawn from charter's service. These actions in personam will begin with clause of foreign attachment, and appearance enforced by seizure of funds within this jurisdiction. Before any steps in the actions other than appearing and giving security for the seized property had been taken, these motions were made.

The charter party of each steamer contained the following very ordinary clause:

"19. Any dispute arising under this charter shall be settled in London by arbitration, the owners and charterers each appointing an arbitrator, and the two so chosen, if they do not agree, shall appoint an umpire, the decision of whom shall be final. Should either party refuse or neglect to appoint an arbitrator within 21 days of being required to do so by the other party, the arbitrator appointed may make a final decision alone, and this decision shall be binding upon both parties. For the purpose of enforcing any award, this agreement shall be made a rule of court."

There can be no doubt that this was a submission to arbitration, and for that reason was a contract between the parties to this action: District of Columbia v. Bailey, 171 U.S. at page 171, 18 S.Ct. 868, 43 L.Ed. 118; citing Whitcher v. Whitcher, 49 N.H. 176, 6 Am.Rep. 486. It is equally plain that under the law of the place of the contract—i. e. England—this arbitration agreement was at the time of making the charter parties entirely valid, and any endeavor to do exactly what libelant has done by bringing these suits would have been restrained by the English courts, acting under authority of the English Arbitration Act of 1889 (chapter 49, 52–53 Victoria). See, also, Manchester Ship Canal Co. v. Pierson & Son [1900] 2 Q. B. 606; Austrian Lloyd Co. v. Gresham, etc., Society [1903] 1 K. B. 249.

The contentions of the parties litigant may therefore be summed up as follows: Respondent urges that the contract for arbitration contained in the charter parties was valid and enforceable when and where it was made, and must consequently be enforced everywhere, unless some positive rule of the law of the forum prevents such recognition and enforcement. Libelant asserts that, whether the contract was or was not good at the time and place of making, it has always been invalid under the law of the United States and most of the states thereof, with the admitted and asserted result that an American may make a solemn contract of this nature in England and repudiate it at will in America with the approbation of the courts of his own country.

There has long been a great variety of available reasons for refusing to give effect to the agreements of men of mature age, and presumably sound judgment, when the intended effect of the agreements was to prevent proceedings in any and all courts and substitute therefor the decision of arbitrators. The remarkably simple nature of this libelant's contract breaking has led me to consider at some length the nature and history of the reasons adduced to justify the sort of conduct, by no means new, but remarkably well illustrated by these libels.

It has never been denied that the hostility of English-speaking courts to arbitration contracts probably originated (as Lord Campbell said in Scott v. Avery, 4 H.L.Cas. 811)—

> "in the contests of the courts of ancient times for extension of jurisdiction—all of them being opposed to anything that would altogether deprive every one of them of jurisdiction."

A more unworthy genesis cannot be imagined. Since (at the latest) the time of Lord Kenyon, it has been customary to stand rather upon the antiquity of the rule than upon its excellence or reason:

> "It is not necessary now to say how this point ought to have been determined if it were res integra—it having been decided again and again," etc. Per Kenyon, J., in Thompson v. Charnock, 8 T.R. 139.

There is little difference between Lord Kenyon's remark and the words of Cardozo, J., uttered within a few months in Meacham v. Jamestown, etc., R. R. Co., 211 N.Y. at page 354, 105 N.E. at page 656:

> "It is true that some judges have expressed the belief that parties ought to be free to contract about such matters as they please. In this state the law has long been settled to the contrary."

Nevertheless the legal mind must assign some reason in order to decide anything with spiritual quiet, and the causes advanced for refusing to compel men to abide by their arbitration contracts may apparently be subdivided as follows:

(a) The contract is in its nature revocable.

(b) Such contracts are against public policy.

(c) The covenant to refer is but collateral to the main contract, and may be disregarded, leaving the contract keeper to his action for damages for breach of such collateral covenant.

(d) Any contract tending to wholly oust the courts of jurisdiction violates the spirit of the laws creating the courts, in that it is not competent for private persons either to increase or diminish the statutory juridical power.

(e) Arbitration may be a condition precedent to suit, and as such valid, if it does not prevent legal action, or seek to determine out of court the general question of liability.

The Doctrine of Revocability

This seems to rest on Vynior's Case, 8 Coke, 81b, and is now somewhat old-fashioned, although it appears in Oregon, etc., Bank v. American, etc., Co. (C.C.) 35 Fed. 23, with due citations of authority; and in Tobey v. County of Bristol, 3 Story, 800, Fed.Cas. No. 14,065, it is treated at great length.

The Public Policy Doctrine

No reason for the simple statement that arbitration agreements are against public policy has ever been advanced, except that it must be against such policy to oust the courts of jurisdiction. This is hardly a variant of the reasoning ascribed by Lord Campbell to the "courts of ancient times":

"Such stipulations [for arbitration] are regarded as against the policy of the common law, as having a tendency to exclude the jurisdiction of the courts." Hurst v. Litchfield, 39 N.Y. 377.

"Such agreements have repeatedly been held to be against public policy and void." Prince Co. v. Lehman (D.C.) 39 Fed. 704, 5 L.R.A. 464.

The above are two examples of the cruder forms of statement; but of late years the higher courts have been somewhat chary of the phrase "public policy," and in Insurance Co. v. Morse, 20 Wall. 457, 22 L.Ed. 365, Hunt, J., quotes approvingly from Story's Commentaries, thus:

"Where the stipulation, though not against the policy of the law, yet is an effort to divest the ordinary jurisdiction of the common tribunals of justice, such as an agreement in case of dispute to refer the same to arbitration, a court of equity will not, any more than a court of law, interfere to enforce the agreement, but will leave the parties to their own good pleasure in regard to such agreements."

But neither the court nor the commentator pointed out any other method by which an arbitration agreement could be against the policy of the law, unless it were by seeking to divest the "ordinary jurisdiction of the common tribunals of justice."

Having built up the doctrine that any contract which involves an "ouster of jurisdiction" is invalid, the Supreme Court of the United States has been able of late years to give decision without ever going behind that statement. Thus in Insurance Co. v. Morse, *supra*, it is said:

"Agreements in advance to oust the courts of the jurisdiction conferred by law are illegal and void."

In Doyle v. Continental Ins. Co., 94 U.S. 535, 24 L.Ed. 148, the case last cited is distinctly reaffirmed. The lower courts have followed, and in Perkins v. United States, etc., Co. (C.C.) 16 Fed. 513, Wallace, J., said:

"It is familiar doctrine that a simple agreement inserted in a contract, that the parties will refer any dispute arising thereunder to arbitration, will not oust courts of law of their ordinary jurisdiction."

Even a partial ouster was held "evidently invalid" when inserted in a bill of lading, in The Etona (D.C.) 64 Fed. 880, citing Slocum v. Western Assurance Co. (D.C.) 42 Fed. 236, and the Guildhall (D.C.) 58 Fed. 796.

The Doctrine That the Covenant to Refer is Collateral Only

This idea is set forth with his customary clearness by Jessel, M. R., in Dawson v. Fitzgerald, 1 Ex.D. 257. It was repeated in Perkins v. United States, etc., Co., supra, and accepted in Crossley v. Connecticut, etc. Co. (C. C.) 27 Fed. 30. The worthlessness of the theory was amply demonstrated in Munson v. Straits of Dover (D.C.) 99 Fed. 787, affirmed 102 Fed. 926, 43 C.C.A. 57, where Judge Brown, accepting without query or comment the doctrine that any agreement which completely ousted the courts of jurisdiction was specifically unenforceable, found himself unable to award more than nominal damages for the breach of the collateral agreement. The opinion for affirmance (102 Fed. 926, 43 C.C.A. 57) is written by Wallace, J., who had himself pointed out in Perkins v. United States, etc., Co., supra, that the action for breach of the collateral agreement to refer was a remedy against the contract breaker who sued when he had promised not to. Comment seems superfluous upon any theory of law (if law be justice) that can come to such conclusions.

The Theory That Arbitration Agreements Violate the Spirit of the Laws Creating the Courts

This is the accepted doctrine in New York, as shown in Meacham v. Jamestown, etc., Railroad, supra. Yet it is surely a singular view of juridical sanctity which reasons that, because the Legislature has made a court, therefore everybody must go to the court.

The Theory That a Limited Arbitration, Not Ousting the Courts of Jurisdiction, May be Valid

This is thought to be the doctrine of Delaware, etc., Co. v. Pennsylvania, etc., Co., 50 N.Y. 265, and it is plainly accepted by the Supreme Court of the United States. Hamilton v. Liverpool, etc., Ins. Co., 136 U.S. at page 255, 10 S.Ct. 945, 34 L.Ed. 419, shows the familiar proviso in an insurance policy by which the *amount* of loss or damage to the property insured shall be ascertained by arbitrators or appraisers, and further that, until such an award should be obtained, the loss should not be payable and no action should lie against the insurer. This makes the appraisal or partial arbitration a condition precedent to suit. Gray, J., said:

> "Such a stipulation, not ousting the jurisdiction of the courts, but leaving the general question of liability to be judicially determined, and simply providing a reasonable method of estimating and ascertaining the amount of the loss, is unquestionably valid, according to the uniform current of authority in England and in this country."

In Hamilton v. Home Insurance Co., 137 U.S. at page 385, 11 S.Ct. at page 138, 34 L.Ed. 708, the same learned Justice said (of a somewhat similar proviso in an insurance policy):

> "If the contract * * * provides that no action upon it shall be maintained until after such an award, * * * the award is a condition precedent to the right of action."

But persons who would thus far avail themselves of compulsory arbitration must be careful, for it has been said:

> "While parties may impose, as a condition precedent to applications to the courts, that they shall first have settled the amount to be recovered by an agreed mode, they cannot entirely close the access to the courts of law. * * * Such stipulations are repugnant to the rest of the contract and assume to divest courts of their established jurisdiction. As conditions precedent to an appeal to the courts, they are void." Stephenson v. Insurance Co., 54 Me. 70, cited in Ins. Co. v. Morse, *supra.*

Finally, in Guaranty, etc., Co. v. Green Cove, etc., R. R. Co., 139 U.S. at page 142, 11 S.Ct. at page 514, 35 L.Ed. 116, Brown, J., considered a proviso in a mortgage to the effect that a sale by the trustee should be "exclusive of all other" methods of sale, and he laid down the law thus:

> "This clause, * * * is open to the objection of attempting to provide against a remedy in the ordinary course of judicial proceedings, and oust the jurisdiction of the courts, which (as is settled by the uniform current of authority) cannot be done."

This decision was filed in 1890. The latest opinion in this circuit known to me is Gough v. Hamburg, etc., Co. (D.C.) 158 Fed. 174, where Adams, J., lays down the rule without comment that any limitation upon the jurisdiction of courts contained in a contract is void.

Whatever form of statement the rule takes, the foregoing citations show that it always amounts to the same thing, viz.: The courts will scarcely permit any other body of men to even partially perform judicial work, and will never permit the absorption of all the business growing out of disputes over a contract by any body of arbitrators, unless compelled to such action by statute. Even such cases as Mittenthal v. Mascagni, 183 Mass. 19, 66 N.E. 425, 60 L.R.A. 812, 97 Am.St.Rep. 404, show no more than a belated acceptance of the right to confine litigation by contract to a particular court, for even that opinion does not recognize the right of mankind to contract themselves out of all courts.[1]

The English Arbitration Act, *supra,* is such a statute. It has compelled the courts of that country to abandon the doctrine that it is wrong or wicked to agree to agree to stay away from the courts when disputes arise. It is highly characteristic of lawyers that, when thus coerced by the Legislature, the wisdom of previous decisions begins to be doubted. In Hamlyn v. Talisker Distillery [1894] App.Cas. 202, Lord Watson said:

> "The rule that a reference to arbitrators not named cannot be enforced does not appear to me to rest on any essential considera-

---

1. For a comparison of earlier cases in Massachusetts with the English cases, see an article on "Arbitration as a Condition Precedent," 11 Harvard Law Rev. 234.

tions of public policy. Even if an opposite inference were deducible from the authorities by which it was established, the rule has been so largely trenched upon by the *legislation* of the last 50 years * * * that I should hesitate to affirm that the policy upon which it was originally based could now be regarded as of cardinal importance."

Neither the Legislature of New York nor the Congress has seen fit thus to modernize the ideas of the judges of their respective jurisdictions.[2]

The question presented by these motions is to be regarded as one of general law; i. e., one wherein the courts of the United States are not bound to follow or conform to the decisions of the state jurisdiction in which they may happen to sit. This was intimated by Dallas, J., in Mitchell v. Dougherty, 90 Fed. 639, 33 C.C.A. 205, and explicitly held in Jefferson Fire Ins. Co. v. Bierce (C.C.) 183 Fed. 588.

Furthermore the question is one of remedy, and not of right. Such was substantially the holding in Mitchell v. Dougherty, *supra;* and in Stephenson v. Ins. Co., *supra,* it is pointed out that:

"The law and not the contract prescribes the remedy; and parties have no more right to enter into stipulations against a resort to the courts for their remedy, in a given case, than they have to provide a remedy prohibited by law."

Finally it has been well said by Cardozo, J., in Meacham v. Jamestown, etc., R. R. Co., *supra,* that:

"An agreement that * * * differences arising under a contract shall be submitted to arbitration relates to the law of remedies, and the law that governs remedies is the law of the forum."

It follows that the final question for determination under these motions is whether the law as laid down by the Supreme Court of the United States permits the enforcement as a remedy of the arbitration clause contained in a contract, assuming that such clause (as here) is intended to oust the courts and all courts of their jurisdiction.

I think the decisions cited show beyond question that the Supreme Court has laid down the rule that such a complete ouster of jurisdiction as is shown by the clause quoted from the charter parties is void in a federal forum. It was within the power of that tribunal to make this rule. Inferior courts may fail to find convincing reasons for it; but the rule must be obeyed, and these motions be severally denied.

Notes and Questions

1. Judge Hough describes the two cases as involving alleged breaches of "charter parties." That term is part of the special language of the law of admiralty—the law of the sea and especially maritime commerce. A charter party is an agreement for the rental of a ship. It is a contract between a shipowner and a person who wishes to

---

2. It has not seemed necessary to pursue this subject beyond the courts of the United States, New York, and Massachusetts; but, with the possible exception of Pennsylvania, the result would not, I think, be different.

use the services of the ship for a voyage or over some period of time. The charterer (United States Asphalt) is also described in the opinion as "the libelant." That, too, is derived from the special terminology of admiralty. The initial pleading (complaint) in an admiralty suit is called a "libel"; the complaining party is thus "the libelant" (plaintiff) while the defending party is "the libelee" (defendant or respondent).

2. It appears from the facts stated by Judge Hough that the ships were in the possession of the charterer, which was operating them in its business. How and by whom and for what purpose do you suppose that the ships were "withdrawn from the charterer's service"?

3. Which party, the owner or the charterer, would be most likely to have demanded the inclusion of the arbitration clause in the charter party? Why? Do you think that the inclusion of such clause may have been a material element of the bargain, affecting such things as the willingness of either party to enter the charter and also the price charged for the charter? If so, is it fair to let one party repudiate that term of the agreement and bring this suit in a U.S. court?

4. The parties provided for submission of disputes to arbitration. Does it appear that they also specified a body of law or customs the arbitrators were to follow in reaching decisions? What sources do you suppose a maritime arbitrator would look to for guidance regarding the decision of a case like this?

5. Does the opinion suggest where the federal judge is to look for guidance in the decision of this case? Would it be the law of Great Britain or the law of the United States? If the parties had specified that all disputes regarding the charter were to be resolved in accordance with British law, would that have been binding on the U.S. court?

6. Judge Hough rather reluctantly concludes that his court has jurisdiction over this case. Why do you suppose he might have preferred to remit the parties to arbitration?

7. If you were a state court judge in a state which had adopted the Uniform Commercial Code, would you favor arbitration as a device to resolve disputes in commercial cases such as Oscar Schlegel? Why?

8. Is judicial enforcement of arbitration clauses more or less likely to facilitate voluntary arrangements in commerce? Why?

9. The common law hostility to enforcement of arbitration clauses in contracts has been very largely dissipated in the years since Judge Hough rendered his rather reluctant opinion in United States Asphalt. State legislatures led the way by adopting arbitration statutes directing their judges to honor arbitration provisions in contracts. The first such statute was adopted in New York in 1920, and a federal arbitration act was adopted in 1925. The adoption of these statutes encouraged judges to be supportive of arbitration agreements. See, *e. g.*, Gil-

bert v. Burnstine, 255 N.Y. 348, 174 N.Y.S. 706 (1931), where the New York Court of Appeals sustained an arbitration agreement in which a New York resident in a contract made in New York had agreed to submit all contract disputes to arbitration in London, England. Arbitration is now very extensively used to resolve a wide range of disputes, particularly in commerce and, as we shall see, in labor-management relations cases.

Judge Hough's opinion introduced the idea that an agreement, or term of an agreement, may be unenforceable because a term or the whole agreement may be "against public policy." That is a rather vague and slippery concept, requiring careful elaboration in situations where it is invoked. Following is an example of a famous modern case in which that concept is invoked and in which the reasons for so doing are clearly articulated.

HENNINGSEN v. BLOOMFIELD MOTORS INC.

[The statement of facts in this case and Part I of the opinion are reprinted *supra* at p. 560 ff. Review those pages before reading the portions of the opinion reprinted below.]

The purchase order was a printed form of one page. On the front it contained blanks to be filled in with a description of the automobile to be sold, the various accessories to be included, and the details of the financing. The particular car selected was described as a 1955 Plymouth, Plaza "6", Club Sedan. The type used in the printed parts of the form became smaller in size, different in style, and less readable toward the bottom where the line for the purchaser's signature was placed. The smallest type on the page appears in the two paragraphs, one of two and one-quarter lines and the second of one and one-half lines, on which great stress is laid by the defense in the case. These two paragraphs are the least legible and the most difficult to read in the instrument, but they are most important in the evaluation of the rights of the contesting parties. They did not attract attention and there is nothing about the format which would draw the reader's eye to them. In fact, a studied and concentrated effort would have to be made to read them. De-emphasis seems the motive rather than emphasis. More particularly, most of the printing in the body of the order appears to be 12 point block type, and easy to read. In the short paragraphs under discussion, however, the type appears to be six point script and the print is solid, that is, the lines are very close together.

The two paragraphs are:
"The front and back of this Order comprise the entire agreement affecting this purchase and no other agreement or understanding of any nature concerning same has been made or entered into, or will be recognized. I hereby certify that no credit has been extended to me for the purchase of this motor vehicle except as appears in writing on the face of this agreement.

"I have read the matter printed on the back hereof and agree to it as a part of this order the same as if it were printed above my signature. I certify that I am 21 years of age, or older, and hereby acknowledge receipt of a copy of this order."

On the right side of the form, immediately below these clauses and immediately above the signature line, and in 12 point block type, the following appears:

"CASH OR CERTIFIED CHECK ONLY ON DELIVERY."

On the left side, just opposite and in the same style type as the two quoted clauses, but in eight point size, this statement is set out:

"This agreement shall not become binding upon the Dealer until approved by an officer of the company."

The two latter statements are in the interest of the dealer and obviously an effort is made to draw attention to them.

The testimony of Claus Henningsen justifies the conclusion that he did not read the two fine print paragraphs referring to the back of the purchase contract. And it is uncontradicted that no one made any reference to them, or called them to his attention. With respect to the matter appearing on the back, it is likewise uncontradicted that he did not read it and that no one called it to his attention.

The reverse side of the contract contains 8½ inches of fine print. It is not as small, however, as the two critical paragraphs described above. The page is headed "Conditions" and contains ten separate paragraphs consisting of 65 lines in all. The paragraphs do not have headnotes or margin notes denoting their particular subject, as in the case of the "Owner Service Certificate" to be referred to later. In the seventh paragraph, about two-thirds of the way down the page, the warranty, which is the focal point of the case, is set forth. It is as follows:

"7. It is expressly agreed that there are no warranties, express or implied, *made* by either the dealer or the manufacturer on the motor vehicle, chassis, or parts furnished hereunder except as follows.

" 'The manufacturer warrants each new motor vehicle (including original equipment placed thereon by the manufacturer except tires), chassis or parts manufactured by it to be free from defects in material or workmanship under normal use and service. Its obligation under this warranty being limited to making good at its factory any part or parts thereof which shall, within ninety (90) days after delivery of such vehicle *to the original purchaser* or before such vehicle has been driven 4,000 miles, whichever event shall first occur, be returned to it with transportation charges prepaid and which its examination shall disclose to its satisfaction to have been thus defective; *this warranty being expressly in lieu of all other warranties expressed or implied, and all other obligations or liabilities on its part,* and it neither assumes nor authorizes any other person to assume for it any other liability in connection with the sale of its vehicles. * * *.' " (Emphasis ours.)

After the contract had been executed, plaintiffs were told the car had to be serviced and that it would be ready in two days. According to the dealer's president, a number of cars were on hand at the time; they had come in from the factory about three or four weeks earlier and at least some of them, including the one selected by the Henningsens, were kept in the back of the shop for display purposes. When sold, plaintiffs' vehicle was not "a serviced car, ready to go." The testimony shows that Chrysler Corporation sends from the factory to the dealer a "New Car Preparation Service Guide" with each new automobile. The guide contains detailed instructions as to what has to be done to prepare the car for delivery. The dealer is told to "Use this form as a guide to inspect and prepare this new Plymouth for delivery." It specifies 66 separate items to be checked, tested, tightened or adjusted in the course of the servicing, but dismantling the vehicle or checking all of its internal parts is not prescribed. The guide also calls for delivery of the Owner Service Certificate with the car.

This Certificate, which at least by inference is authorized by Chrysler, was in the car when released to Claus Henningsen on May 9, 1955. It was not made part of the purchase contract, nor was it shown to him prior to the consummation of that agreement. The only reference to it therein is that the dealer "agrees to promptly perform and fulfill all terms and conditions of the owner service policy." The Certificate contains a warranty entitled "Automobile Manufacturers Association Uniform Warranty." The provisions thereof are the same as those set forth on the reverse side of the purchase order, except that an additional paragraph is added by which the dealer extends that warranty to the purchaser in the same manner as if the word "Dealer" appeared instead of the word "Manufacturer."

* * *

The terms of the warranty are a sad commentary upon the automobile manufacturers' marketing practices. Warranties developed in the law in the interest of and to protect the ordinary consumer who cannot be expected to have the knowledge or capacity or even the opportunity to make adequate inspection of mechanical instrumentalities, like automobiles, and to decide for himself whether they are reasonably fit for the designed purpose. Greenland Develop. Corp. v. Allied Heat. Prod. Co., 184 Va. 588, 35 S.E.2d 801, 164 A.L.R. 1312 (Sup.Ct.App.1945); 1 Williston, supra, pp. 625, 626. But the ingenuity of the Automobile Manufacturers Association, by means of its standardized form, has metamorphosed the warranty into a device to limit the maker's liability. To call it an "equivocal" agreement, as the Minnesota Supreme Court did, is the least that can be said in criticism of it. Federal Motor Truck Sales Corporation v. Shamus, 190 Minn. 5, 250 N.W. 713, 714 (Sup.Ct.1933).

The manufacturer agrees to replace defective parts for 90 days after the sale or until the car has been driven 4,000 miles, whichever is first to occur, *if the part is sent to the factory, transportation charges prepaid, and if examination discloses to its satisfaction that the part is defective.* It is difficult to imagine a greater burden on the consumer, or less satisfactory remedy. Aside from imposing on the buyer the trouble of removing and shipping the part, the maker has sought to retain the uncontrolled discretion to decide the issue of defectiveness. Some courts have removed much of the force of that reservation by declaring that the purchaser is not bound by the manufacturer's decision. [Citations omitted.]

* * *

Moreover, the guaranty is against defective workmanship. That condition may arise from good parts improperly assembled. There being no defective parts to return to the maker, is all remedy to be denied? One court met that type of problem by holding that where the purchaser does not know the precise cause of inoperability, calling a car a "vibrator" would be sufficient to state a claim for relief. It said that such a car is not an uncommon one in the industry. The general cause of the vibration is not known. Some part or parts have been either defectively manufactured or improperly assembled in the construction and manufacture of the automobile. In the operation of the car, these parts give rise to vibrations. The difficulty lies in locating the precise spot and cause. Allen v. Brown, 181 Kan. 301, 310 P. 2d 923 (Sup.Ct.1957). But the warranty does not specify what the purchaser must do to obtain relief in such case, if a remedy is intended to be provided. Must the purchaser return the car, transportation charges prepaid, over a great distance to the factory? It may be said that in the usual case the dealer also gives the same warranty and that as a matter of expediency the purchaser should turn to him. But under the law the buyer is entitled to proceed against the manufacturer. Further, dealers' franchises are precarious (see, Automobile Franchise Agreements, Hewitt (1956)). For example, Bloomfield Motors' franchise may be cancelled by Chrysler on 90 days' notice. And obviously dealers' facilities and capacity, financial and otherwise, are not as sufficient as those of the primarily responsible manufacturer in his distant factory.

The matters referred to represent only a small part of the illusory character of the security presented by the warranty. Thus far the analysis has dealt only with the remedy provided in the case of a defective part. What relief is provided when the breach of the warranty results in personal injury to the buyer? (Injury to third persons using the car in the purchaser's right will be treated hereafter.) As we have said above, the law is clear that such damages are recoverable under an ordinary warranty. The right exists whether the warranty sued on is express or implied. See, e. g., Ryan v. Progressive Grocery Stores, supra. And, of course, it has long since been settled that where the buyer or a member of his family driving with his permission suffers injuries because of negligent manufacture or construction of the vehicle, the manufacturer's liability exists. Prosser, supra, §§ 83, 84. But in this instance, after reciting that defective parts will be replaced at the factory, the alleged agreement relied upon by Chrysler provides that the manufacturer's "obligation under this warranty" is limited to that undertaking; further, that such remedy is "in lieu of all other warranties, express or implied, and all other obligations or liabilities on its part." The contention has been raised that such language bars any claim for personal injuries which may emanate from a breach of the warranty. Although not urged in this case, it has been successfully maintained that the exclusion "of all other obligations and liabilities on its part" precludes a cause of action for injuries based on negligence. Shafer v. Reo Motors, 205 F.2d 685 (3 Cir. 1953). Another Federal Circuit Court of Appeals holds to the contrary. Doughnut Mach. Corporation v. Bibbey, 65 F.2d 634 (1 Cir. 1933). There can be little doubt that justice is served only by the latter ruling.

* * *

II.

The Effect of the Disclaimer and Limitation of Liability Clauses on the Implied Warranty of Merchantability.

Judicial notice may be taken of the fact that automobile manufacturers, including Chrysler Corporation, undertake large scale advertising programs over television, radio, in newspapers, magazines and all media of communication in order to persuade the public to buy their products. As has been observed above, a number of jurisdictions, conscious of modern marketing practices, have declared that when a manufacturer engages in advertising in order to bring his goods and their quality to the attention of the public and thus to create consumer demand, the representations made constitute an express warranty running directly to a buyer who purchases in reliance thereon. The fact that the sale is consummated with an independent dealer does not obviate that warranty. [Citations omitted.]

In view of the cases in various jurisdictions suggesting the conclusion which we have now reached with respect to the implied warranty of merchantability, it becomes apparent that manufacturers who enter into promotional activities to stimulate consumer buying may incur warranty obligations of either or both the express or implied character. These developments in the law inevitably suggest the inference that the form of express warranty made part of the Henningsen purchase contract was devised for general use in the automobile industry as a possible means of avoiding the consequences of the growing judicial acceptance of the thesis that the described express or implied warranties run directly to the consumer.

In the light of these matters, what effect should be given to the express warranty in question which seeks to limit the manufacturer's liability to replacement of defective parts, and which disclaims all other warranties express or implied? In assessing its significance we must keep in mind the general principle that, in the absence of fraud, one who does not choose to read a contract before signing it, cannot later relieve himself of its burdens. Fivey v. Pennsylvania R. R. Co., 67 N.J.L. 627, 52 A. 472, (E. & A.1902). And in applying that principle, the basic tenet of freedom of competent parties to contract is a factor of importance. But in the framework of modern commercial life and business practices, such rules cannot be applied on a strict, doctrinal basis. The conflicting interests of the buyer and seller must be evaluated realistically and justly, giving due weight to the social policy evinced by the Uniform Sales Act, the progressive decisions of the courts engaged in administering it, the mass production methods of manufacture and distribution to the public, and the bargaining position occupied by the ordinary consumer in such an economy. This history of the law shows that legal doctrines, as first expounded, often prove to be inadequate under the impact of later experience. In such case, the need for justice has stimulated the necessary qualifications or adjustments. [Citations omitted.]

In these times, an automobile is almost as much a servant of convenience for the ordinary person as a household utensil. For a multitude of other persons it is a necessity. Crowded highways and filled parking lots are a commonplace of our existence. There is no need to look any farther than the daily newspaper to be convinced that when an automobile is defective, it has great potentiality for harm.

No one spoke more graphically on this subject than Justice Cardozo in the landmark case of MacPherson v. Buick Motor Co., 217 N.Y. 382, 111 N.E. 1050, 1053, L.R.A.1916F, 696 (Ct.App.1916):

> "Beyond all question, the nature of an automobile gives warning of probable danger if its construction is defective. This automobile was designed to go 50 miles per hour. Unless its wheels were sound and strong, injury was almost certain. It was as much a thing of danger as a defective engine for a railroad. * * * The dealer was indeed the one person of whom it might be said with some approach to certainty that by him the car would not be used. * * * Precedents drawn from the days of travel by stagecoach do not fit the conditions of travel to-day. The principle that the danger must be imminent does not change, but the things subject to the principle do change. They are whatever the needs of life in a developing civilization require them to be."

In the 44 years that have intervened since that utterance, the average car has been constructed for almost double the speed mentioned; 60 miles per hour is permitted on our parkways. The number of automobiles in use has multiplied many times and the hazard to the user and the public has increased proportionately. The Legislature has intervened in the public interest, not only to regulate the manner of operation on the highway but also to require periodic inspection of motor vehicles and to impose a duty on manufacturers to adopt certain safety devices and methods in their construction. R.S. 39:3-43 et seq., N.J.S.A. It is apparent that the public has an interest not only in the safe manufacture of automobiles, but also, as shown by the Sales Act, in protecting the rights and remedies of purchasers, so far as it can be accomplished consistently with our system of free enterprise. In a society such as ours, where the automobile is a common and necessary adjunct of daily life, and where its use is so fraught with danger to the driver, passengers and the public, the manufacturer is under a special obligation in connection with the construction, promotion and sale of his cars. Consequently, the courts must examine purchase agreements closely to see if consumer and public interests are treated fairly.

What influence should these circumstances have on the restrictive effect of Chrysler's express warranty in the framework of the purchase contract? As we have said, warranties originated in the law to safeguard the buyer and not to limit the liability of the seller or manufacturer. It seems obvious in this instance that the motive was to avoid the warranty obligations which are normally incidental to such sales. The language gave little and withdrew much. In return for the delusive remedy of replacement of defective parts at the factory, the buyer is said to have accepted the exclusion of the maker's liability for personal injuries arising from the breach of the warranty, and to have agreed to the elimination of any other express or implied warranty. An instinctively felt sense of justice cries out against such a sharp bargain. But does the doctrine that a person is bound by his signed agreement, in the absence of fraud, stand in the way of any relief?

In the modern consideration of problems such as this, Corbin suggests that practically all judges are "chancellors" and cannot fail to be influenced by any equitable doctrines that are available. And he opines that "there is sufficient flexibility in the concepts of fraud, duress, misrepresentation and undue influence, not to mention differences in economic bargaining power" to enable the courts to avoid enforcement of unconscionable provisions in long printed standardized contracts. 1 Corbin on Contracts (1950) § 128, p. 188. Freedom of contract is not such an immutable doctrine as to admit of no qualification in the area in which we are concerned. [Citations omitted.]

* * *

The traditional contract is the result of free bargaining of parties who are brought together by the play of the market, and who meet each other on a footing of approximate economic equality. In such a society there is no danger that freedom of contract will be a threat to the social order as a whole. But in present-day commercial life the standardized mass contract has appeared. It is used primarily by enterprises with strong bargaining power and position. "The weaker party, in need of the goods or services, is frequently not in a position to shop around for better terms, either because the author of the standard contract has a monopoly (natural or artificial) or because all competitors use the same clauses. His contractual intention is but a subjection more or less voluntary to terms dictated by the stronger party, terms whose consequences are often understood in a vague way, if at all." Kessler, "Contracts of Adhesion—Some Thoughts About Freedom of Contract," 43 Colum.L.Rev. 629, 632 (1943); Ehrenzweig, "Adhesion Contracts in the Conflict of Laws," 53 Colum.L.Rev. 1072, 1075, 1089 (1953). Such standardized contracts have been described as those in which one predominant party will dictate its law to an undetermined multiple rather than to an individual. They are said to resemble a law rather than a meeting of the minds. Siegelman v. Cunard White Star, 221 F.2d 189, 206 (2 Cir. 1955).

Vold, in the recent revision of his Law of Sales (2d ed. 1959) at page 447, wrote of this type of contract and its effect upon the ordinary buyer:

> "In recent times the marketing process has been getting more highly organized than ever before. Business units have been expanding on a scale never before known. The standardized contract with its broad disclaimer clauses is drawn by legal advisers of sellers widely organized in trade associations. It is encountered on every hand. Extreme inequality of bargaining between buyer and seller in this respect is now often conspicuous. Many buyers no longer have any real choice in the matter. They must often accept what they can get though accompanied by broad disclaimers. The terms of these disclaimers deprive them of all substantial protection with regard to the quality of the goods. In effect, this is by force of contract between very unequal parties. It throws the risk of effective articles on the most dependent party. He has the least individual power to avoid the presence of defects. He also has the least individual ability to bear their disastrous consequences."

The warranty before us is a standardized form designed for mass use. It is imposed upon the automobile consumer. He takes it or leaves it, and he must take it to buy an automobile. No bargaining is engaged in with respect to it. In fact, the dealer through whom it comes to the buyer is without authority to alter it; his function is ministerial—simply to deliver it. The form warranty is not only standard with Chrysler but, as mentioned above, it is the uniform warranty of the Automobile Manufacturers Association. Members of the Association are: General Motors, Inc., Ford, Chrysler,

Studebaker-Packard, American Motors, (Rambler), Willys Motors, Checker Motors Corp., and International Harvester Company. Automobile Facts and Figures (1958 Ed., Automobile Manufacturers Association) 69. Of these companies, the "Big Three" (General Motors, Ford, and Chrysler) represented 93.5% of the passenger-car production for 1958 and the independents 6.5%. Standard & Poor (Industrial Surveys, Autos, Basic Analysis, June 25, 1959) 4109. And for the same year the "Big Three" had 86.72% of the total passenger vehicle registrations. Automotive News, 1959 Almanac (Slocum Publishing Co., Inc.) p. 25.

The gross inequality of bargaining position occupied by the consumer in the automobile industry is thus apparent. There is no competition among the car makers in the area of the express warranty. Where can the buyer go to negotiate for better protection? Such control and limitation of his remedies are inimical to the public welfare and, at the very least, call for great care by the courts to avoid injustice through application of strict common-law principles of freedom of contract. Because there is no competition among the motor vehicle manufacturers with respect to the scope of protection guaranteed to the buyer, there is no incentive on their part to stimulate good will in that field of public relations. Thus, there is lacking a factor existing in more competitive fields, one which tends to guarantee the safe construction of the article sold. Since all competitors operate in the same way, the urge to be careful is not so pressing. See "Warranties of Kind and Quality," 57 Yale L.J. 1389, 1400 (1948).

Although the courts, with few exceptions, have been most sensitive to problems presented by contracts resulting from gross disparity in buyer-seller bargaining positions, they have not articulated a general principle condemning, as opposed to public policy, the imposition on the buyer of a skeleton warranty as a means of limiting the responsibility of the manufacturer. They have endeavored thus far to avoid a drastic departure from age-old tenets of freedom of contract by adopting doctrines of strict construction, and notice and knowledgeable assent by the buyer to the attempted exculpation of the seller. [Citations omitted.] Accordingly to be found in the cases are statements that disclaimers and the consequent limitation of liability will not be given effect if "unfairly procured," [Citations omitted]; if not brought to the buyer's attention and he was not made understandingly aware of it, [Citations omitted]; or if not clear and explicit, [Citations omitted].

* * *

The task of the judiciary is to administer the spirit as well as the letter of the law. On issues such as the present one, part of that burden is to protect the ordinary man against the loss of important rights through what, in effect, is the unilateral act of the manufacturer. The status of the automobile industry is unique. Manufacturers are few in number and strong in bargaining position. In the matter of warranties on the sale of their products, the Automotive Manufacturers Association has enabled them to present a united front. From the standpoint of the purchaser, there can be no arms length negotiating on the subject. Because his capacity for bargaining is so grossly unequal, the inexorable conclusion which follows is that he is not permitted to bargain at all. He must take or leave the automobile on the warranty terms dictated by the maker. He cannot turn to a competitor for better security.

Public policy is a term not easily defined. Its significance varies as the habits and needs of a people may vary. It is not static and the field of application is an ever increasing one. A contract, or a particular provision therein, valid in one era may be wholly opposed to the public policy of another. See Collopy v. Newark Eye & Ear Infirmary, 27 N.J. 29, 39, 141 A.2d 276 (1958). Courts keep in mind the principle that the best interests of society demand that persons should not be unnecessarily restricted in their freedom to contract. But they do not hesitate to declare void as against public policy contractual provisions which clearly tend to the injury of the public in some way. Hodnick v. Fidelity Trust Co., 96 Ind.App. 342, 183 N.E. 488 (App.Ct.1932).

Public policy at a given time finds expression in the Constitution, the statutory law and in judicial decisions. In the area of sale of goods, the legislative will has imposed an implied warranty of merchantability as a general incident of sale of an automobile by description. The warranty does not depend upon the affirmative intention of the parties. It is a child of the law; it annexes itself to the contract because of the very nature of the transaction. Minneapolis Steel & Machinery Co. v. Casey Land Agency, 51 N.D. 832, 201 N.W. 172 (Sup.Ct.1924). The judicial process has recognized a right to recover damages for personal injuries arising from a breach of that warranty. The disclaimer of the implied warranty and exclusion of all obligations except those specifically assumed by the express warranty signify a studied effort to frustrate that protection. True, the Sales Act authorizes agreements between buyer and seller qualifying the warranty obligations. But quite obviously the Legislature contemplated lawful stipulations (which are determined by the circumstances of a particular case) arrived at freely by parties of relatively equal bargaining strength. The lawmakers did not authorize the automobile manufacturer to use its grossly disproportionate bargaining power to relieve itself from liability and to impose on the ordinary buyer, who in effect has no real freedom of choice, the grave danger of injury to himself and others that attends the sale of such a dangerous instrumentality as a defectively made automobile. In the framework of this case, illuminated as it is by the facts and the many decisions noted, we are of the opinion that Chrysler's attempted disclaimer of an implied warranty of merchantability and of the obligations arising therefrom is so inimical to the public good as to compel an adjudication of its invalidity. See 57 Yale L.J., supra, at pp. 1400–1404; proposed Uniform Commercial Code, 1958 Official Text, § 202.

* * *

VII.

Under all of the circumstances outlined above, the judgments in favor of the plaintiffs and against the defendants are affirmed.

Questions

1. Is the liability imposed through the implied warranty based on breach of a promise? Or is it based on breach of the buyer's demonstrated expectations regarding the skill of the manufacturer and the quality of the product? Or is it based on the court's assumptions about buyers' (plural) expectations regarding the products of industry?

Put another way, is the manufacturer held liable for breach of contract? Or is it held liable as if in contract because that is a convenient doctrinal basis for imposing liability for a breach of a legal duty which is derived from the status of manufacturers and dealers in mass produced goods?

2. Why is the disclaimer of liability held to contravene public policy? Which of the court's arguments on this point seems to you to be the most persuasive?

3. What do this and the preceding cases suggest to you are the minimum requirements for a judicial finding that a relationship between two or more persons has given rise to a contract? Does it appear that there is a uniform set of standards—norms—applicable in all cases, or may the standards vary depending on the circumstances of the particular relationship under consideration?

The Uniform Commercial Code, Article Two, offers an alternative formulation for the judicial authority to void all or parts of agreements which offend some perceived social policy.

UNIFORM COMMERCIAL CODE

ARTICLE TWO

§ 2—302. Unconscionable Contract or Clause

(1) If the court as a matter of law finds the contract or any clause of the contract to have been unconscionable at the time it was made the court may refuse to enforce the contract, or it may enforce the remainder of the contract without the unconscionable clause, or it may so limit the application of any unconscionable clause as to avoid any unconscionable result.

(2) When it is claimed or appears to the court that the contract or any clause thereof may be unconscionable the parties shall be afforded a reasonable opportunity to present evidence as to its commercial setting, purpose and effect to aid the court in making the determination.

Official Comment

Purposes:

1. This section is intended to make it possible for the courts to police explicitly against the contracts or clauses which they find to be unconscionable. In the past such policing has been accomplished by adverse construction of language, by manipulation of the rules of offer and acceptance or by determinations that the clause is contrary to public policy or to the dominant purpose of the contract. This section is intended to allow the court to pass directly on the unconscionability of the contract or particular clause therein and to make a conclusion of law as to its unconscionability. The basic test is whether, in the light of the general commercial background and the commercial needs of the particular trade or case, the clauses involved are so one-sided as to be unconscionable under the circumstances existing at the time of the making of the contract. Subsection (2) makes it clear that

it is proper for the court to hear evidence upon these questions. The principle is one of the prevention of oppression and unfair surprise (Cf. Campbell Soup Co. v. Wentz, 172 F.2d 80 (3d Cir. 1948) and not of disturbance of allocation of risks because of superior bargaining power. . . .

2. Under this section the court, in its discretion, may refuse to enforce the contract as a whole if it is permeated by the unconscionability, or it may strike any single clause or group of clauses which are so tainted or which are contrary to the essential purpose of the agreement, or it may simply limit unconscionable clauses so as to avoid unconscionable results.

3. The present section is addressed to the court, and the decision is to be made by it. The commercial evidence referred to in subsection (2) is for the court's consideration, not the jury's. Only the agreement which results from the court's action on these matters is to be submitted to the general triers of the facts.

Questions

1. Would this provision have afforded a statutory basis for the decision in Henningsen? Did Henningsen involve a bargain "so one-sided as to be unconscionable" on the principle of (a) prevention of oppression or (b) prevention of unfair surprise? Or was Henningsen merely a case where "superior bargaining power" was used to attempt to put on the buyer the risk of personal injury loss due to product defects?

2. Some of the cases you have read, e. g., Balfour v. Balfour, Schnell v. Nell, Oscar Schlegel v. Peter Cooper (Court of Appeals), United States Asphalt v. Trinidad Lake Petroleum, suggest a restrictive view of (a) the types of agreements which may be admitted into the regime of enforceable contracts, and (b) the role of judges in implementing voluntary arrangements. Other cases and materials, e. g., Hamer v. Sidway, Oscar Schlegel v. Peter Cooper (Appellate Division), Henningsen v. Chrysler, Restatement § 90, UCC §§ 2–305 and 2–306, suggest a different view regarding these issues. Do the two views seem to you to rest on different conceptions as to (a) individual capacity, competence, and responsibility of both the parties and the courts regarding the making and enforcement of voluntary arrangements, and/or (b) the nature of the market and social contexts of various voluntary arrangements?

SECTION 27. CONTRACT AND THE DISTRIBUTION OF RISKS: HEREIN OF MISTAKES AND UNAN-TICIPATED EVENTS

SECTION 27.1 MUTUAL MISTAKE

WOOD v. BOYNTON

Supreme Court of Wisconsin, 1885.
64 Wis. 265, 25 N.W. 42.

TAYLOR, J. This action was brought in the circuit court for Milwaukee county to recover the possession of an uncut diamond of the alleged value of $1,000. The case was tried in the circuit court, and after hearing all the evidence in the case, the learned circuit judge directed the jury to find a verdict for the defendants. The plaintiff excepted to such instruction, and, after a verdict was rendered for the defendants, moved for a new trial upon the minutes of the judge. The motion was denied, and the plaintiff duly excepted, and after judgment was entered in favor of the defendants, appealed to this court. The defendants are partners in the jewelry business. On the trial it appeared that on and before the twenty-eighth of December, 1883, the plaintiff was the owner of and in the possession of a small stone of the nature and value of which she was ignorant; that on that day she sold it to one of the defendants for the sum of one dollar. Afterwards it was ascertained that the stone was a rough diamond, and of the value of about $700. After hearing this fact the plaintiff tendered the defendants the one dollar, and ten cents as interest, and demanded a return of the stone to her. The defendants refused to deliver it, and therefore she commenced this action.

The only question in the case is whether there was anything in the sale which entitled the vendor (the appellant) to rescind the sale and so revest the title in her. The only reasons we know of for rescinding a sale and revesting the title in the vendor so that he may maintain an action at law for the recovery of the possession against his vendee are (1) that the vendee was guilty of some fraud in procuring a sale to be made to him; (2) that there was a mistake made by the vendor in delivering an article which was not the article sold,—a mistake in fact as to the identity of the thing sold with the thing delivered upon the sale. This last is not in reality a rescission of the sale made, as the thing delivered was not the thing sold, and no title ever passed to the vendee by such delivery.

In this case, upon the plaintiff's own evidence, there can be no just ground for alleging that she was induced to make the sale she did by any fraud or unfair dealings on the part of Mr. Boynton. Both were entirely ignorant at the time of the character of the stone and of its intrinsic value. Mr. Boynton was not an expert in uncut diamonds, and had made no examination of the stone, except to take it in his hand and look at it before he made the offer of one dollar, which was refused at the time, and afterwards accepted without any comment or further examination made by Mr. Boynton.

The appellant had the stone in her possession for a long time, and it appears from her own statement that she had made some inquiry as to its nature and qualities. If she chose to sell it without further investigation as to its intrinsic value to a person who was guilty of no fraud or unfairness which induced her to sell it for a small sum, she cannot repudiate the sale because it is afterwards ascertained that she made a bad bargain. Kennedy v. Panama, etc., Mail Co., L.R. 2 Q.B. 580. There is no pretense of any mistake as to the identity of the thing sold. It was produced by the plaintiff and exhibited to the vendee before the sale was made, and the thing sold was delivered to the vendee when the purchase price was paid. Kennedy v. Panama, etc., Mail Co., supra., 587; Street v. Blay, 2 Barn. & Adol. 456; Gompertz v. Bartlett, 2 El. & Bl. 849; Gurney v. Womersley, 4 El. & Bl. 133; Ship's Case, 2 De G. J. & S. 544. Suppose the appellant had produced the stone, and said she had been told it was a diamond, and she believed it was, but had no knowledge herself as to its character or value, and Mr. Boynton had given her $500 for it, could he have rescinded the sale if it had turned out to be a topaz or any other stone of very small value? Could Mr. Boynton have rescinded the sale on the ground of mistake? Clearly not, nor could he rescind it on the ground that there had been a breach of warranty, because there was no warranty, nor could he rescind it on the ground of fraud, unless he could show that she falsely declared that she had been told it was a diamond, or, if she had been so told, still she knew it was not a diamond. See Street v. Blay, supra.

It is urged, with a good deal of earnestness, on the part of the counsel for the appellant that, because it has turned out that the stone was immensely more valuable than the parties at the time of the sale supposed it was, such fact alone is a ground for the rescission of the sale, and that fact was evidence of fraud on the part of the vendee. Whether inadequacy of price is to be received as evidence of fraud, even in a suit in equity to avoid a sale, depends upon the facts known to the parties at the time the sale is made. When this sale was made the value of the thing sold was open to the investigation of both parties, neither knowing its intrinsic value, and so far as the evidence in this case shows, both supposed that the price paid was adequate. How can fraud be predicated upon such a sale, even though after-investigation showed that the intrinsic value of the thing sold was hundreds of times greater than the price paid? It certainly shows no such fraud as would authorize the vendor to rescind the contract and bring an action at law to recover the possession of the thing sold. Whether that fact would have any influence in an action in equity to avoid the sale we need not consider. See Stettheimer v. Killip, 75 N.Y. 287; Etting v. Bank of U. S., 11 Wheat. 59.

We can find nothing in the evidence from which it could be justly inferred that Mr. Boynton, at the time he offered the plaintiff one dollar for the stone, had any knowledge of the real value of the stone, or that he entertained even a belief that the stone was a diamond. It cannot, therefore, be said that there was a suppression of knowledge on the part of the defendant as to the value of the stone which a court of equity might seize upon to avoid the sale. The following cases show that, in the absence of fraud or warranty, the value of the property sold, as compared with the price paid, is no ground for a rescission of a sale. Wheat v. Cross, 31 Md. 99; Lambert v. Heath, 15 Mees. & W. 487; Bryant v. Pember, 45 Vt. 487; Kuelkamp v.

Hidding, 31 Wis. 503–511. However unfortunate the plaintiff may have been in selling this valuable stone for a mere nominal sum, she has failed entirely to make out a case either of fraud or mistake in the sale such as will entitle her to a rescission of such sale so as to recover the property sold in an action at law.

The judgment of the circuit court is affirmed.

SHERWOOD v. WALKER

Supreme Court of Michigan, 1887.
66 Mich. 568, 33 N.W. 919.

MORSE, J. Replevin [1] for a cow. Suit commenced in justice's court; judgment for plaintiff; appealed to circuit court of Wayne county, and verdict and judgment for plaintiff in that court. The defendants bring error, and set out 25 assignments of the same.

The main controversy depends upon the construction of a contract for the sale of the cow. . . .

The defendants reside at Detroit, but are in business at Walkerville, Ontario, and have a farm at Greenfield, in Wayne county, upon which were some blooded cattle supposed to be barren as breeders. The Walkers are importers and breeders of polled Angus cattle. The plaintiff is a banker living at Plymouth, in Wayne county. He called upon the defendants at Walkerville for the purchase of some of their stock, but found none there that suited him. Meeting one of the defendants afterwards, he was informed that they had a few head upon their Greenfield farm. He was asked to go out and look at them, with the statement at the time that they were probably barren, and would not breed. May 5, 1886, plaintiff went out to Greenfield, and saw the cattle. A few days thereafter, he called upon one of the defendants with the view of purchasing a cow, known as "Rose 2d of Aberlone." After considerable talk, it was agreed that defendants would telephone Sherwood at his home in Plymouth in reference to the price. The second morning after this talk he was called up by telephone, and the terms of the sale was finally agreed upon. He was to pay five and one-half cents per pound, live weight, fifty pounds shrinkage. He was asked how he intended to take the cow home, and replied that he might ship her from King's cattle-yard. He requested defendants to confirm the sale in writing, which they did by sending him the following letter:

"WALKERVILLE, May 15, 1886.

"*T. C. Sherwood, President, etc.*—DEAR SIR: We confirm sale to you of the cow Rose 2d of Aberlone, lot 56 of our catalogue, at five and a half cents per pound, less fifty pounds shrink. We inclose herewith order on Mr. Graham for the cow. You might leave check with him, or mail to us here, as you prefer.
                    "Yours; truly,   HIRAM WALKER & SONS."

1. Replevin was one of the common law   ing disputes regarding the ownership
   forms of action used in cases involv-   of specific property.

The order upon Graham inclosed in the letter read as follows:
"WALKERVILLE, May 15, 1886.

"*George Graham:* You will please deliver at King's cattle-yard to Mr.
T. C. Sherwood, Plymouth, the cow Rose 2d of Aberlone, lot 56 of our catalogue. Send halter with the cow, and have her weighed.

"Yours truly,   HIRAM WALKER & SONS."

On the twenty-first of the same month the plaintiff went to defendants'
farm at Greenfield, and presented the order and letter to Graham, who informed him that the defendants had instructed him not to deliver the cow.
Soon after, the plaintiff tendered to Hiram Walker, one of the defendants,
$80, and demanded the cow. Walker refused to take the money or deliver
the cow. The plaintiff then instituted this suit. After he had secured possession of the cow under the writ of replevin, the plaintiff caused her to be
weighed by the constable who served the writ, at a place other than King's
cattle-yard. She weighed 1,420 pounds.

It appears from the record that both parties supposed this cow was barren and would not breed, and she was sold by the pound for an insignificant
sum as compared with her real value if a breeder. She was evidently sold
and purchased on the relation of her value for beef, unless the plaintiff had
learned of her true condition, and concealed such knowledge from the defendants. Before the plaintiff secured the possession of the animal, the
defendants learned that she was with calf, and therefore of great value, and
undertook to rescind the sale by refusing to deliver her. The question arises
whether they had a right to do so. The circuit judge ruled that this fact
did not avoid the sale and it made no difference whether she was barren or
not. I am of the opinion that the court erred in this holding. I know that
this is a close question, and the dividing line between the adjudicated cases
is not easily discerned. But it must be considered as well settled that a
party who has given an apparent consent to a contract of sale may refuse to
execute it, or he may avoid it after it has been completed, if the assent was
founded, or the contract made, upon the mistake of a material fact,—such
as the subject-matter of the sale, the price, or some collateral fact materially
inducing the agreement; and this can be done when the mistake is mutual
. . .

If there is a difference or misapprehension as to the substance of the
thing bargained for; if the thing actually delivered or received is different
in substance from the thing bargained for, and intended to be sold,—then
there is no contract; but if it be only a difference in some quality or accident, even though the mistake may have been the actuating motive to the
purchaser or seller, or both of them, yet the contract remains binding. "The
difficulty in every case is to determine whether the mistake or misapprehension is as to the substance of the whole contract, going, as it were, to the
root of the matter, or only to some point, even though a material point, an
error as to which does not affect the substance of the whole consideration."
Kennedy v. Panama, etc., Mail Co., L.R. 2 Q.B. 580, 587. It has been held,
in accordance with the principles above stated, that where a horse is bought
under the belief that he is sound, and both vendor and vendee honestly believe him to be sound, the purchaser must stand by his bargain, and pay
the full price, unless there was a warranty.

It seems to me, however, in the case made by this record, that the mistake or misapprehension of the parties went to the whole substance of the agreement. If the cow was a breeder, she was worth at least $750; if barren, she was worth not over $80. The parties would not have made the contract of sale except upon the understanding and belief that she was incapable of breeding, and of no use as a cow. It is true she is now the identical animal that they thought her to be when the contract was made; there is no mistake as to the identity of the creature. Yet the mistake was not of the mere quality of the animal, but went to the very nature of the thing. A barren cow is substantially a different creature than a breeding one. There is as much difference between them for all purposes of use as there is between an ox and a cow that is capable of breeding and giving milk. If the mutual mistake had simply related to the fact whether she was with calf or not for one season, then it might have been a good sale, but the mistake affected the character of the animal for all time, and for its present and ultimate use. She was not in fact the animal, or the kind of animal, the defendants intended to sell or the plaintiff to buy. She was not a barren cow, and, if this fact had been known, there would have been no contract. The mistake affected the substance of the whole consideration, and it must be considered that there was no contract to sell or sale of the cow as she actually was. The thing sold and bought had in fact no existence. She was sold as a beef creature would be sold; she is in fact a breeding cow, and a valuable one. The court should have instructed the jury that if they found that the cow was sold, or contracted to be sold, upon the understanding of both parties that she was barren, and useless for the purpose of breeding, and that in fact she was not barren, but capable of breeding, then the defendants had a right to rescind, and to refuse to deliver, and the verdict should be in their favor.

The judgment of the court below must be reversed, and a new trial granted, with costs of this court to defendants.

CAMPBELL, C. J., and CHAMPLIN, J., concurred.

SHERWOOD, J., (dissenting.) I do not concur in the opinion given by my brethren in this case. I think the judgments before the justice and at the circuit were right. I agree with my Brother MORSE that the contract made was not within the statute of frauds, and the payment for the property was not a condition precedent to the passing of the title from the defendants to the plaintiff. And I further agree with him that the plaintiff was entitled to a delivery of the property to him when the suit was brought, unless there was a mistake made which would invalidate the contract, and I can find no such mistake. There is no pretense there was any fraud or concealment in the case, and an intimation or insinuation that such a thing might have existed on the part of either of the parties would undoubtedly be a greater surprise to them than anything else that has occurred in their dealings or in the case.

As has already been stated by my brethren, the record shows that the plaintiff is a banker and farmer as well, carrying on a farm, and raising the best breeds of stock, and lived in Plymouth, in the county of Wayne, 23 miles from Detroit; that the defendants lived in Detroit, and were also dealers in stock of the higher grades; that they had a farm at Walkerville, in Canada, and also one in Greenfield in said county of Wayne, and upon these farms the defendants kept their stock. The Greenfield farm was about 15 miles from the plaintiff's. In the spring of 1886 the plaintiff, learning that the defendants had some "polled Angus cattle" for sale, was desirous of purchasing some of that breed, and meeting the defendants, or some of them, at Walkerville, inquired about them, and was informed that they had none at Walkerville, "but had a few head left on their farm at Greenfield, and asked the plaintiff to go and see them, stating that in all probability they were sterile and would not breed." In accordance with said request, the plaintiff, on the fifth day of May, went out and looked at the defendants' cattle at Greenfield, and found one called "Rose, Second," which he wished to purchase, and the terms were finally agreed upon at five and a half cents per pound, live weight, 50 pounds to be deducted for shrinkage. The sale was in writing, and the defendants gave an order to the plaintiff directing the man in charge of the Greenfield farm to deliver the cow to plaintiff. This was done on the fifteenth of May. On the twenty-first of May plaintiff went to get his cow, and the defendants refused to let him have her; claiming at the time that the man in charge at the farm thought the cow was with calf, and, if such was the case, they would not sell her for the price agreed upon. The record further shows that the defendants, when they sold the cow, believed the cow was not with calf, and barren; that from what the plaintiff had been told by defendants (for it does not appear he had any other knowledge or facts from which he could form an opinion) he believed the cow was farrow, but still thought she could be made to breed. The foregoing shows the entire interview and treaty between the parties as to the sterility and qualities of the cow sold to the plaintiff. The cow had a calf in the month of October.

There is no question but that the defendants sold the cow representing her of the breed and quality they believed the cow to be, and that the purchaser so understood it. And the buyer purchased her believing her to be of the breed represented by the sellers, and possessing all the qualities stated, and even more. He believed she would breed. There is no pretense that the plaintiff bought the cow for beef, and there is nothing in the record indicating that he would have bought her at all only that he thought she might be made to breed. Under the foregoing facts,—and these are all that are contained in the record material to the contract,—it is held that because it turned out that the plaintiff was more correct in his judgment as to one quality of the cow than the defendants, and a quality, too, which could not by any possibility be positively known at the time by either party to exist, the contract may be annulled by the defendants at their pleasure. I know of no law, and have not been referred to any, which will justify any such holding, and I think the circuit judge was right in his construction of the contract between the parties.

It is claimed that a mutual mistake of a material fact was made by the parties when the contract of sale was made. There was no warranty in the case of the quality of the animal. When a mistaken fact is relied upon as ground for rescinding, such fact must not only exist at the time the contract is made, but must have been known to one or both of the parties. Where there is no warranty, there can be no mistake of fact when no such fact exists, or, if in existence, neither party knew of it, or could know of it; and that is precisely this case. If the owner of a Hambletonian horse had speeded him, and was only able to make him go a mile in three minutes, and should sell him to another, believing that was his greatest speed, for $300, when the purchaser believed he could go much faster, and made the purchase for that sum, and a few days thereafter, under more favorable circumstances, the horse was driven a mile in 2 min. 16 sec., and was found to be worth $20,000, I hardly think it would be held, either at law or in equity, by any one, that the seller in such case could rescind the contract. The same legal principles apply in each case.

In this case neither party knew the actual quality and condition of this cow at the time of the sale. The defendants say, or rather said, to the plaintiff, "they had a few head left on their farm in Greenfield, and asked plaintiff to go and see them, stating to plaintiff that in all probability they were sterile and would not breed." Plaintiff did go as requested, and found there these cows, including the one purchased, with a bull. The cow had been exposed, but neither knew she was with calf or whether she would breed. The defendants thought she would not, but the plaintiff says that he thought she could be made to breed, but believed she was not with calf. The defendants sold the cow for what they believed her to be, and the plaintiff bought her as he believed she was, after the statements made by the defendants. No conditions whatever were attached to the terms of sale by either party. It was in fact as absolute as it could well be made, and I know of no precedent as authority by which this court can alter the contract thus made by these parties in writing,—interpolate in it a condition by which, if the defendants should be mistaken in their belief that the cow was barren, she could be returned to them and their contract should be annulled. It is not the duty of courts to destroy contracts when called upon to enforce them, after they have been legally made. There was no mistake of any material fact by either of the parties in the case as would license the vendors to rescind. There was no difference between the parties, nor misapprehension, as to the substance of the thing bargained for, which was a cow supposed to be barren by one party, and believed not to be by the other. As to the quality of the animal, subsequently developed, both parties were equally ignorant, and as to this each party took his chances. If this were not the law, there would be no safety in purchasing this kind of stock.

I entirely agree with my brethren that the right to rescind occurs whenever "the thing actually delivered or received is different in substance from the thing bargained for, and intended to be sold; but if it be only a difference in some quality or accident, even though the misapprehension may have been the actuating motive" of the parties in making the contract, yet it will remain binding. In this case the cow sold was the one delivered. What might or might not happen to her after the sale formed no element in the contract. The case of Kennedy v. Panama Mail Co., L.R. 2 Q.B. 587, and the extract cited therefrom in the opinion of my brethren, clearly sustains the views I have taken. See, also, Smith v. Hughes, L.R. 6 Q.B. 597; Carter v. Crick, 4 Hurl. & N. 416.

According to this record, whatever the mistake was, if any, in this case, it was upon the part of the defendants, and while acting upon their own judgment. It is, however, elementary law, and very elementary, too, "that the mistaken party, without any common understanding with the other party in the premises as to the quality of an animal, is remediless if he is injured through his own mistake." Leake, Cont. 338; Torrance v. Bolton, L.R. 8 Ch. 118; Smith v. Hughes, L.R. 6 Q.B. 597.

* * *

In this case, if either party had superior knowledge as to the qualities of this animal to the other, certainly the defendants had such advantage. I understand the law to be well settled that "there is no breach of any implied confidence that one party will not profit by his superior knowledge as to facts and circumstances" actually within the knowledge of both, because neither party reposes in any such confidence unless it be specially tendered or required, and that a general sale does not imply warranty of any quality, or the absence of any; and if the seller represents to the purchaser what he himself believes as to the qualities of an animal, and the purchaser buys relying upon his own judgment as to such qualities, there is no warranty in the case, and neither has a cause of action against the other if he finds himself to have been mistaken in judgment.

The only pretense for avoiding this contract by the defendants is that they erred in judgment as to the qualities and value of the animal. I think the principles adopted by CHIEF JUSTICE CAMPBELL in Williams v. Spurr completely cover this case, and should have been allowed to control in its decision. See 24 Mich. 335. See, also, Story, Sales, §§ 174, 175, 382, and Benj. Sales, § 430. The judgment should be affirmed.

Questions

1. Are the facts of this case distinguishable from Wood v. Boynton? Why is the sterility or fertility of Rose 2d of Aberlone a matter which goes to the "whole substance of the agreement"? Why isn't the nature of the stone treated as a matter which goes to the "whole substance of the agreement?"

2. Would it have made any difference to the court if Boynton had known that the stone was a diamond? Should it have made any difference? Why?

3. Suppose Sherwood had sold the cow to X for $100.00 and then her true value was discovered. Should Walker recover $670 from Sherwood? $20? Anything?

4. In Woodworth v. Prudential Ins. Co. of America, 258 A.D. 103, 15 N.Y.S.2d 541 (1939), suit was brought to rescind an annuity contract. Woodworth had bought an annuity from Prudential on May 1, 1936. He paid $100,000 in cash. At the time he made the purchase he was unaware that he was suffering from a terminal illness which made it impossible for him to live for more than two years. He died on July 15, 1937. His executor brought suit to recover $93,-716 (Woodworth had received $6,284 in annuity payments before his death). What result? Why?

LEONARD v. HOWARD

Supreme Court of Oregon, 1913.
67 Or. 203, 135 P. 549.

Department 1. Appeal from Circuit Court, Multnomah County; Gilbert W. Phelps, Judge.

Action by C. M. Leonard, doing business as the Leonard Construction Company, against A. L. Howard and another, doing business as the Howard Plumbing & Heating Company, and the National Surety Company. Judgment for plaintiff, and defendants appeal. Affirmed.

This is an action for damages arising out of an alleged contract, the particulars of which are as follows: In the latter part of October, 1911, the defendants Howard Plumbing & Heating Company were requested by the Leonard Construction Company to bid upon the plumbing to be installed in a building being constructed by the latter company at Sixth and Everett streets in the city of Portland, and known as the Goode Building. Upon receiving this request, the defendant A. L. Howard, who does all the figuring upon bids for work to be done by the Howard Plumbing & Heating Company, procured from the Construction Company a set of the plans or blueprints which purported to show the fixtures required for the plumbing of the Goode Building. After procuring these blueprints, Mr. Howard prepared and submitted to the Leonard Construction Company the following bid:

Portland, Oregon, Oct. 27, 1911.

Leonard Construction Company:

I agree to do the plumbing for Mrs. E. F. Goode, situated on Sixth and Everett streets, for the consideration of forty-nine hundred seventy-five dollars.

Howard Plumbing & Heating Co.,

By A. L. Howard.

Thereafter on the 15th day of November, 1911, while Mr. Howard was absent from the state, the Leonard Construction Company notified the defendant P. Barger that it had accepted the bid of the Howard Plumbing & Heating Company, and requested that he immediately sign a written contract for the plumbing of the building mentioned in such bid. In response to this request Barger went to the office of the Leonard Construction Company, and was there presented with [a] written order, .   .   .

This order was then signed by one Chas. A. Fingal, who wrote his name under the typewritten words "Leonard Construction Co., Not Inc.," and by P. Barger, who wrote the words "Nov. 11th" after the typewritten word "accepted," and the words "Howard Pl. & Heating Co." after the typewritten word "By," and over the words "Howard Plumbing & Heating Co." Mr. Barger also wrote the word "Nov. 11th" and his own name upon one or two copies thereof at this time; but these copies were not signed by any one on behalf of the Leonard Construction Co., Not Inc. Mr. Barger was also requested at this time to sign certain blueprints which he was told were the plans of the building mentioned in the written order, with which request he complied. Thereafter on the 16th day of November, 1911, the Construction Company delivered to Barger certain blueprints purporting to be the plans of the Goode Building to enable the Howard Plumbing & Heating Company to proceed with the installment of the plumbing system provided for in the order. On the 17th day of November, 1911, the Construction Company called for the surety bond provided for in the order, and said bond was on that day executed and delivered to the Construction Company.

Later defendant Barger notified the company that there was a discrepancy between Howard's count of the number of lavatories, toilets, bathtubs, and slop sinks specified in the plans submitted and the number shown on the plans signed by him in this that by Howard's count there were 75 lavatories, 39 toilets, 26 bathtubs, and 3 slop sinks called for on the blueprints submitted to him for the purposes of a bid, while on the prints signed by Barger for the Howard Plumbing & Heating Company the number specified was 113 lavatories, 59 toilets, 48 bathtubs, and 7 slop sinks. The Howard Company, by Barger, then notified the plaintiff that it would not install the plant at the price bid, and thereupon plaintiff made formal demand on the Howard Company and its surety, the National Surety Company, for performance of the contract, and, this being refused, relet the contract at a price $1,852 higher than that bid by the Howard Company, and thereafter brought this action for damages.

* * *

McBride, C. J. (after stating the facts as above). We conclude from the evidence that the plans submitted to Howard were identical with those signed by Barger, and that the discrepancy probably arose from the failure of Howard to properly check up his work when he examined them. For this carelessness or mistake plaintiff cannot be held accountable; the mistake not being mutual, and no fraud on the part of plaintiff being charged or proved. 20 A. & E. Ency. Law, 813, 824, 825. We cannot assent to the proposition that by reason of the mistake made by Howard there was no "meeting of minds" upon a contract. The subject of the contract, the thing to be done, was the plumbing in the Goode Building. As a detail of this a certain number of toilets, lavatories, and sinks were sketched upon the plans submitted to the defendants. They bid upon the contract, but by inattention overlooked some of the details, and bid too low. The case is not different from what it would have been had they correctly counted the articles to be furnished, and by some mistake or oversight miscalculated the cost of them, and thereby been misled into making an unprofitable bid. Had a fraudulent plan been furnished defendants, or had they by any wrongful act or neglect of plaintiff been induced to make the bid, the case would have been different; but in our opinion the evidence shows that the low bid made by them was the result of a mistake, and this mistake the result of Howard's careless examination of the plans. Under such circumstances neither law nor equity will help them. Brown v. Levy, 29 Tex.Civ.App. 389, 69 S.W. 255; Steinmeyer v. Schroeppel, 226 Ill. 9, 80 N.E. 564, 10 L.R.A. (N.S.) 114, 117 Am. St.Rep. 224; Crilly v. Board of Education, 54 Ill.App. 371. There is no such discrepancy between the bid submitted and the next higher bid as would justify us in saying, as a matter of law, that plaintiff was thereby put upon notice that Howard had made a mistake. That bid was $1,852 higher, and another bid was $1,900 higher than that. We are not aware of any rule of law or morals that requires a person soliciting bids for services to be performed to warn the bidder that his bid is so low that he may lose money by complying with its terms.

* * *

In the view that we have taken of the law in this case, the rulings of the lower court are correct, and the judgment should be affirmed.

MOORE, BURNETT, and RAMSEY, JJ., concur.

GEREMIA v. BOYARSKY

Supreme Court of Errors of Connecticut, 1928.
107 Conn. 387, 104 A. 749.

Appeal from Superior Court, New Haven County; Earnest C. Simpson, Judge.

Action to recover damages for breach of building contract by Sylvester Geremia against Morris Boyarsky and others. Judgment for defendants, and plaintiff appeals. No error.

Argued before WHEELER, C. J., and MALTBIE, HAINES, HINMAN, and BANKS, JJ.

BANKS, J. The defendants are carpenters and building contractors, and in April, 1926, the plaintiff requested them to submit bids for the carpenter work and painting for a house that he was building for himself. The defendants met in the evening of April 25th for the purpose of making their estimates, but did not complete their figures, owing to the lateness of the hour. They wrote their estimates on two separate pieces of paper, but did not add the figures. The next morning the plaintiff called upon the defendants, and requested the defendant Boyarsky to stop the work that he was upon and complete the estimate. Boyarsky sat down with the plaintiff at a workbench, and proceeded to add up the various items upon the two sheets. In his haste, he made an error in adding the items on the first sheet, footing them up at $99.10, when the correct footing should have been $859.10. This error, being carried to the second sheet, made the apparent cost of the work $1,450.40, instead of $2,210.40. The plaintiff thereupon awarded the contract to the defendants, and later the same day they executed a written contract to do the work for the sum of $1,450.40. The plaintiff, when the erroneous bid was given, and when he procured the signing of the contract, had good reason to believe and know that there must have been a substantial omission or error in the amount of the bid. That evening the defendants discovered their mistake, and, as soon as they could find the plaintiff, notified him of the mistake, and offered to go forward with the work according to the actual prices carried out in their estimate, and as low as any responsible contractor would do it for, if less than $2,210.40. The plaintiff refused their offer, and insisted that they complete the work for $1,450.40. The sum of $2,375 was a reasonable price for the work covered by the defendants' contract, and the plaintiff thereafter let the contract for the work to other contractors for that sum. The court found that the defendants had made a material mistake in their bid, that it would be inequitable to award the plaintiff damages for a breach of the contract, and that it should be rescinded.

The finding is not subject to correction in any material respect. In paragraph 12 the item $959.10 should be $859.10, and is corrected accordingly.

The finding discloses a case where the defendants, by reason of an error in computation, have obligated themselves to perform a contract for a sum substantially less than the sum which the actual figures of their estimate totaled, and less than the reasonable cost of the work contracted to be done. It is the contention of the plaintiff that equity should not relieve the defendants from the consequences of their mistake, because (a) it was a unilateral mistake; (b) it was not material to the making of the contract; and (c) it resulted from the defendants' own negligence. While the mistake of only one of the parties inducing him to sign a contract cannot be a ground for a reformation of the contract, it may be a ground for its cancellation. Snelling v. Merritt, 85 Conn. 83, 101, 81 A. 1039. Though the mistake was not induced by the conduct of the other party, equity will grant relief, if the latter, when he becomes aware of the mistake, seeks to take an unconscionable advantage of it. Lieberum v. Nussenbaum, 94 Conn. 276, 108 A. 662. The plaintiff, though he is found by the court not to have participated in the mistake, had good reason to believe that one had been made before the contract was signed, was notified of the mistake by the defendants before he had changed his position in any respect, and sought to take unfair advantage of it by insisting upon the performance of the contract at a price upon which the minds of the parties had never met. When the contract is still executory and the parties can be put in statu quo, one party to the contract will not be permitted to obtain an unconscionable advantage merely because the mistake was unilateral. 3 Williston on Contracts, §§ 1578, 1580.

That a mistake through which the defendants agreed to perform the contract for a price one-third less than the total of the actual figures of their estimate was of so essential and fundamental a character that the minds of the parties never met would not seem to require discussion.

As a general rule, a party will not be given relief against a mistake induced by his own culpable negligence. "But the rule is not inflexible, and in many cases relief may be granted although the mistake was not unmixed with some element of negligence, particularly where the other party has been in no way prejudiced." Fountain Co. v. Stein, 97 Conn. 619, 626, 118 A. 47, 49 (27 A.L.R. 976); Petterson v. Weinstock, 106 Conn. 436, 445, 138 A. 433, 437; 21 Corpus Juris, 88. "The conclusion from the best authorities seems to be that the neglect must amount to a violation of a positive legal duty. The highest possible care is not demanded. Even a clearly established negligence may not of itself be a sufficient ground for refusing relief if it appears that the other party was not prejudiced thereby." 2 Pomeroy's Eq.Juris. (4th Ed.) § 856. "If one of the parties through mistake names a consideration that is out of all proportion to the value of the subject of negotiations, and the other party, realizing that a mistake must have been made, takes advantage of it, and refuses to let the mistake be corrected when it is discovered, he cannot under these conditions claim an enforceable contract." 6 R.C.L. 623.

It may be conceded that the error in addition made by the defendant Boyarsky, when he hastily totaled the items of his estimate at the request of the plaintiff, involved some degree of negligence. It would be inequitable under the circumstances to permit the plaintiff, who had good reason to know, before the contract was signed, that there must have been a substantial omission or error in the amount of the bid, to take advantage of such error while the contract was still executory, and he had been in no way prejudiced, and to require the defendants to do the work for an amount much less than the actual cost. In similar situations when a price has been bid which, because of erroneous arithmetical processes, or by the omission of items, was based on a mistake, rescission has been allowed where the contract was still executory, and it would be inequitable to permit the other party to gain an unfair advantage from a mistake which has not prejudiced him in any way. Moffett v. Rochester, 178 U.S. 373, 20 S.Ct. 957, 44 L.Ed. 1108; Bromagin v. Bloomington, 234 Ill. 114, 84 N.E. 700; St. Nicholas Church v. Kropp, 135 Minn. 115, 160 N.W. 500, L.R.A.1917D, 741; Board of School Com'rs v. Bender, 36 Ind.App. 164, 72 N.E. 154; Barlow v. Jones (N.J.Ch.) 87 A. 649; Everson v. Int. Granite Co., 65 Vt. 658, 27 A. 320.

The mistake of the defendants was of so fundamental a character that the minds of the parties did not meet. It was not, under the circumstances, the result of such culpable negligence as to bar the defendants of redress, and the plaintiff, before the contract was signed, had good reason to believe that a substantial error had been made, and, while the contract was still executory, and he had been in no way prejudiced, refused to permit the correction of the error, and attempted to take an unconscionable advantage of it. The defendants were clearly entitled to a decree canceling the contract.

There is no error.

All concur.

Questions

1. What is a "meeting of the minds"? Was there a meeting of the minds in Sherwood v. Walker? In Wood v. Boynton?

2. If Leonard paid no more than a "fair price" for the plumbing as installed, then what was his loss from Howard and Barger's refusal to perform? Did Geremia lose anything?

3. Are Leonard v. Howard and Geremia v. Boyarsky distinguishable on their facts? Note that Leonard was a commercial builder working under contract to another, while Geremia was building the house for himself. Is that difference significant?

[The significance of the issues considered in the preceding cases is illuminated in the following passage taken from Judge Jerome Frank, concurring, in Ricketts v. Pennsylvania R. Co., 153 F.2d 757 (1946). Some footnotes omitted; others are renumbered.]

In the early days of this century a struggle went on between the respective proponents of two theories of contracts, (a) the "actual intent" theory—or "meeting of the minds" or "will" theory—and (b) the so-called "objective" theory.[1] Without doubt, the first theory had been carried

1. Some adherents of the objective theory have suggested that the "actual in- tent" theory was undesirably transplanted into the common law, in the

too far: Once a contract has been validly made, the courts attach legal consequences to the relation created by the contract, consequences of which the parties usually never dreamed—as, for instance, where situations arise which the parties had not contemplated. As to such matters, the "actual intent" theory induced much fictional discourse which imputed to the parties intentions they plainly did not have.

But the objectivists also went too far. They tried (1) to treat virtually all the varieties of contractual arrangements in the same way, and (2), as to all contracts in all their phases, to exclude, as legally irrelevant, consideration of the actual intention of the parties or either of them, as distinguished from the outward manifestation of that intention. The objectivists transferred from the field of torts that stubborn anti-subjectivist, the "reasonable man"; so that, in part at least, advocacy of the "objective" standard in contracts appears to have represented a desire for legal symmetry, legal uniformity, a desire seemingly prompted by aesthetic impulses. Whether (thanks to the "subjectivity" of the jurymen's reactions and other factors) the objectivists' formula, in its practical workings, could yield much actual objectivity, certainty, and uniformity may well be doubted. At any rate, the sponsors of complete "objectivity" in contracts largely won out in the wider generalizations of the Restatement of Contracts and in some judicial pronouncements.

. . . Williston, the leader of the objectivists, insists that, as to all contracts, without differentiation, the objective theory is essential because "founded upon the fundamental principle of the security of business transactions."

He goes to great lengths to maintain this theory, using a variety of rather desperate verbal distinctions to that end. Thus he distinguishes be-

19th century, from Roman-law dominated continental sources. See, e. g., Williston, Contracts (Rev. ed. 1936) §§ 20, 21, 94; cf. Patterson, Equitable Relief for Unilateral Mistake, 28 Col.L. Rev. (1928) 859, 861, 862, 888–890. The historical accuracy of that suggestion seems somewhat questionable to one who reads a 16th century English decision like Thoroughgood's Case, 1582, 2 Co.Rep. 9a, 76 Eng.Reprint 408, relating to a unilateral mistake. Sponsors of the "objective" theory did not, however, rest their case primarily on chauvinistic common law distaste for continental attitudes. Nor could they consistently have done so. For the "reasonable man," dear to the objectivists, seems to have been imported into the common law. Cf. Beidler & Bookmyer, Inc. v. Universal Ins. Co., 2 Cir., 134 F.2d 828, 830.

The "actual intent" theory, said the objectivists, being "subjective" and putting too much stress on unique individual motivations, would destroy that legal certainty and stability which a

modern commercial society demands. They depicted the "objective" standard as a necessary adjunct of a "free enterprise" economic system. In passing, it should be noted that they arrived at a sort of paradox. For a "free enterprise" system is, theoretically, founded on "individualism"; but, in the name of economic individualism, the objectivists refused to consider those reactions of actual specific individuals which sponsors of the "meeting-of-the-minds" test purported to cherish. "Economic individualism" thus shows up as hostile to real individualism. This is nothing new: The "economic man" is of course an abstraction, a "fiction." See Doehler Metal Furniture Co. v. United States, 2 Cir., 149 F.2d 130, 132; cf. Standard Brands v. Smidler, 2 Cir., 151 F.2d 34, 38, notes 6 and 7.

Patterson (loc. cit. 878 note) says that the "direct ancestry of [the objective] theory goes back to Paley, . . . a theological utilitarian, a contemporary of Adam Smith."

tween (1) a unilateral non-negligent mistake in executing an instrument (*i. e.*, a mistake of that character in signing an instrument of one kind believing it to be of another kind) and (2) a similar sort of mistake as to the meaning of a contract which one intended to make. The former, he says, renders the contract "void"; the latter does not prevent the formation of a valid contract. Yet in both instances "the fundamental principle of the security of business transactions" is equally at stake, for there has been the same "disappointment of well-founded expectations." More than that, Williston concedes that a mistaken idea of one party as to the meaning of a valid contract (Williston's second category) "may, under certain circumstances, be ground for relief from enforcement of the contract." But he asserts that (a) such a contract is not "void" but "voidable," and (b) that the granting of such relief is no exception to the objective theory, because this relief "is in its origin equitable," and "equity" does not deny the formation of a valid contract but merely acts "by subsequently . . . rescinding" it. His differentiation, moreover, of "void" and "voidable" has little if any practical significance. He says that a "voidable" contract will be binding unless the mistaken party sets up the mistake as a defense; but the same is obviously true of agreements which (because of unilateral mistakes affecting their "validity") he describes as "wholly void."

It is little wonder that a considerable number of competent legal scholars have criticized the extent to which the objective theory, under Williston's influence, was carried in the Restatement of Contracts. One of them, Whittier, says that the theory, in its application to the formation of contracts, is a generalization from the exceptional cases; he points out that the theory of "actual mutual assent" explains the great majority of the decisions, so that it would be better, he believes, to adhere to it, creating an exception for the relatively few instances where one party has reasonably relied on negligent use of words by the other. "Why not," asks Whittier, "say that actual assent communicated is the basis of 'mutual assent' except where there is careless misleading which induces a reasonable belief in assent?" There may be much in that notion: Williston admits that "the law generally is expressed in terms of subjective assent, rather than of objective expressions . . ." and that "a doctrine which permits the rescission of a contract on account of a unilateral mistake approaches nearly to a contradiction of the objective theory . . ." As able a judge as Cuthbert Pound said, not long ago, "The meeting of minds which establishes contractual relations must be shown."

Another critic suggests that, in general, Williston, because he did not searchingly inquire into the practical results of many of his formulations, assumed, unwarrantably, without proof, that those results must invariably have a general social value, although (as Williston admits as to the objective theory) they are "frequently harsh."

*   *   *

Two approaches have been suggested which diverge from that of Williston and the Restatement but which perhaps come closer to the realities of business experience. (1) The first utilizes the concept of an "assumption of risk": The parties to a contract, it is said, are presumed to undertake the risk that the facts upon the basis of which they entered into the contract might, within a certain margin, prove to be non-existent; accordingly, one who is mistaken about any such fact should not, absent a deliberate assumption by him of that risk, be held for more than the actual expenses caused by his conduct. Otherwise, the other party will receive a windfall to which he is not entitled. (2) The second suggestion runs thus: Business is conducted on the assumption that men who bargain are fully informed as to all vital facts about the transactions in which they engage; a contract based upon a mistake as to any such fact as would have deterred either of the parties from making it, had he known that fact, should therefore be set aside in order to prevent unjust enrichment to him who made the mistake; the other party, on this suggestion also, is entitled to no more than his actual expenses. Each of those suggestions may result in unfairness, if the other party reasonably believing that he has made a binding contract, has lost the benefit of other specific bargains available at that time but no longer open to him. But any such possibility of unfairness [does not exist in all cases] . . .

In short, the *"security of business transactions" does not require a uniform answer to the question when and to what extent the non-negligent use of words should give rise to rights in one who has reasonably relied on them.* . . .

SECTION 27.2 DISTRIBUTION OF THE RISKS OF UNANTICIPATED EVENTS: THE COMMON LAW DOCTRINE OF FRUSTRATION OF PURPOSE

PARADINE v. JANE

King's Bench, 1647.
Aleyn, 26, 82 English Reprint 897.

[Plaintiff had leased some real property to the defendant. The plaintiff had brought suit to recover unpaid rents. The defendant alleged that he had been expelled from the real estate by an invading army, that he had been excluded from the premises, and that he had not been able to realize any income—profits—from the land during the period for which the plaintiff sought to recover the unpaid rent.]

* * *

3. It was resolved, that the matter of the plea was insufficient; for though the whole army had been alien enemies, yet he ought to pay his rent. And this difference was taken, that where the law creates a duty or charge, and the party is disabled to perform it without any default in him, and hath no remedy over, there the law will excuse him. . . . [B]ut when the party by his own contract creates a duty or charge upon himself, he is bound to make it good, if he may, notwithstanding any accident by inevitable necessity, because he might have provided against it by his contract. And therefore if the lessee covenant to repair a house, though it be burnt by lightning, or thrown down by enemies, yet he ought to repair it. Dyer 33. a. 40 E. 3. 6. h. Now the rent is a duty created by the parties . . . and . . . the lessee must have made it good, notwithstanding the interruption by enemies, for the law would not protect him beyond his own agreement, . . . Another reason was added, that

as the lessee is to have the advantage of casual profits, so he must run the hazard of casual losses, and not lay the whole burthen of them upon his lessor; and Dyer 56.6. was cited for this purpose, that though the land be surrounded, or gained by the sea, or made barren by wildfire, yet the lessor shall have his whole rent: and judgment was given for the plaintiff.

TAYLOR v. CALDWELL

Queen's Bench, 1863.
3 Best & Smith 826.

BLACKBURN, J.   In this case the plaintiffs and defendants had, on May 27th, 1861, entered into a contract by which the defendants agreed to let the plaintiffs have the use of the Surrey Gardens and Music Hall on four days, then to come—viz., June 17th, July 15, August 5th, and August 19th, for the purpose of giving a series of four grand concerts, and day and night fetes, at the Gardens and Hall, on those days respectively; and the plaintiffs agreed to take the Gardens and Hall on those days, and pay 100 Pounds for each day.

The parties inaccurately call this a "letting," and the money to be paid, a "rent"; but the whole agreement is such as to show that the defendants were to retain the possession of the Hall and Gardens, so that there was to be no demise of them, and that the contract was merely to give the plaintiffs the use of them on those days. Nothing, however, in our opinion, depends on this. The agreement then proceeds to set out various stipulations between the parties as to what each was to supply for these concerts and entertainments, and as to the manner in which they should be carried on. The effect of the whole is to show that the existence of the Music Hall in the Surrey Gardens, in a state fit for a concert, was essential for the fulfilment of the contract—such entertainments as the parties contemplated in their agreement could not be given without it.

After the making of the agreement, and before the first day on which a concert was to be given, the Hall was destroyed by fire. This destruction, we must take it on the evidence, was without the fault of either party, and was so complete, that in consequence the concerts could not be given as intended. And the question we have to decide is whether, under these circumstances, the loss which the plaintiffs have sustained is to fall upon the defendants. The parties, when framing their agreement, evidently had not present to their minds the possibility of such a disaster, and have made no express stipulation with reference to it, so that the answer to the question must depend upon the general rules of law applicable to such a contract.

There seems no doubt that where there is a positive contract to do a thing, not in itself unlawful, the contractor must perform it or pay damages for not doing it, although in consequence of unforeseen accidents the performance of his contract has become unexpectedly burdensome or even impossible. The law is so laid down in 1 Roll.Abr. 450, Condition (G), and in the note 2 to Walton v. Waterhouse, 2 Wms.Saund. 421a, 6th ed., and is recognized as the general rule by all the judges in the much discussed case of Hall v. Wright, E.B. & E. 746. But this rule is only applicable when the contract is positive and absolute, and not subject to any condition either express or implied; and there are authorities which, as we think, establish the principle that where, from the nature of the contract, it appears that the parties must from the beginning have known that it could not be fulfilled unless when the time for the fulfilment of the contract arrived some particular specified thing continued to exist, so that when entering into the contract, they must have contemplated such continuing existence as the foundation of what was to be done; there, in the absence of any express or implied warranty that the thing shall exist, the contract is not to be construed as a positive contract, but as subject to an implied condition that the parties shall be excused in case, before breach, performance becomes impossible from the perishing of the thing without default of the contractor.

There seems little doubt that this implication tends to further the great object of making the legal construction such as to fulfil the intention of those who entered into the contract. For in the course of affairs men in making such contracts in general would, if it were brought to their minds, say that there should be such a condition. . . .

It may, we think, be safely asserted to be now English law, that in all contracts of loan of chattels or bailments if the performance of the promise of the borrower or bailee to return the things lent or bailed, becomes impossible because it has perished, this impossibility (if not arising from the fault of the borrower or bailee from some risk which he has taken upon himself) excuses the borrower or bailee from the performance of his promise to redeliver the chattel. . . . The principle seems to us to be that, in contracts in which the performance depends on the continued existence of a given person or thing, a condition is implied that the impossibility of performance arising from the perishing of the person or thing shall excuse the performance.

In none of these cases is the promise in words other than positive, nor is there any express stipulation that the destruction of the person or thing shall excuse the performance; but that excuse is by law implied, because from the nature of the contract it is apparent that the parties contracted on the basis of the continued existence of the particular person or chattel. In the present case, looking at the whole contract, we find that the parties contracted on the basis of the continued existence of the Music Hall at the time when the concerts were to be given, that being essential to their performance.

We think, therefore, that the Music Hall having ceased to exist, without fault of either party, both parties are excused, the plaintiffs from taking the gardens and paying the money, the defendants from performing their promise to give the use of the Hall and Gardens and other things. Consequently the rule must be absolute to enter the verdict for the defendants.

Rule absolute.

Questions

1. Is a legal rule applied in Taylor v. Caldwell which is different from that applied in Paradine v. Jane? Are the facts of the two cases distinguishable?

2.   Was it impossible for the defendant to perform in Paradine v. Jane?   Was it impossible for either side to perform, as agreed, in Taylor v. Caldwell?

3.   Who suffered the loss in Paradine v. Jane?   Who suffered the loss in Taylor v. Caldwell?

KRELL v. HENRY

King's Bench.
[1903] 2 K.B. 740.

By a contract in writing of June 20, 1902, the defendant agreed to hire from the plaintiff a flat in Pall Mall for June 26 and 27, on which days it had been announced that the coronation processions would take place and pass along Pall Mall. The contract contained no express reference to the coronation procession, or to any other purpose for which the flat was taken. A deposit was paid when the contract was entered into. As the processions did not take place on the days originally fixed, the defendant declined to pay the balance of the agreed rent.

VAUGHAN WILLIAMS, L. J. read the following written judgment: The real question in this case is the extent of the application in English law of the principle of the Roman law which has been adopted and acted on in many English decisions, and notably in the case of Taylor v. Caldwell (3 B. & S. at p. 833). That case at least makes it clear that "where, from the nature of the contract, it appears that the parties must from the beginning have known that it could not be fulfilled unless, when the time for the fulfilment of the contract arrived, some particular specified thing continued to exist, so that when entering into the contract they must have contemplated such continued existence as the foundation of what was to be done; there, in the absence of any express or implied warranty that the thing shall exist, the contract is not considered a positive contract, but as subject to an implied condition that the parties shall be excused in case, before breach, performance becomes impossible from the perishing of the thing without default of the contractor." Thus far it is clear that the principle of the Roman law has been introduced into the English law. The doubt in the present case arises as to how far this principle extends. The Roman law dealt with obligationes de certo corpore. Whatever may have been the limits of the Roman law, the case of Nickoll v. Ashton, [1901] 2 K.B. 126, makes it plain that the English law applies the principle not only to cases where the performance of the contract becomes impossible by the cessation of existence of the thing which is the subject-matter of the contract, but also to cases where the event which renders the contract incapable of performance is the cessation or non-existence of an express condition or state of things, going to the root of the contract, and essential to its performance. It is said, on the one side, that the specified thing, state of things, or condition the continued existence of which is necessary for the fulfilment of the contract, so that the parties entering into the contract must have contemplated the continued existence of that thing, condition, or state of things as the foundation of what was to be done under the contract, is limited to things which are either the subject-matter of the contract or a condition or state of things, present or anticipated, which is expressly mentioned in the contract. But, on the other side, it is said that the condition or state of things need not be expressly specified, but that it is sufficient if that condition or state of things clearly appears by extrinsic evidence to have been assumed by the parties to be the foundation or basis of the contract, and the event which causes the impossibility is of such a character that it cannot reasonably be supposed to have been in the contemplation of the contracting parties when the contract was made. In such a case the contracting parties will not be held bound by the general words which, though large enough to include, were not used with reference to a possibility of a particular event rendering performance of the contract impossible. I do not think that the principle of the civil law as introduced into the English law is limited to cases in which the event causing the impossibility of performance is the destruction or non-existence of something which is the subject-matter of the contract or of some condition or state of things expressly specified as a condition of it. I think that you first have to ascertain, not necessarily from the terms of the contract, but if required, from necessary inferences, drawn from surrounding circumstances recognized by both contracting parties, what is the substance of the contract, and then to ask the question whether that substantial contract needs for its foundation the assumption of the existence of a particular state of things. If it does, this will limit the operation of the general words, and in such cases, if the contract becomes impossible of performance by reason of the non-existence of the state of things assumed by both contracting parties as the foundation of the contract, there will be no breach of the contract thus limited. Now what are the facts of the present case? The contract is contained in two letters of June 20 which passed between the defendant and the plaintiff's agent, Mr. Cecil Bisgood. These letters do not mention the coronation, but speak merely of the taking of Mr. Krell's chambers, or, rather, of the use of them, in the daytime of June 26 and 27, for the sum of £75, £25, then paid, balance £50 to be paid on the 24th. But the affidavits, which by agreement between the parties are to be taken as stating the facts of the case, show that the plaintiff exhibited on his premises, third floor, 56A, Pall Mall, an announcement to the effect that windows to view the Royal coronation procession were to be let, and that the defendant was induced by that announcement to apply to the housekeeper on the premises, who said that the owner was willing to let the suite of rooms for the purpose of seeing the Royal procession for both days, but not nights, of June 26 and 27. In my judgment the use of the rooms was let and taken for the purpose of seeing the Royal procession. It was not a demise of the rooms, or even an agreement to let and take the rooms. It is a license to use rooms for a particular purpose and none other. And in my judgment the taking place of the processions on the days proclaimed along the proclaimed route, which passed 56A, Pall Mall, was regarded by both parties as the foundation of the contract; and I think it cannot reasonably be supposed to have been in the contemplation of the contracting parties, when the contract was made, that the coronation would not be held on the proclaimed days, or the procession not take place on those days along the proclaimed route; and I think that the words imposing on the defendant the obligation to accept and pay for the use of the rooms for the named days, although general and unconditional, were not used with reference to the possibility of the particular contingency which afterwards occurred. It was suggested in the course of the argument that if the occurrence, on the proclaimed days, of the coronation and the procession in this case were the foundation of the contract, and if the general words are thereby limited or qualified, so that in the event of the non-occurrence of the coronation and procession along the proclaimed route they would discharge both parties from further performance of the contract, it would follow that if a cabman was engaged to take some one to Epsom on Derby Day at a suitable enhanced price for such a journey, say £10, both parties to the contract would be discharged in the contingency of the race at Epsom for some reason becoming impossible; but I do not think this follows, for I do not think that in the cab case the happening of the race would be the foundation of the contract. No doubt the purpose of the engager would be to go to see the Derby, and the price would be proportionally high; but the cab had no special qualifications for the purpose which led to the selection of the cab for the occasion. Any other cab would have done as well. Moreover, I think that, under the cab contract, the hirer, even if the race went off, could have said, "Drive me to Epsom; I will pay you the agreed sum; you have nothing to do with the purpose for which I hired the cab." and that if the cabman refused he would have been guilty of a breach of contract, there being nothing to qualify his promise to drive the hirer to Epsom on a particular day. Whereas in the case of the coronation, there is not merely the purpose of the hirer to see the coronation procession, but it is the coronation procession and the relative position of the rooms which is the basis of the contract as much as for the lessor as the hirer; and I think that if the King, before the coronation day and after the contract, had died, the hirer could not have insisted on having the rooms on the days named. It could not in the cab case be reasonably said that seeing the Derby race was the foundation of the contract, as it was of the license in this case, where the rooms were offered and taken by reason of their peculiar suitability from the position of the rooms for a view of the coronation procession, surely the view of the coronation procession was the foundation of the contract, which is a very different thing from the purpose of the man who engaged the cab—namely, to see the race—being held to be the foundation of the contract. Each case must be judged by its own circumstances. In each case one must ask oneself, first, what, having regard to all the circumstances, was the foundation of the contract? Secondly was the performance of the contract prevented? Thirdly, was the event which prevented the performance of the contract of such a character that it cannot reasonably be said to have been in the contemplation of the parties at the date of the contract? If all these questions are answered in the affirmative (as I think they should be in this case), I think both parties are discharged from further performance of the contract. I think that the coronation procession was the foundation of this contract; and, secondly, I think that the non-happening of the procession, to use the words of Sir James Hannen in Baily v. De Crespigny (L.R. 4 Q.B. 185), was an event "of such a character that it cannot reasonably be supposed to have been in the contemplation of the contracting parties when the contract as made, and that they are not to be held bound by general words which, though large enough to include, were not used with reference to the possibility of the particular contingency which afterwards happened." The test seems to be whether the event which causes the impossibility was or might have been anticipated and guarded against. It seems difficult to say, in a case where both parties anticipated the happening of an event, which anticipation is the foundation of the contract, that either party must be taken to have anticipated and ought to have guarded against, the event which prevented the performance of the contract. . . . I myself am clearly of opinion that in this case, where we have to ask ourselves whether the object of the contract was frustrated by the non-happening of the coronation and its procession on the days proclaimed, parol evidence is admissible to shew that the subject of the contract was rooms to view the coronation procession, and was so to the knowledge of both parties. When once this is established, I see no difficulty whatever in the case. It is not essential to the application of the principle of Taylor v. Caldwell (3 B. & S. 826) that the direct subject of the contract should perish or fail to be in existence at the date of performance of the contract. It is sufficient if a state of things or condition expressed in the contract and essential to its performance perishes or fails to be in evidence at that time. In the present case the condition which fails and prevents the achievement of that which was, in the contemplation of both parties, the foundation of the contract, is not expressly mentioned either as a condition of the contract or the purpose of it; but I think for the reasons which I have given that the principle of Taylor v. Caldwell (3 B. & S. 826) ought to be applied. This disposes of the plaintiff's claim for £50 unpaid balance of the price agreed to be paid for the use of the rooms. The defendant at one time set up a cross-claim for the return of the £25 he paid at the date of the contract. As that claim is now withdrawn it is unnecessary to say anything about it. I have only to add that the facts of this case do not bring it within the principle laid down in Stubbs v. Holywell Ry. Co. ([1867] L.R. 2 Ex. 311) that in the case of contracts falling directly within the rule of Taylor v. Caldwell (3 B. & S. 826) the subsequent impossibility does not affect the rights already acquired, because the defendant had the whole of June 24 to pay the balance, and the public announcement that the coronation and processions would not take place on the proclaimed days was made early on the morning of the 24th, and no cause of action could accrue till the end of that day. I think this appeal ought to be dismissed.

Questions

1.   Was it impossible for either Krell or Henry to perform as agreed?

2.   What is the holding of Krell v. Henry?

3.   Who suffered the loss in Krell v. Henry?

4.   On the basis of Krell v. Henry and Taylor v. Caldwell, can you formulate a standard, or standards, for determining when nonperformance of a contract will be excused because of events subsequent to the formation of the contract?

5.   What, if any, relationship is there between the preceding three cases and the mistake cases (Wood v. Boynton, and Sherwood v. Walker, *supra* pp. 649–656)?

———

[The following is taken from ARTHUR L. CORBIN,* CORBIN ON CONTRACTS, One Volume ed. (St. Paul, Minn., 1952), pp. 1130–1137. Footnotes are omitted.]

* Professor of Law, Emeritus, Yale University.

Risks of Loss—The Assumption of Risk by Voluntary Assent, and the Allocation of Risks by the Law

Whenever a promise is made, there is always some degree of uncertainty that it will be performed, some degree of probability that the promisee will suffer disappointment. Life is full or risks, including the risk of not being able to convince a jury that a promise was made, the risk that the court will not render a favorable decree, and the risk that the sheriff will not be able to collect the amount that the court adjudges to be due. There is some risk that my house will be destroyed by fire. In return for a premium, an insurance company promises me that it will pay me the amount of the loss; it voluntarily assumes the risk that otherwise I would have had to carry, although I must still carry the risk of its unwillingness or inability to indemnify me.

The risks with which we are now dealing are not the risks of non-persuasion of a court or jury, or the risk of non-collection. They are the risks of the occurrence of supervening events that make some performance impossible or illegal or difficult or dangerous or expensive, or worthless, resulting in the frustration of purposes, in the destruction of values, and in the prevention of gains and the causing of losses.

In determining the effect of "supervening events" upon a contractor's legal duty, we must bear in mind that every act of man and every event in nature that occurs after the contract is made is a supervening event. By most of these events a contractor's ability, or even his willingness, to keep his promise is not affected in the least. Most of them do not "frustrate" his purposes in the smallest degree. Many of the events that do affect his ability and willingness, and to some extent frustrate his purposes by affecting the relative value of the agreed performances are the commonly recurring events of life, foreseen (or reasonably foreseeable) when the contract is made and discounted in the process of agreeing upon the bargain. Fruit is perishable, New England weather is variable, the stock market goes down and up, supply and demand are constant variables. Up to a point, such events as these do not cause contractors to ask or to expect relief. But there comes a "point" at which the request is regarded as reasonable and the expectation will not be disappointed. Where is that "point"? Unfortunately, it is a vanishing point; the line that it draws is an invisible line. In any specific case, its location depends upon customary business practice and commonly prevailing opinion. Is the frustration great or small, complete or partial? Is the "event" one that commonly recurs, one that "reasonable" men contemplate as possible and therefore discount in bargaining?

If a supervening event that causes material frustration of purposes is wilfully or negligently caused by one of the parties, he is the one on whom will be put the burden of the injury, including the burden of making compensation for the injuries of others. Often, however, such events occur without the fault of either party, causing losses and preventing gains. Who, then, must stand the loss or bear the disappointment? If a division of losses is to be made, in what proportion? Courts have had to answer these questions. The cases are numerous, various in character, and not wholly consistent in reasoning or in decision. In each case, the court has determined who must bear and who must pay. These cases must be classified; and tentative rules must be drawn, by means of which future decisions can be influenced, and therefore can be predicted. Thus we may judge which party must bear the risk of supervening events. As between lessor and lessee there are the risks of invading armies and of governmental seizures and prohibitions. As between buyer and seller, there is the risk of destruction of goods, the risk of governmental requisition, the risk of a market collapse. Master and servant have the risks of death and illness. There are the innumerable risks arising out of wars and rumors of wars, on sea and on land.

We can not hope to make all-inclusive rules, to foresee all such future events, or to allocate all the risks of life. Cases will still arise in which the court must blaze a new trail, modifying our tentative rules and adopting a new distribution of losses. But this is no reason for not making use of the extensive judicial experience already at hand. If, like an insurer, either party expressing an intention to assume and carry a particular risk, effect will be given to his expression and the loss distributed accordingly. We must know the processes of interpretation by which the courts have discovered such an assumption. If there is no such assumption, what other factors have influenced the courts in allocating the risks and in distributing the losses?

* * *

Frustration of Purpose by a Collateral Event that Affects the Value of a Performance without Making it Impossible— The Coronation Cases

At this point we may as well discuss the Coronation cases, as illustrations of frustration of a contractor's purpose by a collateral event that gravely affects relative values but does not make any of the promised performances either impossible or illegal or dangerous or difficult or expensive. In these cases, the English courts were faced with a new problem; and they made decisions determining which party had to suffer the losses and bear the disappointments. They laid down tentative rules for allocating the risks; it can not be said that the American courts are strictly following these rules.

When Albert Edward succeeded his mother, Queen Victoria, as King Edward VII of England, great Coronation ceremonies were planned. There were to be a review of the great battle fleet at sea and a magnificent processional pageant leading the king to the crowning at Westminster. Ships were chartered for witnessing the review of the fleet; and, along the announced route of the procession, windows and porches and roofs were hired at high rates for the purpose of viewing it. The king became ill. The reviews and processions were indefinitely postponed. Hamlet would not be Hamlet without the Prince of Denmark. The supervening event, frustrating the hopes and purposes of thousands, was the illness of the king. There were losses and there was prevention of expected gain. How should the risks be allocated and who should bear loss and disappointment?

One defendant hired a steamship from its owner, at an agreed rental, for the purpose of a two day excursion to witness the Coronation naval review and to sail around the Isle of Wight. This purpose of the defendant was stated in the contract; but nothing was said about the possible illness of the king. Yet that illness prevented the naval review and prevented passengers from thronging to the ship and paying fares. The illness of the king in no way affected the performances that were mutually promised other than by greatly reducing the value of one of them. The plaintiff was still able and willing to deliver the steamship at the agreed time and place. There was nothing to prevent the defendant from performing the agreed equivalent, the payment of the promised rental. The court held that the defendant must pay the rent in full, even though his ultimate purpose was frustrated and his expected gains from passenger fares were totally prevented. So, the risk of the king's illness, with its resulting financial harm, was held to rest on the hirer of the ship. The plaintiff, on the other hand, did not risk even the loss of the profits of his bargain. He did, indeed, have his ship available for the voyage as intended; but the rental that he received was out of proportion to the rental value of the ship on the two specified days. He got his expected profit, although the play that made it possible was not given. Let us, at least, make the query whether it would not have been better to put both parties in statu quo, denying to the owner his inflated rental just as the events denied to the hirer his inflated fares. There is no one necessary answer to this question. A factor to be considered is that the hirer might have suffered a net loss even if the king had not been ill; also, he might have reaped a handsome profit.

In a second case, the plaintiff hired a room on Pall Mall, "to view the procession," expecting to erect seats for paying guests. The rental was £141, payable in advance; but only £100 was paid on account. The court held that the plaintiff had no right to money back, and gave judgment to the owner for the balance of £41 unpaid. The court based this judgment on the fact that by the contract the entire rental was due and was collectible before the procession was called off. It thought that the law should leave the parties as they were at the moment when the procession was cancelled, but that the parties should be released from performances that were not due until after the happening of the frustrating event. The hirer should not be in a better position by reason of his not having paid when the money was due.

It should be observed that neither of the promised performances ever became impossible. All that the owner promised to do could still be done after the procession was cancelled; and the hirer of the window could and did pay the rental. The hirer bore the entire loss and made nothing of his expected gains. The owner received the whole of his inflated profit. But, according to the dictum of the court, the antecedent risks were divided to some extent. If the procession had been cancelled before any of the rent was due, the owner would have received nothing; the risk of such a relatively early cancellation was all his. If it had been cancelled before one part of the rent was due, the hirer would have been discharged from paying that part; the loss would be divided between the parties in such proportion as chance might prescribe. The risk that the events might be as they in fact turned out was all on the hirer. The court admitted that its stated rule was "to some extent arbitrary." It suggests, also, that the parties might well have agreed that the hirer should have his money back, with compensation to the owner to the extent of any change of position by reason of the contract. This suggestion seems reasonable. The court had power to adopt such a solution, in the absence of agreement by the parties. If this was justice and equity, the court was a court of justice and a court of equity.

There was no antecedent rule even tentatively controlling the case. The court stated its own rule; and it could have stated a different one.

In a third case, the defendant hired a flat on Pall Mall, to view the procession; he paid £25 down and promised to pay £50 more on June 24, prior to the day set for the procession. On the morning of June 24 the procession was cancelled. The hirer abandoned his claim to restitution of the £25 paid; and the court gave judgment that his duty to pay the balance of the rent was discharged. The court said that "performance of the contract was prevented." As in the preceding case, this seems incorrect; and the other comments made above on that case are applicable here. The collateral event—illness of the king—frustrated the purposes of the hirer. It did not prevent performance, although it destroyed rental value.

What effect should the king's illness have upon the thousands of other contracts made at that period? It should have no effect whatever unless the holding of the ceremonies as planned formed what is sometimes called the "basis of the contract," but is more accurately described as the basis on which one of the parties assented to the bargain. It is not such a "basis" unless it creates a major part—an essential part—of the value of one of the performances that the parties agree to exchange, inducing one of the parties and enabling the other to reach the agreement. If it is the planned ceremonies that give value to A's performance in the mind of B, that will enable B to realize a profitable purpose, and that enable A to charge an inflated price in excess of what would otherwise be possible, then they form the "basis of the contract."

A London resident contracts to buy a car; before delivery or full payment the king falls ill. The price must still be paid and the car delivered, because the Coronation plans do not affect the value of the car or the price that was agreed on. A ship is chartered for a voyage to India, the Coronation plans having no influence on values or terms; the king's illness frustrates nobody's purpose, and the contract stands; a ship is chartered in France, to carry crowds of American tourists across the channel to see the procession; the king is ill, and the tourists remain on the Continent. If the agreed rental was at no more than the normal rate, there is no reason for relieving the charterer of the risk of getting few passengers. The king's illness may frustrate his purpose of making profits; but if the owner of the ship knew of this purpose it did not affect the terms of agreement.

If one contracts to buy property for the purpose of making a resale at a profit, his purpose is frustrated when he finds that no one will pay as much as he did or that no one will buy at all. But this fact is not a discharge of his duty to the seller. This is a risk that is customarily carried by the buyer without ever raising the question. His "frustration" is caused by no uncontemplated cataclysm.

The same result obtains even though the buyer's purpose is to export the goods, or to use them to build a house, and later his purpose is frustrated by an embargo against export or by a zoning ordinance preventing such building. Here the "frustration" is caused by an unexpected event; but the value of the goods purchased is not directly dependent upon the buyer's particular purpose, and the seller was not enabled thereby to fix a price beyond the ordinary.

Many cases will be easy to decide. Differences in degree, small in some cases, are seen to be very great in others. No contract can be said to have only one "basis." Motivating reasons for an agreement are always complex. A writer can only respectfully follow the courts as they feel their way along lines so "wavering and blurred."

Variations in the value of a promised performance, caused by the constantly varying factors that affect the bargaining appetites of men, are the rule rather than the exception. Bargainers know this and swallow their losses and disappointments, meantime keeping their promises. Such being the business mores, court decisions that are not in harmony with them will not make for satisfaction or prosperity. Relief from duty, outside of the bankruptcy court, can safely be granted on the ground of frustration of purpose by the rise or fall of values, only when the variation in value is very great and is caused by a supervening event that was not in fact contemplated by the parties and the risk of which was not allocated by them.

The Uniform Commercial Code, Article Two, response to the problem of unanticipated events follows.

§ 2—615. Excuse by Failure of Presupposed Conditions

Except so far as a seller may have assumed a greater obligation . . . .:

(a) Delay in delivery or non-delivery in whole or in part by a seller who complies with paragraphs (b) and (c) is not a breach of his duty under a contract for sale if performance as agreed has been made impracticable by the occurrence of a contingency the non-occurrence of which was a basic assumption on which the contract was made or by compliance in good faith with any applicable foreign or domestic governmental regulation or order whether or not it later proves to be invalid.

(b) Where the causes mentioned in paragraph (a) affect only a part of the seller's capacity to perform, he must allocate production and deliveries among his customers but may at his option include regular customers not then under contract as well as his own requirements for further manufacture. He may so allocate in any manner which is fair and reasonable.

(c) The seller must notify the buyer seasonably that there will be delay or non-delivery and, when allocation is required under paragraph (b), of the estimated quota thus made available for the buyer.

Official Comment

Purposes:

1. This section excuses a seller from timely delivery of goods contracted for, where his performance has become commercially impracticable because of unforeseen supervening circumstances not within the contemplation of the parties at the time of contracting. The destruction of specific goods and the problem of the use of substituted performance on points other than delay or quantity, treated elsewhere in this Article, must be distinguished from the matter covered by this section.

2. The present section deliberately refrains from any effort at an exhaustive expression of contingencies and is to be interpreted in all cases sought to be brought within its scope in terms of its underlying reason and purpose.

3. The first test for excuse under this Article in terms of basic assumption is a familiar one. The additional test of commercial impracticability (as contrasted with "impossibility," "frustration of performance" or "frustration of the venture") has been adopted in order to call attention to the commercial character of the criterion chosen by this Article.

4. Increased cost alone does not excuse performance unless the rise in cost is due to some unforeseen contingency which alters the essential nature of the performance. Neither is a rise or a collapse in the market in itself a justification, for that is exactly the type of business risk which business contracts made at fixed prices are intended to cover. But a severe shortage of raw materials or of supplies due to a contingency such as war, embargo, local crop failure, unforeseen shutdown of major sources of supply or the like, which either causes a marked increase in cost or altogether prevents the seller from securing supplies necessary to his performance, is within the contemplation of this section. . . .

5. Where a particular source of supply is exclusive under the agreement and fails through casualty, the present section applies rather than the provision on destruction or deterioration of specific goods. The same holds true where a particular source of supply is shown by the circumstances to have been contemplated or assumed by the parties at the time of contracting. . . . There is no excuse under this section, however, unless the seller has employed all due measures to assure himself that his source will not fail. . . .

* * *

8. The provisions of this section are made subject to assumption of greater liability by agreement and such agreement is to be found not only in the expressed terms of the contract but in the circumstances surrounding the contracting, in trade usage and the like. Thus the exemptions of this section do not apply when the contingency in question is sufficiently foreshadowed at the time of contracting to be included among the business risks which are fairly to be regarded as part of the dickered terms, either consciously or as a matter of reasonable, commercial interpretation from the circumstances. . . . The exemption otherwise present through usage of trade under the present section may also be expressly negated by the language of the agreement. Generally, express agreements as to exemptions designed to enlarge upon or supplant the provisions of this section are to be read in the light of mercantile sense and reason, for this section itself sets up the commercial standard for normal and reasonable interpretation and provides a minimum beyond which agreement may not go.

* * *

10. Following its basic policy of using commercial practicability as a test for excuse, this section recognizes as of equal significance either a foreign or domestic regulation and disregards any technical distinctions between "law," "regulation," "order" and the like. Nor does it make the present action of the seller depend upon the eventual judicial determination of the legality of the particular governmental action. The seller's good

faith belief in the validity of the regulation is the test under this Article and the best evidence of his good faith is the general commercial acceptance of the regulation. However, governmental interference cannot excuse unless it truly "supervenes" in such a manner as to be beyond the seller's assumption of risk. And any action by the party claiming excuse which causes or colludes in inducing the governmental action preventing his performance would be in breach of good faith and would destroy his exemption.

11. An excused seller must fulfill his contract to the extent which the supervening contingency permits, and if the situation is such that his customers are generally affected he must take account of all in supplying one. Subsections (a) and (b), therefore, explicitly permit in any proration a fair and reasonable attention to the needs of regular customers who are probably relying on spot orders for supplies. Customers at different stages of the manufacturing process may be fairly treated by including the seller's manufacturing requirements. A fortiori, the seller may also take account of contracts later in date than the one in question. The fact that such spot orders may be closed at an advanced price causes no difficulty, since any allocation which exceeds normal past requirements will not be reasonable. However, good faith requires, when prices have advanced, that the seller exercise real care in making his allocations, and in case of doubt his contract customers should be favored and supplies prorated evenly among them regardless of price. Save for the extra care thus required by changes in the market, this section seeks to leave every reasonable business leeway to the seller.

Questions

1. Does § 2–615 apply to situations like that in Paradine v. Jane? Krell v. Henry? The other coronation cases described in the excerpt from Corbin? If the principle of § 2–615 could have been applied to any of those situations, would it have changed the outcome in any of them?

2. Is § 2–615 consistent with Corbin's analysis of frustration of purpose as an excuse for performance? Does it proceed from and extend that analysis?

SECTION 27.3 LIMITS TO THE DOCTRINE OF FRUSTRATION OF PURPOSE AS AN EXCUSE FOR NONPERFORMANCE: EXAMPLES FROM CONTRACT PRACTICES IN INTERNATIONAL TRADE *

The rule of "absolute obligation," as expressed in Paradine v. Jane, has given way to judicial efforts to adjust contract risks and make "equitable" distributions of losses caused by unanticipated

* Most of the material in this section is adapted from an article published in Columbia Law Review. See Berman, "Excuse for Nonperformance in the Light of Contract Practices in International Trade." 63 Columbia Law Rev. 1413, 1414–1420, 1438–1439 (1963).

events. As we have seen, Professor Corbin endorses this development in our law although he suggests that the doctrine of frustration of purpose should be invoked to excuse performance only when the parties have not themselves established a plan for the distribution of contract risks. However, other writers have suggested that the newer doctrines might even override some contractual terms. It is said that there is a "limit of sacrifice," as the German writer Heck puts it, beyond which a party is not bound by his promises.

The chief difficulty with attempts to set out a general theory of excuse of nonperformance by frustration of purpose is that these attempts override a basic consideration in contract doctrine, that the parties should, within some limits, be allowed—indeed encouraged—to make their own arrangements for the future. Furthermore, such theorizing often leads to excessive generalization as to the proper occasions for the application of a liberal doctrine of excuse for nonperformance. It may be quite appropriate for judges to intervene to distribute risks in a case involving the rental of a flat to be used to watch a parade—a situation wherein the parties have probably given little thought to the distribution of risks. But the same considerations do not exist in other kinds of commercial situations, and it is possible that the application of a liberal doctrine of excuse may interfere with contractual planning. A good example of such a situation is found in the case of contracts for the export and import of generic goods.

The choice of export-import contracts to test the doctrines of excuse is appropriate, since in international trade extraordinary obstacles to performance (such as war, governmental intervention of various kinds, currency fluctuations, and the like) are apt to present greater hazards than in domestic transactions. Indeed, a large proportion of the leading cases on excuse have involved international trade transactions. At the same time, the analysis of contract practices in the export and import of generic goods will reveal that the considerations urged for expanding the doctrine of excuse are generally inapplicable to this class of contracts. The reasons for this may suggest limitations to be placed upon the doctrine in other classes of contracts as well.

More specifically, the intent of the parties with respect to the allocation of the risk of liability for nonperformance in international transactions of the type here under consideration can generally be determined by close analysis of the contractual terms in the context of the commercial custom on which they rest. Thus the effort to imply a missing term or to reconstruct the hypothetical intentions of the parties is misguided; and the effect of the liberalization of the doctrine of excuse is to impose a heavy burden of draftsmanship upon the parties, who, having been schooled in a narrower doctrine, are accustomed to insert in their contracts special provisions relating to excuse and to assume that apart from contingencies covered in those clauses the obligor will be absolutely bound.

The *principal justification* advanced for the liberal doctrine of excuse focuses on the lacunae in the contract. It is said to be extremely difficult in many cases, if not impossible, to determine from the contract itself the intent of the parties with respect to the allocation of the risk of a remote contingency. This may be because the parties (a) were unaware of the risk, (b) were unable to formulate it precisely, or (c) chose not to negotiate the question of its allocation for fear that insistence upon a clause covering it might put too great a strain on the negotiation process and thereby cause the deal to fall through. In such cases, it is urged, a broad doctrine of excuse serves the important function of supplementing the contract, either by implying a missing term or by determining what the parties would have provided had they expressly allocated the risk; or, as it is sometimes put, the court or arbitration tribunal must necessarily in such cases make its own determination, independently of intentions manifested in the contract, of which party should in fairness suffer the loss that occurred when the unallocated risk materialized.

Stated thus in broad terms, as a matter of "general contract law," this argument has considerable appeal. It is elementary that contract law as a whole has the function not only of enforcing the parties' manifested intentions but also of providing a just solution for problems that the parties failed to foresee or that they foresaw but left open. Yet this general proposition is quite misleading when put in the form of rules or doctrines to be applied indiscriminately to all types of contracts. Indeed, one may question whether a unitary law of contract exists outside of the first year law school courses. For while there are certainly many types of business transactions in which the parties rely upon common sense—and if necessary judicial or arbitral wisdom—to resolve questions too elusive for negotiation, there are other types of transaction in which the parties themselves allocate responsibility for losses that may result from contingencies not anticipated. With respect to international trade transactions of the kind here under consideration, a study of actual contract practices shows that the parties generally insert special clauses to cover the most varied types of extraordinary risks, and that they take it for granted that the risk of events not specifically referred to shall be borne by the obligor. When this is true there is no need for a doctrine that supplies a missing term, since there is no missing term; and the party that should in fairness suffer the loss is the party who agreed to suffer it.

Above all, the argument of the "missing term" or "gap" fails to take sufficiently into account the problems of drafting an international trade contract. The parties to such a contract almost invariably insert clauses stating that their obligations shall be discharged by the occurrence of contingencies A, B, C, D, or F. A doctrine which permits their obligations also to be discharged by the occurrence of contingencies X, Y, or Z—not mentioned in the contract—imposes an intolerably heavy burden on the draftsman who seeks to provide, in one way or another, for such contingencies. He would have to insert what might be called an anti-frustration clause, stating that neither party shall be excused from liability for nonperformance caused by any events not expressly covered by particular contractual provisions. However, even such a clause would not necessarily withstand a liberal doctrine of excuse. It would therefore be necessary for the draftsman to attempt to specify in detail all the various contingencies under which, regardless of hardship or expense, the risk of nonperformance remains upon the obligor. In view of the large number of extraordinary risks that are apt to impede performance of international trade transactions, such an attempt would be extremely burdensome.

A *second justification* for an expanded doctrine of excuse looks not to the terms (missing or otherwise) of the contract but to considerations of fairness which, it is thought, should override the contract. This justification is rarely stated so bluntly, although the "limit of sacrifice" theory referred to earlier is an example of it. More often it is said that the parties could not have intended what the words of the contract would indicate, or that the parties' intentions must be construed with business sense. Lord McNair did, indeed, state that the doctrine of frustration possesses a "paramount dissolving power" even over an express contractual provision, but he qualified this statement as applicable only "when a purely mechanical application of the clause would have, in the light of what has happened, the effect of imposing a new contract upon the parties." Yet it is possible to detect behind such statements a theory that goes beyond contract interpretation. There is a suggestion, at least, that the harshness of contractual arrangements may require the protection of an overriding principle.

Such a view has no place in the law governing international trade transactions of the type here under consideration. In the first place, the parties to such transactions are, as a rule, substantial business firms which have invested large sums of money in international trade with hopes of large profits and which have entered into their contracts with open eyes. It may well be true that the bargaining power of one party or the other is not sufficiently great to secure the treatment he would like: the steel exporter, for example, may be in a strong enough position to tell the importer, "You may buy my products at my factory, but if you want me to ship them to you on board a vessel you must assume all the risks that may arise, of any kind whatever, from the time the goods leave the factory"; or the shipowner may be able to say to the shipper, "You may charter your own ship on any conditions you wish, but if you want me to carry your goods I will accept the following terms and no others." Ultimately, the conditions of the market and appropriate legislation will resolve such differences in bargaining power. In any event, the parties do not rely upon judicially formulated doctrines of excuse to relieve one side or the other from obligations assumed with open eyes, for profit, at a price that reflects the risks of the undertaking.

In the second place, the loss, whether great or small, must generally fall on one party or the other, usually in the form of the exporter's expenses and lost profits or in the form of the importer's liability to subpurchasers. Even when the importer buys for consumption (as in the case of the manufacturer-importer), his loss, if the seller is excused, is normally no more nor less than what the seller's loss would be if he were not excused—namely, the difference between the contract price and the market price. Moreover, rules concerning mitigation of damages, restitution, substituted performance, duty to notify, duty to cooperate, and the like, should be equally applicable whether or not performance is excused.

Finally, and most important, the parties to an international trade transaction are generally subjects of diverse systems of national law and therefore tend to rely far more heavily upon the terms of their contracts than upon general legal doctrines prevailing in one country or another. Indeed, sanctity of contract is their surest defense against the peculiarities of legal rules developed in particular countries. Hence their own determination of how risks should be allocated between them—even in the absence of perfect equality of bargaining power—should not be overridden except by clear considerations of public policy.

In short, in the typical international trade transaction, in which party autonomy and security of contractual obligations are of primary importance, general doctrines of excuse for nonperformance should yield to express contractual provisions for excuse and should not go beyond them. No general doctrine that speaks in terms of catastrophic expense or changed circumstances should be applicable where the parties have themselves included in their contract special clauses defining under what circumstances their obligations shall be discharged.

In many instances when a court purports to apply a doctrine of excuse to a contract for the sale of generic goods, it is in fact merely applying an excuse clause of the contract itself. The vice of the doctrine of frustration and its analogies lies not so much on their tendency to produce wrong judicial decisions as in their tendency to lead courts and legal scholars into a wrong mode of thought. In reacting against excessive literalism in the interpretation of contracts and in responding to the need for flexibility in judicial remedies, many writers have leaped from the frying pan of absolute obligation into the fire of an equally abstract relativism. Impressed with the changes of modern life and the political and economic upheavals of our time, they have sought refuge in a universal principle of equitable adjustment, without sufficiently taking into account the capacity of businessmen (and their lawyers) in certain areas of economic activity to make their own equitable adjustment through their contracts.

The validity of the argument for confining the doctrine of excuse to the excuse clauses of the contract depends on the possibility of enumerating in a contract the types of events whose occurrence will relieve the parties from liability for nonperformance without imposing too great a strain on the process of negotiation. Are there contingencies that as a practical matter cannot adequately be covered? In answering this question it is proposed first to consider the kinds of terms found in international trade contracts generally, and, second, to examine several standard contracts used in specific types of export and import transactions.

Typically, the parties to an international trade contract seek to allocate certain risks by means of the basic price and delivery term of the contract (c. i. f., f. o. b., f. a. s., etc.[1]). If the contract is on c. i. f. terms, for example, the exporter takes the risk of placing the goods on board (or, when customary, in the hands of) the carrier and of delivering the necessary documents (bill of lading, invoice, marine insurance policy or certificate, letter of credit, etc.) to the importer or his agent. The risk of increases after the contract has been concluded in the prices of freight, insurance, and goods is upon the seller, and the risks of the voyage are upon the buyer. Of course the seller and buyer may by special clauses vary this pattern of allocation of risks, although they must be wary of introducing clauses which are repugnant to the c. i. f. term itself.

There are other risks, however, that fall outside the scope of the basic price and delivery term. These are usually thought of as abnormal risks in the sense that they materialize only very rarely. They include the effects of natural disaster, such as floods and storms; political disasters, such as war, hostilities, and blockade; abnormal production difficulties, such as strikes, fire, explosions, and shortage of fuel; abnormal transportation difficulties, such as failure of transport facilities or abnormal increase of the cost of transportation; governmental restrictions, such as requisition, expropriation, production prohibitions, trade prohibitions, requisition of workers, denial or revocation of export or import licenses, and exchange controls; failure of sources of supply; and abnormal increases in price, taxes, and exchange rates.

---

[1]. These abbreviations refer to customary ways of quoting prices in international trade. C. i. f. (cost, insurance, and freight) means that the buyer is quoted a delivered price including the costs of insurance on the goods in transit, and freight charges to destination. Typically under a c. i. f. contract the seller controls the routing of the goods and chooses the carrier. In f. o. b. (free on board) and f. a. s. (free along side) contracts the price quoted does not include insurance and ocean freight. Once the goods are on board or delivered to ship's tackle, they are the responsibility of the buyer who typically controls the routing and the choice of carrier.

Such abnormal risks are usually allocated by means of a general excuse clause variously labelled *force majeure*, contingencies, excusable delays, exemptions, exceptions, reliefs (*causes d'exonération*), strike clauses, etc., but they are also often allocated by special clauses, such as "subject to license," "subject to shipment," "subject to exchange," and "this order may be cancelled by the seller without liability upon the seller in the event that . . . ." Of course the buyer or seller-broker may avoid all abnormal (as well as normal) risks affecting the transportation of the goods by a "no arrival—no sale" clause, thereby converting the contract from a c. i. f. to a destination contract.

Although *force majeure* is typically defined by legislation or by judicial decision as requiring not mere difficulty (in the sense of excessive cost) of performance, but impossibility (although impossibility is often broadly interpreted as "practical impossibility"), the so-called *force majeure* clause of an international trade contract may speak also in terms of mere difficulty. The older formulation, "the seller shall not be liable for failure to comply with the terms hereof if performance is *prevented by* . . .," has been replaced in many contracts by the formulation, "the seller shall not be liable for failure to comply with the terms hereof if such failure is *due to [or caused by]* . . . ." The contingencies that follow this phrase often include not merely circumstances that might render performance impossible but also circumstances that might render performance excessively costly or otherwise burdensome or impracticable (*e. g.*, "labor shortages," "economic disturbances and upheavals"). Such contract conditions are intended to indicate that, although in the event of a labor shortage the manufacturer-exporter might, by offering exorbitant wages, succeed in performing, he would nevertheless be excused by showing that the labor shortage "caused" him not to perform, in the sense that he could not reasonably have been expected, in the light of the labor shortage, to have made extraordinary expenditures to overcome it. In effect, the parties may thus write the doctrine of commercial impracticability into the contract—limited, however, by the types of contingencies that they list, by the other terms of the contract, and by the general nature of the transaction.

In examining excuse clauses in individual contracts, it is necessary, of course, to bear in mind both the custom of the particular trade (that is, the nature and purpose of the transaction as it would be understood by merchants who engage in similar transactions) and the relative bargaining power of the two parties. The export of grain, for example, is very different from the export of steel products. The grain exporter is usually one of many sellers of virtually identical goods; the grain importer is usually a middleman who may resell the documents of title shortly after he has received them; the parties usually count on the possibility of fairly rapid price fluctuations; and delay or nonperformance by the exporter can generally be partially counteracted by prompt cover on the part of the importer. The steel exporter, on the other hand, generally manufactures his goods to particular specifications; a relatively long period of time elapses between formation of the contract and performance—though not as long as in the case of plant and equipment; his purchaser is often himself a manufacturer; the market is more stable; in the event of delay or nonperformance it may be impossible for the importer to purchase identical goods elsewhere or, if the delay or nonperformance is on the part of the importer, it may be impossible for the exporter to sell the particular goods elsewhere. It is not surprising, therefore, that one finds quite different contract terms relating to excuse in these two types of export trade.

In this connection it is instructive to compare the c. i. f. contract terms of a large American steel export company with the London Corn Trade Association's c. i. f. contract terms for the sale of rye. The term "c. i. f." is understood in both contracts as casting upon the seller the risk of delivering the goods to the carrier and transferring the necessary documents to the buyer, and as casting upon the buyer the risks of the voyage. However, the excuse clauses in the rye export contract differ markedly from the corresponding clauses in the steel export contract. The former provides, under the heading "Prohibition," that

> should the fulfillment of this contract be rendered impossible by prohibition of export, blockade or hostilities, or by any executive or legislative act done by or on behalf of the Government of the country of origin of the goods or of the territory where the port or ports of shipment named herein is/are situate, this contract, or any unfulfilled part thereof, to be cancelled;

and under the heading "Strike Clause," that

> should shipment of the goods . . . be prevented . . . by reason of riots, strikes or lock-outs . . . then Shipper shall be entitled at the resumption of work after termination of such riots, strikes or lock-outs to as much time, not exceeding 28 days, for shipment . . . as was left for shipment under the contract prior to the outbreak of the riots, strikes or lock-outs, and in the event of the time left for shipment under the contract being 14 days or less a minimum extension of 14 days shall be allowed.

The steel export contract, in contrast, under the heading of "Excusable Delays," states:

> The seller shall not be liable for any delay in manufacture or delivery *due to* fires, strikes, *disputes with workmen,* war, civil commotion, epidemics, floods, accidents, *delays in transportation, shortage of cars, shortage of fuel or other material, shortage of labor,* acts, demands, requirements, or

request of the Government of the United States, or of any other State or Government, or to *any other causes beyond the reasonable control* of the seller, or of the manufacturer, notwithstanding such causes of delay are operative at the time of making the contract and the existence of such causes of delay shall justify the suspension of manufacture and shall extend the time of performance on the part of the seller to such extent as may be necessary to enable it tó make delivery in the exercise of reasonable diligence after the causes of delay have been removed. If the performance of the contract by the seller be delayed by reason of any of the causes above mentioned, the purchaser may, *subject to previously obtaining the consent of the seller,* cancel the purchase of such portion of the goods   .   .   .   as   .   .   .   has not been manufactured nor is in process of manufacture at the time the purchaser's request for such cancellation arrives at the manufacturer's works. The provisions of this paragraph shall not be limited nor waived by any other terms of the contract, whether printed or written.

One may read the steel export contract (and especially the portions emphasized above) as providing, in effect, that if, despite the seller's diligence, his performance is rendered commercially impracticable by the occurrence of abnormal events, his obligations shall be suspended, but the buyer is under an absolute obligation regardless of all difficulties. If it is argued that such terms are unduly onerous, the seller's reply is that they are not unusual in the steel export trade (at least during times when there is a seller's market in steel), that steel products are not goods which can simply be taken off the shelf, and that any buyer who does not wish to undertake such risks is free to buy elsewhere or not at all. It is hard to imagine, furthermore, that such a contract is unconscionable or against public policy, for the steel exporter could require, if he wished and if his bargaining position were sufficiently strong, that the buyer take delivery of the steel products at the seller's plant and pay in advance for all steel to be manufactured.

The grain contract, on the other hand, speaks in terms of impossibility of performance caused by a fairly narrow range of circumstances. The parties clearly intend that each side shall bear the risk that *its* performance will be prevented (or rendered excessively burdensome) by an abnormal event other than the ones indicated in the relevant clauses, since otherwise it would not be necessary to include any contingency clause at all. Moreover, in the grain export trade it would be difficult to operate under a broad rule of excuse for nonperformance, for if the exporter were to be excused from liability to the importer on the ground, for example, of shortage of shipping at the port of export, the importer, if subjected to claims under similar contracts with his subpurchasers, would have the burden of prov-

ing such shortage of shipping in a remote port. Indeed, once the element of multiple dealings in documents enters into the picture—and
such multiple dealings are normal in many types of export trade—the
problem of regressive liability becomes acute. Under the broad rule
of excuse each party in the chain of subsales must show that nonperformance by his supplier was justified in order to have the benefit of
the doctrine, or else must turn over to his buyer his rights against
such supplier. When the parties may be spread out in widely separated parts of the globe, not only the difficulties of proof but also
difficulties of litigation in a foreign court make such regressive claims
unduly onerous.

Examination of contract clauses used in other export trades confirms the belief that the parties assume a limited rule of excuse for
nonperformance, that is, take it for granted that nonperformance
will be excused only insofar as the contract so provides. For example,
a contract for multiple sales of wood pulp states that the Buyer or the
Seller may suspend performance for up to thirty days and thereafter
cancel the contract on account of "Force Majeure," which is defined to
include:

> any Act of God, war, mobilization, strike, lockout, drought,
> flood, total or partial fire, obstruction of navigation by ice at
> port of shipment, or loss, damage or detention at sea, or other
> contingency or cause beyond the control of the Seller which
> prevents the manufacture and/or shipment, and/or sea-
> transport of pulp, or beyond the control of the Buyer which
> prevents the manufacture of paper.

Thereafter, as part of the same clause, it is stated: "In case Seller's
stock of pulp is totally or partially destroyed, and/or damaged by fire,
the Seller is entitled to cancel such quantity which as a consequence
cannot be delivered." The addition of this last statement makes it
clear that suspension only, and not immediate cancellation, is permitted in the event of all *force majeure* circumstances except destruction
or damage of pulp by fire. Similarly, the qualification "by fire" after
the word "damaged" in the additional statement indicates that damage
by other means, such as by some disease, though beyond the seller's
control, is not a basis for either suspension or immediate cancellation.
Clearly, it would defeat the intention of the parties to hold that the
seller is entitled, without liability, to suspend performance or cancel
the contract if he is prevented from manufacturing by failure of his
sources of supply.

Even in international trade, however, many contracts do not contain elaborate clauses relating directly to excuse for nonperformance. The standard c. i. f. contract of the American Spice Trade Association, as amended August 1, 1959, simply states: "Force Majeure:
—This contract is subject to force majeure." Other clauses of the
contract relate to export and import duties and taxes, insurance, shipment, risks of the voyage, government standards and import regula-

tions, insolvency, arbitration, consular fees, and a few other matters. Nevertheless, even in such a contract the scope of the term *force majeure* can be determined by analysis of the contract as a whole. The insurance clause, for example, requires the seller to insure in behalf of the buyer at the price of the contract, such insurance to include war risk on the terms prevailing at the time of shipment. If the goods are lost at sea because of military action *not* included under prevailing war risk terms, the fact that such military action would be included in a customary list of *force majeure* circumstances, or that it frustrated the venture, should not excuse the buyer, for the buyer has, under the c. i. f. term, accepted the risks of the voyage subject to the seller's duty to insure in his behalf. The effect of the *force majeure* clause is to meet the older rule that the parties are subject to an absolute liability for nonperformance, absent an express contractual provision to the contrary. The clause indicates that when performance is prevented by catastrophic events that fall within the definition of *force majeure* and the risk of such nonperformance is not allocated by the other terms of the contract, the obligation is discharged. It would apply, for example, to a case in which war prevented the seller from delivering the goods to the carrier.

In searching for the rules of excuse within the four corners of the contract, as understood in the trade, it is necessary to consider the whole transaction which the contract symbolizes. Certain risks may be allocated by the price itself. If a commission agent, for example, is paid a higher than normal percentage of the contract price, this may indicate that he assumed greater than normal risks. Other risks may be allocated by the nature of the promised performance; if a buyer agrees to pay in a particular currency, this may indicate that he assumed the risks of fluctuation in the value of that currency. Other risks may be allocated by the nature of the business; if the contract is for the sale, in effect, of documents, the risk of impossibility of delivery of the goods is on the buyer after valid documents are tendered. In all these situations, contract practices in the particular trade should be decisive.

The study of a wide variety of international trade contracts reveals that every type of excusing contingency that has come before the courts, and indeed every type of contingency that can be imagined, is covered by express provision in one contract or other. The fact that no single contract expressly covers every type of excusing contingency is not attributable to "impossibility" or even to "commercial impracticability," for though it would undoubtedly be awkward in a contract for the sale of hides, for example, to include dozens of clauses in fine print listing dozens of conceivable causes of exoneration, that is in fact what is done without creating undue agitation in a standard charter party. The reasons why international trade contracts for the sale of such commodities as hides, grain, spice, wax, and similar goods can be relatively short are that established commercial custom in all countries attaches a considerable body of meaning to such abbreviated terms as "c. i. f.," "subject to license," etc., and that risks not expressly exempted by a *force majeure* or other excuse clause are generally understood to remain on the obligor.

Many scholars have stressed the fact that courts and legislators, in expanding the doctrine of excuse based on changed circumstances, have been influenced by the great economic and political upheavals of the past two generations. It should also be emphasized, however, that exporters and importers (and their lawyers) have also responded to times of rapid change by expanding the excuse clauses of their contracts. The two coinciding tendencies will have an unfortunate multiplier effect if the courts apply a liberal theory of excuse, devised for situations in which the parties have in fact not contemplated the risk of nonperformance due to the occurrence of abnormal events, to contracts drawn for sophisticated commercial transactions in which clauses concerning such risk are drafted with care. The draftsman must take into account the theory that has been adopted by the courts for cases in which neither contract nor custom can provide an answer; but the courts must also shape their doctrine to the contract and the custom. Otherwise the doctrine will become a convenient trapdoor through which the imprudent or unscrupulous obligor can escape, leaving the innocent obligee to bear not only the loss of expected benefits but also, in many cases, the burden of liability to subpurchasers.

In particular, the courts must recognize that it is far more difficult to draft clauses negating the effect of a broad doctrine of excuse than it is to draft clauses negating the effect of a narrow doctrine of excuse. To list contingencies that will *not* excuse is contrary both to usual commercial practice and to sound principles of draftsmanship. Therefore, the basic rule for interpreting the kinds of contracts that are here under discussion should be the rule of absolute obligation, unless the contract, interpreted in the light of trade custom, provides otherwise.

It is not only the great upheavals of recent decades that have created the tendency toward liberalization of excuse; more crucially, such liberalization is due to the breakdown of our faith in contract itself. A jurisprudence of adjustment, entirely appropriate in the realm of remedies, has been applied to the realm of substantive rights as well. Considerations of social policy have been introduced in matters that in the public interest ought to be left to determination by the parties themselves. A return to the spirit of *clausula rebus sic stantibus* [2] poses special dangers in the sphere of international trade, where the parties understand each other better, on the whole, than they understand each other's legal systems and where they rely not upon an equity that overrides contract but upon the equity of the contract it-

---

2. The doctrine, in international law, that a treaty is intended by the parties to be binding only as long as there is no vital change in the circumstances assumed by the parties at the time of the conclusion of the treaty.

self—an equity that has its source in the body of international commercial custom which traders throughout the world have developed throughout the centuries.

The decline of faith in contract has been accompanied by an increased faith in general overriding principles, and this, too, has contributed to an unwarranted liberalization of excuse. Courts and writers have sought to develop general doctrines applicable to the most diverse kinds of business activity. Leases of land, bailments, contracts for hire of a music hall, letting of rooms from which a coronation may be viewed, charter parties, contracts for the supply of plant and equipment, contracts for the sale of generic goods and a host of other types of transactions, domestic and international, all have been subjected to a few loose formulae. The solution, it is suggested, lies in the opposite direction.

Question

Is § 2–615 of the UCC consistent with the preceding analysis?

Problem

During the 1960s, X corporation, a major manufacturer of power generating equipment and facilities, contracted to build nuclear power plants for over twenty public utility companies throughout the United States. In its contracts X corporation agreed to supply the utilities' requirements for uranium oxide, the fuel used in nuclear generating facilities. The supply agreements were for long terms and the price for the uranium oxide was set in reference to the then prevailing market price of about $6 a pound. That had been the market price for some years prior to the negotiation of the supply agreements, and the price remained at that level for some years thereafter. X corporation did not own any sources of uranium oxide at the time it entered these supply agreements. X corporation's managers expected the open market would continue to provide $6 a pound uranium oxide in quantities sufficient to allow profitable fulfillment of the long term supply contracts.

By 1975 the market price of uranium oxide had risen to $26 a pound. X corporation strongly suspected that this was due to the price fixing activities of an international cartel of uranium producing countries other than the United States. X corporation was unaware of the cartel, if in fact it was in existence, when the supply contracts were negotiated. In September 1975, X corporation repudiated its supply contracts, and invoked § 2–615 of the UCC as grounds for claiming to its customers that the repudiation was proper and not actionable. The suppliers promptly sued X corporation for breach of contract. The price of uranium oxide had risen to $40 a pound by the time the utilities sued X. Documentary evidence of the existence of the cartel was uncovered in 1976, after X had repudiated its contracts. By July 1978 the price had risen to $44 a pound. If the suppliers are permitted to recover full contract damages from X, it is expected that the total damage awards will exceed $600,000,000. $300,000,000 of the damages will be absorbed by the U.S. Government in reduced taxes since X will deduct any damage awards in computing its taxable income. The $300,-000,000 which would be borne by X is a very substantial part of its net worth. Though this would not bankrupt the company, it would cause major financial difficulties and injure the shareholders by substantially reducing the market value of their stock.

Should X corporation be excused from performance under UCC § 2–615?

SECTION 28. REMEDIES FOR BREACH OF CONTRACT

[The following is taken from GEORGE K. GARDNER, "SOME OBSERVATIONS ON THE COURSE IN CONTRACTS" (Unpublished manuscript, Cambridge, Mass., 1934).]

The ethical problems involved in the law of contracts result as I see them from four elementary ideas:—

(1) *The Tort Idea,* i. e. that one ought to pay for the injuries he does to another. As applied to promises this means that one ought to pay for losses which others suffer in reliance on his promises.

(2) *The Bargain Idea,* i. e. that one who gets anything of value by promising to pay an agreed price for it ought to pay the seller the price he agreed.

(3) *The Promissory Idea,* i. e. that promises are binding in their own nature and ought to be kept in all cases.

(4) *The Quasi-Contractual Idea,* i. e. that one who receives anything of value from another ought to pay for it unless it came to him as a voluntary gift.

These ideas, which at first seem trite and wholly harmonious, are in fact profoundly in conflict. The first and fourth proceed from the premise that justice is to be known after the event, and that it is the business of the court to correct whatever consequences of voluntary intercourse between men may be found to have turned out unjustly. The second and third proceed from the premise that justice is to be known before the event in transactions voluntarily entered into, and that it is the parties' business to settle the justice and injustice of their voluntary transactions at the start. The conflict between these two standpoints is perennial; it can be traced throughout the history of the law of contracts and noted in nearly every debatable contract question; there is no reason to think that it can ever be gotten rid of or to suppose that the present compromises of the issue will be any more permanent than the other compromises that have gone before.

[The following is taken from OLIVER WENDELL HOLMES, "THE PATH OF THE LAW," 10 Harvard Law Review 457, 457–462 (1877).]

When we study law we are not studying a mystery but a well known profession. We are studying what we shall want in order to appear before judges, or to advise people in such a way as to keep them out of court. The reason why it'is a profession, why people will pay lawyers to argue for them or to advise them, is that in societies like ours the command of the public force is intrusted to the judges in certain cases, and the whole power of the state will be put forth, if necessary, to carry out their judgments and decrees. People want to know under what circumstances and how far they will run the risk of coming against what is so much stronger than themselves, and hence it becomes a business to find out when this danger is to be feared. The object of our study, then, is prediction, the prediction of the incidence of the public force through the instrumentality of the courts.

* * *

I wish, if I can, to lay down some first principles for the study of this body of dogma or systematized prediction which we call the law, for men who want to use it as the instrument of their business to enable them to prophesy in their turn, and, as bearing upon the study, I wish to point out an ideal which as yet our law has not attained.

The first thing for a business-like understanding of the matter is to understand its limits, and therefore I think it desirable at once to point out and dispel a confusion between morality and law, which sometimes rises to the height of conscious theory, and more often and indeed constantly is making trouble in detail without reaching the point of consciousness. You can see very plainly that a bad man has as much reason as a good one for wishing to avoid an encounter with the public force, and therefore you can see the practical importance of the distinction between morality and law. A man who cares nothing for an ethical rule which is believed and practised by his neighbors is likely nevertheless to care a good deal to avoid being made to pay money, and will want to keep out of jail if he can.

I take it for granted that no hearer of mine will misinterpret what I have to say as the language of cynicism. The law is the witness and external deposit of our moral life. Its history is the history of the moral development of the race. The practice of it, in spite of popular jests, tends to make good citizens and good men. When I emphasize the difference between law and morals I do so with reference to a single end, that of learning and understanding the law. For that purpose you must definitely master its specific marks, and it is for that that I ask you for the moment to imagine yourselves indifferent to other and greater things.

I do not say that there is not a wider point of view from which the distinction between law and morals becomes of secondary or no importance, as all mathematical distinctions vanish in presence of the infinite. But I do say that that distinction is of the first importance for the object which we are here to consider,—a right study and mastery of the law as a business with well understood limits, a body of dogma enclosed within definite lines. I have just shown the practical reason for saying so. If you want to know the law and nothing else, you must look at it as a bad man, who cares only for the material consequences which such knowledge enables him to predict, not as a good one, who finds his reasons for conduct, whether inside the law or outside of it, in the vaguer sanctions of conscience. The theoretical importance of the distinction is no less, if you would reason on your subject aright. The law is full of phraseology drawn from morals, and by the mere force of language continually invites us to pass from one domain to the other without perceiving it, as we are sure to do unless we have the boundary constantly before our minds. The law talks about rights, and duties, and malice and intent, and negligence, and so forth, and nothing is easier, or, I may say, more common in legal reasoning, than to take these words in their moral sense, at some stage of the argument, and so to drop into fallacy.

. . .

The confusion with which I am dealing besets confessedly legal conceptions. Take the fundamental question, What constitutes the law? You will find some text writers telling you that it is something different from what is decided by the courts of Massachusetts or England, that it is a system of reason, that it is a deduction from principles of ethics or admitted axioms or what not, which may or may not coincide with the decisions. But if we take the view of our friend the bad man we shall find that he does not care two straws for the axioms or deductions, but that he does want to know what the Massachusetts or English courts are likely to do in fact. I am much of his mind. The prophecies of what the courts will do in fact, and nothing more pretentious, are what I mean by the law.

* * *

Nowhere is the confusion between legal and moral ideas more manifest than in the law of contract. Among other things, here again the so called primary rights and duties are invested with a mystic significance beyond what can be assigned and explained. The duty to keep a contract at common law means a prediction that you must pay damages if you do not keep it,—and nothing else. If you commit a tort, you are liable to pay a compensatory sum. If you commit a contract, you are liable to pay a compensatory sum unless the promised event comes to pass, and that is all the difference. But such a mode of looking at the matter stinks in the nostrils of those who think it advantageous to get as much ethics into the law as they can.

. . .

[The following is taken from LON L. FULLER AND WILLIAM R. PERDUE, JR., "THE RELIANCE INTEREST IN CONTRACT DAMAGES," 46 Yale Law Journal 52 and 373, 52–66 (1936). Footnotes are omitted.]

The proposition that legal rules can be understood only with reference to the purposes they serve would today scarcely be regarded as an exciting truth. The notion that law exists as a means to an end has been commonplace for at least half a century. There is, however, no justification for assuming, because this attitude has now achieved respectability, and even triteness, that it enjoys a pervasive application in practice. Certainly there are even today few legal treatises of which it may be said that the author has throughout clearly defined the purposes which his definitions and distinctions serve. We are still all too willing to embrace the conceit that it is possible to manipulate legal concepts without the orientation which comes from the simple inquiry: toward what end is this activity directed? Nietzsche's observation, that the most common stupidity consists in forgetting what one is trying to do, retains a discomforting relevance to legal science.

In no field is this more true than in that of damages. In the assessment of damages the law tends to be conceived, not as a purposive ordering of human affairs, but as a kind of juristic mensuration. The language of the decisions sounds in terms not of command but of discovery. We *measure* the *extent* of the injury; we *determine* whether it was *caused* by the defendant's act; we *ascertain* whether the plaintiff has included the *same item* of damage twice in his complaint. One unfamiliar with the unstated premises which language of this sort conceals might almost be led to suppose that Rochester produces some ingenious instrument by which these calculations are accomplished.

It is, as a matter of fact, clear that the things which the law of damages purports to "measure" and "determine"—the "injuries", "items of damage", "causal connections", etc.—are in considerable part its own creations, and that the process of "measuring" and "determining" them is really a part of the process of creating them. This is obvious when courts work on the periphery of existing doctrine, but it is no less true of fundamental and established principles.   .   .   .

The Purposes Pursued in Awarding Contract Damages

It is convenient to distinguish three principal purposes which may be pursued in awarding contract damages. These purposes, and the situations in which they become appropriate, may be stated briefly as follows:

First, the plaintiff has in reliance on the promise of the defendant conferred some value on the defendant. The defendant fails to perform his promise. The court may force the defendant to disgorge the value he received from the plaintiff. The object here may be termed the prevention of gain by the defaulting promisor at the expense of the promisee; more briefly, the prevention of unjust enrichment. The interest protected may be called the *restitution interest.* For our present purposes it is quite immaterial how the suit in such a case be classified, whether as contractual or quasi-contractual, whether as a suit to enforce the contractor or as a suit based upon a rescission of the contract. These questions relate to the superstructure of the law, not to the basic policies with which we are concerned.

Secondly, the plaintiff has in reliance on the promise of the defendant changed his position. For example, the buyer under a contract for the sale of land has incurred expense in the investigation of the seller's title, or has neglected the opportunity to enter other contracts. We may award damages to the plaintiff for the purpose of undoing the harm which his reliance on the defendant's promise has caused him. Our object is to put him in as good a position as he was in before the promise was made. The interest protected in this case may be called the *reliance interest.*

Thirdly, without insisting on reliance by the promisee or enrichment of the promisor, we may seek to give the promisee the value of the expectancy which the promise created. We may in a suit for specific performance actually compel the defendant to render the promised performance to the plaintiff, or, in a suit for damages, we may make the defendant pay the money value of this performance. Here our object is to put the plaintiff in as good a position as he would have occupied had the defendant performed his promise. The interest protected in this case we may call the *expectation interest*.

It will be observed that what we have called the *restitution interest* unites two elements: (1) reliance by the promisee, (2) a resultant gain to the promisor. It may for some purposes be necessary to separate these elements. In some cases a defaulting promisor may after his breach be left with an unjust gain which was not taken from the promisee (a third party furnished the consideration), or which was not the result of reliance by the promisee (the promisor violated a promise not to appropriate the promisee's goods). Even in those cases where the promisor's gain results from the promisee's reliance it may happen that damages will be assessed somewhat differently, depending on whether we take the promisor's gain or the promisee's loss as the standard of measurement. Generally, however, in the cases we shall be discussing, gain by the promisor will be accompanied by a corresponding and, so far as its legal measurement is concerned, identical loss to the promisee, so that for our purposes the most workable classification is one which presupposes in the restitution interest a correlation of promisor's gain and promisee's loss. If, as we shall assume, the gain involved in the restitution interest results from and is identical with the plaintiff's loss through reliance, then the restitution interest is merely a special case of the reliance interest; all of the cases coming under the restitution interest will be covered by the reliance interest, and the reliance interest will be broader than the restitution interest only to the extent that it includes cases where the plaintiff has relied on the defendant's promise without enriching the defendant. . . .

It is obvious that the three "interests" we have distinguished do not present equal claims to judicial intervention. It may be assumed that ordinary standards of justice would regard the need for judicial intervention as decreasing in the order in which we have listed the three interests. The "restitution interest," involving a combination of unjust impoverishment with unjust gain, presents the strongest case for relief. If, following Aristotle, we regard the purpose of justice as the maintenence of an equilibrium of goods among members of society, the restitution interest presents twice as strong a claim to judicial intervention as the reliance interest, since if A not only causes B to lose one unit but appropriates that unit to himself, the resulting discrepancy between A and B is not one unit but two. [Aristotle, *Nicomachean Ethics*, 1132a–1132b.]

On the other hand, the promisee who has actually relied on the promise, even though he may not thereby have enriched the promisor, certainly presents a more pressing case for relief than the promisee who merely demands satisfaction for his disappointment in not getting what was promised him. In passing from compensation for change of position to compensation for loss of expectancy we pass, to use Aristotle's terms again, from the realm of corrective justice to that of distributive justice. The law no longer seeks merely to heal a disturbed status quo, but to bring into being a new situation. It ceases to act defensively or restoratively, and assumes a more active role. With the transition, the justification for legal relief loses its self-evident quality. It is as a matter of fact no easy thing to explain why the normal rule of contract recovery should be that which measures damages by the value of the promised performance. Since this "normal rule" throws its shadow across our whole subject it will be necessary to examine the possible reasons for its existence. It may be said parenthetically that the discussion which follows, though directed primarily to the normal measure of recovery where damages are sought, also has relevance to the more general question, why should a promise which has not been relied on ever be enforced at all, whether by a decree of specific performance or by an award of damages? . . .

Why Should the Law ever Protect the Expectation Interest?

Perhaps the most obvious answer to this question is one which we may label "psychological." This answer would run something as follows: The breach of a promise arouses in the promisee a sense of injury. This feeling is not confined to cases where the promisee has relied on the promise. Whether or not he has actually changed his position because of the promise, the promisee has formed an attitude of expectancy such that a breach of the promise causes him to feel that he has been "deprived" of something which was "his". Since this sentiment is a relatively uniform one, the law has no occasion to go back of it. It accepts it as a datum and builds its rule about it.

The difficulty with this explanation is that the law does in fact go back of the sense of injury which the breach of a promise engenders. No legal system attempts to invest with juristic sanction all promises. Some rule or combination of rules effects a sifting out for enforcement of those promises deemed important enough to society to justify the law's concern with them. Whatever the principles which control this sifting out process may be, they are not convertible into terms of the degree of resentment which the breach of a particular kind of promise arouses. Therefore, though it may be assumed that the impulse to assuage disappointment is one shared by those who make and influence the law, this impulse can hardly be regarded as the key which solves the whole problem of the protection accorded by the law to the expectation interest.

A second possible explanation for the rule protecting the expectancy may be found in the much-discussed "will theory" of contract law. This theory views the contracting parties as exercising, so to speak, a legislative power, so that the legal enforcement of a contract becomes merely an implementing by the state of a kind of private law already established by the parties. If A has made, in proper form, a promise to pay B one thousand dollars, we compel A to pay this sum simply because the rule or *lex* set up by the parties calls for this payment. *Uti lingua nuncupassit, ita jus esto.*

It is not necessary to discuss here the contribution which the will theory is capable of making to a philosophy of contract law. Certainly some borrowings from the theory are discernible in most attempts to rationalize the bases of contract liability. It is enough to note here that while the will theory undoubtedly has some bearing on the problem of contract damages, it cannot be regarded as dictating in all cases a recovery of the expectancy. If a contract represents a kind of private law, it is a law which usually says nothing at all about what shall be done when it is violated. A contract is in this respect like an imperfect statute which provides no penalties, and which leaves it to the courts to find a way to effectuate its purposes. There would, therefore, be no necessary contradiction between the will theory and a rule which limited damages to the reliance interest. Under such a rule the penalty for violating the norm established by the contract would simply consist in being compelled to compensate the other party for detrimental reliance. Of course there may be cases where the parties have so obviously anticipated that a certain form of judicial relief will be given that we can, without stretching things, say that by implication they have "willed" that this relief should be given. This attitude finds a natural application to promises to pay a definite sum of money. But certainly as to most types of contracts it is vain to expect from the will theory a ready-made solution for the problem of damages.

A third and more promising solution of our difficulty lies in an economic or institutional approach. The essence of a credit economy lies in the fact that it tends to eliminate the distinction between present and future (promised) goods. Expectations of future values become, for purposes of trade, present values. In a society in which credit has become a significant and pervasive institution, it is inevitable that the expectancy created by an enforceable promise should be regarded as a kind of property, and breach of the promise as an injury to the property. In such a society the breach of a promise works an "actual" diminution of the promisee's assets—"actual" in the sense that it would be so appraised according to modes of thought which enter into the very fiber of our economic system. That the promisee had not "used" the property which the promise represents (had not relied on the promise) is as immaterial as the question whether the plaintiff in trespass *quare clausum fregit* was using his property at the time it was encroached upon. The analogy to ordinary forms of property goes further, for even in a suit for trespass the recovery is really for an expectancy, an expectancy of possible future uses. Where the property expectancy is limited (as where the plaintiff has only an estate for years) the recovery is reduced accordingly. Ordinary property differs from a contract right chiefly in the fact that it lies within the power of more persons to work a direct injury to the expectancy it represents. It is generally only the promisor or some one working through or upon him who is able to injure the contract expectancy in a direct enough manner to make expedient legal intervention.

The most obvious objection which can be made to the economic or institutional explanation is that it involves a *petitio principii*. A promise has present value, why? Because the law enforces it. "The expectancy," regarded as a present value, is not the cause of legal intervention but the consequence of it. This objection may be reinforced by a reference to legal history. Promises were enforced long before there was anything corresponding to a general system of "credit", and recovery was from the beginning measured by the value of the promised performance, the "agreed price". It may therefore be argued that the "credit system" when it finally emerged was itself in large part built on the foundations of a juristic development which preceded it.

The view just suggested asserts the primacy of law over economics; it sees law not as the creature but as the creator of social institutions. The shift of emphasis thus implied suggests the possibility of a fourth explanation for the law's protection of the unrelied-on expectancy, which we may call *juristic*. This explanation would seek a justification for the normal rule of recovery in some policy consciously pursued by courts and other lawmakers. It would assume that courts have protected the expectation interest because they have considered it wise to do so, not through a blind acquiescence in habitual ways of thinking and feeling, or through an equally blind deference to the individual will. Approaching the problem from this point of view, we are forced to find not a mere explanation for the rule in the form of some sentimental, volitional, or institutional datum, but articulate reasons for its existence.

What reasons can be advanced? In the first place, even if our interest were confined to protecting promisees against an out-of-pocket loss, it would still be possible to justify the rule granting the value of the expectancy, both as a cure for, and as a prophylaxis against, losses of this sort.

It is a cure for these losses in the sense that it offers the measure of recovery most likely to reimburse the plaintiff for the (often very numerous and very difficult to prove) individual acts and forbearances which make up his total reliance on the contract. If we take into account "gains prevented" by reliance, that is, losses involved in foregoing the opportunity to enter other contracts, the notion that the rule protecting the expectancy is adopted as the most effective means of compensating for detrimental reliance seems not at all far-fetched. Physicians with an extensive practice often charge their patients the full office call fee for broken appointments. Such a charge looks on the face of things like a claim to the promised fee; it seems to be based on the "expectation interest". Yet the physician making the charge will quite justifiably regard it as compensation for the loss of the opportunity to gain a similar fee from a different patient. This foregoing of other opportunities is involved to some extent in entering most contracts, and the impossibility of subjecting this type of reliance to any kind of measurement may justify a categorical rule granting the value of the expectancy as the most effective way of compensating for such losses.

The rule that the plaintiff must after the defendant's breach take steps to mitigate damages tends to corroborate the suspicion that there lies hidden behind the protection of the expectancy a concern to compensate the plaintiff for the loss of the opportunity to enter other contracts. Where after the defendant's breach the opportunity remains open to the plaintiff to sell his services or goods elsewhere, or to fill his needs from another source, he is bound to embrace that opportunity. Viewed in this way the rule of "avoidable harms" is a qualification on the protection accorded the expectancy, since it means that the plaintiff, in those cases where it is applied, is protected only to the extent that he has in reliance on the contract foregone other equally advantageous opportunities for accomplishing the same end.

But, as we have suggested, the rule measuring damages by the expectancy may also be regarded as a prophylaxis against the losses resulting from detrimental reliance. Whatever tends to discourage breach of contract tends to prevent the losses occasioned through reliance. Since the expectation interest furnishes a more easily administered measure of recovery than the reliance interest, it will in practice offer a more effective sanction against contract breach. It is therefore possible to view the rule measuring damages by the expectancy in a quasi-criminal aspect, its purpose being not so much to compensate the promisee as to penalize breach of promise by the promisor. The rule enforcing the unrelied-on promise finds the same justification, on this theory, as an ordinance which fines a man for driving through a stop-light when no other vehicle is in sight.

In seeking justification for the rule granting the value of the expectancy there is no need, however, to restrict ourselves by the assumption, hitherto made, that the rule can only be intended to cure or prevent the losses caused by reliance. A justification can be developed from a less negative point of view. It may be said that there is not only a policy in favor of preventing and undoing the harms resulting from reliance, but also a policy in favor of promoting and facilitating reliance on business agreements. As in the case of the stop-light ordinance we are interested not only in preventing collisions but in speeding traffic. Agreements can accomplish little, either for their makers or for society, unless they are made the basis for action. When business agreements are not only made but are also acted on, the division of labor is facilitated, goods find their way to the places where they are most needed, and economic activity is generally stimulated. These advantages would be threatened by any rule which limited legal protection to the reliance interest. Such a rule would in practice tend to discourage reliance. The difficulties in proving reliance and subjecting it to pecuniary measurement are such that the business man knowing, or sensing, that these obstacles stood in the way of judicial relief would hesitate to rely on a promise in any case where the legal sanction was of significance to him. To encourage reliance we must therefore dispense with its proof. For this reason it has been found wise to make recovery on a promise independent of reliance, both in the sense that in some cases the promise is enforced though not relied on (as in the bilateral business agreement) and in the sense that recovery is not limited to the detriment incurred in reliance.

The juristic explanation in its final form is then twofold. It rests the protection accorded the expectancy on (1) the need for curing and preventing the harms occasioned by reliance, and (2) on the need for facilitating reliance on business agreements. From this spelling out of a possible juristic explanation, it is clear that there is no incompatibility between it and the economic or institutional explanation. They view the same phenomenon from two different aspects. The essence of both of them lies in the word "credit." The economic explanation views credit from its institutional side; the juristic explanation views it from its rational side. The economic view sees credit as an accepted way of living; the juristic view invites us to explore the considerations of utility which underlie this way of living, and the part which conscious human direction has played in bringing it into being.

The way in which these two points of view supplement one another becomes clearer when we examine separately the economic implications of the two aspects of the juristic explanation. If we rest the legal argument for measuring damages by the expectancy on the ground that this procedure offers the most satisfactory means of compensating the plaintiff for the loss of other opportunities to contract, it is clear that the force of the argument will depend entirely upon the existing economic environment. It would be most forceful in a hypothetical society in which all values were available on the market and where all markets were "perfect" in the economic sense. In such a society there would be no difference between the reliance interest and the expectation interest. The plaintiff's loss in foregoing to enter another contract would be identical with the expectation value of the contract he did make. The argument that granting the value of the expectancy merely compensates for that loss, loses force to the extent that actual conditions depart from those of such a hypothetical society. These observations make it clear why the development of open markets for goods tends to carry in its wake the view that a contract claim is a kind of property, a conception which—for all the importance he attached to it—MacLeod seemed to regard as the product of a kind of legal miracle. He who by entering one contract passes by the opportunity to accomplish the same end elsewhere will not be inclined to regard contract breach lightly or as a mere matter of private morality. The consciousness of what is foregone reinforces the notion that the contract creates a "right" and that the contract claim is itself a species of property.

If, on the other hand, we found the juristic explanation on the desire to promote reliance on contracts, it is not difficult again to trace a correspondence between the legal view and the actual conditions of economic life. In general our courts and our economic institutions attribute special significance to the same types of promises. The bilateral business agreement is, generally speaking, the only type of informal contract our courts are willing to enforce without proof that reliance has occurred—simply for the sake of facilitating reliance. This is, by no accident, precisely the kind of contract (the "exchange", "bargain", "trade", "deal") which furnishes the indispensable and pervasive framework for the "unmanaged" portions of our economic activity.

The inference is therefore justified that the ends of the law of contracts and those of our economic system show an essential correspondence. One may explain this either on the ground that the law (mere superstructure and ideology) reflects inertly the conditions of economic life, or on the ground that economic activity has fitted itself into the rational framework of the law. Neither explanation would be true. In fact we are dealing with a situation in which law and society have interacted. The law measures damages by the expectancy *in part* because society views the expectancy as a present value; society views the expectancy as a present value *in part* because the law (for reasons more or less consciously articulated) gives protection to the expectancy.

The combined juristic and economic explanation which has just been developed may seem vulnerable to one serious objection. This lies in the fact that the "normal" rule, which measures damages by the expectancy, has been frequently applied to promises of a type having no conceivable relation to "the credit system," the division of labor, or the organization of economic activity. Professor Williston apparently goes so far as to assume that the "normal" rule is the only permissible rule of recovery even in the case of promises made enforceable by § 90 of the Contracts Restatement, that is, in the case of promises for which no price has been given or promised and which are enforced only because they have been seriously relied on.[1] Most of the arguments for the rule measuring damages by the expectancy which we developed under our combined economic and juristic explanation have no application to such promises. The suggestion that the expectation interest is adopted as a kind of surrogate for the reliance interest because of the difficulty of proving reliance can scarcely be applicable to a situation where we actually insist on proof of reliance, and indeed, reliance of a "definite and substantial character." The notion that the expectancy is granted as compensation for foregoing the opportunity to enter other similar contracts is also without application in this situation, if for no other reason than because no contract is here "entered" at all. Finally the policy in favor of facilitating reliance can scarcely be extended to all promises indiscriminately. Any such policy must presuppose that reliance in the particular situation will normally have some general utility. Where. we are dealing with "exchanges" or "bargains" it is easy to discern this utility since such transactions form the very mechanism by which production is organized in a capitalistic society. There seems no basis for assuming any such general utility in the promises coming under § 90, since they are restricted only by a negative definition—they are not bargains.

It is the application of the "normal" rule of damages to non-bargain promises then an unanswerable refutation of the explanation which we have attempted of the rule? We think not. In the first place, it is obviously possible that courts have, through force of habit, given a broader application to the rule than a philosophic inquiry into its possible bases would justify. In the second place, it is by no means clear, from the decisions at any rate, that the rule of recovery in the case of these "non-bargain" promises *is* necessarily that which measures damages by the expectancy. There are, as we shall show in our second installment, cases which indicate the contrary.

It is not difficult to demonstrate. that the judicial treatment accorded contracts is affected by the relation between the particular contract and what we have called "the credit system." The ideal contract from the standpoint of the credit system is the (bargain) promise to pay money. Here we find a combination of legal qualities which reflects the intimate association of this type of contract with the economic institution of credit: free alienation by the creditor; free substitution of another's performance by the debtor; easy convertibility between present and future claims, the difference being measured by interest; damages measured by a mechanical standard which excludes consideration of the peculiarities of the particular situation; finally, damages measured by the expectancy, with no tendency to substitute a different measure.

If it were not for certain complicating cross currents we might expect to find a uniform increase in the tendency to remit the plaintiff to the reliance interest as we progress away from the credit system. This would come about in two ways, both of which may be illustrated in the contract to adopt. (1) The farther removed a contract is from the credit system the more difficult it is to measure the value of the expectancy. (2) The farther removed a contract is from the credit system, the less is judicial incentive to grant the expectancy, the less pressing are the basic policies which justify the granting of the expectancy in the ordinary business agreement. . . .

1. Reprinted *supra* at p. 607.

HAWKINS v. McGEE

Supreme Court of New Hampshire, 1929.
84 N.H. 114, 146 A. 641.

Action by George Hawkins against Edward R. B. McGee. Verdict for plaintiff, which was set aside. Transferred on exceptions. New trial.

Assumpsit against a surgeon for breach of an alleged warranty of the success of an operation. Trial by jury. Verdict for the plaintiff. The writ also contained a count in negligence upon which a nonsuit was ordered, without exception.

Defendant's motions for a nonsuit and for a directed verdict on the count in assumpsit were denied, and the defendant excepted. During the argument of plaintiff's counsel to the jury, the defendant claimed certain exceptions, and also excepted to the denial of his requests for instructions and to the charge of the court upon the question of damages, as more fully appears in the opinion. The defendant seasonably moved to set aside the verdict upon the grounds that it was (1) contrary to the evidence; (2) against the weight of the evidence; (3) against the weight of the law and evidence; and (4) because the damages awarded by the jury were excessive. The court denied the motion upon the first three grounds, but found that the damages were excessive, and made an order that the verdict be set aside, unless the plaintiff elected to remit all in excess of $500. The plaintiff having refused to remit, the verdict was set aside "as excessive and against the weight of the evidence," and the plaintiff excepted.

The foregoing exceptions were transferred by Seammon, J. The facts are stated in the opinion.

* * *

BRANCH, J. [1, 2]. 1. The operation in question consisted in the removal of a considerable quantity of scar tissue from the palm of the plaintiff's right hand and the grafting of skin taken from the plaintiff's chest in place thereof. The scar tissue was the result of a severe burn caused by contact with an electric wire, which the plaintiff received about nine years before the time of the transactions here involved. There was evidence to the effect that before the operation was performed the plaintiff and his father went to the defendant's office, and that the defendant, in answer to the question, "How long will the boy be in the hospital?" replied, "Three or four days, not over four; then the boy can go home and it will be just a few days when he will go back to work with a good hand." Clearly this and other testimony to the same effect would not justify a finding that the doctor contracted to complete the hospital treatment in three or four days or that the plaintiff would be able to go back to work within a few days thereafter. The above statements could only be construed as expressions of opinion or predictions as to the probable duration of the treatment and plaintiff's resulting disability, and the fact that these estimates were exceeded would impose no contractual liability upon the defendant. The only substantial basis for the plaintiff's claim is the testimony that the defendant also said before the operation was decided upon, "I will guarantee to make the hand a hundred per cent perfect hand or a hundred per cent good hand."

The plaintiff was present when these words were alleged to have been spoken, and, if they are to be taken at their face value, it seems obvious that proof of their utterance would establish the giving of a warranty in accordance with his contention.

The defendant argues, however, that, even if these words were uttered by him, no reasonable man would understand that they were used with the intention of entering "into any contractual relation whatever," and that they could reasonably be understood only "as his expression in strong language that he believed and expected that as a result of the operation he would give the plaintiff a very good hand." It may be conceded, as the defendant contends that before the question of the making of a contract should be submitted to a jury, there is a preliminary question of law for the trial court to pass upon, i. e. "whether the words could possibly have the meaning imputed to them by the party who founds his case upon a certain interpretation," but it cannot be held that the trial court decided this question erroneously in the present case. It is unnecessary to determine at this time whether the argument of the defendant, based upon "common knowledge of the uncertainty which attends all surgical operations," and the improbability that a surgeon would ever contract to make a damaged part of the human body "one hundred per cent perfect," would, in the absence of countervailing considerations, be regarded as conclusive, for there were other factors in the present case which tended to support the contention of the plaintiff. There was evidence that the defendant repeatedly solicited from the plaintiff's father the opportunity to perform this operation, and the theory was advanced by plaintiff's counsel in cross-examination of defendant that he sought an opportunity to "experiment on skin grafting," in which he had had little previous experience. If the jury accepted this part of plaintiff's contention, there would be a reasonable basis for the further conclusion that, if defendant spoke the words attributed to him, he did so with the intention that they should be accepted at their face value, as an inducement for the granting of consent to the operation by the plaintiff and his father, and there was ample evidence that they were so accepted by them. The question of the making of the alleged contract was properly submitted to the jury.

2. The substance of the charge to the jury on the question of damages appears in the following quotation: "If you find the plaintiff entitled to anything, he is entitled to recover for what pain and suffering he has been made to endure and for what injury he has sustained over and above what injury he had before." To this instruction the defendant seasonably excepted. By it, the jury was permitted to consider two elements of damage: (1) Pain and suffering due to the operation; and (2) positive ill effects of the operation upon the plaintiff's hand. Authority for any specific rule of damages in cases of this kind seems to be lacking, but, when tested by general principle and by analogy, it appears that the foregoing instruction was erroneous.

"By 'damages,' as that term is used in the law of contracts, is intended compensation for a breach, measured in the terms of the contract." Davis v. New England Cotton Yarn Co., 77 N.H. 403, 404, 92 A. 732, 733. The purpose of the law is "to put the plaintiff in as good a position as he would have been in had the defendant kept his contract." 3 Williston Cont. § 1338; Hardie-Tynes Mfg. Co. v. Easton Cotton Oil Co., 150 N.C. 150, 63 S. E. 676, 134 Am.St.Rep. 899. The measure of recovery "is based upon what the defendant should have given the plaintiff, not what the plaintiff has given the defendant or otherwise expended." 3 Williston Cont. § 1341. "The only losses that can be said fairly to come within the terms of a contract are such as the parties must have had in mind when the contract was made, or such as they either knew or ought to have known would probably result from a failure to comply with its terms." Davis v. New England Cotton Yarn Co., 77 N.H. 403, 404, 92 A. 732, 733, Hurd v. Dunsmore, 63 N.H. 171.

The present case is closely analogous to one in which a machine is built for a certain purpose and warranted to do certain work. In such cases, the usual rule of damages for breach of warranty in the sale of chattels is applied, and it is held that the measure of damages is the difference between the value of the machine, if it had corresponded with the warranty and its actual value, together with such incidental losses as the parties knew, or ought to have known, would probably result from a failure to comply with its terms. [Citations omitted.]

The rule thus applied is well settled in this state. "As a general rule, the measure of the vendee's damages is the difference between the value of the goods as they would have been if the warranty as to quality had been true, and the actual value at the time of the sale, including gains prevented and losses sustained, and such other damages as could be reasonably anticipated by the parties as likely to be caused by the vendor's failure to keep his agreement, and could not by reasonable care on the part of the vendee have been avoided." Union Bank v. Blanchard, 65 N.H. 21, 23, 18 A. 90, 91; Hurd v. Dunsmore, supra; Noyes v. Blodgett, 58 N.H. 502; P.L. ch. 166, § 69, subd. 7. We therefore conclude that the true measure of the plaintiff's damage in the present case is the difference between the value to him of a perfect hand or a good hand, such as the jury found the defendant promised him, and the value of his hand in its present condition, including any incidental consequences fairly within the contemplation of the parties when they made their contract. 1 Sutherland, Damages (4th Ed.) § 92. Damages not thus limited, although naturally resulting, are not to be given.

The extent of the plaintiff's suffering does not measure this difference in value. The pain necessarily incident to a serious surgical operation was a part of the contribution which the plaintiff was willing to make to his joint undertaking with the defendant to produce a good hand. It was a legal detriment suffered by him which constituted a part of the consideration given by him for the contract. It represented a part of the price which he was willing to pay for a good hand, but it furnished no test of the value of a good hand or the difference between the value of the hand which the defendant promised and the one which resulted from the operation.

It was also erroneous and misleading to submit to the jury as a separate element of damage any change for the worse in the condition of the plaintiff's hand resulting from the operation, although this error was probably more prejudicial to the plaintiff than to the defendant. Any such ill effect of the operation would be included under the true rule of damages set forth above, but damages might properly be assessed for the defendant's failure to improve the condition of the hand, even if there were no evidence that its condition was made worse as a result of the operation.

It must be assumed that the trial court, in setting aside the verdict, undertook to apply the same rule of damages which he had previously given to the jury, and, since this rule was erroneous, it is unnecessary for us to consider whether there was any evidence to justify his finding that all damages awarded by the jury above $500 were excessive.

3.   Defendant's requests for instructions were loosely drawn, and were properly denied.   A considerable number of issues of fact were raised by the evidence, and it would have been extremely misleading to instruct the jury in accordance with defendant's request No. 2, that "the only issue on which you have to pass is whether or not there was a special contract between the plaintiff and the defendant to produce a perfect hand."   Equally inaccurate was defendant's request No. 5, which reads as follows: "You would have to find, in order to hold the defendant liable in this case, that Dr. McGee and the plaintiff both understood that the doctor was guaranteeing a perfect result from this operation."   If the defendant said that he would guarantee a perfect result, and the plaintiff relied upon that promise, any mental reservations which he may have had are immaterial.   The standard by which his conduct is to be judged is not internal, but external. [Citations omitted.]

Defendant's request No. 7 was as follows: "If you should get so far as to find that there was a special contract guaranteeing a perfect result, you would still have to find for the defendant unless you also found that a further operation would not correct the disability claimed by the plaintiff."   In view of the testimony that the defendant had refused to perform a further operation, it would clearly have been erroneous to give this instruction. The evidence would have justified a verdict for an amount sufficient to cover the cost of such an operation, even if the theory underlying this request were correct.

4.   It is unlikely that the questions now presented in regard to the argument of plaintiff's counsel will arise at another trial, and therefore they have not been considered.

New trial.

MARBLE, J., did not sit; the others concurred.

Note and Questions

1.   The summary of the case describes it as an "assumpsit". That term refers to one of the common law forms of action out of which the modern law of contracts and contract remedies was developed.   (See § 30 *infra* at p. 748 ff.)   The term is significant in this case because it indicates that Hawkins' attorney pleaded breach of contract as the primary theory of liability and the New Hampshire Supreme Court heard and decided the case in light of that pleading.

2.   As best you can determine, were the following issues submitted to the jury?

(a)   Did the defendant contract with the plaintiff to perform corrective surgery on the plaintiff's hand?

(b)   As part of the inducement for the contract, did the defendant promise that the corrective surgery would "make the hand a hundred percent perfect hand"?

(c) Was the promise as to the outcome of the surgery absolute and unqualified so that any failure of the defendant's performance which yielded less than "a hundred percent perfect hand" was a breach of promise?

Did the appellate court hold that the jury verdict had resolved these issues in favor of the plaintiff?

3. What are the elements of damage and injury alleged by the plaintiff and for which he seeks to recover from the defendant?

Which of these injuries is a consequence of the defendant's breach of the promised performance? Which of these injuries might be seen instead as a result of defendant's failure to perform the surgery with the care and skill expected of a reasonably competent surgeon? Should it make any difference in determining the damages whether or not defendant breached a promise or breached a general standard of care expected of members of his profession?

4. What is the standard the court finds should be applied in measuring the plaintiff's recovery for the breach of promise? Does the court's damage standard rest on the *promissory idea?* The *bargain idea?* The *tort idea?* The *quasi-contractual idea?*

5. If you had been an attorney in New Hampshire *circa* 1929, and you represented a physician or a group of physicians, what advice would you have given your clients in light of Hawkins v. McGee?

PEEVYHOUSE v. GARLAND COAL & MINING CO.

Supreme Court of Oklahoma, 1962.
382 P.2d 109.

JACKSON, JUSTICE.

In the trial court, plaintiffs Willie and Lucille Peevyhouse sued the defendant, Garland Coal and Mining Company, for damages for breach of contract. Judgment was for plaintiffs in an amount considerably less than was sued for. Plaintiffs appeal and defendant cross-appeals.

In the briefs on appeal, the parties present their argument and contentions under several propositions; however, they all stem from the basic question of whether the trial court properly instructed the jury on the measure of damages.

Briefly stated, the facts are as follows: plaintiffs owned a farm containing coal deposits, and in November, 1954, leased the premises to defendant for a period of five years for coal mining purposes. A "stripmining" operation was contemplated in which the coal would be taken from pits on the surface of the ground, instead of from underground mine shafts. In addition to the usual covenants found in a coal mining lease, defendant specifically agreed to perform certain restorative and remedial work at the end of the lease period. It is unnecessary to set out the details of the work to be done, other than to say that it would involve the moving of many thousands of cubic yards of dirt, at a cost estimated by expert witnesses at about $29,000.00. However, plaintiffs sued for only $25,000.00.

During the trial, it was stipulated that all covenants and agreements in the lease contract had been fully carried out by both parties, except the remedial work mentioned above; defendant conceded that this work had not been done.

Plaintiffs introduced expert testimony as to the amount and nature of the work to be done, and its estimated cost. Over plaintiffs' objections, defendant thereafter introduced expert testimony as to the "diminution in value" of plaintiffs' farm resulting from the failure of defendant to render performance as agreed in the contract—that is, the difference between the present value of the farm, and what its value would have been if defendant had done what it agreed to do.

At the conclusion of the trial, the court instructed the jury that it must return a verdict for plaintiffs, and left the amount of damages for jury determination. On the measure of damages, the court instructed the jury that it might consider the cost of performance of the work defendant agreed to do, "together with all of the evidence offered on behalf of either party".

It thus appears that the jury was at liberty to consider the "diminution in value" of plaintiffs' farm as well as the cost of "repair work" in determining the amount of damages.

It returned a verdict for plaintiffs for $5000.00—only a fraction of the "cost of performance", *but more than the total value of the farm even after the remedial work is done.*

On appeal, the issue is sharply drawn. Plaintiffs contend that the true measure of damages in this case is what it will cost plaintiffs to obtain performance of the work that was not done because of defendant's default. Defendant argues that the measure of damages is the cost of performance "limited, however, to the total difference in the market value before and after the work was performed".

It appears that this precise question has not heretofore been presented to this court. In Ardizonne v. Archer, 72 Okl. 70, 178 P. 263, this court held that the measure of damages for breach of a contract to drill an oil well was the reasonable cost of drilling the well, but here a slightly different factual situation exists. The drilling of an oil well will yield valuable geological information, even if no oil or gas is found, and of course if the well is a producer, the value of the premises increases. In the case before us, it is argued by defendant with some force that the performance of the remedial work defendant agreed to do will add at the most only a few hundred dollars to the value of plaintiffs' farm, and that the damages should be limited to that amount because that is all plaintiffs have lost.

Plaintiffs rely on Groves v. John Wunder Co., 205 Minn. 163, 286 N.W. 235, 123 A.L.R. 502. In that case, the Minnesota court, in a substantially similar situation, adopted the "cost of performance" rule as opposed to the "value" rule. The result was to authorize a jury to give plaintiff damages in the amount of $60,000, where the real estate concerned would have been worth only $12,160, even if the work contracted for had been done.

It may be observed that Groves v. John Wunder Co., *supra,* is the only case which has come to our attention in which the cost of performance rule has been followed under circumstances where the cost of performance greatly exceeded the diminution in value resulting from the breach of contract. Incidentally, it appears that this case was decided by a plurality rather than a majority of the members of the court.

Defendant relies principally upon Sandy Valley & E. R. Co. v. Hughes, 175 Ky. 320, 194 S.W. 344; Bigham v. Wabash-Pittsburg Terminal Ry. Co., 223 Pa. 106, 72 A. 318; and Sweeney v. Lewis Const. Co., 66 Wash. 490, 119 P. 1108. These were all cases in which, under similar circumstances, the appellate courts followed the "value" rule instead of the "cost of performance" rule. Plaintiff points out that in the earliest of these cases (Bigham) the court cites as authority on the measure of damages an earlier Pennsylvania *tort* case, and that the other two cases follow the first, with no explanation as to why a measure of damages ordinarily followed in cases sounding in tort should be used in contract cases. Nevertheless, it is of some significance that three out of four appellate courts have followed the diminution in value rule under circumstances where, as here, the cost of performance greatly exceeds the diminution in value.

The explanation may be found in the fact that the situations presented are artificial ones. It is highly unlikely that the ordinary property owner would agree to pay $29,000 (or its equivalent) for the construction of "improvements" upon his property that would increase its value only about ($300) three hundred dollars. The result is that we are called upon to apply principles of law theoretically based upon reason and reality to a situation which is basically unreasonable and unrealistic.

In Groves v. John Wunder Co., *supra,* in arriving at its conclusions, the Minnesota court apparently considered the contract involved to be analogous to a building and construction contract, and cited authority for the proposition that the cost of performance or completion of the building as contracted is ordinarily the measure of damages in actions for damages for the breach of such a contract.

In an annotation following the Minnesota case beginning at 123 A.L.R. 515, the annotator places the three cases relied on by defendant (Sandy Valley, Bigham and Sweeney) under the classification of cases involving "grading and excavation contracts".

We do not think either analogy is strictly applicable to the case now before us. The primary purpose of the lease contract between plaintiffs and defendant was neither "building and construction" nor "grading and excavation". It was merely to accomplish the economical recovery and marketing of coal from the premises, to the profit of all parties. The special provisions of the lease contract pertaining to remedial work were incidental to the main object involved.

Even in the case of contracts that are unquestionably building and construction contracts, the authorities are not in agreement as to the factors to be considered in determining whether the cost of performance rule or the value rule should be applied. The American Law Institute's Restatement of the Law, Contracts, Volume 1, Sections 346(1)(a)(i) and (ii) submits the proposition that the cost of performance is the proper measure of damages "if this is possible and does not involve *unreasonable economic waste*"; and that the diminution in value caused by the breach is the proper measure "if construction and completion in accordance with the contract would involve *unreasonable economic waste*". (Emphasis supplied.) In an explanatory comment immediately following the text, the Restatement makes it clear that the "economic waste" referred to consists of the destruction of a substantially completed building or other structure. Of course no such destruction is involved in the case now before us.

On the other hand, in McCormick, Damages, Section 168, it is said with regard to building and construction contracts that " * * * in cases where the defect is one that can be repaired or cured without *undue expense*" the cost of performance is the proper measure of damages, but where " * * * the defect in material or construction is one that cannot be remedied without *an expenditure for reconstruction disproportionate to the end to be attained*" (emphasis supplied) the value rule should be followed. The same idea was expressed in Jacob & Youngs, Inc. v. Kent, 230 N.Y. 239, 129 N.E. 889, 23 A.L.R. 1429, as follows:

> "The owner is entitled to the money which will permit him to complete, unless the cost of completion is grossly and unfairly out of proportion to the good to be attained. When that is true, the measure is the difference in value."

It thus appears that the prime consideration in the Restatement was "economic waste"; and that the prime consideration in McCormick, Damages, and in Jacob & Youngs, Inc. v. Kent, supra, was the relationship between the expense involved and the "end to be attained"—in other words, the "relative economic benefit".

In view of the unrealistic fact situation in the instant case, and certain Oklahoma statutes to be hereinafter noted, we are of the opinion that the "relative economic benefit" is a proper consideration here. This is in accord with the recent case of Mann v. Clowser, 190 Va. 887, 59 S.E.2d 78, where, in applying the cost rule, the Virginia court specifically noted that " * * * the defects are remediable from a practical standpoint and the costs *are not grossly disproportionate to the results to be obtained*" (emphasis supplied).

23 O.S.1961 §§ 96 and 97 provide as follows:

> "§ 96. * * * Notwithstanding the provisions of this chapter, no person can recover a greater amount in damages for the breach of an obligation, than he would have gained by the full performance thereof on both sides * * *.

> "§ 97. * * * Damages must, in all cases, be reasonable, and where an obligation of any kind appears to create a right to unconscionable and grossly oppressive damages, contrary to substantial justice no more than reasonable damages can be recovered."

Although it is true that the above sections of the statute are applied most often in tort cases, they are by their own terms, and the decisions of this court, also applicable in actions for damages for breach of contract. It would seem that they are peculiarly applicable here where, under the "cost of performance" rule, plaintiffs might recover an amount about nine times the total value of their farm. Such would seem to be "unconscionable and grossly oppressive damages, contrary to substantial justice" within the meaning of the statute. Also, it can hardly be denied that if plaintiffs here are permitted to recover under the "cost of performance" rule, they will receive a greater benefit from the breach than could be gained from full performance, contrary to the provisions of Sec. 96.

An analogy may be drawn between the cited sections, and the provisions of 15 O.S.1961 §§ 214 and 215. These sections tend to render void any provisions of a contract which attempt to fix the amount of stipulated damages to be paid in case of a breach, except where it is impracticable or extremely difficult to determine the actual damages. This results in spite of the agreement of the parties, and the obvious and well known rationale is that insofar as they exceed the actual damages suffered, the stipulated damages amount to a penalty or forfeiture which the law does not favor.

23 O.S.1961 §§ 96 and 97 have the same effect in the case now before us. *In spite of the agreement of the parties,* these sections limit the damages recoverable to a reasonable amount not "contrary to substantial justice"; they prevent plaintiffs from recovering a "greater amount in damages for the breach of an obligation" than they would have "gained by the full performance thereof".

We therefore hold that where, in a coal mining lease, lessee agrees to perform certain remedial work on the premises concerned at the end of the lease period, and thereafter the contract is fully performed by both parties except that the remedial work is not done, the measure of damages in an action by lessor against lessee for damages for breach of contract is ordinarily the reasonable cost of performance of the work; however, where the contract provision breached was merely incidental to the main purpose in view, and where the economic benefit which would result to lessor by full performance of the work is grossly disproportionate to the cost of performance, the damages which lessor may recover are limited to the diminution in value resulting to the premises because of the non-performance.

We believe the above holding is in conformity with the intention of the Legislature as expressed in the statutes mentioned, and in harmony with the better-reasoned cases from the other jurisdictions where analogous fact situations have been considered. It should be noted that the rule as stated does not interfere with the property owner's right to "do what he will with his own" (Chamberlain v. Parker, 45 N.Y. 569), or his right, if he chooses, to contract for "improvements" which will actually have the effect of reducing his property's value. Where such result is in fact contemplated by the parties, and is a main or principal purpose of those contracting, it would seem that the measure of damages for breach would ordinarily be the cost of performance.

The above holding disposes of all of the arguments raised by the parties on appeal.

Under the most liberal view of the evidence herein, the diminution in value resulting to the premises because of nonperformance of the remedial work was $300.00. After a careful search of the record, we have found no evidence of a higher figure, and plaintiffs do not argue in their briefs that a greater diminution in value was sustained. It thus appears that the judgment was clearly excessive, and that the amount for which judgment should have been rendered is definitely and satisfactorily shown by the record.

We are asked by each party to modify the judgment in accordance with the respective theories advanced, and it is conceded that we have authority to do so. 12 O.S.1961 § 952; Busboom v. Smith, 199 Okl. 688, 191 P.2d 198; Stumpf v. Stumpf, 173 Okl. 1, 46 P.2d 315.

We are of the opinion that the judgment of the trial court for plaintiffs should be, and it is hereby, modified and reduced to the sum of $300.-00, and as so modified it is affirmed.

WELCH, DAVISON, HALLEY, and JOHNSON, JJ., concur.

WILLIAMS, C. J., BLACKBIRD, V. C. J., and IRWIN and BERRY, JJ., dissent.

IRWIN, JUSTICE (dissenting).

By the specific provisions in the coal mining lease under consideration, the defendant agreed as follows:

" * * * "7b Lessee agrees to make fills in the pits dug on said premises on the property line in such manner that fences can be placed thereon and access had to opposite sides of the pits.

"c Lessee agrees to smooth off the top of the spoil banks on the above premises.

"7d Lessee agrees to leave the creek crossing the above premises in such a condition that it will not interfere with the crossings to be made in pits as set out in 7b.

* * *

"7f Lessee further agrees to leave no shale or dirt on the high wall of said pits. * * * "

Following the expiration of the lease, plaintiffs made demand upon defendant that it carry out the provisions of the contract and to perform those covenants contained therein.

Defendant admits that it failed to perform its obligations that it agreed and contracted to perform under the lease contract and there is nothing in the record which indicates that defendant could not perform its obligations. Therefore, in my opinion defendant's breach of the contract was wilful and not in good faith.

Although the contract speaks for itself, there were several negotiations between the plaintiffs and defendant before the contract was executed. Defendant admitted in the trial of the action, that plaintiffs insisted that the above provisions be included in the contract and that they would not agree to the coal mining lease unless the above provisions were included.

In consideration for the lease contract, plaintiffs were to receive a certain amount as royalty for the coal produced and marketed and in addition thereto their land was to be restored as provided in the contract.

Defendant received as consideration for the contract, its proportionate share of the coal produced and marketed and in addition thereto, the *right to use* plaintiffs' land in the furtherance of its mining operations.

The cost for performing the contract in question could have been reasonably approximated when the contract was negotiated and executed and there are no conditions now existing which could not have been reasonably anticipated by the parties. Therefore, defendant had knowledge, when it prevailed upon the plaintiffs to execute the lease, that the cost of performance might be disproportionate to the value or benefits received by plaintiff for the performance.

Defendant has received its benefits under the contract and now urges, in substance, that plaintiffs' measure of damages for its failure to perform should be the economic value of performance to the plaintiffs and not the cost of performance.

If a peculiar set of facts should exist where the above rule should be applied as the proper measure of damages, (and in my judgment those facts do not exist in the instant case) before such rule should be applied, consideration should be given to the benefits received or contracted for by the party who asserts the application of the rule.

Defendant did not have the right to mine plaintiffs' coal or to use plaintiffs' property for its mining operations without the consent of plaintiffs. Defendant had knowledge of the benefits that it would receive under the contract and the approximate cost of performing the contract. With this knowledge, it must be presumed that defendant thought that it would be to its economic advantage to enter into the contract with plaintiffs and that it would reap benefits from the contract, or it would have not entered into the contract.

Therefore, if the value of the performance of a contract should be considered in determining the measure of damages for breach of a contract, the value of the benefits received under the contract by a party who breaches a contract should also be considered. However, in my judgment, to give consideration to either in the instant action, completely rescinds and holds for naught the solemnity of the contract before us and makes an entirely new contract for the parties.

In Goble v. Bell Oil & Gas Co., 97 Okl. 261, 223 P. 371, we held:

> "Even though the contract contains harsh and burdensome terms which the court does not in all respects approve, it is the province of the parties in relation to lawful subject matter to fix their rights and obligations, and the court will give the contract effect according to its expressed provisions, unless it be shown by competent evidence proof that the written agreement as executed is the result of fraud, mistake, or accident."

In Cities Service Oil Co. v. Geolograph Co. Inc., 208 Okl. 179, 254 P.2d 775, we said:

> "While we do not agree that the contract as presently written is an onerous one, we think the short answer is that the folly or wisdom of a contract is not for the court to pass on."

In Great Western Oil & Gas Company v. Mitchell, Okl., 326 P.2d 794, we held:

> "The law will not make a better contract for parties than they themselves have seen fit to enter into, or alter it for the benefit of one party and to the detriment of the others; the judicial function of a court of law is to enforce a contract as it is written."

I am mindful of Title 23 O.S.1961 § 96, which provides that no person can recover a greater amount in damages for the breach of an obligation than he could have gained by the full performance thereof on both sides, except in cases not applicable herein. However, in my judgment, the above statutory provision is not applicable here.

In my judgment, we should follow the case of Groves v. John Wunder Company, 205 Minn. 163, 286 N.W. 235, 123 A.L.R. 502, which defendant agrees "that the fact situation is apparently similar to the one in the case at bar", and where the Supreme Court of Minnesota held:

> "The owner's or employer's damages for such a breach (i. e. breach hypothesized in 2d syllabus) are to be measured, not in respect to the value of the land to be improved, but by the reasonable cost of doing that which the contractor promised to do and which he left undone."

The hypothesized breach referred to states that where the contractor's breach of a contract is wilful, that is, in bad faith, he is not entitled to any benefit of the equitable doctrine of substantial performance.

In the instant action defendant has made no attempt to even substantially perform. The contract in question is not immoral, is not tainted with fraud, and was not entered into through mistake or accident and is not contrary to public policy. It is clear and unambiguous and the parties understood the terms thereof, and the approximate cost of fulfilling the obligations could have been approximately ascertained. There are no conditions existing now which could not have been reasonably anticipated when the contract was negotiated and executed. The defendant could have performed the contract if it desired. It has accepted and reaped the benefits of its contract and now urges that plaintiffs' benefits under the contract be denied. If plaintiffs' benefits are denied, such benefits would inure to the direct benefit of the defendant.

Therefore, in my opinion, the plaintiffs were entitled to specific performance of the contract and since defendant has failed to perform, the proper measure of damages should be the cost of performance. Any other measure of damage would be holding for naught the express provisions of the contract; would be taking from the plaintiffs the benefits of the contract and placing those benefits in defendant which has failed to perform its obligations; would be granting benefits to defendant without a resulting obligation; and would be completely rescinding the solemn obligation of the contract for the benefit of the defendant to the detriment of the plaintiffs by making an entirely new contract for the parties.

I therefore respectfully dissent to the opinion promulgated by a majority of my associates.

SUPPLEMENTAL OPINION ON REHEARING

JACKSON, JUSTICE.

In a Petition for Rehearing, plaintiffs Peevyhouse have raised certain questions not presented in the original briefs on appeal.

They insist that the trial court excluded evidence as to the total value of the premises concerned, and, in effect, that they have not had their "day in court". This argument arises by reason of the fact that their farm consists not merely of the 60 acres covered by the coal mining lease, but includes other lands as well.

Plaintiffs originally pleaded two causes of action against the defendant mining company. The first one was for damages for breach of contract; the second one was for damages to the water well and home of plaintiffs, because of the use of excessively large charges of dynamite or blasting powder in close proximity to the home and well.

Numbered paragraph 2 of plaintiffs' petition alleges that they own and live upon 60 acres of land which are specifically described. *This is the only land described in the petition, and there is no allegation as to the ownership or leasing of any other lands.*

Page 4 of the transcript of evidence reveals that near the beginning of the trial, plaintiff Peevyhouse was asked a question concerning improvements he had made to his property. His answer was "For one thing I built a new home on the place in 1951, and along about that time I was building a pasture. And I would say *ninety percent of this 120 acres is in good grass.*" (Emphasis supplied.) Mr. Watts, defense counsel, then objected "to any testimony about the property, other than the 160 acres". (It is obvious that he means "60" instead of "160".) Further proceedings were as follows:

"The Court: The objection will be sustained as to any other part. Go ahead.

"Mr. McConnell (attorney for plaintiffs): Comes now the plaintiff and dismisses the second cause of action without prejudice."

It thus appears that plaintiffs made no complaint as to the court's exclusion of evidence concerning lands other than the 60 acres described in their petition.

Pages 7 and 8 of the transcript show that later during direct examination of Mr. Peevyhouse, the following occurred:

"Q. (By Mr. McConnell) Now, Mr. Peevyhouse, I ask you to step down here and I ask you if you are familiar with this sketch or drawing?

*   *   *   *   *   *

"A. Yes, I've got about 40 acres here, and here would be 20, and there would be 20 on this sketch. And I've got leased land lying in here, 80 acres.

"Mr. Watts: If your Honor please, I object to anything except the 60 acres involved in this lawsuit.

"The Court: Sustained.

"Q. (By Mr. McConnell) Will you point out to the jury, the boundary line shown of your property?

*   *   *   *   *   *

"A. That blue is where the water is actually standing at the present time. Up until a short time ago this area here came over that far. And this spring all of it would run, come in here out this way and through here, spreading over this land and all below it. And at the present time this is washed out here.

"Mr. Watts: If your Honor please, I object to that as not the proper measure of damages.

"The Court: The objection will be sustained."

This testimony of Mr. Peevyhouse is difficult for us to follow, even with the exhibits in the case before us. However, no complaint was made by plaintiffs, or any suggestion that the court was in error in excluding this testimony.

The defendant offered the testimony of five witnesses in the trial court; four of them testified as to "diminution in value". They were not cross examined by plaintiffs.

In their motion for new trial, plaintiffs did not complain that they had been prevented from offering evidence as to the diminution in value of their lands; on the contrary, they affirmatively complained of the trial court's action in admitting evidence of the *defendant* on that point.

In the original brief of plaintiffs in error (Peevyhouse) filed in this court there appears the following language at page 4:

> " * * * Near the outset of the trial plaintiffs dismissed their second cause of action without prejudice: further, it was stipulated * * *. It was further stipulated that the *only issue remaining in the lawsuit* was the proof and *measure of damages* to which plaintiffs were entitled * * *." (Emphasis supplied.)

In the answer brief of Garland Coal & Mining Co., at page 3, there appears the following language:

> "Defendant offered evidence that the total value of the property involved before the mining operation would be $60.00 per acre, and $11.00 per acre after the mining operation (60 acres at $49.00 per acre is $2940.00). Other evidence was that the property was worth $5.00 to $15.00 per acre after the mining, but before the repairs; and would be worth an increase of $2.00 to $5.00 per acre after the repairs had been made (60 acres at $5.00 per acre is $300.00) (Tr. 96–97, 135, 137–138, 138–141, 143–145, 156, 158)."

At page 18 of the same brief there is another statement to the effect that the "amount of diminution in value of the land" was $300.00.

About two months after the answer brief was filed in this court, plaintiffs filed a reply brief. The reply brief makes no reference at all to the language of the answer brief above quoted and *does not deny that the diminution in value shown by the record amounts to $300.00.* On the contrary, it contains the following language at page 5:

> " * * * Plaintiffs in error pointed out in their initial brief that this evidence concerning land values was objectionable as being incompetent and refused to cross-examine or offer rebuttal for the reason that they did not choose to waive their objections to the competency of the evidence by disproving defendant in error's allegations as to land values. We strongly urged at the trial below, and still do, that market value of the land has no application * * *."

Our extended reference to the pleadings, testimony and prior briefs in this case has not been solely for the purpose of showing that plaintiffs failed to complain of the court's rulings. Our purpose, rather, has been to demonstrate the plan and theory upon which plaintiffs tried their case below, and upon which they argued it in the prior briefs on appeal.

The whole record in this case justifies the conclusion that plaintiffs tried their case upon the theory that the "cost of performance" would be the sole measure of damages and that they would recognize no other. In view of the whole record in this case and the original briefs on appeal, we conclude that they so tried it *with notice* that defendant would contend for the "diminution in value" rule. The testimony to which they specifically refer in the petition for rehearing shows that the trial court properly excluded defendant's evidence concerning lands other than the 60 acres described in the petition because such evidence was *not within the scope of the pleadings.* At no time did plaintiffs ask permission to amend their petition, either with or without prejudice to trial, so as to describe *all* of the lands they own or lease, and no evidence was admitted which could broaden the scope of the petition.

Plaintiffs' petition described 60 acres of land only; plaintiffs offered no evidence on the question of "diminution in value" and objected to similar evidence offered by the defendant; their motion for new trial contained no allegation that they had been prevented from offering evidence on this question; in their reply brief they did not controvert the allegation in defendant's answer brief that the record showed a "diminution in value" of only $300.00; and in view of the stipulation they admittedly made in the trial court, their statement in petition for rehearing that the court's instructions on the measure of damages came as a "complete surprise" and "did not afford them the opportunity to prepare and introduce evidence under the 'diminution in value' rule" is not supported by the record.

We think plaintiffs' present position is that of a plaintiff in any damage suit who has failed to prove his damages—opposed by a defendant who has proved plaintiff's damages; and that plaintiffs' complaint that the record does not show the total "diminution in value" to their lands comes too late. It is well settled that a party will not be permitted to change his theory of the case upon appeal. Knox v. Eason Oil Co., 190 Okl. 627, 126 P.2d 247.

Also, plaintiffs' expressed fear that by introducing evidence on the question of "diminution in value" they would have waived their objection to similar evidence by defendant was not justified. Vogel v. Fisher et al., 203 Okl. 657, 225 P.2d 346; 53 Am.Jur. Trial, Sec. 144.

It is suggested in a brief of amici curiae that our decision in this case has resulted in an impairment of the obligation of the contract of the parties, in violation of Article 1, Section 10, of the Constitution of the United States, and in that connection the only case cited is Sturges v. Crowninshield, 4 Wheat 122, 17 U.S. 1229, 4 L.Ed. 529 (1819). In their brief, amici curiae quote language from the Layer's Edition notes of Mr. Stephen K. Williams, in which he summarized the "points and authorities" of one of the counsel appearing before the U.S. Supreme Court.

Sturges v. Crowninshield was an early case in which the Supreme Court considered the power of a state to enact bankruptcy laws, and the extent, if any, to which such power is limited by Article 1, Section 10 of the Constitution. The contracts concerned consisted of promissory notes executed in March, 1811, and the bankruptcy law under which the promisor claimed a discharge was not enacted until April 3, 1811. In a memorable opinion written by Chief Justice Marshall, the court held that insofar as the bankruptcy law purported to discharge the obligations of contracts executed *before its enactment,* it was unconstitutional and void.

The same situation does not exist here. 23 O.S.1961 §§ 96 and 97, cited in our original opinion, were a part of the Revised Laws of 1910 (R.L.1910) Sections 2889 and 2890, and have been in force in this state, in unchanged form, since that codification was adopted by the legislature in 1911. The lease contract concerned in the case now before us was not executed until 1954.

Nor do we agree that our decision itself (as opposed to the statutes cited therein as controlling) impairs the obligations of the contract concerned. It may be conceded that at one time there was respectable authority for the proposition that the "contract" clause was violated by a judicial decision which overruled prior decisions, upon the strength of which contract rights had been acquired. In this connection, it should be noted that our decision overrules no prior holdings of this court upon which the contracting parties could be said to have relied. Even if it did,

> "* * * it is now definitely and authoritatively settled that such prohibition in federal and state constitutions relate to legislative action and not to judicial decisions. Thus, they do not apply to the decision of a state court, where such decision does not expressly, or by necessary implication, give effect to a subsequent law of the state whereby the obligation of the contract is impaired. * * *" 16 C.J.S. Constitutional Law § 280.

To the same effect, see 12 Am.Jur. Constitutional Law, Sec. 398.

Our decision herein overrules no prior holdings of this court, and it does not give effect to a *subsequent* law of this state. It therefore cannot be said to impair the obligations of the contract of the parties here concerned.

The petition for rehearing is denied.

HALLEY, V. C. J., and WELCH, DAVISON and JOHNSON, JJ., concur.

BLACKBIRD, C. J., and WILLIAMS, IRWIN and BERRY, JJ., dissent.

Questions

1. Does the measure of damages in this case satisfy the *promissory* idea? The *bargain* idea? If the objective of contract damages is to encourage actual performance of promises, what measure of damages would be awarded in this case? If the object of contract damages is to protect the expectation of the promisee, what measure of damages should be applied in this case? Doesn't that depend on how you view the expectation of the promisee? For example, did the Peevyhouses' bargain for the actual return of their land to a condition approximating its pre-contract state? Or did they bargain for Garland to either perform as promised or to pay them "a compensatory sum" for the loss in market value of the leased land which would result from failure to perform as promised? (Review and reconsider the extract from Holmes, "The Path of the Law," *supra* p. 691.)

What would you need to know in order to answer these questions? Does it appear that the majority of the Oklahoma Court is at all interested in the Peevyhouses' particular expectations about the performance of the contract? Or are they concerned instead with finding and applying a general standard by which to measure and protect expectations arising in contract?

2.　Assume that you are a lawyer representing an Oklahoma landowner currently negotiating a lease with Garland Coal. Your client has told you that she wants Garland to fill and grade her land after they have completed the strip mining. Her neighbors, the Peevyhouses, have told her their tale of woe and she wants you to draft her lease to avoid the Peevyhouse outcome. Can you think of a lease provision or provisions which would force Garland either to perform or to pay an amount of money equivalent to the cost of performance?

3.　When Garland Coal repudiated and refused to perform the lease term, the Peevyhouses "went to law" by suing for damages. Would the result in their suit have been different if, upon learning of Garland's repudiation, the Peevyhouses had paid a contractor the $29,-000 to perform the work, and then brought suit against Garland to recover that expenditure as the damages for the breach? Consider the following.

UNIFORM COMMERCIAL CODE
ARTICLE TWO

§ 2—711.　Buyer's Remedies in General; Buyer's Security Interest in Rejected Goods

(1) Where the seller fails to make delivery or repudiates or the buyer rightfully rejects or justifiably revokes acceptance then with respect to any goods involved, and with respect to the whole if the breach goes to the whole contract (Section 2—612), the buyer may cancel and whether or not he has done so may in addition to recovering so much of the price as has been paid

　(a) "cover" and have damages under the next section as to all the goods affected whether or not they have been identified to the contract; or

　(b) recover damages for non-delivery as provided in this Article (Section 2—713).

(2) Where the seller fails to deliver or repudiates the buyer may also

　(a) if the goods have been identified recover them as provided in this Article (Section 2—502); or

　(b) in a proper case obtain specific performance or replevy the goods as provided in this Article (Section 2—716).

(3) On rightful rejection or justifiable revocation of acceptance a buyer has a security interest in goods in his possession or control for any payments made on their price and any expenses reasonably incurred in their inspection, receipt, transportation, care and custody and may hold such goods and resell them in like manner as an aggrieved seller (Section 2—706).

§ 2—712. "Cover"; Buyer's Procurement of Substitute Goods

(1) After a breach within the preceding section the buyer may "cover" by making in good faith and without unreasonable delay any reasonable purchase of or contract to purchase goods in substitution for those due from the seller.

(2) The buyer may recover from the seller as damages the difference between the cost of cover and the contract price together with any incidental or consequential damages as hereinafter defined (Section 2—715), but less expenses saved in consequence of the seller's breach.

(3) Failure of the buyer to effect cover within this section does not bar him from any other remedy.

§ 2—713. Buyer's Damages for Non-Delivery or Repudiation

(1) Subject to the provisions of this Article with respect to proof of market price (Section 2—723), the measure of damages for non-delivery or repudiation by the seller is the difference between the market price at the time when the buyer learned of the breach and the contract price together with any incidental and consequential damages provided in this Article (Section 2—715), but less expenses saved in consequence of the seller's breach.

(2) Market price is to be determined as of the place for tender or, in cases of rejection after arrival or revocation of acceptance, as of the place of arrival.

4. Should UCC §§ 2—712 and 2—713 provide an analogical base for allowing the Peevyhouses to "cover" for Garland's repudiation and sue for the cost of covering for the default? Why? Why not?

JACOB & YOUNGS v. KENT

Court of Appeals of New York, 1921.
230 N.Y. 239, 129 N.E. 889.

CARDOZO, J. The plaintiff built a country residence for the defendant at a cost of upwards of $77,000, and now sues to recover a balance of $3,483.46, remaining unpaid. The work of construction ceased in June, 1914, and the defendant then began to occupy the dwelling. There was no complaint of defective performance until March, 1915. One of the specifications for the plumbing work provides that "all wrought iron pipe must be well galvanized, lap welded pipe of the grade known as 'standard pipe' of Reading manufacture." The defendant learned in March, 1915, that some of the pipe, instead of being made in Reading, was the product of other factories. The plaintiff was accordingly directed by the architect to do the work anew. The plumbing was then encased within the walls except in a few places where it had to be exposed. Obedience to the order meant more than the substitution of other pipe. It meant the demolition at great expense of substantial parts of the completed structure. The plaintiff left the work untouched, and asked for a certificate that the final payment was due. Refusal of the certificate was followed by this suit.

The evidence sustains a finding that the omission of the prescribed brand of pipe was neither fraudulent nor willful. It was the result of the oversight and inattention of the plaintiff's subcontractor. Reading pipe is distinguished from Cohoes pipe and other brands only by the name of the manufacturer stamped upon it at intervals of between six and seven feet. Even the defendant's architect, though he inspected the pipe upon arrival, failed to notice the discrepancy. The plaintiff tried to show that the brands installed, though made by other manufacturers, were the same in quality, in appearance, in market value and in cost as the brand stated in the contract—that they were, indeed, the same thing, though manufactured in another place. The evidence was excluded, and a verdict directed for the defendant. The Appellate Division reversed, and granted a new trial.

We think the evidence, if admitted, would have supplied some basis for the inference that the defect was insignificant in its relation to the project. The courts never say that one who makes a contract fills the measure of his duty by less than full performance. They do say, however, that an omission, both trivial and innocent, will sometimes be atoned for by allowance of the resulting damage, and will not always be the breach of a condition to be followed by a forfeiture. [citations omitted.] The distinction is akin to that between dependent and independent promises, or between promises and conditions (Anson on Contracts [Corbin's ed.], sec. 367; 2 Williston on Contracts, sec. 842). Some promises are so plainly independent that they can never by fair construction be conditions of one another. [citations omitted.] Others are so plainly dependent that they must always be conditions. Others, though dependent and thus conditions when there is departure in point of substance, will be viewed as independent and collateral when the departure is insignificant [citations omitted.] Considerations partly of justice and partly of presumable intention are to tell us whether this or that promise shall be placed in one class or in another. The simple and the uniform will call for different remedies from the multifarious and the intricate. The margin of departure within the range of normal expectation upon a sale of common chattels will vary from the margin to be expected upon a contract for the construction of a mansion or a "skyscraper." There will be harshness sometimes and oppression in the implication of a condition when the thing upon which labor has been expended is incapable of surrender because united to the land, and equity and reason in the implication of a like condition when the subject-matter, if defective, is in shape to be returned. From the conclusion that promises may not be treated as dependent to the extent of their uttermost minutiae without a sacrifice of justice, the progress is a short one to the conclusion that they may not be so treated without a perversion of intention. Intention not otherwise revealed may be presumed to hold in contemplation the reasonable and probable. If something else is in view, it must not be left to implication. There will be no assumption of a purpose to visit venial faults with oppressive retribution.

Those who think more of symmetry and logic in the development of legal rules than of practical adaptation to the attainment of a just result will be troubled by a classification where the lines of division are so wavering and blurred. Something, doubtless, may be said on the score of consistency and certainty in favor of a stricter standard. The courts have balanced such considerations against those of equity and fairness, and found the latter to be the weightier. The decisions in this state commit us to the liberal view, which is making its way, nowadays, in jurisdictions slow to welcome it (Dakin & Co. v. Lee, 1916, 1 K.B. 566, 579). Where the line is to be drawn between the important and the trivial cannot be settled by a formula. "In the nature of the case precise boundaries are impossible" (2 Williston on Contracts, sec. 841). The same omission may take on one aspect or another according to its setting. Substitution of equivalents may not have the same significance in fields of art on the one side and in those of mere utility on the other. Nowhere will change be tolerated, however, if it is so dominant or pervasive as in any real or substantial measure to frustrate the purpose of the contract (Crouch v. Gutmann, 134 N.Y. 45, 51, 31 N.E. 271). There is no general license to install whatever, in the builder's judgment, may be regarded as "just as good" (Easthampton L. & C. Co., Ltd., v. Worthington, 186 N.Y. 407, 412, 79 N.E. 323). The question is one of degree, to be answered, if there is doubt, by the triers of the facts (Crouch v. Gutmann; Woodward v. Fuller, *supra*), and, if the inferences are certain, by the judges of the law (Easthampton L. & C. Co., Ltd., v. Worthington, *supra*). We must weigh the purpose to be served, the desire to be gratified, the excuse for deviation from the letter, the cruelty of enforced adherence. Then only can we tell whether literal fulfilment is to be implied by law as a condition. This is not to say that the parties are not free by apt and certain words to effectuate a purpose that performance of every term shall be a condition of recovery. That question is not here. This is merely to say that the law will be slow to impute the purpose, in the silence of the parties, where the significance of the default is grievously out of proportion to the oppression of the forfeiture. The willful transgressor must accept the penalty of his transgression (Schultze v. Goodstein, 180 N.Y. 248, 251, 73 N.E. 21; Desmond-Dunne Co. v. Friedman-Doscher Co., 162 N.Y. 486, 490, 56 N.E. 995). For him there is no occasion to mitigate the rigor of implied conditions. The transgressor whose default is unintentional and trivial may hope for mercy if he will offer atonement for his wrong (Spence v. Ham, *supra*).

In the circumstances of this case, we think the measure of the allowance is not the cost of replacement, which would be great, but the difference in value, which would be either nominal or nothing. Some of the exposed sections might perhaps have been replaced at moderate expense. The defendant did not limit his demand to them, but treated the plumbing as a unit to be corrected from cellar to roof. In point of fact, the plaintiff never reached the stage at which evidence of the extent of the allowance became necessary. The trial court had excluded evidence that the defect was unsubstantial, and in view of that ruling there was no occasion for the plaintiff to go farther with an offer of proof. We think, however, that the offer, if it had been made, would not of necessity have been defective because directed to difference in value. It is true that in most cases the cost of replacement is the measure (Spence v. Ham, *supra*). The owner is entitled to the money which will permit him to complete, unless the cost of completion is grossly and unfairly out of proportion to the good to be attained. When that is true, the measure is the difference in value. Specifications call, let us say, for a foundation built of granite quarried in Vermont. On the completion of the building, the owner learns that through the blunder of a subcontractor part of the foundation has been built of granite of the same quality quarried in New Hampshire. The measure of allowance is not the cost of reconstruction. "There may be omissions of that which could not afterwards. be supplied exactly as called for by the contract without taking down the building to its foundations, and at the same time the omission may not affect the value of the building for use or otherwise, except so slightly as to be hardly appreciable" (Handy v. Bliss, 204 Mass. 513, 519, 90 N.E. 864. *Cf.* Foeller v. Heintz, 137 Wis. 169, 178, 118 N.W. 543; Oberlies v. Bullinger, 132 N.Y. 598, 601, 30 N.E. 999; 2 Williston on Contracts, sec. 805, p. 1541). The rule that gives a remedy in cases of substantial performance with compensation for defects of trivial or inappreciable importance, has been developed by the courts as an instrument of justice. The measure of the allowance must be shaped to the same end.

The order should be affirmed, and judgment absolute directed in favor of the plaintiff upon the stipulation, with costs in all courts.

MCLAUGHLIN, J. (dissenting). [Opinion omitted].

HISCOCK, CH. J., HOGAN and CRANE, JJ., concur with CARDOZO, J.; POUND and ANDREWS, JJ., concur with MCLAUGHLIN, J.

Order affirmed, etc.

Questions

1. Do you agree with Justice Cardozo's opinion in Jacob & Youngs v. Kent? Do you agree with the opinion in Peevyhouse? If you agree with Cardozo, but not with the court in Peevyhouse, can you reconcile the difference? Explain your answer.

2. Who is plaintiff in this case, and what is the remedy requested?

3. Could the defendant have been the plaintiff, and if so, what remedy would the defendant have been entitled to receive if he had been the plaintiff? Why?

4. Why didn't the Peevyhouses bring a suit in equity requesting the court to order Garland to perform as promised? Consider the following materials on this issue.

Notes on Specific Performance as a Remedy for Breach of Contract

[The following is taken from OLIVER WENDELL HOLMES, THE COMMON LAW (M. D. Howe, editor, Boston, Mass., 1963), pp. 235–236. (Originally published, Boston, Mass., 1881.) Footnotes are omitted.]

If, when a man promised to labor for another, the law made him do it, his relation to his promisee might be called a servitude *ad hoc* with some truth. But that is what the law never does. It never interferes until a promise has been broken, and therefore cannot possibly be performed according to its tenor. It is true that in some instances equity does what is called compelling specific performance. But, in the first place, I am speaking of the common law, and, in the next, this only means that equity compels the performance of certain elements of the total promise which are still capable of performance. For instance, take a promise to convey land within a certain time, a court of equity is not in the habit of interfering until the time has gone by, so that the promise cannot be performed as made. But if the conveyance is more important than the time, and the promise prefers to have it late rather than never, the law may compel the performance of that. Not literally compel even in that case, however, but put the promisor in prison unless he will convey. This remedy is an exceptional one. The only universal consequence of a legally binding promise is, that the law makes the promisor pay damages if the promised event does not come to pass. In every case it leaves him free from interference until the time for fulfilment has gone by, and therefore free to break his contract if he chooses.

[The following is taken from LON L. FULLER, BASIC CONTRACT LAW (St. Paul, Minn., 1947), pp. 26–27.]

Specific Performance of Contracts

In what cases can a plaintiff obtain a decree ordering the defendant to perform his promise *in specie,* and in what cases must he be content with an award of damages? Only a general and summary answer can be given to that question here. Even such an answer requires a brief reference to legal history. . . .

One of the outstanding defects of the [medieval] common-law procedure was that (except in certain extraordinary cases) it did not contemplate *ordering* the defendant to do anything. If a creditor sued his debtor for £10 and got a judgment at common law, the judgment did not take the form of a simple order commanding the debtor to pay his debt. In its traditional form it recited that it was "considered that the plaintiff do recover against the defendant his debt." Enforcement of the judgment was accomplished, not by commanding the defendant tó pay, but by directing the sheriff to levy execution on the defendant's property so that the plaintiff's claim might be satisfied out of this property.

Where the plaintiff was complaining of a breach of contract by the defendant, the outstanding defect of the common law was its inability to order the defendant to perform his promise. Thus, if Seller contracted to convey Blackacre to Buyer and then broke his promise, there was no way in which Buyer could by appealing to the common-law courts get a deed to Blackacre, even though Seller had a perfectly good title to the land and was wholly capable of carrying out his contract. The courts assumed that they neither had power to order Seller to give Buyer a deed, nor to issue a judgment decreeing title to be in Buyer. Accordingly, the only relief Buyer could obtain from a common-law court was an award of money damages which, in the case supposed, would be measured by the difference between the stipulated contract price and the market value of the land. . . .

Where the seller of land, having title, refused to honor his contract to convey to the buyer, the buyer could successfully appeal to a court of equity, alleging that his legal remedy (money damages) was inadequate. Equity would issue a decree ordering the seller to execute a deed in the buyer's favor, and if the seller refused to obey this order he would put himself in contempt of court and be subject to imprisonment.

There are other situations, however, where an appeal to equity to enforce a contract would fail. To put the plainest kind of case, suppose that

Seller has sold and delivered a horse to Buyer for £10, and that Buyer, although having ample funds to do so, refuses to pay the promised price of the horse. Here, conceivably, Seller might get a certain spiritual satisfaction out of an order commanding Buyer to pay his debt, an order that the common-law courts would not issue. On the other hand, the common-law courts would secure the promised price for Seller by a levy of execution on Buyer's goods. Accordingly in this case the "legal remedy" was declared to be "adequate," and a suit by Seller in an equity court would be denied.   .   .   .

In other cases, equity refused to enforce contracts not because the legal remedy was adequate, but because it was considered unwise for various reasons to attempt enforcement *in specie*. For example, a famous opera singer agrees to sing in the plaintiff's theater for three months and then breaks her contract. Here the theater proprietor may with much justice assert that his legal remedy of damages is inadequate; an award of money can scarcely be treated as an adequate substitute for actual performance. At the same time, there are obvious objections to attempting to compel a prima donna to sing against her will. Accordingly, this is a case where a court of equity would deny specific performance despite a recognition that the monetary relief granted by the common-law courts is an inadequate form of relief.

The illustrations given above suffice to give a general view of the way in which the English courts dealt with enforcement of contracts *in specie* at the time our republic began its independent legal existence. Below will be presented an outline of the present treatment of this question in the United States.   .   .   .

Contracts for the sale of land. Here the rule is well settled: either the buyer or seller is entitled to specific performance. The buyer can get a decree ordering the seller to execute a deed in his favor: the seller can get a decree ordering the buyer to take title to the land and pay the agreed price. .   .   . In this case monetary relief in the form of an award of damages for the lost profit is considered to be inadequate for two reasons: (1) the value of land is always to some extent conjectural, since it does not have a clearly defined market price; (2) every piece of land is to some extent unique. The first consideration applies equally to suits by the seller or buyer; the more obvious application of the second is to a suit by the buyer, who cannot with an award of money damages go out on the market and buy a piece of land exactly like that promised him by the defaulting seller.

Contracts for the sale of goods—the inherited rule. The rule inherited from the English system is to the effect that neither the buyer nor the seller can ordinarily get specific performance of a contract for the sale of goods. The explanation for this result is that monetary relief is adequate in this situation and meets the legitimate demands of the plaintiff. To take a simple case, if the seller has broken a contract to deliver 100 bushels of wheat to the buyer, the buyer can cover his needs by buying wheat on the market, and the additional cost of doing so is, of course, the measure of his right to money damages against the seller in an action at law. In keeping with this rationale of the rule, it was held that where a contract was for the sale of a "unique" chattel, such as a rare painting, specific performance might be had in a court of equity.

Contracts for the sale of goods—the right of the buyer to specific performance under American law. Under section 68 of the Uniform Sales Act (first enacted in 1907, and now in force, with some variations, in about 34 states) the courts are given a broad discretion to "direct that the contract [to sell specific and ascertained goods] shall be performed specifically, without giving the seller the option of retaining the goods on payment of damages." Comparatively little use seems to have been made of this section. Its plain intention is to give the courts power to grant specific performance in a proper case, even though the award of damages might, according to traditional standards, be considered "adequate." However, some courts have apparently considered that the section merely enacts the old rule and authorizes specific performance where the chattel is "unique" or "irreplaceable."

. . .

Contracts for the sale of goods—the right of the seller to specific performance under American law. Here the Sales Act (§ 63) gives the seller in certain cases what may be called a short-cut to specific performance. If the buyer refuses to take the goods, the seller may set them aside for the buyer and sue for the promised price. In states where actions at law and suits in equity are kept distinct, the proceeding would be designated an action at law, since the relief sought is merely an ordinary money judgment. This case has been called the exceptional situation of "specific performance at law," because the seller has the power by a kind of self-help to divest himself of title and treat the sale as completed so that the buyer owes him the full price of the goods. The right of the seller to invoke this remedy is, however, subject to significant qualifications in the Act, the most important of which is that the goods must be such that they "cannot readily be resold for a reasonable price."

Employment contracts. Such contracts are not specifically enforced either at the suit of the employee or the employer. . . . The objections to specific performance here do not lie in a notion that monetary relief is an adequate substitute for the promised performance, but primarily in a belief that it is unwise to attempt to extract a performance involving personal relations from an unwilling party.

Construction contracts. In a somewhat attenuated way the same considerations are applicable here that apply to employment contracts. Ordinarily specific performance is denied, emphasis being put on the difficulties of supervision in which the court would become involved in attempting to compel performance. . . .

In many cases where it is still possible for the promisor to perform, the simplest and most direct remedy may be for the court to order specific performance. Nevertheless, in the Anglo-American legal system, specific performance is treated as an extraordinary remedy, which, as Professor Fuller indicates, is available only in a limited number of cases. This limited use of specific performance is a legacy of the common law. Civil law countries follow a different course and, in cases where performance by the promisor is still possible, specific performance is generally regarded as the normal remedy. Nevertheless, there are numerous exceptions to the "normal remedy" in the various continental legal systems, so that the difference is smaller in practice than in theory.

Question. What would you expect the *normal* contract remedy to be in a legal system which bases contractual liability on *the prom-*

issory idea? On *the bargain idea?* On *the tort idea?* On *the quasi-contractual idea?*

HADLEY v. BAXENDALE

In the Court of Exchequer, 1854.
9 Exch. 341.

At the trial before Crompton, J., at the last Gloucester Assizes, it appeared that the plaintiffs carried on an extensive business as millers at Gloucester; and that, on the 11th of May, their mill was stopped by a breakage of the crank shaft by which the mill was worked. The steam-engine was manufactured by Messrs. Joyce & Co., the engineers, at Greenwich, and it became necessary to send the shaft as a pattern for a new one to Greenwich. The fracture was discovered on the 12th, and on the 13th the plaintiffs sent one of their servants to the office of the defendants, who are the well-known carriers trading under the name of Pickford & Co., for the purpose of having the shaft carried to Greenwich. The plaintiff's servant told the clerk that the mill was stopped, and that the shaft must be sent immediately; and in answer to the inquiry when the shaft would be taken, the answer was, that if it was sent up by twelve o'clock any day, it would be delivered at Greenwich on the following day. On the following day the shaft was taken by the defendants, before noon, for the purpose of being conveyed to Greenwich, and the sum of £2, 4s. was paid for its carriage for the whole distance; at the same time the defendants' clerk was told that a special entry, if required, should be made to hasten its delivery. The delivery of the shaft at Greenwich was delayed by some neglect; and the consequence was, that the plaintiffs did not receive the new shaft for several days after they would otherwise have done, and the working of their mill was thereby delayed, and they thereby lost the profits they would otherwise have received.

On the part of the defendants, it was objected that these damages were too remote and that the defendants were not liable with respect to them. The learned Judges left the case generally to the jury, who found a verdict with £25 damages beyond the amount paid into Court.   .   .   .

ALDERSON, B. We think that there ought to be a new trial in this case; but, in so doing, we deem it to be expedient and necessary to state explicitly the rule which the Judge, at the next trial, ought, in our opinion, to direct the jury to be governed by when they estimate the damages.

It is, indeed, of the last importance that we should do this; for, if the jury are left without any definite rule to guide them, it will, in such cases as these, manifestly lead to the greatest injustice.   .   .   .

"There are certain established rules," this Court says, in Alder v. Keighley, 15 M. & W. 117, "according to which the jury ought to find." And the Court, in that case, adds: "and here there is a clear rule, that the amount which would have been received if the contract had been kept, is the measure of damages if the contract is broken."

Now we think the proper rule in such a case as the present is this:—
Where two parties have made a contract which one of them has broken, the

damages which the other party ought to receive in respect of such breach of contract should be such as may fairly and reasonably be considered either arising naturally, i. e., according to the usual course of things, from such breach of contract itself, or such as may reasonably be supposed to have been in the contemplation of both parties, at the time they made the contract, as the probable result of the breach of it. Now, if the special circumstances under which the contract was actually made were communicated by the plaintiffs to the defendants, and thus known to both parties, the damages resulting from the breach of such a contract, which they would reasonably contemplate, would be the amount of injury which would ordinarily follow from a breach of contract under these special circumstances so known and communicated. But, on the other hand, if these special circumstances were wholly unknown to the party breaking the contract, he, at the most, could only be supposed to have had in his contemplation the amount of injury which would arise generally, and in the great multitude of cases not affected by any special circumstances, from such a breach of contract. For, had the special circumstances been known, the parties might have specially provided for the breach of contract by special terms as to the damages in that case; and of this advantage it would be very unjust to deprive them. Now the above principles are those by which we think the jury ought to be guided in estimating the damages arising out of any breach of contract. It is said, that other cases such as breaches of contract in the non-payment of money, or in the not making a good title to land, are to be treated as exceptions from this, and as governed by a conventional rule. But as, in such cases, both parties must be supposed to be cognizant of that well-known rule, these cases may, we think, be more properly classed under the rule above enunciated as to cases under known special circumstances, because there both parties may reasonably be presumed to contemplate the estimation of the amount of damages according to the conventional rule. Now, in the present case, if we are to apply the principles above laid down, we find that the only circumstances here communicated by the plaintiffs to the defendants at the time the contract was made, were, that the article to be carried was the broken shaft of a mill, and that the plaintiffs were the millers of that mill. But how do these circumstances shew reasonably that the profits of the mill must be stopped by an unreasonable delay in the delivery of the broken shaft by the carrier to the third person? Suppose the plaintiffs had another shaft in their possession put up or putting up at the time, and that they only wished to send back the broken shaft to the engineer who made it; it is clear that this would be quite consistent with the above circumstances, and yet the unreasonable delay in the delivery would have no effect upon the intermediate profits of the mill. Or, again, suppose that, at the time of the delivery to the carrier, the machinery of the mill had been in other respects defective, then, also, the same results would follow. Here it is true that the shaft was actually sent back to serve as a model for a new one, and that the want of a new one was the only cause of the stoppage of the mill, and that the loss of profits really arose from not sending down the new shaft in proper time, and that this arose from the delay in delivering the broken one to serve as a model. But it is obvious that, in the great multitude of cases of millers sending off broken shafts to third persons by a carrier under ordinary circumstances, such consequences would not, in all probability, have occurred; and these special circumstances were here never communicated by the plaintiffs to the defendants. It follows, therefore, that the loss of profits here cannot reasonably be considered such a consequence of the breach of contract as could have been fairly and reasonably contemplated by both the parties when they made this contract. For such loss would neither have flowed naturally from the breach of this contract in the great multitude of such cases occurring under ordinary circumstances, nor were the special circumstances, which, perhaps, would have made it a reasonable and natural consequence of such breach of contract, communicated to or known by the defendants. The Judge ought, therefore, to have told the jury, that, upon the facts then before them, they ought not to take the loss of profits into consideration at all in estimating the damages. There must therefore be a new trial in this case.

. . . .

Questions

1. What is the rule of damages formulated by the court?

2. Does the court apply its own standard of foreseeability to the instant case?

3. Is there a discrepancy between the statements of the facts on p. 725, and on p. 726, lines 30–34?

4. Is it in fact "obvious," as the court states, "that, in the great multitude of cases of millers sending off broken shafts to third persons by a carrier under ordinary circumstances, such consequences would not, in all probability, have occurred"?

5. Is "reasonable" foreseeability the same as "normal" or "average" foreseeability? Do ideas of what is "normal" or "average" influence the court's determination of what is "reasonable"? Do the court's ideas of what is "reasonable" influence its ideas of what is "normal" and "average" in this case?

6. Is this decision consistent with *the bargain idea*? With *the tort idea*?

[The following is taken from LON L. FULLER and WILLIAM R. PERDUE, "THE RELIANCE INTEREST IN CONTRACT DAMAGES," 46 Yale Law Journal 52 and 373, pp. 84–87 (1936). Footnotes are omitted.]

The Reliance Interest and Hadley v. Baxendale

Before we discuss the relation between the reliance interest and Hadley v. Baxendale it will be necessary to state briefly what seems to us to be involved in that famous case, considering it not so much as an event in legal history but as the accepted symbol for a set of problems. The case may be said to stand for two propositions: (1) that it is not always wise to make the defaulting promisor pay for all the damage which follows as a consequence of his breach, and (2) that specifically the proper test for determining whether particular items of damage should be compensable is to inquire whether they should have been foreseen by the promisor at the time of the contract. The first aspect of the case is much more important than the second. In its first aspect the case bears an integral relation to the very bases of contract liability. It declares in effect that just as it is wise to refuse enforcement altogether to some promises (considerationless, unaccepted, "social" promises, etc.) so it is wise not to go too far in enforcing those promises which are deemed worthy of legal sanction. The answer to the question of Hadley v. Baxendale (where shall we stop?) must inevitably be as complex as the answer to the question (where shall we begin?) which is implicit in the law of mutual assent, consideration, and the rules governing the formation of contracts generally.

In its second aspect Hadley v. Baxendale may be regarded as giving a grossly simplified answer to the question which its first aspect presents. To the question, how far shall we go in charging to the defaulting promisor the consequences of his breach, it answers with what purports to be a single test, that of foreseeability. The simplicity and comprehensiveness of this test are largely a matter of illusion. In the first place, it is openly branded as inappropriate in certain situations where the line is drawn much more closely in favor of the defaulting promisor than the test of foreseeability as normally understood would draw it. There are, therefore, exceptions to the test, to say nothing of authorities which reject it altogether as too burdensome to the defaulter. In the second place, it is clear that the test of foreseeability is less a definite test itself than a cover for a developing set of tests. As in the case of all "reasonable man" standards there is an element of circularity about the test of foreseeability. "For what items of damage should the court hold the defaulting promisor? Those which he should as a reasonable man have foreseen. But what should he have foreseen as a reasonable man? Those items of damage for which the court feels he ought to pay." The test of foreseeability is therefore subject to manipulation by the simple device of defining the characteristics of the hypothetical man who is doing the foreseeing. By a gradual process of judicial inclusion and exclusion this "man" acquires a complex personality; we begin to know just what "he" can "foresee" in this and that situation, and we end, not with one test but with a whole set of tests. This has obviously happened in the law of negligence, and it is happening, although less obviously, to the reasonable man postulated by Hadley v. Baxendale.

Even if the reasonable man who does the foreseeing is a juristic construct, endowed precisely with those qualities which the court feels he ought to have for the purpose at hand, it does not seem that there is a complete *petitio principii* in the test of foreseeability. When we import into a question of liability the "reasonable man" standard we do at least two things. In the first place we increase the chance that the case will ultimately be determined by the jury. Though the court may define the reasonable man, it cannot be sure that its definition will be regarded by the jury, and any test which speaks of the reasonable man decreases the court's chance of removing the case from the jury. In the second place, whether the case is ultimately decided by the judge or the jury, stating the problem in terms of the reasonable man creates a bias in favor of exempting *normal* or *average* conduct from legal penalties. The reasonable man is not necessarily the average man, but he tends to be, and the notion of what is normal and average puts a bridle on the judicial power of defining reasonableness. But the restraint is far from complete. It becomes illusory in those situations where the concepts "normal" and "average" are without definite content; where the "average man" is as much a juristic construct as the "reasonable man." The restraint is often thrown off even in those fields where, because rather definite lay ways of thought and action are discoverable in them, the notion of the "normal" and "average" has some objectivity reality. The courts have not hesitated to invest the reasonable man with capacities either greater or less than those of the average man. For an example of this judicial autonomy within the reign of fact one need look no further than the case which originated the test of foreseeability, Hadley v. Baxendale itself.

So much for the general implications of Hadley v. Baxendale. Our discussion of the relation between that case and the reliance interest has to do with two distinct problems. First, assuming it is wise to avoid putting too heavy a penalty on breach of contract, are there cases in which the reliance interest may be substituted for the expectation interest as a measure of damages in order to reduce recovery? In this aspect the question is whether the reliance interest may not serve as a kind of substitute for the test of Hadley v. Baxendale. Secondly, what of the problem of Hadley v. Baxendale as it arises inside the reliance interest itself? Should we refuse to grant compensation for acts of reliance where they are not "proximately caused" by the contract, or were not "reasonably foreseeable" by the promisor? We shall discuss these problems in the order given.

In his pioneering article on *culpa in contrahendo* Ihering suggested that the reliance interest (in his terminology, the negative interest) ought to be the proper measure of recovery in a series of situations which we may call "not-quite" contracts. For example, in cases where there is a misunderstanding concerning the terms of the contract and where, accordingly, applying a "subjective" theory of mutual assent, we would arrive at the conclusion that no perfect or complete contract existed, it may nevertheless be found that the misunderstanding was due predominantly to the fault of one party, or that the risk of misunderstanding was created by the act of one of the parties. In this situation it may be just to impose on the party who was at fault, or whose act created the risk of misunderstanding, a liability to compensate the "innocent" party for any actual change of position in reliance on the apparently perfect contract. Here we stop halfway between full contract liability (expectation interest) and a denial of liability altogether. In this aspect the reliance interest bears a resemblance to Hadley v. Baxendale as a compromise between no enforcement and complete but too onerous enforcement of the promise. . . .

SECTION 29.   A REPRISE ON CONTRACT DAMAGES

SULLIVAN v. O'CONNOR

Supreme Court of Massachusetts, 1973.
363 Mass. 579, 296 N.E.2d 183.

[Some footnotes omitted; others renumbered.]

KAPLAN, JUSTICE.

The plaintiff patient secured a jury verdict of $13,500 against the defendant surgeon for breach of contract in respect to an operation upon the plaintiff's nose. The substituted consolidated bill of exceptions presents questions about the correctness of the judge's instructions on the issue of damages.

The declaration was in two counts. In the first count, the plaintiff alleged that she, as patient, entered into a contract with the defendant, a surgeon, wherein the defendant promised to perform plastic surgery on her nose and thereby to enhance her beauty and improve her appearance; that he performed the surgery but failed to achieve the promised result; rather the result of the surgery was to disfigure and deform her nose, to cause her pain in body and mind, and to subject her to other damage and expense. The second count, based on the same transaction, was in the conventional form for malpractice, charging that the defendant had been guilty of negligence in performing the surgery. Answering, the defendant entered a general denial.

On the plaintiff's demand, the case was tried by jury. At the close of the evidence, the judge put to the jury, as special questions, the issues of liability under the two counts, and instructed them accordingly. The jury returned a verdict for the plaintiff on the contract count, and for the defendant on the negligence count. The judge then instructed the jury on the issue of damages.

As background to the instructions and the parties' exceptions, we mention certain facts as the jury cound find them. The plaintiff was a professional entertainer, and this was known to the defendant. The agreement was as alleged in the declaration. More particularly, judging from exhibits, the plaintiff's nose had been straight, but long and prominent; the defendant undertook by two operations to reduce its prominence and somewhat to shorten it, thus making it more pleasing in relation to the plaintiff's other features. Actually the plaintiff was obliged to undergo three operations, and her appearance was worsened. Her nose now had a concave line to about the midpoint, at which it became bulbous; viewed frontally, the nose from bridge to midpoint was flattened and broadened, and the two sides of the tip had lost symmetry. This configuration evidently could not be improved by further surgery. The plaintiff did not demonstrate, however, that her change of appearance had resulted in loss of employment. Payments by the plaintiff covering the defendant's fee and hospital expenses were stipulated at $622.65.

The judge instructed the jury, first, that the plaintiff was entitled to recover her out-of-pocket expenses incident to the operations. Second, she could recover the damages flowing directly, naturally, proximately, and foreseeably from the defendant's breach of promise. These would comprehend damages for any disfigurement of the plaintiff's nose—that is, any change of appearance for the worse—including the effects of the consciousness of such disfigurement on the plaintiff's mind, and in this connection the jury should consider the nature of the plaintiff's profession. Also consequent upon the defendant's breach, and compensable, were the pain and suffering involved in the third operation, but not in the first two. As there was no proof that any loss of earnings by the plaintiff resulted from the breach, that element should not enter into the calculation of damages.

By his exceptions the defendant contends that the judge erred in allowing the jury to take into account anything but the plaintiff's out-of-pocket expenses (presumably at the stipulated amount). The defendant excepted to the judge's refusal of his request for a general charge to that effect, and, more specifically, to the judge's refusal of a charge that the plaintiff could not recover for pain and suffering connected with the third operation or for impairment of the plaintiff's appearance and associated mental distress.[1]

The plaintiff on her part excepted to the judge's refusal of a request to charge that the plaintiff could recover the difference in value between the nose as promised and the nose as it appeared after the operations. However, the plaintiff in her brief expressly waives this exception and others made by her in case this court overrules the defendant's exceptions; thus she would be content to hold the jury's verdict in her favor.

We conclude that the defendant's exceptions should be overruled.

It has been suggested on occasion that agreements between patients and physicians by which the physician undertakes to effect a cure or to bring about a given result should be declared unenforceable on grounds of public policy. See Guilmet v. Campbell, 385 Mich. 57, 76, 188 N.W.2d 601 (dissenting opinion). But there are many decisions recognizing and enforcing such contracts, see annotation, 43 A.L.R.3d 1221, 1225, 1229–1233, and the law of Massachusetts has treated them as valid, although we have had no decision meeting head on the contention that they should be denied legal sanction. Small v. Howard, 128 Mass. 131; Gabrunas v. Miniter, 289 Mass. 20, 193 N.E. 551; Forman v. Wolfson, 327 Mass. 341, 98 N.E.2d 615. These causes of action are, however considered a little suspect, and thus we find courts straining sometimes to read the pleadings as sounding only in tort for negligence, and not in contract for breach of promise, despite sedulous efforts by the pleaders to pursue the latter theory. See Gault v. Sideman, 42 Ill.App.2d 96, 191 N.E.2d 436; annotation, *supra* at 1225, 1238–1244.

It is not hard to see why the courts should be unenthusiastic or skeptical about the contract theory. Considering the uncertainties of medical science and the variations in the physical and psychological conditions of individual patients, doctors can seldom in good faith promise specific results. Therefore it is unlikely that physicians of even average integrity will in fact make such promises. Statements of opinion by the physician with some optimistic coloring are a different thing, and may indeed have therapeutic value. But patients may transform such statements into firm promises in their own minds, especially when they have been disappointed in the event, and testify in that sense to sympathetic juries. If actions for breach of promise can be readily maintained, doctors, so it is said, will be frightened into practising "defensive medicine." On the other hand, if these actions were outlawed, leaving only the possibility of suits for malpractice, there is fear that the public might be exposed to the enticements of charlatans, and confidence in the profession might ultimately be shaken. See Miller, The Contractual Liability of Physicians and Surgeons, 1953 Wash. L.Q. 413, 416–423. The law has taken the middle of the road position of allowing actions based on alleged contract, but insisting on clear proof. Instructions to the jury may well stress this requirement and point to tests of truth, such as the complexity or difficulty of an operation as bearing on the probability that a given result was promised. See annotation, 43 A.L.R.3d 1225, 1225–1227.

---

1. The defendant also excepted to the judge's refusal to direct a verdict in his favor, but this exception is not pressed and could not be sustained.

If an action on the basis of contract is allowed, we have next the question of the measure of damages to be applied where liability is found. Some cases have taken the simple view that the promise by the physician is to be treated like an ordinary commercial promise, and accordingly that the successful plaintiff is entitled to a standard measure of recovery for breach of contract—"compensatory" ("expectancy") damages, an amount intended to put the plaintiff in the position he would be if the contract had been performed, or, presumably, at the plaintiff's election, "restitution" damages, an amount corresponding to any benefit conferred by the plaintiff upon the defendant in the performance of the contract disrupted by the defendant's breach. See Restatement: Contracts § 329 and comment a, §§ 347, 384(1). Thus in Hawkins v. McGee, 84 N.H. 114, 146 A. 641, the defendant doctor was taken to have promised the plaintiff to convert his damaged hand by means of an operation into a good or perfect hand, but the doctor so operated as to damage the hand still further. The court, following the usual expectancy formula, would have asked the jury to estimate and award to the plaintiff the difference between the value of a good or perfect hand, as promised, and the value of the hand after the operation. (The same formula would apply, although the dollar result would be less, if the operation had neither worsened nor improved the condition of the hand.) If the plaintiff had not yet paid the doctor his fee, that amount would be deducted from the recovery. There could be no recovery for the pain and suffering of the operation, since that detriment would have been incurred even if the operation had been successful; one can say that this detriment was not "caused" by the breach. But where the plaintiff by reason of the operation was put to more pain that he would have had to endure, had the doctor performed as promised, he should be compensated for that difference as a proper part of his expectancy recovery. It may be noted that on an alternative count for malpractice the plaintiff in the *Hawkins* case had been nonsuited; but on ordinary principles this could not affect the contract claim, for it is hardly a defence to a breach of contract that the promisor acted innocently and without negligence. The New Hampshire court further refined the *Hawkins* analysis in McQuaid v. Michou, 85 N.H. 299, 157 A. 881, all in the direction of treating the patient-physician cases on the ordinary footing of expectancy. [Citations omitted.]

Other cases, including a number in New York, without distinctly repudiating the *Hawkins* type of analysis, have indicated that a different and generally more lenient measure of damages is to be applied in patient-physician actions based on breach of alleged special agreements to effect a cure, attain a stated result, or employ a given medical method. This measure is expressed in somewhat variant ways, but the substance is that the plaintiff is to recover any expenditures made by him and for other detriment (usually not specifically described in the opinions) following proximately and foreseeably upon the defendant's failure to carry out his promise.

[Citations omitted.] This, be it noted, is not a "restitution" measure, for it is not limited to restoration of the benefit conferred on the defendant (the fee paid) but includes other expenditures, for example, amounts paid for medicine and nurses; so also it would seem according to its logic to take in damages for any worsening of the plaintiff's condition due to the breach. Nor is it an "expectancy" measure, for it does not appear to contemplate recovery of the whole difference in value between the condition as promised and the condition actually resulting from the treatment. Rather the tendency of the formulation is to put the plaintiff back in the position he occupied just before the parties entered upon the agreement, to compensate him for the detriments he suffered in reliance upon the agreement. This kind of intermediate pattern of recovery for breach of contract is discussed in the suggestive article by Fuller and Perdue. The Reliance Interest in Contract Damages, 46 Yale L.J. 52, 373, where the authors show that, although not attaining the currency of the standard measures, a "reliance" measure has for special reasons been applied by the courts in a variety of settings, including noncommercial settings. See 46 Yale L.J. at 396–401.

For breach of the patient-physician agreements under consideration, a recovery limited to restitution seems plainly too meager, if the agreements are to be enforced at all. On the other hand, an expectancy recovery may well be excessive. The factors, already mentioned, which have made the cause of action somewhat suspect, also suggest moderation as to the breadth of the recovery that should be permitted. Where, as in the case at bar and in a number of the reported cases, the doctor has been absolved of negligence by the trier, an expectancy measure may be thought harsh. We should recall here that the fee paid by the patient to the doctor for the alleged promise would usually be quite disproportionate to the putative expectancy recovery. To attempt, moreover, to put a value on the condition that would or might have resulted, had the treatment succeeded as promised, may sometimes put an exceptional strain on the imagination of the fact finder. As a general consideration, Fuller and Perdue argue that the reasons for granting damages for broken promises to the extent of the expectancy are at their strongest when the promises are made in a business context, when they have to do with the production or distribution of goods or the allocation of functions in the market place; they become weaker as the context shifts from a commercial to a noncommercial field. 46 Yale L. J. at 60–63.

There is much to be said, then, for applying a reliance measure to the present facts, and we have only to add that our cases are not unreceptive to the use of that formula in special situations. We have, however, had no previous occasion to apply it to patient-physician cases.

The question of recovery on a reliance basis for pain and suffering or mental distress requires further attention. We find expressions in the decisions that pain and suffering (or the like) are simply not compensable in actions for breach of contract. The defendant seemingly espouses this proposition in the present case. True, if the buyer under a contract for the purchase of a lot of merchandise, in suing for the seller's breach, should claim damages for mental anguish caused by his disappointment in the transaction, he would not succeed; he would be told, perhaps, that the asserted psychological injury was not fairly foreseeable by the defendant as a probable consequence of the breach of such a business contract. See Restatement: Contracts, § 341, and comment a. But there is no general rule barring such items of damage in actions for breach of contract. It is all a question of the subject matter and background of the contract, and when the contract calls for an operation on the person of the plaintiff, psychological as well as physical injury may be expected to figure somewhere in the recovery, depending on the particular circumstances. The point is explained in Stewart v. Rudner, 349 Mich. 459, 469, 84 N.W.2d 816. Cf. Frewen v.

Page, 238 Mass. 499, 131 N.E. 475; McClean v. University Club, 327 Mass. 68, 97 N.E.2d 174. Again, it is said in a few of the New York cases, concerned with the classification of actions for statute of limitations purposes, that the absence of allegations demanding recovery for pain and suffering is characteristic of a contract claim by a patient against a physician, that such allegations rather belong in a claim for malpractice. See Robins v. Finestone, 308 N.Y. 543, 547, 127 N.E.2d 330; Budoff v. Kessler, 2 A.D.2d 760, 153 N.Y.S.2d 654. These remarks seem unduly sweeping. Suffering or distress resulting from the breach going beyond that which was envisaged by the treatment as agreed, should be compensable on the same ground as the worsening of the patient's condition because of the breach. Indeed it can be argued that the very suffering or distress "contracted for"—that which would have been incurred if the treatment achieved the promised result— should also be compensable on the theory underlying the New York cases. For that suffering is "wasted" if the treatment fails. Otherwise stated, compensation for this waste is arguably required in order to complete the restoration of the status quo ante.[2]

In the light of the foregoing discussion, all the defendant's exceptions fail: the plaintiff was not confined to the recovery of her out-of-pocket expenditures; she was entitled to recover also for the worsening of her condition, and for the pain and suffering and mental distress involved in the third operation. These items were compensable on either an expectancy or a reliance view. We might have been required to elect between the two views if the pain and suffering connected with the first two operations contemplated by the agreement, or the whole difference in value between the present and the promised conditions, were being claimed as elements of damage. But the plaintiff waives her possible claim to the former element, and to so much of the latter as represents the difference in value between the promised condition and the condition before the operations.

Plaintiff's exceptions waived.

Defendant's exceptions overruled.

2. Recovery on a reliance basis for breach of the physician's promise tends to equate with the usual recovery for malpractice, since the latter also looks in general to restoration of the condition before the injury. But this is not paradoxical, especially when it is noted that the origins of contract lie in tort. See Farnsworth, The Past of Promise: An Historical Introduction to Contract, 69 Col.L.Rev. 576, 594–596; Breitel, J. in Stella Flour & Feed Corp. v. National City Bank, 285 App. Div. 182, 189, 136 N.Y.S.2d 139 (dissenting opinion). A few cases have considered possible recovery for breach by a physician of a promise to sterilize a patient, resulting in birth of a child to the patient and spouse. If such an action is held maintainable, the reliance and expectancy measures would, we think, tend to equate, because the promised condition was preservation of the family status quo. See Custodio v. Bauer, 251 Cal.App.2d 303, 59 Cal.Rptr. 463; Jackson v. Anderson, 230 So.2d 503 (Fla.App.). Cf. Troppi v. Scarf, 31 Mich.App. 240, 187 N.W.2d 511. But cf. Ball v. Mudge, 64 Wash. 2d 247, 391 P.2d 201; Doerr v. Villate, 74 Ill.App.2d 332, 220 N.E.2d 767; Shaheen v. Knight, 11 Pa.D. & C.2d 41. See also annotation, 27 A.L.R.3d 906.

It would, however, be a mistake to think in terms of strict "formulas." For example, a jurisdiction which would apply a reliance measure to the present facts might impose a more severe damage sanction for the wilful use by the physician of a method of operation that he undertook not to employ.

Questions

1. What is the plaintiff's theory of damages in this case?

2. What is the defendant's theory of damages in this case?

3. What is the court's theory of damages in this case?

4. Would the application of the court's theory of damages change the result in Hawkins v. McGee? Peevyhouse? Hadley v. Baxendale?

SECTION 30. A JURISPRUDENTIAL AND HISTORICAL POSTSCRIPT ON CONTRACT IN THE LEGAL PROCESS

[The following is taken from FRIEDRICH KESSLER, "CONTRACTS OF ADHESION—SOME THOUGHTS ABOUT FREEDOM OF CONTRACT," 43 Columbia Law Review 629, 629–633, 637–638, 640–642 (1943). Footnotes are omitted.]

With the development of a free enterprise system based on an unheard of division of labor, capitalistic society needed a highly elastic legal institution to safeguard the exchange of goods and services on the market. Common law lawyers, responding to this social need, transformed "contract" from the clumsy institution that it was in the sixteenth century into a tool of almost unlimited usefulness and pliability. Contract thus became the indispensable instrument of the enterpriser, enabling him to go about his affairs in a rational way. Rational behavior within the context of our culture is only possible if agreements will be respected. It requires that reasonable expectations created by promises receive the protection of the law or else we will suffer the fate of Montesquieu's Troglodytes, who perished because they did not fulfill their promises. This idea permeates our whole law of contracts, the doctrines dealing with their formation, performance, impossibility and damages.

Under a free enterprise system rationality of the law of contracts has still another aspect. To keep pace with the constant widening of the market the legal system has to place at the disposal of the members of the community an ever increasing number of typical business transactions and regulate their consequences. But the law cannot possibly anticipate the content of an infinite number of atypical transactions into which members of the community may need to enter. Society, therefore, has to give the parties freedom of contract; to accommodate the business community the ceremony necessary to vouch for the deliberate nature of a transaction has to be reduced to the absolute minimum. Furthermore, the rules of the common law of contract have to remain *ius dispositivum*—to use the phrase of the Romans; that is, their application has to depend on the intention of the parties or on their neglect to rule otherwise. (If parties to a contract have failed to regulate its consequences in their own way, they will be supposed to have intended the consequences envisaged by the common law.)

Beyond that the law cannot go. It has to delegate legislation to the contracting parties. As far as they are concerned, the law of contract has to be of their own making.

Thus freedom of contract does not commend itself for moral reasons only; it is also an eminently practical principle. It is the inevitable counterpart of a free enterprise system. As a result, our legal lore of contracts reflects a proud spirit of individualism and of *laissez faire*. This is particularly true for the axioms and rules dealing with the formation and interpretation of contracts, the genuineness and reality of consent. Contract— the language of the cases tells us—is a private affair and not a social institution. The judicial system, therefore, provides only for their interpretation, but the courts cannot make contracts for the parties. There is no contract without assent, but once the objective manifestations of assent are present, their author is bound. A person is supposed to know the contract that he makes. "A mere offer imposes no duty of action upon the offeree; there is no obligation to accept or reject or to take any notice of it." If an offeror does not hear from the offeree about the offer, he is free to make inquiries or to withdraw his offer, but he cannot regard silence as an acceptance. Either party is supposed to look out for his own interests and his own protection. Oppressive bargains can be avoided by careful shopping around. Everyone has complete freedom of choice with regard to his partner in contract, and the privity-of-contract principle respects the exclusiveness of this choice. Since a contract is the result of the free bargaining of parties who are brought together by the play of the market and who meet each other on a footing of social and approximate economic equality, there is no danger that freedom of contract will be a threat to the social order as a whole. Influenced by this optimistic creed, courts are extremely hesitant to declare contracts void as against public policy "because if there is one thing which more than another public policy requires it is that men of full age and competent understanding shall have the utmost liberty of contracting, and that their contracts when entered into freely and voluntarily shall be held sacred and shall be enforced by Courts of justice."

The development of large scale enterprise with its mass production and mass distribution made a new type of contract inevitable—the standardized mass contract. A standardized contract, once its contents have been formulated by a business firm, is used in every bargain dealing with the same product or service. The individuality of the parties which so frequently gave color to the old type contract has disappeared. The stereotyped contract of today reflects the impersonality of the market. It has reached its greatest perfection in the different types of contracts used on the various exchanges. Once the usefulness of these contracts was discovered and perfected in the transportation, insurance, and banking business, their use spread into all other fields of large scale enterprise, into international as well as national trade, and into labor relations. It is to be noted that uniformity of terms of contracts typically recurring in a business enterprise is an important factor in the exact calculation of risks. Risks which are difficult to calculate can be excluded altogether. Unforseeable contingencies affecting performance, such as strikes, fire, and transportation difficulties can be taken care of. The standard clauses in insurance policies are the most striking illustrations of successful attempts on the part of business enterprises to select and control risks assumed under a contract. The insurance business probably deserves credit also for having first realized the full importance of the so-called "juridical risk," the danger that a court or jury may be swayed by "irrational factors" to decide against a powerful defendant. Ingenious clauses have been the result. Once their practical utility was proven, they were made use of in other lines of business. It is highly probable that the desire to avoid juridical risks has been a motivating factor in the widespread use of warranty clauses in the machine industry limiting the common law remedies of the buyer to breach of an implied warranty of quality and particularly excluding his right to claim damages. The same is true for arbitration clauses in international trade. Standardized contracts have thus become an important means of excluding or controlling the "irrational factor" in litigation. In this respect they are a true reflection of the spirit of our time with its hostility to irrational factors in the judicial process, and they belong in the same category as codifications and restatements.

In so far as the reduction of costs of production and distribution thus achieved is reflected in reduced prices, society as a whole ultimately benefits from the use of standard contracts. And there can be no doubt that this has been the case to a considerable extent. The use of standard contracts has, however, another aspect which has become increasingly important. Standard contracts are typically used by enterprises with strong bargaining power. The weaker party, in need of the goods or services, is frequently not in a position to shop around for better terms, either because the author of the standard contract has a monopoly (natural or artificial) or because all competitors use the same clauses. His contractual intention is but a subjection more or less voluntary to terms dictated by the stronger party, terms whose consequences are often understood only in a vague way, if at all. Thus, standardized contracts are frequently contracts of adhesion; . . . standarized contracts have . . . been used to control and regulate the distribution of goods from producer all the way down to the ultimate consumer. They have become one of the many devices to build up and strengthen industrial empires.

And yet the tremendous economic importance of contracts of adhesion is hardly reflected in the great texts on contracts or in the Restatement. As a matter of fact, the term "contract of adhesion" or a similar symbol has not even found general recognition in our legal vocabulary. This will not do any harm if we remain fully aware that the use of the word "contract" does not commit us to an indiscriminate extension of the ordinary contract rules to all contracts. But apparently the realization of the deepgoing antinomies in the structure of our system of contracts is too painful an experience to be permitted to rise to the full level of our consiousness. Consequently, courts have made great efforts to protect the weaker contracting party and still keep "the elementary rules" of the law of contracts intact. As a result, our common law of standardized contracts is highly contradictory and confusing, and the potentialities inherent in the common law system for coping with contracts of adhesion have not been fully developed. . . .

* * *

The task of adjusting in each individual case the common law of contracts to contracts of adhesion has to be faced squarely and not indirectly. This is possible only if courts become fully aware of their emotional attitude with regard to freedom of contract. Here lies the main obstacle to progress, particularly since courts have an understandable tendency to avoid this crucial issue by way of rationalization. They prefer to convince themselves and the community that legal certainty and "sound principles" of contract law should not be sacrificed to dictates of justice or social desirability. Such discussions are hardly profitable.

To be sure, "case law and the feeling of justice are certainly not synonymous;" it is just to obey laws of which one does not approve. But it is equally true that the rules of the common law are flexible enough to enable courts to listen to their sense of justice and to the sense of justice of the community. Just as freedom of contract gives individual contracting parties all the needed leeway for shaping the law of contract according to their needs the elasticity of the common law, with rule and counter-rule constantly competing, makes it possible for courts to follow the dictates of "social desirability." Whatever one may think about the possibility of separating the "law that is" from the "law that ought to be," this much is certain: In the development of the common law the ideal tends constantly to become the practice. And in this process the ideal of certainty has constantly to be weighed against the social desirability of change, and very often legal certainty has to be sacrificed to progress. The inconsistencies and contradictions within the legal system resulting from the uneven growth of the law and from conflicting ideologies are inevitable.

* * *

The individualism of our rules of contract law, of which freedom of contract is the most powerful symbol, is closely tied up with the ethics of free enterprise capitalism and the ideals of justice of a mobile society of small enterprisers, individual merchants and independent craftsmen. This society believed that individual and cooperative action left unrestrained in family, church and market would not lessen the freedom and dignity of man but would secure the highest possible social justice. It was firmly convinced of a natural law according to which the individual serving his own interest was also serving the interest of the community. Profits can be earned only by supplying consumable commodities. Freedom of competition will prevent profits from rising unduly. The play of the market if left to itself must therefore maximize net satisfactions. Justice within this framework has a very definite meaning. It means freedom of property and of contract, of profit making and of trade. Freedom of contract thus receives its moral justification. The "prestabilized harmony" of a social system based on freedom of enterprise and perfect competition sees to it that the "private autonomy" of contracting parties will be kept within bounds and will work out to the benefit of the whole.

With the decline of the free enterprise system due to the innate trend of competitive capitalism towards monopoly, the meaning of contract has changed radically. Society, when granting freedom of contract, does not guarantee that all members of the community will be able to make use of it to the same extent. On the contrary, the law, by protecting the unequal distribution of property, does nothing to prevent freedom of contract from becoming a one-sided privilege. Society, by proclaiming freedom of contract, guarantees that it will not interfere with the exercise of power by contract. Freedom of contract enables enterprises to legislate by contract and, what is even more important, to legislate in a substantially authoritarian manner without using the appearance of authoritarian forms. Standard contracts in particular could thus become effective instruments in the hands of powerful industrial and commercial overlords enabling them to impose a new feudal order of their own making upon a vast host of vassals. This spectacle is all the more fascinating since not more than a hundred years ago contract ideology had been successfully used to break down the last vestiges of a patriarchal and benevolent feudal order in the field of master and servant (Priestley v. Fowler). Thus the return back from contract to status which we experience today was greatly facilitated by the fact that the belief in freedom of contract has remained one of the firmest axioms in the whole fabric of the social philosophy of our culture.

The role played by contract in the destruction of the institutional framework of capitalistic society is constantly obscured to the lawyer by the still prevailing philosophy of law which neglects to treat contract as the most important source of law. According to conventional theory contract is only a convenient label for a number of "operative facts" which have the consequences intended by the parties if the law so ordains. In this respect the great philosophers of natural law thought quite differently: society, in proclaiming freedom of contract—according to their teaching—has delegated to individual citizens a piece of sovereignty which enables them to participate constantly in the law making process. Freedom of contract means that the state has no monopoly in the creation of law. The consent of contracting parties creates law also. The law-making process is decentralized. As a result, law is not an order imposed by the state from above upon its citizens; it is rather an order created from below. This was a realistic insight. Unwarranted, however, was the optimistic belief that capitalism meant a permanent advance over the preceding social system, feudalism, because of the fact that contract and not status had become the chief means of social integration. Nor can we subscribe to the thesis of natural law philosophers that the progress in any society towards freedom is to be measured by the extent to which all political relations can be reduced to contract, "the perfect form of obligation."

In the happy days of free enterprise capitalism the belief that contracting is law making had largely emotional importance. Law making by contract was no threat to the harmony of the democratic system. On the contrary it reaffirmed it. The courts, therefore, representing the community as a whole, could remain neutral in the name of freedom of contract. The deterioration of the social order into the pluralistic society of our days with its powerful pressure groups was needed to make the wisdom of the contract theory of the natural law philosophers meaningful to us. The prevailing dogma, on the other hand, insisting that contracts is *only* a set of operative facts, helps to preserve the illusion that the "law" will protect the public against any abuse of freedom of contract. This will not be the case so long as we fail to realize that freedom of contract must mean different things for different types of contracts. Its meaning must change with the social importance of the type of contract and with the degree of monopoly enjoyed by the author of the standardized contract.

NOTE: A Comparative and Historical Perspective
on the Law of Contract

Roscoe Pound has called it "a jural postulate of civilized society" that "men must be able to assume that those with whom they deal in the general intercourse of the society will carry out their undertakings according to the expectations which the morality of the community attaches thereto." [1]   Indeed, it is a "postulate" of all societies, civilized or uncivilized, that men must be able to rely to some extent upon the expectations created by the words or acts of others.   In even the most simple societies, and in even the most tyrannical, there are mutual undertakings, reciprocal commitments, which are treated as deserving respect and whose breach is in some way met by sanctions.

In many societies, however, security of such mutual commitments is maintained primarily through religion, or through the internal discipline of kinship and similar ties, or through moral pressures, or through sheer force, rather than primarily through law.   It is, indeed, a relatively late development in social evolution when certain kinds of agreements are understood as creating, in and of themselves, *legal* obligations, and a still later development when the remedy for a breach of such agreements is so shaped as to secure for the aggrieved party the promised advantage.

Contract has become so large and so integral a part of our social life that it is hard for us to believe that any society could exist without it.   We must distinguish, however, between agreement-in-fact and the legal aspects of such agreement-in-fact.   By "contract" is not meant agreement-in-fact as such, but rather agreement-in-fact by which certain kinds of legal obligations are created.   Some agreements may give rise to no legal obligations at all—an informal agreement of two friends to write to each other, for example.   Other agreements may give rise to legal obligations which are not, however, "contractual" legal obligations.   Marriage, for example, though based upon agreement, is a status; the obligations involved are fixed not by the agreement but by law, and most of them may not be altered by the parties.

Contract law in primitive societies.   Anthropologists have debated whether contract law exists in primitive (that is, nonliterate) societies.   Much of the debate is obscured by conflicting definitions of what law is and what contract is.   That reciprocity is a fundamental principle of order in many if not all primitive societies, and that reciprocal exchanges of goods and of other values are carried on in primitive societies, are unquestionable facts.   It is equally unques-

---

1. Roscoe Pound, An Introduction to the Philosophy of Law (New Haven, Conn., 1954), p. 133.

tionable, however, that obligations arising from exchanges in primitive societies are not usually seen by members of those societies as examples of a general principle that mutual promises as such are binding in law. Almost invariably those features of primitive institutions which appear to us to be contractual in nature are so inextricably interwoven with noncontractual elements that it is impossible to isolate the one kind from the other. Thus Llewellyn and Hoebel write of contract among the Cheyenne Indians:

> "Bargaining was colored with both reticences and obligations arising from the flavor of more-than-trade. . . . [G]ift exchange rather than explicit bargain was the dominant line of trade. . . . Cheyenne practice shows relatively little of that side of contract which looks to engaging for the future. Assumption of office or of marriage obligation was felt as change of status rather than as the incurring of modern-type contractual duties. Vows one meets from time to time; and some promises, even partaking half as much of bargain as of beneficence. . . ." [2]

Malinowski has emphasized the importance of trade arrangements among the Trobrianders, and the complex network of binding obligations surrounding economic transactions. At the same time he stresses that "barter of goods and services is carried on mostly within a standing partnership, or is associated with definite ties or coupled with a mutuality in non-economic matters. Most if not all economic acts are found to belong to some chain of reciprocal gifts and counter-gifts, which in the long run balance, benefiting both sides equally. . . ." [3]

If we turn to the primitive law of our Germanic ancestors on the European continent and in England we also find protection of exchanges both of economic and of noneconomic values, but the legal obligations surrounding such exchanges arose from ceremonies, and usually from the ceremonial delivery of the thing to be exchanged.[4] In archaic Roman law the earliest enforceable agreements were so-called "formal contracts," in which legal obligations were created by oath, or by a ceremony of question and answer using sacramental words, or by a ceremony with bronze coin and balance in the presence of witnesses.

It should not be thought that in these systems the requirement of a preceding gift, or of a delivery, or of a ceremony, were "mere formalities" which dressed up, so to speak, the contract. They were, rather, the very source of the legal obligation involved, which differed from a contractual obligation based upon promise as such.

2. Karl N. Llewellyn and E. Adamson Hoebel, The Cheyenne Way: Conflict and Case Law in Primitive Jurisprudence (Norman, Okla., 1941, 1953), pp. 236–237.

3. Bronislaw Malinowski, Crime and Custom in Savage Society (Condon, 1926), p. 39.

4. *Cf.* Sir Frederick Pollock and F. W. Maitland, History of English Law (Cambridge, 1898), pp. 184 ff.

Contract in medieval English law. We have seen that in the 11th and 12th centuries the primitive legal systems of the peoples of Europe were transformed and a new system characterized by more rational legal procedures and by more sophisticated legal doctrines was created.[5] The earlier pre-contract law of the Anglo-Saxon system underwent rationalization along with the rest of that system. Particularly, there developed several legal institutions whereby economic exchanges could be more efficiently facilitated and protected. However there still had to be in each case a special reason, apart from the fact of the bargain itself, for assigning legal consequences to a transaction. This development is described in the following pages.

[The following is taken from LON L. FULLER, BASIC CONTRACT LAW (St. Paul, Minn., 1947), p. 304 ff. Footnotes are renumbered.]

Prior to the [16th century] . . . it may be said that the English law recognized two bases of liability which we would classify as "contractual". *First,* a defendant who had promised to pay for goods or services became liable to pay the agreed price (which might be in terms of money or goods) *after* he had received the plaintiff's performance. The appropriate actions to enforce this liability were debt and detinue.[6] *Secondly,* a defendant who had made a promise under seal was liable in an action of debt or covenant.[7] The principles of liability involved in these two contracts of the early law were (1) that a man ought to pay for what he has bargained for and received, and (2) that a formally-made promise shall be binding.

If we compare this early English law of contracts with the modern law we will notice that the most important difference lies in the fact that there was no relief for breach of an informal executory bargain. A and B agree on the sale of a horse for £10. When the time comes for delivery, A,

---

5. See supra, p. 571 ff.

6. Detinue and debt were originally two forms of the same action, debt being allowed where the defendant had promised a sum of money, or a fixed quantity of fungible goods, while detinue was the appropriate form where the defendant had promised to deliver a specific and identified chattel. Detinue was also used against a bailee who wrongfully refused to return the bailed article. By a gradual process of extension, detinue came to be available as a remedy for the wrongful detention of a chattel regardless of the manner in which the defendant came into possession of it. Thus, though in its original form, detinue savored of "contract," being connected with sales and bailments, it later came to be regarded as a tort action, since it was available against anyone wrongfully detaining a chattel belonging to the plaintiff. As a means of enforcing an obligation by the seller to deliver to the buyer a chattel for which the buyer had paid, detinue did not preserve its "contractual" quality since the cases where the action was permitted were cases in which, in terms of later analysis, "title" had passed to the buyer so that his suit to secure possession was conceived to rest on "property" rather than "contract."

7. Originally the distinction between debt and covenant as remedies for breach of a promise under seal was that debt would lie where the promise was to pay a definite sum of money, while covenant would lie in other cases. Later covenant became an alternative remedy to debt even where the promise was to pay a sum certain.

the seller, tenders the horse, and B refuses to accept it. Unless B's promise was under seal, the early law granted no remedy to A in this situation. Suit could be brought for the price of goods delivered or services rendered, but not for "damages" for the other party's refusal to carry out the unsealed executory agreement.

The early English law of contracts was, by modern standards at least, deficient in other important, but less obvious ways. The suit for the price of performance rendered was itself subject to certain limitations, understandable only in the light of the conceptions of legal procedure which prevailed in early English law.

The business of deciding other men's disputes has never been a comfortable one; those charged with judicial functions have in all ages sought means of minimizing their personal responsibility for the decision rendered. The modern judge is likely to depict himself as an inert conduit through which the force of statutes and precedents is communicated. During periods when a general belief in witchcraft and magic exists, another means is open to the judge for obscuring or eliminating his personal responsibility for the decision rendered. This consists in converting the trial into a ritualistic appeal to the supernatural, in which the judge acts as a mere umpire to see that the proper forms are observed and to announce the decision when it has been determined. The modes of trial in early English law which illustrate this conception are trial by battle, by ordeal, and by oath of compurgation. It is disputed whether the conception of procedure, and of the judge's function, embodied in these modes of trial is a general characteristic of primitive justice, or arises only during periods when, for one reason or another, the judge's position has become insecure, either toward those below him or toward the king above him. Apparently in some cases "supernatural" modes of trial originally used only in cases where actual evidence was lacking, were later extended to all cases. Another point of obscurity is the extent to which these modes of trial were manipulated by the judge to procure the result he considered proper "on the merits." In any event, these methods of trial were in wide use at the time when the law of contracts took its beginnings in England, and we may infer from the prominence given them that the judge's rôle was at that time conceived as being not so much that of "deciding" the case as that of supervising a ritualistic and supposedly objective test of the truth of the parties' claims.

This primitive conception of legal procedure inevitably had its repercussions on the substantive law of contracts. It is one thing to have a claim for £10 which can be established by rational proof and which the sheriff will collect out of the debtor's goods, and another to have a claim for £10 which must be vindicated in a judicially supervised duel or by submission to an ordeal. With a change in the conception of legal procedure and the role of the judge, the plaintiff's claim to his debt developed in the direction of the conception which we recognize today. Trial by battle, for example, ceased to be possible in the action of debt at a comparatively early time.

On the other hand, where the plaintiff had to rely on debt or detinue, and the defendant's promise was not under seal, two of the consequences of this primitive conception persisted for several centuries. These were: (1) that the defendant's promise of payment must have been of a "sum certain," or a specified chattel, or fixed quantity of fungible goods; (2) that the defendant might at his option "wage his law" and with the aid of "oath-helpers" escape liability by the process of swearing himself out of it. These two incidents of early procedure were fossilized, as it were, in the actions of debt and detinue and carried down into a period when conceptions of trial had generally advanced beyond the notions which had given rise to them.

The plaintiff in debt had to demand a "sum certain" because otherwise the judge would be called on to determine the amount of the recovery, a determination which would take him out of his passive rôle. A consequence of this requirement was that implied contracts (for "reasonable compensation") could not be enforced. The parties must by agreement have set definitely the price which the plaintiff was to receive for his performance. This requirement of the action of debt remained until the abolition of the distinction between forms of action; in England until 1852.

Though wager of law gradually fell into disuse, it was theoretically possible in England until 1833, when it was abolished by statute. When the defendant "waged his law" he brought into court a number of witnesses (finally set as twelve) who repeated an oath affirming that the defendant's oath was "clean". The theory of this mode of trial seems to have rested partly on rational grounds (If twelve men were willing to swear that the defendant was telling the truth, probably he was), and partly on supernatural grounds (God would intervene to cause the witnesses to trip in repeating the oath if in fact the defendant and his oath helpers were swearing falsely.) The chief importance of wager of law for the history of contract lies in the fact that it constituted a serious defect in the action of debt which gave special impetus to the development of the rival action of assumpsit.

There was still another defect in the remedy which the early law gave to the plaintiff who had performed his side of a bargain. Probably the situation in which the action of debt was originally granted was that where the plaintiff had transferred property to the defendant for which the defendant had agreed to pay. A tangible benefit was conferred directly on the defendant. This was termed in the later cases a *"quid pro quo,"* and there is evidence in the early cases of a struggle to liberate this notion of the *quid pro quo* from the physical conception that originally dominated it. Probably the first development in this direction was that of allowing services rendered to the defendant, instead of a transfer of property, to stand as the *quid pro quo.* Still later, after considerable wavering, it was held that a benefit conferred on a third person at the request of the defendant, and on the defendant's promise to pay for it, could serve as a *quid pro quo* to bind the defendant. But traces of its origin in a physical transfer of value to the defendant remained with the action of debt to the end, though the resulting limitations lost much of their importance after assumpsit had in practice largely superseded the action of debt. It was stated in 1695, for example, that debt could not be maintained for a sum won on a wager. (Walker v. Walker, 5 Mod. 13.) There was here a "sum certain" and an element of bargain involved in the wager itself, but, the *quid pro quo* (a mere chance that the defendant might have won) bore so remote an analogy to that originally involved in debt that the court considered debt an inappropriate action. (It should be observed that at the time of the case cited, the view now prevailing, that wagers are unenforceable as a matter of public policy, had not yet been adopted. The court in fact indicated that suit might have been brought in the appropriate form of assumpsit for the sum won.)

As to the other basis of contractual liability recognized in the early English law (that the formal promise is binding), it should be observed that the seal became in time what may be called a "blanket formality", that is, a device which suffices to make any kind of promise enforceable, except, of course, one which would be denied legal sanction because promotive of an illegal or immoral purpose. Most mature systems of law provide some such blanket formality; in ancient Rome we find the stipulation, and in the modern civil law, the notarial contract.

Because of the pervading "formality" of primitive law, it has been supposed that the notion involved in these devices (that form may bind without reference to content) is a notion of great antiquity. The available facts do not bear out this assumption. In primitive society, formalities and ceremonies are generally known, but are formalities and ceremonies identified with particular transactions of restricted purposes. The notion of a blanket formality seems historically to have been arrived at by the process of broadening the purposes for which a particular ceremony could be used. The formal contract of the Middle Ages in Germanic Europe apparently descended from a transaction originally used only for the purpose of giving hostages in settlement of a blood feud. This transaction came gradually to be used for other purposes, and, by a curious development, it became possible for the debtor to offer himself as a hostage or surety for his own obligation. This notion of self-pledge was on the Continent the source of a formality which became in time a general means of making promises binding.

It is not known when the seal first became a blanket formality in England, though it was certainly by the latter part of the thirteenth century. The actual practice of using seals was introduced by the Norman invaders, so that the binding effect of the seal was not a "product of ancient folk-law." On the other hand, it seems likely that the seal did not originally have an obligatory effect which was independent of the transaction in which it was used. Originally, its significance seems to have been primarily evidentiary, and when a greater effect was first attributed to it, it was apparently on the theory that a seal might make conclusive the acknowledgment of an obligation to pay for something already received. In time, however, by a process which cannot be traced in detail, it came to have the effect which the later common law took for granted, that is, of making a promise, generally speaking, *any* promise, enforceable.

The Development of the Action of Assumpsit. The action of special assumpsit was an off-shoot of the action of trespass on the case, and more particularly of trespass on the case as it was used in suits to recover damages for a negligent injury of the plaintiff or his goods. If the defendant carelessly left a log lying in a darkened road which injured the plaintiff's horse, the plaintiff's remedy would be in trespass on the case, or "case" as it was later called. In this suit there would be no need to include any allegation of an undertaking or promise by the defendant; the defendant was liable for his carelessness and not as a promise-breaker.

The notion of assumpsit was first introduced in cases where the defendant injured a chattel which had been entrusted to him by the plaintiff. The defendant receives the plaintiff's horse for transportation across a river, and negligently causes his boat to overturn so that the horse is lost. Here the plaintiff would allege that the defendant undertook (*assumpsit*) that he would transport the horse safely. Notwithstanding this allegation, the theory of the suit was not that the defendant had broken a promise, but that he had wronged the plaintiff by causing a loss of the horse. Why, then, was the allegation of an undertaking included in the plaintiff's declaration? Apparently it was through a fear that without it the court might consider that the plaintiff was as much to blame for the loss as the defendant, since he voluntarily turned his horse over to the defendant. An analogous case in modern law would be that of a plaintiff who was injured by some remedy suggested during an illness by a lay friend. Unless the friend claimed some special competence, or expressed some definite assurance, probably no liability would be imposed on him. We would say that the plaintiff was injured through his own folly in acting on the medical advice of a layman. At the time when assumpsit was developed, this notion of "plaintiff's folly" was given a broader extension than it is today, and apparently the undertaking of the defendant was first alleged merely to rebut this notion of an assumption of risk by the plaintiff.

So long as the "gist" of the plaintiff's action was not the defendant's breach of his promise, the action of "case in assumpsit" was not a contractual remedy in the modern sense. It became such a remedy by a gradual development which involved: (1) a shift of emphasis from the wrongful act of the defendant to his undertaking or promise; and (2) the introduction of the notion that the defendant could be liable not only for doing something improperly but for neglecting to do what he had promised to do. Case in its original form was allowed only where the defendant had acted unskillfully, not where he had failed to act altogether. Thus it was said that if a carpenter should undertake to build a house, he would be liable for misbuilding it, but not for failing altogether to build it. When case in assumpsit had developed so as to permit recovery against a defendant who had failed to do anything toward the performance of his promise, it had become a contractual action in the modern sense.

The above description of the development of contract law in England during the period from the 11th to the 15th centuries is incomplete in one important respect: it is confined to the development of contract law in the royal courts. Apart from the royal courts, there operated in the Middle Ages—both in England and on the Continent—ecclesiastical courts, manorial courts, borough courts, merchant courts, and other kinds of courts, each with its own kind of law. Thus the ecclesiastical courts, applying canon law, developed the doctrine that a simple formless promise was binding in conscience, and hence could be enforced under the penitential discipline of the ecclesiastical courts.[8] The manorial and borough courts enforced cer-

8. "The canon law recognized as binding the formal contract concluded either by oath or by *fides promissa* [faith pledged] and also the contract formed *solo consensu* [by consent alone]. The basis of the canonical principle, *solus consensus obligat* [consent alone is binding], which conflicted with both Roman and Germanic law, was the theological view that a man who does not keep his promise is guilty of the sin of lying and incurs ecclesiastical penalties. The revolutionary character of their doctrine, and particularly the fact that it was at variance with the Roman maxim *ex nudo pacto actio non oritur* [a bare agreement does not give rise to an

tain kinds of contracts without developing explicit doctrines of contract law. Most important, perhaps, for our purposes is the fact that the merchants throughout Europe, including England, developed their own "law merchant," under which commercial bargains received protection in the mercantile courts of the various countries.[9] It was only

action], led the canonists to formulate a further essential requirement in addition to consent. Finding this requirement in the Roman *causa* the canonists held it immaterial that a pact was *nudum a solemnitate* [bare of solemnity], provided only that it was not *nudum a causa*. Applying this doctrine to both unilateral and bilateral contracts the canonists reached the bold conclusion that all promises supported by *causa* were enforceable. While they held conflicting views as to the nature of *causa* they were all agreed that it involved the necessity of some purpose or result to be attained by the contracting parties, such as a definite legal act; and since the preservation of morality was essential they maintained further that this purpose or object must be reasonable and equitable. From this latter requirement the canonists developed the doctrine of equality in the sphere of contract. This doctrine, which was grounded in their economic notions, they applied not only to the formation and subject matter of contracts but also to their termination. Upon equality they based their prohibition of usury and their ideas of the just wage and the just price; and this same principle of equality led them to hold that if one party did not fulfil his promise the other party was released from, his *non servanti fidem fides non est servanda*.

"In the creation of its law of contract the church, starting from the basic idea of the repression of sin, stressed the importance of the conscience of parties and in fact clothed conscience with legal obligation wherever there were present the two essential elements of consent and *causa*. With the development of the informal consensual contract there was the accompanying emphasis upon the importance of the intention of the parties and of their *bona fides*. There arose, moreover, an interpretation of contracts based on considerations of equity and natural justice. All of these features of the canonical law of contract influenced the secular laws of Europe in the later Middle Ages and in modern times."

They were adopted, in part at least, by the post-glossators and the civilians of the later mediaeval centuries; they passed at an early time into the secular law of Italy, France and other countries; and they helped to shape the growth of a cosmopolitan system of mercantile law."—H. D. Hazeltine, "Canon Law," in Encyclopaedia of the Social Sciences (1937 ed.) Vol. 2, pp. 184–185.

9. The law merchant originated in ancient times in the maritime customs of traders in the seaport towns of the Eastern Mediterranean. It underwent some systematization in the Sea Law of Rhodes (ca. 300 B.C.) and much later in the Code of Amalfi (ca. 1000 A.D.), Barcelona's Consulado del Mar (ca. 1200) and the Laws of Oleron (ca. 1300)—all of which were chiefly concerned with maritime law and carriage of goods by sea. With the growth of the European towns from the 11th century on, merchants dealing in the markets and fairs of Western Europe organized tribunals for settling commercial disputes. In England some of these tribunals came to be called Courts of Piepowder—from the dusty feet (*pied-poudre*) of the merchant-suitors. In the 14th century the English Crown established special courts—called Courts of the Staple—for hearing disputes between English and foreign merchants. The law administered in the various mercantile courts throughout Western Europe constituted a single body of supra-national law and custom. The procedure was relatively informal and speedy. In 1306 Pope Clement V by his bull Saepe contingit defined the duties of judges of mercantile courts to proceed swiftly, plainly and without excessive technicality. See William Mitchell, An Essay on the Early History of the Law Merchant (Cambridge, 1904).

Despite the fact that with the rise of national states in the 16th century the law merchant ultimately became incorporated into the various systems of national law (in England it was absorbed into the common law in the 18th century), it nevertheless retains

in the English royal courts that actions of debt, detinue, covenant, assumpsit, and the like, were developed. On the other hand, although ecclesiastical, manorial, borough and mercantile courts enforced contracts more liberally than the royal courts, none of them developed an explicit theory or doctrine of contract law except the ecclesiastical courts, and theirs was too broad to be suitable for the business world either of the Middle Ages or of modern times.

The development of the modern concept of contract. It was not until the great changes that ushered out the "Middle Ages" and ushered in "modern history" that both in England and on the Continent of Europe there developed the modern notion of contract as "the declared will of a person or persons that some legal result shall follow, to which the law gives the intended effect." [10] More concretely, the idea took shape that a promise given for a promise is legally binding, and the promisor in default is obligated to put the promisee in the position he would have been in had the promise been fulfilled. This idea was one of the great inventions of the 16th century mind, with its faith in the power of the individual will to remake both nature and society.

In England, as has been indicated in the preceding pages, the action of assumpsit was extended in the 15th century to permit the recovery of damages for the nonperformance of a promise. No longer was it necessary that the debt be for a "sum certain," and no longer was it necessary to prove the debt by oath-helpers ("wager of law"). The requirement remained, however, that the plaintiff show that the promise was given for a *quid pro quo*. To this extent, the action of assumpsit, like the older action of debt, remained tied in the 15th century to notions of barter, the exchange of physical things. It was only in the 16th century that English contract law was freed from those notions and became adapted to notions of credit. The way in which this took place was, in rough outline, as follows:

In the 15th century if the defendant agreed to pay for goods or for services and after receiving them failed to do so, the action of debt was an available remedy, but not the action of assumpsit. In other words, assumpsit was restricted to cases in which debt would not lie; if debt could be brought, assumpsit could not. In the 16th century, for the first time, it was held that if *after* the debt was incurred the debtor made a new promise to pay it, the creditor could maintain an action of assumpsit. To this extent, then, assumpsit and debt overlapped and the plaintiff had his choice of either action.

its international character in many important respects. Thus the law of international sales, of bills of exchange (checks, promissory notes, etc.), carriage of goods by sea, marine insurance, bank credits, and the like, continues to some extent to be developed through international treaties and conventions, and out of the customs and practices of merchants, shipowners, marine insurance underwriters, bankers, and others.

10. See Roscoe Pound, "The Role of the Will in Law", 68 Harvard Law Review 1 (1954).

Once the more modern action of assumpsit was permitted to be used to recover a debt where there was a new promise to pay it, pressure mounted to dispense with the necessity of a new promise. The King's Bench yielded to this pressure, partly in order to increase its powers relative to those of other rival courts. Finally in 1602, in Slade's Case, "all the justices of England" were brought together to consider a suit in assumpsit in which the jury by special verdict had found "there was no other promise or assumption but only the said [original] bargain" which had created the debt. The defendant's attorney argued that to deny the defendant wager of law would deprive him of his "birthright." The court held, however, that "every contract executory imports in itself an *assumpsit*"—that is, that the original bargain implied promises by the parties to perform it and such promises would support the action of assumpsit. To reconcile this new principle with the older practice, it became customary after Slade's Case to include in the declaration an allegation that the defendant, "being indebted, promised" (*indebitatus assumpsit*), but this allegation was treated as a fiction and did not have to be proved.

Thus there emerged two forms of assumpsit, the one (called "special assumpsit") available for breach of contract where the bargain was not half-executed, the other (called "general assumpsit") available for breach of contract where the goods had been sold, the money transferred, the work done, or the like.[11] The old action of debt, with its antiquated mode of proof and its theory of liability half possessory (the defendant has something belonging to the plaintiff), half tortious (the defendant has wronged the plaintiff by keeping something from him, or by misleading him into parting with something), receded in favor of an action based on a purely contractual theory of liability, a liability for breach of a promise.

11. The various forms of pleading in general assumpsit (action for goods sold, for money lent, for money paid at defendant's request, for money had and received by defendant to plaintiff's use, for work and labor done by plaintiff at defendant's request)—became known as "the common counts." As the action of special assumpsit was the foundation for the later development of contract law, so the action of general assumpsit, which was an offshoot of special assumpsit, was the foundation for the later development of what is variously called quasi-contract, restitution, or unjust enrichment. In 1657 it was held that the action of (general) assumpsit could be brought to recover money paid by mistake to a person who had no right to receive it. In 1705 the scope of the action was extended to permit recovery of money paid under a contract which had become void. It was not until 1760 that Lord Mansfield, in the case of Moses v. Macferlan, 2 Burr 1005, held that, apart from contract, "If the defendant be under an obligation, from the ties of natural justice, to refund, the law implies a debt, and gives this action, founded in the equity of the plaintiff's case, as it were upon a contract ("quasi ex contractu") as the Roman law expresses it. . . ." The phrase *quasi ex contractu*, which Lord Mansfield borrowed from continental jurists, had been used only occasionally in the sources of classical Roman law. It achieved popularity through the work of medieval glossators of Roman law, but even in the medieval and early modern period, the content of the obligations *quasi ex contractu* was not precisely defined. See Max Radin, "The Roman Law of Quasi-Contract," 23 Virginia Law Review 241 (1937).

By no means every broken promise, however, would support an action of assumpsit. It was the *bargained* promise that was legally protected, and it was the great achievement of English judges in the 16th century that they came to understand that a promise could be bargained, and hence legally binding, if it was given in exchange for another promise. In the terse phrase of an English court in the 16th century, "A promise against a promise will maintain an action." [12] Not merely the half-executed bargain but the executory bargain—I will do this if you will do that—was now seen to be worth something in and of itself, and to be worth something in secular law and not only in faith.

The concept of bargain found expression in the doctrine of "consideration." A "bare" promise to do something was not in itself enforceable, unless it was under seal. If, however, it were given in return for a benefit, or if the promisee in accepting it incurred a detriment, then that benefit or detriment was treated as consideration for the promise and gave it binding effect.

Of course not every kind of benefit to the promisor or detriment to the promisee would make the promise binding. In developing the doctrine of consideration the courts were able to control contract law and to make it conform to social needs and to public policy.

As in England, so in France, Germany, and other countries of Europe there took place in the 16th century a rapid development of contract law. In contrast to the English development, however, the chief instruments of the legal reformation on the Continent of Europe were law professors and civil servants, rather than judges and practicing lawyers. Hence doctrine—what von Mehren calls "speculative and systematic thought" [13]—played a role in Continental legal evolution similar to the role played by procedural innovations and fictions in English legal evolution. The medieval jurists of Germany and France, like their English counterparts, were confronted with an existing law which protected half-executed transactions as well as formal contracts (that is, contracts entered into by means of particular forms and ceremonies). As in England, so on the Continent, only the canon law and the law merchant, within their limited spheres, protected promises in general, promises as such. But in the 16th century the question was posed and debated throughout Continental Europe, Should not the canonists' principle *pacta sunt servanda* ("agreements shall be kept") override the existing divisions among types of enforceable contracts under secular law? Although the principle of the validity of informal executory contracts was not entirely accepted, it made considerable headway. [14]

European jurists also developed doctrines which performed functions similar to those performed by the English doctrine of considera-

---

12. Strangborough and Warner's Case, 1589, 4 Leon. 3.

13. Arthur von Mehren, The Civil Law System (Boston, 1957), p. 359ff.

14. See *ibid.*

tion in denying legal protection to agreements which infringed social interests and public policy. However, the principle of *pacta sunt servanda* had great impact on continental legal thought, and the starting point for modern European contract law has been the doctrine that promises intended to have legal effect shall be enforced; whereas, the starting point for modern Anglo-American contract law has been the doctrine that a promise will be enforced if it is made as part of a bargain.

Both in England and on the Continent one of the main driving forces behind the movement toward a contract law which recognized the enforceability of mutual promises was the expansion of commerce. As Fuller writes:

> "It is, in fact, not difficult to see why the development of open markets for the sale and purchase of goods should lead to a recognition of the binding effect of the executory exchange. Where trade is infrequent, and opportunities for the exchange of goods rare, breach of an executory bargain will be resented only as the destruction of a hope or expectation, unless the disappointed party has in some way changed his position, as by preparing to perform his side of the agreement. But when the channels of trade become more numerous, the mere entry into an executory bargain involves itself a change of position in the sense that the contracting party foregoes the opportunity of covering his needs elsewhere. Suppose A needs a hundred pounds of spices, and B contracts to deliver them to him next month. If in consequence of a rise in the market, B breaks his promise, A may very well feel that he was misled by B in the sense that but for B's promise he would have supplied his needs from another source before the advance in prices. This particular kind of resentment against the promise breaker can only arise where other sources of supply exist. Accordingly, there is probably a causal connection between the economic development of open markets and the legal development of the enforceable executory exchange." [15]

Another principal driving force behind the development of contract law in the 16th century was religious. Closely associated with the Protestant Reformation was the idea that nature could be conquered and social relations could be organized by the exercise of the will of individuals. In law this idea was reflected partly in the development of the "will theory" of contract law—a theory which found its most extreme expression in the 18th and 19th centuries,[16] but

15. Fuller, *op. cit.*, p. 311.

16. ". . . the idea that the end of law was to promote individual liberty, that it was to insure a maximum of free individual self-assertion, limiting the free self-assertion of each only by the like free self-assertion of all others, led to the extreme will theory of Savigny—for example, that notice of revocation of an offer must not only be received by the offeree but must be read by him. Indeed, [one school of European legal thought] . . . undertook to put the whole . . . law of contract in terms of will to bring about a possible and permissible legal result, which will the law recognized and implemented. This doctrine, which I learned in law school in 1889, was even then moribund but has hung on with much persistence here and there

whose origins go back to the 16th and 17th centuries and particularly to Lutheran and Calvinist conceptions of the relations between secular and spiritual life ānd of the autonomy of the individual.

The impact of the contract idea in modern history. As in the formative era of Western legal development from the 11th to the 15th centuries the idea of tort, or wrong (in Norman-English law, "trespass," derived from the Latin *transgressio* or sin), was the central and dominant idea from which new rules and new remedies were created, so in the modern era from the 16th to the 20th centuries the idea of contract has been the central and dominant idea, gradually infiltrating other branches of law, until in the 19th century even labor-management relations were viewed in terms of the contract between the individual worker and his employer. By that time land had to a considerable extent become an article of commerce—that is,. of contract—and the corporation was generally conceived in terms of powers distributed by agreement between the directors and the shareholders.

From the 16th to the 20th centuries the idea of contract has pervaded not only other branches of law but also many aspects of social life. In economics, the institutions of the free market, of middlemen,. of credit, all rest on contract both as an idea and as a legal device. The great flexibility of the contract idea, under which (subject to some important qualifications) promises are, so to speak, fungible, corresponds to the great flexibility of the free market and of the money economy, in which the great variety of different goods and other concrete economic values are rendered commensurable and hence exchangeable as abstract "commodities." So the legal personality—the right-and-duty-bearing unit—became the legal counterpart of economic man.

Likewise in the political sphere contractual concepts came to play an increasingly important role in the West from the 16th century on.. Tradition and heredity gave way to bargain and election as dominant sources of political adjustment and control; and in political theory, government itself appeared to be the result of a contract between the governors and the governed.

Indeed, many writers found contract to be the very foundation of all social life. Sir Henry Maine's famous statement that "the movement of the progressive societies has hitherto been a movement *from Status to Contract*" [17] was widely misinterpreted and used as a slogan of a laissez faire theory of law and society. One prominent 19th-century author wrote:

> In a summary view of the civil order of society, as constituted in accordance with the individualistic ideal, performance of contract presents itself as the chief *positive* element, protection of life

into the present." Roscoe Pound, "The Role of the Will in Law," 68 Harvard Law Review 1, 4 (1954).

17. Sir Henry Maine, Ancient Law (London, 1901), pp. 168–170.

and property being the chief *negative* element. Withdraw contract—suppose that no one can count upon the fulfillment of any engagement—and the members of a human community are atoms that cannot effectively combine, the complex, co-operation and division of employments that are the essential characteristics of modern industry cannot be introduced among such beings. Suppose contracts freely made and effectively sanctioned, and the most elaborate social organisation becomes possible, at least in a society of such human beings as the individualistic theory contemplates—gifted with mature reason, and governed by enlightened self-interest. Of such beings it is prima facie plausible to say that, when once their respective relations to the surrounding material world have been determined so as to prevent mutual encroachment and secure to each the fruits of his industry, the remainder of their positive mutual rights and obligations ought to depend entirely on that coincidence of their free choices, which we call contract. Thoroughgoing individualists would even include the rights corresponding to governmental services, and the obligations to render services to government, which we shall have to consider later: only in this latter case the contract is tacit.[18]

With the crisis of individualism in the 20th century there has been a reaction in many quarters against the predominance of contract conceptions in law as well as in government, economics, and elsewhere. Maine's statement—still misinterpreted—is now sometimes discredited, and it is thought by some that progressive societies move in a cycle from status to contract and back to status. It should be understood, however, that Maine used the word status in a special sense, to signify personal conditions of family life in which relationships are in no way, even remotely, based on contract. He was contrasting, in particular, the substitution of the Individual, as he put it, for the Family "as the unit of which civil laws take account." His statement regarding the movement of the progressive societies is hence applicable to medieval as well as to modern society, since medieval law from the 11th and 12th centuries on treated the personal conditions (the statuses, as we would say) of husband and wife, lord and vassal, master and servant, priest, king, and the like, as based on the consent of individuals. They were lasting relationships from which flowed general rights and duties—in that sense they were like the family relationships of which Maine speaks—but they were assumed by agreement. They were like what Max Weber has called brotherhood-contracts (*Verbrüderungsverträge*), which altered the legal status of the parties, providing that the one shall henceforth be the child, father, wife, brother, lord, slave, clan comrade, battle comrade, protector, client, follower, vassal, subject, friend, and so forth, of another.[19]

Agreements which create permanent relationships, or statuses, should be distinguished from agreements which create transitory rela-

18. Henry Sidgwick, Elements of Politics (2nd ed., London, 1879), p. 82.

19. See Max Weber on Law and Economy in Society, ed. by Max Rhenstein (Cambridge, Mass., 1954), p. 106.

tionships as well as from those which create the obligation to perform specific acts at specific times (what Weber calls specific-purpose-contracts, *Zweckverträge*). The latter types are what we have called here contracts in the modern sense. The feudal "contract" was not a contract; it was an exchange of oaths, a pledge of fealty, creating a status. It was in that sense like the marriage "contract." It established a permanent relationship. The rights and duties flowed from the relationship, and a violation of them was more like a tort or a crime than a breach of contract. The modern contract may by definition be dissolved by the consent of both parties and hence is by definition transitory. Moreover, there is a strong tendency to equate the obligations which it creates with money. Indeed, so far has modern thought made the contract an instrument of specific monetary purposes that some modern writers have defined the obligation created by a contract as the obligation alternatively to perform the contract *or* to pay damages for breach. "The duty to keep a contract at common law means a prediction that you must pay damages if you do not keep it—and nothing else," wrote Holmes in his famous essay "The Path of the Law." "If you commit a tort, you are liable to pay a compensatory sum. If you commit a contract, you are liable to pay a compensatory sum unless the promised event comes to pass, and that is all the difference. But such a mode of looking at the matter stinks in the nostrils of those who think it advantageous to get as much ethics into the law as they can." [20]

In his effort to distinguish law and morals, Holmes failed to differentiate contracts entered into for the purpose of establishing a relationship in which moral (or other non-commercial) obligations play a part from contracts which are entirely concerned with commercial transactions. Indeed, his statement is even inapplicable to many types of commercial transactions in which the promisee may exact specific performance from the defaulting promisor.

The distinction between agreements which create lasting and diffuse relations (such as those of husband and wife, master and servant, and the like) and agreements which create transitory and specific relations (such as those of buyer and seller at an auction) helps to explain the difference between the relationally-oriented law of the period of the 11th or 12th to 15th century, with its emphasis on tort (or trespass) as the growing-point of legal doctrine and legal remedy, and the will-oriented law of the 16th to the 20th centuries, with its emphasis on contract as the growing-point of legal doctrine and legal remedy.

Of course, great changes have taken place in the contract law of the 20th century, not only in socialist societies but also in societies which have not gone over to socialism but which have witnessed a very large increase in state control of economic life and in social control of individual conduct generally.

20. 10 Harvard Law Review 457, 462 (1897).

Apart from socialism, the high degree of organization of economic life today—the growth of large combinations of capital and labor and of legislative and administrative controls over large areas of the economy—has robbed contract of the stamp of individualism to a large extent. "The individual member of the community continuously finds himself involved in contractual obligations, the contents of which are often 'predetermined for him' by statute, public authority or group action. The terms and conditions under which he obtains his supply of electricity and gas will in all likelihood be regulated by a public utility commission. So will his fare, should he use a public conveyance going to work. The rent he will have to pay may be fixed by governmental authority. The price of his food will depend partly on the government's farm support program and not solely on the interplay of demand and supply in a free market. No longer will he be able to have the advantages of simple price-competition in buying many a standard brand used in daily consumption, since prices may well be fixed by arrangement between producer and distributor under price-maintenance requirements with the blessing of statutory approval. The wages he will have to pay or will earn may have been fixed for him beforehand. If he is a businessman, he must also beware of violating the anti-trust laws. . . ."[21]

Contract law in Soviet society. In socialist societies, where the means of production are owned by the state and economic life is subject to relatively strict governmental regulation, the predetermination of contract terms goes much farther than in free economies. Indeed, in a planned economy of the Soviet type the state economic enterprises which manufacture and distribute the most important industrial products are in some cases subject to instructions from central authorities stating which are to enter into contracts with each other and prescribing many of the terms.

Yet contract law continues to play an important role even in a planned economy. Despite the belief of Soviet jurists of the first period of the development of the Soviet state, from 1917 to about 1936, that the system of planning would swallow up the institutions of contract and property, and that law would "wither away," it has been found that plans are not self-executing, and that for their efficient execution a large measure of personal responsibility and personal initiative of managers of state economic enterprises is required. Enterprises have been put on the basis of "economic accountability"; that is, they are responsible for their debts out of their assets. Managers and other personnel receive bonuses based on the enterprise's profits. And within the limits of plans issued from higher organizations, distribution of goods is on the basis of contract. Indeed, probably a

21. Friedrich Kessler and Malcolm P. Sharp, Contracts: Cases and Materials (New York, 1953), p. 9.

million contract disputes between state economic enterprises are litigated in the Soviet Union every year.[22]

Contracts between Soviet state economic enterprises are usually viewed as a means of making general plans more detailed, that is, of allowing the operating enterprises to determine such specific matters as times of delivery, quality of goods, assortment, means of delivery, method of payment, etc. They also, however, serve the important additional function of revealing errors in planning and of informing planners of the actual availability of, and need for, particular products. Indeed, since 1962, in certain industries, the practice has developed of permitting the state economic enterprises to make their contracts in advance of the determination of plans, and of basing the plans upon the contracts that have been concluded.

Where the content of agreements is consciously controlled by governmental authority, the social functions of contract shift. Its functions of facilitating and protecting voluntary transactions remain, but the transactions are no longer conceived as involving merely the parties to the contract; the public interest in the transaction— and in its security—is also explicitly considered. In divorce cases and other matters of domestic relations it is sometimes said that "the state is a third party to the marriage contract." Similarly one might say that in the Soviet Union the state is a third party to commercial contracts between the autonomous state economic enterprises. In the United States, too, there are large areas of social and economic life where contract is not merely a private matter but a social matter, and where, in the securing of contractual obligations, the interest of the public is explicitly taken into account. But the United States has not gone nearly as far as the Soviet Union in regulating contract terms, requiring parties to enter into contracts, and supervising the performance of contracts and enforcing what the Soviets call "contract discipline."

It is a mistake, however, to draw too sharp a contrast between individual and social interests. There never was a time when courts have given absolute protection to private intentions expressed in contract. Not only have they always refused to enforce contracts which are illegal (as where A agrees to pay B to commit a crime) or against public policy (as where the contract unduly restrains competition), but in interpreting valid contracts, and in awarding remedies for breach of contract, they have generally taken into consideration the interests of the business community and of society generally. "There is much in contract law which is non-contractual," said the French sociologist Emile Durkheim. Indeed, security of voluntary arrangements is always to be seen as part of a larger security, the security of law and of society itself.

22. See Berman, Justice in the USSR, rev. ed. (Cambridge, Mass., 1963), p. 97 ff.

Chapter 8

CONTRACT AS A PLANNING PROCESS

People who make arrangements with each other—for example, to sell and to buy particular goods, or to perform and to pay for particular services, or to share responsibility for certain activities—attempt to anticipate future difficulties, resolve uncertainties, eliminate misunderstandings, exchange information, allocate responsibilities, and in short create a workable framework for their future dealings with each other. In many instances it is not the final result of the negotiations called "the contract" which is the important thing, but the mutual understanding which has been reached by the process of negotiation itself. It has been said that the best contract is the one which, once it has been fully negotiated, the parties can put in the drawer and forget.

In a slightly narrower sense, the object of the negotiations is to establish the mutual rights and duties of the parties. By contracting they thus make law for themselves—they engage in a kind of private legislation. The mutual rights and duties thus established have important effects upon the dealings of the parties even though they are never tested by adjudication; indeed, one function of carefully drafting a written statement of the terms of an agreement is to avoid disputes which might arise out of the transaction or relationship which is the subject of the agreement.

Contract thus facilitates the establishment of voluntary arrangements (a) through the process of negotiation, and (b) by the establishment of mutual rights and duties. In addition, (c) the framework of standards and rules set by judges and legislators by which the validity of a contract is tested, its provisions interpreted, remedies provided, *etc.*, also facilitates the establishment of voluntary agreement, at the same time that it sets limits to agreement. By establishing that some kinds of agreements create legal obligations and some do not, that some contracts are binding without various formal requirements (such as writing, seal, witnesses) and some are not, that in one kind of contract certain risks are on the buyer and in another on the seller, and so forth and so forth—contract law not only imposes restrictions upon agreement but also, and more important, provides channels through which agreement may flow. At their best, the rules of contract law transmit group experience and group wisdom regarding which kinds of agreements are likely to prove most useful in promoting the mutual advantage of both parties.

In demonstrating how contract law performs a facilitating function in the ordering of private, voluntary arrangements, we begin with an examination of contract as a planning process, and especially the lawyer's role in that process. Our suggestion is that the lawyer's work as negotiator and draftsman is itself an aspect of law, that the lawyer at work is in fact the law at work, law in action, for it is through the lawyer's offices that not only rules of law but also the experience of bench and bar are made available to the parties to a voluntary arrangement. That experience encompasses countless exposures to similar situations and the problems which can arise out of such situations. If forearmed is forewarned, then this experience may assist in the preparation of a good plan for the arrangement. Furthermore, the lawyer's training in law, in legal method and legal reasoning, may impart to him or her an acuity and objectivity which can greatly assist the parties to express their objectives and arrive at a mutually satisfactory plan.

Of course even the best legal advice will not protect the parties against all the contingencies and uncertainties which may upset the operation of any plan. Every contractual relationship is subject to disruption by unforeseen and unanticipated events which make the performance of part of the bargain either onerous or impossible. To the extent that the contract does not provide for the allocation of the risks of loss due to such events, the judges may be called upon to make adjustments and distribute the losses between the parties.

In the preceding chapter we considered some examples of situations in which judges have been called upon to fill gaps and make after the fact distributions of losses where an agreement was not so carefully planned as to avoid ambiguity and the need for adjudication. (See, § 27, *supra* pp. 649–664.) Those examples graphically illustrate one of the key ways the law facilitates voluntary arrangements by providing both doctrine and process to resolve contract disputes. Those examples also demonstrate how the legal framework itself poses some risks which may need to be taken into account in contract planning. For example, where the law of contract or contract remedies is unclear or incomplete on a particular issue, the parties cannot know how the law will fill a gap in their planning, and they cannot know what consequences will follow from imperfect or incomplete contract planning. (Consider in this regard the sad tale of the Peevyhouses, *supra* pp. 705–716.) Accordingly, one element of careful contract planning is to account for and in some way provide for the legal risks which are posed should it later be necessary to resort to adjudication. (We have already seen some examples of this pheonmenon. Consider in this regard the Rose and Frank and United States Asphalt cases, *supra* pp. 608–613, 631–636.)

The following materials will provide a conclusion for our brief examination of the contract institution, this time largely from the point of view of the drafters and users of contract, rather than from the viewpoint of judges and commentators.

SECTION 31.　CONTRACT AND PLANNING: THE LAWYER'S ROLE IN THE CONTRACT PROCESS

[The following is taken from IAN R. MACNEIL, "A PRIMER OF CONTRACT PLANNING," 48 Southern California Law Review 627, 629–639 (1975). Some footnotes omitted; others are renumbered]

Vertical and Horizontal Economic Ordering

No complex economic system can operate without vast amounts of coordination of economic activity, coordination requiring extensive planning. Oversimplifying, it may be said that such coordination and its planning can be achieved vertically, horizontally, or in a combination of the two. Vertical coordination is command coordination: subordinates are instructed in the details of coordinating their activities to achieve goals desired by the commander. Horizontal coordination is exchange coordination: relative equals [1] make arrangements to coordinate their activities in order to achieve mutually acceptable goals through exchange of effort or property.

Contractual transactions and relations are the techniques whereby horizontal coordination is accomplished. . . .

* * *

A solid understanding of the nature of horizontal ordering of economic activity through contract is essential to successful contract planning. Many avenues lead to such understanding: much of the law school curriculum is devoted to various aspects of contractual ordering, and inevitably lawyers develop a sophisticated, if perhaps unarticulated, understanding through the day-to-day practice of law. One should not, however, overlook the insights to be found not only in the many academic overviews of contract, but also often in the nooks and crannies of more directly practical works on particular kinds of contracts.

Discrete and Relational Agreements

Contractual ordering of economic activity takes place along a spectrum of transactional and relational behavior, a spectrum which justifies distinguishing the discrete transactions lying at one end of the spectrum from the contractual relations lying at the other.

> [Discrete transactions] are contracts of short duration, with limited personal interactions, and with precise party measurements of easily measured objects of exchange, for example money and grain. They are transactions requiring a minimum of future cooperative behavior between the parties and not requiring a sharing of benefits or burdens. They bind the two parties tightly and precisely. The parties view such transactions as deals free of entan-

---

1. Equal at least in the sense that each has some choice whether to make the arrangements with the other party or not, a choice not available to a subordinate in a command structure as long as he remains in it, and does not subvert it.

gling strings, and they certainly expect no altruism. The parties see virtually everything connected with such transactions as clearly defined and presentiated.[2] If trouble is anticipated at all, it is anticipated only if someone or something turns out unexpectably badly. The epitome of discrete contract transactions: two strangers come into town from opposite directions, one walking and one riding a horse. The walker offers to buy the horse, and after brief dickering a deal is struck, in which delivery of the horse is to be made at sundown upon the handing over of $10. The two strangers expect to have nothing to do with each other between now and sundown, they expect never to see each other thereafter, and each has as much feeling for the other as has a Viking trading with a Saxon.[3]

Contractual relations, being more diverse in nature than the well-honed discrete transaction, are more difficult to describe concisely, but the following typical characteristics will convey the concept:

> The relations are of significant duration (for example, franchising). Close whole person relations form an integral aspect of the relation (employment). The object of exchange typically includes both easily measured quantities (wages) and quantities not easily measured (the projection of personality by an airline stewardess). Many individuals with individual and collective poles of interest are involved in the relation (industrial relations). Future cooperative behavior is anticipated (the players and management of the Oakland Raiders). The benefits and burdens of the relation are to be shared rather than divided and allocated (a law partnership). The bindingness of the relation is limited (again a law partnership in which in theory each member is free to quit almost at will). The entangling strings of friendship, reputation, interdependence, morality and altruistic desires are integral parts of the relation (a theatrical agent and his clients). Trouble is expected as a matter of course (a collective bargaining agreement). Finally, the participants never intend or expect to see the whole future of the relation as presentiated at any single time, but view the relation as an ongoing integration of behavior which will grow and vary with events in a largely unforeseeable future (a marriage; a family business).[4]

A great deal of contractual planning takes place within already existing contractual relations. Much of the detail and perhaps all of the general principles discussed in this Article pertain, albeit with modifications, to relational planning of this kind. Such relations often present many occasions for extensive and highly transactional planning, for example, collective bargaining, which is punctuated periodically by the extremely sharp transactional focusing involved in negotiating a "new" contract. But in this Article the focus is on contract planning in the transactional context, a context

2. To presentiate means "To make or render present in place or time; to cause to be perceived or realized as present." 8 Oxford English Dictionary 1306 (1933). *See generally* Macneil, Restatement (Second) of Contracts and Presentiation, 60 Va.L.Rev. 589 (1974) [hereinafter cited as Macneil, Presentiation].

3. Macneil, Presentiation, *supra* note [2], at 594.

4. *Id.* at 595.

in which the separateness of the parties and discreteness of the contract necessarily force concentrated attention upon the planning of specified and dichotomous rights and duties such as those to be found in a commercial loan or a single sale of goods.

Fundamental Processes and Characteristics of Contract Planning

Two processes are essential to contract planning: determining goals (along with related costs of their attainment) and communication. Two fundamental characteristics of contract planning are a constant interplay between planning and non-planning and a distinction between performance planning and risk planning. Since these four aspects of contract planning constitute the base upon which the remainder of the Article is founded, they will be explored briefly in the following pages.

1. *Determining Goals and Ascertaining Costs*

Although in theory determining goals and ascertaining costs are two separable processes, outside the Garden of Eden they are entirely interrelated— a fact inherent in exchange. Thus, the very act of agreeing to a transaction constitutes a determination by each party that what he will receive (his goal, the other's cost) exceeds in value *to him* what he will surrender (his cost, the other's goal).[5] An aspect of this process is ascertaining facts relating to alternative ways of achieving the goals and meeting the costs of achieving the goals, either through the transaction in question or by some other route.

2. *Communication*

Communication, like goal and cost determination, is an integral facet of any exchange. Anyone planning an exchange must always communicate in some fashion with the other party to accomplish the exchange. This process is not simply additive or sequential to determining goals and ascertaining the costs of attaining them; it is interwoven with those processes and affects them as they affect it. Even the party acting entirely alone, who plans, his goals and ascertains their costs, has to take into account the effect that his desires will have on the other potential party; he is thereby engaging in what might be called anticipatory communication. And, or course, far more active mutuality of planning often occurs in which much actual communica-

---

5. The source of the mutuality of benefit in exchange lies in the fact that different people put different values on the same thing, with the result that exchange—all by itself—can often enhance the wealth of both parties as measured by themselves. Many students of contracts, especially if they lack a background in economics, are puzzled by and indeed may reject the idea that a typical exchange is beneficial to *both* participants. I have never figured out how much of this puzzlement or rejection may be caused by a cynical view that in every human interaction one side exploits the other or how much it may be caused by an introduction in law school to the characteristics of contract market damages which are indeed zero sum measures. But they are zero sum measures precisely because the breach itself—if it was deliberate—indicated that one of the parties had *changed his mind* about the correctness of his original belief that the exchange would be beneficial to him.

The sharp notion that my goals always equal your costs is a discrete-transaction concept. In relational patterns my goals may equal your goals and my costs your costs; while exchange takes place, it is in such circumstances muted in that it is not thought of by participants as a discrete exchange. Consider, for example, any mutually successful making of love.

tion shapes both parties' goals and costs. Finally, some kind of communication will be used in determining that the parties are in some degree of harmony on the allocations of those goals and costs. Even passive receipt of the adhesive planning of someone else constitutes a form of mutual communication in such circumstances.

3.   *Planning and Non-Planning*

A friend who has practiced law for many years wrote in a personal letter not long ago:

> My experience has been of the person struggling to draw the maps of "territories to be" with all the attendant frustrations and anxieties imposed by the assumption that the perfect contract anticipates and disposes of all possible future problems and questions.

The perfect contract to which he refers is, of course, always impossible of achievement, even in the simplest and most transactional of situations. That it may serve as an appropriate goad to the planning lawyer to do his best should not be permitted to obscure the idealistic and unachievable nature of the goal. Every contract is necessarily partially unplanned, not only because of the nature of planning, but also because of the nature of one of the major tools of planning—promises.

Thus, generally speaking the unexecuted portion of every contract contains two parts: the planned and the unplanned. The unplanned part of a viable contract consists of at most an anticipation, vague or otherwise, of future cooperation or lack of it in taking the future actions necessary to make the contract work out satisfactorily with all of the superstructure of hopes, worries, fears, ids, egos, and Freudian syndromes ordinarily involved in such anticipation. The more precise this anticipation is, the more closely it comes to resemble planning.

At least four factors complicate any description of the planned portion of the relationship. First, one party may plan the relationship differently than the other party, or else plan in an unsatisfactory manner a portion left unplanned by the other party. The sources of such difficulties are manifold and are potentially present in every contractual relationship.[6]

---

6.   The general difficulty may be characterized as one of communication.

Communication expressed is not communication received: Limitations on the expressions of communication are by no means the last step in the narrowing process. Undoubtedly the statement: "See that woodpecker on the tree trunk" means more to the person saying it than it does to the person hearing it; at least it does until the hearer sees the woodpecker and the tree trunk. The meaning of the declarer can be viewed only against the wealth of detail which seeing the woodpecker created in his mind. The hearer, on the other hand, may envision a more stereotyped and less detailed picture. Conversely, the communication sometimes evokes a richer picture, because of prior experience or because the hearer enjoys a richer sensitivity and image evoking capacity than the declarer. But even so the imagery will not necessarily match the view the hearer would have had if he had seen the woodpecker in the tree, and it may conflict with the declarer's view.

Very closely related to the narrowing effect of transmission-reception [107] is the inevitable distortion occurring in communications between disparate human beings. There is thus an inherent non-mutuality of promise. The hearer simply does not hear what the declarer says, because what the declarer says is part of one human being and what the hearer hears is part of another and different human being. Therefore,

A second complication in describing planning is that it is not always clear where the unplanned portion of a contract ends and the planning begins. Planning may take the form of establishing frameworks for handling otherwise unplanned aspects of the relationship, such as labor grievance and arbitration structures. But this sort of planning itself may be so vague as to be little more than an expression of hope for future cooperation: "We'll worry about that later and work it out somehow."

A further complication comes from the fact that the human mind focuses on only a limited number of aspects of any given situation at any given time, or even over a range of time. Thus, planning is inevitably interstitial in nature.[7] This interstitiality is increased by the further fact that

there can never be complete communication between people; a promise made and a promise heard are two different things. To the extent that parties recognize this and each strips out those aspects that experience suggests are not mutual, there is yet more narrowing of the truly mutual promise.

In addition to the non-mutuality inherent in the imperfect nature of communication is non-mutuality caused by grosser kinds of nonhearing, such as hearing "seventy" when the declaration was "seventeen." This is by no means uncommon, and relatively many such situations find their way into courtrooms to the misery of the parties.

107. For the sake of simplicity the text focuses on oral communication; everything said on that subject, however, applies even more strongly to written communication; a form introducing its own special narrowing processes, down to and including running out of ink or space on a page, to say nothing of the loss of intonations, gestures, facial expressions and the like which accompany the spoken and viewed word. Moreover, the written word tends to be more formal and precise, and unless more written words are used they will convey less than the oral. What is conveyed tends to be more accurate in a discrete sense, less accurate in a contextual sense.

7. *Promissory expression is fragmentary:* Professor Farnsworth performed an important service to general contract jurisprudence when he linked with contracts the psychological concept of "limited attention," a concept intimately related to the interstitial nature of promises. Humans are incapable of focusing on everything in a situation of any complexity (and *all* human physical and social situations

are complex). They are therefore forced by neural processes to limit their attention to as many facets as they can physically handle. Moreover, although Farnsworth does not mention this specifically, it is doubtless true that typically attention is limited yet further either consciously or by habit, because maximizing the number of open channels of reception will seldom be the most effective way for the person to proceed with whatever he is about. The cacophony would be too much for the receivers to sort out efficiently. Thus in making a promise a person cannot and will not be focusing on everything even in the present situation, and the promise will in fact concern only a fragment, often a very small fragment, of that present situation. This limitation is aggravated by the nature of promise, it being inherently a mechanism for dealing with the future. Because the promissory future includes all of the present plus the additional circumstances of the future, it is therefore even more complex than the present, and the inherent behavioral limitations on attention make promises that much smaller fragments of the overall situation. This difficulty is further aggravated by the inherent unknowability of much of the future.

As Farnsworth points out, a second level of selection occurs when parties seek to reduce their promises to contract language. It is unlikely that everything coming within the sphere of limited attention at the thinking-about-it stage will even be remembered when the time comes to reduce it to promissory communication. And even to the extent it is remembered numerous barriers stand in the way of its being expressed. Expression itself is a form of narrowing things down, of selecting a focus a limited aspect of a situation. (Consider, for example, how much of specification of planning inevitably fails to include all the aspects upon which the parties have focused their minds. As Farnsworth put it:

> [A] second process of selection occurs at the initial stage. Instead of attempting to reduce all of their expectations to contract language, the parties again confine their "limited attention" to a limited number of expectations selected as particularly suitable for inclusion in the contract.[8]

Finally, all planning is complicated by what Professor Fuller describes as "tacit assumptions." These lie "somewhere between the superficial layer of consciousness and the dark inner recesses of the human psyche probed by the psychoanalysts." His example of the absent-minded professor reading a book as he steps out of the office demonstrates well what he means by tacit assumptions: the professor assumes that the hall floor is still there, although consciously he never gives any thought to the matter.

Tacit assumptions are as important in contract planning as they are in any other human behavior. Just as people constantly make tacit assumptions while they are eating, driving, playing football, operating a computer, or making love, so too they make tacit assumptions when they are planning contractual relationships.

In light of the foregoing complexities any description of the planned portion of a contract must necessarily be a description of an ideal that actual contract planning may approach but certainly never achieve. That ideal is the complete and exact mapping of all "territories to be," totally understood in precisely the same way by all parties with all details in sharp conscious focus at the same time, with all being entirely unaffected by anything external to that mapping, including tacit assumptions of the parties. Such an ideal is as unobtainable as the Holy Grail.

4. *Performance Planning and Risk Planning*

Parties enter contracts to achieve particular known goals at the expense of incurring particular known costs. These particular goals and costs may or may not be planned specifically at the time of making a contract. For example, one goes to a doctor for an examination knowing that the doctor's fee will have to be paid, but often not knowing just what the fee will be. Goals and costs of this nature are central to party purposes in making the

---

the situation actually perceived, *i. e.*, to which the senses have given an already limited attention, is further narrowed in the statement: "See that woodpecker on the tree trunk.") In addition, the kind of expression involved in promissory behavior is not total recall, but is limited by the purposes sought to be achieved. Both consciously and unconsciously this causes a further narrowing of the emanations of communication. Moreover, it takes work to communicate, and humans often sacrifice work in favor of leisure; all of us are in some

measure lazy draftsmen. Thus, in moving from the overall operative situation to expression of promise, a constant narrowing and elimination occurs.

8. Farnsworth, Disputes Over Omission in Contracts, 68 Colum.L.Rev. 860, 869–70 (1968). One must be careful with this excellent article, as Farnsworth's discussion of this kind of human fact is closely intertwined with sophisticated treatment of legal doctrines which are filled with confusing fictions.

contract, and planning for them can usefully be called performance planning. A shorthand way of identifying performance planning is to ask: Will what is planned almost certainly have to be carried out if this contract is to go through to a successful conclusion as planned? An affirmative answer identifies performance planning.

Like any other human activity, engaging in contractual behavior involves risks of loss. Sometimes dealing with risks of loss is the central purpose of the contract, as in the case of insurance. Where this is the case, planning for those risks is performance planning. In many circumstances, however, risks of loss exist which are peripheral to the main purposes of the parties in making the contract in the sense that the contract may be carried to a completely successful conclusion without the cost of such loss ever being incurred. Planning for such risks can usefully be distinguished from performance planning and called risk planning. A shorthand way of identifying risk planning is to ask: Is this contract likely to go through to a successful conclusion without what is being planned having to be carried out? An affirmamtive answer identifies risk planning as that term is used here.

The questions at the end of each of the two preceding paragraphs are not always easy to answer. Just as certainty and uncertainty are part of a single spectrum, so are performance and risk planning. Some risk hovers about even the most certain of human events including the most certain performance planning of contracts, and risk planning *can* often be argued to be central to party purposes. Nevertheless, with these limitations kept in mind, separating the concepts of performance planning and risk planning can be immensely helpful in enhancing understanding of effective contract planning. This is particularly true respecting lawyer functions in contract planning, to which we turn in the next section.

LAWYER FUNCTIONS: THE PROCESSES OF PERFORMANCE AND RISK PLANNING

Many a contract is entered into and carried to some kind of a conclusion without having passed before the eyes of any lawyer. Others may involve massive input by lawyers at planning or other stages. Thus it is possible here to do no more than point out the potential functions of the lawyer in contract planning—administering the agreement process and administering contract performance. This leaves open questions of when those functions are fulfilled by lawyers and when by others. The functions are summarized by the following chart.

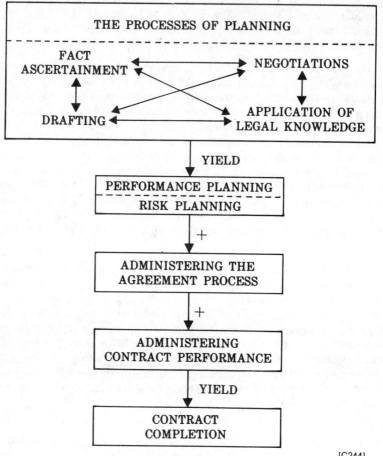

[C244]

Since this is an Article on planning, it will follow the lawyer functions only as far as administering the agreement process, omitting any direct consideration of administering contract performance.

A lawyer engages in four processes in risk and performance planning —ascertaining the facts, negotiation, drafting, and application of legal knowledge. Performance planning and risk planning lend themselves fairly readily to separate treatment, but the four processes constituting them do not. Each of those processes is interlinked with each of the others, and it is virtually impossible to carry out one without carrying out aspects of the others. Nevertheless, each contains a nucleus distinguishing it from the others. The following sections focus on both the nucleus and the interplay with the other processes.

Ascertaining the Facts

The first process to be initiated in contrct planning is ascertaining the facts. The lawyer must determine two distinct, albeit related, kinds of facts in preparation for drafting any contract transaction or relation. One type encompasses the planning goals of the parties: what is it they seek?

The other type encompasses the factual matrix in which the parties' planning goals occur: how will the parties achieve what they seek? Simplistic, but useful, labels for these are, respectively, "goal facts" and "means facts." Thus, for example, if a client asks a lawyer to draft an agreement respecting a business joint venture, the lawyer must ascertain what the client seeks in the way of return, such as allocation of profits—a goal fact. The lawyer must also ascertain what each joint venturer will contribute—both a means fact and a goal fact, not only because in exchanges one person's goal is another person's means, but also because a cost to a party is a "negative" goal, not one desired, but one put up with as necessary to the achievement of other goals. Typically, however, the lawyer must also ascertain much more than goal and means facts as they exist in the minds of the parties if he is to lend realism to the prospects for their realization. Thus, for example, in a joint venture, if one of the other parties is to put up $100,000 cash and a $500,000 line of credit, the lawyer may inquire about the assets and liabilities of that other party to ascertain his capacity to perform, a means fact.

In the process of unearthing both kinds of facts, the lawyer also shapes the facts; he is not simply a computer-like collector of information. This is most obvious respecting the goal facts; the very process of asking a client to explain goals is a shaping process. Often, however, the means facts are also shaped by the lawyer's questions, since focus on them may lead to developing new means, as where a lawyer uncovers shortcomings in prior perceptions of economic reality. These changes in means facts or in the client's perception of them often, of course, change goal facts as well.

Since the lawyer is doing something more in ascertaining the facts than simply ingesting pre-existing and entirely choate information, it is obvious that simply by asking questions he is beginning the representation of his client. He needs, therefore, to be alert, even at this early stage of representation, to possible conflicts of interest among the parties to the contract, conflicts which either preclude his representing everyone, or at least require full notice.

As with other aspects of the planning processes, the ascertainment of facts is a continuing process never safely to be forgotten in any part of planning. While the major portion of the facts may be dug out when the lawyer is first presented with a request to draft a contract, if he sets about his drafting intelligently and diligently he will soon discover that in all but the most routine transactions he does not know everything he needs to know. Moreover, as he acquires more insight into the proposed contract, he will see additional lines of inquiry to be made as he proceeds with the work of specifying the contract. His ignorance is no reflection on his competence; quite the opposite, it is a sign that he is performing an important function. His quest for information may well reveal that inadequate planning has taken place which may still be remediable without serious difficulty, or at least with less difficulty than if discovered later.

Revelation by the lawyer of inadequate performance planning may not bring joy to the client's heart, and the lawyer must be prepared for negative as well as affirmative reactions. A refusal by the client to plan more carefully may or may not be in harmony with the client's real interests. Precise specification of parts of the relationship may be impossible or undesirable for a variety of reasons. Such specification may be too costly (in money or time), or it may jeopardize the prospective relationship between the parties. For example, a couple about to marry may fear the possibly disruptive effect of arms-length negotiations required for specification of performance planning. On the other hand, nonspecification resulting from inadvertence may be undesirable. Examples of that, of course, constitute much of the material in basic contracts casebooks.

Clients may react differently to advice regarding inadequate performance planning than they do to advice regarding inadequate risk planning. The often negative response to the latter may be, as Macaulay points out, a reaction against what is viewed as excessive lawyer concern for remote risks —a concern the client sees as threatening the deal itself. Obviously, discovery of either type of omission calls for the lawyer to be tactful, although not so tactful as to neglect to protect his client's interests properly—in short, on occasion he will be walking a knife edge.

Negotiation

Two law teachers who conducted a course for third year law students in simulated negotiation observed that because few law students have engaged in extensive legal negotiation and few have had much experience in representing the interests of others, reading descriptions of negotiating technique is pointless. Although this observation is a less than accurate over-statement, it would certainly be accurate as to any summation of negotiation—its techniques, its psychology, its pervasiveness—short enough to include in an Article of this nature. Accordingly, no such summation will be made, but rather merely a suggestion that there is indeed merit in reading about negotiation and a reminder that negotiation is conducted in a constant interplay with the other three planning processes: fact ascertainment, drafting, and application of legal knowledge.

Drafting: Reducing Planning to Media of Mutual Communication

Certain common sense principles govern drafting of contractual communications. These principles include paying attention to audience and environment and following certain practices in organizing and composing the contract. Only constant practice will make anyone into a first-class draftsman, but an understanding of these basic principles can help make practice a more effective teacher.

1. *Audience*

As Dickerson points out,[9] one of the main elements of the communication process is the audience to which communication is addressed. All too many contracts are drafted with complete disregard of the audience likely to read them. In most contracts which stay out of serious trouble, and that is most of them, the audience that will actually deal with the contract is not one of lawyers. Rather, the audience consists of people who need the contract documents in order to know what they are expected to do and what they can expect from others.

In more complicated transactions, such as a contract for constructing a large office building, numerous types of personnel may need to know what

9. F. Dickerson, Fundamentals of Legal Drafting 19 (1965) [hereinafter cited as Dickerson, Drafting].

they are expected to do and what they can expect from others. In such cases there are likely to be numerous other communications following the execution of the contract documents. In a construction contract such communications may range in scope from an overall building schedule prepared by the contractor's main office down to an oral direction given by a foreman. At least part of the contract documents themselves may therefore be addressed only to one or a few experts, who in turn will restate the expectations described therein in a form usable by others. In such circumstances, it is, of course, the few experts who are the audience to whom the contract drafter must successfully communicate. Dickerson gives a good statutory example of this—taxation of individual income under the Internal Revenue Code. The Code itself is neither addressed to nor often read by the people who pay taxes. Information needed by taxpayers is instead communicated to them through such methods as instructions to Form 1040, Form 1040 itself, or through accounting or legal advice. The statute can, therefore, be drafted very differently from the form it would have to take were it necessary for most taxpayers to understand it directly. When similar stages of communication are needed in contracts, the nature of the audience is affected, and with it the drafter's task.

Since any contract may run into difficulties involving intervention of lawyers, judges, and lawyer-like people such as Internal Revenue agents, all contract planning, whether performance planning or risk planning, is potentially addressed in part to such an audience. That fact should never, however, be allowed to obscure the nature of the audience which will have to carry out performance of the contract, nor prevent proper communication to that audience.

2. *Environment*

The written words a drafter directs to the audience are simply part of an overall environment of circumstances surrounding the contract—its beginnings, its life, and its termination, if any. Just as the drafter runs great risks if he ignores his audience, he also runs great risks if he ignores those circumstances and writes as if the contract were occurring in some kind of abstract and generalized vacuum. For example, drafting a supply contract while in a state of ignorance about customs of the particular industry is an act of utmost foolhardiness. Not only do *all* circumstances surrounding the contract determine the meanings his audience will attribute to his words, but they will determine the unplanned parts of the contract as well—parts intimately intertwined with the drafted specificities.

3. *Organizing and Composing*

The actual drafting of the document which becomes the contract instrument involves two interrelated functions: organizing and composing. In fact, the lawyer starts performing both functions when he starts inquiring about the facts and thinking about the legal framework in which the relationship will be operating. For instance, the lawyer who, in an organized fashion, has solicited facts concerning a proposed partnership has already purposely or inadvertently gone a long way in organizing the document which will ultimately emerge.

a. *Organizing:* Statements of principles concerning the organization of contract instruments are likely to be so general as to be useless, or, if specific, inapplicable to many contracts. One general principle, however, is worth always keeping in mind: the best organization of a contract document is that which will lead to the accomplishment of the goals of the client. (Trite, but nevertheless, constantly forgotten.) This generalization simply restates the basic principle of lawyering: the lawyer must constantly urge himself to remember what he is trying to accomplish. Few occupations, with the probable exception of teaching, are as subject to forgetfulness on this point as lawyering.

b. *Composing:* Words used by the drafter should be carefully chosen and arranged to convey with clarity and economy the information he wishes to communicate. A contractual document is not the place to display literary style except active, direct, concise, and, one hopes, graceful use of language. Nor is a contractual document a place to show how much useless legal jargon the drafter has absorbed. *Saids, to wits, thereuntos, aforementioneds,* and *whatsoevers* are the works of ancient devils that must be exorcised if contractual writing is to serve its purpose of clear and concise communication.

Ensuring achievement of clear, concise, and complete communication requires a number of actions of diverse nature. Preceding the writing of the first draft is the creation of an initial drafting plan of organization, normally an outline. After writing the first draft, the lawyer should always revise a process which, if properly carried out, will normally create many revised drafts. Revision is probably the most seriously neglected stage in drafting, whether through lack of prior training, laziness, sloppiness, or perhaps a false pride of authorship.

The next stage of composition (interspersed with revision) is what Dickerson calls the "across-the-board check." Across-the-board checks are made in recognition of the fact that instruments are drafted initially vertically from top-to-bottom and step-by-step. In the across-the-board check, the drafter reviews his work horizontally; that is, he checks individually each item of significance that is repeated. These include definitions, cross-references, individual words of significance, and repetitive subject matter such as all the provisions relating to notice, arbitration, times of payment, and the like. For example, in a contract for the sale of abusiness involving two different banks as lending institutions each with different obligations, the drafter should check the entire instrument to make sure that each bank is correctly referred to at each point. Not only does this process tend to uncover ordinary mistakes, but it may also reveal that in the process of drafting step-by-step the drafter has inadvertently changed the meanings of terms, and with them substantive provisions. Moreover, the horizontal check forces the drafter to look at the work from a series of fresh perspectives that may reveal significant defects in the product of the step-by-step approach.

The next stage of composition is also one many lawyers neglect: having the work reviewed by others. This is a step which should be taken in all but the most minor or routine drafting. Pride of authorship and fear of criticism become the greatest evil if they prevent this step. The best drafted contracts are those reviewed by others. Reviewers are, after all, a trial-run audience. Although they may not be typical of the audience that will use the performance provisions of the contract, they provide at least some check on the success (or lack of it) of the drafter's efforts.

Application of Legal Knowledge

The processes of performance and risk planning discussed thus far require no knowledge of principles or rules of law. But a lawyer, or anyone performing these lawyer functions, can deal wisely with what his client wants only if he has an intimate knowledge of the legal framework or milieu in which the contractual relation will take place. This milieu affects fact ascertainment, negotiations, and drafting—*all* the processes yielding contract planning. It also, of course, affects all of the substantive content of the planning, whether it be performance planning or risk planning. The process is so intertwined in the details of the remainder of this Article and lawyers are so alert to this aspect of their functions that nothing further need be said about it here.

Summarizing briefly, four key processes—ascertainment of facts, negotiation, drafting, and application of legal knowledge—constitute the processes of performance and risk planning of contracts. The application of these processes to the preliminary goals and assessments of costs of the parties results in the final substantive content of the particular contract planning. Equally important, it all also affects the substantive content of the unplanned portions of the contract, although by the very nature of nonplanning this effect tends to be far less evident to all concerned than in the case of the planned portions.

———

[The following is taken from "PROFESSIONAL RESPONSIBILITY: REPORT OF THE JOINT CONFERENCE," 44 American Bar Association Journal 1159, 1160–1161 (1958).]

THE LAWYER AS ONE WHO DESIGNS THE FRAMEWORK OF COLLABORATIVE EFFORT

In our society the great bulk of human relations are set, not by governmental decree, but by the voluntary action of the affected parties. Men come together to collaborate and to arrange their relations in many ways: by forming corporations, partnerships, labor unions, clubs and churches; by concluding contracts and leases; by entering a hundred other large and small transactions by which their rights and duties toward one another are defined.

Successful voluntary collaboration usually requires for its guidance something equivalent to a formal charter, defining the terms of the collaboration, anticipating and forfending against possible disputes, and generally providing a framework for the parties' future dealings. In our society the natural architect of this framework is the lawyer.

This is obvious where the transactions or relationship proposed must be fitted into existing law, either to insure legal enforcement or in order not to trespass against legal prohibitions. But the lawyer is also apt to be called upon to draft the by-laws of a social club or the terms of an agreement known to be unenforceable because cancelable by either party at any time. In these cases the lawyer functions, not as an expert in the rules of an existing government, but as one who brings into existence a government for the regulation of the parties' own relations. The skill thus exercised is essentially the same as that involved in drafting constitutions and international treaties.

The fruits of this skill enter in large measure into the drafting of ordinary legal documents, though this fact is obscured by the mistaken notion that the lawyer's only concern in such cases is with possible future litigation, it being forgotten that an important part of his task is to design a framework of collaboration that will function in such a way that litigation will not arise.

As the examples just given have suggested, in devising charters of collaborative effort the lawyer often acts where all of the affected parties are present as participants. But the lawyer also performs a similar function in situations where this is not so, as, for example, in planning estates and drafting wills. Here the instrument defining the terms of collaboration may affect persons not present and often not born. Yet here, too, the good lawyer does not serve merely as a legal conduit for his client's desires, but as a wise counselor, experienced in the art of devising arrangements that will put in workable order the entangled affairs and interests of human beings.

Following is a hypothetical case involving the preliminary steps in the negotiation of lease agreement. The reader is invited to participate in this negotiation, as an armchair quarterback so to speak, to evaluate (and second-guess) the performance of the lawyers in this transaction. It is hoped that through this simulation the reader may develop some insight into the range of considerations which face the lawyer in the planning process and into the opportunities he or she has for shaping economic arrangements.[1]

Mrs. Mona Leeser is a widow, age 45. Her late husband Lorne was a moderately successful real estate broker who met an untimely end in an accident in 1977. Since that time Mrs. Leeser and her three teenage children have lived comfortably, though not extravagantly, on the income from investments left to her and the children by her husband. Mrs. Leeser has taken some interest in the management of this property but she still relies heavily on her late husband's attorney, Malcolm Serjeant to advise her in most of her business dealings.

The Leeser estate includes a building located in a suburban shopping center. The building is presently vacant. Until recently it had been occupied by a branch of the Vielgeld Finance Company, under a ten year lease which is about to expire. During the last three years of the Vielgeld lease Mrs. Leeser had been receiving a rental of $1000 per month. After payment of taxes and maintenance charges she had been realizing $500 per month net. Mrs. Leeser is most anxious to find a new tenant.

Claude Celler, age 40, is a successful salesman. He has travelled extensively as a representative of several manufacturers of hardware and power tools. Celler has tired of his life as a travelling man. He

---

1. The material in this section is suggested by "The case of the jittery landlady" in Henry Hart and Albert Sacks, The Legal Process (tentative ed., 1958), pp. 213–228.

wants to open a retail store in a suburban area where he can experiment with some novel ideas for merchandising hardware, power tools, and related lines. He envisions his store as a kind of department store for "do-it-yourselfers." Celler has approximately $200,000 of his own capital to invest in this venture. He estimates that this is sufficient, with some additional money from borrowing and trade credit, to allow him to furnish and stock a retail store and still have a margin to cover overhead and operating expenses. However, he knows that he will have to shepherd his dollars carefully during the first year or more of his operation until he builds a clientele. He plans an expansive advertising program and he knows that it will take some time for this to begin paying for itself.

Celler has examined the Leeser property. He is satisfied with its location and with the condition of the building. Since he is inexperienced in this phase of business operation he has retained an attorney, Walter Baron, to represent him in negotiating a lease on the property.

The Leeser-Celler negotiations opened with the following correspondence.

June 2, 1978

Malcolm Sergeant, Esq.

Middletown, U.S.A.

Dear Malcolm:

One of my clients, Mr. Claude Celler, is interested in renting the Leeser building. We. discussed the matter with Mrs. Leeser and she has referred us to you.

Mr. Celler has examined the building and, while it is suitable for his needs, he estimates that it will require an expenditure of at least $20,000 to convert the interior for use as a retail hardware store. He is willing to make this investment if he can lease the building for a twenty-year term. He is, of course, quite willing to pay a rental commensurate with going market rates for long-term rentals in this community.

If your client would be interested in entertaining an offer for a lease of this length I will be pleased to discuss the matter with you at your convenience.

Yours Sincerely,

Walter Baron

Immediately after receipt of this letter Serjeant conferred with Mrs. Leeser. She was pleased at the prospect of obtaining another tenant, but she was disappointed at the vague rental proposal. She informed Serjeant that she was anxious to realize a good return on her property inasmuch as her children were approaching an age where expenses for their education would very likely increase considerably. Moreover she was wary about such a long-term lease. She had heard her husband complain that a combination of increasing taxes and maintenance expenses, and diminishing purchasing power of the dollar, made long-term fixed rental leases a bad bargain, and this had been brought home to her during the last years of the Vielgeld lease. Serjeant replied that there were some alternatives that might be arranged to alleviate these risks, and on that assurance Mrs. Leeser authorized him to conduct further negotiations.

Serjeant then made some inquiries about Celler. He learned that Celler had been highly successful as a travelling salesman; that he enjoyed a good credit rating; that he had no real experience in the operation of a retail business; but that he had been in intimate contact with the retail trade during his years as a salesman.

Serjeant also asked a real estate broker, Alfred Prazer, to examine the Leeser property and assess its merits as a location for a retail hardware store. Prazer informed Serjeant that the building was sound and very well located for a retail establishment. Prazer tempered this evaluation by commenting that values in the older part of the shopping center (where the Leeser Building was located) had been slipping of late, after some new buildings had been erected elsewhere in the center. However, Prazer was of the opinion that this could prove to be a temporary condition since most of the buildings near the Leeser Property were about to be refurbished by a new owner, and the erection of the new buildings could very likely lead to a general expansion of the volume of business in the shopping center as a whole. On balance Prazer felt that the Leeser Building should prove to be a very valuable site for the type of store Celler planned to open.

Fortified with this information, Serjeant arranged to meet with Celler and Baron. Serjeant informed Celler and Baron that Mrs. Leeser was reluctant to enter such a long-term lease as it entailed some risks she did not wish to assume. Celler, on the other hand, was adamant regarding the twenty-year term. He said that he expected to invest considerable money in building a clientele and he wanted to have ample time to realize on that investment if his venture proved successful. The discussion then turned to the subject of the appropriate rental. Baron opened this subject by proposing a gross rental of $1500 per month on the condition that the landlord would bear all costs of maintenance and repair except for any damage caused by intentionally injurious or negligent acts of the tenant. Baron also indicated that his client would entertain alternative proposals regarding the allocation of building expenses such as maintenance, repairs, and real property taxes, but that this would necessitate a lower cash rental since Celler could not commit to more than $1500 per month total for his space costs. Celler made it clear that he was very concerned about his cash flow problems during the start up period of his new venture, and that $1500 per month was all he could commit for space during that period. He was also a little wary of entering a long-term lease under a high fixed rental as he had no assurance that his venture would prove successful or that the shopping center would continue to be an attractive location. Serjeant replied that he would inform Mrs. Leeser of this proposal, but he informed Baron and Celler that he would advise her not to enter a long-term lease at that rental. He reminded Baron and Celler that the fixed rental would throw all the risks of inflation on his client at a time when her personal needs required that her investment income keep pace with the general price level. After discussing these problems for an hour or more, Baron suggested that they adjourn the negotiations until he and Celler could reconsider the matter and see what other proposals they might make. Serjeant agreed and said that he in turn would reevaluate the matter in light of their discussion.

A few days after the conference Baron wrote the following letter to Serjeant.

June 21, 1978

Malcolm Serjeant, Esq.

Middletown, U.S.A.

Dear Malcolm:

Following our meeting on the Celler-Leeser matter I discussed the problem with my client and he has agreed to consider several alternatives to his original proposal of a twenty-year, fixed rental lease. These alternatives are as follows:

(1) An initial 5-year lease at $1500 per month, renewable at lessee's option for three successive 5-year terms at an increasing rental: $1750 per month for the first renewal term; $2000 per month for the second renewal term; $2250 per month for the third renewal term; landlord to pay all maintenance expenses and real property taxes.

(2) A 5-year net lease with the tenant to bear all maintenance charges and real property taxes, at an initial rental of $750 per month, renewable at lessee's option for three successive 5-year terms, the net rental to be renegotiated by the parties at the beginning of each renewal term; in the event the parties cannot reach agreement on the renewal rental, the rent will be set, by arbitration, at the fair rental value of the premises.

(3) A percentage lease with the rental to be based on an agreed percentage of gross sales from the premises.

The first and second alternatives are deemed acceptable by my client, but he much prefers the percentage lease. I concur with him in this judgment. I think it meets his special needs and at the same time probably comes closest to satisfying your client's desire to be protected against inflation and rising costs.

Yours Sincerely,
Walter Baron

Immediately upon receipt of this letter Serjeant conferred with Mrs. Leeser. She was intrigued by the mechanics of the first two proposals but the percentage lease caught her fancy. When she first met Celler she had been much impressed by him and by his plans for a suburban hardware store. As a longtime suburbanite and inveterate "do it yourselfer" she was strongly attracted by Celler's idea and she felt certain that it would prove successful. Moreover, she felt that Celler had the drive and personality to put such a venture across. The idea that she might participate in the success of his business was very appealing. On the other hand, she was fretful that the percentage lease might not produce income adequate to meet taxes and maintenance costs while Celler was getting under way. Moreover, she was troubled by the possibility that Celler might not succeed. Serjeant assured her that he would take these considerations into account in negotiating the lease and she authorized him to pursue the percentage lease proposal.

After his conference with Mrs. Leeser, Serjeant asked Alfred Prazer for some advice regarding the economic feasibility of a percentage lease on the premises. Prazer was hard-pressed to develop an estimate of the potential gross sales at the store, inasmuch as Celler was proposing an operation which was novel to the Middletown area. However, Prazer thought that Celler would need to generate average sales of $20,000 per month in order to make a go of his business, and that if he ran a really successful operation, sales could average as high as $40,000 per month. Prazer also suggested that a rental of from 3 to 5 percent of gross sales would be proper. He based this on a survey by the National Association of Real Estate Boards which showed that the applicable percentage on hardware store leases averaged 4 to 5 percent, while appliance stores paid 3 to 4 percent.

Shortly thereafter the following exchange of correspondence took place.

June 28, 1978

Walter Baron, Esq.

Middletown, U.S.A.

Dear Walter:

Thank you for your recent letter regarding the Celler-Leeser matter. I have discussed your proposals with my client. She is quite interested in exploring the possibility of a percentage lease. I will prepare a preliminary draft of the lease and submit it to you. There are certain provisions I would like to have incorporated in the lease and I have listed these below.

Upkeep

A standard covenant for the tenant to keep and maintain the premises in good repair, and return the premises in the condition received subject only to normal wear and tear.

City Ordinances

A standard covenant for the tenant to keep the building and its uses in compliance with all applicable ordinances.

Taxes

A covenant for the tenant to pay all real property taxes during the lease term.

Assignment and Alteration

A standard covenant restricting the assignment of the premises or any alteration of the premises without the written consent of the landlord.

Casualty Loss

A provision regarding the risk of casualty loss, allowing the tenant to abate the rent pending repair of the damage caused by the casualty, and authorizing termination of the lease in the event the landlord determines not to repair or rebuild.

Default

A forfeiture provision allowing termination of the lease upon default on any lessee's covenant and after 10 days notice of the landlord's intention to terminate.

Bankruptcy

A provision authorizing termination of the lease upon 5 days notice from the lessor in the event the tenant declares bankruptcy or commits an act of bankruptcy.

We have discussed the rental terms with an appraiser and he advised us that 5% of the monthly gross is a reasonable figure for hardware and appliance store leases. Since, however, this is a new and uncertain venture I think it would be prudential for us also to provide for termination of the lease in the event rentals fall below an average of $750 per month after the first two years of operation.

Yours sincerely,
Malcolm Serjeant

July 3, 1978

Malcolm Serjeant, Esq.

Middletown, U.S.A.

Dear Malcolm:

I have your letter of June 28, 1978 and I am most pleased that your client is interested in discussing a percentage lease.

The provisions you suggest for inclusion in the lease are generally acceptable although I think some small revision will be necessary.

(1) The provision restricting lessee's power to alter or remodel will have to be modified to account for my client's plans to convert the building for use as a retail store. Furthermore, it is possible that some small alterations may be necessary from time to time to allow my client to install new equipment, etc. I think we can cure this difficulty by adding a provision that the lessor will not unreasonably withhold consent to a request for permission to make alterations.

(2) If at any time during the first ten years of the lease, the premises are destroyed by casualty and if the lessor elects not to rebuild, the lessee should be given the option of purchasing the site at the then fair market value. My client expects to build a neighborhood clientele and it may be important for him to preserve his interest in the building site against loss by casualty.

(3) I would prefer that the lessee be allowed a more reasonable period, say 30 days, within which to cure defaults on the lease. 10 days is very short notice, especially for minor defaults regarding such items as maintenance or compliance with ordinances.

The proposal of a rental of 5% of gross sales is not acceptable in light of other terms set out in your letter. You have proposed a net lease in which my client will bear the risks of increased maintenance costs and real property taxes. Moreover, your "recapture" proposal effectively provides for a guaranteed net cash rental of $750 monthly after the first two years. Under these arrangements your client will not be sharing in the risks to the same extent as would be the case under a straight percentage lease. Accordingly, we do not feel that she is entitled to receive 5% of gross sales. We feel that 3% would be a more appropriate figure.

Yours sincerely,

Walter Baron

Following this exchange of letters, Serjeant called Baron and arranged for a conference with him and with Celler. A meeting was held on July 28, 1978 at which time the final details of the lease were hammered out. Mrs. Leeser agreed to the terms, and the lease was executed and recorded on August 4, 1978. Celler held his grand opening on October 1, 1978. The Leeser-Celler lease is reported below.

This Lease, made this *4th* day of *August, 1978*, between *129 Prospect Street*, Inc., a corporation, known herein as Lessor, and *Claude Celler*, known herein as Lessee.*

Witnesseth, That the Lessor does hereby lease to the Lessee the premises known as *129 Prospect Street* in the City of *Bison, New York*, and fronting approximately twenty-five (25) feet on *Prospect* Street and being the store space heretofore occupied by the *Vielgeld Finance Company*, for the term of twenty years, beginning the *18th* day of *August, 1978*, to be occupied as a hardware and machine tool store and not otherwise, paying therefor the sum of 3 percent of the gross cash received from sales and money collected on accounts on business done from the leased premises during the first two years of the lease term and 4 percent of the said gross cash received for the last 18 years of the said term, upon the following conditions and covenants:

1. Upkeep

The Lessee shall take good care of the property and its fixtures, and suffer no waste; keep the plumbing work, closets, pipes,

* This sample lease is adapted from a form for a percentage store lease in Belsheim, Modern Legal Forms (Kansas City, 1962), Sec. 5071.

and fixtures belonging thereto in repair; keep the water pipes and connections free from ice and other obstructions to the satisfaction of the municipal and police authorities; and at the end or other expiration of the term deliver up the premises in good order and condition, natural deterioration and damage by fire and the elements only excepted. All alterations, additions, and improvements, except trade fixtures, put in at the expense of Lessee shall be the property of the Lessor and shall remain upon and be surrendered with the premises as a part thereof at the termination of this lease.

2. Statement of Cash Receipts

It is further agreed that the rental shall be paid by the Lessee to the Lessor monthly on the 10th day of each calendar month for the preceding month; and that the Lessee shall furnish to the Lessor a monthly statement of cash register readings of gross cash receipts by the Lessee; and that should the Lessor at any time be not satisfied with the said readings, he may at his own expense audit and check the Lessee's books and reports.

3. City Ordinances

The Lessee shall promptly execute and fulfill all the ordinances of the city corporation applicable to the premises and all orders and requirements imposed by the Board of Health, Sanitary and Police Departments, for the correction, prevention and abatement of nuisances in or upon or connected with the premises during the term, at Lessee's expense.

4. Assignment

The Lessee shall not assign this agreement or underlet the premises, or any part thereof, (except as may be mentioned herein) or make any alteration in the building (except as may be mentioned herein), without the consent of the Lessor in writing; or occupy or permit or suffer the same to be occupied for any business or purpose deemed extra-hazardous on account of fire. Lessor will not unreasonably withhold consent to Lessee's requests for consent to assign, underlet, or alter the premises.

5. Casualty Losses

In case of damage by fire or tornado the Lessee shall give immediate notice to the Lessor, who shall thereupon cause the damage to be repaired forthwith and allow the Lessee a fair abatement or diminution of rental in proportion to the extent to which the premises are untenantable; but if the leased premises or the buildings of which the leased premises are a part, are so damaged as to be unfit for occupancy, the Lessor or Lessee may terminate the lease, in which case the rent shall be paid to the time of the fire or tornado, provided, however, that in the event the Lessor elects to terminate the lease under this provision, the Lessee shall have the option to purchase the premises at their then fair market value, such option to be exercised no later than 30 days following receipt of written notice of the Lessor's intention to terminate the lease.

6. Taxes and Fire Insurance

Lessee shall pay all state, city, and county taxes and special assessments which may be levied on the property.

Lessee shall procure and maintain during the lease term a standard form policy or policies of fire and comprehensive casualty insurance and owner's liability insurance for the benefit of the Lessor. Such policy or policies shall insure the building to its full fair market value, and shall provide for the indemnity of any owner's casualty liability claim owed to any third party as a result of the ownership or maintenance and operation of the premises, to the extent of 5 times the fair market value of the premises. Such policy or policies shall name the Lessor as the insured, and shall be deposited with an escrow agent named by Lessor.

7. Utilities

Lessee shall pay for all water, gas, heat, light, power, telephone, waste disposal, and all other services provided to the premises.

8. Default

Except as provided in paragraph 12 below, in case of default in any of the covenants herein the Lessor may enforce the performance of this lease in any modes provided by law, and this lease may be forfeited at the Lessor's discretion if such default continue for a period of ten days after the Lessor notifies the Lessee of such default and his intention to declare the lease forfeited, such notice to be sent by the Lessor by mail or otherwise to the demised premises; and thereupon (unless Lessee shall have completely removed or cured said default) this lease shall cease and come to an end as if that were the day originally fixed herein for the expiration of the term hereof, and Lessor's agent or attorney shall have the right, without further notice to demand, to re-enter and remove all persons and Lessee's property therefrom without being deemed guilty of any manner of trespass. If, on account of breach or default by the Lessee of any of the Lessee's obligations hereunder, it shall become necessary for the Lessor to employ an attorney to enforce or defend any of the Lessor's rights or remedies hereunder, then, in any such event, any reasonable amount incurred by the Lessor as attorney's fee shall be paid by the Lessee.

9. Bankruptcy

In the event that the Lessee shall become bankrupt or shall make a voluntary assignment for the benefit of creditors, or in the event that a receiver of the Lessee shall be appointed, then, at the option of the Lessor and upon five (5) days' notice to the Lessee of the exercise of such option, this lease shall cease and come to an end.

10. Repairs

It is further agreed that Lessor warrants and represents the building to be in first class condition and in a good state of repair

at the commencement of the lease term and the Lessee hereby covenants and warrants to maintain the same at his expense in good
state of repair and good condition during the term of this lease;
and that there shall be no liabilities on the Lessor, for any upkeep
and repair the need for which is not caused by Lessor's negligence
or breach of warranty; the Lessor agrees to replace any broken
plate-glass windows; the Lessee agrees to paint said store both inside and outside at the beginning of this lease and thereafter as
needed.

11. Recapture of Premises

If after the first two years of this lease, the cash rentals paid
to the Lessor average less than $800 per month for any period of
24 consecutive months, the Lessor may, at its option, terminate
this lease upon 30 days notice to the Lessee. In the event that the
Lessor elects to terminate the lease under this provision, the Lessee shall have the option to purchase the premises at their then
fair market value, such option to be exercised not later than 30
days following receipt of written notice of the Lessor's intention to
terminate the lease.

12. Arbitration

Disputes between Lessor and Lessee regarding paragraphs 1,
2, 4, 5, 6, 7, 10, and 11 shall be arbitrated. For this purpose each
party shall select an arbitrator; and the two arbitrators so selected shall select a third arbitrator. The three arbitrators shall hear
and determine the dispute. Their decisions shall be binding on the
parties, who agree to divide the costs of arbitration equally between them.

Questions

1. Which of the lease provisions represent performance planning by the attorneys?

2. Which of the lease provisions represent risk planning by the
attorneys?

3. Can you think of additional risks for which the attorneys have
not planned or for which they have incompletely planned?

4. In your opinion, is the Leeser-Celler arrangement one which
should be respected and enforced through the legal process? Should,
for example, either of the parties be entitled to some legal remedy in
the event the other party breaches one or more of the terms of the
agreement? If so, specifically what is there about this arrangement
that leads you to believe that it is a legally enforceable arrangement?
List those aspects and elements of the arrangement that you think call
for it to be afforded legal sanction.

––––––

The Uniform Commercial Code Article 2 governs transactions in
personal property, *e. g.*, carbon paper, cars, foodstuffs and other mov-

able consumable goods. As such it is not directly applicable to transactions involving real estate, *i. e.*, land and attached improvements and structures. Is the spirit of the UCC nonetheless present in the following case? Recall in this regard the excerpts from the UCC reprinted at pp. 622 and 647 *supra*.

MUTUAL LIFE INSURANCE CO. OF NEW YORK v. TAILORED WOMAN, INC.

Court of Appeals of New York, 1955.
309 N.Y. 248, 128 N.E.2d 401.

Cross appeals from a judgment, entered February 23, 1955, upon a resettled order of the Appellate Division of the Supreme Court in the first judicial department, which modified, on the law and facts, and, as modified, affirmed a judgment of the Supreme Court, entered in New York County upon a decision of the court after a trial at Special Term (GREENBERG, J.), granting judgment in favor of plaintiff. The modification consisted of reducing the amount of the judgment in favor of plaintiff. Stated findings of fact and conclusions of law contained in the opinion of the court at Special Term were reversed and new findings made by the Appellate Division in lieu thereof.

DESMOND, J. The facts of this controversy, and the issues, are set forth and discussed in the Appellate Division opinion. We will limit ourselves to a statement of our views on the principal questions of law.

Since plaintiff is suing for additional percentage rental under the 1939 ten-year lease of the three lower floors of 742 Fifth Avenue, New York City, it must base its claim on the covenants of that lease. Two only of those covenants are pertinent. We take them up in turn. The 4% percentage rental was to be paid on all sales made "on, in, and from the demised premises". After, by separate leases made in 1945, defendant had taken over from plaintiff part of the fifth floor (and the eighth floor, not involved here), defendant made it a practice to pay commissions, on fur sales made on the fifth floor, to salespeople on the lower floor who sent customers to the fifth-floor fur department. We think it not unreasonable to hold, with the Appellate Division, that such sales were, within the lease's intent, made "from" the main store and so subject to percentage rent. Such sales may be considered "main store" sales, as if a clerk in response to a telephone call took merchandise to a customer's home, and there effected a sale. It would be going too far, though, to hold that all fur sales were made "from" the lower store simply because, as hereinafter more fully explained, the fur department was moved up to the fifth floor after that floor had been "integrated" with the main store.

By the other language (of the 1939 percentage lease) which we find pertinent, the tenant promised that the store it would conduct in the lower three floors would "at all times contain a stock of first class merchandise" and would "be conducted and maintained in a manner substantially similar to the Tenant's present store at #729 Fifth Avenue" (that is, the store across the street from which defendant was moving). That verbiage is to be read with the purpose clause (of that same 1939 lease) which prescribed the sale of all kinds of women's apparel and accessories. Here, again, we agree with the Appellate Division that no more was intended than an agree-ment that there should be conducted, on the three lower floors of 742 Fifth Avenue, under the percentage lease, a woman's clothing shop of the same general character as defendant's store across the street. If plaintiff had desired further restrictions as to kinds of merchandise, etc., it should have insisted on them. Absent fraud or trickery (and the findings properly say there was none), defendant could carry on its business in the way that suited it so long as it did not deviate from those very broad and general lease specifications.

In 1945, defendant, needing more space, bought out a custom-made dress business which had been conducted in part of the fifth floor by an-other concern and made with plaintiff a new lease of that space, at a flat no-percentage rent. Again, the lease terms went no further as to purpose than to state that the added space was to be used for the sale of female wearing apparel and accessories and for workrooms. The fifth-floor custom-made dress department was not successful and was soon discontinued. De-fendant then made such physical changes in the building that two elevators, which had theretofore served the first three floors from inside the main store, now could be, and were, used to carry passengers inside the store not only to and from the first three floors but to and from the fifth floor, also (and the eighth floor, although that is not important here). The re-sult was that the first, second, third and fifth floors were, as the phrase goes, "integrated" into one store fronting on Fifth Avenue and served by elevators reached through the main store from the Fifth Avenue entrances. Formerly, the fifth floor could be reached by the use of two other elevators only, to which elevators entrance was from the side street lobby on the 57th Street side of the building. Then defendant moved its fur department to the fifth floor, and thereafter paid no percentage rent on fur sales.

Trial Term held that plaintiff did not acquiesce in these changes. The Appellate Division held that it did. The question of fact is a close one but, acquiescence or not, we think the undisputed facts forbade a re-covery here by plaintiff of more than the percentage on certain fur sales, hereinbefore described as made on the fifth floor, but "from" the lower floors. There is nothing in the main lease to forbid the moving of the fur department and when plaintiff made the second, or fifth floor, lease, it again failed to include any restrictions as to particular kinds of mer-chandise to be sold in one or the other part of the building. It is clear enough that plaintiff did not contemplate, when it leased the fifth and eighth floors for a flat rental, that the fifth floor would be "integrated" with the lower floors into one store but such lack of foresight does not create rights or obligations. True, the second lease said that it would "not have any effect" on the earlier lease but the effect of the two leases, read together and enforcing both, was that defendant had the right to sell all kinds of women's apparel, etc., in any part of the four floors, so long as no other use was made of the premises. As we see it, defendant merely ex-ercised that right when it moved the fur department. As to changing the elevator doors, if that were a violation of any implied covenants (certainly not of an express covenant) redress could be had by injunction or, perhaps, by the landlord putting the elevator doors back as they had been and charg-ing the expense to the tenant. But such violations (if they were violations) could not result in a liability for additional rent not promised in the lease. Except as to the fur sales to customers sent upstairs, there were no additional sales "on, in or from" the premises covered by the percentage lease, even though certain activities with respect to furs continued to be carried on in the lower store.

In the view we take of the case, it is unnecessary to engage in interesting but unproductive computations or speculations as to whether or not the new "integrated" store actually produced more percentage rent for plaintiff than if the fur department and the elevators had not been changed. It is the fact, though, that plaintiff proved no loss in that respect.

In deciding this case as we do, we are not moving away from the good old rule that there is in every contract an implied covenant of fair dealing (Kirke La Shelle Co. v. Armstrong Co., 263 N.Y. 79, 188 N.E. 163). Defendant, as we see it, was merely exercising its rights. Nor do we reject such authorities as Cissna Loan Co. v. Baron (149 Wash. 386, 270 P. 1022) which penalize unconscionable diversion of business from percentage-lease premises to others. The present case does not fit into that pattern.

The judgment should be affirmed, without costs.

BURKE, J. (dissenting). The defendant is liable for additional percentage rental under the 1939 ten-year lease of the premises 742 Fifth Avenue, New York City, for sales of furs made on the fifth floor, as they were sales made on, in and from the main premises.

This appeal involves conflicting constructions of two leases entered into between the plaintiff and defendant.

The defendant was the lessee under a 1939 lease of three floors with the exclusive use of a Fifth Avenue entrance, an entrance on 57th Street and two passenger elevators. Those premises, known as 742 Fifth Avenue, were leased at a fixed rental, plus 4% of the gross receipts in excess of $1,200,000. "Gross receipts" is defined in the lease as including "all sales . . . on, in or from the demised premises". In the spring of 1945, the proprietor of a retail custom dress business, the tenant of half of the fifth floor at 1 West 57th Street, offered her business for sale. The defendant purchased the custom dress business and thereafter, under a fixed rental lease commencing June 1, 1945, the defendant rented the same space on the fifth floor in the premises known as 1 West 57th Street, New York City, "for the sale, display of all types of wearing apparel accessories, worn or carried by women or misses, and as workrooms, and for no other purpose". Such lease provided (1) that the space on the fifth floor in 1 West 57th Street was to be serviced by the elevators in the 57th Street lobby at the landlord's expense "on business days from 8 A.M. to 6 P.M. except on Saturdays when the hours shall be from 8 A.M. to 1 P.M."; (2) that no alterations could be made without the written consent of the landlord; (3) that failure to require strict performance was not to be deemed a waiver, and (4) that the receipt of the rent with the knowledge of a breach was not to be deemed a waiver. The defendant in a short time altered the fifth floor of 1 West 57th Street, so as to give access through the private elevators of 742 Fifth Avenue.

The plaintiff alleges two causes of action. The first cause of action is based upon the theory that the fur sales were made "on, in or from" the main premises. All of the activities of the defendant from the initiation of the alterations to the actual sales were designed to hold out to the public that the fur department was part of the premises 742 Fifth Avenue. The physical layout, the advertising, the window displays, the storage of the furs, and the use of the main store personnel characterized the fur department as an integral part of the main store operations. The second cause of action seeks damages upon the theory that if fur sales were not made "on, in or from" the main premises, nevertheless, the defendant, in removing the fur department from the main premises, violated express and implied covenants of the main lease against diversion of sales. It is implicit in every percentage rental agreement that the tenant has an obligation to conduct its business with regard for the landlord's interest in the tenant's gross receipts. "A promise may be lacking, and yet the whole writing may be 'instinct with an obligation,' imperfectly expressed". (Wood v. Duff-Gordon, 222 N.Y. 88, 91, 118 N.E. 214; Alexander v. Equitable Life Assur. Soc., 233 N.Y. 300, 306, 135 N.E. 509, 511). Unless a percentage rental agreement is so interpreted, the percentage requirement would have no meaning.

The question to be resolved is whether under the terms of the leases and the proof adduced at the trial, the plaintiff is entitled to recover on one or both causes of action. Both causes of action are well founded.

There is no doubt that the sales were made "on, in or from" the main premises. The evidence shows that the furs were delivered to the basement of the main store, prepared for display there, stored in the basement of the main store, packed and shipped out from the main store premises. The entire fur business was administered and conducted in the Fifth Avenue premises, yet the defendant would have us construe the leases so as to permit it to operate a fur department as part of a main store in a space with an address different from the address set forth in the lease of that space, doing a business with average annual gross receipts of over $600,000, for a fixed rental of $3,800 a year free from the percentage provisions of the main store lease. The leases fail to disclose such an authorization. The 742 Fifth Avenue lease limited the exclusive use of the entrances and elevators to three floors and basement. The 1 West 57th Street lease prohibited alterations without consent, and also prohibited any interference with the premises 742 Fifth Avenue.

We can perceive no distinction between the customer who was sent to the fifth-floor fur department by salespeople on the lower floors, and the customers who responded to the advertisements or displays that proclaimed that the defendant's fur department was located at 742 Fifth Avenue. All of these customers were patrons of the Fifth Avenue Tailored Woman store, and were attracted to that store by the advertisements and window displays using the Fifth Avenue address. Therefore, it necessarily follows that the terms of the lease of 742 Fifth Avenue must apply to all transactions taking place at that address.

Moreover in every contract there is an implied covenant that neither party shall do anything which shall have the effect of injuring or destroying the right of the other party to receive the fruits of the contract. (Kirke La Shelle Co. v. Armstrong Co., 263 N.Y. 79, 188 N.E. 163.) The defendant cannot make a virtue of a violation of the lease. It made alterations without the written consent of the landlord of 1 West 57th Street. It violated the prohibition in paragraph 36 of the 1945 lease that the said lease was not to have any effect on the lease dated June 29, 1939, between the Mutual Life Insurance Co. of New York and the Tailored Woman, Inc. (1) by moving its fur department to the fifth-floor space from a lower floor, and (2) by advertising that the fifth-floor space described in the lease as space in the building known as 1 West 57th Street was located at 742 Fifth Avenue. The consequence of these violations was to bring about the condition wherein the defendant was using a Fifth Avenue address and sales space for the sale of furs at a rental rate of a side-street office salesroom.

Furthermore, under the terms of the 742 Fifth Avenue lease, the defendant agreed to maintain a business substantially similar to that which it had maintained at 729 Fifth Avenue, where the defendant had a fur department. As a result of the removal of the fur department to the fifth floor, the plaintiff was deprived of a substantial portion of the fruits of the contract. By excluding the fur sales from the calculations required by the percentage terms of the lease, the defendant excluded almost 20% of the average gross receipts collected at the premises 742 Fifth Avenue. Such an act constitutes an unreasonable diversion of business from the percentage leased premises to the fixed rental premises.

The intent of the parties as expressed in the two leases was that the fifth-floor space at 1 West 57th Street would be operated independently of the main premises. For example, the landlord by lease restricted the use of the elevators in 1 West 57th Street by providing that they would operate only until 1:00 P.M. on Saturdays and 6:00 P.M. on business days, whereas the elevators in 742 Fifth Avenue were within the absolute control of the defendant and could operate until 6:00 P.M. or later on Saturdays, business days and legal holidays only to the third floor.

The rent fixed for the fifth-floor space reflects the restrictions imposed on doing business in an off-street office salesroom space which is not serviced on Saturday afternoons or on legal holidays. Such restrictions are not incompatible with the use permitted by the 1 West 57th Street lease, i. e., the sale and display of women's wearing apparel. Such uses are commonly so restricted. In this very case the former tenant on the fifth floor was engaged in the women's wearing apparel business. The limitation of the use of the elevators to five and one-half days as well as the necessity of sharing the use of the elevators with the other tenants in 1 West 57th Street make it clear that any permitted diversion of business from the main store was intended to be confined to a five and one-half day operation with all the inconvenience of sharing public elevators. Naturally, these conditions in themselves forbid the transfer of a major department from the main store to the off-street office salesroom.

Since the defendant, in order to avoid the restrictions of the 1 West 57th Street lease, elected, in violation of the provisions of the leases, to operate part of the fifth floor as an integral part of the main premises and to make fur sales on, in and from the main premises, it has subjected the gross receipts collected from these operations to the percentage rental terms of the main store lease. Such a conclusion is supported by the evidence, by a common-sense interpretation of the leases, and by the prevailing law in other jurisdictions. (Cissna Loan Co. v. Baron, 149 Wash. 386, 270 P. 1022; Gamble-Skogmo, Inc., v. McNair Realty Co., D.C.Mont., 98 F.Supp. 440, affirmed 193 F.2d 876; Dunham & Co. v. 26 East State Realty Co., 134 N.J.Eq. 237, 35 A.2d 40.)

The judgment of the Appellate Division should be reversed and the judgment of the Trial Term reinstated.

DYE, FULD, FROESSEL and VAN VOORHIS, JJ., concur with DESMOND, J.; BURKE, J., dissents in an opinion in which CONWAY, Ch. J., concurs.

Judgment affirmed.

Questions

1.   Does the majority hold that the plaintiff should have anticipated this situation and protected himself against it?

2.   Could a good lawyer have guarded against this situation by drafting a better lease (or leases) for the landlord? Draft a clause which would have prevented this situation. Do you think your draft would have been acceptable to either the landlord or the tenant?

3.   Do you think that "the good old rule that there is in every contract an implied covenant of fair dealing," facilitates the making of voluntary arrangements? What risks does such a rule impose on the parties to an agreement?

4.   Did Leeser and Celler deal with the Tailored Woman problem in their percentage lease?

SECTION 32. LEGAL ORDER AND PRIVATE ORDER: THE USE AND NON-USE OF CONTRACT IN PLANNING AND IMPLEMENTING EXCHANGE RELATIONSHIPS

[The following is taken from STEWART MACAULAY,* "NON-CONTRACTUAL RELATIONS IN BUSINESS: A PRELIMINARY STUDY," 28 American Sociological Review 55 (1963). Footnotes are omitted.]

This research is only the first phase in a scientific study. The primary research technique involved interviewing 68 businessmen and lawyers representing 43 companies and six law firms. The interviews ranged from a 30-minute brush-off where not all questions could be asked of a busy and uninterested sales manager to a six-hour discussion with the general counsel of a large corporation. Detailed notes of the interviews were taken and a complete report of each interview was dictated, usually no later than the evening after the interview. All but two of the companies had plants in Wisconsin; 17 were manufacturers of machinery but none made such items as food products, scientific instruments, textiles or petroleum products. Thus the likelihood of error because of sampling bias may be considerable. However, to a great extent, existing knowledge has been inadequate to permit more rigorous procedures—as yet one cannot formulate many precise questions to be asked a systematically selected sample of "right people." Much time has been spent fishing for relevant questions or answers, or both.

Reciprocity, exchange or contract has long been of interest to sociologists, economists and lawyers. Yet each discipline has an incomplete view of this kind of conduct. This study represents the effort of a law teacher to

* **Professor of Law, University of Wisconsin.**

draw on sociological ideas and empirical investigation. It stresses, among other things, the functions and dysfunctions of using contract to solve exchange problems and the influence of occupational roles on how one assesses whether the benefits of using contract outweigh the costs.

To discuss when contract is and is not used, the term "contract" must be specified. This term will be used here to refer to devices for conducting exchanges. Contract is not treated as synonymous with an exchange itself, which may or may not be characterized as contractual. Nor is contract used to refer to a writing recording an agreement. Contract, as I use the term here, involves two distinct elements: (a) Rational planning of the transaction with careful provision for as many future contingencies as can be foreseen, and (b) the existence or use of actual or potential legal sanctions to induce performance of the exchange or to compensate for non-performance.

These devices for conducting exchanges may be used or may exist in greater or lesser degree, so that transactions can be described relatively as involving a more contractual or a less contractual manner (a) of creating an exchange relationship or (b) of solving problems arising during the course of such a relationship. For example, General Motors might agree to buy all of the Buick Division's requirements of aluminum for ten years from Reynolds Aluminum. Here the two large corporations probably would plan their relationship carefully. The plan probably would include a complex pricing formula designed to meet market fluctuations, an agreement on what would happen if either party suffered a strike or a fire, a definition of Reynolds' responsibility for quality control and for losses caused by defective quality, and many other provisions. As the term contract is used here, this is a more contractual method of creating an exchange relationship than is a homeowner's casual agreement with a real estate broker giving the broker the exclusive right to sell the owner's house which fails to include provisions for the consequences of many easily foreseeable (and perhaps even highly probable) contingencies. In both instances, legally enforceable contracts may or may not have been created, but it must be recognized that the existence of a legal sanction has no necessary relationship to the degree of rational planning by the parties, beyond certain minimal legal requirements of certainty of obligation. General Motors and Reynolds might never sue or even refer to the written record of their agreement to answer questions which come up during their ten-year relationship, while the real estate broker might sue, or at least threaten to sue, the owner of the house. The broker's method of *dispute settlement* then would be more contractual than that of General Motors and Reynolds, thus reversing the relationship that existed in regard to the "contractualness" of the *creation* of the exchange relationships.

TENTATIVE FINDINGS

It is difficult to generalize about the use and nonuse of contract by manufacturing industry. However, a number of observations can be made with reasonable accuracy at this time. The use and nonuse of contract in creating exchange relations and in dispute settling will be taken up in turn.

The creation of exchange relationships. In creating exchange relationships, businessmen may plan to a greater or lesser degree in relation to several types of issues. Before reporting the findings as to practices in creating such relationships, it is necessary to describe what one can plan about in a bargain and the degrees of planning which are possible.

People negotiating a contract can make plans concerning several types of issues: (1) They can plan what each is to do or refrain from doing; e. g., S might agree to deliver ten 1963 Studebaker four-door sedan automobiles to B on a certain date in exchange for a specified amount of money. (2) They can plan what effect certain contingencies are to have on their duties; e. g., what is to happen to S and B's obligations if S cannot deliver the cars because of a strike at the Studebaker factory? (3) They can plan what is to happen if either of them fails to perform; e. g., what is to happen if S delivers nine of the cars two weeks late? (4) They can plan their agreement so that it is a legally enforceable contract—that is, so that a legal sanction would be available to provide compensation for injury suffered by B as a result of S's failure to deliver the cars on time.

As to each of these issues, there may be a different degree of planning by the parties. (1) They may carefully and explicitly plan; e. g., S may agree to deliver ten 1963 Studebaker four-door sedans which have six cylinder engines, automatic transmissions and other specified items of optional equipment and which will perform to a specified standard for a certain time. (2) They may have a mutual but tacit understanding about an issue; e. g., although the subject was never mentioned in their negotiations, both S and B may assume that B may cancel his order for the cars before they are delivered if B's taxi-cab business is so curtailed that B can no longer use ten additional cabs. (3) They may have two inconsistent unexpressed assumptions about an issue; e. g., S may assume that if any of the cabs fails to perform to the specified standard for a certain time, all S must do is repair or replace it. B may assume S must also compensate B for the profits B would have made if the cab had been in operation. (4) They may never have thought of the issue; e. g., neither S nor B planned their agreement so that it would be a legally enforceable contract. Of course, the first and fourth degrees of planning listed are the extreme cases and the second and third are intermediate points. Clearly other intermediate points are possible; e. g., S and B neglect to specify whether the cabs should have automatic or conventional transmissions. Their planning is not as careful and explicit as that in the example previously given.

The following diagram represents the dimensions of creating an exchange relationship just discussed with "X's" representing the example of S and B's contract for ten taxi-cabs.

	Definition of Performances	Effect of Contingencies	Effect of Defective Performances	Legal Sanctions
Explicit and careful	X			
Tacit agreement		X		
Unilateral assumptions			X	
Unawareness of the issue				X

Most larger companies, and many smaller ones, attempt to plan carefully and completely. Important transactions not in the ordinary course of business are handled by a detailed contract. For example, recently the Empire State Building was sold for $65 million. More than 100 attorneys, representing 34 parties, produced a 400 page contract. Another example is found in the agreement of a major rubber company in the United States to give technical assistance to a Japanese firm. Several million dollars were involved and the contract consisted of 88 provisions on 17 pages. The 12 house counsel—lawyers who work for one corporation rather than many clients—interviewed said that all but the smallest businesses carefully planned most transactions of any significance. Corporations have procedures so that particular types of exchanges will be reviewed by their legal and financial departments.

More routine transactions commonly are handled by what can be called standardized planning. A firm will have a set of terms and conditions for purchases, sales, or both printed on the business documents used in these exchanges. Thus the things to be sold and the price may be planned particularly for each transaction, but standard provisions will further elaborate the performances and cover the other subjects of planning. Typically, these terms and conditions are lengthy and printed in small type on the back of the forms, for example, 24 paragraphs in eight point type are printed on the back of the purchase order form used by the Allis Chalmers Manufacturing Company. The provisions: (1) describe, in part, the performance required, e. g., "DO NOT WELD CASTINGS WITHOUT OUR CONSENT"; (2) plan for the effect of contingencies, e. g., ". . . in the event the Seller suffers delay in performance due to an act of God, war, act of the Government, priorities or allocations, act of the Buyer, fire, flood, strike, sabotage, or other causes beyond Seller's control, the time of completion shall be extended a period of time equal to the period of such delay if the Seller gives the Buyer notice in writing of the cause of any such delay within a reasonable time after the beginning thereof"; (3) plan for the effect of defective performances, e. g., "The buyer, without waiving any other legal rights, reserves the right to cancel without charge or to postpone deliveries of any of the articles covered by this order which are not shipped in time reasonably to meet said agreed dates"; (4) plan for a legal sanction, e. g., the clause "without waiving any other legal rights," in the example just given.

In larger firms such "boiler plate" provisions are drafted by the house counsel or the firm's outside lawyer. In smaller firms such provisions may be drafted by the industry trade association, may be copied from a competitor, or may be found on forms purchased from a printer. In any event, salesmen and purchasing agents, the operating personnel, typically are unaware of what is said in the fine print on the back of the forms they use. Yet often the normal business patterns will give effect to this standardized planning. For example, purchasing agents may have to use a purchase order form so that all transactions receive a number under the firm's accounting system. Thus, the required accounting record will carry the necessary planning of the exchange relationship printed on its reverse side. If the seller does not object to this planning and accepts the order, the buyer's "fine print" will control. If the seller does object, differences can be settled by negotiation.

This type of standardized planning is very common. Requests for copies of the business documents used in buying and selling were sent to approximately 6,000 manufacturing firms which do business in Wisconsin. Approximately 1,200 replies were received and 850 companies used some type of standardized planning. With only a few exceptions, the firms that did not reply and the 350 that indicated they did not use standardized planning were very small manufacturers such as local bakeries, soft drink bottlers and sausage makers.

While businessmen can and often do carefully and completely plan, it is clear that not all exchanges are neatly rationalized. Although most businessmen think that a clear description of both the seller's and buyer's performances is obvious common sense, they do not always live up to this ideal. The house counsel and the purchasing agent of a medium size manufacturer of automobile parts reported that several times their engineers had committed the company to buy expensive machines without adequate specifications. The engineers had drawn careful specifications as to the type of machine and how it was to be made but had neglected to require that the machine produce specified results. An attorney and an auditor both stated that most contract disputes arise because of ambiguity in the specifications.

Businessmen often prefer to rely on "a man's word" in a brief letter, a handshake, or "common honesty and decency"—even when the transaction involves exposure to serious risks. Seven lawyers from law firms with business practices were interviewed. Five thought that businessmen often entered contracts with only a minimal degree of advance planning. They complained that businessmen desire to "keep it simple and avoid red tape" even where large amounts of money and significant risks are involved. One stated that he was "sick of being told, 'We can trust old Max,' when the problem is not one of honesty but one of reaching an agreement that both sides understand." Another said that businessmen when bargaining often talk only in pleasant generalities, think they have a contract, but fail to reach agreement on any of the hard, unpleasant questions until forced to do so by a lawyer. Two outside lawyers had different views. One thought that large firms usually planned important exchanges, although he conceded that occasionally matters might be left in a fairly vague state. The other dissenter represents a large utility that commonly buys heavy equipment and buildings. The supplier's employees come on the utility's property to install the equipment or construct the buildings, and they may be injured while there. The utility has been sued by such employees so often that it carefully plans purchases with the assistance of a lawyer so that suppliers take this burden.

Moreover, standardized planning can break down. In the example of such planning previously given, it was assumed that the purchasing agent would use his company's form with its 24 paragraphs printed on the back and that the seller would accept this or object to any provisions he did not like. However, the seller may fail to read the buyer's 24 paragraphs of fine print and may accept the buyer's order on the seller's own acknowledgment-of-order form. Typically this form will have ten to 50 paragraphs favoring the seller, and these provisions are likely to be different from or inconsistent with the buyer's provisions. The seller's acknowledgment form may be received by the buyer and checked by a clerk. She will read the *face* of the acknowledgment but not the fine print on the back of it because she has neither the time nor ability to analyze the small print on the 100 to 500 forms she must review each day. The face of the acknowledgment—where the goods and the price are specified—is likely to correspond with the face of the purchase order. If it does, the two forms are filed away. At this point, both buyer and seller are likely to assume they have planned an exchange and made a contract. Yet they have done neither, as they are in disagreement about all that appears on the back of their forms. This practice is common enough to have a name. Law teachers call it "the battle of the forms."

Ten of the 12 purchasing agents interviewed said that frequently the provisions on the back of their purchase order and those on the back of a supplier's acknowledgment would differ or be inconsistent. Yet they would assume that the purchase was complete without further action unless one of the supplier's provisions was really objectionable. Moreover, only occasionally would they bother to read the fine print on the back of suppliers' forms. On the other hand, one purchasing agent insists that agreement be reached on the fine print provisions, but he represents the utility whose lawyer reported that it exercises great care in planning. The other purchasing agent who said that his company did not face a battle of the forms problem, works for a division of one of the largest manufacturing corporations in the United States. Yet the company may have such a problem without recognizing it. The purchasing agent regularly sends a supplier both a purchase order and another form which the supplier is asked to sign and return. The second form states that the supplier accepts the buyer's terms and conditions. The company has sufficient bargaining power to force suppliers to sign and return the form, and the purchasing agent must show one of his firm's auditors such a signed form for every purchase order issued. Yet suppliers frequently return this buyer's form *plus* their own acknowledgment form which has conflicting provisions. The purchasing agent throws away the supplier's form and files his own. Of course, in such a case the supplier has not acquiesced to the buyer's provisions. There is no agreement and no contract.

Sixteen sales managers were asked about the battle of the forms. Nine said that frequently no agreement was reached on which set of fine print was to govern, while seven said that there was no problem. Four of the seven worked for companies whose major customers are the large automobile companies or the large manufacturers of paper products. These customers demand that their terms and conditions govern any purchase, are careful generally to see that suppliers acquiesce, and have the bargaining power to have their way. The other three of the seven sales managers who have no battle of the forms problem, work for manufacturers of special industrial machines. Their firms are careful to reach complete agreement with their customers. Two of these men stressed that they could take no chances because such a large part of their firm's capital is tied up in making any one machine. The other sales manager had been influenced by a law suit against one of his competitors for over a half million dollars. The suit was brought by a customer when the competitor had been unable to deliver a machine and put it in operation on time. The sales manager interviewed said his firm could not guarantee that its machines would work perfectly by a specified time because they are designed to fit the customer's requirements, which may present difficult engineering problems. As a result, contracts are carefully negotiated.

A large manufacturer of packaging materials audited its records to determine how often it had failed to agree on terms and conditions with its customers or had failed to create legally binding contracts. Such failures cause a risk of loss to this firm since the packaging is printed with the customer's design and cannot be salvaged once this is done. The orders for five days in four different years were reviewed. The percentages of orders where no agreement on terms and conditions was reached or no contract was formed were as follows:

1953	75.0%
1954	69.4%
1955	71.5%
1956	59.5%

It is likely that businessmen pay more attention to describing the performances in an exchange than to planning for contingencies or defective performances or to obtaining legal enforceability of their contracts. Even when a purchase order and acknowledgment have conflicting provisions printed on the back, almost always the buyer and seller will be in agreement on what is to be sold and how much is to be paid for it. The lawyers who said businessmen often commit their firms to significant exchanges too casually, stated that the performances would be defined in the brief letter or telephone call; the lawyers objected that nothing else would be covered. Moreover, it is likely that businessmen are least concerned about planning their transactions so that they are legally enforceable contracts. For example, in Wisconsin requirements contracts—contracts to supply a firm's requirements of an item rather than a definite quantity—probably are not legally enforceable. Seven people interviewed reported that their firms regularly used requirements contracts in dealings in Wisconsin. None thought that the lack of legal sanction made any difference. Three of these people were house counsel who knew the Wisconsin law before being interviewed. Another example of a lack of desire for legal sanctions is found in the relationship between automobile manufacturers and their suppliers of parts. The manufacturers draft a carefully planned agreement, but one which is so designed that the supplier will have only minimal, if any, legal rights against the manufacturers. The standard contract used by manufacturers of paper to sell to magazine publishers has a pricing clause which is probably sufficiently vague to make the contract legally unenforceable. The house counsel of one of the largest paper producers said that everyone in the industry is aware of this because of a leading New York case concerning the contract, but that no one cares. Finally, it seems likely that planning for contingencies and defective performances are in-between cases —more likely to occur than planning for a legal sanction, but less likely than a description of performance.

Thus one can conclude that (1) many business exchanges reflect a high degree of planning about the four categories—description, contingencies, defective performances and legal sanction—but (2) many, if not most, exchanges reflect no planning, or only a minimal amount of it, especially concerning legal sanctions and the effect of defective performances. As a result, the opportunity for good faith disputes during the life of the exchange relationship often is present.

The adjustment of exchange relationships and the settling of disputes. While a significant amount of creating business exchanges is done on a fairly noncontractual basis, the creation of exchanges usually is far more contractual than the adjustment of such relationships and the settlement of disputes. Exchanges are adjusted when the obligations of one or both parties are modified by agreement during the life of the relationship. For example, the buyer may be allowed to cancel all or part of the goods he has ordered because he no longer needs them; the seller may be paid more than the contract price by the buyer because of unusual changed circumstances. Dispute settlement involves determining whether or not a party has performed as agreed and, if he has not, doing something about it. For example, a court may have to interpret the meaning of a contract, determine what the alleged defaulting party has done and determine what, if any, remedy the aggrieved party is entitled to. Or one party may assert that the other is in default, refuse to proceed with performing the contract and refuse to deal ever again with the alleged defaulter. If the alleged defaulter, who in fact may not be in default, takes no action, the dispute is then "settled."

Business exchanges in non-speculative areas are usually adjusted without dispute. Under the law of contracts, if B orders 1,000 widgets from S at $1.00 each, B must take all 1,000 widgets or be in breach of contract and liable to pay S his expenses up to the time of the breach plus his lost anticipated profit. Yet all ten of the purchasing agents asked about cancellation of orders once placed indicated that they expected to be able to cancel orders freely subject to only an obligation to pay for the seller's major expenses such as scrapped steel. All 17 sales personnel asked reported that they often had to accept cancellation. One said, "You can't ask a man to eat paper [the firm's product] when he has no use for it." A lawyer with many large industrial clients said,

Often businessmen do not feel they have "a contract"—rather they have "an order." They speak of "cancelling the order" rather than "breaching our contract." When I began practice I referred to order cancellations as breaches of contract, but my clients objected since they do not think of cancellation as wrong. Most clients, in heavy industry at least, believe that there is a right to cancel as part of the buyer-seller relationship. There is a widespread attitude that one can back out of any deal within some very vague limits. Lawyers are often surprised by this attitude.

Disputes are frequently settled without reference to the contract or potential or actual legal sanctions. There is a hesitancy to speak of legal rights or to threaten to sue in these negotiations. Even where the parties have a detailed and carefully planned agreement which indicates what is to happen if, say, the seller fails to deliver on time, often they will never refer to the agreement but will negotiate a solution when the problem arises apparently as if there had never been any original contract. One purchasing agent expressed a common business attitude when he said,

> if something comes up, you get the other man on the telephone and deal with the problem. You don't read legalistic contract clauses at each other if you ever want to do business again. One doesn't run to lawyers if he wants to stay in business because one must behave decently.

Or as one businessman put it, "You can settle any dispute if you keep the lawyers and accountants out of it. They just do not understand the give-and-take needed in business." All of the house counsel interviewed indicated that they are called into the dispute settlement process only after the businessmen have failed to settle matters in their own way. Two indicated that after being called in house counsel at first will only advise the purchasing agent, sales manager or other official involved; not even the house counsel's letterhead is used on communications with the other side until all hope for a peaceful resolution is gone.

Law suits for breach of contract appear to be rare. Only five of the 12 purchasing agents had ever been involved in even a negotiation concerning a contract dispute where both sides were represented by lawyers; only two of ten sales managers had ever gone this far. None had been involved in a case that went through trial. A law firm with more than 40 lawyers and a large commercial practice handles in a year only about six trials concerned with contract problems. Less than 10 per cent of the time of this office is devoted to any type of work related to contracts disputes. Corporations big enough to do business in more than one state tend to sue and be sued in the federal courts. Yet only 2,779 out of 58,293 civil actions filed in the United States District Courts in fiscal year 1961 involved private contracts. During the same period only 3,447 of the 61,138 civil cases filed in the principal trial courts of New York State involved private contracts. The same picture emerges from a review of appellate cases. Mentschikoff has suggested that commercial cases are not brought to the courts either in periods of business prosperity (because buyers unjustifiably reject goods only when prices drop and they can get similar goods elsewhere at less than the contract price) or in periods of deep depression (because people are unable to come to court or have insufficient assets to satisfy any judgment that might be obtained). Apparently, she adds, it is necessary to have "a kind of middle-sized depression" to bring large numbers of commercial cases to the courts. However, there is little evidence that in even "a kind of middle-sized depression" today's businessmen would use the courts to settle disputes.

At times relatively contractual methods are used to make adjustments in ongoing transactions and to settle disputes. Demands of one side which are deemed unreasonable by the other occasionally are blocked by reference to the terms of the agreement between the parties. The legal position of the parties can influence negotiations even though legal rights or litigation are never mentioned in their discussions; it makes a difference if one is demanding what both concede to be a right or begging for a favor. Now and then a firm may threaten to turn matters over to its attorneys, threaten to sue, commence a suit or even litigate and carry an appeal to the highest court which will hear the matter. Thus, legal sanctions, while not an everyday affair, are not unknown in business.

One can conclude that while detailed planning and legal sanctions play a significant role in some exchanges between businesses, in many business exchanges their role is small.

TENTATIVE EXPLANATIONS

Two questions need to be answered: (A) How can business successfully operate exchange relationships with relatively so little attention to detailed planning or to legal sanctions, and (B) Why does business ever use contract in light of its success without it?

Why are relatively non-contractual practices so common? In most situations contract is not needed. Often its functions are served by other devices. Most problems are avoided without resort to detailed planning or legal sanctions because usually there is little room for honest misunderstandings or good faith differences of opinion about the nature and quality of a seller's performance. Although the parties fail to cover all foreseeable contingencies, they will exercise care to see that both understand the primary obligation on each side. Either products are standardized with an accepted description or specifications are written calling for production to certain tolerances or results. Those who write and read specifications are experienced professionals who will know the customs of their industry and those of the industries with which they deal. Consequently, these customs can fill gaps in the express agreements of the parties. Finally, most products can be tested to see if they are what was ordered; typically in manufacturing industry we are not dealing with questions of taste or judgment where people can differ in good faith.

When defaults occur they are not likely to be disastrous because of techniques of risk avoidance or risk spreading. One can deal with firms of good reputation or he may be able to get some form of security to guarantee performance. One can insure against many breaches of contract where the risks justify the costs. Sellers set up reserves for bad debts on their books and can sell some of their accounts receivable. Buyers can place orders with two or more suppliers of the same items so that a default by one will not stop the buyer's assembly lines.

Moreover, contract and contract law are often thought unnecessary because there are many effective non-legal sanctions. Two norms are widely accepted. (1) Commitments are to be honored in almost all situations; one does not welsh on a deal. (2) One ought to produce a good product and stand behind it. Then, too, business units are organized to perform commitments, and internal sanctions will induce performance. For example, sales personnel must face angry customers when there has been a late or defective performance. The salesmen do not enjoy this and will put pressure on the production personnel responsible for the default. If the production personnel default too often, they will be fired. At all levels of the two business units personal relationships across the boundaries of the two organizations exert pressures for conformity to expectations. Salesmen often know purchasing agents well. The same two individuals occupying these roles may have dealt with each other from five to 25 years. Each has something to give the other. Salesmen have gossip about competitors, shortages and price increases to give purchasing agents who treat them well. Salesmen take purchasing agents to dinner, and they give purchasing agents Christmas gifts hoping to improve the chances of making sale. The buyer's engineering staff may work with the seller's engineering staff to solve problems jointly. The seller's engineers may render great assistance, and the buyer's engineers may desire to return the favor by drafting specifications which only the seller can meet. The top executives of the two firms may know each other. They may sit together on government or trade committees. They may know each other socially and even belong to the same country club. The interrelationships may be more formal. Sellers may hold stock in corporations which are important customers; buyers may hold stock in important suppliers. Both buyer and seller may share common directors on their boards. They may share a common financial institution which has financed both units.

The final type of non-legal sanction is the most obvious. Both business units involved in the exchange desire to continue successfully in business and will avoid conduct which might interfere with attaining this goal. One is concerned with both the reaction of the other party in the particular exchange and with his own general business reputation. Obviously, the buyer gains sanctions insofar as the seller wants the particular exchange to be completed. Buyers can withhold part or all of their payments until sellers have performed to their satisfaction. If a seller has a great deal of money tied up in his performance which he must recover quickly, he will go a long way to please the buyer in order to be paid. Moreover, buyers who are dissatisfied may cancel and cause sellers to lose the cost of what they have done up to cancellation. Furthermore, sellers hope for repeat orders, and one gets few of these from unhappy customers. Some industrial buyers go so far as to formalize this sanction by issuing "report cards" rating the performance of each supplier. The supplier rating goes to the top management of the seller organization, and these men can apply internal sanctions to salesmen, production supervisors or product designers if there are too many "D's" or "F's" on the report card.

While it is generally assumed that the customer is always right, the seller may have some counterbalancing sanctions against the buyer. The seller may have obtained a large downpayment from the buyer which he will want to protect. The seller may have an exclusive process which the buyer needs. The seller may be one of the few firms which has the skill to make the item to the tolerances set by the buyer's engineers and within the time available. There are costs and delays involved in turning from a supplier one has dealt with in the past to a new supplier. Then, too, market conditions can change so that a buyer is faced with shortages of critical items. The most extreme example is the post World War II gray market conditions when sellers were rationing goods rather than selling them. Buyers must build up some reserve of good will with suppliers if they face the risk of such shortage and desire good treatment when they occur. Finally, there is reciprocity in buying and selling. A buyer cannot push a supplier too far if that supplier also buys significant quantities of the product made by the buyer.

Not only do the particular business units in a given exchange want to deal with each other again, they also want to deal with other business units in the future. And the way one behaves in a particular transaction, or a series of transactions, will color his general business reputation. Blacklisting can be formal or informal. Buyers who fail to pay their bills on time risk a bad report in credit rating services such as Dun and Bradstreet. Sellers who do not satisfy their customers become the subject of discussion in the gossip exchanged by purchasing agents and salesmen, at meetings of purchasing agents' associations and trade associations, or even at country clubs or social gatherings where members of top management meet. The American male's habit of debating the merits of new cars carries over to industrial items. Obviously, a poor reputation does not help a firm make sales and may force it to offer great price discounts or added services to remain in business. Furthermore, the habits of unusually demanding buyers become known, and they tend to get no more than they can coerce out of suppliers who choose to deal with them. Thus often contract is not needed as there are alternatives.

Not only are contract and contract law not needed in many situations, their use may have, or may be thought to have, undesirable consequences.

Detailed negotiated contracts can get in the way of creating good exchange relationships between business units. If one side insists on a detailed plan, there will be delay while letters are exchanged as the parties try to agree on what should happen if a remote and unlikely contingency occurs. In some cases they may not be able to agree at all on such matters and as a result a sale may be lost to the seller and the buyer may have to search elsewhere for an acceptable supplier. Many businessmen would react by thinking that had no one raised the series of remote and unlikely contingencies all this wasted effort could have been avoided.

Even where agreement can be reached at the negotiation stage, carefully planned arrangements may create undesirable exchange relationships between business units. Some businessmen object that in such a carefully worked out relationship one gets performance only to the letter of the contract. Such planning indicates a lack of trust and blunts the demands of friendship, turning a cooperative venture into an antagonistic horse trade. Yet the greater danger perceived by some businessmen is that one would have to perform his side of the bargain to its letter and thus lose what is called "flexibility." Businessmen may welcome a measure of vagueness in the obligations they assume so that they may negotiate matters in light of the actual circumstances.

Adjustment of exchange relationships and dispute settlement by litigation or the threat of it also has many costs. The gain anticipated from using this form of coercion often fails to outweigh these costs, which are both monetary and non-monetary. Threatening to turn matters over to an attorney may cost no more money than postage or a telephone call; yet few are so skilled in making such a threat that it will not cost some deterioration of the relationship between the firms. One businessman said that customers had better not rely on legal rights or threaten to bring a breach of contract law suit against him since he "would not be treated like a criminal" and would fight back with every means available. Clearly actual litigation is even more costly than making threats. Lawyers demand substantial fees from larger business units. A firm's executives often will have to be transported and maintained in another city during the proceedings, if, as often is the case, the trial must be held away from the home office. Top management does not travel by Greyhound and stay at the Y.M.C.A. Moreover, there will be the cost of diverting top management, engineers, and others in the organization from their normal activities. The firm may lose many days work from several key people. The non-monetary costs may be large too. A breach of contract law suit may settle a particular dispute, but such an action often results in a "divorce" ending the "marriage" between the two businesses, since a contract action is likely to carry charges with at least overtones of bad faith. Many executives, moreover, dislike the prospect of being cross-examined in public. Some executives may dislike losing control of a situation by turning the decision-making power over to lawyers. Finally, the law of contract damages may not provide an adequate remedy even if the firm wins the suit; one may get vindication but not much money.

Why do relatively contractual practices ever exist? Although contract is not needed and actually may have negative consequences, businessmen do make some carefully planned contracts, negotiate settlements influenced by their legal rights and commence and defend some breach of contract law suits or arbitration proceedings. In view of the findings and explanation presented to this point, one may ask why. Exchanges are carefully planned when it is thought that planning and a potential legal sanction will have more advantages than disadvantages. Such a judgment may be reached when contract planning serves the internal needs of an organization involved in a business exchange. For example, a fairly detailed contract can serve as a communication device within a large corporation. While the corporation's sales manager and house counsel may work out all the provisions with the customer, its production manager will have to make the product. He must be told what to do and how to handle at least the most obvious contingencies. Moreover, the sales manager may want to remove certain issues from future negotiation by his subordinates. If he puts the matter in the written contract, he may be able to keep his salesmen from making concessions to the customer without first consulting the sales manager. Then the sales manager may be aided in his battles with his firm's financial or engineering departments if the contract calls for certain practices which the sales manager advocates but which the other departments resist. Now the corporation is obligated to a customer to do what the sales manager wants to do; how can the financial or engineering departments insist on anything else?

Also one tends to find a judgment that the gains of contract outweigh the costs where there is a likelihood that significant problems will arise. One factor leading to this conclusion is complexity of the agreed performance over a long period. Another factor is whether or not the degree of injury in case of default is thought to be potentially great. This factor cuts two ways. First, a buyer may want to commit a seller to a detailed and legally binding contract, where the consequences of a default by the seller would seriously injure the buyer. For example, the airlines are subject to law suits from the survivors of passengers and to great adverse publicity as a result of crashes. One would expect the airlines to bargain for carefully defined and legally enforceable obligations on the part of the airframe manufacturers when they purchase aircraft. Second, a seller may want to limit his liability for a buyer's damages by a provision in their contract. For example, a manufacturer of air conditioning may deal with motels in the South and Southwest. If this equipment fails in the hot summer months, a motel may lose a great deal of business. The manufacturer may wish to avoid any liability for this type of injury to his customers and may want a contract with a clear disclaimer clause.

Similarly, one uses or threatens to use legal sanctions to settle disputes when other devices will not work and when the gains are thought to outweigh the costs. For example, perhaps the most common type of business contracts case fought all the way through to the appellate courts today is an action for an alleged wrongful termination of a dealer's franchise by a manufacturer. Since the franchise has been terminated, factors such as personal relationships and the desire for future business will have little effect; the cancellation of the franchise indicates they have already failed to maintain the relationship. Nor will a complaining dealer worry about creating a hostile relationship between himself and the manufacturer. Often the dealer has suffered a great financial loss both as to his investment in building and equipment and as to his anticipated future profits. A cancelled automobile dealer's lease on his showroom and shop will continue to run, and his tools for servicing, say, Plymouths cannot be used to service other makes of cars. Moreover, he will have no more new Plymouths to sell. Today there is some chance of winning a law suit for terminating a franchise in bad faith in many states and in the federal courts. Thus, often the dealer chooses to risk the cost of a lawyer's fee because of the chance that he may recover some compensation for his losses.

An "irrational" factor may exert some influence on the decision to use legal sanctions. The man who controls a firm may feel that he or his organization has been made to appear foolish or has been the victim of fraud or bad faith. The law suit may be seen as a vehicle "to get even" although the potential gains, as viewed by an objective observer, are outweighed by the potential costs.

The decision whether or not to use contract—whether the gain exceeds the costs—will be made by the person within the business unit with the power to make it, and it tends to make a difference who he is. People in a sales department oppose contract. Contractual negotiations are just one more hurdle in the way of a sale. Holding a customer to the letter of a contract is bad for "customer relations." Suing a customer who is not bankrupt and might order again is poor strategy. Purchasing agents and their buyers are less hostile to contracts but regard attention devoted to such matters as a waste of time. In contrast, the financial control department—the treasurer, controller or auditor—leans toward more contractual dealings. Contract is viewed by these people as an organizing tool to control operations in a large organization. It tends to define precisely and to minimize the risks to which the firm is exposed. Outside lawyers—those with many clients—may share this enthusiasm for a more contractual method of dealing. These lawyers are concerned with preventive law—avoiding any possible legal difficulty. They see many unstable and unsuccessful exchange transactions, and so they are aware of, and perhaps overly concerned with, all of the things which can go wrong. Moreover, their job of settling disputes with legal sanctions is much easier if their client has not been overly casual about transaction planning. The inside lawyer, or house counsel, is harder to classify. He is likely to have some sympathy with a more contractual method of dealing. He shares the outside lawyer's "craft urge" to see exchange transactions neat and tidy from a legal standpoint. Since he is more concerned with avoiding and settling disputes than selling goods, he is likely to be less willing to rely on a man's word as the sole sanction than is a salesman. Yet the house counsel is more a part of the organization and more aware of its goals and subject to its internal sanctions. If the potential risks are not too great, he may hesitate to suggest a more contractual procedure to the sales department. He must sell his services to the operating departments, and he must hoard what power he has, expending it on only what he sees as significant issues.

The power to decide that a more contractual method of creating relationships and settling disputes shall be used will be held by different people at different times in different organizations. In most firms the sales department and the purchasing department have a great deal of power to resist contractual procedures or to ignore them if they are formally adopted and to handle disputes their own way. Yet in larger organizations the treasurer and the controller have increasing power to demand both systems and compliance. Occasionally, the house counsel must arbitrate the conflicting positions of these departments; in giving "legal advice" he may make the business judgment necessary regarding the use of contract. At times he may ask for an opinion from an outside law firm to reinforce his own position with the outside firm's prestige.

Obviously, there are other significant variables which influence the degree that contract is used. One is the relative bargaining power or skill of the two business units. Even if the controller of a small supplier succeeds within the firm and creates a contractual system of dealing, there will be no contract if the firm's large customer prefers not to be bound to anything. Firms that supply General Motors deal as General Motors wants to do business, for the most part. Yet bargaining power is not size or share of the market alone. Even a General Motors may need a particular supplier, at least temporarily. Furthermore, bargaining power may shift as an exchange relationship is first created and then continues. Even a giant firm can find itself bound to a small supplier once production of an essential item begins, for there may not be time to turn to another supplier. Also, all of the factors discussed in this paper can be viewed as *components* of bargaining power— for example, the personal relationship between the presidents of the buyer and the seller firms may give a sales manager great power over a purchasing agent who has been instructed to give the seller "every consideration." Another variable relevant to the use of contract is the influence of third parties. The federal government, or a lender of money, may insist that a contract be made in a particular transaction or may influence the decision to assert one's legal rights under a contract.

Contract, then, often plays an important role in business, but other factors are significant. To understand the functions of contract the whole system of conducting exchanges must be explored fully. More types of business communities must be studied, contract litigation must be analyzed to see why the nonlegal sanctions fail to prevent the use of legal sanctions and all of the variables suggested in this paper must be classified more systematically.

Questions

1. Why might a relationship which is created in a highly "contractual" manner, result in dispute resolution which is not "contractual"? And, why might a relationship which is not very "contractual" in origin lead to highly "contractual" dispute resolution?

2. Of the following types of arrangements, which would you expect to originate in a highly "contractual" procedure?

   a. An agreement for the construction of a skyscraper.

   b. The sale of corporate stock on the New York stock exchange.

   c. The purchase of a Plymouth sedan.

   d. The sale of a house.

   e. The lease of an apartment.

   f. The hiring of employees for a large factory.

   g. The hire of a taxicab.

   h. An agreement regarding the repair of a car (or a stagecoach).

   i. An agreement regarding the repair of an airplane.

3. Do you think that more or fewer exchange relationships would be established if the law insisted that parties make a detailed plan as a precondition to legal protection of the relationship?

4. To what extent does law impose limits on private ordering through contract? To what extent should law encourage private ordering through contract? How best can law facilitate such private ordering?

5. Could the informal, "non-legal," customs and institutions described by Professor Macaulay exist if there were no body of contract law? Or does the existence of such customs and institutions indicate that contract law has lost touch with the realities, and the needs, of commerce?

6. In Section 27.3 *supra*, it was suggested that it is the custom in international trade for the parties to treat contracts as absolutely binding, except as provided otherwise by the terms of the contract. On the other hand, according to Professor Macaulay, in some domestic trades it is taken for granted that the parties will be excused where performance becomes burdensome, regardless of contract terms. What reasons can you suggest to explain this difference between international trade and some domestic trades? (Note that contract practices are conditioned by culture as well as by the needs of commerce. For example, Japanese businessmen, even in foreign trade transactions, often assume that contract obligations are subject to the continuation of circumstances rendering the contract mutually profitable, and that if there are substantial price fluctuations or other changes in economic circumstances, they may insist on cancellation of the contract, or, if it is the other party who is disadvantaged, will accept his cancellation as a matter of course.)

7. In what sense might you view contract as a means for integrating different legal systems? Does the extract from Professor Macaulay, and the section on contract practices in international trade, indicate how custom and contract may be the means to transcend barriers raised by different legal systems, or by the limits of national jurisdiction?

Part Four

LAW AS A PROCESS OF RESOLVING ACUTE SOCIAL CONFLICT: ILLUSTRATIONS FROM LABOR LAW AND THE LAW REGARDING RACIAL DISCRIMINATION

In preceding chapters we have viewed law in terms of certain of its broad social functions—its function of restoring order to society when that order has been disrupted, its function of giving historical continuity and doctrinal consistency to social life, its function of protecting and facilitating voluntary arrangements.[1] To illustrate these functions we have presented certain aspects of a few branches of law —civil and criminal procedure, the development of the doctrine of manufacturers' liability in tort, the law of contract. The selection and classification of materials have been determined primarily by the desire to present crucial problems inherent in our legal system, and perhaps in any legal system—such as the problems posed by an adversary system of pleading and proof, the problems inherent in the comparison of an existing case with previous cases, the problems of providing criteria for the enforcement of promises, and the like.

Our final chapters are somewhat different in nature. The primary materials are drawn from the history of an acute social conflict, the conflict between workers and employers in the United States during the past 100 years. Additional materials are drawn from the history of the law regarding racial discrimination in the United States. Although our primary concern is with the legal response to social conflict, it is the social conflict which throws up the problems for solution. Strikes, picketing, unionization, wages, working conditions, seniority, labor discipline—these are the elements of conflict demanding resolution; each of them has a legal aspect, and the kind of resolution upon which we shall focus is a legal resolution, but the conflict is far broader than a legal conflict and the problems are much more than legal problems. The law as to race relations during these same 100 years also reflects an underlying social conflict, though of a somewhat different character. Introduction of this topic as a counterpoint to the labor law material affords an opportunity to compare and contrast the ways in which law 'and legal institutions responded to different but contemporaneous social conflicts. Moreover, the race relations material affords an especially effective vehicle for exploring aspects of the educational function

1. On the use of the term "function," see
supra, p. 28 ff.

803

of law in shaping mores and attitudes, especially through carefully structured litigation. Also, comparison of the legal strategies of organized labor with those of civil rights organizations demonstrates alternative uses of law as a device to channel social change. Finally, in light of these materials, one may ask, without necessarily answering, "Is it possible for legal techniques for resolving one kind of social conflict, to be transposed and applied in the resolution of a very different kind of conflict?" This comparison and contrast may then afford additional insights into the scope and limits of law.

The purpose of selecting acute social conflicts for analysis in legal terms is threefold. First, it will thereby be possible to view the various elements of the legal system operating together. Not only does the history of labor law throw into sharp relief some of the most crucial questions of civil and criminal procedure, constitutional law, tort, contract, judicial remedies, and other fields of law which we have touched upon earlier, but also it introduces important questions of legislation and administrative law—questions which should not be omitted from any introduction to law for students of the arts and sciences—and in addition it brings in two alternatives to adjudication as a mode of settlement of conflict, namely, collective bargaining and arbitration. Thus a study of labor law makes it possible to see a very large range of legal techniques and legal ideals in operation more or less at once and more or less as a complex unity.

The study of race relations law also affords insights into legal institutions and processes affecting social conflict and social change, though it is somewhat more difficult to draw firm conclusions as to the efficacy of law in limiting, channeling, or resolving social conflict regarding race relations.

Second, by studying the law's response to an acute social conflict we are brought to a fuller awareness that it is one important function of law to help resolve acute social conflicts, that is, conflicts between groups or classes as contrasted with conflicts between individuals.

Third, legal processes of resolving acute social conflicts almost inevitably involve a conscious effort to influence the moral and legal conceptions and attitudes of the community. If two neighbors quarrel over the boundary line dividing their respective parcels of land, a court to which the quarrel is brought is not apt to express its concern with their beliefs and attitudes regarding property or regarding each other or regarding the community, or its concern with the community's beliefs and attitudes; the court's concern with these matters, and the law's concern with these matters, will usually be implicit rather than explicit in such a case. The presence of acute social conflict, however, makes it virtually impossible for courts, legislatures or other official bodies to act without more or less explicit reference to the influence of their acts upon the way the people involved, and the community in general, think and feel. If the quarrel over the boundary line involves, for example, a restrictive racial covenant, there will almost inevitably be involved a question of the effect of any decision upon the moral and legal values of the community, and not merely a question of the definition and delimitation of the rights and interests of the parties.

Of course it is a function of law generally to influence the moral and legal ideas and attitudes of the community, including those of the litigants and other participants in a judicial proceeding. The law of contract not only enables people to enter into contracts and to give remedies for breach of contract but also inculcates into the minds of people the idea that it is honorable to keep one's promises. Without a law of contract it would be harder to sustain that idea—at least in a society in which law is respected. Similarly, the law of procedure helps to teach people the difference between fairness and arbitrariness in the resolution of controversies; this is one of its characteristic tendencies, one of its latent functions, at least, if not one of its manifest functions or purposes. Likewise it is a social function of the law of torts to teach people what standards of care they ought to observe and what their obligations are toward those whom they injure. Criminal law also provides numerous examples of the educational role of law; so do constitutional law and other branches of public law.

That it is a function of law in general to help educate and improve the morality of the people is an idea at least as old as Justinian's Digest.[2] This idea was almost lost, however, in the age of rugged individualism. It came to be assumed by many that the persons to whom law is addressed, so to speak, the *subjects* of law, are independent, mature adults whose moral and legal consciousness has already been formed. "Legal man" was conceived as the counterpart of "economic man," a man of prudence who stands or falls by his own claim or defense and is presumed to have intended the natural and probable consequences of his acts. The task of law was seen (and still is seen by many) as *only* that of enforcing existing rights and duties, or defining and delimiting (or "balancing") interests, and not as including that of shaping people's concepts of their rights and duties and interests.

Such a concept of law is appropriate to a society of independent businessmen, whose legal relationships are expressed in terms of contract and ownership. It is hardly appropriate to a society of interdependent groups and organizations, whether economic, political or so-

2. The Digest, published in 533 A.D., is one of three works comprising the Corpus Juris Civilis of the Byzantine Emperor Justinian. The other two are the Institutes, a short educational handbook, and the Codex, a codification of Imperial constitutions. The Digest, is a collection of excerpts or fragments from earlier jurists arranged systematically. In the opening paragraphs of the Digest, the mission of the jurist is compared with that of a priest. *Cf.* A. P. d'Entreves, Natural Law (London, 1951), p. 19.

cial. "Where, today, are the economically self-sufficient households and neighborhoods, where is the economically self-sufficient, versatile, restless, self-reliant man, freely making a place for himself by free self-assertion . . . ?" asked Roscoe Pound in 1930. "Where, indeed, but in our legal thinking in which it is so decisive an element." [3]

In a society of interdependent groups, whose internal and external relationships are founded not only on power but also on ideas, attitudes, loyalties, values, it is essential that law be understood as an important vehicle for shaping these intellectual and moral factors, and not merely as a reflection of them.

Such an idea of law involves substantial dangers. The lawmaker or judge or administrator who conceives it as his or her task to remake the moral and legal consciousness of the community may do far more harm than good. The concept of law as a parent or teacher presupposes a concept of legal man as a child or youth to be disciplined and educated. These are concepts implicit, and to a certain extent explicit, in authoritarian systems, in which the state consciously uses law as a means of training people to fulfill the enormous responsibilities imposed on them.[4]

Yet whether we be totalitarians or democrats, the fact is that in the past generation a whole new set of social relationships has been created in virtually all the major cultures of the world, and that law has played a dynamic role in the creation of these social relationships, not only by defining new policies, establishing new sanctions, and creating channels for new kinds of activities, but also by substantially influencing, and indeed in many instances reshaping, people's beliefs and attitudes on important social issues.[5]

It is the failure to utilize legal institutions to create new forms and new concepts of cooperation between labor and management which is the most discouraging aspect of the early history of labor law in America. The emergence of acute social conflict in labor relations in the period after the Civil War was probably inevitable. Was it inevitable, however, that the courts should respond by exercising their equity jurisdiction to enjoin strikes and picketing even in the absence of violence? Clearly not in all cases, for not all courts so responded. Yet what were the alternatives? It was tempting to invoke equity

3. Roscoe Pound, "The New Feudal System," Kentucky Law Journal, Vol. 19, p. 6 (1930).

4. See Harold J. Berman, Justice in the U.S.S.R. (Cambridge, Mass., rev. ed., 1963), Part III. See also, footnote 33, p. 34 *supra*.

5. Dicey saw this function of law very clearly: "The true importance of laws lies far less in their direct result than in their effect upon the sentiment or convictions of the public." A. V. Dicey, Lectures on the Relation between Law and Public Opinion in England during the Nineteenth Century (2nd ed., London, 1914), p. 42. Cf. also: "Laws are . . . among the most potent of the many cases which create legislative opinion; the legislation of collectivism . . . has itself contributed to produce the moral and intellectual atmosphere in which socialist ideas flourish and abound." *Id.*, pp. 301–302.

powers in order to prohibit conflict and disorder—though the prohibition could not be effective in the long run. It was tempting to maintain the consistency of tort doctrine—though the doctrine had been developed for quite different social situations. It was tempting to protect freedom of contract—though the inequality of bargaining power between the employer and the individual worker made contract a caricature. The alternative was to attempt to use the equity powers of the court to bring labor and management together, to frame a positive decree requiring negotiation and establishing a framework of cooperation. This, of course, is more easily said than done. In many instances it could not possibly have worked, for passions ran too high. Even where it might have worked it required more imagination than most of our judges commanded.

The inadequacy of traditional doctrines of crime and tort and contract, and traditional remedies of fine, damages, and negative injunctions, to meet the problems raised by the acute social conflict between workers and employers in the last half of the 19th and the first third of the 20th centuries, is connected with the inadequacy of then prevailing concepts of the functions of law. If the economic, social and psychological problems of an industrial labor force were to be met, it was necessary that law be used to help create new sentiments and convictions on the part of the participants in labor disputes as well as on the part of the public. The inadequacy of the judicial response to this challenge led eventually to important legislative restrictions upon the powers of the judiciary in labor cases, as well as to the creation of a system of administrative regulation of collective bargaining. It is an explicit function of the newer labor legislation, and of the administrative controls which it established, to encourage new attitudes of cooperation between labor and management.

The interaction of legislation, administration, and adjudication is a crucial element in the legal response to the problems of labor-management relations. The Norris-La Guardia Act of 1932, the National Labor Relations Act of 1935, and the Taft-Hartley Amendments of 1947, are not isolated measures but aspects of a single process in which the courts and the executive also have played and continue to play integral parts. In laying down the conditions under which injunctions may or may not be granted in labor disputes, for example, the legislature has built on past judicial decisions and at the same time has laid a foundation upon which future judicial decisions are to be built. In establishing a framework of investigation of complaints of unfair labor practices, the legislature has set the larger framework within which the administrative agencies must act, and hence the legislature, too, in a real sense administers.

Legislation, administration and adjudication do not exhaust the types of legal processes available for resolution of labor-management problems. Collective bargaining is another such process. Here the role of legal officials is confined to determinations of what is the "good faith" in bargaining required by the N.L.R.A., what are unfair practices by labor or by management, and similar questions; the bargaining itself is carried on by the parties.

Finally, the arbitration of grievances arising under collective bargaining agreements is one of the most interesting and important legal innovations for resolution of disputes between labor and management. To what extent should the arbitrator act like a judge called upon to interpret a contract which the defendant is alleged to have broken? What difference should it make, if any, that workers and management must go on living together after the grievance is disposed of? Should the arbitrator assume the function of educating the parties as to their mutual responsibilities toward each other? To what extent are the answers to such questions as these conditional upon the type of industry involved, the stability of labor relations within it, and the maturity of the union and of management?

Woven through the materials on legislation, adjudication, administration, and arbitration in labor law are excerpts dealing with the application of the same or related legal means to the task of improving race relations, or, at least, ending racial discrimination. These materials are very tentative in that they raise preliminary questions regarding the likelihood that experience gained in legal responses to one type of social conflict may provide a basis for effective legal action regarding another type of social conflict. The answers to those questions are not yet known.

With the study of labor arbitration our treatment of the nature and functions of law comes to an end—at a point full circle from where it began, but on a different level. An analysis of the limitations and potentialities of labor arbitration is illumined by, and illumines, the earlier analysis of the limitations and potentialities of adjudication as a process of resolution of disputes.

———

Much material in this part is taken from ARCHIBALD COX, CASES ON LABOR LAW, 3rd ed. (Brooklyn, N. Y. 1953) and from ARCHIBALD COX and DEREK C. BOK, CASES ON LABOR LAW, 5th ed. (Brooklyn, N. Y., 1962), 7th ed. (Mineola, N. Y., 1969), and 8th ed. (Mineola, N. Y., 1977) co-authored by Robert A. Gorman. The authors are respectively, Professor of Law, and Professor of Law and President of Harvard University, and Professor of Law, University of Pennsylvania.

Chapter 9

THE ORIGINS OF AMERICAN LABOR LAW

SECTION 33. THE RISE OF THE LABOR MOVEMENT

[The following is taken from COX and BOK, CASES ON LABOR
LAW (7th ed.), pp. 9–13, 14–16, 18–19, 20–22. Footnotes are omitted.]

The years between the Civil War and World War I were the time of
building industrial empires. In 1865 the technological developments of the
industrial revolution invited large scale enterprise. Textiles had been on
a factory basis since the 1820's and in 1855 the Bessemer process had become commercially feasible. Vast natural resources—timber, coal, oil, iron
ore, copper and precious metals—awaited exploitation. The expansion of
transportation facilities opened wider markets. The profits of the wartime
years supplied ample capital while quantities of workers stood waiting in
Europe and Asia to be carried at bargain rates to the railroad camps, mines
and mills. Gould, Vanderbilt, Harriman and James J. Hill built their railway empires; Rockefeller organized the Standard Oil Company; Armour
& Company was formed; and under the guiding hand of Andrew Carnegie
the billion dollar United States Steel Corporation came into existence.

The statistics document what the names recall. Between 1860 and 1910
the amount of capital invested in manufacturing increased twelvefold;
the annual value of manufactured products increased fifteenfold; and
5,500,000 wage earners came to be employed in industry instead of 1,500,000.
The statistics also reveal the rising importance of large scale industrial
establishments and the increasing concentration of economic power, which
seem scarcely to have been slowed by the passage of the Sherman Act and
the "trust-busting" campaigns of Theodore Roosevelt. Between 1899 and
1909 the number of manufacturing establishments increased approximately
30 per cent; the number of wage earners increased 40 per cent in the same
period. Not only were more workers becoming employed in each industrial
establishment but the very large establishments were coming to occupy an
increasingly important position and were employing a larger proportion of
the workers. In 1904 establishments whose annual product was valued in
excess of $1,000,000, already employed 25 per cent of the wage earners and
produced 38 per cent of the total annual products. A decade later the percentages had risen to 35 per cent of the wage earners and 48 per cent of
the total annual product.

The growth of the large corporation had many significant consequences
for workers, two of which require mention here. First, it put an end to
the personal relationship between employer and employee which was possible in small establishments. Second, the bargaining power of the individ-

ual worker dwindled until individual bargaining became an empty slogan. "A single employee was helpless in dealing with an employer. He was dependent ordinarily on his daily wage for the maintenance of himself and family. If the employer refused to pay him the wages that he thought fair, he was nevertheless unable to leave the employ and to resist arbitrary and unfair treatment. Union was essential to give laborers an opportunity to deal on equality with their employer."

Concurrently with the growing industrialization of the country other conditions developed which stimulated the rise of a strong labor movement and profoundly influenced its form. Labor unions, whether formed along craft or industrial lines, depend upon group action, and group action is impossible unless the members of the group have a keen enough awareness of their common interest to give them internal solidarity. Before the Civil War there was no class consciousness on the part of American wage earners. Under the social and economic conditions then prevailing a wage earner one day might be a property owner or entrepreneur a few months later. To the West the abundance of free land offered proprietorship to anyone willing to undergo the hardships of frontier life. Everywhere the extraordinarily rapid growth of industry and commerce held out opportunities for personal advancement. Workers tended to identify themselves with the propertied classes and when times were bad, to join with farmers and other debtors in support of political movements seeking to restore freedom of opportunity instead of forming economic organizations concerned with the interests of employees. Since the tide of immigration brought workers of many different nationalities to America, it gave the labor force a heterogeneity which also helps to explain the absence of class feeling before the Civil War. In the post-war period, however, conditions became more favorable to unionization.

Second, the increase in the population and the disappearance of the frontier hastened the growth of cities. As urban dwellers, workers became completely dependent on their wages whereas earlier they were able to lessen the impact of wage cuts or layoffs by keeping small gardens and perhaps a few cows. City life also increased social intercourse; more and more workers learned the strength of their economic ties with other employees in the same occupation. Thus, urbanization proved conducive to the growth of labor unions.

Third, the changed character of the immigrants who began to arrive after 1880 stimulated organization of the skilled workers. The immigrants formed a growing reservoir of unskilled labor which was a threat to the craftsmen both because it increased the competition for existing jobs and because it offered constant encouragement to employers to adapt jobs to the capacities of the semi-skilled or unskilled. In self-protection the skilled employees sought to secure "job ownership" and control over access to their trades. But although immigration encouraged organization of the skilled workers it discouraged unionization on a wider basis. Racial antagonisms, language difficulties, and differences in custom and point of view continued to separate the unskilled workers. "The fact that many of the newer immigrants, arriving in the United States with backgrounds of racial or class oppression, had developed habits of docility rendered easier the introduction of employer policies in which there was little place for collective dealing and labor organization and at the same time sincerely convinced many of the trade-union leaders that to attempt to organize the unskilled was, save in exceptional cases, a task of insurmountable difficulty."

Fourth, the nucleus of a strong trade union movement already existed. There had been periods of great trade union activity before the Civil War, but they were followed in the main by depression, disappointment and collapse. When organization took place, it was confined to the skilled trades, in which the necessary group consciousness most naturally developed. Two carpenters, two machinists or two electricians could find a bond in their common calling, which would be strengthened, no doubt, by common pride in their craftsmanship. The discovery of similar problems would soon focus attention on their identity of interest. Thus the bootmakers, carpenters, painters, iron molders and other skilled workers formed their local trade (i. e., craft) organizations. At the end of the 1860's more than thirty national trade unions were in existence and total union membership was not much below 300,000. Nine new national trade unions appeared during the three years 1870–1873. These unions, despite their inability to survive depressions, created a tradition of trade union activity to be quickened by the economic changes and turmoil of the post war decades.

The "triumph of business enterprise" and the conditions just mentioned not only explain the emergence of a strong labor movement during the period 1870–1914, but they shaped the philosophy and structure of the American Federation of Labor, which gave the movement leadership. For the most part the unionism of this period was organized along craft lines. It foreswore reform and political action in order to seek the immediate improvement of the wage earner's status by economic methods. Yet before the American workers were ready to embrace "business unionism", they flocked once more in the 1880's to the banner of panacea and reform.

THE KNIGHTS OF LABOR

Through the depression of the mid-seventies and its violent unsuccessful strikes, a secret society of workingmen grew steadily. Founded in 1869 by Uriah S. Stephens and six other Philadelphia tailors, the Noble Order of the Knights of Labor dropped its secrecy in 1879 when its membership was 20,000. For another two years the membership remained constant, but during the next six years the Knights enjoyed spectacular success. Its 20,000 members in 1881 had more than doubled a year later only to redouble themselves in the ensuing two-year period. In the summer of 1885 the paid up membership had become 104,000. During the next fourteen months it increased to roughly 700,000. Then the bubble burst. By 1888 the membership in good standing dropped to 222,000, in 1890 to 100,000; in 1893 the number was only 75,000.

A number of circumstances contributed to the success of the Knights of Labor. The time was ripe for an upheaval. People were shocked by political corruption and financial scandals. As prices and freight rates mounted, an outcry swelled against the trusts and railroad monopolies that was later to lead to the Interstate Commerce Act, the Sherman Act and the "trust-busting" campaigns of Theodore Roosevelt. But although its constitution decried, and its national leaders sought to discourage, the use of strikes and boycotts, the greatest appeal of the Knights lay in the spectacular successes which they scored with these weapons. In 1884 direct strike action failed to halt the wage cuts brought on by a minor depression and labor turned to the boycott as a weapon. In 1885 there were seven times as many boycotts as in 1884, most of which were instituted or taken up by the Knights of Labor. Many were successful, but the most spectacular victory was won in 1885 when Jay Gould, the most powerful capitalist in the country, met the Executive Board in conference and satisfied its demands. For the first time in American history a labor organization had forced a business and financial magnate to meet and deal with it on an equal footing.

Despite the Knights' success in conducting strikes and boycotts, it cannot be sufficiently emphasized that the movement was reformist and broadly humanitarian, seeking panaceas which would restore equality of opportunity and lift the wage earners out of their class. The Knights saw no conflict between employers and workers as such; the conflict was between the producing and non-producing classes. The Knights clung to the premise that no man need remain a wage earner, an ideal real enough while there were cheap lands to the west and ample opportunities to establish a small business in some rapidly growing community. The 1884 platform reveals the Knights' preoccupation with political measures and reform. In addition to listing such labor objectives as the eight hour day and the abolition of child labor, the platform laid great stress on direct representation and legislation, taxation of the unearned increment in land, abrogation of all laws not resting equally upon employers and employees, compulsory arbitration, compulsory education and free textbooks, income and inheritance taxes, government ownership of railroads and telegraph lines and a cooperative industrial system. The ultimate goal was "the abolishment of the wage system." Thus in the Knights of Labor the American worker had a final fling at what Professors Millis and Montgomery have called "the more romantic, reformist type of unionism. The arousing of a great hope, accompanied by a proportionately great disappointment, was perhaps necessary before he was willing to abandon the type of unionism for which he had manifested profound affection for almost a century." Many of the dominant characteristics of the American Federation of Labor are attributable to the reflections of trade union leaders on the causes of the Knights' collapse.

THE AMERICAN FEDERATION OF LABOR

Trade union membership grew slowly but steadily during the years in which workers were flocking to the Knights. Many individuals belonged both to the Knights and to the trade union organization of their craft. In other instances trade union locals were accepted into the Knights as complete assemblies, in which their separate identity was maintained. All told the trade unions could count 250,000 members in 1886 when a committee of five issued a call to a convention in Columbus, Ohio, "for the purpose of forming an American Federation or alliance of all national and international trades unions." At this convention the American Federation of Labor was formed. Samuel Gompers became the first president and remained in office, with one brief interruption, until his death in 1924.

The dominant characteristics of the New American Federation of Labor were the reverse of the Knights'. Where the Knights was a humanitarian, reformist movement, the AFL developed what Selig Perlman termed "a philosophy of pure wage consciousness" in order to signify "a labor movement reduced to an opportunistic basis, accepting the existence of capitalism and having for its object the enlarging of the bargaining power of the wage earner in the sale of his labor." The term also implied "an attitude of· aloofness from all those movements which aspire to replace the wage system by cooperation, whether voluntary or subsidized by government, whether greenbackism, socialism or anarchism." . . .

Where the Knights had looked ultimately to political action, the AFL unions relied on economic power. This is not to imply that the AFL did not support social and labor legislation; it did so repeatedly, but it concentrated on short-run objectives, steered clear of political entanglements and refused to allow its energies to be diverted from the task of improving the immediate economic position of its members.

This effort to improve the position of the wage earner "here and now", within the existing economic system, led the AFL unions under Gompers' leadership to put chief reliance on collective bargaining. They realized that the individual employee was usually helpless in dealing with his employer and sought to increase the workers' bargaining power by substituting collective strength for individual weakness. This approach also had a strong theoretical foundation. Gompers, Strasser, and other leaders who guided AFL in its formative years had too much background in Marxist and socialist doctrine to deny that there were points of conflict between employers and employees. Their early experience in the Cigar Workers Union convinced them, however, that regardless of the theoretical merits or demerits of the Marxist conception of the class struggle, immediate improvements in wages, hours and working conditions would have to be achieved within the existing form of society. Thus they saw each collective bargaining agreement as one of a series of treaties negotiated between the employers and the organized employees through which, for the time being, they would adjust their differences.

During the 1880's collective agreements became fairly common in the building trades, and during the 1890's national agreements were signed in the stove and glass container industries. In 1898 the United Mine Workers negotiated a contract covering the important bituminous coal fields and shortly later obtained a similar agreement applicable to anthracite. The form and content of collective bargaining agreements has always varied so widely that generalization is dangerous but it seems fair to say that the AFL collective bargaining agreements were usually conceived as contracts under which the employer would hire workers and the unions would man the jobs. After union recognition, wages, hours and job security were most important. The prevailing conception seems to have been one of a bargain and sale of labor, and it was not until the 1930's when union organization spread into the mass production industries that a philosophy of collective bargaining developed which speaks of "industrial democracy" and sees in the collective agreement and grievance procedures the substantive and procedural rules for the government of industrial workers. Even today there is a marked difference in this respect between many craft agreements and the industrial union contracts in basic industries.

In 1886 the principle of craft organization fitted comfortably into the new philosophy of business unionism. If the bargaining power of the workers was to be increased by substituting collective strength for individual weakness, it was imperative to organize into one group all the workers in the same occupation; they were the ones, and the only ones, who would destroy labor standards by underbidding each other. In addition, by establishing "job ownership" or "job control", the organized workers could achieve a fair degree of security, which must have appealed to many of them not only as a form of insurance against unemployment during hard times but also as a defense against the threatening competition of unskilled labor.

In the AFL philosophy craft autonomy was closely allied to the principle of craft organization. In 1886 and for years thereafter the chief problem of American unionism seemed to be to stay organized. Trade union leaders concluded that the internal solidarity of the craft group should not be risked by the loss of its identity in larger units—the industry, the AFL, the world labor movement—where solidarity would grow less as the size of the unit increased. Nor was a close knit organization required. A national organization of the whole trade union movement was useful chiefly to formulate broad policies, to unite the crafts in spreading organization into new fields, and to act as spokesman, especially on political issues affecting labor. In securing immediate economic objectives experience seemed to show that reliance should be placed on the independent action of the craft unions which had their own solidarity and knew their own needs.

The problem of staying organized also gave rise to the ruthless opposition to dual unionism which has played so important a role in American trade union history. The concurrent existence of the Knights and the trade unions, both in the same field, had resulted in dual authority and divided loyalty, which sapped the trade unions' strength. Thus the AFL became devoted to the principle that in each recognized field of activity there should be but one union, chartered by the AFL, which would have exclusive jurisdiction.

The organizational structure of the American Federation of Labor paralleled its philosophy. As the name implied, it was a federation of trade unions. The dominant units were autonomous International Unions which were "affiliated" with the American Federation of Labor. Under each International were the local unions it had chartered. It was in the locals that individual workers held their memberships.

With this philosophy and internal structure, the trade union movement experienced a period of solid, and sometimes spectacular, growth. For ten years after it was founded in 1886, the AFL's membership remained virtually constant. This was a truly remarkable success, for a depression occurred in 1893, and in every previous depression, as Gompers noted in 1899, the trade unions had been "literally mowed down and swept out of existence. Here for the first time the unions manifested their stability and permanence." In 1897 AFL entered a period of rapid growth. Between 1897 and 1900 memberships arose from something less than 275,000 to 548,000. By 1903 the number of members was 1,465,000, five and one half times the membership only a decade before. AFL membership then remained fairly constant until 1910 when it again began to rise. By 1914 there were more than 2,000,000 AFL members.

The increase in membership was concentrated in the skilled trades and a few industries. More than half was attributable to the phenomenal growth of unions among coal miners, railroad workers and building trades employees. The great mass of semi-skilled and unskilled workers remained unorganized. Yet despite this limitation, union membership in 1914 was perhaps nine times greater than in 1869. The post-Civil War era was marked—in Charles A. Beard's phrase—by the "Triumph of Business Enterprise." But the years are no less significant for the rise of a permanent labor movement.

It was impossible that corporate industry should triumph, or that a strong labor movement should be born, without conflict and upheaval. In the eyes of the workers and debtor classes the monopolists were tightening their hold upon society, enriching themselves and impoverishing "the common people". Greenbackism, the violence and lawlessness which marked the depression of the mid-seventies, the Granger movement, the Knights of Labor and later the Populist uprising were among the consequences; and the trade unions profited from the discontent. To businessmen, property owners and their associates, however, these events not only challenged American ways of life but smacked of violent revolution. It is not difficult to imagine the shock which the business community felt when it watched the Knights of Labor bring Jay Gould to terms, and the stories circulated by the press must have aroused the fears of many readers. In 1885 the New York Sun reported: "Five men in this country control the chief interests of five hundred thousand workingmen, and can at any moment take the means of livelihood from two and a half millions of souls. . . . They can stay the nimble touch of almost every telegraph operator; can shut up most of the mills and factories, and can disable the railroads. . . . They can array labor against capital, putting labor on the offensive or the defensive, for quiet and stubborn self-protection, or for angry, organized assault, as they will."

* * *

In spreading organization unions relied on three kinds of weapons:

(1) Their chief reliance was on a wide variety of arguments, persuasion and social pressures aimed directly at converting workers to ardent union membership.

(2) When this was not enough—or when enough employees had been organized, but an employer refused to recognize the union—unions resorted to strikes, boycotts and picketing. Some were peaceful. Violence crept into others simply because emotions ran high and working men do not observe the niceties of the parlor. Sometimes violence was deliberately planned even to the point of pitched battles.

(3) Labor unions also sought the support of public opinion. Their appeal was to intellectuals and reformers of all kinds. Such support has recently declined but at least until the mid-1950's most "liberals" and "progressives" were sympathetic to the cause of organized labor.

EMPLOYER OPPOSITION

Probably it was inevitable that employers would oppose the rise of labor organizations, some bitterly. Unions not only increased the power of employees to demand and secure higher wages, shorter hours and other benefits increasing labor costs, and so seemed to threaten the company's profits; they also curtailed the power of corporate management to make unilateral decisions. Few men like to surrender power, and the more absolute their authority has been, the more reluctant they are to let it go. Perhaps it is for this reason that in later years disputes over the functions or prerogatives of management, which arose when unions pressed collective bargaining into new fields, began to stir more heated emotions than controversies over wage rates. In any event employers did fight unionization. They resorted to three kinds of measures:

(1) Employers, like unions, used the weapons of self-help. Threats of reprisals were often enough to discourage an incipient union. Labor spies were hired to report on any movement toward organization and to give the names of active leaders. Union leaders were discharged and often they were put on black lists circulated by trade associations. Many of the top union officials today are men whose attitudes were molded by years of working under assumed names, moving on from town to town as their identity was discovered. During World War I and again early in the 1930's some employers sought to prevent the growth of bona fide labor organizations by setting up works councils and company unions that would give employees the forms of union organization without the substance. Perhaps it is unnecessary also to recall the professional strikebreakers supplied by Pinkerton's and other detective agencies.

(2) The second group of weapons used by employers were various methods of appealing to and organizing public opinion. Since the techniques are as much a part of the mores of our times as of yesterday, it is unnecessary to say more than that unionization ran counter to the American tradition of individualism, and this more than anything else led distinguished citizens, including President Eliot of Harvard, to glorify the strikebreaker as a modern American hero.

(3) Employers sought and obtained government aid through the courts. Their requests gave rise to the first major phase in the development of labor law—the rise and decline of the labor injunction.

Later, organized labor also turned to the government not so much for direct social and economic legislation, as in continental Europe, but to clear the way for self-help through collective bargaining. Labor's first political objective, in point of emphasis as well as time, was to persuade the legislative branch of the government to stop the judicial intervention into labor disputes which was impeding unionization. Second, organized labor gradually turned to the government for affirmative assistance through legal recognition of the rights to self-organization and collective bargaining.

These two threads—the rise and decline of the labor injunction and the emergence of the legally protected rights to organize and bargain collectively—run through the development of the law of labor management relations from 1880 until 1947.

Note

The preceding extract deals primarily with the rise of American "business unionism" as exemplified by the AFL. We should note that this does not recount the full story of the American labor movement in that it tends to exclude consideration of the more radical elements of that movement. For example, the mercurial rise and decline of the International Workers of the World—"the Wobblies"— is a fascinating chapter in labor radicalism with equally important legal implications. The Wobblies, however, did not succeed in establishing an effective labor movement; they did not capture public sentiment or political support; and they did not succeed in bringing the law in line with their ideals. Indeed, the law was used so successfully against the Wobblies after World War I, that they ceased to be an effective element of the labor movement. Aspects of this kind of unionism, and legal responses to it, provide additional insights regarding law and social conflict.

SECTION 34. JUDICIAL INTERVENTION IN LABOR-MANAGEMENT DISPUTES

Throughout most of the nineteenth century the law regarding labor-management relations was developed by judges (both state and federal) in the exercise of their jurisdiction to resolve disputes. The problems engendered by the rising labor movement were new, and the courts shaped new law to deal with these problems. Consistent with the traditions of English and American judges, the new law was adapted from old law, primarily the common law of "conspiracy."

A conspiracy, as defined at common law, is a combination of persons organized to commit a criminal act (such as murder or theft) or to realize a criminal objective (such as overthrow of government or thwarting the workings of the courts). The very act of combining for an unlawful purpose is a crime, for which the conspirators can be tried and punished even though no further steps were taken to commit the unlawful acts or to achieve the unlawful objectives.

The common law did not develop similar concepts concerning the civil liability of conspirators. A private person bringing suit to recover damages from conspirators normally had to show actual injury and this was likely to occur only after the conspirators took steps to implement their plan, thereby committing some tortious act beyond the formation of the conspiracy. Thus at the beginning of the nineteenth century the common law of conspiracy was primarily criminal law relating to combinations to perpetrate criminal acts or to achieve objectives proscribed by the criminal law. From this criminal law origin, judges evolved a rationale for the grant of civil remedies, primarily the injunction, to restrain many activities of organized labor.

SECTION 34.1 THE EARLY HISTORY OF THE LABOR INJUNCTION

[The following is taken from FELIX FRANKFURTER (later Justice Frankfurter) and NATHAN GREENE, THE LABOR INJUNCTION (New York, 1930), pp. 1–5. Footnotes are omitted.]

On May 27, 1895, the Supreme Court of the United States for the first time in its history passed on the scope and validity of an injunction in a labor controversy. Yet the very next year this modern application of an ancient procedure was made a party issue, and since then has maintained itself at the forefront of American political problems. "Government by injunction" was the slogan by which the Democratic platform of 1896 inveighed against the practice of issuing labor injunctions. After 1908, the Republican Party also proposed the correction of abuses due to judicial intervention in labor conflicts. In response to this agitation, important federal legislation was enacted in 1914. But the hopes in which it was conceived soon foundered. Protest revived and grew. And so, in the campaign of 1928 both parties acknowledged the existence of abuses and committed themselves to the need of further legislation. What is true of the nation is true of the states. In 1896, the Chief Justice of Massachusetts remarked that the "practice of issuing injunctions in cases of this kind is of very recent origin." Since then the practice has grown widely, giving rise to vigorous counter-agitation. State legislatures have followed Congress in corrective legislation, but proposals for curbing resort to labor injunctions continue to be urged by Democratic and Republican governors alike.

Here, as elsewhere in the law, a full understanding of the history of a legal institution under scrutiny is necessary to wise reform. How labor injunctions came to be and how they operate in practice, the uses which they serve and the abuses to which they have given rise, must be known if we are to determine whether the labor injunction in action represents a desirable social policy.

Two conceptions which, prior to modern legislation, dominated the attitude of English law towards collective action by labor—the doctrines of conspiracy and of restraint of trade—worked themselves permanently into American law. The earliest American case declared with untroubled simplicity that "A combination of workmen to raise their wages may be considered in a two fold point of view: one is to benefit themselves . . . the other is to injure those who do not join their society. The rule of law condemns both." While this idea appears in later cases, it was short-lived. When joint action by laborers was attacked for the first time in New York, the prosecution dipped into the precedents of a bygone age—R. v. Journeymen-Taylors of Cambridge; R. v. Eccles; the specious Tubwomen's Case— and drew therefrom their familiar wisdom, then supported also by the authority of Hawkins' Pleas of the Crown: "A conspiracy of any kind is illegal, although the matter about which they conspired might have been lawful for them, or any of them to do, if they had not conspired to do it." "Conspiracy is the gist of the charge; and even to do a thing which is *lawful* in itself, by *conspiracy*, is *unlawful*." But early we find the court charging the jury in terms which foreshadowed the later standard definition of conspiracy: "He observed there were two points of view in which the offence of a conspiracy might be considered; the one where there existed a combination to do an act, unlawful in itself, to the prejudice of other persons; the other where the act done, or the object of it, was not unlawful, but *unlawful means* were used to accomplish it." During the next three decades there followed a series of indictments and convictions for criminal conspiracy; but nearly all of them presented elements of coercion and intimidating practices.

In 1840 came the clarifying opinion of the great Chief Justice Shaw of Massachusetts in Commonwealth v. Hunt. In this case the indictment averred that the defendant and others formed themselves into a society and agreed not to work for any person who employed a non-member of this society. The trial court ruled that such a combination constituted a conspiracy. Conviction followed, only to be set aside on appeal. This reversal by the Supreme Judicial Court of Massachusetts is noteworthy because it permanently arrested the tendency to identify a labor organization as such with a criminal conspiracy, but not less so because Shaw's opinion brought together the isolated materials of earlier cases and gave them formulation and direction. When Shaw said, after a study of the purpose of the organization in the Hunt Case, "Such a purpose is not unlawful," he indicated purpose or motive as one vital consideration. When he said "The legality of such an association will therefore depend upon the means to be used for its accomplishment," he pierced to the second fighting issue. Commonwealth v. Hunt did not altogether stop prosecutions for criminal conspiracy against trade unions because they were trade unions. Some states tried to achieve the result of the Hunt Case by legislation, but with dubious success. Moreover, "conspiracy" and "restraint of trade," as will soon appear, survived as convenient grab-bag terms for illegal group activities. But, on the whole, since Commonwealth v. Hunt, American legal history is a steady accumulation of instances where the line has been drawn between purposes and acts permitted, and purposes and acts forbidden. The "end" of labor activities and the "means" by which they are pursued constitute the chief inquiries of labor law.

[The following is taken from COX, CASES ON LABOR LAW (3rd ed.), pp. 18–20. Footnotes are omitted.]

. . . The struggle between the workers seeking to organize and the employers, especially large corporations, seeking to block unionization was continuous; but it flared up in several incidents which [had a great] influence upon labor law.

The first was the great railway strike of 1877. In 1873 a financial panic swept the country, precipitated by the failure of Jay Cooke and Co., New York's largest banking house. The New York Stock Exchange closed. Commercial failures increased to 6,000 in 1874, 8,000 in 1875 and 9,000 in 1876. Railroad construction came to a standstill. Industrial plants shut down and as the depression deepened, breadlines formed. In 1877 the four eastern trunk lines jointly announced a second 10 per cent cut in wages. Some employees of the Baltimore and Ohio stopped work in protest, and the strike spontaneously spread to other railroads. For a week rail transportation was paralyzed. The militia was mobilized and as the army of unemployed, hungry and desperate, came to the support of the strikers, pitched battles were fought in the key cities. Responsibility for the violence doubtless lay on both sides. In St. Louis a crowd of labor sympathizers jeered at the police; the police retaliated by arresting the trade union delegates who were assembled at the central labor hall. In Columbus striking workmen used threats and force to close industrial establishments on every side. In Baltimore, Pittsburgh and Chicago numerous strikers and bystanders were killed, not to mention the lesser casualties and the large amounts of property which were destroyed.   Eventually order was restored by federal troops threatening to make "a sharp use of the bayonet and musket."   To the historian looking back the great railway strike of 1877 marks the emergence of "the labor problem."   To the property owners and rising entrepreneurs of the 1870's, it smacked of a rebellion stirred by foreign agitators.   In a sense they were right—for a week or more law and order hung in balance.

In Indianapolis a mob seized the railway station preventing the movement of trains over various railway lines which were in receivership in the federal court.   United States District Judge Walter Q. Gresham, fearing (as he declared) "that society was disintegrating, if it had not dissolved," held a mass meeting in his court room at which he organized a vigilance committee and called for military volunteers.   When the Governor of Indiana rejected his services, Judge Gresham instructed the United States marshal to use the troops as a posse.   The marshal read a proclamation at the railway station telling the members of the mob that they were in contempt of court. The mob disbanded and the trains were permitted to move.   Some of the leaders in the strike, however, were arrested and tried for contempt before Circuit Judge Drummond who sentenced them as well as other strikers in Illinois for interfering with the performance of the court orders directing the receivers to operate the trains.   In his opinion Judge Drummond declared—

> "Every man . . . has a right to leave the service of his employer . . . but men ought not to combine together and cause at once a strike among all railway employees. . . . These railroads are among the principal means of modern civilization by which the business of the country is transacted.   Therefore when a man interferes with a property whose object is so important, which affects so materially all the relations of society, he commits as great an offense against the rights of individuals and against the rights of the public as can well be imagined. . . . A public example must be made, and it must be made emphatically. . . . It is . . . indispensably necessary that the court should not tolerate any interference, however slight, with the management of the railroads . . . in its custody. . . . This thing must be stopped, and, so far as this court has the power to do it, it shall be stopped."

Although this was the first occasion in the United States on which the equity power had been used to terminate a strike, the force of the precedent did not go unobserved.   President Scott of the Pennsylvania Railroad wrote shortly later: "The laws which give the Federal courts the summary process of *injunction* to restrain so comparatively trifling a wrong as infringement of a patent right certainly must have been intended or ought to give the United States authority to prevent a wrongdoing which not only destroys a particular road but also paralyzes the commerce of the country and wastes the national wealth."

It seems plain, however, that in these cases and those which shortly followed the judges intervened to strike down what they conceived to be a challenge to civil government and not merely to protect business against loss. There is no reason to question Judge Gresham's explanation of what occurred for both he and Judge Drummond demonstrated on other occasions that they would not hesitate to thwart financial interests. Nevertheless, in the middle eighties Judge Gresham issued five injunctions in new railway strikes. Eight more were issued in Missouri; and others in Kansas, Texas and Arkansas. Significantly, the injunctions and sentences for contempt were no longer confined to receivership cases. Out of upheaval and conflict new law was being made.

It was inevitable that the government should be called upon to intervene, at least to some degree, in the conflict of interest between employers and employees. The function of all law is to achieve some accommodation of the conflicting interests in society either by direct government determination in one form or another, by providing a framework for the negotiation of private adjustments, or by some combination of the two. Labor law in the United States has sometimes taken one direction; sometimes another. One principal characteristic of the law which grew out of the railway strikes of the 1880's was that it was exclusively judicial intervention. It was law made and enforced by the courts. A second characteristic of the new body of law was that it was couched entirely in terms of prohibitions upon the conduct of employees. Through the labor injunction the courts attempted to deal with the conflicts of interest between employers and employees by defining: (1) the occasions on which employees might engage in concerted activities in pursuit of their interests, (2) the objectives which employees might lawfully pursue by concerted action, and (3) the tactics which employees might lawfully use. . . .

The following cases are illustrative of the judicial inquiry regarding the means and the objectives the emergent labor movement might lawfully pursue:

UNLAWFUL MEANS

VEGELAHN v. GUNTNER

Supreme Judicial Court of Massachusetts.
167 Mass. 92, 44 N.E. 1077 (1896).

After a preliminary hearing upon the bill of complaint an injunction issued *pendente lite* restraining the respondents "from interfering with the plaintiff's business by patrolling the sidewalk or street in front or in the vicinity of the premises occupied by him, for the purpose of preventing any person or persons who now are or may hereafter be in his employment, or desirous of entering the same, from entering it, or continuing in it; or by obstructing or interfering with such persons, or any others, in entering or leaving the plaintiff's said premises; or by intimidating, by threats or otherwise, any person or persons who now are or may hereafter be in the employment of the plaintiff, or desirous of entering the same, from entering it, or continuing in it; or by any scheme or conspiracy among themselves or with others, organized for the purpose of annoying, hindering, interfering with, or preventing any persons who now are or may hereafter be in the employment of the plaintiff, or desirous of entering it, or from continuing therein."

The hearing on the merits was before Holmes, J., who reported the case for the consideration of the full court, as follows:

"The facts admitted or proved are that, following upon a strike of the plaintiff's workmen, the defendants have conspired to prevent the plaintiff from getting workmen, and thereby to prevent him from carrying on his business unless and until he will adopt a schedule of prices which has been exhibited to him, and for the purpose of compelling him to accede to that schedule, but for no other purpose. If he adopts that schedule he will not be interfered with further. The means adopted for preventing the plaintiff from getting workmen are, (1) in the first place, persuasion and social pressure. And these means are sufficient to affect the plaintiff disadvantageously, although it does not appear, if that be material, that they are sufficient to crush him. I ruled that the employment of these means for the said purpose was lawful, and for that reason refused an injunction against the employment of them. If the ruling was wrong, I find that an injunction ought to be granted.

"(2) I find also, that, as a further means for accomplishing the desired end, threats of personal injury or unlawful harm were conveyed to persons seeking employment or employed, although no actual violence was used beyond a technical battery, and although the threats were a good deal disguised, and express words were avoided. It appeared to me that there was danger of similar acts in the future. I ruled that conduct of this kind should be enjoined.

"The defendants established a patrol of two men in front of the plaintiff's factory, as one of the instrumentalities of their plan. The patrol was changed every hour, and continued from half-past six in the morning until half-past five in the afternoon, on one of the busy streets of Boston. The number of men was greater at times, and at times showed some little inclination to stop the plaintiff's door, which was not serious, but seemed to me proper to be enjoined. The patrol proper at times went further than simple advice, not obtruded beyond the point where the other person was willing to listen, and conduct of that sort is covered by (2) above, but its main purpose was in aid of the plan held lawful in (1) above. I was satisfied that there was probability of the patrol being continued if not enjoined. I ruled that the patrol, so far as it confined itself to persuasion and giving notice of the strike, was not unlawful, and limited the injunction accordingly.

"There was some evidence of persuasion to break existing contracts. I ruled that this was unlawful, and should be enjoined."

ALLEN, J. The principal question in this case is whether the defendants should be enjoined against maintaining the patrol. . . . The patrol was maintained as one of the means of carrying out the defendants' plan, and it was used in combination with social pressure, threats of personal injury or unlawful harm, and persuasion to break existing contracts. It was thus one means of intimidation, indirectly to the plaintiff, and directly to persons actually employed, or seeking to be employed, by the plaintiff, and of rendering such employment unpleasant or intolerable to such persons. Such an act is an unlawful interference with the rights both of employer and of employed. An employer has a right to engage all persons who are willing to work for him, at such prices as may be mutually agreed upon, and persons employed or seeking employment have a corresponding right to enter into or remain in the employment of any person or corporation willing to employ them. These rights are secured by the constitution itself. [Citations omitted.] No one can lawfully interfere by force or intimidation to prevent employers or persons employed or wishing to be employed from the exercise of these rights. It is in Massachusetts, as in some other states, even made a criminal offense for one, by intimidation or force, to prevent, or seek to prevent, a person from entering into or continuing in the employment of a person or corporation. Pub.St., c. 74, § 2. Intimidation is not limited to threats of violence or of physical injury to person or property. It has a broader signification, and there also may be a moral intimidation which is illegal. Patrolling or picketing, under the circumstances stated in the report, has elements of intimidation like those which were found to exist in Sherry v. Perkins, 147 Mass. 212, 17 N.E. 307. It was declared to be unlawful in Reg. v. Druitt, 10 Cox, Cr.Cas. 592; Reg. v. Hibbert, 13 Cox, Cr.Cas. 82; Reg. v. Bauld, Id. 282. It was assumed to be unlawful in Trollope v. Trader's Fed. (1875) 11 L.T. 228, though in that case the pickets were withdrawn before the bringing of the bill. The patrol was unlawful interference both with the plaintiff and with the workmen, within the principle of many cases; and, when instituted for the purpose of interfering with his business, it became a private nuisance. [Citations omitted.]

The defendants contend that these acts were justifiable, because they were only seeking to secure better wages for themselves, by compelling the plaintiff to accept their schedule of wages. This motive or purpose does not justify maintaining a patrol in front of the plaintiff's premises, as a means of carrying out their conspiracy. A combination among persons merely to regulate their own conduct is within allowable competition, and is lawful, although others may be indirectly affected thereby. But a combination to do injurious acts expressly directed to another, by way of intimidation or constraint, either of himself or of persons employed or seeking employment from him, is outside of allowable competition, and is unlawful. . . .

A question is also presented whether the court should enjoin such interference with persons in the employment of the plaintiff who are not bound by contract to remain with him, or with persons who are not under any existing contract, but who are seeking or intending to enter into his employment. A conspiracy to interfere with the plaintiff's business by means of threats and intimidation, and by maintaining a patrol in front of his premises, in order to prevent persons who are in his employment from continuing therein, is unlawful, even though such persons are not bound by contract to enter into or to continue in his employment; and the injunction should not be so limited as to relate only to persons who are bound by existing contracts. . . . We therefore think that the injunction should be in the form as originally issued. So ordered.

FIELD, C. J. (dissenting). . . .

HOLMES, J. (dissenting). In a case like the present, it seems to me that, whatever the true result may be, it will be of advantage to sound thinking to have the less popular view of the law stated, and therefore, although, when I have been unable to bring my brethren to share my convictions, my almost invariable practice is to defer to them in silence, I depart from that practice in this case, notwithstanding my unwillingness to do so, in support of an already rendered judgment of my own.

In the first place, a word or two should be said as to the meaning of the report. I assume that my brethren construe it as I meant it to be construed, and that, if they were not prepared to do so, they would give an opportunity to the defendants to have it amended in accordance with what I state my meaning to have been. There was no proof of any threat or danger of a patrol exceeding two men, and as, of course, an injunction is not granted except with reference to what there is reason to expect in its absence, the question on that point is whether a patrol of two men should be enjoined. Again, the defendants are enjoined by the final decree from intimidating by threats, express or implied, of physical harm to body or property, any person who may be desirous of entering into the employment of the plaintiff, so far as to prevent him from entering the same. In order to test the correctness of the refusal to go further, it must be assumed that the defendants obey the express prohibition of the decree. If they do not, they fall within the injunction as it now stands, and are liable to summary punishment. The important difference between the preliminary and the final injunction is that the former goes further, and forbids the defendants to interfere with the plaintiff's business "by any scheme . . . organized for the purpose of . . . preventing any person or persons who now are or may hereafter be . . . desirous of entering the [plaintiff's employment] from entering it." I quote only a part, and the part which seems to me most objectionable. This includes refusal of social intercourse, and even organized persuasion or argument, although free from any threat of violence, either express or implied. And this is with reference to persons who have a legal right to contract or not to contract with the plaintiff, as they may see fit. Interference with existing contracts is forbidden by the final decree. I wish to insist a little that the only point of difference which involves a difference of principle between the final decree and the preliminary injunction, which it is proposed to restore, is what I have mentioned, in order that it may be seen exactly what we are to discuss. It appears to me that the opinion of the majority turns in part on the assumption that the patrol necessarily carries with it a threat of bodily harm. That assumption I think unwarranted, for the reasons which I have given. Furthermore, it cannot be said, I think, that two men, walking together up and down a sidewalk, and speaking to those who enter a certain shop, do necessarily and always thereby convey a threat of force. I do not think it possible to discriminate, and to say that two workmen, or even two representatives of an organization of workmen, do; especially when they are, and are known to be, under the injunction of this court not to do so. See Stimson, Labor Law § 60, especially pages 290, 298–300; Reg. v. Shepherd, 11 Cox, Cr.Cas. 325. I may add that I think the more intelligent workingmen believe as fully as I do that they no more can be permitted to usurp the state's prerogative of force than can their opponents in their controversies. But, if I am wrong, then the decree as it stands reaches the patrol, since it applies to all threats of force. With this I pass to the real difference between the interlocutory and the final decree.

I agree, whatever may be the law in the case of a single defendant (Rice v. Albee, 164 Mass. 88, 41 N.E. 122), that when a plaintiff proves that several persons have combined and conspired to injure his business, and have done acts producing that effect, he shows temporal damage and a cause of action, unless the facts disclose or the defendants prove some ground of excuse or justification; and I take it to be settled, and rightly settled, that doing that damage by combined persuasion is actionable, as well as doing it by falsehood or by force. [Citations omitted.]

Nevertheless, in numberless instances the law warrants the intentional infliction of temporal damage, because it regards it as justified. It is on the question of what shall amount to a justification, and more especially on the nature of the considerations which really determine or ought to determine the answer to that question, that judicial reasoning seems to me often to be inadequate. The true grounds of decision are considerations of policy and of social advantage, and it is vain to suppose that solutions can be attained merely by logic and general propositions of law which nobody disputes. Propositions as to public policy rarely are unanimously accepted, and still more rarely, if ever, are capable of unanswerable proof. They require a special training to enable any one even to form an intelligent opinion about them.

In the early stages of law, at least, they generally are acted on rather as inarticulate instincts than as definite ideas, for which a rational defense is ready.

To illustrate what I have said in the last paragraph: It has been the law for centuries that a man may set up a business in a small country town, too small to support more than one, although thereby he expects and intends to ruin some one already there, and succeeds in his intent. In such a case he is not held to act "unlawfully and without justifiable cause," as was alleged in Walker v. Cronin and Rice v. Albee. The reason, of course, is that the doctrine generally has been accepted that free competition is worth more to society than it costs, and that on this ground the infliction of the damage is privileged. Com. v. Hunt, 4 Metc. (Mass.) 111, 134. Yet even this proposition nowadays is disputed by a considerable body of persons, including many whose intelligence is not to be denied, little as we may agree with them.

I have chosen this illustration partly with reference to what I have to say next. It shows without the need of further authority that the policy of allowing free competition justifies the intentional inflicting of temporal damage, including the damage of interference with a man's business by some means, when the damage is done, not for its own sake, but as an instrumentality in reaching the end of victory in the battle of trade. In such a case it cannot matter whether the plaintiff is the only rival of the defendant, and so is aimed at specially, or is one of a class all of whom are hit. The only debatable ground is the nature of the means by which such damage may be inflicted. We all agree that it cannot be done by force or threats of force. We all agree, I presume, that it may be done by persuasion to leave a rival's shop, and come to the defendant's. It may be done by the refusal or withdrawal of various pecuniary advantages, which, apart from this consequence, are within the defendant's lawful control. It may be done by the withdrawal of, or threat to withdraw, such advantages from third persons who have a right to deal or not to deal with him either as customers or servants. Com. v. Hunt, 4 Metc. (45 Mass.) 111, 112, 133; Bowen v. Matheson, 14 Allen (96 Mass.) 499; Heywood v. Tillson, 75 Me.

225; Steamship Co. v. McGregor [1892] App.Cas. 25. I have seen the suggestion made that the conflict between employers and employed was not competition, but I venture to assume that none of my brethren would rely on that suggestion. If the policy on which our law is founded is too narrowly expressed in the term "free competition," we may substitute "free struggle for life." Certainly, the policy is not limited to struggles between persons of the same class, competing for the same end. It applies to all conflicts of temporal interests.

I pause here to remark that the word "threats" often is used as if, when it appeared that threats had been made, it appeared that unlawful conduct had begun. But it depends on what you threaten. As a general rule, even if subject to some exceptions, what you may do in a certain event you may threaten to do—that is, give warning of your intention to do—in that event, and thus allow the other person the chance of avoiding the consequence. So, as to "compulsion," it depends on how you "compel." Com. v. Hunt, 4 Metc. (45 Mass.) 111, 133. So as to "annoyance" or "intimidation." [Citation omitted.] In Sherry v. Perkins, 147 Mass. 212, 17 N.E. 307, it was found as a fact that the display of banners which was enjoined was part of a scheme to prevent workmen from entering or remaining in the plaintiff's employment, "by threats and intimidation." The context showed that the words as there used meant threats of personal violence and intimidation by causing fear of it.

So far, I suppose, we are agreed. But there is a notion, which latterly has been insisted on a good deal, that a combination of persons to do what any one of them lawfully might do by himself will make the otherwise lawful conduct unlawful. It would be rash to say that some as yet unformulated truth may not be hidden under this proposition. But, in the general form in which it has been presented and accepted by many courts, I think it plainly untrue, both on authority and principle. Com. v. Hunt, 4 Metc. (45 Mass.) 111; Randall v. Hazelton, 12 Allen (94 Mass.) 412, 414. There was combination of the most flagrant and dominant kind in Bowen v. Matheson, and in the Steamship Co. Case, and combination was essential to the success achieved. But it is not necessary to cite cases. It is plain from the slightest consideration of practical affairs, or the most superficial reading of industrial history, that free competition means combination, and that the organization of the world, now going on so fast, means an ever-increasing might and scope of combination. It seems to me futile to set our faces against this tendency. Whether beneficial on the whole, as I think it, or detrimental, it is inevitable, unless the fundamental axioms of society, and even the fundamental conditions of life, are to be changed.

One of the eternal conflicts out of which life is made up is that between the effort of every man to get the most he can for his services, and that of society, disguised under the name of capital, to get his services for the least possible return. Combination on the one side is patent and powerful. Combination on the other is the necessary and desirable counterpart, if the battle is to be carried on in a fair and equal way. I am unable to reconcile Temperton v. Russell [1893] 1 Q.B. 715, and the cases which follow it, with the Steamship Co. Case. But Temperton v. Russell is not a binding authority here, and therefore I do not think it necessary to discuss it.

If it be true that working men may combine with a view, among other things, to getting as much as they can for their labor, just as capital may combine with a view to getting the greatest possible return, it must be true that, when combined, they have the same liberty that combined capital has, to support their interests by argument, persuasion, and the bestowal or refusal of those advantages which they otherwise lawfully control. I can remember when many people thought that, apart from violence or breach of contract, strikes were wicked, as organized refusals to work. I suppose that intelligent economists and legislators have given up that notion today. I feel pretty confident that they equally will abandon the idea that an organized refusal by workmen of social intercourse with a man who shall enter their antagonist's employ is unlawful, if it is dissociated from any threat of violence, and is made for the sole object of prevailing, if possible, in a contest with their employer about the rate of wages. The fact that the immediate object of the act by which the benefit to themselves is to be gained is to injure their antagonist does not necessarily make it unlawful, any more than when a great house lowers the price of goods for the purpose and with the effect of driving a smaller antagonist from the business. Indeed, the question seems to me to have been decided as long ago as 1842, by the good sense of Chief Justice Shaw, in Com. v. Hunt, 4 Metc. (45 Mass.) 111. I repeat at the end, as I said at the beginning, that this is the point of difference in principle, and the only one, between the interlocutory and final decree; and I only desire to add that the distinctions upon which the final decree was framed seem to me to have coincided very accurately with the results finally reached by legislation and judicial decision in England, apart from what I must regard as the anomalous decisions of Temperton v. Russell and the cases which have followed it. Reg. v. Shepherd, 11 Cox, Cr.Cas. 354. . . .

The general question of the propriety of dealing with this kind of case by injunction I say nothing about, because I understand that the defendants have no objection to the final decree if it goes no further, and that both parties wish a decision upon the matters which I have discussed.

Notes

The Prima Facie Theory of Torts; the Yellow Dog Contract

The prima facie theory of torts. Plaintiff's case is based on a tort theory (see *supra* p. 495). His claim is that the patrol was instituted and maintained for the purpose of injuring him in his business dealings, and that the intentional causing of harm to another is a tort for which a legal remedy should be granted.

In the early labor cases the courts struggled with the question of how to treat the intentional infliction of harm caused by concerted activities of employees. The common law did not at that time provide an adequate doctrinal base for the resolution of this problem for the common law never evolved a unified theory of tort law. There was a "law of torts," in the sense that the courts had created "forms of action" to deal with some kinds of wrongs, but each wrong—for which there was a form of action—was treated as *sui generis* and little effort was made to articulate a legal theory which would serve as the basis for a law of tort—as opposed to a law of torts. However, together with the reform of civil procedure in the nineteenth century there developed a considerable interest in systematizing the law. Professor (later Judge and then Justice)

Holmes and Professor Wigmore were leaders in the effort to systematize tort law. They developed the so-called prima facie theory of torts. The gist of this theory and its relation to labor cases is succinctly stated in the following passage.

> "The best articulated approach to the problem of determining the legality of a labor objective grew out of the scholarly systemization of tort law which Holmes and Wigmore were attempting during the closing decades of the nineteenth century. They found one unifying principle in the doctrine that every intentional infliction of harm upon another is *prima facie* tortious and may be the subject of an action unless justified. If A beat B, the beating is *prima facie* a tort, but A may show that it was privileged because A was protecting his family or property. If A erects a blank wall shutting off B's view, there may be a *prima facie* wrong but A may justify by showing that the wall was for the purpose of erecting a warehouse on the property. So in a labor dispute the question would be whether the injury which the workers intentionally inflicted on the employer was a tort because unjustified, or was privileged because of the interests which the workers were seeking to advance." Cox, Cases on Labor Law (3rd ed.), p. 63.

Question. Does Judge Holmes utilize the prima facie theory of torts in his dissenting opinion in Vegelahn v. Guntner?

The "yellow dog contract." There are several references in the case to attempts by the defendants to persuade other workmen to break existing contracts of employment with the plaintiff. Both Holmes and the majority concur in the view that such conduct is unlawful and should be enjoined, since at common law it is a tort to induce a party to break a valid contract. This doctrine was adapted by employers—and their attorneys—to raise a barrier to the organizational efforts of labor unions. Many employers required, as a condition of employment, that a workman expressly promise to refrain from supporting or participating in union activities. This promise was treated as part of the contractual arrangement between employer and employee. When a union attempted to organize a firm whose employees were parties to such an arrangement, the employer could claim that the union was inducing his employees to break their contracts, thus establishing tortious conduct and the basis for a legal remedy.

In the argot of the labor movement, such agreements were called "yellow dog contracts."

Questions

1. What unlawful acts were committed by the defendants in Vegelahn v. Guntner? Which of their acts were criminal? Which of their acts were tortious?

2.　Did Judge Allen hold that the combination of the defendants constituted a conspiracy?　If so, was it because they combined to commit unlawful acts?　Or did he hold that the acts that they combined to commit were unlawful because of the conspiracy?

3.　Did the injunction proposed by Judge Holmes prohibit the unlawful acts of the defendants?

4.　Did the injunction issued by the court prohibit the defendants from using any means whatsoever to persuade others not to work for the plaintiff?

UNLAWFUL OBJECTIVES

PLANT v. WOODS

Supreme Judicial Court of Massachusetts.
176 Mass. 492, 57 N.E. 1011 (1900).

HAMMOND, J.　This case arises out of a contest for supremacy between two labor unions of the same craft, having substantially the same constitution and by-laws.　The chief difference between them is that the plaintiff union is affiliated with a national organization having its headquarters in Lafayette, in the state of Indiana, while the defendant union is affiliated with a similar organization having its headquarters in Baltimore, in the state of Maryland.　The plaintiff union was composed of workmen who, in 1897, withdrew from the defendant union.　.　.　.

The contest became active early in the fall of 1898.　In September of that year the members of the defendant union declared "all painters not affiliated with the Baltimore headquarters to be nonunion men," and voted "to notify bosses" of that declaration.　.　.　.

A duly authorized agent of the defendants would visit a shop where one or more of the plaintiffs were at work, and inform the employer of the action of the defendant union with reference to the plaintiffs, and ask him to induce such of the plaintiffs as were in his employ to sign applications for reinstatement in the defendant union.　As to the general nature of these interviews the master finds that the defendants have been courteous in manner, have made no threats of personal violence, have referred to the plaintiffs as nonunion men, but have not otherwise represented them as men lacking good standing in their craft; that they have not asked that the Lafayette men be discharged, and in some cases have expressly stated that they did not wish to have them discharged, but only that they sign the blanks for reinstatement in the defendant union.　The master, however, further finds, from all the circumstances under which those requests were made, that the defendants intended that employers of Lafayette men should fear trouble in their business if they continued to employ such men, .　.　. and as a means to this end they caused strikes to be instituted in the shops where strikes would seriously interfere with the business of the shops, and in all other shops they made such representations as would lead the proprietors thereof to expect trouble in their business.　We have, therefore, a case where the defendants have conspired to compel the members of the plaintiff union to join the defendant union, and, to carry out their purpose, have resolved upon such coercion and intimidation as naturally may be caused by threats of loss of property by strikes and boycotts, to induce the employers either to get the plaintiffs to ask for reinstatement in the defendant union, or, that failing, then to discharge them. It matters not that this request to discharge has not been expressly made. There can be no doubt, upon the findings of the master and the facts stated in his report, that the compulsory discharge of the plaintiffs in case of noncompliance with the demands of the defendant union is one of the prominent features of the plan agreed upon. It is well to see what is the meaning of this threat to strike, when taken in connection with the intimation that the employer may "expect trouble in his business." It means more than that the strikers will cease to work. That is only the preliminary skirmish. It means that those who have ceased to work will by strong, persistent, and organized persuasion and social pressure of every description do all they can to prevent the employer from procuring workmen to take their places. It means much more. It means that, if these peaceful measures fail, the employer may reasonably expect that unlawful physical injury may be done to his property; that attempts in all the ways practiced by organized labor will be made to injure him in his business, even to his ruin, if possible; and that by the use of vile and opprobrious epithets and other annoying conduct, and actual and threatened personal violence, attempts will be made to intimidate those who enter or desire to enter his employ; and that whether or not all this be done by the strikers or only by their sympathizers, or with the open sanction and approval of the former, he will have no help from them in his efforts to protect himself. However mild the language or suave the manner in which the threat to strike is made under such circumstances as are disclosed in this case, the employer knows that he is in danger of passing through such an ordeal as that above described, and those who make the threat know that as well as he does. Even if the intent of the strikers, so far as respects their own conduct and influence, be to discountenance all actual or threatened injury to person or property or business except that which is the direct necessary result of the interruption of the work, and even if their connection with the injurious and violent conduct of the turbulent among them or of their sympathizers be not such as to make them liable criminally, or even answerable civilly in damages to those who suffer, still, with full knowledge of what is to be expected, they give the signal, and in so doing must be held to avail themselves of the degree of fear and dread which the knowledge of such consequences will cause in the mind of those—whether their employer or fellow workmen—against whom the strike is directed; and the measure of coercion and intimidation imposed upon those against whom the strike is threatened or directed is not fully realized until all those probable consequences are considered. Such is the nature of the threat, and such the degree of coercion and intimidation involved in it. If the defendants can lawfully perform the acts complained of in the city of Springfield, they can pursue the plaintiffs all over the state in the same manner, and compel them to abandon their trade, or bow to the behests of their pursuers. . . . [T]his is not a case between the employer and employed, or, to use a hackneyed expression, between capital and labor, but between laborers all of the same craft, and each having the same right as any one of the others to pursue his calling. In this as in every other case of equal rights the right of each individual is to be exercised with due regard to the similar right of all others, and the right of one be said to end where that of another begins. The right involved is the right to dispose of one's labor with full freedom. This is a legal right, and it is entitled to legal protection. . . .

The defendants contend that they have done nothing unlawful, and in support of that contention they say that a person may work for whom he pleases, and, in the absence of any contract to the contrary, may cease to work when he pleases, and for any reason whatever, whether the same be good or bad; that he may give notice of his intention in advance, with or without stating the reason; that what one man may do several men acting in concert may do, and may agree beforehand that they will do, and may give notice of the agreement; and that all this may be lawfully done, notwithstanding such concerted action may, by reason of the consequent interruption of the work, result in great loss to the employer and his other employees, and that such a result was intended. In a general sense, and without reference to exceptions arising out of conflicting public and private interests, all this may be true. It is said also that, where one has the lawful right to do a thing, the motive by which he is actuated is immaterial. One form of this statement appears in the first headnote in Allen v. Flood, as reported in (1898) App.Cas. 1, as follows: "An act lawful in itself is not converted, by a bad or malicious motive, into an unlawful act, so as to make the doer of the act liable to a civil action." If the meaning of this and similar expressions is that, where a person has the lawful right to do a thing irrespective of his motive, his motive is immaterial, the proposition is a mere truism. If, however, the meaning is that where a person, if actuated by one kind of a motive, has a lawful right to do a thing, the act is lawful when done under any conceivable motive, or that an act lawful under one set of circumstances is therefore lawful under every conceivable set of circumstances, the proposition does not commend itself to us as either logically or legally accurate. In so far as a right is lawful it is lawful, and in many cases the right is so far absolute as to be lawful whatever may be the motive of the actor,—as, where one digs upon his own land for water (Greenleaf v. Francis, 18 Pick. (35 Mass.) 117), or makes a written lease of his land for the purpose of terminating a tenancy at will (Groustra v. Bourges, 141 Mass. 7, 4 N.E. 623); but in many cases the lawfulness of an act which causes damage to another may depend upon whether the act is for justifiable cause, and this justification may be found sometimes in the circumstances under which it is done, irrespective of motive, sometimes in the motive alone, and sometimes in the circumstances and motive combined. . . .

Still standing for solution is the question, under what circumstances, including the motive of the actor, is the act complained of lawful, and to what extent? In cases somewhat akin to the one at bar this court has had occasion to consider the question how far acts manifestly coercive and intimidating in their nature, which cause damage and injury to the business or property of another, and are done with intent to cause such injury, and partly in reliance upon such coercion, are justifiable. . . . On the other hand, it was held in Carew v. Rutherford, 106 Mass. 1, that a conspiracy against a mechanic—who is under the necessity of employing workmen in order to carry on his business—to obtain a sum of money from him, which he is under no legal obligation to pay, by inducing his workmen to leave him, or by deterring others from entering into his employ, or by threatening to do this, so that he is induced to pay the money demanded under a reasonable apprehension that he cannot carry on his business without yielding to the demands, is illegal, if not criminal, conspiracy; that the acts done under it are illegal, and that the money thus obtained may be recovered back. Chapman, C. J., speaking for the court, says that "there is no doubt that, if the parties under such circumstances succeed in injuring the business of the mechanic, they are liable to pay all the damages done to him." That case bears a close analogy to the one at bar. The acts there threatened were like those in this case, and the purpose was, in substance, to force the plaintiff to give his work to the defendants, and to extort from him a fine because he had given some of his work to other persons. Without now indicating to what extent workmen may combine, and in pursuance of an agreement may act by means of strikes and boycotts to get the hours of labor reduced, or their wages increased, or to procure from their employers any other concession directly and immediately affecting their own interests, or to help themselves in competition with their fellow workmen, we think this case must be governed by the principles laid down in Carew v. Rutherford, ubi supra. . . . It was not the intention of the defendants to give fairly to the employer the option to employ them or the plaintiffs, but to compel the latter against their will to join the association, and to that end to molest and interfere with them in their efforts to procure work by acts and threats well calculated by their coercive and intimidating nature to overcome the will. The defendants might make such lawful rules as they please for the regulation of their own conduct, but they had no right to force other persons to join them. The necessity that the plaintiffs should join this association is not so great, nor is its relation to the rights of the defendants, as compared with the right of the plaintiffs to be free from molestation, such as to bring the acts of the defendant under the shelter of the principles of trade competition. Such acts are without justification, and therefore are malicious and unlawful, and the conspiracy thus to force the plaintiffs was unlawful. Such conduct is intolerable, and inconsistent with the spirit of our laws. . . . As the plaintiffs have been injured by these acts, and there is reason to believe that the defendants contemplate further proceedings of the same kind, which will be likely still more to injure the plaintiffs, equity lies to enjoin the defendants. Vegelahn v. Guntner, ubi supra.

HOLMES, C. J. (dissenting). . . . If the decision in the present case simply had relied upon Vegelahn v. Guntner, I should have hesitated to say anything, although I might have stated that my personal opinion had not been weakened by the substantial agreement with my views to be found in the judgments of the majority of the house of lords in Allen v. Flood. But, much to my satisfaction, if I may say so, the court has seen fit to adopt the mode of approaching the question which I believe to be the correct one, and to open an issue which otherwise I might have thought closed. The difference between my Brethren and me now seems to be a difference of degree, and the line of reasoning followed makes it proper for me to explain where the difference lies.

I agree that the conduct of the defendants is actionable unless justified. [Citation omitted.] I agree that the presence or absence of justification may depend upon the object of their conduct; that is, upon the motive with which they acted. Vegelahn v. Guntner, 167 Mass. 92, 105, 106, 44 N.E. 1077, 35 L.R.A. 722. I agree, for instance, that, if a boycott or a strike is intended to override the jurisdiction of the courts by the action of a private association, it may be illegal. [Citation omitted.] On the other hand, I infer that a majority of my Brethren would admit that a boycott or strike intended to raise wages directly might be lawful, if it did not embrace in its scheme or intent violence, breach of contract, or other conduct unlawful on grounds independent of the mere fact that the action of the defendants was combined. A sensible workingman would not contend that the courts should sanction a combination for the purpose of inflicting or threatening violence, or the infraction of admitted rights. To come directly to the point, the issue is narrowed to the question whether, assuming that some purposes would be a justification, the purpose in this case of the threatened boycotts and strikes was such as to justify the threats. That purpose was not directly concerned with wages. It was one degree more remote. The immediate object and motive was to strengthen the defendants' society as a preliminary and means to make a better fight on questions of wages or other matters of clashing interests.

I differ from my Brethren in thinking that the threats were as lawful for this preliminary purpose as for the final one to which strengthening the union was a means. I think that unity of organization is necessary to make the contest of labor effectual, and that societies of laborers lawfully may employ in their preparation the means which they might use in the final contest.

Although this is not the place for extended economic discussion, and although the law may not always reach ultimate economic conceptions, I think it well to add that I cherish no illusions as to the meaning and effect of strikes. While I think the strike a lawful instrument in the universal struggle of life, I think it pure phantasy to suppose that there is a body of capital of which labor, as a whole, secures a larger share by that means.

The annual product, subject to an infinitesimal deduction for the luxuries of the few, is directed to consumption by the multitude, and is consumed by the multitude always. Organization and strikes may get a larger share for the members of an organization, but, if they do, they get it at the expense of the less organized and less powerful portion of the laboring mass. They do not create something out of nothing.

It is only by divesting our minds of questions of ownership and other machinery of distribution, and by looking solely at the question of consumption,—asking ourselves what is the annual product, who consumes it, and what changes would or could we make,—that we can keep in the world of realities.

But, subject to the qualifications which I have expressed, I think it lawful for a body of workmen to try by combination to get more than they now are getting, although they do it at the expense of their fellows, and to that end to strengthen their union by the boycott and the strike.

Note

Compare Vegelahn v. Guntner and Plant v. Woods with the following cases.

Bowen v. Matheson, 14 Allen (96 Mass.) 499 (1867). Plaintiff and defendants were competitors engaged in the business of furnishing seamen to vessels sailing from the Port of Boston. For the purpose of controlling the entire business and destroying competitors who did not comply with their terms, defendants entered into a combination by which they agreed, among other things, not to furnish seamen to any vessel which shipped men furnished by the plaintiff. On demurrer to these allegations *held*, for defendants. "If the effect is to destroy the business of shipping masters who are not members of the association, it is such a result as in the competition of business often follows from a course of proceeding that the law permits. New inventions and new methods of transacting business often destroy the business of those who adhere to old methods. Sometimes associations break down the business of individuals. . . . As the declaration sets forth no illegal acts on the part of defendants, the demurrer must be sustained."

Mogul Steamship Company v. McGregor, Gow, & Co., 23 Q.B.Div. 598 (1889). Defendants, a number of shipowners, formed themselves into a combination for the purpose of driving the plaintiffs and other competitors from the field and thereby securing control of the carriage of tea from certain Chinese ports. In order to accomplish this object defendants during the tea harvest of 1885 combined to offer very low freight rates with a view to "smashing" the rates and thereby rendering it unprofitable for the plaintiffs to send their ships to those ports. Defendants offered a 5 per cent rebate to all shippers and agents who would deal exclusively with defendants' vessels, and any agent who broke the condition forfeited his entire rebate on all shipments made on behalf of all his principals during the whole year. Plaintiffs brought this action for damages and an injunction against the continuance of the conspiracy. *Held*, for defendants. Acts which intentionally damage another's trade are actionable if done without just cause or excuse. Here, just cause or excuse is to be found in the defendants' right "to carry on their own trade freely in the mode and manner that best suits them, and which they think best calculated to secure their advantage. . . . It is urged, however, on the part of the plaintiffs, that even if the acts complained of would not be wrongful had they been committed by a single individual, they became actionable when they are the result of concerted action among several. . . . [It is impossible] to acquiesce in the view that the English law places any such restriction on the combination of capital as would be involved in the recognition of such a distinction. . . . The truth is, that the combination of capital for purposes of trade and competition is a very different thing from such a combination of several persons against one, with a view to harm him, as falls under the head of an indictable conspiracy. There is no just cause or excuse in the latter class of cases. There is just cause or excuse in the former. There are cases in which the very fact of a combination is evidence of a design to do that which is hurtful without just cause—is evidence—to use a technical expression—of malice. But it is perfectly legitimate, as it seems to me, to combine capital for all the mere purposes of trade for which capital may, apart from combination, be legitimately used in trade. To limit combinations of capital, when used for purposes of competition, in the manner proposed by the argument of the plaintiffs, would in the present day, be impossible—would be only another method of attempting to set boundaries to the tides."

Questions

1. Do the facts, as found by the master in chancery, indicate that an employer who refuses to yield to the defendants can reason-

ably expect "strong, persistent, and organized persuasion and social pressure . . . to prevent [him] from procuring workmen"? Is there evidence in the master's findings to indicate that "if [the defendant's] peaceful methods fail, the employer may reasonably expect that unlawful physical violence may be done to his property; . . . and that by . . . actual and threatened personal violence, attempts will be made to intimidate those who enter or desire to enter his employ"?

2. Judge Hammond stated that the defendant's acts were "without justification, and therefore are malicious and unlawful . . . ." What are the grounds on which he based this conclusion?

3. In his dissent in Vegelahn v. Guntner, Judge Holmes said, "It is on the question of what shall amount to a justification, and more especially on the nature of the considerations which really determine or ought to determine the answer to that question, that judicial reasoning seems to me often to be inadequate. The true grounds of decision are considerations of policy and social advantage, ... Propositions as to public policy rarely are unanimously accepted . . . (it requires) special training to enable anyone even to form an intelligent opinion about them." Does this statement imply that judges may not possess that special training necessary to formulate and critically evaluate propositions as to public policy?

4. Judge Holmes states in Plant v. Woods that the difference between him and the majority is "a difference of degree." Was it a difference as to the interpretation and application of the law, or was it a difference regarding considerations of "policy and social advantage"?

5. Can Plant v. Woods be reconciled with Bowen v. Matheson and with Mogul S. S. Co. v. McGregor, Gow, & Co.?

6. Are you persuaded by Judge Holmes' argument that although strikes are futile from the point of view of society (or even the working classes) as a whole, nevertheless in the universal struggle of life employees should have the same right as employers to combine and fight for larger shares of the spoils? Is there a relationship between an economic theory and a legal theory implicit in this analysis?

7. Although sharp conflicts can be found among the courts of different states, the dominant trend in judicial rulings, in the absence of legislative and constitutional developments to be discussed later, has been to permit strikes and picketing by employees where the immediate purpose is to improve wages or working conditions, but to prohibit them where the immediate purpose is to unionize the shop, or to institute collective bargaining, or to induce the hiring of one type of worker as against another for a particular kind of job. Also picketing by persons not employees—so-called "stranger

picketing"—has generally been held tortious at common law. In terms of the functional approach suggested in the Introduction and amplified in Parts I–III, consider to what extent such decisions can contribute to the (a) restoration of social order which has been disrupted, (b) preservation of historical continuity and consistency of legal doctrine, (c) protection and facilitation of voluntary arrangements, and (d) improvement of moral and legal conceptions of the community.

Note
The Philosophy of the Judges

The preceding cases present a small sample of judicial opinion regarding the legal status of organized labor at the turn of this century. The sample fairly accurately reflects the general response to the rise of the labor movement. This response was made in the adjudication of cases where private parties or public officials sought judicial remedies for injuries occasioned by labor union conduct. In the process of adjudicating these cases it fell to the courts to formulate new law to govern the relations between employers and organizations of employees. It is readily apparent that the law as formulated by the judges was disadvantageous to organized labor. This is the more significant since such judge-made law comprised practically the whole of legal doctrine regarding organized labor, in the years between the Civil War and World War I.

The legal restraint of organized labor in that era was viewed by the majority of judges as a proper application of common law principles, and especially the law of conspiracy. Holmes and others offered an alternative formulation of the problem, in which combinations of labor were viewed as the analogue of combinations of capital, *e. g.*, the business corporation, and the struggle between organized labor and the business firm was, in the Holmesian view, the free struggle for life. Thus the judicial response to the burgeoning labor movement can be seen as the product of a choice between competing analogies, and the more persuasive analogy was that which compared the combination of labor to a conspiracy.

But why was that analogy more persuasive to the judges than any other alternative? The following are some of the factors which may have contributed to tipping the judicial balance against organized labor.

1. There is an inherent conservatism in the common law. As we have seen, the common law is a means to maintain stability through a process oriented to the preservation of historical continuity. A social change must achieve some permanence before it is given recognition in common law, and such changes are accorded recognition through an adaptive process of case by case development. As a social evolution takes place, the cases presented in court

will reflect limited aspects of that evolution within the confines of individual disputes, and over time the judges will, in the process of resolving the individual conflicts, evolve general principles which are adapted to the underlying social changes.

However, the rise of organized labor was more nearly a social revolution than a social evolution. It was a massive response to rapid changes in the economic organization of society, and it involved a sharp conflict between social classes over the right to control conditions of work and over the division of the product of economic activity. But the judges, when presented with individual cases which embodied some small part of that conflict, were not asked to plumb these fundamental questions of social justice, but were instead presented with an individual conflict in which an employer or government official sought relief from some immediate injury flowing from some specific acts through which labor was seeking an immediate and limited goal. In such a context the judicial inquiry was directed primarily to the issues raised by the immediate dispute and the immediate injury to the employer or the public. The underlying problems of a massive class conflict resulting from very rapid social change tended, perhaps, to be obscured and, in the context of the individual cases, preservation of the existing order may have seemed the wiser course.

2. The common law embodied some elements of an economic philosophy which was not wholly sympathetic to the acts and objectives of the labor movement. For at least two centuries the common law had been much concerned with the establishment and preservation of individual property rights. It had been the vehicle through which a feudal property system, in which land was held of the crown, evolved into a system in which land was held primarily as a matter of private right. The evolution of the doctrine of free contract further extended the economic liberty of the individual and, together with private property, was one of the prime legal institutions on which the English and American economies rested. These institutions, which afforded mobility to the factors of production, were given strong support in the writings of 19th century economists, the heirs to the laissez faire philosophy of Adam Smith. The judges were not insensitive to this economic philosophy, and they were cognizant of the economic development which was occurring under the existing legal order. Thus both legal and economic theory influenced them to react against a movement which appeared to strike at rights of private property and which threatened interference with individual contracts between employers and individual employees.

3. The social, economic, and political background of American judges in the late 19th and early 20th centuries was not such as to predispose them to give legal protection to the rising labor movement. Drawn primarily from the middle class, most judges, both through upbringing and through professional experience, absorbed the then-dominant beliefs in the sacredness of private property and

contract and in "rugged individualism." The most common routes to judicial appointment were then, as they are now, success in law practice, effective public service, or some preeminence in politics. In the years after the Civil War, attainments in any or all of these fields tended to make judges identify themselves primarily with business interests rather than with the interests of organized labor.

Thus the judiciary, when faced with the necessity of choosing from the competing analogies and policies advocated in a labor case, were influenced not only by legal rules and concepts but also by more subtle factors of legal history, political and economic philosophy, and social background. Indeed, some judges viewed organized labor as a subversive force entirely alien to American life. This reaction, in turn, encouraged some labor leaders and workers to view law as a force entirely alien to their class interests. The history of the adjudication of labor disputes thus furnishes us with a striking and in many ways an extreme example of the effect of extra-legal factors upon judicial decisions. This history also demonstrates the stresses and strains placed upon the judicial process by acute social conflict.

Chapter 10

LEGISLATION AND LABOR LAW: 1890–1921

In preceding sections we have considered some aspects of legislation relevant to particular topics, but our prime focus has been on the judicial process as a source of law. This chapter begins an examination of legislation as a source of law.

We would note at the outset that our primary concern here is not with legislative process, in the sense of the process through which public policy positions are written into statutes. Rather we are concerned with the impact of statutes on the judicial process and on lawyers and litigants subject to that process.

A statute is law in the abstract until such time as judges, public officials, lawyers, and private citizens act with respect to it. When such action takes place, the statute becomes law in action, a part of law viewed not in the abstract but as a process.

The following sections are concerned with the impact of statutes on judges and the manner in which judges respond to statutory law; and with the impact of statutes on lawyers and their clients, who rely on the statutory law as relevant to the resolution of disputes or to obtain guidance in choosing among alternative modes of conduct. Our objective is to provide some insights into the significance of legislation as a means through which law is adapted to social change so as to facilitate the legal resolution of intense social conflict.

SECTION 35. LEGISLATION RESTRICTING ORGANIZED LABOR: THE SHERMAN ANTITRUST ACT OF 1890

[The following is taken from WILLIAM LETWIN,* LAW AND ECONOMIC POLICY IN AMERICA (New York, 1964), pp. 11–12.]

The process of making and then enforcing a law in America creates a strong likelihood that those who wanted the law will be less than satisfied with its effects. It would be different if the wishes of some could by fiat instantly force others to do this or that. A representative democracy whose legal order stems from the common-law tradition is exactly the opposite. The will of the people is first narrowed to a focus, slowly, by successive stages of abstraction; at the focus stands the statute, a number of words printed on

* Professor of Economic History, Massachusetts Institute of Technology.

paper; and then the words are laboriously translated, case by case, into rules of action, which after some long time spread their influence over the actions or lives of all the people. It is a process, one might say, shaped like an hourglass.

The process begins when many citizens become perturbed about something, perhaps without being able clearly to identify the cause of their irritation, or, having identified it, advocating no cure more concrete than "a law against it." To be able to identify exactly where the rub comes is one function of the professional politician; if he lacks the necessary sensitivity he cannot succeed in a vigorously democratic community; but if he is skillful he will be able to point out more sharply than the citizens themselves have ever conceived it the sources of their concern. The politician's first task, then, is to begin arranging and bringing toward convergence the loose, shapeless, spread-out grains of public sentiment. In time, enough of this may have been done so that the party, the administration, or—as often happens—one or two congressmen feel that they have a clear commission to prepare a statute. A bill is introduced in Congress. Most bills are stillborn, because they deal with evils felt and remedies welcomed by none but their sponsors. If, however, the bill is of some general interest, it is considered by a standing committee, which may at its discretion report the bill to the house. The house may then debate the bill—members extolling, criticizing, and offering amendments—during sittings spread out over weeks or months, or during one hectic hour, after which the bill may, if it has attracted sufficiently strong sponsorship, be brought to a vote. If it passes, it is then sent to the other house, where it goes through a similar process of scrutiny by committee, debate, and vote. But even after both houses have voted favorably, the bill may yet be far from law, for the two houses may have passed bills which are nearly the same but not exactly the same. The discrepant bills are now delivered to a conference committee, charged wih inventing a compromise draft. The bill, in its new version, is reconsigned to each house for further action. If passed by both houses, and if signed by the President, the bill finally becomes law.

In this, the first political chapter of law, a great work of condensation has taken place. The diverse and inchoate sentiments that make up public opinion in its early unformed stage have been marshalled into the conflicting positions of congressmen; these in turn are reduced to order by debate and negotiation—that is, by persuasion, bargaining, hectoring, charming, and voting; and finally all is crystallized in a few abstract words.

[The following is taken from CHARLES O. GREGORY,* LABOR AND THE LAW, second revised edition (Chicago, 1958), pp. 201–205.]

The Sherman Act, passed in 1890, is exceedingly simple in statement. The gist of the act appears in its first two sections, which read, in part, as follows:

"Section 1. Every contract, combination in the form of trust or otherwise, or conspiracy, in restraint of trade or commerce among the several

* Lecturer, University of Connecticut School of Law, and Professor of Law, *Emeritus*, University of Virginia.

States, or with foreign nations, is hereby declared to be illegal. Every person who shall make any such contract or engage in any such combination or conspiracy, shall be deemed guilty of a misdemeanor, . . ."

"Section 2. Every person who shall monopolize, or attempt to monopolize, or combine or conspire with any other person or persons, to monopolize any part of the trade or commerce among the several States, or with foreign nations, shall be deemed guilty of a misdemeanor, . . ."

The federal courts are then given jurisdiction to enforce this act, and the attorney general is empowered to initiate criminal prosecutions or to secure injunctive relief against violations. All persons injured by violations of others are allowed to maintain civil suits for triple damages against those who violated the terms of the act.

From what has been quoted above, this act must seem to be fairly simple. In order to appreciate what Section 1 does, all you have to know is the meaning of the phrase "in restraint of trade or commerce." Unfortunately, this phrase has the delusive exactness of a good many other well-known words and phrases of general import current in our language. It is probably easier to understand the phrase, "to monopolize any part of the trade or commerce," appearing in Section 2 of the act, yet that phrase is not crystal clear itself. Justice Holmes is said to have thought these two sections so general in their coverage that they were almost meaningless, amounting to little, if anything, more than a fiat from Congress to the federal courts to do right by the consuming public in protecting it from the depredations of big enterprise. It set forth no economic program at all and took no position, implying at most what English and American courts had thought as a matter of common law to be the meaning of the phrase "restraint of trade." This invitation to the courts to exploit their own economic philosophy in controlling big enterprises of all sorts Holmes is said to have considered so vague and irresponsible as to merit being declared unconstitutional.

Everyone knew why the act was passed in 1890. It was in response to popular demand aroused by the fear of gigantic industrial and commercial enterprises which threatened to seize control of the manufacturing and marketing of consumer goods of all kinds. The public perceived safety of an economic nature only in what it called competition—that grand weasel word productive of so much confusion and misunderstanding. Sympathetic politicians, and economists who were sorely afraid of what was happening to our economic life, were convinced that national economic health and the security of consumers could be possible only if something called freedom of competition prevailed. This they apparently envisaged as a multiplicity of small productive and commercial enterprises continually vying with each other for the patronage of the public by shaving costs and prices, in order that each might make his merchandise more sought after than that of his competitors. Their philospohy was rather shortsighted—albeit it reflected a most commendable social ideal—in that it presupposed natural boundaries to the practices of competition.

The boldest of our big business leaders, on the other hand, recognized no such boundaries. Through collective action and high finance their aim was to eliminate un-co-operative competitors or buy them up, in order that thereafter they might govern particular commodity markets through strict control over the amounts of goods produced and over the pricing of such goods as were released to the public. These techniques they thought of as competition—a sort of commercial conflict with other enterprisers vying with them for the same markets. And since they themselves asked no quarter, they could not understand why they should be expected to pull their punches— especially since the aim of the act was to preserve the process of competition, in which they believed themselves to be busily engaged.

Competition, of course, is a question-begging term. A state of unlimited competition in a free enterprise society logically leads to the centralizing of control in the hands of the strongest, usually through combinations and mergers of formerly separated units which had carried on independently of each other. Thus, competition carried to its logical extreme paradoxically results in the antithesis of competition—or no competition. This result has led some of our leading economists to affirm that there is no such thing as real competition in the idealistic sense of a multiplicity of small units vying for the patronage of the consumer by offering the lowest possible prices for their goods. The legalistic definition of competition which appears in the court reports is this—it is a categorical justification for inflicting damage on others while in the pursuit of self-interest and gain, so far as the means employed do not constitute a violation of any settled category of tort or crime. If this definition is accepted, it might be thought that the proponents of the Sherman Act had in mind the preservation of something quite different from the idealistic competition discussed above. It seems certain, however, that the popular conception was that they were really trying to prevent much that our courts regarded as competition, and hoped to preserve an economy of relatively small units of production and distribution.

The courts at common law had traditionally maintained a prohibition against what they called restraint of trade. This was a negative control, in that it consisted merely of a refusal to enforce contracts in furtherance of restraints of trade and did not imply any punishment or liability in damages. Such restraints commonly occurred after combinations among enterprisers had seized control of markets through the exercise of ruthless competitive practices. For instance, a group of manufacturers of a particular commodity might combine to control the supply and price of this commodity in accordance with a contract among themselves, which provided a penalty against any one of them not observing the arrangement. This contract, and the combination supporting it, effected what is known as a restraint of trade—for it negatived the freedom of economic independence of enterprise that is the kind of competition epigrammatically spoken of as the life of trade.

As long as the combination in question remained mutually co-operative and retained the economic power to discourage independent enterprise in the same industrial field, its members could charge what they wished for the commodity involved. This arrangement the courts thought bad—but not bad enough to deserve the criminal and tort penalties of punishment, triple damages and injunction. It was bad because consumers suffered as a consequence of these production and marketing controls. But the courts, albeit there were historical precedents for punishments of a criminal nature, showed their displeasure only in refusing to enforce the contract holding the combination together when one of its members, in order to promote his own welfare, violated it. The courts considered this negative concession to the interests of consumers, together with the constant theoretical possibility of new enterprise entering the field, to be ample protection for the public.

Events preceding the Sherman Act indicated that this was not so. The public simply did not agree with this optimism. If the courts would not help out combinations and trusts to keep recalcitrant members in line, these organizations had other ways of enforcing their own arrangements through the exercise of economic pressures. As for the influx of new enterprise designed to compete with the combination, that was usually either eliminated or taken in, most handily. In view of all this, it seems fairly clear that what the proponents of the Sherman Act had in mind was merely by statute to supplant the traditional negative sanction against restraints of trade with the positive penalties of criminal punishment, liability in damages and the injunction, and to empower the federal courts to substitute these positive measures in dealing with restraints of trade formerly regarded as only nonenforceable in the courts. To be more explicit, it seems that what Congress did in the Sherman Act was to make expressly unlawful those undertakings which the courts, as a matter of common law and without legislation, had always tolerated as insufficiently evil to punish but only bad enough to ignore.

If this analysis is correct—and there is much evidence in that direction—it explains the ambiguity of sections 1 and 2 of the Sherman Act. Congress apparently presupposed a fairly definite body of common law, covering those types of situations involving monopolies and market controls through combinations, trusts, mergers and agreements, which the courts thought were undesirable. Instead of trying to define in fairly express legislative terms just what these situations were, it merely comprised them in the phrase restraint of trade or commerce and gave the federal courts three clubs to use against restrainers of trade, where before they had had available only the frown of disapproval. This discussion does not relate in detail what was comprised under common-law restraints of trade, as that is an undertaking not particularly necessary in this book. Suffice it to say that the phrase "restraint of trade" implied at common law the denial and suppression of freedom of independent and uncontrolled enterprise by contract and combination, and the control of supply and price of commodities through the same means. Hence it necessarily, or surely would seem to have, meant that violators of the act must have been engaged in the production or marketing of commodities. In any event, this observation is important, if it be true, when we come to deal with labor cases arising under the Sherman Act.

[The following is taken from WILLIAM LETWIN, *op. cit.*, pp. 95–99.]

LAW AND POLICY IN THE SHERMAN ACT

The Sherman Act was as good an antitrust law as the Congress of 1890 could have devised. Congressmen had been called on to give the Federal Government novel powers to control, directly and generally, the organization of economic life. They had little experience to teach them how such a law should be written or to inform them how the courts might interpret it. They realized from the beginning that whatever law they composed would be imperfect. Its strongest advocates frankly admitted that it would be "experimental," and in the end the whole of Congress was reconciled to the limitation Sherman recognized when he said, "All that we, as lawmakers, can do is to declare general principles." Yet if the Sherman Act was an experiment, it was the safest one Congress could make, and if it only declared general principles, they were at least the familiar ones of the common law. Sherman had repeatedly said that his bill was based on a tried formula: "It does not announce a new principle of law, but applies old and well-recognized principles of the common law to the complicated jurisdiction of our State and Federal Government." Edmunds, principal author of the Judiciary Committee bill, and Hoar, who guided it through debate on the floor, said the same. Of the eighty-two senators, sixty-eight were lawyers, and as one of them said, "I suppose no lawyer needs to have argument made to him that these combinations and trusts are illegal without statute." They could not tell how the courts would construe a statute that gave the government power to indict and sue the offenders, but they believed that the courts would experience little difficulty in recognizing the offense.

Congress had reason to think, further, that the Act aimed at the proper goals. On the one hand, it satisfied the public demand for an antitrust law. It prohibited trusts in so many words: it declared illegal "every contract, combination in the form of a trust or otherwise, or conspiracy, in restraint of trade or commerce among the several States or with foreign nations." This specific mention of "trusts" had almost been omitted, for Edmunds so strongly desired to define the offense in "terms that were well known to the law already" that his draft of the section used only the common-law words, "contract," "combination," and "conspiracy." But a majority of his colleagues on the Judiciary Committee had seen the political value of adding a term that was well known to the public and had agreed to insert Evart's phrase, "in the form of a trust or otherwise."

On the other hand, the Act did not go farther than Congress thought it should. Congressmen were no more in favor of unlimited competition than the economists were. Sherman, in his great address, had emphasized that many combinations were desirable. He was sure that they had been an important cause of America's wealth, and he had no intention of prohibiting them. It was only "the unlawful combination, tested by the rules of common law and human experience, that is aimed at by this bill, and not the lawful and useful combination." Edmunds and Hoar later said they had the same intention. A majority of the representatives who conferred with senators about the House amendment opposed it for similar reasons. They said that the bill's "only object was the control of trusts, so called," but that the scope of the amendment was broader, and indeed too broad: "It declares illegal any agreement for relief from the effects of competition in the two industries of transportation and merchandising, however excessive or destructive such competition may be." Senator Teller meant the same, although he used impolitic language, when he said that "a trust may not always be an evil. A trust for certain purposes, which may mean simply a combination of capital, may be a favorable thing to the community and the country." Perhaps the clearest statement of this view, held by many congressmen as well as by many economists of the period, was that of Representative Stewart of Vermont:

> [T]here are two great forces working in human society in this country to-day, and they have been contending for the mastery on one side or the other for the last two generations. Those two great forces are competition and combination. They are cor-

rectives of each other, and both ought to exist.   Both ought to
be under restraint.   Either of them, if allowed to be unrestrained,
is destructive of the material interests of this country.

The common law was a perfect instrument for realizing the policy supported by Congress.   It prohibited some monopolies but not all combinations,
and congressmen felt that a statute based on it would have equally qualified
effects.

Though the pattern of the law was sound, there were nevertheless defects in detail.   Various ambiguities had crept in because so many men
had taken part in drafting it, because they wanted it to be simple and general, and because they wanted to use common-law terms to define the offenses.   In order to keep the law broad, Congress did not specifically exclude labor unions from its scope or include railroad pools.   So far as their
sentiments were expressed in debates and bills, they had favored unions or
wanted to leave them immune from this law.   Sherman said they should
be specifically exempted and many agreed with him.   Edmunds almost
alone spoke against a specific exemption, because he thought that labor
unions should be treated like any other combination.   But when he came to
write the bill he was mainly concerned with keeping it unqualified.   His
colleagues seem to have been convinced by his arguments in favor of simplicity.   Although during the debates four of the eight members of the
Judiciary Committee spoke for exempting labor unions, they all voted for
Edmunds' draft, probably because they agreed that the law should not
be cluttered with details and felt that, in any case, it would not be construed against unions.   Reasoning of the same sort explains why railroad
pools were not specifically named as offenders, for Senator Vest, a member
of the Judiciary Committee, in commenting on the House amendment said
that he too had wanted to add an explicit prohibition, until the other committeemen convinced him it would be redundant.   In order to make the
Act more inclusive, Congress introduced another note that added to its
ambiguity.   "Restraints of trade," as the common law understood them, could
only come about through agreement between persons; but the Judiciary
Committee felt that the Act should also condemn any individual who restrained trade by himself, and they therefore drafted a section making
it illegal for any individual to "monopolize."   Hoar and Edmunds assured
the Senate that the word had a well-known meaning at common law, and
their advice was followed, although the word meant little more at common
law than the engrossing of a local food supply.   These were only a few
of the blemishes that marred the Act; the courts in time found many more.
But to have drawn up a more satisfactory solution for a new and difficult
problem, congressmen would have had to be much more adept, much more
remote from public opinion, and much more unanimous in their own views
than the lawmakers of a democracy ever can be.

LOEWE v. LAWLOR (THE DANBURY HATTERS' CASE)

Supreme Court of the United States, 1908.
208 U.S. 274, 28 S.Ct. 301.

[Plaintiff Loewe was engaged in the business of manufacturing
felt hats at a plant located in Danbury, Connecticut.   The defendants
were all members of the United Hatters of North America, a union

affiliated with the A.F. of L. The hatters' union was attempting to organize all large manufacturers of felt hats in the United States. Local strikes against Loewe had failed to bring him to an agreement with the union, so the hatters organized a national boycott of Loewe's products, as a result of which union members and their sympathizers refused to purchase Loewe's hats or to do business with merchants who sold them. This was a so-called secondary boycott, the union attempting to interfere with Loewe's business by bringing pressure to bear on persons not parties to the primary dispute, in this case Loewe's customers, the hat merchants. The boycott caused a decline in Loewe's sales. He brought suit in the Federal District Court in Connecticut claiming that the boycott constituted a combination in restraint of trade, unlawful under the Sherman Act, and he asked the court to award him treble damages. The District Court dismissed the complaint, holding the Sherman Act inapplicable to the union conduct. Loewe appealed to the Circuit Court of Appeals which in turn certified the case to the Supreme Court. The question presented to the Court was whether the Sherman Act applied to combinations of labor so as to support a treble damage action. Pertinent parts of the Court's opinion follow.]

In our opinion, the combination described in the declaration is a combination "in restraint of trade or commerce among the several states," in the sense in which those words are used in the act, and the action can be maintained accordingly.

And that conclusion rests on many judgments of this court, to the effect that the act prohibits any combination whatever to secure action which essentially obstructs the free flow of commerce between the states, or restricts, in that regard, the liberty of a trader to engage in business.

The combination charged falls within the class of restraints of trade aimed at compelling third parties and strangers involuntarily not to engage in the course of trade except on conditions that the combination imposes; and there is no doubt that (to quote from the well-known work of Chief Justice Erle on Trade Unions) "at common law every person has individually, and the public also has collectively, a right to require that the course of trade should be kept free from unreasonable obstruction." But the objection here is to the jurisdiction, because, even conceding that the declaration states a case good at common law, it is contended that it does not state one within the statute. Thus, it is said that the restraint alleged would operate to entirely destroy plaintiffs' business and thereby include intrastate trade as well; that physical obstruction is not alleged as contemplated; and that defendants are not themselves engaged in interstate trade.

We think none of these objections are tenable, and that they are disposed of by previous decisions of this court.

United States v. Trans-Missouri Freight Asso., 166 U.S. 290, 41 L.Ed. 1007, 17 Sup.Ct.Rep. 540; United States v. Joint Traffic Asso., 171 U.S. 505, 43 L.Ed. 259, 19 Sup.Ct.Rep. 25; and Northern Securities Co. v. United States, 193 U.S. 197, 48 L.Ed. 679, 24 Sup.Ct.Rep. 436, hold, in effect, that the anti-trust law has a broader application than the prohibition of restraints of trade unlawful at common law. Thus, in the Trans-Missouri Case it was said that, "assuming that agreements of this nature are not void at common law, and that the various cases cited by the learned courts below show it, the answer to the statement of their validity now is to be found in the terms of the statute under consideration;" and, in the Northern Securities Case, that the act declares "illegal every contract, combination or conspiracy, in whatever form, of whatever nature, and whoever may be parties to it, which directly or necessarily operates in restraint of trade or commerce among the several states."

The averments here are that there was an existing interstate traffic between plaintiffs and citizens of other states, and that, for the direct purpose of destroying such interstate traffic, defendants combined not merely to prevent plaintiffs from manufacturing articles then and there intended for transportation beyond the state, but also to prevent the vendees from reselling the hats which they had imported from Connecticut, or from further negotiating with plaintiffs for the purchase and intertransportation of such hats from Connecticut to the various places of destination. So that, although some of the means whereby the interstate traffic was to be destroyed were acts within a state, and some of them were, in themselves as a part of their obvious purpose and effect, beyond the scope of Federal authority, still as we have seen, the acts must be considered as a whole, and the plan is open to condemnation, notwithstanding a negligible amount of intrastate business might be affected in carrying it out. If the purposes of the combination were, as alleged, to prevent any interstate transportation at all, the fact that the means operated at one end before physical transportation commenced, and, at the other end, after the physical transportation ended, was immaterial.

Nor can the act in question be held inapplicable because defendants were not themselves engaged in interstate commerce. The act made no distinction between classes. It provided that "every" contract, combination, or conspiracy in restrain of trade was illegal. The records of Congress show that several efforts were made to exempt, by legislation, organizations of farmers and laborers from the operation of the act, and that all these efforts failed, so that the act remained as we have it before us.

In an early case (United States v. Workingmen's Amalgamated Council, 26 L.R.A. 158, 4 Inters.Com.Rep. 831, 54 Fed. 994) the United States filed a bill under the Sherman act in the circuit court for the eastern district of Louisiana, averring the existence of "a gigantic and widespread combination of the members of a multitude of separate organizations for the purpose of restraining the commerce among the several states and with foreign countries," and it was contended that the statute did not refer to combinations of laborers. But the court, granting the injunction, said:

"I think the congressional debates show that the statute had its origin in the evils of massed capital; but, when the Congress came to formulating the prohibition, which is the yardstick for measuring the complainant's right to the injunction, it expressed it in these words: 'Every contract or combination in the form of trust, or otherwise in restraint of trade or commerce among the several states or with foreign nations, is hereby declared to be illegal.' The subject had so broadened in the minds of the legislators that the source of the evil was not regarded as material, and the evil in its entirety is dealt with. They made the interdiction include combinations of labor as well as of capital; in fact, all combinations in restraint of commerce, without reference to the character of the persons who entered into them. It is true this statute has not been much expounded by judges, but, as it seems to me, its meaning, as far as relates to the sort of combinations to which it is to apply, is manifest, and that it includes combinations which are composed of laborers acting in the interest of laborers.

* * *

"It is the successful effort of the combination of the defendants to intimidate and overawe others who were at work in conducting or carrying on the commerce of the country, in which the court finds their error and their violation of the statute. One of the intended results of their combined action was the forced stagnation of all the commerce which flowed through New Orleans. This intent and combined action are none the less unlawful because they included in their scope the paralysis of all other business within the city as well."

The case was affirmed on appeal by the circuit court of appeals for the fifth circuit. 6 C.C.A. 258, 13 U.S.App. 426, 57 Fed. 85.

Subsequently came the litigation over the Pullman strike and the decisions Re Debs, 5 Inters.Com.Rep. 163, 64 Fed. 724, 745, 755, 158 U.S. 564, 39 L.Ed. 1092, 15 Sup.Ct.Rep. 900. The bill in that case was filed by the United States against the officers of the American Railway Union, which alleged that a labor dispute existed between the Pullman Palace Car Company and its employees; that thereafter the four officers of the railway union combined together and with others to compel an adjustment of such dispute by creating a boycott against the cars of the car company; that, to make such boycott effective, they had already prevented certain of the railroads running out of Chicago from operating their trains; that they asserted that they could and would tie up, paralyze, and break down any and every railroad which did not accede to their demands, and that the purpose and intention of the combination was "to secure unto themselves the entire control of the interstate, industrial, and commercial business in which the population of the city of Chicago and of the other communities along the lines of road of said railways are engaged with each other, and to restrain any and all other persons from any independent control or management of such interstate, industrial, or commercial enterprises, save according to the will and with the consent of the defendants."

The circuit court proceeded principally upon the Sherman anti-trust law, and granted an injunction. In this court the case was rested upon the broader ground that the Federal government had full power over interstate commerce and over the transmission of the mails, and, in the exercise of those powers, could remove everything put upon highways, natural or artificial, to obstruct the passage of interstate commerce, or the carrying of the mails. But, in reference to the anti-trust act, the court expressly stated:

"We enter into no examination of the act of July 2, 1890, chap. 647, 26 Stat. at L. 209, U.S.Comp.Stat. 1901, p. 3200, upon which the circuit court relied mainly to sustain its jurisdiction. It must not be understood from this that we dissent from the conclusions of that court in reference to the scope of the act, but simply that we prefer to rest our judgment on the broader ground which has been discussed in this opinion, believing it of importance that the principles underlying it should be fully stated and affirmed."

And, in the opinion, Mr. Justice Brewer, among other things, said:

"It is curious to note the fact that in a large proportion of the cases in respect to interstate commerce brought to this court the question presented was of the validity of state legislation in its bearings upon interstate commerce, and the uniform course of decision has been to declare that it is not within the competency of a state to legislate in such a manner as to obstruct interstate commerce. If a state, with its recognized powers of sovereignty, is impotent to obstruct interstate commerce, can it be that any mere voluntary association of individuals within the limits of that state has a power which the state itself does not possess?"

The question answers itself; and, in the light of the authorities, the only inquiry is as to the sufficiency of the averments of fact. We have given the declaration in full in the margin, and it appears therefrom that it is charged that defendants formed a combination to directly restrain plaintiffs' trade; that the trade to be restrained was interstate; that certain means to attain such restraint were contrived to be used and employed to that end; that those means were so used and employed by defendants, and that thereby they injured plaintiffs' property and business.

[The Court then found that Loewe had been injured by an unlawful combination in restraint of trade and that he should be awarded treble damages. The case was remanded to the District Court, the sole issue remaining for that court being the determination of the amount of the damages. On remand the District Court awarded Loewe more than half a million dollars, which award could be satisfied out of the assets of Lawlor and the other individual union members who were joined as defendants in the action.]

Questions

1. What was the restraint of trade which the Court found had been effectuated by the hatters? Was it interference with Loewe's business? With the business of the hat merchants? With the interstate shipment of hats?

2. If the immediate objective of the union was restraint of the interstate shipment of hats, what was the ultimate objective?

3. Assuming that the union activities here comprised a restraint of trade, does a literal reading of the Sherman Act afford a rationale for the Court's decision?

4. Did the Supreme Court examine the legislative history of the Sherman Act? Should courts indulge in such examinations of legislative history as an aid to statutory construction or should they limit their inquiry to the language of the statute and from that language alone decide what the legal effect of the statute shall be?

Note

The Supreme Court's opinion in the Danbury Hatters' case established the applicability of the Sherman Act to union conduct which restrained interstate commerce. Since the Sherman Act empowered the Department of Justice to bring criminal charges and to obtain injunctions against violators of the act, the decision could have opened the door to a rash of actions by the United States against organized labor. This prospect did not materialize, in part because Congress acted to prevent the application of the Sherman Act against labor in proceedings brought by the United States. The first such action was taken in 1913. In that year the act appropriating monies to support the Justice Department contained the following proviso: "Provided, however, that no part of this money shall be spent in the prosecution of any organization or individual for entering into any combination or agreement having in view the increasing of wages, shortening of hours, or bettering the conditions of labor, or for any act done in furtherance thereof, not in itself unlawful." The same proviso was included in the bills appropriating funds to the Justice Department in each year from 1913 through 1923. This effectively eliminated public actions against organized labor under the Sherman Act during that period, but it did not eliminate the private treble damage proceeding as a possible threat to organized labor. This was more than an idle threat in light of the substantial award in Loewe v. Lawlor. Furthermore that case established that membership in a union was a sufficient basis for the imposition of individual liability on a member who had not himself directly participated in acts injurious to the plaintiff, the theory being that the officers and members who did actively direct the union activity were acting as agents on behalf of all the members. Thus the possible application of the Sherman Act against labor not only discouraged some forms of union activity, but also tended to discourage membership in a union. Congress was called upon to pass legislation completely revising the federal antitrust law with respect to labor. The next section of material deals with that topic.

SECTION 36.   LEGISLATIVE RESTRICTIONS ON THE USE OF THE LABOR INJUNCTION

SECTION 36.1   PUBLIC OPINION AND THE LABOR MOVEMENT

[The following is taken from COX & BOK, CASES ON LABOR LAW (7th ed.) pp. 52–54. Footnotes are omitted.]

THE ENACTMENT OF THE CLAYTON ACT

Throughout the years 1886–1914 there gradually developed, despite the hostile attitude of the courts and the organized opposition of employers, a strong body of opinion which held that the workers should be granted the right to organize unions without employer interference, and that the employers should be required to recognize and deal with their employees' unions. As early as 1894, the United States Strike Commission, which had been investigating the causes of the Pullman strike, criticized the attitude of some of the courts and urged employers to recognize and bargain with labor organizations. In 1902 a report made by the Industrial Commission to Congress ridiculed the suggestion that individual freedom was lost under a system of collective agreements and stressed their effectiveness in promoting industrial peace. It declared—

"The chief advantage which comes from the practice of periodically determining the conditions of labor by collective bargaining directly between employers and employees is, that thereby each side obtains a better understanding of the actual state of the industry, of the conditions which confront the other side, and of the motives which influence it. Most strikes and lockouts would not occur if each party understood exactly the position of the other. Where representatives of employers and employees can meet personally together and discuss all the considerations on which the wage scale and the conditions of labor would be based, a satisfactory agreement can, in the great majority of instances, be reached.   .   .   .

"It is not to be supposed that the introduction of joint conferences and arbitration committees in a trade will render strikes and lockouts thereafter impossible.   .   .   .   Nevertheless experience both in England and in our own country shows that where these practices have once become fairly well established they greatly reduce the number of strikes and lockouts, and in many trades do away with them altogether for long periods of time. Even when a cessation of employment does intervene, the experience of the beneficial effects of peaceful methods usually leads to their reestablishment."

Another federal commission found the Anthracite Coal strike in 1902 was caused partly by the question of union recognition, and called attention to a truth demonstrated by experience which is still too often ignored:

"Experience shows that the more full the recognition given to a trades union, the more businesslike and responsible it becomes. Through dealing with business men in business matters, its more intelligent, conservative, and responsible members come to the front and gain general control and direction of its affairs. If the energy of the employer is directed to discouragement and repression of the union, he need not be surprised if the more radically inclined members are the ones most frequently heard."

In 1915 another Commission on Industrial Relations made a similar report to Congress. It was not unanimous because the three employer members filed a separate report stating that the majority report unfairly blamed employers for practically all the industrial unrest, forgetting the responsibility of labor. But they also declared—

"There has been an abundance of testimony submitted to prove to our satisfaction that some employers have resorted to questionable methods to prevent their workers from organizing in their own self-interest; that they have attempted to defeat democracy by more or less successfully controlling courts and legislatures; that some of them have exploited women and children and unorganized workers; that some have resorted to all sorts of methods to prevent the enactment of remedial industrial legislation; that some have employed gunmen in strikes, who were disreputable characters, and who assaulted innocent people and committed other crimes most reprehensible in character; that some have paid lower wages than competitive conditions warranted, worked their people long hours and at the expense of free labor; that some have been contract breakers with labor; that some have at times attempted, through the authorities, to suppress free speech and the right of peaceful assembly; **and that** some have deliberately, for selfish ends, bribed representatives of labor. All these things, we find, tend to produce industrial unrest, with all its consequent and far-reaching ills.

"There is, therefore, no gainsaying the fact that labor has had many grievances, and that it is thoroughly justified in organizing and in spreading organization in order better to protect itself against exploitation and oppression."

This 1915 report of the Industrial Commission was undoubtedly a symptom of the new spirit which moved through the country after 1910. In politics it found expression in the Bull Moose campaign and the "New Freedom" of Woodrow Wilson. When Wilson was elected his ideas took shape in legislation.

SECTION 36.2   THE CLAYTON ACT OF 1914

The apparent hostility of the law to organized labor was, as we have seen, primarily the result of judicial decisions. Even the application of the Sherman Act to restrain labor was the product of judicial interpretation which probably came as a surprise to most legislators. Thus thwarted in the courts, labor turned to the legislature for relief.

The elected representatives of the people were susceptible to public opinion and to the political muscle of organized labor. They were also aware, however, of the dangers inherent in legislation which might give to labor a preferred position under the law and which might result in the removal of any legal check on the power and practices of unions. Thus the first legislative efforts to accommodate the law to the demands of labor were rather tentative measures which attempted to strike some balance between and among the competing and conflicting interests of organized labor, employers, and the general public. The limitations in the appropriations for the Justice Department from 1913 to 1923 (see note *supra* p. 849) were one such tentative step, but more direct action was taken in the Clayton Act of 1914.

The Clayton Act made extensive additions to federal antitrust law. The general statements in the Sherman Act provided a legislative base for judicial development of law restraining the "trusts" and, in the main, the federal courts had performed that task to the satisfaction of Congress. However, both Congress and the executive (notably Presidents Roosevelt and Wilson) considered that some further refinement of the law was necessary in order to make more precise the legal limitations on the activities of industrial firms and combinations. Accordingly most of the Clayton Act was devoted to the proscription of specific business practices which might ".   .   .   substantially lessen competition or tend to create a monopoly." But in the extended debate on the proposals which ultimately emerged as the Clayton Act, much time was also devoted to the consideration of the demands of organized labor and organizations of farmers that they be granted exemption from the antitrust law. In addition, labor pressed for legislative relief from the "oppression" of "government by injunction." Sections 6 and 20 of the Clayton Act embodied Congress' response to these demands. These sections are set out below.

PUBLIC LAW 63–212, 38 STAT. 730, APPROVED OCTOBER 15, 1914.

Be it enacted by the Senate and House of Representatives of the United States of America in Congress assembled, . . .

Sec. 6. That the labor of a human being is not a commodity or article of commerce. Nothing contained in the anti-trust laws shall be construed to forbid the existence and operation of labor, agricultural, or horticultural organizations, instituted for the purposes of mutual help, and not having capital stock or conducted for profit, or to forbid or restrain individual members of such organizations from lawfully carrying out the legitimate objects thereof; nor shall such organizations, or the members thereof, be held or construed to be illegal combinations or conspiracies in restraint of trade, under the anti-trust laws.

* * *

Sec. 20. That no restraining order or injunction shall be granted by any court of the United States, or a judge or the judges thereof, in any case between an employer and employees, or between employers and employees, or between employees, or between persons employed and persons seeking employment, involving, or growing out of, a dispute concerning terms or conditions of employment, unless necessary to prevent irreparable injury to property, or to a property right, of the party making the application, for which injury there is no adequate remedy at law, and such property or property right must be described with particularity in the application, which must be in writing and sworn to by the applicant or by his agent or attorney.

And no such restraining order or injunction shall prohibit any person or persons, whether singly or in concert, from terminating any relation of employment, or from ceasing to perform any work or labor, or from recommending, advising or persuading others by peaceful means so to do; or from attending at any place where any such person or persons may lawfully be, for the purpose of peacefully obtaining or communicating information, or from peacefully persuading any person to work or to abstain from working; or from ceasing to patronize or to employ any party to such dispute, or from recommending, advising, or persuading others by peaceful and lawful means so to do; or from paying or giving to, or withholding from, any person engaged in such dispute, any strike benefits or other moneys or things of value; or from peaceably assembling in a lawful manner, and for lawful purposes; or from doing any act or thing which might lawfully be done in the absence of such dispute by any party thereto; nor shall any of the acts specified in this paragraph be considered or held to be violations of any law of the United States.

There was extensive debate in Congress on the provision which finally emerged as Section 20 of the Clayton Act. One of the prime issues debated was whether or not the Section legalized the "secondary boycott." That term has no precise referent but in general it relates to union activities which have the effect of disturbing relations between an employer and suppliers or customers. For example, the union boycott in the Danbury Hatters' case had this effect insofar as it prevented or discouraged hat merchants from selling Loewe's products. As was demonstrated in that case, the courts developed an especial concern regarding the lawfulness of such conduct. Although the union objective was to resolve a dispute between itself and an employer—the primary dispute—the union tactics brought direct pressure to bear on parties who were not involved in the primary dispute. Judicial concern for the protection of such secondary parties was coupled with a recognition of the effects of such conduct on interstate traffic and also the devastating effects of such boycotts on the primary employer's business, so that the "secondary boycott" was generally treated as an unlawful means. This taint of illegality was so strong that the classification of any form of conduct as a "secondary boycott" was tantamount to deciding that such conduct was unlawful.

[The following is taken from FELIX FRANKFURTER and NATHAN GREENE, THE LABOR INJUNCTION (New York, 1930), pages 161–166. Footnotes are omitted.]

[The debate on Section 20 revealed] a cross-fire of opposition—"nothing whatsoever for labor's benefit" would be accomplished because it was operative only between an employer and employees, a relationship that terminated in case of strike or lockout; too much was accomplished because prohibition of injunctions against "ceasing to patronize . . . or persuading others by peaceful means so to do" legalized the secondary boycott. The argument in support of the section was briefly that "everything set forth in [it] is the law to-day" and that the section was not intended to legalize the secondary boycott.

We have already had occasion to note the diversity of meanings which has overlaid the label "secondary boycott." The debates on this measure illustrate these accretions of ambiguity. The leaders on both sides, Mr. Webb in support, and Mr. Volstead in opposition, were in accord in their abhorrence of a "secondary boycott." But while the latter rhetorically asked "Can it be questioned that . . . [section 20] will legalize the secondary boycott?" —the former was so "perfectly satisfied" that the section did not authorize the secondary boycott, that he declined to accept an amendment to clarify the point further. The statute itself scrupulously avoided the words "secondary boycott" which would unavoidably have imported ambiguity. The words used were descriptive of conduct, and not a phrase that to many conveyed inseparably the significance of illegality.

The bill, as amended, passed the House on June 5, 1914. In the Senate, it was promptly referred to its Judiciary Committee, reported out on July 22, 1914, and with some modifications of phraseology it was finally passed on

September 2, 1914. The conferees of the two Houses submitted their report which was accepted by the Senate, October 5, 1914, and by the House three days later. By President Wilson's signature on October 15, 1914, the measure known to history as the Clayton Act became law.

This completes in barest outline a sketch of legislative proposals to curb equity jurisdiction, which, from 1894 to 1914, engaged the attention of every Congressional session but one. If such continuous effort and travail in the evolution of a single measure reveal any deliberate purpose, they justify the presumption that Congress was long conscious of abuses in issuing injunctions and that this legislation embodied a solution. Five days after its enactment, however, the then President of the American Bar Association, in his annual address, gave warning of impending pitfalls:

> "All these provisions have been called the charter of liberty of labor. We have seen that the changes from existing law they make are not broadly radical and that most of them are declaratory merely of what would be law without the statute. This is a useful statute in definitely regulating procedure in injunctions and in express definition of what may be done in labor disputes. But what I fear is that when the statute is construed by the courts it will keep the promise of the labor leaders to the ear and break it to the hope of the ranks of labor."

This prophet was himself destined to become Chief Justice of the Court that gave final meaning to the Clayton Act and determined the limits of legislative power in prescribing remedies for injunctive abuses.

Between 1916 and 1920, in thirteen cases in which opinions are reported, lower federal courts applied section 20 of the Clayton Act. In ten of these cases, the statute was held not to stand in the way of an injunction. This surprising result was based on two independent and inconsistent constructions: first, that section 20 did not change the pre-existing law; second, that the section did create new privileges but extremely limited in scope. Thus, the statute was held inapplicable when the strike was to unionize a factory or, generally, for a purpose other than immediate betterment of working conditions. To refuse to work upon non-union products was deemed a strike "for a whim", not sheltered by the Clayton Act and subjecting the defendants to "those settled principles respecting organized picketing." Again, the Act could not be invoked when once the employer had refilled vacancies: persons who continued to strike and picket thereafter were no longer "employees" protected by the Clayton Act. Finally, hostility to all picketing was too deeply ingrained in the mental habits of some of the federal judges to yield to the language of the Clayton Act. Instead, it continued to supply canons of interpretation. An attitude deriving from assumptions like this—"practical people question the possibility of peaceful persuasion through the practice of picketing", found no difficulty in clothing every reasonably effective strike activity in language synonymous with illegality.

Not until 1921 did litigation reach the Supreme Court calling for its pronouncement upon the Clayton Act. . . .

DUPLEX PRINTING PRESS CO. v. DEERING

Supreme Court of the United States, 1921.
254 U.S. 443, 41 S.Ct. 172.

MR. JUSTICE PITNEY* delivered the opinion of the Court.

This was a suit in equity brought by appellant in the District Court for the Southern District of New York for an injunction to restrain a course of conduct carried on by defendants in that district and vicinity in maintaining a boycott against the products of complainant's factory, in furtherance of a conspiracy to injure and destroy its good will, trade, and business—especially to obstruct and destroy its interstate trade. . . . Complainant is a Michigan corporation, and manufactures printing presses at a factory in Battle Creek, in that state, employing about 200 machinists in the factory, in addition to 50 office employees, traveling salesmen, and expert machinists or road men, who supervise the erection of the presses for complainant's customers at their various places of business. . . . [It] conducts its business on the "open shop" policy, without discrimination against either union or non-union men. The individual defendants and the local organizations of which they are the representatives are affiliated with the International Association of Machinists, an unincorporated association having a membership of more than 60,000, and are united in a combination, to which the International Association also is a party, having the object of compelling complainant to unionize its factory and enforce the "closed shop," the eight-hour day, and the union scale of wages, by means of interfering with and restraining its interstate trade in the products of the factory. Complainant's principal manufacture is newspaper presses of large size and complicated mechanism, varying in weight from 10,000 to 100,000 pounds, and requiring a considerable force of labor and a considerable expenditure of time—a week or more—to handle, haul, and erect them at the point of delivery. These presses are sold throughout the United States and in foreign countries; and, as they are especially designed for the production of daily papers, there is a large market for them in and about the city of New York. They are delivered there in the ordinary course of interstate commerce; the handling, hauling, and installation work at destination being done by employees of the purchaser under the supervision of a specially skilled machinist supplied by complainant. The acts complained of and sought to be restrained have nothing to do with the conduct or management of the factory in Michigan, but solely with the installation and operation of the presses by complainant's customers. None of the defendants is or ever was an employee of complainant, and complainant at no time has had relations with either of the organizations that they represent. In August, 1913 (eight months before the filing of the bill), the International Association called a strike at complainant's factory in Battle Creek, as a result of which union machinists to the number of about 11 in the factory and 3 who supervised the erection of presses in the field left complainant's employ. But the defection of so small

---

* Justice Mahlon Pitney was appointed to the Supreme Court of the United States by President Taft in 1912. A member of the New Jersey bar, he served as a member of Congress (1894–1898), and as U. S. Senator (1898–1901). He was a member of the Supreme Court of New Jersey (1901–1908), and Chancellor of New Jersey (1908–1912). Justice Pitney resigned from the Supreme Court in 1922, and he died in 1924.

a number did not materially interfere with the operation of the factory, and sales and shipments in interstate commerce continued.

The acts complained of made up the details of an elaborate programme adopted and carried out by defendants and their organizations in and about the city of New York as part of a country-wide programme adopted by the International Association, for the purpose of enforcing a boycott of complainant's product. The acts embraced the following, with others: Warning customers that it would be better for them not to purchase, or having purchased, not to install, presses made by complainant, and threatening them with loss should they do so; threatening customers with sympathetic strikes in other trades; notifying a trucking company, usually employed by customers to haul the presses, not to do so, and threatening it with trouble if it should; inciting employees of the trucking company, and other men employed by customers of complainant, to strike against their respective employers in order to interfere with the hauling and installation of presses, and thus bring pressure to bear upon the customers; notifying repair shops not to do repair work on Duplex presses; coercing union men, by threatening them with loss of union cards and with being blacklisted as "scabs" if they assisted in installing the presses; threatening an exposition company with a strike if it permitted complainant's presses to be exhibited; and resorting to a variety of other modes of preventing the sale of presses of complainant's manufacture in or about New York City, and delivery of them in interstate commerce, such as injuring and threatening to injure complainant's customers and prospective customers, and persons concerned in hauling, handling, or installing the presses. In some cases the threats were undisguised; in other cases polite in form, but none the less sinister in purpose and effect.

* * *

All the judges of the Circuit Court of Appeals concurred in the view that defendants' conduct consisted essentially of efforts to render it impossible for complainant to carry on any commerce in printing presses between Michigan and New York and that defendants had agreed to do and were endeavoring to accomplish the very thing pronounced unlawful by this court in Loewe v. Lawlor, 208 U.S. 274, 28 S.Ct. 301, 52 L.Ed. 488, 13 Ann.Cas. 815, and Lawlor v. Loewe, 235 U.S. 522, 35 S.Ct. 170, 59 L.Ed. 341. The judges also agreed that the interference with interstate commerce was such as ought to be enjoined, unless the Clayton Act of October 15, 1914, forbade such injunction.

The act was passed after the beginning of the suit, but more than two years before it was brought to hearing. We are clear that the courts below were right in giving effect to it; the real question being whether they gave it the proper effect. In so far as the act (a) provided for relief by injunction to private suitors, (b) imposed conditions upon granting such relief under particular circumstances, and (c) otherwise modified the Sherman Act, it was effective from the time of its passage, and applicable to pending suits for injunction. Obviously, this form of relief operates only in futuro, and the right to it must be determined as of the time of the hearing.

That complainant's business of manufacturing printing presses and disposing of them in commerce is a property right, entitled to protection against unlawful injury or interference; that unrestrained access to the channels of interstate commerce is necessary for the successful conduct of the business; that a widespread combination exists, to which defendants and the associations represented by them are parties, to hinder and obstruct complainant's interstate trade and commerce by the means that have been indicated; and that as a result of it complainant has sustained substantial damage to its interstate trade, and is threatened with further and irreparable loss and damage in the future—is proved by clear and undisputed evidence. Hence the right to an injunction is clear if the threatened loss is due to a violation of the Sherman Act as amended by the Clayton Act.

Looking first to the former act, the thing declared illegal by its first section (26 Stat. 209 [Comp.St. § 8820]) is:
"Every contract, combination in the form of trust or otherwise, or conspiracy, in restraint of trade or commerce among the several states, or with foreign nations." . . .

In Loewe v. Lawlor, 208 U.S. 274, 28 S.Ct. 301, 52 L.Ed. 488, 13 Ann. Cas. 815, where there was an effort to compel plaintiffs to unionize their factory by preventing them from manufacturing articles intended for transportation beyond the state, and also by preventing vendees from reselling articles purchased from plaintiffs and negotiating with plaintiffs for further purchases, by means of a boycott of plaintiffs' products and of dealers who handled them, this court held that there was a conspiracy in restraint of trade actionable under section 7 of the Sherman Act (section 8829), ... And when the case came before the court a second time, 235 U.S. 522, 534, 35 S.Ct. 170, 59 L.Ed. 341, it was held that the use of the primary and secondary boycott and the circulation of a list of "unfair dealers," intended to influence customers of plaintiffs and thus subdue the latter to the demands of the defendants, and having the effect of interfering with plaintiffs' interstate trade, was actionable. . . .

Upon the question whether the provisions of the Clayton Act forbade the grant of an injunction under the circumstances of the present case, the Circuit Court of Appeals was divided; the majority holding that under section 20, "perhaps in conjunction with section 6," there could be no injunction. . . .

As to section 6, it seems to us its principal importance in this discussion is for what it does not authorize, and for the limit it sets to the immunity conferred. The section assumes the normal objects of a labor organization to be legitimate, and declares that nothing in the anti-trust laws shall be construed to forbid the existence and operation of such or organizations or to forbid their members from *lawfully* carrying out their *legitimate* objects.

The principal reliance is upon section 20. This regulates the granting of restraining orders and injunctions by the courts of the United States in a designated class of cases, with respect to (a) the terms and conditions of the relief and the practice to be pursued, and (b) the character of acts that are to be exempted from the restraint, and in the concluding words it declares (c) that none of the acts specified shall be held to be violations of any law of the United States. All its provisions are subject to a general qualification respecting the nature of the controversy and the parties affected. It is to be a "case between an employer and employees, or between employers and employees, or between employees, or between persons employed and persons seeking employment, involving, or growing out of, a dispute concerning terms or conditions of employment."

The first paragraph merely puts into statutory form familiar restrictions upon the granting of injunctions already established and of general application in the equity practice of the courts of the United States. It is but declaratory of the law as it stood before. The second paragraph declares that "no such restraining order or injunction" shall prohibit certain conduct specified—manifestly still referring to a "case between an employer and employees, . . . involving, or growing out of, a dispute concerning terms or conditions of employment," as designated in the first paragraph. It is very clear that the restriction upon the use of the injunction is in favor only of those concerned as parties to such a dispute as is described. The words defining the permitted conduct include particular qualifications consistent with the general one respecting the nature of the case and dispute intended; and the concluding words, "nor shall any of the acts specified in this paragraph be considered or held to be violations of any law of the United States," are to be read in the light of the context, and mean only that those acts are not to be so held when committed by parties concerned in "a dispute concerning terms or conditions of employment." If the qualifying words are to have any effect, they must operate to confine the restriction upon the granting of injunctions, and also the relaxation of the provisions of the anti-trust and other laws of the United States, to parties standing in proximate relation to a controversy such as is particularly described.

The majority of the Circuit Court of Appeals appears to have entertained the view that the words "employers and employees," as used in section 20, should be treated as referring to "the business class or clan to which the parties litigant respectively belong," and that, as there had been a dispute at complainant's factory in Michigan concerning the conditions of employment there—a dispute created, it is said, if it did not exist before, by the act of the Machinists' Union in calling a strike at the factory—section 20 operated to permit members of the Machinists' Union elsewhere, some 60,000 in number, although standing in no relation of employment under complainant, past, present, or prospective, to make that dispute their own and proceed to instigate sympathetic strikes, picketing, and boycotting against employers wholly unconnected with complainant's factory and having relations with complainant only in the way of purchasing its product in the ordinary course of interstate commerce, and this where there was no dispute between such employers and their employees respecting terms or conditions of employment.

We deem this construction altogether inadmissible. Section 20 must be given full effect according to its terms as an expression of the purpose of Congress; but it must be borne in mind that the section imposes an exceptional and extraordinary restriction upon the equity powers of the courts of the United States and upon the general operation of the anti-trust laws, a restriction in the nature of a special privilege or immunity to a particular class, with corresponding detriment to the general public; and it would violate rules of statutory construction having general application and far-reaching importance to enlarge that special privilege by resorting to a loose construction of the section, not to speak of ignoring or slighting the qualifying words that are found in it. Full and fair effect will be given to every word if the exceptional privilege be confined—as the natural meaning of the words confines it—to those who are proximately and substantially concerned as parties to an actual dispute respecting the terms or conditions of their own employment, past, present, or prospective. . . .

The qualifying effect of the words descriptive of the nature of the dispute and the parties concerned is further borne out by the phrases defining the conduct that is not to be subjected to injunction or treated as a violation of the laws of the United States, that is to say:

(a) "Terminating any relation of employment, . . . or persuading others by peaceful means so to do;" (b) "attending at any place where any such person or persons may lawfully be, for the purpose of peacefully obtaining or communicating information, or from peacefully persuading any person to work or to abstain from working;" (c) "ceasing to patronize or to employ any party to such dispute, or . . . recommending, advising, or persuading others by peaceful and lawful means so to do;" (d) "paying or giving to, or withholding from, any person engaged in such dispute, any strike benefits; . . ." (e) "doing any act or thing which might lawfully be done in the absence of such dispute by any party thereto."

The emphasis placed on the words "lawful" and "lawfully," "peaceful" and "peacefully," and the references to the dispute and the parties to it, strongly rebut a legislative intent to confer a general immunity for conduct violative of the anti-trust laws, or otherwise unlawful. The subject of the boycott is dealt with specifically in the "ceasing to patronize" provision, and by the clear force of the language employed the exemption is limited to pressure exerted upon a "party to such dispute" by means of "peaceful and *lawful*" influence upon neutrals. There is nothing here to justify defendants or the organizations they represent in using either threats or persuasion to bring about strikes or a cessation of work on the part of employees of complainant's customers or prospective customers, or of the trucking company employed by the customers, with the object of compelling such customers to withdraw or refrain from commercial relations with complainant, and of thereby constraining complainant to yield the matter in dispute. To instigate a sympathetic strike in aid of a secondary boycott cannot be deemed "peaceful and lawful" persuasion. In essence it is a threat to inflict damage upon the immediate employer, between whom and his employees no dispute exists, in order to bring him against his will into a concerted plan to inflict damage upon another employer who is in dispute with his employees.

The majority of the Circuit Court of Appeals, very properly treating the case as involving a secondary boycott, based the decision upon the view that it was the purpose of section 20 to legalize the secondary boycott "at least in so far as it rests on or consists of refusing to work for any one who deals with the principal offender." Characterizing the section as "blindly drawn," and conceding that the meaning attributed to it was broad, the court referred to the legislative history of the enactment as a warrant for the construction adopted. Let us consider this.

By repeated decisions of this court it has come to be well established that the debates in Congress expressive of the views and motives of individual members are not a safe guide, and hence may not be resorted to, in ascertaining the meaning and purpose of the lawmaking body. . . . But reports of committees of House or Senate stand upon a more solid footing, and may be regarded as an exposition of the legislative intent in a case where otherwise the meaning of a statute is obscure. . . . And this has been extended to include explanatory statements in the nature of a supplemental report made by the committee member in charge of a bill in course of passage.

In the case of the Clayton Act, the printed committee reports are not explicit with respect to the meaning of the "ceasing to patronize" clause of what is now section 20. See House Rept. No. 627, 63d Cong., 2d Sess., pp. 33–36; Senate Rept. No. 698, 63d Cong., 2d Sess., pp. 29–31; the latter being a reproduction of the former. But they contain extracts from judicial opinions and a then recent text-book sustaining the "primary boycott," and expressing an adverse view as to the secondary or coercive boycott, and, on the whole, are far from manifesting a purpose to relax the prohibition against restraints of trade in favor of the secondary boycott.

Moreover, the report was supplemented in this regard by the spokesman of the House committee (Mr. Webb) who had the bill in charge when it was under consideration by the House. The question whether the bill legalized the secondary boycott having been raised, it was emphatically and unequivocally answered by him in the negative.

The extreme and harmful consequences of the construction adopted in the court below are not to be ignored. The present case furnishes an apt and convincing example. An ordinary controversy in a manufacturing establishment, said to concern the terms or conditions of employment there, has been held a sufficient occasion for imposing a general embargo upon the products of the establishment and a nationwide blockade of the channels of interstate commerce against them, carried out by inciting sympathetic strikes and a secondary boycott against complainant's customers, to the great and incalculable damage of many innocent people far remote from any connection with or control over the original and actual dispute—people constituting, indeed, the general public upon whom the cost must ultimately fall, and whose vital interest in unobstructed commerce constituted the prime and paramount concern of Congress in enacting the anti-trust laws, of which the section under consideration forms after all a part.

Reaching the conclusion, as we do, that complainant has a clear right to an injunction under the Sherman Act as amended by the Clayton Act, it becomes unnecessary to consider whether a like result would follow under the common law or local statutes; there being no suggestion that relief thereunder could be broader than that to which complainant is entitled under the acts of Congress. . . .

MR. JUSTICE BRANDEIS,* dissenting, with whom MR. JUSTICE HOLMES and MR. JUSTICE CLARKE, concur.

* Justice Louis Dembitz Brandeis was appointed to the Supreme Court of the United States by President Wilson in 1916. Born in Kentucky in 1856, he studied law at Harvard and then practiced law in Boston for some forty years. Highly successful in practice, he earned a reputation as an ardent advocate of the interests of workingmen (and their unions), small investors, and consumers. His appointment to the Court was bitterly contested and he nearly failed to receive the approval of the Senate. On the Court he often joined Justice Holmes in dissent. Many of his dissenting opinions expressed what, at a later day, would come to be the majority view. He retired from the court in 1939 and died in 1941.

The Duplex Company, a manufacturer of newspaper printing presses, seeks to enjoin officials of the machinists' and affiliated unions from interfering with its business by inducing their members not to work for plaintiff or its customers in connection with the setting up of presses made by it. Unlike Hitchman Coal & Coke Co. v. Mitchell, 245 U.S. 229, 38 S.Ct. 65, 62 L.Ed. 260, L.R.A.1918C, 497, Ann.Cas.1918B, 461, there is here no charge that defendants are inducing employees to break their contracts. Nor is it now urged that defendants threaten acts of violence. But plaintiff insists that the acts complained of violate both the common law of New York and the Sherman Act, and that, accordingly, it is entitled to relief by injunction under the state law and under section sixteen of the Clayton Act, October 15, 1914, c. 323, 38 Stat. 730, 737.

The defendants admit interference with plaintiff's business but justify on the following ground: There are in the United States only four manufacturers of such presses; and they are in active competition. Between 1909 and 1913 the machinists' union induced three of them to recognize and deal with the union, to grant the eight-hour day, to establish a minimum wage scale, and to comply with other union requirements. The fourth, the Duplex Company, refused to recognize the union; insisted upon conducting its factory on the open shop principle; refused to introduce the eight-hour day and operated, for the most part, ten hours a day; refused to establish a minimum wage scale; and disregarded other union standards. Thereupon two of the three manufacturers, who had assented to union conditions, notified the union that they should be obliged to terminate their agreements with it unless their competitor, the Duplex Company, also entered into the agreement with the union, which, in giving more favorable terms to labor, imposed correspondingly greater burdens upon the employer. Because the Duplex Company refused to enter into such an agreement, and in order to induce it to do so, the machinists' union declared a strike at its factory, and in aid of that strike instructed its members and the members of affiliated unions not to work on the installation of presses which plaintiff had delivered in New York. Defendants insisted that by the common law of New York, where the acts complained of were done, and where this suit was brought, and also by section 20 of the Clayton Act, 38 Stat. 730, 738, the facts constitute a justification for this interference with plaintiff's business.

First. As to the rights at common law: Defendants' justification is that of self-interest. They have supported the strike at the employer's factory by a strike elsewhere against its product. They have injured the plaintiff, not maliciously, but in self-defense. They contend that the Duplex Company's refusal to deal with the machinists' union and to observe its standards threatened the interest, not only of such union members as were its factory employees, but even more of all members of the several affiliated unions employed by plaintiff's competitors and by others whose more advanced standards the plaintiff was, in reality, attacking; and that none of the defendants and no person whom they are endeavoring to induce to refrain from working in connection with the setting up of presses made by the plaintiff is an outsider, an interloper. In other words, that the contest between the company and the machinists' union involves vitally the interest of every person whose co-operation is sought. May not all with a common interest join in refusing to expend their labor upon articles whose very production constitutes an attack upon their standard of living and the institution which they are convinced supports it? Applying common law principles the answer should, in my opinion, be: Yes, if as a matter of fact those who so co-operate have a common interest.

The change in the law by which strikes once illegal and even criminal are now recognized as lawful was effected in America largely without the intervention of legislation. This reversal of a common-law rule was not due to the rejection by the courts of one principle and the adoption in its stead of another, but to a better realization of the facts of industrial life. It is conceded that, although the strike of the workmen in plaintiff's factory injured its business, the strike was not an actionable wrong; because the obvious self-interest of the strikers constituted a justification. See Pickett v. Walsh, 192 Mass. 572, 78 N.E. 753, 6 L.R.A.,N.S., 1067, 116 Am.St. Rep. 272, 7 Ann.Cas. 638. Formerly courts held that self-interests could not be so served. Commons, History of Labor in the United States, vol. 2, c. 5. But even after strikes to raise wages or reduce hours were held to be legal because of the self-interest, some courts held that there was not sufficient causal relationship between a strike to unionize a shop and the self-interest of the strikers to justify injuries inflicted. [Citations omitted.] But other courts, repeating the same legal formula, found that there was justification, because they viewed the facts differently. [Citations omitted.]

When centralization in the control of business brought its corresponding centralization in the organization of workingmen, new facts had to be appraised. A single employer might, as in this case, threaten the standing of the whole organization and the standards of all its members; and when he did so the union, in order to protect itself, would naturally refuse to work on his materials wherever found. When such a situation was first presented to the courts, judges concluded that the intervention of the purchaser of the materials established an insulation through which the direct relationship of the employer and the workingmen did not penetrate; and the strike against the material was considered a strike against the purchaser by unaffected third parties. [Citations omitted.] But other courts, with better appreciation of the facts of industry, recognized the unity of interest throughout the union, and that, in refusing to work on materials which threatened it, the union was only refusing to aid in destroying itself. [Citations omitted.]

So, in the case at bar, deciding a question of fact upon the evidence introduced and matters of common knowledge, I should say, as the two lower courts apparently have said, that the defendants and those from whom they sought cooperation have a common interest which the plaintiff threatened.

In my opinion, therefore, plaintiff had no cause of action by the common law of New York.

Second. As to the anti-trust laws of the United States: [The Clayton Act] was the fruit of unceasing agitation, which extended over more than 20 years and was designed to equalize before the law the position of workingmen and employer as industrial combatants. Aside from the use of the injunction, the chief source of dissatisfaction with the existing law lay in the doctrine of malicious combination, and in many parts of the country, in the judicial declarations of the illegality at common law of picketing and persuading others to leave work. The grounds for objection to the latter are obvious. The objection to the doctrine of malicious combinations requires some explanation. By virtue of that doctrine, damage resulting from conduct such as striking or withholding patronage or persuading others to do either, which without more might be damnum absque injuria because the result of trade competition, became actionable when done for a purpose which a judge considered socially or economically harmful and therefore branded as malicious and unlawful. It was objected that, due largely to environment, the social and economic ideas of judges, which thus became translated into law, were prejudicial to a position of equality between workingman and employer; that due to this dependence upon the individual opinion of judges great confusion existed as to what purposes were lawful and what unlawful; and that in any event Congress, not the judges, was the body which should declare what public policy in regard to the industrial struggle demands.

By 1914 the ideas of the advocates of legislation had fairly crystalized upon the manner in which the inequality and uncertainty of the law should be removed. It was to be done by expressly legalizing certain acts regardless of the effects produced by them upon other persons. As to them Congress was to extract the element of injuria from the damages thereby inflicted, instead of leaving judges to determine according to their own economic and social views whether the damage inflicted on an employer in an industrial struggle was damnum absque injuria, because an incident of trade competition, or a legal injury, because in their opinion, economically and socially objectionable. This idea was presented to the committees which reported the Clayton Act. The resulting law set out certain acts which had previously been held unlawful, whenever courts had disapproved of the ends for which they were performed; it then declared that, when these acts were committed in the course of an industrial dispute, they should not be held to violate any law of the United States. In other words the Clayton Act substituted the opinion of Congress as to the propriety of the purpose for that of differing judges; and thereby it declared that the relations between employers of labor and workingmen were competitive relations, that organized competition was not harmful and that it justified injuries necessarily inflicted in its course. Both the majority and the minority report of the House committee indicate that such was its purpose. If, therefore, the act applies to the case at bar, the acts here complained of cannot "be considered or held to be violations of any law of the United States," and hence do not violate the Sherman Act.

The Duplex Company contends that section 20 of the Clayton Act does not apply to the case at bar, because it is restricted to cases "between an employer and employees, or between employers and employees, or between employees, or between persons employed and persons seeking employment, involving, or growing out of, a dispute concerning terms or conditions of employment"; whereas the case at bar arises between an employer in Michigan and workingmen in New York not in its employ, and does not involve their conditions of employment. But Congress did not restrict the provision to employers and workingmen in their employ. By including "employers and employees" and "persons employed and persons seeking employment" it showed that it was not aiming merely at a legal relationship between a specific employer and his employees. Furthermore, the plaintiff's contention proves too much. If the words are to receive a strict technical construction, the statute will have no application to disputes between employers of labor and workingmen, since the very acts to which it applies sever the continuity of the legal relationship. Iron Moulders' Union v. Allis-Chalmers Co., 166 F. 45, 52–53, 91 C.C.A. 631, 20 L.R.A.,N.S., 315. Louisville etc. Ry. Co. v. Wilson, 138 U.S. 501, 505, 11 S.Ct. 405, 34 L. Ed. 1023; Cf. Rex v. Neilson, 44 N.S. 488, 491. The further contention that this case is not one arising out of a dispute concerning the conditions of work of one of the parties is, in my opinion, founded upon a misconception of the facts.

Because I have come to the conclusion that both the common law of a·state and a statute of the United States declare the right of industrial combatants to push their struggle to the limits of the justification of self-interest, I do not wish to be understood as attaching any constitutional or moral sanction to that right. All rights are derived from the purposes of the society in which they exist; above all rights rises duty to the community. The conditions developed in industry may be such that those engaged in it cannot continue their struggle without danger to the community. But it is not for judges to determine whether such conditions exist, nor is it their function to set the limits of permissible contest and to declare the duties which the new situation demands. This is the function of the legislature which, while limiting individual and group rights of aggression and defense, may substitute processes of justice for the more primitive method of trial by combat.

Note

[A succinct analysis of the Duplex opinion is contained in the following extract taken from FRANKFURTER and GREENE, *op. cit.*, pp. 167–169. Footnotes are omitted.]

In Duplex Printing Press Co. v. Deering, an injunction was sought to restrain the Machinists' and affiliated unions from interfering with plaintiff's business by inducing their members not to work for the Duplex Company, or its customers, in connection with the hauling, installation and repair of printing presses made by the Company. There was a strike pending against the Company to secure the closed shop, an eight-hour day, and a union scale of wages. The decision of the District Court dismissing the bill was affirmed by a majority of the Circuit Court of Appeals for the Second Circuit. Judge Hough was clear that section 20, if applicable to the litigation, forbade the granting of an injunction. His only doubt was as to the applicability of the section: "Is the present litigation one between employers and employés, or *an* employer and employés, growing out of a dispute concerning terms *or* conditions of employment?" He held it was. There was a dispute; it concerned conditions of labor; it was a dispute between employer and employees, although only "a dozen or so" of the plaintiff's own employees were on strike. "In strict truth", wrote Judge Hough,

> "this is a dispute between two masters, the union, or social master, and the paymaster; but, unless the words 'employers and employés', as ordinarily used, and used in this statute, are to be given a strained and unusual meaning, they must refer to the business class or clan to which the parties litigant respectively belong."

Meaning that to Judge Hough was "strained and unusual" a majority of the Supreme Court found easy and obvious, and all his conclusions were rejected. Their reasoning took this course: irreparable injury "to property or to a property right" includes injury to an employer's business; the privileges of section 20 did not extend to defendants who had never been in the relationship of employee to the plaintiff or sought employment with him, because it did not apply "beyond the parties affected in a proximate and substantial, not merely a sentimental or sympathetic, sense by the cause of the dispute"; furthermore, analyzing the specific exemption invoked—"ceasing to patronize . . . or persuading others by peaceful and lawful means so to do"—the Court concluded that the instigation of a strike against an employer who was at peace with his own employees, solely to compel such employer to withdraw his patronage from the plaintiff with whom there was a dispute "cannot be deemed 'peaceful and lawful' persuasion." The dissenting opinion of Mr. Justice Brandeis (in which Holmes and Clarke, JJ., concurred) refused to confine the scope of the exemptions of section 20 merely within the area of a legal relationship between a specific employer and his employees, both by reason of the wording of the statute and by virtue of the fact that "the very acts to which it applies sever the continuity of the legal relationship." Finding that the economic relation of the parties brought them within section 20, the dissenting Justices concluded that it did exempt from injunctive process instigation to strike in aid of persons with whom there is a unity of economic interest. Such unity was disclosed by the actual circumstances of the case. After a detailed analysis of the facts, the minority of the Court thus summarized the economic justification for conduct which the majority held subject to an injunction: ". . . in refusing to work on materials which threatened it, the union was only refusing to aid in destroying itself."

Thus ended the litigation which gave the pitch to all future readings of the Clayton Act. How much of the life of a statute dealing with contentious social issues is determined by the general outlook with which judges view such legislation, lies on the very surface of the Duplex Case. Thirteen federal judges were called upon to apply the Clayton Act to the particular facts of this case. Six found that the law called for a hands-off policy in the conflict between the Duplex Printing Company and the Machinists; seven found that the law called for interference against the Machinists. The decision of the majority of the Supreme Court is, of course, the authoritative ruling. But informed professional opinion would find it difficult to attribute greater intrinsic sanction for the views of the seven judges, White, McKenna, Day, Van Devanter, Pitney, McReynolds and Rogers than for the opposing interpretation of the six judges, Holmes, Brandeis, Clarke, Hough, Learned Hand and Manton.

Questions

1. The Court's decision that the boycott was unlawful was based, in part, on this finding: "To instigate a sympathetic strike in aid of a secondary boycott cannot be deemed 'peaceful and lawful' persuasion. In essence it is a threat to inflict damage upon the immediate employer, between whom and his employees no dispute exists, in order to bring him against his will into a concerted plan to inflict damage upon another employer [Duplex] who is in dispute with his employees."

a. If the employees of a firm which handles Duplex products desire the firm to cease handling those products, and if the management refuses to do so, why does that not constitute a dispute between that employer and his or her employees?

b. Was there any evidence cited to support the conclusion that such sympathetic strikes were not "peaceful"?

c. Why are such sympathetic strikes not "lawful"? Is it because they cause injury to the secondary employer?

d. Should Duplex have standing to raise the injury to its customers, resulting from the boycott, as a basis for the grant of an injunction against the boycott?

2. Can you think of any reasons why the Supreme Court should be reluctant to look to the debates in Congress "as a guide . . . in ascertaining the meaning and purpose of the lawmaking body"?

3. Can you think of any reasons why "reports of committees of House or Senate stand upon a more solid footing, and may be regarded as an exposition of the legislative intent in a case where otherwise the meaning of a statute is obscure"? Should more weight or less weight be attached, in this connection, to "explanatory statements in the nature of a supplemental report made by the committee in charge of a bill in course of passage"?

4. Reread Section 20 of the Clayton Act. Is the meaning of that section obscure? Why?

5. Should a statute mean (a) what legislators think it means; or (b) what lawyers think it means; or (c) what laymen think it means? Does a statute mean what judges say it means?

SECTION 37. DUE PROCESS OF LAW: CONSTITUTIONAL LIMITS TO LEGISLATIVE REGULATION OF EMPLOYMENT CONTRACTS

In Part One of the book, we considered the Constitution as a supreme law, which limits the action and discretion of public officials. We saw there that the constitutional limitation on law enforcement officers is made meaningful and effective primarily as the result of judicial interpretation of the Constitution in justiciable controversies between the state and persons accused of committing crimes.

The supervisory power of the judges in our constitutional framework of criminal procedure rests primarily on the assumption that the Constitution is a source of law upon which the judges must rely in the adjudication of many cases. But acceptance of the idea that the Constitution is a source of law for the adjudication of civil and criminal cases should be tempered by the knowledge that the Constitution is concerned also with the establishment of a political structure which distributes governmental authority both within the federal government and between that government and the governments of the several states. As regards the federal government, the Constitution contemplates a tripartite division of authority, with the Legislature, Executive and Judiciary operating as co-equal agencies, all subordinate to the supreme law of the Constitution. If one agency of the government is vested with the responsibility for making authoritative interpretations of the Constitution as regards the conduct of another agency, may not the supremacy of the law of the Constitution also impart some degree of political supremacy to the authoritative interpreter?

Since the Congress is subordinate to the law of the Constitution, it should, before legislating, decide whether the proposed legislation is constitutionally proper. The question then arises whether a determination by the Congress that its legislation is constitutional should be binding on the other two branches of government. Or, when legislation is the basis for claim or defense in an adjudication, should a court have jurisdiction to entertain argument that the statute is void because it conflicts with the Constitution? When first presented with this question the United States Supreme Court, in a unanimous opinion delivered by Chief Justice John Marshall, found that it did have jurisdiction to declare an act of Congress void when, in the Court's view, the act is in conflict with the Constitution (see Marbury v. Madison, 1 Cranch 137, 5 U.S. 137 (1803)). Thus the Supreme Court of the United States decided that it is the final arbiter of the meaning of the Constitution as it relates to legislation, subject—as we have seen—to the limitation that such judicial review of the constitutionality of legislation can be performed only in the context of a case or controversy.

An understanding of the law of the Constitution requires much more than a study of the judicial function of reviewing the constitutionality of legislation, but for our limited purposes such a study should provide some additional insights regarding constitutional law and, in particular, the relation of that law to the resolution of problems associated with social change and social conflicts. As we shall see, to state that the courts have the power to refuse to enforce unconstitutional laws is only the beginning of wisdom, for the crucial questions concern the criteria for exercising that power. We shall explore some of those questions as they appear in cases where the Supreme Court applied the concept of "due process of law" as a test of the validity of legislation regarding employment contracts.

The Fifth and Fourteenth Amendments to the United States Constitution contain identical commands that "no person . . . be deprived of life, liberty, or property, without due process of law;". These commands are directed to the federal and state governments respectively and impose a general limit on official action so that persons may not be penalized or otherwise interfered with by government except in accordance with law. (See Section 10, *supra* p. 211 ff.)

The inclusion of the due process requirement in the Fifth Amendment reflected a commitment to the concept of the supremacy of law over government, in this case the federal government. This was prompted, in part, by memories of arbitrary acts against persons and property which had been committed by British troops and colonial officials prior to the American Revolution.

The extension of the due process requirement against state government was a product of the Civil War. The Thirteenth, Fourteenth, and Fifteenth Amendments were a reconstructionist attempt to establish greater federal checks on the independence of the states. The immediate objective underlying these "Civil War Amendments" was the protection of the emancipated slaves. This is most clearly seen in the Thirteenth Amendment—which prohibits slavery—and in the Fifteenth Amendment—which prohibits abridgement of the right to vote "on account of race, color, or previous condition of servitude." The constitutional concern for Negro civil rights is not so clearly the objective of the Fourteenth Amendment, for it refers to the rights of citizens, and persons, in general. The historical context of the amendment, however, gives strong support to the view that the Fourteenth Amendment was intended chiefly (though not exclusively) to restrain racially discriminatory state acts.

Ironically the Fourteenth Amendment did not really emerge as a significant source of constitutional protection for Negro civil rights until the middle of the twentieth century. Prior to this modern development of the amendment, it was invoked mainly as a limitation on government interference with property rights and economic liberty, and the "due process" clause became a prime legal foundation for the development of American capitalism in the years after the Civil War.

The Supreme Court was first called upon to interpret the Fourteenth Amendment in the so-called "Slaughterhouse Cases." [1] The appellants in the case were butchers in New Orleans, Louisiana. They appealed to the Supreme Court asking reversal of a Louisiana court decision which had upheld an act of the Louisiana legislature granting a monopoly of the slaughterhouse business in New Orleans to a corporation chartered by the legislature. The federal issue advanced as grounds for reversal was that the several provisions of the Fourteenth Amendment were abridged by the statute. A majority of five justices held that the amendment, though general in its terms, was intended primarily for the protection of the emancipated

1. 16 Wall 36 (1873).

slaves, and that it should not be invoked to defeat a legislative decision regarding the conduct and organization of the slaughterhouse business, which decision was ostensibly made to protect the health and welfare of the people of New Orleans. Four dissenting justices argued for a more expansive interpretation of the amendment. They relied on the generality of its language as support for the position that the amendment was intended to have a broader impact than merely to limit state acts discriminatory against racial minorities. Mr. Justice Field was particularly vehement in dissent, arguing that the act operated to deprive citizens of protected privileges and immunities and to deny them the equal protection of the laws. The following is a passage from his dissent.

> "The privileges and immunities designated are those which of right belong to the citizens of all free governments. Clearly among these must be placed the right to pursue a lawful employment in a lawful manner, without other restraint than such as equally affects all persons. . . . This equality of right, with exemption from all disparaging and partial enactments, in the lawful pursuits of life, . . . is the distinguishing privilege of citizens of the United States. . . . The Fourteenth Amendment, in my judgment makes it essential to the validity of the legislation of every state that this equality of right should be respected."

Three years after the Slaughterhouse decision the Supreme Court again examined the relationship between the Fourteenth Amendment and state regulation of business. In Munn v. Illinois,[2] the Court was asked to declare unconstitutional an act of the Illinois legislature which fixed the charges for storage in grain elevators and public warehouses, and required the operators of such establishments to obtain a state license. Munn and others were convicted for violating the statute by refusing to obtain a license. On appeal to the Supreme Court, Munn argued that the act contravened the Fourteenth Amendment in that the fixing of charges for his business constituted a deprivation of property, without due process of law, and that it denied him the equal protection of the law. The Court again rejected the attempt to utilize the Fourteenth Amendment to limit state regulation of business, but for reasons significantly different from those advanced in the majority opinion in the Slaughterhouse case. In Munn, the Court did not deny that the Fourteenth Amendment was relevant to this kind of dispute; it thus abandoned the so-called "Negro race theory" of Slaughterhouse. The Court found, however, that there was ample precedent in English and American law for the right of the state to regulate charges in the warehouse and storage business, and accordingly the majority was unwilling to find that the amendment was intended to proscribe this kind of state regulation. Once again Justice Field dissented:

2. 94 U.S. 113 (1877).

"No State shall deprive any person of life, liberty, or property without due process of law, says the Fourteenth Amendment to the Constitution. By the term 'life,' as here used, something more is meant than mere animal existence. The inhibition against its deprivation extends to all those limbs and faculties by which life is enjoyed. The provision equally prohibits the mutilation of the body by the amputation of an arm or leg, or the putting out of an eye, or the destruction of any other organ of the body through which the soul communicates with the outer world. The deprivation not only of life, but of whatever God has given to every one with life, for its growth and enjoyment, is prohibited by the provision in question, if its efficacy be not frittered away by judicial decision.

"By the term 'liberty,' as used in the provision, something more is meant than mere freedom from physical restraint or the bounds of a prison. It means freedom to go where one may choose, and to act in such manner, not inconsistent with the equal rights of others, as his judgment may dictate for the promotion of his happiness; that is, to pursue such callings and avocations as may be most suitable to develop his capacities, and give to them their highest enjoyment.

"The same liberal construction which is required for the protection of life and liberty, in all particulars in which life and liberty are of any value, should be applied to the protection of private property. If the legislature of a State, under pretence of providing for the public good, or for any other reason, can determine, against the consent of the owner, the uses to which private property shall be devoted, or the prices which the owner shall receive for its uses, it can deprive him of the property as completely as by a special act for its confiscation or destruction. If, for instance, the owner is prohibited from using his building for the purposes for which it was designed, it is of little consequence that he is permitted to retain the title and possession; or, if he is compelled to take as compensation for its use less than the expenses to which he is subjected by its ownership, he is, for all practical purposes, deprived of the property, as effectually as if the legislature had ordered his forcible dispossession. If it be admitted that the legislature has any control over the compensation, the extent of that compensation becomes a mere matter of legislative discretion. The amount fixed will operate as a partial destruction of the value of the property, if it fall below the amount which the owner would obtain by contract, and, practically, as a complete destruction, if it be less than the cost of retaining its possession. There is, indeed, no protection of any value under the constitutional provision, which does not extend to the use and income of the property, as well as to its title and possession. . . ."

It seems clear—today, at least—that the protections of the Fourteenth Amendment encompass economic aspects of life and liberty.

But it does not follow from this that every state interference with economic life or liberty necessarily contravenes the Fourteenth Amendment. The constitutional limitation is qualified, not absolute. Not all deprivations of life, liberty or property are proscribed. It is the deprivation of life or liberty without "due process of law" which is forbidden. Thus Justice Field's contention that the Illinois statute was constitutionally invalid depended on some implicit assumptions regarding the nature of "due process of law." In time, the content of these assumptions was made clear in numerous Supreme Court decisions in which Justice Field's understanding of the Fourteenth amendment was adopted as the majority view.

The judicial definition of "due process" which Field foreshadowed in Slaughterhouse and Munn did not fully emerge until the last decade of the nineteenth century. As it was finally articulated by the Court the "due process" requirement meant the following:

(1) government must legislate and regulate in accordance with the *law of the land*;

(2) implicit in the *law of the land* are certain higher principles, one of which is that the regulatory power—police power—must be exercised in a *reasonable* manner;

(3) in order to be held reasonable, regulatory legislation must be necessary to protect the public health, safety, welfare, or morals and the regulation must be designed to satisfy that need and no more. In sum, "due process of law" required that regulatory legislation "bear a rational [reasonable] relation to a constitutionally permissible [reasonable] objective." Furthermore it was held to be an essential element of due process that the judiciary pass on the reasonableness of a statute challenged on due process grounds. Thus the due process requirement of the Fourteenth Amendment came to be the foundation for a general supervisory power in the judiciary to censor state legislation in accordance with its views as to what was reasonable. The due process clause of the Fifth Amendment was given a like interpretation, so that federal legislation was also subjected to the supervision of the judges. This power was given considerable exercise with respect to state and federal legislation regarding labor-management relations.

Note

In preceding materials—Chapter 3, *supra*—we saw that the "due process" concept is applied by the courts to regulate state and federal criminal procedure. That usage of the "due process" clauses is sometimes called "procedural due process." The application of the "due process" clauses in economic regulation cases is sometimes called "substantive due process."

Question. What does this application of the procedure/substance dichotomy to the "due process" concept suggest to you regarding possible alternative uses of that concept?

THE ERDMAN ACT OF 1898

Act of June 1, 1898. 30 Stat. 424.

[The following is taken from COX and BOK, CASES ON LABOR LAW (5th ed.), p. 74.]

The U. S. Strike Commission's recommendation for conciliation of railway disputes, followed by a form of compulsory arbitration, led to extensive discussions in Congress out of which developed the so-called Erdman Act. The Act applied only to employees engaged in the actual operation of interstate trains, but it contained the seeds of the later development of most railway labor legislation including the present law. Its chief features were as follows:

(1) Labor unions were recognized as the spokesmen of employees and drawn into the statutory procedures. For this reason, and because attacks upon unions were deemed a cause of strikes, section 10 prohibited discharging, or threatening to discharge, an employee because of his union membership.

(2) Upon request of "either party to the controversy", the chairman of the Interstate Commerce Commission and the Commissioner of Labor were required to "put themselves in communication with the parties to such controversy, and shall use their best efforts, by mediation and conciliation, to amicably settle the same . . . ."

(3) If such efforts were unsuccessful, the mediators should endeavor to induce the parties voluntarily to submit the dispute to arbitration in accordance with a detailed procedure afforded by the Act.

Before 1906 the Erdman Act was ineffective because the carriers held the upper hand. From 1906 until the railroads were taken over by the government during World War I the statutory procedure, which was strengthened by the Newlands Act in 1913, operated effectively, save in one dramatic instance. In 1916 a nationwide strike was threatened over the Brotherhoods' demand for a basic eight hour day with time and a half for overtime. Six days before the effective date of the strike President Wilson appeared before a special session of Congress, which promptly enacted the Adamson eight-hour law.

Despite considerable use of the Erdman Act in the settlement of disputes, many carriers refused to accept the right of their employees to organize in labor unions. Litigation resulted which drew in question the power of Congress to utilize union organization and collective bargaining as a framework for bringing about negotiated adjustments of conflicts between employer and employee interests.

ADAIR v. UNITED STATES

Supreme Court of the United States, 1908.
208 U.S. 161, 28 S.Ct. 277.

MR. JUSTICE HARLAN* delivered the opinion of the court:

This case involves the constitutionality of certain provisions of the act of Congress of June 1st, 1898 [the Erdman Act], concerning carriers engaged in interstate commerce and their employees. . . . The 10th section, upon which the present prosecution is based, is in these words:

"That any employer subject to the provisions of this act, and any officer, agent, or receiver of such employer, who shall require any employee, or any person seeking employment, as a condition of such employment, to enter into an agreement, either written or verbal, not to become or remain a member of any labor corporation, association or organization; *or shall threaten any employee with loss of employment, or shall unjustly discriminate against any employee because of his membership in such a labor corporation, association, or organization;* . . . is hereby declared to be guilty of a misdemeanor, and, upon conviction thereof in any court of the United States of competent jurisdiction in the district in which such offense was committed, shall be punished for each offense by a fine of not less than one hundred dollars and not more than one thousand dollars."

* * *

The present indictment was in the district court of the United States for the Eastern district of Kentucky against the defendant, Adair. . . . the criminal offense charged in the count of the indictment upon which the defendant was convicted was, in substance and effect, that being an agent of a railroad company engaged in interstate commerce, and subject to the provisions of the above act on June 1st, 1898, he discharged one Coppage from its service *because of his membership in a labor organization,* —no other ground for such discharge being alleged. [From the judgment of conviction defendant appealed.]

May Congress make it a criminal offense against the United States— as, by the 10th section of the act of 1898, it does—for an agent or officer of an interstate carrier, having full authority in the premises from the carrier, to discharge an employee from service simply because of his membership in a labor organization?

This question is admittedly one of importance, and has been examined with care and deliberation. And the court has reached a conclusion which, in its judgment, is consistent with both the words and spirit of the Constitution, and is sustained as well by sound reason.

---

* Justice John Marshall Harlan was appointed to the Supreme Court by President Hayes in 1877. He commanded a regiment in the Union Army during the Civil War, and then practiced law in Kentucky, where he was a leading figure in the Republican party. During his thirty-four years on the Court he was often cast in the role of dissenter. Perhaps his most forceful, and prophetic, dissent was delivered in Plessy v. Ferguson, in which he urged—although he was the lone southerner on the Court— that enforced segregation of the races violated the Fourteenth Amendment. Justice Harlan died in 1911.

The first inquiry is whether the part of the 10th section of the act of 1898 upon which the first count of the indictment was based is repugnant to the 5th Amendment of the Constitution, declaring that no person shall be deprived of liberty or property without due process of law. In our opinion that section, in the particular mentioned, is an invasion of the personal liberty, as well as of the right of property, guaranteed by that Amendment. Such liberty and right embrace the right to make contracts for the purchase of the labor of others, and equally the right to make contracts for the sale of one's own labor; each right, however, being subject to the fundamental condition that no contract, whatever its subject-matter, can be sustained which the law, upon reasonable grounds, forbids as inconsistent with the public interests, or as hurtful to the public order, or as detrimental to the common good. This court has said that "in every well-ordered society, charged with the duty of conserving the safety of its members, the rights of the individual in respect of his liberty may, at times, under the pressure of great dangers, be subjected to such restraint, to be enforced by reasonable regulations, as the safety of the general public may demand." Jacobson v. Massachusetts, 197 U.S. 11, 29, 49 L.Ed. 643, 651, 25 S.Ct. 358, 362, and authorities there cited. Without stopping to consider what would have been the rights of the railroad company under the 5th Amendment, had it been indicted under the act of Congress, it is sufficient in this case to say that, as agent of the railroad company, and, as such, responsible for the conduct of the business of one of its departments, it was the defendant Adair's right—and that right inhered in his personal liberty, and was also a right of property—to serve his employer as best he could, so long as he did nothing that was reasonably forbidden by law as injurious to the public interests. It was the right of the defendant to prescribe the terms upon which the services of Coppage would be accepted, and it was the right of Coppage to become or not, as he chose, an employee of the railroad company upon the terms offered to him. Mr. Cooley, in his treatise on Torts, p. 278, well says: "It is a part of every man's civil rights that he be left at liberty to refuse business relations with any person whomsoever, whether the refusal rests upon reason, or is the result of whim, caprice, prejudice, or malice. With his reasons neither the public nor third persons have any legal concern. It is also his right to have business relations with anyone with whom he can make contracts and, if he is wrongfully deprived of his right by others, he is entitled to redress." . . .

While, as already suggested, the right of liberty and property guaranteed by the Constitution against deprivation without due process of law is subject to such reasonable restraints as the common good or the general welfare may require, it is not within the functions of government—at least, in the absence of contract between the parties—to compel any person, in the course of his business and against his will, to accept or retain the personal services of another, or to compel any person, against his will, to perform personal services for another. The right of a person to sell his labor upon such terms as he deems proper is, in its essence, the same as the right of the purchaser of labor to prescribe the conditions upon which he will accept such labor from the person offering to sell it. So the right of the employee to quit the service of the employer, for whatever reason, is the same as the right of the employer, for whatever reason, to dispense with the services of such employee. It was the legal right of the defendant,

Adair,—however unwise such a course might have been,—to discharge Coppage because of his being a member of a labor organization, as it was the legal right of Coppage, if he saw fit to do so,—however unwise such a course on his part might have been,—to quit the service in which he was engaged, because the defendant employed some persons who were not members of a labor organization. In all such particulars the employer and the employee have equality of right, and any legislation that disturbs that equality is an arbitrary interference with the liberty of contract which no government can legally justify in a free land. These views find support in adjudged cases . . . .

As the relations and the conduct of the parties towards each other was not controlled by any contract other than a general employment on one side to accept the services of the employee and a general agreement on the other side to render services to the employer,—no term being fixed for the continuance of the employment,—Congress could not, consistently with the 5th Amendment, make it a crime against the United States to discharge the employee because of his being a member of a labor organization.

But it is suggested that the authority to make it a crime for an agent or officer of an interstate carrier, having authority in the premises from his principal, to discharge an employee from service to such carrier, simply be-cause of his membership in a labor organization, can be referred to the power of Congress to regulate interstate commerce, without regard to any question of personal liberty or right of property arising under the 5th Amendment. This suggestion can have no bearing in the present discussion unless the statute, in the particular just stated, is within the meaning of the Constitution, a regulation of commerce among the states. If it be not, then clearly the government cannot invoke the commerce clause of the Constitution as sustaining the indictment against Adair.

Let us inquire what is commerce, the power to regulate which is given to Congress?

This question has been frequently propounded in this court, and the answer has been—and no more specific answer could well have been given—that commerce among the several states comprehends traffic, intercourse, trade, navigation, communication, the transit of persons, and the transmission of messages by telegraph,—indeed every species of commercial intercourse among the several states,—but not that commerce "completely internal, which is carried on between man and man, in a state or between different parts of the same state, and which does not extend to or affect other states." The power to regulate interstate commerce is the power to prescribe rules by which such commerce must be governed. Of course, as has been often said, Congress has a large discretion in the selection or choice of the means to be employed in the regulation of interstate commerce, and such discretion is not to be interfered with except where that which is done is in plain violation of the Constitution. . . . But what possible legal or logical connection is there between an employee's membership in a labor organization and the carrying on of interstate commerce? Such relation to a labor organization cannot have, *in itself* and in the eye of the law, any bearing upon the commerce with which the employee is connected by his labor and services. Labor associations, we assume, are organized for the general purpose of improving or bettering the conditions and conserving the interests of its members as wage-earners,—

an object entirely legitimate and to be commended rather than condemned. But surely those associations, as labor organizations, have nothing to do with interstate commerce, as such. One who engages in the service of an inter-state carrier will, it must be assumed, faithfully perform his duty, whether he be a member or not a member of a labor organization. His fitness for the position in which he labors and his diligence in the discharge of his du-ties cannot, in law or sound reason, depend in any degree upon his being or not being a member of a labor organization. It cannot be assumed that his fitness is assured, or his diligence increased, by such membership, or that he is less fit or less diligent because of his not being a member of such an organization. It is the employee as a man, and not as a member of a labor organization, who labors in the service of an interstate carrier. Will it be said that the provision in question had its origin in the apprehension, on the part of Congress, that, if it did not show more consideration for members of labor organizations than for wage-earners who were not mem-bers of such organizations, or if it did not insert in the statute some such provision as the one here in question, members of labor organizations would, by illegal or violent measures, interrupt or impair the freedom of com-merce among the states? We will not indulge in any such conjectures, nor make them, in whole or in part, the basis of our decision. We could not do so consistently with the respect due to a coordinate department of the government. We could not do so without imputing to Congress the purpose to accord to one class of wage-earners privileges withheld from another class of wage-earners, engaged, it may be, in the same kind of labor and serving the same employer. Nor will we assume, in our consideration of this case, that members of labor organizations will, in any considerable numbers, resort to illegal methods for accomplishing any particular object they have in view.

Looking alone at the words of the statute for the purpose of ascer-taining its scope and effect, and of determining its validity, we hold that there is no such connection between interstate commerce and membership in a labor organization as to authorize Congress to make it a crime against the United States for an agent of an interstate carrier to discharge an employee because of such membership on his part. If such a power exists in Congress it is difficult to perceive why it might not, by absolute regula-tion, require interstate carriers, under penalties, to employ, in the con-duct of its interstate business, *only* members of labor organizations, or *only* those who are *not* members of such organizations,—a power which could not be recognized as existing under the Constitution of the United States. No such rule of criminal liability as that to which we have referred can be regarded as, in any just sense, a regulation of interstate commerce. We need scarcely repeat what this court has more than once said, that the power to regulate interstate commerce, great and paramount as that power is, cannot be exerted in violation of any fundamental right secured by other provisions of the Constitution. Gibbons v. Ogden, 9 Wheat. 1, 196, 6 L.Ed. 23, 70; Lottery Case (Champion v. Ames) 188 U.S. 321, 353, 47 L.Ed. 492, 500, 23 S.Ct. 321.

It results, on the whole case, that the provision of the statute under which the defendant was convicted must be held to be repugnant to the 5th Amendment, and as not embraced by nor within the power of Congress to regulate interstate commerce, but, under the guise of regulating interstate commerce, and as applied to this case, it arbitrarily sanctions an illegal invasion of the personal liberty as well as the right of property of the defendant, Adair. . . .

MR. JUSTICE MOODY did not participate in the decision of this case.

MR. JUSTICE MCKENNA,* dissenting:

The opinion of the court proceeds upon somewhat narrow lines and either omits or does not give adequate prominence to the considerations which, I think, are determinative of the questions in the case. The principle upon which the opinion is grounded is, as I understand it, that a labor organization has no legal or logical connection with interstate commerce, and that the fitness of an employee has no dependence or relation with his membership in such organization. It is hence concluded that to restrain his discharge merely on account of such membership is an invasion of the liberty of the carrier guaranteed by the 5th Amendment of the Constitution of the United States. The conclusion is irresistible if the propositions from which it is deduced may be viewed as abstractly as the opinion views them. May they be so viewed?

A summary of the act is necessary to understand § 10. Detach that section from the other provisions of the act and it might be open to condemnation.

The 1st section of the act designates the carriers to whom it shall apply. The 2d section makes it the duty of the chairman of the Interstate Commerce Commission and the Commissioner of Labor, in case of a dispute between carriers and their employees which threatens to interrupt the business of the carriers, to put themselves in communication with the parties to the controversy and use efforts to "mediation and conciliation." If the efforts fail, then § 3 provides for the appointment of a board of arbitration,—one to be named by the carrier, one by the labor organization to which the employees belong, and the two thus chosen shall select a third.

There is a provision that if the employees belong to different organizations they shall concur in the selection of the arbitrator. The board is to give hearings; power is vested in the board to summon witnesses, and provision is made for filing the award in the clerk's office of the circuit court of the United States for the district where the controversy arose. Other sections complete the scheme of arbitration thus outlined, and make, as far as possible, the proceedings of the arbitrators judicial, and, pending them, put restrictions on the parties, and damages for violation of the restrictions.

Even from this meager outline may be perceived the justification and force of § 10. It prohibits discrimination by a carrier engaged in interstate commerce, in the employment under the circumstances hereafter mentioned, or the discharge from employment of members of labor organi-

---

* Justice Joseph McKenna was appointed to the Supreme Court by President McKinley in 1898. A member of the California bar, he was a county attorney (1866–1870), a member of the California Legislature (1875), a member of the U. S. Congress, (1885–1892), a member of the U. S. Court of Appeals for the Ninth Circuit (1892), and Attorney General of the U. S. (1897). Justice McKenna resigned from the Supreme Court in 1925, and died in 1926.

zations *"because of such membership."* This the opinion condemns. The actions prohibited, it is asserted, are part of the liberty of a carrier, protected by the Constitution of the United States from limitation or regulation. I may observe that the declaration is clear and unembarrassed by any material benefit to the carrier from its exercise. It may be exercised with reason or without reason, though the business of the carrier is of public concern. This, then, is the contention, and I bring its elements into bold relief to submit against them what I deem to be stronger considerations based on the statute and sustained by authority.

I take for granted that the expressions of the opinion of the court, which seems to indicate that the provisions of § 10 are illegal because their violation is made criminal, are used only for description and incidental emphasis, and not as the essential ground of the objections to those provisions.

I may assume at the outset that the liberty guaranteed by the 5th Amendment is not a liberty free from all restraints and limitations, and this must be so or government could not be beneficially exercised in many cases. Therefore, in judging of any legislation which imposes restraints or limitations, the inquiry must be, What is their purpose, and is the purpose within one of the powers of government? Applying this principle immediately to the present case, without beating about in the abstract, the inquiry must be whether § 10 of the act of Congress has relation to the purpose which induced the act, and which it was enacted to accomplish, and whether such purpose is in aid of interstate commerce, and not a mere restriction upon the liberty of carriers to employ whom they please, or to have business relations with whom they please. . . .

The provisions of the act are explicit and present a well co-ordinated plan for the settlement of disputes between carriers and their employees, by bringing the disputes to arbitration and accommodation, and thereby prevent strikes and the public disorder and derangement of business that may be consequent upon them. I submit no worthier purpose can engage legislative attention or be the object of legislative action, and, it might be urged, to attain which the congressional judgment of means should not be brought under a rigid limitation and condemned, if it contribute in any degree to the end, as a "gross perversion of the principle" of regulation, the condition which, it was said in United States v. Joint Traffic Asso., supra, might justify an appeal to the courts.

We are told that labor associations are to be commended. May not, then, Congress recognize their existence? Yes, and recognize their power as conditions to be counted with in framing its legislation? Of what use would it be to attempt to bring bodies of men to agreement and compromise of controversies if you put out of view the influences which move them or the fellowship which binds them,—maybe controls and impels them, whether rightfully or wrongfully, to make the cause of one the cause of all? And this practical wisdom Congress observed,—observed, I may say, not in speculation or uncertain prevision of evils, but in experience of evils,—an experience which approached to the dimensions of a national calamity. The facts of history should not be overlooked nor the course of legislation. The act involved in the present case was preceded by one enacted in 1888 of similar purport. 25 Stat. at L. 501, chap. 1063. That act did not recognize labor associations, or distinguish between the members of such associations and the other employees of carriers. It failed in its purpose, whether from defect in its provisions or other cause we may only conjecture. At any rate, it did not avert the strike at Chicago in 1894. Investigation followed, and, as a result of it, the act of 1898 was finally passed. Presumably its provisions and remedy were addressed to the mischief which the act of 1888 failed to reach or avert. It was the judgment of Congress that the scheme of arbitration might be helped by engaging in it the labor associations. Those associations unified bodies of employees in every department of the carriers, and this unity could be an obstacle or an aid to arbitration. It was attempted to be made an aid; but how could it be made an aid if, pending the efforts of "mediation and conciliation" of the dispute, as provided in § 2 of the act, other provisions of the act may be arbitrarily disregarded, which are of concern to the members in the dispute? How can it be an aid, how can controversies which may seriously interrupt or threaten to interrupt the business of carriers (I paraphrase the words of the statute) be averted or composed if the carrier can bring on the conflict or prevent its amicable settlement by the exercise of mere whim and caprice? I say mere whim or caprice, for this is the liberty which is attempted to be vindicated as the constitutional right of the carriers. And it may be exercised in mere whim and caprice. If ability, the qualities of efficient and faithful workmanship, can be found outside of labor associations, surely they may be found inside of them. Liberty is an attractive theme, but the liberty which is exercised in sheer antipathy does not plead strongly for recognition. . . .

Counsel also makes a great deal of the difference between direct and indirect effect upon interstate commerce, and assert that § 10 is an indirect regulation at best, and not within the power of Congress to enact. Many cases are cited, which it is insisted, sustain the contention. I cannot take time to review the cases. I have already alluded to the contention, and it is enough to say that it gives too much isolation to § 10. . . . To contend otherwise seems to me to be an oversight of the proportion of things. A provision of law which will prevent, or tend to prevent, the stoppage of every wheel in every car of an entire railroad system, certainly has as direct influence on interstate commerce as the way in which one car may be coupled to another, or the rule of liability for personal injuries to an employee. It also seems to me to be an oversight of the proportions of things to contend that, in order to encourage a policy of arbitration between carriers and their employees which may prevent a disastrous interruption of commerce, the derangement of business, and even greater evils to the public welfare, Congress cannot restrain the discharge of an employee. . . .

MR. JUSTICE HOLMES, dissenting:

I also think that the statute is constitutional, and, but for the decision of my brethren, I should have felt pretty clear about it.

As we all know, there are special labor unions of men engaged in the service of carriers. These unions exercise a direct influence upon the employment of labor in that business, upon the terms of such employment, and upon the business itself. Their very existence is directed specifically to the business, and their connection with it is, at least, as intimate and important as that of safety couplers, and I should think, as the liability of master to servant,—matters which, it is admitted, Congress might regulate, so far as they concern commerce among the states. I suppose that it hardly would be denied that some of the relations of railroads with unions of railroad employees are closely enough connected with commerce to justify legislation by Congress. If so, legislation to prevent the exclusion of such unions from employment is sufficiently near.

The ground on which this particular law is held bad is not so much that it deals with matters remote from commerce among the states, as that it interferes with the paramount individual rights secured by the 5th Amendment. The section is, in substance, a very limited interference with freedom of contract, no more. It does not require the carriers to employ anyone. It does not forbid them to refuse to employ anyone, for any reason they deem good, even where the notion of a choice of persons is a fiction and wholesale employment is necessary upon general principles that it might be proper to control. The section simply prohibits the more powerful party to exact certain undertakings, or to threaten dismissal or unjustly discriminate on certain grounds against those already employed. I hardly can suppose that the grounds on which a contract lawfully may be made to end are less open to regulation than other terms. So I turn to the general question whether the employment can be regulated at all. I confess that I think that the right to make contracts at will that has been derived from the word "liberty" in the Amendments has been stretched to its extreme by the decisions; but they agree that sometimes the right may be restrained. Where there is, or generally is believed to be, an important ground of public policy for restraint, the Constitution does not forbid it, whether this court agrees or disagrees with the policy pursued. It cannot be doubted that to prevent strikes, and, so far as possible, to foster its scheme of arbitration, might be deemed by Congress an important point of policy, and I think it impossible to say that Congress might not reasonably think that the provision in question would help a good deal to carry its policy along. But suppose the only effect really were to tend to bring about the complete unionizing of such railroad laborers as Congress can deal with, I think that object alone would justify the act. I quite agree that the question what and how much good labor unions do, is one on which intelligent people may differ; I think that laboring men sometimes attribute to them advantages, as many attribute to combinations of capital disadvantages, that really are due to economic conditions of a far wider and deeper kind; but I could not pronounce it unwarranted if Congress should decide that to foster a strong union was for the best interest, not only of the men, but of the railroads and the country at large.

Note

The applicability of the Fourteenth Amendment due process clause to state legislation similar to the Erdman Act, was tested in Coppage v. Kansas, 236 U.S. 1, 35 S.Ct. 240 (1915). Coppage was employed by the St. Louis and San Francisco Railway Company as superintendent of the company's division in Fort Scott, Kansas. In July, 1911, Coppage requested one Hedges, a switchman employed by the railroad, to sign the following statement: "We the undersigned, have agreed to withdraw from the Switchmen's Union, while in the service of the Frisco Company." Hedges refused to sign the statement and to withdraw from the union. Coppage, acting in his supervisory capacity, discharged Hedges from the employ of the Frisco Line.

By act of the Kansas legislature in 1903, it was declared to be a misdemeanor "for . . . any agent, officer or employee of any company or corporation, to coerce, require, demand, or influence any person or persons to enter into any agreement, either written or verbal, not to join or become or remain a member of any labor organization or association, as a condition of such person or persons securing employment, or continuing in the employment of such . . . , firm, or corporation." Coppage was convicted of violating that act, and his conviction was sustained by the Supreme Court of Kansas. Coppage appealed this decision to the Supreme Court of the United States.

The Supreme Court, in an opinion by Justice Pitney, adhered to the interpretation enunciated in Adair and struck down the Kansas statute. Justices Holmes and Day dissented.

Questions

1. Is the applicable section of the act unconstitutional because Congress seeks to attain an objective barred by the Constitution? Or is the statute unconstitutional because the statutory scheme of regulation does not bear any rational relation to a constitutionally permissible objective?

2. Compare and contrast the dissenting opinions of Justice Holmes and Justice McKenna. Are their reasons for dissenting significantly different?

Chapter 11

LEGISLATION AND LABOR LAW: 1932–1947

In spite of the adoption of the Clayton Act in 1914 the development of American labor law was to remain the province of the judiciary for another two decades.

World War I and its aftermath absorbed legislative and executive attention through 1920, and by the time the Duplex decision was handed down the political and economic environment in the United States was changing to the disadvantage of organized labor. With the return of the Republican Party to power, labor lost the strategic advantage it had obtained during the Wilson administration. The political strength of the labor movement was further weakened by a Communist scare which swept the country following the Bolshevik takeover of the Russian revolution, for a red label was hung on much of organized labor. Then too, the relative economic prosperity which prevailed in the middle and late twenties produced some improvement in wages and other benefits for industrial workers and this, coupled with the militant anti-union stand of management, put a damper on the growth of the labor movement and further limited its political clout. As a result of these and other factors, Congress in this period showed little concern for the problems of organized labor. With the notable exception of the Railway Labor Act (see *infra* p. 888), no comprehensive labor legislation was adopted and the judiciary continued to evolve law and policy substantially as it had done prior to 1914.

In 1932, however, the bubble burst. The nation was plunged into the depths of a massive economic depression. The federal government was called upon to provide some deliverance from this economic disaster, and in the presidential election of 1932 the Democratic Party swept into office, led by Franklin Delano Roosevelt and committed to his promise of a "new deal." The New Deal Congresses would do much to restructure the role of government in economic affairs, especially in the area of labor-management relations. Indeed, just prior to the New Deal era an important transition was made in the Norris-LaGuardia Act of 1932.

SECTION 38. THE NORRIS–LaGUARDIA ACT

The Norris-LaGuardia Act, and corresponding state statutes (so-called "little Norris-LaGuardia Acts"), signalled the end of the era of "government by injunction" and presaged even more significant developments in American labor law which were soon to come.

The Act, in pertinent part, is set out below:

NORRIS–LaGUARDIA ACT

Public Law 72–65, 47 Stat. 70, approved March 23, 1932.

Be it Enacted by the Senate and House of Representatives of the United States of America in Congress Assembled.

Sec. 1. That no court of the United States, as herein defined, shall have jurisdiction to issue any restraining order or temporary or permanent injunction in a case involving or growing out of a labor dispute, except in a strict conformity with the provisions of this Act; nor shall any such restraining order or temporary or permanent injunction be issued contrary to the public policy declared in this Act.

Sec. 2. In the interpretation of this Act and in determining the jurisdiction and authority of the courts of the United States, as such jurisdiction and authority are herein defined and limited, the public policy of the United States is hereby declared as follows:

Whereas under prevailing economic conditions, developed with the aid of governmental authority for owners of property to organize in the corporate and other forms of ownership association, the individual unorganized worker is commonly helpless to exercise actual liberty of contract and to protect his freedom of labor, and thereby to obtain acceptable terms and conditions of employment, wherefore, though he should be free to decline to associate with his fellows, it is necessary that he have full freedom of association, self-organization, and designation of representatives of his own choosing, to negotiate the terms and conditions of his employment, and that he shall be free from the interference, restraint, or coercion of employers of labor, or their agents, in the designation of such representatives or in self-organization or in other concerted activities for the purpose of collective bargaining or other mutual aid or protection; therefore, the following definitions of, and limitations upon, the jurisdiction and authority of the courts of the United States are hereby enacted.

Sec. 3. Any undertaking or promise, such as is described in this section, or any other undertaking or promise in conflict with the public policy declared in section 2 of this Act, is hereby declared to be contrary to the public policy of the United States, shall not be enforceable in any court of the United States and shall not afford any basis for the granting of legal or equitable relief by any such court, including specifically the following:

Every undertaking or promise thereafter made, whether written or oral, express or implied, constituting or contained in any contract or agreement of hiring or employment between any individual, firm, company, association, or corporation, and any employee or prospective employee of the same, whereby

(a) Either party to such contract or agreement undertakes or promises not to join, become, or remain a member of any labor organization or of any employer organization; or

(b) Either party to such contract or agreement undertakes or promises that he will withdraw from an employment relation in the event that he joins, becomes, or remains a member of any labor organization or of any employer organization.

Sec. 4.   No court of the United States shall have jurisdiction to issue any restraining order or temporary or permanent injunction in any case involving or growing out of any labor dispute to prohibit any person or persons participating or interested in such dispute (as these terms are herein defined) from doing, whether singly or in concert, any of the following acts:

(a) Ceasing or refusing to perform any work or to remain in any relation of employment;

(b) Becoming or remaining a member of any labor organization or of any employer organization, regardless of any such undertaking or promise as is described in section 3 of this Act;

(c) Paying or giving to, or withholding from, any person participating or interested in such labor dispute, any strike or unemployment benefits or insurance, or other moneys or things of value;

(d) By all lawful means aiding any person participating or interested in any labor dispute who is being proceeded against in, or is prosecuting, any action or suit in any court of the United States or of any State;

(e) Giving publicity to the existence of, or the facts involved in, any labor dispute, whether by advertising, speaking, patrolling, or by any other method not involving fraud or violence;

(f) Assembling peaceably to act or to organize to act in promotion of their interests in a labor dispute;

(g) Advising or notifying any person of an intention to do any of the acts heretofore specified;

(h) Agreeing with other persons to do or not to do any of the acts heretofore specified; and

(i) Advising, urging, or otherwise causing or inducing without fraud or violence the acts heretofore specified, regardless of any such undertaking or promise as is described in section 3 of this Act.

Sec. 5.   No court of the United States shall have jurisdiction to issue a restraining order or temporary or permanent injunction upon the ground that any of the persons participating or interested in a labor dispute constitute or are engaged in an unlawful combination or conspiracy because of the doing in concert of the acts enumerated in section 4 of this Act.

Sec. 6.   No officer or member of any association or organization, and no association or organization participating or interested in a labor dispute, shall be held responsible or liable in any court of the United States for the unlawful acts of individual officers, members, or agents, except upon clear proof of actual participation in, or actual authorization of, such acts, or of ratification of such acts after actual knowledge thereof.

Sec. 7.   No court of the United States shall have jurisdiction to issue a temporary or permanent injunction in any case involving or growing out of a labor dispute, as herein defined, except after hearing the testimony of witnesses in open court (with opportunity for cross-examination) in support of the allegations of a complaint made under oath, and testimony in opposition thereto, if offered, and except after findings of fact by the court, to the effect—

(a) That unlawful acts have been threatened and will be committed unless restrained or have been committed and will be continued unless restrained, but no injunction or temporary restraining order shall be issued on account of any threat or unlawful act excepting against the person or persons, association, or organization making the threat or committing the unlawful act or actually authorizing or ratifying the same after actual knowledge thereof;

(b) That substantial and irreparable injury to complainant's property will follow;

(c) That as to each item of relief granted greater injury will be inflicted upon complainant by the denial of relief than will be inflicted upon defendants by the granting of relief;

(d) That complainant has no adequate remedy at law; and

(e) That the public officers charged with the duty to protect complainant's property are unable or unwilling to furnish adequate protection.

* * *

Sec. 13. When used in this Act, and for the purposes of this Act—

(a) A case shall be held to involve or to grow out of a labor dispute when the case involves persons who are engaged in the same industry, trade, craft, or occupation; or have direct or indirect interests therein; or who are employees of the same employer; or who are members of the same or an affiliated organization of employers or employees; whether such dispute is (1) between one or more employers or association of employers and one or more employees or associations of employees; (2) between one or more employers or associations of employers and one or more employers or associations of employers; or (3) between one or more employees or associations of employees and one or more employees or associations of employees; or when the case involves any conflicting or competing interests in a "labor dispute" (as hereinafter defined) or "persons participating or interested" therein (as hereinafter defined).

(b) A person or association shall be held to be a person participating or interested in a labor dispute if relief is sought against him or it, and if he or it is engaged in the same industry, trade, craft, or occupation in which such dispute occurs, or has a direct or indirect interest therein, or is a member, officer, or agent of any association composed in whole or in part of employers or employees engaged in such industry, trade, craft, or occupation.

(c) The term "labor dispute" includes any controversy concerning terms or conditions of employment, or concerning the association or representation of persons in negotiating, fixing, maintaining, changing, or seeking to arrange terms or conditions of employment, regardless of whether or not the disputants stand in the proximate relation of employer and employee.

(d) The term "court of the United States" means any court of the United States whose jurisdiction has been or may be conferred or defined or limited by Act of Congress, including the courts of the District of Columbia.

Questions

[Before answering these questions review Section 20 of the Clayton Act, *supra* p. 853.]

1. What is the significance of Section 2 of the Norris-La-Guardia Act? What reasons can you give to explain the inclusion of this section in the Act? Should this section be of special interest to a federal judge? Why?

2. What is the apparent objective of Section 3 of the Act? Is the section adequate for that purpose?

3. Do Sections 1, 4, and 7 of the Act—when considered together—say anything substantially different than what was said in Section 20 of the Clayton Act? Do these sections remedy defects in the prior law? If so, how?

4. What are the apparent objectives of sections 5 and 6 of the Act? Do you think the sections are adequate for those purposes?

5. Sections 1, 4, 5, 6, and 7 all purport to be concerned with the jurisdiction of courts. Why was the Act couched in jurisdictional terms? Was it solely because Congress wished to limit the activities of federal courts? Could the act also provide some guidance to the courts in labor cases where their jurisdiction was not impaired by the act?

6. What is the significance of Section 13 of the Act?

7. Compare the extracts from the Norris-LaGuardia Act, with Sections 1 and 2 of the Sherman Act, and Sections 6 and 20 of the Clayton Act. What, if any, significant differences are there in the *form* of the Norris-LaGuardia Act as compared to the *form* of the other two acts?

8. To what extent were the courts free to have developed independently the same or similar rules as those set out in the Norris-LaGuardia Act?

9. Assuming that the rules laid down by the Act reflect sound policy, what advantages and what disadvantages inhere in their taking the form of legislation rather than emerging solely from judicial decisions?

SECTION 39.　THE NATIONAL LABOR RELATIONS
ACT OF 1935 [1]

[The following is taken from COX and BOK, CASES ON LABOR
LAW (7th ed.), pp. 88–89, 92–98.　Footnotes are omitted.]

The passage of the National Labor Relations Act was the culmination
of a long period of development.　In 1895 the United States Strike Commission declared that the Pullman Company's refusal to recognize and bargain
with labor organizations placed it "behind the age" and that Congress in
the Erdman Act of 1898 sought to protect railway labor unions and draw
them into machinery for the settlement of disputes.　In 1902 and again
in 1916 federal commissions pointed out that such conduct was a prolific
source of industrial strife.　During World War I the interests of the workers in self-organization and collective bargaining received government protection, although not formal legal recognition (see p. 55, supra).　Then the
pendulum swung back.　Collective bargaining was rejected by business and
discountenanced by Republican administrations.　The wartime practices
took root in the transportation industry, however, and after the great
Railway Shopmen's strike of 1922, they were embodied albeit in a watered-
down form, in the Railway Labor Act of 1926.

The provisions of the Railway Labor Act were agreed upon in advance
through private negotiations between the railroads and the interested unions, and little change was made by the Congress.　In general, the emphasis
of the Act was on the peaceful settlement of labor disputes, thus reflecting
the strategic importance of the transportation industry in the national
economy.　Adjustment boards were to be established by agreement of the
carriers and the men to settle differences over the interpretation of contracts and to decide minor disputes over working conditions.　More elaborate
provisions were included to assist in resolving disputes over the negotiation
of wages and working conditions.　Section 2 of the Act imposed a duty on
both sides to make "every reasonable effort to make and maintain agreements concerning rates of pay, rules, and working conditions ＊ ＊ ＊"
In addition, a mediation board was established consisting of five members
appointed by the President.　In the event of a break-down in the contract
negotiations between unions and carriers, the dispute could be referred
to this board, or the board could proffer its services on its own motion.
The Board could then seek to mediate or otherwise assist the negotiations
between the parties.　While no solution was to be imposed upon the parties by the government, the mediation board was empowered to encourage
the parties to arbitrate their differences and procedures were established
whereby both sides might easily agree to submit to final and binding arbitration.　If the controversy could not be settled by these techniques, the
mediation board was empowered to notify the President if the dispute
threatened to disrupt interstate commerce to such a point that any section

1.　In tribute to its chief architect,
Senator Robert Wagner of New York,
the Act of 1935 is commonly referred
to as the Wagner Act, and we shall
hereafter refer to it as such.

of the country would be deprived of essential transport services. The President could then appoint a board to investigate and report on the dispute within thirty days. Neither party was allowed to change the conditions out of which the dispute arose for another thirty days following the making of the report. Thereafter, the parties were free to resort to economic warfare to settle their differences.

The provisions requiring that the status quo be maintained for as much as sixty days represented a substantial concession on the part of the unions. In return, labor obtained a guarantee against interference by the railroads in the process of union organization. Hence, the Act declared that the representatives or parties to railway disputes should be designated "by the respective parties in such manner as may be provided in their corporate organization or unincorporated association, or by other means of collective action, without interference, influence or coercion exercised by either party over the self-organization or designation of representatives by the other." After the enactment of this statute the Texas & N. O. R. Co. resorted to inducement and coercion, including discriminatory discharges, to set up on its lines a company union in lieu of the Brotherhood of Railway and Steamship Clerks. The resulting litigation ended in a landmark decision of the United States Supreme Court. Texas & N. O. R. Co. v. Brotherhood of Railway & S. S. Clerks, 281 U.S. 548, 50 S.Ct. 427, 74 L.Ed. 1034 (1930). [The Court held the Act to be constitutional.]

The Philosophy of the Wagner Act

In every respect American trade union history after 1933 stood in contrast with the twenties. A few facts epitomize what occurred. In 1933 less than 3,000,000 workers were members of trade unions. Early in the 1940's 12,000,000 workers were organized. Between 1937 and 1940 the great industrial giants of the steel, automobile, rubber and electrical manufacturing industries were forced to begin adapting themselves to the ways of collective bargaining.

These events were part of the New Deal revolution. Their explanation lies in the conditions which gave it birth. The stock market panic of 1929 and the deep depression of the early and middle thirties stirred intellectual, social and economic ferment. During the first third of the century the mass of the American people were not ready to listen to those who criticized existing institutions. The collapse of the economic system after 1929 dispelled the worker's faith in welfare capitalism and made the middle classes more sympathetic towards the objectives of organized labor. The challenge which the unions presented to corporate employers was strengthened by the attack of the Roosevelt administration upon "entrenched greed." The new Keynesian economics with its emphasis on mass purchasing power and consumption was favorable to any movement which would increase the bargaining power of the workers. Political power shifted away from business to farm and labor groups. Outside the labor field there was written such far-reaching legislation as the Securities Act, the Securities and Exchange Commission Act, the Public Utilities Holding Company Act, the Federal Deposit Insurance Corporation Act, the Agricultural Adjustment Acts, the Agricultural Marketing Agreement Act of 1937 and the Bituminous Coal Act. In the field of labor legislation, the National Labor Relations Act and federal wage and hour, child labor and social security laws

were enacted.   Labor leaders were regularly consulted by the President upon important issues and were often given representation on government
commissions concerned with labor policy and social welfare.   The labor
movement had always had a considerable following among intellectuals,
but now it commanded the services of enthusiastic young men who found
in the unions opportunities to use their native ability and education.   More
important than all these factors, however, were two others: (1) the federal government's policy of giving active encouragement to unionization
and collective bargaining and (2) the formation of the Congress of Industrial Organizations.

The impetus for general legislation aiding unionization came from the
search for measures to halt the deepening depression which followed the
stock market panic of 1929.

The grand scheme of the National Industrial Recovery Act was to organize industry through trade associations and codes of fair competition
that would eliminate cut-throat competition and other wasteful practices
and so stabilize, if not raise, the price level.   On the side of employees, fair
labor standards were to be established by raising wages, shortening hours,
and eliminating industrial home work, child labor and other sweatshop practices.   Perhaps the latter branch of the NIRA philosophy was considered
even more important than the organization of industry, for this was the day
of Keynesian economics when the way to speed up economic activity was
supposed to be to increase mass purchasing power.

There were two ways to deal with the slow starvation resulting from
constantly shrinking payrolls and to build up mass purchasing power.   One
was to enact legislation fixing minimum wages and maximum hours low
enough to divide the available work and so spread employment.   The other
was to enable employees to help themselves by encouraging the development
of labor organizations strong enough to assert true bargaining power in
dealing with employers.

Measures of the second type offered several advantages.   Unions might
raise wages above the minimum.   They could police the contracts they negotiated without the same need for government action which results from
direct regulation.   There was at least some reason to hope that legislation
assuring freedom to organize would not be subject to the same constitutional
limitations as might invalidate wage and hour laws.   Accordingly, Section
7(A) of the National Industrial Recovery Act declared—

> "That employees shall have the right to organize and bargain col-
> lectively through representatives of their own choosing, and shall be
> free from the interference, restraint, or coercion of employers of labor
> or their agents, in the designation of such representatives or in self-
> organization or in other mutual aid or protection; [and] that no em-
> ployee and no one seeking employment shall be required as a condition
> of employment to join any company union or to refrain from joining,
> organizing, or assisting a labor organization of his own choosing."

In 1935 the NIRA collapsed partly as a result of its own weight although the immediate occasion was a Supreme Court decision holding the
basic statute unconstitutional.   The administration policy toward business
turned away from the philosophy of cartelization to the older tradition of
enforced competition, but it scarcely slackened its interest in building up

the bargaining power of employees.   The Wagner Act of 1935 [2] established on a permanent foundation the legally protected right of employees to organize and bargain collectively through representatives of their own choosing.   The basic idea reaches back before 1900 but much of its elaboration was the work of the NIRA period.

The heart of the Wagner Act was Section 7, which originally provided—

"Employees shall have the right to self-organization, to form, join or assist labor organizations, to bargain collectively through representatives of their own choosing, and to engage in concerted activities for the purpose of collective bargaining or other mutual aid or protection."

There are three parts to the right guaranteed by Section 7—perhaps one should say that three rights are created. *First,* employees are to be secured freedom to form, join, or assist labor organizations. *Second,* they are guaranteed freedom to bargain collectively with the employer, which means to bargain through the union. *Third,* they are also guaranteed the right to engage in concerted activities, i. e., strikes and picketing for the purpose of wielding their collective bargaining power.   It is doubtful whether the right to bargain collectively without the right to engage in strikes and picketing would be more than an empty slogan.

The other provisions of the original National Labor Relations Act were concerned with the implementation and enforcement of the threefold right guaranteed by Section 7.

Section 8(1) [3] declared it to be an unfair labor practice for an employer "to interfere with, restrain, or coerce employees in the exercise of rights guaranteed in Section 7."   This provision covers generally such anti-union tactics as beating up labor organizers, locking the employees out to destroy incipient unions, industrial espionage and other use of the employer's economic power to prevent unionization.   Threats of economic reprisal or promises of benefit are unfair labor practices.   Section 8(1) also forbids subtler antiunion tactics such as wage increases carefully timed to show the employees that nothing would be gained by joining a union.

Subsections (2), (3) and (4) of Section 8 proscribe specifically some of the more offensive anti-union tactics in which employers had engaged. During the NLRA period many companies had formed "Representation Plans" or "Works Councils" carefully controlled to give employees the forms of organization without the substance.   Subsection (2) outlaws these so-called "company unions."   Subsection (3) prohibits discrimination in hiring or firing.   Subsection (4) attempts to furnish protection against reprisals for asserting rights under the NLRA.

The provisions just summarized continue to apply after a union has become the bargaining representative, but their importance is greatest during what may be called the organizational phase of labor management

2. The official title of the act was the National Labor Relations Act.   The colloquial name is used here to distinguish the act in its original form from the present National Labor Relations Act which contains provisions derived from the original act and others added by the Taft-Hartley Act in 1947.

3. As a result of the Taft-Hartley amendments of 1947, the provisions referred to here as Sections 8(1), 8(2), etc. now appear as Sections 8(a) (1), 8(a) (2), etc.

relations—the period in which employees are taking steps to form a union or in which an outside union is seeking to persuade them to organize. For it is at this time that employees need the most protection and the employer is most likely to attack the union.

Section 8(5) relates primarily to the period after the employees have organized and are seeking to engage in collective bargaining. It imposes on an employer an affirmative duty to bargain collectively with the representatives designated by its employees "subject to the provisions of Section 9(a)." Section 9(a) provides—

"Representatives designated or selected for the purposes of collective bargaining by the majority of the employees in a unit appropriate for such purposes, shall be the exclusive representatives of all the employees [in the appropriate bargaining unit]. * * *"

Thus Section 9(a) brought into labor relations the principle of majority rule. This section, in conjunction with Section 8(5), not only requires the employer to bargain with representatives designated by the majority, but through the word "exclusive" it forbids him to deal with any other union.

The principle of majority rule obviously requires not only a procedure for ascertaining what representatives, if any, have been chosen by a majority but also a method for determining the employees among whom to conduct the count. The designated group is called the appropriate bargaining unit because it contains the employees whom the union will represent if designated by the majority.

Section 9 confers on the National Labor Relations Board the authority to resolve these questions. Section 9(c) makes provision for conducting an election within the appropriate unit. At the end of the proceeding the Board issues a formal certification to any union which receives a majority of the valid votes cast. Such certifications are unreviewable orders which carry no legal sanctions. If an employer refuses to bargain with the certified union, the case must then be handled as a violation of Section 8(5).

To enforce the substantive measures just outlined Congress established the kind of administrative agency which was becoming an increasingly common method of implementing New Deal legislation. Sections 3 and 4 created a National Labor Relations Board with exclusive jurisdiction over both unfair labor practices and questions of representation. Under Section 10, which regulates NLRB procedure in unfair labor practice cases, the Board issued complaints of violations, its staff prosecuted the complaints and with the aid of other staff officials the Board passed upon the merits of the case. Judicial enforcement and review were authorized under Section 10(e) and (f) upon petition to an appropriate federal court of appeals. While the courts were authorized to review most questions of law, their power with respect to findings of fact was restricted to determining whether the findings were "supported by evidence." These provisions gave rise to bitter controversy and the Taft-Hartley amendments later made significant changes in both NLRB organization and the scope of judicial review.

Although the Wagner Act was partly an economic measure designed to enable industrial workers to raise their wages and improve their standard of living, it also embodied a conscious, carefully articulated program for minimizing labor disputes. Its sponsors held, and still believe, that enforcement of the guarantees of the rights to organize and bargain collectively is the best method of achieving industrial peace without undue sacrifice of personal and economic freedom. The reasons for their belief that the Act reduces strikes and other forms of industrial unrest may be summarized as follows:

First. The prohibition of employer unfair labor practices and the legal compulsion to recognize and bargain with any union designated by a majority of the employees in an appropriate unit should tend to eliminate strikes for those purposes. Previously, when an employer refused to bargain with a union, its only recourse was to strike. U.S. Department of Labor statistics showed that a substantial proportion of the man days lost from strikes resulted from strikes to secure recognition and bargaining rights. This cause of strikes might be removed if employers were required to bargain. There was also evidence of widespread discriminatory discharges, espionage, black lists and other repressive tactics which caused resentment and unrest and which the prevention of employer unfair labor practices would eliminate.

> "The denial by employers of the right of employees to organize and the refusal to accept the procedure of collective bargaining lead to strikes and other forms of industrial strife or unrest, which have the intent or the necessary effect of burdening or obstructing commerce."

Second. Collective bargaining itself tends to reduce the number of strikes and lockouts. Four points may be made in support of this proposition.

(1) Collective bargaining enables employers and employees to dig behind their prejudices and exchange their views to such an extent that on many points they reach agreement while on others they discover that the area of disagreement is so narrow that it is cheaper to compromise than to do battle. The Industrial Commission reported in 1902—

> "The chief advantage which comes from the practice of periodically determining the conditions of labor by collective bargaining directly between employers and employees is that thereby each side obtains a better understanding of the actual state of the industry, of the conditions which confront the other side, and of the motives which influence it. Most strikes and lockouts would not occur if each party understood exactly the position of the other."

(2) Recognition, experience in bargaining, and the resulting maturity bring a sense of responsibility to labor unions. As early as 1906 another federal commission found—

> "Experience shows that the more full the recognition given to a trades union, the more businesslike and responsible it becomes. Through dealing with businessmen in business matters its more intelligent, conservative, responsible members come to the front and gain general control and direction of its affairs. If the energy of the employer is directed to discouragement and repression of the union, he need not be surprised if the more radically inclined members are the ones most frequently heard."

(3) Collective action substitutes the strength of the group for the weakness of the individual in dealing with a corporate employer and thereby enables employees to raise wages and improve labor standards. Since such

conditions are causes of strikes, their elimination tends to reduce such stoppages.

(4) Collective bargaining substitutes what may be called industrial democracy for the arbitrary power of the employer. Where collective bargaining is the practice, wages and other conditions of employment are the product of consent, for they are governed by a collective bargaining agreement negotiated between the employer and the representatives of the employees instead of being established by the employer's fiat. Moreover, the collective agreement establishes a rule of law; it is the measure of both the employer's and employees' rights and obligations.

Although the Wagner Act was intended to provide a foundation for a comprehensive system of industrial relations, it was not a complete labor code. The sponsors dealt only with the labor problems which seemed most urgent in 1935, leaving others to state law or to the future. Three limitations are especially significant.

First. The Wagner Act was primarily concerned with the organizational phases of labor relations. The aim was to prevent practices which interfered with the growth of labor unions and the development of collective bargaining. Once the union was organized and the employer accorded it recognition as the representative of his employees, the function of the statute, as originally conceived, was completed. Even the duty to bargain with the majority representatives was imposed by Section 8(5) chiefly because the refusal to bargain was a method of destroying the union. (In this respect the development of the law has departed significantly from the original conception.)

Second. The Wagner Act was concerned exclusively with the activities of employers which were thought to violate the rights guaranteed by Section 7. Unions were not beyond reproach, but most of them were so weak that their misconduct raised no serious national problems until the 1940's. Hence the original statute did not deal with their activities.

Third. The Wagner Act left substantive terms and conditions of employment entirely to private negotiation. The Act did not fix wages, hours or other conditions of employment. It did not authorize any administrative tribunal to fix them. When a dispute arose concerning substantive terms and conditions of employment, the Act provided no governmental machinery for its adjustment. The basic theory of the law in its original form, as today, was that the arrangement of substantive terms and conditions of employment was a private responsibility from which the government should stand apart. It was hoped that the processes of collective bargaining would result in a lessening of industrial strife, but no one supposed that strikes would not occur. In the end the force which makes management and labor agree is often an awareness of the costs of disagreement. The strike is the motive power which makes collective bargaining operate. Freedom to strike, the threat of a strike and possibly a number of actual strikes are, therefore, indispensable parts of a national labor policy based upon the establishment of wages, hours and other terms and conditions of employment by private collective bargaining.

Questions

1. In what ways does the Wagner Act represent a basically different approach to the legal resolution of labor-management conflict from that manifested in the Norris-LaGuardia Act?

2. In what respect, if any, do the Wagner Act and the Norris-LaGuardia Act embody the same theory of the role of law and government in the resolution of labor-management conflict?

SECTION 40. THE JUDICIAL RESPONSE TO THE NEW LABOR LAWS: 1937–1947

F.D.R.'s first term in office was a period of tremendous activity in which the Presidential role as legislative leader was firmly established. The Congress acted swiftly to give the President the various reform measures he sought.

The principal problem of the day was the great depression and, not surprisingly, much of the early New Deal legislation was directed to economic reform. (Some of these developments are recounted and analyzed in the preceding section of the materials.) The Congress was generally receptive to President Roosevelt's legislative program and it provided him with many of the measures he requested.

The position of the Supreme Court with respect to the New Deal legislation was a different matter. The political and economic maelstrom of 1932–33 had left untouched the Court and the constitutional doctrine of due process of law in economic regulation. But, to paraphrase Justice Holmes, the calm which surrounds the Supreme Court is very much like the eye of a hurricane, and a constitutional storm of great magnitude was soon to sweep over the Court.

If there was doubt in 1933 as to how the Court would react to constitutional attacks on New Deal legislation, this doubt was dispelled by 1935. In a series of landmark decisions the Court declared unconstitutional some of the key measures in the New Deal recovery formula. Perhaps the most striking of these decisions was the determination made in the Schecter case, that the National Industrial Recovery Act was constitutionally invalid. (See the Cox extract in the preceding section for an outline of the provisions of the N.I.R.A.) This act had been the keystone in the Roosevelt plans for industrial recovery. It is now generally thought to have been ill-advised legislation but, in 1935, the Supreme Court interdiction of the act was deemed a major blow to the New Deal and to hopes for economic recovery. Some of the flavor of the constitutional crisis precipitated by the demise of the N.I.R.A. is captured in the following passage.

———

[The following is taken from THURMAN ARNOLD, THE SYMBOLS OF GOVERNMENT (New Haven, 1935), p. 172.]

In the summer of 1935, screaming headlines announced that the N.R.A. had been declared unconstitutional. The members of the vast organization spread all over the country found themselves without salaries and without a place in the scheme of things. Accepting the decision as "law," the public was greatly puzzled to explain how an unconstitutional organization could have existed unchecked for two years. Blame was variously apportioned to Congress, the President, the executive officers of the Government, the brain trust, radicals, and others, but it occurred to no one that the Supreme Court of the United States might possibly have had something to do with the delay. New laws were advocated to move litigation faster and moral lessons were read to everyone except the Court. It was assumed without question that it would have been impossible for the Court to have said the law was unconstitutional any sooner than it actually did.

President Roosevelt sent up a trial balloon in which he accepted the decision in its broadest interpretation as preventing any further exercise of national power over commerce than we were accustomed to in the "horse and buggy" days. He told people that his hands were tied. Immediately, another storm of criticism arose because it was heresy to claim that such a good constitution interpreted by such a learned court could tie anyone's hands. To interpret the N.R.A. case in this way was simply another attack of a different kind on the Constitution. The public wanted to think of the Constitution as tending to restrict such things as tyranny and bureaucracy without interfering with any necessary exercise of national power.

Upon the failure of this trial balloon the President took the opposite course and urged laws about which there was some doubt in the light of the N.R.A. decision. Immediately, conservative newspapers began bitterly to remind the President of his oath to support the Constitution. The New York Herald-Tribune printed the President's oath to support the Constitution, and under it, as a complete contradiction, his very sensible statement to Congress that the only method of determining whether a doubtful law was constitutional was to pass it and let the Supreme Court decide.

Finally, when lawyers began to study the decision, it appeared that it might be given either a broad or a narrow scope and that actually no one could predict the next case with any certainty. Disturbed by this the New York Herald-Tribune recommended that a commission of experts be appointed to study the decision and that the President take their advice on the exact limits of his powers.

This strange situation brought into the limelight by the public interest in New Deal legislation is repeated every day on a smaller scale whenever judicial sanction in legislative or business practice is required.

———

Here indeed was a pretty pickle. The country, caught in the depths of depression, had given a mandate for change to its new political leaders, only to find that the supreme law of the land barred many of the most significant measures of the New Deal. Arnold suggests that the public conception of the problem was especially troublesome because the dilemma involved an interaction of our most treasured political-legal institutions, so that any attempt to assess responsibility for the dilemma meant at least implied criticism of: (a) a popular President, or (b) a popular legislature; or (c) a learned and respected court; or (d) the Constitution itself. But if the public had difficulty in assessing responsibility for the constitutional crisis, it soon became apparent that the President was not similarly troubled.

F.D.R. was reelected in 1936 in an electoral landslide—he received the electoral votes of all but two states. Fortified by this political triumph, and supported in the Congress by a substantial Democratic majority, he set out to clear the constitutional road blocks to the New Deal. His approach was simple and direct. The problem was not in the Constitution but in a superannuated Supreme Court. It was the "nine old men" who had gone astray, perhaps due to the burden of their years. With the problem stated in this simple form, a simple answer followed. Provision would be made for the appointment of additional justices to help carry the load. The President therefore proposed that Congress exercise its constitutional power to legislate regarding the structure of the Federal Courts. The gist of the proposal was that the President be authorized to make additional appointments to the federal bench, so that one additional judicial position would be created for each position which was then filled by a judge who (a) had been in office at least ten years, (b) was at least seventy years old, and (c) was eligible to retire. The proposal made no specific reference to the Supreme Court but applied to the federal bench generally. As the Court was then constituted, however, the President would have been able to make six appointments to the Court upon adoption of his proposal.

The plan was artfully drawn to avoid constitutional difficulties and to afford a plausible justification for its adoption. But the artifice was too transparent. The proposal was labeled a "Court-packing plan" whereby F.D.R. would attempt to remake constitutional doctrine through Presidential appointments. In the uproar which followed, the President and the Congress joined issue in an epochal conflict over constitutional politics. The plan was rejected by the Congress in what marked a stunning defeat to F.D.R.

Even while that conflict was raging, however, the Court was engaged in a separate struggle over the course of constitutional doctrine, the results of which were revealed in a series of landmark decisions in the spring of 1937. One of these decisions came in the first case in which the Court had occasion to pass on the constitutionality of the Wagner Act.

SECTION 40.1   THE CONSTITUTIONALITY OF THE WAGNER ACT

N. L. R. B. v. JONES & LAUGHLIN STEEL CORP.

Supreme Court of the United States, 1937.
301 U.S. 1, 57 S.Ct. 615.

MR. CHIEF JUSTICE HUGHES* delivered the opinion of the Court. [Footnotes are omitted.]

In a proceeding under the National Labor Relations Act of 1935 the National Labor Relations Board found that the respondent, Jones & Laughlin Steel Corporation, had violated the act by engaging in unfair labor practices affecting commerce. The proceeding was instituted by the Beaver Valley Lodge No. 200, affiliated with the Amalgamated Association of Iron, Steel and Tin Workers of America, a labor organization. The unfair labor practices charged were that the corporation was discriminating against members of the union with regard to hire and tenure of employment, and was coercing and intimidating its employees in order to interfere with their self-organization. The discriminatory and coercive action alleged was the discharge of certain employees.

The National Labor Relations Board, sustaining the charge, ordered the corporation to cease and desist from such discrimination and coercion, to offer reinstatement to ten of the employees named, to make good their losses in pay, and to post for thirty days notices that the corporation would not discharge or discriminate against members or those desiring to become members, of the labor union. As the corporation failed to comply, the Board petitioned the Circuit Court of Appeals to enforce the order. The court denied the petition holding that the order lay beyond the range of federal power. 83 F.2d 998. We granted certiorari. 299 U.S. 534, 57 S.Ct. 119, 81 L.Ed. 393.

* * *

Second.   The Unfair Labor Practices in Question.—The unfair labor practices found by the Board are those defined in section 8, subdivisions (1) and (3). These provide:

"Sec. 8.   It shall be an unfair labor practice for an employer—

"(1) To interfere with, restrain, or coerce employees in the exercise of the rights guaranteed in section 7 [section 157 of this title].   * * *

"(3) By discrimination in regard to hire or tenure of employment or any term or condition of employment to encourage or discourage membership in any labor organization."

---

* Chief Justice Charles Evans Hughes was twice appointed to the Supreme Court, first by President Taft in 1910 (he resigned in 1916) and later by President Hoover in 1930. Justice Hughes had practiced law in New York and was Governor of New York when he was appointed to the Court in 1910. He resigned from the Court to run as the Republican candidate in the 1916 presidential election. He was defeated by Woodrow Wilson and he resumed the practice of law. From 1921 to 1924 he served as Secretary of State to Presidents Harding and Coolidge. As Chief Justice, from 1930 to 1941, Hughes led the Court through the constitutional crisis of the mid-thirties. He retired from the Court in 1941, and he died in 1948.

Section 8, subdivision (1), refers to section 7, which is as follows:

"Section 7. Employees shall have the right to self-organization, to form, join, or assist labor organizations, to bargain collectively through representatives of their own choosing, and to engage in concerted activities, for the purpose of collective bargaining or other mutual aid or protection."

Thus, in its present application, the statute goes no further than to safeguard the right of employees to self-organization and to select representatives of their own choosing for collective bargaining or other mutual protection without restraint or coercion by their employer.

That is a fundamental right. Employees have as clear a right to organize and select their representatives for lawful purposes as the respondent has to organize its business and select its own officers and agents. Discrimination and coercion to prevent the free exercise of the right of employees to self-organization and representation is a proper subject for condemnation by competent legislative authority. Long ago we stated the reason for labor organizations. We said that they were organized out of the necessities of the situation; that a single employee was helpless in dealing with an employer; that he was dependent ordinarily on his daily wage for the maintenance of himself and family; that, if the employer refused to pay him the wages that he thought fair, he was nevertheless unable to leave the employ and resist arbitrary and unfair treatment; that union was essential to give laborers opportunity to deal on an equality with their employer. American Steel Foundries v. Tri-City Central Trades Council, 257 U.S. 184, 209, 42 S.Ct. 72, 78, 66 L.Ed. 189, 27 A.L.R. 360. We reiterated these views when we had under consideration the Railway Labor Act of 1926, 44 Stat. 577. Fully recognizing the legality of collective action on the part of employees in order to safeguard their proper interests, we said that Congress was not required to ignore this right but could safeguard it. Congress could seek to make appropriate collective action of employees an instrument of peace rather than of strife. We said that such collective action would be a mockery if representation were made futile by interference with freedom of choice. Hence the prohibition by Congress of interference with the selection of representatives for the purpose of negotiation and conference between employers and employees, "instead of being an invasion of the constitutional right of either, was based on the recognition of the rights of both." Texas & N. O. R. Co. v. Railway & S. S. Clerks, supra. We have reasserted the same principle in sustaining the application of the Railway Labor Act as amended in 1934 (45 U.S.C.A. § 151 et seq.). Virginian Railway Co. v. System Federation, No. 40, supra.

* * *

Fifth. The Means Which the Act Employs.—Questions under the Due Process Clause and Other Constitutional Restrictions.—Respondent asserts its right to conduct its business in an orderly manner without being subjected to arbitrary restraints. What we have said points to the fallacy in the argument. Employees have their correlative right to organize for the purpose of securing the redress of grievances and to promote agreements with employers relating to rates of pay and conditions of work. Texas & N. O. R. Co. v. Railway S. S. Clerks, supra; Virginian Railway Co. v. System Federation No. 40. Restraint for the purpose of preventing an unjust interference with that right cannot be considered arbitrary or capricious. The provision of section 9(a) that representatives, for the purpose of collective bargaining, of the majority of the employees in an appropriate unit shall be the exclusive representatives of all the employees in that unit, imposes upon the respondent only the duty of conferring and negotiating with the authorized representatives of its employees for the purpose of settling a labor dispute. This provision has its analogue in section 2, Ninth, of the Railway Labor Act, as amended (45 U.S.C.A. § 152, subd. 9), which was under consideration in Virginian Railway Co. v. System Federation No. 40, supra. The decree which we affirmed in that case required the railway company to treat with the representative chosen by the employees and also to refrain from entering into collective labor agreements with any one other than their true representative as ascertained in accordance with the provisions of the act. We said that the obligation to treat with the true representative was exclusive and hence imposed the negative duty to treat with no other. We also pointed out that, as conceded by the government, the injunction against the company's entering into any contract concerning rules, rates of pay and working conditions except with a chosen representative was "designed only to prevent collective bargaining with any one purporting to represent employees" other than the representative they had selected. It was taken "to prohibit the negotiation of labor contracts, generally applicable to employees" in the described unit with any other representative than the one so chosen, "but not as precluding such individual contracts" as the company might "elect to make directly with individual employees." We think this construction also applies to section 9(a) of the National Labor Relations Act 29 U.S.C.A. § 159(a).

The act does not compel agreements between employers and employees. It does not compel any agreement whatever. It does not prevent the employer "from refusing to make a collective contract and hiring individuals on whatever terms" the employer "may by unilateral action determine." The act expressly provides in section 9(a) that any individual employee or a group of employees shall have the right at any time to present grievances to their employer. The theory of the act is that free opportunity for negotiation with accredited representatives of employees is likely to promote industrial peace and may bring about the adjustments and agreements which the act in itself does not attempt to compel. As we said in Texas & N. O. R. Co. v. Railway & S. S. Clerks, supra, and repeated in Virginian Railway Co. v. System Federation No. 40, the cases of Adair v. United States, 208 U.S. 161, 28 S.Ct. 277, 52 L.Ed. 436, 13 Ann.Cas. 764, and Coppage v. Kansas, 236 U.S. 1, 35 S.Ct. 240, 59 L.Ed. 441, L.R.A.1915C, 960, are inapplicable to legislation of this character. The act does not interfere with the normal exercise of the right of the employer to select its employees or to discharge them. The employer may not, under cover of that right, intimidate or coerce its employees with respect to their self-organization and representation, and, on the other hand, the Board is not entitled to make its authority a pretext for interference with the right of discharge when that right is exercised for other reasons than such intimidation and coercion. The true purpose is the subject of investigation with full opportunity to show the facts. It would seem that when employers freely recognize the right of their employees to their own organizations and their unrestricted right of representation there will be much less occasion for controversy in respect to the free and appropriate exercise of the right of selection and discharge.

The act has been criticized as one-sided in its application; that it subjects the employer to supervision and restraint and leaves untouched the abuses for which employees may be responsible; that it fails to provide a more comprehensive plan,—with better assurances of fairness to both sides and with increased chances of success in bringing about, if not compelling, equitable solutions of industrial disputes affecting interstate commerce. But we are dealing with the power of Congress, not with a particular policy or with the extent to which policy should go. We have frequently said that the legislative authority, exerted within its proper field, need not embrace all the evils within its reach. The Constitution does not forbid "cautious advance, step by step," in dealing with the evils which are exhibited in activities within the range of legislative power. Carroll v. Greenwich Insurance Co., 199 U.S. 401, 411, 26 S.Ct. 66, 50 L.Ed. 246; Keokee Coke Co. v. Taylor, 234 U.S. 224, 227, 34 S.Ct. 856, 58 L.Ed. 1288; Miller v. Wilson, 236 U.S. 373, 384, 35 S.Ct. 342, 59 L.Ed. 628, L.R.A.1915F, 829; Sproles v. Binford, 286 U.S. 374, 396, 52 S.Ct. 581, 588, 76 L.Ed. 1167. The question in such cases is whether the Legislature, in what it does prescribe, has gone beyond constitutional limits.

The procedural provisions of the act are assailed. But these provisions, as we construe them, do not offend against the constitutional requirements governing the creation and action of administrative bodies. See Interstate Commerce Commission v. Louisville & Nashville R. Co., 227 U.S. 88, 91, 33 S.Ct. 185, 57 L.Ed. 431. The act establishes standards to which the Board must conform. There must be complaint, notice and hearing. The Board must receive evidence and make findings. The findings as to the facts are to be conclusive, but only if supported by evidence. The order of the Board is subject to review by the designated court, and only when sustained by the court may the order be enforced. Upon that review all questions of the jurisdiction of the Board and the regularity of its proceedings, all questions of constitutional right or statutory authority are open to examination by the court. We construe the procedural provisions as affording adequate opportunity to secure judicial protection against arbitrary action in accordance with the well-settled rules applicable to administrative agencies set up by Congress to aid in the enforcement of valid legislation. It is not necessary to repeat these rules which have frequently been declared. None of them appears to have been transgressed in the instant case. Respondent was notified and heard. It had opportunity to meet the charge of unfair labor practices upon the merits, and by withdrawing from the hearing it declined to avail itself of that opportunity. The facts found by the Board support its order and the evidence supports the findings. Respondent has no just ground for complaint on this score.

The order of the Board required the reinstatement of the employees who were found to have been discharged because of their "union activity" and for the purpose of "discouraging membership in the union." That requirement was authorized by the act. Section 10(c), 29 U.S.C.A. § 160(c). In Texas & N. O. R. Co. v. Railway & S. S. Clerks, supra, a similar order for restoration to service was made by the court in contempt proceedings for the violation of an injunction issued by the court to restrain an interference with the right of employees as guaranteed by the Railway Labor Act of 1926. The requirement of restoration to service of employees discharged in violation of the provisions of that act was thus a sanction imposed in the enforcement of a judicial decree. We do not doubt that Congress could impose a like sanction for the enforcement of its valid regulation. The fact that in the one case it was a judicial sanction, and in the other a legislative one, is not an essential difference in determining its propriety.

Respondent complains that the Board not only ordered reinstatement but directed the payment of wages for the time lost by the discharge, less amounts earned by the employee during that period. This part of the order was also authorized by the act. Section 10(c). It is argued that the requirement is equivalent to a money judgment and hence contravenes the Seventh Amendment with respect to trial by jury. The Seventh Amendment provides that "In suits at common law, where the value in controversy shall exceed twenty dollars; the right of trial by jury shall be preserved." The amendment thus preserves the right which existed under the common law when the amendment was adopted. Shields v. Thomas, 18 How. 253, 262, 15 L.Ed. 368; In re Wood, 210 U.S. 246, 258, 28 S.Ct. 621, 52 L.Ed. 1046; Dimick v. Schiedt, 293 U.S. 474, 476, 55 S.Ct. 296, 79 L.Ed. 603, 95 A.L.R. 1150; Baltimore & Carolina Line v. Redman, 295 U.S. 654, 657, 55 S.Ct. 890, 891, 79 L.Ed. 1636. Thus it has no application to cases where recovery of money damages is an incident to equitable relief even though damages might have been recovered in an action at law. Clark v. Wooster, 119 U.S. 322, 325, 7 S.Ct. 217, 30 L.Ed. 392; Pease v. Rathbun-Jones Engineering Co., 243 U.S. 273, 279, 37 S.Ct. 283, 61 L.Ed. 715, Ann.Cas.1918C, 1147. It does not apply where the proceeding is not in the nature of a suit at common law. Guthrie National Bank v. Guthrie, 173 U.S. 528, 537, 19 S.Ct. 513, 43 L.Ed. 796.

The instant case is not a suit at common law or in the nature of such a suit. The proceeding is one unknown to the common law. It is a statutory proceeding. Reinstatement of the employee and payment for time lost are requirements imposed for violation of the statute and are remedies appropriate to its enforcement. The contention under the Seventh Amendment is without merit.

Our conclusion is that the order of the Board was within its competency and that the act is valid as here applied. The judgment of the Circuit Court of Appeals is reversed and the cause is remanded for further proceedings in conformity with this opinion. It is so ordered.

Reversed and remanded.

[JUSTICE MCREYNOLDS * dissented and delivered an opinion in which he was joined by JUSTICES VAN DEVANTER, SUTHERLAND, and BUTLER. A portion of the opinion is reprinted below. Footnotes are omitted.]

The things inhibited by the Labor Act relate to the management of a manufacturing plant—something distinct from commerce and subject to

---

* Justice James C. McReynolds was appointed to the Supreme Court by President Wilson in 1914. At the time of his appointment he was Attorney General of the U. S. His tenure on the Court was marked by controversy with Holmes and Brandeis regarding the application of the "due process" concept in economic regulation cases. With Justices Sutherland, Van Devanter, and Butler he led the Court which was to become the object of President Roosevelt's "court-packing plan." After 1937, the climate on the Court was hostile to Justice McReynolds' views but, with characteristic tenacity, he remained in office until 1941 and he was the last of the "four horsemen" (see *infra* p. 905) to leave the Court. He died in 1946.

the authority of the state. And this may not be abridged because of some vague possibility of distant interference with commerce.

* * *

Texas & New Orleans Railroad Co. et al., v. Brotherhood of Railway & Steamship Clerks et al., 281 U.S. 548, 50 S.Ct. 427, 434, 74 L.Ed. 1034, is not controlling. There the Court, while considering an act definitely limited to common carriers engaged in interstate transportation over whose affairs Congress admittedly has wide power, declared: "The petitioners invoke the principle declared in Adair v. United States, 208 U.S. 161, 28 S.Ct. 277, 52 L.Ed. 436, 13 Ann.Cas. 764, and Coppage v. Kansas, 236 U.S. 1, 35 S.Ct. 240, 59 L.Ed. 441, L.R.A.1915C, 960, but these decisions are inapplicable. The Railway Labor Act of 1926 does not interfere with the normal exercise of the right of the carrier to select its employees or to discharge them. The statute is not aimed at this right of the employers but at the interference with the right of employees to have representatives of their own choosing. As the carriers subject to the act have no constitutional right to interfere with the freedom of the employees in making their selections, they cannot complain of the statute on constitutional grounds."

Adair's Case, supra, presented the question—"May Congress make it a criminal offense against the United States—as, by the 10th section of the act of 1898 [30 Stat. 428], it does—for an agent or officer of an interstate carrier, having full authority in the premises from the carrier, to discharge an employee from service simply because of his membership in a labor organization?" The answer was no. "While, as already suggested, the right of liberty and property guaranteed by the Constitution against deprivation without due process of law is subject to such reasonable restraints as the common good or the general welfare may require, it is not within the functions of government—at least, in the absence of contract between the parties—to compel any person, in the course of his business and against his will, to accept or retain the personal services of another, or to compel any person, against his will, to perform personal services for another. The right of a person to sell his labor upon such terms as he deems proper is, in its essence, the same as the right of the purchaser of labor to prescribe the conditions upon which he will accept such labor from the person offering to sell it. So the right of the employee to quit the service of the employer, for whatever reason, is the same as the right of the employer, for whatever reason, to dispense with the services of such employee. It was the legal right of the defendant, Adair,—however unwise such a course might have been,—to discharge Coppage because of his being a member of a labor organization, as it was the legal right of Coppage, if he saw fit to do so, however unwise such course on his part might have been—to quit the service in which he was engaged, because the defendant employed some persons who were not members of a labor organization. In all such particulars the employer and the employee have equality of right, and any legislation that disturbs that equality is an arbitrary interference with the liberty of contract which no government can legally justify in a free land." "The provision of the statute under which the defendant was convicted must be held to be repugnant to the 5th Amendment, and as not embraced by nor within the power of Congress to regulate interstate commerce, but, under the guise of regulating interstate commerce, and as applied to this case, it arbitrarily sanctions an illegal invasion of the personal liberty as well as the right of property of the defendant, Adair."

Coppage v. Kansas, following the Adair Case held that a state statute, declaring it a misdemeanor to require an employee to agree not to become a member of a labor organization during the time of his employment, was repugnant to the due process clause of the Fourteenth Amendment.

The right to contract is fundamental and includes the privilege of selecting those with whom one is willing to assume contractual relations. This right is unduly abridged by the act now upheld. A private owner is deprived of power to manage his own property by freely selecting those to whom his manufacturing operations are to be entrusted. We think this cannot lawfully be done in circumstances like those here disclosed.

It seems clear to us that Congress has transcended the powers granted.

Note

The relation of the Court-packing plan to the shift in judicial opinion in 1937 has been a topic of some controversy. One school of thought argues that the Supreme Court reevaluated its constitutional doctrines under the pressure of the Roosevelt plan, and that the decisions in cases such as Jones & Laughlin were motivated by a desire to preserve the existing court structure, and, more important, the political independence of the Court. Some wags have referred to this as "the shift in time that saved nine." [1] Another school of thought has it that the shift by the Court was already underway prior to the submission of the reorganization plan to the Congress.[2]

We do not propose to offer any resolution to this controversy. However, the chronology of the events surrounding the Roosevelt plan and the course of judicial decision in 1936–37 is worth examining.

The personnel of the Court in 1936–37 was as follows: Chief Justice Hughes, Associate Justices Brandeis, Cardozo, Roberts, Stone, Butler, McReynolds, Sutherland, and Van Devanter. The latter four justices made up a coalition which consistently held to a very restrictive view regarding the constitutional propriety of government intervention into economic affairs. The consistency of their approach in these cases resulted in their being dubbed "the four horsemen." They made up the hard core of the Court majorities which had struck down New Deal legislation.

On June 1, 1936, the Court handed down its decision in Morehead v. New York ex rel. Tipaldo, 298 U.S. 587, 56 S.Ct. 918. At issue in the case was the constitutionality of the New York Minimum Wage Law. A like question had been presented to the Court in

---

1. For a forceful, and entertaining, expression of this view see Rodell, Nine Men (1955), pp. 247–249.

2. See for example, Frankfurter, Mr. Justice Roberts, 104 University of Pennsylvania Law Review, 311, 313–317 (1955).

Adkins v. Children's Hospital, 261 U.S. 525, 43 S.Ct. 394 (1923). In Adkins, the Court had found that the District of Columbia minimum wage law for women violated the due process requirement of the Fifth Amendment. In Tipaldo, the Court reaffirmed the ruling in the Adkins case, though with respect to the due process requirement of the Fourteenth Amendment, and accordingly held the New York law unconstitutional. The Court's decision in Tipaldo was carried by a five-justice majority consisting of the "four horsemen" and Justice Roberts, with the Chief Justice, and Justices Brandeis, Cardozo and Stone in dissent. Shortly thereafter the Court went into recess for the summer.

On August 17, 1936, the appeal in West Coast Hotels v. Parrish, 300 U.S. 379, 57 S.Ct. 578 (1937), was filed. At issue in the case was the constitutionality of the Washington Minimum Wage Law. The Supreme Court of Washington had held the act to be constitutional under the Fourteenth Amendment.

The Parrish appeal was argued to the Court on December 16, and 17, 1936—a month after Roosevelt's overwhelming victory over Alfred Landon.

F.D.R.'s plan for reorganizing the judiciary was submitted to the Congress on February 5, 1937.

The decision in West Coast Hotel v. Parrish was handed down on March 29, 1937. A majority consisting of the Chief Justice, and Justices Brandeis, Cardozo, Roberts, and Stone voted to affirm the decision of the Supreme Court of Washington, and to overrule Adkins v. Children's Hospital. Justices Butler, McReynolds, Sutherland and Van Devanter dissented.

On April 12, 1937, the Court handed down its decision in the Jones & Loughlin case.

Justice Van Devanter retired from the Court on June 2, 1937.

On July 22, 1937, the Senate voted to recommit the bill authorizing Presidential enlargement of the courts (S 1392) to the Committee on the Judiciary. This action was taken pursuant to a motion by Senator Logan, acting on behalf of the Committee on the Judiciary. The purpose of the motion was to provide a graceful means for the Senate to kill the Court-packing plan, for the Committee had agreed prior to the submission of the motion that if the bill were recommitted to it, no further consideration of the plan would be undertaken. This was made known to the Senate at the time the motion was made. The motion carried by a vote of 70 to 20.

Although the President was roundly defeated in his effort to "pack the Court," fate was to provide him with the opportunity the Congress denied him. The retirement of Van Devanter was followed by that of Sutherland in January 1938. Cardozo died in July of the same year. Brandeis retired in February of 1939, and Butler died in November of that year. McReynolds retired in February 1941. Thus, within a span of four years after the Court-packing plan was introduced, President Roosevelt was given the opportunity to appoint six new justices to the Court. The persons he chose to fill the vacancies on the Court were all staunch supporters of the New Deal.

Questions

1. In light of the last sentence of the preceding note, can it be said that President Roosevelt did in fact pack the Supreme Court?

2. Justice Roberts has been singled out as the key man in the constitutional revolution of 1937, for it was his vote which marked the difference between the Tipaldo and Parrish decisions, and which presumably provided the majority in the Jones & Loughlin case. It is alleged that his shift in position was a response to a plea from the Chief Justice who feared that Roosevelt might succeed in his plan unless the Court made a change.[1] This allegation has been heatedly denied, notably by Justice Frankfurter, who wrote that Justice Roberts had determined to vote with the Parrish majority prior to the announcement of the Court-packing plan and out of motives that had no relation to that plan.[2]

Do you consider that the allegation is a slur to Justice Roberts' judicial record? Why?

3. Does the majority opinion in Jones & Loughlin demonstrate to your satisfaction that the case is substantially different from Adair v. United States (*supra* p. 874) and Coppage v. Kansas (*supra* p. 881)?

SECTION 40.2   THE CONSTITUTIONALITY OF ANTI-PICKETING LEGISLATION

THORNHILL v. ALABAMA

Supreme Court of the United States, 1940.
310 U.S. 88, 60 S.Ct. 736.

MR. JUSTICE MURPHY delivered the opinion of the Court.

Petitioner, Byron Thornhill, was convicted in the Circuit Court of Tuscaloosa County, Alabama, of the violation of Section 3448 of the State Code of 1923. The Code Section reads as follows: "§ 3448. Loitering or picketing forbidden.—Any person or persons, who, without a just cause or legal excuse therefor, go near to or loiter about the premises or place of business of any other person, firm, corporation, or association of people, en-

---

1. See note *supra* p. 904.   2. See note *supra* p. 904.

gaged in a lawful business, for the purpose, or with intent of influencing, or inducing other persons not to trade with, buy from, sell to, have business dealings with, or be employed by such persons, firm, corporation, or association, or who picket the works or place of business of such other persons, firms, corporations, or associations of persons, for the purpose of hindering, delaying, or interfering with or injuring any lawful business or enterprise of another, shall be guilty of a misdemeanor; but nothing herein shall prevent any person from soliciting trade or business for a competitive business."

The complaint against petitioner, which is set out in the margin, is phrased substantially in the very words of the statute. The first and second counts charge that petitioner, without just cause or legal excuse, did "go near to or loiter about the premises" of the Brown Wood Preserving Company with the intent or purpose of influencing others to adopt one of the enumerated courses of conduct. In the third count, the charge is that petitioner "did picket" the works of the Company "for the purpose of hindering, delaying or interfering with or injuring [its] lawful business".

The proofs consist of the testimony of two witnesses for the prosecution. It appears that petitioner on the morning of his arrest was seen "in company with six or eight other men" "on the picket line" at the plant of the Brown Wood Preserving Company. Some weeks previously a strike order had been issued by a Union, apparently affiliated with The American Federation of Labor, which had as members all but four of the approximately one hundred employees of the plant. Since that time a picket line with two picket posts of six to eight men each had been maintained around the plant twenty-four hours a day. The picket posts appear to have been on Company property, "on a private entrance for employees, and not on any public road." One witness explained that practically all of the employees live on Company property and get their mail from a post office on Company property and that the Union holds its meetings on Company property. No demand was ever made upon the men not to come on the property. There is no testimony indicating the nature of the dispute between the Union and the Preserving Company, or the course of events which led to the issuance of the strike order, or the nature of the effort for conciliation.

The Company scheduled a day for the plant to resume operations. One of the witnesses, Clarence Simpson, who was not a member of the Union, on reporting to the plant on the day indicated, was approached by petitioner who told him that "they were on strike and did not want anybody to go up there to work." None of the other employees said anything to Simpson, who testified: "Neither Mr. Thornhill nor any other employee threatened me on the occasion testified to. Mr. Thornhill approached me in a peaceful manner, and did not put me in fear; he did not appear to be mad." "I then turned and went back to the house and did not go to work." The other witness, J. M. Walden, testified: "At the time Mr. Thornhill and Clarence Simpson were talking to each other, there was no one else present, and I heard no harsh words and saw nothing threatening in the manner of either man." For engaging in some or all of these activities, petitioner was arrested, charged, and convicted as described. [By appropriate motions he raised and the courts below ruled on the constitutional questions considered herein.]

First. The freedom of speech and of the press, which are secured by the First Amendment against abridgment by the United States, are among the fundamental personal rights and liberties which are secured to all persons by the Fourteenth Amendment against abridgment by a state.

The safeguarding of these rights to the ends that men may speak as they think on matters vital to them and that falsehoods may be exposed through the processes of education and discussion is essential to free government. . . .

Second. The section in question must be judged upon its face.

The finding against petitioner was a general one. It did not specify the testimony upon which it rested. The charges were framed in the words of the statute and so must be given a like construction. The courts below expressed no intention of narrowing the construction put upon the statute by prior state decisions. In these circumstances, there is no occasion to go behind the face of the statute or of the complaint for the purpose of determining whether the evidence, together with the permissible inferences to be drawn from it, could ever support a conviction founded upon different and more precise charges. "Conviction upon a charge not made would be sheer denial of due process." [Citations omitted.] The State urges that petitioner may not complain of the deprivation of any rights but his own. It would not follow that on this record petitioner could not complain of the sweeping regulations here challenged.

There is a further reason for testing the section on its face. Proof of an abuse of power in the particular case has never been deemed a requisite for attack on the constitutionality of a statute purporting to license the dissemination of ideas. [Citations omitted.] The cases when interpreted in the light of their facts indicate that the rule is not based upon any assumption that application for the license would be refused or would result in the imposition of other unlawful regulations. Rather it derives from an appreciation of the character of the evil inherent in a licensing system. The power of the licensor against which John Milton directed his assault by his "Appeal for the Liberty of Unlicensed Printing" is pernicious not merely by reason of the censure of particular comments but by reason of the threat to censure comments on matters of public concern. It is not merely the sporadic abuse of power by the censor but the pervasive threat inherent in its very existence that constitutes the danger to freedom of discussion. [Citation omitted.] One who might have had a license for the asking may therefore call into question the whole scheme of licensing when he is prosecuted for failure to procure it. [Citation omitted.] A like threat is inherent in a penal statute, like that in question here, which does not aim specifically at evils within the allowable area of State control but, on the contrary, sweeps within its ambit other activities that in ordinary circumstances constitute an exercise of freedom of speech or of the press. The existence of such a statute, which readily lends itself to harsh and discriminatory enforcement by local prosecuting officials, against particular groups deemed to merit their displeasure, results in a continuous and pervasive restraint on all freedom of discussion that might reasonably be regarded as within its purview. It is not any less effective or, if the restraint is not permissible, less pernicious than the restraint on freedom of discussion imposed by the threat of censorship. An accused, after arrest and conviction under such a statute, does not have to sustain the burden of demonstrating that the State could not constitutionally have written a different and specific statute covering his activities as disclosed by the charge and the evidence introduced against him. [Citation omitted.] Where regulations of the liberty of free discussions are concerned, there are special reasons for observing the rule that it is the statute, and not the accusation or the evidence under it, which prescribes the limits of permissible conduct and warns against transgression. [Citations omitted.]

Third. Section 3448 has been applied by the State courts so as to prohibit a single individual from walking slowly and peacefully back and forth on the public sidewalk in front of the premises of an employer, without speaking to anyone, carrying a sign or placard on a staff above his head stating only the fact that the employer did not employ union men affiliated with the American Federation of Labor; the purpose of the described activity was concededly to advise customers and prospective customers of the relationship existing between the employer and its employees and thereby to induce such customers not to patronize the employer. [Citation omitted.] The statute as thus authoritatively construed and applied leaves room for no exceptions based upon either the number of persons engaged in the proscribed activity, the peaceful character of their demeanor, the nature of their dispute with an employer, or the restrained character and the accurateness of the terminology used in notifying the public of the facts of the dispute.

The numerous forms of conduct proscribed by Section 3448 are subsumed under two offenses: the first embraces the activities of all who "without a just cause or legal excuse" "go near to or loiter about the premises" of any person engaged in a lawful business for the purpose of influencing or inducing others to adopt any of certain enumerated courses of action; the second, all who "picket" the place of business of any such person "for the purpose of hindering, delaying, or interfering with or injuring any lawful business or enterprise of another." It is apparent that one or the other of the offenses comprehends every practicable method whereby the facts of a labor dispute may be publicized in the vicinity of the place of business of an employer. The phrase "without a just cause or legal excuse" does not in any effective manner restrict the breadth of the regulation; the words themselves have no ascertainable meaning either inherent or historical. [Citation omitted.] The courses of action, listed under the first offense, which an accused—including an employee—may not urge others to take, comprehends those which in many instances would normally result from merely publicizing, without annoyance or threat of any kind, the facts of a labor dispute. An intention to hinder, delay or interfere with a lawful business, which is an element of the second offense, likewise can be proved merely by showing that others reacted in a way normally expectable of some upon learning the facts of a dispute. The vague contours of the term "picket" are nowhere delineated.[1] Employees

---

1. See Hellerstein, Picketing Legislation and the Courts (1931) 10 No.Car. L.Rev. 158, 186n:

"A picketer may: (1) Merely observe workers or customers. (2) Communicate information, e. g., that a strike is in progress, making either true, untrue or libelous statements. (3) Persuade employees or customers not to engage in relations with the employer: (a) through the use of banners, without speaking, carrying true, untrue or libelous legends; (b) by speaking, (i) in a calm, dispassionate manner, (ii) in a heated, hostile manner, (iii) using abusive epithets and profanity, (iv) yelling loudly, (v) by persisting in making arguments when employees or customers refuse to listen; (c) by offering money or similar inducements to strike breakers. (4) Threaten employees or customers: (a) by the mere presence of the picketer; the presence may be a threat of, (i) physical violence, (ii) social ostracism, being branded in the community as a 'scab', (iii) a trade or employees' boycott, i. e., preventing workers from securing employ-

or others, accordingly, may be found to be within the purview of the term and convicted for engaging in activities identical with those prescribed by the first offense. In sum, whatever the means used to publicize the facts of a labor dispute, whether by printed sign, by pamphlet, by word of mouth or otherwise, all such activity without exception is within the inclusive prohibition of the statute so long as it occurs in the vicinity of the scene of the dispute.

Fourth. We think that Section 3448 is invalid on its face.

The freedom of speech and of the press guaranteed by the Constitution embraces at least the liberty to discuss publicly and truthfully all matters of public concern without previous restraint or fear of subsequent punishment. The exigencies of the colonial period and the efforts to secure freedom from oppressive administration developed a broadened conception of these liberties as adequate to supply the public need for information and education with respect to the significant issues of the times. The Continental Congress in its letter sent to the Inhabitants of Quebec (October 26, 1774) referred to the "five great rights" and said: "The last right we shall mention, regards the freedom of the press. The importance of this consists, besides the advancement of truth, science, morality, and arts in general, in its diffusion of liberal sentiments on the administration of Government, its ready communication of thoughts between subjects, and its consequential promotion of union among them, whereby oppressive officers are shamed or intimidated, into more honourable and just modes of conducting affairs." Journal of the Continental Congress, 1904 Ed., vol. I, pp. 104, 108. Freedom of discussion, if it would fulfill its historic function in this nation, must embrace all issues about which information is needed or appropriate to enable the members of society to cope with the exigencies of their period.

In the circumstances of our times the dissemination of information concerning the facts of a labor dispute must be regarded as within that area of free discussion that is guaranteed by the Constitution. [Citation of two cases omitted.] See Senn v. Tile Layers Union, 301 U.S. 468, 478, 57 S.Ct. 857, 862, 81 L.Ed. 1229. It is recognized now that satisfactory hours and wages and working conditions in industry and a bargaining position which makes these possible have an importance which is not less than the interests of those in the business or industry directly concerned. The health of the present generation and of those as yet unborn may depend on these matters, and the practices in a single factory may have economic repercussions upon a whole region and affect widespread systems of marketing. The merest glance at State and Federal legislation on the subject demonstrates the force of the argument that labor relations are not matters of mere local or private concern. Free discussion concerning the conditions in industry and the causes of labor disputes appears to us indispensable to the effective and intelligent use of the processes of popular government to shape the destiny of modern

ment and refusing to trade with customers (iv) threatening injury to property; (b) by verbal threats. (5) Assaults and use of violence. (6) Destruction of property. (7) Blocking of entrances and interference with traffic. The picketer may engage in a combination of any of the types of conduct enumerated above. The picketing may be carried on singly or in groups; it may be directed to employees alone or to customers alone or to both. It may involve persons who have contracts with the employer or those who have not or both."

industrial society. The issues raised by regulations, such as are challenged here, infringing upon the right of employees effectively to inform the public of the facts of a labor dispute are part of this larger problem. We concur in the observation of Mr. Justice Brandeis, speaking for the Court in Senn's case (301 U.S. at page 478, 57 S.Ct. at page 862, 81 L.Ed. 1229): "Members of a union might, without special statutory authorization by a state, make known the facts of a labor dispute, for freedom of speech is guaranteed by the Federal Constitution."

It is true that the rights of employers and employees to conduct their economic affairs and to compete with others for a share in the products of industry are subject to modification or qualification in the interests of the society in which they exist. This is but an instance of the power of the State to set the limits of permissible contest open to industrial combatants. [Citation omitted.] It does not follow that the State in dealing with the evils arising from industrial disputes may impair effective exercise of the right to discuss freely industrial relations which are matters of public concern. A contrary conclusion could be used to support abridgement of freedom of speech and of the press concerning almost every matter of importance to society.

The range of activities proscribed by Section 3448, whether characterized as picketing or loitering or otherwise, embraces nearly every practicable, effective means whereby those interested—including the employees directly affected—may enlighten the public on the nature and causes of a labor dispute. The safeguarding of these means is essential to the securing of an informed and educated public opinion with respect to a matter which is of public concern. It may be that effective exercise of the means of advancing public knowledge may persuade some of those reached to refrain from entering into advantageous relations with the business establishment which is the scene of the dispute. Every expression of opinion on matters that are important has the potentiality of inducing action in the interests of one rather than another group in society. But the group in power at any moment may not impose penal sanctions on peaceful and truthful discussion of matters of public interest merely on a showing that others may thereby be persuaded to take action inconsistent with its interests. Abridgement of the liberty of such discussion can be justified only where the clear danger of substantive evils arises under circumstances affording no opportunity to test the merits of ideas by competition for acceptance in the market of public opinion. We hold that the danger of injury to an industrial concern is neither so serious nor so imminent as to justify the sweeping proscription of freedom of discussion embodied in Section 3448.

The State urges that the purpose of the challenged statute is the protection of the community from the violence and breaches of the peace, which, it asserts, are the concomitants of picketing. The power and the duty of the State to take adequate steps to preserve the peace and to protect the privacy, the lives, and the property of its residents cannot be doubted. But no clear and present danger of destruction of life or property, or invasion of the right of privacy, or breach of the peace can be thought to be inherent in the activities of every person who approaches the premises of an employer and publicizes the facts of a labor dispute involving the latter. We are not now concerned with picketing en masse or otherwise conducted which might occasion such imminent and aggravated danger to these interests as to justify a statute narrowly drawn to cover the precise situation giving rise to the danger. [Citation omitted.] Section 3448 in question here does not aim specifically at serious encroachments on these interests and does not evidence any such care in balancing these interests against the interest of the community and that of the individual in freedom of discussion on matters of public concern.

It is not enough to say that Section 3448 is limited or restricted in its application to such activity as takes place at the scene of the labor dispute. "[The] streets are natural and proper places for the dissemination of information and opinion; and one is not to have the exercise of his liberty of expression in appropriate places abridged on the plea that it may be exercised in some other place." [Citations omitted.] The danger of breach of the peace or serious invasion of rights of property or privacy at the scene of a labor dispute is not sufficiently imminent in all cases to warrant the legislature in determining that such place is not appropriate for the range of activities outlawed by Section 3448.

Reversed.

MR. JUSTICE MCREYNOLDS is of opinion that the judgment below should be affirmed.

Questions

[Questions 1, 2, and 3 are taken from COX, CASES ON LABOR LAW (3rd ed.), p. 820.]

1. In appraising a case like Thornhill v. Alabama it is necessary to consider: (1) the reasoning in the opinion, (2) the philosophy underlying the opinion and the extent to which it is embraced by other justices, and (3) the minimum holding to which the Court must adhere unless it is prepared to overrule the precedent. What is the minimum holding of Thornhill's case?

2. May it be important in future cases to distinguish between (a) picketing of a retail establishment whose primary appeal is to the public at large and (b) picketing of a warehouse or factory which is addressed to its employees or employees of other employers who are engaged in picking up and delivering goods, the sole purpose of which is to notify them that they may not cross the picket line without incurring either (i) union discipline or (ii) displeasure and resulting social ostracism by fellow workers?

3. Under Thornhill's case may the objective of the picketing be material?

4. What result would follow from the application of Thornhill to the facts in Vegelahn v. Guntner, and Plant v. Woods?

SECTION 40.3   THE PRECEDENT OF A STATUTE

UNITED STATES v. HUTCHESON

Supreme Court of the United States, 1940.
312 U.S. 219, 61 S.Ct. 463.

MR. JUSTICE FRANKFURTER delivered the opinion of the Court.

. . . Anheuser-Busch, Inc., operating a large plant in St. Louis, contracted with Borsari Tank Corporation for the erection of an additional facility. The Gaylord Container Corporation, a lessee of adjacent property from Anheuser-Busch, made a similar contract for a new building with the Stocker Company. Anheuser-Busch obtained the materials for its brewing and other operations and sold its furnished products largely through interstate shipments. The Gaylord Corporation was equally dependent on interstate commerce for marketing its goods, as were the construction companies for their building materials. Among the employees of Anheuser-Busch were members of the United Brotherhood of Carpenters and Joiners of America and of the International Association of Machinists. The conflicting claims of these two organizations, affiliated with the American Federation of Labor, in regard to the erection and dismantling of machinery had long been a source of controversy between them. Anheuser-Busch had had agreements with both organizations whereby the Machinists were given the disputed jobs and the Carpenters agreed to submit all disputes to arbitration. But in 1939 the president of the Carpenters, their general representative, and two officials of the Carpenters' local organization, the four men under indictment, stood on the claims of the Carpenters for the jobs. Rejection by the employer of the Carpenters' demand and the refusal of the latter to submit to arbitration were followed by a strike of the Carpenters, called by the defendants against Anheuser-Busch and the construction companies, a picketing of Anheuser-Busch and its tenant, and a request through circular letters and the official publication of the Carpenters that union members and their friends refrain from buying Anheuser-Busch beer.

These activities on behalf of the Carpenters formed the charge of the indictment as a criminal combination and conspiracy in violation of the Sherman Law. Demurrers denying that what was charged constituted a violation of the laws of the United States were sustained (D.C., 32 F.Supp. 600) and the case came here under the Criminal Appeals Act.

Section 1 of the Sherman Law on which the indictment rested is as follows: "Every contract, combination in the form of trust or otherwise, or conspiracy, in restraint of trade or commerce among the several States, or with foreign nations, is hereby declared to be illegal." The controversies engendered by its application to trade union activities and the efforts to secure legislative relief from its consequences are familiar history. The Clayton Act of 1914 was the result. Act of October 15, 1914, 38 Stat. 730. "This statute was the fruit of unceasing agitation, which extended over more than 20 years and was designed to equalize before the law the position of workingmen and employer as industrial combatants." Duplex Printing Press Co. v. Deering, 254 U.S. 443, 484, 41 S.Ct. 172, 182, 65 L.Ed. 349, 16 A.L.R. 196. Section 20 of that Act . . . withdrew from the general interdict of the Sherman Law specifically enumerated practices of labor unions by prohibiting injunctions against them—since the use of the injunction had been the major source of dissatisfaction—and also relieved such practices of all illegal taint by the catch-all provision, "nor shall any of the acts specified in this paragraph be considered or held to be violations of any law of the United States". The Clayton Act gave rise to new litigation and to renewed controversy in and out of Congress regarding the status of trade unions. By the generality of its terms the Sherman Law had necessarily compelled the courts to work out its meaning from case to case. It was widely believed that into the Clayton Act courts read the very beliefs which that Act was designed to remove. Specifically the courts restricted the scope of § 20 to trade union activities directed against an employer by his own employees. Duplex Printing Press Co. v. Deering, supra. Such a view it was urged, both by powerful judicial dissents and informed lay opinion, misconceived the area of economic conflict that had best be left to economic forces and the pressure of public opinion and not subjected to the judgment of courts. Id., 254 U.S. at pages 485, 486, 41 S.Ct. at page 183, 65 L.Ed. 349, 16 A.L.R. 196. Agitation again led to legislation and in 1932 Congress wrote the Norris-LaGuardia Act. Act of March 23, 1932, 47 Stat. 70, 29 U.S.C. §§ 101–115, 29 U.S.C.A. §§ 101–115.

The Norris-LaGuardia Act removed the fetters upon trade union activities, which according to judicial construction § 20 of the Clayton Act had left untouched, by still further narrowing the circumstances under which the federal courts could grant injunctions in labor disputes. More especially, the Act explicity formulated the "public policy of the United States" in regard to the industrial conflict and by its light established that the allowable area of union activity was not to be restricted, as it had been in the Duplex case, to an immediate employer-employee relation. Therefore, whether trade union conduct constitutes a violation of the Sherman Law is to be determined only by reading the Sherman Law and § 20 of the Clayton Act and the Norris-LaGuardia Act as a harmonizing text of outlawry of labor conduct.

Were then the acts charged against the defendants prohibited or permitted by these three interlacing statutes? If the facts laid in the indictment come within the conduct enumerated in § 20 of the Clayton Act they do not constitute a crime within the general terms of the Sherman Law because of the explicit command of that section that such conduct shall not be "considered or held to be violations of any law of the United States". So long as a union acts in its self-interest and does not combine with non-labor groups, the licit and the illicit under § 20 are not to be distinguished by any judgment regarding the wisdom or unwisdom, the rightness or wrongness, the selfishness or unselfishness of the end of which the particular union activities are the means. There is nothing remotely within the terms of § 20 that differentiates between trade union conduct directed against an employer because of a controversy arising in the relation between employer and employee, as such, and conduct similarly directed but ultimately due to an internecine struggle between two unions seeking the favor of the same employer. Such strife between competing unions has been an obdurate conflict in the evolution of so-called craft unionism and has undoubtedly been one of the potent forces in the modern development of industrial unions. These conflicts have intensified industrial tension but there is not the slightest warrant for saying that Congress has made § 20 inapplicable to trade union conduct resulting from them.

In so far as the Clayton Act is concerned, we must therefore dispose of this case as though we had before us precisely the same conduct on the part of the defendants in pressing claims against Anheuser-Busch for increased wages, or shorter hours, or other elements of what are called working conditions. The fact that what was done was done in a competition for jobs against the Machinists rather than against, let us say, a company union is a differentiation which Congress has not put into the federal legislation and which therefore we cannot write into it.

It is at once apparent that the acts with which the defendants are charged are the kind of acts protected by § 20 of the Clayton Act. The refusal of the Carpenters to work for Anheuser-Busch or on construction work being done for it and its adjoining tenant, and the peaceful attempt to get members of other unions similarly to refuse to work, are plainly within the free scope accorded to workers by § 20 for "terminating any relation of employment", or "ceasing to perform any work or labor", or "recommending, advising or persuading others by peaceful means so to do". The picketing of Anheuser-Busch premises with signs to indicate that Anheuser-Busch was unfair to organized labor, a familiar practice in these situations, comes within the language "attending at any place where any such person or persons may lawfully be, for the purpose of peacefully obtaining or communicating information, or from peacefully persuading any person to work or to abstain from working". Finally, the recommendation to union members and their friends not to buy or use the product of Anheuser-Busch is explicitly covered by "ceasing to patronize * * * any party to such dispute, or from recommending, advising, or persuading others by peaceful and lawful means so to do."

Clearly, then, the facts here charged constitute lawful conduct under the Clayton Act unless the defendants cannot invoke that Act because outsiders to the immediate dispute also shared in the conduct. But we need not determine whether the conduct is legal within the restrictions which Duplex Printing Press Co. v. Deering gave to the immunities of § 20 of the Clayton Act. Congress in the Norris-LaGuardia Act has expressed the public policy of the United States and defined its conception of a "labor dispute" in terms that no longer leave room for doubt. * * * Such a dispute, § 13(c), 29 U.S.C.A. § 113(c), provides, "includes any controversy concerning terms or conditions of employment, or concerning the association or representation of persons in negotiating, fixing, maintaining, changing, or seeking to arrange terms or conditions of employment, regardless of whether or not the disputants stand in the proximate relation of employer and employee". And that § 13(b) a person is "participating or interested in a labor dispute" if he "is engaged in the same industry, trade, craft, or occupation in which such dispute occurs, or has a direct or indirect interest therein, or is a member, officer, or agent of any association composed in whole or in part of employers or employees engaged in such industry, trade, craft, or occupation".

To be sure, Congress expressed this national policy and determined the bounds of a labor dispute in an act explicitly dealing with the further withdrawal of injunctions in labor controversies. But to argue, as it was urged before us, that the Duplex case still governs for purposes of a criminal prosecution is to say that that which on the equity side of the court is allowable conduct may in a criminal proceeding become the road to prison. It would be strange indeed that although neither the Government nor Anheuser-Busch could have sought an injunction against the acts here challenged, the elaborate efforts to permit such conduct failed to prevent criminal liability punishable with imprisonment and heavy fines. That is not the way to read the will of Congress, particularly when expressed by a statute which, as we have already indicated, is practically and historically one of a series of enactments touching one of the most sensitive national problems. Such legislation must not be read in a spirit of mutilating narrowness. On matters far less vital and far less interrelated we have had occasion to point out the importance of giving "hospitable scope" to Congressional purpose even when meticulous words are lacking. Keifer & Keifer v. Reconstruction Finance Corporation, 306 U.S. 381, 391, 59 S.Ct. 516, 519, 83 L.Ed. 784, and authorities there cited. The appropriate way to read legislation in a situation like the one before us, was indicated by Mr. Justice Holmes on circuit: "A statute may indicate or require as its justification a change in the policy of the law, although it expresses that change only in the specific cases most likely to occur to the mind. The Legislature has the power to decide what the policy of the law shall be, and if it has intimated its will, however indirectly, that will should be recognized and obeyed. The major premise of the conclusion expressed in a statute, the change of policy that induces the enactment may not be set out in terms, but it is not an adequate discharge of duty for courts to say: We see what you are driving at, but you have not said it, and therefore we shall go on as before." Johnson v. United States, 1 Cir., 163 F. 30, 32, 18 L.R.A.,N.S., 1194.

The relation of the Norris-LaGuardia Act to the Clayton Act is not that of a tightly drawn amendment to a technically phrased tax provision. The underlying aim of the Norris-LaGuardia Act was to restore the broad purpose which Congress thought it had formulated in the Clayton Act but which was frustrated, so Congress believed, by unduly restrictive judicial construction. This was authoritatively stated by the House Committee on the Judiciary. "The purpose of the bill is to protect the rights of labor in the same manner the Congress intended when it enacted the Clayton Act, October 15, 1914, 38 Stat.L. 738, which act, by reason of its construction and application by the Federal courts, is ineffectual to accomplish the congressional intent." H.Rep.No.669, 72d Congress, 1st Session, p. 3. The Norris-LaGuardia Act was a disapproval of Duplex Printing Press Co. v. Deering, supra, and Bedford Cut Stone Co. v. Journeyman Stone Cutters' Association, 274 U.S. 37, 47 S.Ct. 522, 71 L.Ed. 916, 54 A.L.R. 791, as the authoritative interpretation of § 20 of the Clayton Act, for Congress now placed its own meaning upon that section. The Norris-LaGuardia Act reasserted the original purpose of the Clayton Act by infusing into it the immunized trade union activities as redefined by the later Act. In this light § 20 removes all such allowable conduct from the taint of being "violations of any law of the United States", including the Sherman Law. . . .

MR. JUSTICE MURPHY took no part in the disposition of this case.

MR. JUSTICE STONE* (concurring).

As I think it clear that the indictment fails to charge an offense under the Sherman Act, as it has been interpreted and applied by this Court, I find no occasion to consider the impact of the Norris-LaGuardia Act on the definition of participants in a labor dispute in the Clayton Act, as construed by this Court in Duplex Printing Press Co. v. Deering, 254 U.S. 443, 41 S.Ct. 172, 65 L.Ed. 349, 16 A.L.R. 196—an application of the Norris-LaGuardia Act which is not free from doubt and which some of my brethren sharply challenge. . . .

MR. JUSTICE ROBERTS.**

I am of opinion that the judgment should be reversed. . . .

Without detailing the allegations of the indictment, it is sufficient to say that they undeniably charge a secondary boycott, affecting interstate commerce.

This court, and many state tribunals, over a long period of years, have held such a secondary boycott illegal. In 1908 this court held such a secondary boycott, instigated to enforce the demands of a labor union against an employer, was a violation of the Sherman Act and could be restrained at the suit of the employer. It is a matter of history that labor unions insisted they were not within the purview of the Sherman Act but this court held to the contrary. As a result of continual agitation the Clayton Act was adopted. That Act, as amended, became effective October 15, 1914. Subsequently suits in equity were brought to restrain secondary boycotts similar to those involved in earlier cases. The contention was made that the Clayton Act exempted labor organizations from such suits. That contention was not sustained. Upon the fullest consideration, this court reached the conclusion that the provisions of Section 20 of the Clayton Act governed not the substantive rights of persons and organizations but merely regulated the practice according to which, and the conditions

---

* Chief Justice Harlan Fiske Stone was appointed to the Supreme Court by President Coolidge in 1925. He had been Professor of Law and Dean of the Law School of Columbia University and he served as Attorney General of the U. S. in 1924. As an Associate Justice of the Supreme Court he often joined Holmes and Brandeis in dissent. He remained on the Court to see many of those dissenting positions become the majority view. When Chief Justice Hughes retired, in 1941, President Roosevelt elevated Stone to the Chief Justiceship, which office he held until his death in 1946.

** Justice Owen J. Roberts was appointed to the Supreme Court by President Hoover in 1930. He was an instructor and Professor of Law at the Law School of the University of Pennsylvania (1898–1918), and he practiced law in Pennsylvania (1904–1930). In 1937, Justice Roberts joined with Chief Justice Hughes, and Justices Brandeis, Cardozo, and Stone to form the majority which upheld the constitutionality of the National Labor Relations Act, over the dissents of Justices Butler, McReynolds, Sutherland, and Van Devanter (see *supra* p. 898). Justice Roberts retired from the Supreme Court in 1945, and he died in 1955.

under which, equitable relief might be granted in suits of this character. Section 6 has no bearing on the offense charged in this case.

This court also unanimously held that a conspiracy such as is charged in the instant case renders the conspirators liable to criminal prosecution by the United States under the anti-trust acts.

It is common knowledge that the agitation for complete exemption of labor unions from the provisions of the anti-trust laws persisted. Instead of granting the complete exemption desired, Congress adopted, March 23, 1932, the Norris-LaGuardia Act. The title and the contents of that Act, as well as its legislative history, demonstrate beyond question that its purpose was to define and to limit the jurisdiction of federal courts sitting in equity. The Act broadens the scope of labor disputes as theretofore understood, that is, disputes between an employer and his employees with respect to wages, hours, and working conditions, and provides that before a federal court can enter an injunction to restrain illegal acts certain preliminary findings, based on evidence, must be made. The Act further deprives the courts of the right to issue an injunction against the doing of certain acts by labor organizations or their members. It is unnecessary to detail the acts as to which the jurisdiction of a court of equity is abolished. It is sufficient to say, what a reading of the Act makes letter clear, that the jurisdiction of actions for damages authorized by the Sherman Act, and of the criminal offenses denounced by that Act, are not touched by the Norris-LaGuardia Act.

By a process of construction never, as I think, heretofore indulged by this court, it is now found that, because Congress forbade the issuing of injunctions to restrain certain conduct, it intended to repeal the provisions of the Sherman Act authorizing actions at law and criminal prosecutions for the commission of torts and crimes defined by the anti-trust laws. The doctrine now announced seems to be that an indication of a change of policy in an Act as respects one specific item in a general field of the law, covered by an earlier Act, justifies this court in spelling out an implied repeal of the whole of the earlier statute as applied to conduct of the sort here involved. I venture to say that no court has ever undertaken so radically to legislate where Congress has refused so to do.

The construction of the act now adopted is the more clearly inadmissible when we remember that the scope of proposed amendments and repeals of the anti-trust laws in respect of labor organizations has been the subject of constant controversy and consideration in Congress. In the light of this history, to attribute to Congress an intent to repeal legislation which has had a definite and well understood scope and effect for decades past, by resurrecting a rejected construction of the Clayton Act and extending a policy strictly limited by the Congress itself in the Norris-LaGuardia Act, seems to me a usurpation by the courts of the function of the Congress not only novel but fraught, as well, with the most serious dangers to our constitutional system of division of powers.

THE CHIEF JUSTICE joins in this opinion.

Questions

[Before answering these questions review the article by Judge Walter V. Schaefer *supra* p. 568 ff. These questions are taken from COX, CASES ON LABOR LAW (3rd ed.), p. 130.]

1. Were the defendant's activities the kind of acts protected by Section 20 of the Clayton Act?

2. If you were counsel for the government, how would you have sought to convince the Court that the Clayton Act was irrelevant?

3. How did Mr. Justice Frankfurter meet this argument? On what principle of statutory interpretation is this part of the opinion predicated? Compare Landis, Statutes and The Sources of Law (1934), pp. 214 *et seq.*

4. In considering the foregoing questions note the following excerpts from arguments presented in support of the Norris-LaGuardia Act while its proposed enactment was a public issue:

(a) "But the immunity accorded is circumscribed: It is not immunity from legal as distinguished from equitable remedies,—hitherto unlawful conduct remains unlawful   *   *   *.   Section 9 of the proposed bill [which became Section 13] settles all of these questions so far as application for equitable relief is concerned. Immunity from injunctions extends to all the categories that we have described, save alone as to persons who are not engaged in the same industry with the complainant."—Frankfurter and Greene, The Labor Injunction (1930), pp. 215–216.

(b) "*Is the denial of all adequate judicial remedies in case of an illegal strike a denial of due process of law?* This question is not pertinent for the bill only withdraws the remedy of injunction. Civil action for damages and criminal prosecution remain available instruments. Illegal strikes are not made legal."—Frankfurter and Greene, Congressional Power Over the Labor Injunction, 31 Col.L.Rev. 385, 408 (1931).

5. The Hutcheson case grew out of a program envisaged by Assistant Attorney-General Arnold for dealing with the problems of jurisdictional strikes, alleged "featherbedding" and other labor union abuses by prosecutions under the Sherman Act. See Arnold, The Bottlenecks of Business (1940), ch. XI. Was the program sound policy?

SECTION 41. THE RETURN OF THE LABOR INJUNCTION

SECTION 41.1   THE JUDICIAL PRELUDE

UNITED STATES v. UNITED MINE WORKERS OF AMERICA

Supreme Court of the United States, 1947.
330 U.S. 258, 67 S.Ct. 677.

[In October, 1946, the United States was in possession of and operating most of the nation's bituminous coal mines. The government seizure of the mines had been made pursuant to a Presidential order which was based on authority granted the President by the War Labor Disputes Act. The President had determined that labor disputes were interrupting the production of bituminous coal and that this was detrimental to the national economy during the critical period at the end of World War II.

The responsibility for the control and operation of the mines was delegated to the Secretary of the Interior, Louis Krug. Subsequent to the seizure, Secretary Krug negotiated an agreement with John L. Lewis, then President of the United Mine Workers, the terms of which were to regulate the terms and conditions of employment in the mines during the period of government control.

On October 21, 1946, Lewis wrote to Krug asking for a conference to negotiate a new agreement. Lewis contended that the Lewis-Krug agreement provided for such a conference to be held at the request of either party and that either party could terminate the current agreement fifteen days after the beginning of such a conference.

The government denied that the Lewis-Krug agreement included such a provision. The government suggested that the union negotiate their wage and hour demands with the mine owners. The union refused. The government then agreed to confer with the union, but maintained its position that there was no provision for termination of the agreement. After 15 days of conference the union announced that it would exercise its alleged option and terminate the agreement on November 20, 1946. Notice to this effect was circulated to the mine workers.

On November 18, the government filed suit against the union in the District Court for the District of Columbia. The suit was brought under the Declaratory Judgment Act and sought judgment that the union had no power to terminate the Lewis-Krug agreement. The United States requested a temporary restraining order, pending resolution of its claim.

The court immediately issued an ex parte order restraining the defendants (Lewis and the union) from continuing the November 15 notice to the workers, or from encouraging them to strike. The complaint and order were served on the defendants on November 18. The order was to extend until November 27, at which date a hearing on the preliminary order was to be held. The miners commenced a walkout on November 18, and by November 20 a full strike was in progress.

On November 21, the United States filed a petition for an order against the defendants requiring them to show cause why they should not be punished for contempt for willfully violating the initial order. The show cause order was issued and on November 27, trial on the contempt charge was scheduled to begin.

By motion filed November 26, the defendants contended that the court was without power to issue such a restraining order. Their contention was based on the Norris-LaGuardia Act. After hearings on November 27, and 29, the court held that it had power to issue the order. Defendants then pleaded not guilty to the contempt charge. Trial on this charge commenced and at its conclusion on December 3, the court found the defendants guilty of civil and criminal contempt. On December 4 the court entered judgment against the defendants and assessed fines of $10,000 against Lewis and $3,500,000 against the Union. Defendants filed notice of appeal from the judgments of contempt. Both parties subsequently filed petitions for certiorari and the Supreme Court granted certiorari pursuant to § 240(a) of the judicial code which in certain cases authorized the use of certiorari prior to judgment in the Circuit Court of Appeals. The following opinion was handed down on March 6, 1947.]

MR. CHIEF JUSTICE VINSON delivered the opinion of the Court.

I.

Defendants' first and principal contention is that the restraining order and preliminary injunction were issued in violation of the Clayton and Norris-LaGuardia Acts. We have come to a contrary decision.

It is true that Congress decreed in § 20 of the Clayton Act that "no such restraining order or injunction shall prohibit any person or persons * * * from recommending, advising, or persuading others * * *" to strike. But by the Act itself this provision was made applicable only to cases "between an employer and employees, or between employers and employees, or between employees, or between persons employed and persons seeking employment * * *." For reasons which will be explained at greater length in discussing the applicability of the Norris-LaGuardia Act, we cannot construe the general term "employer" to include the United States, where there is no express reference to the United States and no evident affirmative grounds for believing that Congress intended to withhold an otherwise available remedy from the Government as well as from a specified class of private persons.

Moreover, it seems never to have been suggested that the proscription on injunctions found in the Clayton Act is in any respect broader than that in the Norris-LaGuardia Act. Defendants do not suggest in their argument that it is. This Court, on the contrary, has stated that the Norris-LaGuardia Act "still further * * * [narrowed] the circumstances under which the federal courts could grant injunctions in labor disputes." Consequently, we would feel justified in this case to consider the application of the Norris-LaGuardia Act alone. If it does not apply, neither does the less comprehensive proscription of the Clayton Act; if it does, defendant's reliance on the Clayton Act is unnecessary.

By the Norris-LaGuardia Act, Congress divested the federal courts of jurisdiction to issue injunctions in a specified class of cases. It would probably be conceded that the characteristics of the present case would be such as to bring it within that class if the basic dispute had remained one between defendants and a private employer, and the latter had been the plaintiff below. So much seems to be found in the express terms of §§ 4 and 13 of the Act, set out in the margin. The specifications in § 13 are in general terms and make no express exception for the United States. From these premises, defendants argue that the restraining order and injunction were forbidden by the Act and were wrongfully issued.

Even if our examination of the Act stopped here, we could hardly assent to this conclusion. There is an old and well-known rule that statutes which in general terms divest pre-existing rights or privileges will not be applied to the sovereign without express words to that effect. It has been stated, in cases in which there were extraneous and affirmative reasons for believing that the sovereign should also be deemed subject to a restrictive statute, that this rule was a rule of construction only. Though that may be true, the rule has been invoked successfully in cases so closely similar to the present one, and the statement of the rule in those cases has been so explicit, that we are inclined to give it much weight here. Congress was not ignorant of the rule which those cases reiterated; and, with knowledge of that rule, Congress would not, in writing the Norris-LaGuardia Act, omit to use "clear and specific [language] to that effect" if it actually intended to reach the Government in all cases.

But we need not place entire reliance in this exclusionary rule. Section 2, which declared the public policy of the United States as a guide to the Act's interpretation, carries indications as to the scope of the Act. It predicates the purpose of the Act on the contrast between the position of the "individual unorganized worker" and that of the "owners of property" who have been permitted to "organize in the corporate and other forms of ownership association", and on the consequent helplessness of the worker "to exercise actual liberty of contract * * * and thereby to obtain acceptable terms and conditions of employment." The purpose of the Act is said to be to contribute to the worker's "full freedom of association, self-organization, and designation of representatives of his own choosing, to negotiate the terms and conditions of his employment, and that he shall be free from the interference, restraint, or coercion of employers of labor, or their agents, in the designation of such representatives * * * for the purpose of collective bargaining * * *" These considerations, on their face, obviously do not apply to the Government as an employer or to relations between the Government and its employees.

If we examine §§ 4 and 13, on which defendants rely, we note that they do not purport to strip completely from the federal courts all their pre-existing powers to issue injunctions, that they withdraw this power only in a specified type of case, and that this type is a case "involving or growing out of any labor dispute." Section 13, in the first instance, declares a case to be of this type when it "involves persons" or "involves any conflicting or competing interests" in a labor dispute of "persons" who stand in any one of several defined economic relationships. And "persons" must be involved on both sides of the case, or the conflicting interests of "persons" on both sides of the dispute. The Act does not define "persons". In common usage that term does not include the sovereign, and statutes employing it will ordinarily not be construed to do so. Congress made express provision, R.S. § 1, 1 U.S.C. § 1, 1 U.S.C.A. § 1, for the term to extend to partnerships and corporations, and in § 13 of the Act itself for it to extend to associations. The absence of any comparable provision extending the term to sovereign governments implies that Congress did not desire the term to extend to them.

Those clauses in § 13(a) and (b) spelling out the position of "persons" relative to the employer-employee relationship affirmatively suggest that the United States, as an employer, was not meant to be included. Those clauses require that the case involve persons "who are engaged in the same industry, trade, craft or occupation", who "have direct or indirect interests therein", who are "employees of the same employer", who are "members of the same or an affiliated organization of employers or employees", or who stand in some one of other specified positions relative to a dispute over the employer-employee relationship. Every one of these qualifications in § 13(a) and (b) we think relates to an economic role ordinarily filled by a private individual or corporation, and not by a sovereign government. None of them is at all suggestive of any part played by the United States in its relations with its own employees. We think that Congress' failure to refer to the United States or to specify any role which it might commonly be thought to fill is strong indication that it did not intend that the Act should apply to situations in which United States appears as employer.

In the type of case to which the Act applies, § 7 requires certain findings of fact as conditions precedent to the issuance of injunctions even for the limited purposes recognized by the Act. One such required finding is that "the public officers charged with the duty to protect complainant's property are unable or unwilling to furnish adequate protection." Obviously, such finding could never be made if the complainant were the United States, and federal property were threatened by federal employees, as the responsibility of protection would then rest not only on state officers, but also on all federal civil and military forces. If these failed, a federal injunction would be a meaningless form. This provision, like those in §§ 2, 4 and 13, already discussed, indicates that the Act was not intended to affect the relations between the United States and its employees.

Defendants maintain that certain facts in the legislative history of the Act so clearly indicate an intent to restrict the Government's use of injunctions that all the foregoing arguments to the contrary must be rejected.

Representative Beck of Pennsylvania indicated in the course of the House debates that he thought the Government would be included within the prohibitions of the Act. Mr. Beck was not a member of the Judiciary Committee which reported the bill, and did not vote for its passage. We do not accept his views as expressive of the attitude of Congress relative to the status of the United States under the Act.

Representative Blanton of Texas introduced an amendment to the bill which would have made an exception to the provision limiting the injunctive power "where the United States Government is the petitioner", and this amendment was defeated by the House. But the first comment made on this amendment, after its introduction, was that of Representative LaGuardia, the House sponsor of the bill, who opposed it, not on the ground that such an exception should not be made, but rather on the ground that the express exception was unnecessary. Mr. LaGuardia read the definition of a person "participating or interested in a labor dispute" in § 13(b), referred to the provisions of § 13(a), and then added: "I do not see how in any possible way the United States can be brought in under the provisions of this bill." When Mr. Blanton thereupon suggested the necessity of allowing the Government to use injunctions to maintain discipline in the army and navy, Mr. LaGuardia pointed out that these services are not "a trade, craft or occupation". Mr. Blanton's only answer to Mr. LaGuardia's opposition was that the latter "does not know what extensions will be made." A vote was then taken and the amendment defeated. Obviously this incident does not reveal a Congressional intent to legislate concerning the relationship between the United States and its employees.

In the debates in both Houses of Congress numerous references were made to previous instances in which the United States had resorted to the injunctive process in labor disputes between private employers and private employees, where some public interest was thought to have become involved. These instances were offered as illustrations of the abuses flowing from the use of injunctions in labor disputes and the desirability of placing a limitation thereon. The frequency of these references and the attention directed to their subject matter are compelling circumstances. We agree that they indicate that Congress, in passing the Act, did not intend to permit the United States to continue to intervene by injunction in purely private labor disputes.

But whether Congress so intended or not is a question different from the one before us now. Here we are concerned only with the Government's right to injunctive relief in a dispute with its own employees. Although we recognize that Congress intended to withdraw such remedy in the former situation, it does not follow that it intended to do so in the latter. The circumstances in which the Government sought such remedy in 1894 and 1922 were vastly different from those in which the Government is seeking to carry out its responsibilities by taking legal action against its own employees, and we think that the references in question have only the most distant and uncertain bearing on our present problem. Indeed, when we look further into the history of the Act, we find other events which unequivocally demonstrate that injunctive relief was not intended to be withdrawn in the latter situation.

When the House had before it a rule for the consideration of the bill, Representative Michener, a ranking minority member of the Judiciary Committee and spokesman for the minority party on the Rules Committee, made a general statement in the House concerning the subject matter of the bill and advocating its immediate consideration. In this survey he clearly stated that the Government's rights with respect to its own employees would not be affected:

"Be it remembered that this bill does not attempt to legislate concerning Government employees. I do not believe that the enactment of this bill into law will take away from the Federal Government any rights which it has under existing law, to seek and obtain injunctive relief where the same is necessary for the functioning of the Government."

In a later stage of the debate, Representative Michener repeated this view in the following terms:

"This deals with labor disputes between individuals, not where the Government is involved. It is my notion that under this bill the Government can function with an injunction, if that is necessary in order to carry out the purpose of the Government. I should like to see this clarified, but I want to go on record as saying that under my interpretation of this bill the Federal Government will not at any time be prevented from applying for an injunction, if one is necessary in order that the Government may function."

Representatives Michener and LaGuardia were members of the Judiciary Committee which reported and recommended the bill to the House. They were the most active spokesmen for the Committee, both in explaining the bill and advocating its passage. No member of the House who voted for the bill challenged their explanations. At least one other member expressed a like understanding. We cannot but believe that the House accepted these authoritative representations as to the proper construction of the bill. The Senate expressed no contrary understanding, and we must conclude that Congress in passing the Act, did not intend to withdraw the Government's existing rights to injunctive relief against its own employees.

If we were to stop here, there would be little difficulty in accepting the decision of the District Court upon the scope of the Act. And the cases in this Court express consistent views concerning the types of situations to which the Act applies. They have gone no farther than to follow Congressional desires by regarding as beyond the jurisdiction of the District Courts the issuance of injunctions sought by the United States and directed to persons who are not employees of the United States. None of these cases dealt with the narrow segment of the employer-employee relationship now before us.

But regardless of the determinative guidance so offered, defendants rely upon the opinions of several Senators uttered in May, 1943, while debating the Senate version of the War Labor Disputes Act. The debate at that time centered around a substitute for the bill, S. 796, as originally introduced. Section 5 of the substitute, as amended, provided, "The district courts of the United States and the United States Courts of the Territories or possessions shall have jurisdiction, for cause shown, but solely upon application by the Attorney General or under his direction * * * to restrain violations or threatened violations of this act." Following the rejection of other amendments aimed at permitting a much wider use of injunctions and characterized as contrary to the Norris-LaGuardia Act, several Senators were of the opinion that § 5 itself would remove some of the protection given employees by that Act, a view contrary to what we have just determined to be the scope of the Act as passed in 1932. Section 5 was defeated and no injunctive provisions were contained in the Senate bill.

We have considered these opinions, but cannot accept them as authoritative guides to the construction of the Norris-LaGuardia Act. They were expressed by Senators, some of whom were not members of the Senate in 1932, and none of whom was on the Senate Judiciary Committee which reported the bill. They were expressed eleven years after the Act was passed and cannot be accorded even the same weight as if made by the same individuals in the course of the Norris-LaGuardia debates. Moreover, these opinions were given by individuals striving to write legislation from the floor of the Senate and working without the benefit of hearings and committee reports on the issues crucial to us here. We fail to see how the remarks of these

Senators in 1943 can serve to change the legislative intent of Congress expressed in 1932 and we accordingly adhere to our conclusion that the Norris-LaGuardia Act did not affect the jurisdiction of the Courts to issue injunctions when sought by the United States in a labor dispute with its own employees.

* * *

We do not find convincing the contention of the defendants that in seizing and operating the coal mines the Government was not exercising a sovereign function and that, hence, this is not a situation which can be excluded from the terms of the Norris-LaGuardia Act. In the Executive Order which directed the seizure of the mines, the President found and proclaimed that "the coal produced by such mines is required for the war effort and is indispensable for the continued operation of the national economy during the transition from war to peace; that the war effort will be unduly impeded or delayed by * * * interruptions [in production]; and that the exercise * * * of the powers vested in me is necessary to insure the operation of such mines in the interest of the war effort and to preserve the national economic structure in the present emergency * * *." Under the conditions found by the President to exist, it would be difficult to conceive of a more vital and urgent function of the Government than the seizure and operation of the bituminous coal mines. We hold that in a case such as this, where the Government has seized actual possession of the mines, or other facilities, and is operating them, and the relationship between the Government and the workers is that of employer and employee the Norris-LaGuardia Act does not apply.

II.

Although we have held that the Norris-LaGuardia Act did not render injunctive relief beyond the jurisdiction of the District Court, there are alternative grounds which support the power of the District Court to punish violations of its orders as criminal contempt.

* * *

In the case before us, the District Court had the power to preserve existing conditions while it was determining its own authority to grant injunctive relief. The defendants, in making their private determination of the law, acted at their peril. Their disobedience is punishable as criminal contempt.

Although a different result would follow were the question of jurisdiction frivolous and not substantial, such contention would be idle here. The applicability of the Norris-LaGuardia Act to the United States in a case such as this had not previously received judicial consideration, and both the language of the Act and its legislative history indicated the substantial nature of the problem with which the District Court was faced.

Proceeding further, we find impressive authority for the proposition that an order issued by a court with jurisdiction over the subject matter and person must be obeyed by the parties until it is reversed by orderly and proper proceedings. This is true without regard even for the constitutionality of the Act under which the order is issued.   In Howat v. Kansas, 1922, 258 U.S. 181, 189, 190, 42 S.Ct. 277, 280, 281, 66 L.Ed. 550, this Court said:

"An injunction duly issuing out of a court of general jurisdiction with equity powers, upon pleadings properly invoking its action, and served upon persons made parties therein and within the jurisdiction, must be obeyed by them, however erroneous the action of the court may be, even if the error be in the assumption of the validity of a seeming, but void law going to the merits of the case.   It is for the court of first instance to determine the question of the validity of the law, and until its decision is reversed for error by orderly review, either by itself or by a higher court, its orders based on its decision are to be respected, and disobedience of them is contempt of its lawful authority, to be punished."

Violations of an order are punishable as criminal contempt even though the order is set aside on appeal, Worden v. Searls, 1887, 121 U.S. 14, 7 S.Ct. 814, 30 L.Ed. 853, or though the basic action has become moot.   Gompers v. Buck's Stove & Range Co., 1911, 221 U.S. 418, 31 S.Ct. 492, 55 L.Ed. 797, 34 L.R.A.,N.S., 874.

We insist upon the same duty of obedience where, as here, the subject matter of the suit, as well as the parties, was properly before the court; where the elements of federal jurisdiction were clearly shown; and where the authority of the court of first instance to issue an order ancillary to the main suit depended upon a statute, the scope and applicability of which were subject to substantial doubt.   The District Court on November 29 affirmatively decided that the Norris-LaGuardia Act was of no force in this case and that injunctive relief was therefore authorized.   Orders outstanding or issued after that date were to be obeyed until they expired or were set aside by appropriate proceedings, appellate or otherwise.   Convictions for criminal contempt intervening before that time may stand.

* * *

Assuming, then, that the Norris-LaGuardia Act applied to this case and prohibited injunctive relief at the request of the United States, we would set aside the preliminary injunction of December 4 and the judgment for civil contempt; but we would, subject to any infirmities in the contempt proceedings or in the fines imposed, affirm the judgments for criminal contempt as validly punishing violations of an order then outstanding and unreversed.

* * *

In the light of these principles, we think the record clearly warrants a fine of $10,000 against defendant Lewis for criminal contempt.   A majority of the Court, however, does not think that it warrants the unconditional imposition of a fine of $3,500,000 against the defendant union.   A majority feels that, if the court below had assessed a fine of $700,000 against the defendant union, this, under the circumstances, would not be excessive as punishment for the criminal contempt theretofore committed; and feels that, in order to coerce the defendant union into a future compliance with the court's order, it would have been effective to make the other $2,800,000 of the fine conditional on the defendant's failure to purge itself within a reasonable time.   Accordingly, the judgment against the defendant union is held to be excessive.   It will be modified so as to require the defendant union to pay a fine of $700,000, and further, to pay an additional fine of $2,800,000 unless the defendant union, within five days after the issuance of the mandate herein, shows that it has fully complied with the temporary restraining order issued November 18, 1946, and the preliminary injunction issued December 4, 1946. . . .

MR. JUSTICE JACKSON joins in this opinion except as to the Norris-La-Guardia Act which he thinks relieved the courts of jurisdiction to issue injunctions in this class of case.

MR. JUSTICE FRANKFURTER, concurring in the judgment.

The historic phrase "a government of laws and not of men" epitomizes the distinguishing character of our political society.   When John Adams put that phrase into the Massachusetts Declaration of Rights, pt. 1, art. 30, he was not indulging in a rhetorical flourish.   He was expressing the aim of those who, with him, framed the Declaration of Independence and founded the Republic.   "A government of laws and not of men" was the rejection in positive terms of rule by fiat, whether by the fiat of governmental or private power.   Every act of government may be challenged by an appeal to law, as finally pronounced by this Court.   Even this Court has the last say only for a time.   Being composed of fallible men, it may err.   But revision of its errors must be by orderly process of law.   The Court may be asked to reconsider its decisions, and this has been done successfully again and again throughout our history.   Or, what this Court has deemed its duty to decide may be changed by legislation, as it often has been, and, on occasion, by constitutional amendment.

But from their own experience and their deep reading in history, the Founders knew that Law alone saves a society from being rent by internecine strife or ruled by mere brute power however disguised.   "Civilization involves subjection of force to reason, and the agency of this subjection is law."   The conception of a government by laws dominated the thoughts of those who founded this Nation and designed its Constitution, although they knew as well as the belittlers of the conception that laws have to be made, interpreted and enforced by men.   To that end, they set apart a body of men, who were to be the depositories of law, who by their disciplined training and character and by withdrawal from the usual temptations of private interest may reasonably be expected to be "as free, impartial, and independent as the lot of humanity will admit".   So strongly were the framers of the Constitution bent on securing a reign of law that they endowed the judicial office with extraordinary safeguards and prestige.   No one, no matter how exalted his public office or how righteous his private motive, can be judge in his own case.   That is what courts are for.   And no type of controversy is more peculiarly fit for judicial determination that a controversy that calls into question the power of a court to decide.   Controversies over "jurisdiction" are apt to raise difficult technical problems.   They usually involve judicial presuppositions, textual doubts, confused legislative history, and like factors hardly fit for final determination by a self-interest of a party.

Even when a statute deals with a relatively uncomplicated matter, and the "words in their natural sense as they would be read by the common man" would appear to give an obvious meaning, considerations underlying the statute have led this Court to conclude that "the words cannot be taken quite so simply."   See Alexander Milburn Co. v. Davis-Bournonville Co., 270 U.S. 390, 400, 46 S.Ct. 324, 70 L.Ed. 651.   How much more true this is of legislation like the Norris-LaGuardia Act. This Act altered a long process of judicial history, but altered it by a scheme of complicated definitions and limitations.

The Government here invoked the aid of a court of equity in circumstances which certainly were not covered by the Act with inescapable clarity. Colloquially speaking, the Government was "running" the mines. But it was "running" them not as an employer, in the sense that the owners of the coal mines were the employers of the men the day before the Government seized the mines. Nor yet was the relation between the Government and the men like the relation of the Government to the civil service employees in the Department of the Interior. It would be naive or wilful to assert that the scope of the Norris-LaGuardia Act in a situation like that presented by this bill raised a question so frivolous that any judge should have summarily thrown the Government out of court without day. Only when a court is so obviously traveling outside its orbit as to be merely usurping judicial forms and facilities, may an order issued by a court be disobeyed and treated as though it were a letter to a newspaper. Short of an indisputable want of authority on the part of a court, the very existence of a court presupposes its power to entertain a controversy, if only to decide, after deliberation, that it has no power over the particular controversy. Whether a defendant may be brought to the bar of justice is not for the defendant himself to decide.

To be sure, an obvious limitation upon a court cannot be circumvented by a frivolous inquiry into the existence of a power that has unquestionably been withheld. Thus, the explicit withdrawal from federal district courts of the power to issue injunctions in an ordinary labor dispute between a private employer and his employees cannot be defeated, and an existing right to strike thereby impaired, by pretending to entertain a suit for such an injunction in order to decide whether the court has jurisdiction. In such a case, a judge would not be acting as a court. He would be a pretender to, not a wielder of, judicial power.

That is not this case. It required extended arguments, lengthy briefs, study and reflection preliminary to adequate discussion in conference, before final conclusions could be reached regarding the proper interpretation of the legislation controlling this case. A majority of my brethren find that neither the Norris-LaGuardia Act nor the War Labor Disputes Act limited the power of the district court to issue the orders under review. I have come to the contrary view. But to suggest that the right to determine so complicated and novel an issue could not be brought within the cognizance of the district court, and eventually of this Court, is to deny the place of the judiciary in our scheme of government. And if the district court had power to decide whether this case was properly before it, it could make appropriate orders so as to afford the necessary time for fair consideration and decision while existing conditions were preserved. To say that the authority of the court may be flouted during the time necessary to decide is to reject the requirements of the judicial process.

It does not mitigate such defiance of law to urge that hard-won liberties of collective action by workers were at stake. The most prized liberties themselves pre-suppose an independent judiciary through which these liberties may be, as they often have been, vindicated. When in a real controversy, such as is now here, an appeal is made to law, the issue must be left to the judgment of courts and not the personal judgment of one of the parties. This principle is a postulate of our democracy.

And so I join the opinion of the Court insofar as it sustains the judgment for criminal contempt upon the broad ground of vindicating the process of law. The records of this Court are full of cases, both civil and criminal, involving life or land or small sums of money, in which the Court proceeded to consider a federal claim that was not obviously frivolous. It retained such cases under its power until final judgment, though the claim eventually turned out to be unfounded and the judgment was one denying the jurisdiction either of this Court or of the court from which the case came. In the case before us, the District Court had power "to preserve the existing conditions" in the discharge of "its duty to permit argument, and to take the time required for such consideration as it might need" to decide whether the controversy involved a labor dispute to which the Norris-LaGuardia Act applied. United States v. Shipp, 203 U.S. 563, 573, 27 S.Ct. 165, 166, 51 L.Ed. 319, 8 Ann.Cas. 265 and Howat v. State of Kansas, 258 U.S. 181, 42 S.Ct. 277, 66 L.Ed. 550.

In our country law is not a body of technicalities in the keeping of specialists or in the service of any special interest. There can be no free society without law administered through an independent judiciary. If one man can be allowed to determine for himself what is law, every man can. That means first chaos, then tyranny. Legal process is an essential part of the democratic process. For legal process is subject to democratic control by defined, orderly ways which themselves are part of law. In a democracy, power implies responsibility. The greater the power that defies law the less tolerant can this Court be of defiance. As the Nation's ultimate judicial tribunal, this Court, beyond any other organ of society, is the trustee of law and charged with the duty of securing obedience to it.

It only remains to state the basis of my disagreement with the Court's views on the bearing of the Norris-LaGuardia Act, 47 Stat. 70, 29 U.S.C. § 101, 29 U.S.C.A. § 101, and the War Labor Disputes Act, 57 Stat. 163, 50 U.S.C.App. § 1501, 50 U.S.C.A. Appendix, § 1501. As to the former, the Court relies essentially on a general doctrine excluding the Government from the operation of a statute in which it is not named, and on the legislative history of the Act. I find the countervailing considerations weightier. The Norris-LaGuardia Act deprived the federal courts of jurisdiction to issue injunctions in labor disputes except under conditions not here relevant. The question before a court of equity therefore is whether a case presents a labor dispute as defined by the Act. Section 13(c) defines "labor disputes":

"The term 'labor dispute' includes any controversy concerning terms or conditions of employment * * * regardless of whether or not the disputants stand in the proximate relation of employer and employee."

That the controversy before the district court comes within this definition does not need to be labored. The controversy arising under the Lewis-Krug contract concerned "terms or conditions of employment" and was therefore a "labor dispute", whatever further radiations the dispute may have had. The Court deems it appropriate to interpolate an exception regarding labor disputes to which the Government is a party. It invokes a canon of construction according to which the Government is excluded from the operation of general statutes unless it is included by explicit language.

* * *

[But], the rule proves too much. If the United States must explicitly be named to be affected, the limitations imposed by the Norris-LaGuardia Act upon the district court's jurisdiction could not deprive the United States of the remedies it therefore had. Accordingly, the courts would not be limited in their jurisdiction when the United States is a party and the Act would not apply in any proceeding in which the United States is complainant. It would mean that, in order to protect the public interest, which may be jeopardized just as much whether an essential industry continued under private control or has been temporarily seized by the Government, a court could, at the behest of the Attorney General of the United States, issue an injunction as courts did when they issued the Debs, the Hayes and the Railway Shopmen's injunctions. But it was these very injunctions, secured by the Attorney General of the United States under claim of compelling public emergency, that gave the most powerful momentum to the enactment of the Norris-LaGuardia Act. This history is too familiar to be rehearsed. It is surely surprising to conclude that when a long and persistent effort to take the federal courts out of the industrial conflict, insofar as the labor injunction put them into it, found its way to the statute books, the Act failed to meet the grievances that were most dramatic and deepest in the memory of those most concerned with the legislation.

[Justice Frankfurter then turned to an examination of the legislative history of the Norris-LaGuardia Act. In his view the remarks of Representatives LaGuardia and Michener were, at best, equivocal on the issue of whether the act applied in cases where the federal government was a party. He closed this part of his opinion as follows.]

. . . The experience which gave rise to the Norris-LaGuardia Act only underscores the unrestricted limitation upon the jurisdiction of the courts, except in situations of which this is not one. To find implications in the fact that in the course of the debates it was not explicitly asserted that the district courts could not issue an injunction in a labor controversy even at the behest of the Government is to find the silence of Congress more revealing than the natural meaning of legislation and the history which begot it. The remarks of Mr. LaGuardia and Mr. Michener ought not to be made the equivalent of writing an amendment into the Act. It is one thing to draw on all relevant aids for shedding light on the dark places of a statute. To allow inexplicit remarks in the give-and-take of debate to contradict the very terms of legislation and the history behind it is to put out the controlling light on meaning shed by the explicit provisions of an Act in its setting.

[In the balance of his opinion JUSTICE FRANKFURTER argued that the coal miners were not "government employees" in the normal sense of those words, hence the implied exception to the Norris-LaGuardia Act should not apply to them. Moreover, he argued that the War Labor Disputes Act did not contemplate the injunction as a remedy for interference with government operation of property seized pursuant to the Act.]

[JUSTICES BLACK and DOUGLAS joined in the Court's finding that the Norris-LaGuardia Act did not apply in this case, but they dissented from the decision to assess the fines unconditionally. A portion of their dissenting opinion follows.]

* * *

In determining whether criminal punishment or coercive sanction should be employed in these proceedings, the question of intent—the motivation of the contumacy—becomes relevant. Difficult questions of law were presented by this case. It is plain that the defendants acted willfully for they knew that they were disobeying the court's order. But they appear to have believed in good faith, though erroneously, that they were acting within their legal rights. Many lawyers would have so advised them. This does not excuse their conduct; the whole situation emphasized the duty of testing the restraining order by orderly appeal instead of disobedience and open defiance. However, as this Court said in Cooke v. United States, 267 U.S. 517, 538, 45 S.Ct. 390, 395, 69 L.Ed. 767, "the intention with which acts of contempt have been committed must necessarily and properly have an important bearing on the degree of guilt and the penalty which should be imposed."

We think it significant that the conduct which was prohibited by the restraining order for violation of which these defendants have been punished for contempt is also punishable under the War Labor Disputes Act. That Act provides a maximum punishment of $5,000 fine and one year imprisonment for those who interfere with the operation of mines taken over by the United States. Had the defendants been tried under that statute, their punishment would have been limited thereby and in their trial they would have enjoyed all the constitutional safeguards of the Bill of Rights. Whatever constitutional safeguards are required in a summary contempt proceeding, whether it be for criminal punishment, or for the imposition of coercive sanction, we must be ever mindful of the danger of permitting punishment by contempt to be imposed for conduct which is identical with an offense defined and made punishable by statute. In re Michael, 326 U.S. 224, 226, 66 S.Ct. 78, 79.

The situation of grave emergency facing the country when the District Court acted called for the strongest measures—measures designed to produce quick and unqualified obedience of the court's order. If the $10,000 fine on defendant Lewis and the $3,500,000 fine on the defendant union be treated as coercive fines, they would not necessarily be excessive. For they would then be payable only if the defendants continued to disobey the court's order. Defendants could then avoid payment by purging themselves. The price of continued disobedience would be the amount of the fines. See Doyle v. London Guaranty & Accident Co., supra, 204 U.S. at page 602, 27 S.Ct. at page 313, 51 L.Ed. 641. The fines would be fixed so as to produce the greatest likelihood that they would compel obedience.

We should modify the District Court's decrees by making the entire amount of the fines payable conditionally. On December 7, 1946, Mr. Lewis directed the mine workers to return to work until midnight, March 31, 1947. But, so far as we are aware, the notice which purported to terminate the contract has not been withdrawn. Thus, there has been, at most, only a partial compliance with the temporary injunction.

Hence our judgment should provide that the defendants pay their respective fines only in the event that full and unconditional obedience to the temporary injunction, including withdrawal of the notice which purported to terminate the contract, is not had on or before a day certain.

MR. JUSTICE MURPHY, dissenting.

An objective reading of the Norris-LaGuardia Act removes any doubts as to its meaning and as to its applicability to the facts of this case. Section

4 provides in clear, unmistakable language that "No court of the United States shall have jurisdiction to issue any restraining order or temporary or permanent injunction in any case involving or growing out of any labor dispute * * *." That language, which is repeated in other sections of the Act, is sufficient by itself to dispose of this case without further ado. But when proper recognition is given to the background and purpose of the Act, it becomes apparent that the implications of today's decision cast a dark cloud over the future of labor relations in the United States.

Due recognition must be given to the circumstances that gave rise to this case. The Government was confronted with the necessity of preserving the economic health of the nation; dire distress would have eventuated here and abroad from a prolonged strike in the bituminous coal mines. It was imperative that some effective action be taken to break the stalemate. But those factors do not permit the conversion of the judicial process into a weapon for misapplying statutes according to the grave exigencies of the moment. That can have tragic consequences even more serious and lasting than a temporary dislocation of the nation's economy resulting from a strike of the miners.

* * *

The crux of this case is whether the fact that the Government took over the possession and operation of the mines changed the private character of the underlying labor dispute between the operators and the miners so as to make inapplicable the Norris-LaGuardia Act. The answer is clear. Much has been said about the Government's status as employer and the miners' status as Government employees following the seizure. In my opinion, the miners remained private employees despite the temporary gloss of Government possession and operation of the mines; they bear no resemblance whatever to employees of the executive departments, the independent agencies and the other branches of the Government. But when all is said and done, the obvious fact remains that this case involves and grows out of a labor dispute between the operators and the miners. Government seizure of the mines cannot hide or change that fact. Indeed, the seizure took place only because of the existence of the dispute and because it was thought some solution might thereafter result. The dispute, however, survived the seizure and is still very much alive. And it still retains its private character, the operators on the one side and the coal miners on the other.

The important point, and it cannot be overemphasized, is that Congress has decreed that strikes and labor disturbances growing out of private labor disputes are to be dealt with by some means other than federal court restraining orders and injunctions. Further confirmation, if any be needed, is to be found in the terms and in the history of the War Labor Disputes Act. To this clearly enunciated policy of making "government by injunction" illegal, Congress has made no exception where the public interest is at stake or where the Government has seized the private properties involved. Congress can so provide. But it has not done so as yet; until it does, we are not free to sanction the use of restraining orders and injunctions in a case of this nature.

* * *

Since in my view the restraining order and the temporary injunction in this case are void and without effect, there remains for me only the contention that the defendants are guilty of criminal contempt for having willfully ignored the void restraining order. It is said that the District Court had the power to preserve existing conditions while it was determining its own authority to grant injunctive relief; hence the defendants acted at their own peril in disobeying the restraining order. Eloquent pleas are made for the supremacy of the judiciary over the individual and the requirement that a person obey court orders until they are reversed by orderly and proper proceedings. Heavy emphasis is placed upon United States v. Shipp, 203 U.S. 563, 27 S.Ct. 165, 51 L.Ed. 319, 8 Ann.Cas. 265.

These arguments have a seductive attractiveness here. Ordinarily, of course, it is better policy to obey a void order than run the risk of a contempt citation. And as a general proposition, individuals cannot be allowed to be the judges of the validity of court orders issued against them. But the problem raised by the violation of the restraining order in this case must be viewed against the background and language of the Norris-LaGuardia Act.

Unlike most other situations, this Act specifically prohibits the issuance of restraining orders except in situations not here involved. There is no exception in favor of a restraining order where there is some serious doubt about the court's jurisdiction; indeed, the prohibition against restraining orders would be futile were such an exception recognized for the minds of lawyers and judges are boundless in their abilities to raise serious jurisdictional objections. And so Congress has flatly forbidden the issuance of all restraining orders under this Act. It follows that when such an order is issued despite this clear prohibition, no man can be held in contempt thereof. however unwise his action may be as a matter of policy. When he violates the void order, 28 U.S.C. § 385, 28 U.S.C.A. § 385, comes into operation, forbidding punishment for contempt except where there has been disobedience of a "lawful writ, process, order, rule, decree, or command" of a court.

This absolute outlawry of restraining orders in cases involving private labor disputes is not without reason. The issuance of such orders prior to the adoption of the Norris-LaGuardia Act had a long and tortured history. Time and again strikes were broken merely by the issuance of a temporary restraining order, purporting to maintain the status quo. Because of the highly fluid character of labor disputes, the delay involved in testing an order of that nature often resulted in neutralizing the rights of employees to strike and picket. And too often, these orders did more than stabilize existing conditions; they called for affirmative change. The restraining order in the instant case is but one example of this. While purporting to preserve the status quo, it actually commands the defendants to rescind the strike call—thereby affirmatively interfering with the labor dispute.

Congress was well aware of this use of restraining orders to break strikes. After full consideration it intentionally and specifically prohibited their use, with certain exceptions not here relevant. We are not free to disregard that prohibition. . . .

It has been said that the actions of the defendants threatened orderly constitutional government and the economic and social stability of the nation. Whatever may be the validity of those statements, we lack any power to ignore the plain mandates of Congress and to impose vindictive fines upon the defendants. They are entitled to be judged by this Court according to the sober principles of law. A judicial disregard of what Congress has decreed may seem justified for the moment in view of the crisis which gave birth to this case. But such a disregard may ultimately have more disastrous and lasting effects upon the economy of the nation than any action of an aggressive labor leader in disobeying a void court order. The cause of orderly constitutional government is ill-served by misapplying the law as it is written, inadequate though it may be, to meet an emergency situation, especially where that misapplication permits punitive sanctions to be placed upon an individual or an organization.

MR. JUSTICE RUTLEDGE, dissenting.

This case became a *cause célèbre* the moment it began. No good purpose can be served by ignoring that obvious fact. But it cannot affect our judgment save only perhaps to steel us, if that were necessary, to the essential and accustomed behavior of judges.[1] In all cases great or small this must be to render judgment evenly and dispassionately according to law, as each is given understanding to ascertain and apply it.

No man or group is above the law. Nor is any beyond its protection. In re Yamashita, 327 U.S. 1, dissenting opinion 41, 66 S.Ct. 340, 359. These truths apply equally to the Government. When its power is exerted against the citizen or another in the nation's courts, those tribunals stand not as partisans, but as independent and impartial arbiters to see that the balance between power and right is held even. In discharging that high function the courts themselves, like the parties, are subject to the law's majestic limitations. We are not free to decide this case, or any, otherwise than as in conscience we are enabled to see what the law commands.

[The balance of JUSTICE RUTLEDGE'S opinion is omitted.]

Questions

1. What is a canon of construction?

2. What justification is there for the rule that "statutes which in general terms divest pre-existing rights or privileges will not be applied to the sovereign without express words to that effect?"

3. The majority argues that: (a) Congress was not ignorant of the rule of construction; and (b) "with knowledge of that rule, Congress would not, in writing the Norris-LaGuardia Act, omit to use 'clear and specific language to that effect' if it actually intended to reach the Government in all cases." Do you find this argument persuasive?

4. Do you agree that the various considerations set forth in Section 2 of the Act "obviously do not apply to the Government as an employer or to relations between the Government and its employees"?

5. Does Section 13 of the Act require that there be "persons" on both sides of a case before the case can be held to involve a labor dis-

---

1. "Great cases, like hard cases, make bad law. For great cases are called great, not by reason of their real importance in shaping the law of the future, but because of some accident of immediate overwhelming interest which appeals to the feelings and distorts the judgment. These immediate interests exercise a kind of hydraulic pressure which makes what previously was clear seem doubtful, and before which even well settled principles of law will bend." Holmes, J., dissenting, in Northern Securities Co. v. United States, 193 U.S. 197, 400–401, 24 S.Ct. 436, 468, 48 L.Ed. 679.

pute? Does Section 13 require that the plaintiff and the defendant in a case be "persons" before the case can be held to involve a labor dispute? Would you argue that the Secretary of the Interior is a "person" with a direct or indirect interest in the bituminous coal industry and that his interest competes or conflicts with the interest of "persons participating or interested" in a labor dispute?

6. Are the following statements canons of construction?

(a) " . . . the debates in Congress expressive of the views and motives of individual members are not a safe guide, and hence may not be resorted to, in ascertaining the meaning and purpose of the law-making body."

(b) "But reports of committees of House or Senate stand upon a more solid footing, and may be regarded as an exposition of the legislative intent in a case where otherwise the meaning of a statute is obscure. And this has been extended to include explanatory statements in the nature of a supplemental report made by the committee member in charge of a bill in course of passage."

Was the majority's use of legislative history consistent with either of these propositions?

What merit is there in these propositions?

7. In what sense, if at all, is it meaningful to suggest that there is a "legislative intent" which is the motivation for a statute?

Why should "legislative intent" be sought in an attempt to establish the meaning of statutory language?

8. Is the U.M.W. case one where "words in their natural sense as they would be read by the common man" appear to give an obvious meaning, but considerations underlying the statute require that "the words cannot be taken quite so simply?"

9. Do either the majority or Justice Frankfurter give any clear guide as to when, if at all, it is permissible to violate a court order?

10. Does the solution proposed by Justices Black and Douglas provide a suitable vindication of the judicial interests in fidelity to law and the integrity of court orders?

11. Do you believe that Justice Murphy was warranted in asserting that "An objective reading of the Norris-LaGuardia Act removes any doubts as to its meaning and as to its applicability to the facts of the case"?

SECTION 41.2   LEGISLATIVE REVIVAL OF THE LABOR INJUNCTION: THE TAFT-HARTLEY ACT [1]

[The following is taken from COX and BOK, CASES ON LABOR LAW (5th ed.), pp. 142–146, 705–707.]

From 1935 until 1947 the national labor policy was founded upon the Norris-LaGuardia and Wagner Acts supplemented by wartime emergency measures. The Norris-LaGuardia Act established the predicate that peaceful, concerted activities—strikes, boycotts, or picketings—should not be enjoinable by law. "So long as a union acts in its self-interest and does not combine with non-labor groups, the licit and the illicit . . . are not to be distinguished by any judgment regarding the wisdom or unwisdom, the rightness or unrightness, the selfishness or unselfishness, of the end of which the particular union activities are the means." The Wagner Act established the twin rights to organize and bargain collectively and made it government policy to encourage unionization and collective bargaining.

Both statutes made permanent contributions to our national labor policy, but their fundamental assumptions were modified by the enactment of the Taft-Hartley Act in 1947. The Taft-Hartley bill was bitterly opposed by organized labor and most so-called "liberals." It was vetoed by President Truman and passed over his veto. Since the political controversy still continues, this is scarcely the place to hazard a judgment on the merits, and the student will have a chance to form his own opinion as specific problems are raised in the ensuing passages. It may be helpful, however, to say a few words about the background of the act and the new trends which it introduced into labor law.

The Spread of Unions and Collective Bargaining

Between 1935 and 1947 labor unions grew and collective bargaining spread rapidly with the aid and encouragement of the federal government. In 1935 only three million workers belonged to labor unions. In 1947 there were nearly fifteen million union members—roughly five times as many. Two thirds of the workers in manufacturing were covered by union agreements and about one third in non-manufacturing industries outside of agriculture and the professions. In some industries, such as coal mining, construction, railroading, and trucking, over four fifths of the employees worked under collective bargaining agreements.

Although government policies scarcely explain this phenomenal development, they exerted important influence. One factor was the Wagner Act and the work of the NLRB. The bare legal protection curbed antiunion tactics. For the government to prosecute an employer for unfair labor practices gave psychological impetus to unionization. Furthermore the NLRB in both Washington and the regional offices was staffed by enthusiasts burning with zeal for organized labor.

---

1. The Wagner Act was substantially amended in 1947 by the Taft-Hartley Act. Further consideration is afforded this important legislation in succeeding materials (see *infra* p. 1105 ff.)

For the moment we are concerned only with the relation of Taft-Hartley to the use of the injunction in cases arising out of labor disputes.

A second factor was the federal government's wartime labor policy. The United States could not become the arsenal of democracy without the whole-hearted cooperation of organized labor, and the surest method of obtaining cooperation was to give unions a permanent role in directing the mobilization and allocation of our national resources. Before Pearl Harbor Sidney Hillman, the president of the Amalgamated Clothing Workers, C.I.O., shared with William Knudson of General Motors Corporation the direction of the Office of Defense Mobilization. Labor representatives were attached to subordinate units. Similar policies prevailed in the organization of the War Production Board. President Roosevelt made it plain that high officials in the labor movement had quick access to the White House. Their pictures were often taken on the White House steps and in company with the President. Their views on policy were prominently solicited (although there are some who say that they were given little weight in making decisions).

Labor's role in government reached a peak in the organization of the War Labor Board. After Pearl Harbor the country could not safely tolerate any interruption in the production and distribution of goods. Organized labor gave a pledge not to resort to strikes provided that all labor management controversies not resolved in collective bargaining were submitted to a War Labor Board for final decision. The War Labor Board was tripartite; the public, industry and organized labor were equally represented.

The psychological impact of these measures was tremendous. The union organizer could plausibly argue "It is patriotic to join a union. The President wants you to become a union member." The role of unions in government and the high praise regularly heaped upon organized labor by government officials seemed to prove his point.

The third important factor was the policies of the War Labor Board. The public members of the War Labor Board and many of the employer members were staunch believers in strong unions and collective bargaining. Their policies and decisions gave it encouragement. Still more important, once a union had organized a plant War Labor Board policies encouraged the development of procedures confirming and strengthening the union's role in the plant—use of company bulletin boards, preferential seniority for shop stewards, strong grievance machinery controlled by the union, and arbitration of unsettled grievances. Unfortunately the tripartite character of the War Labor Board also enabled union officials to reap improper advantages. Wage rates could not be changed without War Labor Board approval. The volume of applications was too great to keep up with. Many turned upon delicate judgments. Applications filed by unions whose officials were War Labor Board members sometimes had a way of getting processed more quickly and without encountering the objections raised against applications filed by unorganized firms or independent unions.

Reasons for the Enactment of the Taft-Hartley Act

By 1947 the labor movement had achieved great power. Sumner Slichter wrote, "The trade unions are the most powerful economic organizations in the community—in fact, they are the most powerful economic organizations which the community has ever seen." Yet it would be a mistake to suppose that power of labor unions was evenly distributed. In the South and in many agricultural states organized labor was weak indeed. Unions were much stronger, by and large, in manufacturing and mining than in wholesale and retail distribution or among office and clerical workers. The United Mine Workers could defy public opinion but most unions were still vulnerable to shifts in the wind of public sentiment.

The public was worried about the power of unions. Its worry was partly an irrational but widespread fear of "the labor bosses." John L. Lewis and the United Mine Workers had carried on two long strikes during wartime in defiance of the government ending only when the government granted substantial concessions. In 1946 there was a great wave of strikes which shut down the steel mills, automobile assembly plants, packing-houses, electrical products industry, the East and West Coast seaports and a few public utilities. Today it seems plain that this wave of strikes simply marked release from wartime restrictions. In 1947 there were many who saw the danger of nationwide stoppages as a threat to the social system.

But if some of the fear was irrational, there were also careful observers sympathetic to organized labor who perceived the need for measures halting the abuse of power. Their bill of particulars might have included seven specific criticisms.

(1) Too many strikes were called under circumstances threatening serious injury to the public health or safety—in the coal mines and in public utilities for example.

(2) Although corruption had not been uncovered as high in the union movement as during the Senate investigation of 1957, it was all too plain that some so-called "labor unions" were primarily rackets.

(3) Strikes and picketing were too often marked by violence organized and promoted by union leaders when peaceful measures failed to achieve their objective.

(4) During the war many building trades unions refused to admit new members and charged exorbitant fees for issuing working permits to the new employees attracted to the industry by defense construction. This practice generated ill will among workers who might otherwise have remained sympathetic to organized labor.

(5) The construction industry was also hampered by strikes resulting from jurisdictional disputes. Should the forms into which concrete was poured be taken down by carpenters or laborers? Should riggers move furnaces and air conditioning units off the trucks or freight cars and set them in place in the construction of a new building or should this work be done by plumbers? Large projects were often tied up for days while labor unions disputed each other's right to job assignments.

(6) The secondary boycott had become an exceedingly powerful weapon in the hands of certain unions. The International Brotherhood of Teamsters could tie up any business dependent upon trucking for supplies and outgoing shipments. The United Brotherhood of Carpenters through its control of construction projects could boycott materials produced by any firm on which it desired to impose economic pressure. . . .

(7) The emphasis which organized labor in the United States places upon closed and union shop contracts has engendered controversy almost as long as there have been labor unions. In 1947 exponents of the open shop collected many instances of the unions' abuse of the power which the closed

and union shop confer upon them. In a few unions the membership rolls were closed and the resulting monopoly of jobs was passed from father to son. Individual employees were expelled for such improper reasons as refusing to take part in political activities, criticizing union officials, refusing to join in an organized slowdown, and testifying adversely to the union in an arbitration proceeding. No doubt the cases cited were extraordinary but the publicity given them lent force to the attack upon all union security contracts and even those who saw the merit in closed and union shop agreements felt the need for safeguards against abuse.

In analyzing the background of the Taft-Hartley Act one must also give a prominent place to anti-unionism. Many business concerns continued to make war on all unions despite the National Labor Relations Act. Others accepted the forms of collective bargaining under legal and economic compulsion hoping that the tide would turn and they might some day be free from "the union."

The irreconcilables were strengthened by the changing frontiers of union organization. By the end of the war most of the big industrial concerns in the Northeast and Midlands had been organized as well as on the Pacific Coast. Union organizers were now seeking to enlist distributive and clerical workers many of whom were employed in small enterprises where they worked in close contact with the boss. People who genuinely sympathized with the plight of unorganized workers in mines, mills and factories doubted the need for unions in wholesale and retail trades or office buildings where the business itself was smaller and economically weaker than the union.

By the mid-forties organized labor was also ready to invade the South where unionization had lagged far behind older industrial areas but where rapid industrialism presented an increasing competitive threat to union labor standards. Operation Dixie encountered an entire social and political system quite unlike the older milieu and one which sometimes seemed impenetrable by ordinary organizing methods.

In sum, the Taft-Hartley Act was the product of diverse forces—the off-spring, a critic might say, of an unhappy union between the opponents of all collective bargaining and the critics of the unions' abuses of power. The former group was probably the more influential of the two in writing the Taft-Hartley amendments, for organized labor's unfortunate decision to oppose all legislation left its sympathetic critics in a dilemma.

* * *

The philosophy behind the labor legislation of the nineteen thirties was deeply rooted in the disappointing experience of half a century of legal intervention into industrial conflicts. The use of fines and prison sentences to enforce a judicial edict against large numbers of employees is out of the question. In a democracy sanctions can be invoked only against occasional wrongdoers. The effectiveness of law depends upon its acceptance by the governed, either because they approve the policy which it expresses or because it is the law. There was, and is, no such consensus of opinion about the propriety of labor's weapons and objectives. The personal preferences and judgments of social and economic policy are too obvious for judicial decisions to command acquiescence merely because they are law. Even legislation suffers from the same weaknesses where the community is divided and feeling runs high. Furthermore, the legal weapons for dealing with labor issues are often cumbersome and blunt. Hence Congress turned to reliance upon negotiation between employers and labor organizations strong enough to bargain effectively for the employees. . . .

In 1947 Congress swung back to the view that the injunction has proper uses as a weapon of labor policy. Numerous forces contributed to the change. The Norris-LaGuardia Act seemed to protect unions in practices which were clearly reprehensible. Picketing to compel employers to commit unfair labor practices is one illustration. . . . During World War II there were a number of widely publicized strikes which appeared to interfere with the production of vital war materials. Public resentment was increased by a waive of major strikes in 1945 and 1946.

Although the problems created by such emergency disputes are of a different order from those which result from the ordinary strike or boycott, the public demand for action against emergency disputes was easily turned into a demand for action on other fronts against the labor unions. By no means the least active of the proponents of new legislation were those who had never accepted the philosophy of collective bargaining and wished to weaken the unions and prevent their spread into unorganized areas. Out of the melange emerged the Taft-Hartley Act and a mass of State legislation. . . .

Prior to its amendment by the Taft-Hartley Act in 1947, the National Labor Relations Act listed as "unfair labor practices" certain acts of employers relating to interference with the exercise by employees of their right to self-organization and to collective bargaining through representatives of their own choosing. Among the proscribed practices were discrimination in regard to hire or tenure of employment or any term or condition of employment to encourage or discourage membership in any labor organization, as well as refusal to bargain collectively with the representatives of employees. The Taft-Hartley Act modifies only slightly the list of employer's unfair labor practices, but adds a list of unfair labor practices with which labor organizations or their agents may be charged. Among them are restraint or coercion of employees in the exercise of their right to self-organization or to collective bargaining, or of an employer in the selection of his representatives for collective bargaining or adjustment of grievances; attempting to cause an employer to discriminate against an employee to encourage or discourage membership in any labor organization; refusal to bargain collectively with an employer; and engaging in strikes or similar activity in order to require an employer to recognize or bargain with a particular labor organization instead of the organization which he has previously properly recognized, or in order to require some other employer to recognize or bargain with a labor organization not certified as the representative of his employees et cetera.

If the National Labor Relations Board finds that an unfair labor practice is being committed either by an employer or by a labor organization or its agents, it may petition a federal court for a restraining order or injunction prohibiting it.

In addition, the Taft-Hartley Act provides that whenever the President of the United States considers that a threatened or actual strike or lockout affecting a substantial part of an industry engaged in interstate commerce will imperil the national health or safety, he may appoint a board of inquiry to report to him and receiving its report he may direct the Attorney General to petition a district court of the United States to enjoin the strike or lock-out, and the court shall have jurisdiction to do so.

Thus the provisions of the Norris-LaGuardia Act are now made specifically inapplicable to certain types of practices of labor organizations or their agents and to situations (called, in the Act, "national emergencies") in which the "national health or safety" is imperilled.

Although the State legislation enacted in the period 1945–1947 was often more restrictive, the role of the labor injunction under the Taft-Hartley Act differs in at least three important respects from its use prior to 1930:

First, instead of attempting to develop a detailed code of justified and unjustifiable strikes and boycotts, the injunction is available only against what were regarded as extremes of employee misconduct. Perhaps Congress went too far—the editor [*i. e.*, Professor Cox] believes that it did—but at worst it must be conceded that most of the concerted activities made enjoinable by [the Act] are intolerable. There is no reason why the law should compel an employer to bargain with one union yet withhold protection against economic reprisals from a competing union which seeks to be the exclusive representative. Although it is hard to see how jurisdictional strikes can be settled by law, the resulting economic waste convinced most people that they should be prevented. Secondary boycotts take too many forms to permit generalization, but the activities of [some unions] surely represent an abuse of the power of organized labor. Within these extremes the national labor policy continued to rely primarily on private adjustments of conflicting interests—the policy of the Norris-LaGuardia and Wagner Acts—instead of determination by law.

Second, under the Taft-Hartley Act the principle questions of policy were resolved by the legislature instead of being left to judicial determination.

Third, control of the proceedings is vested in a government agency; the injunction is presented more as the expression of the public's impartial condemnation of the defendant's conduct than as a weapon in a private, economic quarrel. . . .

SECTION 41.3   CONSTITUTIONAL PROTECTION OF PICKETING REVISITED

INTERNATIONAL BROTHERHOOD OF TEAMSTERS, CHAUFFEURS, WAREHOUSEMEN & HELPERS UNION, LOCAL 309 v. HANKE

Supreme Court of the United States, 1950.
339 U.S. 470, 70 S.Ct. 773.

MR. JUSTICE FRANKFURTER announced the judgment of the Court and an opinion in which THE CHIEF JUSTICE, MR. JUSTICE JACKSON and MR. JUSTICE BURTON concurred.

These two cases raise the same issues and are therefore disposed of in a single opinion. The question is this: Does the Fourteenth Amendment of the Constitution bar a State from use of the injunction to prohibit the picketing of a business conducted by the owner himself without employees in order to secure compliance by him with a demand to become a union shop?

In No. 309, respondents A. E. Hanke and his three sons, as co-partners, engaged in the business of repairing automobiles, dispensing gasoline and automobile accessories, and selling used automobiles in Seattle. They conducted their entire enterprise themselves, without any employees. At the time the senior Hanke purchased the business in June, 1946, which had theretofore been conducted as a union shop, he became a member of Local 309 of the International Brotherhood of Teamsters, which includes in its membership persons employed and engaged in the gasoline service station business in Seattle. Accordingly, the Hankes continued to display in their show windows the union card of their predecessor. Local 309 also included the Hankes' business in the list of firms for which it urged patronage in advertisements published in the Washington organ of the International Brotherhood of Teamsters, distributed weekly to members. As a result of the use of the union shop card and these advertisements, the Hankes received union patronage which they otherwise would not have had.

Automobile Drivers and Demonstrators Local 882, closely affiliated with Local 309 and also chartered by the International Brotherhood of Teamsters, includes in its membership persons engaged in the business of selling used cars and used car salesmen in Seattle. This union negotiated an agreement in 1946 with the Independent Automobile Dealers Association of Seattle, to which the Hankes did not belong, providing that used car lots be closed by 6 p. m. on weekdays and all day on Saturdays, Sundays and eight specified holidays. This agreement was intended to be applicable to 115 used car dealers in Seattle, all except ten of which were self-employers with no employees.

It was the practice of the Hankes to remain open nights, week-ends and holidays. In January, 1948, representatives of both Locals called upon the Hankes to urge them to respect the limitation on business hours in the agreement or give up their union shop card. The Hankes refused to consent to abide by the agreement, claiming that it would be impossible to continue in business and do so, and surrendered the union shop card. The name of the Hankes' business was thereafter omitted from the list published by Local 309 in its advertisements.

Soon afterwards the Local sent a single picket to patrol up and down peacefully in front of the Hankes' between the hours of 8:30 a. m. and 5 p. m., carrying a "sandwich sign" with the words "Union People Look for the Union Shop Card" and a facsimile of the shop card. The picket also wrote down the automobile license numbers of the Hankes' patrons. As a result of the picketing, the Hankes' business fell off heavily and drivers for supply houses refused to deliver parts and other needed materials. The Hankes had to use their own truck to call for the materials necessary to carry on their business.

To restrain this conduct, the Hankes brought suit against Local 309 and its officers. The trial court granted a permanent injunction against the picketing and awarded a judgment of $250, the sum stipulated by the parties to be the amount of damage occasioned by the picketing. The Supreme Court of Washington affirmed. 33 Wash.2d 646, 207 P.2d 206.

The background in No. 364 is similar. . . . In both these cases we granted certiorari to consider claims of infringement of the right of freedom of speech as guaranteed by the Due Process Clause of the Fourteenth Amendment. 338 U.S. 903, 70 S.Ct. 305. . . .

Here as in Hughes v. Superior Court, 339 U.S. 460, 70 S.Ct. 718, 94 L. Ed. 985 we must start with the fact that while picketing has an ingredient of communication it cannot dogmatically be equated with the constitutionally protected freedom of speech. Our decisions reflect recognition that picketing is "indeed a hybrid." Freund, On Understanding the Supreme Court 18 (1949). See also Jaffe, In Defense of the Supreme Court's Picketing Doctrine, 41 Mich.L.Rev. 1037 (1943). The effort in the cases has been to strike a balance between the constitutional protection of the element of communication in picketing and "the power of the State to set the limits of permissible contest open to industrial combatants." Thornhill v. State of Alabama, 310 U.S. 88, 104, 60 S.Ct. 736, 745, 84 L.Ed. 1093. A State's judgment on striking such a balance is of course subject to the limitations of the Fourteenth Amendment. Embracing as such a judgment does, however, a State's social and economic policies, which in turn depend on knowledge and appraisal of local social and economic factors, such judgment on these matters comes to this Court bearing a weighty title of respect.

These two cases emphasize the nature of a problem that is presented by our duty of sitting in judgment on a State's judgment in striking the balance that has to be struck when a State decides not to keep hands off these industrial contests. Here we have a glaring instance of the interplay of competing social-economic interests and viewpoints. Unions obviously are concerned not to have union standards undermined by non-union shops. This interest penetrates into self-employer shops. On the other hand, some of our profoundest thinkers from Jefferson to Brandeis have stressed the importance to a democratic society of encouraging self-employer economic units as a counter-movement to what are deemed to be the dangers inherent in excessive concentration of economic power. "There is a widespread belief . . . that the true prosperity of our past came not from big business, but through the courage, the energy, and the resourcefulness of small men . . . and that only through participation by the many in the responsibilities and determinations of business can Americans secure the moral and intellectual development which is essential to the maintenance of liberty." Mr. Justice Brandeis, dissenting in Ligget Co. v. Lee, 288 U.S. 517, 541, 580, 53 S.Ct. 481, 502, 77 L.Ed. 929, 85 A.L.R. 699.

Whether to prefer the union or a self-employer in such a situation, or to seek partial recognition of both interests, and, if so, by what means to secure such accommodation, obviously presents to a State serious problems. There are no sure answers, and the best available solution is likely to be experimental and tentative, and always subject to the control of the popular will. That the solution of these perplexities is a challenge to wisdom and not a command of the Constitution is the significance of Senn v. Tile Layers Protective Union, 301 U.S. 468, 57 S.Ct. 857, 81 L.Ed. 1229. Senn, a self-employed tile layer who occasionally hired other tile layers to assist him, was picketed when he refused to yield to the union demand that he no longer work himself at his trade. The Wisconsin court found the situation to be within the State's anti-injunction statute and denied relief. In rejecting the claim that the restriction upon Senn's freedom was a denial of his liberty under the Fourteenth Amendment, this Court held that it lay in the domain of policy for Wisconsin to permit the picketing: "Whether it was wise for the state to permit the unions to do so is a question of its public policy—not our concern." 301 U.S. at page 481, 57 S.Ct. at page 863.

This conclusion was based on the Court's recognition that it was Wisconsin, not the Fourteenth Amendment, which put such picketing as a "means of publicity on a par with advertisements in the press." 301 U.S. at page 479, 57 S.Ct. at page 862. If Wisconsin could permit such picketing as a matter of policy it must have been equally free as a matter of policy to choose not to permit it and therefore not to "put this means of publicity on a par with advertisements in the press." If Wisconsin could have deemed it wise to withdraw from the union the permission which this Court found outside the ban of the Fourteenth Amendment, such an action by Washington cannot be inside that ban.

Washington here concluded that even though the relief afforded the Hankes and Cline entailed restriction upon communication that the unions sought to convey through picketing, it was more important to safeguard the value which the State placed upon self-employers, leaving all other channels of communication open to the union. The relatively small interest of the unions considerably influenced the balance that was struck. Of 115 used car dealers in Seattle maintaining union standards all but ten were self-employers with no employees. "From this fact," so we are informed by the Supreme Court of Washington, "the conclusion seems irresistible that the union's interest in the welfare of a mere handful of members (of whose working conditions no complaint at all is made) is far outweighed by the interests of individual proprietors and the people of the community as a whole, to the end that little businessmen and property owners shall be free from dictation as to business policy by an outside group having but a relatively small and indirect interest in such policy." 207 P.2d at page 213.

We are, needless to say, fully aware of the contentious nature of these views. It is not our business even remotely to hint at agreement or disagreement with what has commended itself to the State of Washington, or even to intimate that all the relevant considerations are exposed in the conclusions reached by the Washington Court. They seldom are in this field, so deceptive and opaque are the elements of these problems. That is precisely what is meant by recognizing that they are within the domain of a State's public policy. Because there is lack of agreement as to the relevant factors and divergent interpretations of their meaning, as well as differences in assessing what is the short and what is the long view, the clash of fact and opinion should be resolved by the democratic process and not by the judicial sword. Invalidation here would mean denial of power to the Congress as well as to the forty-eight States.

It is not for us to pass judgment on cases not now before us. But when one considers that issues not unlike those that are here have been similarly viewed by other States [footnote omitted] and by the Congress of the United States [footnote omitted], we cannot conclude that Washington, in holding the picketing in these cases to be for an unlawful object, has struck a balance so inconsistent with rooted traditions of a free people that it must be found an unconstitutional choice. Mindful as we are that a phase of picketing is communication, we cannot find that Washington has offended the Constitution.

We need not repeat the considerations to which we adverted in Hughes v. Superior Court that make it immaterial, in respect to the constitutional issue before us, that the policy of Washington was expressed by its Supreme Court rather than by its legislature. The Fourteenth Amendment leaves the States free to distribute the powers of government as they will between their legislative and judicial branches. [Citations omitted.] "[R]ights under that amendment turn on the power of the state, no matter by what organ it acts." [Citation omitted.]

Nor does the Fourteenth Amendment require prohibition by Washington also of voluntary acquiescence in the demands of the union in order that it may choose to prohibit the right to secure submission through picketing. In abstaining from interference with such voluntary agreements a State may rely on self-interest. In any event, it is not for this Court to question a State's judgment in regulating only where an evil seems to it most conspicuous.

What was actually decided in American Federation of Labor v. Swing, 312 U.S. 321, 61 S.Ct. 568, 85 L.Ed. 855; Bakery & Pastry Drivers & Helpers Local 802 v. Wohl, 315 U.S. 769, 62 S.Ct. 816, 86 L.Ed. 1178, and Cafeteria Employees Union, Local 302 v. Angelos, 302 U.S. 293, 64 S.Ct. 126, 88 L.Ed. 58, does not preclude us from upholding Washington's power to make the choice of policy she has here made. In those cases we held only that a State could not proscribe picketing merely by setting artificial bounds, unreal in the light of modern circumstances, to what constitutes an industrial relationship or a labor dispute. See Cox, Some Aspects of the Labor Management Relations Act, 1947, 61 Harv.L.Rev. 1, 30 (1947). The power of a State to declare a policy in favor of self-employers and to make conduct restrictive of self-employment unlawful was not considered in those cases. Indeed in Wohl this Court expressly noted that the State courts had not found that the picketing there condemned was for a defined unlawful object. 315 U.S. 774, 62 S.Ct. 818, 86 L.Ed. 1178.

When an injunction of a State court comes before us it comes not as an independent collocation of words. It is defined and confined by the opinion of the State court. The injunctions in these two cases are to be judged here with all the limitations that are infused into their terms by the opinions of the Washington Supreme Court on the basis of which the judgments below come before us. So read, the injunctions are directed solely against picketing for the ends defined by the parties before the Washington court and this court. To treat the injunctions otherwise—to treat them, that is, outside the scope of the issues which they represent—is to deal with a case that is not here and was not before the Washington court. In considering an injunction against picketing recently, we had occasion to reject a similar claim of infirmity derived not from the record but from unreality. What we then said is pertinent now: "What is before us . . . is not the order as an isolated, self-contained writing but the order with the gloss of the Supreme Court of Wisconsin upon it." [Citation omitted.] Our affirmance of these injunctions is in conformity with the reading derived from the Washington court's opinions. If astuteness may discover argumentative excess in the scope of the injunctions beyond what we constitutionally justify by this opinion, it will be open to petitioners to raise the matter, which they have not raised here, when the cases on remand reach the Washington court.

Affirmed.

MR. JUSTICE CLARK concurs in the result.

MR. JUSTICE BLACK dissents for substantially the reasons given in his dissent in Carpenters & Joiners Union of America, Local No. 213 v. Ritter's Cafe, 315 U.S. 722, 729–732, 62 S.Ct. 807, 810–812, 86 L.Ed. 1143.

MR. JUSTICE DOUGLAS took no part in the consideration or decision of these cases.

MR. JUSTICE MINTON,* with whom MR. JUSTICE REED joins, dissenting.

Petitioners in each of these cases were "permanently restrained and enjoined from in any manner picketing" the places of business of respondents. The picketing here was peaceful publicity, not enmeshed in a pattern of violence as was true in Milk Wagon Drivers Union of Chicago, Local 753 v. Meadowmoor Dairies, 312 U.S. 287, 61 S.Ct. 552, 85 L.Ed. 836, 132 A.L.R. 1200; nor was there violence in the picketing, as in Hotel & Restaurant Employees' International Alliance, Local No. 122 v. Wisconsin E. R. B., 315 U.S. 437, 62 S.Ct. 706, 86 L.Ed. 946. The decrees entered in the instant cases were not tailored to meet the evils of threats and intimidation as Cafeteria Employees Union, Local 302 v. Angelos, 320 U.S. 293, 295, 64 S.Ct. 126, 88 L.Ed. 58, indicates they might have been; nor were they limited to restraint of picketing for the purpose of forcing the person picketed to violate the law and public policy of the state, as were the decrees in Giboney v. Empire Storage & Ice Co., 336 U.S. 490, 69 S.Ct. 684, 93 L.Ed. 834, and Building Service Employees Union v. Gazzam, 339 U.S. 532, 70 S.Ct. 784, 94 L.Ed. 1045. The abuses of picketing involved in the above cases were held by this Court not to be protected by the Fourteenth Amendment from state restraint.

It seems equally clear to me that peaceful picketing which is used properly as an instrument of publicity has been held by this Court in Thornhill v. State of Alabama, 310 U.S. 88, 60 S.Ct. 736, 84 L.Ed. 1093; Carlson v. People of State of California, 310 U.S. 106, 60 S.Ct. 746, 84 L.Ed. 1104; American Federation of Labor v. Swing, 312 U.S. 321, 61 S.Ct. 568, 85 L.Ed. 855; Bakery & Pastry Drivers & Helpers Local 802 v. Wohl, 315 U.S. 769, 62 S. Ct. 816, 86 L.Ed. 1178; and Cafeteria Employees Union, Local 302 v. Angelos, 320 U.S. 293, 64 S.Ct. 126, 88 L.Ed. 58, to be protected by the Fourteenth Amendment. I do not understand that in the last three mentioned cases this Court, as the majority in its opinion says, "held only that a State could not proscribe picketing merely by setting artificial bounds, unreal in the light of modern circumstances, to what constitutes an industrial relationship or a labor dispute." If the states may set bounds, it is not for this Court to say where they shall be set, unless the setting violates some provision of the Federal Constitution. I understand the above cases to have found violations of the federal constitutional guarantee of freedom of speech, and the picketing

* Justice Sherman Minton was appointed to the Supreme Court by President Truman in 1949. He practiced law in Indiana and was U. S. Senator from that state (1935–1941). He served as a judge on the U. S. Court of Appeals for the Seventh Circuit from 1941 until his appointment to the Supreme Court. Justice Minton retired from the Supreme Court in 1956.

could not be restrained because to do so would violate the right of free speech and publicity. This view is plainly stated by this Court in Cafeteria Employees Union, Local 302 v. Angelos, 320 U.S. at page 295, 64 S.Ct. at page 127: "In Senn v. Tile Layers Protective Union, Local No. 5, 301 U.S. 468, 57 S.Ct. 857, 81 L.Ed. 1229, this Court ruled that members of a union might, 'without special statutory authorization by a state, make known the facts of a labor dispute, for freedom of speech is guaranteed by the Federal Constitution,' 301 U.S. at page 478, 57 S.Ct. at page 862, 81 L.Ed. 1229. Later cases applied the Senn doctrine by enforcing the right of workers to state their case and to appeal for public support in an orderly and peaceful manner regardless of the area of immunity as defined by state policy. A. F. of L. v. Swing, 312 U.S. 321, 61 S.Ct. 568, 85 L.Ed. 855; Bakery and Pastry Drivers and Helpers Local 802 v. Wohl, 315 U.S. 769, 62 S.Ct. 816, 86 L.Ed. 1178."

All the recent cases of this Court upholding picketing, from Thornhill to Angelos, have done so on the view that "peaceful picketing and truthful publicity" (see 320 U.S. at page 295, 64 S.Ct. at page 127, 88 L.Ed. 58) is protected by the guaranty of free speech. This view stems from Mr. Justice Brandeis' statement in Senn that "Members of a union might without special statutory authorization by a state, make known the facts of a labor dispute, for freedom of speech is guaranteed by the Federal Constitution." 301 U.S. 468, 478, 57 S.Ct. 857, 862, 81 L.Ed. 1229. In that case Justice Brandeis was dealing with action of Wisconsin that *permitted* picketing by a labor union of a one-man shop. Of course, as long as Wisconsin allowed picketing, there was no interference with freedom of expression. By permitting picketing the State was allowing the expression found in "peaceful picketing and truthful publicity." There was in that posture of the case no question of conflict with the right of free speech. But because Wisconsin could permit picketing, and not thereby encroach upon freedom of speech, it does not follow that it could forbid like picketing; for that might involve conflict with the Fourteenth Amendment. It seems to me that Justice Brandeis, foreseeing the problem of the converse, made the statement above quoted in order to indicate that picketing could be protected by the free speech guaranty of the Federal Constitution. Whether or not that is what Justice Brandeis meant, I think this Court has accepted that view, from Thornhill to Angelos. It seems to me too late now to deny that those cases were rooted in the free speech doctrine. I think we should not decide the instant cases in a manner so alien to the basis of prior decisions.

The outlawing of picketing for all purposes is permitted the State of Washington by the upholding of these broad decrees. No distinction is made between what is legitimate picketing and what is abusive picketing. "[H]ere we have no attempt by the state through its courts to restrict conduct justifiably found to be an abusive exercise of the right to picket." Angelos case, 320 U.S. at page 295, 64 S.Ct. at page 127, 88 L.Ed. 58.

Because the decrees here are not directed at any abuse of picketing but at all picketing, I think to sustain them is contrary to our prior holdings, founded as they are in the doctrine that "peaceful picketing and truthful publicity" is protected by the constitutional guaranty of the right of free speech. I recognize that picketing is more than speech. That is why I think an abuse of picketing may lead to a forfeiture of the protection of free speech. Tested by the philosophy of prior decisions, no such forfeiture is justified here.

I would reverse the judgments in these two cases.

Notes

1. In Hughes v. Superior Court, cited in the principal case, the employer, Lucky Stores, Inc., operated a chain of grocery stores including a store in Richmond, California. About 50% of its customers at the Richmond store were Negroes, but few if any of its employees were Negroes. Progressive Citizens of America picketed the store in order to put pressure on the employer to give Negroes a preference in hiring new clerks until the proportion of Negro clerks was equivalent to the proportion of Negroes among the store's customers. A California county court issued a preliminary injunction against the picketing and when PCA continued to picket in spite of the injunction, the court cited the pickets for contempt. They appealed from the contempt citation on the ground that the injunction violated the Fourteenth Amendment. Their conviction was affirmed in the California Supreme Court and, on certiorari, in the United States Supreme Court.

2. In Giboney v. Empire Storage & Ice Co., cited in the principal case, Teamsters Local No. 953, having organized 160 of the 200 retail ice peddlers in Kansas City, Missouri, requested the wholesale ice distributors to agree not to sell ice to nonunion peddlers. Empire refused. Local No. 953 thereupon picketed Empire's places of business, and most of the truck drivers employed by Empire's retail customers refused to cross the picket line. An injunction restraining Local 953 from "placing pickets or picketing around or about [Empire's] buildings" was affirmed by the Missouri Supreme Court on the ground that the purpose of the picketing was to compel Empire to become a party to a combination in restraint of trade in violation of a 1939 Missouri statute outlawing the closed shop. The United States Supreme Court, on certiorari, affirmed the decision, holding that it did not violate the Fourteenth Amendment of the United States Constitution.

3. In Building Service Employees International Union v. Gazzam, cited in the principal case, the union requested a small hotel in Bremerton, Washington, which employed 15 persons, to recognize the union as the bargaining agent of the employees and to enter into a closed shop contract. The owner gave the union permission to solicit members, which it did, but the employees voted against union representation. The union then requested the owner to agree to require all new employees to join and remain members of the union, and when the owner refused the union placed the hotel on its "unfair" list and caused it to be picketed peacefully by one picket at a time. An injunction was issued restraining the union "from endeavoring to compel plaintiff to coerce his employees to join the defendant union or to designate defendant as their representative for collective bargaining,

by picketing the hotel premises of plaintiff. . . . " The Supreme Court of Washington upheld the injunction on the basis of a State anti-injunction law which declared that the individual employee "shall be free from interference, restraint, or coercion of employers of labor, or their agents, in the designation of such representatives [for the purpose of negotiating terms and conditions of employment] or in self-organization or in other concerted activities . . . " The Supreme Court of the United States affirmed.

Questions

1.   Note that the Giboney case holds that there is no constitutional right to strike for an objective outlawed by a valid state statute; and the Gazzam case holds that there is no constitutional right to strike for an objective not illegal but contrary to the public policy of a state as declared by state statute; and the Hughes case holds that the same rule applies where the objective is contrary to policies declared by state courts. Is the union's objective in the Hanke case contrary to any public policies of the state? Putting the question another way, if the contract sought by the union had been freely agreed to by Hanke, would the Washington courts have refused to enforce it? If not, does not the Hanke case uphold the constitutional right of a state to forbid concerted activities as a means of attaining an otherwise legitimate aim? See Cox, "Strikes and Picketing," 4 Vanderbilt Law Review 574, 586 (1951).

2.   What, if anything, is left of Thornhill v. Alabama?

3.   Is the right to picket peacefully protected by the United States constitution in the following situations:

(a) Picketing by a Negro organization of a restaurant which refuses to serve Negroes?

(b) Picketing by the Catholic War Veterans of a movie theater showing a picture which they consider immoral?

(c) Picketing by anti-Zionists of the French Embassy protesting the supplying of arms by the French government to Israeli armies?

(d) Picketing by Quakers of a federal court building in which a conscientious objector is being tried for advising other conscientious objectors not to register for the draft?

4.   What are the proper functions of the injunction as a means of controlling labor disputes? What are the limits of its effectiveness?

5.   Preceding materials suggested that a statute may have precedential value, (a) as a guide to the development of common law principle (see Henningsen v. Chrysler, *supra* p. 560); and (b) as a guide to the interpretation of another statute (see U. S. v. Hutcheson, *supra* p. 913).

In what way, if at all, can a statute have precedential value as a guide to constitutional interpretation? Do you think that the National Labor Relations Act might have served as such a precedent in the Hanke case?

SECTION 42. SUMMARY

The material in this and the preceding two chapters presented a capsule history of the evolution of American labor law. This historical excursus has afforded an opportunity to examine many facets of the legal process in the context of one body of legal doctrine. But while each of these many facets is itself worthy of extensive independent consideration, an effort should be made to relate these discrete elements to some more general and inclusive insights into the legal process. We believe that these materials are especially valuable as a source of insight into two related questions: 1) what difficulties does rapid social change pose for the legal process? and 2) what are the limitations of the legal process as a means for resolving the intense conflicts so often associated with rapid social change?

We believe that the student will be assisted in formulating answers to these two basic questions by proposing answers to the following sets of further questions.

I.

1. Is there a substantial element of ambiguity in Sections 1 and 2 of the Sherman Act and in Sections 6 and 20 of the Clayton Act?

2. Is it significant that ambiguity in a statute may afford judges alternative, yet reasonable, interpretations of a statute? (See Loewe v. Lawlor, *supra* p. 845, and Duplex v. Deering, *supra* p. 856.)

3. Might a legislature purposely draft an ambiguous statute? Why?

4. Can you think of any reasons why Congress might purposefully have injected ambiguities in the Sherman Act or the Clayton Act?

5. If legislatures do make use of purposeful ambiguity in the language of a statute, what does that indicate about the relationship of courts and legislatures in the development of law and policy?

[Compare Sections 6 and 20 of the Clayton Act, *supra* p. 853, to the extracts from the Norris-LaGuardia Act, *supra* p. 884. Does this comparison provide insights relevant to the inquiry set out in questions 1–5 above?]

II.

6.   Do the materials on the development of labor law demonstrate that law sometimes lags behind social change?

7.   Assuming that such lags occur, can they be explained as the result of: (a) a failure by one or more participants in the legal process to recognize the nature and extent of a social change; or (b) a conflict or uncertainty as to what is the most efficacious response to a social change; or (c) an attempt by one or more of the participants in the legal process to slow the pace of social change?

8.   Is it desirable that the legal process impose some restraint on the process of social change?

9.   Is the judiciary the agency in the legal process which is most likely to impose restraint on the process of social change?

10.   Is a written constitution likely to be the doctrinal source from which emanates legal restraint on social change?   Why?

III.

11.   Is it fair to assume that law must adapt itself to social change?

12.   Is legislation an especially effective means to adapt law to rapid social change?

13.   Is the legislature a particularly appropriate and competent body to initiate the adaptation of law to social change?

14.   Is legislation a source of judicial insight into the nature of social change?

15.   Are adjudicators necessary participants in the process of adapting law to social change?

16.   Is a written constitution likely to be a doctrinal source from which is drawn a rationale for the adaptation of law to social change?

Chapter 12

CIVIL RIGHTS FOR BLACK AMERICANS: SOME NOTES ON RACE RELATIONS LAW IN THE UNITED STATES, 1865–1965

The legal and social triumph of organized labor in the century after the Civil War was paralleled, in time at least, by the quest of Black Americans for equality and social justice. The following synoptic view of the Black Civil Rights movement will perforce oversimplify issues, but some exposure to the legal history of this movement, compared and contrasted with the material on labor law, reveals much about the relationship of law to social change in the United States.

SECTION 43. EMANCIPATION AND RECONSTRUCTION

BY THE PRESIDENT OF THE UNITED STATES OF AMERICA:

A Proclamation

Whereas on the 22nd day of September A.D. 1862, a proclamation was issued by the President of the United States, containing among other things, the following, to wit:

That on the 1st day of January, A.D., 1863, all persons held as slaves within any State or designated part of a State the people whereof shall then be in rebellion against the United States shall be then, thenceforward, and forever free; and the executive government of the United States including the military and naval authority thereof, will recognize and maintain the freedom of such persons and will do no act or acts to repress such persons, or any of them, in any efforts they may make for their actual freedom.

That the executive will on the 1st day of January aforesaid, by proclamation, designate the States and parts of States, if any, in which the people thereof, respectively, shall then be in rebellion against the United States; and the fact that any State or the people thereof shall on that day be in good faith represented in the Congress of the United States by members chosen thereto at elections wherein a majority of the qualified voters of such States shall have participated shall, in the absence of strong countervailing testimony, be deemed conclusive evidence that such State and the people thereof are not then in rebellion against the United States.

Now, therefore, I, Abraham Lincoln, President of the United States, by virtue of the power in me vested as Commander-in-Chief of the Army and

Navy of the United States in time of actual armed rebellion against the authority and government of the United States, and as a fit and necessary war measure for suppressing said rebellion, do on this 1st day of January, A.D. 1863, and in accordance with my purpose so to do, publicly proclaimed for the full period of one hundred days from the first day above mentioned, order and designate as the States and parts of States wherein the people thereof, respectively, are this day in rebellion against the United States, the following, to wit:

Arkansas, Texas, Louisiana (except the parishes of St. Bernard Plaquemines, Jefferson, St. John, St. Charles, St. James, Ascension, Assumption, Terrebonne, Lafourche, St. Mary, St. Martin, and Orleans, including the city of New Orleans), Mississippi, Alabama, Florida, Georgia, South Carolina, North Carolina, and Virginia (except the forty-eight counties designated as West Virginia and also the counties of Berkeley, Accomac, Northhampton, Elizabeth City, York, Princess Anne, and Norfolk, including the cities of Norfolk and Portsmouth), and which excepted parts are for the present left precisely as if this proclamation were not issued.

And by virtue of the power and for the purpose aforesaid, I do order and declare that all persons held as slaves within said designated States and parts of States are, and henceforward shall be, free; and that the Executive Government of the United States, including the military and naval authorities thereof, will recognize and maintain the freedom of said persons.

And I hereby enjoin upon the people so declared to be free to abstain from all violence, unless in necessary self-defense; and I recommend to them that, in all cases when allowed, they labor faithfully for reasonable wages.

And I further declare and make known that such persons of suitable condition will be received into the armed service of the United States to garrison forts, positions, stations, and other places, and to man vessels of all sorts in said service.

And upon this act, sincerely believed to be an act of justice, warranted by the Constitution upon military necessity, I invoke the considerate judgment of mankind and the gracious favor of Almighty God.

Questions

1. Did President Lincoln make law in the Emancipation Proclamation?

2. If such an order makes law, in what sense does it do so? For example, would a federal judge be bound by the Proclamation with respect to civil or criminal cases in which the status of one of the parties, *i.e.*, as slave or freeman, were in issue? Would a state court be bound in a similar case? Would a federal attorney be bound by the Proclamation with regard to the performance of the duties of his office, and if so, how? Would a state attorney be similarly bound?

3. What was the source of legal authority upon which President Lincoln based the Proclamation?

4. Do you think that the Emancipation Proclamation alone would have been sufficient to remove legal sanction from the institution of slavery?

5.   What practical purposes may be served by an executive order such as the Emancipation Proclamation?

———

The step first taken by presidential order in the Emancipation Proclamation became part of the fundamental law of the United States upon the ratification of the Thirteenth Amendment to the Constitution in 1865.

ARTICLE XIII

SECTION 1.   Neither slavery nor involuntary servitude, except as a punishment for crime whereof the party shall have been duly convicted, shall exist within the United States, or any place subject to their jurisdiction.

SECTION 2.   Congress shall have power to enforce this article by appropriate legislation.

———

[The following is taken from MILTON R. KONVITZ and THEODORE LESKES, A CENTURY OF CIVIL RIGHTS (New York, 1961), pp. 51–52. Footnotes are omitted.]

* * *

Lee surrendered to Grant at Appomattox Court House on April 9, 1865. Less than a month before this event, Congress had passed an act to establish the Freedmen's Bureau, that was to be in existence for the remainder of the war and one year thereafter. The act provided for the appointment of a commissioner who was to be head of the bureau, and of assistant commissioners in the Southern states. The bureau was to have charge of the freedmen and to provide for their needs, including the assignment to each freedman of forty acres of abandoned or confiscated land for a term of three years, with an option to purchase the land within that period.

When Congress met at the end of 1865, the Republican majority excluded the members-elect from the Southern states and set up the Joint Committee of Fifteen on Reconstruction. This was the beginning of Reconstruction. . . .

. . . Congress passed (on March 13, 1866) an act entitled: "An Act to Protect All Persons in the United States in Their Civil Rights, and Furnish the Means of Their Vindication."

The act was, in its intentions, one of the most far-reaching in congressional history. It declared all persons born in the United States to be citizens of the United States, and that all citizens, "of every race and color, without regard to any previous condition of slavery or involuntary servitude," shall have the same right in every state and territory "as is enjoyed by white citizens," to sue, be parties, give evidence; to inherit, purchase, lease, sell, hold, and convey real and personal property; "and to full and equal benefit of all laws and proceedings for the security of person and property"; and to be subject to "like punishment, pains, and penalties, and to none other, any law, statute, ordinance, regulation, or custom to the contrary notwithstanding."

The act made it a criminal offense for any person, acting "under color of any law, statute, ordinance, regulation, or custom," to subject or cause to be subjected any inhabitant to the deprivation of any right secured or protected by the act, or to different punishment, pains or penalties, by reason of color or race. It gave federal courts jurisdiction to try all crimes and offenses committed against the act. Federal officers were given the right to proceed against all persons violating the act, and were directed to afford "protection to all persons in their constitutional rights of equality before the law, without distinction of race or color, or previous condition of slavery or involuntary servitude."

President Johnson vetoed the bill, but the Senate repassed it by vote of 33 to 15, and the House of Representatives by vote of 122 to 41; so the bill became law on April 9, 1866.

* * *

The Fourteenth Amendment

Although President Johnson's veto message failed to convince Congress, it had the effect of stimulating the national legislators to prepare a constitutional amendment that would remove all or most of the President's constitutional objections to the act. Two months after the Civil Rights Act became law, the Senate passed the Fourteenth Amendment, on June 8, 1866, and a few days later (June 13) the amendment was passed by the House. Ratification was completed on July 9, 1868. Before Reconstruction governments took over the states of the South, the amendment was rejected in late 1866 and early 1867 by all the Southern states but Tennessee. The action rejecting the amendment by the legislatures of the ten states is summarized in the following table.

State	House	Senate	Date
Texas	70 to 5	21 to 1	Oct. 13, 1866
Georgia	147 to 2	38 to 0	Nov. 9, 1866
Florida	49 to 0	20 to 0	Dec. 3, 1866
Alabama	66 to 8	28 to 3	Dec. 7, 1866
North Carolina	93 to 10	45 to 1	Dec. 13, 1866
Arkansas	68 to 2	24 to 1	Dec. 17, 1866
South Carolina	95 to 1	rejected	Dec. 20, 1866
Virginia	74 to 1	27 to 0	Jan 9, 1867
Mississippi	88 to 0	27 to 0	Jan. 25, 1867
Louisiana	unanimous	unanimous	Feb. 5, 1867

Following these actions, Congress passed the first Reconstruction Act on March 2, 1867. It made readmission of representatives from the Southern states to Congress conditional upon each of these states holding a constitutional convention of delegates elected by all citizens without regard to race or color, except those disfranchised for participation in the rebellion; on each adopting a constitution with a suffrage provision in similar terms; on ratification of the new state constitution by persons enjoying the suffrage as thus defined; and on ratification of the Fourteenth Amendment by the new state legislature. The reconstructed state legislatures all ratified the amendment as shown in the following table.

State	House	Senate	Date
Arkansas	56 to 0	23 to 0	April 6, 1868
Florida	23 to 6	10 to 3	June 8, 1868
North Carolina	82 to 19	34 to 2	July 2, 1868
South Carolina	108 to 12	23 to 5	July 9, 1868
Louisiana	ratified	22 to 11	July 9, 1868
Alabama	94 to 3	33 to 0	July 13, 1868
Georgia	89 to 71	ratified	July 21, 1868
Virginia	126 to 6	34 to 4	Oct. 7, 1869
Mississippi	87 to 6	23 to 2	Jan. 7, 1870
Texas	ratified	ratified	Feb. 18, 1870

The full text of the amendment follows.

ARTICLE XIV

SECTION 1. All persons born or naturalized in the United States, and subject to the jurisdiction thereof, are citizens of the United States and of the State wherein they reside. No State shall make or enforce any law which shall abridge the privileges or immunities of citizens of the United States; nor shall any State deprive any person of life, liberty, or property, without due process of law; nor deny to any person within its jurisdiction the equal protection of the laws.

SECTION 2. Representatives shall be apportioned among the several States according to their respective numbers, counting the whole number of persons in each State, excluding Indians not taxed. But when the right to vote at any election for the choice of electors for President and Vice President of the United States, Representatives in Congress, the Executive and Judicial officers of a State, or the members of the Legislature thereof, is denied to any of the male inhabitants of such State, being twenty-one years of age, and citizens of the United States, or in any way abridged, except for participation in rebellion, or other crime, the basis of representation therein shall be reduced in the proportion which the number of such male citizens shall bear to the whole number of male citizens twenty-one years of age in such State.

SECTION 3. No person shall be a Senator or Representative in Congress, or elector of President and Vice President, or hold any office, civil or military, under the United States, or under any State, who, having previously taken an oath, as a member of Congress, or as an officer of the United States, or as a member of any State legislature, or as an executive or judicial officer of any State, to support the Constitution of the United States, shall have engaged in insurrection or rebellion against the same, or given aid or comfort to the enemies thereof. But Congress may by a vote of two-thirds of each House, remove such disability.

SECTION 4. The validity of the public debt of the United States, authorized by law, including debts incurred for payment of pensions and bounties for services in suppressing insurrection or rebellion, shall not be questioned. But neither the United States nor any State shall assume or pay any debt or obligation incurred in aid of insurrection or rebellion against the United States, or any claim for the loss or emancipation of any slave; but all such debts, obligations and claims shall be held illegal and void.

SECTION 5. The Congress shall have power to enforce, by appropriate legislation, the provisions of this article.

———

The last of the so-called Civil War Amendments was passed by Congress in February, 1869, and was ratified in 1870.

ARTICLE XV

SECTION 1. The right of citizens of the United States to vote shall not be denied or abridged by the United States or by any State on account of race, color, or previous condition of servitude.

SECTION 2. The Congress shall have power to enforce this article by appropriate legislation.

———

[The following is taken from KONVITZ and LESKES, op. cit., pgs. 57–63.]

The Civil Rights Act of 1870

Several months after ratification of the Fifteenth Amendment had been completed, Congress enacted a new Civil Rights Act, "to enforce the right of citizens of the United States to vote in the several States of this Union, and for other purposes." The act dealt with voting rights and with civil rights.

It declared that all citizens of the United States who are otherwise entitled to vote in any election in any state, municipality, or other territorial subdivision, shall be "entitled and allowed" to vote without distinction of race, color, or previous condition of servitude, "any constitution, law, custom, usage, or regulation of any State or Territory, or by or under its authority, to the contrary notwithstanding."

If any act should be required as a prerequisite for voting under the authority of a state, it would be the duty of officials to give to all citizens "the same and equal opportunity to perform such prerequisite, and to become qualified to vote, without distinction of race, color, or previous condition of servitude." Violation of this provision was made a misdemeanor, and subjected the offender also to the payment of $500 damages to the aggrieved party.

If a person, otherwise qualified to vote, offered to fulfill the prerequisites, but was kept from qualifying by the wrongful act or omission of the official in charge, his offer to perform was to be deemed a performance, and he would be entitled to vote by presenting an affidavit to the officer whose duty it was to receive and count the votes. A refusal to permit voting under these circumstances was made a misdemeanor and also subjected the election official to the payment of $500 damages to the aggrieved party.

Any interference with an attempt to qualify to vote was made a criminal offense and subjected the offender to a suit for damages.

If any person should interfere with the right to vote guaranteed by the Fifteenth Amendment, "by means of bribery, threats, or threats of depriving such person of employment or occupation, or of ejecting such person from rented house, lands, or other property, or by threats of refusing to renew leases or contracts for labor, or by threats of violence to himself or family," he would be guilty of a misdemeanor.

An anti-Ku Klux Klan provision stated that if two or more persons banded or conspired together, or went in disguise upon the public highway or upon the premises of another, with intent to violate any of the provisions of the act, or to injure, oppress, threaten, or intimidate any citizen with intent to prevent or hinder his free exercise or enjoyment of any right or privilege granted or secured to him by the Constitution or laws of the United States or because of his having exercised the same, those persons would be guilty of felony.

Federal courts were given exclusive jurisdiction of all cases, criminal and civil, arising under the act.

Federal circuit courts were given power to designate commissioners "to afford a speedy and convenient means for the arrest and examination of persons charged with a violation of this act."

The President was authorized to use such part of the armed forces as would be necessary "to aid in the execution of judicial process issued under this act."

All persons were to have the same right in every state to make and enforce contracts, to sue, be parties, give evidence, and to the full and equal benefit of all law proceedings for the security of person and property as was enjoyed by white persons, and should be subject to like punishment, licenses, and exactions of every kind, and none other, "any law, statute, ordinance, regulation, or custom to the contrary notwithstanding."

Any person who, "under color of any law, statute, ordinance, regulation or custom," subjected or caused to be subjected any person to the deprivation of any right secured or protected by this act, or to different punishment or pains, by reason of his color or race, would be guilty of a misdemeanor.

The Civil Rights Act of 1866 was re-enacted.

It was made a crime for any person to prevent a qualified voter "from freely exercising the right of suffrage" by "force, threat, menace, intimidation, bribery, reward, or offer, or promise thereof," or by such means to induce any voter to refuse to exercise such right. The same provision applied to voting registration for an election for Congress.

The act passed the Senate on May 25, 1870, by a vote of 48 yeas and 11 nays. It is notable that of the negative votes, six were from the senators of the loyal but former slave states of Delaware, Maryland, and Kentucky. The senators from the "reconstructed" states, except one senator from Virginia, voted for the measure. In the House of Representatives the vote was 133 yeas and 58 nays, with the division along partisan as well as sectional lines.

The Civil Rights Acts of 1871

Congress was not satisfied with its enactments; it seemed to have a passion for turning out statutes that would assure to the Negro full and equal rights. Never before in the history of any people was there such an obsessive concern with the establishment of fundamental rights for a minority which, until then, had had no rights at all. Congress was intent on not merely passing laws giving rights to the Negro but on the vindication and enforcement of these rights against the former masters of slaves in sixteen states.

On February 28, 1871, Congress passed yet another act, to protect the Negro in his voting rights. It was a long, detailed statute. Its more significant provisions were the following.

It made it a crime for any person, by force, threat, menace, intimidation, or other unlawful means, to prevent or hinder any person, having a lawful right to register to vote, from exercising such right.

In cities having 20,000 or more inhabitants, two persons, prior to an election for Congress, could request a federal circuit court judge to appoint commissioners to guard and scrutinize the process of registration or an election. The judge was to appoint two commissioners (known as election supervisors) for each voting precinct. The commissioners were to belong to different political parties. They were to attend the registration and voting places and have broad powers to assure "the truth or fairness" of the process. The United States marshal and his special deputies were required to keep the peace at registration and polling places and protect the election supervisors.

The federal judge was to designate a chief election supervisor from among the commissioners named by him.

All votes in a congressional election were to be by written or printed ballot.

Several months later—on April 20, 1871—Congress enacted an act which contained the following provisions.

Any person who, "under color of any law, statute, ordinance, custom, or usage of any State," subjected any person to the deprivation of any rights, privileges, or immunities secured by the Constitution would be liable to the party injured in the federal courts.

If two or more persons (a) conspired to oppose by force the authority of the federal government, or by force, intimidation, or threat prevent, hinder or delay the execution of any law of the United States; or (b) went in disguise on the highway or on the premises of another person for the purpose of depriving any person or class of persons of equal protection of the laws or of equal privileges or immunities under the law; or (c) conspired for the purpose of impeding, hindering, obstructing, or defeating the due course of justice with intent to deny to any United States citizen due and equal protection of the laws; or (d) by force, intimidation, or threat tried to prevent any United States citizen, lawfully entitled to vote, from supporting the election of a presidential elector or a candidate for Congress, those persons would be guilty of a high crime, and in addition, subject to an action for damages in the federal courts.

In case insurrection, domestic violence, unlawful combination, or conspiracy were to so obstruct or hinder execution of the laws of the state and of the United States as to deprive any portion or class of any of the rights, privileges, or immunities or protection named in the Constitution and secured by this act, and the constituted authorities of the state should be unable, or should fail or refuse to protect the people in such rights, then the state would be deemed to have denied equal protection, and the President must take measures necessary for the suppression of the violence, combination, or conspiracy.

When a combination was so numerous and powerful as to defy the state authorities and the federal authorities within the state, "or when the constituted [state] authorities are in complicity with, or shall connive at the unlawful purposes of, such powerful and armed combinations," and when conviction of the offenders and the preservation of public safety had become impracticable, an insurrection should be deemed to have taken place, and the President might then suspend the writ of habeas corpus.

The Civil Rights Act of 1875

One of the broadest civil rights acts adopted by Congress was entitled "An Act to Protect All Citizens in Their Civil and Legal Rights." It was passed on March 1, 1875. The preamble or "whereas" clause with which the act opened is notable for its echo of some phrases in the Declaration of Independence. It read:

Whereas, it is essential to just government we recognize the equality of all men before the law, and hold that it is the duty of government in its dealings with the people to meet out equal and exact justice to all of whatever nationality, race, color, or persuasion, religious or political; and it being the appropriate object of legislation to enact great fundamental principles into law . . .

This was followed by a brief first section, providing:

That all persons within the jurisdiction of the United States shall be entitled to the full and equal enjoyment of the accommodations, advantages, facilities, and privileges of inns, public conveyances on land or water, theaters, and other places of public amusement; subject only to the conditions and limitations established by law and applicable alike to citizens of every race and color, regardless of any previous condition of servitude.

Then the act further provided that any person who violated the foregoing section

by denying to any citizen except for reasons by law applicable to citizens of every race and color, and regardless of any previous condition of servitude, the full enjoyment of any of the accommodations, advantages, or privileges in said section enumerated, or by aiding or inciting such denial

would be liable to criminal and civil penalties in the federal courts. It also said, however, that the aggrieved person might elect to seek his common law remedy or that provided by state statute in the state courts.

Section 4 provided that no citizen, otherwise qualified, would be disqualified for service on a grand or petit jury, in any federal or state court, on account of race, color, or previous condition of servitude.

The Civil Rights Act of 1875 was the last piece of pro-Black civil rights legislation to pass Congress until 1957. Reconstruction effectively came to an end in 1877, with the election of Rutherford

B. Hayes.   Hayes' victory over Samuel J. Tilden was made possible
by the so-called Compromise of 1877 in which Southern Democrats
joined with Republicans to resolve in Hayes' favor a contest over
the electoral votes of Florida, Louisiana, and South Carolina so that
Hayes received one hundred eighty-five electoral votes to Tilden's
one hundred eighty-four.   (Tilden held a 250,000 vote margin in the
popular vote.)

Southern Democratic participation in the Compromise was secured by the promises of Hayes' supporters that the last vestiges of
Radical Reconstruction in the South would be terminated after his
election.   The federal garrisons which afforded military support to
"carpet bag" state governments were withdrawn by President Hayes,
and Reconstruction came to an end.[1]   During the next two decades
the new leaders of the South would provide some protection of the
civil rights of Negroes.   The nadir of Negro civil rights, in both
the North and South, did not come until the end of the nineteenth
century.   The law and customs known as "Jim Crow" emerged at
that time.

SECTION 44.   SEPARATE BUT EQUAL: THE RISE OF THE LAW OF JIM CROW

PLESSY v. FERGUSON

Supreme Court of the United States, 1896.
163 U.S. 537, 16 S.Ct. 1138.

[In 1890, Louisiana adopted a statute requiring segregation of
the races in railway coaches.   Plessy, "a person of color", was charged
with violating the statute by refusing to move from a car reserved for
whites.   He was convicted in a Louisiana court, which denied his claim
that the statute was unconstitutional.]

JUSTICE BROWN.

* * *

That [the Louisiana Statute] does not conflict with the thirteenth
amendment, which abolished slavery and involuntary servitude, except as a
punishment for crime, is too clear for argument.   Slavery implies involuntary servitude,—a state of bondage; the ownership of mankind as a chattel, or, at least, the control of the labor and services of one man for the
benefit of another, and the absence of a legal right to the disposal of his
own person, property, and services.   This amendment . . . was regarded by the statesmen of that day as insufficient to protect the colored

---

1. See e. g., J. G. Randall and David
Donald, The Civil War and Recon-
struction, Second Revised Edition
(Lexington, Mass.1969), pp. 687–701.

See also, C. Vann Woodward, Reunion
and Reconstruction, Second Revised
Edition (Garden City, New York 1956).

race from certain laws which had been enacted in the Southern states, imposing upon the colored race onerous disabilities and burdens, and curtailing their rights in the pursuit of life, liberty, and property to such an extent that their freedom was of little value; and . . . the fourteenth amendment was devised to meet this exigency. . . .

The object of the amendment was undoubtedly to enforce the absolute equality of the two races before the law, but, in the nature of things, it could not have been intended to abolish distinctions based upon color, or to enforce social, as distinguished from political, equality, or a commingling of the two races upon terms unsatisfactory to either. Laws permitting, and even requiring, their separation, in places where they are liable to be brought into contact . . . have been generally, if not universally, recognized as within the competency of the state legislatures in the exercise of their police power. The most common instance of this is connected with the establishment of separate schools for white and colored children, which have been held to be a valid exercise of the legislative power even by courts of states where the political rights of the colored race have been longest and most earnestly enforced.

One of the earliest of these cases is that of Roberts v. City of Boston, 5 Cush. 198 [1849], in which the supreme judicial court of Massachusetts held that the general school committee of Boston had power to make provision for the instruction of colored children in separate schools established exclusively for them, and to prohibit their attendance upon the other schools, "The great principle," said Chief Justice Shaw, "advanced by the learned and eloquent advocate for the plaintiff [Mr. Charles Sumner], is that, by the constitution and laws of Massachusetts, all persons, without distinction of age or sex, birth or color, origin or condition, are equal before the law. * * * But, when this great principle comes to be applied to the actual and various conditions of persons in society, it will not warrant the assertion that men and women are legally clothed with the same civil and political powers, and that children and adults are legally to have the same functions and be subject to the same treatment; but only that the rights of all, as they are settled and regulated by law, are equally entitled to the paternal consideration and protection of the law for their maintenance and security." It was held that the powers of the committee extended to the establishment of separate schools for children of different ages, sexes and colors, and that they might also establish special schools for poor and neglected children, who have become too old to attend the primary school, and yet have not acquired the rudiments of learning, to enable them to enter the ordinary schools. Similar laws have been enacted by congress under its general power of legislation over the District of Columbia, . . . as well as by the legislatures of many of the states, and have been generally, if not uniformly, sustained by the courts. State v. McCann, 21 Ohio St. 210; Lehew v. Brummell (Mo.Sup.) 15 S.W. 765; Ward v. Flood, 48 Cal. 36; Bertonneau v. Directors of City Schools, 3 Woods, 177, Fed.Cas.No. 1,361 [La.]; People v. Gallagher, 93 N.Y. 438; Cory v. Carter, 48 Ind. 337; Dawson v. Lee, 83 Ky. 49.

Laws forbidding the intermarriage of the two races may be said in a technical sense to interfere with the freedom of contract, and yet have been universally recognized as within the police power of the state. State v. Gibson, 36 Ind. 389.

The distinction between laws interfering with the political equality of the negro and those requiring the separation of the two races in schools, theaters, and railway carriages has been frequently drawn by this court. . . . Strauder v. West Virginia. [S]tatutes for the separation of the two races upon public conveyances were held to be constitutional in Railroad v. Miles, 55 Pa.St. 209; Day v. Owen, 5 Mich. 520; Railway Co. v. Williams, 55 Ill. 185; Railroad Co. v. Wells, 85 Tenn. 613, 4 S.W. 5; Railroad Co. v. Benson, 85 Tenn. 627, 4 S.W. 5; The Sue, 22 Fed. 843; Logwood v. Railroad Co., 23 Fed. 318; McGuinn v. Forbes, 37 Fed. 639; People v. King (N.Y.App.) 18 N.E. 245; Houck v. Railway Co, 38 Fed. 226; Heard v. Railroad Co., 3 Inter St. Commerce Com.R. 111, 1 Inter St. Commerce Com.R. 428.

It is claimed that the same argument that will justify the state legislature in requiring railways to provide separate accommodations for the two races will also authorize them to require separate cars to be provided for people whose hair is of a certain color, or who are aliens, or who belong to certain nationalities, or to enact laws requiring colored people to walk upon one side of the street, and white people upon the other, or requiring white men's houses to be painted white, and colored men's black, or their vehicles or business signs to be of different colors, upon the theory that one side of the street is as good as the other, or that a house or vehicle of one color is as good as one of another color. The reply to all this is that every exercise of the police power must be reasonable, and extend only to such laws as are enacted in good faith for the promotion of the public good, and not for the annoyance or oppression of a particular class. . . .

So far, then, as a conflict with the fourteenth amendment is concerned, the case reduces itself to the question whether the statute of Louisiana is a reasonable regulation, and with respect to this there must necessarily be a large discretion on the part of the legislature. In determining the question of reasonableness, it is at liberty to act with reference to the established usages, customs, and traditions of the people, and with a view to the promotion of their comfort, and the preservation of the public peace and good order. Gauged by this standard, we cannot say that . . . is unreasonable, or more obnoxious to the fourteenth amendment than the acts of congress requiring separate schools for colored children in the District of Columbia, the constitutionality of which does not seem to have been questioned, or the corresponding acts of state legislatures.

We consider the underlying fallacy of the plaintiff's argument to consist in the assumption that the enforced separation of the two races stamps the colored race with a badge of inferiority. If this be so, it is not by reason of anything found in the act, but solely because the colored race chooses to put that construction upon it. The argument necessarily assumes that if, as has been more than once the case, and is not unlikely to be so again, the colored race should become the dominant power in the state legislature, and should enact a law in precisely similar terms, it would thereby relegate the white race to an inferior position. We imagine that the white race, at least, would not acquiesce in this assumption. The argument also assumes that social prejudices may be overcome by legislation, and that equal rights cannot be secured to the negro except by an enforced commingling of the two races. We cannot accept this proposition. If the two races are to meet upon terms of social equality, it must be the result of natural affinities, a mutual appreciation of each other's merits, and a voluntary consent of individuals. . . . Legislation is powerless to eradicate racial instincts, or to abolish distinctions based upon physical differences, and the attempt to do so can only result in accentuating the difficulties of the present situation. If the civil and political rights of both races be equal, one cannot be inferior to the other civilly or politically. If one race be inferior to the other socially, the constitution of the United States cannot put them upon the same plane. . . .

Affirmed.

MR. JUSTICE BREWER did not hear the argument or participate in the decision of this case.

MR. JUSTICE HARLAN dissenting. . . .

In respect of civil rights, common to all citizens, the constitution of the United States does not, I think, permit any public authority to know the race of those entitled to be protected in the enjoyment of such rights. Every true man has pride of race, and under appropriate circumstances, when the rights of others, his equals before the law, are not to be affected, it is his privilege to express such pride and to take such action based upon it as to him seems proper. But I deny that any legislative body or judicial tribunal may have regard to the race of citizens when the civil rights of those citizens are involved. Indeed, such legislation as that here in question is inconsistent not only with that equality of rights which pertains to citizenship, national and state, but with the personal liberty enjoyed by every one within the United States.

The thirteenth amendment does not permit the withholding or the deprivation of any right necessarily inhering in freedom. It not only struck down the institution of slavery as previously existing in the United States, but it prevents the imposition of any burdens or disabilities that constitute badges of slavery or servitude. . . . It was followed by the fourteenth [and fifteenth] amendment[s], which added greatly to the dignity and glory of American citizenship, and to the security of personal liberty . . . .

It was said in argument that the statute of Louisiana does not discriminate against either race, but prescribes a rule applicable alike to white and colored citizens. But this argument does not meet the difficulty. Every one knows that the statute in question had its origin in the purpose, not so much to exclude white persons from railroad cars occupied by blacks, as to exclude colored people from coaches occupied by or assigned to white persons. . . . No one would be so wanting in candor as to assert the contrary. The fundamental objection, therefore, to the statute, is that it interferes with the personal freedom of citizens. "Personal liberty," it has been well said, "consists in the power of locomotion, of changing situation, or removing one's person to whatsoever places one's own inclination may direct, without imprisonment or restraint, unless by due course of law." 1 Bl.Comm. 134. If a white man and a black man choose to occupy the same public conveyance on a public highway, it is their right to do so; and no government, proceeding alone on grounds of race, can prevent it without infringing the personal liberty of each.

. . . If a state can prescribe, as a rule of civil conduct, that whites and blacks shall not travel as passengers in the same railroad coach, why . . . may it not require sheriffs to assign whites to one side of a court room, and blacks to the other? And why may it not also prohibit the commingling of the two races in the galleries of legislative halls or in public assemblages convened for the consideration of the political questions of the day? Further, if this statute of Louisiana is consistent with the personal liberty of citizens, why may not the state require the separation in railroad coaches of native and naturalized citizens of the United States, or of Protestants and Roman Catholics? . . .

The white race deems itself to be the dominant race in this country. And so it is, in prestige, in achievements, in education, in wealth, and in power. So, I doubt not, it will continue to be for all time, if it remains true to its great heritage, and holds fast to the principles of constitutional liberty. But in view of the constitution, in the eye of the law, there is in this country no superior, dominant, ruling class of citizens. There is no caste here. Our constitution is color-blind, and neither knows nor tolerates classes among citizens. . . .

In my opinion, the judgment this day rendered will, in time, prove to be quite as pernicious as the decision made by this tribunal in the Dred Scott Case . . . that the descendants of Africans who were imported into this country, and sold as slaves, were not included nor intended to be included under the word "citizens" in the constitution; . . . that, at the time of the adoption of the constitution, they were "considered as a subordinate and inferior class of beings, who had been subjugated by the dominant race, and, whether emancipated or not, yet remained subject to their authority, and had no rights or privileges but such as those who held the power and the government might choose to grant them." 19 How. 393, 404. The recent amendments of the constitution, it was supposed, had eradicated these principles from our institutions. But it seems that we have yet, in some of the states, a dominant race,—a superior class of citizens,— which assumes to regulate the enjoyment of civil rights, common to all citizens, upon the basis of race. The present decision, it may well be apprehended, will not only stimulate aggressions, more or less brutal and irritating, upon the admitted rights of colored citizens, but will encourage the belief that it is possible by means of state enactments, to defeat the beneficent purposes which the people of the United States had in view when they adopted the recent amendments of the constitution. . . . What can more certainly arouse race hate, what more certainly create and perpetuate a feeling of distrust between these races, than state enactments which, in fact, proceed on the ground that colored citizens are so inferior and degraded that they cannot be allowed to sit in public coaches occupied by white citizens? That, as all will admit, is the real meaning of such legislation as was enacted in Louisiana.

. . . This question is not met by the suggestion that social equality cannot exist between the white and black races in this country . . . for social equality no more exists between two races when traveling in a passenger coach or a public highway than when members of the same races sit by each other in a street car or in the jury box, or stand or sit with each other in a political assembly. . . .

If evils will result from the commingling of the two races upon public highways established for the benefit of all, they will be infinitely less than those that will surely come from state legislation regulating the enjoyment of civil rights upon the basis of race. We boast of the freedom enjoyed by our people above all other peoples. But it is difficult to reconcile that boast with a state of the law which, practically, puts the brand of servitude and degradation upon a large class of our fellow citizens,—our equals before the law. The thin disguise of "equal" accommodations for passengers in railroad coaches will not mislead any one, nor atone for the wrong this day done. . . .

I do not deem it necessary to review the decisions of state courts to which reference was made in argument. Some, and the most important, of them, are wholly inapplicable, because rendered prior to the adoption of the last amendments of the constitution, when colored people had very few rights which the dominant race felt obliged to respect. Others were made at a time when public opinion, in many localities, was dominated by the institution of slavery; when it would not have been safe to do justice to the black man; and when, so far as the rights of blacks were concerned, race prejudice was, practically, the supreme law of the land. Those decisions cannot be guides in the era introduced by the recent amendments of the supreme law, which established universal civil freedom . . . .

Questions

1.   The Louisiana statute required "equal but separate" facilities for Blacks. Does the majority opinion suggest that the requirement of equality was essential to the finding of the constitutional validity of the statute?

2.   What practical problems are presented by a "separate but equal" test for a valid segregation statute?

3.   "Legislation is powerless to eradicate racial instincts, or to abolish distinctions based upon physical differences . . . If one race be inferior to the other socially, the Constitution of the United States cannot put them upon the same plane . . ." Are such assertions verifiable? Are they arguments in support of the decision? Do they tend to explain the result in this case?

4.   How does Justice Harlan meet the argument that segregation of the races is supported by the authority of numerous state court opinions? Do you find his argument persuasive? How would you answer him on this point?

5.   "It was said in argument that the statute . . . [applies] . . . alike to white and colored citizens . . . Everyone knows that the statute in question had its origin in the purpose . . . to exclude colored people from coaches occupied by . . . white people". Is the legislative purpose relevant to the determination of the constitutional issue in this case? Or is it only the effect of the statute which is germane to that issue?

The remains of Reconstruction were interred by federal courts and Congress soon after the Compromise of 1877. A restrictive interpretation of the Civil War Amendments was presaged in the Slaughterhouse Cases, 83 U.S. 36 (1873) and United States v. Cruikshank, 92 U.S. 542 (1875), and elaborated in the Civil Rights Cases, 109 U.S. 3, 3 S.Ct. 18 (1883). Other decisions, notably United States v. Reese, 92 U.S. 214 (1876), United States v. Harris, 106 U.S. 629, 1 S.Ct. 601 (1883), and Baldwin v. Franks, 120 U.S. 678, 7 S.Ct. 656 (1887), reinforced judicial limitations on the scope of federal power under those amendments. Congress made its own contribution to this development in the Acts of 1894 [1] and 1909 [2] which repealed the voting rights sections of the Civil Rights Acts of 1870 and 1871. This emasculation of federal law regarding racial discrimination was accompanied by the rise of a body of state law and associated custom which was to be a distinctive feature of race relations in the United States throughout the first half of the twentieth century.

Plessy v. Ferguson opened the door to this use of law to enforce the segregation of the races, but like many other "leading cases" it only put judicial approval on social and political developments which had been gathering momentum prior to the decision itself.

[The following is taken from C. VANN WOODWARD, THE STRANGE CAREER OF JIM CROW, Second Revised Edition (New York, 1966) pp. 67–74, 81–83.]

Up to the year 1898 South Carolina had resisted the Jim Crow car movement which had swept the western states of the South completely by that time. In that year, however, after several attempts, the proponents of the Jim Crow law were on the eve of victory. The Charleston *News and Courier*, the oldest newspaper in the South and a consistent spokesman of conservatism, fired a final broadside against extremists in behalf of the conservative creed of race policy.

'As we have got on fairly well for a third of a century, including a long period of reconstruction, without such a measure,' wrote the editor, 'we can probably get on as well hereafter without it, and certainly so extreme a measure should not be adopted and enforced without added and urgent cause.' He then called attention to what he considered the absurd consequences to which such a law might lead once the principle of the thing were conceded. 'If there must be Jim Crow cars on the railroads, there should be Jim Crow cars on the street railways. Also on all passenger boats. . . . If there are to be Jim Crow cars, moreover, there should be Jim Crow waiting saloons at all stations, and Jim Crow eating houses. . . . There should be Jim Crow sections of the jury box, and a separate Jim Crow dock and witness stand in every court—and a Jim Crow Bible for colored witnesses to kiss. It would be advisable also to have a Jim Crow section in county auditors' and treasurers' offices for the accommodation of colored taxpayers. The two races are dreadfully mixed in these

1. 28 Stat. 36.　　　　　　　　　2. 35 Stat. 1092.

offices for weeks every year, especially about Christmas. . . . There should be a Jim Crow department for making returns and paying for the privileges and blessings of citizenship. Perhaps, the best plan would be, after all, to take the short cut to the general end . . . by establishing two or three Jim Crow counties at once, and turning them over to our colored citizens for their special and exclusive accommodation.'

In resorting to the tactics of *reductio ad absurdum* the editor doubtless believed that he had dealt the Jim Crow principle a telling blow with his heavy irony. But there is now apparent to us an irony in his argument of which the author was unconscious. For what he intended as a *reductio ad absurdum* and obviously regarded as an absurdity became in a very short time a reality, and not only that but a reality that was regarded as the only sensible solution to a vexing problem, a solution having the sanction of tradition and long usage. Apart from the Jim Crow counties and Jim Crow witness stand, all the improbable applications of the principle suggested by the editor in derision had been put into practice— down to and including the Jim Crow Bible.

The South's adoption of extreme racism was due not so much to a conversion as it was to a relaxation of the opposition. All the elements of fear, jealousy, proscription, hatred, and fanaticism had long been present, as they are present in various degrees of intensity in any society. What enabled them to rise to dominance was not so much cleverness or ingenuity as it was a general weakening and discrediting of the numerous forces that had hitherto kept them in check. . . .

* * *

The acquiescence of Northern liberalism in the Compromise of 1877 defined the beginning, but not the ultimate extent, of the liberal retreat on the race issue. The Compromise merely left the freedman to the custody of the conservative Redeemers upon their pledge that they would protect him in his constitutional rights. But as these pledges were forgotten or violated and the South veered toward proscription and extremism, Northern opinion shifted to the right, keeping pace with the South, conceding point after point, so that at no time were the sections very far apart on race policy. The failure of the liberals to resist this trend was due in part to political factors. Since reactionary politicians and their cause were identified with the bloody-shirt issue and the demagogic exploitation of sectional animosities, the liberals naturally felt themselves strongly drawn toward the cause of sectional reconciliation. And since the Negro was the symbol of sectional strife, the liberals joined in deprecating further agitation of his cause and in defending the Southern view of race in its less extreme forms. It was quite common in the 'eighties and 'nineties to find in the *Nation, Harper's Weekly,* the *North American Review,* or the *Atlantic Monthly* Northern liberals and former abolitionists mouthing the shibboleths of white supremacy regarding the Negro's innate inferiority, shiftlessness, and hopeless unfitness for full participation in the white man's civilization. Such expressions doubtless did much to add to the reconciliation of North and South, but they did so at the expense of the Negro. Just as the Negro gained his emancipation and new rights through a falling out between white men, he now stood to lose his rights through the reconciliation of white men.

The cumulative weakening of resistance to racism was expressed also in a succession of decisions by the United States Supreme Court between 1873 and 1898 that require no review here.   .   .   .

[Professor Woodward refers here to Plessy v. Ferguson, supra, p. 962, and to other cases noted on p. 968, supra.]

For a short time after the Supreme Court decision of 1883 that held the restrictive parts of the Civil Rights Act unconstitutional, Northern legislatures showed a disposition to protect the rights of Negroes by state action.   In the mid-'eighties thirteen states adopted civil rights laws of this sort.   In Indiana, however, a study by Emma Lou Thornbrough finds that "In practice the law proved to be ineffectual in accomplishing its state purpose, and racial patterns [of segregation] remained unchanged by its passage."   The same historian goes further to say that "Throughout the North there was not only acquiescence among the white population in the 'Southern Way' of solving the race problem but a tendency to imitate it in practice."

Then, in the year 1898, the United States plunged into imperialistic adventures overseas under the leadership of the Republican party.   These adventures in the Pacific and the Caribbean suddenly brought under the jurisdiction of the United States some eight million people of the colored races, "a varied assortment of inferior races," as the *Nation* described them, "which, of course, could not be allowed to vote."   As America shouldered the White Man's Burden, she took up at the same time many Southern attitudes on the subject of race.   "If the stronger and cleverer race," said the editor of the *Atlantic Monthly*, "is free to impose its will upon 'new-caught, sullen peoples' on the other side of the globe, why not in South Carolina and Mississippi?"   .   .   .

At the dawn of the new century the wave of Southern racism came in as a swell upon a mounting tide of national sentiment and was very much a part of that sentiment.   Had the tide been running the other way, the Southern wave would have broken feebly instead of becoming a wave of the future.

* * *

If the psychologists are correct in their hypothesis that aggression is always the result of frustration, then the South toward the end of the 'nineties was the perfect cultural seedbed for aggression against the minority race.   Economic, political, and social frustrations had pyramided to a climax of social tensions.   No real relief was in sight from the long cyclical depression of the 'nineties, an acute period of suffering that had only intensified the distress of the much longer agricultural depression.   Hopes for reform and the political means employed in defiance of tradition and at great cost to emotional attachments to effect reform had likewise met with cruel disappointments and frustration.   There had to be a scapegoat.   And all along the line signals were going up to indicate that the Negro was an approved object of aggression.   These "permissions-to-hate" came from sources that had formerly denied such permission.   They came from the federal courts in numerous opinions, from Northern liberals eager to conciliate the South, from Southern conservatives who had abandoned their race policy of moderation in their struggle against the Populists, from the Populists in their mood of disillusionment with their former Negro allies, and from a national temper suddenly expressed by imperialistic adventures and aggressions against colored peoples in distant lands.

The resistance of the Negro himself had long ceased to be an important deterrent to white aggression. But a new and popular spokesman of the race, its acknowledged leader by the late 'nineties, came forward with a submissive philosophy for the Negro that to some whites must have appeared an invitation to further aggression. It is quite certain that Booker T. Washington did not intend his so-called "Atlanta Compromise" address of 1895 to constitute such an invitation. But in proposing the virtual retirement of the mass of Negroes from the political life of the South and in stressing the humble and menial role that the race was to play, he would seem unwittingly to have smoothed the path to proscription.

Having served as the national scapegoat in the reconciliation and reunion of North and South, the Negro was now pressed into service as a sectional scapegoat in the reconciliation of estranged white classes and the reunion of the Solid South. The bitter violence and blood-letting recrimination of the campaigns between white conservatives and white radicals in the 'nineties had opened wounds that could not be healed by ordinary political nostrums and free-silver slogans. The only formula powerful enough to accomplish that was the magical formula of white supremacy, applied without stint and without any of the old conservative reservations of paternalism, without deference to any lingering resistance of Northern liberalism, or any fear of further check from a defunct Southern Populism.

The first step in applying the formula was the total disfranchisement of the Negro. In part this was presented as a guarantee that in the future neither of the white factions would violate the white man's peace by rallying the Negro's support against the other. In part disfranchisement was also presented as a progressive reform, the sure means of purging Southern elections of the corruption that disgraced them. The disgrace and public shame of this corruption were more widely and keenly appreciated than the circuitous and paradoxical nature of the proposed reform. To one Virginian, however, it did seem that disfranchising the Negroes "to prevent the Democratic election officials from stealing their votes" would be "to punish the man who has been injured"—a topsy-turvy justice at best. In no mood for paradoxes, Southerners generally accepted Negro disfranchisement as a reform, without taking second thought. . . .

In full flower, Jim Crow Laws mandated the separation of the races in most public places, and went as well to such essentially private matters as marriage and the choice of residences. Professor Woodward's account of the *reductio ad absurdum* in race relations law (*supra* p. 969) gives a sense of the extent to which this law was ultimately developed during the first third of this century. The law became a framework for a rigid code of behavior. The interstices of the law were filled by customs which further relegated "persons of color" to an inferior social status, that of a lower caste. However, the bedrock on which Jim Crow stood consisted of the laws which decreed segregation.

Professor Woodward concludes that the aggression against Blacks was perhaps a product of the economic, political, and social frustrations of Southerners, a people defeated in a bloody war and by events in its aftermath, which included severe economic depression. He notes that the American legal system played a critical role in legitimating that aggression.

This century has also seen law used in another Western society to identify and subjugate a scapegoat population. In Hitler's Germany Jewish people were singled out for segregation and repression in a process which in its early stages at least, bore some similarities to the rise of Jim Crow. The infamous Nurenburg Laws of 1935 were, in a sense, Nazi Germany's version of the Jim Crow laws which had arisen some 40 to 50 years earlier in the United States. Nazi Germany pursued its policy of segregation and repression to an extreme, an ultimate solution, which far exceeded American Jim Crowism. While the American experience involved systematic attempts at spiritual and psychological repression of a people, Germany under Hitler went to the extreme of attempting the physical annihilation of a people. But in both experiences, law was one of the tools used to lift social sanctions against racial and religious/ethnic animosity. In both societies, law and lawyers participated in giving "permission to hate". In both societies, law would also become a means for people to reconstruct and make some amends for horrors perpetrated in the name of law.

SECTION 45.   SEPARATE BUT EQUAL: THE ATTACK ON JIM CROW

Although law and public institutions both supported and enforced racial segregation and discrimination, the libertarian ideals embodied in the United States Constitution, and especially the Fourteenth Amendment, were to provide a basis for the assault on the legality of Jim Crowism. That assault was to be mounted largely in the courts since access to the legal process through litigation was easier and more promising, in the main, than appeals to Congress or to state legislatures.

The use of litigation as a means to achieve social justice for a class of people poses special problems. Individual members of the class may resort to the courts in their own behalf and, if successful, may produce incidental benefits for the whole class. But such random litigation may be slow to produce coherent and consistent principles to establish rights and remedies for the whole class. Moreover, success in litigation may depend on the availability of skilled counsel. Individual members of an outcast class may have difficulty in finding and funding adequate counsel, especially in cases raising fundamental issues as to the legal and social status of the outcast class. These strategic and tactical considerations militate in favor of joint action by members of the class and such other supporters as they can muster. The following materials sketch the role of one such joint action organization, the NAACP, in the attack on Jim Crow.

[The following excerpts are taken from PETER M. BERGMAN (ed.), THE CHRONOLOGICAL HISTORY OF THE NEGRO IN AMERICA (New York, 1969), pp. 357–358.]

In response to the Springfield, Ill. riots which occurred a year before, William Walling, a wealthy Southerner and Socialist settlement worker, author of the article, *Race War in the North;* Mary White Ovington, a Socialist humanitarian who had worked among New York City Negroes, and Dr. Henry Moskowitz, a social worker, met and decided to launch a campaign to help the Negro. Oswald Garrison Villard joined the group and on Feb. 12 wrote their call for a conference: "We call upon all believers in democracy to join in a national conference for the discussion of present evils, the voicing of protests and the renewal of the struggle for civil and political liberty." The group was expanded and made biracial when Lillian Wald, Florence Kelly (founders of the National Women's Trade Union League), Bishop Alexander Walter of the AMEZ Episcopal Methodist Church, and William Henry Brooks of St. Marks Methodist Episcopal Church were invited to join. Between May 31 and June 1, the National Negro Conference met in New York City. . . . In addition to the original group, some other participants in the conference were Jane Addams, William Dean Howells, Livingston Farrand, John Dewey, John Milholland, W. E. B. Du Bois, and Oswald Garrison Villard. The members decided to incorporate as a National Committee for the Advancement of the Negro Race. Before final incorporation, the name was changed to the National Association for the Advancement of Colored People (NAACP). They demanded equal civil, political, and educational rights, an end to segregation, the right to work, the right to protection from violence and intimidation, and criticized the nonenforcement of the 14th and 15th Amendments. A permanent committee of 40 was established to administer the affairs of the organization.

In May, despite factional disputes, a refusal of support from Booker T. Washington, lack of funds, and resignations, the formal organization of the NAACP was completed, primarily through the efforts of Oswald Garrison Villard. Moorfield Storey of Boston was elected president, William English Walling chairman of the executive committee, Francis Blascoer national secretary, Oswald Garrison Villard assistant treasurer, and W. E. B. Du Bois, the only Negro officer, director of publicity and research, and editor of *Crisis*. A national committee of 100 and an executive committee of 30 from its members were planned. The presence of W. E. B. Du Bois on the staff branded the organization as radical from the beginning . . . It was denounced by many white philanthropists, and even some Negroes thought it unwise. In November, Joel Spingarn was elected to the executive committee. His brother Arthur, a lawyer, joined the New York branch when it was organized in January, 1911. The first local branch of the NAACP was established at Chicago. By 1912, nine branches had been established.

The number of branches doubled in the years 1913 and 1914. Oswald Garrison Villard helped cover the expenses of the fledgling organization with rental fees from the New York Evening Post building. Voluntary contributions and membership fees were the principal sources of income. The NAACP's first program advocated the widening of industrial opportunities for Negroes, sought greater police protection for Negroes in the South, and crusaded against lynching and lawlessness. It planned to hire lawyers to contest prejudicial laws.

* * *

Between 1910 and 1954 the NAACP and, later, the NAACP Legal Defense Fund piled up an impressive string of courtroom victories in cases dealing with racial discrimination in such matters as housing, voting and criminal procedure. In addition, the NAACP mounted a strenuous though largely unsuccessful effort to re-establish civil rights legislation at both the state and federal level. A prime example of this was the attempt to secure a federal anti-lynching law. Several anti-lynching bills were introduced in both houses of Congress between 1920 and 1940, and were either killed in committee or succumbed to filibusters in the Senate. These defeats served some purpose, however, in that they publicized the worst aspects of racial discrimination in the United States while at the same time strengthening claims that only judicial or executive action could be effective to secure the civil rights promised in the Civil War Amendments. Moreover, the experience gained in lobbying for these bills was to prove valuable in subsequent campaigns for civil rights legislation.

On another front, the NAACP was instrumental in securing executive action against racial discrimination. Notable successes here were President Roosevelt's decision in Executive Order 8802 (1941) to forbid employment discrimination in government and defense industries; President Truman's Executive Order 9808 (1946) establishing a Presidential Commission on Civil Rights, which then investigated racial discrimination in the United States and made sweeping recommendations for Federal action against discrimination in its famous report "To Secure These Rights" (1947); President Truman's Executive Order 9981 (1948) barring racial segregation in the Armed Forces. The courts, however, were to provide the NAACP with its largest gains in the assault on Jim Crow.

[The following is taken from LOREN MILLER, THE PETITIONERS (New York, 1966), pp. 259–262.]*

* Member of the bar, California and Kansas; Municipal Court Judge, Los Angeles, California. Judge Miller has been active in the Civil Rights movement throughout his distinguished career. He has been an officer of both the Urban League and the NAACP.

The decision of the NAACP to utilize the courts as the major weapon in its intensified campaign for equality was not a whimsical one. The program was national in scope and purpose, and Congress was so thoroughly dominated by southern Democrats through the seniority system for committee chairmanships in both houses and the filibuster privilege in the Senate that there was no hope for passage of civil rights legislation. A Democratic chief executive could, or would, undertake only a minimum of racial reforms, in light of the political necessity of keeping southern Democrats pacified and willing participants in the delicately balanced South-Labor-Negro political alliance upon which his power rested. Republican Presidents were so beguiled with the hope of breaking the Solid South that they, too, were unwilling to favor the Negro's demands. There was practically no place to turn except to the courts.

Beyond the practical considerations lay the fact that the Negroes had never abandoned the belief that the Civil War Amendments had made them free men and that all that was needed to restore that freedom was Supreme Court enforcement of those amendments according to their original intent and purpose. Reconstruction was fancifully remembered as a Golden Age, and the constitutional problem was assayed as that of inducing the Supreme Court to recant the errors that had led to the undoing of Reconstruction and into which it had been led by evil men. The Great Dream was that the Court by a process of interpretation could restore the Thirteenth, Fourteenth, and Fifteenth Amendments to their pristine glory and thus strike off the shackles of second-class citizenship.

Parenthetically, it is well to observe here that the NAACP did not abandon its work at state and local levels, or its nonlegal tasks. Increased political power in northern and western cities and states meant that Negro councilmen and legislators, representing ghetto constituencies, joined by liberal and labor counterparts, pressed for and secured reforms in ordinances and statutes. In southern states, where there was little chance for more than amelioration of the worst aspects of the Jim Crow system, the NAACP kept up a drum fire of equalitarian propaganda, as it did in the areas of the North and West where legal change was impossible.

Inextricably interwoven with the belief and hope that the Supreme Court could restore the Civil War Amendments to their meaning and efficacy was the knowledge that, for better or worse, the Negro was the ward of the Court and that the prospect for immediate relief lay in inducing it to grant relief from the more onerous restrictions it had laid on his exercise of constitutional rights. There was the additional fact that the Court was under heavy attack by liberals and labor leaders, both professing friendship with the Negro's aspirations. The Court was being derided as a collection of nine old men, most of whom were out of step with their times. The NAACP calculation was that the Court was on the eve of change in both personnel and attitude on social issues. Negro leaders hoped that during the process of that change they could press their own case and secure some of the changes they desired.

Another circumstance of inestimable importance was the rise of a corps of talented and resourceful young Negro lawyers, social scientists, and educators—all chafing under racial discrimination and ready to contribute their learning and skill to an assault on the restrictions that hemmed them in. When Margold left the NAACP in 1933 to take a government post, he was replaced by Charles H. Houston, Harvard-trained, second-generation Negro lawyer, a man of vast creative skill and ability. He expanded and improved Margold's original blueprint for legal action and recruited Negro lawyers from all over the nation to assist in the assault on segregationist bastions. As Dean of the Howard University Law School, he turned that law school into a laboratory for civil rights which trained new classes of militant Negro lawyers. Working closely with him was the erudite William H. Hastie, his cousin, as militant as he was learned in the ways of the law.

One of the Howard Law School trainees was Thurgood Marshall, who ultimately replaced Houston as the NAACP's special counsel and head of its legal program. A bluff and brilliant trial lawyer, he was to translate the "impractical" theories of intellectual lawyers and social scientists into effective courtroom tactics. He expanded the NAACP legal committee to take in more and more gifted lawyers and established liaison with law school professors throughout the nation who were willing to help with research into intricate constitutional problems.

A new day dawned, in which southern attorneys general and lawyer-spokesmen for segregationists everywhere found themselves matched against opponents of superb legal skill and determination. Their names would become bywords in constitutional law, and their pleadings would be accorded great judicial respect. In time, these Negro lawyers and social scientists would become judges, diplomats, college and university presidents, legislators, and men high in the echelons of government.

Changes in legal and constitutional interpretations are not wrought by skilled advocacy alone, nor solely through depth of preparation or new insights into problems. These are but the tools without which opportunity may be lost or frittered away. Without them, little is possible; even with them, little may be gained. There are other factors. Judicial interpretations change as the social climate changes. Vast changes, far beyond the ability of any man to foresee in 1930, were to sweep over the United States, and the world, in the area of race relations, in the swift-moving decades after 1930. Old ideas perished, and new and revolutionary concepts replaced them. An appreciable part of the genius of the NAACP lawyers lay in their acute perception of the depth and direction of these changes, and their ability to take them at their flood and translate them into constitutional concepts palatable to Supreme Court justices, who were at once propelled in new directions by social change and architects of that change. NAACP lawyers could not have won the constitutional victories that lay ahead of them without their technical and legal skills, even in the context of the changing climate of the times. But with the greatest of skill and preparation, they could not have prevailed in an unchanged climate or in a closed society.

The NAACP was not always able to follow its legal blueprint. There were setbacks and defeats. Sometimes events moved too fast, sometimes too slowly. On other occasions, aggressive segregationists acted before the NAACP was ready for the fray. There was an ebb and flow in the generally favorable climate of public opinion that required adjustment and readjustment. But it is hard to overestimate the tactical advantage that lay in the fact that, beginning in the 1930's, Negroes were on the offensive, whereas they had been on the defensive prior to that time. Their lawyers could and did exploit every advantage that lies with having the intiative.

It is against this background that we must examine the story of the Negro and the Supreme Court of the United States as it unfolded after the early 1930's.

Two primary targets were picked for the well-planned campaign of anti-Jim Crow litigation which commenced in the mid-thirties. One target was segregated public education; the other was discrimination in housing secured through racial restrictive covenants in which white property owners entered mutual agreements not to sell or lease real property to Blacks. Through such agreements, which had been held to be enforceable in Corrigan v. Buckley, 271 U.S. 323, 46 S.Ct. 521 (1926), private persons could achieve the same results that had been denied to local governments in Buchanan v. Worley, supra, p. 62.

[The following is taken from CLEMENT E. VOSE,* "N.A.A.C.P. STRATEGY IN THE COVENANT CASES," 6 Western Reserve Law Review 101 (1955). Some footnotes omitted; others are renumbered.]

The NAACP has won more victories in the Supreme Court than any other single organization. From 1915 to January, 1948, when the *Restrictive Covenant Cases* were argued, 23 of 25 sponsored cases were won by the Association. In the face of failures to gain concessions from Congress, due in large part to the power wielded by the Southern delegation, particularly in the Senate, Negroes turned to the judiciary. Furthermore, many of the problems faced by Negroes were appropriate to settlement in the courts.

* * *

In spite of the plain fact of NAACP activity in litigation before the Supreme Court in terms of money spent, legal talent applied, and results gained, it has no credit lines in the official Court reports. Nor have legal historians or commentators given recognition to the role of the NAACP in forging recent constitutional development. An explanation of this neglect may be the presupposition of the American legal system that society is composed of free individuals and that cases reach the Supreme Court through individual actions alone. Court reports do not show the presence of groups even where an organization like the NAACP sponsors and manages the appeal and pays the expenses involved. The pressure of interest groups on the courts is thus ignored.

* * *

The 1945 Chicago Conference

The crop of restrictive covenant cases sprouting over the country in 1944 and 1945 was tended by Negro lawyers in their own areas. But the situation was regarded as a national problem and the National Association for the Advancement of Colored People called a conference to consider the

* John E. Andrus Professor of Political Science, Wesleyan University.

difficulties which might be solved by mutual legal work. Thirty-three persons attended meetings in Chicago on July 9 and 10, 1945. . . .

* * *

From long hours of discussion emerged a clear-cut blue-print for attacking racial restrictive covenants. Every conceivable opportunity of attack was suggested and the advantages of aggressiveness in and out of the courtroom were pointed out. There were comments on the trials, which cases to select for appeal, what issues to raise, how to win in the Supreme Court, and how to exploit public opinion to advantage. . . .

A successful test in the Supreme Court of the United States was what everyone was hoping for. Working for this involved a number of considerations. There are many unforeseeable factors in the passage of a case through the judicial process to the Supreme Court, but one—the decision on what case to carry up—was in the hands of these lawyers. However, there was disagreement among them. Loring Moore believed that the test case should come from a big city in the north like Los Angeles, Detroit or his own Chicago. The public policy of northern states was officially against segregation, while that of the South supported segregation. Believing that "the Supreme Court decision may turn on whether it will sustain a state policy," Moore reasoned that they should "get a case where public policy is favorable." It should come from a section where there has been "some tradition of freedom." He had worked to break a restrictive covenant in Kentucky, but declared: "I would not think of that case being appealed to the U.S. Supreme Court."

Echoing this argument, Irving Mollison raised special objections to appealing cases from Washington, D. C. He recalled that in the recently decided *Mays* case the Circuit Court there had "referred to the rules of law upholding restrictive covenants in the District as almost rules of real property law." The Court did not wish to unsettle affairs in the Capital where large amounts of real estate had been acquired in faith and reliance on the old rule. This led Mollison to the conviction that cases for an ultimate test should be selected from outside the District of Columbia. Here he added a seldom revealed thought on the full nature of the problem.

> . . . As a practical matter, considering some of the things about judges, is it desirable that we have applications for certiorari so immediately close to the home and the real estate investments of the judges of the Supreme Court? I don't believe they can properly separate themselves from their expensive homes and the terrain. We should select cases with greater care and take only a very excellent case up. But future applications should come from a state which on the face of it, by its law and constitution, has at least some outward expression against racial discrimination.

Leaders of the NAACP like William Hastie and Thurgood Marshall disagreed with this viewpoint. Hastie emphasized that restrictive covenants must be broken everywhere in the nation. But he said, "The Supreme Court will not forget that a decision from Illinois will affect Georgia and Mississippi." Thurgood Marshall also cautioned against "putting too much stress on the public policy angle alone." Eighty percent of the Negro people live in states where public policy is against them respecting segregation. The loss of a case on this basis in a northern state like Illinois "immediately becomes a precedent for enforcement in every other state."

Non-lawyers present were greatly interested in applying [Charles] Houston's idea of using the courts as educational forums for moulding national opinion. Homer Jack, a Unitarian minister from Evanston, Illinois, representing two organizations, the Chicago Council Against Discrimination and the American Civil Liberties Union, argued for a publicity campaign.

> . . . in the line of public relations it would be awfully important to ballyhoo a case similar to the Scottsboro Case and get the rank and file of NAACP and other organizations to highlight and understand the process of carrying it out and even though it is lost and there is a terrible let down, it would be terrifically educational and you should get public opinion on it. Even if it is an artificial case, it would be important to spend a good deal of money to build a case and try to decide it on constitutional issues. . . .

At the conclusion of this two day conference in 1945 Thurgood Marshall announced that the national office of the NAACP would devote special attention to the problem of restrictive covenants. He promised a campaign of publicity against "the evils of segregation and racial restrictive covenants." Marshall would recommend that the Association maintain a full-time staff member on housing. Most important of all, he said, would be keeping in touch. Frequent conferences like the present one were important, he declared, and more were promised.

The Sociology of Law

Before Negroes could effectively register their claims against the validity of racial restrictive covenants they had to await the development of favorable social and economic theories. They could know, however, that once new data was available and widely known it could serve as a persuasive factor in reshaping the judicial mind. The growing political power of Negroes and their increasing effectiveness in pressure politics had to be supported by facts and theories. The interpretation of the Negroes' position in American society by sociologists after 1920 placed the race problem in an environmental setting and proved to be potent assistance in the struggle toward a higher status for colored people.[1]

* * *

At the time restrictive covenants were first applied in the United States, dominant social theory favored the segregation of the races.[2] It was commonly thought that the white race, whether termed "Nordic," "Caucasian," "Teutonic," or "Aryan," was superior and that it should protect itself from the corrupting influence of darker people. Social Darwinism, the interpretation of society in terms of the survival of the fittest, was in vogue.[3] The

1. For a history of these cases see NAACP Legal Defense and Educational Fund, Inc., Equal Justice Under Law. The two lost cases were Corrigan v. Buckley, 271 U.S. 323, 46 S.Ct. 521 (1926) a racial restrictive covenant case, and Lyons v. Oklahoma, 322 U.S. 596, 64 S.Ct. 1208 (1944) a confession and torture case.

2. For an extended analysis of the political theory of race supremacy in the United States, see David Spitz, Patterns of Anti-Democratic Thought 137 (1949).

3. An historical treatment of Darwinian influence on theories of racial superiority in the United States, particularly in reference to justifications of imperialism, may be found in Richard Hofstadter, Social Darwinism in American Thought, 1860–1915 (1945) pp. 146–73.

notion that Caucasians were in a position of power because of biological superiority was held not only by Southern intellectuals like Charles Wallace
Collins, but was widely believed in the North, as well. The literature of sociology was dominated by the view that Negroes were inferior to the white
race in every way.[4] This position of scholars both reflected and reinforced
popular beliefs.[5] Thus a study of public attitudes toward Negroes in 1923
showed that the mental capacity of Negroes was ranked far below that of
whites. This was related to the notion that Negroes were predisposed to a
life of crime, immorality, and emotional instability. The existence of this
image in the popular mind was closely associated with justifications of segregation. The most important defense of the white race was established
through state miscegenation laws which made it a crime for white and colored persons to marry. Residential segregation was the next most important
means of maintaining racial purity. Thus the restrictive covenant can be
viewed as a method of enforcing a social theory.

* * *

[Professor Vose discusses sociological research on race relations
conducted between 1910 and 1930, and also the findings of the Chicago Commission on Race Relations, which studied conditions leading
to the Chicago race riots of 1919. According to Vose the Commission found that the depressed state of Negro life in American cities
was the result of racial discrimination in housing and employment.
This tended to discredit Social Darwinism and biological theories of
race relations. In Professor Vose's opinion, sociological research
"confirmed the findings of the Chicago Commission on Race Relations
and (after 1930) placed the main weight of the Sociology profession
on the side of a sympathetic environmental explanation of the urban
Negro's position."]

* * *

New Legal Theory

In March, 1945 the *California Law Review* featured an article with the
assertive title, "Racial Residential Segregation by State Court Enforcement of Restrictive Agreements, Covenants or Conditions in Deeds is Unconstitutional." This conclusion was reached by the author, Professor D. O.
McGovney of the California Law School, through two steps in reasoning.
First, he argued that state enforcement of restrictive covenants is state
action under the Fourteenth Amendment and, second, that this is forbidden
because it denies Negroes the equal protection of the laws.

McGovney's approach gave the Negroes a new theory with which to
blast the constitutional logjam built up behind the Supreme Court's decision
in Corrigan v. Buckley. There a racial restrictive agreement was found to
be perfectly proper because the Constitution did not prohibit "private in-

4. E. B. Reuter, Racial Theory, 50 Am.
    J. of Soc. 452 (1945).

5. The Chicago Commission on Race
    Relations, The Negro in Chicago; A

Study of Race Relations and a Race
Riot 445 (1922). The background of
prevailing popular beliefs concerning
Negroes is presented.

dividuals from entering into contracts respecting the control and disposition of their own property." Now, taking a new sight on the problem, McGovney agreed that individuals can make such a contract but stressed that the enforcement of a restriction brought the state into the picture. This amounted to state action. The situation did not parallel the problem of the *Civil Rights Cases* which held that private action unaided and unsupported by the state government could not be limited by federal statutes enacted under the authority of the Fourteenth Amendment.

Professor McGovney carefully distinguished between the private action of making a restrictive covenant and the state action of enforcing one.

> The discriminatory agreements, conditions or covenants in deeds that exclude Negroes or other racial minorities from buying or occupying residential property so long as they remain purely private agreements are not unconstitutional. So long as they are voluntarily observed by the covenanters or the restricted grantees no action forbidden by the Constitution has occurred. But when the aid of the state is invoked to compel observance and the state acts to enforce observance, the state takes forbidden action. The deed to the colored buyer cannot be cancelled by purely private action. The Negro cannot be ousted from occupancy by purely private action. When a state court cancels the deed or ousts the occupant, the state through one of its organs is aiding, abetting, enforcing the discrimination.

The claim that the enforcement of restrictive covenants was a violation of the Equal Protection Clause was based on a broad view of the line of cases beginning with Buchanan v. Warley, which had disapproved of the enforcement of racial segregation by city ordinance or state legislation. The result in segregation was reached through either method, the legislative or the judicial. If a statute or ordinance enforcing segregation was unconstitutional, enforcement by a court was also.

* * *

As Charles Evans Hughes once said, "in confronting any serious problems, a wide-awake and careful judge will at once look to see if the subject has been discussed, or the authorities collated and analyzed, in a good law periodical." The Supreme Court of the United States has often followed the law reviews. In 1943, the Court reversed its 1940 position on the Jehovah's Witness flag salute problem. The first decision was the subject of sharp legal criticism which was marshalled by Professor Zechariah Chafee, Jr. of the Harvard Law School and brought to the Supreme Court's attention through an *amicus curiae* brief filed for the Committee on the Bill of Rights of the American Bar Association in the second case. Justice Jackson referred to these law review articles in his opinion. Earlier, in 1938, when the Supreme Court changed its position on the question of taxing the income of a federal judge, Justice Frankfurter took into account the fact that the first decision "met wide and steadily growing disfavor from legal scholarship and professional opinion."

Viewed against these results the legal criticisms after 1945 of the judicial enforcement of racial restrictive covenants had an importance beyond the edification of the bar. Favoring the Negro position as they did, these law review articles could be expected to carry some weight with judges, when brought to their attention.

* * *

Potential Test Cases

During 1945 and 1946 numerous restrictive covenant cases were developing throughout the country. Negroes lost them all and yet thereby came closer to an ultimate test of the constitutionality of judicial enforcement in the United States Supreme Court. On January 26, 1947, Negro leaders met for the third time, now at Howard University in Washington, to evaluate their progress in ending the power of racial restrictions in housing. Because the Supreme Court had refused certiorari in Mays v. Burgess [6] only two years before, William Hastie agreed with Thurgood Marshall that if another failure was to be avoided, "the next record on which we apply for certiorari would have to contain something substantially stronger." All eighteen persons present subscribed to the sensible plan of seeking the best possible case in which to apply for a writ of certiorari.

Loring Moore, active as a leader of the National Bar Association, an organization of Negro lawyers, told the conference of the basic components of a case he was working on in Chicago. From this he presented an analysis of the ideal record to build for presentation to the United States Supreme Court.

(1) Testimony of an economist on the effects of covenants upon availability of housing;

(2) Testimony of a sociologist as to the effect of overcrowded slum conditions and black ghettos upon both the victim of discrimination and their fellow citizens;

(3) Introduction of a map of racial occupancy in the community;

(4) Superimposed upon (the map) . . . a map of the restrictive covenants indicating the extensiveness of the restrictions;

(5) Thereafter, further testimony by a sociologist as to the effect of the type of restriction proved by the two maps upon housing conditions;

(6) Evidence as to the effect that thirty or more other restrictive covenant cases are pending in the community to show that the effect of enforcement would be extensive private zoning in the areas.

Actually, Moore's ideal was a mustering of the standard approaches used by Negro lawyers in a number of contemporary cases. The trial record was important, and appeals to higher state courts or intermediate federal courts were planned with care. Nevertheless, failures in these tribunals did not necessarily prejudice Negro chances in the United States Supreme Court. Consequently, NAACP leaders bore in mind the ultimate goal of obtaining a decision on the broad constitutional question from the Supreme Court. When the Howard University conference was held in

<hr/>

6. 147 F.2d 869 (1945), cert. denied 325 U.S. 868, 65 S.Ct. 1406 (1945).

January, 1947, in addition to the Chicago litigation, cases in six cities showed promise of serving as constitutional tests.

* * *

[Four of these cases were Shelley v. Kraemer, Sipes v. McGhee, Hurd v. Hodge, and Urciolo v. Hodge. Their facts are summarized in the opinion in Shelley v. Kraemer, infra p. 991, and the note which follows that case, infra p. 996.]

Before another meeting of NAACP lawyers was held the St. Louis attorney, George Vaughn, took unilateral action by filing a petition for certiorari with the Supreme Court of the United States in Shelley v. Kraemer, on April 21, 1947. This provoked NAACP leaders in New York into taking hasty action and so on May 10 a petition was also filed for the *Mc-Ghee* case. On the last Monday of the term, the Supreme Court agreed to consider these two cases by granting writs of certiorari to the supreme courts of Missouri and Michigan. Charles Houston's Washington cases were not decided by the Circuit Court until May 26 and he did not file petitions for certiorari with the Supreme Court until August. On October 20th, early in the new term, certiorari was granted in the cases of Hurd v. Hodge and Urciolo v. Hodge. Following common practice the Court ordered that these federal cases be consolidated with the two state cases for its consideration. Briefs were to be filed before December 1 and oral arguments in the four cases were set for January 16 and 17, 1948. . . .

NAACP and the Trial Lawyers

Consolidation of the four restrictive covenant cases by the Supreme Court meant that there would have to be some coordination in brief writing and oral argument by the Negro attorneys in the different cases if final success was to be gained. In fact a cooperative spirit was established and maintained even though the NAACP had somewhat different relations with the lawyers in charge of the four cases. The national office entered the Michigan case as *amicus curiae* at the state supreme court level. The two Detroit lawyers, Graves and Dent, were willing to allow the national office of the NAACP to prepare the brief in the United States Supreme Court. Their names appeared on the briefs but Thurgood Marshall and his associates in New York prepared the case.

Shelley v. Kraemer was not an NAACP case in the strict sense and rapport between the national office and the trial lawyer, George Vaughn, was never good. Diplomatic relations were carried on but cordiality was lacking. . . .

In the Washington cases there was instinctive cooperation between Charles Houston and his local helpers and the national office of the NAACP. Houston was a close friend of Thurgood Marshall and they moved in the same direction at about the same pace without antagonism. In Washington, furthermore, there was a group of interested people who cooperated closely with Houston in getting the Hodge case to the Supreme Court. One was Phineas Indritz, an attorney who worked in the Office of the Solicitor of the Department of the Interior. He sought the help of Charles Abrams of New York, recognized expert in the field of housing and a leader in the attack on segregated housing in the New York area.

Inviting Abrams to a meeting in Washington, Indritz wrote, on July 23, that a group of District of Columbia lawyers, economists, sociologists and race relations experts, cooperating with Charles Houston "think it would be most helpful to the Supreme Court if a comprehensive study of the prevalence and effect of private zoning through operation of the restrictive covenants . . . could be presented to the Supreme Court at the time of the argument." If this could be completed, perhaps the study could be published by the Russell Sage Foundation.

Indritz reported progress when he wrote again on August 14:

> During the past two days, working past midnight, Houston (Spottswood) Robinson and I have whipped into shape and sent to the printer petitions for writs of certiorari and brief for submission to the Supreme Court of the United States in the cases of Hurd and Urciolo v. Hodge. We expect to file them next week. . . . We shall begin preparing the briefs on the merits, on the assumption that the writs of certiorari will be granted.

Indritz stressed the need to support the attack in the Supreme Court with a "full sociological presentation." And he hoped that Robert Weaver, who had already published studies on the effects of racial restrictive covenants, and others who were expert in the field would help.

> . . . Houston and I feel that the brief should be accompanied by a separate appendix reprinting all the major articles, or excerpts, dealing with the effects of these covenants. Although the Justices might have the library send to them the articles and books to which we make reference, there would be greater likelihood of their reading the references if we place such a compilation before them.

Flooding the Law Reviews

If the Negroes were to win the restrictive covenant cases they had carried to the Supreme Court in the 1947 Term they would have to rely heavily on non-judicial material. The precedents favored the Caucasians overwhelmingly. To offset this advantage the Negroes would try to persuade the Court that judicial enforcement of covenants was state action which violated the Fourteenth Amendment, as Professor McGovney had suggested. They would also point to the social results of the practice of enforcement. But reasoning by itself is not enough, nor are raw statistics considered to be sufficient for presentation in legal briefs. Citations of articles and books where the facts and ideas had been published would surely make a better appeal to the learned justices. At least this was the theory of the lawyers involved in these cases. In order to meet this and other problems, Thurgood Marshall sent out a call for another NAACP conference for the fall of 1947.

* * *

The first round of discussion at the conference centered upon the twin problem of preparing sociological material and getting it published so that it could be used in briefs to be presented to the Supreme Court. Phineas Indritz suggested that the maps he had might be copyrighted, although he felt it "would be much better if they were published by a reputable magazine." Charles Houston urged that "evidence and data which is not already in the record should be published and put in some acceptable form." Marian Wynn Perry of the New York office of the NAACP commented: "Among the organizations here represented there must be a great many publications. We should get our joint public relations committees together and tell them that we want it published in the best kind of space available in the October issues." This was agreed to by Harold Kahen of Chicago, who had published an article against the validity of the judicial enforcement of covenants in 1945. He believed that "the sociologists should gather the material and get it published in some journals and then supply it to a group of lawyers."

The NAACP had already published some material. It had sponsored a pamphlet, *Race Bias in Housing* by Charles Abrams, together with the American Council on Race Relations and the American Civil Liberties Union. Abrams had also attacked covenants in the monthly magazine, *Commentary*, published by the American Jewish Committee. These blasts served the purpose of bringing the evils of racial restrictive covenants to the attention of the public. However, the object of future publication would be to gain new sources which might be cited in the briefs to be filed with the Supreme Court.

So much independent work had been done in assembling sociological material that the leaders of the movement to end restrictive covenants hoped to coordinate work by appointing a committee to handle the problem. Dr. Louis Wirth of the University of Chicago, who was not present at the meeting, was made chairman. Others agreeing to serve on the committee were Loring Moore, Robert Ming, Harold Kahen, Bryon Miller and Dr. Robert Weaver, all of Chicago, Ruth Weyand of Washington, James T. Bush of St. Louis, and Annette Peyser of New York.

Soon a great flood of writing condemning the existence and application of racial restrictions in housing flowed from the presses of the nation. Numerous case notes and comments appeared. Full-length articles turned up in *The Annals, Yale Law Journal, University of Chicago Law Review, National Bar Journal, Architectural Forum, National Lawyers Guild Review, Journal of Land and Public Utility Economics*, and *Survey Graphic*. Two books on the subject were also published: *The Negro Ghetto* by Dr. Robert Weaver and *People vs. Property: Race Restrictive Covenants in Housing* by Herman H. Long and Charles S. Johnson of Fisk University. Quite clearly the writing public was aroused; the NAACP could tell the Supreme Court.

NAACP's "Friends of the Court"

With plans made to prepare sociological data for use in the briefs, the NAACP conference of September 6, 1947, turned to the question of *amici curiae* briefs. Charles Houston took a poll of the organizational representatives in attendance and found that fourteen planned to file briefs as friends of the court. These were: the American Jewish Congress, American Jewish Committee, Protestant Council of New York City, Japanese American Citizens' League, National Bar Association, Anti-Defamation League, American Civil Liberties Union, Negro Elks, Congress of Industrial Organizations (CIO), Anti-Nazi League, Board of Home Missions of the Congregational Church, National Lawyers Guild, American Indian Association and the American Indian Council.

* * *

Although the minutes of the New York meeting show that consensus was reached on limiting the number of briefs and coordinating their content, little was done afterwards to insure this. As counsel for the parties, the NAACP lawyers had to give consent for the filing of each *amicus curiae* brief but no thought was given to formally restricting misguided friends who wanted to help. The lawyers for the white property owners likewise had to give permission to all friends of the court; they did so willingly.

The NAACP did not wish to alienate any of the groups so eager to provide assistance but some gentle hints were made to gain limited coordination. Thus when Thurgood Marshall granted consent to file a brief *amicus curiae* to William Strong of the American Indian Citizens League of California he included these suggestions:

> . . . I believe that it would be very helpful if you would check with Mr. Loren Miller, of your city, (Los Angeles) who will join in arguing this case before the Supreme Court, so that you will be familiar with the points raised and the general discussion which has occurred among the attorneys for various organizations interested in filing briefs *amicus*. We are particularly anxious, in securing the cooperation of attorneys for organizations who are interested in filing briefs *amicus*, to eliminate as much as possible the repetition of arguments which are fully presented in other briefs. This does not mean, of course, that we do not want briefs filed but rather that we are hoping that each brief can present a new angle of the case.

So far as is known the NAACP took no other measures to see that the *amici curiae* briefs favoring them were worked up together. Thurgood Marshall and his staff were fully occupied with the preparation of the main brief in the *McGhee* case. Eventually a total of nineteen briefs were filed by friends of the court which argued for the Negro position but except for the fact that those interested could draw from the same published sources and could correspond among themselves for information and ideas these briefs were not coordinated.

* * *

Some broad problems of what should be said in a brief and who should say it are illuminated by the experiences of the New York housing consultant, Charles Abrams, in connection with the *amicus curiae* briefs filed in the covenant cases by two organizations. The American Civil Liberties Union had entered numerous Supreme Court cases and therefore had the experience and know-how to write its own brief, but sought Abrams' advice and asked him to sign it. In the meantime, Newman Levy of the American Jewish Committee sought Abrams' comments on the brief Levy was writing for that organization. In November, 1947 Abrams responded with a letter setting forth his ideas on the proper function of the *amicus curiae* brief.

> I have just completed reading your brief. I just couldn't reach it earlier, and hope it isn't too late for suggestions.
>
> It is an excellent "main brief" written with your fine straight style. But I question the adequacy of its emphasis as a brief *amici*.

I have always viewed the function of the *amici* to take up and emphasize those points which are novel or which, if stressed in the main brief, might dilute or weaken the main forceful arguments.

I never thought there was much cumulative force in the repetition of logic by eighteen briefs. Unlike good poetry, repeated it has a tendency to bore. But a weak legal argument, with a moral quality, forcefully presented by an "outsider" will not detract from the force of the main argument. If it creates a healthy doubt or insinuates even a slight justification for itself on moral grounds, it may bend the judge toward adopting the law advocated in the main brief.

Novel arguments in a brief *amici* may serve another purpose. Sometimes the court is ready to adopt the arguments of the main brief. In our case for example it may entail upsetting Corrigan v. Buckley. Or it might be loath to annul a contract between private parties or impinge upon the states' rights doctrine.

The *amici* should be providing the arguments that will salvage the judges' consciences or square with their prepossessions should they lean toward holding for us.

The TVA decision (Ashwander v. Tennessee Valley Authority) is a case in point. Upholding TVA as an exercise of the War Power is about as reasonable an analogy as the Laws of Mohammed are to our law of Domestic Relations. But the Court did not then wish to expand the welfare power so drew upon the war power, which surprised everybody.

In conclusion, Abrams suggested that sociological arguments were useful for furnishing the moral background for a judicial holding.

. . . play up what entailment of all land would mean socially. Use the relevant references by Gunnar Myrdal; give the British background for exclusion of non-conformists and their migration to America where the freehold and the fee simple became one of our earliest and greatest traditions. Show how Jefferson and the States immediately after Independence adopted laws excluding primogeniture and entail. Quote from these constitutions and the debates that prompted their enactment. What if covenants in Washington, D. C., become as common as in Chicago and Los Angeles? Will that not bar Negroes, Jews or other Americans from holding office? May people band together to bar a race from food and clothing? These are a few of the important irrelevancies that occur to me.*

---

* Editors' Note:

Entailment of land and primogeniture were devices in the English law of real property which were used to maintain ownership of land in a family over many generations. Dynastic control of real property was rejected in the United States—hence the reference to Jefferson and to state laws barring entails and primogeniture. Dynastic control of land was also sharply curtailed in England in a series of steps culminating in 19th and early 20th Century legislation.

Judges trained in the Anglo-American law of real property would be fully aware of this history, and probably convinced of the soundness of policies which fostered the free transferability of land. Mr. Abrams' suggestion of these historical analogies probably reflects his view that American judges could be moved to strike down racial covenants because of their impact on the marketability of property. See in this regard the note on Buchanan v. Worley, supra p. 62.

Why desert all these rich and adventurous passages to jam the safe waters that should be reserved for the main advocates?

There can be little quarrel with these sentiments as an expression of the ideal *amicus curiae* brief, but the various organizations had their own interests at heart, and these did not necessarily coincide with Abrams' ideal. Newman Levy explained this problem in an answer to Abrams.

I enjoyed your letter and I wish that time permitted me to adopt your suggestions. As you know the briefs have to be filed before Dec. 1 so I have to send mine to the printer next week.

I thoroughly agree with everything that you say about the function of an *amicus* brief. So far as the court is concerned I am inclined to think that it is pretty much like an endorsement on a note. Its purpose is to tell the court that we agree with the appellant and we hope that it will decide in his favor. I got a note from Proskauer (Joseph Proskauer of the American Jewish Committee) last summer when I first started the brief, in which he said that *amicus* briefs aren't worth a damn because courts don't read them anyway.

There is another function in the present case which perhaps I shouldn't discuss, and which, in fact, I hope you won't repeat. I mean that horrible thing called "public relations." Many of these briefs, I regret to say, are being filed as a sort of organizational propaganda. Although I worked hard on mine it is quite possible that the decision would be the same even if I didn't file it. In the Vashti McCollum case involving released time in the schools, we recently submitted a combined brief, and the American Jewish Congress has ordered 1500 copies to distribute to its admirers around the country. . .

When this brief was first contemplated I discussed it with my legal committee, and they agreed that I should confine myself exclusively to the constitutional question. That was why I omitted the sociological stuff, the United Nations Charter and the rest of it. You see, if the Supreme Court should happen to mention in its decision that restrictive covenants are illegal upon the authority of Buchanan v. Warley, we all will be able to say to our members, "Isn't that exactly what we told the Court?"

Even though the brief was not changed, Abrams consented to having his name appear on the brief.

The Department of Justice as Amicus Curiae

The winter of 1947–1948 appeared to be a propitious one in official Washington for Negroes hoping to see the enforcement of restrictive covenants ended. The Report of President Truman's Committee on Civil

Gunnar Myrdal is an eminent economist-sociologist, and Nobel laureate. A Swedish national and University Professor, Myrdal devoted an extended period of his professional life to the study of race relations in America. In 1945 he published his first great study of that subject, An American Dilemma. Myrdal's findings regarding the corrosive impact of racial discrimination on the social fabric of this country were extensively cited in post-World War II attacks on Jim Crow. His work, along with that of other sociologists, was cited by the Supreme Court to support the view that racial segregation in the public schools was deleterious to Negro children and inherently unequal treatment of them. See e. g., note 7, infra, p. 1005.

Rights appeared in October and the President's sweeping, and controversial civil rights program, so favorable to Negroes, was sent to Congress in February. The Committee had been created at the suggestion of Walter White, Secretary of the NAACP, and others who called on President Truman at the White House in the fall of 1946. Composed of fifteen civic, business, educational and religious leaders, the Committee's chairman was Charles E. Wilson of General Electric and its executive secretary was Professor Robert K. Carr of Dartmouth College. At its meetings during 1947, the Committee heard some forty witnesses and also had correspondence with "nearly 250 private organizations and individuals." The findings and recommendations were highly pleasing to the NAACP.

The Report of the President's Committee on Civil Rights, entitled *To Secure These Rights,* condemned the use of racial restrictive covenants in no uncertain terms and recommended the following action in order to strengthen the right to equality of opportunity:

> The enactment by the states of laws outlawing restrictive covenants;

> Renewed court attack, with intervention by the Department of Justice, upon restrictive covenants.

> The effectiveness of restrictive covenants depends in the last analysis on court orders enforcing the private agreement. The power of the state is thus utilized to bolster discriminatory practices. The Committee believes that every effort must be made to prevent this abuse. We would hold this belief under any circumstances; under present conditions, when severe housing shortages are already causing hardship for many people of the country, we are especially emphatic in recommending measures to alleviate the situation.

This was a small part of the complete report, but the prestige of the Committee which made the recommendation was great, and anything it said was important.

The position of the President's Committee in opposing the enforcement of racial restrictive covenants was anticipated at the September, 1947, meeting of NAACP lawyers and consultants in New York and thought was given to exploiting this fact. Phineas Indritz, the Interior Department lawyer, suggested that if the Judiciary Branch of the Government was to be persuaded to end the effectiveness of covenants an effort should be made to win the support of the Executive Branch. . . .

The Department of Justice functions as the law office of the United States Government and consequently is charged with enforcing the laws of the United States. Within the Department the Solicitor General's office conducts Government litigation in the Supreme Court. Ordinarily this involves legislation enacted by Congress and administrative action by a Government agency. The Solicitor General during most of President Truman's administration, Philip Perlman, . . . has recently recalled how the decision of the Department of Justice to file a brief *amicus curiae,* on the side of the Negroes, was reached:

> The decision was reached during informal conferences which I had with Attorney General Tom C. Clark at the time and was announced by him during the course of a press conference. There were a number of

letters filed with the Attorney General and also with me by different religious, racial, welfare and civil rights organizations, urging the Government to enter the litigation. I believe it was the first time that the Department of Justice had filed a brief in litigation of this character to which it was not a party. It was also decided, in addition to the filing of a brief, that I should ask the Court for leave to present an oral argument, so that in that case the Government filed a brief and argued the merits.

The friend of the court brief filed by the Department of Justice was a response not only to Negro pressures, the President's Committee on Civil Rights and the President himself but to the wishes of official groups within the Executive Branch. A section of the brief is devoted to repeating specially prepared statements on the conflict between the existence of racial covenants and the ideal of a public policy established on the basis of equality of opportunity. Letters were included from Raymond M. Foley, Administrator, Housing and Home Finance Agency; Surgeon General Thomas Parran; Oscar L. Chapman, Under Secretary of the Interior; and Ernest A. Gross, Legal Advisor to the Secretary of State. The Justice Department brief was published as a book by the Public Affairs Press in the spring of 1948, before the Supreme Court had come to its decision in the covenant cases.

* * *

The Negro briefs made the familiar constitutional and public policy claims. Two basic arguments were made to the Court. The first was that racial restrictive covenants produce undesirable social results and unfairly limit Negroes' access to decent housing. This assertion was supported by a tremendous amount of sociological data with references to the books and articles published on the subject during the previous few years. The segregated slums which resulted, it was claimed, make enforcement of covenants contrary to sound public policy. Secondly, it was argued that when a court acts to enforce a racial restrictive covenant, it is acting for the state in violation of the limitation of the Fourteenth Amendment that no state shall "deny to any person within its jurisdiction the equal protection of the laws." This, too, was bolstered by reference to the recent articles in the law reviews on the subject as well as the decisions of the Supreme Court which had expanded the concept of state action.

The briefs entered by the white property owners bristled with the precedents of state courts which had enforced restrictive covenants over the years. It was natural to rely on precedent for only one law review article had supported the Caucasian position. The federal cases from the District of Columbia were stressed in briefs in the *Hodge* cases and the early Supreme Court decision of Corrigan v. Buckley was repeatedly endorsed. The law of the land on this question was firmly established and should not be tampered with. These briefs were devoted also to answering the Negroes' contentions. It was said that racial restrictions were private agreements; consequently enforcement of them by courts did not deny Negroes any constitutionally-protected right. In fact the action of the courts in these instances supported the contract rights of individual white property owners. The public policy issue again saw the white attorneys relying on precedents. It was added that the position of Congress was a more authoritative expression of public policy than the political speeches of President Truman and the declarations of other executive officials. Congress had refrained from enacting any legislation questioning the wisdom of segregation; rather, it had long supported racial separation in the District of Columbia. From all of this it was urged that the enforcement of racial covenants was in tune with public policy.

Questions

1.   Do the opinions in Plessy v. Ferguson (*supra* p. 962), suggest that Social Darwinism and the sociological theories of race relations (discussed by Professor Vose at p. 980 *supra*) influenced judicial thought in race relations cases?

2.   What purpose was to be served by building an "ideal record" (*supra* p. 982) in the covenant cases? What reasons can you suggest for including sociological data in such a record?

3.   What reasons can you suggest for the emphasis on publishing articles on sociological findings as to the effects of restrictive covenants? Is there special significance in the recommendation that the articles be published in "good journals" and "reputable magazines"?

4.   You have seen numerous extracts from law review articles (*e. g.*, at pp. 238, 266, 396, 465, *supra*). Would you classify these articles as scholarly publications dealing with legal issues, or as examples of a special form of advocacy?

5.   Why might courts be likely to "follow the law reviews"? Do you think law review articles would have more weight with a judge if he tended to view them as "scholarly publications" rather than as a special form of advocacy?

6.   Is the strategy of "flooding the law reviews" more consistent with the view of law review articles as scholarly publications, or with the view that they are a special form of advocacy? How might such a strategy be self-defeating?

7.   What is the apparent purpose of an "amicus curiae" brief? Is there special significance in the appearance of the Solicitor General as an amicus curiae? What sort of persons or organizations would you expect to appear as amici curiae for the Negro parties in these cases? Explain your answer.

SHELLEY v. KRAEMER

Supreme Court of the United States, 1948.
334 U.S. 1, 68 S.Ct. 836.

[Some footnotes omitted; others are renumbered.]

[Shelley v. Kraemer arose in the state courts of Missouri. On Appeal Shelley was consolidated for argument with Sipes v. McGhee, 316 Mich. 614, 25 N.W.2d 638 (1947). Both cases involved suits by white property owners seeking to enjoin Negroes from taking posses-, sion of real property burdened with covenants restricting ownership and use of the premises to whites. The validity of such covenants was sustained in *Shelley* by the Supreme Court of Missouri and in *Sipes* by the Supreme Court of Michigan. Both cases were decided by the United States Supreme Court in the opinion set out below.[1]]

* * *

MR. CHIEF JUSTICE VINSON delivered the opinion of the Court.

It cannot be doubted that among the civil rights intended to be protected from discriminatory state action by the Fourteenth Amendment are the rights to acquire, enjoy, own and dispose of property. Equality in the enjoyment of property rights was regarded by the framers of that Amendment as an essential pre-condition to the realization of other basic civil rights and liberties which the Amendment was intended to guarantee.[2] Thus, § 1978 of the Revised Statutes, derived from § 1 of the Civil Rights Act of 1866 which was enacted by Congress while the Fourteenth Amendment was also under consideration, provides:

> "All citizens of the United States shall have the same right, in every State and Territory, as is enjoyed by white citizens thereof to inherit, purchase, lease, sell, hold, and convey real and personal property."

This Court has given specific recognition to the same principle. Buchanan v. Warley, 245 U.S. 60, 38 S.Ct. 16 (1917).

It is likewise clear that restrictions on the right of occupancy of the sort sought to be created by the private agreements in these cases could not be squared with the requirements of the Fourteenth Amendment if imposed by state statute or local ordinance.

[The Court summarized the holdings in Buchanan v. Warley, and Harmon v. Tyler, 273 U.S. 668, 47 S.Ct. 471 (1927), in support of this proposition.]

The precise question before this Court in both the *Buchanan* and *Harmon* cases involved the rights of white sellers to dispose of their properties free from restrictions as to potential purchasers based on considerations of race or color. But that such legislation is also offensive to the rights of those desiring to acquire and occupy property and barred on grounds of race or color is clear, not only from the language of the opinion in Buchanan v. Warley, supra, but from this Court's disposition of the case of Richmond v. Deans, 281 U.S. 704, 50 S.Ct. 407 (1930). There, a Negro, barred from the occupancy of certain property by the terms of an ordinance similar to that in the *Buchanan* case, sought injunctive relief in the federal courts to enjoin the enforcement of the ordinance on the grounds that its provisions violated the terms of the Fourteenth Amendment. Such relief was granted, and this Court affirmed, finding the cita-

---

1. Editor's note.

2. Slaughter-House Cases, 16 Wall. 36, 70, 81 (1873). See Flack, The Adoption of the Fourteenth Amendment.

tion of Buchanan v. Warley, supra, and Harmon v. Tyler, supra, sufficient to support its judgment.

But the present cases, unlike those just discussed, do not involve action by state legislatures or city councils. Here the particular patterns of discrimination and the areas in which the restrictions are to operate, are determined, in the first instance, by the terms of agreements among private individuals. Participation of the State consists in the enforcement of the restrictions so defined. The crucial issue with which we are here confronted is whether this distinction removes these cases from the operation of the prohibitory provisions of the Fourteenth Amendment.

Since the decision of this Court in the *Civil Rights Cases,* 109 U.S. 3, 3 S.Ct. 18 (1883), the principle has become firmly embedded in our constitutional law that the action inhibited by the first section of the Fourteenth Amendment is only such action as may fairly be said to be that of the States. That Amendment erects no shield against merely private conduct, however discriminatory or wrongful.

We conclude, therefore, that the restrictive agreements standing alone cannot be regarded as violative of any rights guaranteed to petitioners by the Fourteenth Amendment. So long as the purposes of those agreements are effectuated by voluntary adherence to their terms, it would appear clear that there has been no action by the State and the provisions of the Amendment have not been violated. Cf. Corrigan v. Buckley, supra.

But here there was more. These are cases in which the purposes of the agreements were secured only by judicial enforcement by state courts of the restrictive terms of the agreements. The respondents urge that judicial enforcement of private agreements does not amount to state action; or, in any event, the participation of the State is so attenuated in character as not to amount to state action within the meaning of the Fourteenth Amendment. Finally, it is suggested, even if the States in these cases may be deemed to have acted in the constitutional sense, their action did not deprive petitioners of rights guaranteed by the Fourteenth Amendment. We move to a consideration of these matters.

II.

That the action of state courts and judicial officers in their official capacities is to be regarded as action of the State within the meaning of the Fourteenth Amendment, is a proposition which has long been established by decisions of this Court. . . .

[THE CHIEF JUSTICE cited and discussed numerous cases supporting this proposition. These cases involved instances of state judicial and executive action held to be violations of the due process provision of the Fourteenth Amendment.]

But the examples of state judicial action which have been held by this Court to violate the Amendment's commands are not restricted to situations in which the judicial proceedings were found in some manner to be procedurally unfair. It has been recognized that the action of state courts in enforcing a substantive common-law rule formulated by those courts, may result in the denial of rights guaranteed by the Fourteenth Amendment, even though the judicial proceedings in such cases may have been in complete accord with the most rigorous conceptions of procedural due process. Thus, in American Federation of Labor v. Swing, 312 U.S. 321, 61 S.Ct. 568 (1941), enforcement by state courts of the common-law policy of the State, which resulted in the restraining of peaceful picketing, was held to be state action of the sort prohibited by the Amendment's guaranties of freedom of discussion. . . .

* * *

The short of the matter is that from the time of the adoption of the Fourteenth Amendment until the present, it has been the consistent ruling of this Court that the action of the States to which the Amendment has reference includes action of state courts and state judicial officials. Although, in construing the terms of the Fourteenth Amendment, differences have from time to time been expressed as to whether particular types of state action may be said to offend the Amendment's prohibitory provisions, it has never been suggested that state court action is immunized from the operation of those provisions simply because the act is that of the judicial branch of the state government.

III.

Against this background of judicial construction, extending over a period of some three-quarters of a century, we are called upon to consider whether enforcement by state courts of the restrictive agreements in these cases may be deemed to be the acts of those States; and, if so, whether that action has denied these petitioners the equal protection of the laws which the Amendment was intended to insure.

We have no doubt that there has been state action in these cases in the full and complete sense of the phrase. The undisputed facts disclose that petitioners were willing purchasers of properties upon which they desired to establish homes. The owners of the properties were willing sellers; and contracts of sale were accordingly consummated. It is clear that but for the active intervention of the state courts, supported by the full panoply of state power, petitioners would have been free to occupy the properties in question without restraint.

These are not cases, as has been suggested, in which the States have merely abstained from action, leaving private individuals free to impose such discriminations as they see fit. Rather, these are cases in which the States have made available to such individuals the full coercive power of government to deny to petitioners, on the grounds of race or color, the enjoyment of property rights in premises which petitioners are willing and financially able to acquire and which the grantors are willing to sell. The difference between judicial enforcement and nonenforcement of the restrictive covenants is the difference to petitioners between being denied rights of property available to other members of the community and being accorded full enjoyment of those rights on an equal footing.

The enforcement of the restrictive agreements by the state courts in these cases was directed pursuant to the common-law policy of the States as formulated by those courts in earlier decisions. In the Missouri case, enforcement of the covenant was directed in the first instance by the highest court of the State after the trial court had determined the agreement to be invalid for want of the requisite number of signatures. In the Michigan case, the order of enforcement by the trial court was affirmed by the highest state court. The judicial action in each case bears the clear and unmistakable imprimatur of the State. We have noted that previous decisions of this Court have established the proposition that judicial action is not immunized from the operation of the Fourteenth Amendment simply because it is taken pursuant to the state's common-law policy. Nor is the Amendment ineffective simply because the particular pattern of discrimination, which the State has enforced, was defined initially by the terms of a private agreement. State action, as that phrase is understood for the purposes of the Fourteenth Amendment, refers to exertions of state power in all forms. And when the effect of that action is to deny rights subject to the protection of the Fourteenth Amendment, it is the obligation of this Court to enforce the constitutional commands.

We hold that in granting judicial enforcement of the restrictive agreements in these cases, the States have denied petitioners the equal protection of the laws and that, therefore, the action of the state courts cannot stand. We have noted that freedom from discrimination by the States in the enjoyment of property rights was among the basic objectives sought to be effectuated by the framers of the Fourteenth Amendment. That such discrimination has occurred in these cases is clear. Because of the race or color of these petitioners they have been denied rights of ownership or occupancy enjoyed as a matter of course by other citizens of different race or color. The Fourteenth Amendment declares "that all persons, whether colored or white, shall stand equal before the laws of the States, and, in regard to the colored race, for whose protection the amendment was primarily designed, that no discrimination shall be made against them by law because of their color." Strauder v. West Virginia, *supra* 100 U.S. at 307. Only recently this Court had occasion to declare that a state law which denied equal enjoyment of property rights to a designated class of citizens of specified race and ancestry, was not a legitimate exercise of the state's police power but violated the guaranty of the equal protection of the laws. Oyama v. California, 332 U.S. 633, 68 S.Ct. 269 (1948). Nor may the discriminations imposed by the state courts in these cases be justified as proper exertions of state police power. Cf. Buchanan v. Warley, *supra.*

Respondents urge, however, that since the state courts stand ready to enforce restrictive covenants excluding white persons from the ownership or occupancy of property covered by such agreements, enforcement of covenants excluding colored persons may not be deemed a denial of equal protection of the laws to the colored persons who are thereby affected. This contention does not bear scrutiny. The parties have directed our attention to no case in which a court, state or federal, has been called upon to enforce a covenant excluding members of the white majority from ownership or occupancy of real property on grounds of race or color. But there are more fundamental considerations. The rights created by the first section of the Fourteenth Amendment are, by its terms, guaranteed to the individual. The rights established are personal rights. It is, therefore, no answer to these petitioners to say that the courts may also be induced to deny white persons rights of ownership and occupancy on grounds of race or color. Equal protection of the laws is not achieved through indiscriminate imposition of inequalities.

Nor do we find merit in the suggestion that property owners who are parties to these agreements are denied equal protection of the laws if denied access to the courts to enforce the terms of restrictive covenants and to assert property rights which the state courts have held to be created by such agreements. The Constitution confers upon no individual the right to demand action by the State which results in the denial of equal protection of the laws to other individuals. And it would appear beyond question that the power of the State to create and enforce property interests must be exercised within the boundaries defined by the Fourteenth Amendment. Cf. Marsh v. Alabama, 326 U.S. 501, 66 S.Ct. 276 (1946).

The problem of defining the scope of the restrictions which the Federal Constitution imposes upon exertions of power by the States has given rise to many of the most persistent and fundamental issues which this Court has been called upon to consider. That problem was foremost in the minds of the framers of the Constitution, and, since that early day, has arisen in a multitude of forms. The task of determining whether the action of a State offends constitutional provisions is one which may not be undertaken lightly. Where, however, it is clear that the action of the State violates the terms of the fundamental charter, it is the obligation of this Court so to declare.

The historical context in which the Fourteenth Amendment became a part of the Constitution should not be forgotten. Whatever else the framers sought to achieve, it is clear that the matter of primary concern was the establishment of equality in the enjoyment of basic civil and political rights and the preservation of those rights from discriminatory action on the part of the States based on considerations of race or color. Seventy-five years ago this Court announced that the provisions of the Amendment are to be construed with this fundamental purpose in mind. Upon full consideration, we have concluded that in these cases the States have acted to deny petitioners the equal protection of the laws guaranteed by the Fourteenth Amendment. Having so decided, we find it unnecessary to consider whether petitioners have also been deprived of property without due process of law or denied privileges and immunities of citizens of the United States.

For the reasons stated, the judgment of the Supreme Court of Missouri and the judgment of the Supreme Court of Michigan must be reversed.

Reversed.

MR. JUSTICE REED, MR. JUSTICE JACKSON, and MR. JUSTICE RUTLEDGE took no part in the consideration or decision of these cases.

———

In Hurd v. Hodge, 334 U.S. 24, 68 S.Ct. 847, and Uricola v. Hodge, 334 U.S. 24, 68 S.Ct. 847, companion cases to Shelley v. Kraemer, the Court ruled that racial restrictive covenants in the District of Columbia were unenforceable under that portion of the Civil Rights Act of 1866 which stated that "All citizens of the United States shall have the same right, in every State and Territory, as is enjoyed by white citizens thereof to inherit, purchase, lease, sell, hold and convey real and personal property." This resurrection of the Act of 1866 avoided the necessity of answering the question whether judicial enforcement of such covenants violated the due process clause of the Fifth Amendment.

Questions

1. What is the significance, if any, of the Court's finding that the covenants in these cases "standing alone cannot be regarded as violation of any rights guaranteed to petitioners by the Fourteenth Amendment"?

2. How does the Court meet the argument that there is no denial of equal protection if the state even-handedly enforces racial restrictive covenants against both Blacks and whites (*supra* p. 995)? Do you find the Court's response adequate?

3. What is (are) the legal principle (principles) supporting the judgment in this case?

4. What result if the principle or principles of *Shelley* are applied to the following cases?

   a. A religious denomination builds a retirement village and sells homes in the village to elderly members of that denomination. The sales agreements include a covenant restricting resale only to members of the denomination. Adjoining homeowners seek to enforce this covenant against another homeowner who proposes to sell to a member of another denomination.

   b. A fraternal organization builds an apartment house and leases apartments only to its own members, and includes a provision in each lease restricting sub-leases also to members of the organization. The fraternal organization sues to enforce the restrictive sublease provision? A, who is not a member, sues to force the organization to lease him an apartment? Is it important to the latter action that the organization is chartered as a private corporation by the state, and the apartment building is licensed under the multiple dwelling laws of the state? Would it make a difference if A were Black and the organization restricted its members to whites only?

5. Can you formulate a principle (or principles) which provides for the result in *Shelley* but which also allows religious or fraternal organizations to discriminate in favor of their own members?

6. Does it appear from the opinion in *Shelley* that sociological data and theories had any bearing on the outcome of the case? Does it appear from the opinion that the Court "followed" law reviews or was influenced by publications in "reputable journals or magazines?"

7. Would the relevance of sociological data and theories, including statistical data on the effects of restrictive covenants, depend on the nature of the legal principle(s) relied on in reaching a decision in such a case?

The carefully managed NAACP campaign against racial restrictive covenants which culminated in Shelley v. Kraemer was part of an overall attack on racial segregation in which the key target was segregation in public education. The campaign opened in 1934 with the filing by the NAACP of suits challenging racial segregation in graduate and professional education. This strategy was chosen since, at that time, the limited demand for such education (primarily in law and medicine) made it difficult for state governments to provide separate facilities for non-whites. Accordingly segregation meant there was no access to publicly supported professional education in many states.

This initial assault achieved some notable successes between 1934 and 1954. Decisions favorable to the NAACP position were handed down in Missouri ex rel. Gaines v. Canada, 305 U.S. 337 (1938), Sipuel v. Board of Regents, 332 U.S. 631 (1948), McLaurin v. Oklahoma, 339 U.S. 637 (1950) and Sweatt v. Painter, 339 U.S. 629 (1950). In each of these cases the Supreme Court ruled that Negro applicants were to be admitted to state supported law schools. Although the holding of Plessy v. Ferguson was not disturbed, the Court weakened the force of that opinion by making clear that a state could have segregated public education only if equal facilities were provided for Blacks. Moreover, the Court adopted such strict standards regarding the quality of the separate facilities that, as a matter of law at least, segregated professional schools were no longer practical. Despite these courtroom victories, segregated professional education persisted through the 1950s. However, these cases set the stage for the main event in the NAACP assault on Jim Crow education.

[The following is taken from LOREN MILLER, THE PETITIONERS, *op. cit.*, pp. 342–346]:

A dozen years elapsed between the decisions in the Gaines and Sweatt cases, but events moved much faster in the 1950's. Less than four short years after the Sweatt case had been decided, the Supreme Court was ready to announce its sweeping decision in cases involving segregation in elementary and secondary schools. The quickened tempo was due to the fact that the NAACP was better organized and better equipped to press its litigation, that restless Negroes were less inclined to wait for vindication of their claimed civil rights, and that the Supreme Court's decisions favorable to the exercise of those rights had brightened the national climate of public opinion and pricked the conscience of the American people. An increasing number of Americans had looked through the separate-but-equal rule and had seen it for what it was: a device to stigmatize Negroes and fix a brand of inferiority on them.   Troubled and troublesome international events played their part; the nation had assumed a stance as the defender of the free world, and all over the globe other people looked askance at the manifestations of racism in the United States.

A year after Herman Sweatt entered the University of Texas law school, cases were on file in four states and the District of Columbia asking four federal and one state court to apply the qualitative test of the Sweatt case to elementary and secondary schools, and declare that the separate-but-equal rule had no validity in the area of public education.   The four states involved were Kansas, South Carolina, Virginia, and Delaware.   Ultimately, the four state cases were grouped together and decided as Brown v. Board of Education of Topeka, and the District of Columbia litigation was decided in a separate case, Bolling v. Sharpe.   All were decided on May 17, 1954.

The first of the cases to actually reach the Supreme Court was a suit by Harry Briggs, Jr., and 66 other Negro children, who sued the Clarendon County, South Carolina, School Board No. 22, in a case known as Harry Briggs, Jr. v. R. W. Elliott, charging that Clarendon County's Negro schools were far inferior to its schools for white children.   They asked a three-judge federal court to hold that South Carolina's separate school laws and constitutional provisions were invalid under the equal-protection clause of the Fourteenth Amendment.   The federal judges agreed that the schools for Negroes were inferior to those maintained for white children, and ordered the board to equalize the school systems and report back in six months as to the progress it had made.   The judges also ruled that they were bound by Plessy v. Ferguson and that South Carolina's separate school laws were valid.   The Supreme Court agreed to review the case in June, 1951, but on January 28, 1952, sent it back to the three-judge court with instructions to report on what progress had been made toward equalization.   Justices Black and Douglas dissented on the ground that the report was "wholly irrelevant to the constitutional questions presented" and urged that the case be set for argument.   In March, 1952, the three-judge district court found that the Clarendon County board had complied with the equalization order, praised it for its compliance, and again upheld South Carolina segregation laws as valid under the Plessy case.   The Supreme Court then restored the case to its docket.

Meanwhile, Oliver Brown had sued the Topeka, Kansas, Board of Education because his eight-year-old daughter was denied entrance to a white school only 5 blocks from her home and forced to travel 21 blocks to a Negro school.   Kansas laws permitted but did not require cities of more than 15,000 to impose school segregation.   Topeka imposed segregation in its grade schools but not in high school.   On August 3, 1951, a three-judge federal court held that Topeka's Negro and white schools were substantially equal, criticized the separate-but-equal rule but decided it was bound by Plessy v. Ferguson and refused to invalidate Kansas laws.   Mr. Brown lost his case and promptly appealed.   When his appeal reached the Supreme Court in October, 1951, the South Carolina case had been sent back to the district court for the report on equalization plans.   The Court agreed to review Brown's case, and thus it became number one on the list of school segregation cases set for hearing and decision.   Brown won immortality of a sort by securing top billing: the school segregation cases would be forever known as Brown v. Board of Education.

The Virginia case was heard in still another three-judge federal court in that state on March 7, 1952. Dorothy E. Davis and other high-school students sued the county school board of Prince Edward County asking that Virginia's constitutional and statutory provisions imposing segregation be declared invalid or that the county's Negro and white high schools be ordered equalized. The court granted the equalization request but also fell back on the Plessy case to deny the plea for invalidation of the segregation requirements of Virginia's constitution and laws. The case was appealed to the Supreme Court as Davis v. County School Board of Prince Edward County.

The Delaware case was filed in the courts of that state, and on April 1, 1952, Delaware Chancellor Collins J. Seitz found the Negro schools inferior to white schools and enjoined Delaware from enforcing segregation laws because of that inequality. The chancellor expressed his opinion that the "separate but equal doctrine in education should be rejected," but added that rejection must come from the Supreme Court. Delaware's supreme court upheld the injunction on August 28, 1952, but seemed to say that the order should be dissolved as soon as Negro schools were equalized. On November 24, 1952, the Supreme Court added the case, Gebhart v. Bolton, to the list of school cases which it was willing to decide.

Brown v. Board of Education now encompassed the four state cases, each of which presented the question of the application of the separate-but-equal rule to public schools. Each of them rested on the contention that the equal-protection-of-the-laws clause of the Fourteenth Amendment prohibited state-imposed segregation in tax-supported schools. Obviously, they could be argued together and decided together. The Court made such an order.

The Fourteenth Amendment does not apply to the District of Columbia but only to the states. Consequently, there is no equal-protection clause for the District; however, the Fifth Amendment like the Fourteenth, forbids denial of due process of law. Spottswood Bolling, who sued for admission to a Washington high school, claimed that the due-process-of-law clause of the Fifth Amendment was broad enough to forbid segregation in public schools, and he asked the federal courts, which exercise jurisdiction in the District, to invalidate congressional legislation requiring separate schools. His suit was dismissed, and on November 10, 1952, the Supreme Court granted review in his case, known as Bolling v. Sharpe, and set it down for argument at the same time as the four state cases.

There was more to this carefully stage-managed selection of cases for review than meets the naked eye. The Kansas case concerned grade-school children in a northern state with a permissive segregation statute; the Virginia case involved high-school students in a state having compulsory laws and located in the upper tier of southern states; South Carolina represented the Deep South, and Delaware the border states. The state cases all presented the issue of the application of the equal-protection-of-law clause of the Fourteenth Amendment, and the Court could have reached and decided that question in any one of them, but the wide geographical range gave the anticipated decision a national flavor and would blunt any claim that the South was being made a whipping boy. Moreover, the combination of cases included Kansas with its permissive statute, while other cases concerned state constitutional provisions as well as statutes with mandatory segregation requirements. Grade-school students were involved in the Kansas case; high-school students in the Virginia case, and all elementary and secondary students in the Delaware and South Carolina cases. The District of Columbia case drew due process of law into the cases as an issue, in distinction to the equal-protection-of-law clause, and also presented an opportunity for inquiry into the congressional power to impose racial segregation. The NAACP had touched all bases.

Initial arguments were made on December 9, 1952, two-and-a-half years after the Sweatt decision. But the Court reached no decision on the basis of the first briefs and arguments. On June 8, 1953, it issued an order setting the case for reargument that fall, submitting a series of questions to the litigants, and inviting the United States Attorney General to participate in the arguments.

The Court's first question asked what evidence there was that the Congress which submitted and the states which ratified the Fourteenth Amendment contemplated that the amendment would abolish school segregation. It then asked whether Congress had the power to abolish all school segregation, regardless of whether the framers or ratifying states believed that the amendment required its immediate abolition, and what was the reach of the Court's power under those circumstances. Its third inquiry was the extent of the Court's power to abolish school segregation in the event that the answers to the first two questions were inconclusive. The fourth question was that of whether a decree favoring the Negro plaintiffs would carry with it an order directing their immediate admission to state-supported schools or whether the Court could devise a gradualistic scheme for their enrollment—a very obvious, and very curious, inquiry as to whether the rights of Negro grade-school students to attend public schools were *personal and present* (as all constitutional rights are) or whether their exercise could be delayed until a more propitious time. The fifth question concerned the form the decree should take, if the Court decided on a gradualistic abolition of segregation.

Thurgood Marshall, counsel and director of the NAACP Legal Defense & Educational Fund, convoked sessions of lawyers, law school professors, and historians from all over the nation to help find answers to the Court's questions and to fashion briefs and arguments. The hard-pressed states hired John W. Davis, one-time Democratic candidate for the presidency of the United States and one of the nation's leading constitutional lawyers, to head an imposing array of counsel.

Reargument began on December 8, 1953 and continued for three days. Then the Court took all of the cases under submission for later decision.

The showdown had come; judgment day was near for Plessy v. Ferguson in the field of public education.

Questions

What was the purpose and significance of each of the five questions propounded to the attorneys prior to the reargument of Brown v. Board of Education (*supra* pp. 1000–1001)? What does this suggest about the role of adversary argument in constitutional litigation?

BROWN v. BOARD OF EDUCATION
Supreme Court of the United States, 1954.
347 U.S. 483, 74 S.Ct. 686.

[Some footnotes omitted; others are renumbered.]

MR. CHIEF JUSTICE WARREN delivered the opinion of the Court.

* * *

In each of the cases, minors of the Negro race, through their legal representatives, seek the aid of the courts in obtaining admission to the public schools of their community on a nonsegregated basis. In each instance, they had been denied admission to schools attended by white children under laws requiring or permitting segregation according to race. This segregation was alleged to deprive the plaintiffs of the equal protection of the laws under the Fourteenth Amendment. In each of the cases other than the Delaware case, a three-judge federal district court denied relief to the plaintiffs on the so-called "separate but equal" doctrine announced by this Court in Plessy v. Ferguson, 163 U.S. 537. Under that doctrine, equality of treatment is accorded when the races are provided substantially equal facilities, even though these facilities be separate. In the Delaware case, the Supreme Court of Delaware adhered to that doctrine, but ordered that the plaintiffs be admitted to the white schools because of their superiority to the Negro schools.

The plaintiffs contend that segregated public schools are not "equal" and cannot be made "equal," and that hence they are deprived of the equal protection of the laws. Because of the obvious importance of the question presented, the Court took jurisdiction. Argument was heard in the 1952 Term, and reargument was heard this Term on certain questions propounded by the Court.

Reargument was largely devoted to the circumstances surrounding the adoption of the Fourteenth Amendment in 1868. It covered exhaustively consideration of the Amendment in Congress, ratification by the states, then existing practices in racial segregation, and the views of proponents and opponents of the Amendment. This discussion and our own investigation convince us that, although these sources cast some light, it is not enough to resolve the problem with which we are faced. At best, they are inconclusive. The most avid proponents of the post-War Amendments undoubtedly intended them to remove all legal distinctions among "all persons born or naturalized in the United States." Their opponents, just as certainly, were antagonistic to both the letter and the spirit of the Amendments and wished them to have the most limited effect. What others in Congress and the state legislatures had in mind cannot be determined with any degree of certainty.

An additional reason for the inconclusive nature of the Amendment's history, with respect to segregated schools, is the status of public education at that time. In the South, the movement toward free common schools, supported by general taxation, had not yet taken hold. Education of white children was largely in the hands of private groups. Education of Negroes was almost nonexistent, and practically all of the race were illiterate. In fact, any education of Negroes was forbidden by law in some states. Today, in contrast, many Negroes have achieved outstanding success in the arts and sciences as well as in the business and professional world. It is true that public school education at the time of the Amendment had advanced further in the North, but the effect of the Amendment on Northern States was generally ignored in the congressional debates. Even in the North, the conditions of public education did not approximate those existing today. The curriculum was usually rudimentary; ungraded schools were common in rural areas; the school term was but three months a year in many states; and compulsory school attendance was virtually unknown. As a consequence, it is not surprising that there should be so little in the history of the Fourteenth Amendment relating to its intended effect on public education.

In the first cases in this Court construing the Fourteenth Amendment, decided shortly after its adoption, the Court interpreted it as proscribing all state-imposed discriminations against the Negro race.[1] The doctrine of "separate but equal" did not make its appearance in this Court until 1896 in the case of Plessy v. Ferguson, supra, involving not education but transportation.[2] American courts have since labored with the doctrine for over half a century. In this Court, there have been six cases involving the "separate but equal" doctrine in the field of public education.[3] In Cumming v. County Board of Education, 175 U.S. 528, 20 S.Ct. 197, and Gong Lum v. Rice, 275 U.S. 78, 48 S.Ct. 91, the validity of the doctrine itself was not challenged.[4] In more recent cases, all on the graduate school level, inequality was found in that specific benefits enjoyed by white students were denied to Negro students of the same educational qualifications. Missouri ex rel. Gaines v. Canada, 305 U.S. 337, 59 S.Ct. 232; Sipuel v. Oklahoma, 332 U.S. 631, 68 S.Ct. 299; Sweatt v. Painter, 399 U.S. 629, 70 S.Ct. 848; McLaurin v. Oklahoma State Regents, 399 U.S. 637, 70 S.Ct. 851. In none of these cases was it necessary to re-examine the doctrine to grant relief to the Negro plaintiff. And in Sweatt v. Painter, supra, the Court expressly reserved decision on the question whether Plessy v. Ferguson should be held inapplicable to public education.

In the instant cases, that question is directly presented. Here, unlike Sweatt v. Painter, there are findings below that the Negro and white schools involved have been equalized, or are being equalized, with respect

1. Slaughter-House Cases, 16 Wall. 36, 67–72 (1873); Strauder v. West Virginia, 100 U.S. 303, 307–308 (1880).

2. The doctrine apparently originated in Roberts v. City of Boston, 59 Mass. 198, 206 (1850), upholding school segregation against attack as being violative of a state constitutional guarantee of equality. Segregation in Boston public schools was eliminated in 1855. Mass. Acts 1855 c. 256. But elsewhere in the North segregation in public education has persisted in some communities until recent years. It is apparent that such segregation has long been a nationwide problem, not merely one of sectional concern.

3. See also Berea College v. Kentucky, 211 U.S. 45, 29 S.Ct. 33 (1908).

4. In the Cumming case, Negro taxpayers sought an injunction requiring the defendant school board to discontinue the operation of a high school for white children until the board resumed operation of a high school for Negro children. Similarly, in the Gong Lum case, the plaintiff, a child of Chinese descent, contended only that state authorities had misapplied the doctrine by classifying him with Negro children and requiring him to attend a Negro school.

to buildings, curricula, qualifications and salaries of teachers, and other "tangible" factors.[5] Our decision, therefore, cannot turn on merely a comparison of these tangible factors in the Negro and white schools involved in each of the cases. We must look instead to the effect of segregation itself on public education.

In approaching this problem, we cannot turn the clock back to 1868 when the Amendment was adopted, or even to 1896 when Plessy v. Ferguson was written. We must consider public education in the light of its full development and its present place in American life throughout the Nation. Only in this way can it be determined if segregation in public schools deprives these plaintiffs of the equal protection of the laws.

Today, education is perhaps the most important function of state and local governments. Compulsory school attendance laws and the great expenditures for education both demonstrate our recognition of the importance of education to our democratic society. It is required in the performance of our most basic public responsibilities, even service in the armed forces. It is the very foundation of good citizenship. Today it is a principal instrument in awakening the child to cultural values, in preparing him for later professional training, and in helping him to adjust normally to his environment. In these days, it is doubtful that any child may reasonably be expected to succeed in life if he is denied the opportunity of an education. Such an opportunity, where the state has undertaken to provide it, is a right which must be made available to all on equal terms.

We come then to the question presented: Does segregation of children in public schools solely on the basis of race, even though the physical facilities and other "tangible" factors may be equal, deprive the children of the minority group of equal educational opportunities? We believe that it does.

In Sweatt v. Painter, supra, in finding that a segregated law school for Negroes could not provide them equal educational opportunities, this Court relied in large part on "those qualities which are incapable of objective measurement but which make for greatness in a law school." In McLaurin v. Oklahoma State Regents, supra, the Court, in requiring that a Negro admitted to a white graduate school be treated like all other students, again resorted to intangible considerations: ". . . his ability to study, to engage in discussions and exchange views with other students, and, in general, to learn his profession." Such considerations apply with added force to children in grade and high schools. To separate them from others of similar age and qualifications solely because of their race generates a feeling of inferiority as to their status in the community that may affect their hearts and minds in a way unlikely ever to be undone. The effect of this separation on their educational opportunities was well stated by a finding in the

---

5. In the Kansas case, the court below found substantial equality as to all such factors. 98 F.Supp. 797, 798. In the South Carolina case, the court below found that the defendants were proceeding "promptly and in good faith to comply with the court's decree." 103 F.Supp. 920, 921. In the Virginia case, the court below noted that the equalization program was already "afoot and progressing" (103 F. Supp. 337, 341); since then, we have been advised, in the Virginia Attorney General's brief on reargument, that the program has now been completed. In the Delaware case, the court below similarly noted that the state's equalization program was well under way. 91 A.2d 137, 139.

Kansas case by a court which nevertheless felt compelled to rule against the Negro plaintiffs:

"Segregation of white and colored children in public schools has a detrimental effect upon the colored children. The impact is greater when it has the sanction of the law; for the policy of separating the races is usually interpreted as denoting the inferiority of the negro group. A sense of inferiority affects the motivation of a child to learn. Segregation with the sanction of law, therefore, has a tendency to [retard] the educational and mental development of negro children and to deprive them of some of the benefits they would receive in a racial[ly] integrated school system." [6]

Whatever may have been the extent of psychological knowledge at the time of Plessy v. Ferguson, this finding is amply supported by modern authority.[7] Any language in Plessy v. Ferguson contrary to this finding is rejected.

We conclude that in the field of public education the doctrine of "separate but equal" has no place. Separate educational facilities are inherently unequal. Therefore, we hold that the plaintiffs and other similarly situated for whom the actions have been brought are, by reason of the segregation complained of, deprived of the equal protection of the laws guaranteed by the Fourteenth Amendment. This disposition makes unnecessary any discussion whether such segregation also violates the Due Process Clause of the Fourteenth Amendment.

Because these are class actions, because of the wide applicability of this decision, and because of the great variety of local conditions, the formulation of decrees in these cases presents problems of considerable complexity. On reargument, the consideration of appropriate relief was necessarily subordinated to the primary question—the constitutionality of segregation in public education. We have now announced that such segregation is a denial of the equal protection of the laws. In order that we may have the full assistance of the parties in formulating decrees, the cases will be restored to the docket, and the parties are requested to present further argument on Questions 4 and 5 previously propounded by the Court for the reargument this Term.[8]

---

6. A similar finding was made in the Delaware case: "I conclude from the testimony that in our Delaware society, State-imposed segregation in education itself results in the Negro children, as a class, receiving educational opportunities which are substantially inferior to those available to white children otherwise similarly situated." 87 A.2d 862, 865.

7. K. B. Clark, Effect of Prejudice and Discrimination on Personality Development (Midcentury White House Conference on Children and Youth, 1950); Witmer and Kotinsky, Personality in the Making (1952) c. VI; Deutscher and Chein, The Psychological Effects of Enforced Segregation: A Survey of Social Science Opinion, 26 J.Psychol. 259 (1948); Chein, What are the Psychological Effects of Segregation Under Conditions of Equal Facilities?, 3 Int.J. Opinion and Attitude Res. 229 (1949); Brameld, Educational Costs in Discrimination and National Welfare (MacIver, ed., 1949), 44–48; Frazier, The Negro in the United States (1949), 674–681. And see generally Myrdal, An American Dilemma (1944).

8. "4. Assuming it is decided that segregation in public schools violates the Fourteenth Amendment

"(a) would a decree necessarily follow providing that, within the limits set by normal geographic school districting, Negro children should forthwith be admitted to schools of their choice, or

"(b) may this Court, in the exercise of its equity powers, permit an effective gradual adjustment to be brought about from existing segregated sys-

The Attorney General of the United States is again invited to participate. The Attorneys General of the states requiring or permitting segregation in public education will also be permitted to appear as amici curiae upon request to do so by September 15, 1954, and submission of briefs by October 1, 1954.

It is so ordered.

Questions

1. Was the result in *Brown* predicated on a finding that segregated schools are detrimental to Negro children?

2. What is the relationship, if any, between the Court's citation of authority at footnote 7 (p. 1005 *supra*), and the District Court's findings as to the effects of segregation on Negro children?

3. Is the use of psychological and sociological evidence necessary to the result in this case? Does the relevance of such evidence depend on the legal principle(s) announced in the case?

4. What legal principle(s) explain(s) the result in this case?

5. Did *Brown* overrule Plessy v. Ferguson?

6. Does *Brown* articulate a principle broad enough to explain subsequent decisions by the Supreme Court (per curiam, and without opinion) holding segregation unlawful in: public parks and golf courses, Muir v. Louisville Park Ass'n, 347 U.S. 971, 74 S.Ct. 783 (1954), Holmes v. City of Atlanta, 350 U.S. 879, 76 S.Ct. 141 (1955), and New Orleans City Park Improvement Ass'n, v. Detiege, 358 U.S. 54, 79 S.Ct. 99 (1958); public beaches, Mayor of Baltimore v. Dawson, 350 U.S. 877, 76 S.Ct. 133 (1955); buses, Gayle v. Browder, 352 U.S. 903, 77 S.Ct. 145 (1956); courtrooms, Johnson v. Virginia, 373 U.S. 61, 83 S.Ct. 1053 (1963)? Explain your answers.

BOLLING v. SHARPE

Supreme Court of the United States, 1954.
347 U.S. 497, 74 S.Ct. 693, 98 L.Ed. 884.

MR. CHIEF JUSTICE WARREN delivered the opinion of the Court.

This case challenges the validity of segregation in the public schools of the District of Columbia. The petitioners, minors of the Negro race, allege

tems to a system not based on color distinctions?

"5. On the assumption on which questions 4(a) and (b) are based, and assuming further that this Court will exercise its equity powers to the end described in question 4(b),

"(a) should this Court formulate detailed decrees in these cases;

"(b) if so, what specific issues should the decrees reach;

"(c) should this Court appoint a special master to hear evidence with a view to recommending specific terms for such decrees;

"(d) should this Court remand to the courts of first instance with directions to frame decrees in these cases, and if so what general directions should the decrees of this Court include and what procedures should the courts of first instance follow in arriving at the specific terms of more detailed decrees?"

that such segregation deprives them of due process of law under the Fifth Amendment. They were refused admission to a public school attended by white children solely because of their race. They sought the aid of the District Court for the District of Columbia in obtaining admission. That court dismissed their complaint. The Court granted a writ of certiorari before judgment in the Court of Appeals because of the importance of the constitutional question presented. 344 U.S. 873, 73 S.Ct. 173.

We have this day held that the Equal Protection Clause of the Fourteenth Amendment prohibits the states from maintaining racially segregated public schools. The legal problem in the District of Columbia is somewhat different, however. The Fifth Amendment, which is applicable in the District of Columbia, does not contain an equal protection clause as does the Fourteenth Amendment which applies only to the states. But the concepts of equal protection and due process, both stemming from our American ideal of fairness, are not mutually exclusive. The "equal protection of the laws" is a more explicit safeguard of prohibited unfairness than "due process of law," and, therefore, we do not imply that the two are always interchangeable phrases. But, as this Court has recognized, discrimination may be so unjustifiable as to be violative of due process.

Classifications based solely upon race must be scrutinized with particular care, since they are contrary to our traditions and hence constitutionally suspect. As long ago as 1896, this Court declared the principle "that the constitution of the United States, in its present form, forbids, so far as civil and political rights are concerned, discrimination by the general government, or by the states, against any citizen because of his race." And in Buchanan v. Warley, 245 U.S. 60, 38 S.Ct. 16, the Court held that a statute which limited the right of a property owner to convey his property to a person of another race, was, as an unreasonable discrimination, denial of due process of law.

Although the Court has not assumed to define "liberty" with any great precision, that term is not confined to mere freedom from bodily restraint. Liberty under law extends to the full range of conduct which the individual is free to pursue, and it cannot be restricted except for a proper governmental objective. Segregation in public education is not reasonably related to any proper governmental objective, and thus it imposes on Negro children of the District of Columbia a burden that constitutes an arbitrary deprivation of their liberty in violation of the Due Process Clause.

In view of our decision that the Constitution prohibits the states from maintaining racially segregated public schools, it would be unthinkable that the same Constitution would impose a lesser duty on the Federal Government. We hold that racial segregation in the public schools of the District of Columbia is a denial of the due process of law guaranteed by the Fifth Amendment to the Constitution.

For the reasons set out in Brown v. Board of Education, this case will be restored to the docket for reargument on Questions 4 and 5 previously propounded by the Court. 345 U.S. 972, 73 S.Ct. 1114.

It is so ordered.

Questions

1. How does racial segregation constitute a denial of due process of law? Does the Opinion in Bolling v. Sharpe provide an adequate answer to this question?

2. Is the due process clause used in the same way in Bolling v. Sharpe as it was used in Adair v. United States (*supra* p. 874)?

BROWN v. BOARD OF EDUCATION

(Second Decision)

Supreme Court of the United States, 1955.
349 U.S. 294, 75 S.Ct. 753, 99 L.Ed. 1083.

Mr. CHIEF JUSTICE WARREN delivered the opinion of the Court.

These cases were decided on May 17, 1954. The opinions of that date, declaring the fundamental principle that racial discrimination in public education is unconstitutional, are incorporated herein by reference. All provisions of federal, state, or local law requiring or permitting such discrimination must yield to this principle. There remains for consideration the manner in which relief is to be accorded.

Because these cases arose under different local conditions and their disposition will involve a variety of local problems, we requested further argument on the question of relief. In view of the nationwide importance of the decision, we invited the Attorney General of the United States and the Attorneys General of all states requiring or permitting racial discrimination in public education to present their views on that question. The parties, the United States, and the States of Florida, North Carolina, Arkansas, Oklahoma, Maryland, and Texas filed briefs and participated in the oral argument.

These presentations were informative and helpful to the court in its consideration of the complexities arising from the transition to a system of public education freed of racial discrimination. The presentations also demonstrated that substantial steps to eliminate racial discrimination in public schools have already been taken, not only in some of the communities in which these cases arose, but in some of the states appearing as amici curiae, and in other states as well. Substantial progress has been made in the District of Columbia and in the communities in Kansas and Delaware involved in this litigation. The defendants in the cases coming to us from South Carolina and Virginia are awaiting the decision of this Court concerning relief.

Full implementation of these constitutional principles may require solution of varied local school problems. School authorities have the primary responsibility for elucidating, assessing, and solving these problems; courts will have to consider whether the action of school authorities constitutes good faith implementation of the governing constitutional principles. Because of their proximity to local conditions and the possible need for further hearings, the courts which originally heard these cases can best perform this judicial appraisal. Accordingly, we believe it appropriate to remand the cases to those courts.

In fashioning and effectuating the decrees, the courts will be guided by equitable principles. Traditionally, equity has been characterized by a practical flexibility in shaping its remedies [4] and by a facility for adjusting and reconciling public and private needs.[5] These cases call for the exercise of these traditional attributes of equity power. At stake is the personal interest of the plaintiffs in admission to public schools as soon as practicable on a nondiscriminatory basis. To effectuate this interest may call for elimination of a variety of obstacles in making the transition to school systems operated in accordance with the constitutional principles set forth in our May 17, 1954, decision. Courts of equity may properly take into account the public interest in the elimination of such obstacles in a systematic and effective manner. But it should go without saying that the vitality of these constitutional principles cannot be allowed to yield simply because of disagreement with them.

While giving weight to these public and private considerations, the courts will require that the defendants make a prompt and reasonable start toward full compliance with our May 17, 1954, ruling. Once such a start has been made, the courts may find that additional time is necessary to carry out the ruling in an effective manner. The burden rests upon the defendants to establish that such time is necessary in the public interest and is consistent with good faith compliance at the earliest practicable date. To that end, the courts may consider problems related to administration, arising from the physical condition of the school plant, the school transportation system, personnel, revision of school districts and attendance areas into compact units to achieve a system of determining admission to the public schools on a nonracial basis, and revision of local laws and regulations which may be necessary in solving the foregoing problems. They will also consider the adequacy of any plans the defendants may propose to meet these problems and to effectuate a transition to a racially nondiscriminatory school system. During this period of transition, the courts will retain jurisdiction of these cases.

The judgments below, except that in the Delaware case, are accordingly reversed and the cases are remanded to the District Courts to take such proceedings and enter such orders and decrees consistent with this opinion as are necessary and proper to admit to public schools on a racially nondiscriminatory basis with all deliberate speed the parties to these cases. The judgment in the Delaware case—ordering the immediate admission of the plaintiffs to schools previously attended only by white children—is affirmed on the basis of the principles stated in our May 17, 1954, opinion, but the case is remanded to the Supreme Court of Delaware for such further proceedings as that Court may deem necessary in the light of this opinion.

It is so ordered.

---

4. See Alexander v. Hillman, 296 U.S. 222, 239, 56 S.Ct. 204, 209.

5. See Hecht Co. v. Bowles, 321 U.S. 321, 329–330, 64 S.Ct. 587, 591–592.

Note and Questions

[Before answering these questions, review the excerpt from Loren Miller, The Petitioners, *supra* at pp. 998–1001.]

1. What reasons does the Court give for prescribing that there be "a reasonable start toward full compliance" with the ruling in Brown I, and that "the parties to these cases" be admitted "to public schools on a nondiscriminating basis with all deliberate speed"?

2. Do those reasons persuade you that the Court should not have ordered that "the parties to these cases" be admitted immediately to public schools formerly reserved only for white students?

3. What other reasons can you suggest for the choice of a remedy requiring "a reasonable start towards full compliance" and admission to public schools on a nondiscriminatory basis with all deliberate speed rather than immediate admission to schools formerly reserved only for white students?

4. The prescription of desegregation with all deliberate speed proved to be a very slow acting remedy. A new prescription was announced in Alexander v. Holmes County Board of Education, 396 U.S. 19, 90 S.Ct. 29 (1969). Part of the per curiam opinion in that case follows:

> These cases come to the Court on a petition for certiorari to the Court of Appeals for the Fifth Circuit. The petition was granted on October 9, 1969, and the case set down for early argument. The question presented is one of paramount importance, involving as it does the denial of fundamental rights to many thousands of school children, who are presently attending Mississippi schools under segregated conditions contrary to the applicable decisions of this Court. Against this background the Court of Appeals should have denied all motions for additional time because continued operation of segregated schools under a standard of allowing "all deliberate speed" for desegregation is no longer constitutionally permissible. Under explicit holdings of this Court the obligation of every school district is to terminate dual school systems at once and to operate now and hereafter only unitary schools. Griffin v. County School Board, 377 U.S. 218, 234, 84 S.Ct. 1226, 1235, 12 L.Ed.2d 256 (1964); Green v. County School Board of New Kent County, 391 U.S. 430, 438–439, 442, 88 S.Ct. 1689, 1694–1695, 1696, 20 L.Ed.2d 716 (1968).

SECTION 46. A JURISPRUDENTIAL POSTSCRIPT TO THE DEMISE OF JIM CROW LAWS

[The following is taken from HERBERT WECHSLER, "TOWARD NEUTRAL PRINCIPLES OF CONSTITUTIONAL LAW," 73 Harvard Law Review 1, 19–20, 26–35 (1959). Some footnotes omitted; others are renumbered.]

. . . The courts have both the title and the duty when a case is properly before them to review the actions of the other branches in the light of constitutional provisions, even though the action involves value choices, as invariably action does. In doing so, however, they are bound to function otherwise than as a naked power organ; they participate as courts of law. This calls for facing how determinations of this kind can be asserted to have any legal quality. The answer, I suggest, inheres primarily in that they are— or are obliged to be—entirely principled. A principled decision, in the sense I have in mind, is one that rests on reasons with respect to all the issues in the case, reasons that in their generality and their neutrality transcend any immediate result that is involved. When no sufficient reasons of this kind can be assigned for overturning value choices of the other branches of the Government or of a state, those choices must, of course, survive. Otherwise, as Holmes said in his first opinion for the Court, "a constitution, instead of embodying only relatively fundamental rules of right, as generally understood by all English-speaking communities, would become the partisan of a particular set of ethical or economical opinions . . . ." [1]

The virtue or demerit of a judgment turns, therefore, entirely on the reasons that support it and their adequacy to maintain any choice of values it decrees, or, it is vital that we add, to maintain the rejection of a claim that any given choice should be decreed.

* * *

. . . I turn to the decisions that for me provide the hardest test of my belief in principled adjudication, those in which the Court in recent years has vindicated claims that deprivations based on race deny the equality before the law that the fourteenth amendment guarantees. The crucial cases are, of course, those involving the white primary,[2] the enforcement of racially restrictive covenants,[3] and the segregated schools.[4]

The more I think about the past the more skeptical I find myself about predictions of the future. . . . But skeptical about predictions as I am, I still believe that the decisions I have mentioned—dealing with the primary, the covenant, and schools—have the best chance of making an enduring contribution to the quality of our society of any that I know in recent years. It is in this perspective that I ask how far they rest on neutral

---

1. Otis v. Parker, 187 U.S. 606, 609, 23 S.Ct. 168, 170 (1903).

2. Smith v. Allwright, 321 U.S. 649, 64 S.Ct. 756 (1944).

3. Shelley v. Kraemer, 334 U.S. 1, 68 S.Ct. 836 (1948); Barrows v. Jackson, 346 U.S. 249, 73 S.Ct. 1031 (1953).

4. Brown v. Board of Educ., 347 U.S. 483, 74 S.Ct. 686 (1954).

principles and are entitled to approval in the only terms that I acknowledge to be relevant to a decision of the courts.

The primary and covenant cases present two different aspects of a single problem—that it is a state alone that is forbidden by the fourteenth amendment to deny equal protection of the laws, as only a state or the United States is precluded by the fifteenth amendment from denying or abridging on the ground of race or color the right of citizens of the United States to vote. It has, of course, been held for years that the prohibition of action by the state reaches not only an explicit deprivation by a statute but also action of the courts or of subordinate officials, purporting to exert authority derived from public office.[5]

* * *

[Professor Wechsler first discusses the white primary cases.]

The case of the restrictive covenant presents for me an even harder problem. Assuming that the Constitution speaks to state discrimination on the ground of race but not to such discrimination by an individual even in the use or distribution of his property, although his freedom may no doubt be limited by common law or statute, why is the enforcement of the private covenant a state discrimination rather than a legal recognition of the freedom of the individual? That the action of the state court is action of the state, the point Mr. Chief Justice Vinson emphasizes in the Court's opinion [6] is, of course, entirely obvious. What is not obvious, and is the crucial step, is that the state may properly be charged with the discrimination when it does no more than give effect to an agreement that the individual involved is, by hypothesis, entirely free to make. Again, one is obliged to ask: What is the principle involved? Is the state forbidden to effectuate a will that draws a racial line, a will that can accomplish any disposition only through the aid of law, or is it a sufficient answer there that the discrimination was the testator's and not the state's?[7] May not the state employ its law to vindicate the privacy of property against a trespasser, regardless of the grounds of his exclusion, or does it embrace the owner's reasons for excluding if it buttresses his power by the law? Would a declaratory judgment that a fee is determinable if a racially restrictive limitation should be violated represent discrimination by the state upon the racial ground?[8] Would a judgment of ejectment?

* * *

Many understandably would like to perceive in the primary and covenant decisions a principle susceptible of broad extension, applying to the other power aggregates in our society limitations of the kind the Constitution has imposed on government. My colleague A. A. Berle, Jr., has, indeed, pointed to the large business corporation, which after all is chartered by the state and wields in many areas more power than the government, as uniquely

---

5. See, e. g., Ex parte Virginia, 100 U.S. 339, 347 (1880); Hale, Freedom Through Law ch. xi (1952).

6. See Shelley v. Kraemer, 334 U.S. 1, 14–23, 68 S.Ct. 836, 842–847 (1948).

7. Cf. Gordon v. Gordon, 332 Mass. 197, 210, 124 N.E.2d 228, 236, cert. denied 349 U.S. 947, 75 S.Ct. 875 (1955).

8. See Charlotte Park & Recreation Comm'n v. Barringer, 242 N.C. 311, 88 S.E.2d 114 (1955), cert. denied 350 U.S. 983, 76 S.Ct. 469 (1956).

suitable for choice as the next subject of such application. I doubt that the courts will yield to such temptations; and I do not hesitate to say that I prefer to see the issues faced through legislation, where there is room for drawing lines that courts are not equipped to draw. If this is right the two decisions I have mentioned will remain, as they now are, *ad hoc* determinations of their narrow problems, yielding no neutral principles for their extension or support.

Lastly, I come to the school decision, which for one of my persuasion stirs the deepest conflict I experience in testing the thesis I propose. Yet I would surely be engaged in playing Hamlet without Hamlet if I did not try to state the problems that appear to me to be involved.

The problem for me, I hardly need to say, is not that the Court departed from its earlier decisions holding or implying that the equality of public educational facilities demanded by the Constitution could be met by separate schools. I stand with the long tradition of the Court that previous decisions must be subject to reexamination when a case against their reasoning is made. Nor is the problem that the Court disturbed the settled patterns of a portion of the country; even that must be accepted as a lesser evil than nullification of the Constitution. Nor is it that history does not confirm that an agreed purpose of the fourteenth amendment was to forbid separate schools or that there is important evidence that many thought the contrary; the words are general and leave room for expanding content as time passes and conditions change. Nor is it that the Court may have miscalculated the extent to which its judgment would be honored or accepted; it is not a prophet of the strength of our national commitment to respect the judgments of the courts. Nor is it even that the Court did not remit the issue to the Congress, acting under the enforcement clause of the amendment. That was a possible solution, to be sure, but certainly Professor Freund is right that it would merely have evaded the claims made.

The problem inheres strictly in the reasoning of the opinion, an opinion which is often read with less fidelity by those who praise it than by those by whom it is condemned. The Court did not declare, as many wish it had, that the fourteenth amendment forbids all racial lines in legislation, though subsequent per curiam decisions may, as I have said, now go that far. Rather, as Judge Hand observed, the separate-but-equal formula was not overruled "in form" but was held to have "no place" in public education on the ground that segregated schools are "inherently unequal," with deleterious effects upon the colored children in implying their inferiority, effects which retard their educational and mental development. So, indeed, the district court had found as a fact in the Kansas case, a finding which the Supreme Court embraced, citing some further "modern authority" in its support.

Does the validity of the decision turn then on the sufficiency of evidence or of judicial notice to sustain a finding that the separation harms the Negro children who may be involved? There were, indeed, some witnesses who expressed that opinion in the Kansas case, as there were also witnesses in the companion Virginia case, including Professor Garrett of Columbia, whose view was to the contrary. Much depended on the question that the witness had in mind, which rarely was explicit. Was he comparing the position of the Negro child in a segregated school with his position in an integrated school where he was happily accepted and regarded by the whites;

or was he comparing his position under separation with that under integration where the whites were hostile to his presence and found ways to make their feelings known? And if the harm that segregation worked was relevant, what of the benefits that it entailed: sense of security, the absence of hostility? Were they irrelevant? Moreover, was the finding in Topeka applicable without more to Clarendon County, South Carolina, with 2,799 colored students and only 295 whites? Suppose that more Negroes in a community preferred separation than opposed it? Would that be relevant to whether they were hurt or aided by segregation as opposed to integration? Their fates would be governed by the change of system quite as fully as those of the students who complained.

I find it hard to think the judgment really turned upon the facts. Rather, it seems to me, it must have rested on the view that racial segregation is, in principle, a denial of equality to the minority against whom it is directed; that is, the group that is not dominant politically and, therefore, does not make the choice involved. For many who support the Court's decision this assuredly is the decisive ground. But this position also presents problems. Does it not involve an inquiry into the motive of the legislature, which is generally foreclosed to the courts? Is it alternatively defensible to make the measure of validity of legislation the way it is interpreted by those who are affected by it? In the context of a charge that segregation *with equal facilities* is a denial of equality, is there not a point in *Plessy* in the statement that if "enforced separation stamps the colored race with a badge of inferiority" it is solely because its members choose "to put that construction upon it"? Does enforced separation of the sexes discriminate against females merely because it may be the females who resent it and it is imposed by judgments predominantly male? Is a prohibition of miscegenation a discrimination against the colored member of the couple who would like to marry?

For me, assuming equal facilities, the question posed by state-enforced segregation is not one of discrimination at all. Its human and its constitutional dimensions lie entirely elsewhere, in the denial by the state of freedom to associate, a denial that impinges in the same way on any groups or races that may be involved. I think, and I hope not without foundation, that the Southern white also pays heavily for segregation, not only in the sense of guilt that he must carry but also in the benefits he is denied. In the days when I was joined with Charles H. Houston in a litigation in the Supreme Court, before the present building was constructed, he did not suffer more than I in knowing that we had to go to Union Station to lunch together during the recess. Does not the problem of miscegenation show most clearly that it is the freedom of association that at bottom is involved, the only case, I may add, where it is implicit in the situation that association is desired by the only individuals involved? I take no pride in knowing that in 1956 the Supreme Court dismissed an appeal in a case in which Virginia nullified a marriage on this ground, a case in which the statute had been squarely challenged by the defendant, and the Court, after remanding once, dismissed per curiam on procedural grounds that I make bold to say are wholly without basis in the law.

But if the freedom of association is denied by segregation, integration forces an association upon those for whom it is unpleasant or repugnant. Is this not the heart of the issue involved, a conflict in human claims of high dimension, not unlike many others that involve the highest freedoms—conflicts that Professor Sutherland has recently described. Given a situation where the state must practically choose between denying the association to those individuals who wish it or imposing it on those who would avoid it, is there a basis in neutral principles for holding that the Constitution demands that the claims for association should prevail? I should like to think there is, but I confess that I have not yet written the opinion. To write it is for me the challenge of the school-segregation cases.

Having said what I have said, I certainly should add that I offer no comfort to anyone who claims legitimacy in defiance of the courts. This is the ultimate negation of all neutral principles, to take the benefits accorded by the constitutional system, including the national market and common defense, while denying it allegiance when a special burden is imposed. That certainly is the antithesis of law.

Questions

1. Can you provide a principled resolution of the problems posed by Professor Wechsler in the will and trespass cases, *supra* p. 1012?

2. What response can you give to Professor Wechsler's query (*supra* p. 1014) regarding the reaction of Blacks (and possibly women) to discrimination imposed by a politically dominant majority? Is there any point in the statement he quotes from Plessy v. Ferguson (*supra* p. 1014)?

3. Professor Wechsler suggests that courts do not generally concern themselves with the motives underlying legislative decisions. Can you think of reasons why that should be so?

4. Does Professor Wechsler suggest that there is no neutral principle which will support the result in *Brown*, or only that the *Brown* opinion does not state such a principle?

5. How would you answer Professor Wechsler regarding the matter of freedom of association and the impact of either segregation laws or the *Brown* decision on that freedom (*supra* p. 1014)? Numerous scholars have responded to Professor Wechsler's doubts about the principles (or lack thereof) in *Shelley* and *Brown*. Extracts from two of these responses are set out below. See if you think either or both of them adequately meet the issues raised by Professor Wechsler.

[The following is taken from CHARLES L. BLACK, JR., "THE LAWFULNESS OF THE SEGREGATION DECISIONS," 69 Yale Law Journal 421 (1960). Some footnotes omitted; others are renumbered.]

If the cases outlawing segregation were wrongly decided, then they ought to be overruled. One can go further: if dominant professional opinion ever forms and settles on the belief that they were wrongly decided, then they will be overruled, slowly or all at once, openly or silently. The insignificant error, however palpable, can stand, because the convenience of settlement outweighs the discomfort of error. But the hugely consequential error cannot stand and does not stand.

There is pragmatic meaning then, there is call for action, in the suggestion that the segregation cases cannot be justified.[1] In the long run, as a corollary, there is practical and not merely intellectual significance in the question whether these cases were rightly decided. I think they were rightly decided, by overwhelming weight of reason, and I intend here to say why I hold this belief.

My liminal difficulty is rhetorical—or, perhaps more accurately, one of fashion. Simplicity is out of fashion, and the basic scheme of reasoning on which these cases can be justified is awkwardly simple. First, the equal protection clause of the fourteenth amendment should be read as saying that the Negro race, as such, is not to be significantly disadvantaged by the laws of the states. Secondly, segregation is a massive intentional disadvantaging of the Negro race, as such, by state law. No subtlety at all. Yet I cannot disabuse myself of the idea that that is really all there is to the segregation cases. If both these propositions can be supported by the preponderance of argument, the cases were rightly decided. If they cannot be so supported, the cases are in perilous condition.

As a general thing, the first of these propositions has so far as I know never been controverted in a holding of the Supreme Court. I rest here on the solid sense of The Slaughterhouse Cases and of Strauder v. West Virginia, where Mr. Justice Strong said of the fourteenth amendment:

> It ordains that no State shall make or enforce any laws which shall abridge the privileges or immunities of citizens of the United States (evidently referring to the newly made citizens, who, being citizens of the United States, are declared to be also citizens of the State in which they reside). It ordains that no State shall deprive any person of life, liberty, or property, without due process of law, or deny to any person within its jurisdiction the equal protection of the laws. What is this but declaring that the law in the States shall be the same for the black as for the white; that all persons, whether colored or white, shall stand equal before the laws of the States, and, in regard to the colored race, for whose protection the amendment was primarily designed, that no discrimination shall be made against them by law because of their color? The words of the amendment, it is true, are prohibitory, but they contain a necessary implication of a positive immunity, or right, most valuable to the colored race,—the right to exemption from unfriendly legislation against them distinctively as colored,—exemption from legal discriminations, implying inferiority in civil society, lessening the security of their enjoyment of the rights which others enjoy, and discriminations which are steps towards reducing them to the condition of a subject race.

If Plessy v. Ferguson be thought a faltering from this principle, I step back to the principle itself. But the *Plessy* Court clearly conceived it to be

---

1. See Wechsler, Toward Neutral Principles of Constitutional Law, 73 Harv. L.Rev. 1, 34 (1959). The present Article was immediately suggested by Professor Wechsler's questionings. It is not, however, to be looked on as formal "reply," since I cover here only one part of the ground he goes over, and since my lines of thought are only partly responsive in terms to the questions as he sees them.

its task to show that segregation did not really disadvantage the Negro, except through his own choice. There is in this no denial of the *Slaughterhouse* and *Strauder* principle; the fault of *Plessy* is in the psychology and sociology of its minor premise.

The lurking difficulty lies not in "racial" cases but in the total philosophy of "equal protection" in the wide sense. "Equal protection," as it applies to the whole of state law, must be consistent with the imposition of disadvantage on some, for all law imposes disadvantage on some; to give driver's licenses only to good drivers is to disadvantage bad drivers. Thus the word "reasonable" necessarily finds its way into "equal protection," in the application of the latter concept to law in general. And it is inevitable, and right, that "reasonable," in this broader context, should be given its older sense of "supportable by reasoned considerations." "Equal" thereby comes to mean not really "equal," but "equal unless a fairly tenable reason exists for inequality."

But the whole tragic background of the fourteenth amendment forbids the feedback infection of its central purpose with the necessary qualifications that have attached themselves to its broader and so largely accidental radiations. It may have been intended that "equal protection" go forth into wider fields than the racial. But history puts it entirely out of doubt that the chief and all-dominating purpose was to ensure equal protection for the Negro. And this intent can hardly be given the self-defeating qualification that necessity has written on equal protection as applied to carbonic gas. If it is, then "equal protection" for the Negro means "equality until a tenable reason for inequality is proffered." On this view, Negroes may hold property, sign wills, marry, testify in court, walk the streets, go to (even segregated) school, ride public transportation, and so on, only in the event that no reason, not clearly untenable, can be assigned by a state legislature for their not being permitted to do these things. That cannot have been what all the noise was about in 1866.

What the fourteenth amendment, in its historical setting, must be read to say is that the Negro is to enjoy equal protection of the laws, and that the fact of his being a Negro is not to be taken to be a good enough reason for denying him this equality, however "reasonable" that might seem to some people. All possible arguments, however convincing, for discriminating against the Negro, were finally rejected by the fourteenth amendment.

Then does segregation offend against equality? Equality, like all general concepts, has marginal areas where philosophic difficulties are encountered. But if a whole race of people finds itself confined within a system which is set up and continued for the very purpose of keeping it in an inferior station, and if the question is then solemnly propounded whether such a race is being treated "equally," I think we ought to exercise one of the sovereign prerogatives of philosophers—that of laughter. The only question remaining (after we get our laughter under control) is whether the segregation system answers to this description.

Here I must confess to a tendency to start laughing all over again. I was raised in the South, in a Texas city where the pattern of segregation was firmly fixed. I am sure it never occurred to anyone, white or colored, to question its meaning. The fiction of "equality" is just about on a level with the fiction of "finding" in the action of trover. I think few candid southerners deny this. Northern people may be misled by the entirely sincere protestations of many southerners that segregation is "better" for the Negroes, is not intended to hurt them. But I think a little probing would demonstrate that what is meant is that it is better for the Negroes to accept a position of inferiority, at least for the indefinite future.

But the subjectively obvious, if queried, must be backed up by more public materials. What public materials assure me that my reading of the social meaning of segregation is not a mere idiosyncracy?

First, of course, is history. Segregation in the South comes down in apostolic succession from slavery and the *Dred Scott* case. The South fought to keep slavery, and lost. Then it tried the Black Codes, and lost. Then it looked around for something else and found segregation. The movement for segregation was an integral part of the movement to maintain and further "white supremacy"; its triumph (as Professor Woodward has shown) represented a triumph of extreme racialist over moderate sentiment about the Negro. It is now defended very largely on the ground that the Negro as such is not fit to associate with the white.

History, too, tells us that segregation was imposed on one race by the other race; consent was not invited or required. Segregation in the South grew up and is kept going because and only because the white race has wanted it that way—an incontrovertible fact which in itself hardly consorts with equality. This fact perhaps more than any other confirms the picture which a casual or deep observer is likely to form of the life of a southern community—a picture not of mutual separation of whites and Negroes, but of one in-group enjoying full normal communal life and one out-group that is barred from this life and forced into an inferior life of its own. When a white southern writer refers to the woes of "the South," do you not know, does not context commonly make it clear, that he means "white southerners"? When you are in Leeville and hear someone say "Leeville High," you know he has reference to the white high school; the Negro school will be called something else—Carver High, perhaps, or Lincoln High to our shame. That is what you would expect when one race forces a segregated position on another, and that is what you get.

Segregation is historically and contemporaneously associated in a functioning complex with practices which are indisputably and grossly discriminatory. I have in mind especially the long-continued and still largely effective exclusion of Negroes from voting. Here we have two things. First, a certain group of people is "segregated." Secondly, at about the same time, the very same group of people, down to the last man and woman, is barred, or sought to be barred, from the common political life of the community—from all political power. Then we are solemnly told that segregation is not intended to harm the segregated race, or to stamp it with the mark of inferiority. How long must we keep a straight face?

* * *

The various items I have mentioned differ in weight; not every one would suffice in itself to establish the character of segregation. Taken together they are of irrefragable strength. The society that has just lost the Negro as a slave, that has just lost out in an attempt to put him under quasi-servile "Codes," the society that views his blood as a contamination and his name as an insult, the society that extralegally imposes on him every humiliating mark of low caste and that until yesterday kept him in line by lynching—this society, careless of his consent, moves by law, first to exclude him from voting, and secondly to cut him off from mixing in the general public life of the community. The Court that refused to see inequality in this cutting off would be making the only kind of law that can be warranted outrageous in advance—law based on self-induced blindness, on flagrant contradiction of known fact.

I have stated all these points shortly because they are matters of common notoriety, matters not so much for judicial notice as for the background knowledge of educated men who live in the world. A court may advise itself of them as it advises itself of the facts that we are a "religious people," that the country is more industrialized than in Jefferson's day, that children are the natural objects of fathers' bounty, that criminal sanctions are commonly thought to deter, that steel is a basic commodity in our economy, that the imputation of unchastity is harmful to a woman. Such judgments, made on such a basis, are in the foundations of all law, decisional as well as statutory; it would be the most unneutral of principles, improvised *ad hoc,* to require that a court faced with the present problem refuse to note a plain fact about the society of the United States—the fact that the social meaning of segregation is the putting of the Negro in a position of walled-off inferiority—or the other equally plain fact that such treatment is hurtful to human beings. Southern courts, on the basis of just such a judgment, have held that the placing of a white person in a Negro railroad car is an actionable humiliation; must a court pretend not to know that the Negro's situation there is humiliating?

I think that some of the artificial mist of puzzlement called into being around this question originates in a single fundamental mistake. The issue is seen in terms of what might be called the metaphysics of sociology: "Must Segregation Amount to Discrimination?" That is an interesting question; someday the methods of sociology may be adequate to answering it. But it is not our question. Our question is whether discrimination inheres in that segregation which is imposed by law in the twentieth century in certain specific states in the American Union. And that question has meaning and can find an answer only on the ground of history and of common knowledge about the facts of life in the times and places aforesaid.

Now I need not and do not maintain that the evidence is all one way; it never is on issues of burning, fighting concern. Let us not question here the good faith of those who assert that segregation represents no more than an attempt to furnish a wholesome opportunity for parallel development of the races; let us rejoice at the few scattered instances they can bring forward to support their view of the matter. But let us then ask which balance-pan flies upward.

The case seems so onesided that it is hard to make out what is being protested against when it is asked, rhetorically, how the Court can possibly advise itself of the real character of the segregation system. It seems that what is being said is that, while no actual doubt exists as to what segregation is for and what kind of societal pattern it supports and implements, there is no ritually sanctioned way in which the Court, as a Court, can permissibly learn what is obvious to everybody else and to the Justices as individuals. But surely, confronted with such a problem, legal acumen has only one proper task—that of developing ways to make it permissible for the Court to use what it knows; any other counsel is of despair. And, equally surely, the fact that the Court has assumed as true a matter of common knowledge in regard to broad societal patterns, is (to say the very least) pretty far down the list of things to protest against.

I conclude, then, that the Court had the soundest reasons for judging that segregation violates the fourteenth amendment. These reasons make up the simple syllogism with which I began: The fourteenth amendment commands equality, and segregation as we know it is inequality.

* * *

[I]t is doubtless true that the *School Segregation Cases,* and perhaps others of the cases on segregation, represented a choice between two kinds of freedom of association. Freedom from the massive wrong of segregation entails a corresponding loss of freedom on the part of the whites who must now associate with Negroes on public occasions, as we all must on such occasions associate with many persons we had rather not associate with. It is possible to state the competing claims in symmetry, and to ask whether there are constitutional reasons for preferring the Negroes' desire for merged participation in public life to the white man's desire to live a public life without Negroes in proximity.

The question must be answered, but I would approach it in a way which seems to me more normal—the way in which we more usually approach comparable symmetries that might be stated as to all other asserted rights. The fourteenth amendment forbids inequality, forbids the disadvantaging of the Negro race by law. It was surely anticipated that the following of this directive would entail some disagreeableness for some white southerners. The disagreeableness might take many forms; the white man, for example, might dislike having a Negro neighbor in the exercise of the latter's equal right to own a home, or dislike serving on a jury with a Negro, or dislike having Negroes on the streets with him after ten o'clock. When the directive of equality cannot be followed without displeasing the white, then something that can be called a "freedom" of the white must be impaired. If the fourteenth amendment commands equality, and if segregation violates equality, then the status of the reciprocal "freedom" is automatically settled.

I find reinforcement here, at least as a matter of spirit, in the fourteenth amendment command that Negroes shall be "citizens" of their States. It is hard for me to imagine in what operative sense a man could be a "citizen" without his fellow citizens' once in a while having to associate with him. If, for example, his "citizenship" results in his election to the School Board, the white members may (as recently in Houston) put him off to one side of the room, but there is still some impairment of their freedom "not to associate." That freedom, in fact, exists only at home; in public, we have to associate with anybody who has a right to be there. The question of our right not to associate with him is concluded when we decide whether he has a right to be there.

I am not really apologetic for the simplicity of my ideas on the segregation cases. The decisions call for mighty diastrophic change. We ought to call for such change only in the name of a solid reasoned simplicity that takes law out of artfulness into art. Only such grounds can support the nation in its resolve to uphold the law declared by its Court; only such grounds can reconcile the white South to what must be. *Elegantia juris* and conceptual algebra have here no place. Without pretending either to completeness or to definitiveness of statement, I have tried here to show reasons for believing that we as lawyers can without fake or apology present to the lay community, and to ourselves, a rationale of the segregation decisions that rises to the height of the great argument.

These judgments, like all judgments, must rest on the rightness of their law and the truth of their fact. Their law is right if the equal protection clause in the fourteenth amendment is to be taken as stating, without arbitrary exceptions, a broad principle of practical equality for the Negro race, inconsistent with any device that in fact relegates the Negro race to a position of inferiority. Their facts are true if it is true that the segregation system is actually conceived and does actually function as a means of keeping the Negro in a status of inferiority. I dare say at this time that in the end the decisions will be accepted by the profession on just that basis. Opinions composed under painful stresses may leave much to be desired [2] it may be that the per curiam device has been unwisely used. But the judgments, in law and in fact, are as right and true as any that ever was uttered.

[The following is taken from ALEXANDER M. BICKEL, THE LEAST DANGEROUS BRANCH (New York, 1962), pp. 56–57, 59.]

As Mr. Wechsler concedes, the *School Segregation Cases,* read in conjunction with certain brief orders that followed after them, have made clear that the principle in question is that racial segregation constitutes, *per se,* a denial of equality to the minority group against whom it is directed. That group, Mr. Wechsler adds, is the one "that is not dominant politically and, therefore, does not make the choice involved." Mr. Wechsler suggests several additional considerations. Does not the finding of a denial of equality depend on an estimate of the motive of the legislature? Or, alternatively, does it not make decisive the interpretation placed on the legislation by those who are affected by it? That is, is not segregation a denial of equality only because Negroes subjectively feel it to be such? After all, segregation by sex is not viewed as discriminating against females. For himself, Mr. Wechsler sees segregation statutes as regulations of the freedom to associate. They impair the freedom of whites and Negroes alike, and damage both. But the fact of the matter in the Southern states is that most whites do not wish to associate with Negroes. A legislature must make a choice between abridging Negro freedom to associate and abridging white freedom not to associate, "between denying the association to those individuals who wish it or imposing it on those who would avoid it." To order integration

---

2. I do not mean here to join the hue and cry against the *Brown* opinion. The charge that it is "sociological" is either a truism or a canard—a truism if it means that the Court, precisely like the *Plessy* Court, and like innumerable other courts facing innumerable other issues of law, had to resolve and did resolve a question about social fact; a canard if it means that anything like principal reliance was placed on the formally "scientific" authorities, which are relegated to a footnote and treated as merely cor-roboratory of common sense. It seems to me that the venial fault of the opinion consists in its not spelling out that segregation, for reasons of the kind I have brought forward in this Article, is perceptibly a means of ghettoizing the imputedly inferior race. (I would conjecture that the motive for this omission was reluctance to go into the distasteful details of the southern caste system.) That such treatment is generally not good for children needs less talk than the Court gives it.

is simply to reverse such a legislative choice, not to avoid it or somehow make it unnecessary, for it cannot be avoided. "[I]s there a basis in neutral principles for holding that the Constitution demands that the claims for association should prevail?"

The reply question is this: What, on the score of generality and neutrality, is wrong with the principle that a legislative choice in favor of a freedom not to associate is forbidden, when the consequence of such a choice is to place one of the groups of which our society is constituted in a position of permanent, humiliating inferiority; when the consequence beyond that is to foster in the whites, by authority of the state, self-damaging and potentially violent feelings of racial superiority—feelings that, as Lincoln knew, find easy transference from Negroes to other groups as their particular objects? It may be that this principle is wrong or is on other grounds ill suited for pronouncement and application by the Court. But wherein is it lacking on the score of neutrality, in the terms in which so far we have analyzed that concept?

The point that the Court must necessarily rely on an estimate of legislative motive or of the subjective feelings of Negroes affected by segregation fails, in my judgment, entirely. Granted that it would be relatively novel, and in that degree *ad hoc*, as well as extremely difficult for the Court so to rely. But it is unnecessary. To determine that segregation establishes a relationship of the inferior to the superior race is to take objective notice of a fact of our national life and of experience elsewhere in the world, now and in other times, quite without reference to legislative motives and without reliance on subjective and perhaps idiosyncratic feelings. It is no different from a similarly experiential judgment that official inquiries into private associations inhibit the freedom to join, or that hearsay evidence, reported at second or third hand, has a tendency to become distorted. . . .

* * *

Earlier we saw the rule of the neutral principles as foreclosing *ad hoc* constitutional judgments which express merely the judge's transient feeling of what is fair, convenient, or congenial in the particular circumstances of a litigation. . . .

A neutral principle, by contrast, is an intellectually coherent statement of the reason for a result which in like cases will produce a like result, whether or not it is immediately agreeable or expedient. Now the demand for neutral principles is carried further. It is that the Court rest judgment only on principles that will be capable of application across the board and without compromise, in all relevant cases in the foreseeable future: absolute application of absolute—even if sometimes flexible—principles. The flexibility, if any, must be built into the principle itself, in equally principled fashion. Thus a neutral principle is a rule of action that will be authoritatively enforced without adjustment or concession and without let-up. If it sometimes hurts, nothing is better proof of its validity. If it must sometimes fail of application, it won't do. Given the nature of a free society and the ultimate consensual basis of all its effective law, there can be but very few such principles.

SECTION 47. LEGISLATIVE INTERMENT OF JIM CROW

It is not possible to establish cause and effect relationships in such matters, but it seems fair to suggest that the *Brown* decision triggered other responses to the problem of race relations in the United States. A new assertiveness and self-assurance in the matter of civil rights developed both in the Black community and among significant numbers of white Americans sympathetic to its cause. This mood was reflected in a series of legal and political developments in the decade after Brown. Perhaps the most significant of these developments was the passage of major federal civil rights legislation in 1957, 1960, and 1964.

[The following summaries of the major provisions of the Civil Rights Acts of 1957, 1960 and 1964 are taken from "REVOLUTION IN CIVIL RIGHTS", a special publication of the Congressional Quarterly Service (1966), pages 28, 34, 71–74.]

Provisions of Civil Rights Act of 1957

TITLE I

Created an executive Commission on Civil Rights composed of six members, not more than three from the same political party, to be appointed by the President with the advice and consent of the Senate.

Established rules of procedure for the Commission.

Authorized the Commission to receive in executive session any testimony that might defame or incriminate anyone.

Provided that penalties for unauthorized persons who released information from executive hearings of the Commission would apply only to persons whose services were paid for by the Government.

Barred the Commission from issuing subpenas for witnesses who were found, resided or transacted business outside the state in which the hearing would be held.

Placed the pay for Commissioners at $50 per day—plus $12 per day for expenses away from home.

Empowered the Commission to investigate allegations that U. S. citizens were being deprived of their right to vote and have that vote counted by reason of color, race, religion, or national origin; to study and collect information concerning legal developments constituting a denial of equal protection of the laws under the Constitution; to appraise the laws and policies of the Federal Government with respect to equal protection of the laws.

Directed the Commission to submit interim reports to the President and Congress and a final report of its activities, findings and recommendations not later than two years following enactment of the bill.

Authorized the President, with the advice and consent of the Senate, to appoint a full-time staff director of the Commission whose pay would not exceed $22,500 a year.

Barred the Commission from accepting or utilizing the services of voluntary or uncompensated personnel.

TITLE II

Authorized the President to appoint, with the advice and consent of the Senate, one additional Assistant Attorney General in the Department of Justice.

TITLE III

Extended the jurisdiction of the district courts to include any civil action begun to recover damages or secure equitable relief under any act of Congress providing for the protection of civil rights, including the right to vote.

Repealed a statute of 1866 giving the President power to employ troops to enforce or to prevent violation of civil rights legislation.

TITLE IV

Prohibited attempts to intimidate or prevent persons from voting in general or primary elections for federal offices.

Empowered the Attorney General to seek an injunction when an individual was deprived or about to be deprived of his right to vote.

Gave the district courts jurisdiction over such proceedings, without requiring that administrative remedies be exhausted.

Provided that any person cited for contempt should be defended by counsel and allowed to compel witnesses to appear.

TITLE V

Provided that in all criminal contempt cases arising from the provisions of the Civil Rights Act of 1957, the accused, upon conviction, would be punished by fine or imprisonment or both.

Placed the maximum fine for an individual under those provisions at $1,000 or six months in jail.

Allowed the judge to decide whether a defendant in a criminal contempt case involving voting rights would be tried with or without a jury.

Provided that in the event a criminal contempt case was tried before a judge without a jury and the sentence upon conviction was more than $300 or more than 45 days in jail, the defendant could demand and receive a jury trial.

Stated that the section would not apply to contempts committed in the presence of the court or so near as to interfere directly with the administration of justice, nor to the behavior or misconduct of any officer of the court in respect to the process of the court.

Provided that any U. S. citizen over 21 who had resided for one year within a judicial district would be competent to serve as a grand or petit juror unless: (1) he had been convicted of a crime punishable by imprisonment for more than one year and his civil rights not restored; (2) he was unable to read, write, speak and understand the English language; (3) he was incapable, either physically or mentally, to give efficient jury service.

Provisions of Civil Rights Act of 1960

TITLE I

Provided that persons who obstructed or interfered with any order issued by a federal court, or attempted to do so, by threats or force, could be punished by a fine of up to $1,000, imprisonment of up to one year, or both. Such acts could also be prevented by private suits seeking court injunctions against them.

TITLE II

Made it a federal crime to cross state lines to avoid prosecution or punishment for, or giving evidence on, the bombing or burning of any building, facility or vehicle, or an attempt to do so. Penalties could be a fine of up to $5,000, or imprisonment of up to five years, or both.

Made it a federal crime to transport or possess explosives with the knowledge or intent that they would be used to blow up any vehicle or building. Allowed the presumption, after any bombing occurred, that the explosives used were transported across state lines (therefore allowing the FBI to investigate any bombing case), but stipulated that this would have to be proved before the person could be convicted. Penalties could be imprisonment of up to one year and/or $1,000 fine; if personal injury resulted, 10 years and/or $10,000 fine; if death resulted, life imprisonment or a death penalty if recommended by a jury.

Made it a federal crime to use interstate facilities, such as telephones, to threaten a bombing or give a false bomb-scare, punishable by imprisonment of up to one year or a fine of up to $1,000, or both.

TITLE III

Required that voting records and registration papers for all federal elections, including primaries, must be preserved for 22 months. Penalties for failing to comply or for stealing, destroying or mutilating the records could be a fine of up to $1,000, and/or imprisonment for one year.

Directed that the records, upon written application, be turned over to the Attorney General "or his representative" at the office of the records' custodian.

Unless directed otherwise by a court, the Justice Department representative must not disclose the content of the records except to Congress, a government agency, or in a court proceeding.

TITLE IV

Empowered the Civil Rights Commission, which was extended for two years in 1959, to administer oaths and take sworn statements.

TITLE V

Stated that arrangements might be made to provide for the education of children of members of the armed forces when the schools those children regularly attended had been closed to avoid integration and the U. S. Commissioner of Education had decided that no other educational agency would provide for their schooling. Amended the laws on aid to impacted school districts (PL 81–815, PL 81–874) to this effect.

TITLE VI

Provided that after the Attorney General won a civil suit brought under the 1957 Civil Rights Act to protect Negroes' right to vote, he could then ask the court to hold another adversary proceeding and make a separate finding that there was a "pattern or practice" of depriving Negroes of the right to vote in the area involved in the suit.

If a court found such a "pattern or practice," any Negro living in that area could apply to the court to issue an order declaring him qualified to vote if he proved (1) he was qualified to vote under state law; (2) he had tried to register after the "pattern or practice" finding; and (3) he had not been allowed to register or had been found unqualified by someone acting under color of law. The court would have to hear the Negro's application within 10 days and its order would be effective for as long a period as that for which he would have been qualified to vote if registered under state law.

State officials would be notified of the order, and they would then be bound to permit the person to vote. Disobedience would be subject to contempt proceedings.

To carry out these provisions, the court may appoint one or more voting referees, who must be qualified voters in the judicial district. The referees would receive the applications, take evidence, and report their findings to the court. The referee must take the Negro's application and proof in an *ex parte* proceeding (without cross-examination by opponents) and the court may set the time and place for the referee's hearing.

The court may fix a time limit of up to 10 days, in which state officials may challenge the referee's report. Challenges on points of law must be accompanied by a memorandum and on points of fact by a verified copy of a public record or an affidavit by those with personal knowledge of the controverting evidence. Either the court or the referee may decide the challenges in accordance with court-directed procedures. Hearings on issues of fact could be held only when the affidavits show there is a real issue of fact.

If a Negro has applied for a court certificate 20 or more days before the election, his application is challenged, and the case is not decided by election day, the court must allow him to vote provisionally, provided he is "entitled to vote under state law," and impound his ballot pending a decision on his application. If he applies within 20 days before the election, the court has the option of whether or not to let him vote.

The court would not be limited in its powers to enforce its decree that these Negroes be allowed to vote and their votes be counted and may authorize the referee to take action to enforce it.

The referees would have the powers conferred on court masters by rule 53(c) of the Federal Rules of Civil Procedure. (Rule 53(c) gives masters the right to subpena records, administer oaths and cross-examine witnesses.)

In any suit instituted under these provisions, the state would be held responsible for the actions of its officials and, in the event state officials resign and are not replaced, the state itself could be sued.

Provisions of Civil Rights Act of 1964

TITLE I—VOTING RIGHTS

In voting for federal elections, HR 7152 added to the Civil Rights Act of 1957's provisions against denial of voting rights the following:

barred unequal application of voting registration requirements;

prohibited denial of the right to vote because of immaterial errors or omissions by applicants on records of application;

required that all literacy tests be administered in writing, and that for a period of 22 months the individual may, on request, receive a copy of the papers within 25 days; gave the Attorney General authority to enter into agreements with state or local authorities that their literacy tests are fairly administered and need not be given in writing;

made a sixth-grade education (if in English) a rebuttable presumption of literacy.

When the Attorney General, under authority granted by the 1957 Civil Rights Act, files a voting rights suit and requests a finding of a pattern or practice of discrimination against voters, HR 7152 authorized him, at the time he filed the suit, to request that it be heard by a three-judge federal court (decisions of three-judge courts are immediately appealable to the Supreme Court). One of the judges must be a member of a federal circuit court and another a district judge in the district where the complaint is brought. A defendant also was authorized to request a three-judge court within 20 days after the suit was filed.

In pattern or practice suits—whether a three-judge court is requested or not—or in suits against intimidation of those attempting to register, required the courts to expedite the cases.

TITLE II—PUBLIC ACCOMMODATIONS

Barred discrimination on grounds of race, color, religion or national origin in public accommodations enumerated below, if discrimination or segregation in such an accommodation is supported by state laws or official action, if lodgings are provided to transient guests or interstate travelers are served, or if a substantial portion of the goods sold or entertainment presented moves in interstate commerce.

Covered restaurants, cafeterias, lunch rooms, lunch counters, soda fountains, gasoline stations, motion picture houses, theaters, concert halls, sports arenas, stadiums, or any hotel, motel or lodging house except owner-occupied units with five or less rooms for rent (the "Mrs. Murphy" clause). Also covered any public establishment within or containing an accommodation otherwise covered (for example, a store containing a lunch counter, or a barber shop in a hotel). Not specifically covered: barber shops, retail stores, bars, small places of amusement such as bowling alleys. Specifically exempted were private clubs, except to the extent that they offer their facilities to patrons of covered establishments (such as hotels).

Made it unlawful to deny any person access to these facilities because of race, color, religion or national origin, to threaten or intimidate anyone seeking his rights under this title, or to punish any person for exercising his rights under this title.

Permitted anyone denied his rights under this title to sue in court for preventive relief through a civil injunction, and authorized the courts, in their discretion, to permit the Attorney General to intervene in the private suit; also permitted the court to appoint an attorney for the complainant.

If the alleged discriminatory practice takes place in a state or local area which has a law prohibiting such acts and establishing methods of seeking relief, prohibited the suit from being brought until the state or local authority has had 30 days' notice. Allowed the court to stay proceedings further, pending termination of state or local enforcement proceedings.

If the alleged action takes place in a state which has no public accommodations law, permitted the courts to refer the matter to the Community Relations Service (established in Title X) for 60 to 120 days, if there was a reasonable chance of obtaining voluntary compliance.

Authorized the Attorney General to bring a civil action when he "has reasonable cause to believe" that a person or group of persons is engaged in a pattern or practice of resistance to granting the rights under this title. (No waiting period was required.)

Authorized the Attorney General to request a three-judge court to hear the case, the request to be accompanied by a certificate that the case is of "general public importance."

Directed the courts to expedite suits by the Attorney General.

Permitted the courts to order the payment of the attorney's fee of the winning party, unless it is the Government.

TITLE III—DESEGREGATION OF PUBLIC FACILITIES

Upon written complaint of aggrieved individuals, permitted Justice Department suits to secure desegregation of state or locally owned, operated or managed public facilities, when the Attorney General believes that the complaint is "meritorious" and certifies that the aggrieved persons are unable to initiate and maintain legal proceedings because of financial limitations or potential economic or other injury to themselves or their families.

TITLE IV—DESEGREGATION OF PUBLIC EDUCATION

Required the U.S. Office of Education to make a survey and report to Congress within two years on the progress of desegregation of public schools at all levels.

Authorized the Office to give technical and financial assistance, if requested, to local public school systems planning or going through the process of desegregation. The assistance could be:

technical assistance in the form of information on effective methods of coping with special problems arising out of desegregation, or making available Office of Education or other personnel equipped to handle such problems;

arrangements, through grants or contracts, with colleges and universities for special institutes to train school personnel to deal with desegregation problems, and payment of stipends to those who attend the institutes on a full-time basis;

grants to a school board to pay for the cost of giving school personnel special training or employing specialists.

Authorized the Attorney General to file suit for the desegregation of public schools and colleges if he receives a signed complaint, believes that the complaint is meritorious, and certifies that the aggrieved individuals are unable to initiate and maintain legal proceedings, and that the action would "materially further" orderly school desegregation; provided that the suit may be filed only after he has notified the local school board or college authority of the complaint and given them a reasonable time to adjust the conditions.

Made clear that this law did not authorize any U.S. officials or courts to issue any order seeking to achieve racial balances in schools by transporting children from one school to another, nor did it enlarge the courts' existing powers to ensure compliance with constitutional standards.

Made clear that this title did not prohibit classification and assignment of students for reasons other than race, color, religion or national origin.

TITLE V—CIVIL RIGHTS COMMISSION

Wrote into law a number of requirements for Commission procedures, covering the summoning and taking testimony from witnesses, giving notice of hearings, confidentiality of proceedings, and bipartisanship in its activities.

Broadened the duties of the Commission by authorizing it to serve as a national clearinghouse on civil rights information, and to investigate vote frauds as well as denials of the right to vote.

Barred the Commission from investigating the membership practices or internal practices of any fraternal organizations, college sororities and fraternities, private clubs or religious organizations.

Extended the life of the Commission for four years, through Jan. 31, 1968, and required it to file a final report at that time, with such interim reports as the Commission, Congress or the President deem desirable.

TITLE VI—NONDISCRIMINATION IN FEDERALLY ASSISTED PROGRAMS

Barred discrimination under any program or activity receiving federal assistance against any person because of his race, color or national origin.

Directed each federal department or agency extending financial assistance to any program or activity through grants, loans or most kinds of contracts, except contracts of insurance or guaranty, to issue rules or regulations, to be approved by the President, to carry out the purposes of this title.

Required that to enforce the title, agencies must first seek voluntary compliance, but if it is not forthcoming, authorized the agencies, after making a finding on the record, and giving opportunity for hearing, and after giving the appropriate legislative committees 30 days' notice, to cut off the federal program involved from the particular recipient or political entity involved.

Made any action cutting off assistance subject to judicial review.

Made clear that this section was not to be used to enforce equal employment practices, except where a primary purpose of the federal program is to provide employment.

Stated that nothing in this title added to or subtracted from any existing federal authority.

TITLE VII—EQUAL EMPLOYMENT OPPORTUNITY

Outlawed the following employment practices if based on grounds of race, color, religion, sex or national origin:

failure or refusal to hire or fire any person, or discrimination against him with respect to pay or terms and conditions of employment; or, in the case of an employment agency or hiring hall, failure or refusal to refer a worker;

segregation, classification or any limitation of an employee in a way that would deprive him of equal employment opportunities;

exclusion or expulsion from union membership;

segregation, classification or limitation in union membership, or failure or refusal to refer for employment;

a union's causing or attempting to cause an employer to discriminate against a worker;

discrimination in any apprenticeship or training programs;

discrimination against employees or applicants for employment because they have challenged employment practices outlawed by this section;

printing or publishing any job notices indicating preferences because of race, color, religion, sex or national origin, unless these are bona fide job qualifications.

Coverage: HR 7152 provided a one-year delay before any employees would be covered by this section and full coverage would not be in effect for five years. In the second year after enactment, employers in industries affecting commerce with 100 or more employees for 20 weeks in a year, unions in industries affecting commerce with 100 or more members, union hiring halls and employment agencies would be covered. In the third year, industries and unions with 75 workers would be covered; in the fourth year, those with 50; and in the fifth year and thereafter, those with 25 workers.

Exemptions: Made the following exemptions from coverage:

employers' alien workers outside the U.S.;

employment by religious groups of individuals to carry out their religious activities;

hiring for educational activities by educational institutions;

hiring or classification on the grounds of religion, sex, or national origin where these are bona fide occupational qualifications;

hiring by schools supported, controlled, or managed by a particular religion or persons of that religion;

discrimination against Communists or members of Communist-front organizations (as determined by the federal Subversive Activities Control Board);

preferential treatment for Indians living on or near reservations in enterprises on or near reservations;

refusing to hire, or firing those who do not meet Government security requirements;

the United States Government, and state and local governments, government-owned corporations, Indian tribes and non-profit private membership clubs (fraternal organizations, social clubs, country clubs, etc.); however, the section stated that it shall be the policy of the U.S. to insure equal employment opportunities in federal employment.

Made it clear that this section did not outlaw seniority or merit systems, or the setting of different standards of compensation or terms of employment, or the giving of professionally developed ability tests, as long as such actions were not with intent to discriminate because of race, color, religion, sex or national origin.

Stated that this section was not to be used to require quotas in employment, unions, or training programs on the grounds of race, color, religion, sex or national origin.

EEOC: Created a five-member Equal Employment Opportunity Commission, with no more than three members of the same political party, and all members to be appointed by the President and confirmed by the Senate.

Required the Commission to report to Congress and the President at the end of each fiscal year.

Authorized the Commission to: work with state and local agencies, public and private; furnish technical assistance to those covered under this section, on request, to help them with compliance; assist in conciliation, on request; make technical studies; refer matters to the Attorney General for legal action, and advise and assist the Attorney General.

Enforcement: Authorized the Commission to investigate written charges of unlawful employment practices filed by an aggrieved individual or a member of the Commission, and to attempt to settle the problem by informal methods of conference, conciliation and persuasion.

Required that such proceedings remain confidential, and stipulated that an officer or employee of the EEOC who revealed any information would be guilty of a misdemeanor.

If the alleged act of discrimination took place in a state or local area with an equal employment law, covering the alleged unlawful practice, barred the filing of a charge with the EEOC until 60 days after the complaint was presented to the local agency (120 days in the first year of a state or local law).

Required that the individual must file his complaint with the EEOC within 90 days after the alleged unlawful practice took place, unless state or local agencies were handling the matter. In this case, he was given 210 days to bring the complaint (90 days plus the 120 days for local proceedings), or up to 30 days after receiving notice that the local agency's proceedings had terminated, whichever was earlier.

Gave the EEOC up to 60 days to seek voluntary compliance, and, if that failed, authorized the aggrieved individual to bring a civil suit.

Authorized the courts, at their discretion, to appoint an attorney for the complainant, and permit the Attorney General to intervene.

Allowed the courts, on request, to stay the proceedings for another 60 days if state or local proceedings were continuing, or the EEOC was still seeking voluntary compliance.

Permitted the suits to be brought in the judicial district where the alleged practice was committed, where the relevant employment records were kept, or where the plaintiff would have worked but for the alleged practice. If the respondent was not to be found in any of these districts, suit could be filed in the district where he had his main office.

If the court found that the respondent had "intentionally" engaged in the unlawful act, the court was authorized to order cessation of the unlawful practice and to order reinstatement or hiring of employees, with or without back pay (payable by the employer, union or employment agency responsible for the practice).

Permitted the EEOC to commence legal proceedings if a court order was flouted.

Made these proceedings subject to appeal.

Authorized the courts to pay the attorney's fees of the prevailing party, other than the Government or the EEOC.

Authorized the Attorney General to file a civil suit whenever he had reasonable cause to believe that a person or group of persons was engaged in a pattern or practice of resistance to this title, with intent to deny the rights if guaranteed. (The Attorney General was not required to submit to the waiting periods prescribed for private suits.)

Authorized the Attorney General to request a three-judge court to hear these suits, if he certifies that the case is of general public importance; and required the courts to expedite the suits, whether or not a three-judge court is requested.

Miscellaneous: Gave the EEOC access to the evidence of any person being investigated or proceeded against that is relevant to the charge under investigation.

Authorized the EEOC to utilize the services of state and local agencies carrying out local employment practices laws, with their consent; and to enter into agreements with these agencies specifying types of cases under their jurisdiction that will not be processed or prosecuted by the EEOC or taken to court by individuals.

Required those covered by the title to keep records as prescribed by regulations of the EEOC, to be drawn up after public hearing; if the requirements caused an undue hardship, anyone covered could seek an exemption from the EEOC or sue in court. Those in states with fair employment practices laws were exempted from keeping additional records, to the extent that the state or local requirements paralleled the federal regulations. Also exempted were Government contractors already required to keep similar records.

Required employers, employment agencies and unions to post notices prepared or approved by the EEOC setting forth the provisions of this title.

Directed the Secretary of Labor to study factors which result in discrimination in employment because of age and of the effects of such discrimination on the economy and the individuals involved, and to report to Congress with recommendations by June 30, 1965.

Directed the President, as soon as feasible, to convene one or more conferences of labor and business leaders and representatives of state and local and interested Government agencies to prepare for wide understanding and effective administration of this title.

TITLE VIII—REGISTRATION AND VOTING STATISTICS

Directed the Census Bureau to gather registration and voting statistics based on race, color and national origin in such areas and to the extent recommended by the Civil Rights Commission, both on primary and general elections to the U.S. House since Jan. 1, 1960.

Required such information on a nationwide scale in connection with the 1970 Census.

Made clear that persons could not be compelled to disclose race, color and national origin, or questioned about party affiliation or how they voted.

TITLE IX—INTERVENTION AND REMOVAL OF CASES

Made reviewable in higher federal courts the action of federal district courts in remanding a civil rights case to state courts.

Authorized the Attorney General to intervene in private suits where persons have alleged denial of equal protection of the laws under the 14th Amendment and where he certifies that the case is of "general public importance."

TITLE X—COMMUNITY RELATIONS SERVICE

Created a Community Relations Service in the Department of Commerce to aid communities in resolving disputes relating to discriminatory practices based on race, color or national origin.

Authorized the Service to offer its services either on its own accord or in response to a request from a state or local official or other interested person; directed the Service to seek the cooperation of other agencies and to carry out its conciliation activities without publicity.

Stipulated that the Service be headed by a director, to be appointed by the President and confirmed by the Senate for a four-year term; and authorized the director to appoint whatever staff was necessary.

Required the director to file a report with Congress by Jan. 31 of each year.

TITLE XI—MISCELLANEOUS

Provided that in any criminal contempt case arising under the Act, except voting rights cases, defendants are entitled to a jury trial upon demand, with a limit on the sentences of six months in prison and a $1,000 fine. (Voting rights cases were still covered by the 1957 jury trial provision that a judge may try a case without a jury, but in that instance the sentences would be limited to $300 and 45 days in prison, and in any case to six months and $1,000.)

Prohibited any one person from being subjected to *both* criminal prosecution and criminal contempt proceedings in federal courts for the same act or omission under the Act.

Provided that no one could be convicted for criminal contempt under the Act unless it is proved that the act or omission was intentional.

Provided that nothing in the law was to restrict existing powers of the Attorney General or the Government or any of its agencies to institute or intervene in any action or proceeding.

Stated that it was not the intent of this law to preempt or invalidate state laws in the same field, unless they were inconsistent with any of the purposes of the Act.

Authorized appropriation of whatever sums necessary to carry out the Act.

The passage of these Civil Rights Acts was, like the decisions in *Shelley* and *Brown*, both an end and a beginning in the legal responses to changing social conditions. Some implications and effects of aspects of this legislation will be explored in the next chapter.

Chapter 13

SECURING FUNDAMENTAL RIGHTS

Preceding chapters have recounted, in brief outline, the stormy history of the first stages in the growth of American labor law. That history demonstrates some of the limitations of law as a means of resolving intense social conflict, for the early legal responses to the problem probably tended to exacerbate rather than mitigate labor-management antagonism. However the unceasing efforts of judges and legislators to find some acceptable pattern of legal responses to the problems raised by the emergence of organized labor—whether or not such efforts were successful—were themselves part of a larger movement to contain the growing class struggle and to reaffirm the supremacy of the national interest in legality. If there had been no attempt to give legal recognition and protection to the labor movement, it is at least conceivable that the final outcome would have been an explosive revolution.

We have also traced, once again in brief outline, legal responses to race relations in the United States since the Civil War. Like organized labor, Black Americans succeeded, albeit much more slowly, to establish the legitimacy of their claims for social justice. The legal strategies and tactics of the Black civil rights movement differed in many respects from those of the labor movement, and the roles and uses of courts and legislatures were also notably different in the two areas, but ultimately both judicial and legislative action succeeded in establishing, at least in theory, the fundamental rights of Black Americans to the equal protection of the law. Once again the national interest in legality was asserted, and that may have lessened the level of racial conflict. Nevertheless, as the history of the 1960s shows, this legal development did not eliminate major disruptions and individual terrorist acts inspired by racial tensions.

Ultimately, the solution to labor-management conflict required not merely the adaptation of older legal forms and concepts but also the creation of new legal forms and concepts. In particular, a newly expanding branch of law—administrative law—was put to use in the regulation of labor organization and labor-management relations; and a new form of self-regulation—collective bargaining—was given legal protection and legal definition, along with such related procedures as conciliation, mediation, and arbitration. Similarly, various administrative and judicial proceedings have been established to shape the future course of race relations. Many of these procedures have aspects in common with those developed in the labor field. In this final chapter, we shall consider aspects of legal procedures and remedies in labor-management and race relations cases in order to inquire further regarding the effectiveness of law as a means of resolving social conflict.

The materials in the preceding chapters of this part dealt with attempts by organized labor and by Black Americans to establish the legitimacy of their respective rights; on the one hand to organize for collective economic and social action; on the other to be relieved of the burden of racial segregation enforced by law. Each group was ultimately successful in its striving for legitimation of its fundamental claims. Ultimately each group turned the law in its favor. The labor injunction, the yellow dog contract, the treatment of unions as conspiracies in restraint of trade, all yielded to the new law which restricted the use of injunctions and protected the right to organize and bargain collectively. Similarly "Jim Crow" laws were dispatched to the ash can of history, and judicial opinions and state and federal civil rights laws promised equal treatment regardless of race, sex or religion. But it is one thing for opinions and statutes to state new ground rules regarding social and economic relations, and quite another thing for those rules to be implemented and made effective. The old law of labor relations and the law of "Jim Crow" were very much a reflection of deeply engrained attitudes and behaviors. In order for the new rights of organized labor and Black Americans to become effective, those attitudes and behaviors would have to change or be changed. The materials in this chapter deal, in part, with the role of law as a teacher of values, and as a means to shape attitudes and alter behaviors. This role of law is both difficult and controversial, particularly in a democratic society. In this closing chapter we will explore briefly some means, some techniques, which our legal system has evoked and evolved in its not entirely successful efforts to perform this role in the fields of labor-management and race relations.

SECTION 48. SELF HELP, AND LEGAL RESPONSES TO SELF HELP

Labor's legislative victory in the passage of the Wagner Act, and the NAACP's victory in Brown v. Board of Education and subsequent federal court cases, and in Congress, signalled new eras in labor and race relations. These events did not, however, immediately change social attitudes and behaviors which had built up over many years. While both labor and Blacks continued to successfully press their claims in legal fora, they also found it necessary and possible to take more direct actions to further their causes. Some of these actions, such as the sit-down strike and the sit-in, raised difficult issues of legality. On the one hand they were aimed at people who allegedly were violating newly won legal rights or status of the demonstrators, but the demonstrators were at the same time violating general laws aimed at securing public peace, in particular the laws against trespass on privately owned real property. Our brief study of the process of securing fundamental rights begins with materials on these episodes in labor-management and race relations.

SECTION 48.1   SIT–DOWN

[The following is taken from FOSTER RHEA DULLES, LABOR IN AMERICA, 2d rev. ed. (1960), pp. 303–308.]

* * *

There were some scattered strikes during the summer of 1936 and by late fall the United Automobile Workers—some 30,000 strong—was coming out in the open, prepared to demand recognition from the giants of the industry —General Motors, Chrysler, and Ford. "We don't want to be driven; we don't want to be spied on," was the workers' new refrain. But the companies, defying the provisions of the Wagner Act, were not yet willing to make any concessions. When Martin asked the officers of General Motors for a conference on collective bargaining, William S. Knudsen, vice-president, merely suggested that if the workers had any grievances they should take them up with local plant managers. The reply of the union was a strike which began in the Fisher Body plants of the company at Flint, Michigan, in January, 1937 and then gradually spread to Detroit, Cleveland, Toledo, and other parts of the country. Production in General Motors came to a standstill with some 112,000 of its 150,000 workers idle.

This strike was something new under the sun. It took the form in Flint of a sit-down. There had been some earlier use of this radical technique, notably among the rubber workers at Akron, but the General Motors strike marked its first use on a really wide scale. The automobile workers refused to leave the plant; they just sat at their work benches. It was not an act of violence but one of passive resistance, doubly effective in that such a strike could be broken only by the forcible removal of the workers from company premises.

Excitement ran high in Flint and neighboring Detroit. General Motors management and the Flint Alliance, a company-sponsored association supposedly made up of loyal employes, assailed the sit-down as an unlawful invasion of property rights and called for the immediate ejection of the strikers. Martin * countered with charges that General Motors proposed to invade the property rights of the workers.

---

* Homer S. Martin, then President of the
UAW.

"What more sacred property right is there in the world today," he demanded, "than the right of a man to his job? This property right involves the right to support his family, feed his children and keep starvation away from the door. This . . . is the very foundation stone of American homes . . . the most sacred, most fundamental property right in America."

The C.I.O. at first looked upon the strike with misgivings and was anything but enthusiastic over the sit-down. Deeply involved in the organizing drive in steel, whose success was considered basic to the whole program of industrial unionism, the outbreak in automobiles was highly embarrassing. But support could not be withheld and the C.I.O. undertook to do everything it could to aid the General Motors employes. "You men are undoubtedly carrying on through one of the most heroic battles that has ever been undertaken by strikers in an industrial dispute," Lewis declared. "The attention of the entire American public is focussed upon you. . . ."

The latter part of his statement was unquestionably true, and became even more so as violence broke out in Flint and the strikers showed their stubborn determination not to be dislodged from the occupied plants. The cutting off of all heat—even though it was the dead of winter—made no difference. When the police tried to rush Fisher Body Plant No. 2, they were met by a hail of missiles—coffee mugs, pop bottles, iron bolts and heavy automobile door hinges. When they then returned to the attack with tear-gas bombs, the strikers retaliated by turning streams of water on them from the plant fire hoses. The forces of law and order were finally compelled to make a hasty retreat in what the exultant workers promptly termed the "Battle of the Running Bulls."

The strike dragged on from week to week as the General Motors employes continued to sit it out with food and other supplies brought in to them through the picket lines. Discipline was rigid. "Brilliantly lighted," reads a contemporary description by a union organizer, "this vast plant was heavily guarded inside and outside—to keep strikebreakers and other interlopers from entering and to protect the building and its contents. Especially did these strikers guard the company's dies. No liquor was permitted on the premises, and smoking was prohibited on all production floors. Forty-five men were assigned to police patrol duty inside. Their word was law."

Both the company and the Flint Alliance now demanded that the state militia be mobilized to clear the plants since the police had failed to do so. But Governor Murphy of Michigan, sympathetic with the automobile workers and fearful of the bloodshed that would certainly result, refused to take this step. Finally, however, General Motors obtained a court order setting 3:00 P.M. on February 3 as the deadline for evacuation of the plants under penalty of imprisonment and fines. The strikers were undismayed. "We the workers," they wired the governor, ". . . have carried on a stay-in strike over a month to make General Motors Corporation obey the law and engage in collective bargaining. . . . Unarmed as we are, the introduction of the militia, sheriffs or police with murderous weapons will mean a blood-bath of unarmed workers. . . . We have decided to stay in the plant."

Realizing that the strikers meant what they said, Murphy frantically summoned a peace conference. John L. Lewis rushed to Detroit ("Let there be no moaning at the bar when I put out to sea," he cryptically told reporters as he entrained in Washington) and began negotiations with Vice-President Knudsen, whom Governor Murphy had prevailed upon to meet him. But the morning of February 3 arrived without any settlement having been reached. The sit-downers were barricaded in the factories, armed with iron bolts and door hinges, and protected against the expected tear and vomiting gas with slight cheesecloth masks. Outside the besieged plants, thousands of sympathetic workers and members of women's emergency brigades milled about as sound trucks blared forth the slogan of "Solidarity Forever."

The zero hour approached—and passed. Governor Murphy refused to order the national guardsmen to enforce the court order. In spite of mounting popular pressure, he remained unwilling to make a move that would have precipitated violence on an unpredictable scale.

The next day President Roosevelt added his request for a continuation of negotiations to that of Governor Murphy, and the Lewis-Knudsen talks (with other representatives of both General Motors and the strikers present) were resumed. For a full week, while the sit-downers grimly held the fort, the conference proceeded until at long last, the weary, haggard governor was able to announce that agreement had been reached. General Motors undertook to recognize the United Automobile Workers as the bargaining agent for its members, to drop injunction proceedings against the strikers, not to discriminate in any way against union members, and to take up such grievances as the speed-up and other matters.

It was not a complete victory for the union. The U.A.W. had sought sole bargaining privileges for all General Motors employes, a uniform minimum wage and the thirty-hour week. But as in the case of the S.W.O.C. settlement with "Big Steel," another anti-union stronghold had been captured. Organized labor had taken the first step toward what was to become the complete unionization of the entire automobile industry. Whatever might be said of the legality or ethics of a sit-down strike, the results spoke for its effectiveness.

With the success of the automobile workers in General Motors, sit-down strikes spread through union ranks in all parts of the country. The employes of the Chrysler Corporation soon followed suit, and after a relatively brief sit-down in comparison with the forty-four day strike at General Motors, succeeded in winning recognition for the union and a collective bargaining agreement comparable to that exacted from General Motors. Indeed, only Ford continued to hold out among the automobile companies, successfully resisting all attempts of the United Automobile Workers to organize its plants for another four years.

Other industries also felt the impact of labor's new weapon. Between September, 1936, and June, 1937, almost 500,000 workers were involved in sit-down strikes. Rubber workers, glass workers and textile workers sat at their benches; striking Woolworth clerks stayed behind their counters but would not wait on customers; pie bakers, opticians, dressmakers and apartment house janitors sat down. The longest strike of this kind was that of some 1800 electrical workers in Philadelphia. Two bridegrooms sat out their honeymoons and the wives of six other married strikers greeted their returning husbands with newly born babies.

As workers throughout the country eagerly took up this militant strategy to force anti-union employers into line, they enthusiastically sang their song of revolt:

When they tie the can to a union man,
Sit down! Sit down!
When they give him the sack, they'll take him back,
Sit down! Sit down!
When the speed-up comes, just twiddle your thumbs,
Sit down! Sit down!
When the boss won't talk, don't take a walk,
Sit down! Sit down!

These strikes aroused increasing popular resentment. Conservative newspapers grew hysterical in condemning such a flagrant invasion of property rights and there was little support for the sit-downs from any quarter. While Upton Sinclair wrote from California that "for seventy-five years big business has been sitting down on the American people, and now I am delighted to see the process reversed," even among labor sympathizers there were few to echo this sentiment. The A.F. of L. explicitly disavowed the sit-down and while the C.I.O. had supported the automobile workers, official approval was never given to its general use. After lively and acrimonious debate, the Senate resolved that such strikes were "illegal and contrary to public policy," and the courts eventually outlawed them as constituting trespass on private property.

For all the excitement it occasioned during the first half of 1937, the sit-down strike in fact proved to be a temporary phenomenon and was abandoned almost as quickly as it had been adopted. It had been the quick and ready response of new and impatient union members fighting for recognition in the strongholds of anti-unionism and embittered by the refusal of employers to comply with the provisions of the Wagner Act. When the law was sustained and the N.L.R.B. empowered to hold elections for collective bargaining units, the sit-downs were given up.

Before this happened, however, the strikes of early 1937 had greatly aroused public opinion and labor as a whole bore the brunt of popular condemnation of the sit-down. Gallup poll reports showed that an overwhelming majority of persons interviewed opposed the use of labor's new weapon, while seventy per cent of those questioned were convinced that new regulatory laws were needed to curb the unions. Sit-down strikes might be explained as no more contrary to law than the refusal of industry to heed cease and desist orders issued by the N.L.R.B., but they awoke fears and alarms that were not easily stilled.

Note and Questions

1. What, according to Professor Dulles, was the ostensible objective of the G. M. sit-down strike?

2. Was that a lawful objective?

3. Did the sit-down strikers have a reasonable claim that their action was at least morally right in light of the Wagner Act? Did G. M. have adequate legal grounds for alleging that the sit-down strikers were perpetrating a wrong? What injury did G. M. suffer

as a result of the sit-down and the strikers' holding possession of the plants?

4. Did Governor Murphy act lawfully regarding the use of troops to enforce the court order? Did the Wagner Act give at least moral support to Governor Murphy's decision in this regard?

5. Governor Murphy was defeated in his bid for re-election in 1938. Subsequently President Roosevelt appointed him Attorney General of the United States, and later Associate Justice of the United States Supreme Court.

SECTION 48.2   SIT–IN

[The following is taken from ARTHUR I. WASKOW, FROM RACE RIOT TO SIT IN (1966), pp. 225–227. Footnotes are omitted.]

It was not until the early 1960s that another generation of "new Negroes" forced its way to national attention. That generation invented the sit-ins, and its members were both far more vigorous and far less violent than the generation of 1919.* Where the unorganized rioters of 1919 had fought back violently against violent attack, the organized sit-in movement initiated action instead of defensively responding, carried its protest against racial hierarchy into the camp of the enemy—but did so under a strict discipline of avoiding violence.

What the new generation of Negroes was like can best be understood in the words of one of its members. Asked whom she thought of as participants in the new civil-rights movement, she smiled and answered, "Anybody who's black—and glad." Millions of Negro Americans have throughout our history been black and sad; the Negro rioters of 1919 were black and bitter; many civil-rights workers for many decades have tried to act like angry whites. But only in the 1960s did large numbers of Negroes embrace their blackness and channel their ancient anger into joyful protest.

The new techniques of the sit-in generation brought to fruition James Weldon Johnson's bare hint of "creative disorder." Since 1919, Johnson's own NAACP had concentrated on what may be called "the politics of order" in courtroom, legislative lobby, and newspaper column—the same kind of politics that the NAACP had pursued in response to the 1919 riots. What may be called "the politics of violence" had also been used in American racial conflicts since 1919—notably when race riots erupted in Detroit, Harlem, and Los Angeles during 1943 and when enforcement of court orders for school desegregation brought mob uprisings and military occupations to parts of the South in the 1950s. But the thorough application of a third kind of politics, neither orderly nor violent, had to await the emergence of the "new Negro" generation of the 1960s.

---

* The references to 1919 relate to the
Chicago race riots of that year.

The first act of that generation was the invention of the sit-in on February 1, 1960, in Greensboro, North Carolina. Four Negro college freshmen sat down at a lunch counter where Negroes had never been served, refused to leave although they were denied service, and attracted both shouted curses and whispered support from increasing numbers of white bystanders. Their act at once reverberated in their own college, and within six weeks across the South. Two major events of the previous decade had helped bring the students to the point of action: the 1954 decision by the Supreme Court that public schools should be desegregated, and the subsequent failure of the schools they attended to be desegregated; and the 1958 boycott of segregated buses led by the Reverend Martin Luther King, Jr., in Montgomery, Alabama. The one event had bred first a major heightening of expectations and then a deep frustration and anger at the failure of those expectations to be fulfilled; the other event had offered both a hero and a basic approach—Martin Luther King and Gandhian "non-violence"—to these Negro adolescents.

BELL v. MARYLAND

Supreme Court of the United States, 1964.
378 U.S. 226, 84 S.Ct. 1814.

[Most footnotes are omitted.]

MR. JUSTICE BRENNAN delivered the opinion of the Court.

Petitioners, 12 Negro students, were convicted in a Maryland state court as a result of their participation in a "sit-in" demonstration at Hooper's restaurant in the City of Baltimore in 1960. The convictions were based on a record showing in summary that a group of 15 to 20 Negro students, including petitioners, went to Hooper's restaurant to engage in what their counsel describes as a "sit-in protest" because the restaurant would not serve Negroes. The "hostess," on orders of Mr. Hooper, the president of the corporation owning the restaurant, told them, "solely on the basis of their color," that they would not be served. Petitioners did not leave when requested to by the hostess and the manager; instead they went to tables, took seats, and refused to leave, insisting that they be served. On orders of Mr. Hooper the police were called, but they advised that a warrant would be necessary before they could arrest petitioners. Mr. Hooper then went to the police station and swore out warrants, and petitioners were accordingly arrested.

The statute under which the convictions were obtained was the Maryland criminal trespass law, § 577 of Art. 27 of the Maryland Code, 1957 edition, under which it is a misdemeanor to "enter upon or cross over the land, premises or private property of any person or persons in this State after having been duly notified by the owner or his agent not to do so." The convictions were affirmed by the Maryland Court of Appeals, 227 Md. 302, 176 A.2d 771 (1962), and we granted certiorari. 374 U.S. 805, 83 S.Ct. 1691.

We do not reach the questions that have been argued under the Equal Protection and Due Process Clauses of the Fourteenth Amendment. It appears that a significant change has taken place in the applicable law of Maryland since these convictions were affirmed by the Court of Appeals. Under this Court's settled practice in such circumstances, the judgments must consequently be vacated and reversed and the case remanded so that the state court may consider the effect of the supervening change in state law.

Petitioners' convictions were affirmed by the Maryland Court of Appeals on January 9, 1962. Since that date, Maryland has enacted laws that abolish the crime of which petitioners were convicted. These laws accord petitioners a right to be served in Hooper's restaurant, and make unlawful conduct like that of Hooper's president and hostess in refusing them service because of their race. On June 8, 1962, the City of Baltimore enacted its Ordinance No. 1249, adding § 10A to Art. 14A of the Baltimore City Code (1950 ed.). The ordinance, which by its terms took effect from the date of its enactment, prohibits owners and operators of Baltimore places of public accommodation, including restaurants, from denying their services or facilities to any person because of his race. A similar "public accommodations law," applicable to Baltimore City and Baltimore County though not to some of the State's other counties, was adopted by the State Legislature on March 29, 1963. Art. 49B Md.Code § 11 (1963 Supp.). This statute went into effect on June 1, 1963, as provided by § 4 of the Act, Acts 1963, c. 227. The statute provides that:

> "It is unlawful for an owner or operator of a place of public accommodation or an agent or employee of said owner or operator, because of the race, creed, color, or national origin of any person, to refuse, withhold from, or deny to such person any of the accommodations, advantages, facilities and privileges of such place of public accommodation. For the purpose of this subtitle, a place of public accommodation means any hotel, restaurant, inn, motel or an establishment commonly known or recognized as regularly engaged in the business of providing sleeping accommodations, or serving food, or both, for a consideration, and which is open to the general public . . . ." [1]

It is clear from these enactments that petitioners' conduct in entering or crossing over the premises of Hooper's restaurant after being notified not to do so because of their race would not be a crime today; on the contrary, the law of Baltimore and of Maryland now vindicates their conduct and recognizes it as the exercise of a right, directing the law's prohibition not at them but at the restaurant owner or manager who seeks to deny them service because of their race.

[Justice Brennan then turned to a discussion of the effect that these new statutes might have on the convictions of the petitioners. He found that under Maryland law "the supervening enactment" of such statutes might cause "the Maryland Court of Appeals at this time to reverse the convictions and order the indictments dismissed." That

1. Another public accommodations law was enacted by the Maryland Legislature on March 14, 1964, and signed by the Governor on April 7, 1964. This statute re-enacts the quoted provision from the 1963 enactment and gives it statewide application, eliminating the county exclusions. The new statute was scheduled to go into effect on June 1, 1964, but its operation has apparently been suspended by the filing of petitions seeking a referendum. See Md.Const., Art. XVI; Baltimore Sun, May 31, 1964, p. 22, col. 1. Meanwhile, the Baltimore City ordinance and the 1963 state law, both of which are applicable to Baltimore City, where Hooper's restaurant is located, remain in effect.

finding was based on a review of Maryland cases which suggested that Maryland "follows the universal common-law rule that when the legislature repeals a criminal statute or otherwise removes the state's condemnation from conduct that formerly was ruled criminal, this action requires the dismissal of a pending criminal proceeding charging such conduct." Justice Brennan noted, however, that Maryland also had a "general savings clause statute which in certain circumstances 'saves' state convictions from the common-law effect of supervening enactments." He also, found that, under Maryland law, there was a substantial question as to the applicability of the savings clause statute in the case at hand. That in turn raised for him, and the Justices who joined in his opinion, the issue as to whether or not the Supreme Court should attempt to resolve this "open and arguable" issue of state law or remand the case to the Maryland Courts so that they could determine whether or not the petitioner's convictions should be sustained or reversed on the grounds of the supervening enactment doctrine.

Citing the tradition of federal court deference to the state courts in such cases, the majority decided to vacate the judgment of the Maryland Court of Appeals and remand the case to that court.]

Reversed and remanded.

MR. JUSTICE DOUGLAS, with whom MR. JUSTICE GOLDBERG concurs as respects Parts II–V, for reversing and directing dismissal of the indictment.

I.

I reach the merits of this controversy. The issue is ripe for decision and petitioners, who have been convicted of asking for service in Hooper's restaurant, are entitled to an answer to their complaint here and now.

On this the last day of the Term, we studiously avoid decision of the basic issue of the right of public accommodation under the Fourteenth Amendment, remanding the case to the state court for reconsideration in light of an issue of state law.

This case was argued October 14 and 15, 1963—over eight months ago. The record of the case is simple, the constitutional guidelines well marked, the precedents marshalled. Though the Court is divided, the preparation of opinions laying bare the differences does not require even two months, let alone eight. Moreover, a majority reach the merits of the issue. Why then should a minority prevent a resolution of the differing views?

The laws relied on for vacating and remanding were enacted June 8, 1962, and March 29, 1963—long before oral argument. We did indeed not grant certiorari until June 10, 1963. Hence if we were really concerned with this state law question, we would have vacated and remanded for reconsideration in light of those laws on June 10, 1963. By now we would have had an answer and been able to put our decision into the mainstream of the law at this critical hour. If the parties had been concerned, they too might have asked that we follow that course. Maryland adverted to the new law merely to show why certiorari should not be granted. At the argument and at our conferences we were not concerned with that question, the issue being deemed frivolous. Now it is resurrected to avoid facing the constitutional question.

The whole Nation has to face the issue; Congress is conscientiously considering it; some municipalities have had to make it their first order of concern; law enforcement officials are deeply implicated, North as well as South; the question is at the root of demonstrations, unrest, riots, and violence in various areas. The issue in other words consumes the public attention. Yet we stand mute, avoiding decision of the basic issue by an obvious pretense.

The clash between Negro customers and white restaurant owners is clear; each group claims protection by the Constitution and tenders the Fourteenth Amendment as justification for its action. Yet we leave resolution of the conflict to others, when, if our voice were heard, the issues for the Congress and for the public would become clear and precise. The Court was created to sit in troubled times as well as in peaceful days.

* * *

We have in this case a question that is basic to our way of life and fundamental in our constitutional scheme. No question preoccupies the country more than this one; it is plainly justiciable; it presses for a decision one way or another; we should resolve it. The people should know that when filibusters occupy other forums, when oppressions are great, when the clash of authority between the individual and the State is severe, they can still get justice in the courts. When we default, as we do today, the prestige of law in the life of the Nation is weakened.

For these reasons I reach the merits; and I vote to reverse the judgments of conviction outright.

II.

The issue in this case, according to those who would affirm, is whether a person's "personal prejudices" may dictate the way in which he uses his property and whether he can enlist the aid of the State to enforce those "personal prejudices". With all respect, that is not the real issue. The corporation that owns this restaurant did not refuse service to these Negroes because "it" did not like Negroes. The reason "it" refused service was because "it" thought "it" could make more money by running a segregated restaurant.

+ + +

Here, as in most of the sit-in cases before us, the refusal of service did not reflect "personal prejudices" but business reasons. Were we today to hold that segregated restaurants, whose racial policies were enforced by a State, violated the Equal Protection Clause, all restaurants would be on an equal footing and the reasons given in this and most of the companion cases for refusing service to Negroes would evaporate. Moreover, when corporate restaurateurs are involved, whose "personal prejudices" are being protected? The stockholders'? The directors'? The officers'? The managers'? The truth is, I think, that the corporate interest is in making money, not in protecting "personal prejudices."

IV.

The problem in this case, and in the other sit-in cases before us, is presented as though it involved the situation of "a private operator conducting his own business on his own premises and exercising his own judgment" as to whom he will admit to the premises.

The property involved is not, however, a man's home or his yard or even his fields. Private property is involved, but it is property that is serving the public. As my Brother GOLDBERG says, it is a "civil" right, not a "social" right, with which we deal. Here it is a restaurant refusing service to a Negro. But so far as principle and law are concerned it might just as well be a hospital refusing admission to a sick or injured Negro (cf. Simkins v. Moses H. Cone Memorial Hospital, 323 F.2d 959), or a drugstore refusing antibiotics to a Negro, or a bus denying transportation to a Negro, or a telephone company refusing to install a telephone in a Negro's home.

The problem with which we deal has no relation to opening or closing the door of one's home. The home of course is the essence of privacy, in no way dedicated to public use, in no way extending an invitation to the public. Some businesses, like the classical country store where the owner lives overhead or in the rear, make the store an extension, so to speak, of the home. But such is not this case. The facts of these sit-in cases have little resemblance to any institution of property which we customarily associate with privacy.

Joseph H. Choate, who argued the Income Tax Cases (Pollock v. Farmers' Loan & Trust Co., 157 U.S. 429, 534, 15 S.Ct. 673), said:

"I have thought that one of the fundamental objects of all civilized government was the preservation of the rights of private property. I have thought that it was the very keystone of the arch upon which all civilized government rests, and that this once abandoned, everything was at stake and in danger. That is what Mr. Webster said in 1820, at Plymouth, and I supposed that all educated, civilized men believed in that."

Charles A. Beard had the theory that the Constitution was "an economic document drawn with superb skill by men whose property interests were immediately at stake." An Economic Interpretation of the Constitution of the United States (1939), p. 188. That school of thought would receive new impetus from an affirmance of these judgments. Seldom have modern cases (cf. the ill-starred *Dred Scott* decision, 19 How. 393) so exalted property in suppression of individual rights. We would reverse the modern trend were we to hold that property voluntarily serving the public can receive state protection when the owner refuses to serve some solely because they are colored.

* * *

V.

The requirement of equal protection, like the guarantee of privileges and immunities of citizenship, is a constitutional command directed to each State.

State judicial action is as clearly "state" action as state administrative action. Indeed, we held in Shelley v. Kraemer, 334 U.S. 1, 20, 68 S.Ct. 836, 845, that "State action, as that phrase is understood for the purposes of the Fourteenth Amendment, refers to exertions of state power in all forms."

* * *

Maryland's action against these Negroes was as authoritative as any case where the State in one way or another puts its full force behind a policy. The policy here was segregation in places of public accommodation; and

Maryland enforced that policy with her police, her prosecutors, and her courts.

* * *

The preferences involved in Shelley v. Kraemer and its companion cases were far more personal than the motivations of the corporate managers in the present case when they declined service to Negroes. Why should we refuse to let state courts enforce *apartheid* in residential areas of our cities but let state courts enforce *apartheid* in restaurants? If a court decree is state action in one case, it is in the other. Property rights, so heavily underscored, are equally involved in each case.

The customer in a restaurant is transitory; he comes and may never return. The colored family who buys the house next door is there for keeps— night and day. If "personal prejudices" are not to be the criterion in one case they should not be in the other. We should put these restaurant cases in line with Shelley v. Kraemer, holding that what the Fourteenth Amendment requires in restrictive covenant cases it also requires from restaurants.

Segregation of Negroes in the restaurants and lunch counters of parts of America is a relic of slavery. It is a badge of second-class citizenship. It is a denial of a privilege and immunity of national citizenship and of the equal protection guaranteed by the Fourteenth Amendment against abridgment by the States. When the state police, the state prosecutor, and the state courts unite to convict Negroes for renouncing that relic of slavery, the "State" violates the Fourteenth Amendment.

I would reverse these judgments of conviction outright, as these Negroes in asking for service in Hooper's restaurant were only demanding what was their constitutional right.

[The appendices to Justice Douglas' opinion are omitted. The concurring opinion of Justice Goldberg is omitted.]

Mr. Justice Black, with whom Mr. Justice Harlan and Mr. Justice White join, dissenting.

[In Parts I and II of his opinion Justice Black argued that the Court should reach the merits of the case, and uphold the convictions and the constitutionality of the Maryland trespass statute.]

III.

Section 1 of the Fourteenth Amendment provides in part:

"No State shall . . . deprive any person of life, liberty, or property, without due process of law; nor deny to any person within its jurisdiction the equal protection of the laws."

This section of the Amendment, unlike other sections, is a prohibition against certain conduct only when done by a State—"state action" as it has come to be known—and "erects no shield against merely private conduct, however discriminatory or wrongful." Shelley v. Kraemer, 334 U.S. 1, 13, 68 S.Ct. 836, 842 (1948). This well-established interpretation of section 1 of the Amendment—which all the parties here, including the petitioners and the Solicitor General, accept—means that this section of the Amendment does not of itself, standing alone, in the absence of some cooperative state action or compulsion, forbid property holders, including restaurant owners, to ban people from entering or remaining upon their premises, even if the owners act out of racial prejudice. But "the prohibitions of the amendment extend to all action of the State denying equal protection of the laws" whether "by its legislative, its executive, or its judicial authorities." Virginia v. Rives, 100 U.S. 313, 318 (1880). The Amendment thus forbids all kinds of state action, by all state agencies and officers, that discriminate against persons on account of their race. It was this kind of state action that was held invalid in Brown v. Board of Education, 347 U.S. 483, 74 S.Ct. 686 (1954), Peterson v. City of Greenville, 373 U.S. 244, 83 S.Ct. 1133 (1963), Lombard v. Louisiana, 373 U.S. 267, 83 S.Ct. 1122 (1963), and Griffin v. County School Board, 377 U.S. 218, 84 S.Ct. 1226 (1964), and that this Court today holds invalid in Robinson v. Florida, *ante,* p. 153, 84 S.Ct. 1693.

Petitioners, but not the Solicitor General, contend that their conviction for trespass under the state statute was by itself the kind of discriminatory state action forbidden by the Fourteenth Amendment. This contention, on its face, has plausibility when considered along with general statements to the effect that under the Amendment forbidden "state action" may be that of the Judicial as well as of the Legislative or Executive Branch of Government. But a mechanical application of the Fourteenth Amendment to this case cannot survive analysis. The Amendment does not forbid a State to prosecute for crimes committed against a person or his property, however prejudiced or narrow the victim's views may be. Nor can whatever prejudice and bigotry the victim of a crime may have be automatically attributed to the State that prosecutes. Such a doctrine would not only be based on a fiction; it would also severely handicap a State's efforts to maintain a peaceful and orderly society. Our society has put its trust in a system of criminal laws to punish lawless conduct. To avert personal feuds and violent brawls it has led its people to believe and expect that wrongs against them will be vindicated in the courts. Instead of attempting to take the law into their own hands, people have been taught to call for police protection to protect their rights wherever possible. It would betray our whole plan for a tranquil and orderly society to say that a citizen, because of his personal prejudices, habits, attitudes, or beliefs, is cast outside the law's protection and cannot call for the aid of officers sworn to uphold the law and preserve the peace. The worst citizen no less than the best is entitled to equal protection of the laws of his State and of his Nation. None of our past cases justifies reading the Fourteenth Amendment in a way that might well penalize citizens who are law-abiding enough to call upon the law and its officers for protection instead of using their own physical strength or dangerous weapons to preserve their rights.

In contending that the State's prosecution of petitioners for trespass is state action forbidden by the Fourteenth Amendment, petitioners rely chiefly on Shelley v. Kraemer, *supra.* That reliance is misplaced.

* * *

It seems pretty clear that the reason judicial enforcement of the restrictive covenants in *Shelley* was deemed state action was not merely the fact that a state court had acted, but rather than it had acted to "deny to petitioners, on the grounds of race or color, the enjoyment of property rights in premises which petitioners are willing and financially able to acquire and which the grantors are willing to sell." 334 U.S., at 19, 68 S.Ct. at 845. In other words, this Court held that state enforcement of the covenants had the effect of denying to the parties their federally guaranteed right to own, occupy, enjoy, and use their property without regard to race or color. Thus, the line of cases from *Buchanan* through *Shelley* establishes these propositions: (1) When an owner of property is willing to sell and a would-be purchaser is willing to buy, then the Civil Rights Act of 1866, which gives all persons the same right to "inherit, purchase, lease, sell, hold, and convey" property, prohibits a State, whether through its legislature, executive, or judiciary, from preventing the sale on the grounds of the race or color of one of the parties. Shelley v. Kraemer, *supra*, 334 U.S., at 19, 68 S.Ct. at 845. (2) Once a person has become a property owner, then he acquires all the rights that go with ownership: "the free use, enjoyment, and disposal of a person's acquisitions without control or diminution save by the law of the land." Buchanan v. Warley, *supra*, 245 U.S., at 74, 38 S.Ct. at 18. This means that the property owner may, in the absence of a valid statute forbidding it, sell his property to whom he pleases and admit to that property whom he will; so long as *both* parties are willing parties, then the principles stated in *Buchanan* and *Shelley* protect this right. But equally, when one party is unwilling, as when the property owner chooses *not* to sell to a particular person or *not* to admit that person, then, as this Court emphasized in *Buchanan*, he is entitled to rely on the guarantee of due process of law, that is, "law of the land," to protect his free use and enjoyment of property and to know that only by valid legislation, passed pursuant to some constitutional grant of power, can anyone disturb this free use. But petitioners here would have us hold that, despite the absence of any valid statute restricting the use of his property, the owner of Hooper's restaurant in Baltimore must not be accorded the same federally guaranteed right to occupy, enjoy, and use property given to the parties in *Buchanan* and *Shelley*; instead, petitioners would have us say that Hooper's federal right must be cut down and he must be compelled—though no statute said he must—to allow people to force their way into his restaurant and remain there over his protest. We cannot subscribe to such a mutilating, one-sided interpretation of federal guarantees the very heart of which is equal treatment under law to all. We must never forget that the Fourteenth Amendment protects "life, liberty, or property" of all people generally, not just some people's "life," some people's "liberty," and some kinds of "property."

* * *

IV.

[Part IV of Justice Black's opinion is addressed to the arguments in Justice Goldberg's concurring opinion. The issue between them was the extent to which the Fourteenth Amendment, standing alone, was intended to bar discrimination in public accommodations.] *

V.

Petitioners, but not the Solicitor General, contend that their convictions for trespass deny them the right of freedom of expression guaranteed by the Constitution. They argue that their

> "expression (asking for service) was entirely appropriate to the time and place at which it occurred. They did not shout or obstruct the conduct of business. There were no speeches, picket signs, handbills or

* Editor's note.

other forms of expression in the store possibly inappropriate to the time
and place. Rather they offered to purchase food in a place and at a
time set aside for such transactions. Their protest demonstration was
a part of the 'free trade in ideas' (Abrams v. United States, 250 U.S.
616, 630, 40 S.Ct. 17, 22, Holmes, J., dissenting) . . . ."

Their argument comes down to this: that since petitioners did not shout,
obstruct Hooper's business (which the record refutes), make speeches, or display picket signs, handbills, or other means of communication, they had a
perfect constitutional right to assemble and remain in the restaurant, over
the owner's continuing objections, for the purpose of expressing themselves
by language and "demonstrations" bespeaking their hostility to Hooper's
refusal to serve Negroes. This Court's prior cases do not support such a
privilege growing out of the constitutional rights of speech and assembly.
Unquestionably petitioners had a constitutional right to express these views
wherever they had an unquestioned legal right to be. Cf. Marsh v. Alabama,
supra. But there is the rub in this case. The contention that petitioners
had a constitutional right to enter or to stay on Hooper's premises against
his will because, if there, they would have had a constitutional right to express their desire to have restaurant service over Hooper's protest, is a boot-
strap argument. The right to freedom of expression is a right to express
views—not a right to force other people to supply a platform or a pulpit. It
is argued that this supposed constitutional right to invade other people's
property would not mean that a man's home, his private club, or his church
could be forcibly entered or used against his will—only his store or place
of business which he has himself "opened to the public" by selling goods or
services for money. In the first place, that argument assumes that Hooper's
restaurant *had* been opened to the public. But the whole quarrel of petitioners with Hooper was that instead of being open to all, the restaurant
refused service to Negroes. Furthermore, legislative bodies with power to
act could of course draw lines like this, but if the Constitution itself fixes
its own lines, as is argued, legislative bodies are powerless to change them,
and homeowners, churches, private clubs, and other property owners would
have to await case-by-case determination by this Court before they knew
who had a constitutional right to trespass on their property. And even if
the supposed constitutional right is confined to places where goods and services are offered for sale, it must be realized that such a constitutional rule
would apply to all businesses and professions alike. A statute can be drafted to create such exceptions as legislators think wise, but a constitutional
rule could as well be applied to the smallest business as to the largest, to the
most personal professional relationship as to the most impersonal business,
to a family business conducted on a man's farm or in his home as to businesses carried on elsewhere.

A great purpose of freedom of speech and press is to provide a forum
for settlement of acrimonious disputes peaceably without resort to intimidation, force, or violence. The experience of ages points to the inexorable
fact that people are frequently stirred to violence when property which the
law recognizes as theirs is forcibly invaded or occupied by others. Trespass laws are born of this experience. They have been, and doubtless still
are, important features of any government dedicated, as this country is, to
a rule of law. Whatever power it may allow the States or grant to the
Congress to regulate the use of private property, the Constitution does not

confer upon any group the right to substitute rule by force for rule by law. Force leads to violence, violence to mob conflicts, and these to rule by the strongest groups with control of the most deadly weapons. Our Constitution, noble work of wise men, was designed—all of it—to chart a quite different course: to "establish Justice, insure domestic Tranquility . . . and secure the Blessings of Liberty to ourselves and our Posterity." At times the rule of law seems too slow to some for the settlement of their grievances. But it is the plan our Nation has chosen to preserve both "Liberty" and equality for all. On that plan we have put our trust and staked our future. This constitutional rule of law has served us well. Maryland's trespass law does not depart from it. Nor shall we.

We would affirm.

Notes and Questions

1. Does Shelley v. Kraemer provide support for defendants' constitutional arguments in Bell? Did Justice Black adequately meet the argument based on *Shelley* (*supra* p. 1048)?

2. Why do you think Justice Douglas wished to reach the merits of this case? Do the extracts from Justice Black's dissent suggest reasons why he wished to reach the merits of the case?

3. What result do you suppose the Court might have reached if it had decided the case on its merits? Why?

4. Do any of Justice Douglas's arguments meet Justice Black's argument regarding the likely emotional responses of owners to sit-ins on their property?

5. Suppose Maryland recognized a common law right of an owner to self help in the removal of trespassers. Suppose further that the owner here, through employees, forcibly removed the people in the sit-in from the store. Would it be racially discriminatory state action for the Maryland courts to recognize the owner's right of self help as a defense to a criminal charge or civil action based on a claim by the sit-ins that they were assaulted by the employees?

6. Did the evolution of state and federal law after 1954 give at least moral support to the actions of the defendants in Bell v. Maryland?

7. Bell v. Maryland was the culmination of a series of sit-in cases which came before the Court in the early 1960's. Garner v. Louisiana, 368 U.S. 157, 82 S.Ct. 248 (1961); Taylor v. Louisiana, 370 U.S. 154, 82 S.Ct. 1188 (1962); Shuttlesworth v. Birmingham, 373 U.S. 262, 83 S.Ct. 1130 (1963); Peterson v. Greenville, 373 U.S. 244, 83 S.Ct. 1119 (1963); Lombard v. Louisiana, 373 U.S. 267, 83 S.Ct. 1122 (1963);

Barr v. City of Columbia, 378 U.S. 146, 84 S.Ct. 1734 (1964); Robinson v. Florida, 378 U.S. 153, 84 S.Ct. 1693 (1964); Griffin v. Maryland, 378 U.S. 130, 84 S.Ct. 1770 (1964); Bouie v. City of Columbia, 378 U.S. 347, 84 S.Ct. 1697 (1964). In these cases the Court assiduously avoided the constitutional issues regarding the propriety of convicting the participants in civil rights sit-ins, while at the same time finding procedural grounds upon which to reverse their convictions. While the Court was dealing with the sit-in issue in this deliberate and cautious way, the Congress was also hard at work trying to deal with the underlying causes of the problem, namely Jim Crow laws which decreed segregation of the races in public places, and the proclivity of businessmen, particularly but not exclusively in the South, to deny Blacks equal or any accommodations in restaurants, hotels and other eating and lodging establishments. Congress finally chose to deal with the issues in Title II of the Civil Rights Act of 1964, summarized *supra* at pp. 1027–1028. The passage of Title II, and comparable state statutes (e. g., the Maryland statutes cited in Bell v. Maryland) pretty much brought an end to the attempts to secure judicial determinations that the Fourteenth Amendment itself barred the various forms of segregated public facilities.

Was it in some sense better or more appropriate for this issue to be resolved by statute rather than through adjudication applying the U.S. Constitution? If so, why?

8. On October 22, 1964 the Court of Appeals of Maryland announced its decision on the remand of Bell v. Maryland. The Maryland Court affirmed the trespass convictions, holding that Maryland's saving clause preserved the convictions of Bell et al. which had been affirmed in the Maryland Court of Appeals in January 1962, over a year prior to the adoption of the Maryland and Baltimore public accommodations law and ordinance. According to the Maryland Court, the savings clause preserved prior convictions against subsequent enactments except where the legislature gave a clear direction to the contrary. The Court could find nothing in the public accommodations law to indicate that the Maryland legislature intended to overturn prior convictions for trespass in cases, like Bell v. Maryland, which antedated the adoption of the public accommodations law. One judge dissented. See Bell v. State, 236 Md. 356, 204 A.2d 54 (1964).

SECTION 48.3 SIT–DOWN AND SIT–IN: A COMPARISON

[The following is taken from SIDNEY FINE, SIT–DOWN (1970), pp. 338–341.]

The sit-down strike phase of the labor upheaval of the 1930's, of which the GM strike serves as the best example, was the equivalent in some ways of the civil-rights upheaval that began with the Montgomery bus boycott of 1955-56. In his analysis of the civil-rights movement, Arthur I. Waskow has coined the phrase "creative disorder" to describe the pursuit of change by disorderly but non-violent means such as sit-ins. Insofar as the politics of disorder seeks change, he has argued, "it is generally invented by people who are 'outside' a particular system of political order, and want to bring change about so that they can enter. In doing so, they tend to use new techniques that make sense to themselves out of their own experience, but that look disorderly to people who are thinking and acting inside the system."

The technique of disorder, Waskow contends, is apt to be tolerated or even encouraged to the extent that the "outside" group using it is pursuing ends deemed legitimate. When the state refuses to use its power against the perpetrators of disorder and prevents the use of violence against them, it in effect legitimizes disorder. In the instance of the civil-rights trespassers, Congress and the Department of Justice, quite apart from any belief in the worthiness of the goals sought by the civil-rights movement, tolerated non-violent disorder because the imposition of order might have led to violence.

The GM sit-down had many of the characteristics Waskow associates with the concept of creative disorder—the Congress of Racial Equality, as a matter of fact, "apparently derived" the sit-in technique from the sit-down strikes in the automobile industry. The sit-down strikers, like the civil-rights trespassers, were seeking change by "disorderly" but non-violent means. They were employing a technique that certainly made "sense" to workers familiar with the technology of automobile production; and, like the civil-rights demonstrators, they were "outsiders" insofar as representation in the automobile industry was concerned and were seeking entry into the "system."

Since the sit-downers were pursuing objectives sanctioned by law but denied them by their employer, their unconventional behavior was tolerated by large sections of the public. Governor Murphy, sympathetic with the goals of the strikers and seeking above all to avoid the outbreak of major violence that might have resulted from a no-nonsense law-and-order approach, refused to employ the power of the state to dislodge the sit-downers and forestalled the use of force against them by others, thus ensuring that some non-violent way out of the struggle would have to be found. Murphy and others apparently assumed that the sit-down strike would some day be accepted among the authorized methods of industrial warfare, just as the outside strike and, to a lesser degree, picketing had gained legitimacy by that time after having previously been considered illegal, but this turned out to be an incorrect judgment.

In other respects, also, the sit-down strike movement of the 1930's, and especially the GM strike, anticipated the civil-rights movement of the 1950's and 1960's. College students involved themselves in both movements, and songs—"We Shall Not Be Moved" was sung in Flint in 1937 and in the South in the early 1960's—were used as a morale builder by both UAW and civil-rights organizers. The UAW-CIO drive for recognition was a challenge to the conservative AFL leadership of the labor movement and brought new labor leaders to the fore nationally and locally—"Leaders are popping up everywhere," Travis said about Flint a month after the GM strike—just as the later civil-rights movement was, in some degree, a revolt against the conservatism of the established and dominant Negro organizations and led to the emergence of new leadership elements in local communities and in the nation as a whole. The UAW addressed its appeal to the mass of the semiskilled and unskilled workers in the automobile plants and not just to an elite of the skilled in the same way that the new civil-rights organizations a generation later sought to bestir the mass of the Negroes and not just "the talented tenth" to join in their protests.

Finally, the GM strike was the beginning of a brief period in the history of the American labor movement when workers saw themselves, or at least were so seen by liberal reformers, as seeking not just to better their own condition but also to better the nation, a moment when group interest and the national interest seemed to merge, when the union was not just another organization but was "a social and moral force." In this sense, too, the labor upheaval of the 1930's suggests the civil-rights movement of the 1950's and 1960's at its height.

Although there were obvious dissimilarities, echoes of the sit-down strikes of the 1930's were heard in 1968 and 1969 when college students, conscious of the tactics of civil disobedience practiced by the civil-rights movement for more than a decade, occupied college and university buildings in an effort to wrest concessions from administrative authorities. University administrators, like the public officials confronted with factory sit-downs in the 1930's, like Governor Murphy, had to decide whether to tolerate the trespass upon university property, to secure the abandonment of the tactic by denying food and utility service to the trespassers, to seek court injunctions against the sit-ins, or to eject the offending students by the use of force. Like GM and other companies in the 1930's some university authorities hesitated to employ force to dislodge the strikers lest it result in damage to university property and win support for the sit-downers from those who opposed or were indifferent to their behavior.

The sit-ins at Columbia University and elsewhere were conducted by a minority of militants who by their action sometimes prevented the majority of students from attending classes, just as the GM sit-downers forestalled the majority of the corporation's employees from going to their jobs. The student sit-downers, like the factory sit-downers, commonly wished to share in the decision-making that affected their lives, but their cry for "participatory democracy," "student power," or "black power" lacked the concreteness of labor's demand for collective bargaining and union power. Like the automotive sit-downers, student sit-downers were disposed to argue that the ends that they were seeking justified the means that they employed, especially since less disorderly tactics had allegedly proved unavailing; and just as the GM strikers insisted that the corporation withdraw the injunction directed against the trespass upon its property, so the student strikers demanded amnesty for their behavior. The most radical of the student leaders in 1968 and 1969 hoped to "radicalize" the campus just as the far left in the UAW in 1937 desired, in vain, to radicalize the union.

The sit-ins on college campuses in the late 1960s and early 1970s produced other echoes from the history of the labor movement. The sit-in tactic tried the patience and ingenuity of academic administrators who needed some peaceful means to evict the demonstrators and thus to placate alumni, faculty, parents, students, trustees and others who were inconvenienced or irritated by sit-ins. Peaceful means were required because the resort to force, i. e., eviction of demonstrators by police action, almost always produced violence, radicalization of more students and mobilization of faculty opinion against the administrators who called in the police. Legal counsel found in the civil injunction a non-violent but effective form of coercion to threaten demonstrators and dislodge their hold on campus facilities. Many courts were persuaded to issue *ex parte* injunctions threatening demonstrators with the contempt penalty for violation of very broad orders designed to secure peace on the campus and return facilities to the control of faculty and administrative officers. In many cases, such orders had an *in terrorem* effect which was quite striking, and quite reminiscent of the effects of the injunctions which were issued in the early days of the organized labor movement. The legal issues posed by this modern day revival of the *ex parte* injunction to restore order on campuses are explored in the following excerpt.

[The following is taken from an unsigned student note, "EQUITY ON THE CAMPUS: THE LIMITS OF INJUNCTIVE REGULATION OF UNIVERSITY PROTEST," 80 Yale Law Journal 987 (1971).]

Chairman Ichord, during his committee's hearings on SDS, commented that "most university administrators have concluded the best way to control campus disturbances is the injunction or temporary restraining order method." Administrators who have reached this conclusion base their judgment on factors other than the traditional tests for equitable jurisdiction and a concern for the protection of First Amendment freedoms. From the perspective of a beleaguered administration quick recourse to the injunctive process may seem advantageous for a variety of purely strategic reasons. An authoritative declaration that the conduct of the demonstrators is unlawful can help gain community and student support for the administration's position. It may forestall vigilante action on the part of those opposed to the demonstrators. Perhaps it will help insulate the university from the second wave of disturbances which seek to coerce amnesty for students arrested in earlier disruptions. If the order is obeyed, it may avert the indiscriminate application of force and the open hostility that so often accompany the presence of police on campus. Of course, these appealing items must be balanced against certain legal complications which may attend the enforcement of an injunction on campus. For example, difficulties may arise in binding nonparties, serving the order, and acquiring jurisdiction over juveniles. In addition, the limited and confused character of the defenses available to alleged contemnors may place the injunction defendants in an unfair position.

Thus if injunctions are framed in the light of the equitable and constitutional principles described earlier, their use on campus presents tactical rather than legal problems. Of all the strategic considerations that have been outlined, the most important by far is the hope that voluntary compliance with the injunction will avoid the prospect of the campus' being turned into an exercise in riot control. Inversely, the gravest problem with the use of the injunctive process is that posed by the spectre of widespread defiance of court orders. Accordingly, advocates of the campus injunction point out that many of the early orders issued to terminate building seizures were successful in clearing the buildings without resort to police; in the words of one administrator, the use of injunctions has had "a great tranquilizing effect." Yet, unqualified success has not been forthcoming, and the prospects for continued voluntary compliance are diminishing.

The probability that a court order will be complied with voluntarily is a function of at least three variables. First, thus far, injunctive relief is an extraordinary remedy, imbued with more judicial majesty than a riot stick can command. In this respect its use, as one radical group pointed out, is "psychological warfare." If so, as the novelty of the invocation of injunctions wears off at particular campuses, prospects for voluntary compliance will dwindle. Already, at those institutions where multiple resort to injunctive relief has been had, growing numbers of students have become increasingly less cooperative with the process. Apparently, "[y]oung blood doth not obey an old decree."

Second, for the injunction defendants the order is a specific weapon pointing directly at them. This factor has its maximum impact on those named in the order, and by clearly announcing what activity is intolerable, has a secondary effect on those not named. Nonetheless, the possibility that an injunction defendant will risk a contempt citation is by no means chimeric. Many protesting student groups have excellent legal advice, and, as further use of the injunction is made, these students will be informed of differences between state injunction statutes and criminal laws. When they realize that with the recent barrage of criminal statutes trained on the campus a contempt conviction will often result in a sentence less severe than that imposed for a criminal violation, they will be less hesitant to defy a court's authority.

Third, to the extent that students perceive the administration's use of the injunction as "illegitimate," they will be disinclined to honor it. From the standpoint of the demonstrators, the injunctive process is but a judicial subterfuge purporting to resolve the crisis but avoiding the underlying issues; the court acts as a lackey of the university, attempting to legitimize the administration's inaction or rejection of the protestors' grievances. If the university repeatedly seeks the aid of the courts, especially in instances where the complaints voiced by the dissenting students have substantial support among the campus community, this analysis is likely to prevail among more moderate students as well. Therefore, rather than "tranquilizing" students, interposition of the court may polarize resistance to university discipline and generate animosity toward the judiciary. If demands for vague and overbroad orders persist, and if improper resort to the injunction is made for the purpose of restraining First Amendment freedoms, it may, as the ABA cautioned, "result in lower court denials or appellate court reversals embarrassing to the university, and may contribute to the arguments of dissidents that the university does not respect basic constitutional rights."

For such reasons one administrator recently expressed the fear that if the proliferation of campus injunctions continues unchecked, in a year or so the tactic will no longer be potent in inducing voluntary compliance. Although this prognosis may be overly pessimistic, slogans like the one in vogue at George Washington University in 1970—LIFT THE RESTRAINING ORDER NOW! JOIN US!—will undoubtedly attract more adherents in the coming years.

To summarize, it would be a serious mistake to believe that injunctive control will automatically defuse a campus crisis. Whatever their constitutional and equitable merits, the success of injunctions in dislodging students from barricaded buildings and curtailing other militant tactics has varied considerably, sometimes effecting immediately compliance and, increasingly, evoking mass defiance. Considering the three major factors which appear to influence the efficacy of injunctive relief, three parallel principles should guide its deployment. First, if familiarity is not to breed contempt, relief should be sought sparingly, and reserved for major confrontations in which seriously disruptive conduct well beyond the limits of the First Amendment has already occurred. Second, it should not be used prospectively, as a prior restraint on protest, but should be restricted to ongoing, unprotected, disruptive actions. Finally, it should be obtained only when the rallying potential of the issues advocated by the demonstrators is small. Otherwise, if these admonitions are ignored and the device displayed too frequently, campus injunctions will be flaunted by students, police or patience will be necessary to weather the crisis, respect for the administrations' positions will have been undermined, and the moral force of the courts squandered.

By the time this note was published the issues posed by student demonstrations had been put in a very different perspective. In the Spring of 1970, students at Kent State University had been wounded, or crippled or killed in a crackle of gunfire from beleaguered National Guardsmen. That watershed event was followed by the gradual demise of campus sit-ins, thus eliminating the occasions for testing the predictions made in the Yale Law Journal note.

SECTION 48.4   SELF HELP AND FREE SPEECH

[The following is taken from HARRY KALVEN, JR., "THE CONCEPT OF THE PUBLIC FORUM: COX v. LOUISIANA," 1965 Supreme Court Review 1, 10–12, 23–25, 26–27. Most footnotes are omitted.

[This article attempts to reconcile differences in the opinions in Edwards v. South Carolina, 372 U.S. 229, 83 S.Ct. 680, and Cox v. Louisiana, 379 U.S. 536, 85 S.Ct. 453 (1965), two cases in which the Supreme Court struck down convictions in criminal cases arising out of civil rights demonstrations. We have excerpted only a small portion of Professor Kalven's excellent text. In order to put this excerpt in context, we first reprint excerpts from the opinions in Edwards and Cox describing the respective demonstrations leading to those cases. Both passages were reprinted by Professor Kalven in his article in order, as he put it, to "establish the style of the two protests".]

Late in the morning of March 2, 1961, the petitioners, high school and college students of the Negro race, met at the Zion Baptist Church in Columbia. From there at about noon they walked in separate groups of about 15 to the South Carolina State House grounds, an area of two city blocks open to the general public. Their purpose was to "submit a protest to the citizens of South Carolina, along with the Legislative Bodies of South Carolina, our feelings and our dissatisfaction with present conditions of discriminatory actions against Negroes, in general, and to let them know we were dissatisfied and that we would like for the laws which prohibited Negro privileges in this State to be removed."

Already on the State House grounds when petitioners arrived, were some 30 or more law enforcement officers who had advance knowledge that petitioners were coming. Each group of petitioners entered the grounds through a driveway and parking area known in the record as the "horseshoe." As they entered they were told by the law enforcement officials that they had a right as a citizen to go through the State House grounds as any other citizen has, as long as they were peaceful. During the next half hour or 45 minutes, the petitioners in the same small groups walked single file or two abreast in an orderly way through the grounds, each group carrying placards bearing such messages as "I'm proud to be a Negro" and "Down with segregation." *

On December 14, 1961, 23 students from Southern University, a Negro college, were arrested in downtown Baton Rouge, Louisiana, for picketing stores that maintained segregated lunch counters. . . . [After a mass meeting on campus that night,] the students resolved to demonstrate the next day in front of the courthouse in protest of segregation and the arrest and imprisonment of the picketers who were being held in the parish jail located on the upper floor of the courthouse building.

[Next day the students left the campus in mass and marched five miles to Baton Rouge. The student leader having been arrested for violation of an anti-noise statute while using a sound truck, the defendant Cox, a Congregational minister, field secretary of CORE, and adviser to the student movement, came to "pick up this leadership and keep things orderly."] When Cox arrived 1,500 of the 2,000 students were assembling at the site of the old State Capitol building two and one half blocks from the courthouse. Cox walked up and down cautioning the students to keep to one side of the sidewalk while getting ready for their march to the courthouse. The students circled the block in a file two or three abreast occupy-

---

* From the opinion of Justice Stewart in
Edwards v. South Carolina.

ing about one-half the sidewalk. . . . They walked in an orderly and peaceful file, two or three abreast, one block east, stopping on the way for a red traffic light. . . .

[The students were joined by another group and came to a halt in the next block opposite the courthouse. A colloquy with police officials followed.] The students were then directed by Cox to the west sidewalk across from the courthouse, 101 feet from its steps. They were lined up on this sidewalk about five deep and spread almost the entire length of the block. The group did not obstruct the street. [Several hundred onlookers gathered on the sidewalk near the courthouse and some 75 to 80 police and members of the fire department also turned out.]

Several of the students took from beneath their coats picket signs similar to those which had been used the day before. The signs bore legends such as "Don't buy discrimination for Christmas," "Sacrifice for Christ, don't buy," and named stores which were proclaimed "unfair." They then sang "God Bless America," pledged allegiance to the flag, prayed briefly, and sang one or two hymns, including "We Shall Overcome." The 23 students who were locked in jail cells in the courthouse building out of the sight of the demonstrators responded by themselves singing; this, in turn, was greeted with cheers and applause by the demonstrators.**

[Following are the excerpts from Professor Kalvin's Text.]

It may prove helpful to risk the pretentiousness of distinguishing among three closely related gestures of protest often lumped together in popular discussions of the civil rights movement: revolution, civil disobedience, and protest. A revolutionary gesture is intended as direct defiance of law and order; it is a declaration of open war; it is coercive and obstructive. It may well be morally justifiable, but only under the stringent conditions by which Western tradition has measured a right of revolution. The suggestion, for example, that Negroes let their water taps run in New York to aggravate the water shortage is just such a revolutionary gesture.

Civil disobedience is deliberate violation of law for the sake of protest and as a matter of individual conscience. It is a gesture we associate with Socrates, Thoreau, and conscientious objectors. In the famous formula of Plato's *Apology* and *Crito* this gesture requires that the actor accept the punishment. It is a refusal to obey the law coupled with a willingness to accept the legal consequences. Insofar as it is symbolic, it is also an intense form of protest. To an uncertain extent, especially in the sit-in demonstrations, the Negro movement has in this sense courted arrest. The important point is that civil disobedience claims exemption from the obligation to obey particular laws on moral grounds but not immunity from punishment.

Finally, there are the various forms of mass protest in public places using parades, picketing, and so on. Here the essential feature is appeal to public opinion. The intention is not to violate the law, and the claim is one of privilege in the exercise of basic rights. Most of the civil rights demonstrations to date, as I see it, fall in this category. This has been one of the extraordinary achievements of the movement. It is this gesture of protest that I am concerned with in this essay. These distinctions are

** From the opinion of Justice Goldberg
in Cox v. Louisiana.

undoubtedly difficult to draw from the facts, and the Negro movement has not itself always been clear about which strategy it was pursuing. The Negro movement shares with the rest of us the task of working out the appropriate forms for its protest.

It is simplistic, if tempting, to reduce the issue to a choice between order and anarchy. I suggest three interrelated propositions for examination. First, that in an open democratic society the streets, the parks, and other public places are an important facility for public discussion and political process. They are in brief a public forum that the citizen can commandeer; the generosity and empathy with which such facilities are made available is an index of freedom. Second, that only confusion can result from distinguishing sharply between "speech pure" and "speech plus." And, third, that what is required is in effect a set of Robert's Rules of Order for the new uses of the public forum, albeit the designing of such rules poses a problem of formidable practical difficulty. As will be apparent, there is much in *Cox* that bears on these three points. . . .

* * *

[At this point Professor Kalven discusses a number of relevant precedents, particularly Hague v. C. I. O., 307 U.S. 496, 59 S.Ct. 954 (1939), Jamison v. Texas, 318 U.S. 413, 63 S.Ct. 669 (1943), and Talley v. California, 362 U.S. 60, 80 S.Ct. 536 (1960). Hague involved a dispute between the then Mayor of Jersey City, New Jersey and the C. I. O. regarding labor organizing activities in Jersey City. Of special interest in that case was a dictum of Justice Roberts:

> Wherever the title of street and parks may rest, they have immemorially been held in trust for the use of the public and time out of mind, have been used for purposes of assembly, communicating thoughts between citizens, and discussing public questions. Such use of the streets and public places has from ancient times, been a part of the privileges, immunities, rights, and liberties of citizens.

Jamison and Talley dealt with attempts by cities to limit distribution of leaflets by religious and civil rights organizations. In both cases the Court upheld the defendant's right to distribute leaflets on city streets. Professor Kalven points out that the Court in such cases and in Cox attempted to develop a distinction between "speech pure" *e.g.*, a newspaper article, and "speech plus", *i.e.*, a combination of speech and other activity. Picketing with signs is one example of speech plus.]

* * *

To begin with, I would suggest that all speech is necessarily "speech plus." If it is oral, it is noise and may interrupt someone else; if it is written, it may be litter. Indeed this is why the leaflet cases were an appropriate model: they involved speech with collateral consequences that invited regulation. But the leaflets were not simply litter; they were litter with ideas.

Perhaps this is the time to bring into the discussion a classic distinction in speech theory. It is the distinction between regulations like Robert's Rules of Order and regulation of content. No one has ever argued that speech should be free of the restraints of reasonable parliamentary rules, and any concessions on this front should not be taken as relevant to the questions most central to speech theory—questions of control of content.

The point then is that, in any theory, speech has always been dependent on some commitment to order and etiquette. There is, therefore, nothing novel in the vulnerability of protest speech to regulation on this score. This is not, as the Court was willing to assume in *Cox*, a characteristic setting it apart from traditional speech and hence summarily subject to regulation.

Listen for a moment to Alexander Meiklejohn describing a town meeting:

> In the town meeting the people of a community assemble to discuss and to act upon matters of public interest—roads, schools, poorhouses, health, external defense, and the like. Every man is free to come. They meet as political equals. Each has a right and a duty to think his own thoughts, to express them, and to listen to the arguments of others. The basic principle is that the freedom of speech shall be unabridged. And yet the meeting cannot even be opened unless, by common consent, speech is abridged. A chairman or moderator is, or has been, chosen. He "calls the meeting to order." And the hush which follows that call is a clear indication that restrictions upon speech have been set up. The moderator assumes, or arranges, that in the conduct of the business, certain rules of order will be observed. Except as he is overruled by the meeting as a whole, he will enforce those rules. His business on its negative side is to abridge speech. For example, it is usually agreed that no one shall speak unless "recognized by the chair." Also, debaters must confine their remarks to "the question before the house." If one man "has the floor," no one else may interrupt him except as provided by the rules. The meeting has assembled, not primarily to talk, but primarily by means of talking to get business done. And the talking must be regulated and abridged as the doing of the business under actual conditions may require. If a speaker wanders from the point at issue, if he is abusive or in other ways threatens to defeat the purpose of the meeting, he may be and should be declared "out of order." He must then stop speaking, at least in that way. And if he persists in breaking the rules, he may be "denied the floor" or, in the last resort, "thrown out" of the meeting. The town meeting, as it seeks for freedom of public discussion of public problems, would be wholly ineffectual unless speech were thus abridged. . . .

These speech-abridging activities of the town meeting indicate what the First Amendment to the Constitution does not forbid. When self-governing men demand freedom of speech they are not saying that every individual has an inalienable right to speak whenever, wherever, however he chooses. They do not declare that any man may talk as he pleases, when he pleases, about what he pleases, about whom he pleases, to whom he pleases. The common sense of any reasonable society would deny the existence of that unqualified right. No one, for example, may, without consent of nurse, or doctor, rise up in a sickroom to argue for his principles or his candidate. In the sickroom, that question is not "before the house." The discussion is, therefore, "out of order." To you who now listen to my words, it is allowable to differ with me, but it is not allowable for you to state that difference in words until I have finished my reading. Anyone who would thus irresponsibly interrupt the activities of a lecture, a hospital, a concert hall, a church, a machine shop, a classroom, a football field, or a home, does not thereby exhibit his freedom. Rather, he shows himself to be a boor, a public nuisance, who must be abated, by force if necessary.

The Meiklejohn passage demonstrates that there is something askew in the distinction between "speech pure" and "speech plus." Certainly his recalcitrant participant at the town meeting is engaged in "speech plus"; but if he is, who is not? And surely it is sobering to note that the call for regulation of such activity on behalf of the rational use of speech resources comes from the champion of the position that the First Amendment is an abolute.

* * *

Admittedly there is a difference between the town meeting and the street. In the former the only problems of order and competing use relate to speakers, and the problem can be solved under a formula seeking to provide the maximum opportunity for speech at the meeting. The streets on the other hand, although a meeting place for free men from time out of mind, are also dedicated to other uses, such as travel. Hence, the speech interests compete in this instance with non-speech interests and the appropriate accommodation is more difficult. Despite this difference it strikes me that Robert's Rules are a happy analogy because they make it so clear that the concern ought not to be with censorship, or with the content of what is said; what is needed is a phasing or timing of the activity, not a ban on it. It remains to be seen, of course, whether even under this generous view, the protest movement may not generate sharp controversies by asking for "prime time." But so long as the intention is not obstruction or harassment, as in general it has not been in the past demonstrations, it should be possible, if difficult, to work out mutually satisfactory arrangements.

Notes and Questions

1.　What are the various purposes you ascribe to political speech?

2.　What reasons can you suggest for choosing the public forum as a place to present speech?

3.　What reasons can you suggest for choosing a peaceful mass demonstration in the public forum as a way of presenting speech?

4.　Would you say that a purpose of political speech can be to convey both ideas *and* an impression of the intensity with which those ideas are held by the speaker?

5.　Can the manner of presenting speech affect both the likelihood that it will be widely disseminated and that it will influence the thinking of the audience? If so, will not regulation of the mode of presentation also affect the substance of the communication?

6.　Does the idea of "speech pure" suggest a conception of political speech as an essentially intellectual process?

7.　Can political speech also attempt to invoke essentially emotional and impressionistic responses in addition to or in place of intellectual reactions?

8. Can you suggest reasons why the law might strongly protect the intellectual aspects of speech, but be less protective of other aspects of speech?

9. Do you think that relatively lenient rules of order regarding peaceful political demonstrations in the public forum aid or hamper the resolution of social conflict?

10. How extensive is the public forum? Consider the following problems:

(a) Logan Valley Plaza, Inc. owned and operated a shopping plaza in Altoona, Pennsylvania. Weis Markets, Inc. operated a food market in the plaza. Amalgamated Food Employees, Local 590, picketed Weis at the plaza as part of its efforts to organize the employees of Weis Markets, which was then a non-union shop. All the picketing was conducted on land, roadways and parking lots, owned by Logan Valley. Weis and Logan Valley sought and obtained an injunction barring further picketing. The trial court found that the injunction should issue because Local 590 was unlawfully coercing Weis' employees, and that the picketing was a trespass on private property. On appeal the Pennsylvania Supreme Court affirmed, solely on the trespass issue. What result should follow on appeal in the United States Supreme Court? See Amalgamated Food Employees v. Logan Valley Plaza, 391 U.S. 308, 88 S.Ct. 1601 (1967).

(b) Lloyd Corporation, Ltd. (Lloyd) owned a shopping center in Portland, Oregon. The center had a perimeter of some one and one-half miles bounded by public streets and adjacent sidewalks. Some public streets and sidewalks also crossed through the center. The main structure in the center was an enclosed mall. The mall housed all the stores in the center. Some of the stores had entrances which opened directly on to the public sidewalks, but most could be reached only through the interior of the mall. Lloyd allowed use of the common areas and public spaces in the center and mall for various community service programs and organizations. Among other things, Lloyd had permitted parades through the mall on Veteran's Day and also speeches by representatives of Veteran's organizations, and it had allowed the American Legion some access to solicit donations from mall patrons. Political campaigning was barred in the mall, except that Lloyd had allowed presidential candidates to speak in the mall. Distribution of handbills in the mall was strictly forbidden, and there were no exceptions to this policy.

On November 14, 1968, one Tanner and four other young people entered the mall for the purpose of distributing handbills inviting people to a meeting to protest the draft and the war in Vietnam. Security guards employed by Lloyd informed Tanner et al. that they would be arrested unless they stopped distributing handbills in the mall. The guards suggested that the five go out on to the adjacent public sidewalks and distribute the handbills. The five left the mall and continued handbilling on the adjacent sidewalks. Subsequently they brought suit in Federal District Court seeking a declaratory judgment that they were entitled to handbill in the mall, and an injunction to implement that declaration of rights. How should the District Court have decided this case? See Lloyd Corp. v. Tanner, 407 U.S. 551, 92 S.Ct. 2219 (1971).

(c) Scott Hudgens owned a shopping center in a suburb of Atlanta, Georgia. The center consisted of an enclosed mall building surrounded by parking lots which could accommodate over 2500 cars. The parking lots abutted on public streets and highways on which there were entrances to the lots. The mall housed 60 stores, including one which was leased to the Butler Shoe Company, which had eight other retail stores in the Atlanta area, all of which were served from one central warehouse. Some of the warehouse employees went on strike in January, 1971. The strikers decided to picket not only at the warehouse but also at the nine retail stores in the Atlanta area. On January 22, 1971 four of the strikers entered Hudgen's shopping center carrying placards which read "Butler Shoe Warehouse on Strike, AFL-CIO, Local 315." The shopping center manager threatened to have them arrested if they attempted to picket in the mall or in the parking lot. The strikers left the mall but returned shortly and commenced picketing inside the mall adjacent to the Butler Shoe store. After a half-hour of the picketing the manager repeated his threat and the strikers departed. The warehouse employee's union then filed an unfair labor practice charge with the NLRB, alleging that Hudgens had violated rights guaranteed to the warehousemen by § 7 of the National Labor Relations Act, which provides, in pertinent part, that:

"Employees shall have the right to self-organization, to form, join, or assist labor organizations, to bargain collectively through organizations of their own choosing, and to engage in other concerted activities for the purpose of collective bargaining or other mutual aid or protection . . ." 29 U.S.C. § 157. How should the NLRB have decided this case? See Hudgens v. N.L.R.B., 424 U.S. 507, 96 S.Ct. 1029 (1976).

SECTION 49. ADMINISTRATIVE REGULATION OF LABOR MANAGEMENT RELATIONS AND RACIAL DISCRIMINATION IN EMPLOYMENT

The Wagner Act established some new norms to govern the behavior of organized labor and management, but perhaps more significant were the processes established for the administration of the new law. The responsibility for the administration and enforcement of the law was vested in the National Labor Relations Board, an agency created by the Wagner Act and established as a governmental unit to function independent of direct control by either Congress or the President. The organization and function of the Board will be examined after a brief survey of the subject of administrative law.

Congress also established administrative agencies to implement various of the Civil Rights Acts adopted since 1954. The Equal Employment Opportunity Commission is an example we shall examine briefly in this section.

SECTION 49.1   A PREVIEW OF ADMINISTRATIVE LAW

[The following is taken from KENNETH CULP DAVIS, ADMINISTRATIVE LAW TEXT (St. Paul, 1959), pp. 1–5, 8–17, 23–29. Footnotes are omitted.]

What Is Administrative Law?

Administrative law is the law concerning the powers and procedures of administrative agencies, including especially the law governing judicial review of administrative action. An administrative agency is a governmental authority, other than a court and other than a legislative body, which affects the rights of private parties through either adjudication or rule making.[1] An administrative agency may be called a commission, board, authority, bureau, office, officer, administrator, department, corporation, administration, division, or agency. Nothing of substance hinges on the choice of name, and usually the choices have been entirely haphazard. When the President, or a governor, or a municipal governing body exercises powers of adjudication or rule making, he or it is to that extent an administrative agency.

The administrative process is the complex of methods by which agencies carry out their tasks of adjudication, rule making, and related functions. The administrative process is often compared or contrasted with the judicial process, the executive process, and the legislative process.   .   .   .

The three large segments of administrative law relate to transfer of power from legislatures to agencies, exercise of power by the agencies, and review of administrative action by the courts. As recently as a quarter

---

1. Rule making is the procedure through which an agency promulgates orders and directives which apply generally to the persons or firms subject to the regulatory jurisdiction of the agency. These orders are a form of law analogous to legislation both in terms of their formulation and application. Thus rules and rule making stand in the same relation to administrative agencies, as statutes and legislating relate to legislatures.

Adjudication by an administrative agency, is the process through which an agency makes decisions regarding the application of a statute or administrative rules to specific persons or firms. It is analogous to the functions traditionally performed by the courts.

of a century ago, the subject was still largely limited to the first and third of these, with concentration upon the doctrines of separation of powers and non-delegation. But as of the middle of the century, the theory of separation of powers, while still guiding the drafters of constitutions, has hardly any influence upon administrative arrangements or activities. The problems of delegation are tending to disappear from federal law and are of sharply diminishing importance in state law.

* * *

The Place of Administrative Action in Our Governmental and Legal Systems

MR. JUSTICE JACKSON asserted in a formal opinion in 1952: "The rise of administrative bodies probably has been the most significant legal trend of the last century and perhaps more values today are affected by their decisions than by those of all the courts, review of administrative decisions apart."

A statistical measure of the place of administrative law in Supreme Court litigation has recently been set forth by MR. JUSTICE FRANKFURTER, on the basis of analysis of cases of two recent terms of the Supreme Court (348–351 U.S.): "Review of administrative action, mainly reflecting enforcement of federal regulatory statutes, constitutes the largest category of the Court's work, comprising one-third of the total cases decided on the merits." Constitutional law, including "cases with constitutional undertones," was in second place, with less than one-fourth of the cases.

The average person is much more directly and much more frequently affected by the administrative process than by the judicial process. The ordinary person probably regards the judicial process as somewhat remote from his own problems; a large portion of all people go through life without even being a party to a lawsuit. But the administrative process affects nearly every one in many ways nearly every day. The pervasiveness of the effects of the administrative process on the average person can quickly be appreciated by running over a few samples of what the administrative process protects against: excessive prices of electricity, gas, telephone, and other utility services; unreasonableness in rates, schedules, and services of airlines, railroads, street cars, and buses; disregard for the public interest in radio and television and chaotic conditions for broadcasting; unwholesome meat and poultry; adulteration in food; fraud or inadequate disclosure in sale of securities; physically unsafe locomotives, ships, airplanes, bridges, elevators; unfair labor practices by either employers or unions; false advertising and other unfair or deceptive practices; inadequate safety appliances; uncompensated injuries related to employment; cessation of income during temporary unemployment; subminimum wages; poverty in old age; industrial plants in residential areas; loss of bank deposits; and (perhaps) undue inflation or deflation. Probably the list could be expanded to a thousand or more items that we are accustomed to take for granted.

The volume of the legislative output of federal agencies far exceeds the volume of the legislative output of Congress. The Code of Federal Regulations is considerably larger than the United States Code. The Federal Register, the accumulation of less than one-quarter of a century, fills much more shelf space than the Statutes at Large, the accumulation of nearly a century and three-quarters. The quantity of state and local administrative regulations is hard to estimate, but the administrative codes of the states that codify their regulations seem to approach in size the unannotated statutes.

The quantity of adjudication in federal agencies is probably many times the quantity of adjudication in federal courts. Statements of responsible people to this effect have become very common, but the statements are typically about as vague as the one just made. A rare statement having some degree of precision is that "There are now between 3 and 4 times as many matters coming before the administrative agencies as are presented in our Federal courts today, and they are of great importance to the country and to the Nation." The Director of the Office of Administrative Procedure is more cautious: "It is estimated that the administrative business today may exceed in volume the civil business in all of our courts."

* * *

Even the relatively simple question of how many federal agencies have powers of either adjudication or rule making is quite elusive, for this question involves not only locating the boundaries of adjudication and rule making but also deciding what segment of the government constitutes an agency. Is an executive department an agency, or each major unit of the department an agency, or is each bureau within each major unit an agency? The Bureau of Old Age and Survivors Insurance handles two million claims a year—is it an agency? Or is the agency the Social Security Administration including Public Assistance, the Children's Bureau, and Federal Credit Unions? Or is the proper segment to count the Department of Health, Education, and Welfare, which includes the Public Health Service, the Office of Education, the Food and Drug Administration, the Office of Vocational Rehabilitation, St. Elizabeths Hospital, and Howard University? If Howard University makes rules that are binding on students, is it properly counted as a rule-making agency?

In 1941 the Attorney General's Committee on Administrative Procedure found that by taking the largest possible units as agencies, there were nine executive departments and eighteen independent agencies, but that by taking subdivisions of departments the number of agencies was increased from 27 to 51, of which 22 were outside the executive departments and 29 within them.

The Code of Federal Regulation contains the codification of administrative rules and regulations, classified by the names of issuing agencies. Each volume of the CFR contains a list of this classification of agencies. The list in the 1949 edition includes 155 agencies.

The simple question whether we have 27 or 51 agencies; as the Attorney General's Committee found, or at least 155 agencies, as the compilers of the CFR have found, cannot be answered except by saying that the answer depends on the size of the units that are counted.

The average state probably has more than one hundred agencies with powers of adjudication or rule making or both. A count of the agencies in Mississippi, one of our least industrial states, shows at least seventy-five.

Nearly all states have major agencies such as public service commissions, insurance commissioners, workmen's compensation tribunals, zoning agencies, unemployment compensation commissions, departments of agriculture, departments of labor, and many others. Every state has a large and growing number of occupational licensing agencies.

No one knows how many administrative agencies have been created by municipalities and other units of local government. The number may be in the tens of thousands. Anyone who tries to count them in a single city will quickly discover the insuperable problems of classification.

Reasons for Growth of the Administrative Process

The fundamental reason for resort to the administrative process is the undertaking by government of tasks which from a strictly practical standpoint can best be performed through that process. When the predecessors agency of the present Veterans' Administration was created in 1789 the fundamental pattern was set that has been followed ever since; the job of determining which claimants were entitled to be paid was assigned to an agency other than the courts because what was needed was a staff of low-paid clerks, not a few high-paid judges with all the cumbersome trappings of the courtroom. Similar reasons explain the establishment of collectors of customs in 1789, a fore-runner of the Patent Office in 1790, the Office of Indian Affairs in 1796, and the General Land Office in 1812. No one was thinking in terms of judiciary versus bureaucracy, capitalism versus socialism, or laissez-faire versus governmental interference. The early agencies were created because practical men were seeking practical answers to immediate problems.

Precisely the same approach was dominant in 1887 when the Interstate Commerce Commission, the first great regulatory agency, was created. The railroads before 1870 had been free from governmental interference, except for statutory prohibitions enforceable through prosecuting attorneys and courts, and except for common-law actions by shippers for refund of unreasonable charges. But as abuses multiplied—discriminations and preferences, exorbitant rates, irresponsible financial manipulation—the realization grew that legislatures and courts were inadequate. What was needed was a governmental authority having power not merely to adjudicate but to initiate proceedings, to investigate, to prosecute, to issue regulations having force of law, to supervise. Between 1871 and 1875, the legislatures of Iowa, Michigan, Minnesota, Missouri, and Wisconsin, spurred by aroused farmers, established regulatory commissions. Then the Supreme Court in 1886 held the states without power to regulate interstate rates, and the creation of a federal commission became inevitable, since three-fourths of railroad tonnage was interstate, and since Congress and the courts could not themselves accomplish what the state commissions had been accomplishing.

* * *

The legislative process and the judicial process, which are the principal alternatives to the administrative process, frequently fall far short of providing what is needed. A legislative body is at its best in determining the direction of major policy, and in checking and supervising administration. It is ill-suited for handling masses of detail, or for applying to shifting and continuing problems the ideas supplied by scientists or other professional advisers. Experience early proved the inability of Congress to prescribe detailed schedules of rates for railroads, or to keep abreast of changing needs concerning the levels of import duties. Gradually our legislative bodies developed the system of legislating only the main outlines of programs requiring constant attention, and leaving to administrative agencies the tasks of working out subsidiary policies. This system facilitated not merely the promulgation of law through rules and regulations but the correlation of rule making with such other necessary activities as adjudication, investigating, prosecuting, and supervising.

Somewhat less compelling are the reasons for developing systems of administrative adjudication instead of transferring cases to the courts whenever specific issues are crystallized which call for the finding of facts and the application of law or policy. Even if an ICC is needed which will make rules, supervise, investigate, administer, and do other things courts cannot do, why should not the courts still decide individual controversies? Even if a social security administration must use a staff of nearly eighteen thousand to pay two million claims annually for old age and survivors insurance, why should not the courts step in whenever an issue arises for adjudication? The same question is pertinent for every other agency.

The reasons are numerous and variable. Some apply to some agencies and some to others. Some are convincing, some are not, and some may be in need of reexamination.

Perhaps the most important reason why, as a matter of historical fact, we have not sent all controversies to the courts, is that adjudication of issues naturally grows directly out of the administrative handling of cases. For instance, ninety-nine veterans are admitted to a veterans' hospital, and only in the hundredth case does a controversy arise. Even if a hearing or something like a hearing is called for, the hospital officials or members of their immediate organization may most conveniently conduct the proceeding; the adjudication is virtually a part of the administrative work of admitting the hundred veterans. This is so, even if the issues when isolated from the administrative work are entirely appropriate for judicial determination. The reasons are often about the same whether the subject matter is the award of a benefit, the granting of a license, the approval of a rate, or the issuance of a cease and desist order. Thus, even when courts are well qualified to adjudicate some classes of controversies, administrative adjudication has often been preferred mostly for reasons of convenience.

But much of the substance of administrative adjudication is, or at the crucial time has been thought to be, outside the area of judicial competence. Courts are not qualified to fix rates or to determine what practices related to rates are to be preferred. Even a simple process of granting or denying licenses, on the basis of a record of evidence, has been held so far beyond the competence of courts that a statute requiring courts to perform this task is held unconstitutional. Judges rather obviously cannot furnish the skills in law, accounting, and engineering supplied by the staff of a relatively simple agency like the FCC, to say nothing of a more complex agency like the ICC, which requires the assistance of rate men, locomotive inspectors, railroad reorganization specialists, explosives experts, valuation engineers, tariff interpreters, accountants, specialists in long-and-short-haul problems, and experts on problems of rail traffic congestion. With all the specialized personnel available on the Commission's staff, it would be odd, even when specific issues are fully crystallized, to transfer a case to a court made up of judges who are not expected to have the needed specialized experience and who are not advised by specialists.

Even when issues are of a type that courts can competently handle, such as claims for old age insurance, the advantages of specialization may be a crucial consideration. Among the eighteen thousand government workers who handle such claims are units which specialize in particular types of problems; even when the subject matter is of a type on which judges are especially well qualified, such as questions of law—say, marriage and divorce law—the specialized unit in the Bureau of Old Age and Survivors Insurance may best handle the case; the specialized unit may dispose of hundreds of such cases a week, whereas it might take a judge a week for a handful of such cases.

* * *

Another major reason for the legislative preference for the administrative process has been the belief that the judicial process is unduly awkward, slow, and expensive. The public has demanded a speedy, cheap, and simple procedure, a procedure which keeps the role of the lawyers to a minimum. Of course, the administrative process is by no means always fast and inexpensive, but the prevailing belief has been that it is.

* * *

Another significant reason for using agencies instead of courts for some types of adjudications has to do with the traditional passiveness of courts, which typically have no machinery for initiating proceedings or for taking other action in absence of a moving party. This characteristic of courts has combined with the recognized need for public representation of large numbers of little people—consumers, usually—none of whom is sufficiently affected to assert his own interests in a judicial proceeding. President Roosevelt made this point in his veto message: "Wherever a continuing series of controversies exist between a powerful and concentrated interest on one side and a diversified mass of individuals, each of whose separate interests may be small, on the other side, the only means of obtaining equality before the law has been to place the controversy in an administrative tribunal." Another way, of course, would be to have courts do the adjudicating, and to have sufficiently alert prosecutors to represent the public interest.

Another major reason for resort to the administrative process has been the widespread belief, whether or not justifiable, that the biases of the judges disqualify them to administer the new programs that have been committed to administrative agencies. Whatever the proper interpretation of the facts might be, the opinion was often dominant among sponsors of reform legislation that judges during the first third of the twentieth century frequently construed away sound and necessary reform legislation. In many of the regulatory programs the fundamental cleavage was believed to be between private rights and social objectives. The assumptions were that the primary business of courts was to decide controversies involving private rights and not to further legislative policies, that judges have been typically influenced by legal training toward conservative attitudes and accustomed through experience as advocates at the bar to favoring the interests of property, and that judges were therefore biased in favor of protection of private rights against governmental interference. When the primary purpose of the sponsors of regulatory legislation was to alter what was regarded as the accustomed judicial protection of private rights, the choice was naturally made in favor of tribunals other than courts to administer the regulatory programs.

* * *

A good example of the political point of view that led to rejection of the courts for administering new legislation is a 1914 statement of a Senate Committee, recommending establishment of the Federal Trade Commission because: "The people of this country will not permit the courts to declare a policy for them with respect to this subject." Of course, this attitude outrages those who are inclined to emphasize the desirability of protecting established rights from bureaucratic interference. But, right or wrong, this attitude is historically one of the prime reasons for the growth of the administrative process.

Of course, reasons for the growth of the administrative process must include not only reasons for establishment of the agencies but also reasons for keeping them once they have been established. The record here is especially impressive. Although much shifting of functions from one agency to another has occurred, probably no federal peacetime agency having significant powers of adjudication or rule making has ever been abolished. Professor Willard Hurst, in a context of discussion of state agencies, pointed out in 1950: "No important administrative agency seems ever to have been destroyed because of objections to its distinctive characteristics as an administrative agency."

The reasons, however, for the retention of agencies are by no means entirely favorable to the administrative process. That many agencies are continued because they successfully do the jobs assigned to them is clear, as probably nearly everyone would agree with respect to, say, the Internal Revenue Service, the Veterans' Administration, and perhaps most local zoning boards. But some of the most important regulatory agencies may be kept, not because of their success, but because the degree of their failure is approved by politically powerful interests that are regulated. An ineffective regulatory agency often goes through the motions of regulating, thereby silencing the sponsors of the legislation that brought the agency into existence, but at the same time the agency is careful for the most part to regulate in the interest of the regulated, thereby silencing them. And we go on and on with our mixture of regulatory agencies, all of them varying somewhat from time to time in their effectiveness, some rather fully dominated most of the time by regulated parties, others semi-effective some of the time or much of the time, and hardly any fully effective over sustained periods.

All in all, the political outlook is for a long-term continued growth of the administrative process. Few informed people of any political persuasion are likely to disagree with a 1955 statement by the Attorney General for the most conservative national administration we have had since 1933: "Administrative agencies have become an established part of our constitutional government, accepted by Congress, the judiciary and the people as an essential part of the government structure. They were created as a necessary means for protecting public interests which could not be suitably protected by the courts or other means. . . . Administrative agencies must be enabled and permitted to function efficiently and effectively if the public interest, which is their primary concern, is to be preserved."

* * *

Separation of Powers

Probably the principal doctrinal barrier to the development of the administrative process has been the theory of separation of powers. In 1881 the Supreme Court declared in Kilbourn v. Thompson that all powers of government are divided into executive, legislative and judicial, and that it is "essential to the successful working of this system that the persons intrusted with power in any one of these branches shall not be permitted to encroach upon the powers confided to the others, but that each shall by the law of its creation be limited to the exercise of the powers appropriate to its own department and no other . . ." This dictum was founded upon doctrine stemming from Plato, Aristotle, Polybius, Cicero, Machiavelli, Harrington, Locke, and Montesquieu. The basic principle had been stated by Blackstone a century before the Kilbourn case: "In all tyrannical governments, the supreme magistracy, or the right both of making and enforcing the laws is vested in one and the same man, or one and the same body of men; and wherever these two powers are united together, there can be no public liberty." Most state constitutions contain explicit provisions having something in common with the Kilbourn statement.

The Federal Constitution, however, contains no specific provision that the three kinds of powers shall be kept separate. It goes no further than to provide separately for each of the three branches of the government: "All legislative powers herein granted shall be vested in a Congress . . ." "The executive power shall be vested in a President . . ." "The judicial power shall be vested in one Supreme Court and in . . . inferior courts . . ."

Since a typical administrative agency exercises many types of power, including executive, legislative, and judicial power, a strict application of the theory of separation of powers would make the very existence of such an agency unconstitutional. Various authorities from time to time have taken the position that the fundamental structure of the administrative system is unconstitutional. For instance, the President's Committee on Administrative Management reported in 1937 that the agencies "constitute a headless 'fourth branch' of the Government, a haphazard deposit of irresponsible agencies and uncoordinated powers. They do violence to the basic theory of the American Constitution that there should be three major branches of the Government and only three." This view surprisingly won the support of President Franklin D. Roosevelt. Others have taken a similar position that combination of powers in the agencies violates the theory of separation of powers and is therefore unconstitutional.

Of course, the plain fact is that the forces that have brought about the creation of administrative agencies have overridden any and all interpretations of the doctrine of separation of powers that have been inconsistent with the development of the administrative process. The Supreme Court held as early as 1855 that "there are matters involving public rights, which may be presented in such form that the judicial power is capable of acting on them, and which are susceptible of judicial determination, but which congress may or may not bring within the cognizance of the courts of the United States, as it may deem proper." More recently the Supreme Court has held that judicial powers may be conferred upon agencies, and, of course, it has usually assumed this. The Court, without disapproval, said of the Federal Trade Commission in 1935: "To the extent that it exercises any executive function—as distinguished from executive power in the constitutional sense—it does so in the discharge and effectuation of its quasi-legislative or quasi-judicial powers, or as an agency of the legislative or judicial departments of the government."

The realities of the law about separation of powers, along with some delightful innuendoes about its unrealities, have been beautifully captured in an authoritative statement by Mr. Justice Jackson: "They (administrative bodies) have become a veritable fourth branch of the government, which has deranged our three-dimensional thinking. Courts have differed in assigning a place to these seemingly necessary bodies in our constitutional system. Administrative agencies have been called quasi-legislative, quasi-executive, or quasi-judicial, as the occasion required, in order to validate their functions within the separation-of-powers scheme of the Constitution. The mere retreat to the qualifying 'quasi' is implicit with confession that all recognized classifications have broken down, and 'quasi' is a smooth cover which we draw over our confusion as we might use a counterpane to conceal a disordered bed."

The basic idea that executive, legislative and judicial power should to a considerable extent be separated from each other still prevails in our dominant theoretical thinking. If today we were framing a new Constitution, we would no doubt assume the validity of that idea and we would build on it. Even a superficial examination of totalitarian regimes in other lands brings an appreciation of the advantages of avoiding concentration of power in the hands of any officer or group of officers.

When, however, we are not framing a Constitution but we are making relatively small arrangements within a framework already established, the idea that the three kinds of power should not at any level be blended in any one set of hands becomes so impracticable that our legislative bodies, with later judicial approval, have generally had no hesitation in rejecting it. After all, the philosophers who developed the theory of separation of powers were not thinking in terms of the practical problems of fitting administrative powers into the existing structure of national and state governments; they had no conception of such modern problems as what kind of governmental machinery is desirable, within our overall framework of government, for the regulation of airlines or of television. What we have discussed in facing such problems—and we have by now had a good deal of experience—is that the true principle that should guide the allocation of power within the general framework is not the principle of separation of the three kinds of power but is the principle of check.

In the organic arrangements that we have been making in recent decades in the establishment and control of administrative agencies, the principle that has guided us is the principle of check, not the principle of separation of powers. We have had little or no concern for avoiding a mixture of three or more kinds of powers in the same agency; we have had much concern for avoiding or minimizing unchecked power. The very identifying badge of the modern administrative agency has become the combination of judicial power (adjudication) with legislative power (rule making). But we have taken pains to see that the agencies are appointed and reappointed by the executive, and that the residual power of check remains in the judiciary.

The principle whose soundness has been confirmed by both early and recent experience is the principle of check. We have gone far beyond Montesquieu. We have learned that danger of tyranny or injustice lurks in unchecked power, not in blended power.

Questions

1. Does the Davis extract suggest parallels between reasons for the growth of administrative law and the proliferation of administrative agencies, and the evolution of Equity (*supra* pp. 73–76)?

2. Which of the various reasons advanced by Professor Davis in explanation of the growth of the administrative process may also explain Congress' decision to invest an administrative agency with the responsibility to enforce the National Labor Relations Act, and to adjudicate cases arising under the Act?

SECTION 49.2   UNFAIR LABOR PRACTICE PROCEDURES BEFORE THE NATIONAL LABOR RELATIONS BOARD

NATIONAL LABOR RELATIONS ACT

§ 10

Prevention of Unfair Labor Practices

(a) The Board is empowered, as hereinafter provided, to prevent any person from engaging in any unfair labor practice (listed in section 8) affecting commerce.

(b) Whenever it is charged that any person has engaged in or is engaging in any such unfair labor practice, the Board, or any agent or agency designated by the Board for such purposes, shall have power to issue and cause to be served upon such person a complaint stating the charges in that respect, and containing a notice of hearing before the Board or a member thereof, or before a designated agent or agency, at a place therein fixed, not less than five days after the serving of said complaint: *Provided,* That no complaint shall issue based upon any unfair labor practice occurring more than six months prior to the filing of the charge with the Board and the service of a copy thereof upon the person against whom such charge is made, unless the person aggrieved thereby was prevented from filing such charge by reason of service in the armed forces, in which event the six-month period shall be computed from the day of his discharge. Any such complaint may be amended by the member, agent, or agency conducting the hearing or the Board in its discretion at any time prior to the issuance of an order based thereon. The person so complained of shall have the right to file an answer to the original or amended complaint and to appear in person or otherwise and give testimony at the place and time fixed in the complaint. In the discretion of the member, agent, or agency conducting the hearing or the Board, any other person may be allowed to intervene in the said proceeding and to present testimony. . . . Any such proceeding shall, so far as practicable, be conducted in accordance with the rules of evidence applicable in the district courts of the United States under the rules of civil procedure for the district courts of the United States . . ..

(c) The testimony taken by such member, agent, or agency or the Board shall be reduced to writing and filed with the Board. Thereafter, in its discretion, the Board upon notice may take further testimony or hear argument. If upon the preponderance of the testimony taken the Board shall be of the opinion that any person named in the complaint has engaged in or is engaging in any such unfair labor practice, then the Board shall state its findings of fact and shall issue and cause to be served on such person an order requiring such person to cease and desist from such unfair labor practice, and to take such affirmative action including reinstatement of employees with or without back pay, as will effectuate the policies of this Act. . . .

[The following is taken from COX, BOK and GORMAN, CASES ON LABOR LAW, 8th ed., pp. 113–122.]

NLRB Organization and Procedure

Although it is customary to speak of "the Board" as if the National Labor Relations Board and its large staff of employees thought and acted as a single person, this usage is highly misleading. In reality, the NLRB is composed of various categories of persons exercising quite different responsibilities. The adjudicative responsibilities of the agency are ultimately entrusted to the five members of the Board, appointed by the President of the United States for five-year terms by and with the consent of the Senate. In the course of the Taft-Hartley amendments of 1947, the Congress also established the office of General Counsel, appointed to a four-year term by the President by and with the consent of the Senate. The General Counsel has authority to investigate charges of unfair labor practices, to decide whether complaints should be issued on the basis of these charges and to direct the prosecution of such complaints. The General Counsel also represents the Board in court proceedings to enforce or review Board decisions.

To assist the Board members and the General Counsel in discharging their responsibilities, a large staff has been created. Organizationally, the staff is divided between the Washington office and over thirty Regional Offices. The Regional Offices are under the general supervision of the General Counsel. Each Regional Office is under the direction of a Regional Director aided by a Regional Attorney. Their staff consists principally of Field Examiners, who investigate charges and conduct elections, and attorneys, who prosecute complaints at hearings before Administrative Law Judges (called Trial Examiners prior to August 1972) and act as legal counsel to the Regional Director.

1. Unfair Labor Practice Cases.

The General Counsel may issue a complaint only upon a formal charge that the employer or the union has engaged in an unfair labor practice. Such a charge may be filed by any person or employer or qualified labor organization in the office for the region in which the alleged unfair labor practice occurred. Section 10(b) of the Act requires that a charge be filed and served upon the charged party within six months of the alleged unfair labor practice. When a charge is filed, the Regional Director normally requires the person making the charge to submit the supporting evidence in the form of affidavits, lists of witnesses, etc. The charged party (respondent) may or may not be asked to submit a reply. In either case, a Field Examiner then makes a thorough investigation of the facts and surrounding circumstances. For example, if a charge is filed against the employer, the Field Examiner interviews the union officials and employees concerned, locates other witnesses, goes to the plant and may discuss the case with company officials.

If this preliminary investigation discloses that the charge is without foundation, the case is likely to be dropped forthwith. Otherwise, further investigation may ensue and there will commonly be an informal conference at the local office of the Board, attended by both the respondent and the charging party, at which the alleged unfair practices are thoroughly discussed and possible settlements considered. The nature of any particular settlement depends, of course, on the circumstances of the case. Where the charge is that the company has violated Section 8(a)(1) by unlawful activities of foremen and other supervisors—threatening those who join the union with reprisals, circulating anti-union petitions, threatening the closing of the plant if it is organized, etc.—the normal remedy after a complaint and hearing would be an order to cease and desist from such interference and to post appropriate notices informing the employees that the company will not interfere with, restrain or coerce them in the exercise of their right of self-organization. Consequently, if informal conferences convince the officials of a company that acts of interference have occurred, or if the company is doubtful whether there has been interference but sincerely desires its employees to have the freedom guaranteed by the Act, then it is usually possible to convince the Regional Offices and the union of the company's good faith and to work out in the informal conferences a satisfactory form of announcement to be posted in the plant. Sometimes cases are settled in this manner even though the employer is convinced that there have been no unfair labor practices, for making the desired announcement may be far less burdensome than litigation before the Board. On the other hand, when a case involves an allegation that an employee was discharged for engaging in union activities, the employer may have strong reasons for refusing to accede to the Board's normal demand that it reinstate the discharged employee with back pay. It is important, for example, for an employer who has not violated the Act to maintain the authority of its supervisory staff and show that union membership is no protection against punishment for breaches of plant discipline. Even this kind of case, however, is often settled without a hearing. The investigation of the Field Examiner may convince the company officials that some inferior supervisor has in fact acted unfairly, and in that event it is as sound industrial relations promptly to correct the error as it is to maintain the supervisor's prestige by backing him up when he is right. Conversely, the investigation of the Field Examiner or the explanation made by the company may convince the Regional Director that the discharge was justified. In that event, the Regional Director may persuade the union to withdraw its charge or else, if the union refuses, he may decline to issue a complaint.

It is important to emphasize the informality of these investigations, conferences and settlements. Except for such steps as are required by sound administration, including the reduction to writing of any settlement agreement, the entire procedure up to this point is conducted with all possible informality and an eye to amicable adjustments. In the past, most unfair labor practice cases were disposed of in one way or another in the Regional Offices by these informal personal negotiations. In the fiscal year ending June 30, 1975, for example, 94% of all unfair labor practice cases were disposed of prior to a formal hearing. (Approximately one-third were disposed of by dismissing the charge involved, one-third by voluntary withdrawal of the charge, and one-quarter by settlement.)

If it is impossible to dispose of an unfair labor practice case in the Regional Office, formal proceedings are commenced by the filing of a complaint. The General Counsel has delegated to the Regional Directors authority to issue complaints except in cases "involving novel and complex issues." Should the Regional Director refuse to issue a complaint, the matter may be appealed to the General Counsel. If the General Counsel declines to issue a complaint, it is generally understood that the charging party has no further recourse. Vaca v. Sipes, 386 U.S. 171, 87 S.Ct. 903, 17 L.Ed.2d 842 (1967). However, once a complaint has issued, the charging party may be entitled to an evidentiary hearing on his objections to a negotiated settlement. Leeds & Northrup Co. v. NLRB, 357 F.2d 527 (3d Cir. 1966).

Upon the issuance of a complaint the Board may petition the district court, under Section 10(j) of the Act, for appropriate interlocutory relief preventing continuance of the unfair labor practice. These requests are made rather infrequently. Between 1947 and the middle of 1971, an average of only nine injunctions each year were sought under section 10(j); in the next three years, the requests averaged fifteen each year. Of the injunction requests formally acted upon by the district courts in recent years, an injunction has been issued in roughly one-half to two-thirds of the cases in any given year. Section 10(j) injunctions have been issued against unions as well as employers, the more common employer violations being discriminatory discharges, recognition of minority unions and bad faith or "surface" bargaining, and the more common union violations involving strike violence and hiring-hall discrimination.

The complaint, which is drafted by the Regional Attorney or a member of his staff, specifies the violations of the Act which the company is alleged to have committed and contains a notice of the time and place of hearing. Under the Board rules the time of hearing need not be more than ten days after service of the complaint but although the notice of hearing may fix a short period, it is nearly always possible to secure one or more extensions before the hearing is held.

The Act and the Board's rules give the respondent the right to answer a complaint. The answer is filed with the Regional Director, as are all motions made prior to the hearing. Normally, the answer is to be filed within ten days from service of the complaint, but extensions may be granted on the Regional Director's own motion or for good cause shown by any party. The Board's rules provide that failure to deny an allegation will be taken to admit it, and Board representatives have sometimes capitalized upon this provision. More often, however, the Board has chosen not to rely on this provision and has introduced evidence on all the issues.

The hearing is usually held in the city or town where the alleged violation occurred before an Administrative Law Judge appointed from the Division of Administrative Law Judges in Washington (or by the Associate Chief Administrative Law Judge in San Francisco when the case arises in certain regions located in the Far West). The case is prosecuted for the Board by an attorney from the Regional Office. The charging party is permitted to intervene, and its attorneys may take part in the proceedings. The respondent, of course, may and usually does appear by an attorney as in the normal court proceeding. Section 10(b) of the Act provides that unfair labor practice proceedings "shall, so far as practicable, be conducted in accordance with the rules of evidence applicable in the district courts" under the rules of civil procedure adopted by the Supreme Court. Evidence is introduced through witnesses and documents, just as in an ordinary civil trial. At the conclusion of the hearing both parties are entitled as a matter of right to argue orally before the Administrative Law Judge and file a written brief. In practice, however, it has not been customary for either party to make an oral argument.

After the hearing is completed, the Administrative Law Judge prepares a decision containing proposed findings of fact and recommendations for the disposition of the case. The Administrative Law Judge's decision is then filed with the Board, and a copy is served on the respondent and any other parties. Within twenty days after service of the Administrative Law Judge's decision, counsel for any party or for the Board may file exceptions together with a brief in support thereof. Cross exceptions may then be filed within the succeeding ten days by any party who has not previously filed exceptions. Permission to argue orally before the Board itself must be specially requested in writing, and it is granted only in unusual cases. If no exceptions are filed, the Board normally adopts the decision of the Administrative Law Judge.

Although minor changes are made from time to time, the Board's procedure after the filing of exceptions, briefs and oral argument, if permitted, has recently been as follows. When the record is complete, the Executive Secretary assigns cases among the five Board members in rotation. A case assigned to Member A is transmitted to his Chief Legal Assistant who thereupon assigns it to some junior legal assistant on Member A's staff. The latter examines the record and decides whether the case is one which the full Board should consider or is sufficiently routine for decision by a three-member panel. Thereafter one of A's legal assistants prepares a draft decision—or in doubtful and very important cases a memorandum— which is reviewed by his superiors and then transmitted to the Board members who will participate. Under the panel system copies also go to the two members who were not on the panel so that they or one of their legal assistants can check the draft and decide whether the case is sufficiently important to ask for consideration by the full Board. Any member may ask to have a case referred to the full Board.

In routine cases the members of the three-member panel go over the draft opinion and approve it—or suggest changes—without the need for a formal conference. Member A may read it either before it is sent to his colleagues or while they have it under consideration. Where there is a difference of opinion or important issues are at stake, a conference is held. In cases sufficiently important for decision by the full Board there is always a conference. Thereafter the opinion is prepared, approved by the members and issued by the Board.

The five members of the Board decide in this fashion more than one hundred unfair labor practice cases a month. It is obvious that in most of them the basic responsibility rested on the trial examiner and the legal assistants who prepared draft decisions for the Board. Only a relatively small number of really important cases could receive full consideration from the members themselves, however conscientiously they attended to their duties.

The Rules and Regulations issued by the Board provide for handling a charge that labor organization has violated Section 8(b) in the same manner that the Board handles charges against employers. In the case of strikes and other concerted activities alleged to violate Sections 8(b)(4), 8(b)(7), or 8(e), however, the Regional Office must give its investigation precedence over all other cases not of the same character. If there is reason to believe that the charge is true, the Regional Director files a petition for "appropriate injunctive relief pending the final adjudication of the Board" (Section 10(*l*)). The proceeding before the Board is then expedited and upon the Board's final decision, any order of the district court expires.

Board orders carry no sanctions, although every Regional Office includes a compliance officer who determines whether Board orders are being complied with and endeavors to secure voluntary compliance. If the respondent does not comply with a Board order, the Board must secure enforcement by filing a petition in a federal court of appeals; this action is taken on behalf of the Board by its Enforcement Division (which is a part of the Office of the General Counsel), and the enforcement petition is uniformly filed in the circuit in which the unfair labor practice was committed. The Board may in fact secure such an enforcement order even when there has been no refusal to comply. Similarly, if the respondent desires to have the Board's order reviewed and set aside, it may file a petition for that purpose since under Section 10(f) it is a "person aggrieved." That section gives such a person a choice of courts of appeals, for review may be sought where the unfair labor practice was committed, or where the person does business or in the Court of Appeals for the District of Columbia. Respondents frequently avail themselves of the right to seek review without waiting for the Board to file a petition for enforcement, particularly since this will give the respondent the power to select the circuit for review, a choice sometimes thought to be significant in the ultimate outcome of the case. If the decision of the Board denies relief in whole or in part to the charging party, that party becomes a "person aggrieved" who may also seek appellate review. The Supreme Court has also held that a party who is not aggrieved by the Board's decision, and whose position is sustained by the Board, may nonetheless intervene to protect its interests in the event another party petitions for review or for enforcement. UAW Local 283 v. Scofield, 382 U.S. 205, 86 S.Ct. 373 (1965).

Upon the filing of a petition for enforcement or for review by a court of appeals the pleadings, testimony and transcript of proceedings before the Board are certified to the court, and the case is put on its ordinary appellate docket. No objection that has not been urged before the Board may be considered by the court, save in exceptional cases. In such proceedings, the court is authorized to enter a decree setting aside, enforcing, or modifying the order and enforcing it as so modified. Review of the decree of a court of appeals may be had in the Supreme Court upon the granting of a petition for a writ of certiorari in the same manner as other cases.

In reviewing an order issued by the NLRB, courts must accept the Board's findings of fact "if supported by substantial evidence on the record considered as a whole" (Section 10(f)). This general standard of review eludes precise definition. "Substantial evidence" requires more than a scintilla; taking account of the facts and inferences on both sides of the issue, there must be enough evidence to support the agency's conclusion in a reasonable and reasoning mind. In other words, the court must not freely substitute its judgment for the Board's, yet it need not approve findings that the judges consider unreasonable or unfair. The deference given to the Board's findings is based in part on the fact that the hearing examiner of the Board is in a position to observe the witnesses at first hand. It is also partly due to the fact that the Board is "one of those agencies presumably equipped or informed by experience to deal with a specialized field of knowledge, whose findings within that field carry the authority of an expertness which courts do not possess and therefore must respect." Universal Camera Corp. v. NLRB, 340 U.S. 474, 71 S.Ct. 456 (1951). The degree of deference which the courts will pay to the "expertness" of the Board tends to vary according to the nature of the question involved. In particular, if the issue is a highly technical one, far removed from the ordinary experience of the judge, the court will be less likely to disturb the Board's findings, particularly if the Board has set forth the basis for its findings with reasonable clarity and if its reasoning and conclusions do not appear inconsistent with its decisions in related cases.

In defining the scope and nature of judicial review, courts have traditionally distinguished between questions of law and questions of fact. In practice, this distinction is often difficult to draw with precision. Certain decisions, for example, involve "mixed questions of law and fact," as in NLRB v. Hearst Publications, 322 U.S. 111, 64 S.Ct. 851 (1944), where the Board was interpreting the statutory term "employee" but in so doing considered various factual questions, such as the business relationship of newsboys to the newspaper and the economic power of the former in dealing with the latter. Other decisions which appear to involve pure questions of fact, may actually contain principles of law. For example, if the Board should conclude that employers who grant a wage increase during a representation campaign interfere with the free choice of the employees in voting for or against the union, the Board is not merely deciding the factual question of the effect of the increase upon the minds of the employees; the Board is also laying down a principle of law that the risk of interference in the generality of cases is sufficiently large that such increases should be prohibited entirely without requiring the burdensome and perhaps impractical task of investigating the effects of the employer's action in each case.

One may question how much actually turns on formal distinctions between questions of law, questions of fact, and mixed questions of law and fact. Where elements of law are involved in the issues under review, the Supreme Court has at times freely substituted its own judgment for that of the administrative agency while at other times it has declared that "the judicial function is exhausted when there is found to be a rational basis for the conclusions approved by the administrative body." Rochester Tel. Corp. v. United States, 307 U.S. 125, 59 S.Ct. 754 (1939). The degree of deference accorded by the courts has not seemed to turn necessarily on any formal definition regarding the nature of the question involved. Instead, though it is difficult to generalize on the question, courts have tended to assume greater responsibility in passing upon issues of law where (1) they require a weighing of other statutes or policies not confided to the special jurisdiction of the Board; (2) they involve common-law or constitutional considerations rather than "technical" matters requiring administrative expertise; (3) they involve controversial questions which demand the prestige of judicial resolution; or (4) they require the interpretation of statutory language in the light of legislative history rather than specialized judgments of a kind which the agency is peculiarly qualified to make.

The principles which guide appellate courts in reviewing questions of law and fact are plainly of a very general nature leaving much to the discretion of the judges involved. In exercising this discretion, courts will presumably be influenced to some degree by such other factors as the respect they hold for the capabilities and impartiality of the Board and the cogency and comprehensiveness of the arguments made by that agency in support of its conclusions. These factors are unavoidably subjective and may therefore cause considerable variation from one court to another concerning the nature of review. It is for this reason, perhaps, that during one five-year period, the Court of Appeals for the Fifth Circuit refused to affirm findings of fact of administrative agencies in 55% of the cases it reviewed while the Second Circuit took similar action in only 11% of the cases coming before it. Statistics such as these suggest that the principles governing the scope and nature of judicial review should be taken as providing only the most general indication of the nature of review to be accorded by any given court in a particular case.

Since the order made by the federal court of appeals in a proceeding under the Act is an equity decree, it may be enforced by proceedings for contempt. The Board has been held to have exclusive authority to prosecute civil contempts with the result that neither unions nor employers may petition the court for this purpose.

2. Representation Cases.

In addition to the work that the Regional Office does in unfair labor practice cases, it also plays the most important day-to-day role in processing representation cases. Election petitions are filed in the Regional Office, and the bulk of these seek the holding of a representation election in order to determine the desires of the employees concerning the selection of a union for collective bargaining. (Other elections may be held to decertify a union already representing employees in bargaining.) Such representation petitions may be filed either by an employer upon whom a demand for recognition and bargaining has been made by a union, or by a union seeking to represent employees (and demonstrating that it has what is known as a "showing of interest" from thirty percent of the employees within the bargaining, unit, generally evidenced by signed cards authorizing that union to be bargaining agent).

The regional staff investigates the petition, in order to determine such questions as whether the employer and the union are covered by the National Labor Relations Act and whether the group of employees within which the election is sought constitute "an appropriate bargaining unit." In most cases, these issues are resolved through the consent of the parties, either on their own initiative or after an investigation and conference in the Regional Office. If these matters are contested, they will be made the subject of a hearing conducted by a hearing officer from the Regional Office. The transcript of the hearing is then transferred to the Regional Director, who makes decisions on issues such as the Board's jurisdiction and the appropriate bargaining unit, and (eventually, after an election is conducted) the eligibility of voters and objections to the validity of the election. His decisions on such matters, both those which are made prior to the election and those which are made after the election, are subject to appeal in a limited set of circumstances to the National Labor Relations Board—not, as in complaint cases, to the General Counsel. The Regional Director has the power to issue an order setting the time and place of the election, to rule on objections and to certify the election results. All of the election issues discussed above were, until 1961, determined in the first instance by the Board itself; in that year Section 3(b) of the Labor Act was amended to authorize their delegation to the Regional Directors.

Decisions made by the NLRB in representation proceedings can normally not be challenged directly by judicial review. The Labor Act in its terms provides for judicial review, in the courts of appeals, only of final orders in unfair labor practice cases. If a person is aggrieved by a Board decision in a representation case, the appropriate manner for precipitating court action is for that person to commit an unfair labor practice, challenge within the unfair labor practice proceeding the decision made by the Board in the representation case (which the Board will normally reaffirm in the unfair labor practice case), and only then seek review in a court of appeals. Most commonly, this is done by an employer—seeking review, for example, of a Board appropriate-unit decision—by refusing to bargain with a union recently certified after a Board election. The purpose of this seemingly circuitous review mechanism, contemplated under Section 9(d) of the Act, is to prevent obstructive recourse to the courts at various stages of the representation proceeding and long delay in the determination of employee preferences on the matter of unionization. In certain extraordinary cases, however—to be explored further in the materials below (pp. 342–51)—a federal district court may have jurisdiction directly to enjoin the Board or a Regional Director from implementing a decision in the context of a representation proceeding.

Questions

1. Outline the process for adjudicating an unfair labor practice case under the National Labor Relations Act. How does this compare with the process for adjudicating a civil action in a federal court?

2. What aspects, if any, of the unfair labor practice procedure reflect the various reasons for preferring administrative to judicial adjudication of labor cases? See in this regard, the Davis extract (*supra* pp. 1068–1071) and review your answer to Question 2 on p. 1074 *supra*.

SECTION 49.3 ADMINISTRATIVE ENFORCEMENT OF TITLE VII OF THE CIVIL RIGHTS ACT OF 1964 BY THE EQUAL EMPLOYMENT OPPORTUNITY COMMISSION

[The provisions of Title VII are summarized at pp. 1030–1033, *supra*. The following is taken from an unsigned student note, "EMPLOYMENT DISCRIMINATION AND TITLE VII OF THE CIVIL RIGHTS ACT OF 1964," 84 Harvard Law Review 1109, 1195–1199, 1216–1219, 1222–1236, 1239–1241 (1971). Some footnotes omitted; others are renumbered.]

Introduction

Title VII proscribes discrimination based on race, religion, color, sex, or national origin in practically every phase of the employment relationship. Although the substantive provisions of the Act appear quite sweeping, closer analysis reveals a number of tensions inherent in this product of political compromise. Underlying Title VII is the public interest in eliminating employment discrimination in order to guarantee to minorities the economic status necessary to a free society and to insure maximum utilization of human potential. But the Act also reflects the private individual's interest in securing equal employment opportunity. Similarly, there is a tension between the judgment that informal, private, and local methods of eliminating employment discrimination are preferable,[1] and the desire for prompt, judicial redress of discrimination grievances.[2]

These tensions are apparent in the Act's procedural mechanisms. The Act provides for three instrumentalities of enforcement: the aggrieved individual; the Equal Employment Opportunity Commission (EEOC); and the Attorney General. The aggrieved party bears the primary responsibility for enforcing Title VII through the mechanism of a private action in

---

1. *See* Act § 706(a) and (b), 42 U.S.C. § 2000e–5(a) and (b).

2. *See* Act §§ 706(e), 707(a), 42 U.S.C. §§ 2000e–5(e), 2000e–6(a).

federal district court.[3] The EEOC, which as the bill was originally conceived [4] bore the primary enforcement responsibility, lost its adjudicatory and coercive enforcement powers through a series of political compromises.[5] This shift in responsibility for enforcement of the Act has been characterized as a

> basic change in the philosophy of the title . . . [which] implied an appraisal of discrimination in employment as a private rather than a public wrong, a wrong, to be sure, which entitles the damaged party to judicial relief, but not one so injurious to the community as to justify the intervention of the public law enforcement authorities.

But the private action inherited a large measure of public interest. It is unlikely that the shift in enforcement responsibility, designed to make the bill more politically palatable, is indicative of a pervasive congressional purpose to deny a public interest in Title VII. Indeed, the private action was specifically endowed with public interest characteristics. The provision for Justice Department intervention,[6] the provision for appointment of counsel in the discretion of the court [7] and for the discretionary award of attorney's fees to victorious litigants,[8] and the provision for discretionary relief in the form of affirmative action and back pay were all designed to protect the public interest.[9] The interplay of the public and private aspects of the Act has played a significant role in the courts' interpretations of the Act's procedural requirements.

Moreover, the Attorney General is directly empowered to protect the public interest by bringing suit in the government's name when discrimination occurs in the form of a pattern or practice of resistance.[10] Finally, the

---

3. Act § 706(e), 42 U.S.C. § 2000e–5(e).

4. As the enforcement scheme was originally conceived in the House, the EEOC was to be empowered to issue complaints, conduct hearings, and issue enforceable cease and desist orders much like the National Labor Relations Board. H.R. 405 §§ 9(c), 9(j), 10(a), 88th Cong., 1st Sess. (1963). For a discussion of the merits of such a proposal, see pp. 1270–75 *infra*.

5. The House Committee on the Judiciary stripped the EEOC of its enforcement powers and substituted a power to institute a court action in its own name against the discriminator when attempts at settlement had failed. H.R. 7152, 88th Cong., 1st Sess. (1963). The reasons suggested for the change were: the belief that a de novo court action would facilitate more rapid and more frequent settlements, the belief that a court would be a fairer forum for the employer or union to establish innocence, and the fear that the EEOC would impose forced racial balance according to rigid mathemati-

cal formulae. *See* Hearings on H.R. Res. 789 Before the House Comm. on Rules, 88th Cong., 2d Sess. 19 (1964).

In the Senate, the so-called "leadership compromise," which was made to secure enough Republican votes to achieve the two-thirds majority necessary to obtain cloture over the civil rights filibuster, resulted in the elimination of the power of the EEOC to enforce the Title by bringing civil actions in its own name.

6. Act § 706(e), 42 U.S.C. § 2000e–5(e).

7. Act § 706(e), 42 U.S.C. § 2000e–5(e).

8. Act § 706(k), 42 U.S.C. § 2000e–5(k).

9. Act § 706(g), 42 U.S.C. § 2000e–5(g).

10. Act § 707(a), 42 U.S.C. § 2000e–6(a). The power of the Attorney General to bring suit in cases of a pattern or practice of resistance intended to deny full exercise of Title VII rights originated in the Senate as a quid pro quo to satisfy the proponents of a strong EEOC when the EEOC's power to bring suits was eliminated.

EEOC has power to utilize "conference, conciliation, and persuasion" [11] in attempting to eliminate unlawful discrimination.[12] Although these powers are relatively weak, Congress apparently considered them so important that it subordinated to some degree the prompt vindication of Title VII rights to the informal conciliatory measures undertaken by the EEOC. Therein lies the second tension inherent in the Act, and the extent and importance of this subordination has been the subject of much of the procedural litigation occurring under Title VII.

The Procedural Scheme

"A person claiming to be aggrieved" [13] begins the enforcement process when he files a charge with the EEOC alleging a violation of Title VII. If the occurrence giving rise to the charge took place in a state "which has a State or local law prohibiting the unlawful employment practice alleged and establishing or authorizing a State or local authority to grant or seek relief from such practice," [14] the EEOC may not act on the charge until at least sixty days [15] have elapsed since the commencement of proceedings under state or local law, unless these proceedings terminated earlier.[16] If the alleged discrimination occurred in a state without state or local enforcement mechanisms, the charge must be filed with the EEOC within ninety days of the violation.[17] In a state with such enforcement, the aggrieved party must file his charge within thirty days after receiving notice that the state or local agency has terminated its proceedings, but in no event later than 210 days from the date of occurrence.[18]

When the aggrieved party files a charge, the EEOC investigates to determine whether there is "reasonable cause to believe that the charge is true," [19] and if it finds such reasonable cause, attempts to eliminate the unlawful practice through "informal methods of conference, conciliation, and persuasion." [20] If the EEOC is unable to obtain voluntary compliance with Title VII, it notifies the person aggrieved accordingly and informs him that he may at any time within the following thirty days bring a civil action in federal district court.[21] Upon finding a violation of the Act, "the court may enjoin the respondent from engaging in such unlawful employment practice, and order such affirmative action as may be appropriate, which may include reinstatement or hiring of employees, with or without back pay."

11. Act § 706(a), 42 U.S.C. § 2000e–5(a).

12. After a court order is issued in favor of a complainant, however, the EEOC may sue to compel compliance with the decree. Act § 706(i), 42 U.S.C. § 2000e–5(i).

13. Act § 706(a), 42 U.S.C. § 2000e–5(a).

14. Act § 706(b), 42 U.S.C. § 2000e–5(b).

15. During the first year after the effective date of the state fair employment practices law, the period is 120 days. Id.

16. Id.

17. Act § 706(d), 42 U.S.C. § 2000e–5(d).

18. Id.

19. Act § 706(a), 42 U.S.C. § 2000e–5(a).

20. Id.

21. Act § 706(e), 42 U.S.C. § 2000e–5(e). This section also provides for the appointment of an attorney and commencement of the action without payment of fees, costs, or security, in order to facilitate enforcement of the Title by indigent individuals.

A Commissioner of the EEOC may also file a charge with the Agency if he has reasonable cause to believe that a violation of Title VII has occurred. This self-starting procedure has been utilized in cases in which the EEOC receives an anonymous complaint or where the aggrieved party is unwilling to sign a sworn charge for fear of reprisal. It may also be invoked when other violations are observed during an investigation of charges filed by an individual or when any reliable source passes on information as to the existence of unfair employment practices. Although the number of these "Commissioner charges" has been increasing, the EEOC has not emphasized this aspect of its activity because of its inability to handle adequately the number of individual charges which it receives and to which it gives priority.

If the EEOC finds reasonable cause to believe that the violations alleged in the Commissioner's charge are true, it will undertake conciliation efforts. If these efforts fail, two further courses remain open to the Agency, although neither guarantees enforcement in the courts. The EEOC must notify the allegedly aggrieved person of his right to sue in federal court. In addition, the EEOC may recommend to the Attorney General that he bring a pattern and practice suit.

* * *

The Complaint

The Title VII enforcement process is often begun by a simple letter from the most unlettered layman. The courts have been quite liberal in construing the language to make out an effective charge. "All that is required is that the [charge] give sufficient information to enable EEOC to see what the grievance is about." Technical requirements of the statute, such as the "under oath" requirement of section 706(a), may be satisfied by later amendments. Later amendments can also amplify the scope of the charge, with the amendments relating back to the date of the original filing. The courts have also been quite liberal in construing the charge presented to the EEOC when deciding whether the complaint in subsequent litigation goes beyond the charge considered by the Agency. Courts taking this stance have argued that the complainant is frequently ignorant of "the full panoply of discrimination which he may have suffered" and may often be "ignorant of or unable to thoroughly describe the discriminatory practices to which [he is] subjected." Additionally, a rigid standard restricting the plaintiff's complaint to the precise issues raised in his charge would discourage conciliation since the respondent would realize that an issue which became apparent only during investigation could not be included in court action.

But the conciliation policy could be argued to cut the other way as well. A liberal construction of the charge might mean that an issue which had never been subjected to conciliation could be litigated. Since this argument ignores the reality that the EEOC is usually unable to seek any conciliation at all within the time limit allowed, it is not surprising that it has not tipped the scales in favor of a strict rule. It is now settled that the complaint may encompass any discrimination like or reasonably related to the allegations of the charge or growing out of such allegations during the pendency of the charge before the EEOC.

Class Actions

Although most Title VII actions are brought by private individuals, there is also a public interest in the outcome of the lawsuit. While this public interest should not unduly delay the complainant from getting his private remedy if that is all he seeks, a qualified complainant who wishes to represent a broader class should be permitted to do so. Moreover, since a violation of the Act is by definition a class-wide discrimination, even the purely private litigant almost always represents interests larger than his own. For these reasons class-wide relief is almost always an appropriate remedy.

* * *

Government Enforcement of Title VII

I. The Pattern or Practice Power.—The compromise that facilitated the passage of the Civil Rights Act stripped the EEOC of virtually all its enforcement powers, leaving it essentially with only its responsibility for attempting to effect a voluntary settlement between the parties. The great bulk of governmental power to enforce Title VII was given to the Attorney General by the authorization of suits against a "pattern or practice" of discrimination.[22]

Effective use of the pattern or practice suit is an essential element in the fight against discrimination. Experience has shown that the individual complaint mechanism is an inadequate vehicle for eliminating job discrimination. Too often, victims of job discrimination fail to file charges: they may be reluctant to be branded as troublemakers; they may, with some justification, fear retaliation; or they may lack firm evidence to support their suspicions. In addition, many victims of discrimination will fail to file charges because they are ignorant of their legal rights. Black workers may be "cynical about the prospect of their rights being enforced against whites by white authority." In fact, it is likely that complaints are not filed against many of the worst offenders of Title VII: in some cases, workers, realizing that there is little hope of obtaining employment, will not make the futile effort of applying for work required before a charge alleging hiring discrimination can be filed; in others, workers who do apply for work are not even aware that they have been the subject of unlawful discrimination. To attack the many cases of discrimination that the complaint process does not reach, an enforcement mechanism which allows the government to initiate its own action is required. The pattern or practice suit provides this mechanism.

The pattern or practice action has functional virtues other than the reaching of those employers against whom a complaint might otherwise not be filed. It enables the Government to mount a coordinated attack on the largest or most flagrant violators of Title VII. Such systematic attack would be almost impossible if private actions were the only mode of enforcement; the necessarily random selection of defendants in private actions would allow many offenders to escape prosecution. And whereas the private suit challenges the employment practices of only a single employer or a single union, the pattern or practice suit can be used to attack industrywide discriminatory practices.

22. Act § 707(a), 42 U.S.C. § 2000e–6(a).

In addition, the pattern or practice suit avoids many of the procedural obstacles to the private suit: there is no requirement that either state FEPC's or the EEOC have an opportunity to consider the case or attempt conciliation prior to suit. Rather, Congress has directed that the pattern or practice suit be assigned for hearing at the earliest practicable date and that the case "be in every way expedited." To that end, it has also provided for the convening of a three-judge district court, with its concomitant right of direct appeal to the Supreme Court, in cases certified by the Attorney General to be of "general public importance."

Despite the potential value of this enforcement mechanism, however, the Justice Department has made only limited use of it. To be sure, each Title VII litigation is exceedingly long and complex, and consumes a tremendous amount of Department resources. And the Civil Rights Division has been hampered by its small size and inadequate funding, and by its inability to train and retain attorneys sufficiently experienced to handle complex Title VII litigation. Yet even within these constraints, the Justice Department has failed to assume an effective role in Title VII enforcement.

During the first two and one-half years of Title VII's existence (through the end of 1967), a total of only ten pattern or practice suits was brought by the Attorney General. In part, this slow beginning can be attributed to the relatively low priority accorded by the Department to employment cases. For several years following passage of the Civil Rights Act, the Attorney General concentrated on the enforcement of school desegregation and voting rights laws, granting lowest priority to Title VII cases. This failure to devote substantial attention to employment discrimination cases was apparently corrected by a change in Department policy in late 1967. Yet the backlog caused by the delay remains a serious problem: the Justice Department has been unable to file many pattern or practice actions in 1969 or 1970 because its resources have been almost totally committed to litigating the belated rush of cases filed in late 1968 and early 1969.

More importantly, the Justice Department has taken a restrictive view of its role in Title VII enforcement. It has seen a significant part of its role to be securing favorable court interpretations of the statute, while deferring in large part to the EEOC and the Office of Federal Contract Compliance for actual enforcement of the Act. Within the limited role it has defined for itself, the Justice Department has done an excellent job; it claims not to have lost a case, obtaining reversal on appeal of its few losses in the district courts. Yet it makes little sense for the Justice Department to leave to the EEOC a primary enforcement role under the Act, for that agency has almost no enforcement powers.

*   *   *

In an effort to remedy many of these deficiencies, there has been an unsuccessful attempt to transfer the power to bring pattern or practice actions to the EEOC.[23] This effort surely reflects, at least in part, the grow-

---

23. S. 2453, 91st Cong., 2d Sess. (1970), which provided for the transfer of the pattern or practice authority to the EEOC in three years upon the approval of the Attorney General and three Commissioners, passed the Senate. 116 Cong.Rec. 16,913 (daily ed. Oct. 1, 1970). However, its companion bill, H.R. 17,555, died a slow death in the House Rules Committee. 29 Cong.Q. 39 (Jan. 8, 1971). The proposed transfer was to be postponed three years to allow the EEOC to first establish its proposed cease and desist machinery. Senate Comm. on Labor and Public Welfare, Equal Employment Oppor-

ing recognition that the Justice Department's many other responsibilities under the civil rights laws have detracted from its enforcement of Title VII. In contrast, the EEOC clearly can devote all of its attention to the single goal of equal employment opportunities. In this regard, many commentators have noted how effective such a dedicated, single-minded agency, armed with sufficient enforcement powers, could be. Further, the EEOC could coordinate the use of such enforcement power with its other activities, thereby increasing the effectiveness of its Commissioner charges and the conciliation process for private complaints.

Providing enforcement powers for the EEOC should not, however, necessitate stripping the Justice Department of its present powers under Title VII. To the contrary, it seems likely that the more independent bodies there are attacking employment discrimination, the more effective enforcement will be. Certainly, the pervasiveness of discriminatory employment practices is such that there is enough work for both the EEOC and the Justice Department. In addition, Title VII, unlike, for example, the Interstate Commerce Act, is not a law which requires the development of a coherent system of regulation by a single agency. Instead, it is more in the nature of a remedial provision directed at the eradication of particular unlawful employment practices. To the extent that the agencies' philosophies differ on what problems are critical, the net result may be a more diverse and broader scale attack on discrimination in employment.

Perhaps the most substantial danger of coordinate enforcement jurisdiction is that each agency will assume that the other will carry the brunt of the enforcement duties. But this result seems unlikely considering the EEOC's enthusiasm for its mission. In addition, conceding that such a danger is real, it nonetheless appears to be more than outweighed by the possibility that a single enforcement agency could be immobilized by political pressures. One major reason at times advanced for transferring the Justice Department's enforcement responsibility to the EEOC is the view that by doing so governmental enforcement of Title VII would then be insulated from the political process. The possibility of the neutralization of Title VII by political forces should indeed be a weighty consideration in an area such as the elimination of employment discrimination where it is apparent that some of the most powerful interests in the nation may have to be challenged. The staggered five-year terms of the Commissioners, who most likely cannot be removed at the will of the President, undoubtedly make them more independent from the Executive will than is the Attorney General. Still, it is ultimately impossible to isolate the EEOC from significant political pressures. For while largely independent of the Executive, the agency remains continually at the mercy of Congress through its power of the purse. Each enforcement authority, then, is to some degree susceptible to political pressures. But the duplication of power inherent in a coordinate enforcement scheme should substantially decrease the possibility that the entire governmental Title VII enforcement mechanism can be immobilized by outside pressure.

2. EEOC Enforcement.—(a) Compliance Power Under Section 706(i). —General responsibility for the enforcement of Title VII having been lodged in the Attorney General, only section 706(i) of the version of the

tunities Enforcement Act, S.Rep. No. 91–1137, 91st Cong., 2d Sess. 15 (1970)   [hereinafter cited as S.Rep. No. 91–1137].

Act finally passed provides for any form of direct enforcement by the EEOC: it allows the Commission to commence contempt proceedings in the district courts to compel compliance with a court order issued in a prior private action. This provision has been rarely used, primarily because the Commission lacks the manpower to effectively monitor compliance in all private actions, but it is potentially significant as a means of policing compliance with conciliation agreements through the device of consent decrees.

* * *

(c) Other Commission Enforcement Efforts.—Ironically, the one enforcement mechanism that the EEOC has utilized to a significant degree, appearing as amicus curiae in private actions, was not specifically authorized by Title VII. The courts have adopted the attitude that the Commission's brief would be a useful aid to decision and to framing relief and despite the lack of statutory authorization, have seen no reason to refuse the EEOC such an appearance. The Commission has had some success through these appearances in persuading the courts to adopt its view, particularly in the area of remedies and procedural technicalities. Still, appearances as amicus curiae are not an adequate substitute for more enforcement powers; the EEOC must rely on an individual to bring the action, and the Commission has no control over the course of the litigation or the right to appeal.

Central to such EEOC activity is the question of what weight the courts will give to EEOC opinion, not only in its amicus briefs, but also as embodied in its interpretative rulings and Guidelines. The courts have generally acknowledged the Supreme Court's command to "show great deference to the interpretation given the statute by the officers or agency charged with its administratiom." But at the same time, the courts have also remained cognizant of the fact that the EEOC's opinion cannot be binding on them, and have felt free to disregard it when they disagree. Perhaps the most revealing statement of the weight courts will give to the EEOC's interpretations and Guidelines is the Supreme Court's discussion of the effect of an "interpretative bulletin" of the Wage and Hour Administrator under the Fair Labor Standards Act:

> The rulings, interpretations, and opinions of the Administrator under this Act, while not controlling upon the courts by reason of their authority, do constitute a body of experience and informed judgment to which courts and litigants may properly resort for guidance. The weight of such a judgment in a particular case will depend upon the thoroughness evident in its consideration the validity of its reasoning, its consistency with earlier and later pronouncements, and all those factors which give it power to persuade, if lacking power to control.[24]

Finally, the EEOC has recently added another enforcement role to its arsenal of non-powers: petitioning other administrative agencies for permission to intervene in their proceedings in an effort to persuade these agencies to consider the employment practices of the firms which they are regulating. The Commission finds the statutory authority to take such action by virtue of section 705(g), which empowers the EEOC "to cooperate with . . . other agencies." While EEOC officials are enthusiastic

---

24. Skidmore v. Swift & Co., 323 U.S. 134, 140, 65 S.Ct. 161, 164 (1944).

about the potential of this enforcement mechanism, the extent of Commission activity of this sort will depend in large part upon what the Federal Communications Commission does with the first effort, an EEOC challenge of the employment practices of the American Telephone and Telegraph Company.

Notes and Questions

1. Although Title VII emphasized the private action as a primary enforcement device, it also limited the use of the private action to situations where the complaining party had first sought the assistance of EEOC or of comparable state agencies. Accordingly, a valid private action under Title VII could be filed only after the complainant had filed a complaint with EEOC and then waited 60 days to allow EEOC to pursue its investigation and conciliation attempts. Similarly, if the discriminatory practice occurred in a state or municipality where law or local ordinance provided administrative remedies against employment discrimination, a complainant was required to file a discrimination charge with the appropriate agency and then wait 60 days before commencing a federal court Title VII action upon that charge. These prerequisites to suit are described in the Harvard Law Review note at p. 1085.

2. Compare and contrast the unfair labor practice procedure as described by Cox, Bok and Gorman (p. 1075 *supra*) with the procedures under Title VII, as described by the Harvard Law Review editors.

3. Is the unfair labor practice procedure a stronger or weaker enforcement procedure than the procedures under Title VII? Explain your answer.

4. Do the differences in the procedures suggest different congressional objectives regarding resolution of these different employment problems? Explain your answer.

5. Can you explain the differences in the two procedures in terms of basic differences between the types of problems posed by an unfair labor practice charge as compared to a racial discrimination charge?

6. Do the enforcement powers of the EEOC reflect any of the special advantages and competence of administrative agencies which reputedly justify the establishment of such agencies? (See Davis, *supra* pp. 1068–1071 and Question 2 *supra* p. 1074). Does the existence of EEOC and its Title VII powers seem to hold particular promise for assisting individuals who have been denied employment on racial grounds?

7. How, if at all, would you change the enforcement procedures and remedies of Title VII to secure equal employment opportunity for all? What problems are posed by any amendments you propose?

The Harvard Law Review editors assumed, along with many other commentators, that the EEOC's limited powers to force compliance with the Civil Rights Act was one significant deficiency in the Act's enforcement scheme. Comparison between the EEOC and the NLRB and its enforcement powers provided one focus for the debate over proposals to amend Title VII to extend more power to EEOC. Many commentators argued that EEOC should have the authority to hold administrative hearings on Title VII charges brought by EEOC staff, and to issue cease and desist orders in much the same way that the NLRB hears and decides unfair labor practice cases. Other advocates favored strengthening the EEOC by empowering it to initiate Civil Rights actions in Federal District Courts, rather than by authorizing it to perform the adjudicatory function of the NLRB and other federal agencies. In the end, Congress expanded the enforcement powers of EEOC in an interesting compromise. EEOC was authorized to initiate suits in Federal District Court, rather than being given the administrative adjudicating power, but, like the NLRB, EEOC was to have an independent General Counsel appointed by the President, and who would have the authority to decide which cases to prosecute. This expansion of EEOC authority was accomplished in the Equal Employment Opportunity Act of 1972. 86 Stat. 103, Title 42 U.S.C. § 2000e–5(f)(1).

Questions

1. What arguments would you advance in favor of giving the EEOC power to adjudicate employment discrimination charges brought before it by EEOC attorneys? Would you also argue that EEOC should be empowered to hear employment discrimination cases brought before it by private parties? If the EEOC did have the power to adjudicate employment discrimination cases, what remedies should it be able to employ? Awards of money damages? Orders to cease and desist discriminatory practices? Mandatory orders to put specific persons into jobs, or to require procedures for opening jobs to members of minority groups? Would the EEOC proceedings be subject to judicial review? If so, what standards should judges apply in reviewing the proceedings? Would EEOC findings be presumptively valid, only entitled to some deference, or be subject to full evidentiary review?

2. What arguments can you suggest in favor of denying EEOC administrative adjudicatory power and instead giving it the authority to prosecute employment discrimination cases directly in Federal District Courts?

3. Which solution do you prefer? Why? Is your answer affected by the history of judicial involvement in the development of race relations law in the 20th century? Does that history distinguish the race relations field from the labor relations field with regard to the choice of the remedial procedures and forums to be used to implement the law in each field?

Before finally formulating your answers to the preceding questions, consider the following extract.

[The following is taken from CORNELIUS J. PECK,* "THE EQUAL EMPLOYMENT OPPORTUNITY COMMISSION: DEVELOPMENTS IN THE ADMINISTRATIVE PROCESS 1965–1975," ** 51 Washington Law Review 831, 831–846, 858–860 (1976). Most footnotes omitted; others renumbered.]

From an administrative point of view, the most significant development in the ten-year history of the Equal Employment Opportunity Commission (EEOC) has been the demonstration that, at least with respect to certain subjects, courts may be trusted to give novel legislation an expansive and favorable development which traditional learning suggests can be obtained only through the administrative process. . . .

Another major development in the ten-year history of the EEOC has been the demonstration of the means by which a weak and nearly powerless agency can broker its way into being a formulator of policy and a significant force in bringing about compliance with legislation which invalidated long-standing employer and union practices. . . .

I. JUDICIAL DEVELOPMENT OF TITLE VII AND THE ROLE OF THE EEOC

That the judicial branch would give supportive treatment to legislation designed to eliminate discrimination in employment should have been no surprise to those familiar with court decisions in the labor field during the years immediately preceding enactment of Title VII of the Civil Rights Act. Ten years before the Supreme Court's famous decision in Brown v. Board of Education, which held "separate but equal" public educational facilities to be unconstitutional, that Court had read into the Railway Labor Act a duty that a union give equal representation to those it represented without regard to race.[1] The Court went further and held that the duty protected Negro employees from a loss of work threatened by an agreement which a union that did not represent them had made with their employer. The duty of fair representation established under the Railway Labor Act was subsequently extended to unions whose activities were subject to the National Labor Relations Act.[2] Thus the Court had revealed a sensitivity to problems of discrimination in employment well before it undertook to eliminate discrimination in public education.

One year after its first momentous decision in *Brown*, the Court turned its attention to the practical problems of eliminating entrenched discriminatory practices in education. Recognizing that courts would become involved

---

* Professor of Law. University of Washington.

** Address given at A Symposium in Observance of the 10th Aniversary of the U.S. Equal Employment Opportunity Commission, at Rutgers School of Law, November 28, 1975, sponsored by the EEOC. The EEOC retains the right to publish this article, or to authorize others to do so. This article is the property of the United States Government: there is no copyright on the material.

1. Steele v. Louisville & Nashville R.R. 323 U.S. 192, 65 S.Ct. 226 (1944).

2. Syres v. Local 23, Oil Workers, 223 F.2d 739 (5th Cir. 1955), rev'd and remanded per curiam, 350 U.S. 892, 76 S.Ct. 152 (1956). It is of interest that the courts thus demonstrated a concern for racial discrimination in employment well before the NLRB gave consideration to the question of whether a union owes a duty of fair representation to employees it represents. See, e. g., Hughes Tool Co., 104 N.L.R.B. 318 (1953).

in problems of school administration, it concluded that the trial courts should retain jurisdiction of the pending cases. That elimination of racial discrimination would require both strength and involvement on the part of the judiciary must have been impressed upon the Court in its concern with enforcement of desegregation in Little Rock, Arkansas. The commitment thus made presaged a willingness of the Supreme Court that the judiciary engage in an on-going supervision of activities more traditionally associated with the administrative process. In accepting this new role for the judiciary, the Court acted on its own and without the benefit of supporting legislation. The judicial branch was thus well ahead of the legislative branch at the time Title VII was enacted.

A. *Avoidance of Technicalities*

The procedural provisions of Title VII as enacted included the potential for impossible barriers to relief had the courts taken the technical approach which has been attributed to them in contrast to the approach used by administrative agencies. A charge alleging unlawful employment practices had to be filed with EEOC within 90 days after the alleged unlawful practice occurred. Exceptions to this time limitation were made for cases of unlawful employment practices occurring in states or political subdivisions of states which had laws prohibiting the practices and providing relief from such practices. In those cases a complicated formula for deferral to the state or local agency was established. When such a charge had been filed, the statute provided that the EEOC "shall determine" whether there was reasonable cause to believe that the charge is true; if it did, the statute provided that the EEOC "shall endeavor to eliminate any such unlawful employment practice by informal methods of conference, conciliation, and persuasion."

The statute originally provided that the EEOC had 30 days to obtain voluntary compliance with the Act, a period which the EEOC was authorized to and did extend to 60 days. If the attempt to obtain voluntary compliance was unsuccessful the EEOC was directed to inform the person claiming to be aggrieved, and that person then had 30 days within which to file suit against the party charged. Implicit in the statutory provisions was the possibility that the EEOC might not determine that there was reasonable cause to find a violation of the Act, but nothing was stated in the statute concerning the effect of such a determination. Likewise, unmentioned in the statute was the effect to be given to the availability of a remedy through arbitration under the terms of a collective bargaining agreement, a process which had been made a "king-pin" of the national labor policy. The Supreme Court and lower courts have not permitted these technicalities to become barriers to remedies for the prohibited employment practices.

The courts have generally held that the filing of a charge with the EEOC is a jurisdictional prerequisite to suit under the Act. Not all parties to a class action, however, need to have filed a charge with the EEOC. Moreover, the concept of systematic or continuing violations of the Act has been utilized by courts to permit attack upon employment practices instituted more than 90 days prior to the filing of a charge. Nor does the charge have to be stated with a precision not likely to be obtained by a layman; instead, suit may be brought on any charges which are similar or reasonably related to the charge filed with the EEOC. In what must be recognized as a creative decision, the Court of Appeals for the Fifth Circuit held that the statutory limitation periods are tolled when an employee first pursues his remedies under the grievance and arbitration provisions of a collective bargaining agreement. Complications might have arisen for persons filing charges for which there might be a remedy before a state or local authority. The complications included not only those of what constituted the institution and termination of a state or local proceeding, but the possibility that some portions of a charging party's complaint might be remediable by the state or local agency and other portions not so remediable. EEOC attempted to eliminate the problem by a procedural rule providing for automatic referral of a charge to an appropriate state or local agency and an automatic refiling with the EEOC 60 days after receipt of the charge by the state or local agency. The Supreme Court gave its approval to the procedures established, noting that procedural "technicalities are particularly inappropriate in a statutory scheme in which laymen, unassisted by trained lawyers, initiate the process."

The EEOC soon developed an enormous caseload, and the backlog of unresolved charges grew to such an extent that a holding that investigation and attempted conciliation by the EEOC were mandatory would have prevented litigation by a substantial proportion of the private parties who wished to assert rights under the Act. The language of the statute was susceptible, under the traditional rule of construction that the word "shall" is mandatory, to a reading which made the reasonable cause finding and the attempted conciliation jurisdictional requirements for further proceedings under the Act. The EEOC responded to the problem by making provision in its procedural rules that after the expiration of 60 days following the filing of a charge an aggrieved person could demand that a notice be issued that the EEOC had not been able to obtain voluntary compliance with the Act. Some district courts found that an actual attempt at conciliation by the EEOC was a jurisdictional requisite to a private civil action. But those decisions were reversed by the courts of appeals. In 1973 the Supreme Court gave its approval to the related rule developed by lower courts that the absence of an EEOC finding of reasonable cause does not bar a suit by a private party under Title VII.

More recently, judicial resistance to an EEOC practice of sending two notices to a charging party, one of which informed the party that conciliation efforts had failed and the other of which was to constitute a formal notice of the right to sue developed in the district courts. The practice created a period during which the charging party might obtain counsel before the 90 day limitation period on filing suit began to run. EEOC has changed its practice in response to these decisions and now gives notice of the failure of conciliation and the right to sue by letter sent following investigation of the charge by its General Counsel. The changed practice of EEOC thus accepts limitations upon the development of private suits which a court of appeals would not require by a decision reversing a district court judgment and upholding the earlier two-notice practice.

Comparable technicalities might have been developed with respect to the power to sue granted EEOC by amendment in 1972. For example, those amendments provide that the EEOC might bring suit if it were not able to secure a conciliation agreement within 30 days after the filing of a charge, and further provide that if within 180 days after the filing of a charge the Commission has not filed suit, it should notify the person who has filed the charge. That person then has 90 days within which to file a private suit. Argument could thus be made that EEOC has but 180 days within which to file suit and, if it does not, that then a charged party is subject to suit for no more than the 90 day period for private actions. Three courts of appeals have rejected this argument.

As indicated above, it was suggested to the courts that the availability or utilization of arbitration procedures established by a collective bargaining agreement should constitute a non-statutory barrier to relief. While some courts accepted the election of remedies argument, however, the Supreme Court ultimately adopted the conclusion reached by most courts that the doctrine of election of remedies did not apply to suits under Title VII. At the time that it did so, the Supreme Court also rejected an argument that federal courts should defer to arbitration decisions on discrimination claims in a manner similar to that followed by the NLRB. The consequence is that one who believes a prohibited discrimination has occurred may successively utilize two forums in the attempt to obtain a remedy.

Other examples might be given of judicial rejection of technicalities which, if adopted, might have seriously interfered with the assertion of statutory rights in suits under Title VII. What has been presented, however, should suffice to demonstrate that courts were as sensitive as any administrative agency could be to the necessity of simplifying procedures so as to make them useable by laymen. The judicial attitude was expressed forcefully by the Court of Appeals for the Fifth Circuit in a case dealing with the limitation period for filing charges with EEOC. That court said, "It is, therefore, the duty of the courts to make sure that the Act works, and the intent of Congress is not hampered by a combinátion of a strict construction of the statute and a battle with semantics."

B. Class Actions

Judicial liberality with procedural requirements has not been limited to the provisions of Title VII. Perhaps one of the most dramatic and hopeful areas of judicial development has been in the use of class actions to remedy violations of the Act. As mentioned previously, the courts have concluded that a person who has filed a charge may maintain a class action for the benefit of other victims of discrimination even though the other victim-members of the class have not filed charges. Of course, the requirements of rule 23 of the Federal Rules of Civil Procedure must be met.

The Court of Appeals for the Fifth Circuit, again asserting a position of leadership, has established a number of precedents which facilitate the use of class actions for suits under Title VII. In so doing, it noted that a suit under Title VII should be viewed as more than a private claim for particular relief; it should be viewed as an action with heavy overtones of public interest for effectuating the policies of the Act. In a series of decisions, that court of appeals has established the principle that the propriety of a class action to remedy unlawful employment practices may be ascertainable only after all the evidence, or a substantial part of it, has been heard, and the determination of the class or sub-classes may therefore be deferred beyond the initial pleading stages. This conclusion may seem at odds with the direction of rule 23(c)(1) that the court determine "as soon as practicable" whether an action brought as a class action may be so maintained. But the Court of Appeals for the Fifth Circuit concluded that a court operating under rule 23 "has the duty, and ample powers, both in the conduct of the trial and relief granted to treat common things in common and to distinguish the distinguishable." The Court of Appeals for the Fourth Circuit has recently demonstrated a similar willingness to exercise supervisory powers over district courts which too severely limit the use of class actions.

Perhaps most indicative of the willingness to permit the use of class actions to vindicate the policies of Title VII are those decisions which allow the maintenance of such an action by a plaintiff who has failed on the merits to establish his own case. Such a plaintiff must not have interests adverse to the class or interests which would otherwise disqualify him. If he does not, however, the suit may continue despite the lack of personal interest. The obvious question of whether such an individual has the legal standing to present a case or controversy for judicial resolution has thus been resolved in favor of allowing the litigation to proceed.

A similar recognition of the usefulness of class suits in producing massive remedial action underlies those decisions permitting the awarding of back pay for unnamed members of the class. Other courts have not been as receptive to class actions to enforce Title VII, as illustrated by a district court holding that a group of 184 individuals was not so numerous as to make appropriate a class action. But ultimately, other courts should follow the progressive leadership of the Court of Appeals for the Fifth Circuit.

By virtue of the numbers involved, class actions offer opportunities for departure from the individualized determinations associated with the judicial process in litigation between two parties. In providing such mass justice, courts have found it necessary to devise remedies which have a simplicity in application. But although the terminology is that of fashioning a remedy, courts in this area have engaged in the use of power comparable to the rule making powers of administrative agencies. In dealing with questions of entitlement to back pay or transfer rights of the thousands of employees who were victims of unlawful employment practices the courts face problems not unlike that encountered by the Federal Power Commission (FPC) in the 1950's and 1960's when it struggled with the problem of fixing the price at which natural gas producers could sell gas to the interstate pipelines. Ultimately the FPC found it necessary to resort to rule-making in an area price-fixing procedure to handle what would otherwise have been an impossible number of individualized determinations. Courts, like administrative agencies, are utilizing class actions as a practical solution to handling claims which would produce an overwhelming caseload if treated on an individual basis.

Thus, in dealing with the problems of computing back-pay in a class action the Court of Appeals for the Fifth Circuit noted the impossibility of determining with exactitude how an employee's work career would have developed absent discrimination, and established what it called "guidelines" for determination of the amounts of back pay. It said that the trial court should limit its inquiries to objective factors which are both ascertainable and provable. Although it did not attempt to list all of the factors which a trial court should consider, it said that an employee who proved that he had been hired prior to a certain critical date and had been frozen into a racially segregated department, had established a prima facie case for back pay. It was then for the employer to show that other factors would have prevented the employee from transferring to more desirable employment.

In a "pattern or practice" suit brought the the Department of Justice, the Court of Appeals for the Fifth Circuit concluded that the district judge had established three classes of discriminatees because he believed that there had to be proof of individualized discrimination and prejudice. The court of appeals believed that, a pattern and practice having been established, "it would defy reason and waste precious judicial resources for the Court either to require or permit individualized proof for every member of a class here numbering nearly 400 but frequently involving thousands." Accordingly, it disapproved the trial court's tripartite classification system for the determination of transfer rights stating that whatever evidentiary hearings were required for individuals could be postponed to the remedy.

More recently, in giving its approval to the terms of consent decrees worked out in the pattern and practice suit against the steel industry, the same court gave its approval to the rough justice of awarding an average sum of $500.00 to those victims of discrimination who executed releases of claims for back pay due them under Title VII, rather than making individualized determinations. The court noted that individuals who accepted the sums and executed a waiver of statutory rights might nevertheless maintain individual suits for additional injunctive relief or to prevent future discrimination. But the principal consideration underlying the decision was the necessity of utilizing the product of negotiations as a practical means of achieving compliance with the Act rather than having the EEOC pursue each claim individually. Indeed, the general approval given by the courts to the use of temporary preferential quotas in the context of discriminatory hiring practices may appropriately be characterized as the use of rule-making powers to devise a remedy operative in the future for a generalized problem which would not be dealt with satisfactorily after the event on a case-by-case basis.

C. Support for Litigation

1. Court-appointed administrators. Courts have been willing to retain jurisdiction of Title VII cases so as to permit the on-going supervision of the remedial program established by a decree. In exercising such on-going supervision they perform functions previously thought to be a unique advantage of the administrative process. In so doing, courts have displayed ingenuity in organizing the supervisory apparatus, employing a variety of court-appointed administrators and committees to perform the day-to-day work of checking on compliance efforts.

2. Attorney's fees. In developing their expansive role in the enforcement of Title VII, the courts have been much assisted by the provision made in Title VII for the awarding of attorney's fees to the prevailing party. They have recognized that the purposes to be served by the awarding of attorney's fees are not limited to discouraging the advancement of frivolous defenses, but include encouragement of plaintiffs to bring suits, thereby vindicating the public interest embodied in the Act. Accordingly, courts have from time to time awarded attorney's fees which are very substantial and even exceed the amount of damages recovered by the individual plaintiffs. Perhaps the lesson to be learned is that provision for attorney's fees in court actions should be considered as a meaningful alternative to the establishment of an administrative agency.

D.   Judicial Elevation of EEOC

In addition to performing an expansive role themselves, courts have assisted the EEOC in developing a role in the administration of Title VII that took the Commission considerably beyond the function of conciliator. Probably the most important assistance given the EEOC was in the weight given by the courts to EEOC guidelines. The Supreme Court has characterized the guidelines as "[t]he administrative interpretation of the Act by the enforcing agency," which are consequently entitled to "great deference." [3] The Court of Appeals for the Fifth Circuit adopted the narrow interpretation given by EEOC guidelines to the bona fide occupational qualification defense established in Title VII. Other courts have recognized a responsibility to defer to other provisions of the guidelines.

In traditional administrative law analysis, greatest deference will be given to rules promulgated by an agency in the exercise of legislative powers conferred on the agency by Congress, but the EEOC was given no legislative powers by Congress. Its authority to make rules is limited to the making of procedural rules and to establishing reporting requirements for employers and unions. A back-handed statutory authorization for the issuance of interpretative rulings may be found in a provision making it a defense to have relied in good faith on any written interpretation or opinion of the Commission. Interpretations developed by an adjudicating body are entitled to greater deference by the courts than are those of an officer engaged only in enforcement. The theory is that the officer or body charged with the duty of deciding feels the responsibility of being fair, just, and "right." He, she, or it is therefore less expansive in questions of interpretation than is an officer or body charged with prosecuting, it being proper in the latter case to attempt to utilize all plausible constructions of the legislation. But at the time the EEOC developed its guidelines it did not have power to adjudicate. It did not even have power to prosecute. Insofar as action by the EEOC was concerned, the guidelines could serve only to advise parties as to when the EEOC would find reasonable cause to believe a violation had occurred, leading it to undertake conciliation. If, as is likely the case, a conciliator might act where a prosecutor would not, the progression would lead to a further reduction in the deference due the guidelines.

At the present time the EEOC guidelines on discrimination because of sex and the guidelines on employment selection procedures cite as authority

---

3. Griggs v. Duke Power Co., 401 U.S. 424, 433–34, 91 S.Ct. 849, 854–55 (1971). *See also* Albemarle Paper Co. v. Moody, 422 U.S. 405, 431, 95 S.Ct. 2362, 2378 (1975).

the provision of Title VII making it a defense to have relied in good faith on a written interpretation of the Commission. The guidelines on discrimination because of religion and the guidelines on discrimination because of national origin do not cite authority for their issuance. Now that EEOC has power to sue, its guidelines can be recognized as what the enforcer agrees is not a violation of the Act, but certainly would not on general principles be recognized as what is required by the Act.

Perhaps the deference shown to EEOC guidelines will diminish. Last year in a concurring opinion, Justice Blackmun noted that the guidelines have not been subjected to the test of adversary comment,[4] and Chief Justice Burger, dissenting and concurring in the same case, noted that the guidelines were not federal regulations which have been submitted to the public comment and scrutiny required by the Administrative Procedure Act. Earlier the Supreme Court refused to defer to the EEOC guideline on discrimination because of national origin which it believed to be inconsistent with Congressional intent not to regulate the practice of requiring citizenship as a condition of employment. Whatever the final result, the deference accorded EEOC guidelines by the courts to date must have significantly increased the impact of those guidelines on employment practices.

It would unduly lengthen this article to undertake a review of the substantive law developed by the courts to determine whether it has been as expansive as that which might have developed in an administrative process. I believe the conclusion would be that, while there is a difference in their reading of the substantive protection of Title VII today, courts generally have given those substantive provisions a liberal interpretation. It is worth pointing out, as an important example, that on the question of how seniority rights had to be reshaped to meet the requirements of Title VII the courts at an early date took positions more advanced than those previously accepted by the EEOC.

This review suggests that it may have been no loss to the cause of eliminating discrimination in employment that EEOC did not originally or in 1972 obtain power to issue cease and desist orders. Very probably judges, like other people, prefer to lead rather than be pushed. What the EEOC might have gained from a power to find facts, subject to the limits of review of the substantial evidence test, or from the power to formulate policy through adjudication, might well have been offset by a generalized skepticism when it sought enforcement of its orders by a judiciary which had not been directly involved in developing the meaning and reach of the statute. An effective technique of advocacy is to persuade a judge that the idea or view of the case springs from his insights and is not something forced into his faltering intellectual apparatus by learned counsel. EEOC's original role of conciliator, and its current role of enforcer, may thus produce a more expansive and favorable interpretation of Title VII than would have resulted if the judiciary had been limited to accepting or rejecting a decision on the merits made by EEOC. Also, the greater prestige of the

4. Albemarle Paper Co. v. Moody, 422 U.S. 405, 449, 95 S.Ct. 2362, 2389 (1975).

courts probably has made more acceptable to the general public the very great changes in employment practices required by Title VII than would be the case if those changes were first directed by an agency which both prosecuted and decided.

*   *   *

III.   EEOC'S FAILURE TO EXPLOIT NEW POWERS

Prior to 1972, EEOC had no power of its own to institute enforcement proceedings. Under the Civil Rights Act of 1964, EEOC could make recommendations to the Attorney General that he file suit based upon a pattern or practice of discrimination or that he, not the EEOC, intervene in a suit initiated by a private person. A grudging grant of access to the courts was made in a provision which permitted the EEOC to commence proceedings to compel a respondent to comply with an order of a court issued in a civil action initially brought by an aggrieved person. EEOC's role in the courts was limited to that of amicus curiae. During its first years EEOC was represented in litigation instituted by private parties by the Department of Justice, but subsequently appeared through its own counsel as amicus curiae. During its third year EEOC participated as intervenor or amicus curiae in 22 private civil suits; during its fifth year such activity had increased substantially and EEOC participated in 167 private civil suits. Throughout this period EEOC officials argued that its lack of enforcement powers was the principal reason that its attempts at conciliation had been frustrated.

A.   *Use of the Power to Sue*

Finally, in 1972 EEOC received authorization to bring a civil action against private parties to remedy violations of Title VII. There had been disagreement as to whether EEOC should be given power to issue cease and desist orders or whether its power should be limited to a power to bring suit in court. Although the power to bring civil actions was thought of by some not to be as potent as the power to issue cease and desist orders, the 1972 change might nevertheless have been expected to bring about great changes in the activities of EEOC. Those changes have not occurred.

As mentioned previously, one year after EEOC had obtained power to file suit, there were vacancies in almost 40 percent of the positions authorized in the Office of the General Counsel. By the end of its 1972 fiscal year EEOC had filed only five suits, and by March 31, 1975, it had filed only 290 suits, intervened in 60 cases, and sought preliminary injunctions in 18 cases. As of August, 1974, more than 40 percent of the suits filed were against respondents having work forces of 300 or fewer employees, and only 34 percent were against respondents having 1,000 or more employees. The litigation record is not a good one, and what activity has occurred has not been concentrated in the rewarding areas involving large employers or patterns for practices of discrimination. In statistics alone the litigation accomplishments seem little different from those achieved through appearances as amicus curiae.

On March 24, 1972, EEOC acquired concurrent power with the Department of Justice to institute "pattern or practice" suits, and on March 24,

1974, EEOC assumed all the functions formerly performed by the Attorney General with respect to such suits. The use of this power in conjunction with Commissioner charges could have become a major means of establishing priorities of Commission work and more effectively eliminating unlawful employment practices. But EEOC never utilized its concurrent power, and during fiscal 1975 it had filed only one suit under its exclusive power to institute such litigation.

In conferring enforcement powers on EEOC, Congress expected that use of that power would become the primary means of compelling compliance with the law. But this did not happen. The importance of litigation by private parties is illustrated by the fact that in its 1973 fiscal year EEOC filed 116 cases, whereas it estimated that private parties had filed 800 suits. EEOC has continued to stress the importance of litigation by aggrieved parties, instituting training programs for private attorneys to represent them. It appears, however, that only in Los Angeles has EEOC developed a panel of private attorneys adequate to meet the needs for representation.

Section 204(b) of Title II of the Civil Rights Act of 1964 [42 U.S. C. § 2000a–3(b)] reads as follows:

> **(b) Attorneys' fees.** In any action commenced pursuant to this title the court, in its discretion, may allow the prevailing party, other than the United States, a reasonable attorney's fee as part of the costs, and the United States shall be liable for costs the same as a private person.

Section 706(k) of Title VII of the Act [42 U.S.C. § 2000e–5(k)] is substantially the same as § 204(b) and it reads as follows:

> **(k) Attorney's fee.** In any action or proceeding under this title the court, in its discretion, may allow the prevailing party, other than the Commission or the United States, a reasonable attorney's fee as part of the costs, and the Commission and the United States shall be liable for costs the same as a private person.

NEWMAN v. PIGGIE PARK ENTERPRISES, INC.

Supreme Court of the United States, 1968.
390 U.S. 400, 88 S.Ct. 964, 19 L.Ed.2d 1263.

PER CURIAM.

The petitioners instituted this class action under Title II of the Civil Rights Act of 1964, § 204(a), 78 Stat. 244, 42 U.S.C. § 2000a–3(a), to enjoin racial discrimination at five drive-in restaurants and a sandwich shop owned and operated by the respondents in South Carolina. The District Court held that the operation of each of the respondents' restaurants affected commerce within the meaning of § 201(c)(2), 78 Stat. 243, 42 U.S.C. § 2000a(c)(2), and found, on undisputed evidence, that Negroes had been discriminated against at all six of the restaurants. 256 F.Supp. 941, 947, 951. But the District Court erroneously concluded that Title II does not cover drive-in restaurants of the sort involved in this case. 256 F.Supp., at 951–953. Thus the court enjoined racial discrimination only at the respondents' sandwich shop. Id., at 953.

The Court of Appeals reversed the District Court's refusal to enjoin discrimination at the drive-in establishments, 377 F.2d 433, 435–436, and then directed its attention to that section of Title II which provides that "the prevailing party" is entitled to "a reasonable attorney's fee" in the court's "discretion." § 204(b), 78 Stat. 244, 42 U.S.C. § 200a–3(b). In remanding the case, the Court of Appeals instructed the District Court to award counsel fees only to the extent that the respondents' defenses had been advanced "for purposes of delay and not in good faith." 377 F.2d, at 437. We granted certiorari to decide whether this subjective standard properly effectuates the purposes of the counsel-fee provision of Title II of the Civil Rights Act of 1964. · · · We hold that it does not.

When the Civil Rights Act of 1964 was passed, it was evident that enforcement would prove difficult and that the Nation would have to rely in part upon private litigation as a means of securing broad compliance with the law.[1] A Title II suit is thus private in form only. When a plaintiff brings an action under that Title, he cannot recover damages. If he obtains an injunction, he does so not for himself alone but also as a "private attorney general," vindicating a policy that Congress considered of the highest priority.[2] If successful plaintiffs were routinely forced to bear their own attorneys' fees, few aggrieved parties would be in a position to advance the public interest by invoking the injunctive powers of the federal courts. Congress therefore enacted the provision for counsel fees—not simply to penalize litigants who deliberately advance arguments they know to be untenable but, more broadly, to encourage individuals injured by racial discrimination to seek judicial relief under Title II.[3]

It follows that one who succeeds in obtaining an injunction under that Title should ordinarily recover an attorney's fee unless special circumstances would render such an award unjust. Because no such circumstances

---

1. In this connection, it is noteworthy that 42 U.S.C. § 2000a–3(a) permits intervention by the Attorney General in privately initiated Title II suits "of general public importance" and provides that, "in such circumstances as the court may deem just," a district court may "appoint an attorney for [the] complainant and may authorize the commencement of the civil action without the payment of fees, costs, or security." Only where a "pattern or

practice" of discrimination is reasonably believed to exist may the Attorney General himself institute a civil action for injunctive relief. 42 U.S.C. § 2000a–5.

2. See S.Rep. No. 872, 88th Cong., 2d Sess., pt. 1, at 11, 24 (1964); HR Rep. No. 914, 88th Cong., 1st Sess., pt. 1, at 18 (1963); HR Rep. No. 914, 88th Cong., 1st Sess., pt. 2 at 1–2 (1963).

are present here, the District Court on remand should include reasonable counsel fees as part of the costs to be assessed against the respondents. As so modified, the judgment of the Court of Appeals is

Affirmed.

MR. JUSTICE MARSHALL took no part in the consideration or decision of this case.

The Piggie Park case involved an action under Title II for the desegregation of public accommodations. In Albemarle Paper Co. v. Moody, 422 U.S. 405, 95 S.Ct. 2362 (1975), the Court made it clear that the Piggie Park standard for awarding attorney's fees also applies in Title VII actions.

Query. Does this suggest an additional reason why private civil actions in court may be a satisfactory alternative to extensive administrative enforcement of the Civil Rights Act of 1964? See, *e. g.,* the excerpt from Peck at pp. 1093–1101 *supra.*

SECTION 50. SECURING FUNDAMENTAL RIGHTS THROUGH ADJUDICATION: SHAPING DOCTRINE AND REMEDIES TO COMMAND AND PERSUADE CHANGED BEHAVIOR

The following materials trace certain episodes in the development of labor law and race relations law following major legislative and judicial breakthroughs, such as the Wagner Act and Brown v. Board of Education. The materials deal tentatively with the movement of law from the broad policy level to the action level in administrative and judicial adjudication.

SECTION 50.1   EVOLUTION OF THE DUTY TO BARGAIN UNDER THE WAGNER AND TAFT-HARTLEY ACTS

The Wagner Act created a legal duty that labor and management bargain with each other. In studying some of the problems that have arisen in connection with this duty, we shall have an opportunity to consider more sharply the larger issue of the educational function of law.

---

3. If Congress' objective had been to authorize the assessment of attorneys' fees against defendants who make completely groundless contentions for purposes of delay, no new statutory provision would have been necessary for it has long been held that a federal court may award counsel fees to a successful plaintiff where a defense has been maintained "in bad faith, vexatiously, wantonly, or for oppressive reasons." 6 Moore's Federal Practice, 1352 (1966 ed.).

It is apparent, as we have suggested earlier, that all law performs —or can perform—an educational function. Thus, for example, the legal proscription of most homicides—backed by criminal sanctions— performs an educational function by establishing norms of morality. Similarly, legal rules concerning remedies for breach of contract help to teach people that contracts are supposed to be performed. Yet commands of the state supported by coercive sanctions, while often effective in inducing the intended behavior, do not necessarily bring about the internalization of the standards imposed by law. Indeed, it is argued by some that law should not concern itself with such an internalization—that its proper role is to regulate behavior, and not to attempt to shape people's attitudes and beliefs.

The legal duty to bargain, however, does presuppose something more than behavior. Just going through the motions of bargaining, without a desire to reach a genuine resolution of differences, is presumably not enough.

At the same time, the duty to bargain must be considered in the light of the historical background set out in the preceding chapters. That experience provided the unique context for the subsequent development of the law, and the nature of that experience posed two distinct though interrelated problems for the law: the one was to educate both sides to the possibility of a legal means to resolve their conflict; the other was to begin to shape attitudes and beliefs in such way as to afford some prospect for a voluntary accommodation of the conflicting interests of labor and management. Resolution of the first educational task was a necessary prelude to fulfillment of the second.

As we consider the educational function of law, however, we must keep in mind that the law as teacher is not divorced from the law as student. A good teacher will help students to learn, but as they learn they change, and the teacher must be aware of these changes and adapt to them lest the students outstrip their teacher. So it is with the law. If it is successful as teacher, the characteristics of the contest and the contestants will be changed so that the law must continue to learn and change at the same time that it teaches, if it is to continue to play a meaningful role in mitigating and resolving the ongoing controversy.

PUBLIC LAW 74–198, 49 STAT. 449, APPROVED JULY 5, 1935. [The Wagner Act.] Section 8. It shall be an unfair labor practice for an employer—

* * *

(5) to refuse to bargain collectively with the representatives of his employees, . . .

J. I. CASE CO. v. NATIONAL LABOR RELATIONS BOARD

Supreme Court of the United States, 1944.
321 U.S. 332, 64 S.Ct. 576, 88 L.Ed. 762.

MR. JUSTICE JACKSON delivered the opinion of the Court.

This cause was heard by the National Labor Relations Board on stipulated facts which so far as concern present issues are as follows:

The petitioner, J. I. Case Company, at its Rock Island, Illinois, plant, from 1937 offered each employee an individual contract of employment. The contracts were uniform and for a term of one year. The Company agreed to furnish employment as steadily as conditions permitted, to pay a specified rate, which the Company might redetermine if the job changed, and to maintain certain hospital facilities. The employee agreed to accept the provisions, to serve faithfully and honestly for the term, to comply with factory rules, and that defective work should not be paid for. About 75% of the employees accepted and worked under these agreements.

According to the Board's stipulation and finding, the execution of the contracts was not a condition of employment, nor was the status of individual employees affected by reason of signing or failing to sign the contracts. It is not found or contended that the agreements were coerced, obtained by any unfair labor practice, or that they were not valid under the circumstances in which they were made.

While the individual contracts executed August 1, 1941 were in effect, a C.I.O. union petitioned the Board for certification as the exclusive bargaining representative of the production and maintenance employees. On December 17, 1941 a hearing was held, at which the Company urged the individual contracts as a bar to representation proceedings. The Board, however, directed an election, which was won by the union. The union was thereupon certified as the exclusive bargaining representative of the employees in question in respect to wages, hours, and other conditions of employment.

The union then asked the Company to bargain. It refused, declaring that it could not deal with the union in any manner affecting rights and obligations under the individual contracts while they remained in effect. It offered to negotiate on matters which did not affect rights under the individual contracts, and said that upon the expiration of the contracts it would bargain as to all matters. Twice the Company sent circulars to its employees asserting the validity of the individual contracts and stating the position that it took before the Board in reference to them.

The Board held that the Company had refused to bargain collectively, in violation of § 8(5) of the National Labor Relations Act, 29 U.S.C.A. § 158 (5); and that the contracts had been utilized, by means of the circulars, to impede employees in the exercise of rights guaranteed by § 7 of the Act, 29 U.S.C.A. § 157, with the result that the Company had engaged in unfair labor practices within the meaning of § 8(1) of the Act. It ordered the Company to cease and desist from giving effect to the contracts, from extending them or entering into new ones, from refusing to bargain and from interfering with the employees; and it required the Company to give notice accordingly and to bargain upon request. . . .

Contract in labor law is a term the implications of which must be determined from the connection in which it appears. Collective bargaining between employer and the representatives of a unit, usually a union, results in an accord as to terms which will govern hiring and work and pay in that unit. The result is not, however, a contract of employment except in rare cases; no one has a job by reason of it and no obligation to any individual ordinarily comes into existence from it alone. The negotiations between union and management result in what often has been called a trade agreement, rather than in a contract of employment. Without pushing the analogy too far, the agreement may be likened to the tariffs established by a carrier, to standard provisions prescribed by supervising authorities for insurance policies, or to utility schedules of rates and rules for service, which do not of themselves establish any relationships but which do govern the terms of the shipper or insurer or customer relationship whenever and with whomever it may be established. Indeed, in some European countries, contrary to American practice, the terms of a collectively negotiated trade agreement are submitted to a government department and if approved become a governmental regulation ruling employment in the unit.

After the collective trade agreement is made, the individuals who shall benefit by it are identified by individual hirings. The employer, except as restricted by the collective agreement itself and except that he must engage in no unfair labor practice or discrimination, is free to select those he will employ or discharge. But the terms of the employment already have been traded out. There is little left to individual agreement except the act of hiring. This hiring may be by writing or by word of mouth or may be implied from conduct. In the sense of contracts of hiring, individual contracts between the employer and employee are not forbidden, but indeed are necessitated by the collective bargaining procedure.

But, however engaged, an employee becomes entitled by virtue of the Labor Relations Act somewhat as a third party beneficiary to all benefits of the collective trade agreement, even if on his own he would yield to less favorable terms. The individual hiring contract is subsidiary to the terms of the trade agreement and may not waive any of its benefits, any more than a shipper can contract away the benefit of filed tariffs, the insurer the benefit of standard provisions, or the utility customer the benefit of legally established rates.

Concurrent existence of these two types of agreement raises problems as to which the National Labor Relations Act makes no express provision. We have, however, held that individual contracts obtained as the result of an unfair labor practice may not be the basis of advantage to the violator of the Act nor of disadvantage to employees. National Licorice Co. v. National Labor Relations Board, 309 U.S. 350, 60 S.Ct. 569, 84 L.Ed. 799. But it is urged that where, as here, the contracts were not unfairly or unlawfully obtained, the court indicated a contrary rule in National Labor Relations Board v. Jones & Laughlin Steel Corp., 301 U.S. 1, 44, 45, 57 S.Ct. 615, 627, 628, 81 L.Ed. 893, 108 A.L.R. 1352, and Virginian R. Co. v. System Federation, 300 U.S. 515, 57 S.Ct. 592, 81 L.Ed. 789. Without reviewing those cases in detail, it may be said that their decision called for nothing and their opinions contain nothing which may be properly read to rule the case before us. The court in those cases recognized the existence of some scope for individual contracts, but it did not undertake to define it or to consider the relations between lawful individual and collective agreements, which is the problem now before us.

Care has been taken in the opinions of the Court to reserve a field for the individual contract, even in industries covered by the National Labor Relations Act, not merely as an act or evidence of hiring, but also in the sense of a completely individually bargained contract setting out terms of employment, because there are circumstances in which it may legally be used, in fact, in which there is no alternative. Without limiting the possibilities, instances such as the following will occur: Men may continue work after a collective agreement expires and, despite negotiation in good faith, the negotiation may be deadlocked or delayed; in the interim express or implied individual agreements may be held to govern. The conditions for collective bargaining may not exist; thus a majority of the employees may refuse to join a union or to agree upon or designate bargaining representatives, or the majority may not be demonstrable by the means prescribed by the statute, or a previously existent majority may have been lost without unlawful interference by the employer and no new majority have been formed. As the employer in these circumstances may be under no legal obligation to bargain collectively, he may be free to enter into individual contracts.

Individual contracts, no matter what the circumstances that justify their execution or what their terms, may not be availed of to defeat or delay the procedures prescribed by the National Labor Relations Act looking to collective bargaining, nor to exclude the contracting employee from a duly ascertained bargaining unit; nor may they be used to forestall bargaining or to limit or condition the terms of the collective agreement. "The Board asserts a public right vested in it as a public body, charged in the public interest with the duty of preventing unfair labor practices." National Licorice Co. v. National Labor Relations Board, 309 U.S. 350, 364, 60 S.Ct. 569, 577, 84 L.Ed. 799. Wherever private contracts conflict with its functions, they obviously must yield or the Act would be reduced to a futility.

It is equally clear since the collective trade agreement is to serve the purpose contemplated by the Act, the individual contract cannot be effective as a waiver of any benefit to which the employee otherwise would be entitled under the trade agreement. The very purpose of providing by statute for the collective agreement is to supersede the terms of separate agreements of employees with terms which reflect the strength and bargaining power and serve the welfare of the group. Its benefits and advantages are open to every employee of the represented unit, whatever the type or terms of his pre-existing contract of employment.

But it is urged that some employees may lose by the collective agreement, that an individual workman may sometimes have, or be capable of getting, better terms than those obtainable by the group and that his freedom of contract must be respected on that account. We are not called upon to say that under no circumstances can an individual enforce an agreement more advantageous than a collective agreement, but we find the mere possibility that such agreements might be made no ground for holding generally that individual contracts may survive or surmount collective ones. The practice and philosophy of collective bargaining looks with suspicion on such individual advantages. Of course, where there is great variation in circumstances of employment or capacity of employees, it is possible for the collective bargain to prescribe only minimum rates or maximum hours or expressly to leave certain areas open to individual bargaining. But except as so provided, advantages to individuals may prove as disruptive of industrial peace as disadvantages. They are a fruitful way of interfering with organization and choice of representatives; increased compensation, if individually deserved, is often earned at the cost of breaking down some other standard thought to be for the welfare of the group, and always creates the suspicion of being paid at the long-range expense of the group as a whole. Such discriminations not infrequently amount to unfair labor practices. The workman is free, if he values his own bargaining position more than that of the group, to vote against representation; but the majority rules, and if it collectivizes the employment bargain, individual advantages or favors will generally in practice go in as a contribution to the collective result. We cannot except individual contracts generally from the operation of collective ones because some may be more individually advantageous. Individual contracts cannot subtract from collective ones, and whether under some circumstances they may add to them in matters covered by the collective bargain, we leave to be determined by appropriate forums under the laws of contracts applicable, and to the Labor Board if they constitute unfair labor practices.

It also is urged that such individual contracts may embody matters that are not necessarily included within the statutory scope of collective bargaining, such as stock purchase, group insurance, hospitalization, or medical attention. We know of nothing to prevent the employee's, because he is an employee, making any contract provided it is not inconsistent with a collective agreement or does not amount to or result from or is not part of an unfair labor practice. But in so doing the employer may not incidentally exact or obtain any diminution of his own obligation or any increase of those of employees in the matters covered by collective agreement. Hence we find that the contentions of the Company that the individual contracts precluded a choice of representatives and warranted refusal to bargain during their duration were properly overruled. It follows that representation to the employees by circular letter that they had such legal effect was improper and could properly be prohibited by the Board. . . .

As so modified [in details not here material] the decree is
Affirmed.

MR. JUSTICE ROBERTS is of opinion that the judgment should be reversed.

Questions

1. In light of the history of the evolution of American labor law, can you suggest some reasons why the Supreme Court would be disposed to disfavor individual contracts of employment?

2. Did the Court imply that a collective bargaining agreement is not a contract, or only that it is a peculiar kind of contract?

3. What difficulty is posed in this case if a collective bargaining agreement is determined to be *only* a contract?

4. In what sense is the relation between a statute and the Constitution analogous to the relation between an individual employment contract and a collective bargaining agreement?

5. By the time this case was argued to the Supreme Court, all the individual employment contracts in effect at the start of the proceedings had expired. Was this a moot case in the Supreme Court? Was the decision in this case necessary to resolve a dispute or was it calculated to clarify a total situation?

6. Is it essential to the educational function of law that courts, on occasion, undertake to clarify a total situation?

NATIONAL LABOR RELATIONS BOARD v. MONTGOMERY WARD & CO.

United States Circuit Court of Appeals, Ninth Circuit, 1943.
133 F.2d 676.

GARRECHT, CIRCUIT JUDGE. . . . Clerks began organizing Ward's retail employees in February or March, 1940, and by August 6 of that year claimed a majority of Ward's retail clerks, which claim apparently was accepted by Wards, and is not disputed. The Warehousemen was certified by the Board, on August 10, 1940, as the proper and exclusive bargaining representative of the unit of Ward's warehouse employees. Wards, through its West coast labor representative, W. B. Powell (assisted at times by the manager of the Portland retail store and the manager of the mail order house), engaged in bargaining conferences with Clerks on September 19, and October 22, 1940; with Warehousemen on November 12, 1940; and in a joint conference with both Clerks and Warehousemen on November 25, 1940. Subsequent to the commencement of the strike further conferences were conducted for the avowed purpose of negotiating agreements. Prior to the first conferences each union submitted to Wards a proposed written contract. No stenographic transcript was taken of the discussions at the conferences, due to objection by Wards, but there is no substantial conflict in the testimony respecting what transpired at these meetings. In advancing a reason for his objection thereto Wards' representative suggested that the taking of a stenographic transcript would impair the flexibility of the discussions. At no time did Wards offer in writing any proposed contracts to which it would agree, or offer any written counter proposals. Wards' representative took the position that Wards was seeking nothing from the unions and that the unions were obliged to submit to it contracts with which it would agree.

In general outline, the conferences proceeded with a reading of the unions' proposed contracts, article by article or section by section to which Wards' representative would reply and state the company's position or objection. On some occasions the union representative would comment respecting the objections, but on others, the article or section was simply passed and the next article or section read. The unions did not present or propose new written contracts following the conferences, but at such meeting presented the contracts originally proposed, notwithstanding knowledge of the company's objection to certain sections.

The Board found "that on September 19, 1940, and at all times thereafter [Wards] has refused to bargain with the Retail Clerks and the Warehousemen as the exclusive representatives of its employees in appropriate units with respect to rates of pay, wages, hours of employment, and other conditions of employment, and that the respondent has thereby interfered with, restrained, and coerced its employees in the exercise of the rights guaranteed in Section 7 of the Act." The Board held that there had been "a refusal to bargain" and that Wards was guilty of an "unfair labor practice," under Section 8 of the Act. . . .

Since the only remaining question to be decided is whether or not Wards was guilty of a refusal to bargain collectively with the representatives of its employees, it is necessary to determine the meaning of the term "refusal to bargain." The Act itself contains no precise definition of the term. Looking to the cases for enlightenment, we find that the phrase "collective bargaining" has been considered by many courts and uniformly interpreted. Wilson & Co., Inc., v. NLRB, 8 Cir., 115 F.2d 759, 763, contains an excellent and well-documented discussion on the subject of "collective bargaining." We quote:

"The petitioner relies heavily upon the language of the Chief Justice Hughes in the case of National Labor Relations Board v. Jones & Laughlin Steel Corp., hereinbefore quoted [301 U.S. 1], to the effect that the act does not compel agreements between employers and employees and does not compel any agreement whatever. That language, of course, sustains petitioner's contention that it could not be compelled to enter into any written agreement which incorporated provisions unacceptable to it; but the language does not sustain petitioner's contention that bare collective bargaining, without any willingness on its part to reduce understandings reached to writing, constitutes the kind of bargaining which the law requires. Obviously, the purpose of the act is to require collective bargaining to the end that contracts satisfactory to both employer and employees may be reached. [Citations omitted.] The act does not specifically require that the results of collective bargaining be reduced to writing, but a refusal to do what reasonable and fair-minded men are ordinarily willing to do, upon request, may certainly be taken to be an indication of a lack of proper intent and good faith in collective bargaining. . . .

"Without attempting complete accuracy, we think that the applicable rules of law are, in substance, as follows: While the act does not compel that employer and employees shall agree, it contemplates that agreements will be reached as the result of collective bargaining. [Citations omitted.] It obligates the employer to bargain in good faith both collectively and exclusively with the chosen representative of a majority of his employees with respect to all matters which affect his employees as a class, including wages, hours of employment, and working conditions. [Citations omitted.] It does not, however, prohibit individual employees or groups of employees from negotiating with the employer concerning grievances. [Citations omitted.] The employer is not required to take the initiative in seeking a contract with his employees or with their chosen representative, nor is he required to enter into negotiations with third parties not representing his employees. [Citations omitted.] When an employer has reached an agreement with his employees, he is under the further duty of bargaining collectively before making changes in existing contracts. [Citations omitted.] The requirements which are imposed by the act upon the employer can only be satisfied by an honest and sincere compliance. [Citations omitted.] When collective bargaining results in agreement, a good-faith compliance with the law requires that the agreement be reduced to writing, unless both parties desire that it remain oral, or unless some other justifiable ground exists for not putting it in writing. [Citations omitted.]" . . .

The Board found that "Pursuant to its hypertechnical approach, the respondent [Wards] was willing to meet with the Unions when requested, listen to their demands, and explain its position thereon. Further than this the respondent refused to go. . . . The Board also found that Wards adhered to the view that "the obligation of taking further steps rested upon the Unions alone" and that Wards "was opposed to submitting to the Unions genuine counter-proposals."

There were four major obstacles upon which the conferences reached an impasse: (1) Union or closed shop; (2) increased wages; (3) seniority; and (4) arbitration. In the contract proposed by each union there was a clause which provided, substantially, that the company either would give preference of employment to unemployed union members, or that if nonmembers were employed they must make application within a specified time for membership in the particular union. Each of the proposed contracts contained a section relative to seniority—that is, that in slack seasons or in the event of lack of work, lay-offs and rehiring should be on the basis of seniority, those with the greater length of service should be laid off later than those with lesser periods of service and that rehiring should be made in the inverse order. Also, each of the proposed contracts made provision for wage increases applicable to the various classifications of employees within the several bargaining units. In addition, the contracts proposed by each of the three unions provided for arbitration of disputes by a "Board of Adjustment," which would have the power to decide questions respecting the meaning or enforcement of the proposed agreement and to settle disputes arising out of discharge of an employee where such employee alleges the discharge to be unjust and to settle disputes on other questions concerning the contracts.

Wards and the unions also disagreed upon other matters contained in the proposed contracts. Wards refused to agree to the inclusion of exclusive-recognition and nondiscrimination clauses in the "binding" parts of the proposed agreements. The company based its refusal upon the ground that neither of these questions was a bargaining matter—that both questions were controlled by the Act, 29 U.S.C.A. §§ 158 and 159—but offered to include recognition as a preliminary "whereas" clause in the agreement.

None of the "bargainers" exhibited any intention to, nor did any of them, recede from the original position taken, until December 13, 14, and 16, 1940, at meetings presided over by one Ashe a conciliator of the United States Department of Labor, when the unions appeared to waver. At the

December 13 conference, counsel for the unions asked Powell, Wards' representative, whether Wards would be willing to arbitrate "the question of what clauses should be included in the contract" if the unions should withdraw their request for a "union shop." The reply was in the negative. The unions then made further proposals for arbitration and concluded with a request to Powell that the company take up the proposed contracts, section by section, and write them out and delete from, and add to, the proposed sections as it desired. Powell replied that it was up to the unions to make proposals which would please the company; that the company had no affirmative duty to do anything. On the following day Wards' representative was asked if the company would be willing to sign an agreement which merely set out its present policies and practices. Powell replied that the question of the form of the agreement—verbal or written— was premature at the time; that if an agreement could be reached upon substantial provisions, that question should then be considered. In answer to a question whether Wards would sign an agreement Powell replied that discussion on the question was premature. Obviously, the primary question asked Powell remained unanswered. Neither did Wards change its attitude on the occasion of the last meeting, December 16, 1940; it took the same position as always upon the principal points of dispute.

We think we may say that no contention is made that the facts found do not conform to the evidence. After carefully reviewing all the testimony in the record, we are satisfied that facts found are in accordance therewith. This seems to be agreed: The dispute is as to the inferences which may be drawn from these facts. The Board drew the inference that Wards by its conduct during the course of the conferences and negotiations demonstrated a want of good faith and was, therefore, guilty of a refusal to bargain collectively, as required so to do by the National Labor Relations Act. . . .

Wards argue that "The duty to bargain collectively is no less nor more than the duty to recognize the authority of the employee representative, to participate in such discussion as is necessary to avoid mutual misunderstanding, and to enter into binding agreements on such terms, if any, as are mutually acceptable." Unquestionably, Wards recognized the unions as bargaining agents for its employees, and it did meet with them, listen to their demands, and explain its position thereon. But no agreement was entered into by Wards, and nothing in the nature of a binding contract was put in writing by Wards, nor was any document purporting to be a binding agreement signed by it. We think, also, that Wards' understanding of the connotation of the phrase "duty to bargain collectively" is acceptable, insofar as it goes, but that it is incomplete. As we view the statute, it is the obligation of the parties to participate actively in the deliberations so as to indicate a present intention to find a basis for agreement, and a sincere effort must be made to reach a common ground. As was said in NLRB v. Reed & Prince Mfg. Co., 1 Cir., 118 F.2d 874, 885: "The respondent, following the beginning of the strike, was legally bound to confer and negotiate sincerely with the representatives of its employees. It was required to do so with an open mind and a sincere desire to reach an agreement in a spirit of amity and cooperation. The cases setting forth this obligation are many, and it is well settled that a mere formal pretence at collective bargaining with a completely closed mind and without this spirit of cooperation and good faith is not a fulfillment of his duty. [Citations omitted.]"

As illustrative of the attitude with which Wards approached and conducted the bargaining conferences, and from which, among other factors, the Board might have inferred that Wards exhibited a want of good faith, we shall briefly refer to a few matters which arose out of the conferences.

It appears from the findings of the Board that Wards never, at any time in the course of the negotiations, directly promised to sign a written contract, although its representative was asked on several occasions whether or not he would do so. Always the reply was that the question was "premature," that it had best be answered when agreement was reached. Considering as immaterial the fact that the "parties had not yet reached complete understanding," the Board concluded that this type of answer "was tantamount to a refusal to bargain altogether." Certainly the answer was evasive and not calculated to reveal whether or not the Company would sign an agreement if any was reached, and may well have had a discouraging influence. The significance of the answer becomes apparent when we consider that the Supreme Court's decision in H. J. Heinz Co. v. NLRB, 311 U.S. 514, 526, 61 S.Ct. 320, 85 L.Ed. 309—which settled once and for all that it is a "refusal to bargain" to decline to sign an agreement entered into—was not filed until some weeks after the negotiations here had broken down. We believe the Board was entitled to consider the failure of Wards to state that it would put into writing any contract to which it might agree as a pertinent circumstance on the issue of refusal to bargain. Hartsell Mills Co. v. NLRB, 4 Cir., 111 F.2d 291, 292.

The Board regarded as an additional factor in a design to refuse to bargain the action of Ward's representative respecting a provision of the proposed contracts. The proposed contracts contained provisions that if the employees were worked in excess of five hours without a meal period, the excess time should be paid for at the overtime rate. Ward's representative insisted that the word "five" be changed to "six" to conform to existing practice. The record reveals, however, that he had been advised by his superior at the home office that "under normal conditions an employee should not be worked more than five consecutive hours without a meal period." Not even Wards doubted the reasonableness of such a demand; nevertheless Powell, its representative, stood firm. No court in the land could hold that the Board was not justified in drawing an inference unfavorable to Wards from its conduct respecting this provision. A reasonable man might conclude that it refused to agree to this provision because it had no intention of entering into a contract, or of binding itself at all.

The McGowan activity, discussed heretofore, was also regarded by the Board as a pertinent circumstance tending to show the Company's lack of good faith in conducting negotiations.

A further circumstance which supports the Board in drawing the inference that Wards was "stalling," arose out of the conference of November 25, between Wards and Warehousemen. At this meeting Estabrook, secretary for Warehousemen, suggested that he would fly to Chicago for a conference with Barr, Powell's superior, in an effort to induce

Wards to change its policy respecting "union shop." Powell's report of this discussion is contained in his letter of November 26, addressed to Barr, and which reads in part as follows: ". . . Mr. Estabrook then suggested he would be glad to fly to Chicago to talk with you, if there were some possibility that our policy could be changed. At first they insisted we give them a reply within twenty-four hours, but later agreed to allow us until noon on Thursday, November 28. *I will wait until Thursday morning at which time I will call Mr. White* [a union representative] in San Francisco and explain that you will be glad to meet with union representatives in Chicago and listen to their argument, . . ." (Emphasis supplied.)

From this it appears that Powell *knew* on the 25th, or, at the latest, the 26th, what his answer was going to be, and deliberately refrained from informing White until the 28th—and this in face of the union's desire for an immediate answer. Unquestionably the Board was privileged to draw from these delaying tactics an inference unfavorable to Wards' "good faith" in the negotiations.

The Board, in reviewing the various acts of Wards as a non-performance or mis-performance of its duty to bargain, appears to attach especial significance to the refusal of Wards to submit counterproposals to the unions at any time during the course of the negotiations. Wards was not bound to offer a counterproposal (NLRB v. Express Pub. Co., 5 Cir., 111 F.2d 588, 589), but when one is asked for, it ought to be made, although not indispensable (Globe Cotton Mills v. NLRB, 5 Cir., 103 F.2d 91, 94). A counterproposal would, no doubt, have put Wards' willingness to bargain beyond question, and in the absence thereof the Board may not be condemned for drawing the opposite conclusion. While the Act places upon the employees the burden of instituting the bargaining proceedings and no burden in this respect upon the employer, it is not incumbent upon the employees continually to present new contracts until ultimately one meets the approval of the company. M. H. Ritzwoller Co. v. NLRB, 7 Cir., 114 F.2d 432, 436.

The incidents just discussed, while perhaps, not controlling in and of themselves, in cumulative effect give impetus and decisiveness to the Board's conclusions. They are simply manifestations of an attitude— intent, if you will—persisted in by Wards, a negative attitude which amounted to, in its result, a refusal to bargain. In its brief, Wards says, "The duty [to bargain] is to do nothing or say nothing which would make agreement on those terms [mutually acceptable] impossible." This is not a carrying of the burden of the duty to bargain, for, in effect, it means to do nothing or say nothing to make agreement possible. Throughout the conferences there is apparent a studied design of aloofness, of disinterestedness, of unwillingness to go forward, upon the part of Wards, which found its answer in the Board's conclusion of refusal to bargain.

Wards' conduct throughout the conferences was an all too literal adherence to the rule formulated by itself as a fulfillment of the duty to bargain collectively: "to participate in such discussion as is necessary to avoid mutual misunderstanding." To do this and nothing more is to fall far short of the accomplishment of the statutory duty to bargain collectively, because the affirmative efforts of both parties are required—there must be, in a real sense, active cooperation. The cases, supra, defining "collective bargaining" sustain this view. See, also, NLRB v. George P. Pilling & Son Co., 3 Cir., 119 F.2d 32, 37. In Singer Mfg. Co. v. NLRB, 7 Cir., 119 F.2d 131, 134, the court said: ". . . The greatest of rascals may solemnly affirm his honesty of purpose; that does not foreclose a jury from finding from the evidence submitted that he possesses no trace of such innocent quality. We think the Board had full authority to determine as a fact whether petitioner was acting in good faith or whether its actions amounted to a mere superficial pretense at bargaining,—whether it had actually the intent to bargain, sincerely and earnestly,—whether the negotiations were captious and accompanied by an active purpose and intent to defeat or obstruct real bargaining. [Citations omitted.]" . . .

Questions

1. Considering all the evidence summarized by Judge Garrecht, would you conclude that Wards had refused to bargain?

2. What purpose is served by introducing the concept of "good faith" into the law regarding collective bargaining? Is it necessary to the disposition of this case?

3. What problems in administration and enforcement of the law may result from reliance on a "good faith" standard? Illustrate your answer by reference to the Wards case.

4. Does the evolution of a "good faith" standard support the suggestion that the law may perform, or attempt to perform, an educational function?

THE DUTY TO BARGAIN EXTENDED: THE TAFT-HARTLEY ACT

[Review pp. 891–892, supra.]

PUBLIC LAW 80–101, 61 STAT. 136, APPROVED JUNE 23, 1947. [Taft-Hartley Act]

Section 8. (a) It shall be an unfair labor practice for an employer—

* * *

(5) to refuse to bargain collectively with the representatives of his employees, . . .

(b) It shall be an unfair labor practice for a labor organization or its agents—

* * *

(3) to refuse to bargain collectively with an employer, provided it is the representative of his employees . . .

* * *

(d) For the purpose of this section, to bargain collectively is the performance of the mutual obligation of the employer and the representative of the employees to meet at reasonable times and confer in good faith with respect to wages, hours, and other terms and conditions of employment, or

the negotiation of an agreement, or any question arising thereunder, and the execution of a written contract incorporating any agreement reached if requested by either party, but such obligation does not compel either party to agree to a proposal or require the making of a concession:
. . .

Questions

1. Are the requirements of Section 8(d) significantly different than the rules regarding the duty to bargain as summarized by Judge Garrecht in the Ward's case? See pp. 1111–1112 *supra*.

2. Does the codification in Section 8(d) of standards evolved by the Board and the Courts constitute legislative commendation of the administrative and judicial efforts in this area? How might the enactment of 8(d) be interpreted to be a reprimand to the Board and the Courts?

3. Assuming that the Taft-Hartley Act was directed against labor how would you explain the inclusion of 8(b) (3) and 8(d) in the Act? Does the adoption of these amendments offer any insight into a) business attitudes toward collective bargaining as of 1947; and b) the relative bargaining strength of labor and management in 1947?

4. Sections 8(b) (3) and 8(d) were both an endorsement of the Wagner Act and the beginning of a more legally sophisticated approach to collective bargaining. Do you agree with this assertion?

MATTER OF TRUITT MFG. CO.

National Labor Relations Board, 1955.
110 NLRB 856.

[During negotiations upon the reopening of a collective bargaining agreement the company offered a 2½ cents an hour increase. The union rejected the proposal in writing and asserting that the company could afford to pay a 10 cents an hour general increase, requested permission to have a certified public accountant examine the company's financial records to ascertain the merit of its assertion that it was unable to meet the union's proposal. The company refused on the ground that "confidential financial information concerning the affairs of this Company is not a matter of bargaining or discussing with the Union. The Company's position throughout the recent negotiations and in previous sessions with you and the Union, has been that the question of granting a wage increase concerns our competitive bidding for jobs to keep the plant operating." The letter then went on to argue that Truitt's average wage was already higher than the average wage of competing companies in the area. There was further correspondence but neither side substantially changed its position. In the oral discussions Truitt's officers referred to the company's precarious financial condition and said it would "break the company" to increase wages 10 cents an hour. The union struck for five days but Truitt remained firm and the men returned to work. The union then filed unfair labor practice charges.]

Decision and Order of the NLRB

* * *

We agree with the Trial Examiner that the Respondent failed to bargain in good faith with respect to wages in violation of Section 8(a) (5) of the Act. We do not, however, mean to imply, nor do we adopt the statement of the Trial Examiner, that the Respondent's failure to substantiate its economic position as to wages obligates the Respondent to accede to the Union's wage demands. On the other hand, it is settled law, that when an employer seeks to justify the refusal of a wage increase upon an economic basis, as did the Respondent herein, good-faith bargaining under the Act requires that upon request the employer attempt to substantiate its economic position by reasonable proof. In the present case, we are satisfied that the Respondent has failed to submit such reasonable proof. We shall, therefore, order that the Respondent bargain collectively with the Union.

Upon the entire record in the case, and pursuant to Section 10(c) of the National Labor Relations Act, the National Labor Relations Board hereby orders that the Respondent, Truitt Manufacturing Co., Greensboro, North Carolina, its officers, agents, successors, and assigns, shall:

* * *

(b) Upon request furnish Shopmen's Local 729, International Association of Bridge, Structural and Ornamental Iron Workers of America, A.F.L., with such statistical and other information as will substantiate the Respondent's position of its economic inability to pay the requested wage increase and will enable the Shopmen's Local No. 729, International Association of Bridge, Structural and Ornamental Iron Workers of America, A.F.L., to discharge its functions as the statutory representative of the employees in the unit found appropriate by the Board.

Notes and Questions

1. Is it reasonable to infer that the refusal to disclose the records in Truitt was a manifestation of lack of good faith? Is it necessary to conclude that the failure to disclose the records manifested lack of good faith?

2. What are the advantages and disadvantages of a rule of law which establishes that a particular set of facts, *e. g.*, a refusal to disclose financial records to support a bargaining position, is necessarily —per se—an unfair labor practice?

3. Truitt appealed from the Board decision and order to the Fourth Circuit Court of Appeals, which set aside the order, Matter of Truitt Mfg. Co., 224 F.2d 869 (4th Cir. 1955). The Union carried the appeal to the United States Supreme Court. The Court, in an opinion by Justice Black, reversed the Circuit Court and reinstated the Board order. Matter of Truitt Mfg. Co., 351 U.S. 149, 76 S.Ct. 753 (1956).

NATIONAL LABOR RELATIONS BOARD v. KATZ

Supreme Court of the United States, 1962.
369 U.S. 736, 82 S.Ct. 1107, 8 L.Ed.2d 230.

MR. JUSTICE BRENNAN delivered the opinion of the Court.

Is it a violation of the duty "to bargain collectively" imposed by § 8(a)
(5) of the National Labor Relations Act for an employer, without first consulting a union with which it is carrying on bona fide contract negotiations,
to institute changes regarding matters which are subjects of mandatory
bargaining under § 8(d) and which are in fact under discussion? The
National Labor Relations Board answered the question affirmatively in
this case, in a decision which expressly disclaimed any finding that the
totality of the respondents' conduct manifested bad faith in the pending
negotiations. 126 N.L.R.B. 288. A divided panel of the Court of Appeals for
the Second Circuit denied enforcement of the Board's cease-and-desist order,
finding in our decision in Labor Board v. Insurance Agents' Union, 361
U.S. 477, 80 S.Ct. 419, a broad rule that the statutory duty to bargain cannot
be held to be violated, when bargaining is in fact being carried on, without
a finding of the respondent's subjective bad faith in negotiating. 289 F.2d
700. The Court of Appeals said:

"We are of the opinion that the unilateral acts here complained of, occurring as they did during the negotiating of a collective bargaining agreement, do not *per se* constitute a refusal to bargain collectively and *per se* are
not violative of § 8(a) (5). While the subject is not generally free from
doubt, it is our conclusion that in the posture of this case a necessary requisite of a Section 8(a) (5) violation is a finding that the employer failed to
bargain in good faith." 289 F.2d, at 702–703.

We granted certiorari, 368 U.S. 811, in order to consider whether the
Board's decision and order were contrary to Insurance Agents. We find
nothing in the Board's decision inconsistent with *Insurance Agents* and hold
that the Court of Appeals erred in refusing to enforce the Board's order.

The respondents are partners engaged in steel fabricating under the
firm name of Williamsburg Steel Products Company Following a consent
election in a unit consisting of all technical employees at the company's plant,
the Board, on July 5, 1956, certified as their collective bargaining representative Local 66 of the Architectural and Engineering Guild, American Federation of Technical Engineers, AFL–CIO. The Board simultaneously certified
the union as representative of similar units at five other companies which,
with the respondent company, were members of the Hollow Metal Door &
Buck Association. The certifications related to separate units at the several
plants and did not purport to establish a multi-employer bargaining unit.

On July 11, 1956, the union sent identical letters to each of the six companies, requesting collective bargaining. Negotiations were invited on either
an individual or "association wide" basis, with the reservation that wage
rates and increases would have to be discussed with each employer separately.
A follow-up letter of July 19, 1956, repeated the request for contract negotiations and enumerated proposed subjects for discussion. Included were merit
increases, general wage levels and increases, and a sick-leave proposal.

The first meeting between the company and the union took place on August 30, 1956. On this occasion, as at the ten other conferences held between October 2, 1956, and May 13, 1957, all six companies were in attendance and represented by the same counsel. It is undisputed that the subject of merit increases was raised at the August 30, 1956, meeting although there is an unresolved conflict as to whether an agreement was reached on joint participation by the company and the union in merit reviews, or whether the subject was simply mentioned and put off for discussion at a later date. It is also clear that proposals concerning sick leave were made. Several meetings were held during October and one in November, at which merit raises and sick leave were each discussed on at least two occasions. It appears, however, that little progress was made.

On December 5, a meeting was held at the New York State Mediation Board attended by a mediator of that agency, who was at that time mediating a contract negotiation between the union and Aetna Steel Products Corporation, a member of the Association bargaining separately from the others; and a decision was reached to recess the negotiations involved here pending the results of the Aetna negotiation. When the mediator called the next meeting on March 29, 1957, the completed Aetna contract was introduced into the discussion. At a resumption of bargaining on April 4, the company, along with the other employers, offered a three-year agreement with certain initial and prospective automatic wage increases. The offer was rejected. Further meetings with the mediator on April 11, May 1, and May 13, 1957, produced no agreement, and no further meetings were held.

Meanwhile, on April 16, 1957, the union had filed the charge upon which the General Counsel's complaint later issued. As amended and amplified at the hearing and construed by the Board, the complaint's charge of unfair labor practices particularly referred to three acts by the company: unilaterally granting numerous merit increases in October 1956 and January 1957; unilaterally announcing a change in sick-leave policy in March 1957; and April 1957. As the ensuing litigation has developed, the company has defended against the charges along two fronts: First, it asserts that the unilateral changes occurred after a bargaining impasse had developed through the union's fault in adopting obstructive tactics. According to the Board, however, "the evidence is clear that the Respondent undertook its unilateral actions before negotiations were discontinued in May 1957, or before, as we find on the record, the existence of any possible impasse." 126 N.L.R.B., at 289–290. There is ample support in the record considered as a whole for this finding of fact, which is consistent with the Examiner's Intermediate Report. 126 N.L.R.B., at 295–296, and which the Court of Appeals did not question.

The second line of defense was that the Board could not hinge a conclusion that § 8(a)(5) had been violated on unilateral actions alone, without making a finding of the employer's subjective bad faith at the bargaining table; and that the unilateral actions were merely evidence relevant to the issue of subjective good faith. This argument prevailed in the Court of Appeals which remanded the cases to the Board saying:

"although we might . . . be justified in denying enforcement without remand, . . . since the Board's finding of an unfair labor practice impliedly proceeds from an erroneous view that specific unilateral acts, regardless of bad faith, may constitute violations of § 8(a) (5), the case should be remanded to the Board in order that it may have an opportunity to take additional evidence, and make such findings as may be warranted by the record." 289 F.2d, at 709.

The duty "to bargain collectively" enjoined by § 8(a) (5) is defined by § 8(d) as the duty to "meet . . . and confer in good faith with respect to wages, hours, and other terms and conditions of employment." Clearly, the duty thus defined may be violated without a general failure of subjective good faith; for there is no occasion to consider the issue of good faith if a party has refused even to negotiate *in fact*—"to meet . . . and confer"—about any of the mandatory subjects. A refusal to negotiate *in fact* as to any subject which is within § 8(d), and about which the union seeks to negotiate, violates § 8(a) (5) though the employer has every desire to reach agreement with the union upon an over-all collective agreement and earnestly and in all good faith bargains to that end. We hold that an employer's unilateral change in conditions of employment under negotiation is similarly a violation of § 8(a) (5), for it is a circumvention of the duty to negotiate which frustrates the objectives of § 8(a) (5) much as does a flat refusal.

The unilateral actions of the respondent illustrate the policy and practical considerations which support our conclusion.

We consider first the matter of sick leave. A sick-leave plan had been in effect since May 1956, under which employees were allowed ten paid sick-leave days annually and could accumulate half the unused days, or up to five days each year. Changes in the plan were sought and proposals and counter-proposals had come up at three bargaining conferences. In March 1957, the company, without first notifying or consulting the union, announced changes in the plan, which reduced from ten to five the number of paid sick-leave days per year, but allowed accumulation of twice the unused days, thus increasing to ten the number of days which might be carried over. This action plainly frustrated the statutory objective of establishing working conditions through bargaining. Some employees might view the change to be a diminution of benefits. Others, more interested in accumulating sick-leave days, might regard the change as an improvement. If one view or the other clearly prevailed among the employees, the unilateral action might well mean that the employer had either uselessly dissipated trading material or aggravated the sick-leave issue. On the other hand, if the employees were more evenly divided on the merits of the company's changes, the union negotiators, beset by conflicting factions, might be led to adopt a protective vagueness on the issue of sick leave, which also would inhibit the useful discussion contemplated by Congress in imposing the specific obligation to bargain collectively.

Other considerations appear from consideration of the respondents' unilateral action in increasing wages. At the April 4, 1957 meeting, the employers offered, and the union rejected, a three-year contract with an immediate across-the-board increase of $7.50 per week, to be followed at the end of the first year and again at the end of the second by further increases of $5 for employees earning less than $90 at those times. Shortly thereafter, without having advised or consulted with the union, the company announced a new system of automatic wage increases whereby there would be an increase of $5 every three months up to $74.99 per week; an increase of $5 every six months between $75 and $90 per week; and a merit review every six months for employees earning over $90 per week. It is clear at a glance that the automatic wage increase system which was instituted unilaterally was considerably more generous than that which had shortly theretofore been offered to and rejected by the union. Such action conclusively manifested bad faith in the negotiations, Labor Board v. Crompton-Highland Mills, 337 U.S. 217, 69 S.Ct. 960, and so would have violated § 8(a) (5) even on the Court of Appeals' interpretation, though no additional evidence of bad faith appeared. An employer is not required to lead with his best offer; he is free to bargain. But even after an impasse is reached he has no license to grant wage increases greater than any he has ever offered the union at the bargaining table, for such action is necessarily inconsistent with a sincere desire to conclude an agreement with the union.

The respondents' third unilateral action related to merit increases, which are also a subject of mandatory bargaining. Labor Board v. Allison & Co., 165 F.2d 766. The matter of merit increases had been raised at three of the conferences during 1956 but no final understanding had been reached. In January 1957, the company, without notice to the union, granted merit increases to 20 employees out of the approximately 50 in the unit, the increases ranging between $2 and $10. This action too must be viewed as tantamount to an outright refusal to negotiate on that subject, and therefore as a violation of § 8(a) (5), unless the fact that the January raises were in line with the company's long-standing practice of granting quarterly or semi-annual merit reviews—in effect, were a mere continuation of the status quo—differentiates them from the wage increases and the changes in the sick-leave plan. We do not think it does. Whatever might be the case as to so-called "merit raises" which are in fact simply automatic increases to which the employer has already committed himself, the raises here in question were in no sense automatic, but were informed by a large measure of discretion. There simply is no way in such a case for a union to know whether or not there has been a substantial departure from past practice, and therefore the union may properly insist that the company negotiate as to the procedures and criteria for determining such increases.

It is apparent from what we have said why we see nothing in Insurance Agents contrary to the Board's decision. The union in that case had not in any way whatever foreclosed discussion of any issue, by unilateral actions or otherwise. The conduct complained of consisted of partial-strike tactics designed to put pressure on the employer to come to terms with the union negotiators. We held that Congress had not, in § 8(b) (3), the counterpart of § 8(a) (5), empowered the Board to pass judgment on the legitimacy of any particular economic weapon used in support of genuine negotiations. But the Board *is* authorized to order the cessation of behavior which is in effect a refusal to negotiate, or which directly obstructs or inhibits the actual process of discussion, or which reflects a cast of mind against reaching agreement. Unilateral action by an employer without prior discussion with the union does amount to a refusal to negotiate about the affected conditions of employment under negotiation, and must of necessity obstruct bargaining, contrary to the congressional policy. It will often disclose an unwillingness to agree with the union. It will rarely be justified by any reason of substance. It follows that the Board may hold such unilateral action to be an unfair labor practice in violation of § 8(a) (5), without also finding the employer guilty of overall subjective bad faith. While we do not foreclose the possibility that there might be circumstances which the Board could or should accept as excusing or justifying unilateral action, no such case is presented here.

The judgment of the Court of Appeals is reversed and the case is remanded with direction to the court to enforce the Board's order.

It is so ordered.

MR. JUSTICE FRANKFURTER took no part in the decision of this case.

MR. JUSTICE WHITE took no part in the consideration or decision of this case.

Questions

1. Was the Board's ruling in this case based on a finding that the company representative's behavior: (a) was in effect a refusal to negotiate; or (b) directly obstructed or inhibited the actual process of negotiation; or (c) reflected a cast of mind against reaching an agreement?

2. How, if at all, could a Board order requiring the cessation of certain behavior influence the subjective intent which motivated that behavior? Would the application of punitive sanctions for a refusal to bargain in good faith be more or less likely to shape the attitudes of bargainers to a "right" subjective intent? When the law demands of a person that he act in "good faith" is this an attempt to legislate morality?

3. Why did the Board conclude that the company negotiators had refused to bargain, rather than finding a failure to bargain in good faith? If the Board had concluded on the basis of the whole record that the company negotiators had refused to bargain in good faith, do you think Justice Brennan would have upheld that finding?

4. Isn't it clearly a fiction to hold that the company negotiators refused to bargain in this case? Would it not be more honest to say that the company's behavior was improper because it tended to make it more difficult for the Union negotiators to realize their objectives at the bargaining table and tended to disrupt the solidarity of the organized employees? But could or should the Board—or the courts— legitimately conclude that behavior having such effects constitutes a *per se* unfair labor practice? Would the policy of the Wagner Act support such a finding? Would the provisions of the Taft-Hartley Act support such a finding?

5. Would you say that decisions such as Katz tend to compel agreement rather than merely compelling bargaining?

6. Does a decision such as Katz indicate that the law has succeeded in establishing good faith as the standard in collective bargaining?

NATIONAL LABOR RELATIONS BOARD v. WOOSTER DIVISION OF BORG–WARNER CORP.

Supreme Court of the United States, 1958.
356 U.S. 342, 78 S.Ct. 718, 2 L.Ed.2d 823.

MR. JUSTICE BURTON* delivered the opinion of the Court.

In these cases an employer insisted that its collective-bargaining contract with certain of its employees include: (1) a "ballot" clause calling for a pre-strike secret vote of those employees (union and non-union) as to the employer's last offer, and (2) a "recognition" clause which excluded, as a party to the contract, the International Union which had been certified by the National Labor Relations Board as the employees' exclusive bargaining agent, and substituted for it the agent's uncertified local affiliate. The Board held that the employer's insistence upon either of such clauses amounted to a refusal to bargain, in violation of § 8(a) (5) of the National Labor Relations Act, as amended. The issue turns on whether either of these clauses comes within the scope of mandatory collective bargaining as defined in § 8(d) of the Act. For the reasons hereafter stated, we agree with the Board that neither clause comes within that definition. Therefore, we sustain the Board's order directing the employer to cease insisting upon either clause as a condition precedent to accepting any collective-bargaining contract.

Late in 1952, the International Union, United Automobile, Aircraft and Agricultural Implement Workers of America, CIO (here called International) was certified by the Board to the Wooster (Ohio) Division of the Borg-Warner Corporation (here called the company) as the elected representative of an appropriate unit of the company's employees. Shortly thereafter, International chartered Local No. 1239, UAW–CIO (here called the Local). Together the unions presented the company with a comprehensive collective-bargaining agreement. In the "recognition" clause, the unions described themselves as both the "International Union, United Automobile, Aircraft and Agricultural Implement Workers of America and its Local Union No. 1239, U. A. W.–C. I. O. * * *."

The company submitted a counter-proposal which recognized as the sole representative of the employees "Local Union 1239, affiliated with the International Union, United Automobile, Aircraft and Agricultural Implement Workers of America (UAW–CIO)." The unions' negotiators objected because such a clause disregarded the Board's certification of International as the employees' representative. The negotiators declared that the employees would accept no agreement which excluded International as a party.

The company's counterproposal also contained the "ballot" clause, · · · In summary, this clause provided that, as to all nonarbitrable issues (which eventually included modification, amendment or termination of the contract), there would be a 30-day negotiation period after which, before the union could strike, there would have to be a secret ballot taken

* Justice Harold H. Burton was appointed to the Supreme Court by President Truman in 1945. He practiced law in Cleveland, Ohio from 1918 to 1935. He was active in politics, serving as Mayor of Cleveland (1935–1940), and U. S. Senator from Ohio (1941–1945). Justice Burton resigned from the Supreme Court in 1958, and he died in 1964.

among all employees in the unit (union and non-union) on the company's last offer. In the event a majority of the employees rejected the company's last offer, the company would have an opportunity, within 72 hours, of making a new proposal and having a vote on it prior to any strike. The unions' negotiators announced they would not accept this clause "under any conditions."

From the time that the company first proposed these clauses, the employees' representatives thus made it clear that each was wholly unacceptable. The company's representatives made it equally clear that no agreement would be entered into by it unless the agreement contained both clauses. In view of this impasse, there was little further discussion of the clauses, although the parties continued to bargain as to other matters. The company submitted a "package" proposal covering economic issues but made the offer contingent upon the satisfactory settlement of "all other issues * * *." The "package" included both of the controversial clauses. On March 15, 1953, the unions rejected that proposal and the membership voted to strike on March 20 unless a settlement were reached by them. None was reached and the unions struck. Negotiations, nevertheless, continued. On April 21, the unions asked the company whether the latter would withdraw its demand for the "ballot" and "recognition" clauses if the unions accepted all other pending requirements of the company. The company declined and again insisted upon acceptance of its "package," including both clauses. Finally, on May 5, the Local, upon the recommendation of International, gave in and entered into an agreement containing both controversial clauses.

In the meantime, International had filed charges with the Board claiming that the company, by the above conduct, was guilty of an unfair labor practice within the meaning of § 8(a) (5) of the Act. The trial examiner found no bad faith on either side. However, he found that the company had made it a condition precedent to its acceptance of any agreement that the agreement include both the "ballot" and the "recognition" clauses. For that reason, he recommended that the company be found guilty of a *per se* unfair labor practice in violation of § 8(a) (5). He reasoned that, because each of the controversial clauses was outside of the scope of mandatory bargaining as defined in § 8(d) of the Act, the company's insistence upon them, against the permissible opposition of the unions, amounted to a refusal to bargain as to the mandatory subjects of collective bargaining. The Board, with two members dissenting, adopted the recommendations of the examiner. 113 N.L.R.B. 1288, 1298. In response to the Board's petition to enforce its order, the Court of Appeals set aside that portion of the order relating to the "ballot" clause, but upheld the Board's order as to the "recognition" clause. 236 F.2d 898.

Because of the importance of the issues and because of alleged conflicts among the Courts of Appeals, we granted the Board's petition for certiorari in No. 53, relating to the "ballot" clause, and the company's cross-petition in No. 78, relating to the "recognition" clause. 353 U.S. 907, 77 S.Ct. 661, 1 L.Ed.2d 662.

We turn first to the relevant provisions of the statute. · · ·

Read together, [Section 8(a) (5) and Section 8(d)] establish the obligation of the employer and the representative of its employees to bargain with each other in good faith with respect to "wages, hours, and other terms and conditions of employment * * *." The duty is limited to those subjects, and within that area neither party is legally obligated to yield. National Labor Relations Board v. American Insurance Co., 343 U.S. 395, 72 S.Ct. 824, 96 L.Ed. 1027. As to other matters, however, each party is free to bargain or not to bargain, and to agree or not to agree.

The company's good faith has met the requirements of the statute as to the subjects of mandatory bargaining. But that good faith does not license the employer to refuse to enter into agreements on the ground that they do not include some proposal which is not a mandatory subject of bargaining. We agree with the Board that such conduct is, in substance, a refusal to bargain about the subjects that are within the scope of mandatory bargaining. This does not mean that bargaining is to be confined to the statutory subjects. Each of the two controversial clauses is lawful in itself. Each would be enforceable if agreed to by the unions. But it does not follow that, because the company may propose these clauses, it can lawfully insist upon them as a condition to any agreement.

Since it is lawful to insist upon matters within the scope of mandatory bargaining and unlawful to insist upon matters without, the issue here is whether either the "ballot" or the "recognition" clause is a subject within the phrase "wages, hours, and other terms and conditions of employment" which defines mandatory bargaining. The "ballot" clause is not within that definition. It relates only to the procedure to be followed by the employees among themselves before their representative may call a strike or refuse a final offer. It settles no term or condition of employment—it merely calls for an advisory vote of the employees. It is not a partial "no-strike" clause. A "no-strike" clause prohibits the employees from striking during the life of the contract. It regulates the relations between the employer and the employees. See National Labor Relations Board v. American Insurance Co., supra, 343 U.S. at page 408, n. 22, 72 S.Ct. at page 831, 96 L.Ed. 1027. The "ballot" clause, on the other hand, deals only with relations between the employees and their unions. It substantially modifies the collective-bargaining system provided for in the statute by weakening the independence of the "representative" chosen by the employees. It enables the employer, in effect, to deal with its employees rather than with their statutory representative. Cf. Medo Photo Corp. v. National Labor Relations Board, 321 U.S. 678, 64 S.Ct. 830, 88 L.Ed. 1007.

The "recognition" clause likewise does not come within the definition of mandatory bargaining. The statute requires the company to bargain with the certified representative of its employees. It is an evasion of that duty to insist that the certified agent not be a party to the collective-bargaining contract. The Act does not prohibit the voluntary addition of a party, but that does not authorize the employer to exclude the certified representative from the contract.

Accordingly, the judgment of the Court of Appeals in No. 53 is reversed and the cause remanded for disposition consistent with this opinion. In No. 78, the judgment is affirmed.

No. 53—Reversed and remanded.

No. 78—Affirmed.

MR. JUSTICE FRANKFURTER joins this opinion insofar as it holds that insistence by the company on the "recognition" clause, in conflict with the provisions of the Act requiring an employer to bargain with the representative of his employees, constituted an unfair labor practice. He agrees with the views of MR. JUSTICE HARLAN regarding the "ballot" clause. The subject matter of that clause is not so clearly outside the reasonable range of industrial bargaining as to establish a refusal to bargain in good faith, and is not prohibited simply because not deemed to be within the rather vague scope of the obligatory provisions of § 8(d).

MR. JUSTICE HARLAN, whom MR. JUSTICE CLARK and MR. JUSTICE WHITTAKER join, concurring in part and dissenting in part.

I agree that the company's insistence on the "recognition" clause constituted an unfair labor practice, but reach that conclusion by a different route from that taken by the Court. However, in light of the finding below that the company bargained in "good faith," I dissent from the view that its insistence on the "ballot" clause can support the charge of an unfair labor practice. · · ·

Preliminarily, I must state that I am unable to grasp a concept of "bargaining" which enables one to "propose" a particular point, but not to "insist" on it as a condition to agreement. The right to bargain becomes illusory if one is not free to press a proposal in good faith to the point of insistence. Surely adoption of so inherently vague and fluid a standard is apt to inhibit the entire bargaining process because of a party's fear that strenuous argument might shade into forbidden insistence and thereby produce a charge of an unfair labor practice. This watered-down notion of "bargaining" which the Court imports into the Act with reference to matters not within the scope of § 8(d) appears as foreign to the labor field as it would be to the commercial world. To me all of this adds up to saying that the Act limits *effective* "bargaining" to subjects within the three fields referred to in § 8(d), that is "wages, hours, and other terms and conditions of employment," even though the Court expressly disclaims so holding.

* * *

Questions

1. Isn't it clearly a fiction to hold in Wooster Division that the company refused to bargain? Would it not be more honest to find that the company committed an unfair labor practice because it was attempting to force negotiation on a matter not properly subject to bargaining? But should the Board—or the courts—make the determination that there are matters not properly subject to bargaining—other than those matters proscribed by the NLRA?

2. Do decisions like Katz and Wooster Division indicate that the concepts of bargaining and bargaining in good faith are being altered to serve different ends than those originally intended for them? Is it

possible that these concepts have served an educational function so well, that it is now possible to use them as a vehicle for advancing to the consideration of a new level of problems? Before answering this question, read the following excerpt.

NATIONAL LABOR RELATIONS BOARD v. GENERAL ELECTRIC CO.

United States Court of Appeals, Second Circuit, 1969.
418 F.2d 736.

[Footnotes omitted.]

IRVING R. KAUFMAN, CIRCUIT JUDGE.

Almost ten years after the events that gave rise to this controversy, we are called upon to determine whether an employer may be guilty of bad faith bargaining, though he reaches an agreement with the union, albeit on the company's terms. We must also decide if the company committed three specific violations of the duty to bargain by failing to furnish information requested by the union, by attempting to deal separately with IUE locals, and by presenting a personal accident insurance program on a take-it-or-leave-it basis.

I.

THE PRIOR PROCEEDINGS

In the wake of what it regarded as unsatisfactory negotiations with the General Electric Company (GE) during the summer and fall of 1960, the International Union of Electrical, Radio and Machine Workers, AFL–CIO (IUE) filed unfair labor practice charges with the National Labor Relations Board. The General Counsel, on April 12, 1961, filed a complaint alleging that GE had committed unfair labor practices in violation of sections 8(a)(1), 8(a)(3), and 8(a)(5) of the National Labor Relations Act, 29 U.S.C. §§ 158(a)(1), 158(a)(3), and 158(a)(5) (1964). Hearings were held before a trial examiner between July, 1961, and January, 1963, and included testimony, oral argument, and submission of briefs. The Trial Examiner issued his Intermediate Report on April 1, 1963, which found GE guilty of several unfair labor practices. GE and the IUE filed exceptions to the Intermediate Report, and on December 16, 1964, the NLRB agreed with the Trial Examiner. 150 N.L.R.B. 192 (1964).

There followed the race to the courthouse that is an unhappy feature too often encountered in these matters. See Carrington, Crowded Dockets and the Courts of Appeals: The Threat to the Function of Review and the National Law, 82 Harv.L.Rev. 542, 598–600 (1969). Since GE does business in every state, every court of appeals has jurisdiction, if GE's petition for review is first filed there. See 29 U.S.C. § 160(f) (1964); 28 U.S.C. § 2112 (1964). The IUE claimed that it filed in the District of Columbia Circuit 14 seconds before GE handed its petition to the clerk in the Seventh Circuit. GE's version of course differed. The NLRB, admitting its confusion (not without reason, it would seem), suggested that since the question of timing was incapable of rational solution, the Second Circuit, where the unfair labor practices complained of occurred, would be the logical place to begin. The District of Columbia and Seventh Circuits agreed. IUE v. NLRB, 120 U.S.App.D.C. 45, 343 F.2d 327 (1965); GE v. NLRB, 58 LRRM 2694 (7th Cir. 1965). Another year was required to determine that the Union's proper status in the action was that of intervenor. NLRB v. General Electric Co., 59 LRRM 2094, 2095 (2d Cir. 1965), vacated and remanded, IUE v. NLRB, 382 U.S. 366, 86 S.Ct. 528, 15 L.Ed.2d 420 (1966), modified on remand NLRB v. General Electric Co., 358 F.2d 292 (2d Cir.), certiorari denied, 385 U.S. 898, 87 S.Ct. 201, 17 L.Ed.2d 130 (1966). See International-al Union, United Auto., Aerospace, etc., Local 283 v. Scofield, 382 U.S. 205, 86 S.Ct. 373, 15 L.Ed.2d 272 (1965).

In order for the action to reach its present state of ripeness, this court consolidated GE's petition for review (No. 29576) with the Board's petition for enforcement (No. 29502). NLRB v. General Electric Co., 358 F.2d 292 (2d Cir. 1966), certiorari denied 385 U.S. 898, 87 S.Ct. 201 (1966). Another year and a half passed while the parties attempted to settle the case without recourse to further litigation. When a satisfactory settlement proved too elusive, they reentered the fray with renewed vigor, undiminished by the passage of time, two successive collective bargaining contracts (1963 and 1966), and by another suit over proper representation arising out of the 1966 negotiations. McLeod for and on Behalf of NLRB v. General Electric Co., 257 F.Supp. 690 (S.D.N.Y.), reversed 366 F.2d 847 (2d Cir. 1966), remanded 385 U.S. 533, 87 S.Ct. 637, 17 L.Ed.2d 588 (1967). See also General Electric Co. v. NLRB, 412 F.2d 512 (2d Cir., June 9, 1969).

II.

THE BARGAINING BACKGROUND

General Electric, a New York corporation, is the largest and perhaps best known manufacturer of electrical equipment, appliances, and the like. Its products—manufactured in all the 50 states—range from refrigerators to atomic energy plants, from submarines to light bulbs. In 1960, it employed about 250,000 men and women; of these only 120,000 were unionized. The IUE is an international union, affiliated with the AFL–CIO, and had a total membership of about 300,000. In 1960 it represented some 70,000 of the 120,000 unionized GE employees, formally grouped in more than 105 bargaining units, and was far and away the largest single union with whom GE dealt. The next largest, the United Electrical Workers (UE), represented only 10,000 members, and the remaining 50,000 unionized employees were split among some 100-odd other unions or bargaining agents who dealt independently with GE. A high proportion of GE employees are supervisory or managerial personnel, who are available to the company in the event of a strike.

The present action has its roots deep in the history of prior negotiations and bargaining relationships. Before 1950, the major union was the UE. In 1946, negotiations reached an impasse and resulted in a serious and crippling strike. GE eventually capitulated, and agreed to a settlement that it later characterized as a "debacle," and beyond the company's ability to meet.

GE's response came in the form of a new approach to employee relations, urged by one of its vice presidents, Lemuel R. Boulware. Although GE generally objects to use of the term, describing it as a "hostile label," the tactic of "Boulwareism" associated with his name soon became the hallmark of the company's entire attitude towards its employees.

In many respects, GE's negotiating policy after the 1946 strike followed a predictable course. The Company had been concerned over the antipathy many of the employees displayed during the strike. It decided that it was no longer enough to act in a manner that it thought becoming for a "good" employer; it had to insure that the employees recognized and appreciated the Company's efforts in their behalf. The problem was perceived as a failure to apply GE's highly successful consumer product merchandising techniques to the employment relations field.

The new plan was threefold. GE began by soliciting comments from its local management personnel on the desires of the work force, and the type and level of benefits that they expected. These were then translated into specific proposals, and their cost and effectiveness researched, in order to formulate a "product" that would be attractive to the employees, and within the Company's means. The last step was the most important, most innovative, and most often criticized. GE took its "product"—now a series of fully-formed bargaining proposals—and "sold" it to its employees and the general public. Through a veritable avalanche of publicity, reaching awesome proportions prior to and during negotiations, GE sought to tell its side of the issues to its employees. It described its proposals as a "fair, firm offer," characteristic of its desire to "do right voluntarily," without the need for any union pressure or strike. In negotiations, GE announced that it would have nothing to do with the "blood-and-threat-and-thunder" approach, in which each side presented patently unreasonable demands, and finally chose a middle ground that both knew would be the probable outcome even before the beginning of the bargaining. The Company believed that such tactics diminished the company's credibility in the eyes of its employees, and at the same time appeared to give the union credit for wringing from the Company what it had been willing to offer all along. Henceforth GE would hold nothing back when it made its offer to the Union; it would take all the facts into consideration, and make that offer it thought right under all the circumstances. Though willing to accept Union suggestions based on facts the Company might have overlooked, once the basic outlines of the proposal had been set, the mere fact that the Union disagreed would be no ground for change. When GE said firm, it meant firm, and it denounced the traditional give and take of the so-called auction bargaining as "flea bitten eastern type of cunning and dishonest but pointless haggling."

To bring its position home to its employees, GE utilized a vast network of plant newspapers, bulletins, letters, television and radio announcements, and personal contacts through management personnel.

Side by side with its policies of "doing right voluntarily" through a "firm, fair offer," GE also pursued a policy of guaranteeing uniformity among unions, and between union and non-union employees. Thus all unions received substantially the same offer, and unrepresented employees were assured that they would gain nothing through representation that they would not have had in any case. Prior to 1960, GE held up its proposed benefits for unrepresented employees until the unions agreed, or until the old contract with the Union expired.

The IUE split off from the UE in 1950, when the UE was expelled from the CIO for alleged Communist domination. Since 1950, the IUE and GE have bargained on a multi-unit basis, despite the presence of separate unit certifications for IUE locals. The pattern was continued in successive 1951, 1952, 1954, and 1955 renewal contracts. In practice, the IUE has dealt with the company through its General Electric Conference Board, composed of delegates elected from IUE locals. Under the Union constitution, the Conference Board may call strikes, make contract proposals, and conclude agreements, regardless of an individual local's consent. GE has dealt with, and recognized the status of, the Conference Board since 1950, although the national agreements frequently provided that some matters, usually minor, would be left to local agreement.

The 1955 Contract, which was to run for five years, contained a provision allowing the Union to reopen in 1958, solely on the issue of employment security. The union did so, but was unable either to gain concessions from the Company, or to elicit enough support for a strike.

III.

THE 1960 NEGOTIATIONS

Under the 1955 Contract, the earliest date that either party could compel the beginning of negotiations was August 16, 1960, 45 days before the end of the contract. Both sides, however, were anxious to take at least some preliminary steps before they were required to.

The IUE set up a loose alliance with several other AFL–CIO unions who bargained with GE, and they jointly polled their members on proposals. Before the actual beginning of formal negotiations, the IUE also began preparing its members through information about some of the possible demands that appeared likely to be presented to GE.

Since the linchpin of the "Boulware approach" was to bring GE's side of the story home to its employees and to the general public, it began in the latter part of 1959 to advise its Employment Relations Managers of the subjects that they should be prepared to discuss with employees. This was effected through various media, including plant publications and personal contact. General arguments in favor of keeping GE competitive through low costs, and the advantage of receiving GE benefits without having to wait for Union officials to approve them, were among the suggestions presented.

Informal meetings were first held in January, 1960, and Union and Company subsequently joined in preparing a body of information. Neither side felt any inclination to complain of want of cooperation at this stage. GE, in fact, took pains to suggest alternate information when the precise form the Union desired was unavailable.

Before another planned informal meeting in June, 1960, GE notified the IUE by letter that as of July it would institute a contributory group accident and life insurance plan for all employees, but if the Union objected, only unrepresented employees would receive the benefits. The Union protested that the Company had to bargain before making such a unilateral change, but GE insisted that the 1955 IUE–GE ,Pension and Insurance agreement waived all such requirements. The Union still objected, and the program was put into effect only for unrepresented employees.

At the June meeting, the Union stated its proposals, as they then stood. Without much discussion, other than some minor clarifications, Philip D. Moore, GE's Union Relations Service Manager and chief negotiator, called the proposals "astronomical" in cost, "ridiculous," and not designed for early settlement.

Following the presentation of these proposals, the early publicity phase of the Boulware approach swung into high gear. Employing virtually all media, from television and radio, to newspaper, plant publications and personal contact, the Company urged employees and the public to regard the Union demands as "astronomical" (then and later a favored Company term), and likely to cost many GE employees their jobs through increased foreign competition. GE, on the other hand, announced it would in time make a fair and "firm" offer that would give employees no reason to allow union leadership to impose a strike. The basic theme was that the Company, and not the Union, was the best guardian and protector of the employees' interests.

The IUE also tried its hand at publicity, including an "IUE Caravan" that travelled from city to city, and occasional articles in the International Union's newspaper. In scope and effectiveness, however, they were far outshadowed by the Company's massive campaign.

From July 19 to August 11, the Union presented its specific proposals on employment security, to which the Company replied with general expressions of disapproval, or simply rejected. GE spent the next five meetings delivering prepared presentations on the general causes of economic instability, which the Union branded as a waste of time.

In subsequent meetings, the Company's posture remained unchanged. It would comment generally on some Union demands, and consider them in formulating its offer, but would not commit itself in any way. While it complained that the IUE proposals were excessive, it replied to Union requests for cost estimates with "we talk about the level of benefits," or that the proposals cost "a lot." GE would not indicate the total cost of a settlement it considered reasonable ("we talk level of benefits"); the Union in turn refused to rank its demands by priority, describing them all as "musts." Indeed the entire early period—and the later negotiations as well —were characterized by an air of rancor on both sides, which provided each with welcome opportunities to downgrade the other in communications to Union members.

GE finally revealed its own proposal informally on August 29. While expressing distress at some features of the offer, Union negotiators urged the Company to delay publicizing its "firm, fair" offer, so that its position would not be frozen before the IUE had an opportunity to examine it and offer changes. GE refused, agreeing only to hold up most of the prepared and packaged publicity until after formal presentation of the offer on the next day.

Union officials frequently renewed their requests for cost information during the ensuing month of negotiations. GE consistently refused to estimate the cost of its proposal or of any of its elements, so that the Union might reallocate its demands. When pressed for some of the highly-touted GE cost studies, Moore frequently slipped into the "level of benefits" format, and generally showed no interest in presenting alternate information that was available and would have served the Union's needs.

There were few modifications made in the original GE offer. The Company did propose an extra week's vacation after 25 years in exchange for a smaller wage increase; but Union officials had indicated at the outset that they were uninterested in paring down what they considered an already inadequate wage offer. Despite this, and in the face of the departure by Union officials for their national conference, GE publicized the "new" offer heavily in employee communications.

After declaring late in September that the "whole offer" was "on the table," GE contrary to prior practice, brought its position home by making its three per cent wage increase offer effective for unrepresented employees before the end of the contract or IUE acceptance. Two days later GE also puts its pension and insurance proposals into effect, despite IUE President James Carey's complaint that this would "inhibit" any subsequent modifications.

On September 21, Federal Mediation Service officials began to sit in on the negotiations at the request of the Union. Their presence does not appear to have measurably aided the negotiations. The Union, in response to Company complaints that the IUE proposals were too costly, submitted a written request for information on the cost per employee of the GE pension and insurance plans, as well as the number of employees who could be expected to benefit from GE's vacation and income extension proposals. The request was refused in part, and the remainder was not complied with until after the strike, when the information would be of no substantial value to the Union.

Similar difficulties confronted the Union in its efforts to change the effective date of the pension and insurance plans. The Company proposed a January 1 date for the first increase in pension and insurance benefits; the Union in turn suggested that the increase in benefits should coincide with the beginning of the contract. GE shifted its ground back and forth: first it claimed that the earlier date would be too costly; then it said that it was talking "level of benefits" and not cost; then it argued that prior contracts had always provided for pension increases on the first of the year. When this last ground proved to be incorrect, one GE negotiator promised to "consider" the October date, although he insisted the January date was "appropriate." During that afternoon, however, even this concession was withdrawn, and later explanations included describing January again as "appropriate," and "the time that you make all the resolutions for the New Year."

Union officials complained that "it is just because we request something that you would refuse to give it," and subsequent Company explanations served to support, rather than to undercut, this feeling. On September 28, with three scheduled meetings left before the end of the contract, a Union negotiator, seeking to salvage something of the earlier IUE Supplemental Unemployment Benefits proposal, suggested a local option plan under which some of the funds the Company had allocated to wage increases and its income extension offer could be diverted to supplement unemployment compensation. He was clear that nothing was to be added to the Company's costs. Moore responded, "After all our month of bargaining and after telling the employees before they went to vote that this is it, we would look ridiculous to change it at this late date; and secondly the answer is no." A few moments later Moore reiterated his belief that "we would look ridiculous if we changed it." Hilbert, for GE, later gave three reasons why the Company would not consider the proposal—and two of them were that it would make GE "look foolish in the eyes of employees and others. * * *"

GE on September 29 rejected a Union offer to maintain the status quo under the old contract until a new one was signed, specifically refusing the cost-of-living escalator clause, and stating that it would "consider" later Union-related terms such as dues checkoff. A strike (which took place on October 2, except for the Schenectady Local, which joined October 6) was clearly imminent. Although claiming to be uncertain about truce terms with national IUE negotiators, GE headquarters on September 29 authorized its Schenectady Employee Relations Manager, Stevens, to offer all the pre-existing terms of the contract (except for the cost-of-living term) to the local. Stevens did so in statements to Union members to the local Business Agent, Jandreau. A similar offer was made to the Pittsfield local, and broadly publicized there.

By October 10, the Company (after the Union had filed an unfair labor practice charge) made the same offer to the Union's national negotiators, for any locals that returned to work. Despite rejection by the Union at the national level, the Company proceeded to deal directly with local officials, and to urge acceptance of the offer. When local officials demurred, as, for example, at Lynn, Massachusetts, publicity was aimed at the employees themselves, criticizing the local officials' stand on the "truce." Similar events occurred at Waterford, Louisville, Bridgeville, and Syracuse.

Throughout the course of the strike, GE communications to the employees emphasized the personal character of the Union leaders' conduct, and threatened loss of jobs to plants that returned to work late. Negotiations were held during the strike until October 19, when the Company declared that an impasse had been reached. During that period, GE refused to give the IUE definitive contract language until the Union had chosen which of the options it preferred, and until it gave its unqualified approval of the Company proposal.

On October 21, it became clear that Union capitulation was near. The Company, which had previously refused to delete the retraining provision from its offer, felt free to relax its position, and granted the Union's request to permit a local option on retraining. While refusing a joint strike settlement agreement, which both parties would sign, GE did propose a unilateral "letter of intent," indicating that it was in agreement with most of the Union settlement proposals. On October 22, the Union capitulated completely, signing a short form memorandum agreement (they had not yet seen the complete contract language to which they were agreeing), and the Company alone issued its letter of intent. The strike ended on October 24.

Two matters were left open for settlement: seniority for transferred employees, and dues checkoffs. Neither, when finally settled, represented more than an adjustment to take account of NLRB decisions that rendered the original form of the agreement of dubious legality. Some minor changes also followed, none of any considerable significance.

The only other events of importance occurred at the Augusta, Georgia plant. On October 5, the plant manager sent a letter to the four employees on strike (at that time the only ones), warning them that their employment would be terminated and replacements hired if they did not return to work. On October 13, however, he sent them telegrams, retracting the earlier letter as to job termination, but indicating the replacements would be hired. More employees (twenty in all) joined the strike after October 5, and on October 24 the Company refused their unconditional offer to return to work. It did, however, give physical examinations to three of the employees, and rehired the two who passed.

[The Court went on to hold that G.E. had failed to bargain in good faith; both as a general matter on the basis of the whole record in the case, and specifically with respect to the insurance proposal, the refusal to supply information regarding the costs to the company of the union contract demands, and as to the company's direct bargaining with local unions.

Judge Waterman concurred with Judge Kauffman, and Judge Friendly dissented.]

———

The report of the NLRB trial examiner in the G.E. case is found in 150 NLRB 192 (1964). The following excerpts from the trial examiner's report set out the remedies and order which he recommended, and which the NLRB confirmed, and which the Second Circuit Court of Appeals affirmed.

THE REMEDY

Having found that the Respondent has engaged in unfair labor practices in violation of Section 8(a)(1), (3), and (5) of the Act, I shall recommend that it cease and desist therefrom and take certain affirmative action designed to effectuate the policies of the Act.

It has been found that the Respondent, at its Augusta, Georgia, plant, discriminatorily refused reinstatement to the employees listed in the attached Appendix A on October 24, 1960. It will accordingly be recommended that the Respondent offer each of such employees—except W. A. Chalker and Lonnie M. Usry—immediate and full reinstatement to his former or a substantially equivalent position, without prejudice to his seniority or other rights and privileges. It is further recommended that the Respondent make each of the employees listed in Appendix A whole for any loss of pay he may have suffered by reason of the discrimination from October 24, 1960, until the date of the Respondent's offer of full reinstatement or earlier grant thereof, in a manner consistent with Board policy as set forth in F. W. Woolworth Company, 90 NLRB 289, with interest as provided in Isis Plumbing & Heating Co., 138 NLRB 716.

With respect to the 8(a)(5) violations found, it is not believed that the circumstances of this case require an affirmative order in addition to the cease-and-desist order provided for, except with regard to the furnishing of information, and this only to the extent that the Union's request for relevant and necessary information has not already been complied with.

With respect to the cease-and-desist provisions of the Recommended Order relating to the refusal-to-bargain remedy, certain clarifying comments are in order. *First*: The Recommended Order is not to be construed as disturbing the appropriate unit findings made in the representation proceedings referred to in Appendix A, as amended, attached to the complaint. *Second*: The Recommended Order assumes that the Respondent will continue to engage in national level or multiunit bargaining with the Union on a consensual basis. The Respondent has indicated no desire to withdraw from that arrangement. Whether in the light of the historical pattern of bargaining, the Respondent may withdraw in the future, and insist upon entire separate bargaining on a unit-by-unit basis, and, if so, at what time and under what circumstances it may appropriately do so, is a matter not decided here. The purpose of this Order is to remedy the violation that has occurred, not to anticipate other contexts which may arise in the future as to which determination may be required of questions not specifically litigated in this case. *Third*: It is not the purpose of this Order to enlarge or limit the subjects that are to be assigned respectively to national level or to local level bargaining. These are matters to be hammered out by the parties themselves in negotiations, subject, however, to the requirements of good-faith bargaining, taking into account among other considerations, but not necessarily giving controlling weight to, the pattern of bargaining as it has evolved over the course of years.

*   *   *

RECOMMENDED ORDER

Upon the basis of the foregoing findings of fact and conclusions of law, and upon the entire record in this proceeding. I recommend that the Respondent, General Electric Company, its officers, agents, successors, and assigns, shall:

1. Cease and desist from:

(a) Refusing—in national level bargining—to bargain collectively in good faith with the IUE (through its General Electric Conference Board), (a) on behalf of the IUE as the certified representative of employees of the Company in appropriate bargaining units represented on the IUE–GE Conference Board for purposes of national level bargaining with the Company, and (b) on behalf of IUE constituent locals which (i) are certified representatives of employees of the Company in appropriate bargaining units, (ii) are represented on the IUE–GE Conference Board for purposes of national level bargaining with the Company, and (iii) have duly authorized the IUE (through its GE Conference Board) by virtue of union constitutional requirement or otherwise to bargain on their behalf with respect to rates of pay, wages, hours of employment, and other terms and conditions of employment.

(b) Failing or refusing upon request, timely to furnish the IUE with information necessary or relevant to bargaining issues involved in national level collective bargaining.

(c) Bargaining directly or attempting to bargain directly—while engaged in national level negotiations—with IUE locals which are duly represented for the purposes of national bargaining by the IUE (through its GE Conference Board) concerning subjects then involved in national level negotiations; or offering separately any such IUE local concerning any such subject more favorable terms and conditions of employment than offered to the IUE national level negotiators.

(d) Discouraging membership in the IUE, or in any IUE local, or in any other labor organization of its employees, by refusing to reinstate, upon their unconditional request, any of its employees engaged in concerted activity as unfair labor practice strikers.

(e) In any like or related manner interfering with, restraining, or coercing its employees in the exercise of their right to self-organization, to form labor organizations, to join or assist the IUE, its affiliated local unions, or any other labor organization, to bargain collectively through representatives of their own choosing, and to engage in concerted activities for the purpose of collective bargaining or other mutual aid or protection, or to refrain from any or all such activity, except to the extent that such right may be affected by an agreement requiring membership in a labor organization as a condition of employment as authorized in Section 8(a)(3) of the Act.

2. Take the following affirmative action which it is found will effectuate the policies of the Act:

(a) Upon request, furnish to the IUE the following information: (1) the cents per month premium, per employee, and also for employee dependents, of each insurance benefit improvement added to the insurance plan provided for in the 1960–63 agreement relating thereto; (2) the estimated monthly average net cost per employee, and also for employee dependents, to the Company of each such insurance benefit improvement, computed from the cost estimates prepared and maintained by the Company for its own use in making calculations of that kind; and (3) the estimated average cost in cents per hour per employee of each added increment in pension plan benefits provided for in the 1960–63 agreement relating thereto, computed from the cost estimates prepared and maintained by the Company for its own use in making calculations of that kind.

(b) Offer to the employees named in the attached Appendix A, except W. A. Chalker and Lonnie M. Usry, immediate and full reinstatement to their former or substantially equivalent positions, without prejudice to their seniority or other rights and privileges.

(c) Make whole all the employees listed in the attached Appendix A in the manner set forth in the section entitled "The Remedy," for any loss of pay each may have suffered by reason of the Respondent's discrimination against him.

(d) Preserve and, upon request, make available to the Board or its agents, for examination and copying, all payroll records, social security payment records, timecards, personnel records and reports, and all other records necessary to analyze the amounts of backpay due under the terms of this Recommended Order.

(e) Post at all its plants, installations, and other places of business in the United States, at which bargaining units represented by the IUE or any of its constituent locals are located, copies of the attached notice marked "Appendix B." Copies of said notice, to be furnished by the Regional Director for Region 2, shall, after being duly signed by the Respondent's representative, be posted by the Respondent immediately upon receipt thereof, and be maintained by it for a period of at least 60 consecutive days thereafter, in conspicuous places, including all places where notices to employees are customarily posted. Reasonable steps shall be taken by the Respondent to insure that such notices are not altered, defaced, or covered by any other material.

(f) Notify the said Regional Director, in writing, within 20 days from the receipt of this report, what steps the Respondent has taken to comply therewith.

Questions

1.   What management attitudes toward unions and collective bargaining seem to you to be reflected in the management behavior in the Wooster Division and General Electric cases?

2.   Is the remedy fashioned by the trial examiner, approved by the NLRB, and affirmed by the Circuit Court in General Electric intended to or likely to correct for injuries done to employees? the union? Is it intended to or likely to affect the future relationship between company and union?

3.   What purposes were served by the litigation of this case for almost a decade after the strike ended? Who won?

4.   What theory of labor-management relations is implicit in the reasoning of Wooster Division and General Electric? Is that consis-

tent with the underlying theory of the National Labor Relations Act? Is that theory consistent with the theory of economic relations expounded by Judge Holmes in Vegelahn v. Guntner and Plant v. Woods, *supra*, pp. 821–833?

Congress maintains continuing oversight of the law governing labor-management relations, if for no other reason than the regular efforts of both labor and management to secure amendments favorable to their respective interests. Recent legislative hearings on proposals for further amendments to the NLRA provide additional insights regarding the problem of using law as a tool to change attitudes and behavior.

[The following is taken from REPORT OF THE HOUSE COMMITTEE ON EDUCATION AND LABOR, on HR 8410, The Labor Reform Act of 1977, 95th Congress, 1st Session, House Report 95–637, pp. 19–24.]

THE WITNESSES

Perhaps the most compelling testimony heard before the Labor-Management Relations Subcommittee during the hearings on H.R. 8410 was that presented by working men and women who were the victims of the law's current inadequacies. Here are the words of Paul Grammont, a supporter of the new 7-year long, still not successful, effort by employees of Dayton Tire and Rubber Co., a subsidiary of Firestone Tire and Rubber Co., to determine by free and uncoerced election whether to be represented by the United Rubber Workers Union:

> I was the 66th clock card employee hired by Dayton Tire on January 27, 1970. If I were still there, I would now be the most senior employee. I set production records as a tire builder and advanced to the highest rate in setup man classification in record time.
>
> I was the first employee to wear a union T-shirt and one of the first employees to sign a URW authorization card and distribute pro-union handbills. I served as a union observer in three of the NLRB elections at our plant.
>
> I thought the law would protect me from the company discriminating against me. I was wrong. The company has harassed and humiliated me in every way possible. The discrimination against me has destroyed my finances and has interfered with my health and with my family.
>
> After the company was found to have committed an unfair labor practice by not giving me a job I deserved, I was ridiculed in front of my fellow workers. The company tried to force me to quit. I am not a quitter.
>
> In January 1973, I hurt my back at work. The Company doctor said I had to do light-duty work. I was found to be disabled but the company contested my workmen's compensation claim. It

took me 17 weeks to get any benefits. In 1974 my doctor said I could return to work but the company illegally refused to let me return.

I have now been refused employment by Dayton Tire for over 3 years despite NLRB and court orders to allow me to work. I have not received a penny of back pay. The promise of back pay won't put food on my table and won't pay the bills. I am currently unemployed but have worked some jobs to sustain my family and me. I have driven a school bus, built miniature windmills out of sticks for sale as arts and crafts, and have made picture frames in my garage. The money I have received is a mere fraction of what I should be making.

When Dayton Tire finally decides to comply with the law and rehire me, I will go back to work and I will try to get a union for my fellow workers. We need representation to fight this vicious employer. I only hope that by then the law will be strong enough to stop the company from harassing and firing other union supporters or me.

A similar tale of frustration was told by Pauline Frazier, who began work at Craftool in Fort Worth, Tex., in 1973. This is how Mrs. Frazier became interested in the United Brotherhood of Carpenters (UBC), and what happened after she and her fellow workers elected the UBC to represent them.

It was · · · unfair treatment that led me and a fellow worker to talking about a union. Many other employees including my leadwoman were talking union. We decided that to get anywhere this organizing had to include both black and white employees, and we talked it over with a black fellow worker who later joined our bargaining committee.

We asked a number of employees we trusted to come, and about 10 came to the first meeting. We were told about how the NLRB would protect us in our organizing activities and how authorization cards would start the ball rolling. Before we moved, the union representative hand-billed the plant publicly so we would be protected by the openness of our group activity.

The union filed a petition for election on March 20, 1975. We met with management at the NLRB, and agreed to election matters.

Then the employer began a really nasty campaign of threats. The NLRB issued a complaint. This case was settled and Craftool was required to post a notice to stop these threats.

The election was held on May 28, 1975, and the union was certified by the NLRB on June 5, 1975.

We began to negotiate with the employer and he insisted on meetings about 1 month apart. We had these meetings and complained, and he said he was out of town, like in Tahiti, on vacation and other places. In August 1975, the plant foreman told me we were wasting our time and would never get a contract. We agreed in January 1976 to a 1-year contract. But when it came to putting it in writing, the employer insisted that it was only a 3-month contract, due to expire on the anniversary date of our certification.

The day after we ratified the contract in January 1976, the general manager told two employees to push to get the union decertified on company time. They were given petitions and told to get them signed and return them to the employer.

The decertification was dismissed by the NLRB because they were gotten up by the employer and were false and produced by threats. So the employer simply ignored the NLRB and refused to meet with us any more. Now a year has gone by, the NLRB found the employer's refusal to meet with us is against the law, but the employer ignored the NLRB order and the case is now in court.

We have been cheated and the NLRB has yet to get one of its many orders enforced. We are out on a limb and the employer is sawing it off. I feel more should be done to protect me and my fellow employees when we set out, as we have done, to protect each other from abuse on the job.

While it is the lowest-paid, most vulnerable workers who bear the brunt of management lawlessness, our hearings revealed that the prominent and the better-paid have also been victimized by justice delayed. Kermit Alexander, former officer of the NFL Players Association (NFLPA), told us how an illegal discharge for union activity ended his career despite his eventual "paper" vindication in 8(a)(3) proceedings before the NLRB:

As a former officer of the NFLPA during and after our unsuccessful strike of 1974, I can assure you that delay is the enemy of justice. I was cut by Philadelphia because of my position in the union, but I was hopeful that quick action by the NLRB would allow me to return within a year. I kept in shape and hoped that I could play in 1975, but as I watched the NLRB proceedings drag on because the NFL wanted them to drag on, I began to lose all hope of ever playing again.

It took the NLRB almost a year to issue a complaint. That delay probably ended any realistic hope of my playing again. A 44-day hearing during the 1975 season made it ridiculous to even think about football again. When the decision came out June 30, 1975, I had mixed emotions. It was good that we had finally exposed the illegal practices of the NFL, but the 2 years it took had made it clear to friends and former teammates that the NLRB was not the answer. Players learned that the law would not protect them.

Had H.R. 8410 been enacted in 1974, I honestly believe that we would have achieved a fair collective bargaining agreement that year. The double back pay provision would have eliminated the trades and cuts of our representatives and officers. The expedited procedures would have brought about bargaining. It is tough as a union leader to ask your people to get involved when you know that you can't protect them if they lose their careers in the battle.

Maybe I'm naive, but I thought the National Labor Relations Board was designed to promote industrial peace, not to create turmoil by rewarding those who violate the law.

* * *

CASE STUDIES

During the years of oversight hearings, the committee has received innumerable case studies of employers who, through manipulation of the existing law, have frustrated the right of self organization. The 1976 staff report of the Labor-Management Relations Subcommittee describes many of these in detail.

What follows are three examples of the impotence of the existing law against a company that is determined to unlawfully deprive its employees of their rights.

The J. P. Stevens Case

The ultimate symbol of the law's ineffectiveness is J. P. Stevens. Even as this Committee was holding hearings on labor law reform, the United States Court of Appeals for the Second Circuit issued a decision unprecedented in labor law experience in its expression of judicial despair at the workings of the Nation's labor laws. In this case, which the Court described as "perhaps destined to be bleakly denominated as *Stevens* XVIII in the long list of Stevens litigation" (NLRB v. J. P. Stevens and Co., 563 F. 2d 8, C.A.2, August 31, 1977), the Nation's "most notorious recidivist" has been found for a second time in contempt of outstanding orders of the Court. What this means in the driest legal terms is that twice Stevens was charged with extensive unfair labor practices, twice found to have violated the Act by the NLRB, twice the Court of Appeals for the Second Circuit has agreed, and, yet, in the Court's words, "Stevens has acted in contempt of our court decrees not once but twice, involving over thirty individual violations. Its violations have been described as 'massive,' and 'cynical,' and 'flagrantly contemptuous.' "

And then the Court concluded by stating the ultimate reason for this bill:

> The case . . . has been a troubling one not only because of the violations of the rights of the employees involved, but also because it raises grave doubts about the ability of the courts to make the provision of the Federal labor law work in the face of persistent violations.

The decision of the Second Circuit Court is simply the most recent in a series of unfair labor practice violations that stretch back over 14 years. These violations have included coercive interrogations, illegal surveillance of union supporters, threats of plants closing and a wide range of economic reprisals for union activity. During this period, J. P. Stevens has been found guilty of illegally firing 184 employees for their union activity.

Despite having been found in violation of the law by Federal courts 13 times, J. P. Stevens has shown no indication of any relaxation in its patently illegal multi-state campaign to keep the Textile Workers Union of America from representing workers in any of its 85 plants. Even in Roanoke Rapids, N.C., where the workers managed to hold a representation election and vote in favor of the union, Stevens has refused to sign a contract. The NLRB issued a complaint charging the company with bad faith bargaining, which has been tried, and is now pending before an Administrative Law Judge. Thus, this latest charge is again subject to the very same time-consuming delays and ineffective remedies so characteristic of the other J. P. Stevens cases.

One of the principal reasons for the ineffectiveness of each of these court orders is that it simply pays for J. P. Stevens to violate the law. It has been estimated that the company has been ordered to pay its workers over $1.3 million in back wages. These tax-deductible payments are certainly less expensive than what the company would have had to pay in higher wages and decent working conditions if the workers had secured a collective bargaining agreement.

The Darlington case

In March of 1956 the approximately 550 workers at Deering Milliken's plant in Darlington, S.C. began efforts to organize a local union of the Textile Workers Union of America, AFL–CIO. Not only were these efforts effectively thwarted by illegal company actions, but today, 21 years later, these workers and their families remain uncompensated for the harms they suffered.

An NLRB conducted election was held on September 6, 1956. Despite the six months of threats from managerial personnel that the plant would be shut down if the employees voted for union representation, a majority of the workers voted for the union. Two months later the mill was shut down and the 550 workers were unemployed. The Supreme Court ruled this violated the Act (Textile Workers v. Darlington Co., 380 U.S. 263, 85 S.Ct. 994 (1965)).

Because of administrative delays and repeated company appeals, 12½ years were required to obtain a supposedly effective order of reinstatement and backpay for the 550 discharges. That occurred on January 13, 1969 when the Supreme Court denied Deering Milliken's petition for certiorari from the decision of the circuit court enforcing the NLRB's order of reinstatement and back pay. (165 NLRB 1074 (1967) enf'd 397 F.2d 760 (4th Cir. 1968), cert. den. 393 U.S. 1023 (1969)).

Upon denial of the company's petition, Deering Milliken was under a duty to offer reinstatement to all employees still living and qualified to work and to award backpay to those employees who lost their jobs as a result of the shutdown. Of 96 requests for reinstatement, 54 were made job offers, but none of the 54 accepted, many claiming that the job offers violated the Board's order that they be substantially equivalent to their prior jobs. Backpay has yet to be awarded to even one worker, since the company is still contesting the case in a backpay specification hearing.

The case of Darlington represents one of the low water marks in the history of enforcement of this country's National Labor Relations Act. The prolonged proceedings have all been at the expense of Darlington's workers. The lack of effective remedies for the company's initial violation failed to deter both the wrongful conduct and the unconscionable footdragging of Deering Milliken in litigating the case. Finally, if and when Darlington's workers are awarded compensation, it will hardly be sufficient to right the wrong that was done.

The Case of Sumpter Plywood Company

The case of Virginia Ingram, Barbara Ward and May Ezell, employees of Sumpter Plywood Company, well illustrates the burden shouldered by the individual worker when seeking enforcement of his or her rights under the Act.

The three women participated in efforts to organize their fellow workers in order to obtain better working conditions. In a deliberate move to frustrate these efforts and to sound a clear warning to other employees, the Company misled the women into breaking a rarely enforced rule and then fired them. This was on March 8, 1973. The case was tried before an Administrative Law Judge, appealed to the NLRB and finally to a United States Court of Appeals, all of which held in favor of the three women. However, it was not until June of 1977, after Sumpter had contested the amount of backpay to which each of the three women were entitled, that they agreed to settle the case for backpay awards of $8,054.97, $6,186.26 and $8,278.23 respectively. The women had been urged to accept the employer's offer to settle for less than they were entitled to avoid years of further litigation.

Barabara Ward accepted the company's offer of reinstatement, but soon thereafter she was once again fired. The case followed an identical path to the Court of Appeals where the Board decision, which found another violation of her rights, is yet to be enforced.

The award of backpay and the offer of reinstatement in no way compensated Ward, Ingram and Ezell for the costs of their unemployment and the many other human costs of being without work.

The committee heard testimony about workers who had their homes foreclosed and cars repossessed while waiting an ultimately favorable disposition of their case. Clearly, in addition to failing to deter violations of the act, remedies under existing law also fail to compensate the victims of such illegal conduct.

FINDINGS OF EARLIER COMMITTEE REPORTS

H.R. 8410 does not contain new concepts; it reflects the accumulated wisdom of the prior studies. Here is what the Cox panel said about remedies in February 1960:

A major weakness in the labor-management relations law is the long delay in contested NLRB proceedings. In labor-management relations justice delayed is often justice denied.

HR 8410 proposed a number of remedies to deal with some of the problems disclosed in the testimony and case studies. These remedies included authorizing awards of double back pay upon reinstatement of an unlawfully discharged employee; authorizing the NLRB to secure preliminary injunctions to order immediate reinstatement of employees allegedly discharged for organizational activities; authorizing the NLRB to award monetary compensation (i. e., damages) to employees whose employers unlawfully refuse to bargain; and barring repeated NLRA violators from receiving federal contracts.

Query: Do the proposed remedies seem to you likely to resolve the type of problems disclosed in the excerpts from the House Committee Report?

SECTION 50.2　REMEDIES AGAINST RACIAL DISCRIMINATION IN EMPLOYMENT

Preceding sections of this chapter provided an overview of the procedures available under Title VII of the Civil Rights Act of 1964 to persons whose employment opportunities have been impaired by racial discrimination. In this section we shall consider examples demonstrating the kinds of remedies which courts have fashioned to implement Title VII. We should note, however, that racial discrimination in employment has also been successfully attacked under other older laws. In Steele v. Louisville and Nashville Ry. Co., 323 U.S. 192, 65 S.Ct. 226 (1944), the Supreme Court found that the Railway Labor Act imposed on labor organizations "the duty to represent all employees . . . without discrimination because of their race" in cases where a labor organization was an exclusive bargaining agent for employees under the terms of that act. On the same day Steele was decided, the Court held in Wallace Corp. v. N. L. R. B., 323 U.S. 248, 65 S.Ct. 238 (1944), that the National Labor Relations Act imposed an identical duty of "fair representation" on labor unions which are exclusive bargaining agents under the terms of that act. Thus, a decade before Brown v. Board of Education, the Court took aim on Jim Crowism in the labor movement. Subsequent decisions in lower federal courts have extended the "fair representation" doctrine and supported NLRB findings that racially discriminatory union practices or actions may be held to be an unfair labor practice. See, e. g., Local 12, Rubber Workers v. N. L. R. B., 5th Cir. 1967, 368 F.2d 12. It has also been held that "an employer's policy and practice of invidious discrimination on account of race or national origin" can be an unfair labor practice for which the NLRB may "order an appropriate remedy." See United Packinghouse, Food and Allied Workers Int. U. v. N. L. R. B., D.C.Cir. 1969, 416 F.2d 1126.

Even more venerable statutes have been infused with new life in employment discrimination cases.

Title 42　United States Code

§ 1981.　Equal rights under the law

All persons within the jurisdiction of the United States shall have the same right in every State and Territory to make and enforce contracts, to sue, be parties, give evidence, and to the full and equal benefit of all laws and proceedings for the security of persons and property as is enjoyed by white citizens, and shall be subject to like punishment, pains, penalties, taxes, licenses, and exactions of every kind, and to no other.

§ 1982. Property rights of citizens

All citizens of the United States shall have the same right, in every State and Territory, as is enjoyed by white citizens thereof to inherit, purchase, lease, sell, hold, and convey real and personal property.

§ 1983. Civil action for deprivation of rights

Every person who, under color of any statute, ordinance, regulation, custom, or usage, of any State or Territory, subjects, or causes to be subjected, any citizen of the United States or other person within the jurisdiction thereof to the deprivation of any rights, privileges, or immunities secured by the Constitution and laws, shall be liable to the party injured in an action at law, suit in equity, or other proper proceeding for redress.

These sections of the United States Code are derived from a post-Civil War statute, the Civil Rights Act of 1866. In the Civil Rights Cases, 109 U.S. 3, 3 S.Ct. 18 (1883), the Supreme Court severely restricted the application of these statutes by holding, among other things, that these provisions could not be invoked to restrain racial discrimination by private persons. That limitation was abandoned by the Court in Jones v. Alfred H. Mayer Co., 392 U.S. 409, 88 S.Ct. 2186 (1968), in which the Court held that § 1982 would support a remedy against racial discrimination in the sale of real property. By implication, the Court also provided a basis for remedies against private parties in cases brought under § 1981. Even before that decision, lower federal courts had allowed remedies for employment discrimination under §§ 1981 and 1983. In Ethridge v. Rhodes, S.D.Ohio 1967, 268 F.Supp. 83, the court found that the plaintiffs were denied admission to unions as a result of their race; that this effectively precluded them from employment on major public projects since the contractors on such jobs hired exclusively through the unions; that the responsible public officials were aware of this pattern of discrimination against Negroes; and that no effective steps had been taken to overcome this discrimination. The court then concluded that the acquiescence of state officials in this practice constituted "state action", and that the contractors, as joint participants with the state in public construction projects, could be liable to remedial action under §§ 1981 and 1983.

The Supreme Court has since affirmed that § 1981 affords a basis for a federal remedy against racial discrimination in private employment. See Johnson v. Railway Express Agency, Inc., 421 U.S. 454, 95 S.Ct. 1716 (1975), and McDonald v. Santa Fe Trail Transp. Co., 427 U.S. 273, 96 S.Ct. 2574 (1976). In Johnson the Court made it clear that Title VII of the Civil Rights Act of 1964 did not preclude alternative procedures and remedies under other federal statutes such as 42 U.S.C. §§ 1981, 1982, and 1983. It is also clear, however, that Title VII affords the most comprehensive body of federal law on the subject of employment discrimination, and we turn now to the problem of remedies under Title VII.

REMOVING BARRIERS TO ENTRY: HEREIN OF TESTS, QUOTAS, GOALS, AND TIMETABLES

GRIGGS v. DUKE POWER CO.

Supreme Court of the United States, 1970.
401 U.S. 424, 91 S.Ct. 849.

Mr. Chief Justice Burger delivered the opinion of the Court.

We granted the writ in this case to resolve the question whether an employer is prohibited by the Civil Rights Act of 1964, Title VII, from requiring a high school education or passing of a standardized general intelligence test as a condition of employment in or transfer to jobs when (a) neither standard is shown to be significantly related to successful job performance, (b) both requirements operate to disqualify Negroes at a substantially higher rate than white applicants, and (c) the jobs in question formerly had been filed only by white employees as part of a longstanding practice of giving preference to whites.[1]

Congress provided, in Title VII of the Civil Rights Act of 1964, for class actions for enforcement of provisions of the Act and this proceeding was brought by a group of incumbent Negro employees against Duke Power Company. All the petitioners are employed at the Company's Dan River Steam Station, a power generating facility located at Draper, North Carolina. At the time this action was instituted, the Company had 95 employees at the Dan River Station, 14 of whom were Negroes; 13 of these are petitioners here.

The District Court found that prior to July 2, 1965, the effective date of the Civil Rights Act of 1964, the Company openly discriminated on the basis of race in the hiring and assigning of employees at its Dan River plant. The plant was organized into five operating departments: (1) Labor, (2) Coal Handling, (3) Operations, (4) Maintenance, and (5) Laboratory and Test. Negroes were employed only in the Labor Department where the highest paying jobs paid less than the lowest paying jobs in the other four "operating" departments in which only whites were employed.[2]

---

1. The Act provides:

    "Sec. 703. (a) It shall be an unlawful employment practice for an employer—

    .   .   .   .   .   .

    "(2) to limit, segregate, or classify his employees in any way which would deprive or tend to deprive any individual of employment opportunities or otherwise adversely affect his status as an employee, because of such individual's race, color, religion, sex, or national origin.

    .   .   .   .   .

    "(h) Notwithstanding any other provision of this title, it shall not be

    an unlawful employment practice for an employer . . . to give and to act upon the results of any professionally developed ability test provided that such test, its administration or action upon the results is not designed, intended or used to discriminate because of race, color, religion, sex or national origin. . . ."
    78 Stat. 255, 42 U.S.C. § 2000e–2.

2. A Negro was first assigned to a job in an operating department in August 1966, five months after charges had been filed with the Equal Employment Opportunity Commission. The em-

Promotions were normally made within each department on the basis of job seniority. Transferees into a department usually began in the lowest position.

In 1955 the Company instituted a policy of requiring a high school education for initial assignment to any department except Labor, and for transfer from the Coal Handling to any "inside" department (Operations, Maintenance, or Laboratory). When the Company abandoned its policy of restricting Negroes to the Labor Department in 1965, completion of high school also was made a prerequisite to transfer from Labor to any other department. From the time the high school requirement was instituted to the time of trial however, white employees hired before the time of the high school education requirement continued to perform satisfactorily and achieve promotions in the "operating" departments. Findings on this score are not challenged.

The Company added a further requirement for new employees on July 2, 1965, the date on which Title VII became effective. To qualify for placement in any but the Labor Department it became necessary to register satisfactory scores on two professionally prepared aptitude tests, as well as to have a high school education. Completion of high school alone continued to render employees eligible for transfer to the four desirable departments from which Negroes had been excluded if the incumbent had been employed prior to the time of the new requirement. In September 1965 the Company began to permit incumbent employees who lacked a high school education to qualify for transfer from Labor or Coal Handling to an "inside" job by passing two tests—the Wonderlic Personnel Test, which purports to measure general intelligence, and the Bennett Mechanical Comprehension Test. Neither was directed or intended to measure the ability to learn to perform a particular job or category of jobs. The requisite scores used for both initial hiring and transfer approximated the national median for high school graduates.[3]

The District Court had found that while the Company previously followed a policy of overt racial discrimination in a period prior to the Act, such conduct had ceased. The District Court also concluded that Title VII was intended to be prospective only and, consequently, the impact of prior inequities was beyond the reach of corrective action authorized by the Act.

The Court of Appeals was confronted with a question of first impression, as are we, concerning the meaning of Title VII. After careful analysis a majority of that court concluded that a subjective test of the employer's intent should govern, particularly in a close case, and that in this case there was no showing of a discriminatory purpose in the adoption of the diploma and test requirements. On this basis, the Court of Appeals concluded there was no violation of the Act.

The Court of Appeals reversed the District Court in part, rejecting the holding that residual discrimination arising from prior employment practices was insulated from remedial action.[4] The Court of Appeals noted,

ployee, a high school graduate who had begun in the Labor Department in 1953, was promoted to a job in the Coal Handling Department.

3. The test standards are thus more stringent than the high school require-

ment, since they would screen out approximately half of all high school graduates.

4. The Court of Appeals ruled that Negroes employed in the Labor Department at a time when there was no

however, that the District Court was correct in its conclusion that there was no showing of a racial purpose or invidious intent in the adoption of the high school diploma requirement or general intelligence test and that these standards had been applied fairly to whites and Negroes alike. It held that, in the absence of a discriminatory purpose, use of such requirements was permitted by the Act. In so doing, the Court of Appeals rejected the claim that because these two requirements operated to render ineligible a markedly disproportionate number of Negroes, they were unlawful under Title VII unless shown to be job related.[5] We granted the writ on these claims. 399 U.S. 926, 90 S.Ct. 2238 (1970).

The objective of Congress in the enactment of Title VII is plain from the language of the statute. It was to achieve equality of employment opportunities and remove barriers that have operated in the past to favor an identifiable group of white employees over other employees. Under the Act, practices, procedures, or tests neutral on their face, and even neutral in terms of intent, cannot be maintained if they operate to "freeze" the status quo of prior discriminatory employment practices.

The Court of Appeals' opinion, and the partial dissent, agreed that, on the record in the present case, "whites register far better on the Company's alternative requirements" than Negroes.[6] 420 F.2d 1225, 1239 n. 6. This consequence would appear to be directly traceable to race. Basic intelligence must have the means of articulation to manifest itself fairly in a testing process. Because they are Negroes, petitioners have long received inferior education in segregated schools and this Court expressly recognized these differences in Gaston County v. United States, 395 U.S. 285, 89 S.Ct. 1720 (1969). There, because of the inferior education received by Negroes in North Carolina, this Court barred the institution of a literacy test for voter registration on the ground that the test would abridge the right to vote indirectly on account of race. Congress did not intend by Title VII, however, to guarantee a job to every person regardless of qualifications. In short, the Act does not command that any person be hired simply because

high school or test requirement for entrance into the higher paying departments could not now be made subject to those requirements, since whites hired contemporaneously into those departments were never subject to them. The Court of Appeals also required that the seniority rights of those Negroes be measured on a plantwide, rather than a departmental, basis. However, the Court of Appeals denied relief to the Negro employees without a high school education or its equivalent who were hired into the Labor Department after institution of the educational requirement.

5. One member of that court disagreed with this aspect of the decision, maintaining, as do the petitioners in this Court, that Title VII prohibits the use of employment criteria that operate in a racially exclusionary fashion and do not measure skills or abilities necessary to performance of the jobs for which those criteria are used.

6. In North Carolina, 1960 census statistics show that, while 34% of white males had completed high school, only 12% of Negro males had done so. U. S. Bureau of the Census, U. S. Census of Population: 1960, Vol. 1, Characteristics of the Population, pt. 35, Table 47.

Similarly, with respect to standardized tests, the EEOC in one case found that use of a battery of tests, including the Wonderlic and Bennett tests used by the Company in the instant case, resulted in 58% of whites passing the tests, as compared with only 6% of the blacks. Decision of EEOC, CCH Empl. Prac. Guide, ¶ 17,304.53 (Dec. 2, 1966). See also Decision of EEOC 70–552, CCH Empl. Prac. Guide, ¶ 6139 (Feb. 19, 1970).

he was formerly the subject of discrimination, or because he is a member of a minority group. Discriminatory preference for any group, minority or majority, is precisely and only what Congress has proscribed. What is required by Congress is the removal of artificial, arbitrary, and unnecessary barriers to employment when the barriers operate invidiously to discriminate on the basis of racial or other impermissible classification.

Congress has now provided that tests or criteria for employment or promotion may not provide equality of opportunity merely in the sense of the fabled offer of milk to the stork and the fox. On the contrary, Congress has now required that the posture and condition of the jobseeker be taken into account. It has—to resort again to the fable—provided that the vessel in which the milk is proffered be one all seekers can use. The Act proscribes not only overt discrimination but also practices that are fair in form, but discriminatory in operation. The touchstone is business necessity. If an employment practice which operates to exclude Negroes cannot be shown to be related to job performance, the practice is prohibited.

On the record before us, neither the high school completion requirement nor the general intelligence test is shown to bear a demonstrable relationship to successful performance of the jobs for which it was used. Both were adopted, as the Court of Appeals noted, without meaningful study of their relationship to job-performance ability. Rather, a vice president of the Company testified, the requirements were instituted on the Company's judgment that they generally would improve the overall quality of the work force.

The evidence, however, shows that employees who have not completed high school or taken the tests have continued to perform satisfactorily and make progress in departments for which the high school and test criteria are now used.[7] The promotion record of present employees who would not be able to meet the new criteria thus suggests the possibility that the requirements may not be needed even for the limited purpose of preserving the avowed policy of advancement within the Company. In the context of this case, it is unnecessary to reach the question whether testing requirements that take into account capability for the next succeeding position or related future promotion might be utilized upon a showing that such long-range requirements fulfill a genuine business need. In the present case the Company has made no such showing.

The Court of Appeals held that the Company had adopted the diploma and test requirements without any "intention to discriminate against Negro employees." 420 F.2d, at 1232. We do not suggest that either the District Court or the Court of Appeals erred in examining the employer's intent; but good intent or absence of discriminatory intent does not redeem employment procedures or testing mechanisms that operate as "built-in headwinds" for minority groups and are unrelated to measuring job capability.

The Company's lack of discriminatory intent is suggested by special efforts to help the undereducated employees through Company financing of two-thirds the cost of tuition for high school training. But Congress di-

---

7. For example, between July 2, 1965, and November 14, 1966, the percentage of white employees who were promoted but who were not high school graduates was nearly identical to the percentage of nongraduates in the entire white work force.

rected the thrust of the Act to the *consequences* of employment practices, not simply the motivation. More than that, Congress has placed on the employer the burden of showing that any given requirement must have a manifest relationship to the employment in question.

The facts of this case demonstrate the inadequacy of broad and general testing devices as well as the infirmity of using diplomas or degrees as fixed measures of capability. History is filled with examples of men and women who rendered highly effective performance without the conventional badges of accomplishment in terms of certificates, diplomas, or degrees. Diplomas and tests are useful servants, but Congress has mandated the commonsense proposition that they are not to become masters of reality.

The Company contends that its general intelligence tests are specifically permitted by § 703(h) of the Act.[8] That section authorizes the use of "any professionally developed ability test" that is not "designed, intended *or used* to discriminate because of race . . . ." (Emphasis added.)

The Equal Employment Opportunity Commission, having enforcement responsibility, has issued guidelines interpreting § 703(h) to permit only the use of job-related tests.[9] The administrative interpretation of the Act by the enforcing agency is entitled to great deference. See, *e. g.*, United States v. City of Chicago, 400 U.S. 8, 91 S.Ct. 18 (1970); Udall v. Tallman, 380 U.S. 1, 85 S.Ct. 792 (1965); Power Reactor Co. v. Electricians, 367 U. S. 396, 81 S.Ct. 1529 (1961). Since the Act and its legislative history support the Commission's construction, this affords good reason to treat the guidelines as expressing the will of Congress.

Section 703(h) was not contained in the House version of the Civil Rights Act but was added in the Senate during extended debate. For a period, debate revolved around claims that the bill as proposed would prohibit all testing and force employers to hire unqualified persons simply because they were part of a group formerly subject to job discrimination.[10] Propo-

---

8. Section 703(h) applies only to tests. It has no applicability to the high school diploma requirement.

9. EEOC Guidelines on Employment Testing Procedures, issued August 24, 1966, provide:

"The Commission accordingly interprets 'professionally developed ability test' to mean a test which fairly measures the knowledge or skills required by the particular job or class of jobs which the applicant seeks, or which fairly affords the employer a chance to measure the applicant's ability to perform a particular job or class of jobs. The fact that a test was prepared by an individual or organization claiming expertise in test preparation does not, without more, justify its use within the meaning of Title VII."

The EEOC position has been elaborated in the new Guidelines on Employee Selection Procedures, 29 CFR § 1607, 35 Fed.Reg. 12333 (Aug. 1, 1970). These guidelines demand that employers using tests have available "data demonstrating that the test is predictive of or significantly correlated with important elements of work behavior which comprise or are relevant to the job or jobs for which candidates are being evaluated." Id., at § 1607.4(c).

10. The congressional discussion was prompted by the decision of a hearing examiner for the Illinois Fair Employment Commission in Myart v. Motorola Co. (The decision is reprinted at 110 Cong.Rec. 5662.) That case suggested that standardized tests on which whites performed better than Negroes could never be used. The decision was taken to mean that such tests could never be justified even if the needs of the business required them. A number of Senators feared that Title VII might produce a similar result. See remarks of Senators Ervin, 110 Cong. Rec. 5614–5616; Smathers, id., at 5999–6000; Holland, id., at 7012–7013; Hill,

nents of Title VII sought throughout the debate to assure the critics that the Act would have no effect on job-related tests. Senators Case of New Jersey and Clark of Pennsylvania, comanagers of the bill on the Senate floor, issued a memorandum explaining that the proposed Title VII "expressly protects the employer's right to insist that any prospective applicant, Negro or white, *must meet the applicable job qualifications.* Indeed, the very purpose of Title VII is to promote hiring on the basis of job qualifications, rather than on the basis of race or color." 110 Cong.Rec. 7247.[11] (Emphasis added.) Despite these assurances, Senator Tower of Texas introduced an amendment authorizing "professionally developed ability tests." Proponents of Title VII opposed the amendment because, as written, it would permit an employer to give any test, "whether it was a good test or not, so long as it was professionally designed. Discrimination could actually exist under the guise of compliance with the statute." 110 Cong.Rec. 13504 (remarks of Sen. Case).

The amendment was defeated and two days later Senator Tower offered a substitute amendment which was adopted verbatim and is now the testing provision of § 703(h). Speaking for the supporters of Title VII, Senator Humphrey, who had vigorously opposed the first amendment, endorsed the substitute amendment, stating: "Senators on both sides of the aisle who were deeply interested in title VII have examined the text of this amendment and have found it to be in accord with the intent and purpose of that title." 110 Cong.Rec. 13724. The amendment was then adopted.[12]

id., at 8447; Tower, id., at 9024; Talmadge, id., at 9025–9026; Fulbright, id., at 9599–9600; and Ellender, id., at 9600.

11. The Court of Appeals majority, in finding no requirement in Title VII that employment tests be job related, relied in part on a quotation from an earlier Clark-Case interpretative memorandum addressed to the question of the constitutionality of Title VII. The Senators said in that memorandum:

"There is no requirement in title VII that employers abandon bona fide qualification tests where, because of differences in background and education, members of some groups are able to perform better on these tests than members of other groups. An employer may set his qualifications as high as he likes, he may test to determine which applicants have these qualifications, and he may hire, assign, and promote on the basis of test performance." 110 Cong. Rec. 7213.

However, nothing there stated conflicts with the later memorandum dealing specifically with the debate over employer testing, 110 Cong.Rec. 7247 (quoted from in the text above), in which Senators Clark and Case explained that tests which measure "applicable job qualifications" are permissible under Title VII. In the earlier memorandum Clark and Case assured the Senate that employers were not to be prohibited from using tests that determine *qualifications.* Certainly a reasonable interpretation of what the Senators meant, in light of the subsequent memorandum directed specifically at employer testing, was that nothing in the Act prevents employers from requiring that applicants be fit for the job.

12. Senator Tower's original amendment provided in part that a test would be permissible "if . . . in the case of any individual who is seeking employment with such employer, such test is designed to determine or predict whether such individual is suitable or trainable with respect to his employment in the particular business or enterprise involved . . . ." 110 Cong.Rec. 13492. This language indicates that Senator Tower's aim was simply to make certain that job-related tests would be permitted. The opposition to the amendment was based on its loose wording which the proponents of Title VII feared would be susceptible of misinterpretation.

From the sum of the legislative history relevant in this case, the conclusion is inescapable that the EEOC's construction of § 703(h) to require that employment tests be job related comports with congressional-intent.

Nothing in the Act precludes the use of testing or measuring procedures; obviously they are useful. What Congress has forbidden is giving these devices and mechanisms controlling force unless they are demonstrably a reasonable measure of job performance. Congress has not commanded that the less qualified be preferred over the better qualified simply because of minority origins. Far from disparaging job qualifications as such, Congress has made such qualifications the controlling factor, so that race, religion, nationality, and sex become irrelevant. What Congress has commanded is that any tests used must measure the person for the job and not the person in the abstract.

The judgment of the Court of Appeals is, as to that portion of the judgment appealed from, reversed.

MR. JUSTICE BRENNAN took no part in the consideration or decision of this case.

Questions

1. Aptitude, achievement, and skills tests are widely used as gatekeeping devices in a variety of settings, e.g., college and university entrance examinations, public employer civil service examinations. Is it possible for such examinations to prevent or limit racial, ethnic, social, economic or religious bias and discrimination in the selection of new entrants? Do such tests reflect egalitarian and meritocratic attitudes regarding access to education and employment? What qualifications does the *Griggs* opinion impose on the use of such tests in situations governed by Title VII? Is that a reasonable qualification in light of the ostensible purpose of such examinations? Does that qualification impinge on the potential anti-discrimination function of such tests?

2. How did Duke Power "limit, segregate, or classify" employees, like Griggs, so as to deprive them of employment opportunities on the basis of race? In answering this question specify the evidence and process of inference through which Duke Power can be found to have discriminated in violation of section 703(a)(2) of Title VII.

3. In what sense, if at all, can it be said that Duke Power intentionally discriminated against Griggs et al.? Does § 703(a) call for any finding as to the employer's intent in this regard?

4. What does § 703(h) mean? How does it modify § 703(a)? What line of reasoning does the Court follow in reaching its answer to this question?

5. What is the past discrimination which the remedy in this case is intended to correct? How is Duke Power's test program related to that discrimination?

The final amendment, which was acceptable to all sides, could hardly have required less of a job relation than the first.

CONTRACTORS ASS'N OF EASTERN PA. v. SECRETARY OF LABOR

Third Circuit Court of Appeals, 1969.
442 F.2d 159.

[Some footnotes omitted; others renumbered.]

OPINION OF THE COURT

GIBBONS, CIRCUIT JUDGE.

The original plaintiff, the Contractors Association of Eastern Pennsylvania (the Association) and the intervening plaintiffs,[1] construction contractors doing business in the Philadelphia area (the Contractors), appeal from an order of the district court which denied their motion for summary judgment, granted the motion of the federal defendants[2] to dismiss the Association complaint for lack of standing, and granted the cross-motion of the federal defendants for summary judgment.[3]

*   *   *

The complaint challenges the validity of the Philadelphia Plan, promulgated by the federal defendants under the authority of Executive Order No. 11246. That Plan is embodied in two orders issued by officials of the United States Department of Labor, dated June 27, 1969 and September 23, 1969, respectively. . . . In summary, they require that bidders on any federal or federally assisted construction contracts for projects in a five-county area around Philadelphia, the estimated total cost of which exceeds $500,000, shall submit an acceptable affirmative action program which includes specific goals for the utilization of minority manpower in six skilled crafts: ironworkers, plumbers and pipefitters, steamfitters, sheetmetal workers, electrical workers, and elevator construction workers.

Executive Order No. 11246 requires all applicants for federal assistance to include in their construction contracts specific provisions respecting fair employment practices, including the provision:

"The contractor will take affirmative action to ensure that applicants are employed, and that employees are treated during employment, without regard to their race, color, religion, sex or national origin."

The Executive Order empowers the Secretary of Labor to issue rules and regulations necessary and appropriate to achieve its purpose. On June 27, 1969 Assistant Secretary of Labor Fletcher issued an order implementing the Executive Order in the five-county Philadelphia area. The order re-

1. James D. Morrissey, Inc.; The Conduit & Foundation Corp.; Glasgow, Inc.; Buckley & Company; The Nyleve Company; Erb Engineering & Constr. Co.; Perkins, Kanak, Foster, Inc.; and Lansdowne Constructors, Inc.

2. The Secretary of Labor, George P. Shultz; The Assistant Secretary of Labor, Arthur A. Fletcher; The Director, Office of Federal Contract Compliance, John L. Wilks; The Secretary of Agriculture, Clifford M. Hardin.

3. An additional defendant, the General State Authority of the Commonwealth of Pennsylvania, has not participated in this appeal.

quired bidders, prior to the award of contracts to submit "acceptable affirmative action" programs "which shall include specific goals of minority manpower utilization." The order contained a finding that enforcement of the "affirmative action" requirement of Executive Order No. 11246 had posed special problems in the construction trades. Contractors and subcontractors must hire a new employee complement for each job, and they rely on craft unions as their prime or sole source for labor. The craft unions operate hiring halls. "Because of the exclusionary practices of labor organizations," the order finds "there traditionally has been only a small number of Negroes employed in these seven trades." The June 27, 1969 order provided that the Area Coordinator of the Office of Federal Contract Compliance, in conjunction with the federal contracting and administering agencies in the Philadelphia area, would determine definite standards for specific goals in a contractor's affirmative action program. After such standards were determined, each bidder would be required to commit itself to specific goals for minority manpower utilization. The order set forth factors to be considered in determining definite standards including:

"(1) The current extent of minority group participation in the trade.

(2) The availability of minority group persons for employment in such trade.

(3) The need for training programs in the area and/or the need to assure demand for those in or from existing training programs.

(4) The impact of the program upon the existing labor force."

Acting pursuant to the June 29, 1969 order, representatives of the Department of Labor held public hearings in Philadelphia on August 26, 27 and 28, 1969. On September 23, 1969, Assistant Secretary Fletcher made findings with respect to each of the listed factors and ordered that the following ranges be established as the standards for minority manpower utilization for each of the designated trades in the Philadelphia area for the following four years:

Identification of Trade	Range of Minority Group Employment			
	Until 12/31/70	for 1971	for 1972	for 1973
Ironworkers	5%–9%	11%–15%	16%–20%	22%–26%
Plumbers & Pipefitters	5%–8%	10%–14%	15%–19%	20%–24%
Steamfitters	5%–8%	11%–15%	15%–19%	20%–24%
Sheetmetal workers	4%–8%	9%–13%	14%–18%	19%–23%
Electrical workers	4%–8%	9%–13%	14%–18%	19%–23%
Elevator construction workers	4%–8%	9%–13%	14%–18%	19%–23%

The order of September 23, 1969 specified that on each invitation to bid each bidder would be required to submit an affirmative action program. The order further provided:

"4. No bidder will be awarded a contract unless his affirmative action program contains goals falling within the range set forth * * * above. * * *

* * *

6. The purpose of the contractor's commitment to specific goals as to minority manpower utilization is to meet his affirmative action obligations under the equal opportunity clause of the contract. This commitment is not intended and shall not be used to discriminate against any qualified applicant or employee. Whenever it comes to the bidder's attention that the goals are being used in a discriminatory manner, he must report it to the Area Coordinator of the Office of Federal Contract Compliance of the U. S. Department of Labor in order that appropriate sanction proceedings may be instituted.

* * *

8. The bidder agrees to keep such records and file such reports relating to the provisions of this order as shall be required by the contracting or administering agency."

In November, 1969, the General State Authority of the Commonwealth of Pennsylvania issued invitations to bid for the construction of an earth dam on Marsh Creek in Chester County, Pennsylvania. Although this dam is a Commonwealth project, part of the construction cost, estimated at over $3,000,000 is to be funded by federal monies under a program administered by the Department of Agriculture. The Secretary of Agriculture, one of the federal defendants, as a condition for payment of federal financial assistance for the project, required the inclusion in each bid of a Philadelphia Plan Commitment in compliance with the order of September 23, 1969. On November 14, 1969, the General State Authority issued an addendum to the original invitation for bids requiring all bidders to include such a commitment in their bids. It is alleged and not denied that except for the requirement by the Secretary of Agriculture that the Philadelphia Plan Commitment be included, the General State Authority would not have imposed such a requirement on bidders.

The Association consists of more than eighty contractors in the five-county Philadelphia area who regularly employ workers in the six specified crafts, and who collectively perform more than $150,000,000 of federal and federally assisted construction in that area annually. Each of the contractor plaintiffs is a regular bidder on federal and federally assisted construction projects. The complaint was filed prior to the opening of bids on the Marsh Creek dam. It sought injunctive relief against the inclusion of a Philadelphia Plan Commitment requirement in the invitation for bids. By virtue of a stipulation that the General State Authority would issue a new and superseding invitation for bids if the district court held the Plan to be unlawful, the parties agreed that bids could be received without affecting the justiciability of the controversy. Bids were received on January 7, 1970. One of the intervening contractor plaintiffs submitted a low bid and appeared at the time of the district court decision to be entitled to an award of the contract.

The complaints of the Association and the Contractors refer to the fact that the Comptroller General of the United States has opined that the Philadelphia Plan Commitment is illegal and that disbursement of federal funds for the performance of a contract containing such a promise will be treated as unlawful.[4] The plaintiffs point out that the withholding of funds after a contractor has commenced performance would have catastrophic consequences, since contractors depend upon progress payments, and are in no position to complete their contracts without such payments. They allege that the Philadelphia Plan is illegal and void for the following reasons:

1. It is action by the Executive branch not authorized by the constitution or any statute and beyond Executive power.

2. It is inconsistent with Title VII of the Civil Rights Act of 1964.

3. It is inconsistent with Title VI of the Civil Rights Act of 1964.

4. It is inconsistent with the National Labor Relations Act.

5. It is substantively inconsistent with and was not adopted in procedural accordance with Executive Order No. 11246.

6. It violates due process because

    a) it requires contradictory conduct impossible of consistent attainment;

    b) it unreasonably requires contractors to undertake to remedy an evil for which the craft unions, not they, are responsible;

    c) it arbitrarily and without basis in fact singles out the five-county Philadelphia area for discriminatory treatment without adequate basis in fact or law; and

    d) it requires quota hiring in violation of the Fifth Amendment.

* * *

Executive Power

The plaintiffs contend that the Philadelphia Plan is social legislation of local application enacted by the Executive without the benefit of statutory or constitutional authority. They point out, probably correctly, that the Plan imposes on the successful bidder on a project of the Commonwealth of Pennslyvania record keeping and hiring practices which violate Pennslyvania law. If the Plan was adopted pursuant to a valid exercise of presidential power its provisions would, of course, control over local law. [Citations omitted.] But, say the plaintiffs, where there is neither statutory authorization nor constitutional authority for the Executive action, no substantive federal requirements may be imposed upon a contract between the Commonwealth and its contractor.

---

4. Comp.Gen.Op., Letter to Sec. of Labor George P. Shultz, August 5, 1969, 115 Cong.Rec. 17,201–04 (daily ed. Dec. 18, 1969). The Comptroller General had objected to earlier efforts at implementing the "affirmative action" aspect of Exec.Order No. 11246 on the ground that these plans failed to inform prospective bidders of definite minimum standards for acceptable programs. In his negative opinion letter in response to the original Philadelphia Pre-Award Plan, he had also adverted to the possibility of conflict with Title VII of the Civil Rights Act of 1964. . . . The Title VII objections became the heart of the opinion of August 5, 1969 which challenged the validity of the Revised Philadelphia Plan.

The district court's answer is that the federal government "has the unrestricted power to fix the terms, conditions and those with whom it will deal." For this proposition it cites Perkins v. Lukens Steel Co., 310 U.S. 113, 60 S.Ct. 869 (1940) ánd King v. Smith, 392 U.S. 309, 333, 88 S.Ct. 2128 (1968). Neither case is in point, however on the issue of Executive as distinguished from federal power.

*   *   *

The federal defendants and several amici contend that Executive power to impose fair employment conditions incident to the power to contract has been upheld in this circuit and in the Fifth Circuit. They cite Farmer v. Philadelphia Electric Company, 329 F.2d 3 (3d Cir. 1964) and Farkas v. Texas Instrument, Inc., 375 F.2d 629 (5th Cir.), certiorari denied 389 U.S. 977, 88 S.Ct. 480 (1967). Both cases discussed the Executive Order program for achieving fair employment in the context of Government contracts rather than federally assisted state contracts, and both assumed the validity of the Executive Order then applicable. Both cases held that even assuming the validity of the Executive Order, it did not give rise to a private cause of action for damages by a party subjected to discrimination. Discussion of the validity of the Executive Order was in each case dictum. Moreover, both *Farmer* and *Farkas* refer to 40 U.S.C. § 486(a) as the source of the Executive power to issue the order. That subsection authorizes the President to prescribe such policies and directives as he deems necessary to effectuate the provisions of Chapter 10 of Title 40 and Chapter 4 of Title 41. These chapters deal with procurement of Government property and services, not with federal assistance programs. Thus even if *Farmer* and *Farkas* were holdings rather than dicta as to Executive power, the holdings would not reach the instant case. The validity of the Executive Order program as applied to the construction industry in state government contracts by virtue of federal assistance has not been litigated, so far as we have been able to determine, in any case reaching the courts of appeals. Certainly no case has arisen which considers Executive power to impose, by virtue of federal assistance, contract terms in a state construction contract which are at variance with state law.

The limitations of Executive power have rarely been considered by the courts. One of those rare instances is Youngstown Sheet & Tube Co. v. Sawyer, 343 U.S. 579, 72 S.Ct. 863 (1952). From the six concurring opinions and one dissenting opinion in that case, the most significant guidance for present purposes may be found in that of Justice Jackson:

"We may well begin by a somewhat oversimplified grouping of practical situations in which a President may doubt, or others may challenge, his powers, and by distinguishing roughly the legal consequences of this factor of relativity.

1. When the President acts pursuant to an express or implied authorization of Congress, his authority is at its maximum, for it includes all that he possesses in his own right plus all that Congress can delegate. In these circumstances, and in these only, may he be said (for what it may be worth) to personify the federal sovereignty. If his act is held unconstitutional under these circumstances, it usually means that the Federal Government as an undivided whole lacks power. A seizure executed by the President

pursuant to an Act of Congress would be supported by the strongest of presumptions and the widest latitude of judicial interpretation, and the burden of persuasion would rest heavily on any who might attack it.

2.   When the President acts in absence of either a congressional grant or denial of authority, he can only rely upon his own independent powers, but there is a zone of twilight in which he and Congress may have concurrent authority, or in which its distribution is uncertain.   Therefore, congressional inertia, indifference or quiescence may sometimes, at least as a practical matter, enable, if not invite, measures on independent presidential responsibility.   In this area, any actual test of power is likely to depend on the imperatives of events and contemporary imponderables rather than on abstract theories of law.

3.   When the President takes measures incompatible with the expressed or implied will of Congress, his power is at its lowest ebb, for then he can rely only upon his own constitutional powers minus any constitutional powers of Congress over the matter. Courts can sustain exclusive presidential control in such a case only by disabling the Congress from acting upon the subject. Presidential claim to a power at once so conclusive and preclusive must be scrutinized with caution, for what is at stake is the equilibrium established by our constitutional system."

Plaintiffs contend that the Philadelphia Plan is inconsistent with the will of Congress expressed in several statutes.   We deal with these statutory contentions hereinafter.   Thus for the moment we may set to one side consideration of Justice Jackson's third category, and turn to category (1), action expressly or impliedly authorized, and category (2), action in which the President has implied power to act in the absence of congressional preemption.   To determine into which category the Philadelphia Plan falls a review of Executive Orders in the field of fair employment practices is helpful.

The first such order, Executive Order No. 8802, was signed by President Roosevelt on June 25, 1941.   It established in the Office of Production Management a Committee on Fair Employment Practice, and it required that all Government contracting agencies include in all defense contracts a covenant not to discriminate against any worker because of race, creed, color, or national origin.   The order contained no specific statutory reference, and describes the action "as a prerequisite to the successful conduct of our national defense production effort."   In December 1941 Congress enacted "An Act to expedite the prosecution of the war effort," and on December 27, 1941, pursuant to that Act the President issued Executive Order No. 9001 which granted to the War and Navy Departments and the Maritime Commission broad contracting authority   This order among other provisions stated that a non-discrimination clause would be deemed incorporated by reference in all such contracts.   On May 27, 1943, Executive Order No. 8802 was amended by Executive Order No. 9346 which established in the Office for Emergency Management of the Executive Office of the President a Committee on Fair Employment Practice. This order required the antidiscrimination clause in all government contracts rather than in defense contracts only. Still, the order was quite clearly bottomed on the President's war mobilization powers and was by its terms directed toward enhancing the pool of workers available for defense production.

On December 18, 1945, President Truman signed Executive Order No. 9664, which continued the Committee established by Executive Orders Nos. 8802 and 9346 "for the periods and subject to the conditions stated in the National War Agencies Appropriation Act, 1946 (Public Law 156, 79th Cong., 1st Sess., approved July 17, 1945)." On February 2, 1951, the President signed Executive Order No. 10210, which transferred to the Department of Defense the contracting powers referred to in Executive Order No. 9001. The order continued the provision that a non-discrimination clause would be deemed incorporated by reference in all defense contracts. It referenced the First War Powers Act, 1941, as amended. By a subsequent series of Executive Orders, Executive Order No. 10210 was extended to other Government agencies engaged in defense related procurement. On December 3, 1951 the President signed Executive Order No. 10308, creating the Committee on Government Contract Compliance, which was charged with the duty of obtaining compliance with the non-discrimination contract provisions. The statutory authorities referenced in Executive Order No. 10308 are the Defense Production Act of 1950 and 31 U.S.C. § 691. Reference to the Defense Production Act of 1950 shows that the President was still acting, pursuant to his national defense powers, to assure maximum utilization of available manpower.

President Eisenhower on August 13, 1953, by Executive Order No. 10479 revoked Executive Order No. 10308 and transferred the compliance functions of the Committee on Government Contract Compliance to the Government Contract Committee. In this order for the first time there is no mention of defense production. For the first time the Committee is authorized to receive complaints of violations, and to conduct activities not directly related to federal procurement. On September 3, 1954, by Executive Order No. 10557 the required form of Government contract provision was revised. The new provision was much more specific, required the imposition of the contractor's obligation on his subcontractors, and required the posting of appropriate notices. The Eisenhower orders, while they did not refer to defense production and did authorize the Compliance Committee to encourage nondiscrimination outside the field of Government contracts, were still restricted in direct application to federal government procurement. While the orders do not contain any specific statutory reference other than the appropriations statute, 31 U.S.C. § 690, they would seem to be authorized by the broad grant of procurement authority with respect to Titles 40 and 41. No less than in the case of defense procurement it is in the interest of the United States in all procurement to see that its suppliers are not over the long run increasing its costs and delaying its programs by excluding from the labor pool available minority workmen. In the area of Government procurement Executive authority to impose non-discrimination contract provisions falls in Justice Jackson's first category: action pursuant to the express or implied authorization of Congress.

Executive Order No. 10925 signed by President Kennedy on March 6, 1961, among other things enlarged the notice requirements and specified that the President's Committee on Equal Employment Opportunity could by rule, regulation or order impose sanctions for violation. Coverage still extended only to federal government contracts. Significantly for purposes of this case, however, the required contract language was amended to add the provision:

> "The Contractor will take affirmative action to ensure that applicants are employed, and that employees are treated during employment, without regard to their race, creed, color, or national origin."

The Philadelphia Plan is simply a refined approach to this "affirmative action" mandate. Applied to federal procurement the affirmative action clause is supported by the same Presidential procurement authority that supports the non-discrimination clause generally.

The most significant change in the Executive Order program for present purposes occurred on June 22, 1963 when the President signed Executive Order No. 11114, which amended Executive Order No. 10925 by providing that the same non-discrimination contract provisions heretofore required in all federal procurement contracts must also be included in all federally assisted construction contracts. By way of Executive Order No. 11246 issued in 1965, President Johnson transferred to the Secretary of Labor the functions formerly specified in Executive Order Nos. 10925 and 11114, and he continued both the affirmative action requirement and the coverage of federally assisted construction contracts.

While all federal procurement contracts must include an affirmative action covenant, the coverage on federally assisted contracts has been extended to construction contracts only. This choice is significant, for it demonstrates that the Presidents were not attempting by the Executive Order program merely to impose their notions of desirable social legislation on the states wholesale. Rather, they acted in the one area in which discrimination in employment was most likely to affect the cost and the progress of projects in which the federal government had both financial and completion interests. In direct procurement the federal government has a vital interest in assuring that the largest possible pool of qualified manpower be available for the accomplishment of its projects. It has the identical interest with respect to federally assisted construction projects. When the Congress authorizes an appropriation for a program of federal assistance, and authorizes the Executive branch to implement the program by arranging for assistance to specific projects, in the absence of specific statutory regulations it must be deemed to have granted to the President a general authority to act for the protection of federal interests. In the case of Executive Order Nos. 11246 and 11114 three Presidents have acted by analogizing federally assisted construction to direct federal procurement. If such action has not been authorized by Congress (Justice Jackson's first category), at the least it falls within the second category. If no congressional enactments prohibit what has been done, the Executive action is valid. Particularly is this so when Congress, aware of Presidential action with respect to federally assisted construction projects since June of 1963, has continued to make appropriations for such projects. We conclude, therefore, that unless the Philadelphia Plan is prohibited by some other congressional enactment, its inclusion as a pre-condition for federal assistance was within the implied authority of the President and his designees. We turn, then to a consideration of the statutes on which plaintiffs rely.

The Civil Rights Act of 1964

Plaintiffs suggest that by enacting Title VII of the Civil Rights Act of 1964, 42 U.S.C. § 2000e et seq. which deals comprehensively with discrimination in employment, Congress occupied the field. The express reference in that statute to Executive Order No. 10925 or any other Executive Order prescribing fair employment practices for Government contractors, 42 U.S.C. § 2000e–8(d), indicates, however, that Congress contemplated continuance of the Executive Order program. Moreover we have held that the remedies established by Title VII are not exclusive. Young v. International Telephone & Telegraph Co., 438 F.2d 757 (3d Cir. 1971).

But while Congress has not prohibited Presidential action in the area of fair employment on federal or federally assisted contracts, the Executive is bound by the express prohibitions of Title VII. The argument most strenuously advanced against the Philadelphia Plan is that it requires action by employers which violates the Act. Plaintiffs point to § 703(j), 42 U.S.C. § 2000e–2(j):

> "Nothing contained in this subchapter shall be interpreted to require any employer * * * [or] labor organization * * * to grant preferential treatment to any individual or to any group because of the race * * * of such individual or groups on account of an imbalance which may exist with respect to the total number or percentage of persons of any race * * * employed * * * in comparison with the total number or percentage of persons of such race * * * in the available work force in any community * * * or other area."

The Plan requires that the contractor establish specific goals for utilization of available minority manpower in six trades in the five-county area. Possibly an employer could not be compelled, under the authority of Title VII, to embrace such a program, although § 703(j) refers to percentages of minorities in an area work force rather than percentages of minority tradesmen in an available trade work force. We do not meet the issue here, however, for the source of the required contract provision is Executive Order No. 11246. Section 703(j) is a limitation only upon Title VII not upon any other remedies, state or federal.

Plaintiffs, and more particularly the union amici, contend that the Plan violates Title VII because it interferes with a bona fide seniority system. Section 703(h), 42 U.S.C. § 2000e–2(h), provides:

> "Notwithstanding any other provision of this subchapter, it shall not be an unlawful employment practice for an employer to employ different standards of compensation, or different terms, conditions, or privileges of employment pursuant to a bona fide seniority or merit system * * * ."

The unions, it is said, refer men from the hiring halls on the basis of seniority, and the Philadelphia Plan interferes with this arrangement since few minority tradesmen have high seniority. Just as with § 703(j), however, § 703(h) is a limitation only upon Title VII, not upon any other remedies.

Plaintiffs contend that the Plan, by imposing remedial quotas, requires them to violate the basic prohibitions of Section 703(a), 42 U.S.C. § 2000e–2(a):

"It shall be an unlawful employment practice for an employer—

   (1) to fail or refuse to hire * * * any individual * * * because of such individual's race * * * or

   (2) to * * * classify his employees in any way which would deprive * * * any individual of employment opportunities * * * because of such individual's race * * *."

Because the Plan requires that the contractor agree to specific goals for minority employment in each of the six trades and requires a good faith effort to achieve those goals, they argue, it requires (1) that they refuse to hire some white tradesmen, and (2) that they classify their employees by race, in violation of § 703(a). This argument rests on an overly simple reading both of the Plan and of the findings which led to its adoption.

The order of September 23, 1969 contained findings that although overall minority group representation in the construction industry in the five-county Philadelphia area was thirty per cent, in the six trades representation was approximately one per cent. It found, moreover, that this obvious underrepresentation was due to the exclusionary practices of the unions representing the six trades. It is the practice of building contractors to rely on union hiring halls as the prime source for employees. The order made further findings as to the availability of qualified minority tradesmen for employment in each trade, and as to the impact of an affirmative action program with specific goals upon the existing labor force. The Department of Labor found that contractors could commit to the specific employment goals "without adverse impact on the existing labor force." Some minority tradesmen could be recruited, in other words, without eliminating job opportunities for white tradesmen.

To read § 703(a) in the manner suggested by the plaintiffs we would have to attribute to Congress the intention to freeze the status quo and to foreclose remedial action under other authority designed to overcome existing evils. We discern no such intention either from the language of the statute or from its legislative history. Clearly the Philadelphia Plan is color-conscious. Indeed the only meaning which can be attributed to the "affirmative action" language which since March of 1961 has been included in successive Executive Orders is that Government contractors must be color-conscious. Since 1941 the Executive Order program has recognized that discriminatory practices exclude available minority manpower from the labor pool. In other contexts color-consciousness has been deemed to be an appropriate remedial posture. Porcelli v. Titus, 302 F.Supp. 726 (D.N.J. 1969), affirmed 431 F.2d 1254 (3d Cir. 1970); Norwalk CORE v. Norwalk Redevelopment Agency, 395 F.2d 920, 931 (2d Cir. 1968); Offermann v. Nitkowski, 378 F.2d 22, 24 (2d Cir. 1967). It has been said respecting Title VII that "Congress did not intend to freeze an entire generation of Negro employees into discriminatory patterns that existed before the Act." Quarles v. Philip Morris, Inc., *supra*, 279 F.Supp. at 514. The *Quarles* case rejected the contention that existing, nondiscriminatory seniority arrangements were so sanctified by Title VII that the effects of past discrimination in job assignments could not be overcome. We reject the contention that Title VII prevents the President acting through the Executive Order program from attempting to remedy the absence from the Philadelphia construction labor of minority tradesmen in key trades.

What we have said about Title VII applies with equal force to Title VI of the Civil Rights Act of 1964, 42 U.S.C. § 2000d et seq. That Title prohibits racial and other discrimination in any program or activity receiving federal financial assistance. This general prohibition against discrimination cannot be construed as limiting Executive authority in defining appropriate affirmative action on the part of a contractor.

We hold that the Philadelphia Plan does not violate the Civil Rights Act of 1964.

The National Labor Relations Act

The June 27, 1969 order, par. 8(b) provides:

"It is no excuse that the union with which the contractor has a collective bargaining agreement failed to refer minority employees. Discrimination in referral for employment, even if pursuant to provisions of a collective bargaining agreement, is prohibited by the National Labor Relations Act and the Civil Rights Act of 1964. It is the longstanding uniform policy of OFCC that contractors and subcontractors have a responsibility to provide equal employment opportunity if they want to participate in federally involved contracts. To the extent they have delegated the responsibility for some of their employment practices to some other organization or agency which prevents them from meeting their obligations pursuant to Executive Order 11246, as amended, such contractors cannot be considered to be in compliance with Executive Order 11246, as amended, or the implementing rules, regulations and orders."

The union amici vigorously contend that the Plan violates the National Labor Relations Act by interfering with the exclusive union referral systems to which the contractors have in collective bargaining agreements bound themselves. Exclusive hiring hall contracts in the building and construction industry are validated by Section 8(f) of the National Labor Relations Act, 29 U.S.C. § 158(f). In Teamsters Local 357 v. NLRB, 365 U.S. 667, 81 S. Ct. 835 (1961), the Supreme Court held that the National Labor Relations Board could not proscribe exclusive hiring hall agreements as illegal per se since Congress had not chosen to prohibit hiring halls. It is argued that the President is attempting to do what the Supreme Court said the National Labor Relations Board could not do—prohibit a valid hiring hall agreement. Of course collective bargaining agreements which perpetuate the effects of past discrimination are unlawful under Title VII. Local 189, United Papermakers & Paperworkers v. United States, *supra*; United States v. Sheet Metal Workers, Local 36, 416 F.2d 123, 132 (8th Cir. 1969). The findings of past discrimination which justified remedial action in these cases were made in judicial proceedings, however. See 42 U.S.C. § 2000e–5(g). The amici contend that the Assistant Secretary's nonjudicial finding of prior exclusionary practices is insufficient to support the Plan's implied requirement that the contractor look to other sources for employees if the unions fail to refer sufficient minority group members.

It is clear that while hiring hall arrangements are permitted by federal law they are not required. Nothing in the National Labor Relations Act purports to place any limitation upon the contracting power of the federal government. We have said hereinabove that in imposing the affirmative action requirement on federally assisted construction contracts the President acted within his implied contracting authority. The assisted agency may either agree to do business with contractors who will comply with the affirmative action covenant, or forego assistance. The prospective contractors may either agree to undertake the affirmative action covenant, or forego bidding on federally assisted work. If the Plan violates neither the Constitution nor federal law, the fact that its contractual provisions may be at variance with other contractual undertakings of the contractor is legally irrelevant. Factually, of course, that variance is quite relevant. Factually it is entirely likely that the economics of the marketplace will produce an accommodation between the contract provisions desired by the unions and those desired by the source of the funds. Such an accommodation will be no violation of the National Labor Relations Act.

The absence of a judicial finding of past discrimination is also legally irrelevant. The Assistant Secretary acted not pursuant to Title VII but pursuant to the Executive Order. Regardless of the cause, exclusion from the available labor pool of minority tradesmen is likely to have an adverse effect upon the cost and completion of construction projects in which the federal government is interested. Even absent a finding that the situation found to exist in the five-county area was the result of deliberate past discrimination, the federal interest in improving the availability of key tradesmen in the labor pool would be the same. While a court must find intentional past discrimination before it can require affirmative action under 42 U.S.C. § 2000e–5(g), that section imposes no restraint upon the measures which the President may require of the beneficiaries of federal assistance. The decision of his designees as to the specific affirmative action which would satisfy the local situation did not violate the National Labor Relations Act and was not prohibited by 42 U.S.C. § 2000e–5(g).

Consistency with Executive Order No. 11246

The plaintiffs argue that the affirmative action mandate of § 202 of Executive Order No. 11246 is limited by the more general requirement in the same section, "The contractor will not discriminate against any employee or applicant for employment because of race, creed, color, or national origin." They contend that properly construed the affirmative action referred to means only policing against actual present discrimination, not action looking toward the employment of specific numbers of minority tradesmen.

Section 201 of the Executive Order provides:
"The Secretary of Labor shall be responsible for the administration of Parts II [Government contracts] and III [federal assistance] of this Order and shall adopt such rules and regulations and issue such orders as he deems necessary and appropriate to achieve the purposes thereof."

Acting under this broad delegation of authority the Labor Department in a series of orders of local application made it clear that it interpreted "affirmative action" to require more than mere policing against actual present discrimination. Administrative action pursuant to an Executive Order is invalid and subject to judicial review if beyond the scope of the Executive Order. Peters v. Hobby, 349 U.S. 331, 75 S.Ct. 790 (1955). But the courts should give more than ordinary deference to an administrative agency's interpretation of an Executive Order or regulation which it is charged to administer. Udall v. Tallman, 380 U.S. 1, 85 S.Ct. 792 (1965); Bowles v. Seminole Rock & Sand Co., 325 U.S. 410, 413, 65 S.Ct. 1215 (1945). The Attorney General has issued an opinion that the Philadelphia Plan is valid, and the President has continued to acquiesce in the interpretation of the Executive Order made by his designee. The Labor Department interpretation of the affirmative action clause must, therefore, be deferred to by the courts.

Plaintiffs also contend that the signing of the June 27, 1969 and September 23, 1969 orders by an assistant secretary rather than by the Secretary of Labor makes those orders procedurally invalid. Here they rely on § 401 which provides:

> "The Secretary of Labor may delegate to any officer, agency, or employee in the Executive branch of the Government, any function or duty of the Secretary under Parts II and III of this Order, except authority to promulgate rules and regulations of a general nature."

The Plan, they say, is a rule or regulation of a general nature, and could have been issued only by the Secretary. In the first place the Plan is not general. It is based upon findings as to the available construction manpower in a specific labor market. Moreover, the interpretation of § 401 made by the administrator requires the same deference from the courts as is required toward his other interpretations of the order. We will not second guess his delegation to the Assistant Secretary of the duty of enforcing the affirmative action covenant.

The Due Process Contentions

Plaintiffs urge that the Plan violates the Due Process Clause of the Fifth Amendment in several ways.

First, they allege that it imposes on the contractors contradictory duties impossible of attainment. This impossibility arises, they say, because the Plan requires both an undertaking to seek achievement of specific goals of minority employment and an undertaking not to discriminate against any qualified applicant or employee, and because a decision to hire any black employee necessarily involves a decision not to hire a qualified white employee. This is pure sophistry. The findings in the September 23, 1969 order disclose that the specific goals may be met, considering normal employee attrition and anticipated growth in the industry, without adverse effects on the existing labor force. According to the order the construction industry has an essentially transitory labor force and is often in short supply in key trades. The complaint does not allege that these findings misstate the underlying facts.

Next the plaintiffs urge that the Plan is arbitrary and capricious administrative action, in that it singles out the contractors and makes them take action to remedy the situation created by acts of past discrimination by the craft unions. They point to the absence of any proceedings under Title VII against the offending unions, and urge that they are being discriminated against. This argument misconceives the source of the authority for the affirmative action program. Plaintiffs are not being discriminated against. They are merely being invited to bid on a contract with terms imposed by the source of the funds. The affirmative action covenant is no different in kind than other covenants specified in the invitation to bid. The Plan does not impose a punishment for past misconduct. It exacts a covenant for present performance.

Some amici urge that selection of the five-county Philadelphia area was arbitrary and capricious and without basis in fact. The complaint contains a conclusive allegation to this effect. No supporting facts are alleged. It is not alleged, for example, that the specific goals for minority manpower utilization would be different if more or fewer counties were to be included in the September 23, 1969 order. The union amici do question the findings made by the Assistant Secretary of Labor, but the complaint, fairly read, does not put these findings in issue. We read the allegation with respect to the five-county area as putting in issue the legal authority of the Secretary to impose a specific affirmative action requirement in any separate geographic area. The simple answer to this contention is that federally assisted construction contracts are performed at specific times and in specific places. What is appropriate affirmative action will vary according to the local manpower conditions prevailing at the time.

Finally, the plaintiffs urge that the specific goals specified by the Plan are racial quotas prohibited by the equal protection aspect of the Fifth Amendment. See Shapiro v. Thompson, 394 U.S. 618, 641–642, 89 S.Ct. 1322 (1969); Schneider v. Rusk, 377 U.S. 163, 84 S.Ct. 1187 (1964); Bolling v. Sharpe, 347 U.S. 497, 74 S.Ct. 693 (1954). The Philadelphia Plan is valid Executive action designed to remedy the perceived evil that minority tradesmen have not been included in the labor pool available for the performance of construction projects in which the federal government has a cost and performance interest. The Fifth Amendment does not prohibit such action.

* * *

The judgment of the district court will be affirmed.

Questions

1. The opinion details the long history of Executive Orders attempting to deal with racial discrimination by federal contractors. (*Supra* pp. 1157–1161.) What is the federal interest which the court finds is the basis for upholding the validity of these Executive Orders?

2. Why is the validity of the Executive Order program significant to the outcome in this case? See the discussion of §§ 703(j) and (h) at pp. 1162–1163, *supra*.

3. What is the remedy against racial discrimination provided in the Philadelphia Plan? What (whose) discriminatory acts are the

subject of that remedy? Is the remedy designed to compensate for past discrimination? Prevent future discrimination? To do both?

4. What is the basis for the employers' and the unions' argument that § 703(a) bars the Philadelphia Plan? See pp. 1163–1164, *supra.* Do they argue that Title VII requires an employer to be color blind in selecting persons for employment? Are there statutory grounds for that argument? Does the history of race relations law support that argument? What is the counter argument?

5. What costs, both private and social, may be incurred through implementation of a Philadelphia Plan? Who will bear those costs? Who should bear those costs? How and by whom should such decisions be made?

———

Griggs and Contractors Association illustrate the expansive reading federal courts have given to Title VII in the years since its adoption. It should be apparent, however, that this line of judicial development puts the law regarding employment discrimination on a potential collision course with the results of national law and policy regarding collective bargaining. For example, orderly hiring, advancement and termination procedures are normal subjects of collective bargaining. Thus in Contractors Association employers and unions had negotiated a contract calling for employment of tradesmen to be arranged through union hiring halls utilizing seniority in the trade as the basic criterion for selection. Since past discrimination by both employers and unions had kept minority workers out of the construction trades, they obviously had low or no seniority in employment. Accordingly, efforts to expand minority employment in those trades would be inconsistent with the seniority principle in any period when the jobs available were less than the number of tradesmen on the seniority list. Since advancement in employment can be conditioned on seniority, efforts to open higher skilled trades or supervisory positions to minority workers also run counter to the seniority principle, and if minority workers are to be afforded job security then seniority may have to yield to some other criteria for deciding who will be laid off in periods of employment contraction.

The courts have grappled with this problem with somewhat mixed results. In Franks v. Bowman Transp. Co., 424 U.S. 751, 96 S.Ct. 1251 (1976), the Supreme Court held that federal courts have the authority, in some cases, to accord seniority rights to minority employees who have suffered employment discrimination *after* the adoption of the Civil Rights Act of 1964.

In the term following its decision in Franks v. Bowman the Court was required to deal with an issue not addressed in that case. Franks dealt only with the grant of seniority as a remedy for acts of unlawful discrimination committed *after* the adoption of the Civil Rights Act of

1964. In International Bhd. of Teamsters v. U. S., 431 U.S. 324, 97 S. Ct. 1843 (1977), a lower court had awarded seniority to minority group employees on the basis that the seniority system negotiated between the union (Teamsters) and an employer (T.I.M.E.–D.C., Inc.) unlawfully perpetuated the effects of "pre-act" discrimination. The lower court had been persuaded by the Justice Department's arguments that no seniority system which perpetuated the effects of "pre-act" discrimination could be held to be a bona fide system entitled to the immunity afforded by § 703(h). That section of Title VII provides that "it shall not be an unlawful employment practice for an employer to apply different standards of compensation, or different terms, conditions, or privileges of employment pursuant to a bona fide seniority . . . system" where the differential treatment was not the result of an intention to discriminate on the basis of race. The Supreme Court reversed, finding that:

> In sum, the unmistakable purpose of § 703(h) was to make clear that the routine application of a bona fide seniority system would not be unlawful under Title VII. As the legislative history shows, this was the intended result even where the employer's pre-Act discrimination resulted in whites having greater existing seniority rights than Negroes. Although a seniority system inevitably tends to perpetuate the effects of pre-Act discrimination in such cases, the congressional judgment was that Title VII should not outlaw the use of existing seniority lists and thereby destroy or water down the vested seniority rights of employees simply because their employer had engaged in discrimination prior to the passage of the Act.
>
> To be sure, § 703(h) does not immunize all seniority systems. It refers only to "bona fide" systems, and a proviso requires that any differences in treatment not be "the result of an intention to discriminate because of race . . . or national origin . . . ." But our reading of the legislative history compels us to reject the Government's broad argument that no seniority system that tends to perpetuate pre-Act discrimination can be "bona fide." To accept the argument would require us to hold that a seniority system becomes illegal simply because it allows the full exercise of the pre-Act seniority rights of employees of a company that discriminated before Title VII was enacted. It would place an affirmative obligation on the parties to the seniority agreement to subordinate those rights in favor of the claims of pre-Act discriminatees without seniority. The consequence would be a perversion of the congressional purpose. We cannot accept the invitation to disembowel § 703(h) by reading the words "bona fide" as the Government would have us do. Accordingly, we hold that an otherwise neutral, legitimate seniority system does not become unlawful under Title VII simply because it may perpetuate pre-Act discrimination. Congress did not intend to make it illegal for employees with vested seniority

rights to continue to exercise those rights, even at the expense of pre-Act discriminatees.

In dissent Justices Marshall and Brennan, pointed out that the majority finding with respect to § 703(h) ran against the weight of authority. They noted that in over 30 cases six of the Circuit Courts of Appeals had decided "that § 703(h) does not immunize seniority systems that perpetuate the effects of prior [unlawful] discrimination," that the EEOC had reached the same conclusion in a long line of cases where it had made findings, and that "the overwhelming weight of scholarly opinion" supported the Circuit Courts and EEOC on this issue. 431 U.S. 324, at footnotes 2–5. The dissenters also suggested that Teamsters represented a retreat by the Court from its prior expressed opinion that the interpretations of the EEOC are "entitled to great deference," see Griggs v. Duke Power Co., *supra* at p. 1151. The majority decision in Teamsters may indicate that at least in the Supreme Court, Title VII may not continue to receive quite "the expansive and favorable development" chronicled in Professor Peck's accounting for the decade 1965–1975. See Peck, *supra* p. 1093.

Doubt about the future course of the law regarding remedies for racial discrimination was also raised by the Court's decision in Bakke v. Board of Regents of the University of California, 438 U.S. 265, 98 S.Ct. 2733 (1978). Plaintiff-respondent Bakke twice applied for and was denied admission to the medical school of the University of California at Davis. Each year the medical school enrolled a class of 100 first year students. Sixteen places in the class were reserved for special admissions of Black-Americans, Mexican-Americans, Asian-Americans, and American Indians. Bakke alleged that this affirmative action program violated his Fourteenth Amendment right to Equal Protection against discriminatory state action. He sued in the Superior Court of California, seeking to enjoin the Cal-Davis affirmative action program and for an order that he be admitted to the medical school. The Court found for Bakke and granted the requested injunction but not the order for his admission. Both Bakke and the Regents appealed to the California Supreme Court. That Court affirmed the findings of the Superior Court but modified the judgment to order Bakke's admission to medical school. The Regents petitioned the Supreme Court for review, and the petition was granted. In what is surely one of the most difficult and hotly debated decisions and series of opinions recently rendered by the Court, Bakke's admission to medical school was confirmed; the Supreme Court affirmed so much of the order of the California Courts as barred the absolute affirmative action quota of the Cal-Davis medical school; but the Court reversed the California Courts' order which barred the medical school from taking account of race in its admissions decisions. Four justices, Burger, Stewart, Rehnquist and Stevens concurred in the first two aspects of this judgment, but they found that Title VI of the Civil Rights Act of 1964 bars the use of race as a criteria for admission to federally supported educational programs. They did not find it necessary to rule on the constitutional issues in dissenting from the last part of the Court's judgment. Four justices, Brennan, White, Marshall and Blackmun, concurred in the last part of the judgment, but dissented from the partial affirmance of the California Courts' orders. They found the Cal-Davis affirmative action quota to be both constitutional and valid under Title VI. Justice Powell delivered the judgment of the Court in a separate opinion in which he joined Burger, Stewart, Rehnquist, and Stevens for the partial affirmance. Powell also joined Brennan, White, Marshall, and Blackmun to provide the majority for the partial reversal. His basic position was that neither the Fourteenth Amendment or Title VI barred institutions of higher learning from using race as "a factor" in admissions decisions, although he found the absolute quota system to be improper. Needless to say, the 1–4–4 division, with a judgment but no opinion from the Court, disappointed those who had hoped this case would set down clearer guidelines regarding the propriety of various affirmative action programs. Does the following opinion shed some light on this subject?

KAISER ALUMINUM AND CHEMICAL CORPORATION
v. WEBER

Supreme Court of the United States, 1979.
— U.S. —, 99 S.Ct. 2721.
[Some footnotes omitted; others renumbered.]

MR. JUSTICE BRENNAN delivered the opinion of the Court.

Challenged here is the legality of an affirmative action plan—collectively bargained by an employer and a union—that reserves for black employees 50% of the openings in an in-plant craft training program until the percentage of black craft workers in the plant is commensurate with the percentage of blacks in the local labor force. The question for decision is whether Congress, in Title VII of the Civil Rights Act of 1964 as amended, 42 U.S.C. § 2000e, left employers and unions in the private sector free to take such race-conscious steps to eliminate manifest racial imbalances in traditionally segregated job categories. We hold that Title VII does not prohibit such race-conscious affirmative action plans.

I

In 1974 petitioner United Steelworkers of America (USWA) and petitioner Kaiser Aluminum & Chemical Corporation (Kaiser) entered into a master collective-bargaining agreement covering terms and conditions of employment at 15 Kaiser plants. The agreement contained, *inter alia*, an affirmative action plan designed to eliminate conspicuous racial imbalances in Kaiser's then almost exclusively white craft work forces. Black craft hiring goals were set for each Kaiser plant equal to the percentage of blacks in the respective local labor forces. To enable plants to meet these goals, on-the-job training programs were established to teach unskilled production workers—black and white—the skills necessary to become craft workers.

The plant reserved for black employees 50% of the openings in these newly created in-plant training programs.

This case arose from the operation of the plan at Kaiser's plant in Gramercy, La. Until 1974 Kaiser hired as craft workers for that plant only persons who had had prior craft experience. Because blacks had long been excluded from craft unions,[1] few were able to present such credentials. As a consequence, prior to 1974 only 1.83% (five out of 273) of the skilled craft workers at the Gramercy plant were black, even though the work force in the Gramercy area was approximately 39% black.

Pursuant to the national agreement Kaiser altered its craft hiring practice in the Gramercy plant. Rather than hiring already trained outsiders, Kaiser established a training program to train its production workers to fill craft openings. Selection of craft trainees was made on the basis of seniority, with the proviso that at least 50% of the new trainees were to be black until the percentage of black skilled craft workers in the Gramercy plant approximated the percentage of blacks in the local labor force. See 415 F. Supp. 761, 764.

During 1974, the first year of the operation of the Kaiser-USWA affirmative action plan, 13 craft trainees were selected from Gramercy's production work force. Of these, 7 were black and 6 white. The most junior black selected into the program had less seniority than several white production workers whose bids for admission were rejected. Thereafter one of those white production workers, respondent Brian Weber, instituted this class action in the United States District Court for the Eastern District of Louisiana.

The complaint alleged that the filling of craft trainee positions at the Gramercy plant pursuant to the affirmative action program had resulted in junior black employees receiving training in preference to more senior white employees, thus discriminating against respondent and other similarly situated white employees in violation of §§ 703(a)[2] and (d)[3] of Title VII.

---

1. Judicial findings of exclusion from crafts on racial grounds are so numerous as to make such exclusion a proper subject for judicial notice. See, e. g., United States v. International Union of Elevator Constructors, 538 F.2d 1012 (CA3 1976); Associated General Contractors of Massachusetts v. Altshuler, 490 F.2d 9 (CA1 1973); Southern Illinois Builders Association v. Ogilve, 471 F.2d 680 (CA7 1972); Contractors Association of Eastern Pennsylvania v. Secretary of Labor, 442 F. 2d 159 (CA3 1971); Local 53 of International Association of Heat & Frost, etc. v. Vogler, 407 F.2d 1047 (CA5 1969); Buckner v. Goodyear, 339 F. Supp. 1108 (ND Ala.1972), aff'd without opinion, 476 F.2d 1287 (CA5 1973). See also United States Commission on Civil Rights, The Challenge Ahead: Equal Opportunity in Referral Unions 58–94 (1976), (summarizing judicial findings of discrimination by craft un-

ions); G. Myrdal, An American Dilemma (1944) 1079–1124; R. Marshall and V. Briggs, The Negro and Apprenticeship (1967); S. Spero and A. Harris, The Black Worker (1931): United States Commission on Civil Rights, Employment 97 (1961), State Advisory Committee, United States Commission on Civil Rights, 50 States Report 209 (1961); Marshall, "The Negro in Southern Unions," in The Negro and the American Labor Movement (ed. Jacobson, Anchor 1968) p. 145; App., 63, 104.

2. Section 703(a), 42 U.S.C. § 2000e–2 (a), provides:

"(a) It shall be an unlawful employment practice for an employer—

"(1) to fail or refuse to hire or to discharge any individual, or otherwise to discriminate against any individual with respect to his compensation,

3. See note 3 on page 1173.

The District Court held that the plan violated Title VII, entered a judgment in favor of the plaintiff class, and granted a permanent injunction prohibiting Kaiser and the USWA "from denying plaintiffs, Brian F. Weber and all other members of the class, access to on-the-job training programs on the basis of race." 415 F.Supp. 761 (1976). A divided panel of the Court of Appeals for the Fifth Circuit affirmed, holding that all employment preferences based upon race, including those preferences incidental to bona fide affirmative action plans, violated Title VII's prohibition against racial discrimination in employment. 563 F.2d 216 (1978). We granted certiorari. —— U.S. —— (1979). We reverse.

II

We emphasize at the outset the narrowness of our inquiry. Since the Kaiser-USWA plan does not involve state action, this case does not present an alleged violation of the Equal Protection Clause of the Constitution. Further, since the Kaiser-USWA plan was adopted voluntarily, we are not concerned with what Title VII requires or with what a court might order to remedy a past proven violation of the Act. The only question before us is the narrow statutory issue of whether Title VII *forbids* private employers and unions from voluntarily agreeing upon bona fide affirmative action plans that accord racial preferences in the manner and for the purpose provided in the Kaiser-USWA plan. That question was expressly left open in McDonald v. Santa Fe Trail Trans. Co., 427 U.S. 273, 281 n. 8 (1976) which held, in a case not involving affirmative action, that Title VII protects whites as well as blacks from certain forms of racial discrimination.

Respondent argues that Congress intended in Title VII to prohibit all race-conscious affirmative action plans. Respondent's argument rests upon a literal interpretation of § 703(a) and (d) of the Act. Those sections make it unlawful to "discriminate . . . because of . . . race" in hiring and in the selection of apprentices for training programs. Since, the argument runs, McDonald v. Santa Fe Trans. Co., supra, settled that Title VII forbids discrimination against whites as well as blacks, and since the Kaiser-USWA affirmative action plan operates to discriminate against white employees solely because they are white, it follows that the Kaiser-USWA plan violates Title VII.

Respondent's argument is not without force. But it overlooks the significance of the fact that the Kaiser-USWA plan is an affirmative action plan voluntarily adopted by private parties to eliminate traditional patterns

terms, conditions, or privileges of employment, because of such individual's race, color, religion, sex, or national origin; or

"(2) to limit or classify his employees or applicants for employment in any way which would deprive or tend to deprive any individual of employment opportunities or otherwise adversely affect his status as an employee, because of such individual's race, color, religion, sex, or national origin."

3. Section 703(d), 42 U.S.C. § 2000e–2 (d), provides:

    "It shall be an unlawful employment practice for any employer, labor organization, or joint labor-management committee controlling apprenticeship or other training or retraining, including on-the-job training programs to discriminate against any individual because of his race, color, religion, sex, or national origin in admission to, or employment in, any program established to provide apprenticeship or other training."

of racial segregation. In this context respondent's reliance upon a literal construction of § 703(a) and (d) and upon *McDonald* is misplaced. See McDonald v. Santa Fe Trail Trans. Co., supra, at 281 n. 8. It is a "familiar rule, that a thing may be within the letter of the statute and yet not within the statute, because not within its spirit, nor within the intention of its makers." Holy Trinity Church v. United States, 143 U.S. 457, 459 (1892). The prohibition against racial discrimination in § 703(a) and (d) of Title VII must therefore be read against the background of the legislative history of Title VII and the historical context from which the Act arose. See Train v. Colorado Public Interest Research Group, 426 U.S. 1, 10 (1976); Woodworkers v. NLRB, 386 U.S. 612, 620 (1967); United States v. American Trucking Assns., 310 U.S. 534, 543–544 (1940). Examination of those sources makes clear that an interpretation of the sections that forbade all race-conscious affirmative action would "bring about an end completely at variance with the purpose of the statute" and must be rejected. United States v. Public Utilities Comm'n, 345 U.S. 295, 315 (1953). See Johansen v. United States, 343 U.S. 427, 431 (1952); International Union v. Juneau Spruce Corp., 342 U.S. 237, 243 (1952); Texas & Pacific R. Co. v. Abilene Oil Co., 204 U.S. 426 (1907).

Congress' primary concern in enacting the prohibition against racial discrimination in Title VII of the Civil Rights Act of 1964 was with "the plight of the Negro in our economy." 110 Cong.Rec. 6548 (remarks of Sen. Humphrey). Before 1964, blacks were largely relegated to "unskilled and semi-skilled jobs." Id., at 6548 (remarks of Sen. Humphrey); id., at 7204 (remarks of Sen. Clark); id., at 7279–7280 (remarks of Sen. Kennedy). Because of automation the number of such jobs was rapidly decreasing. See 110 Cong.Rec., at 6548 (remarks of Sen. Humphrey); id., at 7204 (remarks of Sen. Clark). As a consequence "the relative position of the Negro worker [was] steadily worsening. In 1947 the non-white unemployment rate was only 64 percent higher than the white rate; in 1962 it was 124 percent higher." Id., at 6547 (remarks of Sen. Humphrey). See also id., at 7204 (remarks of Sen. Clark). Congress considered this a serious social problem. As Senator Clark told the Senate:

> "The rate of Negro unemployment has gone up consistently as compared with white unemployment for the past 15 years. This is a social malaise and a social situation which we should not tolerate. That is one of the principal reasons why this bill should pass." Id., at 7220.

Congress feared that the goals of the Civil Rights Act—the integration of blacks into the mainstream of American society—could not be achieved unless this trend were reversed. And Congress recognized that that would not be possible unless blacks were able to secure jobs "which have a future." Id., at 7204 (remarks to Sen. Clark). See also id., at 7279–7280 (remarks of Sen. Kennedy). As Senator Humphrey explained to the Senate.

> "What good does it do a Negro to be able to eat in a fine restaurant if he cannot afford to pay the bill? What good does it do him to be accepted in a hotel that is too expensive for his modest income? How can a Negro child be motivated to take full advantage of integrated educational facilities if he has no hope of getting a job where he can use that education?" Id., at 6547.

* * *

"Without a job, one cannot afford public convenience and accommodations. Income from employment may be necessary to further a man's education, or that of his children. If his children have no hope of getting a good job, what will motivate them to take advantage of educational opportunities." Id., at 6552.

These remarks echoed President Kennedy's original message to Congress upon the introduction of the Civil Rights Act in 1963.

"There is little value in a Negro's obtaining the right to be admitted to hotels and restaurants if he has no cash in his pocket and no job." Id., at 11159.

Accordingly, it was clear to Congress that "the crux of the problem [was] to open employment opportunities for Negroes in occupations which have been traditionally closed to them," id., at 6548 (remarks of Sen. Humphrey), and it was to this problem that Title VII's prohibition against racial discrimination in employment was primarily addressed.

It plainly appears from the House Report accompanying the Civil Rights Act that Congress did not intend wholly to prohibit private and voluntary affirmative action efforts as one method of solving this problem. The Report provides:

"No bill can or should lay claim to eliminating all of the causes and consequences of racial and other types of discrimination against minorities. There is reason to believe, however, that national leadership provided by the enactment of Federal legislation dealing with the most troublesome problems *will create an atmosphere conducive to voluntary or local resolution of other forms of discrimination.*" H.R.Rep.No.914, 88th Cong., 1st Sess. (1963), at 18. (Emphasis supplied.)

Given this legislative history, we cannot agree with respondent that Congress intended to prohibit the private sector from taking effective steps to accomplish the goal that Congress designed Title VII to achieve. The very statutory words intended as a spur or catalyst to cause "employers and unions to self-examine and to self-evaluate their employment practices and to endeavor to eliminate, so far as possible, the last vestiges of an unfortunate and ignominious page in this country's history," Albemarle v. Moody, 422 U.S. 405, 418 (1975), cannot be interpreted as an absolute prohibition against all private, voluntary, race-conscious affirmative action efforts to hasten the elimination of such vestiges.[4] It would be ironic indeed if a law triggered by a Nation's concern over centuries of racial injustice and intended to improve the lot of those who had "been excluded from the American dream for so long." 110 Cong.Rec., at 6552 (remarks of Sen. Humphrey), constituted the first legislative prohibition of all voluntary, private, race-conscious efforts to abolish traditional patterns of racial segregation and hierarchy.

---

4. The problem that Congress addressed in 1964 remains with us. In 1962 the nonwhite unemployment rate was 124% higher than the white rate. See 110 Cong.Rec. 6547 (remarks of Sen. Humphrey). In 1978 the black unemployment rate was 129% higher. See Monthly Labor Review, U. S. Department of Labor Bureau of Labor Statistics 78 (Mar. 1979).

Our conclusion is further reinforced by examination of the language and legislative history of § 703(j) of Title VII.[5] Opponents of Title VII raised two related arguments against the bill. First, they argued that the Act would be interpreted to *require* employers with racially imbalanced work forces to grant preferential treatment to racial minorities in order to integrate. Second, they argued that employers with racially imbalanced work forces would grant preferential treatment to racial minorities, even if not required to do so by the Act. See 110 Cong.Rec. 8618–8619 (remarks of Sen. Sparkman). Had Congress meant to prohibit all race-conscious affirmative action, as respondent urges, it easily could have answered both objections by providing that Title VII would not require or *permit* racially preferential integration efforts. But Congress did not choose such a course. Rather Congress added § 703(j) which addresses only the first objection. The section provides that nothing contained in Title VII "shall be interpreted to *require* any employer . . . to grant preferential treatment . . . to any group because of the race . . . of such . . . group on account of" a de facto racial imbalance in the employer's work force. The section does *not* state that "nothing in Title VII shall be interpreted to *permit*" voluntary affirmative efforts to correct racial imbalances. The natural inference is that Congress chose not to forbid all voluntary race-conscious affirmative action.

The reasons for this choice are evident from the legislative record. Title VII could not have been enacted into law without substantial support from legislators in both Houses who traditionally resisted federal regulation of private business. Those legislators demanded as a price for their support that "management prerogatives and union freedoms . . . be left undisturbed to the greatest extent possible." H.R.Rep.No.914, 88th Cong., 1st Sess., Pt. 2 (1963), at 29. Section 703(j) was proposed by Senator Dirksen to allay any fears that the Act might be interpreted in such a way as to upset this compromise. The section was designed to prevent § 703 of Title VII from being interpreted in such a way as to lead to undue "Federal Government interference with private businesses because of some Federal employee's ideas about racial balance or imbalance." 110 Cong.Rec., at 14314 (remarks of Sen. Miller). See also Id., at 9881 (remarks of Sen. Allott); set low enough to permit the employer to prove it without obligating him-

---

5. Section 703(j) of Title VII, 42 U.S.C. § 2000e–2(j), provides:

"Nothing contained in this subchapter shall be interpreted to require any employer, employment agency, labor organization, or joint labor-management committee subject to this subchapter to grant preferential treatment to any individual or to any group because of the race, color, religion, sex, national origin of such individual or group on account of an imbalance which may exist with respect to the total number or percentage of persons of any race, color, religion, sex, or national origin employed by any employer, referred or classified for employment by any employment agency or labor organization, or admitted to, or employed in, any apprenticeship or other training program, in comparison with the total number or percentage or persons of such race, color, religion, sex, or national origin in any community, State, section, or other area, or in the available work force in any community, State, section, or other area."

Section 703(j) speaks to substantive liability under Title VII, but it does not preclude courts from considering racial imbalance as evidence of a Title VII violation. See Teamsters v. United States, 431 U.S. 324, 339–340, n. 20 (1977). Remedies for substantive violations are governed by § 706(g), 42 U.S.C. § 2000e–5(g).

self to pay a damage award. The inevitable tendency would be to avoid hairsplitting litigation by simply concluding that a mere disparity between the racial composition of the employer's work force and the composition of the qualified local labor force would be an "arguable violation," even though actual liability could not be established on that basis alone. See Note, 57 N.C.L.Rev. 695, 714–719 (1979).

B. The Court also departs from the "arguable violation" approach by permitting an employer to redress discrimination that lies wholly outside the bounds of Title VII. For example, Title VII provides no remedy for pre-Act discrimination, Hazelwood School District v. United States, 433 U.S. 299, 309–310 (1977); yet the purposeful discrimination that creates a "traditionally segregated job category" may have entirely predated the Act. More subtly, in assessing a prima facie case of Title VII liability, the composition of the employer's work force is compared to the composition of the pool of workers who meet valid job qualifications. Hazelwood, 433 U.S., at 308, and n. 13; Teamsters v. United States, 431 U.S., at 339–340, and n. 20 (1977). When a "job category" is traditionally segregated, however, that pool will reflect the effects of segregation, and the Court's approach goes further and permits a comparison with the composition of the labor force as a whole, in which minorities are more heavily represented.

Strong considerations of equity support an interpretation of Title VII that would permit private affirmative action to reach where Title VII itself does not. The bargain struck in 1964 with the passage of Title VII guaranteed equal opportunity for white and black alike, but where Title VII provides no remedy for blacks, it should not be construed to foreclose private affirmative action from supplying relief. It seems unfair for respondent Weber to argue, as he does, that the asserted scarcity of black craftsmen in Louisiana, the product of historic discrimination, makes Kaiser's training program illegal because it ostensibly absolves Kaiser of all Title VII liability. Brief for Respondents 60. Absent compelling evidence of legislative intent, I would not interpret Title VII itself as a means of "locking in" the effects of segregation for which Title VII provides no remedy. Such a construction, as the Court points out, would be "ironic," given the broad remedial purposes of Title VII.

The dissent, while it focuses more on what Title VII does not require than on what Title VII forbids, cites several passages that appear to express an intent to "lock in" minorities. In mining the legislative history anew, however, the dissent, in my view, fails to take proper account of our prior cases that have given that history a much more limited reading than that adopted by the dissent. For example, in Griggs v. Duke Power Co., 401 U.S. 424, 434–436, and n. 11 (1971), the Court refused to give controlling weight to the memorandum of Senators Clark and Case which the dissent now finds so persuasive. See post, at 21–24. And in quoting a statement from that memorandum that an employer would not be "permitted . . . to prefer Negroes for future vacancies," post, at 22, the dissent does not point out that the Court's opinion in Teamsters v. United States, 431 U.S. 324, 349–351 (1977), implies that that language is limited to the protection of established seniority systems. Here seniority is not in issue because the craft training program is new and does not involve an abrogation of pre-existing seniority rights. In short, the passages marshaled by the dissent are not so compelling as to merit the whip hand over the obvious equity of permitting employers to ameliorate the effects of past discrimination for which Title VII provides no direct relief.

III

I also think it significant that, while the Court's opinion does not foreclose other forms of affirmative action, the Kaiser program it approves is a moderate one. The opinion notes that the program does not afford an absolute preference for blacks, and that it ends when the racial composition of Kaiser's craft work force matches the racial composition of the local population. It thus operates as a temporary tool for remedying past discrimination without attempting to "maintain" a previously achieved balance. See University of California Regents v. Bakke, 438 U.S. 265, 342 n. 17 (1978) (BRENNAN, WHITE, MARSHALL, and BLACKMUN, JJ.). Because the duration of the program is finite, it perhaps will end even before the "stage of maturity when action along this line is no longer necessary." Id., at 403 (BLACKMUN, J.). And if the Court has misperceived the political will, it has the assurance that because the question is statutory Congress may set a different course if it so chooses.

MR. CHIEF JUSTICE BURGER, dissenting.

The Court reaches a result I would be inclined to vote for were I a Member of Congress considering a proposed amendment of Title VII. I cannot join the Court's judgment, however, because it is contrary to the explicit language of the statute and arrived at by means wholly incompatible with long-established principles of separation of powers. Under the guise of statutory "construction," the Court effectively rewrites Title VII to achieve what it regards as a desirable result. It "amends" the statute to do precisely what both its sponsors and its opponents agreed the statute was *not* intended to do.

When Congress enacted Title VII after long study and searching debate, it produced a statute of extraordinary clarity, which speaks directly to the issue we consider in this case. In § 703(d) Congress provided:

> "It shall be an unlawful employment practice for any employer, labor organization, or joint labor-management committee controlling apprenticeship or other training or retraining, including on-the-job training programs to discriminate against any individual because of his race, color, religion, sex, or national origin in admission to, or employment in, any program established to provide apprenticeship or other training." 42 U.S.C. § 2000e–2(d).

Often we have difficulty interpreting statutes either because of imprecise drafting or because legislative compromises have produced genuine ambiguities. But here there is no lack of clarity, no ambiguity. The quota embodied in the collective-bargaining agreement between Kaiser and the Steelworkers unquestionably discriminates on the basis of race against individual employees seeking admission to on-the-job training programs. And, under the plain language of § 703(d), that is "an *unlawful* employment practice."

Oddly, the Court seizes upon the very clarity of the statute almost as a justification for evading the unavoidable impact of its language. The

Court blandly tells us that Congress could not really have meant what it said, for a "literal construction" would defeat the "purpose" of the statute—at least the congressional "purpose" as five Justices divine it today. But how are judges supposed to ascertain the *purpose* of a statute except through the words Congress used and the legislative history of the statute's evolution? One need not even resort to the legislative history to recognize what is apparent from the face of Title VII—that it is specious to suggest that § 703 (j) contains a negative pregnant that permits employers to do what § 703 (a) and (d) unambiguously and unequivocally *forbid* employers from doing. Moreover, as MR. JUSTICE REHNQUIST'S opinion—which I join—conclusively demonstrates, the legislative history makes equally clear that the supporters and opponents of Title VII reached an agreement about the statute's intended effect. That agreement, expressed so clearly in the language of the statute that no one should doubt its meaning, forecloses the reading which the Court gives the statute today.

Arguably, Congress may not have gone far enough in correcting the effects of past discrimination when it enacted Title VII. The gross discrimination against minorities to which the Court adverts—particularly against Negroes in the building trades and craft unions—is one of the dark chapters in the otherwise great history of the American labor movement. And, I do not question the importance of encouraging voluntary compliance with the purposes and policies of Title VII. But that statute was conceived and enacted to make discrimination against *any* individual illegal, and I fail to see how "voluntary compliance" with the no-discrimination principle that is the heart and soul of Title VII as currently written will be achieved by permitting employers to discriminate against some individuals to give preferential treatment to others.

Until today, I had thought the Court was of the unanimous view that "discriminatory preference for any group, minority or majority, is precisely and only what Congress has proscribed" in Title VII. Griggs v. Duke Power Co., 401 U.S. 424, 431 (1971). Had Congress intended otherwise, it very easily could have drafted language allowing what the Court permits today. Far from doing so, Congress expressly *prohibited* in § 703(a) and (d) the discrimination against Brian Weber the Court approves now. If "affirmative action" programs such as the one presented in this case are to be permitted, it is for Congress, not this Court, to so direct.

It is often observed that hard cases make bad law. I suspect there is some truth to that adage, for the "hard" cases always tempt judges to exceed the limits of their authority, as the Court does today by totally rewriting a crucial part of Title VII to reach a desirable result. Cardozo no doubt had this type of case in mind when he wrote:

> "The judge, even when he is free, is still not wholly free. He is not to innovate at pleasure. He is not a knight-errant, roaming at will in pursuit of his own ideal of beauty or of goodness. He is to draw his inspiration from consecrated principles. He is not to yield to spasmodic sentiment, to vague and unregulated benevolence. He is to exercise a discretion performed by tradition, methodized by analogy, disciplined by system, and subordinated to 'the primordial necessity of order in the social life.' Wide enough in all conscience is the field of discretion that remains." B. Cardozo, The Nature of the Judicial Process 141 (1921).

What Cardozo tells us is beware the "good result," achieved by judicially unauthorized or intellectually dishonest means on the appealing notion that the desirable ends justify the improper judicial means. For there is always the danger that the seeds of precedent sown by good men for the best of motives will yield a rich harvest of unprincipled acts of others also aiming at "good ends."

———

MR. JUSTICE REHNQUIST, with whom THE CHIEF JUSTICE joins, dissenting.

In a very real sense, the Court's opinion is ahead of its time: it could more appropriately have been handed down five years from now, in 1984, a year coinciding with the title of a book from which the Court's opinion borrows, perhaps subconsciously, at least one idea. Orwell describes in his book a governmental official of Oceania, one of the three great world powers, denouncing the current enemy, Eurasia, to an assembled crowd:

> "It was almost impossible to listen to him without being first convinced and then maddened. . . . The speech had been proceeding for perhaps twenty minutes when a messenger hurried onto the platform and a scrap of paper was slipped into the speaker's hand. He unrolled and read it without pausing in his speech. Nothing altered in his voice or manner, or in the content of what he was saying, but suddenly the names were different. Without words said, a wave of understanding rippled through the crowd. Oceania was at war with Eastasia! . . . The banners and posters with which the square was decorated were all wrong!
> . . .
>   "[T]he speaker had switched from one line to the other actually in mid-sentence, not only without a pause, but without even breaking the syntax." G. Orwell, Nineteen Eighty-Four, 182–183 (1949).

Today's decision represents an equally dramatic and equally unremarked switch in this Court's interpretation of Title VII.

The operative sections of Title VII prohibit racial discrimination in employment *simpliciter*. Taken in its normal meaning, and as understood by all Members of Congress who spoke to the issue during the legislative debates, see infra, at ——, this language prohibits a covered employer from considering race when making an employment decision, whether the race be black or white. Several years ago, however, a United States District Court held that "the dismissal of white employees charged with misappropriating company property while not dismissing a similarly charged Negro employee does not raise a claim upon which Title VII relief may be granted." McDonald v. Santa Fe Trail Transp. Co., 427 U.S. 273, 278 (1976). This Court unanimously reversed, concluding from the "uncontradicted legislative history" that "Title VII prohibits racial discrimination against the white petitioners in this case upon the same standards as would be applicable were they Negroes . . . ." 427 U.S., at 280.

We have never waivered in our understanding that Title VII "prohibits *all* racial discrimination in employment, without exception for any particular employees." Id., at 283 (emphasis in original). In Griggs v. Duke Power Co., 401 U.S. 424, 429 (1971), our first occasion to interpret Title VII, a unanimous court observed that "[d]iscriminatory preference, for any group, minority or majority, is precisely and only what Congress has proscribed." And in our most recent discussion of the issue, we uttered words seemingly dispositive of this case: "It is clear beyond cavil that the obligation imposed by Title VII is to provide an equal opportunity for *each* applicant regardless of race, without regard to whether members of the applicant's race are already proportionately represented in the work force." Furnco Construction Corp. v. Waters, 438 U.S. 567, —— (1978) (emphasis in original).[1]

Today, however, the Court behaves much like the Orwellian speaker earlier described, as if it had been handed a note indicating that Title VII would lead to a result unacceptable to the Court if interpreted here as it was in our prior decisions. Accordingly, without even a break in syntax, the Court rejects "a literal construction of § 703(a)" in favor of newly discovered "legislative history," which leads it to a conclusion directly contrary to that compelled by the "uncontradicted legislative history" unearthed in *McDonald* and our other prior decisions. Now we are told that the legislative history of Title VII shows that employers are free to discriminate on the basis of race; an employer may, in the Court's words, "trammel the interests of white employees" in favor of black employees in order to eliminate "racial imbalance." Ante, at 12. Our earlier interpretations of Title VII, like the banners and posters decorating the square in Oceania, were all wrong.

As if this were not enough to make a reasonable observer question this Court's adherence to the oft-stated principle that our duty is to construe rather than rewrite legislation, United States v. Rutherford, slip op., at 9 (June —, 1979), the Court also seizes upon § 703(j) of Title VII as an independent, or at least partially independent, basis for its holding. Totally ignoring the wording of that section, which is obviously addressed to those charged with the responsibility of interpreting the law rather than those who are subject to its proscriptions, and totally ignoring the months of legislative debates preceding the section's introduction and passage, which demonstrate clearly that it was enacted to prevent precisely what occurred in this case, the Court infers from § 703(j) that "Congress chose not to forbid all voluntary race-conscious affirmative action." Ante, at 10.

Thus, by a *tour de force* reminiscent not of jurists such as Hale, Holmes, and Hughes, but of escape artists such as Houdini, the Court eludes clear statutory language, "uncontradicted" legislative history and uniform precedent in concluding that employers are, after all, permitted to consider race in making employment decisions. It may be that one or more of the principal sponsors of Title VII would have preferred to see a provision allowing preferential treatment of minorities written into the bill. Such a provision, however, would have to have been expressly or impliedly excepted from Title VII's explicit prohibition on all racial discrimination in employment. There is no such exception in the Act. And a reading of the legislative debates concerning Title VII, in which proponents and opponents alike

---

1. Our statements in *Griggs* and *Furnco Construction*, patently inconsistent with today's holding, are not even mentioned, much less distinguished, by the Court.

uniformly denounced discrimination in favor of, as well as discrimination against, Negroes, demonstrates clearly that any legislator harboring an unspoken desire for such a provision could not possibly have succeeded in enacting it into law.

I

Kaiser opened its Gramercy, La., plant in 1958. Because the Gramercy facility had no apprenticeship or in-plant craft training program, Kaiser hired as craft workers only persons with prior craft experience. Despite Kaiser's efforts to locate and hire trained black craftsmen, few were available in the Gramercy area, and as a consequence, Kaiser's craft positions were manned almost exclusively by whites. In February 1974, under pressure from the Office of Federal Contract Compliance to increase minority representation in craft positions at its various plants, and hoping to deter the filing of employment discrimination claims by minorities, Kaiser entered into a collective-bargaining agreement with the United Steelworkers of America (Steelworkers) which created a new on-the-job craft training program at 15 Kaiser facilities, including the Gramercy plant. The agreement required that no less than one minority applicant be admitted to the training program for every nonminority applicant until the percentage of blacks in craft positions equaled the percentage of blacks in the local work force. Eligibility for the craft training programs was to be determined on the basis of plant seniority, with black and white applicants to be selected on the basis of their relative seniority within their racial group.

Brian Weber is white. He was hired at Kaiser's Gramercy plant in 1969. In April 1974 Kaiser announced that it was offering a total of nine positions in three on-the-job training programs for skilled craft jobs. Weber applied for all three programs, but was not selected. The successful candidates—five black and four white applicants—were chosen in accordance with the 50% minority admission quota mandated under the 1974 collective-bargaining agreement. Two of the successful black applicants had less seniority than Weber. Weber brought the instant class action in the United States District Court for the Eastern District of Louisiana, alleging that use of the 50% minority admission quota to fill vacancies in Kaiser's craft training programs violated Title VII's prohibition on racial discrimination in employment. The District Court and the Court of Appeals for the Fifth Circuit agreed, enjoining further use of race as a criterion in admitting applicants to the craft training programs.

II

Were Congress to act today specifically to prohibit the type of racial discrimination suffered by Weber, it would be hard pressed to draft language better tailored to the task than that found in § 703(d) of Title VII:

"It shall be an unlawful employment practice for any employer, labor organization, or joint labor-management committee controlling apprenticeship or other training or retraining, including on-the-job training programs to discriminate against any individual because of his race, color, religion, sex, or national origin in admission to, or employment in, any program established to provide apprenticeship or other training." 43 U.S.C. § 2000e–2(d).

Equally suited to the task would be § 703(a)(2), which makes it unlawful for an employer to classify his employees "in any way which would deprive or tend to deprive any individual of employment opportunities or otherwise adversely affect his status as an employee, because of such individual's race, color, religion, sex, or national origin." 42 U.S.C. § 2000e–2(a)(2).

Entirely consistent with these two express prohibitions is the language of § 703(j) of Title VII, which provides that the Act is not to be interpreted "to require any employer . . . to grant preferential treatment to any individual or to any group because of the race . . . of such individual or group" to correct a racial imbalance in the employer's work force. 42 U.S.C. § 2000e–2(j). Seizing on the word "require," the Court infers that Congress must have intended to "permit" this type of racial discrimination. Not only is this reading of § 703(j) outlandish in the light of the flat prohibitions of § 703(a) and (d), but, as explained Part III, it is totally belied by the Act's legislative history.

Quite simply, Kaiser's racially discriminatory admission quota is flatly prohibited by the plain language of Title VII. This normally dispositive fact, however, gives the Court only momentary pause. An "interpretation" of the statute upholding Weber's claim would, according to the Court, " 'bring about an end completely at variance with the purpose of the statute.' " Ante, at 6, quoting United States v. Public Utilities Comm'n, 345 U.S. 295, 315 (1953). To support this conclusion, the Court calls upon the "spirit" of the Act, which it divines from passages in Title VII's legislative history indicating that enactment of the statute was prompted by Congress' desire "to open employment opportunities for Negroes in occupations which [had] been traditionally closed to them." Ante, at 8, quoting 110 Cong.Rec. 6548 (1964) (remarks of Sen. Humphrey). But the legislative history invoked by the Court to avoid the plain language of § 703(a) and (d) simply misses the point. To be sure, the reality of employment discrimination against Negroes provided the primary impetus for passage of Title VII. But this fact by no means supports the proposition that Congress intended to leave employers free to discriminate against white persons. In most cases, "[l]egislative history . . . is more vague than the statute we are called upon to interpret." United States v. Public Utilities Comm'n, 345 U.S. 295, 321 (1954) (Jackson, J., concurring). Here, however, the legislative history of Title VII is as clear as the language of § 703(a) and (d), and it irrefutably demonstrates that Congress meant precisely what it said in § 703(a) and (d)—that *no* racial discrimination in employment is permissible under Title VII, not even preferential treatment of minorities to correct racial imbalance.

III

In undertaking to review the legislative history of Title VII, I am mindful that the topic hardly makes for light reading, but I am also fearful that nothing short of a thorough examination of the congressional debates will fully expose the magnitude of the Court's misinterpretation of Congress' intent.

A

Introduced on the floor of the House of Representatives on June 20, 1963, the bill—H.R. 7152—that ultimately became the Civil Rights Act of 1964 contained no compulsory provisions directed at private discrimination in employment. The bill was promptly referred to the Committee on the Judiciary, where it was amended to include Title VII. With two exceptions, the bill reported by the House Judiciary Committee contained § 703(a) and (d) as they were ultimately enacted. Amendments subsequently adopted on the House floor added § 703's prohibition against sex discrimination and § 703(d)'s coverage of "on the job training."

After noting that "[t]he purpose of [Title VII] is to eliminate . . . discrimination in employment based on race, color, religion, or national origin," the Judiciary Committee's report simply paraphrased the provisions of Title VII without elaboration. H.R.Rep. No. 914, 88th Cong., 1st Sess., 26 (1963) (hereinafter H.R.Rep.). In a separate Minority Report, however, opponents of the measure on the Committee advanced a line of attack which was reiterated throughout the debates in both the House and Senate and which ultimately led to passage of § 703(j). Noting that the word "discrimination" was nowhere defined in H.R. 7152, the Minority Report charged that the absence from Title VII of any reference to "racial imbalance" was a "public relations" ruse and that "the administration intends to rely upon its own construction of 'discrimination' as including the lack of racial balance . . . ." H.R.Rep., at 67–68. To demonstrate how the bill would operate in practice, the Minority Report posited a number of hypothetical employment situations, concluding in each example that the employer *"may be forced to hire according to race,* to 'racially balance' those who work for him *in every job classification* or be in violation of Federal law." *Id.,* at 69 (emphasis in original).

When H.R. 7152 reached the House floor, the opening speech in support of its passage was delivered by Representative Celler, Chairman of the House Judiciary Committee and the Congressman responsible for introducing the legislation. A portion of that speech responded to criticism "seriously misrepresent[ing] what the bill would do and grossly distort[ing] its effects":

> "[T]he charge has been made that the Equal Employment Opportunity Commission to be established by title VII of the bill would have the power to prevent a business from employing and promoting the people it wished, and that a 'Federal inspector' could then order the hiring and promotion only of employees of certain races or religious groups. This description of the bill is entirely wrong
> . . . .
>
> *   *   *
>
> "Even [a] court could not order that any preference be given to any particular race, religion or other group, but would be limited to ordering an end of discrimination. The statement that a Federal inspector could order the employment and promotion only of members of a specific racial or religious group is therefore patently erroneous.
>
> *   *   *
>
> ". . . The Bill would do no more than prevent . . . employers from discriminating against *or in favor* of workers because of their race, religion, or national origin.
>
> "It is likewise not true that the Equal Employment Opportunity Commission would have power to rectify existing 'racial or

religious imbalance' in employment by requiring the hiring of certain people without regard to their qualifications simply because
they are of a given race or religion. Only actual discrimination
could be stopped." 110 Cong.Rec. 1518 (1964) (emphasis added).
Representative Celler's construction of Title VII was repeated by several
other supporters during the House debate.

Thus, the battle lines were drawn early in the legislative struggle over
Title VII, with opponents of the measure charging that agencies of the
federal government such as the Equal Employment Opportunity Commission (EEOC), by interpreting the word "discrimination" to mean the
existence of "racial imbalance," would "require" employers to grant preferential treatment to minorities, and supporters responding that the EEOC
would be granted no such power and that, indeed, Title VII prohibits discrimination "in favor of workers because of their race." Supporters of
H.R. 7152 in the House ultimately prevailed by a vote of 290 to 130, and
the measure was sent to the Senate to begin what became the longest debate
in that body's history.

B

The Senate debate was broken into three phases: the debate on sending
the bill to Committee, the general debate on the bill prior to invocation of
cloture, and the debate following cloture.

1

When debate on the motion to refer the bill to Committee opened,
opponents of Title VII in the Senate immediately echoed the fears expressed
by their counterparts in the House, as is demonstrated by the following
colloquy between Senators Hill and Ervin:

"MR. ERVIN. I invite attention to . . . Section [703
(a)] . . . .

"I ask the Senator from Alabama if the Commission could
not tell an employer that he had too few employees, that he had
limited his employment, and enter an order, under [Section 703
(a)], requiring him to hire more persons, not because the employer
thought he needed more persons, but because the Commission wanted to compel him to employ persons of a particular race.

"MR. HILL. The Senator is correct. That power is written
into the bill. The employer could be forced to hire additional persons . . . ." 110 Cong.Rec. 4764 (1964).

Senator Humphrey, perhaps the primary moving force behind H.R. 7152 in
the Senate, was the first to state the proponents' understanding of Title
VII. Responding to a political advertisement charging that federal agencies were at liberty to interpret the word "discrimination" in Title VII to
require racial balance, Senator Humphrey stated: "[T]he meaning of
racial or religious discrimination is perfectly clear. . . . [I]t means
a distinction and treatment given to different individuals because of their
different race, religion, or national origin." Id., at 5423. Stressing that
Title VII "does not limit the employer's freedom to hire, fire, promote,
or demote for any reasons—or no reasons—so long as his action is not
based on race," Senator Humphrey further stated that "nothing in the

bill would permit any official or court to require any employer or labor union to give preferential treatment to any minority group." Ibid.

After 17 days of debate the Senate voted to take up the bill directly, without referring it to a committee. Id., at 6455. Consequently, there is no Committee Report in the Senate.

2

Formal debate on the merits of H.R. 7152 began on March 30, 1964. Supporters of the bill in the Senate had made elaborate preparations for this second round. Senator Humphrey, the Majority Whip, and Senator Kuchel, the Minority Whip, were selected as the bipartisan floor managers on the entire civil rights bill. Responsibility for explaining and defending each important title of the bill was placed on bipartisan "captains." Senators Clark and Case were selected as the bipartisan captains responsible for Title VII. Vass, Title VII: Legislative History, 7 B.C.Indus. & Com. L.Rev. 431, 444–445 (1966) (hereinafter Title VII: Legislative History).

In the opening speech of the formal Senate debate on the bill, Senator Humphrey addressed the main concern of Title VII's opponents, advising that not only does Title VII not require use of racial quotas, *it does not permit* their use. "The truth," stated the floor leader of the bill, "is that this title forbids discriminating against anyone on account of race. This is the simple and complete truth about title VII." 110 Cong.Rec. 6549 (1964). Senator Humphrey continued:

> "Contrary to the allegations of some opponents of this title, there is nothing in it that will give any power to the Commission or to any courts to require hiring, firing, or promotion of employees in order to meet a racial 'quota' or to achieve a certain racial balance.
>
> "That bugaboo has been brought up a dozen times; but it is nonexistent. In fact, *the very opposite is true. Title VII prohibits discrimination.* In effect, it says that race, religion, and national origin are not to be used as the basis for hiring and firing. Title VII is designed to encourage hiring on the basis of ability and qualifications, not race or religion." Ibid. (emphasis added).

At the close of his speech, Senator Humphrey returned briefly to the subject of employment quotas: "It is claimed that the bill would require racial quotas for all hiring, when in fact it provides that race shall not be a basis for making personnel decisions." Id., at 6553.

Senator Kuchel delivered the second major speech in support of H.R. 7152. In addressing the concerns of the opposition, he observed that "[n]othing could be further from the truth" than the charge that "Federal inspectors" would be empowered under Title VII to dictate racial balance and preferential advancement of minorities. Id., at 6563. Senator Kuchel emphasized that seniority rights would in no way be affected by Title VII: "Employers and labor organizations could not discriminate *in favor of or against* a person because of his race, his religion, or his national origin. In such matters   .   .   .   the bill now before us   .   .   .   is color-blind." Id., at 6564 (emphasis added).

A few days later the Senate's attention focused exclusively on Title VII, as Senators Clark and Case rose to discuss the title of H.R. 7152 on which their shared floor "captain" responsibilities. In an interpretative memorandum submitted jointly to the Senate, Senators Clark and Case took pains to refute the opposition's charge that Title VII would result in preferential treatment of minorities. Their words were clear and unequivocal:

> "There is no requirement in title VII that an employer maintain a racial balance in his work force. On the contrary, any deliberate attempt to maintain a racial balance, whatever such a balance may be, would involve a violation of title VII because maintaining such a balance would require an employer to hire or to refuse to hire on the basis of race. It must be emphasized that discrimination is prohibited as to any individual." Id., at 7213.

Of particular relevance to the instant case were their observations regarding seniority rights. As if directing their comments at Brian Weber, the Senators said:

> "Title VII would have no effect on established seniority rights. Its effect is prospective and not retrospective. Thus, for example, if a business has been discriminating in the past and as a result has an all-white working force, when the title comes into effect the employer's obligation would be simply to fill future vacancies on a nondiscriminatory basis. He would not be obliged— *or indeed permitted*—to fire whites in order to hire Negroes, *or to prefer Negroes for future vacancies, or, once Negroes are hired, to give them special seniority rights at the expense of the white workers hired earlier.*" Ibid. (emphasis added).

Thus with virtual clairvoyance the Senate's leading supporters of Title VII anticipated precisely the circumstances of this case and advised their colleagues that the type of minority preference employed by Kaiser would violate Title VII's ban on racial discrimination. To further accentuate the point, Senator Clark introduced another memorandum dealing with common criticisms of the bill, including the charge that racial quotas would be imposed under Title VII. The answer was simple and to the point: "Quotas are themselves discriminatory." Id., at 7218.

Despite these clear statements from the bill's leading and most knowledgeable proponents, the fears of the opponents were not put to rest. Senator Robertson reiterated the view that "discrimination" could be interpreted by a federal "bureaucrat" to require hiring quotas. Id., at 7418–7420. Senators Smathers and Sparkman, while conceding that Title VII does not in so many words require the use of hiring quotas, repeated the opposition's view that employers would be coerced to grant preferential hiring treatment to minorities by agencies of the Federal Government. Senator Williams was quick to respond:

> "Those opposed to H.R. 7152 should realize that to hire a Negro solely because he is a Negro is racial discrimination, just as much as a 'white only' employment policy. Both forms of discrimination are prohibited by title VII of this bill. The language of that title simply states that race is not a qualification for employment.
> . . . Some people charge that H.R. 7152 favors the Negro, at the expense of the white majority. But how can the language of equality favor one race or one religion over another? Equality

can have only one meaning, and that meaning is self-evident to reasonable men. Those who say that equality means favoritism do violence to common sense." Id., at 8921.

Senator Williams concluded his remarks by noting that Title VII's only purpose is "the elimination of racial and religious discrimination in employment." Ibid. On May 25, Senator Humphrey again took the floor to defend the bill against "the well-financed drive by certain opponents to confuse and mislead the American people." Id., at 11846. Turning once again to the issue of preferential treatment, Senator Humphrey remained faithful to the view that he had repeatedly expressed:

> "The title does not provide that any preferential treatment in employment shall be given to Negroes or to any other persons or groups. It does not provide that any quota systems may be established to maintain racial balance in employment. In fact, *the title would prohibit preferential treatment for any particular group,* and any person, whether or not a member of any minority group, would be permitted to file a complaint of discriminatory employment practices." Id., at 11848 (emphasis added).

While the debate in the Senate raged, a bipartisan coalition under the leadership of Senators Dirksen, Mansfield, Humphrey, and Kuchel was working with House leaders and representatives of the Johnson Administration on a number of amendments to H.R. 7152 designed to enhance its prospects of passage. The so-called "Dirksen-Mansfield" amendment was introduced on May 26 by Senator Dirksen as a substitute for the entire House-passed bill. The substitute bill, which ultimately became law, left unchanged the basic prohibitory language of §§ 703(a) and (d), as well as the remedial provisions in § 706(g). It added, however, several provisions defining and clarifying the scope of Title VII's substantive prohibitions. One of those clarifying amendments, § 703(j), was specifically directed at the opposition's concerns regarding racial balancing and preferential treatment of minorities, providing in pertinent part: "Nothing contained in [Title VII] shall be interpreted to require any employer . . . to grant preferential treatment to any individual or to any group because of the race . . . of such individual or group on account of" a racial imbalance in the employer's work force. 42 U.S.C. § 2000e–2(j); quoted in full, at n. 8, supra.

The Court draws from the language of § 703(j) primary support for its conclusion that Title VII's blanket prohibition on racial discrimination in employment does not prohibit preferential treatment of blacks to correct racial imbalance. Alleging that opponents of Title VII had argued (1) that the act would be interpreted to require employers with racially imbalanced work forces to grant preferential treatment to minorities and (2) that "employers with racially imbalanced work forces would grant preferential treatment to racial minorities, even if not required to do so by the Act," ante, at 9, the Court concludes that § 703(j) is responsive only to the opponents' first objection and that Congress therefore must have intended to permit voluntary, private discrimination against whites in order to correct racial imbalance.

Contrary to the Court's analysis, the language of § 703(j) is precisely tailored to the objection voiced time and again by Title VII's opponents.

Not once during the 83 days of debate in the Senate did a speaker, proponent or opponent, suggest that the bill would allow employers *voluntarily* to prefer racial minorities over white persons. In light of Title VII's flat prohibition on discrimination "against any individual . . . because of such individual's race," § 703(a), 42 U.S.C. § 2000e–2(a), such a contention would have been, in any event, too preposterous to warrant response. Indeed, speakers on both sides of the issue, as the legislative history makes clear, recognized that Title VII would tolerate no *voluntary* racial preference, whether in favor of blacks or whites. The complaint consistently voiced by the opponents was that Title VII, particularly the word "discrimination," would be *interpreted* by federal agencies such as the Equal Employment Opportunity Commission to *require* the correction of racial imbalance through the granting of preferential treatment to minorities. Verbal assurances that Title VII would not require—indeed, would not permit—preferential treatment of blacks having failed, supporters of H.R. 7152 responded by proposing an amendment carefully worded to meet, and put to rest, the opposition's charge. Indeed, unlike § 703(a) and (d), which are by their terms directed at entities—*e. g.*, employers, labor unions —whose actions are restricted by Title VII's prohibitions, the language of § 703(j) is specifically directed at entities—federal agencies and courts —charged with the responsibility of interpreting Title VII's provisions.

In light of the background and purpose of § 703(j), the irony of invoking the section to justify the result in this case is obvious. The Court's frequent references to the "voluntary" nature of Kaiser's racially discriminatory admission quota bear no relationship to the facts of this case. Kaiser and the Steelworkers acted under pressure from an agency of the Federal Government, the Office of Federal Contract Compliance, which found that minorities were being "underutilized" at Kaiser's plants. See n. 2, supra. That is, Kaiser's work force was racially imbalanced. Bowing to that pressure, Kaiser instituted an admissions quota preferring blacks over whites, thus confirming that the fears of Title VII's opponents were well founded. Today § 703(j), adopted to allay those fears, is invoked by the Court to uphold imposition of a racial quota under the very circumstances that the section was intended to prevent.

Section 703(j) apparently calmed the fears of most of the opponents; after its introduction complaints concerning racial balance and preferential treatment died down considerably. Proponents of the bill, however, continued to reassure the opposition that its concerns were unfounded. In a lengthy defense of the entire civil rights bill, Senator Muskie emphasized that the opposition's "torrent of words . . . cannot obscure this basic, simple truth: Every American citizen has the right to equal treatment— not favored treatment, not complete individual equality—just equal treatment." 110 Cong.Rec. 12614 (1964). With particular reference to Title VII, Senator Muskie noted that the measure "seeks to afford to all Americans equal opportunity in employment without discrimination. Not equal pay, not 'racial balance.' Only equal opportunity." Id., at 12617.

Senator Saltonstall, Chairman of the Republican Conference of Senators participating in the drafting of the Dirksen-Mansfield amendment, spoke at length on the substitute bill. He advised the Senate that the Dirksen-Mansfield substitute, which included § 703(j), "provides no preferential treatment for any group of citizens. In fact, *it specifically prohibits such treatment.*" Id., at 12691 (emphasis added).

On June 9, Senator Ervin offered an amendment that would entirely delete Title VII from the bill. In answer to Senator Ervin's contention that Title VII "would make the members of a particular race special favorites of the laws," id., at 13079, Senator Clark retorted:

> "The bill does not make anyone higher than anyone else. It establishes no quotas. It leaves an employer free to select whomever he wishes to employ. . . .

> "All this is subject to one qualification, and that qualification, is to state: 'In your activity as an employer . . . you must not discriminate because of the color of a man's skin. . . .'

> "That is all this provision does. . . .   It merely says, 'When you deal in interstate commerce, you must not discriminate on the basis of race . . . .'" Id., at 13080.

The Ervin amendment was defeated, and the Senate turned its attention to an amendment proposed by Senator Cotton to limit application of Title VII to employers of at least 100 employees. During the course of the Senate's deliberations on the amendment, Senator Cotton had a revealing discussion with Senator Curtis, also an opponent of Title VII. Both men expressed dismay that Title VII would prohibit preferential hiring of "members of a minority race in order to enhance their opportunity":

> "MR. CURTIS. Is it not the opinion of the Senator that any individuals who provide jobs for a class of people who have perhaps not had sufficient opportunity for jobs should be commended rather than outlawed?

> "MR. COTTON. Indeed it is." Id., at 13086.

Thus in the only exchange on the Senate floor raising the possibility that an employer might wish to reserve jobs for minorities in order to assist them in overcoming their employment disadvantage, both speakers concluded that Title VII prohibits such, in the words of the Court, "voluntary, private, race-conscious efforts to abolish traditional patterns of racial segregation and hierarchy." Ante, at 9. Immediately after this discussion, both Senator Dirksen and Senator Humphrey took the floor in defense of the 25-employee limit contained in the Dirksen-Mansfield substitute bill, and neither Senator disputed the conclusions of Senators Cotton and Curtis. The Cotton amendment was defeated.

3

On June 10 the Senate, for the second time in its history, imposed cloture on its members. The limited debate that followed centered on proposed amendments to the Dirksen-Mansfield substitute. Of some 24 proposed amendments, only 5 were adopted.

As the civil rights bill approached its final vote, several supporters rose to urge its passage. Senator Muskie adverted briefly to the issue of preferential treatment: "It has been said that the bill discriminates in favor of the Negro at the expense of the rest of us. It seeks to do nothing more than to lift the Negro from the status of inequality to one of *equality* of treatment." 110 Cong.Rec. 14328 (1964) (emphasis added). Senator

Moss in a speech delivered on the day that the civil rights bill was finally passed, had this to say about quotas:

> "The bill does not accord to any citizen advantage or preference— it does not fix quotas of employment or school population—it does not force personal association. What it does is to prohibit public officials and those who invite the public generally to patronize their businesses or to apply for employment, to utilize the offensive, humiliating, and cruel practice of discrimination on the basis of race. In short, the bill does not accord special consideration; it establishes *equality*." Id., at 14484 (emphasis added).

Later that day, June 19, the issue was put to a vote, and the Dirksen-Mansfield substitute bill was passed.

C

The Act's return engagement in the House was brief. The House Committee on Rules reported the Senate version without amendments on June 30, 1964. By a vote of 289 to 126, the House adopted House Resolution 789, thus agreeing to the Senate's amendments of H.R. 7152. Later that same day, July 2, the President signed the bill and the Civil Rights Act of 1964 became law.

IV

Reading the language of Title VII, as the Court purports to do, "against the background of [its] legislative history . . . and the historical context from which the Act arose," ante, at 6, one is led inescapably to the conclusion that Congress fully understood what it was saying and meant precisely what it said. Opponents of the civil rights bill did not argue that employers would be permitted under Title VII voluntarily to grant preferential treatment to minorities to correct racial imbalance. The plain language of the statute too clearly prohibited such racial discrimination to admit of any doubt. They argued, tirelessly, that Title VII would be interpreted by federal agencies and their agents to require unwilling employers to racially balance their work forces by granting preferential treatment to minorities. Supporters of H.R. 7152 responded, equally tirelessly, that the Act would not be so interpreted because not only does it not require preferential treatment of minorities, it does not *permit* preferential treatment of any race for any reason. It cannot be doubted that the proponents of Title VII understood the meaning of their words, for "[s]eldom has similar legislation been debated with greater consciousness for the need for 'legislative history' or with greater care in the making thereof, to guide the courts in interpreting and applying the law." Title VII: Legislative History, at 444.

To put an end to the dispute, supporters of the civil rights bill drafted and introduced § 703(j). Specifically addressed to the opposition's charge, § 703(j) simply enjoins federal agencies and courts from interpreting Title VII to require an employer to prefer certain racial groups to correct imbalances in his work force. The section says nothing about voluntary preferential treatment of minorities because such racial discrimination is plainly proscribed by § 703(a) and (d). Indeed, had Congress intended to except voluntary, race-conscious preferential treatment from the blanket prohibition on racial discrimination in § 703(a) and (d), it surely could have drafted language better suited to the task than § 703(j). It knew how. Section 703(i) provides:

> "Nothing contained in [title VII] shall apply to any business or enterprise on or near an Indian reservation with respect to any publicly announced employment practice of such business or enterprise under which a preferential treatment is given to any individual because he is an Indian living on or near a reservation." § 703 (i), 42 U.S.C. § 2000e–2(i).

V

Our task in this case, like any other case involving the construction of a statute, is to give effect to the intent of Congress. To divine that intent, we traditionally look first to the words of the statute and, if they are unclear, then to the statute's legislative history. Finding the desired result hopelessly foreclosed by these conventional sources, the Court turns to a third source—the "spirit" of the Act. But close examination of what the Court proffers as the spirit of the Act reveals it as the spirit animating the present majority, not the Eighty-eighth Congress. For if the spirit of the Act eludes the cold words of the statute itself, it rings out with unmistakable clarity in the words of the elected representatives who made the Act law. It is *equality*. Senator Dirksen, I think, captured that spirit in a speech delivered on the floor of the Senate just moments before the bill was passed:

> "[T]oday we come to grips finally with a bill that advances the enjoyment of living; but, more than that, it advances the equality of opportunity.
>
> "I do not emphasize the word 'equality' standing by itself. It means equality of opportunity in the field of education. It means equality of opportunity in the field of employment. It means equality of opportunity in the field of participation in the affairs of government .   .   .
>
> "That is it.
>
> "Equality of opportunity, if we are going to talk about conscience, is the mass conscience of mankind that speaks in every generation, and it will continue to speak long after we are dead and gone." 110 Cong.Rec. 14510 (1964).

There is perhaps no device more destructive to the notion of equality than the *numerus clausus*—the quota. Whether described as "benign discrimination" or "affirmative action," the racial quota is nonetheless a creator of castes, a two-edged sword that must demean one in order to prefer another. In passing Title VII Congress outlawed *all* racial discrimination, recognizing that no discrimination based on race is benign, that no action disadvantaging a person because of his color is affirmative. With today's holding, the Court introduces into Title VII a tolerance for the very evil that the law was intended to eradicate, without offering even a clue as to what the limits on that tolerance may be. We are told simply that Kaiser's racially discriminatory admission quota "falls on the permissible side of the line." Ante, at 12. By going not merely *beyond,* but directly *against* Title VII's language and legislative history, the Court has sown the wind. Later courts will face the impossible task of reaping the whirlwind.

Notes and Questions

1. According to Justice Brennan's reading of the legislative history, what was the dominant purpose underlying the adoption of Title VII? Was it to prevent racial discrimination *after* the adoption of the act? Was it to provide remedies for pre-act racial discrimination? Was it to provide job opportunities to racial minorities which had been subjected to discrimination?

2. Suppose that EEOC and the Office of Contract Compliance (OFCC) found that Kaiser had been guilty of racial discrimination, and Kaiser had then entered into a consent agreement with EEOC and OFCC calling for an affirmative action program identical to the program negotiated with the U.S.W. According to Justice Rehnquist's reading of the legislative history, would that consent agreement violate Title VII? According to Justice Rehnquist's reading of the legislative history, would Title VII bar a court from ordering the Kaiser plan as a remedy for past acts of racial discrimination by an employer?

3. Do the various excerpts from the legislative history, cited and quoted in the four opinions, resolve the issues in this case for you? Does the literal language of Title VII resolve the issues for you?

4. Does the Kaiser plan discriminate against white workers? What was the basis for Weber's claim that he had been discriminated against? What was the basis of Weber's claim to access to the apprenticeship program?

5. If Blacks had generally lower seniority at Kaiser due to prior racial discrimination, would Kaiser be vulnerable to a Title VII discrimination charge if it based entry to its craft training program on a strict seniority basis? Compare this problem to the problem in *Griggs* supra p. 1147.

6. Weber raises a question as to the role collective bargaining may play in dealing with the effects of past racial discrimination. That issue is complicated by conflicting policies. Collective bargaining agents are enjoined to give fair representation to minority interests, Steele v. Louisville and Nashville Ry. Co., *supra* p. 1145; collective bargaining agents are also empowered to negotiate for removal of discriminatory practices since those have been held to be unfair labor practices, United Packinghouse, Food and Allied Workers Int. U. v. N. L. R. B., *supra* p. 1145; finally, where there is a collective bargaining agent, minority employees are effectively barred from collective activity against discriminatory practices of the employer, since the bargaining agent has the exclusive authority to bargain for employees regarding all terms and conditions of employment, Emporium Capwell v. Western Addition Community Organization, 420 U.S. 50, 95 S.Ct. 977 (1975). The problem, of course, is that the bargaining agent is chosen by majority vote of employees. As a matter of inter-

nal politics, the union must see to it that the majority of workers is treated fairly, and, perhaps more important, that the majority perceive themselves as being fairly treated. In Weber, the union, pressed by its and the employer's need to comply with federal affirmative action requirements, negotiated a program to improve minority status. That is consistent with the cases cited above, but since Title VII applies generally to all employers the affirmative action plan raised the issue of "reverse discrimination" against the majority of employees. This conflict of policies is clearly the most difficult remaining issue in the law regarding race relations. That we have come to this point in so short a time indicates both how much can be accomplished through legal process and that there are some limitations to the uses of legal process to resolve complex social issues.

SECTION 51. CONTRACT AND CONTRACT REMEDIES UNDER THE WAGNER AND TAFT–HARTLEY ACTS

The Wagner and Taft-Hartley Acts establish collective bargaining as the preferred method for resolving labor-management disputes. This section considers techniques established by law to both facilitate and protect the voluntary agreements which are the end product of collective bargaining. The materials will also raise, without answers, questions regarding the possibility of applying these techniques to other areas of social conflict.

JUDICIAL ENFORCEMENT OF THE COLLECTIVE CONTRACT: SECTION 301 OF THE TAFT–HARTLEY ACT

PUBLIC LAW 80–101, 61 STAT. 136 (1947), [Taft-Hartley Act]

Sec. 301. (a) Suits for violation of contracts between an employer and a labor organization representing employees in an industry affecting commerce as defined in this Act, or between any such labor organizations, may be brought in any district court of the United States having jurisdiction of the parties, without respect to the amount in controversy or without regard to the citizenship of the parties.

(b) Any labor organization which represents employees in an industry affecting commerce as defined in this Act and any employer whose activities affect commerce as defined in this Act shall be bound by the acts of its agents. Any such labor organization may sue or be sued as an entity and in behalf of the employees whom it represents in the courts of the United States. Any money judgment against a labor organization in a district court of the United States shall be enforceable only against the organization as an entity and against its assets, and shall not be enforceable against any individual member or his assets.

[The following is taken from COX and BOK, CASES ON LA-
BOR LAW, 7th ed., pp. 597–598.]

Legal Status of Collective Agreements Prior to LMRA Section 301

Prior to the enactment of Section 301 of the Labor Management Relations Act in 1947 the State courts alone had jurisdiction over suits for breach
of a collective bargaining agreement (except where there was diversity
of citizenship), and any substantive rights and remedies were determined
by State law. Legal rights and remedies were uncertain or ineffective or
both, for a variety of reasons.

A union was not treated as a legal entity. In most jurisdictions a class
action was necessary for the members to sue or be sued. Execution of a
money judgment would have to be levied upon the individual property of
the members.

There was grave doubt whether a collective agreement was enforceable
at all and, if so, by and against whom it was enforceable.

One view was that a collective bargaining contract was only a "gentlemen's agreement" without legal effect.

A second analysis allowed individual employees to sue the employer as
third party beneficiaries of promises made by the employer to the union.

A third view was that the union negotiated as agent for its members
(or perhaps all the employees) as principals, so that the legal obligations ran
directly between employees and employer. Under this view, presumably only
the employees and employer could sue or be sued and the employer and any
individual employee could negotiate different terms and conditions of employment. . . .

A fourth view argued that the agreement between employer and labor
union had the effect of a custom which was to be presumed to be incorporated into each individual employment contract unless the presumption was
negated. The consequences of this view would seem to be much the same
as the results of an agency analysis.

In the national debate upon labor policy leading to enactment of the
Taft Hartley Act many employers and trade associations pressed for a law
that would make collective bargaining agreements binding on unions. It is
unclear whether the demand was a response to genuine need or merely the
outgrowth of psychological frustration engendered by finding that collective bargaining was often a one way street. Employers rarely seek to obtain and collect a large money judgment against the local union with which
they must live and work in a day to day relationship just as, while the marriage lasts, there are few lawsuits between husband and wife. The ability
to get a quick injunction against a strike in breach of contract would be
valuable to an employer, but that remedy would revive fears of the old labor
injunction and require modification of the Norris-LaGuardia Act.

TEXTILE WORKERS UNION v. LINCOLN MILLS
OF ALABAMA

Supreme Court of the United States, 1957.
353 U.S. 448, 77 S.Ct. 923.

MR. JUSTICE DOUGLAS delivered the opinion of the Court. [Footnotes are omitted.]

Petitioner-union entered into a collective bargaining agreement in 1953 with respondent-employer, the agreement to run one year and from year to year thereafter, unless terminated on specified notices. The agreement provided that there would be no strikes or work stoppages and that grievances would be handled pursuant to a specified procedure. The last step in the grievance procedure—a step that could be taken by either party—was arbitration.

This controversy involves several grievances that concern work loads and work assignments. The grievances were processed through the various steps in the grievance procedure and were finally denied by the employer. The union requested arbitration, and the employer refused. Thereupon the union brought this suit in the District Court to compel arbitration.

The District Court concluded that it had jurisdiction and ordered the employer to comply with the grievance arbitration provisions of the collective bargaining agreement. The Court of Appeals reversed by a divided vote. 230 F.2d 81. . . .

The starting point of our inquiry is § 301 of the Labor Management Relations Act of 1947, 61 Stat. 156, 29 U.S.C. § 185, 29 U.S.C.A. § 185, which provides: . . .

There has been considerable litigation involving § 301 and courts have construed it differently. There is one view that § 301(a) merely gives federal district courts jurisdiction in controversies that involve labor organizations in industries affecting commerce, without regard to diversity of citizenship or the amount in controversy. Under that view § 301(a) would not be the source of substantive law; it would neither supply federal law to resolve these controversies nor turn the federal judges to state law for answers to the questions. Other courts—the overwhelming number of them—hold that § 301(a) is more than jurisdictional—that it authorizes federal courts to fashion a body of federal law for the enforcement of these collective bargaining agreements and includes within that federal law specific performance of promises to arbitrate grievances under collective bargaining agreements. Perhaps the leading decision representing that point of view is the one rendered by Judge Wyzanski in Textile Workers Union of America (C.I.O.) v. American Thread Co., D.C., 113 F.Supp. 137. That is our construction of § 301(a), which means that the agreement to arbitrate grievance disputes, contained in this collective bargaining agreement, should be specifically enforced.

From the face of the Act it is apparent that § 301(a) and § 301(b) supplement one another. Section 301(b) makes it possible for a labor organization, representing employees in an industry affecting commerce, to sue and be sued as an entity in the federal courts. Section 301(b) in other words provides the procedural remedy lacking at common law. Section 301(a) certainly does something more than that. Plainly, it supplies the basis upon which the federal district courts may take jurisdiction and apply the procedural rule of § 301(b). The question is whether § 301(a) is more than jurisdictional.

The legislative history of § 301 is somewhat cloudy and confusing. But there are a few shafts of light that illuminate our problem.

The bills, as they passed the House and the Senate, contained provisions which would have made the failure to abide by an agreement to arbitrate an unfair labor practice. S.Rep. No. 105, 80th Cong., 1st Sess., pp. 20–21, 23; H.R.Rep. No. 245, 80th Cong., 1st Sess., p. 21. This feature of the law was dropped in Conference. As the Conference's Report stated, "Once parties have made a collective bargaining contract, the enforcement of that contract should be left to the usual processes of the law and not to the National Labor Relations Board." H.Conf.Rep. No. 510, 80th Cong., 1st Sess., p. 42.

Both the Senate and the House took pains to provide for "the usual processes of the law" by provisions which were the substantial equivalent of § 301(a) in its present form. Both the Senate Report and the House Report indicate a primary concern that unions as well as employees should be bound to collective bargaining contracts. But there was also a broader concern— a concern with a procedure for making such agreements enforceable in the courts by either party. At one point the Senate Report, supra, p. 15, states, "We feel that the aggrieved party should also have a right of action in the Federal courts. Such policy is completely in accord with the purpose of the Wagner Act which the Supreme Court declared was 'to compel employers to bargain collectively with their employees to the end that an employment contract, binding on both parties, should be made . . ..' "

Congress was also interested in promoting collective bargaining that ended with agreements not to strike. The Senate Report, supra, p. 16 states:

"If unions can break agreements with relative impunity, then such agreements do not tend to stabilize industrial relations. The execution of an agreement does not by itself promote industrial peace. The chief advantage which an employer can reasonably expect from a collective labor agreement is assurance of uninterrupted operation during the term of the agreement. Without some effective method of assuring freedom from economic warfare for the term of the agreement, there is little reason why an employer would desire to sign such a contract.

"Consequently, to encourage the making of agreements and to promote industrial peace through faithful performance by the parties, collective agreements affecting interstate commerce should be enforceable in the Federal courts. Our amendment would provide for suits by unions as legal entities and against unions as legal entities in the Federal courts in disputes affecting commerce."

Thus collective bargaining contracts were made "equally binding and enforceable on both parties." Id., p. 15. As stated in the House Report, supra, p. 6, the new provision "makes labor organizations equally responsible with employers for contract violation and provides for suit by either against the other in the United States district courts." To repeat, the Senate Report, supra, p. 17, summed up the philosophy of § 301 as follows: "Statutory recognition of the collective agreement as a valid, binding, and enforceable contract is a logical and necessary step. It will promote a higher degree of responsibility upon the parties to such agreements, and will thereby promote industrial peace."

Plainly the agreement to arbitrate grievance disputes is the *quid pro quo* for an agreement not to strike. Viewed in this light, the legislation does more than confer jurisdiction in the federal courts over labor organizations. It expresses a federal policy that federal courts should enforce these agreements on behalf of or against labor organizations and that industrial peace can be best obtained only in that way.

To be sure there is a great medley of ideas reflected in the hearings, reports, and debates on this Act. Yet, to repeat, the entire tenor of the history indicates that the agreement to arbitrate grievance disputes was considered as *quid pro quo* of a no-strike agreement. And when in the House the debate narrowed to the question whether § 301 was more than jurisdictional, it became abundantly clear that the purpose of the section was to provide the necessary legal remedies. Section 302 of the House bill, the substantial equivalent of the present § 301, was being described by Mr. Hartley, the sponsor of the bill in the House:

"Mr. Barden. Mr. Chairman, I take this time for the purpose of asking the Chairman a question, and in asking the question I want it understood that it is intended to make a part of the record that may hereafter be referred to as history of the legislation.

"It is my understanding that section 302, the section dealing with equal responsibility under collective bargaining contracts in strike actions and proceedings in district courts contemplates not only the ordinary lawsuits for damages but also such other remedial proceedings, both legal and equitable, as might be appropriate in the circumstances; in other words, proceedings could, for example, be brought by the employers, the labor organizations, or interested individual employees under the Declaratory Judgments Act in order to secure declarations from the Court of legal rights under the contract.

"Mr. Hartley. The interpretation the gentleman has just given of that section is absolutely correct." 93 Cong.Rec. 3656–3657.

It seems, therefore, clear to us that Congress adopted a policy which placed sanctions behind agreements to arbitrate grievance disputes, by implication rejecting the common-law rule, discussed in Red Cross Line v. Atlantic Fruit Co., 264 U.S. 109, 44 S.Ct. 274, 68 L.Ed. 582, against enforcement of executory agreements to arbitrate. We would undercut the Act and defeat its policy if we read § 301 narrowly as only conferring jurisdiction over labor organizations.

The question then is, what is the substantive law to be applied in suits under § 301(a)? We conclude that the substantive law to apply in suits under § 301(a) is federal law which the courts must fashion from the policy of our national labor laws. See Mendelsohn, Enforceability of Arbitration Agreements Under Taft-Hartley Section 301, 66 Yale L.J. 167. The Labor Management Relations Act expressly furnishes some substantive law. It points out what the parties may or may not do in certain situations. Other problems will lie in the penumbra of express statutory mandates. Some will lack express statutory sanction but will be solved by looking at the policy of the legislation and fashioning a remedy that will effectuate that policy. The range of judicial inventiveness will be determined by the nature of the problem. See Board of Commissioners of Jackson County v. United States, 308 U.S. 343, 351, 60 S.Ct. 285, 288, 84 L.Ed. 313. Federal interpretation of the federal law will govern, not state law. Cf. Jerome v. United States, 318 U.S. 101, 104, 63 S.Ct. 483, 485, 87 L.Ed. 640. But state law, if compatible with the purpose of § 301, may be resorted to in order to find the rule that will best effectuate the federal policy. See Board of Commissioners of Jackson County v. United States, supra, 308 U.S. at pages 351–352, 60 S.Ct. at pages 288–289. Any state law applied, however, will be absorbed as federal law and will not be an independent source of private rights.

It is not uncommon for federal courts to fashion federal law where federal rights are concerned. See Clearfield Trust Co. v. United States, 318 U.S. 363, 366–367, 63 S.Ct. 573, 574–575, 87 L.Ed. 838; National Metropolitan Bank v. United States, 323 U.S. 454, 65 S.Ct. 354, 89 L.Ed. 383. Congress has indicated by § 301(a) the purpose to follow that course here. There is no constitutional difficulty. Article III, § 2 extends the judicial power to cases "arising under . . . the Laws of the United States . . .." The power of Congress to regulate these labor-management controversies under the Commerce Clause is plain. Houston East & West Texas R. Co. v. United States, 234 U.S. 342, 34 S.Ct. 833, 58 L.Ed. 1341; National Labor Relations Board v. Jones & Laughlin Corp., 301 U.S. 1, 57 S.Ct. 615, 81 L.Ed. 893. A case or controversy arising under § 301(a) is, therefore, one within the purview of judicial power as defined in Article III.

The question remains whether jurisdiction to compel arbitration of grievance disputes is withdrawn by the Norris-LaGuardia Act, 47 Stat. 70, 29 U.S.C. § 101 et seq., 29 U.S.C.A. § 101 et seq. Section 7 of that Act prescribes stiff procedural requirements for issuing an injunction in a labor dispute. The kinds of acts which had given rise to abuse of the power to enjoin are listed in § 4. The failure to arbitrate was not a part and parcel of the abuses against which the Act was aimed. Section 8 of the Norris-La-Guardia Act does, indeed, indicate a congressional policy toward settlement of labor disputes by arbitration, for it denies injunctive relief to any person who has failed to make "every reasonable effort" to settle the dispute by negotiation, mediation, or "voluntary arbitration." Though a literal reading might bring the dispute within the terms of the Act (see Cox, Grievance Arbitration in the Federal Courts, 67 Harv.L.Rev. 591, 602–604), we see no justification in policy for restricting § 301(a) to damage suits, leaving specific performance of a contract to arbitrate grievance disputes to the inapposite procedural requirements of that Act. Moreover, we held in Virginian R. Co. v. System Federation, 300 U.S. 515, 57 S.Ct. 592, 81 L.Ed. 789, and in Graham v. Brotherhood Firemen, 338 U.S. 232, 237, 70 S.Ct. 14, 17, 94 L.Ed. 22, that the Norris-LaGuardia Act does not deprive federal courts of jurisdiction to compel compliance with the mandates of the Railway Labor Act, 45 U.S.C.A. § 151 et seq. The mandates there involved concerned racial discrimination. Yet those decisions were not based on any peculiarities of the Railway Labor Act. We followed the same course in Syres v. Oil Workers International Union, 350 U.S. 892, 76 S.Ct. 152, 100 L.Ed. 785, which was governed by the National Labor Relations Act, 29 U.S.C.A. § 151 et seq. There an injunction was sought against racial discrimination in application of a collective bargaining agreement; and we allowed the injunction to issue. The congressional policy in favor of the enforcement of agreements to arbitrate grievance disputes being clear, there is no reason to submit them to the requirements of § 7 of the Norris-LaGuardia Act. . . .

MR. JUSTICE BLACK took no part in the consideration or decision of this case.

MR. JUSTICE BURTON, whom MR. JUSTICE HARLAN joins, concurring in the result.

This suit was brought in a United States District Court under § 301 of the Labor Management Relations Act of 1947, 61 Stat. 156, 29 U.S.C. § 185, 29 U.S.C.A. § 185, seeking specific enforcement of the arbitration provisions of a collective-bargaining contract. The District Court had jurisdiction over the action since it involved an obligation running to a union—a union controversy—and not uniquely personal rights of employees sought to be enforced by a union. Cf. Association of Westinghouse Salaried Employees v. Westinghouse Elec. Corp., 348 U.S. 437, 75 S.Ct. 489, 99 L.Ed. 510. Having jurisdiction over the suit, the court was not powerless to fashion an appropriate federal remedy. The power to decree specific performance of a collectively bargained agreement to arbitrate finds its source in § 301 itself, and in a Federal District Court's inherent equitable powers, nurtured by a congressional policy to encourage and enforce labor arbitration in industries affecting commerce.

I do not subscribe to the conclusion of the Court that the substantive law to be applied in a suit under § 301 is federal law. At the same time, I agree with Judge Magruder in International Brotherhood v. W. L. Mead, Inc., 1 Cir., 230 F.2d 576, that some federal rights may necessarily be involved in a § 301 case, and hence that the constitutionality of § 301 can be upheld as a congressional grant to Federal District Courts of what has been called "protective jurisdiction."

MR. JUSTICE FRANKFURTER dissented.

Notes and Questions

1. In the light of the history of American labor law, can you see any objections to giving the courts the responsibility of enforcing collective bargaining agreements?

2. Would you prefer that an administrative agency, say the NLRB, be made primarily responsible for adjudicating disputes arising out of collective bargaining agreements?

3. The Textile Workers sought the remedy of specific enforcement of its collective bargaining agreement. Specific enforcement is an equitable remedy for breach of contract (see the note on Law and Equity, *supra* p. 73, and the note on contract remedies, *supra* p. 721), and it entails issuance by a court of an order—an injunction—requiring the defendant to perform the terms of the agreement or be in contempt of court. This aspect of the remedy requested forced the Court to consider the application of the Norris-LaGuardia Act to this case. What reasons does the Court give in support of its finding that

the Norris-La Guardia Act does not bar the specific performance remedy to enforce an arbitration clause in a collective bargaining agreement? Can you offer other reasons to support that finding? What, if any, reasons can you suggest in support of denying specific enforcement of arbitration clauses? of other terms of collective bargaining agreements?

4.   Note that the civil action in federal court has been the preferred method for adjudicating employment discrimination cases under Title VII of the Civil Rights Act of 1964, and that the EEOC has been denied administrative enforcement techniques, and has been remitted to bringing civil actions to enforce Title VII (see Section 49.3, *supra* pp. 1083–1104). Is the Congress's disposition to favor judicial adjudication of civil rights cases and administrative adjudication of labor disputes purely historical, or are there other reasons which favor this selection of the primary forum for resolving each type of dispute?

5.   In Lincoln Mills the plaintiff was a collective bargaining agent seeking injunctive relief against a recalcitrant employer. The Court in Lincoln Mills found the employer subject to specific enforcement of its arbitration agreement. Subsequently the Court was forced to consider the other side of the coin. In Sinclair Refining Co. v. Atkinson, the plaintiff was an employer seeking specific enforcement of a no-strike clause in a collective bargaining agreement. The no-strike clause is a promise from the collective bargaining agent that it will not call or sanction strikes during the term of a collective bargaining agreement. The no-strike clause is usually a *quid pro quo* given by the union in exchange for the grievance machinery, including binding arbitration of grievances. The strike in Sinclair v. Atkinson was over arbitrable grievances and the employer sought an injunction to restrain the strike and compel the union to submit the grievances to arbitration. The Court found that neither § 301 or Lincoln Mills would support an injunction against the union, holding instead that the no injunction policy of the Norris-LaGuardia Act was controlling in such cases. See Sinclair Refining Co. v. Atkinson, 370 U.S. 195, 82 S.Ct. 1328 (1962). Eight years later the Court reconsidered this issue. See Boys Market, Inc. v. Retail Clerk's Union, Local 770, 398 U.S. 235, 90 S.Ct. 1583 (1970). The following is from Mr. Justice Brennan's opinion for the Court:

IV

We have also determined that the dissenting opinion in *Sinclair* states the correct principles concerning the accommodation necessary between the seemingly absolute terms of the Norris-LaGuardia Act and the policy considerations underlying § 301(a). 370 U.S., at 215, 82 S.Ct., at 1339. Although we need not repeat all that was there said, a few points should be emphasized at this time.

The literal terms of § 4 of the Norris-LaGuardia Act must be accommodated to the subsequently enacted provisions of § 301(a) of the Labor Management Relations Act and the purposes of arbitration. Statutory interpretation requires more than concentration upon isolated words; rather, consideration must be given to the total corpus of pertinent law and the policies that inspired ostensibly inconsistent provisions. See Richards v. United States, 369 U.S. 1, 11, 82 S.Ct. 585, 592 (1962); Mastro Plastics Corp. v. NLRB, 350 U.S. 270, 285, 76 S.Ct. 349, 359 (1956); United States v. Hutcheson, 312 U.S. 219, 235, 61 S.Ct. 463, 467 (1941).

The Norris-LaGuardia Act was responsive to a situation totally different from that which exists today. In the early part of this century, the federal courts generally were regarded as allies of management in its attempt to prevent the organization and strenthening of labor unions; and in this industrial struggle the injunction became a potent weapon that was wielded against the activities of labor groups. The result was a large number of sweeping decrees, often issued *ex parte*, drawn on an *ad hoc* basis without regard to any systematic elaboration of national labor policy. See Milk Wagon Drivers' Union, etc. v. Lake Valley Co., 311 U.S. 91, 102, 61 S. Ct. 122, 127 (1940).

In 1932 Congress attempted to bring some order out of the industrial chaos that had developed and to correct the abuses that had resulted from the interjection of the federal judiciary into union-management disputes on the behalf of management. See declaration of public policy, Norris-LaGuardia Act, § 2, 47 Stat. 70. Congress, therefore, determined initially to limit severely the power of the federal courts to issue injunctions "in any case involving or growing out of any labor dispute * * *." § 4, 47 Stat. 70. Even as initially enacted, however, the prohibition against federal injunctions was by no means absolute. See Norris-LaGuardia Act, §§ 7, 8, 9, 47 Stat. 71, 72. Shortly thereafter Congress passed the Wagner Act, designed to curb various management activities that tended to discourage employee participation in collective action.

As labor organizations grew in strength and developed toward maturity, congressional emphasis shifted from protection of the nascent labor movement to the encouragement of collective bargaining and to administrative techniques for the peaceful resolution of industrial disputes. This shift in emphasis was accomplished, however, without extensive revision of many of the older enactments, including the anti-injunction section of the Norris-LaGuardia Act. Thus it became the task of the courts to accommodate, to reconcile the older statutes with the more recent ones.

A leading example of this accommodation process is Brotherhood of Railroad Trainmen v. Chicago River & Ind. R. Co., 353 U.S. 30, 77 S.Ct. 635 (1957). There we were confronted with a peaceful strike which violated the statutory duty to arbitrate imposed by the Railway Labor Act. The Court concluded that a strike in violation of a statutory arbitration duty was not the type of situation to which the Norris-LaGuardia Act was responsive, that an important federal policy was involved in the peaceful settlement of disputes through the statutorily mandated arbitration procedure, that this important policy was imperiled if equitable remedies were not available to implement it, and hence that Norris-LaGuardia's policy of nonintervention by the federal courts should yield to the overriding interest in the successful implementation of the arbitration process.

The principles elaborated in *Chicago River* are equally applicable to the present case. To be sure, *Chicago River* involved arbitration procedures established by statute. However, we have frequently noted, in such cases as *Lincoln Mills,* the *Steelworkers Trilogy,* and *Lucas Flour,* the importance that Congress has attached generally to the voluntary settlement of labor disputes without resort to self-help and more particularly to arbitration as a means to this end. Indeed, it has been stated that *Lincoln Mills,* in its exposition of § 301(a), "went a long way towards making arbitration the central institution in the administration of collective bargaining contracts."

The *Sinclair* decision, however, seriously undermined the effectiveness of the arbitration technique as a method peacefully to resolve industrial disputes without resort to strikes, lockouts, and similar devices. Clearly employers will be wary of assuming obligations to arbitrate specifically enforceable against them when no similarly efficacious remedy is available to enforce the concomitant undertaking of the union to refrain from striking. On the other hand, the central purpose of the Norris-LaGuardia Act to foster the growth and viability of labor organizations is hardly retarded—if anything, this goal is advanced—by a remedial device that merely enforces the obligation that the union freely undertook under a specifically enforceable agreement to submit disputes to arbitration.[55] We conclude, therefore, that the unavailability of equitable relief in the arbitration context presents a serious impediment to the congressional policy favoring the voluntary establishment of a mechanism for the peaceful resolution of labor disputes, that the core purpose of the Norris-LaGuardia Act is not sacrificed by the limited use of equitable remedies to further this important policy, and consequently that the Norris-LaGuardia Act does not bar the granting of injunctive relief in the circumstances of the instant case.

V

Our holding in the present case is a narrow one. We do not undermine the vitality of the Norris-LaGuardia Act. We deal only with the situation in which a collective-bargaining contract contains a mandatory grievance adjustment or arbitration procedure. Nor does it follow from what we have said that injunctive relief is appropriate as a matter of course in every case of a strike over an arbitrable grievance. The dissenting opinion in *Sinclair* suggested the following principles for the guidance of the district courts in determining whether to grant injunctive relief—principles that we now adopt:

"A District Court entertaining an action under § 301 may not grant injunctive relief against concerted activity unless and until

---

55. As well stated by the neutral members of the A.B.A. *Sinclair* committee: " * * * [T]he reasons behind the Norris-LaGuardia Act seem scarcely applicable to the situation * * * [in which a strike in violation of a collective-bargaining agreement is enjoined]. The Act was passed primarily because of widespread dissatisfaction with the tendency of judges to enjoin concerted activities in accordance with 'doctrines of tort law which made the lawfulness of a strike depend upon judicial views of social and economic policy.' * * * Where an injunction is used against a strike in breach of contract, the union is not subjected in this fashion to judicially created limitations on its freedom of action but is simply compelled to comply with limitations to which it has previously agreed. Moreover, where the underlying dispute is arbitrable, the union is not deprived of any practicable means of pressing its claim but is only required to submit the dispute to the impartial tribunal that it has agreed to establish for this purpose." A.B.A. Sinclair Report 242.

it decides that the case is one in which an injunction would be appropriate despite the Norris-LaGuardia Act. When a strike is sought to be enjoined because it is over a grievance which both parties are contractually bound to arbitrate, the District Court may issue no injunctive order until it first holds that the contract *does* have that effect; and the employer should be ordered to arbitrate, as a condition of his obtaining an injunction against the strike. Beyond this, the District Court must, of course, consider whether issuance of an injunction would be warranted under ordinary principles of equity—whether breaches are occurring and will continue, or have been threatened and will be committed; whether they have caused or will cause irreparable injury to the employer; and whether the employer will suffer more from the denial of an injunction than will the union from its issuance." 370 U.S., at 228, 82 S.Ct., at 1346. (Emphasis in original.)

In the present case there is no dispute that the grievance in question was subject to adjustment and arbitration under the collective-bargaining agreement and that the petitioner was ready to proceed with arbitration at the time an injunction against the strike was sought and obtained. The District Court also concluded that, by reason of respondent's violations of its no-strike obligation, petitioner "has suffered irreparable injury and will continue to suffer irreparable injury." Since we now overrule *Sinclair*, the holding of the Court of Appeals in reliance on *Sinclair* must be reversed. Accordingly, we reverse the judgment of the Court of Appeals and remand the case with directions to enter a judgment affirming the order of the District Court.

It is so ordered.

Judgment of Court of Appeals reversed and case remanded with directions.

The Court in Boys Market overruled Sinclair v. Atkinson, insofar as that case had barred the injunction remedy to enforce a no-strike clause where the strike in question was over a clearly arbitrable issue. Two justices dissented. In Buffalo Forge Co. v. U. S. Steelworkers, 428 U.S. 397, 96 S.Ct. 3141 (1976), the Court declined to extend Boys Market to a case where a strike in violation of a no-strike clause did not involve a clearly but only arguably arbitrable dispute. Four Justices dissented.

The last section of these materials (Section 54, *infra*) deals with arbitration as an alternative to judicial or administrative adjudication of labor disputes. See if you think the judicial deference to arbitration, which is manifested in Lincoln Mills and Boys Market, is sufficiently warranted to justify the interpretation that § 301 of the Landrum-Griffin Act overrides the Norris-LaGuardia Act with respect to no-strike clauses in agreements where there is also a binding arbitration clause.

SECTION 52.　CONCILIATION AND MEDIATION

CONCILIATION, MEDIATION AND FACT FINDING IN LABOR DISPUTES

[The following is taken from COX and BOK, CASES ON LABOR LAW, 7th ed., pp. 935–945.]

The organic act of 1913 which established the United States Department of Labor authorized the Secretary of Labor "to appoint Commissioners of Conciliation in labor disputes whenever in his judgment the interests of industrial peace require it to be done." [2] Since that time the importance of the conciliation services of the federal government and the size of the Service have grown enormously. To meet the needs of both industry and labor the Conciliation Service established regional offices in 17 industrial centers, from which the assistance of a trained staff of conciliators could be quickly obtained. In the year prior to the enactment of the Taft-Hartley Act, the Conciliation Service aided in bringing about the voluntary settlement of 13,000 disputes.

The Taft-Hartley Act established a new independent agency, known as the Federal Mediation and Conciliation Service, and transferred to it all the functions of the Conciliation Service of the Department of Labor. As we have already pointed out, sixty days prior to making any change in the terms and conditions of employment fixed by a collective agreement covering employees in an industry affecting interstate commerce, the party desiring a change must give notice to the other party, and 30 days thereafter must notify both the Federal Mediation and Conciliation Service and any State mediation agency. During the 60 day period it is an unfair labor practice to make any change in terms and conditions of employment (except by mutual agreement) or to call a strike. The Service may proffer its services in any labor dispute in an industry affecting interstate commerce—the old Conciliation Service could properly intervene even though interstate commerce was not affected—but it is directed to avoid attempting to mediate disputes having only a minor effect on interstate commerce. In addition, the Service may intervene in grievance cases only in exceptional circumstances. Behind these restrictions lies the belief that State agencies should assume a larger role in settling labor controversies.

Most of the industrial States have also established effective conciliation or mediation agencies. In New York there is a State Board of Mediation, established in the Department of Labor, which is empowered to take "such steps as it may deem expedient to effect a voluntary, amicable and expeditious adjustment and settlement of the differences and issues between employer and employees which have precipitated" a labor dispute. The Board may designate any member or officer of the Board to act in its behalf. It is vested with power to hold public hearings and subpoena witnesses but in fact proceedings are generally conducted with the greatest informality.[3] A Pennsylvania statute provides that whenever the services of the Depart-

---

2. Act of March 4, 1913, § 8, 37 Stat. 738, 5 U.S.C.A. § 619.

3. N.Y.Labor Law, art. 21.

ment of Labor and Industry are invoked by either party to a controversy over the negotiation or application of a collective bargaining agreement, "the department shall promptly put itself in communication with the parties to such controversy, and shall use its best efforts by mediation, through a representative of the Secretary, to bring them in agreement."[4] In other States, as in Massachusetts, the conciliation agency is also empowered by statute to arbitrate disputes which the parties are willing to submit.[5]

In addition to official State and federal services, there are a growing number of voluntary local mediation agencies established through the co-operation of industrial and labor leaders. In Toledo, Ohio, for example, a committee of 18 members drawn from industry, labor and the public was established to halt the industrial warfare which had long plagued the city. The committee formulated a set of principles and working rules, and commenced to settle disputes. The theory behind the plan is that through regular meetings the industry and labor members will develop mutual understanding of each other's problems and, with the help of the public members, they hope also to recommend policies beneficial to the community. Other cities have developed equally promising arrangements which have achieved remarkable success in settling disputes.[6]

Occasionally a distinction is drawn between conciliation and mediation: a conciliator is said to be merely an errand boy carrying messages between the parties whereas a mediator drives affirmatively toward a settlement by making his own proposals. But the difference is largely theoretical. By whatever name they may be called both have one end in view—that of bringing the parties to agree on the terms of a contract or, failing complete agreement, a voluntary submission to arbitration. Like every trade, mediation has its peculiar tricks, but basically the mediator depends on persuasion and on a thorough understanding of industrial relations to enable him to discover some basis for agreement. The general pattern has been summarized as follows:[7]

"1—When he [a conciliator] is called into a dispute he holds a preliminary discussion with each party which is sufficiently extensive so that he understands the major factors in the dispute, the progress that has been made to date, and the stumbling blocks to further progress. At this point he first determines whether he is needed yet or whether he should continue to remain on the sidelines. In these first conferences, also he establishes his impartial and expert position with both parties.

"2—The conciliator then schedules a joint conference. In that conference he acts as the chairman of the negotiations. His first role in the joint negotiations is to keep the discussions at the plane of rational analysis of the issues with the least possible emphasis on personalities and emotions. To the maximum degree, he encourages the parties to continue their own negotiating.

4. Penna.Statutes (Purdon), §§ 211.31–211.39.

5. Mass.General Laws Ann. ch. 150.

6. See Hepner, Local and Unofficial Arrangements for Labor Dispute Settle-

ment, 12 Law and Contemporary Problems 220 (1947).

7. Remarks of W. Ellison Chalmers, U. S. Conciliation Service at Conference on Training Law Students in Labor Relations.

"3—He breaks up the joint conference and conducts separate conferences with the parties at such time as it appears necessary for the separate consideration of each of the problems that have been jointly discussed. As in all his moves, it is not so much what he does but when he does it that determines his effectiveness. His function in the separate conferences is to explore intimately and confidentially all of the factors that have been raised in the joint conference. He never violates the confidences of either party. He induces each party to analyze the stumbling blocks, the obstacles to a settlement, in such a way as to develop compromise approaches that will lead toward a mutually satisfactory agreement.

"4—Not infrequently the conciliator finds that a deadlock has resulted over a misunderstanding concerning basic facts or of the position of the other party. Either in joint or separate conference, part of his role therefore is to correct such misunderstandings.

"5—Occasionally, the differences between the parties rest on either confusions or lack of facts concerning the practices elsewhere, the appropriate laws or administrative rulings. Again, either in separate or joint conferences, as the situation dictates, his role is to supply and develop a realistic use of such factual material.

"6—As the conferences proceed it is frequently the role of the conciliator to suggest compromises or alternative approaches to either side in reaching its own objectives. These are made as tentative suggestions for the consideration of each party, frequently in separate conference, but occasionally made jointly to both. They do not represent any final judgment of the conciliator on the equities in the case, but are efforts to stimulate the thinking and imagination of the two parties who may have beaten such a solid path up blind alleys that they have failed to think of new ways of finding common ground.

"7—Not infrequently the conciliator finds that the deadlock is pretty hopeless as long as the case is handled exclusively by the same negotiators who have been in from the first. One or more of these individuals on the one side or the other may have presented such a personality problem that no further compromise from the other side is possible. Or, the representatives present may have gone the limit of their authority to compromise the situation, and some higher authority on one side or the other is necessary. In such cases the conciliator may appeal to superiors on one or both sides in order to get a change of personalities, a new approach or a broader authority.

"8—Usually the conciliator avoids making any definite and public recommendations for the solution of the dispute. As the Twentieth Century Report well says, 'The conciliator should never indulge in any form of coercion.' The conciliator occasionally finds, however, that both parties would welcome his sponsorship of a compromise proposal. In such circumstances he may explore with each side the terms they would be likely to accept, and then recommend such terms to both parties. In other words, if he makes a formal recommendation it is almost always on the basis of the advance knowledge that it will be accepted by the parties.

"What I have described above is in general terms the standard practice of the individual government conciliator as he seeks to bring the parties together. In a relatively few cases, additional procedures may be invoked in an effort to resolve an otherwise deadlocked dispute. We in the Conciliation Service occasionally add a second or third man along with the original conciliator. We have found that sometimes such a device, by adding a new face and giving a somewhat different perspective to both parties, will break a deadlock; or, combined with this procedure may be a change in location of the conferences in order to achieve a broader perspective for the negotiators.

"Occasionally a conciliator will suggest that the parties refer their dispute to an arbitrator for a final and binding decision. The Conciliation Service maintains an extensive panel of expert arbitrators who have been cleared by both labor and management. If the issue is a grievance or an application of an existing contract, this is our usual procedure. On the other hand, only under exceptional circumstances do we make an arbitration suggestion on new contract terms.

"An agreement arrived at by the parties themselves is more likely to be a realistic evaluation of their own problems than is a solution dictated from a third party, no matter how wise or impartial he may be. It is also clear that such an agreement is much more likely to be fully honored and to be the basis for a constructive development of industrial relations by the very fact that it has been self-determined rather than be imposed by the outside. However, particularly in the area of public utilities disputes where the recourse of a strike would seriously cripple the community, arbitration is suggested by the conciliator where no other peaceful way out appears possible."

Experience demonstrates beyond question that a skilled mediator can generally give invaluable assistance in facilitating collective bargaining. It is to be remembered that mediation is generally invoked when there is reason to fear a breakdown in the negotiations. Frequently, the parties have stiffened in their positions and become angry and distrustful. By keeping the parties apart but going back and forth between them the mediator may bring the discussions back to a less emotional level where compromises can be achieved. At this stage, too, in joint negotiations both parties may seem to stand adamant on every issue, excluding all possibility of adjusting their differences, yet in private conference the experienced mediator can often learn from each party which of its demands it stresses and on which points it would yield.

In many disputes, especially those involving plants or industries in which collective bargaining is new, the mediator may find negotiations are breaking down chiefly because both the management and the local union fail to understand each other's problems and therefore neither comprehends the reasons for the position which the other takes. Surprisingly often, moreover, the parties fail to perceive the full implications of their own arguments. A mediator who has the confidence of the disputants can explain to each, in terms that it will understand, the problems that confront the other; he can point out to each the strengths and weaknesses of its position. In like manner, the skilled mediator may propose acceptable solutions drawn from his own experience but not familiar to the parties. Sometimes the proposal is frankly a compromise. On other occasions it is one of those happy solutions which satisfies the essential interests of both management and labor.

The mediator has a more difficult task when both the company and union are represented by experienced and highly skilled officials; there is little new he can suggest and each side understands the other. But even in such cases the mediator may serve a useful role. Often negotiations are drawn out because neither party knows the other party's breaking point. Management says it will have to shut down if wages are increased, and the union knows, perhaps, that this is an overstatement. At the same time, the union knows that if the demand is too high, the company may in fact not be able to operate if it is granted. Purported demonstrations in terms of profit and loss statements, etc., involve accounting mysteries and are never conclusive on such an issue, even to the expert. Accordingly, the union is often "playing for time" hoping to learn what increase in wages can be absorbed without serious trouble. Conversely, management is trying to find out how serious the union's threats of strike really are, and how much must be discounted as oratorical license. In such a situation a mediator, if his judgment is trusted by the parties, can shorten the negotiations (and perhaps avert a "blow-up" resulting from shortened tempers) by conveying to one of the parties that the other does in fact "mean business." He would naturally hesitate to say that the other does *not* mean what he says, for if he did so he would soon lose the confidence of that party, but his failure to speak may be no less eloquent. In somewhat the same manner, the mediator is sometimes in a position where he estimates the relative economic strength of the disputants and determines the most probable settlement before they themselves are aware of it. The mediator then drives continuously to get agreement at this breaking point, a course which will often expedite the negotiation of an agreement even if a strike has occurred.

No less important, the mediator is able to impress upon both parties the requirements of the public interest. In major disputes a government mediator can sometimes bring such tremendous pressure on both sides that they are compelled in fact, although not in legal theory, to accept the compromises which the mediator sponsors.

* * *

Fact Finding Boards

Considerable reliance has sometimes been placed on fact finding boards to supplement normal conciliation and mediation services, and in the railway labor field they have become an integral part of the collective bargaining process. Under the Railway Labor Act the carriers and the Brotherhoods which represent their employees are required to give at least 30 days' written notice of any intended change in an agreement affecting rates of pay, rules or working conditions. The National Mediation Board established by the Act may intervene in the dispute on its own motion or at the request of either party. The Board first attempts to mediate the dispute. If the effort fails, the Mediation Board seeks to induce the parties voluntarily to submit the controversy to arbitration. If either party refuses arbitration, the Mediation Board gives notice in writing that its mediatory efforts have failed. For 30 days thereafter no change may be made in rates of pay, rules or working conditions. Thereafter, a final step may be taken. If the dispute still threatens to deprive any section of the country of essential transportation service, the President may appoint an Emergency Board "to investigate promptly the facts as to the dispute and make a report thereon to the

President within 30 days". During the 30 day period and for 30 days thereafter, neither party may make any change in the conditions out of which the dispute arises.

The chief reason for the establishment of fact finding boards is the belief that public pressure will force the parties to accept the report of a prominent, impartial body appointed by the President. A second reason is that the intervention of a third person who makes recommendations carrying some measure of public authority may enable the spokesmen of management and labor to make concessions which they would like to make but for which they were afraid to take the responsibility lest they be criticized by other employers or, in the case of union leaders, by the members of their union. For a considerable period the procedures established by the Railway Labor Act appeared to be singularly successful; no important stoppages occurred. In 1941, however, the Brotherhoods refused to accept the report of an Emergency Board, and by using the report as a basis for further negotiations they secured additional concessions from the carriers, which were made under pressure by the President. Since that time the recommendations of fact finding boards have been less effective not only in the transportation field but also in other cases in which they were designated by executive action, notably during the wave of large scale strikes early in 1946.

The objections usually raised to fact finding boards are three in number: First, if they are frequently used, the parties to a dispute may avoid making any offers of compromise until they have gone before the Board and it has made recommendations. There is no bargaining between the parties. In this way unnecessary crises are precipitated. This tendency is very noticeable under the Railway Labor Act. Second, the impact of important fact finding awards extends into other fields regardless of underlying differences. In 1946, for example, the award of the General Motors fact finding board established a national pattern of wage increases which there was enormous pressure on both employers and unions to follow in other industries operating under different conditions. Third, the objection is often made that a process of fact finding and recommendations is virtually compulsory arbitration.

Despite these objections, however, it seems fairly plain that the fact finding board is a sound procedure to have available for occasional use in achieving the settlement of large scale controversies.

Questions

1. What are the respective functions of conciliation, mediation, and fact finding, as described by Cox and Bok?

2. Does adjudication have elements in common with conciliation, mediation or fact finding?

Note: *Mediation and Conciliation in Civil Rights Disputes*

Title VII of the Civil Rights Act of 1964 provided modest enforcement authority to the Equal Employment Opportunity Commissioner. (See, e. g., the materials in § 49.3, supra at pp. 1083–1104.) Title VII instead placed heavy reliance on the use of conciliation by the EEOC as a primary tool for administrative implementation of the Act's employment discrimination provisions. One commentator has succinctly summarized the history of conciliation under Title VII.

[The following is taken from CORNELIUS J. PECK, "THE EQUAL EMPLOYMENT OPPORTUNITY COMMISSION: DEVELOPMENTS IN THE ADMINISTRATIVE PROCESS 1965–1975," 51 Washington Law Review 831, 852–853 (1976).]

1. *The failure of conciliation*

It is ironic that the EEOC has had the success which it has thus far enjoyed with its guidelines when the conciliation process to which they lead has been quite unsuccessful. EEOC has itself said that exclusive reliance upon voluntary methods of negotiation, persuasion, and conciliation to resolve complaints of employment discrimination was misplaced and ineffective. Earlier, a similar scholarly judgment was expressed. EEOC statistics confirm the assessment. In its 1970 fiscal year, EEOC completed conciliation in a total of 1,179 cases, in which it reported that conciliation had been fully successful in 342 cases, partially successful in 105 cases, and unsuccessful in 732 cases. During its 1973 fiscal year, EEOC achieved 1,091 successful Pre-Decision Settlements; and 1,188 successful Post-Decision Settlements, or a total of 2,279 successful settlements out of the total of 4,970 cases in which a settlement effort was made.

The reasons for the failure of the conciliation process established by Title VII are numerous. Among the reasons for the failure was the lack of understanding at the time of the adoption of the Civil Rights Act of the nature of discrimination in employment. Conceivably, conciliation would work more effectively if discrimination in employment consisted of individual and isolated events springing from malice or ill will. The conciliator, by producing understanding and mutual confidence, might achieve successful settlements through "conference, conciliation, and persuasion." But experience has indicated that major problems of discrimination in employment lie in practices which are neutral on their face, such as testing, diploma or accreditation requirements, seniority practices, or even the absence of established recruitment procedures. The practices frequently have been adopted because of belief in their efficacy, justice, and value to the business enterprise and its employees. They are not likely to be abandoned by one who believes he has not discriminated and has no plan to engage in motivated discrimination. One who has abandoned motivated discrimination may conclude enough has been done, and refuse to take action to eliminate present effects of abandoned discrimination.

Moreover, conciliation works only between parties who are in fact negotiating. Dispute settlement negotiations do not take place successfully unless there is a force field which induces parties to accept the negotiated settlement as preferable to the consequence which might be expected if other remedies were pursued to their ultimate conclusion. EEOC's general practice during most of the decade of its existence of treating all charges on a class basis tended to ensure that the product of conciliation would be worse than, or at least no better than, the result of a suit by the charging party, and this discouraged settlements. Similarly, EEOC's concern that a charging party not settle for less than the full measure of statutory rights did not make the settlement process attractive. The charging party's waiver of the right to sue is the greatest bargaining tool for producing settlement, but it is not one that was available to EEOC, because unless the charging party joins in the settlement agreement, that party is not barred from suing because of an agreement made between the EEOC and the party charged.

Title 42 United States Code

(Public Law 88–352, Title X (1964))

SUBCHAPTER VIII.—COMMUNITY RELATIONS SERVICE

§ 2000g.   Establishment of Service; Director of Service: appointment, term; personnel; experts and consultants

There is hereby established in and as a part of the Department of Commerce a Community Relations Service (hereinafter referred to as the "Service"), which shall be headed by a Director who shall be appointed by the President with the advice and consent of the Senate for a term of four years. The Director is authorized to appoint, subject to the civil service laws and regulations, such other personnel as may be necessary to enable the Service to carry out its functions and duties, and to fix their compensation in accordance with the Classification Act of 1949, as amended. The Director is further authorized to procure services as authorized by section 55a of Title 5, but at rates for individuals not in excess of $75 per diem.

§ 2000g—1.   Functions of Service

It shall be the function of the Service to provide assistance to communities and persons therein in resolving disputes, disagreements, or difficulties relating to discriminatory practices based on race, color, or national origin which impair the rights of persons in such communities under the Constitution or laws of the United States or which affect or may affect interstate commerce. The Service may offer its services in cases of such disputes, disagreements, or difficulties whenever, in its judgment, peaceful relations among the citizens of the community involved are threatened thereby, and it may offer its services either upon its own motion or upon the request of an appropriate State or local official or other interested person.

§ 2000g—2.   Cooperation with other agencies; conciliation assistance in confidence and without publicity; information as confidential; restriction on performance of investigative or prosecuting functions; violations and penalties

(a) The Service shall, whenever possible, in performing its functions, seek and utilize the cooperation of appropriate State or local, public, or private agencies.

(b) The activities of all officers and employees of the Service in providing conciliation assistance shall be conducted in confidence and without publicity, and the Service shall hold confidential any information acquired in the regular performance of its duties upon the understanding that it would be so held.   No officer or employee of the Service shall engage in the performance of investigative or prosecuting functions of any department or agency in any litigation arising out of a dispute in which he acted on behalf of the Service.   Any officer or other employee of the Service, who shall make public in any manner whatever any information in violation of this subsection, shall be deemed guilty of a misdemeanor and, upon conviction thereof, shall be fined not more than $1,000 or imprisoned not more than one year.

§ 2000g—3.   Reports to Congress

Subject to the provisions of sections 2000a—4 and 2000g—2(b) of this title, the Director shall, on or before January 31 of each year, submit to the Congress a report of the activities of the Service during the preceding fiscal year.

The Community Relations Service was transferred to the Department of Justice effective April 22, 1966.   The transfer had been recommended by Vice President Humphrey and endorsed by President Johnson.   The transfer was accomplished as part of the executive department Reorganization Plan Number 1 of 1966.   Congress acquiesced in the reorganization, but the reference to the Commerce Department remains in § 2000g–1 since the transfer was accomplished by Executive Order with Congressional approval rather than by amendment of the original statute.

The Community Relations Service has been an active if somewhat low visibility agency of the Justice Department.   Its activities in recent years are reflected in the following excerpts from its annual report for 1976.

[The following is taken from Annual Report 1976, Community Relations Service, Department of Justice.]

* * *

The agency may offer its assistance whenever, in its judgment, racial or ethnic conflict threatens peaceful relations among the citizens of a community.   Assistance can also be requested by State or local officials, or by other interested individuals.

In addition, CRS' services are available to Federal courts as an alternative to resolving disputes through litigation.   For example, district court judges have used the agency's assistance to resolve prison inmate suits under 42 U.S.C. § 1983.

Title II of the 1964 Civil Rights Act provides specific authority and procedure for using CRS' assistance in resolving public accommodation suits, and a small number of referrals continue to be made.   More recently, district court judges have designated the agency to help communities desegregate their school systems peacefully.

CRS carries out its mandate using the techniques of the objective, third-party intervenor.   Essentially, that means defusing tension, opening up a dialog, and providing technical assistance the disputants need to resolve their differences.

The agency separates its peacemaking efforts into two categories: conciliation and mediation. "Conciliation" defines the act of alleviating tension, opening up communications between disputants, and helping to work out an agreement through essentially informal steps.

"Mediation," on the other hand, refers to a formal negotiation process similar to that used in labor disputes. Disputing groups are brought together ultimately around a negotiating table with a CRS mediator acting as facilitator. The objcct is a binding written agreement on the issues involved.

* * *

In 12 years of helping communities overcome racial difficulties, CRS has undergone a number of changes. Possibly the most significant is its emphasis on formal mediation as a means of resolving disputes. During the turbulent 1960's, deeply dissatisfied minorities expressed their frustration in demonstrations often punctuated by disorder and violence. These outbursts were frequently accompanied by sweeping demands labeled as non-negotiable.

But toward the end of the decade, a new trend developed. Outrage was still forcefully expressed, but grievances were spelled out with increasing sophistication. The civil rights controversy was becoming, in effect, a new "ball game."

In the 1970's the trend toward more sophisticated expression of dissent grew stronger. Now, detailed bills of particulars have largely replaced lists of diffuse demands. Minority groups usually trace complaints of discrimination to institutions believed responsible and present representatives of those institutions with detailed proposals to correct the perceived injustices.

During fiscal 1976, CRS gave high priority to initiating formal negotiations between parties caught up in such conflict. Since mediation leads to more indepth exploration of differences—and, consequently, a more lasting resolution—the agency plans to continue expanding its use. CRS now has experienced mediators in all 10 regions, which made possible 50 formal, written agreements this year—compared to 15 in fiscal 1973, the year the effort was begun, and 37 in fiscal 1975.

* * *

If a public poll were taken, most people would probably cite school desegregation as the major racial problem in 1967. It did, of course, cause a great deal of trauma. But, while CRS does not keep comprehensive statistics on racial disputes nationally, most of the school disputes in which the agency interceded had nothing to do with implementing desegregation.

Moreover, the agency responded to more disputes involving minorities and the police—or other elements of the criminal justice system—than all school disputes combined. Specifically, there were 226 cases involving the criminal justice system and 202 school cases, accounting together for more than two-thirds of all disputes worked on.

The remaining cases made up a broad spectrum: job discrimination disputes, biased handling of revenue sharing funds, disputes over social and municipal services, housing discrimination, and others. All the nation's larger minority groups were involved, to some extent, with these problems. However, problems particularly affecting the Spanish-speaking, such as the illegal alien issue, and Native Americans, stemming from their unique status, gave added complexity to the picture.

Overall, CRS actively worked on 630 racial and ethnic "disputes, disagreements, or difficulties": 456 new cases and 174 carryovers from the preceding year. Of the 630 cases in which resolutions were sought—81 more than in fiscal 1975—410 were completed, leaving the outcome still to be determined in 220. Another 530 potential new cases were closed either at the "alert" or "assessment" stages, steps in the process of determining whether CRS will intercede and how.

*   *   *

Minority groups still don't believe justice is blind. This fact is reflected in the continuing high incidence of confrontations between police and minorities, mainly—but not exclusively—blacks, the Spanish-speaking, and American Indians. These groups frequently allege that police routinely harass and use deadly force against them but not against whites.

CRS has moved aggressively toward bringing aggrieved minority groups and the police together to discuss problems causing friction between them. Improved relations and greater racial harmony in communities have often resulted.

During the year, agency troubleshooters conciliated or mediated 200 disputes involving minorities and police—as opposed to other elements of the criminal justice system. In virtually every instance, a mutually distrustful, negative relationship that existed before the flare-up militated against a quick solution.

There is no easy answer to how this situation can be turned around. One obvious step is to build a bridge between police and minorities through community relations programs. Many police departments across the country also are increasing sensitivity training for recruits and veteran officers, but others offer little if any such training.

Still, the quality of relations between police and the public is too important to be left to chance. The significance was graphically stated by a commission the mayor of a southwestern city appointed to look at crime problems, a group which CRS assisted:

> When a police department is believed to be honest, fair, and helpful, its tasks are greatly simplified. The Police Department has a definite, though limited, ability to improve its reputation in the community it serves. Performance is of course basic to both these points, but so are public perceptions and understanding. We should not be satisfied with a police force about which a citizen wrote, " . . . if the officers were better trained and *friendlier*, (emphasis original) they could get more help from citizens. They are at times snappy, rude, and use vulgar language." While we did not find such perceptions widespread, we found them often enough to warrant inclusion here. On the other side of the same coin, a patrolman gave us his view, "The only person who will help a cop is another cop."

Where such attitudes exist, there is obviously potential for problems even if everybody on both sides is white. But a sizable percentage of minorities believe that white police "protect and serve" white neighborhoods and patrol theirs as enemy territory. Consequently, where minorities are involved, the chances of a *disastrous* confrontation are significantly greater.

* * *

Desegregation was a major—but not the sole—cause of school racial tension CRS encountered. As the year began, there was widespread speculation that court-ordered desegregation would trigger major disturbances in "northern" cities—fueled by recent history in Boston and Louisville. However, large-scale disruption proved to be the exception rather than the rule.

Most communities facing desegregation apparently were determined to make it work. School administrators, police, and other officials planned extensively to cope with problems. Civic leaders helped create an attitude of receptivity in communities.

* * *

Since the situation was never exactly the same in any two cities, the precise nature of activities varied case-by-case. But Detroit is essentially typical. U.S. Judge Robert DeMascio requested in April 1975 that CRS "provide assistance to the City of Detroit, to the parties to this litigation, and to the Court in achieving harmonious implementation of a remedial plan to be ordered by the Court and of future long-range plans to eliminate racial segregation to the extent possible."

Even before Judge DeMascio's request, CRS had offered its assistance to Detroit leaders, eliciting a positive response. Given this two-sided mandate and anti-busing sentiment, the agency opened a temporary field office. Staff assigned to it set out immediately to pinpoint potential problems, develop plans to minimize them, and help implement the structure to handle problems that did arise.

Dozens of tasks were completed in the months leading up to the mid-winter implementation of desegregation. For example, Judge DeMascio asked that the school system's student code of conduct and policy on rights and responsibilities be analyzed. The purpose was to determine, based on CRS' experience, whether shortcomings existed that might unnecessarily fuel discontent.

At the police department's request, CRS critiqued its operations plan for a desegregation task force. Agency staff and consultants also conducted a half-day training session for 150 officers assigned to the task force. In addition, police and school officials were brought together for several joint meetings to work out a coordinated response to problems at schools.

Other tasks included: critiquing a community relations program prepared by school officials; providing a citizens' monitoring commission established by the court with information on similar bodies in Denver and elsewhere; helping plan an information and rumor control center; and arranging for an advertising executive who had worked on a media campaign against violence in his own city to meet with Detroit media executives.

Altogether, CRS met with more than 125 local agencies and community groups, including those opposed to desegregation, to discuss ways to minimize disorder. At least one staff member attended more than 300 public meetings to discuss residents' concerns.

As the hour for desegregation neared, seven other conciliators joined the regular two-member Detroit team. On opening day, everything went smoothly. A combination of factors—inclement winter weather, parents' uncertainty about safety, and anti-busing sentiment—led to an absentee rate of about 32 percent. However, it dropped to less than 14 percent on the third day, compared to the 12 percent school officials said was normal.

The consensus among school officials, police, and civic leaders was that the extensive preparation had paid off.

* * *

SECTION 53. GRIEVANCE PROCEDURE AND THE ARBITRATION OF DISPUTES DURING THE TERM OF A COLLECTIVE BARGAINING AGREEMENT

The collective bargaining agreement is a contract which, like all contracts, is a form of law made by the parties to govern aspects of their relationships. In this regard, collective agreements are constitutions which establish the basic framework and terms of the parties' relationship during the life of the agreement.

A collective agreement is not likely to be self-executing. Disputes as to the meaning of the agreement will arise. The employment relationship entails day to day contacts between constituents of the union, *i. e.*, the employees, and representatives of management, *i. e.*, supervisors and foremen. Disputes may arise regarding discipline of employees, behavior of supervisors, and the application of provisions of the agreement. A strike during the contract term is undesirable to both sides, but judicial adjudication of the dispute may be an equally undesirable alternative. A common solution is to include in the collective agreement a "no-strike" clause and a grievance arbitration provision regarding the adjudication of grievances by an arbitrator selected by the parties.

This topic raises issues regarding alternative forms of dispute resolution in social conflict situations, and raises again some of the fundamental questions about the resolution of disputes with which we began our discussion of the nature and functions of law.

GRIEVANCE AND ARBITRATION CLAUSES

AGREEMENT BETWEEN THE TURNER TANNING MACHINERY CO. AND UERMWA–CIO

Dated June 2, 1943.

Article IV.

Grievances: In order to provide an orderly method for handling and disposing of all grievances and disputes, all grievances and disputes shall be taken up in the following manner:

Section (a) Between the aggrieved employee or a representative of the Union or both with the foreman.

Section (b) If a settlement is not reached under Section (a) above within twenty-four hours, between the Grievance Committee of the Union and the superintendent or assistant superintendent. After the operation of this Section grievances shall be briefly stated in writing.

Section (c) If a settlement is not reached under Section (b) above within forty-eight hours, between representatives of the Union and the management of the Company.

The Company agrees that (except in cases in which the Union shall agree that a longer period is desirable) it will announce to the Union its position on each grievance or dispute within one week after the conclusion of discussions under Section (c) hereof.

Article V.

Arbitration: If any grievance or dispute between the Union and the Employer is not adjusted in accordance with Article IV above, the dispute shall go to arbitration in the following manner: The Union and the Employer shall each select an arbitrator, these two to select the third arbitrator. If they fail to agree upon a third arbitrator within forty-eight (48) hours, the third arbitrator from the Conciliation Service of the United States Department of Labor shall be designated by it. The decision of any two arbitrators selected in accordance with this provision shall be final and binding upon both the Union and the Employer.

Note and Questions

No one would suggest that a single form of grievance procedure is equally effective in every establishment. The clause printed above might not be adequate to the needs of labor and management in a large corporation such as U. S. Steel or General Motors. Accordingly, the arbitration clause of a collective bargaining agreement must be tailored to fit the parties. There is no single form of arbitration clause which is better than any other at all times and in all places. Despite this need for variety, however, the questions that have to be considered in drafting such a clause are usually the same and, while they can never be answered abstractly, it is useful to inquire into the considerations which may argue for one form of clause or another. Among the important questions are the following:

1. What are the arguments for and against a clause providing for arbitration of grievances under a collective bargaining agreement? Is their strength the same in the case of a department store as in an automobile assembly plant?

2. How broad should the arbitration clause be? How elaborate an arbitration procedure should be provided for in the arbitration clause, *i. e.*, how much discretion should be left to the arbitrator in structuring the procedure?

3. Should there be a permanent umpire or provision for the appointment of ad hoc arbitrators?

4. Should there be a single arbitrator or tripartite board? If the latter, how are decisions to be reached?

THE ARBITRATOR AT WORK

MATTER OF FORD MOTOR CO. AND UNITED AUTOMOBILE WORKERS

(Opinion A–151, 1944)

SHULMAN, UMPIRE:* The Chairman of the Flat Rock Plant Committee was given a disciplinary lay-off of two weeks. As soon as this became known, a stoppage of work shut the plant down on September 20, 1944. Efforts to persuade the men to return to work proved unavailing. As a final means of effecting a resumption of work, the parties agreed to waive the several steps of the grievance procedure and to bring directly to the Umpire the case of the Plant Chairman and the other employee who was involved in the incident. A hearing at the Umpire's office was scheduled for October 3rd. But on September 30th the plant went down again for a reason related to the Chairman's disciplinary penalty. The plant was still down on October 3rd when the parties appeared for the hearing, and is still down now.

The Company objected to the holding of the hearing while the employees were on strike. It objected, further, to the consideration of the case at all in the expedited manner. It urged that the special agreement to waive the prior steps of the grievance procedure was made for the purpose of restoring production in the plant; that in stopping work on September 30th and continuing the stoppage thereafter, the men destroyed the consideration for the agreement and abandoned the schedule procedure.

These positions must be sustained. The current stoppage, like its predecessor, is, of course, completely unauthorized, in defiance of the Union's regularly constituted leadership, in violation of the Constitution and By-laws of

---

* Mr. Harry Shulman, before his death in 1955, was Dean of the Yale Law School. He was for many years permanent umpire under the agreement between the Ford Motor Company and the United Automobile Workers, CIO.

both the International and the Local, and in disregard of the no-strike pledge. These features should surely condemn the stoppage in the mind of any thinking worker. But the feature bearing more closely upon the Umpire's function is the fact that the stoppage is an outright breach of the parties' Agreement.

When a Union enters a plant, one of its very first concerns is the establishment of a grievance procedure. For the grievance procedure is fundamental in civilized collective bargaining. A Union and its members can choose, if they like, to settle each day-to-day dispute by strike action. They could stop work every time a supervisor or other representative of management did something that they deemed improper. But union men long ago recognized that this method of protest would destroy the Union and their own economy. For this method would necessitate a stoppage nearly every day. Now workers live by production. Strikes are costly to workers as they are to management. In normal times an occasional deliberate test of strength by strikes on matters of major importance may be necessary and desirable. The anticipated victory is then deemed to be worthy of the cost. But wanton and needless use of the strike weapon weakens the weapon itself, casts undue burden on the workers, and threatens to destroy their organization.

The workers who shed their blood and whose families suffered the pain of hunger and privation in order to establish the right of collective bargaining, those workers saw these dangers and rejected this anarchistic method. They asked for a just and civilized reign of order; the collective agreement which states the rights and obligations of the parties for its duration and establishes a regular procedure for their enforcement. They cherished the strike weapon for effective use in crises, when, for example, negotiations for a new contract failed. Even then they sought to preserve the strength of that weapon by permitting its use only after deliberate consideration and decision made by the Union in prescribed ways. Provisions of union constitutions and by-laws state in careful detail how and when authorized strike action is to be taken.

The Ford contract is true to this tradition. It established a grievance procedure which insures final determination in an impartial manner. And it provides that, during its term, the grievance procedure, not strikes or interruptions of production, shall be employed for the adjustment of grievances. This is the rule of order for which generations of working men have struggled. They understood and appreciated it. It should be clearly understood and appreciated now.

It is, of course, entirely obvious that when parties sign a collective agreement, they fully expect that disputes will arise as to its interpretation and application from day to day. That is precisely why the grievance procedure was established. It is the orderly, economic procedure prescribed for those situations in which a violation of agreement is alleged. The obligation to employ this procedure rather than the work stoppage is a solemn contractual obligation which law and honor require to be observed. To employ the stoppage when the grievance procedure is available is to abandon the contract. In no case is the grievance procedure more effective and adequate than in the case of an allegedly improper disciplinary penalty. The aggrieved employee can be fully compensated; and no other employee need suffer any loss. There is no reason for imposing an economic loss on hundreds of employees for the purpose of securing illegally to one of them that which he can get in an orderly, legal manner without loss to any employee.

Questions

What was gained by this ruling? Wouldn't it have been better to act on the controversy and end the strike by disposing of it?

MATTER OF FORD MOTOR CO.

Arbitration Award, 1945. Prentice Hall Lab.Arb.Awards, par. 67,269.

SHULMAN, UMPIRE. The grievances in these two cases protest that promotions were given to two employees with less seniority than the aggrieved and with at least no greater ability.

In the Twin Cities case, J. S. was classified as a Laborer in the Maintenance Department at $1.05 per hour, whose job it was to keep machines supplied with coolant. P. L., a Machine Operator at $1.10 an hour, was promoted to a machine operation paying $1.15. He has either one day or one month less seniority than S.

In the Edgewater case, both employees work on the Chassis Line. P. A. has seniority from 1919 and is a veteran of the first World War. J. M. has seniority from 1936 and is a veteran of the second World War. A vacancy occurred in the classification of Body Hoist Operator. A. wanted the job. The foreman of the department and the committeeman met and the latter urged that A. be given the job as the oldest employee willing to take it and qualified for it. The job, however, was given to M.

Section 53 of the 1942 Agreement (Section 51 of the Supplementary Agreement on Seniority) provides that "promotions to higher paid jobs or better jobs with equal pay are based primarily upon merit and ability, but when these are equal the employee having the greatest seniority will receive preference. Dispute as to merit and ability under this paragraph may be adjusted under the grievance procedure." I have had several occasions in the past to construe and apply the provisions of this Section. (See Opinions A-17, A-83, A-107, A-135 and A-147.) On the whole, the provisions of the Section seem to have been observed satisfactorily. Its dictates are not difficult to observe if supervision and Union representatives consult cooperatively and exercise honest judgment as to relative merit and ability. But here and there troublesome friction seems to exist—largely because of misunderstanding or undue zeal on both sides.

I

On the Union's side there is a tendency to overemphasize seniority and forget merit and ability. That is, of course, wrong.

Seniority controls when merit and ability are substantially equal. Where there is definite superiority, it controls.

There has also been some feeling within the Union that the promotion section is the equivalent of an up-grading program whereby new employees would be hired only in the lowest rated bracket and present employees would be given preference for vacancies in the higher rated brackets. It is, to be sure, wise industrial policy to promote employees to higher paying jobs as far as practicable rather than hire employees directly to them. But clearly Section 53 does not make this requirement. It deals only with the selection of the employee for promotion if and when a promotion is made. (See Opinion A–17.)

The Twin Cities case illustrates another fallacy; the fallacy of unreasonably expanding the group of employees to be considered for the promotion involved. The delimitation of the group to be considered is indeed a problem. Section 53 does not itself make the delimitation. The question can be answered only in the light of the local occupational groupings. If the Company reached into a group of laborers to select one for promotion to one of the higher machine operations, then other laborers or employees in any other classification could properly insist upon consideration for the job.

But it is patently unreasonable to hold that laborers as such can properly complain under Section 53, if, in making a promotion to a machine operation, the Company considered only machine operators and not laborers. And it would be equally unreasonable to hold that in appraising relative merit and ability the Company must go beyond its own records and beyond the employee's performance in its own plant to claimed experience outside. That may be proper in lay-offs, but is not required in promotions.

S. was never a machine operator for the Company. He states that he operated a machine shop in Wisconsin and claims to have broad machine shop experience. Without in any way questioning his claim, it is clear that the Company is not required to make an investigation of its employees' outside experience before determining merit and ability for a promotion. In promoting a machine operator to a higher paying machine operation, without considering the aggrieved who was classified as a laborer and never operated a machine for the Company, Management did not violate Section 53 or act unreasonably otherwise. S's grievance is denied.

II

On the Company's side, there is some tendency to overemphasize supervision's personal judgment of merit and ability and forget seniority. Some members of Management or supervision seem to think that it is sufficient for them to form and assert strongly the belief that one employee is superior to another. That is clearly not enough. They must be able to support this belief with specific, concrete reasons. Section 53 expressly declares that disputes as to merit and ability are subject to the grievance procedure. The several agencies in the grievance procedure, including the Umpire, are thereby given a positive task to perform. The provision is not an empty formalism; and the agencies of the grievance procedure, including the Umpire, are not expected merely to rubber stamp the assertions of one side or the other, or to make decisions merely on the basis of the strength or positiveness of the assertions. To perform their tasks they must be given adequate basis for judgment. A supervisor's testimony that he honestly believes one employee to be superior to another with respect to the promotion is certainly a factor to be considered. It is not, however, either conclusive or sufficient.

The supervisor must be prepared to state the basis for his belief and to support it, not by repeated assertion, but by specific and understandable evidence—evidence which relates to capacity for the job in question, not merely to the employee's general character. I am speaking, of course, only of promotions to jobs within the jurisdiction of the Union. The situation may perhaps be totally different with respect to supervisory, managerial or confidential jobs. They are not here involved and I express no opinion with respect to them.

Another mistake occasionally made on the Company's side in the application of Section 53 is to become unduly obsessed with fear of impairment of efficiency. The safeguarding of efficiency is a proper and highly important concern of Management. No criticism can be levelled against proper attempts in this direction. But the goal of industry is not merely to produce efficiently. Its goal is to produce efficiently with justice to its employees. Or, to put it in other words, efficiency is a product of many forces; and a fair concern for the welfare of the employees tends itself to make a more efficient operation. Section 53 is a provision of this character.

A supervisor may feel that Employee A is more qualified for the job in question than Employee B. He may recognize, however, if he has proper humility, that the question is one of judgment and that he is not altogether infallible. Were he able to put both employees to test in some way which would surely not affect production, he would doubtless readily do so whenever some doubt is raised. But he may hesitate to do so because of a fear that efficiency might be temporarily impaired. That possibility should, of course, be taken into account. But it should not prevent a trial in all circumstances.

The controversy and ill will that may be engendered by the failure to provide a reasonable trial in some cases also affect production and, in the long run, may affect it even more seriously than the trial would. I do not suggest for one moment that a trial should be given in all cases. But surely it should not be denied in all cases. It should not be denied wherever there is a reasonable doubt and where the trial would cause no serious inconvenience. The supervisor should not permit his proper confidence in his own judgment to become a rigid belief in his own infallibility.

The Edgewater case is of this character. A is an old employee who has held a great variety of jobs in the plant. He is strong and rugged. The foreman of the department involved testified that he would gladly give A the hoist operation if he thought A could do it; but he thought that A could not do it. His reasons were vague and difficult to gather but meant apparently that, in his belief, A was not young or supple enough. In reply to a direct question, he testified that by placing A on the job he could tell in less than two hours whether A could handle it. Yet he refused to take this simple expedient and placed on the job an employee with 17 years less seniority.

But there is more to the case which gives it a bad complexion, and tends to support the Union's charge that supervision decided to give the job to M without reference to Section 53. When A's grievance was filed, the foreman in the department, who surely was in a position to give a proper answer, referred it instead to the Rate Department which, in turn, referred it to Labor Relations. The disposition of the Labor Relations officer was that the promotion had been made in accordance with Section 53. The disposition was sustained by the Management representatives on the Appeal Board. The company's brief before me contended only that M had superior merit and ability and was promoted in accordance with Section 53. The foreman of the department testified before me as stated above, that in his judgment M was properly promoted. Then suddenly the General Foreman, who is alleged by the Union to have directed the promotion of M in the first place, blandly announced that neither M nor anyone else had been promoted to the hoist operation job. This information was apparently a surprise to all concerned. And the strange situation has not been explained.

When supervision makes a promotion with honest and reasonable effort to comply with Section 53 and its judgment is subsequently held to be mistaken, the appropriate remedy may be merely to rescind the promotion and require that it be made in the proper manner without retroactive adjustment. (See Memorandum 197.)

But supervision should realize that a promotion not in accordance with Section 53 involves a risk of financial loss to the Company. If the violation of Section 53 is palpable, retroactive adjustment to the employee who should have been promoted is appropriate. And I shall award such retroactive adjustment, should a case like A's of Edgewater come before me in the future.

My award on A's grievance is that he be given the hoist operation now and that he be allowed five working days in which to prove himself on it. The five days are fixed, not as a general standard, but only because of the peculiar circumstances of this particular case.

Questions

1. Dean Shulman is associated with what might be called a "parental" philosophy of labor arbitration, which embraces the views (a) that the arbitrator should not be bound solely by the collective bargaining agreement but may go beyond its terms in order to promote good labor-management relations, (b) that labor arbitration is in some sense an extension of collective bargaining, and (c) that the arbitrator should in some situations seek to mediate a solution to the dispute acceptable to both sides. Are these views implicit in the foregoing opinion?

2. Which, if any, general functions of law are evident in the two Ford Motor cases?

MATTER OF NATHAN MFG. CO.

Arbitration Award, 1947. 7 Lab.Arb.Rep. 3.

SCHEIBER, ARBITRATOR:—The parties have submitted for arbitration grievances arising out of the discharge of J. Grady Blackwell, shop steward, and Sidney Fisher, shop chairman, which submission is pursuant to Article XIII of the contract between the parties dated September 10, 1946.

The matters to be decided by the Arbitrator under the formal submission are as follows:

1.   Whether J. Grady Blackwell . . . [was] discharged for just and sufficient cause;

2.   If such discharges were not for just and sufficient cause, the terms on which they should be reinstated shall be left to the discretion of the arbitrator.

The company's position is that, since under the contract its power to discharge is limited to discharges "for just and sufficient cause only" and since the submission is stated in terms of the contract, the decision to discharge is subject to reversal by the arbitrator only upon finding that "just and sufficient" cause did not exist; if it does exist, he is not empowered under the terms of the contract and of the submission to reverse the determination of the company unless he finds that the action of the company was not in good faith, was arbitrary, capricious, or discriminatory.

The arbitrator is in accord with this contention since any other holding would substitute his opinion for that of management, which is charged in law and by the contract with the efficient management of the plant. It therefore becomes necessary to first determine whether the discharges were "for just and sufficient cause."

The discharge of J. Grady Blackwell is based upon his alleged "interference with workers' assignments, violations of the contract, and subnormal production."

On January 17, 1947, while the workers during their paid cleanup time were engaged in carrying out an order previously given by the foreman to sweep around their machines, Blackwell "instructed" them to drop their brooms. He has testified that, when he gave "instructions", he expected to be obeyed (R. 272).

This was apparently the "precipitating cause" of his discharge or, in the language of the plant manager, "The straw that broke the camel's back."

The following are some of the other claims presented by the company of Blackwell's countermanding orders previously given by the foreman which appear in the record:

1.   January 3, 1946—Blackwell prevented Operator Hill from performing set-ups, contrary to instructions from Foreman Perna. Blackwell was warned by Mr. Boggs that it was a violation of the contract for a steward to countermand a foreman's order without referring the problem to the grievance procedure.

2.   Blackwell, among others again prevented the performance of set-ups by operators in Grades 7 and 8. At the labor-management committee meeting of March 26, 1946, the union admitted the irregularity of this and stated that it would refrain in the future from so doing and would thenceforth act in an advisory capacity only so far as job structure was concerned.

3.   On September 30, 1946, Blackwell again countermanded an order of supervision which this time directed a trades helper to go from one side of the floor to the other to change oil in a machine. Blackwell was again expressly told by Mr. Boggs that the assignment of trades helpers was a matter for the foreman and not his concern.

4.   In October, 1946, Blackwell, despite all prior warnings, instructed the trades helper not to clean a machine on one side of the floor, thus again countermanding Dugan's direct order.   Blackwell was again expressly told that the trades helpers were to obey supervision's orders, that the "agreement" on which he relied was not applicable in the situation presented by the absence of one of the helpers, that the trades helper was to be discharged if he refused to follow Dugan's orders, and that, if Blackwell continued his interference with Dugan's running of the department, he too was to be discharged.

5.   Blackwell stated that, unless the company complied with his ideas as to the performance of a time study, he "would be forced to stop the time study" and demanded of Mr. Asherman "Do you want me to pull piecework out of this department altogether?"

While the top union officials, during the course of the arbitration, and the union's research director sought to give every possible favorable intendment to Blackwell's actions, it was admitted under cross-examination that they could cite no case where a shop steward is authorized to issue orders, and two of the union's top officials concurred that the issuance of orders by a shop steward countermanding those of the foreman were beyond the powers of a shop steward.

Despite this, however, Blackwell reiterated his belief at several points in the testimony that it was his duty as union representative not to permit the employees to perform such work as he believed they were not required to do until after it had been discussed at a labor-management meeting and, further, that he would repeat his action if such situations arose again.

Blackwell's failure to abide by the established grievance machinery as manifested in the various instances where he countermanded orders given by a foreman may have created some doubt or confusion in the plant as to the necessity and importance of the established grievance procedure.

At the sacrifice of brevity but in the hope that the following statements and decisions may clarify this phase of the labor-management relationship and, by bringing a clearer understanding, help the parties in their future relations, attention is directed to the following decisions in point.

While the arbitrator agrees with the union's able research director that as yet there is no settled "labor common law," that such law is in process of evolvement, and that these decisions therefore are not binding on the arbitrator, he feels nevertheless, that the decisions are entitled to some consideration since they do represent the best thought of skilled practitioners in the field of arbitration.

The grievance procedure now a part of labor-management contracts represents an important advance in the industrial field and should therefore be zealously adhered to and carefully guarded.   It is intended for the protection of labor and, when adhered to, advances peaceful and constructive industrial relations with resultant benefits to labor, management, and the public.

When any union leader or worker loses sight of the great gain which a sound grievance procedure affords to labor in the protection of its rights and disregards its provisions, a serious disservice is being done to labor.

This has been recognized by one of this union's leaders, Robert Schrank, in his own book Leadership Training for Stewards, Shop Committeemen and Lodge Officers, where seven pages are devoted to the importance of making grievance machinery work.

Similarly, in an equally interesting volume entitled, The Shop Steward on the Job, published by the United Electrical, Radio and Machine Workers, some 15 pages are devoted by the union to the importance of applying and adhering to the grievance procedure. In Matter of Ampco Metal, Inc., 3 LA 374 (1945), Arbitrator Updegraff sustained the company action in disciplining a union president for leaving his job in violation of a company rule, although that rule violated the contract. The arbitrator declared that the grievance procedure of the contract protected the union and should have been utilized. . . .

Since a union official must not himself flout a company rule or work assignment, it is clear that he must not countermand a foreman's order relating to work assignment. Where the official refuses to follow instructions personally, only one person fails to perform the appointed task; where the union official countermands an order, the result is the failure of an entire group to carry out instructions. This unwarranted interference with plant production and plant efficiency is a case for discharge, especially where, as here, the contract contains a "no cessation of work" clause.

This reasoning finds ample support in the decision of Prof. Harry Shulman, impartial umpire under the Ford-UAW contract in Matter of Ford Motor Company, 3 LA 779 (1944). There, a union committeeman had instructed operators not to comply with an emergency assignment, relying on the union interpretation, of a disputed policy. Prof. Shulman squarely held that it was immaterial whether the foreman's action was in conformity with prior policy. We quote at length from his opinion upholding the company action disciplining the committeeman because it presents an enlightened exposition of effective labor-management relations.

"The undisputed testimony as to the policy of the building and the disputed testimony as to what X's instructions actually were are both premised on the assumption that a committeeman may countermand supervision's orders and instruct employees not to do what supervision requires. That assumption is wrong. And it should be clearly understood that it is wrong.

"No committeeman or other union officer is entitled to instruct employees to disobey supervision's orders no matter how strongly he may believe that the orders are in violation of the agreement. If he believes that an improper order has been issued, his course is to take the matter up with supervision and seek to effect an adjustment. Failing to effect an adjustment, he may file a grievance. But he may not tell the employee to disregard the order.

"The employee himself must also normally obey the order even though he thinks it improper. His remedy is prescribed in the grievance procedure. He may not take it on himself to disobey. To be sure, one can conceive of improper orders which need not be obeyed. An employee is not expected to obey an order to do that which would be criminal or otherwise unlawful. He may refuse to obey an improper order which involves an unusual health hazard or other serious sacrifice. But, in the absence of such justifying factors, he may not refuse to obey merely because the order violates some right of his under the contract. The remedy under the contract for violation of right lies in the grievance procedure and only in the grievance procedure. To refuse obedience because of a claimed contract violation would be to substitute individual action for collective bargaining and to replace the grievance procedure with extra-contractual methods. And such must be the advice of the committeeman if he gives advice to employees. His advice must be that the safe and proper method is to obey supervision's instructions and to seek correction and redress through the grievance procedure. . . .

". . . more important, the grievance procedure is prescribed in the contract precisely because the parties anticipated that there would be claims of violations which would require adjustment. That procedure is prescribed for all grievances and not merely for doubtful ones. Nothing in the contract even suggests the idea that only doubtful violations need be processed through the grievance procedure and that clear violations can be resisted through individual self-help. The only difference between a 'clear' violation and a 'doubtful' one is that the former makes a clear grievance and the latter a doubtful one. But both must be handled in the regular prescribed manner. . . .

"But an industrial plant is not a debating society. Its object is production. When a controversy arises, production cannot wait for exhaustion of the grievance procedure. While that procedure is being pursued, production must go on. And some one must have the authority to direct the manner in which it is to go on until the controversy is settled. That authority is vested in supervision. It must be vested there because the responsibility for production is also vested there; and responsibility must be accompanied by authority. It is fairly vested there because the grievance procedure is capable of adequately recompensing employees for abuse of authority by supervision.

"It should be definitely understood, then, that a committeeman has no authority to direct or advise an employee to disobey supervision's instructions; that his authority is expressed in the duty to take the matter up with supervision and seek an adjustment through negotiations and the grievance procedure; that an employee must obey supervision's instructions pending the negotiations or the processing of his grievance except only in the rare case where obedience would involve an unusual health hazard or similar sacrifice; and that disobedience by the employee, or counsel of disobedience by a committeeman, is proper cause for disciplinary penalty."

The record also indicates that Blackwell has persisted in operating the grievance procedure under his own interpretation of the contract. The company has pointed out numerous occasions where Blackwell has countermanded foreman's instructions to operators on the floor. Although warned repeatedly by the company that such action was a violation of the contract, would not be tolerated, and would lead to his discharge and although informed by the union that he had no power to countermand foreman's orders, Blackwell apparently operated on the theory that the contract gave him that power, and further that he would repeat his action if such situation arose again.

On January 17, 1947, the arbitrator finds that Blackwell countermanded the order of a foreman and prevented the operators in the department from performing the duties enjoined upon them by supervision.

The arbitrator finds that there existed nothing in the past relations between the parties which prevented the foreman from giving such order. However, in the arbitrator's opinion, it is immaterial whether or not the foreman had such power. There exists a detailed grievance procedure in the contract, one which has been operative for a number of years and one which is apparently effective. If supervision exceeded its rights, Blackwell should have allowed the operation to continue but file a grievance. The arbitrator holds that a shop steward is not empowered under this contract to countermand an order of supervision unless such order involves an unusual health hazard or a criminal act. To allow such shop steward to determine for himself when a foreman's order is unauthorized and to permit him on the basis of his own opinion to prevent the functioning of the plant would lead to chaos in the plant and would be harmful to the interests of both the company and the union. . . .

[The arbitrator then found that by reason of Blackwell's repeated violation of the contract, his repeated interference with plant efficiency and his demonstrated inefficiency in performing his regular work, his discharge was for "just and sufficient cause."]

Query: In what sense, if at all, did the arbitrator make use of "precedent" in coming to his decision? Should an arbitrator make use of "precedent" and, if so, how?

———

[The following is reprinted from COX, BOK and GORMAN, CASES ON LABOR LAW, 8th ed., pp. 637–639 (1977).]

FRY'S FOOD STORES, 44 Lab.Arb. 431, 444 (1965):

" * * * *Precedent Value of Prior Awards:* * * * It is recognized widely that prior awards have great value, "Though published awards are not binding on another arbitrator, * * * the thinking of experienced men is often helpful to him" (S. H. Kress and Co., 25 LA 77, 79.) Of great practical significance is the attitude of arbitrators themselves. An extensive survey of labor arbitration disclosed that 77% of the 238 responding arbitrators believe that precedence, even under *other* contracts, should be given "some weight" (Warren and Bernstein, "A Profile of Labor Arbitration", 16 LA 970, 982). The question is not so much whether prior awards are of some precedential value but rather what quantum of force is to be given them.

"Many Arbitrators have held that an award interpreting a collective agreement usually becomes a binding part of the agreement and will be applied by arbitrators thereafter. A view which does not go as far as that first view is one which would give such awards "serious and weighty consideration though not binding" (Arbitrator Rider in 22 LA 605, 606). That view has been emphasized by Arbitrator McCoy, who has said that where "prior decisions involve the interpretation of the identical contract provision, between the same Company and Union, every principle of common sense, policy, and labor relations demands that it stand until the parties annul it by a newly worded contract provision" (Pan American Refining Corp., 2 ALAA par. 67,937, 69,464). Arbitrator

Russell A. Smith has urged that a proper regard for the arbitration process and for stability in collective bargaining relations requires acceptance by an arbitrator, even though he is not technically bound, of any interpretation of the parties' contractual relations rendered by a previous arbitrator, if in point and if based on the same agreement (O & S Bearing Co., 12 LA 132, 135). We see too that if an agreement is renegotiated without materially changing a provision that has been interpreted by an arbitration, the parties may be held to have adopted the award as part of the contract. Indeed, the binding force of an award may even be strengthened by such renegotiation without change. Arbitrator Clark Kerr would place the burden of proof upon the party alleging obvious and substantial errors of fact or law and the lack of fair and full hearing as a justification for refusal to apply the prior award (Waterfront Employers Assn. of Pacific Coast, 7 LA 757, 758).

> "It is therefore correct to say that while prior awards have authoritative force in some situations, and while the great mass of awards are considered to have persuasive force only, it is not correct to say that a prior award, particularly on the same issue involving the same company and the same union, may be dismissed without giving it significant, perhaps strategic, value. * * *"

MERRILL, A LABOR ARBITRATOR VIEWS HIS WORK, 10 Vand.L.Rev. 789, 797–98 (1957):

> "As to decisions of other arbitrators under the same contract between the same parties, I believe that I expressed the correct principle when I wrote, in an unreported decision which I find in my files:
>
>> Unless clearly wrong, and it cannot be said that Arbitrator C was clearly wrong, such a decision should be binding as to the interpretation of the same clause in respect to like situations.
>
> Obviously, contractual provisions should be applied with equality, or justice is denied. Also, if this rule is adhered to generally, it discourages the reprehensible practice of shopping around for the most favorable arbitral opinion. The same principle I have applied to similarly phrased contracts, negotiated by the same union with component corporations of an integrated organization.

> "As to arbitral decisions rendered under other contracts between parties not related to those in the case at hand, usefulness depends upon similarity of the terms and of the situations to which they are to be applied. They must be weighed and appraised, not only in respect to these characteristics, but also with regard to the soundness of the principles upon which they proceed. Certainly, an arbitrator may be aided in formulating his own conclusions by knowledge of how other men have solved similar problems. He ought not to arrogate as his own special virtues the wisdom and justice essential to sound decision. In at least two instances in recent months I have found by investigation that a strong current of arbitral decision had overborne my first impression of the implications of particular language. To yield to this

"common sense of most," especially as, on examination, the reasoning on which it was based carried plausibility, was neither to evade my responsibility nor to sacrifice my intellectual integrity. Contrariwise, it reduced discriminatory application of similar provisions. It enabled me to make use of the wisdom of others at work in the same field. It increased the reliance which draftsmen of future contracts might feel as to the application which would be made of the words which they had chosen. It informed these same draftsmen of words to be avoided if they desired a different result. And it could lessen the need for future arbitrations by adding to the consensus in favor of the particular interpretation of commonly used forms.

"This resort to precedent in aid of interpretation and application does not deserve the scornful appellation of "playing follow-the-leader." One is not to accept a single prior decision elsewhere as binding precedent. Indeed, no number of decisions has such an effect. The resort to the opinions rendered under other contracts is simply for the purpose of making available, for what they are worth, the judgment of informed and able adjudicators and the developing usage of the community. In each instance the arbitrator is to apply his own acumen in valuing the decisions of the past. Certainly, he must use them with due regard to the facts of the case before him, which well may call for a disposition different from that in other instances. Particularly he will need to take into account any light that the negotiations preceding the contract or the practices of the parties may shed on the problem of interpretation. Such factors often dictate a result varying from determinations elsewhere."

SECTION 54. THE FUNCTIONS OF THE LABOR ARBITRATOR

[The following is taken from HARRY SHULMAN, "REASON, CONTRACT, AND LAW IN LABOR RELATIONS," 68 Harvard Law Review 1002, 1002–1024 (1955). Some footnotes omitted; others are renumbered.]

Collective bargaining is today, as Brandeis pointed out, the means of establishing industrial democracy as the essential condition of political democracy, the means of providing for the workers' lives in industry the sense of worth, of freedom, and of participation that democratic government promises them as citizens.[1] The modern industrial worker is not engaged to produce a specific result and left to himself for the performance. He is hired to work under continuous and detailed direction and supervision, in close association with hundreds or thousands of fellow workers, each of whom performs a very minute portion of the work that ultimately results in a finished product. The enterprise requires the continuous co-ordination of

---

1. See Hearings Before the U. S. Commission on Industrial Relations, S.Doc. No. 415, 64th Cong., 1st Sess. 991–1011, 7657–81 (1914–15), reprinted in part in Brandeis, The Course of Bigness 70–95 (Fraenkel ed. 1934).

the work of this multitude of employees; and this poses numerous daily problems whether or not the employees are organized. So elementary a matter as leaving the job for a few minutes "to service the body," as they say in the shop, poses a serious problem which must be carefully analyzed and provided for, otherwise one might find the work of a hundred men held up every time one of them had to leave. Every day a number of employees may be absent or report late. Daily or almost daily some employees have to be laid off for a short period or indefinitely; some employees must be hired; changes must be made in job assignments, either by way of promotion or demotion or otherwise. And daily there are thousands of occasions for friction between employee and supervisor which may erupt in disciplinary action against the employee or a stoppage of work.

These and a host of similar problems are inherent in the necessity of co-ordinating the work of thousands of persons into an efficient operation. Even where there is no union, the employer needs statements of policy to guide the hundreds of persons through whom he must act, though he may be ready to invest them with large powers of discretion. Addition of the union alters the situation in at least two ways: First, the employees, through the union, must participate in the determinations. Second, the acceptance of unions and collective bargaining has increased the employee's confidence and his sense of dignity and importance; where previously there may have been submission, albeit resentful, there is now self-assertion.

One might conceive of the parties engaging in bargaining and joint determination, without an agreement, by considering each case as it arises and disposing of it by *ad hoc* decision. But this is, of course, a wholly impractical method, particularly for a large enterprise. So the parties seek to negotiate an agreement to provide the standards to govern their future action.

In this endeavor they face problems not unlike those encountered wherever attempt is made to legislate for the future in highly complex affairs. The parties seek to foresee the multitude of variant situations that might arise, the possible types of action that might then be available, the practicalities of each and their anticipated advantages or disadvantages. Choice between the suggested possibilities is rendered more difficult by the very process of bargaining and the expected subsequent administration of the bargain. The negotiations are necessarily conducted by representatives removed in variant degrees from direct confrontation with the anticipated situations. They act on the basis partly of their own experience and partly of the more or less incomplete or clashing advice of constituents—the resolutions of councils, subcouncils, unit and departmental meetings in the case of the union, and the suggestions from individuals at the various levels of management in the case of the employer. While each area of problems— vacations, overtime, promotions, layoffs, and the like—must be separately and carefully considered, each is nevertheless but a small part of the total negotiation. The pressure for trade or compromise is ever present.

No matter how much time is allowed for the negotiation, there is never time enough to think every issue through in all its possible applications, and never ingenuity enough to anticipate all that does later show up. Since the parties earnestly strive to complete an agreement, there is almost irresistible pressure to find a verbal formula which is acceptable, even though its meaning to the two sides may in fact differ. The urge to make sure of real consensus or to clarify a felt ambiguity in the language tentatively accepted is at times repressed, lest the effort result in disagreement or in subsequent enforced consent to a clearer provision which is, however, less favorable to the party with the urge. With agreement reached as to known recurring situations, questions as to application to more difficult cases may be tiredly brushed aside on the theory that those cases will never—or hardly ever—arise.

Then there is never, of course, enough time to do an impeccable job of draftsmanship after substantive agreement is reached—apart from the hazard that such an effort might uncover troublesome disagreement. Though the subject matter is complex and the provisions intricate, the language must nevertheless be directed to laymen whose occupation is not interpretation— the workers in the plant, the foremen, the clerks in the payroll office. For it is they whose actions must be guided by the agreement; and indeed, in the case of the union, the membership is asked to ratify or reject what is prior to its action only a proposed agreement. While the interpretations or explanations made at the membership meetings can hardly bind the employer, it is nevertheless important that the agreement be not such as to become a promise to the ear but a disappointment to the hope of the membership.

To be sure, the parties are seeking to bind one another and to define "rights" and "obligations" for the future. But it is also true that, with respect to nonwage matters particularly, the parties are dealing with hypothetical situations that may or may not arise. Both sides are interested in the welfare of the enterprise. Neither would unashamedly seek contractual commitments that would destroy the other. Each has conflicts of interests in its own ranks. Both might be content to leave the future to discretion, if they had full confidence in that discretion and in its full acceptance when exercised. And even when the negotiating representatives have full confidence in each other as individuals, they recognize that it will be many others, not they, who will play major roles in the administration of the agreement. So they seek to provide a rule of law which will eliminate or reduce the areas of discretion. The agreement then becomes a compilation of diverse provisions: some provide objective criteria almost automatically applicable; some provide more or less specific standards which require reason and judgment in their application; and some do little more than leave problems to future consideration with an expression of hope and good faith.

Consider, for example, the role of seniority. Specifically, the parties seek to provide for the selection of employees for promotion, or for layoff should it become necessary to reduce force; and seniority is urged as the touchstone for the selection. Seniority here means not chronological age, or length of service in the particular industry or in industry generally. It means rather length of service for the particular employee in the particular seniority unit of that employer. When the union insists that seniority shall govern promotions to better jobs, it is not because the union does not admit the desirability of recognizing superior ability and encouraging ambition and greater effort; nor is it because the union is unaware that the progress of some of its worthy members will be retarded by a strict seniority rule. Again, when the union demands that layoffs shall be made by strict order of seniority, it is not because of unawareness of the other factors that might appeal, for example, to the social worker. The union is well aware that layoff by seniority may in some instances cause greater hardship than would be the case if other factors were considered. It knows that in a particular case, the senior employee in the given seniority unit may be a relatively young man with no dependents and with considerable mobility that would enable him to find some work elsewhere; while the junior employee may be a relatively old man with a lot of service in the industry, many dependents, and little chance of finding work elsewhere. To be sure, there is the general opinion that long service deserves of itself some reward and preference. But the seniority rules of which I speak apply at all periods of service—to the men with one or two years of service or less, as well as to those with ten, fifteen, or more. And a difference of a day or a week is made determinative in the selection. Moreover, seniority is commonly not a factor in determining the employee's pay for his work. He receives the rate for the job whether he has been on it a year or ten years.

I suggest that the insistence on seniority, like the insistence on single rates of pay for specific jobs, is based in large part on the desire or need for an objective rule which eliminates judgment and discretion in particular cases. And that is not merely because the union is unwilling to lodge discretion in the employer. I daresay that if the employer were willing to grant to the union complete control over promotions and layoffs, the union would adopt the seniority standards in order to curb its own discretion. For the exercise of discretion in these cases is a very difficult task and its fairness or soundness is always subject to attack—more or less violent. When it is recognized that the purpose is not merely that of rewarding seniority, but is also to provide a fair, objective measure which would curtail arbitrary power or discretion, the range of possible adjustments is significantly altered.

Now contrast the different matter of discipline. Here, too, the parties recognize that occasion for disciplinary action will arise and that disciplinary action is something of a necessity. But whereas a reduction of force requires a selection among employees which necessarily means preference of some employees over others, disciplinary action poses no problem of preference. The union can generally seek to protect each employee threatened with disciplinary action without subordinating an interest of other employees. Here that protection requires the exercise of fair and humane judgment and discretion which takes into account all mitigating factors that can be mustered for the particular employee. The problem, at least for the union, is not that of eliminating the pains of discretion, but rather that of confining the employer's power and providing maximum opportunity for the union to challenge the soundness of his exercise of discretion, while for the employer the problem is that of reducing this vulnerability of the disciplinary action taken by him. So most collective agreements do not go much beyond recognizing the employer's power to discipline or discharge and providing that the action shall be for cause, or good cause, and shall be subject to challenge by the employee and the union, subject to a few limitations or exceptions.

The parties recognize, when they make their collective agreement, that they may not have anticipated everything and that, in any event, there will be many differences of opinion as to the proper application of its standards. Accordingly the agreement establishes a grievance procedure or machinery for the adjustment of complaints or disputes during its term. The autonomous rule of law thus established contemplates that the disputes will be adjusted by the application of reason guided by the light of the contract, rather than by force or power.

While the details of the grievance procedure differ from one enterprise to another, its essence is a hierarchy of joint conferences between designated representatives of the employer and the union. But joint conferences even at the highest levels of authority may not, and frequently do not, result in agreement. In the absence of provision for resolution of stalemate, the parties are left to their own devices. Since grievances are almost always complaints against action taken or refused by the employer, a stalemate means that the employer's view prevails. Of course, in the absence of some restraint by contract or otherwise, the union is free to strike in order to reverse the employer's choice. But the union can hardly afford an all out strike every time it feels that a grievance has been unjustly denied. The consequence is either that unadjusted grievances are accumulated until there is an explosion, or that groups of workers, less than the entirety, resort to job action, small stoppages, slowdowns, or careless workmanship to force adjustment of their grievances.

The method employed by almost all industry today for the resolution of stalemates in the adjustment of grievances under the private rule of law established by the collective agreement is private arbitration by a neutral person. The largest enterprises provide for a standing umpire or arbitrator to serve for a stated period of time or so long as he continues to be satisfactory to both sides. The great majority of agreements provide for separate appointment of an arbitrator in each case. And the appointments in any case are made by the parties or by a method agreed upon by them. The wide acceptance of arbitration as a terminal step in the grievance procedure—as contrasted with its relatively limited use in the making of the contract in the first place—is explained generally on the grounds, first, that grievances involve interests of lesser importance than those in contract negotiation and, second, that the discretion of the arbitrator is confined by the agreement under which the grievances arise. Both statements require qualification. As umpire under one collective agreement, I have arbitrated cases ranging all the way from the claim of a single employee for fifteen minutes' pay to that of more than sixty thousand employees for a paid lunch period the direct cost of which was between seven and eight million dollars a year. And the restraining bonds of the collective agreement are found on occasion to be elastic indeed.

The parties do not generally restrict their own joint powers in the grievance procedure. But it is customary for the collective agreements to limit the arbitrator's jurisdiction with apparent strictness. Apart from the specific exclusion of certain subjects, as, for example, rates for new jobs or production standards, he is commonly confined to the resolution of grievances or disputes as to "the interpretation or application of the agreement," or of claims of "violation of the agreement." And quite frequently he is further enjoined not to "add to, subtract from, or modify any of the terms of the agreement." In the agreement with which I am most familiar he is admonished also that he has "no power to substitute his discretion for the Company's discretion in cases where the Company is given discretion" by the agreement, and no power "to provide agreement for the parties in those cases where they have in their contract agreed that further negotiations shall or may provide for certain contingencies." [2]

Doubtless these are wise, perhaps even necessary, safeguards—at least before the parties develop sufficient confidence in their private rule of law to enable them to relax the restriction. And an arbitrator worthy of appointment in the first place must conscientiously respect the limits imposed on his jurisdiction, for otherwise he would not only betray his trust, but also undermine his own future usefulness and endanger the very system of self-government in which he works. But these are hardly provisions which would be inserted in the agreement to control the courts in an action on the contract. The judge, too, must decide only "according to law." Unlike the case of the arbitrator, however, the judge's authority and the law which he must interpret and apply do not derive entirely from the agreement of the litigants before him.

Let me consider some of the difficulties and limitations of the arbitrator's function. Suppose the collective agreement is completely silent on a matter in dispute. Suppose, for example, that the agreement is silent on the question whether acceptance of overtime work is mandatory or optional with the employee. This very issue was reported as the cause of the recent extensive and vexing strikes on the English docks.[3] It is an issue which a number of arbitrators have had to decide under collective agreements. Now it is easy enough to say that the matter is not covered by the agreement. But what follows? May the employer, therefore, require the employees to accept the overtime assignments on pain of disciplinary penalties, such as layoff or discharge, or may the employees properly refuse the assignments? Answer would be aided, of course, if there were a common presupposition as to the effect of the collective agreement. In constitutional law terms, but without pushing the metaphor far, is it a grant of limited powers or is it a set of restrictions on otherwise unlimited powers? If it is the former and the employer is not given the power to command overtime work, then his attempt to discipline employees for failure to accept would be a violation of the contract; if it is the latter, then, since by hypothesis the agreement contains no relevant restriction, the employer would have the "reserved power" to enforce the command.

Partly for the purpose of meeting this difficulty many agreements now include what is generally called a "management prerogative" clause, sometimes more accurately and tactfully called a "management responsibility" or "management functions" clause. This normally lists certain matters as "the sole right" of management or for "sole determination" by management, subject, however, to such restriction as may be provided in the agreement. The inclusion of the management provision in some agreements may raise a question as to the significance of its exclusion in others; and it focuses attention on the precise language of the provision with possible reference to the maxim *inclusio unius est exclusio alterius*. Apart from its specification of items as to which there is normally no question, such as the products to be manufactured, the provision is normally couched in broad phrases like "the right to manage the business" or to "direct the working forces." One

2. Agreement Between Ford Motor Co. and United Automobile Workers, CIO, art. III, § 21 (1949, 1950).

3. See N.Y. Times, Oct. 17, 1954, p. 22, col. 1.

may wonder about the chance of the adoption of an agreement, in some enterprises at least, if it states in unmistakable language that the employer shall have the right to do anything at all with respect to the work of the employees except as he is expressly limited by the agreement.

Courts, if confronted with this problem, would doubtless declare a general principle, whether or not it squared with the conception of the parties in the particular case. But the power of the arbitrator to do so is at least questionable. The obvious alternative is for the arbitrator to refrain from affirmative decision and to remand the dispute to the parties on the ground that it is outside of his jurisdiction. But would not that be in effect a decision supporting the employer's freedom of action? If the validity of the employer's order requiring the overtime work is beyond the arbitrator's jurisdiction, he would seem to have no power to restrain the disciplinary action taken by the employer to enforce the order. On the other hand, if he does restrain the disciplinary action, is he not in effect denying validity to the employer's order? Again, the denial of jurisdiction presumably leaves the dispute for resolution by the parties. But whether the union may properly resort to economic pressure in the effort at resolution may depend upon the construction of the "no strike" provision of the agreement. The obligation not to strike may or may not be coextensive with the arbitrator's jurisdiction.

The question of fundamental presuppositions arises in another way. The parties rarely start with an enterprise from scratch; generally they negotiate an agreement for a going enterprise which has been in operation for some time and which has developed practices or precedents of varying degrees of consistency and force. What is the significance of the claimed "prior practice"?

For example, in the overtime case we have been considering, suppose that evidence is tendered that the employer never sought to compel acceptance of overtime assignments, or that the employees never refused such assignments without good excuse. Or suppose that, though the agreement is silent on the matters, the employer had been giving the employees a rest period of ten minutes in each half of the shift, or a lunch period on the employer's time, or a five minute wash-up period before lunch or at the end of the shift, or a money bonus at Christmas. Or, to vary the nature of the example, suppose the claim is that it had been customary for the employer to assign a rigger to assist pipefitters when they were required to lift pipe of four inches or more in diameter, or to assign an employee to hold the pieces which a welder had to weld. Now suppose that, during the term of the agreement, the employer changes these claimed practices over the union's strenuous objections, which are then carried through the grievance procedure to the umpire. In these cases it is the union which relies on the prior practice. But frequently the position is reversed. For example, an employer directs a punch press operator to paint his press when he has no punching to do; or he asks a crib attendant to paint the walls of his crib. In either case, the employee refuses on the ground that painting is not work in his classification, but rather in that of a painter. And the employer points to a claimed prior practice in accord with his direction.

Again the fundamental question may be asked: Is the agreement an exclusive statement of rights and privileges or does it subsume continuation of existing conditions? And again it may be ventured that courts, if confronted with the question, would probably give a general answer for all cases. For the arbitrator, particularly if his jurisdiction is limited to "interpretation" with a prohibition against "adding to, subtracting from or modifying" the terms of the agreement, a general answer is not so clear.

Some have urged that established practices, at least if they were in existence at the time of the negotiation of the agreement and were not considered in any way during the negotiations, are binding upon the parties and must be continued for the duration of the agreement. This, it is said, is implied in the agreement itself—or in the "logic" of the agreement or in the collective bargaining relationship. Lawyers are familiar with "implied" terms. We used to differentiate between implications "in fact" and implications "in law." Now scholars say the differentiation is not quite valid and the implication in any event is based on morality, common understanding, social policy, and legal duty expressed in tort or quasi-contract. The common understanding of the litigants in the particular action is only one factor in the implication—and not the most important. But the judges' authority for imposing the implication is not the party's will; it is the superior authority of the law, which transcends the party's will.

The arbitrator of whom we are talking does not have such superior authority to impose implied conditions. The implications which he may find are only those which may reasonably be inferred from some term of the agreement. Is there an implication "in fact" in the collective agreement that existing practices must be continued until changed by mutual consent? It may be said parenthetically that the legal duty to bargain is not quite relevant because, apart from the question whether the arbitrator may enforce that duty, the issue is whether the practice may be changed without mutual consent when bargaining has failed to achieve consent.

It is more than doubtful that there is any general understanding among employers and unions as to the viability of existing practices during the term of a collective agreement. There may be some agreements which are negotiated upon a real or tacit assumption of continuance of existing practices except as modified by the agreement. There are certainly some agreements which specifically provide for the continuance of existing practices with variant limitations. But I venture to guess that in many enterprises the execution of a collective agreement would be blocked if it were insisted that it contain a broad provision that "all existing practices, except as modified by this agreement, shall be continued for the life thereof unless changed by mutual consent." And I suppose that execution would also be blocked if the converse provision were demanded, namely, that "the employer shall be free to change any existing practice except as he is restricted by the terms of this agreement." The reasons for the block would be, of course, the great uncertainty as to the nature and extent of the commitment, and the relentless search for cost-saving changes. The larger the enterprise, the more varied its operations, the more dependent it is on technological change, and the keener the competition the greater this uncertainty and search. The agreement between Bethlehem Steel and the United Steelworkers steers a middle course. It provides that if management changes any local practice or custom, an affected employee may file a grievance and in "the disposition of the grievance the burden shall be on Management to justify its action." [4] The agreement does not state, however, what is to constitute justification. That little question is left to future judgment.

Assuming the prior practice to be at least relevant, we may find ourselves in further trouble. I have spoken of the practice as an ascertained or readily ascertainable matter. But commonly it is only a question. Commonly there is widely conflicting evidence as to what was in fact done in the past. Ascertaining the facts with respect to an alleged practice is a difficult task not suggested by the assurance implicit in the word "practice." Nor is it a task which can fortunately be cast on the broad shoulders of a jury. But even after the facts are ascertained, what is their significance? When do they add up to a practice? And what practice?

Suppose that in the pipefitters' case, the employer says: "Sure we've used a rigger in the instances cited. But we did that because we had a rigger available with free time and used him to expedite the work. We still do that. But we never had any notion that we would supply a rigger in other circumstances or that the pipefitters can't be required to work without him." Or take the Christmas bonus. The employer says: "Of course we've paid the bonus. We did it in our discretion when we thought we could afford it and accomplish some good for our business. This year we are convinced that we cannot afford the bonus and, in any event, that it will do us no good." Or consider the union's reply to the company's claim that crib attendants always painted their cribs: "Sure they have. But that was their individual choice—not a collective determination. The union is not out to stir up trouble. So long as nobody objected, we did not look into the question. But when a crib attendant did object, we then took our position. And we say that the attendant has the choice of accepting or rejecting the assignment." Such are the limitations commonly claimed for alleged practices, and their reality cannot be gainsaid merely because they were not recorded at the time or communicated to the other side. One cannot accompany his every act in the course of a busy day with explanations which would avoid prejudice for the future.

I have been discussing situations where the agreement is silent on important phases of the parties' dispute. But frequently the silence so assumed is a conclusion as to the very question in dispute. Generally one or the other of the parties urges strongly that while the agreement may not speak to the issue directly, it speaks to it indirectly but clearly.

A fairly common recurring dispute relates to the employment of independent outside contractors to do work which has been or can be done by the employer's own employees. For example, an employer may decide to engage an independent outside painting contractor to paint the plant, though he has painters in his own work force. Or he may decide to employ an outside contractor to make an electrical installation in the plant though he has his own electricians available for the work. The fact that some

----

4. Agreement Between Bethlehem Steel Co. and United Steelworkers, CIO, art. II, § 3 (1952).

of his own employees may be on layoff while the outside contractor is working aggravates the situation, but is not necessarily controlling on the issue of interpretation involved. The employer's defense of his action in these cases normally runs along these lines: He contends that the determination whether to have particular work done by his own employees or by an outside contractor is part of his reserved "prerogative" which is either unrestrained by the agreement or recognized in the agreement by a provision of the kind mentioned above, leaving to him the "management of the business," the choice of "products to be manufactured," "the schedules of production," the "direction of the working forces," and the like. And he may add, with or without full disclosure of the supporting evidence, that he chose to engage an independent contractor for reasons of economy and business expediency.

The union's reliance is on the agreement. It points to the section, normally called recognition, which usually states that the employer recognizes the union as the collective bargaining agent for his employees in stated categories of work, such as production, or maintenance, or shop clerical and the like. This means, it argues, that work of the stated categories must be done by employees represented by the union. Its representation, it maintains, is not of any specified individuals as of any one time, but of the categories of work in the plant. Unless this meaning is accepted, the argument runs, the employer could drastically reduce or destroy the bargaining unit for which the union was designated.

Of course, if this meaning is accepted, the considerations of economy and business expediency upon which the employer relies become irrelevant. But another possibility is suggested. The recognition clause, it is said, merely establishes the bargaining unit. But good faith, which must be an obligation in all agreements, requires that the employer refrain from deliberately impairing that unit without sufficient justification. In this view the recognition clause is violated only if the letting of the work to the outside contractor is without sufficient business justification.

But if this is the view found to be required by the agreement, then it launches an inquiry for which the agreement provides no guides at all: What is sufficient business justification? To what extent is the employer's own assertion of business judgment significant? How much or what kind of evidence is necessary to bolster his judgment? How much or how little economy is necessary to justify the assumed impairment of the bargaining unit?

Or take the example of employee discipline discussed above. The agreement may be quite clear that the employer has the power to discharge or discipline for cause. It may be quite clear in empowering the arbitrator to pass on grievances protesting the employer's action and even to reduce or modify penalties. But what and where are the guides for his decision? With the advent of grievance procedures and arbitration, discharge has ceased to be regarded as the only available disciplinary measure. Layoffs for various periods are now in general use; and suggestion is made of disciplinary demotions, transfers, reduction of seniority, and the like. What is proper cause for disciplinary action, and more particularly, for discharge rather than for some other penalty? May such measures as demotion or reduction in seniority be properly used for disciplinary purposes? How much weight is to be attached in each case to the employer's judgment, particularly in view of the fact that it is precisely that judgment which is sought to be curbed by the grievance procedure? What significance is to be attached to the personality of the individual employee, his age, his seniority, his prior record, his promise? What consideration, if any, is to be given to probable effects on plant "morale," the morale of supervisors as well as of the workers, and the effects at the time the decision is to be made as well as at the time the penalty is imposed? The frequent instances of stoppage of work in a department or a whole plant because of a disciplinary penalty imposed on a single employee indicate that what is involved is not merely the case of an individual but a group dispute. Factors of this kind should be and doubtless are considered by the parties in the other stages of the grievance procedure. Do they become irrelevant when the case is appealed to the arbitrator?

Here is, of course, the clearest illustration of the arbitrator's role as creative more than interpretive. It would be folly to suggest that all his work is of that character. Despite all platitudes as to the inherent ambiguity of language, there are cases in which the language of the agreement appears compelling and leaves no room for consideration of other evidence of meaning; cases in which the dispute seems frivolous or captious, or patently designed to shift the onus of decision from the party to the arbitrator, or a desperate effort to recapture a confession made in negotiations and subsequently regretted. Assuming, however, a real difference of opinion, what criteria may the arbitrator look to for the choice between conflicting interpretations, each of which is more or less permissible?

Answer in the form of rules or canons of interpretation is neither practical nor helpful. Long experience with statutory interpretation has failed to produce such answer. In the last analysis, what is sought is a wise judgment. It is judgment, said Holmes, that the world pays for.[5] And we can only seek to be aware of the kind of care and preparation that is necessary in forming and pronouncing this judgment.

A proper conception of the arbitrator's function is basic. He is not a public tribunal imposed upon the parties by superior authority which the parties are obliged to accept. He has no general charter to administer justice for a community which transcends the parties. He is rather part of a system of self-government created by and confined to the parties. He serves their pleasure only to administer the rule of law established by their collective agreement. They are entitled to demand that, at least on balance, his performance be satisfactory to them, and they can readily dispense with him if it is not.

To the extent that the parties are satisfied that the arbitrator is properly performing his part in their system of self-government, their voluntary cooperation in the achievement of the purposes of the collective agreement is promoted. When I speak of the satisfaction of the parties, I do not mean only the advocates who may present the case to the arbitrator, or the top echelons of management or union representatives. I mean rather all the persons whose cooperation is required—all the employees in the bar-

5. Holmes, John Marshall, in Speeches
90 (1934).

gaining unit and all the representatives of management who deal with them, from the job foreman up.

Ideally, the arbitrator should be informed as fully as possible about the dispute which he is asked to resolve. He should hear all the contentions with respect to it which either party desires to make. For a party can hardly be satisfied that his case has been fully considered if he is not permitted to advance reasons which to him seem relevant and important.

The more serious danger is not that the arbitrator will hear too much irrelevancy, but rather that he will not hear enough of the relevant. Indeed, one advantage frequently reaped from wide latitude to the parties to talk about their case is that the apparent rambling frequently discloses very helpful information which would otherwise not be brought out. Rules of procedure which assure adequate opportunity to each party to prepare for and meet the other's contentions, or rules designed to encourage full consideration and effort at adjustment in the prior stages of the grievance procedure may be quite desirable. But they should not be such as to prevent full presentation of the controversy to the arbitrator before he is required to make final decision. For that would not only limit his resources for sound judgment, but would tend also to create dissatisfaction with the system.

The arbitrator may have to take a more active part in the investigation than does a trial court. This is not merely because, being charged with the responsibility for decision, he should be satisfied that he knows enough to be able to decide. A judge starts with some legal premises as to burden of proof or burden of going forward, which are presumably known to the lawyers who conduct the litigation and are binding on their clients. Even there these burdens are considerably eased by the modern practice of pretrial examination and discovery. But a collective agreement— the arbitrator's law—rarely states any burden of proof; and the presentation to the arbitrator is not always in the hands of skilled advocates having the same training for the work and operating on common premises. A court's erroneous findings of fact in a particular litigation may work an injustice to the litigants but rarely disturb the future; similar error by an arbitrator may cause more harm by disturbing the parties' continuing relationship than by the injustice in the particular case.

Moreover, notions of burden of proof are hardly applicable to issues of interpretation. Even courts do not confine themselves to the parties' presentations in their search for the meaning of the law. Interpretation of the agreement requires, however, appreciation by the interpreter of relevant facts; and the arbitrator must assure himself as well as he can that he has them.

Finally, in this connection the arbitrator must be quite circumspect in explaining his decision on the ground of inadequate presentation, for his usefulness may depend in large part on the very people so designated for responsibility. And so, for several reasons, the arbitrator cannot simply sit back and judge a debate. He must seek to inform himself as fully as possible and encourage the parties to provide him with the information.

His choice from the more or less permissible interpretations of the language of the agreement, keeping the basic conceptions in mind, requires an appraisal of the consequences of each of the possibilities. Though all the parts of the agreement do not necessarily make a consistent pattern, the interpretation which is most compatible with the agreement as a whole is to be preferred over one which creates anomaly. The effects on efficiency, productivity, and cost are important factors to be considered. So are also the effects on the attitudes and interests of the employees. The two sets of factors are not always in opposition. An apparent increased cost may in some circumstances be more than repaid by the increased productivity resulting from the greater stimulus to voluntary co-operation. Practicality of the interpretation in its day-to-day applications is a related value. The interpretation, no matter how right· in the abstract, is self-defeating and harmful to both sides if its day-to-day application provides further occasion for controversy and irritation.

Appraisal of probable consequences and practicality is no easy task and is not made on the basis of indisputable proof. The parties, too, make the appraisal. They differ with one another and they may differ with the arbitrator. But disagreement with the arbitrator by one or the other of the parties is normal and expectable and, of itself, not at all unhealthy. Indeed, the surprising thing is the extent of agreement that his award may meet within the ranks of both parties. For while a party may speak with one voice at the hearing, the fact is that there may be considerable difference of opinion among the many people who make up the artificial entity called the party.

The important question is not whether the parties agree with the award but rather whether they accept it, not resentfully, but cordially and willingly. Again, it is not to be expected that each decision will be accepted with the same degree of cordiality. But general acceptance and satisfaction is an attainable ideal. Its attainment depends upon the parties' seriousness of purpose to make their system of self-government work, and their confidence in the arbitrator. That confidence will ensue if the arbitrator's work inspires the feeling that he has integrity, independence, and courage so that he is not susceptible to pressure, blandishment, or threat of economic loss; that he is intelligent enough to comprehend the parties' contentions and emphatic enough to understand their significance to them; that he is not easily hoodwinked by bluff or histrionics; that he makes earnest effort to inform himself fully and does not go off half-cocked; and that his final judgment is the product of deliberation and reason so applied on the basis of the standards and the authority which they entrusted to him.

An important factor tending toward such general acceptance is the opinion accompanying the arbitrator's award. It has been urged by some that an arbitrator's award should be made without opinion or explanation in order to avoid the dangers of accumulating precedents and subjecting arbitration to the rigidities of stare decisis in the law. Perhaps this view has merit when the particular arbitration is regarded as solely a means of resolving the particular stalemate and nothing else. It is an erroneous view for the arbitration which is an integral part of the system of self-government and rule of law that the parties establish for their continuing relationship.

In this system opinions are necessary, first to assure the parties that the awards are based on reason applied to the agreement in the manner I have described.[6] To be sure, the opinions may convince the parties that their arbitrator is inadequate and should be replaced. This may work a hardship, and at times even an injustice, on the arbitrator. But that is a risk which the parties are entitled to impose on his occupation and which is a necessary feature of the system.

Secondly, in this system a form of precedent and stare decisis is inevitable and desirable. I am not referring to the use in one enterprise, say United States Steel, of awards made by another arbitrator in another enterprise, say General Motors. Because the publishing business has made arbitration awards generally available, they are being used in this way both by the parties and by arbitrators. But they are not so used in the belief that they are entitled to any precedential value, for they are not so entitled. Their value, if any, lies rather in their suggestion of approach or line of argument, or perhaps in their character of evidence as to practice in other enterprises. As such evidence, it must be used, of course, with great circumspection because of its limited character, and with ample opportunity for the parties to consider it.

But the precedent of which I am now speaking refers to the successive decisions within the same enterprise. Even in the absence of arbitration, the parties themselves seek to establish a form of stare decisis or precedent for their own guidance—by statements of policy, instructions, manuals of procedure, and the like. This is but a means of avoiding the pain of rethinking every recurring case from scratch, of securing uniformity of action among the many people of co-ordinate authority upon whom each of the parties must rely, of assuring adherence in their action to the policies established by their superiors, and of reducing or containing the possibilities of arbitrary or personal discretion.

When the parties submit to arbitration in the system of which I speak, they seek not merely resolution of the particular stalemate, but guidance for the future, at least for similar cases. They could hardly have a high opinion of the arbitrator's mind if it were a constantly changing mind. Adherence to prior decisions, except when departure is adequately explained, is one sign that the determinations are based on reason and are not merely random judgments.

The arbitrator's opinion can help in rationalizing the agreement and the parties' contentions with respect to it and in fostering greater appreciation by them of each other's views and needs with respect to the problem at hand. Its greatest utility lies in its effect, not merely on the advocates who presented the case or the higher authorities in the enterprise, but on what might be called the rank and file—the workers in the shop and their supervisors. It is the rank and file that must be convinced. For the temptation to resort to job action is ever present and is easily erupted. The less their private rule of law is understood by the workers and the more remote from their participation are the decisions made on their grievances, the greater is the likelihood of wildcat stoppages or other restraints on productivity. The likelihood can be decreased by bringing the arbitration close to the shop, not only in the hearings and investigations, but also in the opinion which explains the award.

6. I pass over the desirability of an opinion to assure the arbitrator himself that he has reached his conclusion in that way.

The awards must necessarily set precedents for recurring cases and the opinions must necessarily provide guidance for the future in relating decision to reason and to more or less mutually accepted principle. Consistency is not a lawyers' creation. It is a normal urge and a normal expectation. It is part of the ideal of equality of treatment. The lawyer's contribution, indeed, is his differentiation of rational, civilized consistency from apparent consistency. Let me give you an example. In many appeals from disciplinary penalties imposed by the employer, I heard the union argue earnestly that the penalty should be reduced because of the employee's long service record. I was persuaded and held that the employee's seniority should be considered in fixing the size of his penalty. Then came a case in which two employees committed the same offense at the same time, and one was given a larger penalty than the other. The union protested the larger penalty as being an obvious impairment of the principle of equality. This was not necessarily conscious opportunism, although there is always a good deal of that. A period of education was required to effect the realization, not only by the advocates, but by the rank and file that the equality for which they themselves contended in the area of discipline necessitated different penalties for the same offense whenever factors other than the offense itself were considered.

The arbitrator's opinions may thus be a valuable means of seating reason in labor relations. But the opinions must be carefully restrained. I venture to think that the greater danger to be guarded against is that too much will be said rather than too little. If the opinion wanders too far from the specific problem, in order to rationalize and guide, it runs great risk of error and subsequent embarrassment to the arbitrator himself. Even more unfortunately, it may lead the parties to distrust him because he has gone beyond the necessities of the case and has assumed to regulate their affairs in excess of their consent.

The danger of deciding too much or too early appears in another way. The parties themselves, each confidently expecting a decision its way, may press the arbitrator to decide issues which might better be left undecided or at least delayed until time and experience provide greater assurance of wise judgment. To the dogmatic and the partisan, there is no need for delay; their minds are made up and, to them, delay is confusing and exasperating. The United States Supreme Court has seen the dangers of premature decision and has developed standards for avoiding it, such as the insistence upon a "case or controversy" and the refusal to pass upon a constitutional question when a narrower ground will suffice for the case in hand. The conscientious arbitrator sometimes yearns for similar means of avoiding or delaying decision on issues which he feels unready to decide. For it must be remembered that the arbitrator's decision has a strength and a carry-over which does not exist in the case of an adjustment made by the parties in the lower stages of the grievance procedure.

Consider this example: The agreement sets forth certain classifications with attached rates of pay—ironworker, millwright, crib builder, sashman, belt repairman, and the like. The work of all these classifications is related by features common to all of them. In some plants all the work might be covered by perhaps one or two classifications rather than by a half-dozen. The agreement contains no job descriptions outlining the work of each classification, or if there are job descriptions they are either unilaterally adopted, or sketchy and expressly not exhaustive, or both. Disputes arise as to whether particular assignments made on certain days by supervision fall properly within one or another of the classifications. The particular cases may come to the arbitrator on appeal of disciplinary penalties imposed on employees who refused the assignments on the ground that they were not within the classifications of these employees; or they may come on the grievances of employees claiming that they were deprived of work belonging to their classification when the work was assigned to others. Such cases are vexing indeed, for the parties as well as the arbitrator. Even after long experience, he may find it practically impossible to draw clear and fine lines of demarcation between the several classifications. If he attempts to prick points in a future line by deciding the individual cases as they arise, his task is not much easier because he lacks confidence as to the direction in which he is going and knows that each case may be a prelude to many others. To decide that the issues are beyond his jurisdiction, because the agreement does not demarcate the classifications, is unsatisfactory because that may in effect be a decision for one of the parties and because the fact is that the dispute relates to a provision of the agreement.

In cases of this character, and others in which the arbitrator conscientiously feels baffled, it may be much wiser to permit him to mediate between the parties for an acceptable solution. I do not suggest it for all cases; nor do I urge that settlement is always better than decision. I suggest it only for those cases where decision with confidence seems impossible and where the arbitrator is quite at sea with respect to the consequences of his decision in the operation of the enterprise. In such cases, an adjustment worked out by him with the parties is the most promising course. And the possibility of adjustment is enhanced if he is able to exert the gentle pressure of a threat of decision. In this activity, as in the case of the arbitrator's socializing or meeting with the parties separately, the dangers envisaged with respect to judges or other governmental personnel are not equally applicable. For the parties' control of the process and their individual power to continue or terminate the services of the arbitrator are adequate safeguards against these dangers.

The example I cited comes from my own experience. With the parties' indulgence, though not with their prior consent, I withheld decision and let numerous cases accumulate, meanwhile gaining more illustrations of the scope of the problem and encouraging the parties to search for solution. We finally came up with a mutual understanding which amalgamated the several classifications into one with an appropriate adjustment of rate, reclassified the affected employees, disposed of the accumulated cases, and eliminated the problem for the future. To avoid certain internal difficulties the understanding was recorded not as a signed agreement, but rather as a decision of the umpire, the parties having waived for this case the normal limitations on his jurisdiction.

I have attempted in this paper to sketch the autonomous rule of law and reason which the collective labor agreement establishes. It has, of course, its limitations and its faults. It relies upon wholehearted acceptance by the parties and requires a congenial and adequate arbitrator, as I have explained, who is neither timid nor rash and who feels a responsibility for the success of the system. The arbitration may be resented by either party as an impairment of its authority or power. It is susceptible of use for buck-passing and face-saving. And it may sometimes encourage litigiousness. But when the system works fairly well, its value is great. To consider its feature of arbitration as a substitute for court litigation or as the consideration for a no-strike pledge is to take a foreshortened view of it. In a sense it is a substitute for both—but in the sense in which a transport airplane is a substitute for a stagecoach. The arbitration is an integral part of the system of self-government. And the system is designed to aid management in its quest for efficiency, to assist union leadership in its participation in the enterprise, and to secure justice for the employees. It is a means of making collective bargaining work and thus preserving private enterprise in a free government. . . .

Notes and Questions

1. Are the principles of the parental philosophy of arbitration (see question 1, *supra* p. 1224) expressed or implied in this article?

2. How will the arbitrator's willingness to base his decisions on broad principles of "the efficiency of the plant" and "the welfare of the workers" affect the settlement of disputes in the grievance procedure prior to arbitration and the number of disputes brought to arbitration?

3. How will it affect the acceptability of his decision by the losing side in a given case?

4. Consider the following statements by an opponent of "parental" labor arbitration: "Protestations of intent to balance the equities, to recognize human values and to take a socio-economic approach to labor disputes should be considered as an exercise in semantics employed by self-styled 'liberators' who, once they become entrenched, tend to become tyrants. The parties to a dispute which goes to arbitration do not seek an economic or sociological treatise, but simply want to be told whether or not a violation of the contract occurred and why. . . . The time for legislating expired when the contract was signed. . . . The contract is the frame of reference within which the dispute must be determined. Had either of the parties wanted the arbitrator's advice as to what the substantive rights and obligations of the parties should be, they would have employed the arbitrator as a consultant or negotiator at the time the contract was negotiated.

" . . . Employers and unions need no superhumans who, without intimate knowledge of the industrial situation involved, want to determine their way of 'living together.' When they employ an arbitrator, they hire a judge, not a legislator.

" . . . The place for mediation and compromise is at the bargaining table. The function of arbitration is to determine the rights of the parties without dabbling in their unrelated affairs. If the complaining party sustains the burden of proving he has been denied some right accorded him by the agreement, he should prevail. If not, the case should be dismissed. Arbitrators who insist on going beyond the contractual frame of reference in making an award create more problems than are solved . . .

" . . . Arbitrators who undertake to meddle in industrial affairs beyond or in disregard of the contractual scope of reference become mere politicians without competence to exercise the powers granted them. Good arbitrators will try to emulate good judges, since they too are required to judge. Since arbitration is an adjudicating process, there is every reason why the historical practices which characterize our judicial system should be followed." O. S. Hoebreckx, "In Defense of Judicial Arbitration," Labor Law Journal, Vol. 3, p. 487 (1952).

5. Suppose, as in the example suggested by Mr. Shulman, the contract is silent regarding a right of the employer to require a worker to work overtime, and suppose further that it contains no "management functions" clause. In a case against the employer for disciplining workers who refuse to work 20 hours a week overtime, on what grounds would it be proper for the arbitrator to interpret the contract as prohibiting such disciplining? In a case against the employer for disciplining workers who refuse to work an hour a day overtime for two weeks, on what grounds would it be proper for the arbitrator to interpret the contract as permitting such disciplining? Could the arbitrator properly hold that the silence of the contract regarding the right of management to require overtime work should not be interpreted as conferring or denying that right in all cases, and that the spirit or "logic" of the contract permits management to require a reasonable amount of overtime but no more? Would this differ from "legislating" or "mediating"?

6. Mr. Shulman expressly limits his analysis to the situation of the permanent arbitrator. To what extent is it applicable or inapplicable to the so-called ad hoc arbitrator, called in to decide a single dispute?

7. Mr. Shulman was appointed umpire at Ford after a long period of intensely bitter and often violent labor-management relations had finally resulted in union recognition. Do you believe that his philosophy of the role of the permanent labor arbitrator is better adapted to such a situation than to a situation in which there is a relatively high degree of stability, mutual confidence and maturity on both sides?

8. Is the legitimacy of an arbitrator's decision enhanced by the fact that the parties to the dispute selected him, or specified the process for his selection?

9. Is the legitimacy of the arbitrator's decision enhanced by the fact that it must be based on a law—the collective contract—or customs—"a common law of the shop"—developed by the parties them-

selves, either by express agreement or by established patterns of behavior in a long term relationship?

10.   Does the history of American labor law demonstrate the deep involvement of organized labor and management in the framing and interpretation of the law of labor-management relations? Does that involvement tend to enhance the moral force of decisions made under that law?

11.   Does the historical material on race relations demonstrate a similar deep involvement of Black Americans in the development of the law regarding race relations?

12.   Do the procedures and remedies available in race relations disputes afford the parties a kind or sense of participation in the legal process similar to the procedures and remedies available under the National Labor Relations Act and under collective agreements?

*

BIBLIOGRAPHY

The following is a short list of books which are recommended to readers who wish to pursue further some of the aspects of law introduced in the text. The bibliography is divided into two parts, the first consisting of books which treat principally of legal philosophy, legal history, comparative law, primitive law, or sociology of law, and the second consisting of books which treat principally of the American legal system as a whole or particular parts thereof.

I

Allen, Carleton K., *Law in the Making,* 7th ed. (Oxford, 1964).

Amos, Sheldon, *The Science of Law* (London, 1909).

Aquinas, St. Thomas, *Treatise on Law, Summa Theologica, Questions 90–97,* Gateway Edition (Chicago, 1949).

Arnold, Thurman, *The Symbols of Government* (New Haven, 1935).

Austin, John, *Lectures on Jurisprudence,* 5th ed., revised and edited by Robert Campbell (London, 1885).

Berman, Harold J., *The Interaction of Law and Religion* (New York, 1974) (available from The Council on Religion and Law, P. O. Box 30, Cambridge, Massachusetts).

Berman, Harold J., *Justice in the U.S.S.R.,* rev. ed. (Cambridge, Mass., 1963).

Bodenheimer, Edgar, *Jurisprudence, the Philosophy and Method of the Law* (Cambridge, Mass., 1962).

Boorstin, Daniel J., *The Mysterious Science of the Law; An Essay on Blackstone's Commentaries* (Cambridge, Mass., 1941).

Bowen, Catherine Drinker, *A Yankee from Olympus; Justice Holmes and His Family* (Boston, 1944).

Bowen, Catherine Drinker, *The Lion and the Throne; the Life and Times of Sir Edward Coke* (Boston 1957).

Cahn, Edmund N., *The Moral Decision; right and wrong in the light of American law* (Bloomington, Indiana, 1955).

Cardozo, Benjamin N., *The Growth of the Law* (New Haven, 1924, 1963).

Cardozo, Benjamin N., *The Nature of the Judicial Process* (New Haven, 1928).

Cardozo, Benjamin N., *The Paradoxes of Legal Science* (New York, 1928).

Cardozo, Benjamin N., *Selected Writings,* edited by Margaret E. Hall (New York, 1947).

Cohen, Felix S., *Ethical Systems and Legal Ideals: an essay on the foundations of legal criticism* (New York 1933, 1959).

Cohen, Morris R., and Cohen, Felix S., *Readings in Jurisprudence and Legal Philosophy* (New York, 1951).

Cohen, Morris, R., *Law and the Social Order* (New York, 1933).

Commons, John R., *Legal Foundations of Capitalism* (Madison, Wisconsin, 1957).

d'Entreves, Allisandro P., *Natural Law: An Introduction to Legal Philosophy* (London, 1951).

Devlin, Sir Patrick, *The Enforcement of Morals* (London, 1965).

Dicey, Albert V., *The Relation Between Law and Public Opinion in England in the 19th Century*, 2d ed., with preface by E.C.S. Wade (London, 1962).

Durkheim, Emile, *On the Division of Labor in Society*, translated and edited by George Simpson (New York, 1933).

Ehrlich, Eugene, *Fundamental Principles of the Sociology of Law*, translated by W. L. Moll (Cambridge, Mass., 1936; New York, 1962).

Encyclopedia of the Social Sciences, 1930–1934, articles on Administration of Justice, Crime, Jurisprudence, and Legal Relations, listed in Vol. 15, p. 548 ff.

Fortescue, Sir John, *In Praise of the Laws of England*, translated by Francis Gigor (London, 1917).

Frank, Jerome, *Law and the Modern Mind*, 2d ed. (New York, 1949).

Friedmann, Wolfgang W., *Law in a Changing Society* (London, 1959).

Friedrich, Carl J., *The Philosophy of Law in Historical Perspective*, rev. ed. (Chicago, 1963).

Fuller, Lon L., *The Morality of Law* (New Haven, 1964).

Fuller, Lon L., *The Problems of Jurisprudence*, temp. ed. (Brooklyn, N.Y., 1949).

Gierke, Otto F. von, *Natural Law and the Theory of Society, 1500 to 1800*, translated by Ernest Barker (Cambridge, England, 1934; Boston, 1957).

Gray, John C., *The Nature and Sources of Law* (New York, 1909), paperback ed. (Boston, 1963).

Haar, Charles M., editor, *The Golden Age of American Law* (New York, 1965).

Hall, Jerome, *Theft, Law, and Society*, 2d ed. (Indianapolis, 1952).

Hart, Herbert L. A., and Honore, Antony M., *Causation in the Law* (Oxford, 1962).

Hart, Herbert L. A., *The Concept of Law* (Oxford, 1961).

Havighurst, Harold C., *Nature of Private Contract* (Evanston, Ill., 1961).

Hoebel, E. Adamson, *The Law of Primitive Man* (Cambridge, Mass., 1954).

Holmes, Oliver Wendell, Jr., *The Common Law*, edited by Mark De Wolfe Howe (Boston, 1963).

Honnold, John, editor, *The Life of the Law; readings on the growth of legal institutions* (New York, 1964).

Hurst, James W., *Law and Social Process in U.S. History* (Ann Arbor, Michigan, 1960).

Hurst, James W., *Law and the Conditions of Freedom* (Madison, Wisconsin, 1956).

Hurst, James W., *The Growth of American Law, the Law Makers* (Boston, 1950).

Keeton, George W., *The Norman Conquest and the Common Law* (London, 1966).

Keeton, Robert E., *Legal Cause in the Law of Torts* (Columbus, Ohio, 1963).

Kelsen, Hans, *What is Justice?*, collected essays (Berkeley, California, 1957).

Konefsky, Samuel J., *The Legacy of Holmes and Brandeis: A Study in the Influence of Ideas* (New York, 1956).
Koschaker, Paul, *Europa und das roemische Recht* (Munich, Germany, 1947).

Lerner, Max, *The Mind and Faith of Justice Holmes* (Boston, 1943).
Llewellyn, Karl N. and Hoebel, E. Adamson, *The Cheyenne Way: Conflict and Case Law in Primitive Jurisprudence* (Norman, Okla., 1941, 1953).

Maine, Sir Henry, *Ancient Law: Its Connection with the Early History of Society and Its Relation to Modern Ideas*, rev. ed., with introduction and notes by Sir Frederick Pollock (London, 1930).
Maitland, F. W., *Equity, also the Forms of Action at Common Law*, revised by John Brungate, 2nd ed. (Cambridge, England, 1936).
Mason, Alpheus T., *Brandeis: Lawyer and Judge in the Modern State* (Princeton, N.J., 1953).
Mellinkoff, David, *The Language of the Law* (Boston, 1963).
Mitchell, William, *An Essay on the Early History of the Law Merchant* (Cambridge, England, 1904).
Montesquieu, Charles Louis de Secondat, *The Spirit of the Laws*, translated by T. Nugent (New York, 1949).

Noyes, C. Reinold, *The Institution of Property* (New York, 1936).

Patterson, Edwin W., *Jurisprudence: Men and Ideas of the Law* (Brooklyn, N.Y., 1958).
Plucknett, Theodore F. T., *A Concise History of the Common Law* (5th ed., London, 1956).
Pollock, Sir Frederick, and Maitland, Frederic W., *History of English Law*, 2 vols., 2nd ed. (Cambridge, England, 1898).
Pound, Roscoe, *An Introduction to the Philosophy of Law* (New Haven, 1954).
Pound, Roscoe, *Interpretations of Legal History* (Cambridge, Mass., 1946).
Pound, Roscoe, *Social Control Through Law* (New Haven, 1942).
Pound, Roscoe, *The Formative Era of American Law* (New York, 1938, 1950).
Pound, Roscoe, *The Lawyer from Antiquity to Modern Times* (St. Paul, Minn., 1953).
Pound, Roscoe, *The Spirit of the Common Law* (Boston, 1921).

Radin, Max, *Law as Logic and Experience* (New Haven, 1940).
Renner, Karl, *The Institutions of Private Law and Their Social Functions* (London, 1949).

Savigny, Friedrich K. von, *On the Vocation of Our Age for Legislation and Jurisprudence*, translated by Abraham Hayward (London, 1831).
Smith, Adam, *Inquiry into the Nature and Causes of the Wealth of Nations*, 4th ed. (Edinburgh, 1850).
Smith, Munroe, *The Development of European Law* (New York, 1928).
Sohm, Rudolf, *Institutes of Roman Law*, 3rd ed., translated by J. C. Ledlie (Oxford, 1907).
Stone, Julius, *Human Law and Human Justice* (Stanford, Cal., 1965).
Stone, Julius, *Legal System and Lawyers' Reasonings* (Stanford, Cal., 1964).
Stone, Julius, *The Province and Function of Law* (London, 1947).

Vinogradoff, Sir Paul, *Introduction to Historical Jurisprudence* (Oxford, 1923).

Von Mehren, Arthur T., *The Civil Law System* (Englewood Cliffs, N.J., 1957).

Weber, Max, *On Law in Economy and Society*, edited with introduction and annotations by Max Rheinstein, translated by Max Rheinstein and Edward Shils (Cambridge, Mass., 1954).

Williams, Glanville, *The Criminal Law*, 2d ed. (London, 1961).

II

Association of American Law Schools, *Selected Readings on the Legal Profession* (St. Paul, Minn., 1962).

Auerbach, Carl A., Hurst, Willard, Garrison, Lloyd K., and Mermin, Samuel, *The Legal Process; an introduction to decision-making by judicial, legislative, executive and administrative agencies* (San Francisco, 1961).

Berman, Harold J., editor, *Talks on American Law* (New York, 1961).

Bickel, Alexander M., *The Least Dangerous Branch: the Supreme Court at the Bar of Politics* (New York, 1962).

Black, Charles L., *The People and the Court, Judicial Review in a Democracy* (New York, 1960).

Cheatham, Elliot E., *Cases and Materials on the Legal Profession*, 2nd ed. (Brooklyn, N.Y., 1955).

Clark, Charles E., *Handbook of the Law of Code Pleading*, 2d ed. (St. Paul, Minn., 1947).

Corbin, Arthur L., *Corbin on Contracts, One Volume Edition* (St. Paul, Minn., 1952).

Corwin, Edward S., editor, *The Constitution of the United States of America, Analysis and Interpretation*, 2d ed., edited by Normal J. Small, and Lester S. Jayson (Washington, D.C., Government Printing Office, 1964).

Corwin, Edward S., *The Constitution and What it Means Today*, 12th rev. ed. (Princeton, N.J., 1958).

Cox, Archibald and Bok, Derek, *Cases on Labor Law*, 6th ed. (Brooklyn, N.Y., 1965).

Cozzens, James Gould, *The Just and the Unjust* (New York, 1942).

Curtis, Charles P., *It's Your Law* (Cambridge, Mass., 1954).

Davis, Kenneth Culp, *Administrative Law*, 3 vols. (St. Paul, Minn., 1958).

Donnelly, Richard C., Goldstein, Joseph, and Schwartz, Richard C., *Criminal Law* (New York, 1962).

Elliott, Sheldon D., and Karlen, Delmar, *Cases and Materials on Pleading and Procedure before Trial* (St. Paul, Minn., 1961).

Farnsworth, Allan, *An Introduction to the Legal System of the United States* (New York, 1963).

Field, Richard H., and Kaplan, Benjamin, *Materials for a Basic Course in Civil Procedure* (Brooklyn, N.Y., 1953).

Frank, Jerome, *Courts on Trial* (Princeton, N.J., 1949; New York, 1963).

Frankfurter, Felix, and Greene, Nathan, *The Labor Injunction* (New York, 1930), reprinted (Gloucester, Mass., 1963).

Freund, Paul A., *On Understanding the Supreme Court* (Boston, 1949).

Freund, Paul A., Sutherland, Arthur E., Howe, Mark DeWolfe, and Brown, Ernest J., *Constitutional Law; Cases and Other Problems*, 2 vols. (Boston, 1954; Supplement 1965).

Friedman, Lawrence M., *Contract Law in America: A Social and Economic Case Study* (Madison, Wisconsin, 1965).

Friendly, Henry J., *The Federal Administrative Agencies; the need for better definition of standards* (Cambridge, Mass., 1962).

Fuller, Lon L., and Braucher, Robert, *Basic Contract Law* (St. Paul, Minn., 1964).

Goldstein, Irving, *Trial Technique* (Chicago, 1935).

Gregory, Charles O., *Labor and the Law*, 2d rev. ed., with 1961 supplement (New York, 1961).

Griswold, Erwin N., *Law and Lawyers in the United States; the Common Law Under Stress* (Cambridge, Mass., 1965).

Hall, Livingston, and Kamisar, Yale, *Modern Criminal Procedure* (St. Paul, Minn., 1965).

Harper, Fowler V., and James, Fleming, *The Law of Torts*, 3 vols. (Boston, 1956).

Harvard Law Review, *Selected Essays on the Law of Torts* (Cambridge, Mass., 1948).

Jackson, Robert A., *The Struggle for Judicial Supremacy* (New York, 1941).

Jaffe, Louis L., *Administrative Law: cases and materials*, 2d ed. with Nathaniel L. Nathanson (Boston, 1961).

James, Fleming, *Civil Procedure* (Boston, 1965).

Karlen, Delmar, *Appellate Courts in the United States and England* (New York, 1963).

Karlen, Delmar, *Primer of Procedure* (Madison, Wis., 1950).

Kessler, Friedrich, and Sharp, Malcolm P., *Contracts: Cases and Materials* (Boston, 1964).

Kinnane, Charles H., *A First Book on Anglo-American Law*, 2nd ed. (Indianapolis, 1952).

Kurland, Philip B., *Religion and the Law: of church and state and the Supreme Court* (Chicago, 1962).

Landis, James M., *The Administrative Process* (New Haven, 1938).

Letwin, William, *Law and Economic Policy in America; the evolution of the Sherman Act* (New York, 1965).

Levi, Edward H., *An Introduction to Legal Reasoning* (Chicago, 1949).

Lewis, Anthony, *Gideon's Trumpet* (New York, 1964).

Llewellyn, Karl N., *The Bramble Bush* (New York, 1951).

Llewellyn, Karl N., *The Common Law Tradition: Deciding Appeals* (Boston, 1962).

McCloskey, Robert G., *The American Supreme Court* (Chicago, 1960).

McCormick, Charles T., *Handbook of the Law of Evidence* (St. Paul, Minn., 1954).

Mason, Alpheus T., *Supreme Court; Palladium of Freedom* (Ann Arbor, Mich., 1962).

Mayers, Lewis, *The American Legal System*, rev. ed. (New York, 1964).

Mendelson, Wallace, *Justices Black and Frankfurter: Conflict in the Court* (Chicago, 1961).

Neale, Albert D., *The Antitrust Laws of the U.S.A.* (Cambridge, England 1960).

Orfield, Lester B., *Criminal Procedure from Arrest to Appeal* (New York, 1947).

Pfeffer, Leo, *This Honorable Court: A History of the U.S. Supreme Court* (Boston, 1965).

Phillips, Harlan B., editor, *Felix Frankfurter Reminisces* (New York, 1960).

Porter, Charles O. and Blaustein, Albert P., *The American Lawyer* (Chicago, 1954).

Prosser, William L., *Handbook of the Law of Torts*, 3rd ed. (St. Paul, Minn., 1964).

Rodell, Fred, *Nine Men: A Political History of the Supreme Court from 1790–1955* (New York, 1965).

Rosenberg, Maurice, *The Pre-Trial Conference and Effective Justice* (New York, 1964).

Rostow, Eugene V., *The Sovereign Prerogative; the Supreme Court and the Quest for Law* (New Haven, 1962).

Seavey, Warren A., *Cogitations on Torts* (Lincoln, Nebraska, 1954).

Shartel, Burke, *Our Legal System and How It Operates* (Ann Arbor, Mich., 1951).

Stryker, Lloyd P., *The Art of Advocacy* (New York, 1954).

Sutherland, Arthur E., *Constitutionalism in America; origin and evaluation of its fundamental ideas* (New York, 1965).

S,wisher, Carl Brent, *The Supreme Court in Its Modern Role*, rev. ed. (New York, 1965).

Ulman, Joseph N., *A Judge Takes the Stand* (New York, 1933).

Vanderbilt, Arthur T., *Cases and Other Materials on Modern Procedure and Judicial Administration* (New York, 1952).

Westin, Allan F., *The Anatomy of a Constitutional Law Case* (New York, 1950).

Westin, Allan F., *The Supreme Court; views from inside* (New York, 1961).

Wigmore, John H., *A Student's Textbook of the Law of Evidence* (Chicago 1935).

TABLE OF CASES

Principal cases are in Italic type. Cases discussed or cited are in Roman type. References are to Pages.

*

INDEX TO PERSONS CITED OR QUOTED

Abelard, 577.
Aberlone, Rose 2d, 651, 652.
Alfred the Great, 573, 574.
Allen, Carleton K., quoted 25, 31.
Amos, Sheldon, quoted 20.
Aquinas, St. Thomas, quoted 19.
Aristotle, 482, 576, 694; quoted 19.
Arnold, Thurman, 38; quoted 35; *The Symbols of Government*, excerpts 110–113, 896.
Atkin, Lord, quoted 540; opinions 596, 613.
Ayres, Richard, "Confessions and the Courts," excerpt 279–280.

Barnard, Chester I., quoted 15.
Bartlett, Willard, opinions 513, 522.
Bazelon, David, opinion 332.
Bell, Griffin B., opinion 312.
Bentham, Jeremy, 558; quoted 486.
Bergman, Peter M., *The Chronological History of the Negro in America*, excerpt 973–974.
Bernhard, Arnold, "The Antitrust Convictions in the Electrical Equipment Case," excerpt 140–141.
Bickel, Alexander M., quoted 84; *The Least Dangerous Branch*, excerpt 1021–1022.
Bismark, 471.
Black, Charles L., 85; "The Lawfulness of the Segregation Decisions," excerpt 1015–1021.
Black, Hugo L., opinions 163, 1047.
Blackstone, Sir William, 3; quoted 1, 261.
Blumberg, Abraham, "Lawyers With Convictions," excerpt 335–336.
Bok, Derek C. See Cox and Bok.
Bonaparte, Napoleon, 470.
Bracton, Henry de, 576, 578, 587.
Bramwell, Baron, quoted 435.
Brandeis, Louis D., opinion 861.
Breitel, Charles D., opinion 234.
Brennan, William J., opinions 98, 1042, 1119, 1171, 1201.
Brett (Lord Esher), quoted 518, 535.
Brewer, Justice, opinion 848.
Brougham, Lord, 432.
Brown, Justice, opinion 962.
Burger, Warren E., opinions 1147, 1178.
Burke, Edmund, 10; quoted 1–2, 412, 416, 572.
Burton, Harold H., opinions 1124, 1200.

Cardozo, Benjamin N., 40, 66; quoted 538–539, 643; opinions 63, 516, 718.
Charlemagne, 574, 577.
Chevigny, Paul G., quoted 236–237.
Clark, Charles E., *Handbook of the Law of Code Pleading*, excerpt 169–170; opinion 176.
Clemenceau, Georges, 4.
Cockburn, Lord, quoted 433.
Cohen, Felix S., quoted 180; "Field Theory and Judicial Logic," excerpt 179–180.

Konvitz, Milton R. and Theodore Leskes, *A Century of Civil Rights*, excerpts 955–957, 958–961.

LaFave, Wayne, quoted 210; see, also, Hall, Kamisar, Israel and LaFave.

Landis, James, quoted 569.

Langbein, John H. and Lloyd L. Weinreib, "Continental Criminal Procedure: 'Myth' and Reality," excerpt 349–356.

Langdell, Christopher Columbus, 599.

Leisure, George S., quoted 440.

Leskes, Theodore. See Konvitz and Leskes.

Letwin, William, *Law and Economic Policy in America*, excerpts 839–840, 843–845.

Levi, Edward H., 40; *An Introduction to Legal Reasoning*, excerpt 526–542.

Lincoln, Abraham, quoted 434, 953–954.

Llewellyn, Karl N., 40; quoted 6, 24, 741; *The Bramble Bush*, excerpt 167–168, 487–495.

Macaulay, Stewart, 43; "Non-Contractual Relations in Business: A Preliminary Study," excerpt 787–801.

MacNeil, Ian R., "A Primer of Contract Planning," excerpt 759–771.

McKenna, Joseph, opinion 878.

McNair, Lord, quoted 680.

McReynolds, James C., opinion 902.

Maine, Sir Henry, 21, 556, 559; quoted 554, 557, 558, 752–753.

Maitland, Frederic W., 24, quoted 573.

Malinowski, Bronislaw, quoted 741.

Mansfield, Lord, quoted 587, 589, 747 n. 11.

Marcus, Martin. See Goldstein and Marcus.

Marshall, John, quoted 129.

Mayers, Lewis, *The American Legal System*, excerpt 213–215.

Meiklejohn, Alexander, quoted 1061–1062.

Merton, R. K., 29; quoted 28.

Miller, Loren, *The Petitioners*, excerpts 974–977, 998–1001.

Minton, Sherman, opinion 947.

Murphy, Justice, opinions, 906, 932.

Neale, A. D., *The Antitrust Laws of the U.S.A.*, excerpt 136–139.

Parker, Isaac, quoted 3.

Peck, Cornelius J., "The Equal Employment Opportunity Commission: Developments in the Administrative Process 1965–1975," excerpts 1092–1102, 1211–1212.

Pepper, George W., quoted 441–442.

Perdue, William R. Jr. See Fuller and Perdue.

Pitney, Mahlon, opinion 856.

Ploscowe, Morris, "The Investigating Magistrate (Juge D'Instruction) in European Criminal Procedure," excerpt 344–345.

Plucknett, T. F. T., quoted 74.

Pollock, Sir Frederick, quoted 568.

Pound, Roscoe, 24, 123; quoted 390, 568, 740, 748, 751 n.11, 806.

Rapallo, Judge, opinion 509.

Rehnquist, William H., opinion 1180.

Reich, Charles A., "Police Questioning of Law Abiding Citizens," excerpt 238–239.

Renfrew, Charles B., "The Paper Label Sentences: An Evaluation," excerpt 142–144.

Rhinelander, Philip H., quoted 15.

INDEX

References are to Pages

---

†